The
INTERNATIONAL CRITICAL COMMENTARY
on the Holy Scriptures of the Old and New Testaments

GENERAL EDITORS

G. I. DAVIES, F.B.A.
Emeritus Professor of Old Testament Studies in the University of Cambridge
Fellow of Fitzwilliam College

AND

C. M. TUCKETT
Emeritus Professor of New Testament in the University of Oxford
Fellow of Pembroke College

FORMERLY UNDER THE EDITORSHIP OF

J. A. EMERTON, F.B.A., C. E. B. CRANFIELD, F.B.A.
and G. N. STANTON
General Editors of the New Series

S. R. DRIVER
A. PLUMMER
C. A. BRIGGS
Founding Editors

A CRITICAL AND EXEGETICAL COMMENTARY

ON

EXODUS 1–18

BY

G. I. DAVIES, F.B.A.

*Emeritus Professor of Old Testament Studies in the University of Cambridge
Fellow of Fitzwilliam College*

IN TWO VOLUMES

VOLUME 1

Commentary on Exodus 1–10

t&tclark
LONDON • NEW YORK • OXFORD • NEW DELHI • SYDNEY

T&T CLARK
Bloomsbury Publishing Plc
50 Bedford Square, London, WC1B 3DP, UK
1385 Broadway, New York, NY 10018, USA

BLOOMSBURY, T&T CLARK and the T&T Clark logo are trademarks of
Bloomsbury Publishing Plc

First published in Great Britain 2020
Paperback edition published in 2025

Copyright © G. I. Davies, 2020

G. I. Davies has asserted his right under the Copyright, Designs and Patents Act,
1988, to be identified as the Author of this work.

All rights reserved. No part of this publication may be reproduced or transmitted
in any form or by any means, electronic or mechanical, including photocopying,
recording, or any information storage or retrieval system, without prior permission in
writing from the publishers.

Bloomsbury Publishing Plc does not have any control over, or responsibility for, any
third-party websites referred to or in this book. All internet addresses given in this
book were correct at the time of going to press. The author and publisher regret any
inconvenience caused if addresses have changed or sites have ceased to exist, but
can accept no responsibility for any such changes.

The NewJerusalemU, GraecaU and TranslitLSU fonts used to print this work
are available from Linguist's Software, Inc., PO Box 580, Edmonds,
WA 98020-0580 USA.
Tel (425) 775-1130. www.linguistsoftware.com

A catalogue record for this book is available from the British Library.

A catalog record for this book is available from the Library of Congress.

ISBN: HB: 978-0-5676-8868-2
PB: 978-0-5677-1695-8
ePDF: 978-0-5676-8869-9

Series: International Critical Commentary

Typeset by Forthcoming Publications (www.forthpub.com)

To find out more about our authors and books visit www.bloomsbury.com
and sign up for our newsletters.

UXORI DILECTISSIMAE TOTIQUE FAMILIAE

CONTENTS OF VOLUME I

General Editors' Preface	xi
Preface	xiii
Bibliography	xvii
Abbreviations	xxxv

INTRODUCTION	1
1. Names, Place in the Canon and Contents	1
2. The Text and its Ancient Versions	5
(i) The Hebrew Text	5
a. Medieval Jewish Manuscripts	5
b. The Samaritan Pentateuch	11
c. The Dead Sea Scrolls and Other Ancient Hebrew Sources	18
(ii) The Ancient Versions	27
a. General Considerations	27
b. The Septuagint	31
c. The Targums (or Targumim)	41
d. The Peshiṭta	53
e. The Vulgate	58
3. Main Component Sections and their Plot, Genres and Theological Themes	64
(i) The Exodus Story (1.1–15.21)	65
(ii) The Wilderness Journey (15.22–18.27)	67
(iii) The Sinai Narrative (First Part) (19.1–40.38)	68
(iv) Summary	72
4. Composition of the Book	72
(i) History of Research	73
(ii) Sources and Redaction in Exodus: Principles and Results	87
a. Principles	87
b. Results	91
5. The Contents of Exodus Divided between the Two Main Versions of the Story	113

ISRAEL IN EGYPT AND THE EARLY LIFE OF MOSES
(1.1–2.22)

CHAPTER 1.1-6
RÉSUMÉ: THE BACKGROUND TO THE STORY OF THE EXODUS   117

CHAPTER 1.7-22
THE GROWTH OF ISRAEL DESPITE EGYPTIAN COUNTERMEASURES   131

CHAPTER 2.1-10
THE NAMING OF MOSES   170

CHAPTER 2.11-22
FROM EGYPT TO MIDIAN   193

MOSES' COMMISSIONING
AND APPROACH TO PHARAOH
(2.23–7.13)

CHAPTER 2.23-25
GOD'S CONCERN FOR HIS PEOPLE ISRAEL   215

CHAPTER 3.1-12
MOSES' COMMISSIONING BY GOD   225

CHAPTER 3.13-15
MOSES' QUESTION ABOUT THE NAME OF GOD ANSWERED   266

CHAPTER 3.16-22
YAHWEH'S INSTRUCTIONS TO MOSES   285

CHAPTER 4.1-9
MOSES' FIRST OBJECTION COUNTERED   307

CHAPTER 4.10-17
MOSES' SECOND AND THIRD OBJECTIONS COUNTERED   322

CHAPTER 4.18-31
MOSES' RETURN TO EGYPT   342

CONTENTS

CHAPTER 5.1-23
MOSES AND AARON'S FIRST, FRUITLESS, ENCOUNTER
WITH PHARAOH   373

CHAPTER 6.1-9
GOD'S (RENEWED) PROMISE OF DELIVERANCE
TO MOSES AND ISRAEL   408

CHAPTER 6.10–7.5
MOSES' OBJECTION AND ITS ANSWER
(INCLUDING: GENEALOGY OF AARON AND THE AARONIDES)   427

CHAPTER 7.6-13
STAFFS AND SNAKES   469

MOSES AND AARON BEFORE PHARAOH
(THE FIRST NINE PLAGUES)
(7.14–10.29)

CHAPTER 7.14-25
THE PLAGUE(S) OF WATER TURNED TO BLOOD   484

CHAPTER 7.26–8.11
THE PLAGUE(S) OF FROGS   508

CHAPTER 8.12-15
THE PLAGUE OF LICE   527

CHAPTER 8.16-28
THE PLAGUE OF WORMS(?)   536

CHAPTER 9.1-7
PESTILENCE ON THE ANIMALS   557

CHAPTER 9.8-12
BOILS ON HUMANS AND ANIMALS   570

CHAPTER 9.13-35
THE HAIL AND THE THUNDER   580

CHAPTER 10.1-20
THE PLAGUE OF LOCUSTS 620

CHAPTER 10.21-29
DARKNESS 651

GENERAL EDITORS' PREFACE

Much scholarly work has been done on the Bible since the publication of the first volumes of the International Critical Commentary in the 1890s. New linguistic, textual, historical and archaeological evidence has become available, and there have been changes and developments in methods of study. In the twenty-first century there will be as great a need as ever, and perhaps a greater need, for the kind of commentary that the International Critical Commentary seeks to supply. The series has long had a special place among works in English on the Bible, because it has sought to bring together all the relevant aids to exegesis, linguistic and textual no less than archaeological, historical, literary and theological, to help the reader to understand the meaning of the books of the Old and New Testaments. In the confidence that such a series meets a need, the publishers and the editors are commissioning new commentaries on all the books of the Bible. The work of preparing a commentary on such a scale cannot but be slow, and developments in the past half-century have made the commentator's task yet more difficult than before, but it is hoped that the remaining volumes will appear without too great intervals between them. No attempt has been made to secure a uniform theological or critical approach to the problems of the various books, and scholars have been selected for their scholarship and not for their adherence to any school of thought. It is hoped that the new volumes will attain the high standards set in the past, and that they will make a significant contribution to the understanding of the books of the Bible.

G. I. D.
C. M. T.

PREFACE

Exodus was one of the rather few books of the Bible on which no commentary appeared among the older volumes of the *International Critical Commentary*. It had been assigned (by 1905 at the latest) to A.R.S. Kennedy, Professor of Hebrew and Semitic Languages at the University of Edinburgh, who had already published a pocket-sized edition of the English text of Exodus with a brief introduction and notes in 1901. He also contributed several articles on the 'tabernacle chapters' in the second half of the book to the *Hastings' Dictionary of the Bible* and wrote some commentaries on other biblical books. But no drafts of a commentary for this series (if there ever were any) seem to have survived. The world of Old Testament studies had come to look very different by the late 1980s, when I began to work through Exodus 1–24 in classes for graduate students. This was even more so a dozen years later when I broke ground on this commentary with a seminar paper entitled '"And": The First Word of the Book of Exodus', not fully realising how controversial that word and what it represented was soon to become! Progress has been slower than I would have liked, but work on Exodus has had to compete for time with my other interests and commitments and the pattern of the *ICC*, like other major series, leaves little room for cutting corners. Its breadth of scope and attention to detail are of course its strengths and I cannot say that I have found the requirements onerous, rather the reverse. In one respect I may even have widened the scope, compared with many of the older volumes especially, by including a short concluding reflection on the theological import of each passage (somewhat like the 'Ziel' sections in the *Biblischer Kommentar* series).

I am also one of those who have reverted to the older pattern of beginning with a long general Introduction to the book, in which the evidence for the text and its composition out of older materials are treated in some detail. A table at the end of it indicates broadly the contents of the once separate 'Priestly' and 'Non-Priestly' versions of the narrative, and I have used italics in my translations to distinguish the Priestly sections more precisely from the remainder of the text (see also the explanatory remarks on p. 113). For convenience my overall conclusions about the allocation of passages to the major source-documents can be found on pp. 94 (n. 109: P) and 102-103 (n. 117: J and E). The detailed argument on which these conclusions are built and discussions of the views of other scholars, past and present, appear in the introductions to each section of text. In the commentary itself I begin with a translation of the Masoretic text and linguistic notes on its interpretation (in smaller print). There then follow 'Explanatory Notes', which elucidate the content of the passage and draw attention to signs that it may not be a unified composition. Finally 'Text and Versions' (again in smaller print) provides a close examination of variations in both the other Hebrew witnesses to the text (especially the Samaritan Pentateuch and the scrolls from Qumran and nearby) and the major ancient translations, to consider how they arose and whether they point to an older form of the text or a later modification of it. The writing and revision of the commentary was essentially complete early in 2018 and so only a few references could be made to recently published works such as S. Germany's *The Exodus-Conquest Narrative* and the final fascicles of W.H. Schmidt's commentary.

I could not have written a commentary like this without the training given to me by my classical tutors in Oxford, who introduced me to textual criticism, and my formative teachers in biblical languages and exegesis: Hedley Sparks, John Emerton, Ronald Clements and Sebastian Brock. But along the way many others have given me valuable help and encouragement in a variety of ways. Among them are James Aitken, Andrew Chester, Alan Crown, Katharine Dell, Brian Elfick, Simon Gathercole, Robert Gordon, Alison Gray, William Horbury, Marinus Koster, Drew Longacre, Nathan Macdonald, Andrew Macintosh, Bradley Marsh, Brian Mastin, Alan Millard, Walter Moberly, Ernest Nicholson, Kim Phillips, Stefan Reif, Peter Williams, Hugh Williamson and Naomi Wormell. Many others could have been included in this list – I am truly grateful to them all. I have also benefited greatly from the generous and painstaking help of the staff at the University Library and the Divinity Faculty in Cambridge, the Bodleian Library in Oxford, the British Library and the Beineke Library at Yale. Among the electronic resources that are now available I should mention especially the Accordance software and text modules, which have greatly simplified some aspects of my work.

In the closing stages of the preparation of the typescript Jan Joosten very kindly agreed to read it all through on behalf of the publishers, acting in place of the Old Testament Editor of the series, who could not edit his own work. He made numerous valuable suggestions for improvement and provided information about recent (and not so recent) books and articles that I had missed, and I have been glad to follow his advice in most cases. This help, given in the midst of his other commitments, including the editing of a major journal, was an exceptional and much valued contribution to my work. I am delighted and thankful that we are again able to use the superb fonts and software provided by Linguists' Software for the *ICC*, and my thanks are also due to Dominic Mattos and his colleagues at T&T Clark for their invaluable practical help.

My family, and especially Nicola, have given me remarkable support throughout the writing of the commentary, including the provision of a country cottage to work in and 'leave of absence' for much of the working week since my retirement from the University in 2011. The family has multiplied fourfold since I began – a modest increase compared with the Israelites in Egypt! – and has been a source of immense delight to me. This volume is dedicated to them all in much gratitude and affection.

Graham Davies
Cambridge

BIBLIOGRAPHY

Commentaries on Exodus (marked **) and other frequently cited monographs (marked *) are referred to in the main text by the author's name. Other items listed in this bibliography are cited by short title. For editions of the biblical text see the relevant part of the Introduction, Section 2. Details of some reference works are included in the list of abbreviations. (For additional bibliography on ch. 15 see the Introduction to 15.1-21.)

Abel, F.-M., *Géographie de la Palestine* (Paris, 1933; 2nd ed. 1938).
Aejmalaeus, A., *On the Trail of the Septuagint Translators: Collected Essays* (Kampen, 1993).
Aharoni, Y., *The Land of the Bible: A Historical Geography* (London, 2nd ed., 1979).
Ahuis, F., *Exodus 11,1 – 13,16 und die Bedeutung der Trägergruppen für das Verständnis des Passa* (FRLANT 168; Göttingen, 1996).
Albertz, R., *Religionsgeschichte Israels in alttestamentlicher Zeit* (ATD Ergänzungsreihe 8/1-2; Göttingen, 1992; ET London, 1994).
**— *Exodus 1–18* (ZBK; Zurich, 2012).
Albright, W.F., *Archaeology and the Religion of Israel* (Baltimore, 2nd ed., 1946).
— *Yahweh and the Gods of Canaan* (London, 1968).
Aldred, C., *The Egyptians* (London, rev. ed., 1984).
Alt, A., *Kleine Schriften zur Geschichte des Volkes Israel* (Munich, 1953–64).
— *Essays on Old Testament History and Religion* (Oxford, 1966).
Alter, R., *The Art of Biblical Narrative* (London, 1981).
Amiran, R., *Ancient Pottery of the Holy Land* (New Brunswick, 1970).
Andersen, F.I., *The Hebrew Verbless Clause in the Pentateuch* (JBLMS 14; Nashville and New York, 1970).
— *The Sentence in Biblical Hebrew* (Janua Linguarum, Ser. Pract. 231; The Hague, 1974).
* Anderson, R.T., and T. Giles, *The Samaritan Pentateuch: An Introduction to its Origin, History and Significance for Biblical Studies* (RBS 72: Atlanta, 2012).
Aurelius, E., *Der Fürbitter Israels: eine Studie zum Mosebild im Alten Testament* (CBOT 27; Stockholm, 1988).
Avi-Yonah, M., *The Holy Land from the Persian to the Arab Conquest (536 B.C. – A.D. 640)* (Grand Rapids, 1977).
*Baden, J.S., *J, E and the Redaction of the Pentateuch* (FAT 68; Tübingen, 2009).

— 'The Original Place of the Priestly Manna Story in Exodus 16', *ZAW* 122 (2010), pp. 491-504.
— *The Composition of the Pentateuch: Renewing the Documentary Hypothesis* (New Haven, 2012).
— 'From Joseph to Moses: The Narratives of Exodus 1–2', *VT* 62 (2012), pp. 133-58.
**Baentsch, B., *Exodus–Leviticus–Numeri* (HKAT; Göttingen, 1903).
Baillet, M., 'Corrections à l'édition de von Gall du Pentateuque samaritain', in W.C. Delsman (ed.), *Von Kanaan bis Kerala* (FS J.P.M. van der Ploeg; AOAT 21; Kevelaer, 1982), pp. 23-35.
Baly, D., *The Geography of the Bible* (London, 1957).
Barr, J., *The Semantics of Biblical Language* (Oxford, 1961).
*— *Comparative Philology and the Text of the Old Testament* (Oxford, 1968; enlarged ed. Winona Lake, 1987).
Barthélemy, D., *Les dévanciers d'Aquila* (VTSup 10; Leiden, 1963).
Beer, G., and O. Holtzmann (eds.), *Die Mischna: Text, Übersetzung und ausführliche Erklärung*, 2/3, *Pesachim* (Giessen, 1912).
**Beer, G., and K. Galling, *Exodus* (HAT; Tübingen, 1939).
Bekins, P., 'Non-Prototypical Uses of the Definite Article in Biblical Hebrew', *JSS* 58 (2013), pp. 225-40.
Bergsträsser, G., *Hebräische Grammatik*, 1–2 (Leipzig, 1918, 1929; repr. Hildesheim, 1962).
Berner, C., *Die Exoduserzählung: das literarische Werden einer Ursprungslegende Israels* (FAT 73; Tübingen, 2010).
Besters, A., 'L'expression "fils d'Israël" en *Ex.*, I-XIV. Un nouveau critère pour la distinction des sources', *RB* 74 (1967), pp. 321-55.
Beyerlin, W., *Herkunft und Geschichte der ältesten Sinaitraditionen* (Tübingen, 1961; ET Oxford, 1965).
Bietak, M., and I. Forstner-Müller, 'The Topography of New Kingdom Avaris and Per-Ramesses', in M. Collier and S. Snape (eds.), *Ramesside Studies in Honour of K.A. Kitchen* (Bolton, 2011), pp. 23-50.
*Blenkinsopp, J., *The Pentateuch: An Introduction to the First Five Books of the Bible* (New York, 1992).
Blum, E., *Die Komposition der Vätergeschichte* (WMANT 57; Neukirchen-Vluyn, 1984).
*— *Studien zur Komposition des Pentateuch* (BZAW 189; Berlin and New York, 1990).
— 'Die literarische Verbindung von Erzvätern und Exodus. Ein Gespräch mit neueren Endredaktionshypothesen', in Gertz et al. (eds.), *Abschied*, pp. 119-56.
Boyce, R.N., *The Cry to God in the Old Testament* (SBLDS 103; Atlanta, 1988).
Bright, J., *A History of Israel* (OTL; London, 1960).
Brock, S.P., 'An Early Interpretation of *pāsaḥ*: *'aggēn* in the Palestinian Targum', in J.A. Emerton and S.C. Reif (eds.), *Interpreting the Hebrew Bible* (FS E.I.J. Rosenthal; UCOP 32; Cambridge, 1982).

Brockelmann, C, *Hebräische Syntax* (Neukirchen-Vluyn, 1956).
*— *Syrische Grammatik* (Leipzig, 11th ed., 1968).
Brockington, L.H., *The Hebrew Text of the Old Testament: The Readings Adopted by the Translators of the New English Bible* (Oxford and Cambridge, 1973).
Brueggemann, W., *Theology of the Old Testament: Testimony, Dispute, Advocacy* (Minneapolis, 1997).
— and H.W. Wolff, *The Vitality of Old Testament Traditions* (Atlanta, 1975).
Cansdale, G.S., *Animals of Bible Lands* (Exeter, 1970).
**Carpenter, J.E., and Harford-Battersby, G. (eds.), *The Hexateuch according to the Revised Version arranged according to its Constituent Documents* (London, 1900).
Carr, D., *Reading the Fractures of Genesis: Historical and Literary Approaches* (Louisville, 1996).
**Cassuto, U., *A Commentary on the Book of Exodus* (Jerusalem, 1967 [Heb. 1951]).
Cazelles, H., 'Les localisations de l'Exode et la critique littéraire', *RB* 62 (1955), pp. 321-54, repr. in id., *Autour de l'Exode (Études)* (Sources Bibliques; Paris, 1987), pp. 189-231.
*Chester, A.N., *Divine Revelation and Divine Titles in the Pentateuchal Targumim* (TSAJ 14; Tübingen, 1986).
Charlesworth, J.H., *Graphic Concordance to the Dead Sea Scrolls* (Tübingen and Louisville, 1991).
— (ed.), *The Old Testament Pseudepigrapha* (London, 1983, 1985).
Childs, B.S., 'The Birth of Moses', *JBL* 84 (1965), pp. 109-22.
**— *Exodus* (OTL; London, 1974).
Clements, R.E., *God and Temple: The Idea of the Divine Presence in Ancient Israel* (Oxford, 1965).
**— *Exodus* (CBC; Cambridge, 1972).
Clifford, R.J., *The Cosmic Mountain in Canaan and the Old Testament* (HSM 4; Cambridge MA, 1972).
Clines, D.J.A., *The Theme of the Pentateuch* (JSOTSup 10; Sheffield, 1978; 2nd ed. 1997).
Coats, G.W., 'The Traditio-Historical Character of the Reed Sea Motif', *VT* 17 (1967), pp. 253-65.
— *Rebellion in the Wilderness* (Nashville, 1968).
— 'A Structural Transition in Exodus', *VT* 22 (1972), pp. 129-42.
— 'The Wilderness Itinerary', *CBQ* 34 (1972), pp. 135-52.
— *Moses: Heroic Man, Man of God* (JSOTSup 57; Sheffield, 1988).
**— *Exodus 1–18* (FOTL 2A; Grand Rapids, 1999).
Cody, A., *A History of Old Testament Priesthood* (AnBib 35; Rome, 1969).
Conybeare, F.C., and St.G. Stock, *Grammar of Septuagint Greek* (Boston, 1905; repr. Peabody MA, 1988), pp. 143-99 (introduction, Greek text and commentary on Exod. 1.8–15.21).

Cook, S.L., 'The Tradition of Mosaic Judges', in id. and S.C. Winter (eds.), *On the Way to Nineveh: Studies in Honor of George M. Landes* (ASORB 4; Atlanta, 1999), pp. 286-315.

Cross, F.M., *The Ancient Library of Qumran and Modern Biblical Studies* (London, 1958; 2nd ed. 1961; 3rd ed. Sheffield, 1995).

— *Canaanite Myth and Hebrew Epic: Essays in the History of the Religion of Israel* (Cambridge MA, 1973).

— and D.N. Freedman, *Studies in Ancient Yahwistic Poetry* (SBLDS 21; Missoula, [1950,] 1975).

Crown, A.D., et al. (eds.), *A Companion to Samaritan Studies* (Tübingen, 1993).

— *Samaritan Scribes and Manuscripts* (TSAJ 80; Tübingen, 2001).

Crüsemann, F., *Studien zur Formgeschichte von Hymnus und Danklied in Israel* (WMANT 32; Neukirchen, 1969).

— *Die Tora: Theologie und Sozialgeschichte des alttestamentlichen Gesetzes* (Munich, 1992; ET Minneapolis and Edinburgh, 1996).

Culley, R.C., *Studies in the Structure of Biblical Narrative* (Semeia Supplements; Philadelphia and Missoula, 1976).

Davies, G.F., *Israel in Egypt. Reading Exodus 1–2* (JSOTSup 135; Sheffield, 1992).

Davies, G.I., 'The Wilderness Itineraries: A Comparative Study', *TynB* 25 (1974), pp. 46-81.

*— *The Way of the Wilderness: A Geographical Study of the Wilderness Itineraries in the Old Testament* (SOTSMS 5; Cambridge, 1979).

— 'The Wilderness Itineraries and the Composition of the Pentateuch', *VT* 33 (1983), pp. 1-13.

— 'The Composition of the Book of Exodus: Reflections on the Theses of Erhard Blum', in M.V. Fox et al. (eds.), *Texts, Temples and Traditions: A Tribute to Menahem Haran* (Winona Lake, 1996), pp. 71-85.

— 'K<small>D</small> in Exodus. An Assessment of E. Blum's Proposal', in M. Vervenne and J. Lust (eds.), *Deuteronomy and Deuteronomic Literature* (FS C.H.W. Brekelmans; BETL 133; Leuven, 1997), pp. 407-20.

— 'Was There an Exodus?', in J. Day (ed.), *In Search of Pre-Exilic Israel* (JSOTSup 406; London, 2004), pp. 23-40.

— 'The Exegesis of the Divine Name in Exodus', in R.P. Gordon (ed.), *The God of Israel* (UCOP 64; Cambridge, 2007), pp. 139-56.

— 'The Transition from Genesis to Exodus', in K.J. Dell et al. (eds.), *Genesis, Isaiah and Psalms: A Festschrift to Honour Professor John Emerton for his Eightieth Birthday* (VTSup 135; Leiden, 2010), pp. 59-78.

— 'The Passover as the New Year Festival in P', in J. Kotjatko-Reeb et al. (eds.), *Nichts Neues unter der Sonne? Zeitvorstellungen im Alten Testament* (FS E. Waschke; BZAW 450; Berlin and Boston, 2014), pp. 157-70.

Desilva, D.A., 'Five Papyrus Fragments of Greek Exodus', *BIOSCS* 40 (2007), pp. 1-31.

**Dillmann, A., *Die Bücher Exodus und Leviticus* (2nd ed. of KEH; Leipzig, 1881; 3rd ed. with V. Ryssel, 1897).
Dines, J.M., *The Septuagint* (London, 2004).
*Dotan, A., *Torah, Nevi'im uKhetuvim. Biblia Hebraica Leningradensia* (Peabody, MA, rev. ed., 2001 [1st ed. Tel Aviv, 1973]).
Dozeman, T.D., *God at War: Power in the Exodus Tradition* (New York and Oxford, 1996).
**— *Exodus* (Eerdmans Critical Commentary; Grand Rapids, 2009).
— and K. Schmid (eds.), *A Farewell to the Yahwist? The Composition of the Pentateuch in Recent European Interpretation* (SBLSS 34; Atlanta, 2006).
— et al. (eds.), *The Pentateuch: International Perspectives on Current Research* (FAT 78; Tübingen, 2011).
— et al. (eds.), *The Book of Exodus: Composition, Reception and Interpretation* (VTSup 164; Leiden, 2014).
Driver, G.R., *Problems of the Hebrew Verbal System* (Edinburgh, 1936).
Driver, S.R., *A Treatise on the use of the tenses in Hebrew and some other syntactical questions* (3rd ed; Oxford, 1892).
**— *The Book of Exodus* (CBSC; Cambridge, 1911).
— *An Introduction to the Literature of the Old Testament* (Edinburgh, 9th ed., 1913).
— *Notes on the Hebrew Text of the Books of Samuel* (Oxford, 2nd ed., 1913).
**Durham, J.I., *Exodus* (WBC; Waco, 1987).
*Ehrlich, A.B., *Randglossen zur Hebräischen Bibel: textkritisches, sprachliches und sachliches*, 1 (Leipzig, 1908).
*Eissfeldt, O., *Hexateuch-Synopse. Die Erzählung der fünf Bücher Mose und des Buches Josua mit dem Anfange des Richterbuches* (Leipzig, 1922; repr. Darmstadt, 1987).
— *Baal Zaphon, Zeus Kasios und der Durchzug der Israeliten durchs Meer* (Halle, 1932).
Elfick, B., 'The Staff of Moses in Early Jewish Literature: A Study in Exegetical Creativity' (unpublished MPhil. dissertation, University of Cambridge, 2005).
Evans, T.V., *Verbal Syntax in the Greek Pentateuch: Natural Greek Usage and Hebrew Interference* (Oxford, 2001).
Fichtner, J., 'Die etymologische Ätiologie in den Namengebungen der geschichtlichen Bücher des Alten Testaments', *VT* 6 (1956), pp. 372-96.
Field, F., *Origenis Hexapla quae supersunt* (Oxford, 1875).
Fischer, G., *Jahwe Unser Gott: Sprache, Aufbau und Erzähltechnik in der Berufung des Mose (Ex 3–4)* (OBO 91; Freiburg and Göttingen, 1989).
Fishbane, M., *Biblical Interpretation in Ancient Israel* (Oxford, 1985).
*Flesher, P.V.M., and B.D. Chilton, *The Targums: A Critical Introduction* (Waco, 2011).
Floss, J.P., *Jahwe dienen – Göttern dienen* (BBB 45; Bonn, 1975).
*Fohrer, G., *Überlieferung und Geschichte des Exodus: eine Analyse von Ex 1–15* (BZAW 91; Berlin, 1964).

Fränkel, D., *The Murmuring Stories of the Priestly School: A Retrieval of Ancient Sacerdotal Lore* (VTSup 89; Leiden, 2002).
Frerichs, E.S., and L.H. Lesco (eds.), *Exodus: The Egyptian Evidence* (Winona Lake, 1997).
Freytag, G.W. (ed.), *Lexicon Arabico-Latinum* (4 vols.; Halle, 1830–37).
Friedman, R.E., *Who Wrote the Bible?* (New York, 1987; 2nd ed. 1997).
— *The Hidden Book of the Bible* (San Francisco, 1998).
*Fritsch, C.T., *The Anti-Anthropomorphisms of the Greek Pentateuch* (Princeton, 1943).
*Fritz, V., *Israel in der Wüste* (MTS 7; Marburg, 1970).
Fuss, W., *Die Deuteronomistische Pentateuchredaktion in Exodus 3–17* (BZAW 126; Berlin, 1972).
*von Gall, A., *Der hebräische Pentateuch der Samaritaner* (Giessen, 1918).
Gerhards, M., *Die Aussetzungsgeschichte des Mose* (WMANT 109; Neukirchen-Vluyn, 2006).
Germany, S., *The Exodus-Conquest Narrative: The Composition of the Non-Priestly Narrative in Exodus–Joshua* (FAT 115; Tübingen, 2017).
*Gertz, J.C., *Tradition und Redaktion in der Exoduserzählung. Untersuchungen zur Endredaktion des Pentateuch* (FRLANT 186; Göttingen, 2000).
— et al. (eds.), *Abschied vom Jahwisten: Die Komposition des Hexateuch in der jüngsten Diskussion* (BZAW 315; Berlin and New York, 2002).
Gesenius, W., *Thesaurus Philologicus Criticus Linguae Hebraeae et Chaldaeae Veteris Testamenti* (Leipzig, 1835–58).
Gesundheit (Bar-On), S., *Three Times a Year: Studies on Festival Legislation in the Pentateuch* (FAT 82; Tübingen, 2012).
Gibson, J.C.L., *Davidson's Introductory Hebrew Grammar – Syntax* (Edinburgh, 4th ed., 1994).
Glessmer, U., *Einleitung in die Targume zum Pentateuch* (TSAJ 48; Tübingen, 1995).
Gnuse, R.K., *The Elohist: A Seventh-Century Theological Tradition* (Eugene, 2017).
Gogel, S.L. *A Grammar of Epigraphic Hebrew* (RBS 23; Atlanta, 1998).
*Goldingay, J., and D.F. Payne, *Isaiah 40–55* (ICC; London, 2006).
*Graupner, A., *Der Elohist: Gegenwart und Wirksamkeit des transzendenten Gottes in der Geschichte* (WMANT 97; Neukirchen-Vluyn, 2002).
Greenberg, M., *Understanding Exodus: A Holistic Commentary on Exodus 1–11* (New York, 1969; 2nd ed. Eugene, 2013).
*Gressmann, H., *Mose und seine Zeit: ein Kommentar zu den Mosesagen* (FRLANT 18; Göttingen, 1913).
— *Die Anfänge Israels (von 2. Mosis bis Richter und Ruth)* (SAT; Göttingen, 1914).
Grünwaldt, K., *Exil und Identität: Beschneidung, Passa und Sabbat in der Priesterschrift* (BBB 85; Frankfurt, 1992).

Gunkel, H., *The Legends of Genesis* (Chicago, 1901; repr. New York, 1964: ET of the Introduction to *Genesis* [1st ed., 1901]).
— *Genesis* (HKAT; Göttingen, 3rd ed., 1910).
— *Einleitung in die Psalmen: Die Gattungen der religiösen Lyrik Israels* (Göttingen, 1933).
Haarmann, V., *YHWH-Verehrer der Völker* (ATANT 91; Zurich, 2008).
*Haran, M., *Temples and Temple-Service in Ancient Israel* (Oxford, 1978).
Harel, M., *Mas‘e Sinay* (Heb.; Tel Aviv, 1968).
*Hatch, E., and H.A. Redpath, *A Concordance to the Septuagint and the Other Greek Versions of the Old Testament* (Oxford, 1897, 1906).
Hayward, C.T.R., *Divine Name and Presence: The Memra* (Totowa, 1981).
**Heinisch, P., *Das Buch Exodus* (HSAT; Bonn, 1934).
Herrmann, S., *Israels Aufenthalt in Ägypten* (SBS 40; Stuttgart, 1970; ET SBT 2/27, London, 1973).
Hoffmeier, J.K., *Israel in Egypt* (New York and Oxford, 1997).
— *Ancient Israel in Sinai: The Evidence for the Authenticity of the Wilderness Tradition* (New York, 2005).
**Holzinger, H., *Exodus* (KHAT; Tübingen, 1900).
Houston, W.J., *The Pentateuch* (London, 2013).
**Houtman, C., *Exodus* (Commentar op het Oude Testament; Kampen, 1986–96; cited from the ET, *Exodus*, 1 [HCOT; Kampen, 1993] and *Exodus*, 2 [HCOT; Kampen, 1996]).
— *Der Pentateuch. Die Geschichte seiner Erforschung neben einer Auswertung* (CBET 9; Kampen, 1994).
Humphreys, C.J., *The Miracles of Exodus* (London, 2003).
Hupfeld, H., *Die Quellen der Genesis und die Art ihrer Zusammensetzung* (Berlin, 1853).
**Hyatt, J.P., *Exodus* (NCB; London, 1971).
[Ibn Ezra, Abraham] *Abraham Ibn Ezras Langer Kommentar zum Buch Exodus*, ed. and tr. D.U. Rottzoll (Studia Judaica 17/1-2; Berlin and New York, 2000).
Jackson, B.S., *Wisdom-Laws: A Study of the* Mishpatim *of Exodus 21:1–22:16* (Oxford, 2006).
— 'Law in the Ninth Century: Jehoshaphat's "Judicial Reform"', in H.G.M. Williamson (ed.), *Understanding the History of Ancient Israel* (Oxford, 2007), pp. 369-97.
**Jacob, B., *Das Buch Exodus* [1943] (Stuttgart, 1997; the ET, *The Second Book of the Bible: Exodus* [Hoboken NJ, 1992], is a little paraphrastic).
Jacobson, H., *The Exagoge of Ezekiel* (Cambridge, 1983).
**Janzen, J.G., *Exodus* (Louisville, 1997).
Jarvis, C.S., *Yesterday and Today in Sinai* (Edinburgh, 1931).
*Jastrow, M., *A Dictionary of the Targumim, the Talmud Babli and Yerushalmi, and the Midrashic Literature* (London, 1903).
Jenks, A.W., *The Elohist and North Israelite Traditions* (SBLMS 22; Missoula, 1977).

Jellicoe, S., *The Septuagint in Modern Study* (Oxford, 1968).
Jeremias, J., *Theophanie: Die Geschichte einer alttestamentlichen Gattung* (WMANT 10: Neukirchen, 1965).
Johnstone, W., *Exodus* (OTG; Sheffield, 1990).
— *Chronicles and Exodus: An Analogy and its Application* (JSOTSup 275; Sheffield, 1998).
Joosten, J., *The Verbal System of Biblical Hebrew. A New Synthesis elaborated on the basis of Classical Prose* (JBS 10; Jerusalem, 2012).
Joüon, P. *Grammaire de l'hébreu biblique* (Rome, 1923).
Jülicher, A., *Die Quellen von Exodus I-VII,7. Ein Beitrag zur Hexateuchfrage* (diss. phil. Halle, 1880).
— 'Die Quellen von Exodus VII,8-XXIV,11. Ein Beitrag zur Hexateuchfrage', *JPTh* 8 (1882), pp. 79-127, 272-315.
Kahle, P.E., *Die Masoreten des Ostens: die ältesten punktierten handschriften des Alten Testaments und der Targume* (BWAT 15; Leipzig, 1913).
— *Die Masoreten des Westens* (2 vols., BWAT 33, 50; Stuttgart, 1927, 1930).
— *The Cairo Geniza* (Oxford, 1947; 2nd ed., 1959).
Kartveit, M., *The Origins of the Samaritans* (VTSup 128; Leiden, 2009).
Kaufmann, Y., *The Religion of Israel: From its Beginnings to the Babylonian Exile* (Chicago, 1960 [ET (abridged) of *Toldot ha-emunah ha-Yiśra'elit* (8 vols., Jerusalem, 1937–56)].
Keel, O., *Die Welt der altorientalischen Bildsymbolik und das Alte Testament: Am Beispiel der Psalmen* (Zurich and Neukirchen, 1972; ET New York and London, 1978).
**Keil, C.F., *Biblischer Commentar über die Bücher Mose's* (Leipzig, 1861–62, ET Edinburgh, 1864–65).
Kessler, R., *Die Querverweise im Pentateuch. Überlieferungsgeschichtliche Untersuchung der expliziten Querverbindungen innerhalb des vorpriesterlichen Pentateuchs* (diss. theol., Heidelberg, 1972; BEATAJ 59, Frankfurt, 2015).
King, P.J., and L.E. Stager, *Life in Biblical Israel* (Library of Ancient Israel; Louisville, 2001).
Kitchen, K.A., *Pharaoh Triumphant* (Warminster, 1982).
— 'From the Brickfields of Egypt', *TynB* 27 (1976), pp. 137-47.
*Klein, M., *Genizah Manuscripts of the Palestinian Targum to the Pentateuch* (Cincinnati, 1986).
— *Michael Klein on the Targums: Collected Essays 1972–2002* (ed. A. Shinan et al.; Leiden, 2011).
Klopfenstein, M.A., *Die Lüge nach dem Alten Testament: ihr Begriff, ihre Bedeutung und ihre Beurteilung* (Zurich, 1964).
Knierim, R., 'Exodus 18 und die Neuordnung der mosaischen Gerichtsbarkeit', *ZAW* 73 (1961), pp. 146-71.
**Knobel, A., *Die Bücher Exodus und Leviticus* (KEH; Leipzig, 1857).
— *Die Bücher Numeri, Deuteronomium und Josua* (KEH; Leipzig, 1861).

*Knohl, I., *The Sanctuary of Silence: The Priestly Torah and the Holiness School* (Minneapolis, 1995).
Koch, K., 'Šaddaj. Zum Verhältnis zwischen israelitischer Monolatrie und nordwest-semitischem Polytheismus', *VT* 26 (1976), pp. 299-332.
*König, E., *Historisch-kritisches Lehrgebäude der hebräischen Sprache* (Leipzig, 1881–97).
*Kohata, F., *Jahwist und Priesterschrift in Exodus 3–14* (BZAW 166; Berlin and New York, 1986).
*Koster, M.D., *The Peshiṭta of Exodus: The Development of its Text in the Course of Fifteen Centuries* (Amsterdam, 1977).
*Kratz, R.G., *Die Komposition der erzählenden Bücher des Alten Testaments* (UTB 2157; Göttingen, 2000).
Kraus, H.-J., *Gottesdienst in Israel. Grundriss einer Geschichte des alttestamentlichen Gottesdienstes* (Munich, 2nd ed., 1962; ET Oxford, 1966).
— *Psalmen* (BKAT; Neukirchen, 5th ed., 1978).
Kraus, M.A., 'Jerome, the Book of Exodus and the World of Late Antiquity', in L.M. Teugels and R. Ulmer (eds.), *Midrash and Context* (Judaism in Context 5; Piscataway, 2007), pp. 17-37.
— *Jewish, Christian and Classical Exegetical Traditions in Jerome's Translation of the Book of Exodus* (VCSup 141; Leiden, 2017).
Kuenen, A., *Historisch-kritisch onderzoek naar het ontstaan en de verzameling van de boeken des ouden verbonds* (Leiden, 3rd ed., 1861–65).
— *A Historico-Critical Inquiry into the Origin and Composition of the Hexateuch* (London, 1886).
Laaf, P., *Die Pascha-Feier Israels: eine literarkritische und überlieferungsgeschichtliche Studie* (BBB 36; Bonn, 1970).
Lambert, W.G., and A.R. Millard, *Atra-Ḥasīs: The Babylonian Story of the Flood* (Oxford, 1969).
Lane, E.W., *Arabic–English Lexicon: derived from the best and most copious eastern sources* (London and Edinburgh, 1863–93; repr. Cambridge, 1984).
Lamberty-Zielinski, H., *Das 'Schilfmeer': Herkunft, Bedeutung und Funktion eines alttestamentlichen Exodusbegriffs* (BBB 78; Frankfurt, 1993).
*Lange, A., *Handbuch der Textfunde vom Toten Meer. 1: Die Handschriften biblischer Bücher von Qumran und den anderen Fundorten* (Tübingen, 2009).
— and E. Tov (eds.), *Textual History of the Bible*, 1A, *The Hebrew Bible: Overview Articles* (Leiden, 2016); 1B, *The Hebrew Bible: Pentateuch, Former and Latter Prophets* (Leiden, 2017).
*Le Boulluec, A., and P. Sandevoir, *L'Exode* (BAlex 2; Paris, 1989).
Lee, J.A.L., *A Lexical Study of the Septuagint Version of the Pentateuch* (SCS 14; Chico, 1983).
*Lemmelijn, B., *A Plague of Texts? A Text-Critical Study of the So-Called 'Plagues Narrative' in Exodus 7:14–11.10* (OTS 56; Leiden, 2009).
*Levin, C., *Der Jahwist* (FRLANT 157; Göttingen, 1993).

Levinson, B.M., *"The Right Chorale": Studies in Biblical Law and Interpretation* (FAT 54; Tübingen, 2008, repr. Winona Lake, 2011).
Levy, J., *Chaldäisches Wörterbuch über die Targumim und einen grossen Theil des rabbinischen Schriftthums* (Leipzig, 1867–68).
Lipschitz, O., *Sinai (Part I)* (Tel Aviv, 1978).
Lohfink, N., *Das Hauptgebot: Eine Untersuchung literarischer Einleitungsfragen zu Dtn 5–11* (AnBib 20; Rome, 1963).
— '"Ich bin Jahwe, dein Arzt" (Ex 15,26): Gott, Gesellschaft und menschliche Gesundheit in einer nachexilischen Pentateuchbearbeitung', in H. Merklein and E. Zenger (eds.), *'Ich will euer Gott werden': Beispiele biblischen Redens von Gott* (SBS 100; Stuttgart, 1981), pp. 11-73; ET in Lohfink, *Theology of the Pentateuch: Themes of the Priestly Narrative and Deuteronomy* (Minneapolis, 1994), pp. 35-95.
Longacre, D.G., 'A Contextualized Approach to the Hebrew Dead Sea Scrolls containing Exodus' (doctoral dissertation, Birmingham, 2015; forthcoming in STDJ).
Longman, T., *Fictional Akkadian Autobiography: A Generic and Comparative Study* (Winona Lake, 1991).
Loretz, O., *Habiru-Hebräer* (BZAW 160; Berlin and New York, 1984).
*Lust, J., et al., *A Greek–English Lexicon of the Septuagint* (Stuttgart, 1992, 1996).
McCarthy, C. (ed.), *Deuteronomy* (BHQ 5; Stuttgart, 2007).
McEvenue, S., *The Narrative Style of the Priestly Writer* (AnBib 50; Rome, 1971).
**McNeile, A.H., *The Book of Exodus* (Westminster Commentaries; London, 2nd ed., 1917).
Maiberger, P., *Das Manna: Eine literarische, etymologische und naturkundliche Untersuchung* (ÄUAT 6; Wiesbaden, 1983).
*Mandelkern, S., *Veteris Testamenti Concordantiae Hebraicae atque Chaldaicae* (Jerusalem and Tel Aviv, 9th ed., 1971).
Marx, A., 'La généalogie d'Exode vi 14-25: sa forme, sa fonction', *VT* 45 (1995), pp. 318-36.
Mayes, A.D.H., *Deuteronomy* (NCB; London, 1979).
*Mayser, E., *Grammatik der griechischen Papyri aus der Ptolemäerzeit* (Berlin, 1923–38).
Meyer, E., *Die Israeliten und ihre Nachbarstämme* (Halle, 1906).
*Meyer, R., *Hebräische Grammatik* (Berlin, 3rd ed., 1966–72).
Meyers, C.L., 'Of Drums and Damsels: Women's Performance in Ancient Israel', *BA* 54 (1991), pp. 16-27 (an adapted version ['Miriam the Magician'] appeared in A. Brenner [ed.], *A Feminist Companion to Exodus to Deuteronomy* [Sheffield, 1994], pp. 207-30).
**— *Exodus* (NCBC; Cambridge and New York, 2005).
Milgrom, J., *Leviticus 1–16: A New Translation with Introduction and Commentary* (AB 3; New York, 1991).
— *Leviticus 17–22: A New Translation with Introduction and Commentary* (AB 3A; New York, 2000).

— *Leviticus 23–27: A New Translation with Introduction and Commentary* (AB 3B; New York, 2001).
Miller, P.D., *The Divine Warrior in Early Israel* (HSM 5; Cambridge MA, 1973).
Moberly, R.W.L., *The Old Testament of the Old Testament: Patriarchal Narratives and Mosaic Yahwism* (OBT; Minneapolis, 1992).
Montgomery, J.A., *The Book of Daniel* (ICC; Edinburgh, 1927).
*Moscati, S., *An Introduction to the Comparative Grammar of the Semitic Languages* (Wiesbaden, 1964).
Mowinckel, S., 'Drive and/or Ride in O.T.', *VT* 12 (1962), pp. 278-99.
Muraoka, T., *Emphatic Words and Structures in Biblical Hebrew* (Jerusalem, 1985).
*— *A Greek–English Lexicon of the Septuagint, chiefly of the Pentateuch and the Twelve Prophets* (Leuven, 2002).
Nicholson, E.W., *Exodus and Sinai in History and Tradition* (Oxford, 1973).
*— *The Pentateuch in the Twentieth Century: The Legacy of Julius Wellhausen* (Oxford, 1998).
Nihan, C., *From Priestly Torah to Pentateuch: A Study in the Composition of the Book of Leviticus* (FAT 2, 25; Tübingen, 2007).
— 'The Priestly Covenant, its Reinterpretations, and the Composition of "P"', in Shechtman and Baden (eds.), *Strata*, pp. 87-134.
Noth, M., *Die israelitischen Personennamen im Rahmen der gemeinsemitischen Namengebung* (BWANT 3/10; Stuttgart, 1928).
— *Überlieferungsgeschichte des Pentateuch* (Stuttgart, 1948).
— *Geschichte Israels* (Göttingen, 2nd ed., 1954, ET 1960).
**— *Das zweite Buch Mose, Exodus* (ATD; Göttingen, 1959; ET *Exodus* [OTL; London, 1962]).
— *Das vierte Buch Mose, Numeri* (ATD; Göttingen, 1966; ET *Numbers* [OTL; London, 1968]).
O'Connell, K.J., *The Theodotionic Revision of the Book of Exodus* (HSM 3; Cambridge, MA, 1972).
— 'The List of Seven Peoples in Canaan: A Fresh Analysis', in H.O. Thompson (ed.), *The Answers Lie Below* (FS L.E. Toombs; Lanham and London, 1984), pp. 221-41.
Otto, E., 'Die nachpriesterschrifliche Pentateuchredaktion im Buch Exodus', in Vervenne (ed.), *Studies*, pp. 61-111.
— 'Forschungen zur Priesterschrift', *TR* 62 (1997), pp. 1-50.
— 'Innerbiblische Exegese im Heiligkeitsgesetz Levitikus 17–26', in H.-J. Fabry and H.-W. Jüngling (eds.), *Levitikus als Buch* (BBB 119; Berlin, 1999), pp. 125-96.
Palmer, E.H., *The Desert of the Exodus* (Cambridge, 1871).
Paran, M., *Forms of the Priestly Style in the Pentateuch: Patterns, Linguistic Usages, Syntactic Structures* (Heb.; Jerusalem, 1989).
Penkower, J.S., *New Evidence for the Pentateuch Text in the Aleppo Codex* (Heb.; Ramat Gan, 1992).

Perlitt, L., *Bundestheologie im Alten Testament* (WMANT 36; Neukirchen, 1969).
*Petit, F., *La chaîne sur l'Exode: Édition intégrale* (TEG 9-11; Leuven, 1999, 2000, 2001).
Polzin, R., *Late Biblical Hebrew: Toward an Historical Typology of Biblical Hebrew Prose* (HSM 12; Missoula, 1976).
Propp, W.H.C., 'The Priestly Source Recovered Intact?', *VT* 46 (1996), pp. 458-78.
**— *Exodus 1–18: A New Translation with Introduction and Commentary* (AB 2; New York, 1999).
— *Exodus 19–40: A New Translation with Introduction and Commentary* (AB 2A; New York, 2006).
Pummer, R., 'The Greek Bible and the Samaritans', *REJ* 157 (1998), pp. 269-358.
*Qimron, E., *The Hebrew of the Dead Sea Scrolls* (HSS 29; Atlanta, 1986).
von Rad, G., *Die Priesterschrift im Hexateuch, literarisch untersucht und theologisch gewertet* (BWANT 4/13; Stuttgart, 1934).
— *Der heilige Krieg im alten Israel* (Zurich, 1951).
— *Das erste Buch Mose, Genesis* (ATD; Göttingen, 1956; ET 2nd ed., London, 1963).
Rainey, A.F., *Canaanite in the Amarna Tablets* (HbO 1/25; Leiden, 1996).
[Rashbam] *Rashbam's Commentary on Exodus: An Annotated Translation*, ed. and tr. M.I. Lockshin (Brown Judaic Studies 310; Atlanta, 1997).
[Rashi] *Pentateuch with Targum Onkelos, Haphtaroth and Rashi's Commentary*, with ET and notes by M. Rosenbaum and A.M. Silbermann; *Exodus* (Jerusalem, 1930).
Rendtorff, R., *Die Gesetze in der Priesterschrift: eine gattungsgeschichtliche Untersuchung* (FRLANT NF 44; Göttingen, 1954).
— 'Der "Jahwist" als Theologe? Zur Dilemma der Pentateuchkritik', in J.A. Emerton (ed.), *Congress Volume: Edinburgh* (VTSup 28; Leiden, 1975), pp. 158-66; ET *JSOT* 3 (1977), pp. 2-10.
— *Das überlieferungsgeschichtliche Problem des Pentateuch* (BZAW 147; Berlin and New York, 1977; ET JSOTSup 89; Sheffield, 1990).
— *Die Bundesformel* (SBS 160; Stuttgart, 1995, ET Edinburgh, 1998).
Renz, J., and W. Röllig, *Handbuch der althebräischen Epigraphik* (Darmstadt, 1995, 2003).
Reymond, E.D., *Qumran Hebrew: An Overview of Orthography, Phonology and Morphology* (RBS 76; Atlanta, 2014).
Roberts, B.J., *The Old Testament Text and Versions* (Cardiff, 1951).
Robinson, E., *Biblical Researches in Palestine, Mount Sinai and Arabia Petraea: A Journal of Travels in the year 1838* (London, 1841).
Rösel, M., 'The Reading and Translation of the Divine Name in the Masoretic Tradition and the Greek Pentateuch', *JSOT* 31 (2007), pp. 411-28.
Rothenberg, B., *God's Wilderness: Discoveries in Sinai* (London, 1961).
*Rudolph, W., *Der 'Elohist' von Exodus bis Josua* (BZAW 68; Berlin, 1938).

Ruprecht, E., 'Stellung und Bedeutung der Erzählung vom Mannawunder (Ex 16) im Aufbau der Priesterschrift', *ZAW* 86 (1974), pp. 269-307.

*Sadaqa, A., and R., *Jewish Version and Samaritan Version of the Pentateuch* (Tel Aviv, 1961–65).

Saebø, M., 'Offenbarung oder Verhüllung? Bemerkungen zum Charakter des Gottesnamens in Ex 3, 13-15', in J. Jeremias and L. Perlitt (eds.), *Die Botschaft und die Boten* (FS H.W. Wolff; Neukirchen, 1981), pp. 43-55.

— (ed.), *Hebrew Bible/Old Testament: The History of its Interpretation*, 1/1: *Antiquity* (Göttingen, 1996); 3/1: *The Nineteenth Century* (Göttingen, 2013).

Salvesen, A., *Symmachus in the Pentateuch* (JSSM 15; Manchester, 1991).

— 'Midrash in Greek? An Exploration of the Versions of Aquila and Symmachus in Exodus', in J.K. Aitken et al., *On Stone and Scroll* (FS G.I. Davies; BZAW 420; Berlin and Boston, 2011), pp. 523-36.

Sanders, P., 'The Ashkar-Gilson Manuscript: Remnant of a Proto-Masoretic Model Scroll of the Torah', *JHebS* 14/7 (2014), pp. 1-25.

Sanderson, J.E., *An Exodus Scroll from Qumran: 4QpaleoExod^M and the Samaritan Tradition* (HSS 30; Atlanta, 1986).

Särkio, P., *Exodus und Salomo: Erwägungen zur verdeckten Salomokritik anhand von Ex 1–2; 5; 15 und 32* (Helsinki and Göttingen, 1998).

**Sarna, N.M., *Exodus* (JPS Torah Commentary; Philadelphia, 1991).

Sawyer, J.F.A., *Semantics in Biblical Research: New Methods of Defining Hebrew Words for Salvation* (SBT 2/24; London, 1972).

Schaper, J.L.W., *Priester und Leviten in achämenidischen Juda: Studien zur Kult- und Sozialgeschichte Israels in persischer Zeit* (FAT 31; Tübingen, 2000).

**Scharbert, J., *Exodus* (Neuer Echter Bibel; Würzburg, 1989).

Schart, A., *Mose und Israel im Konflikt: eine redaktionsgeschichtliche Studie zu den Wüstenerzählungen* (OBO 98; Freiburg and Göttingen, 1990).

Shechtman, S. and J.S. Baden (eds.), *The Strata of the Priestly Writings* (AThANT 95; Zurich, 2009).

*Schmid, K., *Erzväter und Exodus: Untersuchungen zur doppelten Begründung der Ursprünge Israels innerhalb der Geschichtsbücher des Alten Testaments* (WMANT 81; Neukirchen, 1999; ET Winona Lake, 2010).

*Schmidt, L., 'Überlegungen zum Jahwisten', *EvTh* 37 (1977), pp. 230-47.

— *Beobachtungen zu der Plagenerzählung in Exodus VII 14 – XI 10* (Studia Biblica 4; Leiden, 1990).

— *Studien zur Priesterschrift* (BZAW 214; Berlin and New York, 1993).

— 'Diachrone und Synchrone Exegese am Beispiel von Exodus 3–4', in his *Gesammelte Aufsätze zum Pentateuch* (BZAW 263; Berlin, 1998), pp. 224-50.

— 'Die vorpriesterliche Verbindung von Erzvätern und Exodus durch die Josefsgeschichte (Gen 37; 39–50*') und Exodus 1', *ZAW* 124 (2012), pp. 19-37.

**Schmidt, W.H., *Exodus* (BKAT 2/1-2; Neukirchen-Vluyn, 1974–2019).

— *Exodus, Sinai und Mose* (Erträge der Forschung 191; Darmstadt, 1983).

— *Einführung in das Alte Testament* (Berlin and New York, 5th ed., 1995; ET of the 2nd ed., London, 1984).

Schmitt, H.-C., '"Priesterliches" und "prophetisches" Geschichtsverständnis in der Meerwundererzählung Ex 13,17–14,31. Beobachtungen zur Endredaktion des Pentateuch', in A.H.J. Gunneweg and O. Kaiser (eds.), *Textgemäss. Aufsätze und Beiträge zur Hermeneutik des Alten Testament* (FS E. Würthwein; Göttingen, 1979), pp. 139-55.

— 'Redaktion des Pentateuch im Geiste der Prophetie: Beobachtungen zur Bedeutung der "Glaubens"-Thematik innerhalb der Theologie des Pentateuch', *VT* 32 (1982), pp. 170-89.

— 'Die Geschichte vom Sieg über die Amalekiter Ex. 17,8-16 als theologische Lehrerzählung', *ZAW* 102 (1990), pp. 335-44.

— 'Das sogenannte vorprophetische Berufungsschema. Zur "geistigen Heimat" des Berufungsformulars von Ex 3,9-12; Jdc 6, 11-24 und I Sam 9,1–10,16', *ZAW* 104 (1992), pp. 202-16.

— 'Die Jahwenamenoffenbarung in Ex 6,2-9* und die zwei Zeiten der Landgabe. Zum Ende der Priesterschrift und zu ihrem Zeitverständnis', in J. Kotjatko-Reeb et al., *Nichts Neues unter der Sonne? Zeitvorstellungen im Alten Testament* (FS E. Waschke; BZAW 450; Berlin and Boston, 2014), pp. 137-55.

Schmitt, R., *Exodus und Passa* (OBO 7; Freiburg and Göttingen, 2nd ed., 1982).

*Schorch, S., 'A Critical *editio maior* of the Samaritan Pentateuch: State of Research, Principles and Problems', *HBAI* 2 (2013), pp. 100-120.

Screnock, J., *Traductor Scriptor: The Old Greek Translation of Exodus 1–14 as Scribal Activity* (VTSup 174; Leiden, 2017).

Seebass, H., 'Pentateuch', in *TRE*, 26 (1997), pp. 185-209.

Segal, J.B., *The Hebrew Passover: from the earliest times to A.D. 70* (London, 1963).

Segal, M.H., *A Grammar of Mishnaic Hebrew* (Oxford, 1927).

Siebert-Hommes, J., *Let the Daughters Live! The Literary Architecture of Exodus 1–2* (BibInt 37; Leiden, 1998).

Sirat, C., *Les papyrus en caractères hébraïques trouvées en Égypte* (Paris, 1985).

*Sivan, D., *A Grammar of the Ugaritic Language* (HbO 1/28; Leiden, 1997).

Ska, J.-L., *Le passage de la mer: étude de la construction, du style et de la symbolique d'Ex 14,1-31* (AnBib 109; Rome, 1986).

Smend, R., *Die Erzählung des Hexateuch: auf ihre Quellen untersucht* (Berlin, 1912).

Smend, R., *Jahwekrieg und Stämmeverband* (FRLANT 84; Göttingen, 1963).

Smith, J. Payne, *A Compendious Syriac Dictionary* (Oxford, 1903).

Smith, M.S., *The Pilgrimage Pattern in Exodus* (JSOTSup 239; Sheffield, 1997).

Sokoloff, M., *Dictionary of Jewish Palestinian Aramaic of the Byzantine Period* (Ramat Gan, 1990; 2nd ed. Ramat Gan and Baltimore, 2002).

Stanley, A.P., *Sinai and Palestine* (London, 1858).

Steingrimsson, S.Ö., *Vom Zeichen zur Geschichte. Eine literar- und formkritische Untersuchung von Ex 6,28–11,10* (CBOT 14; Lund, 1979).

Stevenson, W.B., *Grammar of Palestinian Jewish Aramaic* (Oxford, 2nd ed., 1962).

*Swete, H.B., *An Introduction to the Old Testament in Greek* (Cambridge, 2nd ed., 1902).
Tal, A., *The Samaritan Targum of the Pentateuch: A Critical Edition* (Tel Aviv, 1980–83).
*— *The Samaritan Pentateuch; Edited according to MS. 6(C) of the Shekhem Synagogue* (Heb.) (Tel Aviv, 1994: rev. 2010 with M. Florentin, including the Masoretic text in parallel).
— *A Dictionary of Samaritan Aramaic* (HbO 1/50; Leiden, 2000).
Thompson, R.J., *Moses and the Law in a Century of Criticism since Graf* (VTSup 19; Leiden, 1970).
Tov, E., *Textual Criticism of the Hebrew Bible* (Minneapolis and Assen, 1992; 2nd ed. 2001).
— *Scribal Practices and Approaches Reflected in the Texts from the Judaean Desert* (STDJ 54; Leiden, 2004).
Tov, E., et al. (eds.), *Dead Sea Scrolls Fragments in the Museum Collection* (Publications of Museum of Bible 1; Leiden, 2016).
[Tyndale, William] *Tyndale's Old Testament, being the Pentateuch of 1530, Joshua to 2 Chronicles of 1537, and Jonah*, ed. D. Daniell (New Haven, 1992).
Valentin, H., *Aaron. Eine Studie zur vor-priesterschriftlichen Aaron-Überlieferung* (OBO 18; Freiburg and Göttingen, 1978).
Van Seters, J., *Prologue to History: The Yahwist as Historian in Genesis* (Louisville, 1992).
**— *The Life of Moses: The Yahwist as Historian in Exodus-Numbers* (Louisville, 1994).
— 'The Geography of the Exodus', in J.A. Dearman and M.P. Graham (eds.), *The Land that I Will Show You* (J.M. Miller FS; JSOTSup 343; Sheffield, 1997), pp. 255-76.
de Vaux, R., *Les institutions de l'Ancien Testament* (Paris, 1958, 1960; ET 1961, 2nd ed. 1965).
— *Studies in Old Testament Sacrifice* (Cardiff, 1964).
— 'The Revelation of the Divine Name YHWH', in J.I. Durham and J.R. Porter (eds.), *Proclamation and Presence: Old Testament Essays in Honour of Gwynne Henton Davies* (London, 1970), pp. 63-75.
— *Histoire ancienne d'Israël* (Paris, 1971; ET London, 1978).
Vergote, J., *Joseph en Égypte: Génèse Chap. 37–50 à la lumière des etudes égyptologiques récentes* (Louvain, 1959).
Vermes, G., *Scripture and Tradition in Judaism: Haggadic Studies* (SPB 4; Leiden, 1961).
Vervenne, M., 'The "P" Tradition in the Pentateuch: Document and/or Redaction? The "Sea Narrative" (Exodus 13,17- 14,31) as a Testcase', in C. Brekelmans and J. Lust (eds.), *Pentateuchal and Deuteronomistic Studies* (BETL 94; Leuven, 1990), pp. 67-90.
— (ed.), *Studies in the Book of Exodus: Redaction – Reception – Interpretation* (BETL 126; Leuven, 1996).

Vriezen, T.C., 'Exodusstudien Exodus I', *VT* 17 (1967), pp. 334-53.
de Waard, J., *General Introduction and Megilloth* (*BHQ* 18; Stuttgart, 2004).
Wade, M.L., *Consistency of Translation Techniques in the Tabernacle Accounts of Exodus in the Old Greek* (SCS 49; Atlanta, 2003).
Wagner, M., *Die lexikalischen und grammatikalischen Aramaismen im alttestamentichen Hebräisch* (BZAW 96; Berlin, 1966).
*Walters, P., *The Text of the Septuagint* (Cambridge, 1973).
Watson, W.G.E., *Classical Hebrew Poetry: A Guide to its Techniques* (JSOTSup 26; Sheffield, 1984).
Weimar, P., *Untersuchungen zur priesterschriftlichen Exodusgeschichte* (FzB 9; Würzburg, 1973).
— *Untersuchungen zur Redaktionsgeschichte des Pentateuch* (BZAW 146; Berlin, 1977).
— *Die Berufung des Mose* (OBO 32; Freiburg and Göttingen, 1980).
— 'Exodus 1,1 – 2,10 als Eröffnungskomposition des Exodusbuches', in Vervenne (ed.), *Studies*, pp. 179-208.
Weimar, P., and E. Zenger, *Exodus: Geschichte und Geschichten der Befreiung Israels* (Stuttgart, 1975).
Weinfeld, M., *Deuteronomy and the Deuteronomic School* (Oxford, 1972).
— *Deuteronomy 1–11* (AB 5; New York, 1991).
Weiss, M., 'Weiteres über die Bauformen des Erzählens in der Bibel', *Bib* 46 (1965), pp. 181-206.
*Weitzman, M.P., *The Syriac version of the Old Testament: An Introduction* (UCOP 56; Cambridge, 1999).
Wellhausen, J., 'Die Composition des Hexateuchs', *JDTh* 21 (1876), pp. 392-450, 531-602; 22 (1877), pp. 407-79.
— *Prolegomena zur Geschichte Israels* (2nd ed. of *Geschichte Israels I* [1878]; Berlin, 1883; ET Edinburgh, 1885).
**— *Die Composition des Hexateuchs und der Historischen Bücher des Alten Testaments* (Berlin, 3rd ed., 1899; repr. Berlin, 1963).
Westermann, C., *Das Loben Gottes in den Psalmen* (Göttingen, 3rd ed., 1963; 5th enlarged ed., *Lob und Klage in den Psalmen* [Göttingen, 1977]).
— *Grundformen prophetischer Rede* (BET 31; Munich, 5th ed., 1964; ET *Basic Forms of Prophetic Speech* [London, 1967]).
— *Genesis 12–50* (Erträge der Forschung; Darmstadt, 1975).
— *Genesis 12–36* (BKAT; Neukirchen, 1981; ET London, 1986).
— *Genesis 37–50* (BKAT; Neukirchen, 1982; ET London, 1987).
*Wevers, J.W., *Notes on the Greek Text of Exodus* (SCS 30; Atlanta, 1990).
— *Text History of the Greek Exodus* (MSU 21; Göttingen, 1992).
Wilkinson, J., *Egeria's Travels* (London, 1971; rev. ed. Warminster, 1981).
Wilson, R.R., 'The Hardening of Pharaoh's Heart', *CBQ* 41 (1979), pp. 18-36.
Wolff, H.W., 'Zur Thematik der elohistischen Fragmente im Pentateuch', *EvTh* 29 (1969), pp. 59-72; ET *Int* 26 (1972), pp. 158-73.
— *Anthropologie des Alten Testaments* (Munich, 1973; ET Philadelphia, 1974).

Wormell, N.A., 'The Composition of the Book of Numbers in the Light of Babylonian Educational Practice' (unpublished PhD dissertation, University of Cambridge, 2015).
Wright, G.R.H., *Ancient Building in South Syria and Palestine* (HbO VII.1.2.B3; Leiden, 1985).
Yeivin, I., *Introduction to the Tiberian Masorah* (ET, Masoretic Studies 5; Chico, 1980).
Zenger, E., *Israel am Sinai: Analysen und Interpretationen zu Exodus 17–34* (Altenberge, 2nd ed., 1985).
— and C. Frevel, *Einleitung in das Alte Testament* (Stuttgart, 9th ed., 2015 [1st ed. 1995]).
Zimmerli, W., 'Ich bin Jahwe', in W.F. Albright et al., *Geschichte und Altes Testament* (FS A. Alt; BHT 16; Tübingen, 1953), pp. 179-209; ET in *I Am Yahweh*, pp. 1-28.
— *I Am Yahweh* (Atlanta, 1982).

ABBREVIATIONS

AB	The Anchor Bible
ABD	D.N. Freedman (ed.), *The Anchor Bible Dictionary* (New York, 1992)
ACCS	*Ancient Christian Commentary on Scripture*, Old Testament vol. 3, *Exodus, Leviticus, Numbers, Deuteronomy* (ed. J.T. Lienhard; Downers Grove, 2001)
AGAJU	Arbeiten zur Geschichte des antiken Judentums und des Urchristentums
AGSU	Arbeiten zur Geschichte des Spätjudentums und des Urchristentums
AHI	G.I. Davies, *Ancient Hebrew Inscriptions: Corpus and Concordance* (Cambridge, 1991, 2004)
AHw	W. von Soden, *Akkadisches Handwörterbuch* (Wiesbaden, 1965–81)
AIL	Ancient Israel and its Literature
AJSL	*American Journal of Semitic Languages and Literatures*
Akk.	Akkadian
ALASP	Abhandlungen zur Literatur Alt-Syrien-Palästinas und Mesopotamiens
ALGHJ	Arbeiten zur Literatur und Geschichte des hellenistischen Judentums
ANEP	J.B. Pritchard (ed.), *The Ancient Near East in Pictures relating to the Old Testament* (Princeton, 1954)
ANESSup	Ancient Near Eastern Studies Supplement
ANET	J.B. Pritchard (ed.), *Ancient Near Eastern Texts relating to the Old Testament* (Princeton, 3rd ed., 1969)
ANETS	Ancient Near Eastern Texts and Studies
AnBib	Analecta Biblica
AnOr	Analecta Orientalia
AnPap	*Analecta Papyrologica*
AO	*Archiv für Orientforschung*
AOAT	Alter Orient und Altes Testament
AOS	American Oriental Series
Aq	Aquila
Ar	Arabic (version)
ARAB	*Ancient Records of Assyria and Babylonia* (tr. D.D. Luckenbill; Chicago, 1926–27)

ABBREVIATIONS

Aram.	Aramaic
AramB 2	*The Aramaic Bible. The Targums*, 2: *Targum Neofiti 1: Exodus* (tr., Introduction and Apparatus by M. McNamara and Notes by C.T.R. Hayward); *Targum Pseudo-Jonathan: Exodus* (tr. with Notes by M. Maher) (Edinburgh, 1994)
AramB 7	*The Aramaic Bible. The Targums*, 7: *The Targum Onqelos to Exodus* (tr., Apparatus and Notes by B. Grossfeld) (Edinburgh, 1988)
ARE	*Ancient Records of Egypt* (tr. J.H. Breasted; Chicago, 1906–1907)
ARMT	Archives Royales de Mari: transcriptions et traductions
ASAE	*Annales du Service des Antiquités de l'Égypte*
ASORB	American Schools of Oriental Research Books
ASTI	*Annual of the Swedish Theological Institute*
ATANT	Abhandlungen zur Theologie des Alten und Neuen Testaments
ATD	Das Alte Testament Deutsch
ATS	Arbeiten zu Text und Sprache im Alten Testament
ÄUAT	Ägypten und Altes Testament
ÄUL	*Ägypten und Levante*
AuS	G. H. Dalman. *Arbeit und Sitte in Palästina* (Gütersloh, 1928–42)
AV	The Authorised (King James) Version of the Bible
BA	*The Biblical Archaeologist*
BAG	W. Bauer, W.F. Arndt and F.W. Gingrich, *A Greek–English Lexicon of the New Testament and Other Early Christian Literature* (Chicago, 1957)
BAlex	*La Bible d'Alexandrie*
BAR	*Biblical Archaeology Review*
BARIS	British Archaeological Reports International Series
BASOR	*Bulletin of the American Schools of Oriental Research*
BBB	Bonner Biblische Beiträge
BDB	F. Brown, S.R. Driver and C.A. Briggs, *A Hebrew and English Lexicon of the Old Testament* (Oxford, 1907; reprinted with corrections, 1953)
BDF	F.J. Blass and A. Debrunner, *A Greek Grammar of the New Testament and other Early Christian Literature* (tr. and rev. by R.W. Funk from the 9th–10th German ed.; Chicago, 1961)
BEATAJ	Beiträge zur Erforschung des Alten Testaments und des antiken Judentums
BET	Beiträge zur evangelischen Theologie
BH	*Biblia Hebraica*
BH	Biblical Hebrew

BHQ	*Biblia Hebraica Quinta*
BHS	*Biblia Hebraica Stuttgartensia*
BHT	Beiträge zur historischen Theologie
Bib	*Biblica*
BibInt	Biblical Interpretation
BIFAO	*Bulletin de l'institut français d'archéologie orientale*
BIOSCS	*Bulletin of the International Organization for Septuagint and Cognate Studies*
BJRL	*Bulletin of the John Rylands Library*
BKAT	Biblischer Kommentar Altes Testament
BL	H. Bauer and P. Leander, *Historische Grammatik der hebräischen Sprache des Alten Testamentes* (Halle, 1922, repr. Hildesheim, 1962)
BN	*Biblische Notizen*
BO	*Bibliotheca Orientalis*
BR	*Bible Review*
BRL	K. Galling (ed.), *Biblisches Reallexicon* (Tübingen, 2nd ed., 1977)
BSAEP	British School of Archaeology in Egypt Publications
BTS	Biblisch-theologische Studien
BWANT	Beiträge zur Wissenschaft vom Alten und Neuen Testament
BWAT	Beiträge zur Wissenschaft vom Alten Testament
BZ	*Biblische Zeitschrift*
BZAW	Beihefte zur *ZAW*
CAD	*Chicago Assyrian Dictionary*
CAH	*The Cambridge Ancient History* (vols. I-II; Cambridge, 3rd ed., 1970–75)
CahSA	Cahiers de la Société Asiatique
CAL	The Comprehensive Aramaic Lexicon (online: cal.huc.edu)
CBC	The Cambridge Bible Commentary
CBET	Contributions to Biblical Exegesis and Theology
CBOT	Coniectanea Biblica Old Testament Series
CBQ	*Catholic Biblical Quarterly*
CBSC	Cambridge Bible for Schools and College
CC(SL)	Corpus Christianorum (Series Latina)
CHANE	Culture and History of the Ancient Near East
CHB	*Cambridge History of the Bible*
CML²	J.C.L. Gibson (ed.), *Canaanite Myths and Legends* (Edinburgh, 2nd ed., 1978)
COS	W.W. Hallo and K.L. Younger (eds.), *The Context of Scripture* (Leiden, 1997–2017)
CPA	Christian Palestinian Aramaic

CRAIBL	Comptes Rendus de l'Academie des Inscriptions et Belles Lettres
CRINT	Compendia Rerum Iudaicarum ad Novum Testamentum
DAPT	Deir ʿAlla Plaster Texts (ed. J. Hoftijzer and G. van der Kooij)
DBAT	Dielheimer Blätter zum Alten Testament
DBS	Dictionnaire de la Bible Supplément
DCH	D.J.A. Clines, The Dictionary of Classical Hebrew (Sheffield, 1993–2011)
DDD	Dictionary of Deities and Demons in the Bible (ed. K. van der Toorn et al.; Leiden, 1995)
DJD	Discoveries in the Judaean Desert (various authors/editors, 40 vols; Oxford, 1955–2010)
DMOA	Documenta et Monumenta Orientis Antiqui
DNWSI	J. Hoftijzer and K. Jongeling, Dictionary of the North-West Semitic Inscriptions (HdO 1/21; Leiden, 1995)
DSD	Dead Sea Discoveries
DULAT	G. del Olmo Lete and J. Sanmartin, Dictionary of the Ugaritic Language in the Alphabetic Tradition (HdO 1/67; Leiden, 2nd ed., 2004)
EAEHL	M. Avi-Yonah (ed.), Encyclopedia of Archaeological Excavations in the Holy Land (London and Jerusalem, 1975–78)
Eg.	Egyptian
ESA	Epigraphic South Arabian
ESV	English Standard Version
ET	English translation
Eth	Ethiopic (version)
ETL	Ephemerides Theologicae Lovanienses
EÜ	Einheitsübersetzung (Stuttgart, 1980)
EvTh	Evangelische Theologie
EV(V)	English version(s)
ExpT	The Expository Times
FAT	Forschung zum Alten Testament
FOTL	The Forms of the Old Testament Literature
FRLANT	Forschungen zur Religion und Literatur des Alten und Neuen Testament
FzB	Forschung zur Bibel
GAG	W. von Soden, Grundriss der Akkadischen Grammatik (samt Ergänzungsheft) (AnOr 33 [2nd ed., 47]; Rome, 1969)
Ges18	R. Meyer and H. Donner (eds.), Wilhelm Gesenius. Hebräisches und Aramäisches Handwörterbuch über das Alte Testament. 18.Auflage (Berlin, 1987–2012)

Ges-B	F. Buhl (ed.), *Wilhelm Gesenius' Hebräisches und Aramäisches Handwörterbuch über das Alte Testament* (Leipzig, 12th ed., 1895; 13th ed., 1899; 14th ed., 1905; 15th ed., 1910; 16th ed., 1915)
GK	E. Kautzsch and A.E. Cowley (eds.), *Gesenius' Hebrew Grammar* (Oxford, 2nd ed., 1910)
GSA	R. Macuch, *Grammatik des Samaritanischen Aramäisch* (Studia Samaritana 4; Berlin, 1982)
GSH	R. Macuch, *Grammatik des Samaritanischen Hebräisch* (Studia Samaritana 1; Berlin, 1969)
GTA	Göttinger Theologische Arbeiten
HACL	History, Archaeology and Culture of the Levant
HAL	L. Köhler and W. Baumgartner, *Hebräisches und Aramäisches Lexicon zum Alten Testament* (Leiden, 1967–95)
HAT	Handbuch zum Alten Testament
HBAI	*Hebrew Bible and Ancient Israel*
HBM	Hebrew Bible Monographs
HbO	Handbuch der Orientalistik
HCOT	Historical Commentary on the Old Testament
HDB	*Hastings' Dictionary of the Bible*
Heb.	Hebrew
HKAT	Handkommentar zum Alten Testament
HSAT	Die Heilige Schrift des Alten Testamentes
HSM	Harvard Semitic Monographs
HSS	Harvard Semitic Studies
HTR	*Harvard Theological Review*
HUCA	*Hebrew Union College Annual*
IBD	*The Illustrated Bible Dictionary* (ed. J.D. Douglas, N. Hillyer et al.; Leicester, 1980)
IBHS	B.K. Waltke and M. O'Connor, *An Introduction to Biblical Hebrew Syntax* (Winona Lake, 1990)
IDB(S)	G.A. Buttrick (ed.), *The Interpreter's Dictionary of the Bible* (Nashville and New York, 1962); K. Crim (ed.), *Supplementary Volume* (Nashville, 1976)
IGECBM	*Introductory Guide to the Egyptian Collections of the British Museum* (London, 1964)
Int	*Interpretation*
IOS	*Israel Oriental Studies*
JAEI	*Journal of Ancient Egyptian Interconnections* (online)
JAJSup	Journal of Ancient Judaism Supplements
JAOS	*Journal of the American Oriental Society*

ABBREVIATIONS

JAram	Jewish Aramaic
JB	The Jerusalem Bible
JBL	*Journal of Biblical Literature*
JBLMS	Journal of Biblical Literature Monograph Series
JBS	Jerusalem Biblical Studies
JDTh	*Jahrbücher für Deutsche Theologie*
JE	*The Jewish Encyclopedia* (ed. I. Singer; New York and London, 1901–1906)
JEA	*Journal of Egyptian Archaeology*
JHebS	*Journal of Hebrew Scriptures* (online: www.jhsonline.org)
JJS	*Journal of Jewish Studies*
JM	P. Joüon and T. Muraoka, *A Grammar of Biblical Hebrew* (Subsidia Biblica 14; Rome, 1991)
JNES	*Journal of Near Eastern Studies*
JNSL	*Journal of Northwest Semitic Languages*
JPTh	*Jahrbücher für protestantische Theologie*
JQR	*Jewish Quarterly Review*
JSJ	*Journal for the Study of Judaism*
JSOT	*Journal for the Study of the Old Testament*
JSOTSup	Journal for the Study of the Old Testament Supplements
JSP	*Journal for the Study of the Pseudepigrapha*
JSQ	*Jewish Studies Quarterly*
JSS	*Journal of Semitic Studies*
JSSM	Journal of Semitic Studies Monographs
JTS	*Journal of Theological Studies*
JTVI	*Journal of the Transactions of the Victoria Institute*
KAI	H. Donner and W. Röllig, *Kanaanäische und Aramäische Inschriften* (Wiesbaden, 1962–64; 5th ed. of vol. 1 [texts], 2002)
KAT	Kommentar zum Alten Testament
KB	L. Köhler and W. Baumgartner, *Lexicon in Veteris Testamenti libros* (Leiden, 1953)
KEH	Kurzgefasstes Exegetisches Handbuch zum Alten Testament
KHAT	Kurzer Handcommentar zum Alten Testament
KTU	M. Dietrich, O. Loretz and J. Sanmartin (eds.), *The Cuneiform Alphabetic Texts from Ugarit, Ras ibn Hani and Other Places* (ALASP 8, 2nd enlarged ed. of id., *Die Keilalphabetischen Texte aus Ugarit* [AOAT 24; Neukirchen-Vluyn, 1976]; Münster, 1995)
L	Codex Leningradensis (Petropolitanus) B19a
LAB	*Liber Antiquitatum Biblicarum* (Pseudo-Philo)
LBH	Late Biblical Hebrew
LexAeg	*Lexikon der Ägyptologie*

LS	C.T. Lewis and C. Short, *A Latin Dictionary* (Oxford, 1879)
LSJ	H.G. Liddell, R. Scott and H. Stuart Jones, *A Greek-English Lexicon* (Oxford, 9th ed., 1940); *Revised Supplement*, ed. P.G.W. Glare (Oxford, 1996)
LXX/LXX*	Septuagint (the original text, as reconstructed)
MH	Mishnaic/Middle Hebrew
MPIL	Monographs of the Peshiṭta Institute (Leiden)
MRI	*Mekhilta of Rabbi Ishmael* (ed. and tr. J.Z. Lauterbach; Philadelphia, 1933–35)
MSL	Materialien zum sumerischen Lexikon
MSU	Mitteilungen des Septuaginta-Unternehmens
MT	Masoretic Text
MTS	Marburger Theologische Studien
NBL	*Neues Bibel-Lexikon* (ed. M. Görg and B. Lang; Zurich, 1988–2001)
NCB	New Century Bible
NCHB 1	J.N.B. Carleton Paget and J.L.W. Schaper (eds.), *The New Cambridge History of the Bible*, 1. *From the Beginnings to 600* (Cambridge, 2013)
NEB	The New English Bible
NedTT	*Nederlands Theologisch Tijdschrift*
NERTOT	W. Beyerlin (ed.), *Near Eastern Religious Texts relating to the Old Testament* (OTL; 1978)
NETS	A. Pietersma and B.G. Wright (eds.), *A New English Translation of the Septuagint and the Other Greek Translations Traditionally Included under that Title* (Oxford, 2007; 2nd ed. 2009, also online at ccat.sas.upenn.edu)
NJPS	The New Jewish Publication Society Translation
NRSV	The New Revised Standard Version
NT	*Novum Testamentum*
NTSup	Novum Testamentum Supplements
OBO	Orbis Biblicus et Orientalis
OBT	Overtures to Biblical Theology
OEAE	*The Oxford Encyclopedia of Ancient Egypt* (ed. D.B. Redford; Oxford, 2001)
OffAram	Official (or: Imperial) Aramaic
OG	The 'Old Greek' (=LXX*)
OL	Old Latin (Translation)
OLD	P.G.W. Glare (ed.), *The Oxford Latin Dictionary* (Oxford, 1982)
OLZ	*Orientalistische Literaturzeitung*
OT	Old Testament
OTG	Old Testament Guides

OTL	The Old Testament Library
OTS	*Oudtestamentische Studiën*
Pal Tg(g)	Palestinian Targum(s)
PBA	*Proceedings of the British Academy*
PC	Prefix-conjugation
PEFMS	Palestine Exploration Fund Monograph Series
PEQ	*Palestine Exploration Quarterly*
pers. comm.	personal communication
PJ	*Palästinajahrbuch*
POTT	D.J. Wiseman (ed.), *Peoples of Old Testament Times* (Oxford, 1973)
PRU	*Le Palais Royal d'Ugarit* (ed. C.F.-A. Schaeffer et al.; Paris, 1955–)
PSSSI	Publications of the Society for the Study of Scripture in Israel
P-W	A. Pauly, G. Wissowa and W. Kroll (eds.), *Real-Encyclopädie der classischen Altertumswissenschaft* (Stuttgart, 1894–1980)
RB	*Revue Biblique*
RBS	Resources for Biblical Study
REB	The Revised English Bible
REJ	*Revue des etudes juives*
RGG	*Die Religion in Geschichte und Gegenwart*
RHPR	*Revue d'histoire et de philosophie religieuses*
RITA(NC)	K.A. Kitchen, *Ramesside Inscriptions Translated and Annotated* (Oxford, 1993–2014); *Notes and Commentary* (Oxford, 1993–)
RLA	E. Ebeling et al. (eds.), *Reallexikon der Assyriologie* (Berlin, 1928–)
RQ	*Revue de Qumran*
RSP	L.R. Fisher et al. (eds.), *Ras Shamra Parallels: The Texts from Ugarit and the Hebrew Bible* (AnOr 49-51; Rome, 1972–81)
RSV	The Revised Standard Version
RV	The Revised Version
Sah	Sahidic
SAHD	Semantics of Ancient Hebrew Database (www.sahd.div.ed.ac.uk)
SAT	Die Schriften des Alten Testaments
SBLABS	Society of Biblical Literature Archaeology and Biblical Studies
SBLDS	Society of Biblical Literature Dissertation Series
SBLMS	Society of Biblical Literature Monograph Series
SBLSS	Society of Biblical Literature Symposium Series
SBS	Stuttgarter Bibelstudien
SBT	Studies in Biblical Theology
ScrH	*Scripta Hierosolymitana*

SCS	Septuagint and Cognate Studies
SEÅ	*Svensk Exegetisk Årsbok*
SEL	*Studi Epigrafici e Linguistici*
SJOT	*Scandinavian Journal of the Old Testament*
SNTSMS	Society for New Testament Study Monograph Series
SOTSMS	Society for Old Testament Study Monograph Series
SP	Samaritan Pentateuch
SPB	Studia Post-Biblica
SSLL	Studies in Semitic Languages and Linguistics
StBL	Studies in Biblical Literature
STDJ	Studies in the Texts of the Desert of Judah
StTh	*Studia Theologica*
Sy	Peshitta
Sy^{hex}	Syro-hexaplar Version
Symm	Symmachus
Syr.	Syriac (language)
TAD	*Textbook of Aramaic Documents from Ancient Egypt* (B. Porten and A. Yardeni; Jerusalem, 1986–)
TAVO	*Tübinger Atlas des Vorderen Orients*
TDNT	*Theological Dictionary of the New Testament* (ET of *TWNT*)
TDOT	*Theological Dictionary of the Old Testament* (ET of *TWAT*)
TEG	Traditio Exegetica Graeca
Tg(g)	Targum(s)
Tg^F	Fragment-Targums
Tg^G	Cairo Genizah Targum manuscript(s)
Tg^J	Targum of Pseudo-Jonathan
Tg^N	Targum Neofiti 1
Tg^O	Targum of Onkelos
TGI	K. Galling (ed.), *Textbuch zur Geschichte Israels* (Tübingen, 3rd ed., 1979)
THAT	E. Jenni and C. Westermann (eds.), *Theologisches Handwörterbuch zum Alten Testament* (Munich, 1971, 1976)
Theod	Theodotion
THGE	J.W. Wevers, *Text History of the Greek Exodus* (MSU 21; Göttingen, 1992)
ThT	*Theologisch Tijdschrift*
TLOT	*Theological Lexicon of the Old Testament* (ET of *THAT*)
TLZ	*Theologische Literaturzeitung*
TR	*Theologische Rundschau*
TRE	G. Krause et al. (eds.), *Theologische Realenzyklopädie* (Berlin, 1997–2007)
TSAJ	Texte und Studien zum Antiken Judentum

T.Sim.	Testament of Simeon
TUAT	Texte aus der Umwelt des Alten Testaments (ed. O. Kaiser et al; Gütersloh, 1982–)
TWAT	G.J. Botterweck, H. Ringgren and H.J.Fabry (eds.), *Theologisches Wörterbuch zum Alten Testament* (Stuttgart, 1970–95)
TWNT	G. Kittel, *Theologisches Wörterbuch zum Neuen Testament* (Stuttgart, 1933–78)
TWQ	H.-J. Fabry and U. Dahmen (eds.), *Theologisches Wörterbuch zu den Qumrantexten* (Stuttgart, 2011–16)
TynB	*Tyndale Bulletin*
UCOP	University of Cambridge Oriental Publications
ÜGP	M. Noth, *Überlieferungsgeschichte des Pentateuch* (Stuttgart, 1948)
UF	*Ugarit-Forschungen*
Ug.	Ugaritic
UT	C.H. Gordon, *Ugaritic Textbook* (AnOr 38; Rome, 1965)
UTB	Uni-Taschenbücher
VCSup	Vigiliae Christianae Supplements
VT	*Vetus Testamentum*
VTSup	Vetus Testamentum Supplements
Vulg	Vulgate
WÄS	A. Erman and H. Grapow, *Wörterbuch der Ägyptischen Sprache* (Leipzig and Berlin, 1926–63)
WBC	Word Biblical Commentary
WCJS	*World Congress of Jewish Studies, Proceedings*
WUNT	Wissenschaftliche Untersuchungen zum Neuen Testament
WMANT	Wissenschaftliche Monographien zum Alten und Neuen Testament
WO	*Die Welt des Orients*
ZÄS	*Zeitschrift für Ägyptische Sprache und Altert(h)umskunde*
ZAW	*Zeitschrift für die alttestamentliche Wissenschaft*
ZBK	Zürcher Bibelkommentare
ZDMG	*Zeitschrift der Deutschen Morgenländischen Gesellschaft*
ZDPV	*Zeitschrift des Deutschen Palästina-Vereins*
ZThK	*Zeitschrift für Theologie und Kirche*

INTRODUCTION

1. *Names, Place in the Canon and Contents*

The name 'Exodus', a Latinised form of a Greek word (ἔξοδος: cf. LXX at 19.1) meaning 'departure', reflects the standard designation of the book used in the early Christian Church and in Greek manuscripts such as Codex Vaticanus (Alexandrinus adds Αἰγύπτου, 'from Egypt'): the earliest surviving attestations of 'Exodus' as a title are in Justin's *Dialogue with Trypho* (e.g. 59.1-2: mid-second cent. A.D.) and a list of biblical books attributed to Melito of Sardis (late second cent. A.D.) by Eusebius, *HE* 4.26.12-14.[1] Almost certainly its origin lay in earlier Greek-speaking Judaism, although a different word, Ἐξαγωγή, was favoured by Philo (*Migr.* 14; *Quis Heres* 14, 251; *Somn.* 1.117) and it had already been used by Ezekiel Tragicus as the title of his dramatisation of the narrative in, most likely, the second century B.C.[2] This name, meaning 'bringing out, removal', was arguably more appropriate to the language of the book (ἐξάγω, 'bring out', like the Heb. *hôṣî'* which usually underlies it, is frequent from 3.8 onwards) and to its focus on the human (Moses) and divine agency which secured the Israelites' release. It has been pointed out that neither of these titles takes account of the important themes of the second half of the book, but they do identify its distinctive and even dominant characteristic.

The now traditional Jewish name for the book, '(These are) the names' ([wᵉ'ēlleh] *šᵉmôt*, Shemot), was already in use in the third century A.D. according to Origen's list in his commentary on Psalm 1 which is preserved by Eusebius, *HE* 6.25 (cf. Swete, pp. 198-99): see also Jerome's prologue to his translation of Samuel and Kings (*prologus galeatus*) and the title of Exodus in the Vulgate, *incipit*

---

[1] I owe the Justin references to Dr Simon Gathercole. For the other data see Swete, pp. 198-216. A similar Heb. title to the fuller form appears in *Dikduke Taanim* 57 (tenth cent.).

[2] For discussion of various proposals about the date cf. Jacobson, *Exagoge*, pp. 5-13.

liber ellesmoth id est exodus. It consists of the first two words (or in the more common abbreviated form only the second word) of the Hebrew text of the book, following a pattern with a long pedigree in ancient Near Eastern literature (e.g. *Enuma elish* as the title of the Babylonian Epic of Creation) and one that is also used for the other books of the Pentateuch. Strangely the earliest surviving occurrence in a Hebrew or Aramaic text seems to be in the probably sixth-century midrash *Genesis Rabbah* (ch. 64: so Sarna, p. xi) – the Dead Sea Scrolls introduce quotations from Exodus, if at all, in a different way (see below) – but the accuracy of Origen's information about Jewish practice in his time is confirmed by the correspondence of his Heb. titles for other books of the Pentateuch with the usage of the Mishnah (Yoma 7.1; Sotah 7.7-8).

Within the Hebrew Bible Exodus forms part of the first division of the canon, which has been known from at least the second century B.C. as 'the Law' (*tôrāh*, νόμος: Aristeas 3 and passim; Greek prologue to Ecclesiasticus; cf. Luke 24.44), and this position has been preserved in all the many translations that have been made since. Another early description for the Law was 'the book of Moses', used occasionally in the Dead Sea Scrolls (4QMMT [4Q397, 398] fr. 14-17; probably originally also in 4Qflorilegium [4Q174] fr. 1 i 2-3, where it introduced a quotation of Exod. 15.17-18), in the New Testament (Mk 12.26, with reference to Exod. 3; cf. Luke 20.37) and in the Talmud (b.Baba Bathra 14b-15a). Its division into five separate 'books' evidently preceded the translation into Greek in the third century B.C., as modern study of the translators' methods has confirmed that each of the books as they are known today was translated separately.[3] The Letter of Aristeas refers to 'books' (30-31, 38), 'parchments' and 'rolls' (176-77, 179, 310) in the plural, alongside singular expressions like 'law' and 'book'; as do the Damascus Document from Qumran (though in a passage [6.15] which actually only survives in the medieval copy), Philo (see above) and Josephus (explicitly the 'five' books of Moses [*cAp* 1.39]; likewise Melito). The independence of Exodus as well as its attachment to a wider context is reflected in the biblical manuscripts from Qumran (see further below, Section 2 [i] c). Three manuscripts contained at least either Genesis

---

[3] E.g. Lange, pp. 123-24: see further below in the section on the Septuagint.

(4QGen-Ex^a; 4QpalGen-Ex^l) or Leviticus (4QEx-Lev^f) as well as Exodus, and two of them may have included the whole Pentateuch (Lange, pp. 51, 62). A slightly later manuscript from Wadi Muraba'at (MurGen-Ex,Num) is even more likely to have included the whole Pentateuch, and at least one copy of a parabiblical work, 'Reworked Pentateuch', is known to have done so (4Q365). But for most manuscripts of this time there is no evidence of this and they were probably limited to Exodus (or even just a part of it). At a much later date the copyists of medieval Samaritan manuscripts refer both to Exodus as 'the second book' and to the Pentateuch as a unified whole, *twrh tmymh*, 'the whole ([or perfect?] Law' (von Gall, pp. 206, 438).[4]

Exodus begins with two interwoven sections that link it closely to Genesis: one showing how the small number of tribal families who entered Egypt with Jacob became a great multitude (1.1-5, 7; cf. Gen. 46.8-27; 47.27) and one focusing on Joseph in particular and the accession of a new king who knew nothing of his achievements (1.6, 8; cf. Gen. 37; 39–50). It continues by describing the Egyptians' oppression of the Israelites (1.9-22; cf. 5.23) and the origin of Moses, who receives two very similar commissions from God (3.1–4.17, at Mount Horeb in the desert; 6.2–7.5, apparently in Egypt; cf. 6.28) and demands permission from another king (2.23) of Egypt (Pharaoh) for Israel to leave Egypt to worship God in the desert. When this is refused (5.1–6.1), God causes a series of plagues to fall on the Egyptians, culminating in the death of all their firstborn children and animals, and Pharaoh relents (7.6–12.51). The feast of Passover and other rituals commemorating Israel's liberation from Egypt are inaugurated (12.1-28, 43-49; 13.1-16). The Israelites set out on their journey but are overtaken on the shore of a 'sea' (or lake), which they are able to cross, while their pursuers are drowned (13.20–14.31, with celebratory hymns of praise in 15.1-21). After a short but arduous journey they reach 'the mountain of God', now called Sinai (15.22–19.2), where the remaining narratives of the book (and all of Leviticus and Num. 1.1–10.32) are located.

---

[4] The numeration of the books is found also in titles provided in some Greek and Syriac manuscripts and was adopted in early modern vernacular versions (e.g. Luther, Tyndale).

As a whole the subsequent narratives describe the presence of Israel's God Yahweh in power and splendour at the mountain, his meeting with his people through the mediation of Moses, the making and renewal of a covenant agreement with them, and the revelation in several stages of Yahweh's instructions for their future life and worship. But again two interwoven strands of narrative and law can be discerned here, each with its own inner coherence. One (which is more briefly recounted in Deut. 4.9-20; 5.2-31; 9.8–10.5, 10-11) begins with a theophany accompanied by the phenomena of storm, earthquake and perhaps a volcanic eruption, continues with the revelation of the Ten Commandments and a longer series of detailed laws, and tells of the making of a covenant between Yahweh and Israel on this basis (19.3–24.14). While Moses is up on the mountain receiving the stone tablets on which the Ten Commandments are written, the people, led by Moses' brother Aaron, make an image of a golden calf to represent Yahweh and worship before it. This is Israel's first act of rebellion against Yahweh's law and it threatens to annul the covenant that has been made and Yahweh's promises to the people. But through Moses' intercession and Yahweh's merciful response the covenant is renewed on the basis of a summary of the earlier laws (31.18–34.28).

The other strand of narrative and law has a quite different character and is entirely (apart from the instructions about Sabbath observance in 31.12-17 and 35.2-3) concerned with the building of a portable shrine (the 'tabernacle') and the consecration and clothing of Aaron and his sons as the priests to officiate there. Its first section contains Yahweh's instructions about these matters (25.1–31.11, with 24.15-18 as an introduction), while the second describes the carrying out of these instructions by the people (except for the consecration of the priests, which is deferred until Lev. 8.1–9.24 and carried out by Moses alone) in wording that is for the most part practically identical (though the order of the making of the different furnishings is not) to that of the instructions given earlier (35.4–40.33, with 34.29-35 as its introduction and 40.34-38 as its conclusion). For a critical discussion of the repetitions and variations referred to and their origin see below, Section 4 of the Introduction, 'Composition of the Book'.

2. The Text and its Ancient Versions

(i) The Hebrew Text

a. *Medieval Jewish Manuscripts*

The primary sources for knowledge of the text of Exodus, as of the rest of the Old Testament, continue to be Hebrew manuscripts, Jewish and (for the Pentateuch) Samaritan, from the Middle Ages, although their evidence can be supplemented, confirmed and corrected from other resources to be described below. The medieval manuscripts retain their primacy over against the older manuscripts from the Dead Sea region (and occasionally elsewhere), because the latter are, with rare exceptions, far from complete and they lack the valuable aids to the reader provided by the traditional pronunciation of the text (even if it is not infallible) and the various indications of its sub-division into verses and phrases. Although paragraph divisions are present in them, they do not yet exhibit the classic form of the system(s) in the medieval texts. Equally, the ancient translations which were based directly on a Hebrew original, while of great value for the indirect access which they give to earlier (and in this case complete) forms of the Hebrew text and for the explanations of its meaning which they provide, remain at one remove from the Hebrew itself and depend for their contribution to textual studies upon comparisons (and contrasts) with the medieval manuscripts. Apart from such comparisons their nature as translations, which may and does vary between precise and paraphrasing or expansive, remains unknown and, whatever its aims, a translation cannot even at best represent every aspect of its original. In practice, the translators were also limited by the knowledge of Biblical Hebrew vocabulary and grammar that was available to them and by their ignorance of the cultural differences between their own time and that of the original composition of the biblical text. (See further the 'General Considerations' at the beginning of Section 2 [ii] of this introduction.)

Until the early twentieth century modern knowledge of the medieval Hebrew text(s) and the printed editions used by Christians as well as Jews were for the most part dependent on the second Rabbinic Bible of Jacob ben Chayim (Venice 1524-25), which sought to reproduce the authoritative Ben Asher text from manuscripts that were accessible to him at the time. The text of the first two editions of Rudolf Kittel's *Biblia Hebraica* (1905, 1913) and the Letteris edition of the British and Foreign Bible Society (1852 and reprints to the 1950s) were still based on this foundation. In subsequent editions the aim has still been to present the Ben Asher text (on divergent, less influential medieval texts see below), but the policy has been to give pride of place to manuscripts from the tenth or eleventh century which derive either from the Ben Asher family itself or from a scribe who had direct contact with its work and prove, not surprisingly, to conform more closely to the intended text than the Rabbinic Bible produced several centuries later.[5]

The Hebrew University Bible Project has been able to use the Aleppo Codex (A) as the base text for its editions of Isaiah and Jeremiah: the manuscript includes the claim that Aaron Ben Asher himself was responsible for the vowels, accents and Masorah (which has occasionally been doubted) and, more important, 'there is no doubt that in its closeness to the tradition ascribed to Ben Asher, and also in its accuracy and consistency, this ms. must be considered superior to all other Tiberian mss known to us' (Yeivin, *Introduction*, p. 17). Its production is dated to c. 925–930 A.D. Unfortunately most of its text of the Pentateuch is lost, including the whole of Exodus.[6] The oldest completely surviving manuscript of the Hebrew Bible is known as the Leningrad Codex (L), ms. B19a of the Russian National Library in St Petersburg: it was produced between 1008 and 1013 and its scribe, Samuel ben Jacob, states in a colophon that he corrected it according to manuscripts produced and corrected by Aaron Ben Asher. Careful comparison has shown that it does in fact conform at disputed points to the Ben Asher tradition nearly as often as the Aleppo codex (Yeivin, *Introduction*, pp. 16, 19), although in

---

[5] See further Roberts, *Old Testament Text*, Chapters 4 and 5; Yeivin, *Introduction*, pp. 1-32; Tov, *Textual Criticism*, Chapter 2.1.A (pp. 21-79 of the 1992 ed.); M. Beit-Arieh et al., *Codices Hebraicis Litteris Exarati quo tempore Scripti Fuerint Exhibentes*, 1, Jusqu'à 1020 (Turnhout, 1997); de Waard et al., *General Introduction (BHQ 18)*, pp. vii-xxv; P. Sanders, 'Ashkar-Gilson Manuscript'; Lange and Tov, *Textual History* 1A, pp. 420-29 (§1.5); 1B, pp. 22-72, 126-30 (§§2.2.1-2, 2.3).

[6] There is evidence which enables a plausible reconstruction of the missing text to be made, but this is not the same as possessing the original copy: cf. Penkower, *New Evidence*, and further references in Lange and Tov, *Textual History* 1A, pp. 420-21 (§1.5.2).

certain respects (especially in its divisions of the text) it is less exact. It was brought to scholarly attention by Paul Kahle and at his instigation was selected as the base text for the third edition of Kittel's *Biblia Hebraica* (1937) and subsequently for *BHS* (the edition mainly used in this commentary), *BHQ* and the edition of A. Dotan (1973, rev. ed. 2001).

There are earlier manuscripts which contain just the Pentateuch (or most of it), among which ms. Or. 4445 of the British Library (B) is especially important and highly regarded. The original text of over three-quarters of Genesis and most of Deuteronomy (with any colophons which there may have been) no longer survives (it was replaced in the sixteenth cent.), but the whole of Exodus is intact. It conforms only a little less closely than mss A and L to the Ben Asher pattern. It was once regarded as the very oldest Masoretic manuscript, from the ninth century, and Dotan (who has made a special study of it) still inclines to this view; but others including Yeivin (p. 19) prefer a date c. 925 (for references to some of Dotan's publications see the Bibliography in Lange and Tov, *Textual History* 1A, p. 429 [§1.5]; also his 'Reflections towards a Critical Edition of Pentateuch Codex Or. 4445', in E. Fernández Tejero and M.T. Ortega [eds.], *Estudios Masoréticos* [Tenth Congress of IOMS]; *en memoria de Harry M. Orlinsky* [Madrid, 1993], pp. 39-51: a digital copy of the ms. can be viewed at www.bl.uk/manuscripts/FullDisplay.aspx?ref=Or_4445).

The other manuscripts from the tenth century (or at least possibly so) include a portion of what is known as the 'Exodus Scroll' (not to be confused with the older London/Ashkar-Gilson manuscript, on which see below), containing the unvocalised text of Exod. 10.10–16.15 in five columns,[7] three codices with a less strong Ben Asher affiliation than those mentioned above (Firkovitch II.17 [all Exodus except 23.8–25.1]; Sassoon 507 [the 'Damascus Pentateuch': all Exodus except 18.1-23]; and Sassoon 1053: see Yeivin, *Introduction*, pp. 21-23; de Waard et al., *BHQ*, fasc. 18, pp. xxii-xxv) and one from the Karaite synagogue in Cairo which had its

---

[7] See J.S. Penkower, 'A Sheet of Parchment from a 10th or 11th Century Torah Scroll: Determining its Type among Four Traditions (Oriental, Sefardi, Ashkenazi, Yemenite)', *Textus* 21 (2002), pp. 235-64; Sanders, 'Ashkar-Gilson Manuscript', p. 8: there is a good photograph of the whole sheet at www.menachemmendel.net (see 'Bible Studies')

original Ben Naphtali readings corrected to those of Ben Asher (C3).[8] Since the differences between all these manuscripts are so slight as not to affect the meaning, there is a strong basis for seeing Codex L as preserving essentially the same text of the whole of Exodus that existed a century earlier. For some sections of the book it is possible to go further back, at least for the consonantal text and its layout. In 1959 S.A. Birnbaum published a portion of a scroll with seven columns of the unvocalised text of Exodus (9.18–13.2), known then as the 'London Manuscript', and dated it on palaeographical grounds to the seventh or eighth century A.D. ('A Sheet of an Eighth Century Synagogue Scroll', *VT* 9 [1959], pp. 122-29). Subsequently another sheet of the same scroll, named after its purchasers as the 'Ashkar-Gilson Manuscript', has come to light, containing four columns with the text of Exod. 13.19–16.1: it is inferred that one column of text between the two sheets was occupied by the intervening verses. Those who have studied the text in detail have concluded that it is practically identical to the consonantal text in the major Ben Asher manuscripts and that the latter based their layout of Exod. 15.1-21 and the surrounding text upon it (Birnbaum, p. 123; Sanders, 'Ashkar-Gilson manuscript', pp. 4-18, 20-21). C^{14} dating of the Ashkar-Gilson sheet confirmed the seventh–eighth-century date indicated by palaeography, though the tests were apparently done some time ago (Sanders, p. 2).[9]

---

[8] Cf. Penkower, 'A Tenth-Century Pentateuchal MS from Jerusalem (MS C3), corrected by Mishael ben Uzziel' (Heb.), *Tarbiz* 58 (1988), pp. 49-74, where it is held to be the closest of all the witnesses to the Ben Asher tradition; Tov, *Textual Criticism*, p. 47.

[9] The new sheet is published with discussion in E. Engel and M. Mishor, 'An Ancient Scroll of the Book of Exodus: The Reunion of Two Separate Fragments', *Israel Museum Studies in Archaeology* 7 (2015), pp. 24-60. Subsequently M. Veintrob ('More fragments of early Torah scroll come to light', *Genizah Fragments* 77 [2019], pp. 1-2) has identified 13 more fragments of this scroll, mostly in the Genizah Collection of Cambridge University Library, which contained parts of all the books of the Pentateuch. It was therefore a complete Torah scroll and its provenance was the Cairo Genizah. The following additional passages in Exodus are shown to have survived: 2.14–3.21; 13.2-18; 17.5–18.14. In addition, in 2018 B.M. Outhwaite (to whom I am indebted for this information and for permission to publish it) discovered what seems to be a further piece of a sixth- or seventh-century 'Genesis Scroll' from the Genizah, two sections of which were identified by C. Sirat, M. Dukan and A. Yardeni in the late 1980s

A slightly later fragment (P.10598 Berlin) published by C. Sirat contains parts of Exod. 3.13–4.9 (as established by R. Hendel in Lange and Tov, 1B, p. 61 [2.2.2.1] n. 17: the original attribution to Num. 3–4 in Sirat, *Les papyrus*, pp. 34-35, pl. 9, was perhaps a misprint). The text (again unvocalised) is dated provisionally to the eighth or ninth century A.D. and includes one textual variant (*ʾl bny* in 3.14)[10] and one abbreviation (*yś* for *yśrʾl* in 3.16) as well as four variations in the use of *matres lectionis* (Lange and Tov, 1B, pp. 53-54 [2.2.1.11.3]). It thus falls broadly within the (proto-)Masoretic tradition.

Large numbers of fragments of medieval biblical manuscripts were found in the Cairo Genizah at the end of the nineteenth century and are now held in a variety of libraries and private collections, the chief locations being the University Library at Cambridge, the Bodleian Library at Oxford, the Jewish Theological Seminary in New York and the Russian National Library in St Petersburg.[11] Readings from these manuscripts were included with some specificity in *BH³*, but in *BHS* only the general symbol ꜩ is used. It must be remembered that the Genizah contained documents of very varied origins and character and this applies to the

---

(cf. eaed., 'Rouleaux de la Tora antérieurs à l'an mille', *CRAIBL* 138.4 [1994], pp. 861-87). The new piece preserves Exod. 5.11, 16-23; 6.1-3, 7-25; 7.1-16 and was written by the same scribe as the two Genesis fragments. Whether the three fragments are all part of a single scroll and if so whether it could have contained the whole Torah remains under discussion, but it is a fascinating possibility. There is one textual variant in the Exodus piece (ב in place of MT's על at 7.5, probably a mistake based on the similar expression in 7.4, as Outhwaite has seen) and a few typical orthographic variants.

[10] For the wider attestation of this (probably secondary) variant see Text and Versions on 3.13-15.

[11] Widely accessible surveys were provided by Paul Kahle, both in the Introduction to *BH³*, pp. x-xiii (also in Latin and English), and more fully in the first chapter of his *Cairo Geniza*; for a more recent account see S.C. Reif, *A Jewish Archive from Old Cairo* (Richmond, 2000), especially pp. 98-120, and his 'The Cairo Genizah and its Treasures, with Special Reference to Biblical Studies', in D.R.G. Beattie and M.J. McNamara (eds.), *The Aramaic Bible: Targums in their Historical Context* (Sheffield, 1994), pp. 30-50; and in most detail M.C. Davis and B.M. Outhwaite, *Hebrew Bible Manuscripts in the Cambridge Genizah Collections* (4 vols., Cambridge University Library Genizah Series 2; Cambridge, 1978–2003).

biblical mss too: some are school exercises, for example, which have little if any value for textual criticism. A recent sampling of the high-quality Tiberian mss of Exodus in Cambridge by Dr K.L. Phillips and others revealed only a few very minor deviations from the standard text. But most of the material remains unstudied and new insights into the history of the text could emerge in the future.

One category of manuscripts which has been intensively studied, especially by Kahle, are those with non-Tiberian supralinear vocalisation from both Babylonian and Palestinian schools.[12] Kahle dated these manuscripts from the sixth to the ninth centuries and concluded that they provided access to an earlier stage in the history of vocalisation than the Tiberian system (e.g. in BH^3, pp. x-xi). More recently these dates have been lowered to 'from the ninth to the eleventh centuries' (Tov, *Textual Criticism*, p. 44 n. 20), which would make this evidence contemporary with the earliest Tiberian manuscripts. Even then, the co-existence of a rival system or systems, which might well still be intrinsically of an older origin, warns against any absolute status for the Ben Asher school or whatever tradition lies behind it.[13] This is the more evident from the recognition in the Masorah itself of 'Eastern' ($m^e dinḥā^{\,\prime}ê$) variants in the consonantal text and the parallel system of Ben Naphtali for some features of the pointing of manuscripts (see Tov, *Textual Criticism*, pp. 26-27, 45). On the other hand, the formerly much used collections of variants made especially by B. Kennicott (1776–80) and J.B. de Rossi (1784–88), which were taken from later manuscripts (post-1100), probably derive from scribal errors or 'improvements' and

---

[12] See initially Kahle, *Masoreten des Ostens* and *Masoreten des Westens* 1 and 2; *Cairo Geniza* passim: for summaries and newer studies Roberts, *OT Text*, pp. 47-58, and Tov, *Textual Criticism*, pp. 26-27, 39-49. For comments on the Genizah variants cited in the second part of the *BHS* fascicle which also included Exodus see M. Saebø, 'Bemerkungen zur Textgeschichte von Levitikus. Welchen Wert haben die Varianten aus der Kairoer Geniza?', in E. Blum et al. (eds.), *Die Hebräische Bibel und ihre zweifache Nachgeschichte* (FS R. Rendtorff; Neukirchen, 1990), pp. 131-39. A new four-year project began in October 2017 at the Genizah Research Unit of Cambridge University Library, where Dr K.L. Phillips will re-examine the biblical manuscripts from the Genizah with Palestinian pointing, including their consonantal text.

[13] Such caution is also warranted by the divergent vocalisation attested in the transcriptions of the Hebrew that derive from the second column of Origen's Hexapla (see on this below) and in the works of Jerome, as well as by other earlier evidence.

are no longer regarded as of so much interest as the evidence from the Dead Sea Scrolls, the Samaritan Pentateuch and the ancient translations.[14]

b. *The Samaritan Pentateuch*
'(The Samaritan Pentateuch) is also the most significant Hebrew witness to the textual history of the Pentateuch, aside from the MT' (S. Schorch, 'A Critical *editio maior*', 100). For the completeness of its text and the number of its manuscripts this claim is undoubtedly justified, even if in some other ways (especially their early date) the Dead Sea manuscripts (see 2 [i] c) must be reckoned as of higher value. The existence of a complete parallel text of this part of the Hebrew Bible, which has been preserved independently of the Jewish and Christian traditions for over two thousand years, is of great significance for the antiquity and authenticity of the Pentateuchal text. Even the special characteristics of the Samaritan text to be discussed below do not greatly detract from this significance, which has received fresh recognition since the discovery of several related manuscripts at Qumran.[15]

The existence of a distinctive Samaritan text was already known through a Greek translation of it to such early Christian writers as Origen, Eusebius and Jerome (see Swete, p. 437; more fully Field, *Origenis Hexapla*, pp. lxxxii, lxxxiv, 329-30). But it was only in 1616 that a copy of the Hebrew text was brought to Europe, where it was printed in the seventeenth-century Paris and London Polyglotts and attracted much interest for the places where it agreed with the Septuagint against the Masoretic text. These and other variants were carefully examined and analysed in an early work of Wilhelm

---

[14] They were recorded in much detail in *BH³* and more approximately in *BHS*, but *BHQ* has dispensed with them in its apparatus: see de Waard et al., *BHQ* fasc. 18, p. xiv; Tov, *Textual Criticism*, pp. 35-39. On the practice of *The Hebrew University Bible* (*HUB*) see recently M. Segal, 'The Hebrew University Bible Project', *HBAI* 2 (2013), pp. 38-62 (56-60).

[15] See further von Gall, *Der hebräische Pentateuch*; Sadaqa, *Jewish Version and Samaritan Version*; Tal, *Samaritan Pentateuch*; Macuch, *GSH*; Z. Ben-Hayyim, *The Literary and Oral Tradition of Hebrew and Aramaic amongst the Samaritans*, 4: *The Words of the Pentateuch* (Heb.: Jerusalem, 1977); Crown et al., *Companion*; id., *Samaritan Scribes*; Kartveit, *Origins*, pp. 259-312; S. Schorch, *Die Vokale des Gesetzes: Die samaritanische Lesetradition als Textzeugin der Tora*, 1, *Das Buch Genesis* (BZAW 339; Berlin, 2004); Anderson and Giles, *Samaritan Pentateuch*.

Gesenius (1815), who concluded that they were secondary readings, some of which were deliberately inserted to favour the Samaritan position in their debates with the Jews. This conclusion dampened the earlier enthusiasm for the version, but it continued to play a valued ancillary role in biblical scholarship. Its importance was, however, underlined when early Hebrew biblical manuscripts found (from 1947 onwards) at Qumran and neighbouring sites proved to include some presenting the text in a consistently 'Samaritan' form, though not with the 'sectarian' variants mentioned above (especially 4QpalEx^m, 4QNum^b and mss of 4Q [Reworked] Pentateuch: for fuller details see section 2 [i] c below). These discoveries made it clear that the Samaritan text had an ancient (first cent. B.C. or earlier) origin and, even more surprising, that it had also been known and used by (at least some) Jews for a time.

The complete (or nearly so) Samaritan mss of the Pentateuch date, like their Masoretic counterparts, from the Middle Ages, the earliest of them being from the twelfth century (for lists and details see von Gall, pp. i-lxi, lxxi-xciii; Schorch, 'A Critical *editio maior*', pp. 111-13, no doubt to be amplified in the volumes of his forthcoming *editio maior*). Only one of these, Cambridge University Library Add. 1846, preserves a relatively full text: even it lacks most of Genesis 1–11 and the last two chapters of Deuteronomy, having lost (like other early mss in codex form) its opening and closing pages.[16] From the early thirteenth century on there is an increasing number of such mss, such as Nablus Synagogue 6 (1204), Cambridge University Library Add.713 (beginning of the thirteenth cent.) and Dublin Chester Beatty Library 751 (1225). But the earliest fully preserved mss are from the fourteenth cent. (Schorch, p. 111 n. 38). Comparison of even a selection of these manuscripts makes it clear that they display remarkable consistency among themselves at the macro- or word level with considerable

---

[16] A.D. Crown, *Samaritan Scribes*, pp. 169-70, 495 (where Camb. Add. 713 is dated to 'within a decade of 1167 CE'), cites evidence from the end of its Exodus text for a date shortly before 1149. The famous 'Abisha scroll' from Nablus, which was once thought to be much older than this, was studied from photographs and shown to be a composite of sections with different dates by F. Perez Castro, *Sefer Abiša* (Madrid, 1959), who published the text of its oldest part (from Num. 35 to the end) and dated it to the twelfth century (see also the important review by E. Robertson, *VT* 12 [1962], pp. 228-35; and Crown in id. et al., *Companion*, pp. 4-6).

variation at the micro- or spelling level (similarly Schorch, pp. 102, 110, 112). Both presumably reflect aspects of Samaritan scribal practice and pronunciation: the former suggests a cadre of scribes who were trained to maintain the textual tradition with great care (going back to what Crown has termed in a loose sense a 'Masoretic' tradition of some antiquity: *Samaritan Scribes*, Chapter 12, first published in *BJRL* 67 [1984], pp. 349-81), while the latter arises from simplification and change in spoken Samaritan Hebrew (and Aramaic), which was tolerated even in the written output of the scribe (see, e.g., Macuch, *GSH* §13-17 on the guttural letters). Even here one should not exaggerate: one can read through pages of the better mss and meet only occasional variations in the use of the *matres lectionis*. The vowels are only sporadically marked in the manuscripts: some help can be had from the oral reading tradition, though it is itself not uniform and retains evidence of a complex process of development, with some apparently very ancient elements and others which reflect changes over time (Ben-Hayyim, *Literary and Oral Tradition*, p. 4; Schorch, *Die Vokale*; *GSH* §30).

The differences between the Samaritan and Masoretic texts are of several different kinds, as Gesenius already saw. The following summary of the main categories is based on Tov, *Textual Criticism*, pp. 84-97:

(a) Large harmonising additions, ranging in length from one to ten verses and serving to fill out what were perceived as 'gaps' in a narrative with text from the same book of the Pentateuch or a different one: e.g. in Exodus after 6.9, 7.18, 7.29, 8.1, 8.19, 9.5, 9.19, 10.2, 11.3, 18.24 (in place of v. 25), (20.17), 20.19, 20.21, 27.19, 28.29, 32.10, 39.21. Many of these introduce the fulfilment of a command or, occasionally, a command to do what is subsequently done. The added material in these cases mostly comes from Exodus, but in five cases (after 18.24, 20.17, 20.19, 20.21 and 32.19) from Deuteronomy 1–9, 11, 18 and 27.

(b) Relocation of a passage to match a related context: in Exodus after 26.35 and 29.28, to match the order of the construction of the tabernacle or the ordination of Aaron and his sons.

(c) Short harmonising changes, usually only involving a word or two in the immediate context (e.g. Exod. 8.20; 18.26).

(d) The conversion of rare spellings or morphemes to their standard equivalents (e.g. Exod. 4.9; 15.16; 22.4).

(e) Changes to conform to strict grammatical requirements (e.g. Exod. 17.12; 18.20).

(f) Differences in the content, involving the substitution or addition of a word (e.g. Exod. 2.10; 7.14; 15.3 [perhaps theological]).

(g) Differences which are related to disputes between Jews and Samaritans over the proper place for temple worship (for which John 4.20 provides well-known evidence, but see also Jos., *AJ* 12.10; 13.74-79). The most famous examples are the addition after 20.17, in Deut. 27.4, where the Samaritan text has 'Gerizim' (the Samaritans' holy place) instead of 'Ebal', and in Deut. 12.8 and parallel passages, where the Samaritan reads 'has chosen' instead of 'will choose'. Traditionally the Samaritan readings have been seen as later alterations, but recently some scholars have argued that it is the 'Jewish' readings (which are found already in the Septuagint translation as it has come down to us) which are the result of emendation (see Schorch, *HBAI* 2 [2013], pp. 1041-106: cf. McCarthy, *Deuteronomy* [*BHQ* 5], pp. 122-23*).

(h) Spelling differences, which mainly concern the more extensive use of *matres lectionis* in the Samaritan text and variation in the use of the guttural letters, which is due to the gradual loss of their distinctive sounds in the spoken language.

Most of these kinds of variation are also attested in the Dead Sea Scrolls and are not distinctively Samaritan. The large harmonising additions (a), however, only occur in certain manuscripts (such as 4QpalEx^m and 4QRP) and for obvious reasons the Samaritan readings in (g) do not occur in the biblical texts at all.[17] The same smaller variations as occur in SP are also often found in 4QpalEx^m (from the first cent. B.C.) and other witnesses, so that it can be concluded that a process of 'editorial' improvement of an older text-form was already under way in the last two centuries B.C. It is perhaps no coincidence that it was precisely in this period that the greatest of Homeric scholars in antiquity, Aristarchus (c. 215–143), was busy with editorial work and teaching in Alexandria, the aim

---

[17] The occurrence of 'has chosen' in 4QMMT B 61 (= 4Q394 and 395: cited by Schorch, 'A Critical *editio maior*', p. 105 n. 16) certainly alludes to the Deuteronomic formula, but it occurs in words of the letter-writer himself, who is using the text to affirm Jerusalem's supremacy and from his point of view he naturally uses the past tense for God's choice of it. This says nothing about the wording of his biblical source, which could perfectly well have used the future.

of which was to establish the original (and perfect) text of Greek literary works. He was also the founder of a distinctive school of textual critics.[18] Whether we should attribute this early revision of the Pentateuch to Jews, Samaritans, or both, there is plenty of evidence for contact with Hellenistic culture of other kinds, and not only in Egypt but in Palestine too (see M. Hengel, *Judentum und Hellenismus: Studien zur ihrer Begegnung unter besonderer Berücksichtigung Palästinas bis zur Mitte des 2. Jh.s v.Chr.* [WUNT 10; Tübingen, 2nd ed., 1973, ET 1974], passim; and more recently D.M. Carr, *Writing on the Tablet of the Heart* [New York, 2005], Chapters 7–12, and *The Formation of the Hebrew Bible* [New York, 2011], Chapters 5–6, which come close to the suggestion made here without apparently actually making it).

As for editions of the text, shortly (we may hope) there will be the Exodus volume of the *editio maior* of Stefan Schorch, the principles of which are described in his article 'A Critical *editio maior*'.[19] For the present there remains much valuable information in the edition of A. von Gall, even though its text is often not a reliable guide to what it sought to offer, the original text of the Samaritan version (see especially the critique of Baillet, 'Corrections'; also, for Exod. 4, J.D. Purvis, *The Samaritan Pentateuch and the Origin of the Samaritan Sect* [HSM 2; Cambridge MA, 1968], p. 56). It is a critical edition, based on over twenty manuscripts and numerous fragments, whose readings are cited at length. Several of its sources go back to the thirteenth or even the twelfth century. The more recent editions of Sadaqa and Tal present the text of single manuscripts that were not known to von Gall, the former (for Exodus) 'a manuscript from the eleventh century', and the latter Nablus Synagogue 6, which is dated in 1204. They are therefore free from the distortion caused by von Gall's defective editorial principles, but when used alone they provide only a narrow perspective on the text. In addition to these published resources, I have had access to the draft text of Exodus for the

---

[18] See P.M. Fraser, *Ptolemaic Alexandria* (Oxford, 1972), pp. 462-79; on the intellectual context D. Dawson, *Allegorical Readers and Cultural Revision in Ancient Alexandria* (Berkeley and Los Angeles, 1992), pp. 52-72; and J. Ben-Dov, 'Early Texts of the Torah: Revisiting the Greek Scholarly Context', *JAJ* 4 (2013), pp. 210-34.

[19] The first volume to appear, of Leviticus, was published in 2018.

edition that was being prepared by Alan Crown before his death, which he generously made available to me in the 1990s. It records the readings of two manuscripts used by von Gall (his N and Camb. Add.713: on the date of the latter see above, n. 11) and two not used by him, the Rylands manuscript of 1211 and Dublin Chester Beatty 751 of 1225 (the base text for Schorch's new edition). I have also, through the kind help of Professor Stefan Reif, been able to use a photocopy of the very early manuscript Cambridge University Library Add. 1846. The citations of Samaritan readings in the 'Text and Versions' sections of the commentary are based on a comparison of these sources. Although it has not produced many divergent readings, this provides a much firmer foundation than would otherwise have been possible at the moment for assertions about the predominant text.

There are also old translations of the Samaritan text into Greek, Aramaic and Arabic. In the latter two cases the versions survive in complete form and critical editions of their texts and studies which clarify their origins and history have been published. A. Tal has distinguished three stages in the development of the Aramaic version (Targum), not principally from the age of the surviving manuscripts but from the changing form of the language which they use (see his edition of the text [1980–83], with a lengthy introduction in vol. 3; and his articles 'Aramaic' and 'Targum' in Crown et al., *Companion*, pp. 24-25, 226-28). The earliest stage (best represented in ms. J, BM/BL Or. 7562) takes the origin of the Samaritan Targum back to the third or fourth century A.D.: the language is close to that of Tg^O and Qumran. In character the translation is mainly verbatim and literal, with few exegetical variations, and it remained essentially the same even in mss written in much later forms of the language (Tal, *Targum*, pp. 52-54). The Arabic versions are much later, coming into use after Arabic replaced Aramaic as the Samaritan vernacular in the eleventh cent. For a time a version based on the *Tafsir* of Saʿadya Gaon was used (a copy survives in the parallel column of ms. J mentioned above). A new Samaritan Arabic translation, again very literal, was prepared in the eleventh cent. (it appears in Nablus Synagogue 6) and then in the thirteenth cent. the learned scholar Abū Saʿīd revised the existing translations to match classical Arabic norms and to eliminate 'heretical' elements: his version appears in Paris BN Arabe 5 (see H. Shehadeh, *The Arabic Translation of the Samaritan*

Pentateuch [Jerusalem, 1989, 2002], a critical edition of both these versions, with a brief Foreword in vol. 1, pp. iii-vi; for references to other works of Shehadeh see his article on 'Arabic Versions of the Pentateuch', in Crown et al., *Companion*, pp. 22-24).

The Greek version survives only in fragments, if indeed they do represent a specifically Samaritan translation, which has been disputed.[20] The evidence is of four main kinds: (a) translations of the 'expanded' texts in Exodus and elsewhere, sometimes in the original Greek but mainly in the Syrohexapla, where there are also references to collation with the Samaritan text in colophons and a scholion; (b) marginal variants in Greek manuscripts, especially in Codex Paris BN Coislinianus 1 (M), which either are marked τὸ σαμ(αρειτικόν) or agree with the SamTg; (c) the 'Glaue-Rahlfs' Greek fragments of Deuteronomy (also known as the 'Giessen and Geneva fragments'), which read 'Mount Gerizim' in Deut. 27.4; (d) the Samaritan inscription from Thessalonika published in 1968, which contains a Greek version of Num. 6.22-27 in a form that differs from LXX but agrees with the Samaritan Pentateuch. It might seem that this amply justifies the view that the Samaritans, like the Jews and early Christians, had a Greek version of the Pentateuch, one which matched the distinctive text of their Hebrew Bible. The need for such a translation would come from the existence of Greek-speaking Samaritan communities in Palestine and as far west as Italy (Anderson and Giles, *Samaritan Pentateuch*, pp. 175-78). But questions have been raised about such an inference. Is it certain that the Greek versions in (a) and (b) were made by Samaritans? Could they have been the work of Christian scholars or scribes? Could the Greek text of the 'Glaue-Rahlfs' fragments have been taken from a non-Samaritan source, and likewise the Greek inscription from Thessalonika, which agrees with the Masoretic

---

[20] For fuller details of the evidence and discussion of the competing interpretations see Pummer, 'The Greek Bible and the Samaritans'; also J. Joosten, 'Samareitikon' in Lange and Tov, *Textual History* 1A, pp. 235-38 (1.3.2). The problem has now been addressed in much more detail and depth in the as yet unpublished Oxford D.Phil. dissertation of Bradley Marsh, 'Early Christian Scripture and the Samaritan Pentateuch: A Study in Hexaplaric Manuscript Activity' (2016). A summary will appear in Dr Marsh's contribution to the forthcoming *Oxford Handbook of the Septuagint*. I am grateful to Dr Marsh for providing me with a draft copy of the latter, for reading an earlier version of this paragraph and for drawing my attention to a problem with a phrase in it.

text as well as the Samaritan Pentateuch?[21] Account needs also to be taken of the fact that the Giessen and Thessalonika texts are in places very similar to the LXX (this is also true for some features of the evidence in groups [a] and [b]). Supporters of a Samaritan Greek version therefore often take the view today that it was not a totally new translation but an adaptation of the existing LXX to fit the Samaritan Hebrew text, just like the Jewish revisions of the LXX. On the other hand, the argument for a Samaritan origin of the marginal variants in group (b) is weakened by the fact that they have parallels not only in SamTg but in Jewish sources. There are, however, a few where a Samaritan origin is probable and it remains possible for a number of others. All in all, it seems most likely that τὸ Σαμαρειτικόν does refer to a distinct Greek version of the Pentateuch that was used (and at least adapted) by Samaritans and that other types of evidence derive from it (cf. Pummer, pp. 306-11). In so far as this is correct, it also helps to confirm the antiquity of distinctive Samaritan readings long before the earliest medieval Samaritan manuscripts were written.[22] Of course, as the next section will show, this is also the implication, for some passages at least, of a group of Hebrew texts of Exodus from Qumran.

c. *The Dead Sea Scrolls and Other Ancient Hebrew Sources*
Although the two great Isaiah scrolls from Qumran Cave 1 were among the first discoveries to emerge from the western shoreline of the Dead Sea in 1947 and 1948, it was only with the archaeological excavation of this and other caves, especially Cave 4, that it became clear how much new light on the history of the biblical text was about to appear (cf. Cross, *Ancient Library*, Chapter 4; R. de Vaux, *Archaeology and the Dead Sea Scrolls* [London, rev. Eng. ed., 1975]; Lange, *Handbuch*). It took many years of further study and joining of the fragments before the manuscripts were

---

[21] These two points were pressed especially by E. Tov, in 'Pap.Giessen 13, 19, 22, 26: A Revision of the LXX?', *RB* 78 (1971), pp. 355-83; 'Une inscription grecque d'origine samaritaine trouvée à Thessalonique', *RB* 81 (1974), pp. 394-99.

[22] There are numerous Exodus quotations from SP and SamTg in the older (third–fourth cent. A.D.) sections of Books 1-2 of *Tibat Marqe* (or *Memar Marqah*), which might also be of text-critical interest: see the lists in J. Macdonald (ed. and tr.), *Memar Marqah: The Teaching of Marqah* (BZAW 84; Berlin, 1963) 2, pp. 249-55 and the brief remarks in 1, pp. xxxiv-xxxvi. On the date cf. 1, p. xx, and more precisely A. Tal in Crown et al., *Companion*, pp. 235-36.

all definitively published, but it is now clear that parts of around twenty manuscripts containing the Hebrew text of Exodus have been found in the area, dating from the third cent. B.C. to the early second century A.D. The exact number depends on the affiliation of an as yet unpublished fragment (see n. 26 below) and, more important, on the assessment of a group of manuscripts which were published as 'Biblical Paraphrase: Genesis, Exodus' and 'Reworked Pentateuch' (see below on 4Q158 and 4Q364-366).

The manuscripts are listed below in numerical order, with details of the surviving text from Exodus, any special features of script or orthography and opinions about their date and textual character: for fuller information see the introductions and notes in *DJD* and the recent *Handbuch* of A. Lange on the pages specified.[23] A convenient presentation of all the Qumran texts (except for 4QRP) in one volume can be found in E. Ulrich, *The Biblical Qumran Scrolls: Transcriptions and Textual Variants* (Leiden, 2013) 1, pp. 27-107.

1Q2/1QEx (*DJD* I, pp. 50-51; Lange, pp. 56-57): 16.12-16; 19.24–20.1; 20.5-6; 20.25–21.1; 21.4-5. 1–50 A.D. Affiliation indeterminate (Lange: too few variants) or non-aligned.

2Q2/2QEx^a (*DJD* III, pp. 49-52; Lange, p. 57): 1.11-14; 7.1-4; 9.27-29; 11.3-7; 12.32-41; 21.18-19(20?); 26.11-13; 30.21(?); 30.23-25; 32.32-34. 50–68 A.D. Affiliation non-aligned (Lange), but the strongest association is with LXX.

2Q3/2QEx^b (*DJD* III, pp. 52-55; Lange, pp. 57-58): 4.31; 12.26-27; 18.21-22; 19.9+34.10; 21.37–22.2; 22.15-19; 27.17-19; 31.16-17. 1–68 A.D. 'Qumran practice' orthography, divine name in palaeo-Heb. Affiliation indeterminate (Lange: too few variants): several cases of an expanded text.

2Q4/2QEx^c (*DJD* III, p. 56; Lange, p. 58): 5.3-5. 50–1 B.C.? Affiliation indeterminate.

---

[23] On 'Qumran practice' (the use of distinctively fuller spellings) see Tov, *Scribal Practices*, pp. 261-73; Lange, pp. 6, 10-11. In statements about the manuscripts' affiliation 'indeterminate' means that there is too little evidence to decide, whereas 'non-aligned' means that there is evidence of association with more than one of the major textual traditions (MT, SP, LXX). Where passages are preserved in more than one ms., it is in principle possible to use shared variants to reconstruct relationships between them, and a careful study of this kind for the book of Exodus has been made by D.G. Longacre in his as yet unpublished doctoral dissertation 'A Contextualized Approach to the Hebrew Dead Sea Scrolls containing Exodus' (Birmingham, 2015): see also Text and Versions on 17.1 and 17.7.

4Q1/4QGen-Exª (*DJD* XII, pp. 7-30; Lange, p. 44: at first called 4QEx^b): 1.3-17; 1.22-2.5; 3.8-16; 3.18-21; 4.4-9; 4.26–5.1; 5.3-7; 6.4-21; 6.25; 7.5-13; 7.15-20; 8.20-22; 9.8(?). 125–100 B.C. Affiliation semi-Masoretic (Lange).

4Q11/4QpalGen-Ex^l (*DJD* IX, pp. 17-50; Lange, pp. 51-52): 1.1-5; 2.10; 2.22–3.4; 3.17-21; 8.13-15; 8.19-21; 9.25-29; 9.33–10.5; 11.4–12.12; 12.42-46; 14.15-24; 16.2-7; 16.13-14; 16.18-20; 16.23-31; 16.33–17.3; 17.5-11; 18.17-24; 19.24–20.2; 22.23-24; 23.5-16; 25.7-20; 26.29–27.1; 27.6-14; 28.33-35; 28.40-42; 36.34-36. 100–25 B.C. Written in palaeo-Heb. Affiliation semi-Masoretic (Lange): the ms. apparently lacked the longer expansions of SP and it did not share the latter's placement of the incense-altar pericope after 26.35.

4Q13/4QEx^b (*DJD* XII, pp. 79-95; Lange, pp. 58-59: at first (e.g. by Cross) called 4QEx^a): 1.1-6; 1.10-11 (not in *DJD*: see *RQ* 21 [2003–2004], p. 483); 1.16-21; 2.2-18; 3.13–4.8; 5.3-14. 30 B.C.–20 A.D. Very likely included Genesis too, though nothing survives. Not full 'Qumran practice' but some features of it. Non-aligned but close to LXX (Lange: number of unique readings); the proximity to LXX is greater according to Cross in *DJD*, where superior and inferior readings are distinguished.

4Q14/4QEx^c (*DJD* XII, pp. 97-125; Lange, pp. 59-60): 7.17-23; 7.26–8.1; 8.5-18; 8.22; 9.10-12; 9.15-35; 10.1-9; 10.12-19; 10.23-24; 11.9-10; 12.12-16; 12.31-48; 13.18–14.13; 15.9-21; 17.1–18.12. 50–25 B.C. There are several cases of omission by parablepsis, some of which were later corrected. The manuscript apparently did not include the major expansions of SP. Affiliation non-aligned.

4Q15/4QEx^d (*DJD* XII, pp. 127-28; Lange, pp. 60-61): 13.15-16+15.1 (separated only by a *vacat*). C. 100 B.C. Unless the manuscript had a shorter text of Exodus or a different arrangement of it, the collocation of these two passages suggests that it contained only excerpts from the text, perhaps selected for a liturgical or pedagogical purpose. Affiliation indeterminate.

4Q16/4QEx^e (*DJD* XII, pp. 129-31; Lange, p. 61): 13.3-5. 150–100 B.C. The small size of the ms. suggests that it included only excerpts from the text, in view of the content perhaps for liturgical purposes. Affiliation indeterminate, but there are several divergences from MT.

4Q17/4QEx-Lev^f (*DJD* XII, pp. 133-44; Lange, pp. 61-62): 38.18-22; 39.6-24; 40.8-27. C. 250 B.C.: this is one of the oldest Qumran mss, dating from before the foundation of the settlement. Only one of the four columns is well preserved. The script is described as 'proto-cursive' in *DJD*; *matres lectionis* occur more frequently than in MT, especially in the spelling of את as אות. In the order of the text the placing of ch. 39 agrees with MT and SP against LXX. The evidence of shared readings points to affiliation with the proto- or pre-Samaritan/Palestinian tradition (Cross, *DJD*), but the number of unique variants implies a somewhat loose association with it (hence Lange: 'non-aligned').

4Q18/4QExᵍ (*DJD* XII, pp. 145-46; Lange, pp. 62-63): 14.21-27. C. 50 B.C. Affiliation indeterminate.

4Q19/4QExʰ (*DJD* XII, p. 147; Lange, p. 63): 6.3-6. 50–1 B.C. Affiliation indeterminate.

4Q20/4QExʲ (*DJD* XII, pp. 149-50; Lange, p. 63): 7.29–8.1/2. 1–25 A.D. The divine name is written in palaeo-Heb. The divisions in the text give some support to the presence of the SP expansions and so to a proto- or pre-Samaritan affiliation (*DJD*), but the fragment is too small for certainty (Lange: indeterminate).

4Q21/4QExᵏ (*DJD* XII, p. 151; Lange, pp. 63-64): 36.9-10. C. 50 A.D. (or even later). Affiliation indeterminate.

4Q22/4QpalExᵐ (*DJD* IX, pp. 53-130; Lange, pp. 64-66: see also J.E. Sanderson, *An Exodus Scroll from Qumran: 4QpalaeoExod*ᵐ *and the Samaritan Tradition* [HSS 30; Atlanta, 1986]): 6.25–7.16; 7.16-19; 7.29ᵇ–8.1; 8.12-18; 8.19ᵇ-22; 9.5ᵇ-16; 9.19ᵇ-21; 9.35–10.1; 10.2ᵇ-5; 10.5-12; 10.19-24; 10.25-28; 11.8–12.2; 12.6-8, 13-15, 17-22; 12.31-32, 34-39; 13.3-7, 12-13; 14.3-5, 8-9, 25-26; 15.23–16.1; 16.4-5, 7-8, 31-32; 16.32–17.16; 18.1-21; 18.21–19.1; 19.7-17; 19.23–20.1; 20.18-19; 21.5-6, 13-14, 22-32; 22.3-4, 6-7, 11-13, 16-30; 23.15-16, 29-31; 24.1-4, 6-11; 25.11-12, 20-29, 31-34; 26.8-15, 21-30; 30.10; 27.1-3, 9-14, 18-19ᵇ; 28.3-4, 8-12, 22-24, 26-28, 30-39; 28.39–29.5; 29.20, 22-25, 31-41; 30.12-18, 29-31; 30.34–31.7; 31.7-8, 13-15; 32.2-9, 10-19, 25-30; 33.12-15; 33.16–34.3; 34.10-13, 15-18, 20-24, 27-28; 35.1; 36.21-24; 37.9-16. 100–25 B.C. Written in palaeo-Heb. The orthography is fuller than MT, but not overly so. The scribe distinguishes between מצרים for the land of Egypt and מצריים for the Egyptians as a people, as the Vss often do in their renderings.

This manuscript is one of the most interesting and important of the Qumran biblical scrolls, both because of its script and preserved extent and because it provides, like 4QNumᵇ, clear evidence of the existence of 'Samaritan' expansions and readings in antiquity and knowledge of them in the Jewish community at Qumran (see also below on 4QRP). Parts of 45 out of the original estimated 57 columns survive, though only in (sometimes quite large) fragments. The distribution of the text between columns is aided by the preservation of about one-third of the top and bottom margins, but only in cols 1, 35 and 38 do both the beginnings and ends of lines and (parts of) the first and last lines remain. Evidence of the 'Samaritan' expansions of the text is extant in twelve places (some of these are evident from the superscript 'b' in the list of contents given above) and can be plausibly inferred in three others. It is also clear that the incense-altar pericope appeared not in ch. 30, as in MT, but after 26.35, as in SP. But the long sectarian expansion after 20.17, referring to an altar on Mount Gerizim, was definitely not present in 4QpalExᵐ: there is no room for it among the extant fragments (see *DJD* IX, pp. 101-103). The scroll also includes many of the minor readings (but not all of them) which are characteristic of SP but of no religious significance. These data show that in many matters, both large and small, 4QpalEx^m coincides with the Samaritan text but that it has not undergone the distinct religious editing which is found in the latter. Possibly that editing had already taken place in some copies used by the Samaritans, but if so 4QpalEx^m was copied from an older exemplar that had not been affected by it. For this reason (as well as their discovery in the library or archive of a Jewish religious community) it and the other Qumran mss with similar features cannot be described as 'Samaritan', and terms like 'proto-' or 'pre-Samaritan' or even 'Palestinian' are used for them instead. But it remains of the highest importance that the foundations of the later Samaritan text were laid at the latest in the second or first century B.C., so that the literary conventions which it reflects are predominantly those of the Hellenistic period.

4Q37/4QDeut^j (*DJD* XIV, pp. 75-91; Lange, pp. 92-93): 12.43-51; 13.1-5. C. 50 A.D. Other fragments of the ms. contain passages from Deut. 5, 6, 8, 11 and 32: the contents correspond in part to those of the Qumran phylacteries (see below) and related texts such as 4QDeutⁿ and the Nash papyrus. The Exodus text occupies the last three lines of one column and the whole of the next (14 lines): it appears to have followed Deut. 11.21 directly after a *vacat*. The dimensions of the columns support the view that this is an 'excerpted manuscript'. Affiliation non-aligned.

Mur1/MurGen-Ex,Num^a (*DJD* II.1, pp. 75-78; Lange, p. 55): 4.28-31; 5.3; 6.5-11. Early second cent. A.D. The inclusion of passages from Genesis 32–35 and Numbers 34 and 36 in other fragments and the very large column size (c. 50 lines) suggest that the ms. may originally have contained the whole Pentateuch. Affiliation proto-Masoretic: there are no divergences at all from the standard medieval consonantal text (*DJD*, Lange).

4Q158/4QRP('Reworked Pentateuch')^a (*DJD* V, pp. 1-6 [note also the corrections by J. Strugnell, *RQ* 7 (1970), pp. 168-76]; Lange, p. 37; see also M. Zahn, *Rethinking Rewritten Scripture* [STDJ 95; Leiden, 2011], pp. 25-74, and S. White Crawford, 'Exodus in the Dead Sea Scrolls', in Dozeman et al., *The Book of Exodus*, pp. 305-21 [306-10]): Gen. 32.25-32+Exod. 4.27-28; Exod. 19.17-23; Deut. 5.27+Exod. 20.19b-21+Deut. 5.28b-29+18.18-22; Exod. 20.12-17+Deut. 5.30-31+new text+Exod. 20.22-26; 21.1-10 (fragmentary); 21.15-25 (fragmentary); 21.32–22.13; 3.12+24.4-6 (?+ fr. 14 with more expansion of the promise to Israel's ancestors); 30.32, 34. First cent. B.C. (*RQ* 7 [1970], p. 168). 'Qumran practice' orthography. Most likely this was a heavily expanded version of Exodus, not the whole Pentateuch (Zahn). In Exodus 20 it includes the SP additions, except for the 'Gerizim' expansion after v. 17. The Genesis texts and the related material in frs 4 and 14 have been inserted for theological reasons: '4QReworked Exodus' would be an appropriate designation for this work (cf. Zahn). The extent of the reworking makes this a work of interpretation, but there are enough sections of 'pure' Exodus text (especially in chs. 21–22) to give it value as a textual witness in its own right.

4Q364/4QRP('Reworked Pentateuch')[b] (*DJD* XIII, pp. 187-96 [on 4Q364-367], 197-254; Lange, pp. 37-39; see also M. Segal, '4Q Reworked Pentateuch or 4Q Pentateuch?', in L.H. Schiffman et al. [eds.], *The Dead Sea Scrolls: Fifty Years after their Discovery. Proceedings of the Jerusalem Congress 1997* [Jerusalem, 2000], pp. 391-99, and Zahn and White Crawford as for 4Q158): 21.14-15, 19-22; (19.17) 24.12-14+new text+25.1-2; 26.1; 26.33-35. 75–50 B.C. 'Qumran practice' orthography. Originally the scroll certainly included Genesis, Numbers and Deuteronomy as well, so probably the whole Pentateuch. There are some notable agreements with SP (in harmonising additions after Gen. 30.36 and before Deut. 2.8) which are taken to indicate an underlying 'pre-Samaritan' affiliation. But many other additions and other variants are distinctive and so the final product should be described as 'non-aligned' (Lange). Segal has argued that 4Q364-367 are no more 'rewritten' than the Samaritan Pentateuch and that like it they should simply be regarded as 'biblical' manuscripts. There is certainly a difference between them and a thoroughgoing 'rewriting' of the biblical narrative like the book of Jubilees: but the greater *extent* of the expansions and the use of non-biblical supplementary material in them also distinguish them significantly from the 'biblical' manuscripts. Another question is whether they are four copies of the same work (as argued in *DJD*) or copies of four similar revisions of the Pentateuch. The doubt arises from the fact that, despite the extensive remains that survive (at least of 4Q364 and 4Q365), they overlap at only two points (Exod. 26.34-35 and Lev. 27.34) and share only one distinctive reading (cf. *DJD* XIII, p. 188). However these questions are answered, the four manuscripts (together with 4Q158) show that such elaboration of the biblical text was popular at Qumran alongside more straightforward copying of it.

4Q365/4QRP('Reworked Pentateuch')[c] (*DJD* XIII, pp. 255-318; Lange, pp. 39-42: also Zahn and White Crawford as for 4Q158): 8.13-19; 9.9-12; 10.19-20?; 14.10, 12-21; 15.16-20; new text+15.22-26; 17.3-5; 18.13-15; 26.34-36; 28.16-20; 29.20-22; 30.37–31.3; 35.3-5; 36.32-38; 37.29–38.7; 39.1-5, 8-19. 75–50 B.C. (Lange). 'Qumran practice' orthography. Fragments of all five books of the Pentateuch have survived.[24] Both *DJD* and Lange see 4Q365, like 4Q364, as based on a 'pre-Samaritan' form of the text, but the evidence is much less clear. The most obvious characteristic is the extent of the additional material which has no parallel anywhere (such as the fuller form of the Song of Miriam). This can certainly be attributed to the Qumran reviser, but the absence of 'Samaritan' variants such as harmonising additions

---

[24] The status of what was published as 4Q365a and attributed by the editors to a different work altogether (*DJD* XIII, pp. 319-33) is not directly relevant for Exodus, since the fragments concerned do not correspond to any biblical text and, if they are part of a copy of 4QRP (as Lange and others believe), they would most likely belong in one of the later books of the Pentateuch.

and especially the relocations of text in Exodus 26 and 29 raises serious doubt about the foundation on which the reviser was building. 'Non-aligned' (Lange, for the completed text) might be a safer designation for the manuscript's textual character as a whole.

4Q366/4QRP('Reworked Pentateuch')^d (*DJD* XIII, pp. 355-43; Lange, p. 42): 21.35–22.4. 75–50 B.C. Orthography close to the Masoretic tradition. Other fragments include sections of Leviticus–Deuteronomy, but not Genesis. Overall textual affiliation indeterminate (*DJD*) or non-aligned (Lange), but the (damaged) text of Exod. 22.4 appears to have been close to SP/LXX rather than MT.[25]

Phylacteries and Mezuzot Numerous examples of the tiny copies of extracts from the Pentateuch which were worn or placed on doorways according to the rulings of Exod. 13.9, 16; Deut. 6.8-9 have been found at Qumran and at nearby sites (*DJD* I, pp. 72-76; II, pp. 80-85; III, pp. 149-57; VI, pp. 48-85; XXXVIII, pp. 183-91; *IEJ* 11 [1961], pp. 22-23; Y. Yadin, *Tefillin from Qumran (XQPhyl 1-4)* [Jerusalem, 1969]: Lange, pp. 116-22, includes a list of the individual items and their contents). Precise dating (and even reading) of the small and often semi-cursive script is difficult, but an overall range between the late second century B.C. and the early second cent. A.D. is likely. From Exodus sections of 12.43–13.16 and 20.11 (the latter in a mixed text of the Decalogue) appear in some copies. The passages included sometimes conform to the later rabbinic rulings (Exod. 13.1-10, 11-16; Deut. 6.4-9; 11.13-21), but a larger number (which are often written in 'Qumran practice': Tov) also contain part or all of Exod. 12.43-51; Deut. 5.1–6.3; 10.12–11.12, and in one case sections of Deuteronomy 32. In this group especially there are many small (or even large) variations from the standard forms of the texts, which can be attributed to their being written out from (sometimes faulty) memory. As such they are of only minor interest for textual criticism, but the variations are nevertheless noted in 'Text and Versions' in the commentary.[26]

---

[25] From 4Q367/4QRP('Reworked Pentateuch')^e (*DJD* XIII, pp. 345-51; Lange, p. 42) only fragments of Lev. survive: it may never have included the whole Pentateuch (cf. 4Q158).

[26] Three (possibly four) fragments pertaining to Exodus have come to light in the past twenty years but they have no secure provenance and their authenticity is doubtful: DSS F.Exod3 (Exod. 3.13-15) and DSS F.Exod4 (5.9-14), both published by E. and H. Eshel in *Meghillot* 5-6 (2007), pp. 272-74; DSS F.Exod5 (possibly 16.10) in the Schøyen collection but omitted, like the two previous fragments, from the publication in T. Elgvin et al. (eds.), *Gleanings from the Caves: Dead Sea Scrolls and artefacts from the Schøyen collection* (London and New York, 2016); and DSS F.Exod6 (17.4-7), published in E. Tov et al. (eds.), *Dead Sea Scrolls Fragments in the Museum Collection* (Publications of Museum of Bible 1; Leiden, 2016), pp. 90-109. For discussion of the problems which they raise see K. Davis et al., 'Nine Dubious "Dead Sea Scrolls" Fragments from the Twenty-First Century', *DSD* 24 (2017), pp. 189-228; and K. Davis, 'Caves

Shorter Extracts Isolated verses from Exodus occur in florilegia or as citations in non-biblical scrolls. 4Q174/4QFlor 1-3 I 3+fr. 21 (*DJD* V, pp. 53-57: cf. G.J. Brooke, *Exegesis at Qumran: 4QFlorilegium in its Jewish Context* [JSOTSup 29; Sheffield, 1985]) contains 15.17b-18, while 4Q175/ 4QTest 1-8 (*DJD* V, pp. 57-60) begins with the combination of Deut. 5.28b-29+18.18-19 which is inserted in SP at Exod. 20.21b (with additional text from Deut. 18 following, as also in 4Q158 and presumably in 4QpalEx^m). Citations from Exodus appear in the *Community Rule* (1QS 5.15: Exod. 23.7) and the *Temple Scroll* (11QT^a 2.1-7, 11-15: Exod. 34.10-16; 11QT^a 13.10-13: Exod. 29.38-40).

The Nash Papyrus (see Lange and Tov, *Textual History* 1B, pp. 111-15 [§2.2.5.2]; also conveniently E. Würthwein, *Der Text des Alten Testament* [Stuttgart, 4th ed., 1973; ET 1980], p. 37, with photograph and transcription on pp. 130-31). Although the Nash Papyrus was published nearly fifty years before the Dead Sea Scrolls were discovered, in 1903, it is appropriately treated after them here, as its nature and significance have been greatly, if not entirely, clarified by some of the scrolls. The portions of 24 lines that survive (many of the beginnings and ends of lines are lost) contain the Hebrew text of most of the Decalogue and, after a short introduction, the beginning of the Shema: the text of the latter certainly continued into Deut. 6.5, perhaps further, and there may also have been introductory words before the Decalogue. The manuscript came from Egypt, supposedly from the Fayum, and is now kept in Cambridge University Library. It is dated to the second or first cent. B.C. The wording of the Decalogue is a mixture of the versions in Exodus and Deuteronomy. The motivation for the Sabbath commandment is based on the first creation story, as in Exodus 20, but a number of phrases agree with the text of Deuteronomy and the order of the three short commandments (6, 7 and 8) are in an order (7, 6, 8) which corresponds to the Greek text of

---

of Dispute: Patterns of Correspondence and Suspicion in the Post-2002 "Dead Sea Scrolls" Fragments', ibid., 229-70. They would in any case be of only slight scholarly importance, even if they were genuine, and will not be referred to in the verse-by-verse commentary. Two further fragments of Exodus have been reported to be in the collections of Azusa Pacific University and South-Western Baptist Theological Seminary, but full details of them are not generally available. I am very grateful to Drew Longacre for drawing my attention to the problems with these fragments and the recent bibliography referred to: see also his review of the Museum Collection volume in *JTS* 69 (2018), pp. 265-67.

Deuteronomy and to two passages of Philo (*De Dec.* 36, 51) and three in the New Testament (Luke 18.20; Rom. 13.9; James 2.11) which are dependent upon it. Scholars have disagreed over whether the writer of the papyrus adapted the wording of Exodus to Deuteronomy or vice versa.[27] The scrolls have shown that this may be the wrong question to ask. The papyrus now fits well into the category of 'excerpted manuscripts' like 4Q15, 4Q16 and 4Q37 and the selection of texts in (the preserved section of) it finds a parallel in the wider range of passages in some of the ancient phylacteries and mezuzot. In some of the latter the Exodus version of the Sabbath commandment appears in what is clearly a Deuteronomic context (4QPhylG, 8QPhyl3 and 4QMezA). In fact, the papyrus is not a 'biblical text' in the strict sense at all: it reflects a wider tendency, both in Palestine and in Egypt, to produce copies of specially venerated texts in a form which, where the Decalogue was concerned, could be adapted to retain what were judged to be the best features of the different versions that were available. The choice seems to have been based not merely on the decisions (or memories) of individual scribes, but on wider conventions. Not surprisingly, the latter varied somewhat in their regional circulation: the preference for the Exodus motivation for the Sabbath is attested both in Egypt and in Palestine, whereas the reordering of the short commandments seems to have been limited to Egypt and other places where the Greek Pentateuch was well known and used.

Oxford Heb.d.89(P) i (Sirat, *Les papyrus*, pp. 32, 35, 123; Lange and Tov, *Textual History* 1B, p. 53 [§2.2.1.11.2]): 2.23-25. The fragment[28] contains parts of six lines of text, probably from the beginnings of lines (cf. the precise vertical alignment of the first letter in each line). It was found at Oxyrhyncus in 1905 and was dated by A. Yardeni to the second or third century A.D. (*The Book of Hebrew Script* [Jerusalem, 1997], p. 73). The surviving text

---

[27] I. Himbaza, 'Le Décalogue de Papyrus Nash, Philon, 4QPhylG, 8QPhyl3 et 4QMezA', *RQ* 20 (2001–2002), pp. 411-28, has argued that the papyrus is closest to the *Greek* text of Exodus (or its presumed Heb. *Vorlage*), which shows signs of adaptation to the Heb. Deuteronomy (see also p. 417 nn. 6-7 for a list of the supporters of the two main alternatives).

[28] The secondary literature refers to it as a 'papyrus', but Sirat's edition makes it clear that the fragment was a piece of parchment and that 'papyrus' is being used by her in the wider sense sometimes favoured by archaeologists (p. 17).

corresponds exactly to the MT. The column was much narrower (5-6 cm.) than those of the major Qumran biblical scrolls. Restoration of the context according to MT suggests that v. 23 began a new line, most likely with a division before it (as in MT, SP and 4QpalEx[1]).

(ii) *The Ancient Versions*

a. *General Considerations*

The extensive notes on ancient translations of Exodus which appear in this commentary, as they do in all volumes of the ICC, require some justification and clarification of their purpose. The translations to which attention is chiefly devoted are those which were made, primarily at least, on the basis of a Hebrew text before c. 500 A.D. They are distinguished from the so-called daughter versions such as the Armenian and Ethiopic, which are translations of an older translation (in both these cases a Greek version): these are treated as witnesses to that earlier version's form and history, which may sometimes be of great importance. For example, the first Old Latin translations were made from Greek texts a century or more earlier than the oldest complete Greek manuscripts of the Septuagint that survive and so they can (like the usually more fragmentary early papyri) provide evidence for the development of the Septuagint text closer to its time of origin. But most such secondary translations come from a later period. The translations which occupy pride of place here are the Septuagint, the Targumim (Jewish or Samaritan translations into Aramaic), the Peshiṭta (the earliest translation into Syriac, a dialect of Eastern Aramaic) and the Vulgate. Mention is also made where possible of early Jewish revisions of the Septuagint, such as those attributed to Theodotion, Aquila and Symmachus, and the *Samareitikon* (which has already been dealt with in section [i] [b]), all of which utilised knowledge of the Hebrew language and were already known to Origen in the third century A.D. None of these revisions any longer exists in its entirety and they are known chiefly from isolated quotations by later writers and from marginal notes in manuscripts (especially those of the Syrohexapla), which were derived from Origen's *Hexapla*, a massive compendium which placed the whole of the three (sometimes more) Jewish revisions in parallel columns alongside the Hebrew text and an edited version of the Septuagint itself.

At the time when the original volumes of the ICC were written, the main reason for giving so much attention to the ancient translations was the belief that they had a vital part to play in the correction of errors in the standard (Jewish) Hebrew text. The importance of this consideration has, however, been much diminished (though not eliminated) over the past century. In poetical books, where peculiarities of linguistic expression led in early times to misunderstanding and textual corruption, 'emendation on the basis of the Versions' continues to be a necessary tool of the critical interpreter, but in many prose books like Exodus there is much less scope for it (for one among several examples where it is needed see Text and Versions on 8.19). There are several reasons for the change in approach. There is no doubt that the discovery and study of the biblical manuscripts among the Dead Sea Scrolls has had a major impact, although the implications should not be over-simplified. The sheer availability of Hebrew copies of the biblical books, albeit unvocalised and mainly fragmentary, which are a thousand years older than the earliest medieval Hebrew manuscripts has undercut the older claim that it was only through the ancient translations that there could be access to the pre-Masoretic Hebrew text of the Bible. Moreover, the scrolls in question provide direct access, despite the limitations mentioned, to the text in its original language(s), not just the indirect access provided, potentially, by a translation. Many of these scrolls preserve a text which is close to and even identical with the medieval consonantal text, so that its ancient origin cannot be so readily called in question. But not all do, and the kinds of variant readings and errors which appear are similar in type and sometimes in wording to those reconstructed from the ancient translations. To this extent the scrolls have shown that the biblical texts were indeed vulnerable in antiquity to the same kinds of mistakes in copying or even deliberate alteration as other ancient writings, as had already been inferred from the translations. Prior to c. 100 A.D., at any rate, there was a certain 'fluidity' in the wording of the biblical texts, a feature which becomes more prominent in the eyes of those who allow no sharp distinction to be drawn between them and 'parabiblical' or 'reworked' texts like those of 4QReworked Pentateuch. Even apart from this, the evidence shows that there is just as much need for textual criticism as there was a hundred years ago: the difference is that there is now ancient evidence in Hebrew to take into account, which may act as a control over investigations even of passages where no such new evidence is available.

Emendation generally, whether or not on the basis of the Versions, has also become much less of a first resort when interpreting a difficult text (or even an easy one!) than it used to be, again for several reasons. Three may be mentioned here, which are sometimes combined and sometimes seen as alternatives. Advances in the comparative study of Semitic languages and as a result in knowledge of ancient Hebrew itself have offered new ways (or revived old ones) of explaining unusual items of vocabulary or grammatical features without the need for presuming that a scribal error has occurred. Different scholars have argued for the particular value of Arabic, Akkadian and Ugaritic or all three for elucidating unsolved problems in the text as it stands, or at least with only some change to the medieval vocalisation (cf. Barr, *Comparative Philology*, with some necessary critical remarks; more recently J.A. Emerton, 'Comparative Semitic Philology and Hebrew Lexicography', in id. [ed.], *Congress Volume: Cambridge, 1995* [VTSup 66; Leiden, 1997], pp. 1-24). Secondly, greater attention to the philological commentaries of the medieval rabbis such as Rashi and Ibn Ezra and other 'pre-critical' writers has encouraged more resourcefulness in explaining difficulties from within the semantic possibilities of Hebrew itself, including Mishnaic Hebrew, and this has sometimes been reinforced by insights from the study of modern linguistics. Finally, those who have pursued a more 'literary' (in the general sense) study of the biblical text, whether poetry or prose, have seen 'peculiarities' in a more positive light, to be preserved rather than removed by emendation. Even where their specific proposals are not adopted, the recognition that the biblical authors were, at least in many cases, guided by literary aims and conventions drawn from their wider cultural environment has made interpreters more ready to seek sense and meaning in the text as we have inherited it.

All these factors have been complemented by decades of closer study of the ancient translations themselves. An early note of caution was sounded in the observation that, before such translations were cited in support of emendations of the Hebrew text, it was necessary to study them in their own right as a whole, so as to understand their own aims and methods. Only then would an inference from the wording of a translation to its being based on a different

Hebrew original (or *Vorlage*) be valid. It might, for example, be due to paraphrase, clarification of the original or 'correction' for theological or other reasons. The study of *The Anti-Anthropomorphisms of the Greek Pentateuch* by C.T. Fritsch (Princeton, 1943) uncovered a number of examples of the third kind of change. The Targums especially showed the close nexus between translation and interpretation, some (e.g. Pseudo-Jonathan) more than others, and drew attention to possible edificatory motives in any biblical translator working within and for a faith community. More generally, studies of 'translation technique' have identified linguistic features of particular translations and indeed the translator(s) of one biblical book (or part of a book) as distinct from others. None of this has eliminated the possibility that translators may have used a Hebrew original that was different from the medieval consonantal text, but alternative explanations are now more readily considered before such a conclusion is accepted. Moreover even when, say, the Septuagint does seem to presuppose a different *Vorlage*, it can by no means be assumed that it will be superior to the Masoretic text. As with any kind of variant reading, such reconstructions have to be carefully scrutinized, not only for their appropriateness to the context but to see whether the likely process by which two or more different readings came into being points to the greater originality of the text behind the translation or the traditional Hebrew text. Ancient scribes were as adept at simplifying difficult passages as modern textual critics and the old adage that 'the more difficult reading is to be preferred' frequently applies in such cases.

Paradoxically perhaps, such cautionary remarks mean that more space, not less, now needs to be given in a commentary like this to the examination of the renderings in the ancient translations. In one sense this is merely an extension of the first stage of any study of a work which is preserved in a large number of textual witnesses to embrace the special case of translations of the work in question. This of course includes, when numerous manuscripts of a translation are known (as in the case of the early biblical translations), the critical study of those manuscripts, to determine as far as possible the original and subsequent stages of the textual history of each translation. That is a task where a commentary like this must largely rely on the work of specialists, whose editions and other studies may be more or less complete at the present time.

The attention given here to the ancient translations is, however, not by any means justified only by the (perhaps in the end limited) potential which they offer for reconstructing the original Hebrew text of Exodus. They are worthy of study in their own right and a commentary of this kind is a natural place in which to do this. There are, of course, increasing numbers of studies, modern translations and even commentaries on the individual ancient translations and these have been a valuable resource in the present work. What it can offer, and they usually do not, is an overview of the process of translation into various ancient languages over a period of several centuries, which will indicate both similarities and differences between the different Versions. Whether the similarities are accidental or (perhaps) due to the influence of one translation on another, the material gathered and to some extent explained here may be useful for future more general studies of the individual translations. In addition, precisely because of the nexus between translation and interpretation, which is in some cases (especially the Targums) very prominent, these sections of the commentary can provide a valuable point of entry into the history of biblical interpretation, which was an interest of many of the older commentators who contributed to the ICC. Here no attempt is made to be comprehensive and such references as are included are mainly to writings of the ancient and medieval periods. But because the ancient translations provided 'the biblical text' for centuries afterwards to those who quoted it and interpreted it, the elucidation of their own rationale will often clarify why later developments in interpretation took the course that they did.

b. *The Septuagint*
Understandably, since it is the oldest translation of the Old Testament that we possess, the Septuagint has been a greater focus for study and publication than any of the other Ancient Versions.[29] From a

---

[29] See in general the bibliographies of S.P. Brock et al., *A Classified Bibliography of the Septuagint* (ALGHJ 6; Leiden, 1973), and C. Dogniez, *Bibliography of the Septuagint=Bibliographie de la Septante (1970–1993)* (VTSup 60; Leiden, 1995); the introductions by Swete, Jellicoe and Dines; and more briefly Lange, pp. 122-38, Lange and Tov, *Textual History* 1A, pp. 191-211 (§1.3.1.1), 1B, pp. 135-42 (§2.4.1.2), and A. Salvesen, 'Exodus', in J.K. Aitken (ed.), *Companion to the Septuagint* (London, 2015), pp. 29-42.

text-critical point of view its importance is enhanced, potentially at least, by the fact that it alone originated in the period before about 100 A.D. when there was still some fluidity in the transmission of the Hebrew text. But its own complex textual history, both before and after the production of the great codices of the fourth century A.D., Vaticanus and Sinaiticus (see also below on an important papyrus of Exodus from the same period), has created a continuing challenge for scholarly endeavours to recover the original or at least an early form of the translation as a basis for further investigation. The two Cambridge editions which laid the foundations for modern Septuagintal study were content to print the text of Codex Vaticanus (B) with a larger or smaller listing of variant readings in their apparatus.[30] No attempt was made to group the manuscripts or to relate them to ancient editorial interventions: the editors' aim was (and it was a great achievement to do so) to indicate the extent of the textual problems and to provide the evidence for future examination. The 'pocket' edition of Alfred Rahlfs was a first step towards a critical text: it offered an eclectic text based on the three oldest uncial manuscripts (in Exodus only Vaticanus and the fifth-century Alexandrinus, as Sinaiticus does not survive here), with an apparatus that referred also to Origen's recension and, in later books, to those of Lucian and the Catena manuscripts as well.[31]

Since 1991 students of the Greek Exodus have at last had available to them a full critical edition of the text, prepared by J.W. Wevers and based on meticulous study of a wide range of manuscripts and the linguistic choices of the translator in his Hellenistic context. It was accompanied by two distinct volumes in which the editor's decisions and the translator's own intentions are explained.[32] There

---

[30] H.B. Swete, *The Old Testament in Greek according to the Septuagint* (3 vols., Cambridge, 1887–94); A.E. Brooke and N. McLean (with H.StJ. Thackeray for vol. 2), *The Old Testament in Greek according to Codex Vaticanus* (Cambridge, 1906–40: only the books from Genesis to Tobit were published): the larger edition of Exodus appeared in 1909.

[31] A. Rahlfs, *Septuaginta, id est Vetus Testamentum Graece iuxta LXX Interpretes* (Stuttgart, 1935). A revision, but with only minor corrections, was made by R. Hanhart (Stuttgart, 2006): this is the text provided, with tagging by R.A. Kraft and others, for use with the Accordance computer program.

[32] Wevers, *Septuaginta. Vetus Testamentum Graece*, 2.1: *Exodus* (Göttingen, 1991); *Notes*; *THGE*. There are also now the following annotated translations: Le Boulluec and Sandevoir, *L'Exode* (*BAlex* 2); L.J. Perkins, in *NETS*, pp. 43-81;

are numerous differences, mostly minor, between the texts of Rahlfs and Wevers, because the latter is frequently able to identify features of the fourth-century text as products of the process of textual transmission and so penetrate behind it to an older form of the text. Instances where one might still favour Rahlfs's judgment are rare. A more serious, but currently unanswerable, question is whether even what Wevers has reconstructed is the original translation of Exodus or only the earliest form of it to which we have access. The question arises because a Qumran fragment dated c. 100 B.C. (4QLXXLev[a]: *DJD* IX, pp. 161-65) presents a Greek text of Lev. 26.2-16 which is a less precise rendering of the Heb. than what is found in the later manuscripts, and it has been suggested that this is (or is closer to) the original translation of the passage (E. Ulrich in *DJD* IX, p. 163). No similar evidence exists for any part of Exodus – early papyri of the Greek Exodus are few and tiny – but if the well-known text of Leviticus is only early and not original, the same might be true for Exodus. Of course, such inferences build a lot on a single column of a manuscript which may not have contained the whole of Leviticus, let alone the whole Pentateuch, and one whose peculiarities could conceivably be due to either the existence at one time of multiple versions with different approaches to translation or to a freer 'improvement' of the original text. Another Qumran manuscript of the Greek Leviticus (4QpapLXXLev[b]: *DJD* IX, pp. 167-86), probably from the first cent. B.C., does not diverge substantially from the familiar text except in one particularity: for the divine name it never uses the κύριος (or, less frequently, θεός) of the later manuscripts, but twice has ιαω (3.12; 4.27), a transliteration of the name as it was once pronounced. When taken together with the writing of the divine name in Hebrew characters in some other early Greek biblical manuscripts (such as P. Fouad 266 and 8HevXIIgr: see further Lange, p. 344), this could point to the use of reverential substitutes such as κύριος and θεός being not an original but a later feature of the writing of the Greek text, though not necessarily (as some have suggested) only a Christian development.

W. Kraus and M. Karrer, *Septuaginta Deutsch: Das griechische Alte Testament in deutscher Übersetzung* (2 vols., Translation; Stuttgart, 2009), pp. 56-98 (Exodus); Notes and Commentary (Stuttgart, 2011), pp. 258-324 (on Exodus, by J.L.W. Schaper).

One important new witness to the Greek text of Exodus has come to light since the publication of Wevers' edition, a papyrus codex dated to the fourth (or fifth) century A.D.[33] The date and circumstances of its discovery remain obscure. According to some accounts it was found in the 1970s in the same cache as the manuscript which contained the Coptic Gospel of Judas and two others.[34] Whatever its origin, after several years in the hands of dealers, what is known of it is now divided between several private collections and two American libraries. Five fairly complete leaves are in the collection of Martin Schøyen, one in that of F. Antonovich and one in the Beinecke Library at Yale; a smaller fragment of one leaf is at Ashland Seminary and twelve more are in the possession of an unnamed collector. Further fragments of what is probably the same manuscript are known only from copies of photographs sent in 1982 to the Vatican Library.[35] The Beinecke Library leaf has remained

---

[33] The latest assessment (by Minutoli and Pintaudi [2011–12: see n. 35 below], p. 200) argues for 'the first half of the fourth century', i.e. before Codex Vaticanus. For lists of the meagre papyrus fragments of Exodus known hitherto see Wevers, *Exodus*, pp. 14-15, and L. Hurtado, *The Earliest Christian Artefacts* (Grand Rapids, 2006), pp. 210-11 (adds P865, P896, P993).

[34] The earlier part of this story, when the four manuscripts were still kept together, is summarised, on the basis of the previous accounts, in S.J. Gathercole, *The Gospel of Judas* (Oxford, 2007), pp. 8-16: see also P.M. Head, *TynB* 58 (2007), pp. 3-4; and Minutoli and Pintaudi (2011–12, n. 35 below), pp. 193-95.

[35] For publication of the texts and discussion, mostly with photographs, see (in the order of the list given) D. Minutoli and R. Pintaudi, '*Esodo* (IV 16 – VII 21) in un codice di papiro della collezione Martin Schøyen (*MS* 187)', *AnPap* 23-24 (2011–12), pp. 17-55; O. Munnich, in F. Antonovich, *Les métamorphoses divines d'Alexandre* (Paris, 1996), pp. 401-403 (cf. 224-25) [see also the previous article, pp. 50-55]; R.G. Babcock, 'A Papyrus Codex of Exodus', *Yale University Library Gazette* (Apr. 1997), pp. 163-67; D.A. Desilva with M.P. Adams, 'Seven Papyrus Fragments of a Greek Manuscript of Exodus', *VT* 56 (2006), pp. 143-70; Desilva, 'Five Papyrus Fragments'. Two other important articles are: Minutoli and Pintaudi, 'Un codice biblico su papiro della collezione Schøyen *MS* 187 (Esodo IV 16 – VII 21)', in G. Bastianini and A. Casanova (eds.), *I Papiri Letterari Cristiani* (Studi e Testi di Papirologia 13; Florence, 2011), pp. 193-205; and K. De Troyer, 'The Textual Character of the *Exodus Codex* of the Schøyen Collection (*MS* 187; RA 866)', *AnPap* 23-24 (2011–12), pp. 57-79. On the 1982 copies see A. Rahlfs, *Verzeichnis der griechischen Handschriften des Alten Testaments. Die Überlieferung bis zum VIII. Jahrhundert* (Septuaginta, Supplementum I/1), rev. ed. by D. Fränkel (Göttingen, 2004), pp. 271-72, 323, 447-48, and Minutoli and Pintaudi, 'Un codice biblico, pp. 194-95.

practically unknown to specialists, but it fits perfectly between the first Schøyen leaf and the Antonovich leaf and provides the text of 6.12-27 which is missing from the published sequence. Only the Schøyen leaves have received an official designation, as ms. 866 in the 'Rahlfs' list, but since there is much to suggest that all the scattered leaves and fragments derive from the same codex[36] and there is no agreement about its precise provenance the material as a whole will provisionally be described here and in the commentary as 'papyrus 866'. Part or all of the following verses is preserved: 3.16-18, 21-22; 4.1-3, 16-31; 5.1-23; 6.1-30; 7.1-21; 10.3-5, 8-9, 12-15, 17-22, 24-28; 11.2-5, 7-10; 12.3-6, 9-12, 15-22, 25-34, 37-41, 45-51; 13.3-7; 26.21-25, 30-33; 30.11-15, 18-21; 34.12-15, 20-24; 35.9-17, 22-25 [the 1982 copies show 31.11-15; 32.26-28; 33.1-4, 7-8, 13-15, 21-23; 34.1-3, 5-10, 23-24?, 28-31, 34-35; 35.1-4, but are of poor quality].

Papyrus 866 is by far the most fully preserved early Greek witness to the text of Exodus apart from the major Greek uncial manuscripts, and contains parts of about one-sixth of the verses in the book. Studies of its text-type so far have concluded that it is not closely related to the hexaplaric or Byzantine groups of mss and belongs rather with Vaticanus and Alexandrinus in providing valuable (though not unmixed) evidence of the 'Old Greek' text. One peculiarity is that while the Schøyen leaves and other material from the early part of the book show significant indications of 'pre-hexaplaric' assimilation to the Hebrew (cf. De Troyer, pp. 71-75), this is apparently not the case (with a notable exception in 34.13) in the later chapters (so explicitly Desilva, 'Seven Papyrus Fragments', pp. 153, 164; 'Five Papyrus Fragments', p. 18: differently Fränkel, *Verzeichnis* p. 448, regarding the 'lost' fragments). If this is not a sign that the material comes from two separate but very similar codices (which seems improbable), it would appear that such 'correction' was not evenly applied throughout the text-form represented here. Further study of the material as a whole should clarify the situation: it may also be able to provide a background for the 'stylistic improvement' of the Old Greek which is evident in all parts of the codex, sometimes in agreement with readings only otherwise attested in much later miniscules.

---

[36] Cf. Desilva, 'Five Papyrus Fragments', pp. 1-2.

As has already been mentioned, the Old Latin translation of Exodus (based on Greek original[s] from the second cent. A.D. onwards) gains in importance as a witness to the Septuagint text (and according to some, to the Hebrew text behind it) from the shortage of surviving Greek texts earlier than the fourth century.[37] There is published manuscript evidence of the translation for most of Exodus, supported by quotations in a variety of Latin writers which make possible some clarification of the version's own textual history: Jerome's words *cum apud Latinos tot sint exempla quot codices* indicate (but probably exaggerate) the problem. As yet there is no modern critical edition of the Old Latin text of Exodus, but the resources on which one will be based are contained in the archive of the Vetus Latina Institute at Beuron in Germany and this is now accessible online in some libraries through the publisher Brepols. In addition to its contribution to the textual problems of individual verses, the Old Latin (in the form of a manuscript [104] which in parts seems to be based on an early African text: cf. Billen, pp. 23-30, 41-43, 172-74) may provide the key to the much-discussed problems of the Greek and Hebrew texts of the 'tabernacle' chapters (Exod. 25–31; 35–40).[38]

As for the Greek translation itself, reference has already been made to the conclusion that each of the five books of the Pentateuch was translated separately.[39] This can be deduced from the different character and aims of the translation in each book (so initially Z. Fränkel, *Ueber den Einfluss der palästinischen Exegese auf die*

---

[37] On the manuscripts and other sources for the Old Latin see A.V. Billen, *The Old Latin Texts of the Heptateuch* (Cambridge, 1927), and Wevers, *Exodus*, pp. 21-33; more generally Roberts, *Old Testament Text*, pp. 237-46; E. Schulz-Flügel, 'The Latin Old Testament Tradition', in M. Saebø (ed.), *Hebrew Bible/Old Testament: The History of its Interpretation*, I/1 (Göttingen, 1996), pp. 642-52; P.-M. Bogaert, 'The Latin Bible', in J. Carleton Paget and J.L.W. Schaper (eds.), *The New Cambridge History of the Bible: From the Beginnings to 600* (Cambridge, 2013), pp. 505-26 (esp. 505-14); on Exodus id., 'L'importance de la Septante et du "Monacensis" de la Vetus Latina pour l'exégèse de l'Exode (chap. 35-40)', in Vervenne (ed.), *Studies*, pp. 399-428.

[38] These problems will be treated in the volume of this commentary that covers chs. 25–40.

[39] Lange, *Handbuch*, p. 123, with references in n. 698. On the characteristics of the translation of Exodus in particular see the studies of Lemmelijn, Perkins (in NETS), Salvesen (cf. n. 29) and Screnock, *Traductor*, as well as Wevers, *Notes*, pp. vii-xvi.

alexandrinische Hermeneutik [Leipzig, 1851]; recently among others Dines, *Septuagint*, pp. 14-16). Probably chs. 35–40 were the work of a different translator from chs. 1–34 (Wevers, *THGE*, pp. 117-46; M.L. Wade, *Consistency of Translation Technique in the Tabernacle Accounts of Exodus in the Old Greek* [SCS 49; Atlanta, 2003], pp. 238-45). Several scholars have observed that the Greek of the Exodus translation(s) is good quality *koine*, with ugly Hebraisms generally avoided: 'it soon strikes the reader of his text that he was the one who of all the Pentateuchal translators paid most attention to the requirements of the Greek language' (A. Aejmalaeus, 'What Can We Know about the Hebrew *Vorlage* of the Septuagint?', in id., *On the Trail*, pp. 77-115 [94, with numerous examples on pp. 94-100]). On the whole, it is achieved with a precise understanding of what the Hebrew means and a close representation of it in the Greek idiom. But occasionally the understanding is lacking and the rendering is determined by the context (as in 1.16 and 14.20: cf. Wevers, *THGE*, p. 147) or theological concerns lead the translator to modify the original (as in 24.10-11). More commonly divergences from the familiar Hebrew text (i.e. the MT) are due to expansion and clarification, often to achieve what may be termed 'short-range harmonisation' or 'levelling', as Wevers calls it (*THGE*, p. 148; see also Tov, in Lange and Tov, *Textual History* 1A, p. 201). The origin of such divergences may in principle be explained in two ways. It may lie in the work of the translators themselves, or they may simply have been following a Hebrew original (*Vorlage*) in which the fuller text was already present. The existence of such fuller Hebrew texts is now confirmed not only by the Samaritan Pentateuch but by manuscripts from Qumran. Specialists continue to differ over what the 'default' explanation is likely to be. Some emphasise the 'freedom' and initiative of the translator and presume that for the most part his *Vorlage* was close to MT (Tov, *The Text-Critical Use of the Septuagint in Biblical Research* [JBS 3; Jerusalem, 1981], p. 139; Wevers, *Notes*, pp. xv-xvi; L. Perkins, NETS, pp. 43-51; Lange, *Handbuch*, p. 129). Others are readier to envisage variations in the underlying Hebrew, of which the translator will then have given a 'faithful' rendering (Aejmelaeus, *On the Trail*, pp. 88-92, 100-12; Lemmelijn, *Plague of Texts*, pp. 96-135; Tov, in Lange and Tov, *Textual History* 1A, p. 201). Aejmelaeus in particular has sought to shift the 'burden of proof' from those who infer a variant *Vorlage* to those who would attribute divergences to the translator: 'The scholar who wishes to attribute deliberate changes...to the translator is under the obligation to prove his thesis with weighty arguments and also to show why the divergences cannot have originated with the *Vorlage*' (p. 92). This is implausible: it is surely likely that translators would have had at least as much freedom to elaborate their text as copyists of the Hebrew and there are clear cases where they did so. Each case must be considered on its merits. But in the end the translation is what we have and due caution requires that we hesitate before presuming a Hebrew variant behind it without good reason. Where the variation shows clear signs of being secondary (as many of them do), it ultimately makes little difference whether it occurred at the copying stage or the translation stage, and commentators can (as they often must) be content to rest with uncertainty at this point.

The divergences of the Old Greek Exodus from the form of the Hebrew text which was eventually to become the Masoretic text did not remain unnoticed in antiquity, as the latter gradually assumed a normative status in and after the first cent. A.D. Early evidence of the 'correction' of such variants exists in a Greek fragment of Exodus from Qumran containing parts of 28.4-7 (7QLXXEx: *DJD* IX, pp. 142-43), dated c. 100 B.C., and in a third cent. A.D. papyrus of ch. 40 (ms. 1000).[40] The best known Jewish revisions of the Old Greek are those of 'the Three', Aquila, Symmachus and Theodotion, whose work was taken up by Origen for his Hexapla (see below) and about whom there is some evidence in the Church Fathers (conveniently collected by Swete, pp. 29-53; see also Jellicoe, pp. 74-99, and the specialised studies of O'Connell, *Theodotionic Revision*, which also deals with Aquila, and Salvesen, *Symmachus*). On the basis of this it was initially held that Aquila lived in the reign of Hadrian, Theodotion a little later but before the writing of Irenaeus's *Adversus Haereses* in the 180s and Symmachus at the end of the second cent. (he is not mentioned by Irenaeus with the other two). The dates for Aquila and Symmachus remain the most probable, but the date of Theodotion and his place after Aquila have been called in question by the discovery in a cave near Qumran of a Greek

---

[40] For a more general overview of recent research on such revisions see P. Gentry, 'Pre-Hexaplaric Translations, Hexapla, post-Hexaplaric Translations', in Lange and Tov, *Textual History* 1A, pp. 211-35 (§1.3.1.2). The seminal work in this field was Barthélemy, *Dévanciers*.

version of the Minor Prophets which shares many of Theodotion's characteristics but is dated no later than the first century A.D. and more likely to the first century B.C. (8HevXIIgr: *DJD* VIII; cf. Lange, pp. 343-45). It seems that Aquila took Theodotion's version as the basis for his own much more far-reaching revision (so first Barthélemy, *Dévanciers* [n. 40]; similarly O'Connell, *Theodotionic Revision*, pp. 252-73, and Gentry [n. 40], in Lange and Tov, *Textual History* 1A, p. 227). It has also become clear that a distinction needs to be drawn between the original work of Theodotion and revisions found in a number of Septuagint mss which share some of its characteristics. This will also presumably account for what Wevers and others have described as 'pre-hexaplaric recensional activity' in Exodus and elsewhere (see Wevers, 'Pre-Origen Recensional Activity in the Greek Exodus', in D. Fränkel et al. [eds.], *Studien zur Septuaginta. Festschrift R. Hanhart* [MSU 20; Göttingen, 1990], pp. 121-39: also the observations noted above by De Troyer and Fränkel on Schøyen ms. 187 = Papyrus 866).

Most of the evidence for these revisions comes ultimately or occasionally directly from Origen's *Hexapla*, but a few extracts from Aquila's version have appeared among the Cairo Geniza manuscripts.[41] Both Theodotion and Aquila were primarily concerned to present a translation that was more precisely equivalent than the Old Greek to the Hebrew text known to them, but Aquila took his revision much further in this direction. Symmachus shared this desire but, probably in a reaction against Aquila, combined it with a mastery of contemporary Greek. Like his predecessors, his translation has been shown to reflect aspects of developing rabbinic interpretation of the biblical text in the equivalents used (cf. Salvesen, *Symmachus*, pp. 182-83; 'Midrash in Greek?').

Origen's *Hexapla* was in a sense the Christian equivalent to the work of the three Jewish revisers, although it was both more and less than that. It was more in that its six columns included (1) the unvocalised text of the whole Hebrew Bible; (2) a transliteration of this into Greek characters, including vowels (both of these could be taken for granted by the Jewish revisers); (3) the version of Aquila; (4) the version of Symmachus; and (6) the version of Theodotion,

---

[41] The classic collection of the evidence was Field's *Origenis Hexapla quae supersunt*, which was drawn upon and amplified in the apparatus of the Brooke-McLean and Wevers editions.

as well as (5) a revised text of the Old Greek version. It was less than the Jewish revisions in that Origen ventured no new translation of his own, instead using the Jewish revisions to identify variation between the Hebrew and the Old Greek and where necessary (as it was, for example, in the final chapters of Exodus) to fill gaps in the latter. The added material was mainly taken from Theodotion and it was marked with an asterisk. Where the Greek contained text that had no parallel in the Hebrew it was marked with an 'obelus' or dagger, but the excess text was not removed.[42]

The Hexapla was far too bulky to be copied as a whole and only a few fragments of copies (most notably the Mercati fragment of a number of Psalms, see Jellicoe, pp. 130-33, for a summary) survive to show how it was laid out. What did survive in large numbers were copies of the fifth, revised Old Greek, column, in some of which marginal notes of the readings of Aquila, Symmachus and Theodotion were added. This text was also translated into Syriac by Paul of Tella in the early seventh century, complete with Origen's critical signs and many readings of the Jewish revisers (for editions of the text of the 'Syro-hexapla[r]' see Wevers, *Exodus*, pp. 37-38). It is from this translation and the Greek copies that it has been possible in modern times to reconstruct Origen's fifth column ('the O-text', as it is referred to in the commentary) and, equally if not more important, most of what we know of the work of the Jewish revisers.

In a famous passage of the prologue to his translation of the books of Chronicles Jerome wrote (as he does elsewhere) of two other versions of the Septuagint that were widely used in his time, that of Hesychius in Egypt and that of Lucian 'the Martyr' from Constantinople to Antioch.[43] Of this Hesychius little or nothing is known and attempts to correlate 'his' version with a particular manuscript or Egyptian translation are perhaps mistaken. It may be sufficient to see evidence of what Jerome knew, in a broad sense, in the 'Alexandrian' text of the fourth- and fifth-century uncials and citations that have come down to us. Lucian (c. 240–311 A.D.)

---

[42] The asterisk and obelus were signs that had been used by Greek textual critics since the Hellenistic period to mark respectively authentic and inauthentic portions of text.

[43] Jellicoe, p. 134, provides both the complete Latin text and an English translation. For a thorough discussion (for its time) see ibid., pp. 134-71, 345-48.

is a better known figure and the numerous citations of biblical passages in the writings of the Syrian Church Fathers such as John Chrysostom have made possible the identification of a 'Syrian' or 'Antiochene' text in various parts of the Old Testament textual tradition.[44] But claims to have done so for the Pentateuch (including the notorious case of P. de Lagarde's *Pars Prior* of 1883) have long been controversial, and Wevers's study of 1973[45] and his subsequent critical editions of all five books of the Greek Pentateuch have established a consensus that no continuous manuscript evidence of Lucian's recension of them has survived (if it ever existed, which some have doubted). All that we have are citations in the Syrian Fathers which in cases of multiple attestation that agree may give the wording of a distinctive version which was used by them.[46]

c. *The Targums (or Targumim)*

The Targums are translations of the Hebrew Bible into Aramaic (generally not including the Syriac translations such as the Peshiṭta, although they share some characteristics with the Targums).[47] The word originated in Mishnaic Hebrew (hence the alternative plural form with the Heb. ending -*im*), where it was used already in M.Yad. 4.5 for a written 'translation' (and also, interestingly, for the Aramaic sections of Ezra and Daniel). The related verb *tirgēm*

---

[44] See e.g. J. Ziegler (ed.), *Duodecim Prophetae* (Göttingen, 2nd ed., 1967), pp. 70-89; S.P. Brock, *The Recensions of the Septuagint Version of 1 Samuel* (Quaderni di Henoch 9; Turin, 1996 [doctoral dissertation, Oxford, 1966]); S. Kreuzer and M. Sigismund (eds.), *Der antiochenische Text der Septuaginta in seiner Bezeugung und seiner Bedeuting* (De Septuaginta Investigationes 4; Göttingen, 2013).

[45] 'A Lucianic Recension in Genesis?', *BIOSCS* 6 (1973), pp. 22-35; see also *The Text History of the Greek Genesis* (MSU 11; Göttingen, 1974), pp. 158-75.

[46] One such example, in Exod. 7.1, is mentioned by Wevers, *Notes*, p. 92 (cf. his apparatus ad loc.); the longer text in 2.22 might be another (see further Text and Versions on these two verses). For a cautious but not totally negative assessment see N. Fernandos Marcos, 'Some Reflections on the Antiochian Text of the Septuagint', in D. Fränkel et al. (eds.), *Studien zur Septuaginta, Robert Hanhart zu Ehren* (MSU 20; Göttingen, 1990), pp. 219-29 (220-21).

[47] P.S. Alexander, 'Targum, Targumim', *ABD* 6, pp. 320-31; Flesher and Chilton, *The Targums*; Glessmer, *Einleitung in die Targume*; Lange and Tov, *Textual History* 1A, pp. 239-262 (§1.3.3); Roberts, *Old Testament Text*, pp. 197-213.

occurs once in Biblical Hebrew (Ezra 4.7), where it refers to the translation of a Persian administrative document.[48] Although, as this example shows, the word-group could be used quite generally for any translation into another language, most of its occurrences in rabbinic literature arise from the practice in the early synagogues of providing an oral 'interpretation' (which the word can also mean) of the readings from the Bible, usually in Aramaic (so already in M.Meg. 4.4, 6, 10), which had become a more familiar language to most Jews than Hebrew itself.[49] Eventually written copies of such translations became available (see below): the names of Onkelos and Jonathan are associated with them in the Babylonian Talmud (B.Meg. 3a) and by the ninth century the Targum of Onkelos had received 'official' status in Babylonia at least (cf. Flesher and Chilton, p. 478). It is likely that the Targums were also used in education and private study.

Parts of Aramaic translations of Leviticus and Job have been found at Qumran (4QTgLev/4Q156; 4QTgJob/4Q157; 11QTgJob/ 11Q10 [the most extensive]l cf. Lange, pp. 112-14, 453-57), but not of Exodus. The extant Jewish Targums of Exodus form parts of three larger compositions which covered the whole Pentateuch (except for some texts designed for specific liturgical occasions and, according to some, the 'Fragment Targum').[50] While each has its own distinctive origin and history, there is sufficient common ground between them to indicate some kind (indeed most likely various kinds) of relationship between them. The form of the Aramaic language in which each is written has always played a part in discussions about their origins, but recent work has introduced a fresh paradigm which provides an important new framework for study, although it does not by itself answer all the questions.[51] This paradigm, based on phases of the language distinguished by J.A. Fitzmyer and developed further by S.A. Kaufman and others in the

---

[48] It is probably a loan-word from Babylonian: cf. Akk. *targumannu*, 'translator' (*HAL*, p. 1645; *AHw*, p. 1329).

[49] According to rabbinic tradition (e.g. B.Meg. 3a) the expression 'with interpretation' (Heb. $m^e p\bar{o}r\bar{a}\check{s}$) in Neh. 8.8 is the first reference to an oral Targum, but this is unlikely.

[50] For the threefold division see Glessmer, pp. 82-83, 181-96, and below under 'Pseudo-Jonathan'.

[51] Cf. Glessmer, pp. 4-6, 13-75.

context of work on the *Comprehensive Aramaic Lexicon*, identifies the following sub-divisions in the history of Jewish Aramaic:[52]

1. Imperial or Official Aramaic (c. 700–200 B.C.), which includes the Aramaic portions of Ezra and the Elephantine and other Egyptian Jewish texts.

2. Judaean Aramaic, a branch of Middle Aramaic (c. 200 B.C.–200 A.D.), which is represented by inscriptions, legal documents, administrative letters from the Bar Kochba period and *Megillat Ta'anit*.

3. Jewish Literary Aramaic, which was contemporary with the preceding type, developed from what seem to have been the meagre literary compositions in Imperial Aramaic into a revised and more widely used medium exemplified by the Aramaic portions of Daniel and Qumran Aramaic.

4. Jewish Palestinian Aramaic (c. 200–700 A.D.), which is a branch of Late Aramaic. It includes a range of synagogue and other inscriptions in Galilee, the Jordan valley and Idumaea, the Palestinian Talmud and the midrashim Genesis and Leviticus Rabbah and Pesiqta deRab Kahana, the latter two categories commonly being known as 'Galilaean Aramaic'.

5. Jewish Babylonian Aramaic (c. 200–900 A.D.), the main Aramaic dialect of the Babylonian Talmud.

6. Late Jewish Literary Aramaic (c. 300–1100 A.D.), a mixed dialect combining elements of Jewish Literary Aramaic (especially in its grammar) and Jewish Palestinian Aramaic (in its lexicon, which is also shared with Jewish Babylonian Aramaic and other sources). This is the dialect of the medieval Targums to Psalms, Chronicles and Job and, to an extent, of the Targum to the Megillot.

The *Targum of Onkelos* has already been mentioned as the official Targum to the Pentateuch of the Babylonian Jewish communities (and indeed of their successors to the present day). As a result of this status it is by far the best attested in surviving manuscripts and printed editions. A. Sperber's modern edition, *The Bible in Aramaic* (Leiden, 1959–73; repr. 1992), presents essentially the

---

[52] See further J.A. Fitzmyer, 'The Phases of the Aramaic Language', in his *A Wandering Aramaean: Collected Aramaic Essays* (Missoula, 1979), pp. 57-84; S.A. Kaufman, 'Languages (Aramaic)', *ABD* 4, 173-78; Flesher and Chilton, *Targums*, pp. 267-83.

text of one (vocalised) manuscript with variants from six others and eleven early printed editions in the apparatus, and this is only a small selection from those that are known. One omission from the selection, which has been criticised, is Ms. Ebr.448 of the Vatican Library, an eleventh-century manuscript with Babylonian vocalisation: this was subsequently used as the base text for the Madrid Polyglot and the translation by B. Grossfeld in the *Aramaic Bible* (= *AramB* 7).[53] The Babylonian connections of Targum Onkelos and some features of its language have led some to conclude that it had a Babylonian origin (Kahle, Diez Macho), but this is probably only true for the later stages of its production. In fact the western features of its language are much more central and it fits well into the category of Jewish Literary Aramaic, with a particular linguistic affinity to the Genesis Apocryphon from Qumran. An origin in Palestine is also supported by its haggadic expansions, which look like shorter versions of what appears in the Palestinian Targum (Alexander, p. 321; Flesher and Chilton, pp. 109-19). The 'first edition', which some call Proto-Onkelos, has been dated to the first or second century A.D., with the Babylonian 'redaction' being completed by c. 500. The translation follows closely the wording of its Heb. original, which only rarely shows signs of being different from the later Masoretic text (for one example see Text and Versions on 7.19). Variations from the Heb. are usually due to the influence of rabbinic exegesis, most commonly through rephrasing or the addition of words to 'protect' the transcendence of God from too close a resemblance to or involvement in some human activities ('anti-anthropomorphisms'). Sometimes the intention is to bring the text closer to later Jewish belief or practice (see in general B. Grossfeld in *AramB* 6 [on Genesis], pp. 15-30). An interesting text related to Onkelos which goes a good deal further than this is included in Michael Klein's volumes of *Genizah Manuscripts of the Palestinian Targum to the Pentateuch* (Ms. G, dated to eleventh–foureenth cent.: pp. 248-51, on Exod. 15.6-16).

The texts of the *Palestinian Targum* show much more variation among themselves than those of Onkelos, but are close enough where they overlap for their 'family resemblance' and common

---

[53] On other criticisms of Sperber see R.P. Gordon in a Foreword to the 1992 reprint.

ancestry to be very clear. The variations can plausibly be attributed to their differing age, the lack of any formal official status and a more fluid process of tradition, which matches and perhaps partly derives from an oral stage in the transmission of this version. For centuries the only significant examples of it that were known were both exceptional representatives of the version (and one, the so-called Targum of Pseudo-Jonathan, is increasingly regarded as in a category of its own, as it will be here). But the old name 'Jerusalem Targum' that they were given served at least to indicate the broad provenance of this alternative Targum tradition. Its most typical representatives, however, are relatively recent discoveries and it is they which have made possible the much clearer perception of its character which is possible today. First, as with so many other aspects of medieval Jewish life and literature, the Cairo Genizah proved to contain portions of this kind of Targum text in a number of manuscripts, as was demonstrated by Paul Kahle in the second volume of his *Die Masoreten des Westens* (1930). Secondly, in 1956 a manuscript in the Vatican Library, Codex Neophyti I (also spelt Neofiti), which had been miscatalogued as a manuscript of Onkelos, was recognised by A. Diez Macho to contain, in fact, an almost complete text of the Palestinian Targum. In both cases it was the similarities to the texts already known that made the identification certain.

The evidence now available falls into three main categories:[54]

(1) *Codex Neophyti I.* It is appropriate to begin with the most recent discovery, because it is the most complete. The ms. is dated in 1504, but the origin of its text has been placed much earlier, even in pre-Christian times. The latter view probably places too much weight on correspondences to other examples of early Jewish exegesis, but the interpretations concerned indicate some of the traditions on which the Targum drew and even a more moderate scholar could conclude: 'There are no good grounds for dating anything in *Neof.* later than the 3rd/4th cent. C.E.' (Alexander, p. 323). The language is predominantly Jewish Palestinian Aramaic, as it is of the other Palestinian Targum texts, and the Palestinian

---

[54] A useful synoptic presentation of most of the texts (which also includes Pseudo-Jonathan) is provided in A. Diez Macho et al. (eds.), *Biblia Polyglotta Matritensia. Series IV: Targum Palestinense in Pentateuchum*, 2, *Exodus* (Madrid, 1980).

Talmud is aware of some of its interpretations. This is not to deny that changes were made over the centuries and a closer approximation to the Masoretic text is sometimes evident. In addition, there are large numbers of marginal and interlinear glosses, of varied origin, which record the readings (without specific attribution) of other Targums, known and unknown: these are collectively referred to in the commentary as 'Tg^{Nmg}'.

The translation itself exhibits many additions and changes, large and small, to the underlying Heb. (which again is generally close to the MT). In various ways these frequently reflect rabbinic rulings or midrash, such as the replacement of 'elders' with 'wise men/sages' in 3.18 and elsewhere. Others appear to belong to the translators' own specific milieu, like the addition of 'redeemed' (*pryqyn*) to nearly all instances of the verb *yāṣā'*, 'go out, bring out', and the development of God's Memra into a theological concept that represents, like other more widely used expressions, a means by which God interacts with the world and humanity (see Chester, *Divine Revelation*, pp. 293-324, for a careful assessment of the issues). Perhaps the most famous example is the insertion of 'the Midrash of the Four Nights' after 12.42, where the night of Passover is seen as a stage in the workings of the divine 'economy' from creation and the promise of a son to Abraham until the future 'night' of eschatological redemption (R. Le Déaut, *La Nuit Pascale* [Rome, 1963]; a recent overview of the topic is given by B.D. Chilton, 'The Exodus Theology of the Palestinian Targumim', in Dozeman et al., *The Book of Exodus*, pp. 387-403). The text was edited, with English and Spanish translations, by A. Diez Macho, *Neophyti I. Targum Palestinense*, 2, *Éxodo* (Madrid and Barcelona, 1971). A French translation by Le Déaut is provided in *Targum du Pentateuque. 2, Exode et Lévitique* (Paris, 1979) and a fully annotated English translation by M. McNamara and C.T.R. Hayward in *AramB 2*, pp. 1-158, where details of rabbinic and other parallels can be found.

(2) *The Cairo Genizah manuscripts*. Only those portions of manuscripts which contain parts of the Palestinian Targum of Exodus will be listed here: page references for texts, translations and notes are to Klein, *Genizah Manuscripts*, with occasional additions from later publications. The designations are those used by Klein (who gives additional information): some were taken over from Kahle's earlier publication. The dates given are based on those provided by Professor M. Beit Arié for Klein's edition (see 1, p. xxxvii).

Ms. A (Klein 1, pp. 172-73, 282-97; 2, pp. 53-54, 77-81): 4.7-11; 20.21/24-23/26; 21.1-7, 13-37; 22.1-28; 23.1-3, 8-14. Eight–ninth cent. or even earlier, the earliest Palestinian Targum ms. from the Genizah.

Ms. D (Klein 1, pp. 174-85, 298-305; 2, pp. 54-56, 81-82): 5.20-23; 6.1-10; 7.10-22; 9.21-34. C. 1000. The ms. also contains sections of Genesis and Deuteronomy. In *Sefarad* 49 (1989), p. 132, Klein published further fragments containing parts of 5.6-7, 18-19; 7.15-16, 20, in the latter case confirming the restorations of lacunae proposed by him earlier.

Ms. E (Klein, *Sefarad* 49 [1989], pp. 124-27): 36.8-13, 22-29; 39.32-40; 40.2-12. Ninth-mid-eleventh cent. Hitherto only sections of Genesis from this ms. had been known.

Ms. F (Klein 1, pp. 260-71; 2, pp. 70-75): 19.1-25; 20.1-23/26. C. eleventh cent. The ms. also contains sections of Leviticus and Numbers and is one of the 'Festival-Liturgical Collections'. It appears to have been preserved complete but only includes the Targum of the additional readings for Passover and Weeks (except for the addition of Deut. 34.5-12 by a later scribe: F_2). The scribe apparently did not complete his task, as the colophon on the title-page indicates his intention to include the readings for all the festivals (see Klein 1, pp. xxiii-xxiv, 306-307).

Ms. G (see above under Onkelos)

Ms. J (Klein 1, pp. 224-27, 254-57; 2, pp. 62-63, 68-69): 14.1, 13-14, 29-31; 15.1-2; 17.15-16; 19.1-8. Mid-eleventh to late foureenth cent. All the passages are parts of festival readings, for Passover, Purim and Weeks respectively. More of ch. 17 and 19 may have been written on pages that are now lost, but the text for Passover clearly contains only selected verses, according to the general pattern of the Fragment-Targums but not in exact agreement with the contents of those which have been preserved (on which see below). It is, in Klein's words, a 'hybrid' (1, p. xxiv): quite possibly it originally contained (parts of) readings for other festivals.

Ms. Q (Klein 1, pp. 276-77; 2, pp. 76-77): 20.1-3, 7-8. Mid-eleventh to late fourteenth cent. This is a curious fragment which begins and ends in mid-sentence. What survives 'is a very expansive embroidery, in prose, around an *incomplete* literal translation that resembles Onkelos' (Klein 2, p. 76). Even the 'literal translation' is an amalgam of different versions.

Ms. S (Klein 1, pp. 273-74; 2, p. 76): 19.25; 20.1-13. Mid-eleventh to late fourteenth cent. The only surviving passage is a section of the readings for Weeks, so this is probably part of a 'Festival-Liturgical Collection' (see Klein 1, pp. xxv-xxvi).

Ms. T (Klein 1, pp. xxviii, 238-39). Ninth–tenth to mid-eleventh cent. This is not a Targum as such but an 'Introductory Poem' which is constructed like many others as an acrostic. Such poems are thought to have accompanied the Torah readings for Passover and Weeks and for the Sabbath preceding the 1st day of Nisan. In this case the poem elaborates Moses' 'conflict' with the Sea in Exodus 14–15. It has been shown to be very ancient by its occurrence in a papyrus from the fourth or fifth cent. A.D. The Paris ms. of the

Fragment-Targum incorporates it after Exod. 14.29. Ms. T also includes a similar poem on Moses' death.

Ms. U (Klein 1, pp. 242-43, 258-59; 2, pp. 64-65, 69): 15.3-8; 19.7-14. thirteenth–fourteenth cent. Another 'Festival-Liturgical Collection', this time containing parts of the readings for two festivals, Passover and Weeks.

Ms. W (Klein 1, pp. 244-47; 2, pp. 65-66): 15.7-21. Ninth–tenth to mid-eleventh cent. (?). Probably this is from a 'Festival-Liturgical Collection', but only part of the Passover readings is preserved. It appears to be, like mss Y, AA and HH, one of the earlier surviving texts of this type.

Ms. X (Klein 1, pp. xxvi-xxviii, 222-23, 236-37; 2, pp. 61-62): 13.17. Mid-eleventh to late fourteenth cent. The ms. is a collection of *Toseftot* introduced by words from the Tg and also includes texts related to Genesis and a version of the poem about Moses in ms. T.

Ms. Y (Klein, pp. xxiv, 272; 2, p. 76): 19.1-10. Ninth–tenth to mid-eleventh cent. There is a heading at the beginning. Before it the ms. contains the end of the 'additional reading for Passover' and then, on the attached page, parts of the readings for Weeks and Rosh haShanah: 'all in perfect calendrical order' (Klein). It can be presumed that this 'Festival-Liturgical Collection' originally contained readings for all the major festivals.

Ms. AA (Klein 1, pp. 208-19, 252-53; 2, pp. 57-61, 67-68): 12.1-42; 12.21-34 (repeated); 17.8-16. Ninth–tenth to mid-eleventh cent. An early 'Festival-Liturgical Collection' from which passages in Numbers and Deuteronomy also survive. Oddly the sequence in the ms. follows neither the order of the Bible nor that of the calendar. There are headings to some of the sections. The overlapping extracts from Exod. 12 differ slightly, but could have been copies from the same exemplar. The repetition is to provide for two separate occasions in the period of Passover.

Ms. BB (Klein 1, p. 274; 2, p. 76): 19.25–20.2. Mid-eleventh to late fourteenth cent. The small fragment begins with a heading which identifies it as being from 'Targum Yerushalmi'. It is presumably an extract included in a 'Festival-Liturgical Collection'.

Ms. CC (Klein 1, pp. xxvi-xxvii, 275-76; 2, p. 76): 20.13-14/17. C. eleventh cent. After v. 14/17 (i.e. the end of the Ten Commandments) the ms. continues with the Onkelos version of vv. 15/18-21/24. The explanation seems to be that the Palestinian Targum version of the Commandments was inserted into a copy of Onkelos as a *tosefta*.

Ms. FF (Klein 1, pp. xxvi-xxvii, 172-73, 220-23, 240-41, 254-55, 270-71; 2, pp. 54, 61-62, 64, 68): 4.25-26; 12.42 (the 'Four Nights'); 14.13-14; 17.12, 16; 20.26(?). Mid-eleventh to late fourteenth cent. Some parts of the ms. are damaged: originally it probably included 17.13-15 as well. Passages from Genesis and Leviticus also survive. This is a collection of *toseftot*, probably designed as a supplement to the text of Onkelos – similar in purpose to the Fragment-Targum but different in character, since only expanded passages are included.

Ms. GG (Klein 1, pp. xxviii-xxix, 186-89; 2, p. 56): 12.1-2. Mid-eleventh to late fourteenth cent. Two acrostic poems which each conclude with (and so lead into) the verse in question: one of them is about 'The Contest of the Months'. They clearly belong to the category of 'Introductory Poems'.

Ms. HH (Klein 1, pp. 196-209; 2, pp. 56-57): 12.1-3. Ninth–tenth to mid-fourteenth cent. The ms., which is classed among the 'Festival-Liturgical Collections', contains three acrostic poems about the debate between the months followed by the Targum of 12.1-3, the text to which they relate, on the back cover of the 'booklet'.

Ms. KK (Klein 1, pp. xxix, 192-95): 12.1. Ninth–tenth to mid-eleventh cent. The ms. contains three acrostic poems, one of which is followed by the Targum of 12.1. The poems are related at several points to the debate of the months, but the page begins with the Targum of Gen. 24.3-4.

Ms. MM (Klein 1, pp. 190-91, 234-35). Late eleventh cent. The surviving pages contain the middle of an acrostic poem on the debate of the months, related to Exod. 12.2, and (with no direct connection) another apparently for use with the reading of Exodus 14, though in the extant lines only allusions to earlier chapters appear.

Ms. NN (Klein 1, pp. 256-59; 2, pp. 69-71): 19.1-7. Mid-eleventh to late fourteenth cent. The (sometimes faint) text on the two sides of the leaf is the beginning of the Torah reading for Weeks, so it may well have been part of a 'Festival-Liturgical Collection'.

Ms. PP (Klein 1, pp. xxviii, 226-35): 14.29-31. Mid-eleventh to late fourteenth cent. A long acrostic poem, expanded in places and linked to the Hebrew text and/or Targum of 14.29–15.1, and so to the reading for the seventh day of Passover. The ms. includes other poems which are related to haftara readings.

A great many of the mss contain material for use at the major festivals and so the Targum texts preserved largely come from a limited range of chapters. Some of these mss are mainly composed of acrostic poems and contain little or no actual Targum material. Their relevance is to the wider context of biblical interpretation. The main mss which offer (parts of) a continuous Targum text and a wider selection of passages are A, D and E, all of which are among the older texts from the Genizah. They in particular provide manuscript evidence from an earlier stage of the Palestinian Targum's history than Codex Neophyti and the other sources still to be described.

The general character of the translation in the Genizah manuscripts, however, corresponds closely to what was said earlier about Codex Neophyti. Klein, in his summary (1, pp. xxix-xxxiv), emphasizes the extent of material additional to, or more rarely different from, the Hebrew text. Proper names and explanatory words are often added, the wording may be changed to what it 'should' have been (as in 17.11) and a variety of expressions are used (though not everywhere) to avoid anthropomorphic references to God. In legal passages later interpretation is sometimes incorporated and the preservation of rulings that did not become normative (as in 20.21/24; 21.4, 20; 22.4, 12) is particularly interesting. Finally, the context of synagogue recitation is clearly reflected in the addition of introductory phrases like 'My people, Israelites', as in the Ten Commandments, in Ms. F.

(3) *The Fragment-Targums*. A copy of excerpts from a Palestinian Targum text (the thirteenth-cent. Nuremberg Ms. [N] of modern editions) was already known to Felix Pratensis and reproduced in the First Rabbinic Bible (1516–17). In addition to some examples from the Cairo Genizah (mss Br, DD and J in Klein's listing), several more manuscripts of this kind are now known. Those most commonly cited are in Paris (P), Leipzig (L) and the Vatican Library (V): V and L belong to the same sub-group as N, while P is the sole representative of a separate collection of the same type. Often the extracts overlap, but there are differences between the mss in what they include (V and N are fuller than P, while L is much shorter) and in the wording of otherwise similar passages. The modern edition is again by Michael Klein, *The Fragment-Targums of the Pentateuch according to their Extant Sources* (AnBib 76; Rome, 1980), where fuller information may be found (on the mss see 1, pp. 26-42). Haggadic expansions of the text from the Palestinian tradition predominate in these collections over variant literal renderings and this is probably due to their origin. The modern description of them as 'fragmentary' suggests that they are accidental relics from damaged manuscripts, but this is not how they present themselves and how they are being understood today. The earliest manuscript known (DD from the Cairo Genizah) dates from before 1050, in the period when the Targum of Onkelos was establishing itself as the 'official' Targum for synagogue use. It is therefore plausible to see the 'Fragment-Targum' collections as an attempt made at that time to preserve the distinctive features of the Palestinian Targum for use along with Onkelos in study and public reading. One of the other Genizah mss of about the same date (CC: see above) seems to show how such a Palestinian text (in this case of the Ten

Commandments) might be inserted in a copy of Onkelos. The full Targum from which such extracts were taken would of course be older. Another clue is the fact that Ms. P of the 'Fragment-Targum' includes three much longer extracts, from Genesis 1–2, Exodus 13–15 and Exodus 19–20, all of which were synagogue readings for one of the major festivals (Tabernacles, Passover and Weeks respectively). A better name for these collections might therefore, on the pattern of a similar phenomenon now attested much earlier at Qumran, be 'Excerpted Targums'. In any case they continue to be a valuable witness for the passages included in them, which amount to about one-sixth of the whole Pentateuch. The Aramaic texts are reproduced in Klein's edition, with a translation and notes in a second volume: for Exodus English versions of variants in the extracts can be found in the apparatus of the translation of Targum Neofiti in *AramB* 2, pp. 12-158 (see also pp. 7-8 for a full list of all the extracts in the different mss).

The so-called *Targum of Pseudo-Jonathan* owes its name to a well-known misunderstanding. Like the Fragment-Targum this version was referred to in medieval sources as *Targum Yerushalmi*, 'the [or "a"] Targum of Jerusalem', or *T.Y.* for short, but the '*Y*' was wrongly taken to be an abbreviation for *yônātān*, 'Jonathan', and assumed to refer to the figure who was credited with the standard (and only completely extant) Targum of the Prophets, Jonathan ben Uzziel.[55] This error was perpetuated in the *editio princeps* of 1591, but when it was exposed in the eighteenth-century scholarship could do no better than prefix 'Pseudo' to the name which had by then become traditional and so far no one has produced a more appropriate alternative. Until recently Pseudo-Jonathan has been seen as a representative of the Palestinian Targum tradition, with which it does share numerous haggadic expansions. But its origins are evidently more complex than this, as its composition in the 'Late Jewish Literary Aramaic' dialect, its equally close affinities to Onkelos and the inclusion of additional haggadic material show. So it is increasingly being seen as (so far) the only representative of a third category of Pentateuchal Targum.

---

[55] Some publications still refer to 'Pseudo-Jonathan' as *Targum Yerushalmi I* and to the Fragment-Targums as *Targum Yerushalmi II*.

In Pseudo-Jonathan the tendency to relate the biblical text to later events or phenomena is occasionally taken much further than in the other Targums: mention is made of the orders of Mishnaic tractates (Exod. 26.9; 36.16), Rome and Constantinople (Num. 24.19-24) and even of the wives of Mohammed (Gen. 21.21). The last of these has often been used as an argument for dating Pseudo-Jonathan to the Islamic period, but this could of course be a late addition to a much older work. A stronger case for its late compilation has been based on similarities to early medieval midrash, such as *Pirqe deRabbi Eliezer*. But this argument too has been criticized by C.T.R. Hayward, who has also sought to establish a more rigorous method for the use of rabbinic parallels in dating Targums.[56] He prefers a date in the fourth century for the main body of the work, at the very beginning of the range for Late Jewish Literary Aramaic, and Flesher and Chilton take a similar view.[57] Whether this will become the generally accepted conclusion remains to be seen. One might still argue, as Glessmer does, that the kind of work that Pseudo-Jonathan is, with its integration of Palestinian Targum material and much else into a translation that owes more to Onkelos, is more likely to belong to the 'second phase' of Targumic activity in the early medieval period than the formative stage when each of the main traditions was developing in its own way. The 'learned' character of Pseudo-Jonathan, which does not seem to have any explicit attestation of synagogue use (this may be why only two manuscripts of it are known to have existed: see below), might support such a view.[58] Extensive use of older materials by the compiler could of course be presumed. One such source that is repeatedly drawn upon in Exodus 12-23 is the probably third-century *Mekhilta of Rabbi Ishmael*, which might seem to support an early date, but it was also well known in the medieval period.[59] Another important feature of Pseudo-Jonathan, to which attention has been drawn by B. Mortensen, is the intense preoccupation with

---

[56] See his *Targums and the Transmission of Scripture into Judaism and Christianity* (Leiden, 2010), esp. pp. 172-204, 234-58.

[57] Their treatment in *The Targums*, pp. 159-66, is a valuable guide to the issues and recent discussion of them.

[58] Cf. Glessmer, *Einleitung*, pp. 195-96; Alexander, pp. 322-23; A. Shinan, in Lange and Tov, *Textual History* 1B, pp. 162-63 (§2.4.3.4.1).

[59] G. Stemberger, *Introduction to the Talmud and Midrash* (Edinburgh, 2nd ed., 1996), p. 252.

priestly matters in the material that is unique to Pseudo-Jonathan.[60] Whatever this Targum's date(s) of origin, such concerns could provide some valuable clues to its possible purpose and setting.[61]

The manuscript on which the *editio princeps* had been based was subsequently lost or destroyed, but the printed edition is sometimes referred to as a source of alternative readings. The only extant ms. is British Library (formerly British Museum) Add. 27031 and a new, more accurate transcription was published by E.G. Clarke in connection with the preparation of a computer-generated concordance, which is also included in the volume: *Targum Pseudo-Jonathan of the Pentateuch: Text and Concordance* (Hoboken NJ, 1984). A French translation of the Exodus section by Le Déaut was published in 1979 (see above on Codex Neophyti) and an English translation with extensive notes by M. Maher is included in *AramB* 2, pp. 159-275. A photographic copy of the ms. is now available online at www.bl.uk/manuscripts.

d. *The Peshiṭta*

The Peshiṭta, or 'simple', version is the oldest Syriac translation of the Old Testament and the one which has remained standard in the Syriac churches until the present day.[62] The Syriac language is a dialect of Eastern Aramaic that was originally spoken in Edessa (modern Şanliurfa, 200 km NE of Aleppo) and its hinterland of Osrhoene and spread eastwards with Christianity into northern Mesopotamia and eventually much further afield. Numerous manuscripts containing part or all of the Old Testament survive, ranging in date from the fifth to the nineteenth century A.D.: one of the earliest, now known as 5b1 (see further below), contains the text

---

[60] *The Priesthood in Targum Pseudo-Jonathan* (Leiden, 2006).

[61] On more general questions about the interrelations of the Pentateuch Targums and their development see Roberts, pp. 199-207; Alexander, *ABD* 6, pp. 321-24; Glessmer, *Einleitung*, pp. 8-11; Flesher and Chilton, pp. 91-166 (with the most detail); B. Eco, in Lange and Tov, *Textual History*, pp. 241-51 (§1.3.3).

[62] See, in general, Roberts, *Old Testament Text*, pp. 214-28; S.P. Brock, 'Versions, Ancient (Syriac)', *ABD* 6, pp. 794-99; Weitzman, *Syriac Version*; Flesher and Chilton, *Targums*, pp. 356-68; J.A. Lund, 'Exodus in Syriac', in Dozeman et al., *The Book of Exodus*, pp. 349-69; I. Carbajosa, 'Primary Translations: Peshitta', in Lange and Tov, *Textual History* 1A, pp. 262-78 (§1.3.4); Lund, 'Pentateuch; Primary Translations: Peshitta', in Lange and Tov, *Textual History* 1B, pp. 173-80 (§2.4.5).

of Exodus (along with Genesis, Numbers and Deuteronomy). Early modern editions of the Peshitta were based on relatively recent manuscripts, but the discovery of Codex Ambrosianus B.21 Inferiore (7a1) and its publication in facsimile form in 1876–1883 initiated a new stage of research, in which attention was focused increasingly on the most ancient manuscripts.[63] In 1914 W.E. Barnes published his *Pentateuchus Syriace*, based on sixteen mss, half of which were dated to the eighth century or earlier (see his 'A New Edition of the Pentateuch in Syriac', *JTS* 15 [1914], pp. 41-44). M.D. Koster's edition, published in 1977 as part of the Leiden Peshitta Institute's plan for a comprehensive series of volumes to cover the whole Old Testament and Apocrypha, represented a further major step forward in three respects.[64] It benefited from the Institute's worldwide search for Peshitta manuscripts, which greatly enlarged the available resources; it presented all significant variant readings from mss of the twelfth century and earlier in a critical apparatus; and it enabled Koster, simultaneously, to produce a detailed monograph on the development of the text in the various groups of mss that could be distinguished.[65] What the edition did not provide, in line with the Institute's considered policy, was a critical reconstruction of the original (or earliest accessible) text of the Peshitta: the text printed is that of 7a1 (corrected where it was deemed necessary from other early mss). But the data are there in the apparatus for scholars to form their own view about what the original text may have been.[66]

Koster himself, in his monograph and a number of articles published subsequently, has left readers in no doubt about his own view.[67] In doing so he revived a debate, and a conclusion, which had

---

[63] For fuller details see P.B. Dirksen, *An Annotated Bibliography of the Peshitta of the Old Testament* (MPIL 5; Leiden, 1989).

[64] M.D. Koster (ed.), 'Exodus', in *The Old Testament in Syriac according to the Peshitta Version*, I.1, *Preface; Genesis–Exodus* (Leiden, 1977).

[65] *The Peshitta of Exodus: The Development of its Text in the course of Fifteen Centuries* (Assen/Amsterdam, 1977), esp. pp. 55-114 and 177-97.

[66] The system introduced by the Institute for designating mss indicates the date (7 = seventh cent. A.D.) and contents of each ms. (thus a = a complete or nearly complete Bible; b = the Pentateuch only; h = only one book; l = a lectionary etc.). The final number simply identifies different mss with the same characteristics.

[67] See (e.g.) his 'Redating TR and BTR: The Three Stages at Stake?', *Aramaic Studies* 7 (2009), pp. 1-18.

already emerged in the work on Barnes's edition. Both Barnes and one of his assistants, J. Pinkerton, were well aware that the oldest manuscript, 5b1, differed considerably in its readings for Genesis and Exodus from the other early mss which they consulted. The differences were not random: again and again the readings of 5b1 matched those of the Masoretic text more closely than the others. As Barnes put it, 'It is probable that there are two recensions of the Peshitta of the books of Genesis and Exodus represented respectively in D [his siglum for 5b1] and in A [7a1] B [12a1] E [8b1] H [13b3] l [18b3]' ('New Edition', p. 42). Barnes inclined to the view that 5b1 had been 'accommodated' to the Masoretic text (i.e. revised to agree with it), while the text of 7a1 and 8b1 'may be a more faithful copy of the original Peshitta'. Pinkerton, on the other hand, in a much longer article, gave reasons for taking precisely the opposite view: the original, more literal, translation (probably made by Jews for Jews) was taken over by the Syrian church, which 'gradually amplified and improved the style' of it: 'The best example of this class is, on the whole, the "Codex Ambrosianus"' (p. 41).[68]

It was Pinkerton's view that Koster, with much more data and extensive analysis, found to be in principle correct.[69] Although theoretically both explanations are possible (the oldest manuscript need not necessarily preserve the earliest stage in the text's history that is accessible to us) and at first Koster's conclusion was much debated, recent scholarship seems to be unanimous that he was right to place the 'Masoretic' readings at the beginning of the process (see especially Brock, *ABD* 6, pp. 794-95; Weitzman, *Syriac Version*, pp. 272-88, 300-306; Carbajosa, pp. 268-70; Lund, 'Exodus in Syriac', pp. 352-54). Ephrem in the fourth century already knew a text of this kind;[70] there is no evidence of competence in Hebrew in

---

[68] J. Pinkerton, 'The Origin and the Early History of the Syriac Pentateuch', *JTS* 15 (1914), pp. 14-41.

[69] In 1968 P. Wernberg-Møller had shown that Pinkerton was mistaken to lay so much emphasis on stylistic improvement as the motive of the revisers, while accepting that 5b1 had the more original text ('Some scribal and linguistic features of the Genesis part of the oldest Peshitta manuscript (BM Add 14425)', *JSS* 13 [1968], pp. 136-61). Koster makes clear that other factors, such as the context, were also important to the revisers (*The Peshitta*, pp. 190-95).

[70] Eusebius of Emesa (who was born in Edessa) cites readings of the Peshitta (ὁ Σύρος) in Greek in his Genesis commentary (mid-fourth century) and some

the Syriac-speaking church in the following centuries; and a small number of other manuscripts, both for Exodus and for other books (especially 9a1), present further examples of what must be regarded as original readings closer to the Hebrew than those of most of the manuscripts.

Several important implications follow from this. It now seems likely that in most if not all books the original translation of the Peshitta was very close to the consonantal text of the Masoretic manuscripts. This means that in using the Leiden edition one must not treat the main text printed (basically that of 7a1) as always equivalent to the original translation: one must look to see if there are variants closer to the Hebrew in the apparatus (especially from 5b1) and prefer their reading. In the commentary the siglum 'Sy' represents the Leiden text, but significant variants from 5b1 are regularly noted. Further, any assessment of the translation technique of the Peshitta must now take account of this manuscript as a witness to the original translation. The increasing elaboration of the translation in sixth, seventh and eighth-century mss and even more in later ones can no longer be treated as evidence for the original character of the Peshitta. In fact, 5b1 already includes examples of these later developments and it is being plausibly argued that to reach the original translation emendation would be needed, with or without support from early quotations and relics in later manuscripts (Weitzman, *Syriac Version*, pp. 288-300). The problem is that we have no way of knowing how far this should go: whether, in other words, the original included no additional material (like Aquila's Greek version) or already exhibited some amplification to improve the sense and style.

With this proviso, there is still scope for descriptions of the character of the Peshitta translation of Exodus like those provided by Lund ('Exodus in Syriac', pp. 354-67) and now more generally by Carbajosa (pp. 271-74), in which the variant readings of 5b1 are kept in mind. The translators, while remaining faithful to their Hebrew source, were also attentive to the lexicon and grammatical requirements of Syriac. In an interesting study, which will no

---

of them can also be aligned with 5b1 (R.B. ter Haar Romeny, *A Syrian in Greek Dress: The Use of Greek, Hebrew and Syriac Biblical Texts in Eusebius of Emesa's Commentary on Genesis* [TEG 6; Leuven, 1997], pp. 75-79; cf. Weitzman, *Syriac Version*, pp. 144, 302).

doubt be taken further by others, Weitzman has examined divergent renderings of the same Hebrew word and their use in different books, so as to produce a rough classification of translators as more 'conservative' or 'modern' in their choices: on this scale Exodus emerges as 'transitional' between Genesis and Leviticus–Deuteronomy (*Syriac Version*, pp. 164-86). In view of the likely length of time during which the Peshitta was produced (see further below), such developments may well have occurred quite quickly.

The extent to which the Peshitta was dependent upon older translations such as the Septuagint or an early Targum has been re-evaluated in recent years, partly as a result of the appearance of the Leiden editions (see Weitzman, *Syriac Version*, pp. 68-163; Carbajosa, pp. 274-76). Earlier such dependence was thought to be extensive and scholars such as Kahle and Roberts were particularly insistent on the translators' familiarity with the Palestinian Targum. There is no question now of the original Peshitta being described as a Targum and even direct use of the Jewish texts is no longer thought likely. There certainly are points where interpretations are shared with rabbinic literature, but the explanation for this can be found in a broader familiarity of the Pentateuch translators in particular with Jewish exegetical traditions (see especially Y. Maori, *The Peshitta Version of the Pentateuch and Early Jewish Exegesis* [Heb.: Jerusalem, 1995]). Similarly, many of the agreements with the Septuagint can be ascribed either to a common approach to the task of translation or to much later scribal interventions. In Weitzman's view, however, there remain a few cases where early consultation of the Greek translation remains likely, perhaps to help with the understanding of a difficult passage (e.g. Exod. 25.2: *Syriac Version*, pp. 68-86).

The question of the origin of the Peshitta has deliberately been left till last. There is no reliable tradition about this and scholars have always been faced with the puzzling fact that the translation, which has been preserved only within a Christian church, was evidently made, not from the Septuagint which enjoyed such high prestige in early Christianity, but from the Hebrew original and in such a way that it bears numerous other signs of a Jewish origin, as noted above. An obvious, and widely supported, explanation would be that the Peshitta was originally produced for the use of a Jewish community or communities in northern Mesopotamia and was taken over from them by an adjacent Christian church to avoid unnecessary repetition of the work of translation. Edessa, in the western part of the region where the Syriac language is first attested by inscriptions and from early times a Christian centre there, is the most plausible location for this to have occurred: there is some evidence of a Jewish community too. But some scholars have favoured Adiabene to the east, where Josephus reports the conversion of the royal family to Judaism in the first cent. A.D. (*AJ* 20.34-53). Within such an overall picture Weitzman has proposed that a number of internal features of the translation indicate an origin among a group of non-rabbinic Diaspora Jews whose religious life was centred on the practice of communal prayer. Such a group might have been particularly open to conversion to Christianity and would naturally have brought their translation of the Old Testament with them into their new religious setting (*Syriac Version*, pp. 206-37, 258-62).

The date of the translation is partly determined by its citation in the works of the fourth-century writers Aphrahat and Ephrem and by its influence on the biblical quotations in the Old Syriac Gospels (c. 200 A.D.) and even Tatian's Diatessaron (c. 170 A.D.). An origin in the mid-second century is likely, but a somewhat earlier date cannot be entirely excluded.

e. *The Vulgate*

For the Vulgate the modern scholar is much better placed than for the other ancient translations to give an answer to questions about its origin, background, predecessors, purpose and character. The voluminous writings of Jerome, which include letters, commentaries and even prefaces to the translations, can be supplemented from those of contemporaries such as Augustine and Rufinus to illuminate not only the work of translation itself but its reception in the contemporary Western churches. Not only do we know that Jerome was the translator but we can place his translation from the Hebrew (and even that of Exodus) quite precisely in the sequence of his scholarly work.[71] Jerome's early education had taken him to Rome, where he was baptized in the mid-360s, probably in his late teens.

---

[71] For fuller accounts see F. Stummer, *Einleitung in die lateinische Bibel* (Paderborn, 1928); Roberts, *Old Testament Text*, pp. 247-65; J.N.D. Kelly, *Jerome: His Life, Writings and Controversies* (London, 1975); E. Schulz-Flügel, 'The Latin Old Testament Tradition', in Saebø (ed.), *Hebrew Bible*, 1/1, pp. 643-62; S. Rebenich, *Jerome* (London, 2002); A. Kamesar, 'Jerome', in Carleton-Paget

Around 370, when he spent time in Trier (*Augusta Treverorum*), he was copying the *Treatises on the Psalms* by Hilary of Poitiers for a friend, which would have introduced him to the work and ideas of Origen as well as to 'advanced Christian biblical scholarship', including the problems of translation from Hebrew into Greek and Greek into Latin.[72] In the following years, during stays in Syria and Constantinople, he began to learn Greek, Hebrew and Aramaic for himself and to undertake some translations of Christian writings in Greek. After his return to Rome in 383, with a growing reputation for biblical scholarship, he received the famous commission from Pope Damasus to prepare a revision of the existing Latin translation of the Bible (the 'Old Latin') on the basis of a comparison with Greek manuscripts. It is not certain how much of the Latin Bible Jerome was intended to revise: the original wording of the commission does not survive and Jerome's own summary of his task (in his *Preface to the Gospel*, i.e. the four Gospels) sets the Old Testament to one side, for the time being at least. By the time of Damasus's death late in 384 he had completed only his work on the Gospels and a similar revision of the Psalter: the latter does not survive. The rest of the New Testament was later revised by others.

For a combination of reasons Jerome was forced to leave Rome in mid-385 and he took the opportunity to make a journey to the Holy Land, where he realized his growing ambition to lead a monastic life. He founded a monastery just outside Bethlehem and lived there until his death in 420. It was during these years that his great work of translating and commenting on the Old Testament was carried out. Initially he retranslated several books into Latin using Origen's revised Greek text in the Hexapla, which was accessible to him at Caesarea and in copies which circulated more widely. Among these books was the Psalter and the revision which he produced, known generally as the 'Gallican Psalter', has remained in use to the present day. But since the attraction of Origen's text was its fidelity to the Hebrew, it was a natural step for Jerome to make the Hebrew the immediate basis of his later translation work. In the Holy Land he also had access to Jewish biblical scholarship. The transition can be

---

and Schaper, *NCHB* 1, pp. 653-75; M. Graves, 'Vulgate', in Lange and Tov, 1A, *Textual History*, pp. 279-89 (§1.3.5).

[72] Kamesar, *NCHB* 1, p. 654: see pp. 653-59 for an up-to-date overview of Jerome's biography, and more fully Kelly, *Jerome*, and Rebenich, *Jerome*.

placed quite precisely between 389 and 391 or 392 and a group of Jerome's works that can be dated to these years shows how he moved from one approach to the other (cf. Kelly, *Jerome*, pp. 149-63). His *Commentary on Ecclesiastes* already shows an inclination to translate from the Hebrew, but he was still taking his wording where possible from the Septuagint version: since in Ecclesiastes the latter keeps extremely and even artificially close to the Hebrew wording, this will not have been a major concession. This was followed by two handbooks, the *Onomasticon* and the *Book of Places*, and then by the *Hebrew Questions on Genesis*, with its widespread use of rabbinic scholarship, its constant focus on the meaning of Hebrew words and a *Preface* which, despite Jerome's protestations, undermined the reliability of the old Septuagint translation (and so of Latin versions that were based on it).[73] Although Jerome sometimes implies that it was to be followed by similar works on other books, he had made his point sufficiently and from then on gave his time for much of the next fifteen years to the work of translation from the Hebrew itself.

Surprisingly, Jerome did not go straight on and begin, as might have been expected, with the translation of Genesis and the rest of the Pentateuch. From his 'progress reports' in his letters and prefaces it is clear that he began with Samuel–Kings, the Prophets and the Psalms, though he does not say which of these he did first and there have been different views about it. For most of the twentieth century the dominant view was that Samuel–Kings came first, as its prologue (the so-called *Prologus galeatus*) looks most like an introduction to the whole project. But B. Kedar-Kopfstein's publications on the language and style of Jerome's translations (see further below) have made it more likely that Samuel–Kings came after the Prophets and the Psalms. The recent completion of the Pentateuch is referred to in the *Preface to Joshua* and must fall in 403 or 404, as the same Preface also refers to the death of Jerome's long-standing patron and friend Paula in the latter year. Only Joshua, Judges, Ruth and Esther were completed later, probably in 405. Work on Genesis had begun by 398 and was apparently finished by 401, as Jerome quotes from its Preface in his work *Against Rufinus*, which can be

---

[73] See in detail A. Kamesar, *Jerome, Greek Scholarship and the Hebrew Bible: A Study of the* Quaestiones Hebraicae in Genesim (Oxford, 1993). The *Preface* is translated in Rebenich, *Jerome*, pp. 93-96.

dated then (Graves, 'Vulgate', p. 279). He must have been working on Exodus around 400.

Translation was an activity to which Jerome devoted much of his intellectual energy, even when his efforts met with opposition. It is understandable, therefore, that he several times spelt out in his other writings what qualities a translation should display, from the Preface to his translation of Eusebius of Caesarea's *Chronicon* (380) to his letter to Pammachius (395: *Ep.* 57). Guided by classical forebears (he refers to Cicero as a model more than once), he held that accuracy (*veritas*) needed to be complemented by a 'flavour' (*sapor*) that was appropriate to the text that was being translated (on this Kamesar, *NCHB* 1, pp. 659-70, is masterly). It was deficiencies in the latter as well as the former that he found in the Old Latin and he sought to remedy them both. This helps to account for the fact that he sometimes seems to waver between a translation that reflects the meaning of a text (*ad sensum*) and one that reproduces precisely its wording (*ad verbum*). In one passage, which commentators have found very difficult to understand, he indicates a general preference for *ad sensum* translation, but then appears to make an exception for the Bible (and Origen's *On First Principles*), where even the order of the words can be significant (*Ep.* 57.5: see the different explanations offered by Schulz-Flügel, 'Tradition', pp. 654-55; Kamesar, *NCHB* 1, p. 669; Graves, 'Vulgate', p. 283). Perhaps the reason is that Jerome was always fighting on two fronts, for the accuracy of his new translations against their traditionalist detractors and for stylistic freedom in the face of pagan criticism of the poor literary quality of the Old Latin. Certainly Jerome's statements elsewhere and his actual practice of biblical translation show a strong leaning towards the *ad sensum* approach, but he valued the precision of Aquila as an aid to understanding and in places his translations do follow the wording of the original closely. Close study of his translations from the Hebrew has in fact shown that in them Jerome was gradually moving from greater to less adherence to the wording of the original, so that the translation of Exodus (one of the latest) exhibits, for example, much more freedom in rendering Hebrew phrases in idiomatic Latin and a readiness to avoid what Jerome regarded as unnecessary repetition (e.g. of names).[74]

---

[74] See B. Kedar-Kopfstein, 'The Latin Translations', in M.J. Mulder (ed.), *Mikra: Text, Translation, Reading and Interpretation of the Hebrew Bible in*

Jerome's turn to the Hebrew as the basis for his translation was the product both of his own increasing competence in the language and regard for its importance (cf. Kamesar, *Jerome*, pp. 41-49) and of a growing dissatisfaction with the Septuagint and any version based upon it. Initially he had shared the traditional Christian reverence for the work of the original translators of the Septuagint, a reverence which had been able to deploy in its defence various explanations of the discrepancies between it and the Hebrew text as it now circulated among Jews (Kamesar, *NCHB* 1, p. 662-64). So in his early *Preface to the Gospel* he could write: *sit illa vera interpretatio quam Apostoli probaverunt*. Even around 390 he was still maintaining in his *Preface to Chronicles translated from the Septuagint* that the translators had been inspired by the Holy Spirit and mistakes were due to the later scribes who copied their work: by using Origen's corrected text he could get back to something like the original Greek. Soon afterwards, however, he began to see that even this did not solve all the linguistic problems and in his Prefaces to the translations of Chronicles and Genesis from Hebrew (the latter translated in Rebenich, pp. 101-104) he questions the legend about the seventy translators miraculously producing identical versions through divine inspiration. Later still, in commentaries written towards the end of his life, he was repeatedly to point out deficiencies in the Septuagint translation.[75]

The basis for such criticisms did not simply come from Jerome's own linguistic knowledge. He drew heavily on the later Jewish versions assembled by Origen in the Hexapla, especially Aquila and Symmachus (for the Pentateuch see Salvesen, *Symmachus*, pp. 265-81), and he often mentions the valuable help which he received from Jewish scholars. Some of his interpretations match those in the Targums as a consequence, but there is no evidence that he had or used written copies of them. At times he clearly still has his eye (or perhaps his memory) on the Septuagint and Old Latin

---

Ancient Judaism and Early Christianity (CRINT 2.1; Assen, 1988), pp. 299-338; D.L. Everson, 'The *Vetus Latina* and the Vulgate of the Book of Exodus', in Dozeman et al., *The Book of Exodus*, pp. 370-86.

[75] In *Jerome*, pp. 44-46, Kamesar argued that Jerome already envisaged a translation direct from the Hebrew in the early 380s and had ceased to believe in the inspiration of the Septuagint by then. His account of the matter in *NCHB* 1, pp. 659-64, perhaps significantly, says nothing about the latter point.

versions and the latter sometimes provided him with the language for his translation. Occasionally his choice of words reflects the Christian setting in which he wrote: this is more common in the Psalms, but there are some possible examples in Exodus. Even here Jerome can be seen to be integrating influences from classical culture and Jewish tradition.[76]

The new translation of the Old Testament did not receive the widespread acclaim from his contemporaries for which Jerome must have hoped. Its merits were not obvious to ordinary church-people, who preferred the versions they knew, and it met with disapproval from leading figures such as Augustine and Rufinus who found it wrong-headed. There were exceptions, such as the bishop Chromatius to whom Jerome dedicated his translation of Chronicles, and they were evidently sufficient in number and influence to ensure that Jerome's work survived. But until the seventh century more extant manuscripts of the Old Latin were copied than of Jerome's version. Cassiodorus in the mid-sixth century is thought to have been the first to collect Jerome's versions in a 'pandect' and only the production of Alcuin's edition c. 800 marked their acceptance as the standard version of the western church.

The edition of Alcuin was the foundation for the Paris Bible text of the thirteenth century and the Clementine edition of 1592. (It is only from the sixteenth century [or possibly the thirteenth] that the name 'Vulgate' was applied to Jerome's translation: in his own time it would of course have meant the Old Latin.) Two twentieth-century editions have penetrated behind the Alcuin text by giving the primary place to a group of earlier manuscripts such as Codex Amiatinus, written in Northumbria c. 700. The multi-volume edition of the Roman Benedictines provides the fullest information about the evidence: the volume containing Exodus was published in 1929. The edition of R. Weber is based on this for the Old Testament, with an abbreviated apparatus, but reflects the editor's own critical judgement in the text printed. It has been widely welcomed and is regarded as entirely adequate for general scholarly use.[77] Even the early manuscripts do not present a pure

---

[76] M.A. Kraus, 'Jerome', pp. 17-37 (26-37); now more fully in his *Jewish, Christian and Classical Exegetical Traditions*.

[77] F.A. Gasquet et al. (eds.), *Biblia sacra iuxta latinam vulgatam versionem ad codicum fidem... Cura et studio monachorum Abbatiae Pontificiae Sancti*

text of Jerome's translation, because of contamination from the Old Latin, so there remains an unavoidable element of uncertainty even in critical texts like these.

The Hebrew text used by Jerome was certainly very close in both extent and wording to the consonants of the later Masoretic text. It needs, nevertheless, to be remembered that the *ad sensum* method of translation followed in Exodus inevitably conceals some features of the underlying Hebrew and the minor divergences of Jerome's wording from the Masoretic text are in most cases at least probably due to this. They cannot be used with any confidence to reconstruct a different Hebrew text.

3. *Main Component Sections and their Plot, Genres and Theological Themes*

Exodus is, from a literary point of view, a story, or more precisely part of a story. It begins with the Israelites, or 'Hebrews' as they are also known (e.g. 1.15), in Egypt: how they came to be there and where they came from has been told in the preceding book of Genesis. At the end of Exodus they are at Mount Sinai but their eventual departure from there is not described until Numbers 10. Where the end of this larger story is to be placed is an open question. The canon puts it at the death of Moses in Deuteronomy 34, but the recurrent motif of the possession of the land of Canaan only reaches its climax at the end of the book of Joshua: hence the persistent modern preference for the expression 'Hexateuch' over 'Pentateuch'. Some would extend the story further still, to the end of 2 Kings, since each of the intervening books is at least loosely attached to its predecessor, but this deprives the narrative of the coherence and the tightness of plot which the earlier conclusions preserve.

Major divisions within Exodus are indicated by the changing geographical settings of the narrative: in Egypt, in the wilderness and at Mount Sinai. These are reinforced by the differences in character between the sections so defined: differences in the chief

---

Hieronymi in Urbe Ordinis Sancti Benedicti (18 vols., Rome, 1926–95); R. Weber, (with R. Gryson for more recent revisions), *Biblia sacra iuxta vulgatam versionem* (Stuttgart, 1969; 5th ed. 2007).

participants in the narrative and their roles, as well as the plot, the genres and some of the theological themes. In all probability these variations are related to the settings and use of the material outside its preserved literary framework. There is of course continuity too – these are parts of a connected story – and the complexity of the narrative leads to some blurring of the dividing lines which reinforces this. Although the 'Egypt' section naturally concludes with the failure of Pharaoh's attempt to recapture his fleeing slaves and the celebratory hymns that follow (15.1-21), G.W. Coats pointed out that the 'wilderness itinerary' begins already in 12.37, that the Israelites are already 'in the wilderness' in 13.18 and 14.11 (perhaps also v. 3) and that the 'murmuring motif' in 14.11-12 is more typical of the wilderness narratives.[78] On this view the climax of the 'Egypt' section comes in the final plague in ch. 12. Again, there is some ambiguity about whether the Israelites are already at Mount Sinai when Jethro appears in ch. 18: according to 19.1-2 they only arrive there subsequently, but 18.5 says that they (or at least Moses) were already 'encamped at the mountain of God', an expression which appears to refer to Mount Sinai in 24.13. As the commentary on these passages will show, there are possible solutions to these conundrums, but their 'bivalent' character also points to what can be called their 'transitional' status in the narrative.

(i) *The Exodus Story (1.1–15.21)*

This section as a whole conforms well to the common pattern in which a situation of trouble or distress is eventually, after one or more failed attempts or other kinds of delay, brought to a successful outcome (compare Abraham's quest for a son in Gen. 15–22). The length of the narrative makes it possible for it to incorporate a series of episodes which temporarily create tension before the story can continue on its way. Thus, even when the birth of Moses and his adoption into the Egyptian royal family promise relief for the Israelites from their oppression by the Egyptians, his violent action (2.11-15) leads to his removal from the land. When God appears to Moses at the mountain in the desert and appoints him as his chosen leader for the people, he at first hesitates and raises objections to his choice. But each time they are overcome. When Pharaoh refuses

---

[78] Coats, 'Traditio-Historical Character'.

the demand to let the Israelites leave Egypt, force is applied in the form of the plagues. But still time after time Pharaoh refuses, or qualifies his permission in unacceptable ways. Even when he eventually relents and the Israelites depart from the vicinity of his capital, he changes his mind and pursues them, until his forces are swallowed up in the 'sea' and the liberation is finally complete. Each individual episode is not independent but part of the larger scheme in which Pharaoh and the Egyptians are ranged in conflict with Moses, Israel and their all-powerful God.

The individual episodes nonetheless have their own character, which often enables them to be compared to similar stories elsewhere: for example, Moses' birth-story, his meeting with the daughters of the Midianite priest, his commissioning as the leader of the Israelites, the giving of a (prophetic) sign and, with the fullest development of an existing pattern, the plague-stories (see more fully the introductions to each passage).[79] In the simple form of the latter, a plague occurs which threatens to wipe out a people and it is warded off by the intercession or ritual action of a national leader (cf. Num. 21.5-9; more fully in 2 Sam. 24.15-25). In the Exodus sequence the pattern is modified (in two slightly different ways) to fit the needs of the plot. Pharaoh must be persuaded by the threat of the plague to let the Israelites go and Moses acts as the intercessor on behalf of the Egyptians to bring about its end. In addition to these narrative genres, the Exodus story also includes two genealogies (1.1-5; 6.14-25), ritual ordinances (12.1-28, 43-49; 13.1-16) and two hymns of praise (15.1-18, 21).

The overriding theological theme of the narrative is that Yahweh is the Saviour of his people from their enemies, however powerful they may be, and the giver of the promised land of Canaan. This is already foreshadowed in his words to Moses in 3.7-8, 16-17; 6.2-8 and it is reaffirmed as the narrative proceeds in the ritual ordinances of 12.25-27; 13.3-16 and above all in the account and hymnic celebration of the deliverance at the sea (14.13, 30; 15.1-3, 16-17). The bond between Yahweh and his people is grounded in his relationship with their ancestors, Abraham, Isaac and Jacob, which is sometimes expressed in terms of a covenant (2.24; 6.4-5). He

---

[79] See further the classic work of Gressmann, *Mose*, esp. the summary on pp. 374-86, and the more recent studies of Coats, *Moses* and *Exodus 1–18*.

now deals with them through a chosen leader, Moses, to whom he (through his angel initially) has 'appeared' in the burning bush (3.4, 16; 4.5) and whom he continues to instruct about his intentions and requirements, like a prophet (e.g. 6.1). It is during the long account of the commissioning of Moses that he reveals his name and interprets its meaning as (probably: see the commentary on 3.14) 'I will be who/what I will be'. To him and to Moses the appropriate response of the people is faith (4.1-9, 31; 14.31) and the fear of God (1.17, 21; 14.31). But ritual actions are also expected: worship, including sacrifice (3.18 etc.; 15.1-21); circumcision (4.24-26; 12.43-49); the celebration of Passover, the festival of Unleavened Bread and the dedication of firstborn (chs. 12–13); the dedication of a temple, at which Yahweh will be present (15.13, 17). This God is unique (8.6; 9.29; 15.11), the Everlasting King (15.18).[80]

(ii) *The Wilderness Journey (15.22–18.27)*

Here the literary structure of the narrative is quite different, since it consists of a series of five independent narratives (six if ch. 18 is divided in two), each with a separate topic and, in the case of the first four, a repetition of the pattern already seen at much greater length in the Exodus story itself: distress, delay and an eventually successful outcome. The itinerary-notes which delimit several of these episodes (15.27–16.1; 17.1) reinforce the separation between them by giving it a geographical dimension in these cases. At the same time, like the links of a chain, they give the narrative an external unity which is further underlined by the similar verses which mark its beginning and end (15.22; 19.1-2): the wilderness narrative here is (like the similar sequence of narratives in Num. 10.11–21.20) made explicitly into the story of a journey, in this case the journey from Egypt to Mount Sinai. Closer examination (see below) will show that there are also recurring motifs in the first three episodes which give them an internal unity, though not apparently any real dramatic progression from one to the next. In any case the episode(s) involving Jethro and even the war with Amalek stand somewhat apart from them and each other on thematic grounds.

---

[80] On chs. 1–11 see further Greenberg, *Understanding Exodus*.

It is therefore possible, form-critically, to distinguish the verses which represent portions of an itinerary (on which see my article 'The Wilderness Itineraries: A Comparative Study'; also the Excursus in the introduction to 12.28-42, 50-51) from the (mainly short) narratives which they frame. The first four of these narratives can be categorised as 'stories of deliverance', as already indicated, arising from situations of thirst and hunger or, in the final case, an enemy attack. The two sections of ch. 18 are very different and more difficult to classify, but in general terms vv. 1-12 is a 'description of a cultic celebration' and vv. 13-27 is an 'aetiological didactic narrative' (see the commentary for fuller discussion).

In terms of their main participants and recurring themes the difference between this series of episodes and the Exodus story is equally clear. Pharaoh and the Egyptians are no longer active characters, only the subject of memories. In the first four stories Moses, Israel and Yahweh have the major roles, while in ch. 18 only Moses and Jethro interact, though Yahweh/God is repeatedly the subject in what they say and hear. As for their themes, it is the first three episodes which are the most distinctive. Theologically they have an inherent ambiguity about the relationship between Yahweh and Israel, and consequently about Moses' role as mediator: Yahweh appears now as the provider of Israel's material needs, but this contrasts with negative features that centre on Israel's 'murmurings' (which continue in the later sequence of wilderness narratives in Numbers: see the classic study of Coats, *Rebellion in the Wilderness*) and the (two-way) notion of testing. The second triad have more in common with the other major sections of the book: the Exodus story, in different ways, in the war with Amalek and the first Jethro episode, and some legal texts in the Sinai narrative (especially 23.1-3, 6-9) in the institution of judges to assist Moses, where God appears in a new role as the ultimate source of judicial wisdom.

(iii) *The Sinai Narrative (First Part) (19.1–40.38)*

A narrative framework is maintained throughout this section too, but in extensive portions of it the narrative mode is abandoned in favour of instruction, in the form either of what has traditionally been called 'law' or of instruction about building and ritual matters. Even where narrative prevails it is of a different kind (or kinds) from most of what appears in the earlier parts of Exodus. (The same applies, with some variations, to the remainder of the Sinai narrative in Leviticus and Numbers.)[81] This is only to be expected when the subject-matter is generally so different in character from what has appeared before. Only one sub-section can be classified as a 'deliverance story' (32.1–34.28) and such a description is in great danger of obscuring the special characteristics and complexity of these chapters, even if it has some value. In general the narratives and the other literary patterns conform to a series of themes which are largely new: theophany, covenant, legislation, ritual and worship. One feature which is only partly determined by these themes – for it is quite possible to imagine them being presented in a different way – is the long sections of 'law' and instruction which are introduced as divine speech, even where the grammatical implication of this (the use of the first person singular to refer to God) is not rigorously maintained: 20.1-17; 20.22–23.33; 25.1–31.18; 34.10-27; 40.1-15. In this part of Exodus God (or rather, usually, Yahweh, 'the Lord') is portrayed as the speaker of the text (somewhat as in prophecy) to a much greater extent (over half the text) than anywhere else in the book: the longest such passage in chs. 1–18, by some way, is 12.1-20. Even where he is not the speaker, Yahweh is mentioned in nearly every verse (slightly less in the building account of chs. 35–39). Moses, as a prophet-like leader, mediator and intercessor, is only a little less prominent: beside him Aaron and the craftsman Bezalel are the next most important figures. The Israelite people are generally little more than onlookers, but at decisive moments they speak up (19.8; 20.19; 24.3, 7; 32.1) and bring their gifts (32.3; 35.20-29).

The section begins with a 'report of a theophany', here in the sense of a divine appearance that does not merely (as in the Baal-myth from Ugarit and some biblical poems) create dramatic upheavals in the world of nature but is a means for Yahweh to meet with and speak to his people Israel (19.3–20.21).[82] Embedded within

---

[81] What follows is a preliminary and provisional statement which will need at least some modification after the commentary on chs. 19–40 is complete.

[82] On the distinction between this part of the Sinai narrative (and texts related to it) and examples of the 'description of a theophany' genre see Westermann (who uses the term 'epiphany' for the latter), *Loben Gottes*, pp. 73-76 (5th ed., pp. 73-76); Jeremias, *Theophanie*, pp. 100-11, 118-22.

this is a first series of commands and prohibitions ('apodictic law', or one form of it, in Alt's terminology: 20.1-17), which have formal similarity to both a style of wisdom instruction and the stipulations of ancient Near Eastern treaties. The same form of instruction introduces and concludes the following collection of laws (20.22–23.33) which, however, incorporates a long section of 'ordinances' (most of 21.1–22.16), which instead resemble closely in their form (and sometimes content as well) the 'casuistic' pattern that is typical of other ancient Near Eastern legal collections such as the Code of Hammurabi. In 24.3-8 these laws are (apparently) the basis for an 'account of making a covenant' between Yahweh and Israel. But this section is 'framed' by the two parts of an 'account of a cultic theophany' for the leaders of the people, which takes place at the top of Mount Sinai (24.1-2, 9-11).

The conclusion of this is followed in turn by an 'account of a meeting with God' on the top of the mountain for Moses alone (24.12–31.18, with its conclusion [32.7-16] embedded in the next section of narrative). Apart from brief references to the delivery to Moses of stone tablets inscribed with the words of the law, this account mainly takes the form of 'divine instructions for the building of a (portable) sanctuary'. A plan of this kind is referred to in 1 Chr. 28.11-19 (as much earlier in Gudea Cylinder A) and Ezek. 40.1–43.17 presents one in the context of a vision report.[83] The topics of this account recur in the two following sections of the Sinai narrative, which are very different from one another.

What we earlier referred to as a kind of 'deliverance story' (32.1–34.28) in fact comprises a narrative with several sub-sections which have a character that distinguishes it markedly from the other examples in Exodus. Its overall theme is the contrast between acceptable and unacceptable worship. The 'trouble' which is the point of departure for the rest of the story is Yahweh's anger at Aaron's making of a calf (or bull) image which the people worship (32.1-10). There follows a long central section in which interim acts of punishment occur (including the smashing of the stone tablets as a sign of the broken covenant) and Moses intercedes on behalf of the people (32.11–33.19). The 'outcome' is presented in a further

---

[83] The Temple Scroll from Qumran (11Q19) originally contained such a plan (cols. 3-13), but only fragments of it survive. A brief passage of a similar kind indicates how Noah's ark was to be built (Gen. 6.14-16).

'account of a meeting with God' on the top of the mountain (34.1-28), in which Moses is given a new set of stone tablets, Yahweh 'proclaims his name' as one who is 'merciful and gracious', Moses worships him and makes a final prayer for the forgiveness of the people, and Yahweh unilaterally renews his covenant with them on the basis of (some of) the earlier laws. Corresponding to this very different development of the 'deliverance' pattern, in which the continued existence of Israel as Yahweh's people is called in question, the genres employed for the sub-sections include a 'narrative of divine judgement' (to which there are parallels elsewhere in the Pentateuch), several examples of 'intercessory prayer' and 'divine responses', a generalised 'account of the consultation of a prophet' (33.7-11), a 'declaration of a god's character/name' and another 'account of making a covenant'.

The 'divine instructions for the building of a sanctuary' find their sequel much more straightforwardly in 34.29–40.38, where a 'building report' occupies nearly the whole of the text. Such reports are found elsewhere in the Old Testament, both for royal palaces and for the temple in Jerusalem (the latter in 1 Kgs 5.15–6.38; 7.13–8.13; par. 2 Chr. 1.18–6.2; Ezra 1.1–6.18). They are also a commonplace in other ancient Near Eastern texts, especially in royal building inscriptions for temples and other structures.[84] A text from the sixth century found in the Temple of Shamash at Sippar has a number of similarities to the Exodus account.[85]

(iv) *Summary*

The theology of Exodus at the level of the canonical text thus accumulates through the sequence of the varied literary genres that comprise its narrative. It begins, at first glance, without God, in a

---

[84] For many examples and discussion, including comparisons with Old Testament texts, see V. Hurowitz, *I Have Built You an Exalted House: Temple Building in the Bible in the Light of Mesopotamian and North-West Semitic Writings* (JSOTSup 115; Sheffield, 1992); M.J. Boda and J. Novotny (eds.), *From the Foundations to the Crenellations: Essays on Temple-Building in the Ancient Near East and Hebrew Bible* (AOAT 366; Münster, 2010), especially the essay by Novotny on pp. 109-39.

[85] See my study 'The Priestly Histories in the Bible in the light of the Sun-Temple Inscription from Sippar', in J. Elayi and J.-M. Durand (eds.), *Bible et Proche-Orient. Mélanges André Lemaire, 1* (*Transeuphratène* 44 [2014]), pp. 125-37.

situation of oppression and fear, within which nevertheless human courage and kindness can be seen. God intervenes first as one who remembers, remembers his people, and then as one who is powerful enough to rescue them from the hands of one of the great powers of the day, as the King of kings. On the wilderness journey he provides for their material needs and protects them against enemy attack. Here there is also for a moment a rare sight of a non-Israelite worshipper of Yahweh and teacher, Jethro, participating in the leadership of Yahweh's people. At Sinai Yahweh comes down to meet his people and is presented as a God, first, with legal requirements embracing both community life and worship. On this basis the bond with his people is sealed in a covenant. This holy God also desires to be present among his people and authorises the building of a sanctuary, with a priesthood and daily sacrificial worship. But, as the story of the golden calf shows, it must not be idolatrous worship. This same story adds one final dimension of his character: when his people sin, his anger can give way to mercy, assuaged by the prayers of their leader and mediator, Moses, who also becomes an intercessor. So the book ends with God's presence reaffirmed in his people's midst and them prepared for their onward journey.[86]

4. *Composition of the Book*

In this section of the Introduction 'composition' is used to refer not to the plan and stylistic character of the book (as it might have been used in the previous section), but to the process by which the book as we know it came into being over a lengthy period and with the involvement of a number of different writers. As with other aspects of its study, an enquiry into this process cannot be undertaken without some reference to the fact that Exodus forms part of the Pentateuch as a whole (or, as many have thought, of a Hexateuch that includes the book of Joshua as well). But as far as possible the treatment here will focus on issues about composition in the sense defined as they affect Exodus in particular: the more general issues

---

[86] Each of the underlying sources of Exodus has its own emphasis within this broad theological framework, on which see further Section 4 (ii) below: 'Composition of the Book. Sources and Redaction in Exodus: Principles and Results'.

have been well dealt with many times before.[87] First a brief survey of critical work on Exodus since 1850 is given: the scope of this is necessarily limited mainly to the commentaries and other works to which I most frequently refer and their place in the broader development of research. This is followed by an equally brief resumé and justification of the conclusions reached in my detailed analysis of each passage in Exodus 1–18, with a provisional outline of the implications which seem to follow from this for the composition of chs. 19–40. Here, as in the commentary generally, the principle will be followed that we should not, with the evidence and tools that are available to us, expect to be able to answer all the questions about the text's origins that we might want to pose. It follows from this that it is important to distinguish, as far as possible, between what is more and less certain in our conclusions.

(i) *History of Research*

The turning-point in the analysis of the Pentateuch which is marked, as often noted, by H. Hupfeld's *Die Quellen der Genesis und die Art ihrer Zusammensetzung* (Berlin, 1853) made only a limited (and in part misjudged) immediate contribution to the study of Exodus. Hupfeld did, for good reasons, extend his analysis as far as Exod. 6.9 and to some extent beyond (cf. *Quellen*, pp. 85-86: the passages which he attributed to the *Grundschrift* after Exod. 6.9 are listed in

---

[87] Among more recent treatments the following are particularly helpful and represent a variety of different approaches and points of view: Noth, *ÜGP*; Thompson, *Moses and the Law*; J.W. Rogerson, *Old Testament Criticism in the Nineteenth Century: England and Germany* (London, 1984); Houtman, *Der Pentateuch*; Nicholson, *The Pentateuch*; J.-L. Ska, *Introduction à la lecture du Pentateuque: Clés pour l'interprétation des cinq premiers livres de la Bible* (Brussels, 2000); Dozeman et al. (eds.), *The Pentateuch*; Baden, *Composition*; Houston, *The Pentateuch*; T. Römer, 'Zwischen Urkunden, Fragmenten und Ergänzungen: zum Stand der Pentateuchforschung', *ZAW* 125 (2013), pp. 2-24; idem, '"Higher Criticism": The Historical and Literary-Critical Approach – with special reference to the Pentateuch', in Saebø (ed.), *Hebrew Bible/Old Testament*, 3/1, pp. 393-423; R. Smend, 'The Work of Abraham Kuenen and Julius Wellhausen', ibid., pp. 424-53; E. Zenger, C. Frevel et al., *Einleitung in das Alte Testament* (Stuttgart, 9th ed., 2015), pp. 67-228. I have attempted a brief survey of the issues and theories in 'Introduction to the Pentateuch', in J. Barton and J. Muddiman (eds.), *The Oxford Bible Commentary* (Oxford, 2001), pp. 12-38 (reprinted unchanged in Barton and Muddiman [eds.], *The Pentateuch* [Oxford, 2010], pp. 16-53).

Carpenter/Harford-Battersby 1, p. 48) and his conclusion, that in Genesis the redactor had used three parallel sources[88] to compile his narrative, certainly paved the way for a similar analysis of Exodus which would eventually be quite different from the then popular 'Supplementary Hypothesis' of F. Bleek and F. Tuch.[89] It remained for A.W. Knobel (who can probably be regarded as the author of the first critical commentary on Exodus) to work out, gradually, the details of this. In the Preface to his commentary (1857, p. vi) he drew attention to his new analysis of chs. 3–5, 19–24 and 32–34 and in his lengthy 'Kritik des Pentateuch und Josua' published in 1861 he included full lists of the portions which he assigned to the two independent documents which the 'Jehovist' redactor had used to amplify the original *Grundschrift* (in large measure the Priestly document of later scholars).[90] One of these he named *Das Kriegsbuch* (it corresponds largely to the later 'J') and the other *Das Rechtsbuch* (close to the later 'E'). It was this analysis which lay before the 'revolutionaries' like A. Kuenen and K.H. Graf who built on it their argument that the so-called *Grundschrift* was in fact the latest, not the earliest, of the sources of the Pentateuch.

Wellhausen was the inheritor of the analysis as well as the late dating of the *Grundschrift*, which he renamed Q (for *quattuor*, after its four covenants: 'Composition', p. 392 = *Composition*, p. 1). The latter conclusion, which Wellhausen was to advocate in an even more compelling way than his predecessors in his *Prolegomena* (first published as *Geschichte Israels I* in 1878 and then in an English translation in 1885), of course eliminated any question of the other source-material being a supplement to 'Q'. In his treatment of the analysis in 1876 Wellhausen proceeded with caution, laying the greatest emphasis on the distinction between 'Q' and the remaining material.[91] He called the latter 'JE', taking up the older siglum 'Je'

---

[88] *Quellen*, pp. 193-95.

[89] This theory is often associated with H. Ewald, but this is true only in a modified sense. Once he adopted a critical approach (by 1831) he always gave an important place to originally separate sources in his (increasingly complex) accounts of Pentateuchal origins: cf. Knobel, *Numeri*, pp. 495-96; Thompson, *Moses and the Law*, pp. 27-29; Houtman, *Pentateuch*, pp. 93-95.

[90] *Numeri*, pp. 489-606.

[91] It was Kuenen who introduced the siglum 'P' (Thompson, p. 50). According to Houtman, *Pentateuch*, p. 105 n. 20, this was in 1880 (*TT* 14, pp. 257-81, esp. 273), but already in 1870 Kuenen was referring (without the siglum) to the

for the non-*Grundschrift* ('Jehovist') sections but by capitalisation of the 'E' indicating that in many places (but not e.g. in Gen. 2–11) it could be divided between two older parallel sources distinguished by, among other things, their use of Yahweh and Elohim in Genesis and sometimes later ('Composition', p. 392, 407 = *Composition*, pp. 1-2, 16). The quest for this sub-division is pursued throughout the non-Q material, but not relentlessly. Sometimes uncertainty is allowed to remain (*Composition*, p. 79, on 15.22-26 and ch. 16) and in the Sinai-narrative Wellhausen is prepared to attribute more of the shape of the narrative and more of the text itself (e.g. 33.12-23) to the 'Jehovist', whom he regards as 'the real author of the section', not merely as a redactor (p. 94).

Knobel had died (in 1863) before the views of Kuenen and Graf were fully developed but Dillmann, who published a revised edition of Knobel's commentary in 1880, did not accept the argument for a late date for P and pointedly referred to it as 'A', for the oldest source, with 'B' and 'C' denoting the two parts of JE in place of Knobel's terminology. He was, however, increasingly in a minority among critical scholars. A short-lived star, as far as the Old Testament was concerned, who won Wellhausen's admiration after abandoning an initial enthusiasm for Dillmann, was Adolf Jülicher. He learned Dutch to read the works of Kuenen and his pupil H.H. Oort and wrote a dissertation and a long article on the sources of Exodus 1–24, placing a greater emphasis than others at this time on redactional developments. His work has recently become widely cited, but in his own day it was his later writings on the New Testament which were more highly valued (see R. Smend, 'In the Wake of Wellhausen: The Growth of a Literary-Critical School and its Varied Influence', in Saebø [ed.], *Hebrew Bible/Old Testament*, 3/1, pp. 472-93 [478-79]).

By the time that Baentsch and Holzinger published their commentaries in 1900 (in two parallel series which were another product of the new developments) the period of fresh ideas and debate had given way to one of consolidation and refinement of the broader conclusions that had been reached. This was marked by the production of syntheses such as the Introductions to the Old Testament by

'priesterlijke bestanddeelen' in the Pentateuch and Joshua (*TT* 4, pp. 411, 487ff.), having abandoned his earlier adoption of Ewald's term 'the Book of Origins' (*Onderzoek* [Leiden, 3rd ed., 1861] 1, pp. 76-77).

C.H. Cornill and S.R. Driver (1891) and Holzinger's *Einleitung in den Hexateuch* (1893), as well as the appearance in America of B.W. Bacon's *The Triple Tradition of the Exodus* (1894). With further detailed study the main source-documents, even more than before, came to be seen as complex entities in themselves, each including later supplements as well as an original core. This is particularly evident in the 'Oxford Hexateuch', also published in 1900, which displayed the biblical text in three or four columns as required, one for each source, and distinguished secondary additions by the use of smaller and/or italic type. This pioneering work, which included a lengthy introduction as well as the synopsis and notes, was edited by J.E. Carpenter and G. Harford-Battersby on behalf of a committee which included G.B. Gray, the author of the commentary on Numbers in this series (1903). The opening words of the Preface indicate the sense of achievement which inspired its authors: 'These volumes are intended to place before English readers the principal results of modern enquiry into the composition of the first six books of the Old Testament' (p. v). A foundation had been laid which was to remain in essence the standard critical view of the subject for most of the twentieth century, even if different opinions about particular passages continued to appear. McNeile's Exodus commentary of 1908 (2nd ed. 1917) is an early example of this now 'mainstream' approach, but those of Noth (1959; ET 1962), Hyatt (1971) and Childs (1974) were not substantially different in their analysis and dating of the texts.

This did not mean, however, that fresh thinking about the composition of Exodus ceased. In fact, already in the years just before the first World War two publications introduced some very different paradigms. The elder Rudolf Smend's *Die Erzählung des Hexateuch* (1912) divided the text into four narrative sources (i.e. in addition to Deuteronomy) rather than three. Superficially this involved the division of the J source into two (named J^1 and J^2), but the material for the extra parallel narrative was secured by a wholesale revision of the existing analysis which at least in Exodus left none of the sources unaffected (e.g. in Exod. 3–4 and 14). Although this never became a popular view, it remained part of the scholarly landscape until the 1970s, mainly through its presentation in O. Eissfeldt's *Hexateuch-synopse* (1922, repr. 1987) and the widely used Introductions of Eissfeldt (1st ed. 1934, ET 1965) and G. Fohrer (1st ed. 1965, ET 1968), in the latter case on the strength of Fohrer's fresh examination of Exodus 1–15 (1964). The only significant commentary to adopt it was that of G. Beer and K. Galling (1939), in which the division of P into two parallel strands by G. von Rad (1934) was also influential.

Much more significant for the later study of Exodus was the work of Hugo Gressmann who, following broadly in the footsteps of H. Gunkel's commentary on Genesis (1st ed. 1901), sought to isolate the individual old *Sagen* out of which the compilers (hardly 'authors' on his view) of the written sources in Exodus had composed their narratives. He also gave a much more prominent place (as Gunkel was doing for Genesis and the Psalms) to parallels from elsewhere in the ancient Near East, drawn partly from the collections of texts and pictures which he had edited a few years earlier. His main conclusions about Exodus were worked out in his monograph *Mose und seine Zeit* (1913), but it is somewhat easier to find the treatment of particular passages in *Die Anfänge Israels* (1914). Gressmann was more ambivalent than Gunkel had been about the conclusions of source criticism and (once the Priestly material had been separated off) regarded it as more of a convenience (and sometimes an inconvenience) than an end in itself (cf. *Anfänge*, p. 17). In practice this often meant that he felt free to go his own way in dividing up (and even altering and rearranging) the text if it seemed to suit his own agenda, without necessarily being able to provide much justification for his idiosyncrasies. But in his reproduction of the text the now traditional sigla J (without sub-division) and E continued to be used, with the added help of different typefaces.

Both books, however, emphasised much more the sensitive and imaginative (in both senses of the word) interpretation of the underlying *Sagen*, and it was these 'literary-historical results' which did most to shift the direction of subsequent study of the Exodus narratives (the legal and cultic sections are barely touched) for two generations (*Mose*, pp. 345-92). This is particularly true of the description of the general character of *Sagen*, the emphasis on their original independence from one another and their form-critical classification into different types. In fact Gressmann acknowledged that the different categories often overlap: the same story may be a 'hero' *Sage* (including Moses), a cultic *Sage*, a local *Sage* and an ethnological (i.e. Israel-centred) *Sage*. Gressmann was also interested in identifying groups of *Sagen* linked to particular places or persons (Kadesh; Jethro), which he incorporated into innovative theories about the development of the tradition and early Israelite history.

The new approach to the older Pentateuchal sources had the potential to bring about further upheavals in scholarly thinking. Applied to legal texts like the Decalogue and the Book of the Covenant, it could encourage a quest for their origins behind and even apart from the narratives in which they are now embedded, as Albrecht Alt did in 'The Origins of Israelite Law' (1934, ET 1966). And just as Gressmann had seen it as providing a superior explanation for the 'inconsistencies' which led Smend and others to introduce an extra source (*Mose*, pp. 369-72), a more 'holistic' reading of the texts could raise doubts about whether even the E source was a necessary hypothesis. This does seem to have played a part in the arguments put forward by Paul Volz and Willy Staerck, and they had both been part of the team engaged with Gunkel and Gressmann on the 'Göttingen Bible' (as the series SAT was popularly known). But it is less clearly the case (except at second hand) with Wilhelm Rudolph. He was a (very) junior colleague of Volz at Tübingen and joined him in a critical examination of the supposedly E texts in Genesis in 1933. Five years later he published, on his own, *Der 'Elohist' von Exodus bis Josua*, concluding that there was no separate E source in Exodus (or the following books) either: in many passages there was no duplication and where there was it could be attributed to secondary supplementation rather than the use of a source. It seems that by the time he began his academic career in 1922 he had adopted a cautious and independent stance towards Wellhausen's work and was in other ways tending to favour more conservative positions about Old Testament problems.[92] His Pentateuchal work looks almost like a diversion at the time, as his main interest was already in prophecy and it was on this (and subsequently the later historical books) that his most influential work was to be done. His scepticism about the Elohist, by contrast, had little effect 'for decades', though in noting this in 1987 Smend was able to observe that by then Rudolph's confidence that he was right might finally have been justified.[93]

---

[92] See R. Smend, 'Wilhelm Rudolph (1891–1987)', in *Deutsche Alttestamentler in drei Jahrhunderten* (Göttingen, 1989), pp. 208-25 (213-14, cf. 217-18).
[93] 'Wilhelm Rudolph', p. 218.

The studies of the following years served to give the 'triple tradition' a new lease of life. This was in no small measure due to Martin Noth's *Überlieferungsgeschichte des Pentateuch* (1948, ET 1972), whose primary purpose and chief claim to fame (or notoriety) were quite different, namely his attempt to reconstruct the preliterary history in a more systematic and convincing way than what Gunkel and Gressmann had proposed. But, unlike the Scandinavian scholars who sought to do this without employing source criticism as a foundation, Noth regarded the latter as indispensable and in need only of a 'sehr wichtige Korrektur' (p. 24), for which he gave Volz and Rudolph the main credit. They, he believed, had succeeded in showing that earlier source criticism had worked with the unjustified assumption that the redactor(s) of J and E aimed to preserve their sources in full, so that each section of text had to be divided into two (or even three) strands, however weak the justification for doing so. Noth also took issue with the emphasis placed on supposed inconsistencies and variations between different passages as a basis for distinguishing the components of different sources: once it was recognised that sources were collections of older oral material with its own history, such phenomena were only to be expected (pp. 20-21). In principle it was only the duplication of the same or similar material which could (and should) be used to distinguish J from E, just as it was for the prior distinction of JE and P. And of this there were quite enough examples to justify the hypothesis of two (but only two) continuous, once independent, parallel sources in the non-Priestly material, even if there were certainly places where it was no longer possible to decide finally whether some verses had belonged to one of these sources rather than the other. Since such duplications did not occur everywhere, Noth concluded that the redactor had, on the whole, only drawn on E when it had something important to add to his preferred account, which was J. This general approach was also followed by Noth in his Exodus commentary (1959, ET 1962) as well as in V. Fritz's *Israel in der Wüste* (1970: see its pp. 4-6). An important demonstration that the 'fragments' of E did indeed have a common origin and were extracts from a fuller account was provided by H.W. Wolff, like Rudolph a specialist on the prophets who contributed to Pentateuchal research ('Zur Thematik der elohistichen Fragmente im Pentateuch' [1969, ET 1972]: see also A.W. Jenks, *The Elohist and North Israelite Traditions* [1977]).

Noth's *Überlieferungsgeschichte* also reawakened, as he had intended, attention to the early, pre-monarchic, stage of the Pentateuchal tradition and the history of Israel, in a way that many found very radical. It could seem that scholars now knew, or thought they knew, more about the history of the tradition than they did about the early history of Israel itself. The figure of Moses, so central to the Exodus story as it has been transmitted, became a particular bone of contention, with Noth affirming that all that was certain about Moses was that he died in Transjordan and had a non-Israelite wife (pp. 184-91: on the ensuing discussion see Nicholson, *Exodus and Sinai* [1973] and Schmidt, *Exodus, Sinai und Mose* [1983]). In different ways these questions shaped both commentaries and other studies for the next generation, perhaps most productively in the commentary by W.H. Schmidt (1974–2019), but also in monographs by his pupils F. Kohata (1986) and A. Graupner (2002) and earlier by W. Beyerlin (1961, ET 1965), L. Perlitt (1969) and G.W. Coats (1968, 1988). Childs also gave these questions attention in his commentary (1974), along with source-critical analysis, but his distinctive contribution was to be an early representative of a very different development, by reintroducing into critical scholarship a high regard for the final ('canonical') form of the text and the older history of its interpretation. This tendency to shift the balance away from diachronic investigations also took other forms, such as structuralist interpretation, the treatment of the Pentateuch as a work of literature (as notably in D.J.A. Clines, *The Theme of the Pentateuch* [1978, 2nd ed. 1997]) and various kinds of what is in effect 'reader-response' or 'contextual' interpretation. The commentary of C. Houtman (1986–96, ET 1993–2002), while including a wide range of other valuable linguistic and exegetical material, is written from the same broad perspective, viewing the completed text as the work of a narrator in the exilic period, whose older source-materials can generally not be identified in detail.[94]

---

[94] See the summaries in his *Der Pentateuch* (1994), pp. 421, 423: in this work he examines the history of modern research in great detail, but concludes that the 'Four-Source Theory' is untenable. His standpoint is similar to that of R.N. Whybray, *The Making of the Pentateuch* (JSOTSup 53; Sheffield, 1987), who was equally critical of Rendtorff's ideas (on which see below), and represents a kind of 'Fragment Hypothesis'.

A challenge to the critical consensus from the opposite direction emerged from the heart of German critical scholarship in writings of Rolf Rendtorff from the late 1960s onwards. Initial probes into the relation of tradition history to literary criticism and some specific new ideas about the composition of the Pentateuch appeared first in two articles.[95] Further developments of them can now be seen in a doctoral dissertation completed in Heidelberg, where Rendtorff was teaching, in 1972 but regrettably only published as a book in 2015.[96] The wider impact of the new ideas only began to be felt, however, in a paper delivered by Rendtorff at the 1974 Congress of the International Organization for the Study of the Old Testament in Edinburgh, entitled 'Der "Jahwist" als Theologe? Zur Dilemma der Pentateuchkritik' and amplified in his *Das überlieferungsgeschichtliche Problem des Pentateuch* (1977). This embodied a very direct attack on one of the 'pillars' of recent source criticism, by arguing that the main theological theme of Genesis 12–50, the promises to the patriarchs, had developed quite separately from the Exodus story, so that there was no room for the Yahwist (J) writer as the great shaper of the Pentateuchal traditions into a coherent theological whole. It also set out a different way of investigating the shaping of the traditions by tracing the development of the promise theme in Genesis and beyond through a series of stages, the later ones at least being redactional layers which finally bound the major sections of the Pentateuch (patriarchs, Exodus, wilderness, Sinai and conquest of Canaan) into a narrative and theological unity. In 1990 this fresh approach was applied to Exodus and the following books in E. Blum's *Studien zur Komposition des Pentateuch*, and by this time the 'new way' had assumed a somewhat different form. Central to it now were two successive 'compositions' (so much more than redactional layers), a 'D-composition' and wrapped around it a 'P-composition', which in line with the

---

[95] 'Literarkritik und Traditionsgeschichte', *EvTh* 27 (1967), pp. 138-53 (a lecture given in Uppsala and first published in *SEÅ* 31 [1966], pp. 5-20); 'Traditio-Historical Method and the Documentary Hypothesis', *WCJS (Fifth Congress 1969)* 5/1 (Jerusalem, 1972), pp. 5-11.

[96] R. Kessler, *Die Querverweise im Pentateuch: Überlieferungsgeschichtliche Untersuchung der expliziten Querverbindungen innerhalb des vorpriesterlichen Pentateuchs* (BEATAJ 59; Frankfurt, 2015): there is an introduction by Rainer Albertz. The dissertation was referred to earlier e.g. by Rendtorff (*Problem*, pp. 153, 163) and Blum (*Studien*, p. 19: see also Propp 2, p. 725).

regular dating of the Deuteronomistic and Priestly literature were both dated to the exilic period and later. Much less is said here about the older traditions which preceded them.[97] Blum is in no doubt that there were such earlier traditions (see especially pp. 37-43, 208-18) and he even reckons with remnants of two different versions of the Exodus-Moses traditions, one for example lying behind the later 'D' account in Exod. 3.1–4.18 and the other interrupted by it.

This model, with distinct Deuteronomistic and Priestly 'editions' of the Exodus story (and more), bears a superficial resemblance to the earlier traditio-historical reconstructions of Ivan Engnell, but for him the 'D-work' proper only began in Deuteronomy. Closer to Blum in their use of the model as well as in time are William Johnstone (in his Old Testament Guide [1990]) and more fully in *Chronicles and Exodus* [1998]) and Joseph Blenkinsopp (1992), though the latter apparently still regards P as an independent 'source'. For a time this kind of approach gave way to others (see below), but recently it has reappeared in the commentaries of T.B. Dozeman (2009: with 'Non-P' as a less specific term for the 'D-composition') and Rainer Albertz (2012, 2015: but with the D redaction after and not before the main Priestly layer) and, with a much more complex layering of the text, the monograph of C. Berner (2010) and S. Germany (2017).

Even among those who see the need for drastic changes to earlier views, talk of 'sources' has by no means ceased. A 'Yahwist' is still central to the thinking of Christoph Levin (1993) and John Van Seters (1994), though both see him as a writer of the exilic period, as Van Seters had already proposed twenty years earlier in a study of Genesis (1974: H.H. Schmid's 'sogenannte Jahwist' [1977] was dated only slightly earlier). This may seem at first no different from Blum's exilic 'D-composition', but the point of the nomenclature is to emphasise that, even if this Yahwist was to some extent dependent on Deuteronomic ideas (as Van Seters believes), the overall ethos of his work is quite different in important respects. Levin is also one of those who continue to maintain that P was originally, as in the older theory, an independent source-document, along with David Carr (1996), Propp (in *VT* 1996 as well as in his commentary), E. Otto (1999) and R.G. Kratz (2000). In fact this quickly became a tenet

---

[97] This is in contrast to Blum's earlier study of the patriarchal narratives (1984).

of central importance again, both in Konrad Schmid's argument for a long-lasting separation of the patriarchal and Exodus traditions (1999) and among those, such as J.C. Gertz and Thomas Römer, who joined him in making 'Abschied vom Jahwisten' – farewell to the Yahwist! – the watchword for the 'new way' in Pentateuchal criticism (2002). This does make more of a difference to the study of Exodus than may at first appear, both because the older Exodus story is no longer set in the context of the patriarchal traditions and because texts in Exodus that do refer to them tend in consequence to be regarded as late additions. According to these scholars it was only in an independent Priestly document that the canonical sequence from creation to Sinai (at least) was first established.[98] After the non-Priestly material was joined to this, the final redactor (*Endredaktor*) and even later reworkings (*Bearbeitungen*) came to be credited with substantial harmonising and expansionist additions. It was these late developments (in Exod. 1–14) that were the object of special study in Gertz's *Tradition und Redaktion in der Exoduserzählung* (2000), but on the way to them he made an important fresh analysis of the materials that were available to the late redactors, which is often referred to in this commentary.

The 'recovery' of a place for the Priestly source in innovative Continental scholarship was a notable shift from the position of Rendtorff and Blum and it brought with it two further developments in research. The first, which is less relevant to Exodus than the books that follow it, is the debate about possible end-points for the original Priestly narrative considerably earlier than the end of the Pentateuch: for example at Leviticus 16, or Exodus 40, or even Exodus 29.[99] Only the last of these proposals would, if accepted,

---

[98] For difficulties with this view see my 'The Transition from Genesis to Exodus' and references there. Some further points were made by J.S. Baden, 'The Continuity of the Non-Priestly Narrative from Genesis to Exodus', *Bib* 93 (2012), pp. 161-86. The idea that an independent Priestly narrative was the basis for all other narrative developments is an old one, going back to those who identified it as the *Grundschrift* in the nineteenth century. An early instance of its revival, for the plague-narrative, was Steingrimsson, *Vom Zeichen*.

[99] For some discussion and further references see Blum, 'Issues and Problems in the Contemporary Debate Regarding the Priestly Writings', in Shechtman and Baden (eds.), *The Strata of the Priestly Writings*, pp. 30-44 (39-41); T. Römer, 'The Exodus Narrative according to the Priestly Document', in ibid., pp. 157-74 (159-61).

have a direct impact on the study of Exodus. The other development has taken up again an issue which was already being discussed in the nineteenth century, namely a distinction between the original form of P and additions that were made to it later. The proposal for an earlier ending for P in its first stage clearly adds a fresh edge to this question, but the older identification of additions such as the Holiness Code in Leviticus and the expansions designated as P^s naturally come into play as well. Here passages such as Exod. 6.13-30 and 12.43-51, to name but two, would inevitably be involved. Three main stages in the growth of P are now often distinguished: the original narrative document including the building of the tabernacle and related material; the insertion of the Holiness Code and some similar texts elsewhere (where many would see some influence of Deuteronomic law and theology); and finally the incorporation of a variety of supplementary legislation which is often built upon earlier parts of the Priestly corpus.[100]

In the midst of these fast-moving debates there have also been those who have criticised the main claims of the newer theories and advocated the retention of something very like the older consensus. In Germany they include not only W.H. Schmidt (a final fascicle of his Exodus commentary appeared in 2019) and Graupner, but Horst Seebass (especially in the article 'Pentateuch' in *TRE* [1997]), Ludwig Schmidt and the Zenger-Frevel *Einleitung* in its various editions (with a seventh-century *Jerusalemer Geschichtswerk*). Graupner's positive evaluation of the evidence for an Elohist source (2002) is particularly noteworthy, even though it limits the relevant material by unnecessarily excluding all texts which contain the divine name, even after Exodus 3 (cf. pp. 32-36). Elsewhere Ernest Nicholson's *The Pentateuch in the Twentieth Century* (1998), of which two-thirds is concerned with developments since 1970 (including the work of Van Seters, Martin Rose, Blum, Whybray and Levin) summarised the conclusions of his extensive examination of alternative views as follows: '[G]ranted its shortcomings, [the Documentary Theory] remains the most

---

[100] See J. Nihan, *From Priestly Torah to Pentateuch: A Study in the Composition of the Book of Leviticus* (FAT 2/25; Tübingen, 2007); and his essay 'The Priestly Covenant, its Reinterpretations and the Composition of "P"', in Shechtman and Baden (eds.), *Strata*, pp. 87-134, as well as other essays in the same volume.

comprehensive among all those that have recently been advanced as its replacement' (p. 195); '[T]here are no convincing reasons for doubting the relative chronology of the sources: that J and E are earlier than Deuteronomy and derive from the pre-exilic period; that their combination and redaction likewise preceded the work of the authors of Deuteronomy and the Deuteronomistic History, though this stage of redaction (R^{JE}) may have continued in the period in which they wrote' (pp. 247-48).

In the United States the studies of R.E. Friedman (most readily accessible in his summary his article 'Torah (Pentateuch)' in *ABD* 6 (pp. 605-22), have reached similar conclusions and are cited with approval by Propp in an Appendix to his commentary (2, p. 724: see also his ensuing discussion and 1, pp. 47-52).[101] But both Friedman and Propp have attributed much more of the old Exodus story to E than earlier scholars did. The most prominent recent advocate of the Documentary Theory in America is undoubtedly Joel Baden. His *J, E and the Redaction of the Pentateuch* (2009) endeavoured to establish the unusual thesis that J and E remained uncombined, independent documents until 'the redactor' compiled all four documents together after all of them had been written. Whatever one makes of this thesis, which bears some resemblance to the views of Hupfeld and Dillmann, the book is of much wider importance. For it begins with nearly 100 pages on the history of Pentateuchal research, in which Baden shows a wide knowledge and deep understanding of his predecessors. They include a number of those who have been most critical of the Documentary Theory and a recurring feature of Baden's discussion of them is the use of their criticisms to identify, not weaknesses in the source-critical approach itself but misunderstandings or misrepresentations of it, which he sees as at least partly the responsibility of those who have accepted and practised it. This analysis of the present situation almost required that he should himself attempt a better account of the theory and the reasons for it, which is what he has sought to do in *The Composition*

---

[101] Friedman's longer works are two books written for a wider readership, *Who Wrote the Bible?* (San Francisco, 1987; 2nd ed. 1997), and *The Hidden Book of the Bible* (New York, 1998). R.K. Gnuse's *The Elohist: A Seventh-Century Theological Tradition* (Eugene, 2017; preceded by several articles) envisages an associated group of Elohist 'pools of tradition' and refers to a number of other 'contemporary defenders of the Elohist' (pp. 21-26).

of the Pentateuch: The Renewing of the Documentary Hypothesis (2012). Here he presents a vigorous continuing debate with those who have adopted different explanations for the origins of the Pentateuch alongside a clear argument based on five 'case-studies' which is designed to persuade those who see no reason for any kind of subdivision of the Pentateuch into different sources or layers. The book is true to its sub-title, especially in its rigid limitation to source-analysis (thus ignoring questions about the earlier history of the sources, their dating and 'post-redactional' additions such as the end of Exod. 34) and in its prioritisation of different 'historical claims' (seen in contradictions and inconsistencies of 'fact') and narrative coherence as criteria for analysis and synthesis, rather than relying on distinctions of style and theme. The scope is thus similar to Wellhausen's first study of the subject, 'Die Composition des Hexateuchs': Baden's choice of his own title was evidently deliberate (cf. p. 247). The frequently made assumption that every episode must have been recounted in all the sources is abandoned and as a result a number of narratives which earlier criticism had felt (unjustifiably) compelled to divide into two or three strands can be treated much more simply. In this as in other ways his version of the theory is simpler and more 'economical' than others in its explanation of the data. On the basis of it Baden finds no difficulty in defending the continuity of the J narrative from creation to the death of Moses and the connectedness of the parallel text attributed to E. In the latter case his choice of a different starting-point in the text (Exodus and Numbers rather than Genesis), surprisingly perhaps, contributes significantly to the tightness of the argument that he constructs (pp. 116-28). The general character of Baden's approach can be traced through the work of Baruch Schwartz (to whose inspiring teaching he refers more than once[102]) back to Menahem Haran, who like some other Israeli scholars also distinguished the analytical part of the Documentary Theory, which he accepted, from its dating of P later than D.[103] It is much of the

---

[102] For Exodus see Schwartz's 'The Priestly Account of the Theophany and Lawgiving at Sinai', in M.V. Fox et al. (eds.), *Texts, Temples and Traditions: A Tribute to Menahem Haran* (Winona Lake, 1996), pp. 103-34.

[103] See, for example, his *Temples and Temple-Service in Ancient Israel: An Inquiry into the Characteristics of Cult Phenomena and the Historical Setting of the Priestly School* (Oxford, 1978).

detail, especially in the arguments against other recent scholars, that appears to be new. A weakness of the book is its almost total neglect of the legal portions of the Pentateuch. Baden is by no means alone in this among recent scholars of all persuasions (Eckart Otto is a notable exception), but it does make it easier for him to say that the dating of the sources is only possible with additional information outside the Pentateuch. Others have rightly seen that, while extra-Pentateuchal data provide more precision, the legal texts can by careful comparison establish a plausible sequence on their own both for them and for the documents of which they are part.

(ii) *Sources and Redaction in Exodus: Principles and Results*

a. *Principles*

It is a measure of the current diversity in Old Testament scholarship that, as has been shown above, it can accommodate both those who, for various reasons, resolutely devalue or disregard the methods and conclusions of the older *Literarkritik* and those who pursue analytical endeavours with even greater intensity and innovativeness than before. Anyone who continues, as this commentary does, to enquire into the origins of the text(s) of Exodus that we have in a controlled and convincing way has on the one hand to provide a justification for pursuing such enquiries in the first place and on the other to have appropriate methods and criteria for distinguishing material of a different origin. These methods and criteria must also be used with care, to avoid mistakes and to inspire confidence in the results.

It has recently been argued that a strong justification for identifying material of diverse origins in a text can be found in the very practice of 'close reading' that often sees itself as a superior alternative to such an enterprise, and that this was exactly what guided the pioneering critics of the eighteenth and nineteenth centuries.[104] There is much truth in this, and it will be noted below that 'narrative coherence' continues to be a vital presupposition in the practice

---

[104] See especially John Barton's *The Nature of Biblical Criticism* (Louisville, 2007), but also Joel Baden's statement: 'The critical study of the composition of the Pentateuch begins, in practical terms, and began, in terms of the history of scholarship, with the attempt to *read* the pentateuchal narrative from beginning to end as a unified whole' (Baden, *Composition*, p. 13: my italics).

of Pentateuchal criticism, both where the lack of it points to the combination of originally unrelated material and where its presence provides clues to which sections of the text originally belonged together in a larger narrative whole. Such a justification for critical analysis is particularly persuasive when the reader is faced with 'difficult terrain' such as the Sinai pericope(s) in Exodus (and the Flood story in Genesis). Often in this commentary it is the awkward sequence of statements in a passage which first raises the suspicion that it is of composite origin.

But it is not without reason that both supporters and opponents of such analyses have spoken of them as 'historical-critical' in character, for a concern with historical questions is implicit in them, as well as in the use which can (or cannot, according to their opponents) be made of them. At the simplest level, an enquiry into a text's 'sources' is a question about the earlier history of the text itself. But once those sources have been identified, a comparison between them leads quickly to further questions about the history of the tradition that is differently presented in the sources, and these in turn lead on to the evaluation and use of the earlier accounts to answer questions about the national and perhaps religious history of the people to whom the text refers. One can see these three 'historical' aspects of criticism very clearly in Wellhausen's successive publications on 'The Composition of the Hexateuch', 'The History of Israel Part I' (better known as the *Prolegomena*) and 'Israelite and Judaean History'. Not every scholar manages a book on all three, but the example is sufficient to show how there can be various kinds of historical justification for biblical criticism and that those who turn away from it are in fact depriving themselves of valuable resources for knowledge and insight.

The practice of diachronic literary criticism has to proceed by stages of analysis and synthesis, generally in that order. In both stages evidence, conforming to various 'criteria', is needed to establish the lack of unity in the text as it stands and the association of discrete elements in the text with others which may be some distance away in the narrative. Traditionally, four kinds of criteria for establishing disunity in the text have been appealed to (in addition to the unnatural sequence of statements within a passage): contradictions and inconsistencies; 'doublets' (repeated statements or whole narratives); variations in vocabulary and style; and differences in theological, legal or political points of view. Over time scholars have differed in the weight which they have given to each of these features as criteria and this has been partly responsible for the different conclusions to which they have come. Here the view has been taken that the first two criteria are the most reliable for this purpose, with the other two playing an ancillary role: the argument for division is most powerful where all four coincide. The third and fourth criteria can often, but not always, have their greatest value at the second, synthetic, stage, where the disparate elements are being 'reassembled' in groups comprising earlier source material or redactional layers. It is here that the factor of 'narrative coherence' (or connectivity), mentioned above, also makes a valuable, indeed essential, contribution. A procedure such as the one just outlined is clearly much more sophisticated than the popular conception that sources and other elements in the text are identified simply by the various ways in which the God of Israel is referred to in the Bible. This certainly was a primary criterion in the earliest source-critical work on the Pentateuch and the continued designation (by some at least) of 'Yahwist' (J) and 'Elohist' (E) sources may reinforce the popular conception. But such variations belong to the third and perhaps the fourth kinds of criteria mentioned above, which are less decisive.

The most recent analyses of the Pentateuch have also made much use of a further criterion which may perhaps be called 'dependency', that is, a portion of text (perhaps one verse in a longer passage) is seen, because of its similarity to another passage whose origin is (thought to be) known, as being derived from that other passage and so contemporary with or even later than it. This kind of argument may have been first used in the detection of 'Deuteronomistic' additions to Exodus by the observation of ideas and language which were also found in Deuteronomy. Of late it has been particularly common (to anticipate a later part of this section), and sometimes usefully so, in the identification of secondary elements in the Priestly texts of Exodus and even additions which are later still. It is, however, an argument that needs to be used with some caution. Sometimes it is too quickly assumed that similarity implies a relationship of literary dependence and that the literary relationship can only be in one direction. The problems with this were already exposed by critical discussion of so-called Deuteronomistic passages in Exodus. For example, the argument that references to a covenant in Exodus 19–24 (and 34) were dependent on Deuteronomy too quickly overlooked the differences between these passages and the Deuteronomic Sinai/Horeb narrative and abandoned the older view that the Exodus accounts were (in this respect at least) prior to Deuteronomy. Another problem with the argument for dependency and deductions made from it is that everything hangs on the conclusions reached by a particular scholar about the passage whose influence is detected elsewhere. Sometimes there can be a kind of 'domino effect': passage A is, say, post-Priestly because it depends on passage B, which is post-Priestly because it depends on passage C, and so on. To change the metaphor, doubt may arise whether the links in the 'chain' are strong enough to bear the weight that is placed upon them.

At the level of synthesis there are, as we have noted above, currently serious disagreements, both within the most innovative scholarship (especially over the nature of P) and between it and more traditional approaches (especially about the existence of E as a second continuous old narrative source), between theories which envisage the existence of two or more originally separate parallel narrative sources and those which see one narrative as having been expanded by a series of later additions. This is, formally, a re-run of the debate between supplementary and documentary accounts of Pentateuchal origins in the nineteenth century, but with the important difference that then it was the material now designated as P (or part of it) that was regarded as the *Grundschrift*, whereas now the P material is (by most scholars) placed towards the end of the process of composition. What sort of arguments can be used to justify one or other of these approaches? It is sometimes argued that only the supplementary account fits in with ancient practice. Within the Bible there are certainly analogies for such an explanation in the prophetic and historical books, and the latter are appealed to explicitly as a parallel by William Johnstone. It has also been claimed that redactional expansion is what is attested by the various copies of some works within the Qumran corpus.[105] But at Qumran the case of the Temple Scroll provides a valuable parallel to documentary theories by its interweaving of laws which

---

[105] Cf. R.G. Kratz, 'Reworked Pentateuch and Pentateuchal Theory', in J.C. Gertz et al. (eds.), *The Formation of the Pentateuch: Bridging the Academic Cultures of Europe, Israel and North America* (FAT 111; Tübingen, 2016), pp. 501-24.

we know to have existed earlier in separate parts of the Pentateuch, in the Holiness Code, Deuteronomy and elsewhere. In the historical books, prior to the (first) Deuteronomistic redaction, there are duplications and inconsistencies which probably point to the combination of overlapping versions of the reigns of Saul and David. Outside the Jewish tradition ancient historians have certainly sometimes been able to detect with some confidence the combination of parallel sources in surviving historical works (as in those of Arrian, Livy and Diodorus Siculus). Even though much more source-material will have been available in the Hellenistic and Roman worlds, Israel's history in the biblical period also provided plausible opportunities for both the production and the combination of separate accounts of the people's origins. On a priori grounds both kinds of explanation, as well as a combination of the two, are perfectly possible.

Specific arguments for the supplementation of a single account by the addition of new material emphasise the dependence of the latter on the framework established by the former and the incompleteness of the added text. On the other hand the possibility of discerning two relatively complete accounts in the surviving text speaks strongly for their previous independent existence, as does the presence of serious contradictions between them. Even where such strong pointers are lacking, the nature of the 'alien' text may be such as to suggest that it is more likely to have come from a separate source than from redactional supplementation (see e.g. the introductions below to the commentary on 7.14-25 and 14.1-31).

b. *Results*

General principles of literary analysis like those outlined above have not so far led, in recent critical scholarship, to widespread agreement about how exactly Exodus was composed.[106] This is partly because, as they have been stated, they leave open the possibility of choosing different options at certain points. It is also because, in the nature of the case, it is (as indicated at the beginning)

---

[106] For a fuller examination of the methodological issues, which is designed at least to make bridges across the wide gaps between the opinions of contemporary scholars, see now R.G. Kratz, 'The Analysis of the Pentateuch', *ZAW* 128 (2016), pp. 529-61. Some valuable cautionary notes are sounded by W.H. Schmidt at two points in the second volume of his Exodus commentary (pp. 360-61, 588-93).

the way in which the principles are applied in the detailed study of the text, with its numerous complexities and ambiguities, that leads to the more and less certain conclusions at which each scholar arrives. What follows is a summary of the conclusions reached in this commentary, with a broad indication of the reasoning behind them, and a sketch of each major component of the text and the process by which these components were brought together.

Since the work of Hupfeld and Knobel in the mid-nineteenth century it has been evident (despite changing views about the order of the sources and the nomenclature for them) that the major analytical distinction to be made in Exodus, and in the Pentateuch as a whole, is between what are now recognisable as the Priestly and non-Priestly components of the text. This distinction is particularly clear in the Sinai-narrative in the second half of Exodus (chs. 19–40) and beyond, where the basis for the now standard nomenclature first appears. Some indication has already been given above (in section 3 of this introduction) of the thematic difference within these chapters, between sections which are focused on theophany, law and covenant on the one hand and the building of a portable sanctuary for the priestly activities of Aaron and his sons on the other.[107] The chapters concerned form large blocks without any overlap except at their beginning and end: chs. 19–24 (except for 19.1 and 24.15-18a) and 32–34 (except for 34.29-35) form a coherent narrative about theophany, law and covenant, while chs. 25–31 (except for part of 31.18) and 35–40 deal throughout with the sanctuary and the Aaronide priesthood. The two sequences present the meeting with God at Mount Sinai in two quite different ways, the first corresponding in many respects to the recapitulation of it in Deuteronomy (chs. 5 and 9–10), while the second does not. In addition the Sinai-narrative exhibits doublets for the arrival at Mount Sinai in 19.1-2, for Moses' ascent of the mountain in ch. 24 (vv. 13 and 15) and his

---

[107] The description of the latter sections as distinctively 'Priestly' (P) is not ideal, as priests and cultic matters are also mentioned elsewhere in the Sinai-narrative (e.g. 19.22, 24; 23.14-19; 34.17-26). What is really distinctive about these sections is their almost total concentration on cultic matters and especially the requirement that the priesthood should comprise only Aaron and his sons. The description of them as 'Aaronide' would be more precise: compare Ellis Rivkin's attribution of them (and the completed Pentateuch) to 'The Revolution of the Aaronides' (*The Shaping of Jewish History* [New York, 1971], pp. 21-41.

subsequent descent from it (32.15 and 34.29).[108] There are also two different structures described as 'the tent of meeting', one large and at the centre of the camp, for priestly activities (27.21 etc.), and the other small and outside the camp (33.7) for Moses, with Joshua as his servant, to be consulted by the people. Finally there is a striking contradiction in the way that Moses' brother Aaron is regarded in the two presentations of the narrative: in one he is an idolater who leads the people to make an image and offer sacrifice to it and lies when his wrongdoing is exposed (32.1-6, 21-25, 35), while in the other he is the father/ancestor of all the priests who are authorised by Yahweh through Moses to minister for ever in his holy sanctuary (29.1-9). Neither account makes any reference to the other and it is hard, if not impossible, to see how they could have had a common origin.

In the first half of the book there is a series of similar doublets, which though not in continuous sequences of text nevertheless can be combined to form two connected and almost complete versions of the Exodus story. The most obvious pair are the two accounts of Moses' commissioning to lead Israel out of Egypt to freedom in the land of Canaan (3.1–4.17; 6.2–7.5). Many features, not surprisingly, are shared between them: God's prior relationship with Israel's ancestors, his hearing of Israel's cry for release from bondage and his promise of deliverance; the further promise to bring them to the land of Canaan as their home; the appointment of Moses as their leader with Aaron as his assistant; the warning that Pharaoh will not let Israel go willingly, but only when great divine interventions compel him to do so. But the two versions differ in a number of ways: the first has a complex narrative introduction in which Moses marries the daughter of a Midianite priest and his encounter with God is located at Mount Horeb in the desert, from which he has subsequently to return to Egypt, while the second knows nothing of this and differs in the wording which it uses for the shared features. There is no indication at all that it is intended to record a recommissioning of Moses: the only prior events referred to are those which are also included in the first version.

The other doublets are interwoven with each other to a greater or lesser extent: parallel links to the stories in Genesis (1.1-5, 7; 1.6, 8), parallel reports of the Egyptians' mistreatment of Israel (1.9-12;

---

[108] There is also a doublet for the departure from Mount Sinai in Num. 10.11-12 and 10.33-34, each with a characteristic (and different) surrounding context.

1.13-14), parallel but differently formed accounts of the plagues inflicted on the Egyptians (alternating within 7.14–11.10 continued by 12.29-32), parallel accounts of the institution of Passover, the festival of Unleavened Bread and the dedication of the firstborn (12.1-20 and 13.1-2; 12.21-27 and 13.3-16); a clearly composite account of the deliverance at the 'sea' (14.1-31 continued by 15.1-21). On the details see the introductions to the relevant sections of the commentary. One passage or sequence of passages in each pair (including one of the accounts of Moses' commissioning) forms part of a connected story which is closely linked by both narrative continuity and similar linguistic and theological characteristics to passages earlier and later in the Pentateuch, including those which belong to the 'Priestly' strand in the Sinai-narrative.[109] The other members of the pairs likewise comprise a more or less complete account of the Exodus story which also has strong links to Genesis.[110] The only important episode that is missing from either account is a description of the actual slaying of the Egyptian firstborn in the Priestly strand. It is anticipated in 12.12-13 and presupposed in 12.40-42, 50-51 and some words from it may have been incorporated in 12.29a, but the compiler evidently chose to follow the other version that he had in the main.[111]

Most likely these two parallel accounts once existed separately and were combined together by a redactor who made minor adjustments to smooth the transitions between them. This has been the majority view among critical scholars since the mid-nineteenth century. The main alternative is the proposal that the Priestly account never existed as a separate whole, but was 'built on' (or better 'into') the non-Priestly account, in some cases with the use of already existing parallel versions of certain sections of the narrative to which the authors had access. In recent times this approach has been favoured by scholars such as F.M. Cross, R.E. Friedman, Erhard Blum and John Van Seters and after a gap it has found

---

[109] The full list of the passages assigned to the Priestly writers in this commentary is: 1.1-5, 7 (most of it), 13-14; 2.23aβb-25; 6.2–7.13; 7.19-20a, 21b-22; 8.1-3, 11b, 12-15; 9.8-12; 11.9-10; 12.1-20, 28, 40-51; 13.1-2; 14.1-4, 8, 16aβb-18, 21(most of it)-23, 26-27(the beginning), 28a, 29; 16.1b-3, 6-20, 22-25, 32-36; 19.1; 24.15-18a; 25.1-31.18a; 34.29-40.38.

[110] See my article 'The Transition from Genesis to Exodus'.

[111] Some further clues to the wording of the Priestly version can probably be recovered from the redactional additions in Num. 33.3.

renewed support in the commentary of Rainer Albertz. In the present commentary, especially in the introductions to relevant sections of the text, detailed arguments against this view (and sometime against its converse, that the non-Priestly account is 'built into' the Priestly one) have regularly been marshalled and there is no need to repeat them here. The remarkable completeness of the parallel narratives that can be disentangled by analysis – completeness, that is, in terms of their authors' intentions – in both halves of the book, where the redactors' activity necessarily proceeded in different ways, is nevertheless a powerful first indication that two once separate sources were combined, and the arguments to the contrary are weak, especially in Exodus.[112]

To reach such a conclusion is not, however, to hold that the editorial combination of two extended narratives is all that there is to say about the composition of Exodus (or the Pentateuch more generally). First, within the Priestly account it is possible to identify material of differing origin. 'Strata' within the Priestly legislation were already being identified over a hundred years ago and recent scholarship has rightly given the later layers full recognition (for bibliography see above in nn. 99-100). In Exodus 1–18 they are particularly clear in the Passover ordinances in ch. 12. The 'appendix' in vv. 43-49, with a further 'fulfilment formula' in v. 50 (cf. v. 28) and a recapitulation of the earlier notice of departure from Egypt in v. 51 (cf. v. 41), is clearly a supplement to vv. 1-14a and not a separate Passover regulation, since it does not repeat the central instructions there for the observance of Passover. Among other treatments of the Passover ordinance it seems (with Num. 9.1-14) to be earlier than the Priestly combination of Passover with Unleavened Bread which is found in the Holiness Code and Exod. 12.14b-20. Another passage which has been secondarily added to a Priestly context is 6.14-27, again with a recapitulation of some earlier material after it to bed it in (vv. 28-30; cf. vv. 10-12).[113] In this case the purpose is

---

[112] For more wide-ranging discussions of the 'supplementary' view reference may be made to K. Koch, 'P kein Redaktor! Erinnerung an zwei Eckdaten der Quellenscheidung', *VT* 37 (1987), pp. 446-67; J.A. Emerton, 'The Priestly Writer in Genesis', *JTS* N.S. 39 (1988), pp. 381-400; my 'The Composition of the Book of Exodus'; Propp, 'The Priestly Source Recovered Intact'; and Nicholson, *The Pentateuch*, pp. 196-218.

[113] Verse 13 presupposes the combination of the Priestly and non-Priestly narratives.

to provide an early introduction for the high-priestly line beginning with Aaron and to anticipate the narrative developments, negative (Korah: Num. 16) and positive (Phinehas: Num. 25), in the book of Numbers. This points to an association with one or more of the later Priestly layers that have been detected in Numbers. The same might be true of 13.1-2, the Priestly law on the firstborn, since it is in Numbers that the Israelites' firstborn become important in P (see further Nihan as cited above [in n. 100] and Wormell, 'The Composition of the Book of Numbers in the Light of Babylonian Educational Practice').[114] Finally, the plan for the sanctuary (chs. 25–31) and the report of its building (chs. 35–40) probably both include at least some secondary expansion of the original Priestly account. Since the work of J. Popper (*Der biblische Bericht über die Stiftshütte* [Leipzig, 1862]) it has even been widely held that the whole of the building report in its present form is a later addition. The discussion is complicated by the existence of different versions of these chapters in the Septuagint and the Old Latin. Conclusions about this will have to await a fresh assessment of the textual and redactional issues in a later volume of this commentary.[115]

Within the non-Priestly text there is also reason to discern the combination of material of differing origin, to an even greater extent. We shall limit our detailed discussion to chs. 1–18. Even here we concentrate on the conclusions which have been reached in the commentary, where the argument that lies behind them is explained more fully. The first clear doublets (as distinct from what may well be different ways of opening the Exodus story within chs. 1–2) occur in the call of Moses in ch. 3 and the narrative leading up to it. The duplication between vv. 7-8+16-20 and vv. 9-15 is particularly clear and it is not too difficult, on the basis of the unnecessarily

---

[114] Extensive secondary additions have also often been identified in the Priestly portion of the manna-story in ch. 16 (so again recently C. Berner, 'Der Sabbat in der Mannaerzählung Ex 16 und in den priesterlichen Partien des Pentateuch', *ZAW* 128 [2016], pp. 562-78), but we have only found it necessary to exclude v. 8 (an isolated gloss anticipating v. 12) from the main composition.

[115] Convenient and useful summaries of the problems and some solutions to them, with bibliography, are provided by Childs, pp. 529-37; Dozeman, pp. 594-97; A.G. Salvesen, 'Textual and Literary Criticism and the Book of Exodus: The Role of the Septuagint', in K.J. Dell and P.M. Joyce (eds.), *Biblical Interpretation and Method* (FS J. Barton; Oxford, 2013), pp. 37-51; and H. Utzschneider, 'Tabernacle', in Dozeman et al. (eds.), *The Book of Exodus*, pp. 267-301 (294-99).

repeated speech markers in vv. 5 and 6, to unravel elements of two once separate introductions to the main speech of God, one (like v. 7) using the divine name and one the title 'God' (*ᵉlōhîm*: like vv. 13-15aα). In chs. 2–4 further signs of disunity are the different names given to Moses' Midianite father-in-law – Reuel in 2.18 and Jethro in 3.1 and 4.18 (as well as several times in ch. 18) – and the presence of two different series of questions or objections from Moses about what he is being asked to do, each with God's answers: one series in 3.11-15 which centres on the name of God and the other in 4.1-16 about how Moses can persuade the people that God has appeared to him. In ch. 4 there is also a duplication of staffs, one that belongs to Moses in vv. 1-5 and another one that is given to him by God in vv. 17 and 20. Together with the 'narrative coherence' of other elements and some further unevenness in the sequence of events (e.g. in 4.18-19 and 4.26-27) this makes it possible, with some confidence, to assign most of the rest of chs. 3–4 and the end of ch. 2 to one or other of the two parallel narratives detected at the beginning of ch. 3 (on 4.14aβ-16 and 4.21-23 see below). In ch. 5 there is a further doublet in vv. 1-5, with two parallel approaches to Pharaoh in vv. 1 and 3, and associated with them two different responses from Pharaoh in vv. 2 and 4-5. Verses 4-5 lead on to the actions described in the rest of the chapter and 6.1. Verse 3 clearly continues the strand which included 3.18 (J), so vv. 1-2 presumably belong with the other narrative. These two strands correspond closely to what the older source-critics called J and E on the basis of the ways in which God is referred to by the narrator in each case, a difference which continues to apply up to the first part of ch. 3. From then on, following the naming of God as Yahweh ('the Lord') in 3.15, which is part of the E narrative, it also often employs the divine name, as here and in 4.27, though not exclusively.

In the non-Priestly plague-stories (most of 7.14–11.8) there are further indications of the combination of two non-Priestly narrative sources in the accounts of four of the ten plagues: the turning of water into blood (7.14-25), the thunder and hail (9.13-35), the locusts (10.1-20) and the darkness (10.21-29). In the first three cases the main story follows a broadly similar pattern, though variations are introduced as the sequence develops. But the pattern is disrupted by intrusions which also have recurring features. In the plague of water turned to blood the non-Priestly introduction in vv. 14-18 contains two strands, in one of which Moses' staff plays a key part (most of v. 15, the beginning of v. 16 and the middle of v. 17: likewise the mention of the staff in v. 20), while in the other it is Yahweh who strikes the waters of the Nile and renders them undrinkable and deadly for the fish in them (v. 14, the beginning of v. 15, most of vv. 16-18: likewise the summary in v. 25). The first strand has an explicit connection via Moses' staff to 4.1-5 in v. 15 and to 3.18 (and 5.3) in v. 16a, while the second is linked to 5.1-2 by the expressions 'slow to understand' in v. 14 and 'know (that I am) Yahweh' in v. 17a, and through 5.1-2 to 3.9-12, which is E. Moreover it is this second strand which displays the motif of an attempt to change Pharaoh's mind which is characteristic of the other non-Priestly plague-narratives, including those in which there is no sign of a parallel non-Priestly version. The first strand here, by contrast, is connected by its mention of Moses' staff only to the other plague-stories in which there is evidence of duplication. In 9.13-35 and 10.1-20 there are similar (but more easily recognisable) mentions of the use of Moses' staff which the earlier part of the account has not led the reader to expect (9.22-23a, probably continued by vv. 24a and 25b; 10.12-13a, continued in parts of vv. 14-15): up to this point it is again simply Yahweh himself whose intervention is expected. In 10.21-29 too a similar gesture by Moses is involved in vv. 21-23 (though with the presence of the staff in Moses' 'hand' taken for granted), but this time at the beginning (of the climactic onset of darkness), without any preceding dialogue between Moses and Pharaoh: together with v. 27, these verses form the complete account of the plague. (It is likely – see the commentary – that vv. 24-26 and 28-29 were originally separate and formed the 'bridge' between the longer version of the locust plague and the final 'negotiations' between Moses and Pharaoh in most of 11.3b-8.)

The preservation of the complete form of the darkness 'plague' in 10.21-23+27 probably shows more or less the original structure of the alternative versions of the episodes of water turned to blood, the hail and thunder and the locusts (in the same way as the Priestly plague-narratives that are preserved in full in 8.12-15 and 9.8-12 do for those which have been combined with non-Priestly versions in 7.14-25 and 7.26–8.11). There is here, therefore, an important indication that the variation in four of the non-Priestly plague-narratives is not simply the work of a redactor or supplementer of the longer main versions, as many continue to think, but a series of extracts from a separate full version of the Exodus story. This is exactly the conclusion that emerged above in the links between the two non-Priestly strands in 7.14-25 and passages of different origin earlier in the story. But those links have another, hitherto unsuspected, implication: the main and most familiar version of the plagues is connected, through our analysis of ch. 5, not to the 'J' version of Moses' commissioning but to the 'E' version. In other words, at this point the narrative of E is not, as generally thought, preserved in some rather dubious 'fragments' but in full, or nearly so. Here it is J that exists mainly in fragments, though still sufficient to show that it did have a plagues narrative, albeit one that was probably shorter and less elaborate than that of E. For just this reason, we may well imagine, the redactor who combined J and E gave the main place to the E version here and used the J version where he could to introduce the motif of the use of Moses' staff.[116]

There is a further doublet, though the overlap is not complete, in the account of the Israelites' departure from Egypt. In 12.29-39 they are first given leave by Pharaoh to depart unconditionally (vv. 29-32): this picks up Moses' earlier demands in the main plagues narrative (with the repeated explicit 'as you said' in vv. 31-32) and the timing 'at midnight' (v. 29) which Moses has already set in 11.4. But then 'the Egyptians' urge the Israelites to leave quickly and they do so, taking dough with them which they bake into bread on their journey (vv. 33-34, 37b-39). Each of these strands has an appropriate continuation in the following chapter: the first leads into 13.17-19, which cites Pharaoh's permission explicitly and has long been attributed to the E source because of its reversion to the title 'God'; while the second is directly continued in 13.3-4 (presumably

---

[116] The only scholars known to me who have taken a somewhat similar view of the plagues narrative are Friedman (*ABD* 6, p. 612; *The Hidden Book of the Bible*, p. 398), Propp (pp. 310-17) and earlier Besters, 'L'expression "fils d'Israël"'. According to Friedman (*Hidden Book*, p. 314) he and Propp 'each came to this conclusion, that the non-P version of the plagues is E, not J, independently' (similarly Propp 2, p. 724: 'independently and simultaneously'). But Friedman is unable to identify any J material there and Propp assigns only 11.2-3 (an intrusion into the final confrontation between Moses and Pharaoh before the slaughter of the Egyptian firstborn) to J. In other words they do not use the argument from duplication at all at this point.

from J), the basic instruction for future abstinence from leavened bread on the anniversary of the day of departure (on vv. 5-16 see below). It is also likely that the non-Priestly account of the Passover in 12.21-27 (but on v. 24 see below), which has a similar combination of immediate action and a continued observance on the basis of it, was part of this strand. It has often been found intrusive in the rapid transition from 11.8 to 12.29 in the main narrative, which makes no reference to it, and the blood-ritual recalls the procedure by which Moses' own life was saved in 4.24-26, an element of the earlier narrative which is firmly attributed to J. 13.20-22 presents the divine guidance of the people in a different way from vv. 17-19 and probably also belonged to J.

Some further repetitiveness can be detected in the non-Priestly account of the crossing of the 'sea' in ch. 14 (see the Explanatory Notes on vv. 5, 3-15, 19-20, 24-25 and 30-31), but it is not sufficient to reconstruct two complete versions of the story. Nevertheless even the short elements which are at various points more loosely attached to the main account are designed to amplify it rather than to rewrite it and they exhibit some points of contact with the E narrative elsewhere (Pharaoh's change of mind in v. 5b, the use of the title 'God' in v. 19 and the 'fear' of Yahweh in v. 31). This is probably enough to justify their derivation from a parallel E account of the episode rather than mere editorial expansion of the main (J) narrative here. In any case the compiler of the non-Priestly Exodus narrative seems here to have reverted to his earlier practice of using J as his main framework. There is thus a sequence of duplicate narratives in the non-P parts of Exodus 3–14.

At the beginning and end of Exodus 1–18 it is not possible to speak of true doublets or contradictions in the non-Priestly text and so its division into extracts from two parallel accounts of the Exodus is less certain. But even here some more or less probable inferences can be made in most sections of the text on the basis of features shared (or not shared) with the narratives that have already been discussed. In chs. 1–2 the section 2.11-22 is taken up by 4.19 (cf. 2.15) and not by the strand (E) which calls Moses' father-in-law Jethro (because a different name for him is used in 2.18), to which 2.23aα, as a duplicate of 4.19, may also belong. 2.11-14 in turn presupposes the imposition of heavy labour on the Israelites in 1.8-12. So both of these passages can be attributed to

J. This receives support from connections further back, as 1.8 is most naturally seen as the continuation of 1.6 and this appears to be the 'missing' conclusion to Gen. 50.22 (or 50.22-23), the parallel death-notice for Joseph to what E has in Gen. 50.24-26. The intervening narratives in 1.15-21 and 2.1-10 (which have probably been connected by 1.22) do not in themselves presuppose this specific context and could therefore in theory have been taken from a different account of Israel's oppression by the Egyptians. But it can hardly be said that they are inconsistent with the surrounding narrative and without it they lack both an introduction and a connection to Moses' subsequent appearance in Midian and at the mountain of God. This is not in itself an objection to their having been extracted from a parallel account (presumably E), but it means that there is less direct evidence for it. They could be fresh elaborations of the Exodus story or isolated narratives that were in circulation, as a number of scholars have recently thought. Something can, however, be said on other grounds for their having once formed part of the E source. Even though the story of attempted genocide in 1.15-22 can be seen (as it is in the extant text) as a continuation and intensification of Pharaoh's earlier efforts to deal with a threatening situation in 1.8-12(13-14), the narrative progression is not entirely a smooth one. The way that 1.8-12 ends, with steadily increasing growth in Israel's numbers, makes the further statement to this effect in v. 20 unnecessary and has been held to be difficult to reconcile with the small numbers implied by the presence of only two midwives in v. 15 (so recently Baden in 'From Joseph to Moses', pp. 134, 138-40). When this is combined with the fact that both the use of the title 'God' and the specific expressions 'fear God' (vv. 17, 21) and 'handmaid' (*'āmāh*: 2.5) are elsewhere characteristic of E rather than J, there is a definite case for this pair of narratives (especially 1.15-21) having been taken from the E source. The 'gaps' before and after it in the material from E that has been preserved could readily be attributed to some selectiveness on the part of the redactor who combined the older traditions: the E account itself would have been more complete.

In chs. 15–18 there is again very little evidence of doublets or contradiction to support the sub-division of the non-Priestly material between extracts from different sources. Certainty is impossible but here too connections with the two strands that can more clearly be identified in chs. 3–14 provide a basis for a plausible attribution of all but 15.1-18 to one or other of the main non-Priestly sources (for fuller discussion of the arguments see the commentary). The two poems celebrating the Exodus in 15.1-21 do form a doublet and have often been assigned, with their introductions, to J (vv. 1-18) and E (vv. 20-21: on v. 19 see below). But, although the Song of Moses is in our view an old pre-exilic poem which could have stood in one of the older sources, its introduction in v. 1a is so similar to Num. 21.17a, which introduces another poem at the end of the wilderness journey, that its incorporation into the narrative may be best attributed to a later redactional layer that spanned the whole wilderness story. The Song of Miriam, on the other hand, raises no such problems and we have concluded (in the introduction to 15.1-21) that there are still good reasons for following the old consensus that it was included in E. In the Marah-story in 15.22-26 there is an awkward 'join' in the middle of v. 25, and the theme of God 'testing' Israel links v. 25b to E passages in Gen. 22.1 and Exod. 20.20: vv. 22-25a will therefore probably be from J (on vv. 26-27 see below). The almost complete non-Priestly version of the manna-story in Exodus 16, which is parallel to the much fuller Priestly version of the story, also refers to God testing Israel (v. 4) and so it may well be from E. In ch. 17 each of the main narrative units, the water-story (originally vv. 3-6) and the story of the victory over Amalek (originally vv. 8-13, 15), has an explicit connection with an earlier narrative in Exodus. The staff with which Moses is said to have 'struck the river Nile' (v. 5) is the one in the alternative version of the plague-narratives which appears sporadically in chs. 7–10 (see especially 7.15, 17, 20) and is assigned by us to J; while 'the staff of God' (v. 9) has been mentioned before in 4.20b (part of the E account of Moses' return to Egypt). Chapter 18 (except for redactional additions in v. 2b and perhaps in vv. 21b and 25b, as well as a possible gloss in v. 10) several times names Moses' father-in-law as Jethro, like the E narrative in chs. 3–4, as well as using the title 'God' more often than the divine name (and exclusively in vv. 13-27): this long section must be derived from E too.[117]

---

[117] The full list of passages attributed here (with varying degrees of confidence) to the two non-Priestly sources is therefore:
J: 1.6, 8-12; 2.11-22; 3.2-4a, 5, 7-8, 16-19; 4.1-8, 10-14aα, 19-20a, 24-26, 29-31 (most); 5.3-23 (most); 6.1; 7.15b-16aα, 17 (part), 20aβ; 9.22-23a, 24a, 25b,

INTRODUCTION 103

Some verses and longer passages are unlikely to have formed part of the main sources of the non-Priestly narrative and can be attributed to the scribes who combined them together or to others who studied and copied them. We have taken a conservative view in the identification of such additions, limiting ourselves to cases where there is clear evidence of them and avoiding the temptation to indulge in the wholesale speculation which can be observed in both recent and earlier scholarship. No doubt other changes were made to the text in the process of its transmission, just as they were in other ancient Near Eastern texts, for which multiple copies make this easier to see, and in the later copying of the biblical text itself. But where we only have, for the most part, late and relatively uniform copies of the text, we cannot expect to be able to reconstruct every development in its earlier history and must be content to record the more obvious discrepancies which the work of later scribes has introduced.

The following additions and changes (some of which have been mentioned already) can be identified as such with some confidence, and where possible they will be grouped together according to their connection with one another or common purpose.

(a) Some additions or changes are clearly intended to create a more unified narrative from the combination of the main non-Priestly sources J and E. The reading 'his sons' in 4.20a (a J text) includes Moses' second son, who is not otherwise mentioned until 18.3-4 (4.25 implies that there was only one). Conversely, the addition of 'after she had been sent away' in 18.2b (part of E) is made to explain why Zipporah and her children are brought to Moses from Midian when the J account in 4.20a and 4.24-26 had indicated that Moses took them with him to Egypt. Another example is the insertion of Aaron in the J narrative in 4.29-30 and 5.4, 20-21 on the basis of E's accounts of his meeting with Moses in 4.27-28 and his appearance

---

35; 10.12-13a, 14-15 (part), 20, 21-23, 27; 12.21-23, 25-27, 33-34, 37b-38 (?), 39; 13.3-4, 21-22; 14.5a, 6-7, 10-14, 16aα, 19b-20, 24, 25b, 27b, 28b, 30, 31b; 15.22-25a; 17.3-6;

E: 1.15-22; 2.1-10, 23aα; 3.1, 4b, 6, 9-15; 4.17-18, 20b, 27-28; 5.1-2; 7.14-18 (most), 20b-21a, 23-29; 8.4-11aα, 16-28; 9.1-7, 13-21, 23b, 24b-25a, 26-34; 10.1a, 3-11, 13b, 14-15 (parts), 16-19, 24-26, 28-29; 11.3b-8; 12.29-32; 13.17-19; 14.5b, 9aα, 15, 19a, 21aβ, 25a, 31a; 15.20-21, 25b; 16.4-5, 26, 21, 27-31 (probably); 17.8-13 (most), 15; 18.1-12 (most), 13-27.

in 5.1 and 18.12: the more extensive insertion of Yahweh's provision of Aaron to be Moses' mouthpiece in 4.14aβ-16 is closely associated with this.[118] Possibly the words 'Three days' journey' in 8.23 (E) are an addition from this stage to provide agreement with 3.18 and 5.3 (J). Some other additions which presuppose the combination of the two accounts could have been made later, as they modify the narrative rather than reconciling inconsistencies in it. The three passages about 'the plundering of the Egyptians' which are inserted in J in 3.21-22 and 12.35-36 and in E in 11.1-3a would be a notable case of this: they introduce an assumption, that the Israelites lived among the Egyptians rather than separately, which is not made in either of the main sources. 15.26 is an addition which gives a strongly Deuteronomistic twist in both its theology and its language to the two awkwardly joined parts of the preceding verse ('I am Yahweh your healer' takes up the 'healing' of the waters by divine instruction in v. 25a). The addition of 'in Horeb' (probably a regional term, and taken from E in 3.1) in 17.6, which is part of an episode from J, established the location of Yahweh's appearance as appropriately near to the mountain of God.

(b) Another group of redactional additions made to the combined JE narrative can be taken together because they all form part of an itinerary. These occur in 12.37a, 13.20, 15.27, 16.1a and 17.1 (19.2a also belongs to this sequence) and so are attached to narratives which probably come from both J and E. Further elements of this itinerary appear in Numbers, one in a Deuteronomistic context in ch. 21 which betrays the background for the incorporation of these verses in the wilderness narrative. The wording has probably been taken from a fuller description of the Israelites' journey which was based on ancient Near Eastern practice and underlies the version with Priestly additions in Num. 33.1-49 (see further the excursus on 'The Wilderness Itinerary' in the introduction to 12.28-42, 50-51).

(c) Some further miscellaneous additions are difficult to date precisely. Two which are important for what they convey about the use of the Exodus story in the teaching of children, 10.1b-2 and

---

[118] In the plagues narrative and in 12.31 it is more difficult to determine the origin of the references to Aaron (see the introduction to 7.26–8.11): they may be from E or from the redactor who combined the Priestly and non-Priestly accounts.

13.5-9, 11-16, probably belong together. They need not be as late as Deuteronomy (where the teaching of children is focused on the law: 6.7, 20-25; 11.19-20; cf. 31.11-13), but the second passage seems to draw on both J and E: it is the latter which makes specific reference to the death of the Egyptian firstborn. 15.1a, the introduction of the Song of Moses in 15.1b-18 seems to be designed, among other things, to create a 'frame' around the wilderness narrative with Num. 21.17-18 and could be part of a 'wilderness redaction' which also included the incorporation of the detailed itinerary. But the origin of the material in Num. 21.12-20 is very obscure and these old poems could easily have been introduced into the narrative at an earlier stage. In ch. 18 the unnecessary duplication in v. 10 could be due to the combination of two alternative versions of Jethro's words of praise, but the wording may be imitating the parallelism of hymnic poetry. In vv. 21 and 25 the lists of officials responsible for 'thousands, hundreds, fifties and tens' is less appropriate to the judges with whose appointment Exodus deals than to the leaders with wider responsibilities in the Deuteronomic version of this story (Deut. 1.15). Many commentators have therefore attributed them to clumsy harmonisation with that passage, which is possible, though the argument is not conclusive. Somewhat similar are 17.14 and 16, which may have been added to the Amalek story, respectively, in the light of the wider conquest narrative in Joshua and from the account of Amalek's later defeat in 1 Samuel 15.

(d) Finally, some additions to the non-Priestly account were made after it was combined with the Priestly narrative. 4.9 is probably one case: although the turning of Nile water into blood is a non-Priestly motif (7.17-18, 20-21a), the word used for 'dry ground' (cf. 14.16, 22, 29 in contrast to the different word used in 14.21) is the standard Priestly expression (cf. Gen. 1.9-10). Careful study of 4.21-23 has suggested that it is a late piece that draws on both JE and P to provide a justification in advance for the final plague and we have followed this view. In 12.24 and 13.10 Priestly language is used (cf. 12.14, 17) to underline the permanent validity of the non-P Passover and Unleavened Bread regulations. 14.9aβb draws in Priestly language from elsewhere in the chapter (v. 2; vv. 17-18, 23, 28) to fill out the non-Priestly account of the Egyptian pursuit; and some of the same expressions are used in 15.19 with Priestly language from 14.26-29 to keep in view what the redactor saw as the main theme of the

Song of Moses. In 16.1a and 17.1 Priestly expressions (especially 'the congregation' [*hāʿēdāh*]) have been added to these itinerary-notes to match the extensive Priestly component in the story which they now frame (cf. 16.2, 9-10, 22).[119] Finally, although they do not contain any Priestly language, we have followed the view that 17.2 and 7, with the names Massah and Meribah, were put where they are after being displaced from their original position in Numbers 13 when the Priestly and non-Priestly spies stories were combined (see further the introduction to 17.1-7).

To summarise, the written tradition to which we have access behind the present text would seem to comprise four main elements: two non-Priestly narratives, a Priestly narrative and the Song of Moses. Neither of the non-Priestly narratives survives in its complete original form, but each is sufficiently preserved to indicate the inclusion in it of the major elements of the Exodus story: the presence of Jacob's descendants in Egypt (known as Israel from 1.9 and 3.9 onwards) and their growth into a numerous people, their oppression by the Egyptians, Moses' marriage into the family of a Midianite priest, his encounter with God in the desert and his commissioning to bring the Israelites out of Egypt, Moses' demand that Pharaoh (the king of Egypt) permit them to go out into the desert to celebrate a religious festival, Pharaoh's refusal, the occurrence of a series of plagues sent by God, at the end of which the Israelites depart, the pursuit of the Israelites by an Egyptian military force which is thwarted by God's intervention at a 'sea', the Israelites' journey into the desert and God's special provision for their needs there. Differences in the presentation of these common elements make it likely that these two narratives are based on an outline of the story which formed part of a multi-faceted body of probably oral tradition about Israel's origins, which is largely beyond our reach.[120] But the possibility that one is a revision of the other cannot be entirely ruled out. In addition, what survives of the two non-Priestly narratives (this is an important

---

[119] Later, 20.11 is a similar addition based on a Priestly text, in this case Gen. 2.1-3 in the Priestly creation story.

[120] See the valuable reminder of this important dimension of the biblical tradition, as in other cultures, in R.D. Miller, *Oral Tradition in Ancient Israel* (Eugene, 2011).

qualification, as the redactor who combined them could in some cases have omitted parallel versions altogether) suggests that certain episodes were included in only one of them. For example only E has accounts of the revelation of God's name (though something similar occurs later in 34.5-8, which is often attributed to J), of the protracted negotiations with Pharaoh, of the battle with the Amalekites, of the visit of Jethro to Moses after the Exodus and perhaps of Moses' birth and naming. Conversely, only J has an account of Moses killing an Egyptian (E must have explained his presence in Midian in some other way), of God's attempt to kill him, of the intensification of the Israelites' oppression and of the inauguration of Passover and the festival of Unleavened Bread. Some of these sections may also have been part of the older tradition, while others were fashioned by the authors of these narratives: for discussion see the introductions to the relevant sections.

Older critical scholarship dated the two non-Priestly narratives to the first half of the monarchy period, often on the basis of evidence from Genesis and Numbers which cannot be discussed here. The references to the Israelites as 'Hebrews' in both narratives, especially in Exodus 1–2 but occasionally later, give support to such a date, since the expression occurs predominantly in texts referring to the early period and is probably to be associated with *'prw* in extra-biblical sources (see the Explanatory Note on 1.15). Apart from Exodus 1–10 and the story of Joseph in Genesis, 'Hebrews' occurs mainly (6x) in 1 Samuel. More recently (see section 4a of this introduction) the tendency has been to date these sections of Exodus (or at least material in them) to the seventh century or later, on the basis that they are dependent on classical prophecy and/or Deuteronomy or because of conclusions reached about particular passages. There are certainly features shared with classical prophecy (such as the 'call-narrative' and the 'messenger-formula', but they also occur elsewhere, especially in accounts of pre-classical prophecy, where the analogies are in some respects closer. The description of Moses as a 'prophet' (*nābî'*) is found already in Hosea (12.14), and not only in Deuteronomy (where it is applied to him in a special way in 18.15, 18 and 34.10). Apart from a very few passages which have a redactional origin (see above on 15.26) the claims for Deuteronomic influence remain unproven: on the whole the narratives have a very different character. It has been claimed that 1.11 (Redford,

Schipper), 2.1-10 (Gerhards) and 18.1-12 (Blum, Haarmann) are all for various reasons late in origin. In none of these cases is the argument conclusive (see the introductions and notes to these passages) and for 18.13-27 (which presupposes 18.1-12) a much more plausible case can be and has been made for its origin in the monarchy period (see the introduction to that passage). More generally it has been argued, by Nicholson and Emerton among others, that the non-Priestly narrative sources (especially J) cannot be late, because they show no awareness of the dramatic political and theological developments of the late monarchy and exilic periods.[121]

These two versions of the Exodus story (and the larger narratives of which they probably formed part) must have been merged together at some point and small additions and changes were made to reconcile differences between them. It is not possible to be certain when this occurred, but the old view that the two versions derive from the two kingdoms of Judah and Israel which existed side by side for two hundred years and that the combination of them was made in the seventh century after the fall of the northern kingdom to the Assyrians has much to be said for it.[122] A similar introduction of northern material into the literature of Judah can be observed in psalmodic (e.g. Pss. 77, 80, 81), prophetic (Hosea) and historical (parts of Samuel–Kings) writings about the same time.

Additions to the combined narrative continued to be made, some reflecting familiarity with Deuteronomy (or the tradition behind it), which gave the teaching of the law a much more central place than the Exodus narrative in its religious and educational programme of reform. The Priestly account kept the narrative structure of the older sources, but on a briefer scale in most of the episodes, omitting

[121] Nicholson, *Pentateuch*, pp. 170-71; J.A. Emerton, 'The Date of the Yahwist', in J. Day (ed.), *In Search of Pre-Exilic Israel* (JSOTSup 406; London, 2004), pp. 107-29.

[122] So recently Friedman, *Who Wrote the Bible?*, pp. 60-88. Baden, *J, E and the Redaction*, suggests reasons for holding that J and E remained separate for much longer, until after P and D had been written. It remains to be seen whether this proposal will gain wider acceptance. The closer integration of J and E with each other than with P in large parts of Exodus (and Genesis) could be an indication that they were already combined at an earlier stage. In addition the more selective use of J and E material contrasts with the relatively complete preservation of P and the combined non-P narrative and suggests that different redactors with different priorities were responsible for separate stages in the combination of the sources.

unnecessary and sometimes what it saw as improper detail (such as Moses' marriage to a Midianite woman; cf. Gen. 28.1-2) and concentrating on those episodes where Yahweh's unique glory and faithfulness could most effectively be expounded and appropriate celebration of it could be ensured (the commissioning of Moses, the plague-stories with their very negative portrait of Pharaoh, the rules for Passover and Unleavened Bread, the destruction of the Egyptian army at the sea and the provision of manna and meat with regulations for Sabbath observance). In all of this (except notably in the drama at the sea) Aaron is prominent alongside Moses from his introduction in 7.1-2 onwards: it is he with his staff that actually brings on the plagues one by one, he receives the rules for Passover and Unleavened Bread with Moses and shares in the leadership of the people in the story of the manna and meat. In the latter he is entrusted with a portion of manna to be placed 'before the decree' in the portable sanctuary when it is built (16.33-34). So, the way is being prepared for him to become, with his descendants, the exclusive priesthood in this sanctuary and for evermore, according to the provisions of chs. 28–29.[123]

In the context, then, of its own theology, which is grounded in creation, the covenant with Abraham (2.24; 6.4-5; cf. Gen. 17), the Exodus deliverance, which is based on it, and Yahweh's presence in his sanctuary, P provides a validation for those who could trace their ancestry to Aaron (and as will later emerge, for them alone out of all the tribe of Levi) to officiate as the priests of Yahweh.[124] This is one of several characteristics of P which have formed the basis for establishing the date and circumstances of its origin and, as being the most distinctive of them and the one which takes us most directly to its likely authors, it is of the greatest importance. Within the Old Testament Aaronide priests are mentioned, outside P and a few passages influenced by it, only in the books of Chronicles, Ezra and Nehemiah. On this issue, whatever one may make

---

[123] The author of a later supplement to P in 6.14-30 provided a much fuller introduction for Aaron, before he is first mentioned, in a genealogy which focuses on Aaron's ancestry, his marriage and his immediate descendants (and says nothing about Moses except his name!).

[124] On the theology of P see Albertz, *History* 2, pp. 480-93; E. Gerstenberger, *Israel in der Perserzeit. 5. und 4. Jahrhundert v. Chr.* (BE 8; Stuttgart, 2005), pp. 133-50. On Aaron see further the Excursus on 4.10-17.

of its historicity in other respects, Chronicles can be seen from a comparison with Samuel–Kings to have repeatedly modified the older narrative by giving priests of the monarchy period an Aaronide ancestry (see especially the speech attributed to Abijah in 2 Chr. 13.4-12, which has no parallel in 1 Kings). In actual history all that is certain is that such an ancestry was claimed for priests (specifically the holders of the high-priesthood) in postexilic Jerusalem (1 Chr. 5.29-41; cf. Hag. 1.1; Neh. 10.37; 12.10-11; also Ezra 7.1-6) and at some point by the Samaritans.[125] Prior to this, it would seem, descent from Zadok, David's priest, was sufficient in Jerusalem (cf. Ezek. 44.15). One might well therefore conclude, as most critical scholars have done, that the idea of Aaronide ancestry being the criterion was devised by Jerusalem priests in the exilic or early post-exilic period for their own benefit and that the composition of P derives from them at that time. But other possibilities, allowing a greater antiquity for an Aaronic priesthood, have also been proposed and on this basis (and for other reasons) some scholars envisage a somewhat earlier date for the composition of P.

It has been argued that, since Exodus 32 is very probably directed against the presence of a golden calf-image in the temple at Bethel, the leading role played by Aaron in the manufacture of the calf must mean that his descendants were the priests at Bethel in the monarchic period. Arguments based on inferences from more indirect evidence have been brought forward to suggest that Jerusalem was also in Aaronide hands from the time of David, and specifically that Zadok actually was a descendant of Aaron. From this and from other observations, such as the likely antiquity of many aspects of the cultic regulations in P, the inclusion of some such regulations in Deuteronomy and Ezekiel, signs that Jeremiah and Ezekiel knew parts of P, and more recently arguments based

---

[125] The evidence for Samaritan claims about the origin of their priesthood, however, is unfortunately too late and too variable in its details to provide any clarity about the biblical period. Although Aaron is commonly seen as its ultimate source, there are a number of intermediate figures, such as Uzzi/Ozzi, Seraiah and even Zadok, who might have been thought of as the more immediate founders of the Samaritan line (see in general J. Macdonald, *The Theology of the Samaritans* [NTL; London, 1964], pp. 15-21, 310-13). Though earlier, neither Neh. 13.28 and Jos., *AJ* 11.302-324 is likely to preserve any authentic memory of the Samaritan priesthood.

on the (classical) language of P, it has been deduced that P can be, indeed must be, much older than the exilic or post-exilic period.¹²⁶ These arguments, however, turn out on examination to be much weaker than the total absence of any support for a requirement of Aaronide ancestry for priests in texts that can securely be regarded as pre-exilic or indeed earlier than the period of the Second Temple.¹²⁷ It is revealing that M. Haran, who believed that 'the literary crystallisation of P must have taken place in pre-exilic times' (in fact under Hezekiah) acknowledged in his preface to *Temples and Temple-Service* that 'it was only in the days of Ezra... that P's presence became perceptible in historical reality and began to exercise its influence on the formation of Judaism' (p. v). There is no reason to see Aaron's prominence in Exodus 32 as representative of an Aaronide priesthood at Bethel. If there were, he would have to be also representative of the priesthood at Dan, where there was also a golden calf according to 1 Kgs 12.29-30, but it is clear from Judg. 18.30-31 that the priesthood there was not Aaronide. Other non-Priestly texts likewise give no reason to suppose that Aaron was seen as the ancestor of a hereditary priesthood, or even as a priest. That cultic regulations existed, perhaps even in written form, before the exile need not mean that the compilation of P had already taken place and the prophetic 'allusions' to P concern at most specific passages such as Genesis 1. The fact that P is written in classical Hebrew does not demand a pre-exilic date, since 'Late Biblical Hebrew' did not begin to replace it until the fifth century and even then documents purporting to be ancient may well have been written in the older form of the language.

---

¹²⁶ So especially Y. Kaufmann, *The Religion of Israel*, pp. 193-200; M. Weinfeld, *Deuteronomy and the Deuteronomic School*, pp. 179-89; M. Haran, *Temples and Temple-Service in Ancient Israel* (Oxford, 1978), esp. Chapters 4–6; Friedman, *Who Wrote the Bible?*, pp. 167-216. Cross also maintained (as some earlier scholars had done) that the priests of Bethel and Jerusalem (and Hebron) were Aaronide in the pre-exilic period, but states very clearly his view that, for other reasons (including some features of P's language), 'The Priestly editors of the Tetrateuch wrote in the sixth century' (*Canaanite Myth*, pp. 133, 195-215, 293-325).

¹²⁷ Cf. Nicholson, *Pentateuch*, pp. 218-20; Houston, *Pentateuch*, pp. 102-103, 112-14.

A more plausible origin for the notion of priests descended from Aaron can possibly be found in sixth-century Judah, on the basis of the Levitical city-list in Joshua 21, which assigns cities in the tribal areas of Judah, Simeon and Benjamin to 'the sons of Aaron' (vv. 9-19). These could be the same Levite priests of the Judaean countryside who were, contrary to the provisions of Deut. 18.6-8, refused access to full rights in the Jerusalem temple after Josiah's reform and in the regulations of Ezekiel 40–48 (2 Kgs 23.9; Ezek. 44.10-14). It may be that, when plans for the rebuilding of the temple were well advanced, the authors of P took up this claim and applied it also to the traditional Zadokite priesthood of Jerusalem, thus arriving at an accommodation with this particular group of Levites (Cody, *History*, pp. 158-74; Schaper, *Priester und Leviten*, pp. 26-42, 169-73, takes a somewhat similar view but retains the idea of Aaronides at Bethel for the exilic period).[128]

A full study of the composition of chs. 19–40 can of course only be given after detailed work on the commentary on those chapters is complete and it will appear in a future volume. It remains to be seen whether and how far the conclusions reached for chs. 1–18 will hold good in the later chapters, where the character of the material is very different. The major distinction between P and non-P, as has already been noted, does continue and could be said to be even more evident because of the separation of the disparate material into very large 'blocks' here. Within each account there are also signs of duplication and inconsistency which may be explicable in the same or similar terms as in chs. 1–18.[129] There are further occurrences of 'God' as an alternative designation for Yahweh in chs. 19–24, which

---

[128] Or may it have arisen, a little later, from a wish to establish a common ancestry for the priests of Jerusalem and Mount Gerizim, in the context of the production of a text of the Torah which would be acceptable to both the Jewish and the Samaritan communities? For the possibility of some such inter-communal collaboration see R. Pummer, 'The Samaritans and their Pentateuch', in G.N. Knoppers and B.M. Levinson, *The Pentateuch as Torah* (Winona Lake, 2007), pp. 237-69 (263-69); W.J. Houston, 'Between Salem and Mount Gerizim: The Context of the Formation of the Torah Reconsidered', *JAJ* 5 (2014), pp. 311-34 (esp. 326-28).

[129] It is notable that Baden is sufficiently confident of this to make it (rather than Gen. 12–50) the starting-point for his argument for an independent E source (*Composition*, pp. 103-104, 116-19): cf. Graupner, *Elohist*, pp. 113-37 on chs. 19–24.

may prove as before to be a useful marker of one non-Priestly strand if there is other evidence that supports this. But there are additional complications in the inclusion of collections of laws which may either have still been free-standing or were already incorporated into a narrative context, in more extensive parallels with Deuteronomy and in the second account of covenant-making in 34.10-28 which is not referred to in Deuteronomy or anywhere else.[130] It is not surprising that already in 1974 Childs could comment on 'the extreme difficulty of analyzing the Sinai pericope', adding that 'many of the major problems have resisted a satisfactory solution' (p. 344). In the present situation of Pentateuchal study the task is certainly not going to be any easier.

5. *The Contents of Exodus Divided between the Two Main Versions of the Story*

The following table shows the major distinction between the Priestly and non-Priestly sections of the book of Exodus and what is contained in each. At this level there is considerable agreement among scholars at the present time, as previously, and this distinction is much more important for the interpretation of the book than the further sub-divisions within each part of it, which are where most of the disagreements have existed and continue to exist. Our own view of the latter is not shown here, but is worked out in the introductions to each portion of the text and displayed in the translations that accompany the commentary. In the translations a difference of type-face is used to identify precisely which sections of text are attributed here to the Priestly (italic) and non-Priestly (Roman) narratives and laws.[131] Within each major component of the text square brackets indicate elements which this commentary judges to be, or possibly to be, secondary additions or (in the non-Priestly sections) parts of a parallel version, i.e. extracts from E in a section where J provides the main non-Priestly text and vice versa (the latter [mainly] in 7.14–13.22).

---

[130] For a recent assessment of some of these problems see L. Schmidt, 'Dekalog und Bundesbuch im Kontext von Exodus 19-24', *ZAW* 128 (2016), pp. 579-93.

[131] As in the commentaries of von Rad on Genesis and Noth on Exodus.

The Non-Priestly Version

Israel in Egypt and the Early Life of Moses (…1.6–2.22)
1.6 Resumé: Joseph

1.8-12, 15-22: Oppression of Israel
2.1-22 Moses: his birth, flight to Midian and marriage

Moses' commissioning and approach to Pharaoh (2.23aα–6.1)

2.23aα The death of an Egyptian king
3.1–4.17 Moses' commissioning at the mountain of God
4.18-31 Moses' return to Egypt
5.1-23 Moses and Aaron's first encounter with Pharaoh
6.1 Yahweh's renewed assurance of his powerful help

The series of (seven) plagues (7.14–10.29)
Water turned to blood
Frogs
Flies
Pestilence on the animals
Hail and thunder
Locusts
Darkness

The Priestly Version

Israel in Egypt (…1.1-14)
1.1-5 Resumé: Jacob's family in Egypt
1.7: Growth into a people
1.13-14: Oppression of Israel

Moses' commissioning and approach to Pharaoh (2.23aβb–7.13)

2.23aβb-25 God's concern for his people Israel
6.2 – 7.5 Moses' commissioning

7.6-13 Moses and Aaron's (first) encounter with Pharaoh

The series of (four) plagues (7.19–9.12)
Water turned to blood
Frogs
Gnats
Boils on humans and animals

Passover and Departure (11.1–13.22)

11.1-8 Announcement of the Final Plague
12.21-27 The ordinances for Passover

12.29-39 The final plague makes Pharaoh let Israel go
13.3-16 Rules about Unleavened Bread and the Firstborn
13.17-22 Aspects of Israel's departure

The Deliverance at the Sea (14.5–15.21, part)

14.5-31 Narrative
15.1-18, 20-21 Two hymns of celebration

The Journey to the Mountain of God (15.22–18.27, part)

15.22-27 Water at Marah and Elim
16.1-31 Manna and Sabbath
17.1-7 Water at Rephidim
17.8-16 The Battle with Amalek
18.1-27 Jethro's coming

Theophany at Mount Sinai and the Making of the Covenant (19.2–24.11)

19.2 Arrival
19.3-25 Preparations for meeting and Yahweh's theophany

Passover and Departure (11.9–13.2)

11.9-10 Summary: Pharaoh's Refusal

12.1-20, 28 The ordinances for Passover and Unleavened Bread
12.40-51 Israel's departure and further rules for Passover
13.1-2 Rules about the Firstborn

The Deliverance at the Sea (14.1-29, part)

14.1-29 Narrative

The Journey to the Mountain of God (16.1-36, part)

16.1-36 Manna, meat and Sabbath

Theophany at Mount Sinai (19.1–24.18)

19.1 Arrival
24.(12?)15-18 Moses ascends the mountain and Yahweh's glory appears

20.1-17 God reveals the Decalogue to the people
20.18-21 Preparations for further laws
20.22–23.19 The laws of the covenant given to Moses
23.20-33 The promised land
24.1-11 The making of the covenant
24.12/13-14 Moses ascends the mountain to receive the tablets of law

The Plan for the Sanctuary given to Moses (25.1–31.17/18)

The Rebellion of Israel and the Renewal of the Covenant (31.18–34.28)
31.18 Moses receives the tablets of law
32.1-29, 35 The making of the golden calf and ensuing punishment
32.30-34, 33.1-6 Moses' intercession and the people's response
33.7-11 Moses at the tent of meeting
33.12-13 Moses' further intercession
34.1-28 The renewal of the covenant

The Making of the Sanctuary and the Entry of Yahweh's Glory (34.29–40.38)

ISRAEL IN EGYPT
AND THE EARLY LIFE OF MOSES
(1.1–2.22)

CHAPTER 1.1-6

RÉSUMÉ:
THE BACKGROUND TO THE STORY
OF THE EXODUS

The *definition* of the first textual unit of the book of Exodus is not entirely straightforward, despite the practical unanimity of commentators and translators, as well as the Masoretes, in identifying it as 1.1-7. On formal grounds the break between the list of names, with its conclusion, and the narrative comes after 1.5 (so the paragraphing in NEB, REB). More significant, however, is the fact that the book begins by recapitulating matters already dealt with at the end of Genesis (see the detailed notes below). The boundary between this résumé and the opening of the Exodus story itself is most naturally placed after 1.6, as in the Geneva Bible and the AV.[1] It could be argued that v. 7 also belongs to the résumé, because of its anticipation in Gen. 47.27, but that anticipation is only partial and v. 7 belongs more closely with what follows. The priority of the subject in v. 7 supports the view that it is a new beginning, and the structural arguments of P. Weimar ('Exodus 1,1–2,10', pp. 186-88) against it are not decisive.

The *form* of 1.1-6, despite its uniform function, is twofold. Verses 1-5 are a list with introduction (v. 1) and conclusion (v. 5), which has been compared to Gen. 25.13-16 and 35.22b-26, for example (Schmidt, p. 26). A difference from these, purely genealogical, lists is the specific narrative episode to which the present list is attached by the phrase 'who came to Egypt': this is the reason for the omission

---

[1] So also Coats, 'Structural Transition', p. 130; *Exodus 1–18*, pp. 21-22.

of Joseph's name from the main list and the expanded introduction and conclusion, and the result is that this passage is more tightly woven into its narrative context than at least Gen. 25.13-16: in 35.22b-26 the final words of v. 26 give it a closer link to its narrative setting. In some respects the distinctive features of 1.1-5 are paralleled in Gen. 46.8-27, which has a similar heading, but the contents of that list are much less affected by its specific setting and it resembles the standard genealogical pattern more closely (see further below on the relationship between that passage and this one). 1.1-5 itself exhibits some widespread features of genealogical lists: (a) the introductory formula 'These are (the names of)...', (b) economy of detail in the list itself and (c) a summarizing total. Verse 6, on the other hand, as its beginning with an imperfect consecutive verb indicates, is a typical component of a narrative.

There was long a substantial consensus about the *origin* of these verses: 1-5 come from the Priestly source and 6 from JE, more specifically J. A separation between these two units is already suggested by the formal difference just noted and by the fact that v. 6 (like v. 8) is linked to the parenthetical reference to Joseph in v. 5b rather than the main preoccupation of vv. 1-5 with the people as a whole. The fact that in the remainder of the chapter, as well as in Genesis 48–50, at least two narrative strands are evident (see the introductory section on 1.7-22; also Baden, 'From Joseph to Moses') lends further weight to this view. The vocabulary and style of vv. 1-5 are strongly Priestly (see the detailed notes below), whereas such features are lacking in v. 6.

Noth and Hyatt, it is true, did attribute v. 6 to P, but without citing any argument in support, and Vriezen's comparison of the schema in vv. 6 and 8 with Judg. 2.8-10 ('Exodusstudien', pp. 334-44) has convinced most subsequent commentators that the older view should be retained. Coats ('Structural Transition', pp. 132-33) has pointed out some weaknesses in this comparison and argued that v. 7 rather than v. 8 is the natural continuation of v. 6, but the Joseph-centred focus of v. 6 really fits much better with the Joseph-narrative in Genesis and with v. 8 than with the rather meagre account of P which treats the descendants of Jacob as a single unit. Recently Vriezen's conclusions have been used as an argument for attributing v. 6 (and v. 8) to a Deuteronomistic (or late Yahwist) author (Blum, *Studien*, pp. 102-103; Van Seters, *Life of Moses*, pp. 16-19) but, as Vriezen clearly saw (pp. 339, 344), the two passages are not similar enough to establish a relationship of literary dependence between them (cf. Davies, 'K^D in Exodus', p. 408).

Subsequently more far-reaching doubts have been raised about the antiquity of verses formerly attributed to the older sources in Exodus 1, leading to the conclusion that there was no literary connection between the Exodus story and the patriarchal narratives before the composition of P (see further below in the introduction to 1.7-22). As part of this 'Abschied vom Jahwisten' 1.6 has been attributed to a post-Priestly redactor (Schmid, *Erzväter*, pp. 69-73; Kratz, *Pentateuch*, pp. 286-88; Gertz, *Tradition*, pp. 358-63, who is followed by Blum, 'Literarische Verbindung', pp. 145-51, and Albertz, p. 43). Schmid, for example, sees 1.6 as a duplicate of Gen. 50.26, which he (like Rendtorff) attributed to a very late redactional layer too. Strictly the two verses are not a complete doublet, as they overlap only in the mention of Joseph's death. In any case, even if Gen. 50.26 is a redactional addition, that says nothing about the origin of 1.6, which could perfectly well come from a continuous older narrative source, which probably also included the parallel statement about Joseph's age at death in Gen. 50.22-23 (and perhaps v. 24). Gertz seeks to strengthen the argument for a late origin of 1.6 by claiming that it 'presupposes' (p. 360) the listing of Joseph's brothers in vv. 1-5, but it is just as likely that the mention of the brothers looks back to Genesis 50, where they are central to the non-Priestly narrative from v. 8 onwards. There is nothing in the wording of 1.6 to suggest a late origin and it also links well to 1.8-12 (for a more wide-ranging response to the 'disintegration' of Gen. 50 and Exod. 1 in some recent scholarship see my essay 'The Transition from Genesis', esp. pp. 69-71).

Some scholars have attributed part or all of vv. 1-5 to a redaction subsequent to the main Priestly narrative. Beer and Fohrer (*Überlieferung und Geschichte*, p. 9) associated the whole passage with the late separation of the Pentateuch into individual books, arguing respectively from the repetition of what had already been stated in Genesis 35 and from dependence on Gen. 46.8-27 in v. 5a and the inconsistent use of 'sons of Israel' (*bny yśr'l*) in v. 1 and v. 7 (so also Gertz, *Tradition*, pp. 354-57). Heinisch and Noth regarded v. 5a as dependent on Gen. 46.8-27, and Weimar attributed it to P[s] for this and other reasons (*Untersuchungen*, pp. 24-25). Vriezen argued that most of vv. 1 and 5 was added by the redactor who joined P to the older sources (who was also responsible according to him for the redaction of Gen. 46.8-27: 'Exodusstudien', pp. 347-52), as linking material, and Schmidt derived v. 1b as well as v. 5a from P[s] (see his detailed analysis of the passage, pp. 9-11).

The most pervasive argument among these scholars is that the present form of the text is dependent on, or contemporary with, Gen. 46.8-27, which is now universally regarded as a very late insertion, contradicting in detail not only JE but the narrative of P (cf. Westermann, *Genesis 37–50*, pp. 174, 176). This relationship between the passages is held to be established by the number 'seventy', the very similar headings to the two lists and a series of shared items of vocabulary. Several of the latter are of little significance and show at most that these verses belong to the Priestly texts in a broad sense (e.g. the use of *nepeš* in v. 5). The similar headings perhaps point to some relationship between the passages, but it is just as likely that at this point Genesis 46 is dependent on Exodus 1 as the other way round. The number 'seventy', which is given a precise basis in Gen. 46.8-27 (cf. v. 27 and the sum of the figures in vv. 15, 18, 22 and 25), and the expression translated 'who were descended from Jacob', lit. 'who came out from Jacob's thigh' (*yṣ'y yrk y'qb*: see Note f on the translation), which occurs in a Priestly passage only here and in Gen. 46.26 (*yṣ'y yrkw*), seem at first sight to offer stronger support, but in fact neither feature points decisively towards a post-P origin for Exod. 1.1-5 (or any part of it). 'Seventy' as a round figure for the family of Jacob (compare its other uses noted below) was traditional (cf. Deut. 10.22) and need not presuppose the detailed list of Gen. 46.8-27, which in fact could only be accommodated to it with great difficulty (see the commentaries ad loc. and P. Addinall, 'Genesis XLVI 8-27', *VT* 54 [2004], pp. 289-300, as well as the alternative figure of sixty-six in v. 26). The phrase *yṣ'y yrkw* in Gen. 46.26 is generally recognized to be part of the secondary elaboration of the list and it is more likely that it was borrowed from Exod. 1.5 than *vice versa*. Other shared items of vocabulary could indeed be due to the same process. A return to the older view of Wellhausen (*Composition*, p. 51), Gunkel (*Genesis*, p. 493) and Baentsch (*Exodus*, p. 2), that it is Exod. 1.1-5 (*in toto*) which is the primary text, seems fully justified.

There remain, as possible objections to the attribution of these verses to P^g, the observations of Beer and Fohrer about the repetition of what has already appeared in Genesis 35 and the inconsistency over the meaning of 'sons of Israel' (*bny yśr'l*). Weimar has argued that both of these features are due to the use by P of an older version of the story in Exodus 1–14 (and probably elsewhere), to which 1.1aα, 2-4 belonged (*Untersuchungen*, pp. 18-21). Such an explanation will gain in persuasiveness if it turns out to apply to other passages in Exodus. Schmidt at least is not convinced by it: 'Die Priesterschrift liebt eben Wiederaufnahmen bzw. Wiederholungen und hat bei aller Freiheit im Umgang mit Überlieferung die verschiedenen Geschichtstraditionen nicht ganz zur homogenen Einheit gestalten können, so daß gewisse Unebenheiten bestehen bleiben' (*Einführung*, p. 99, ET, p. 97). Even without this hypothesis, the repetition need not be a major problem.

As it stands, Exod. 1.1-5 does not merely repeat what has been said in Genesis 35: it presents the sons of Jacob as the leaders of a larger body, numbering seventy, who went to Egypt. In a similar way the sons of Noah are mentioned no fewer than three times in Priestly texts (Gen. 5.32; 6.10; 10.1). The use of the expression 'sons of Israel' (*bny yśr'l*) to refer to the sons of Jacob is not only in tension with v. 7 but with Priestly usage generally: even in Genesis 35, immediately after the change of Jacob's name is reported by P, it is not taken up in the list of his sons (v. 22b). Nevertheless, if P's reason for recording the change of name there was to underline the continuity between the patriarch and later Israelites, as seems likely, that reason would also be relevant precisely at this point where, at the conclusion of the Jacob-story (see below), the transition is about to be made to the history of the people.

In the light of our literary-critical conclusions it is possible to consider what *purpose* vv. 6 and 1-5 respectively were intended by their original authors to fulfil. Our view of the purpose (and even the origin) of v. 6 will largely depend on our understanding of the composition of Genesis (48–)50, where a reference to the death of Joseph (but not his brothers or the rest of 'that generation') also appears, in 50.26. Despite the almost total abandonment of source criticism by C. Westermann in the section of his commentary dealing with Genesis 46–50 (see esp. pp. 239-42, ET, pp. 211-14) and by E. Blum in his study of the composition of the patriarchal narratives (*Komposition*, pp. 244-63), the reasons given long ago for viewing the non-Priestly conclusion to the stories of Jacob and Joseph as being derived, in the main, from two parallel accounts (cf. Wellhausen, Gunkel and even von Rad [pp. 351, 360-61, 375-76, ET, pp. 396, 408, 425]) are still weighty, even if the attribution of certain verses remains somewhat uncertain. According to the less far-reaching analyses of Wellhausen and Driver, the whole of Gen. 50.15-26 was derived from E, so that Exod. 1.6 would (so far as the J source is preserved) have followed the account in 50.14 of Joseph's return, with his entourage, from the burial of Jacob in Canaan. Such an abrupt end to the story of Joseph is perhaps possible: it would imply that with the burial of his father Joseph's life-work (and the patriarchal age) was, for the Yahwist, complete. All that remained was briefly to recount the deaths of Joseph himself and his brothers before the story of the oppression of their descendants by the Egyptians began.

But, to leave on one side the unanswerable question whether a section of J may have been omitted at this point in the process of redaction (as has evidently happened with its account of the actual burial of Jacob), there are sufficient signs of duplication in vv. 15-26 to suggest that this passage may not all be from E. Joseph's brothers try two strategies to persuade him to forgive them (vv. 15-17; v. 18), he twice tells them not to be afraid (vv. 19 and 21), and his kindly reassurance of them is stated twice in different words in v. 21.

On this basis the existence of a J version of the final reconciliation between Joseph and his brothers could readily be presumed. Even if vv. 15-21 are regarded as a unity, their attribution to E is not as certain as was once thought. The more recent study of the Joseph-story, to which these verses form a very effective conclusion, has resulted in a widespread recognition that it is essentially a unity, apart from a few additions which derive not from parallel versions of the same story but either, perhaps, from different, probably much briefer accounts of how the ancestors of Israel came to be in Egypt or from redactional expansion of the main narrative. The credit for this 'turning of the tide', if that is what it is, must be given to a brief but characteristically incisive article by R. N. Whybray ('The Joseph Story and Pentateuchal Criticism', *VT* 18 [1968], pp. 522-28). For further references see Westermann, *Genesis 12–50* (EdF; Darmstadt, 1975), pp. 64-66; Blum, *Komposition*, pp. 230-34, esp. 230-31 nn. 3-5; Van Seters, *Prologue*, pp. 311-12.[2] It is implicit in this view that the expressions used for God are not a criterion for source-analysis within the Joseph-story, since 'Yahweh' and 'God' are both found within it. This means that what has in the past been seen as a strong reason for attributing Gen. 50.15-21 to E, e.g. by Gunkel (*Genesis*, p. 487), need not be so, and his other linguistic arguments also lose their force when the essential unity of the Joseph-story is acknowledged. If it is the case (as generally thought) that the Joseph-story was incorporated by J into his work, then these verses too will have formed part of that work.[3]

The case for multiple authorship in vv. 22-26 is arguably stronger than in vv. 15-21, though it is frequently overlooked.[4] Joseph's age

---

[2] The mistake of Whybray in his later work on the Pentateuch, as well as of the earlier critics, was to fail to recognize that the Joseph story is a special case. Acceptance that source criticism does not work in it (or in most of it – the case for two parallel narratives at the beginning and the end is still strong) is no reason for thinking that it will not produce plausible results elsewhere, any more than the opposite is the case: each section of the Pentateuch must be examined for itself, though not in total isolation from other sections.

[3] Rudolph, p. 175, and Van Seters, *Prologue*, pp. 323-24, naturally attribute all these verses (and vv. 22-26) to their J authors.

[4] Most recently by Van Seters, *Prologue*, pp. 323-24. Blum attributed vv. 22-26 initially to '(mehrere?) Redaktionschichten...die weit über die Vätergeschichten, ja über die Genesis hinausreichen' (*Komposition*, p. 255), but having concluded that v. 24 is Deuteronomistic (with Rendtorff), that vv. 24-25 are closely linked (with Lohfink) and likewise vv. 25 and 26b, and that v. 23 picks up the reference to

at his death is twice stated to have been 110 years (vv. 22 and 26), which is presumably why Gunkel, for example, attributed v. 22 to J (*Genesis*, p. 491): it is only surprising that he did not do the same with v. 23, which is closely connected with it. The repetition of 'will show concern' (Heb. *pāqōd yipqōd*) in Joseph's two parting sentences, one addressed to 'his brothers' (v. 24) and the other to the 'sons of Israel' (v. 25), is also unlikely to be due to a single narrator. Carpenter and Harford-Batttersby (p. 79) and Eissfeldt (*Hexateuch-synopse*, p. 106*) attributed v. 24 to J, which might be correct (cf. Exod. 3.16; but note also 13.19). Verses 25-26 have a clear narrative connection with other references to Joseph's bones and burial in later books (Exod. 13.19 and Josh. 24.32) and possibly also with Gen. 33.19, but the statement about Joseph's death duplicates part of Exod. 1.6. The most probable explanation of these features is that vv. 25-26 belong to one account of Joseph's death and vv. 22-23(24) to another, which is concluded by Exod. 1.6.

If this is correct, then Exod. 1.6 rounds off a narrative which has presented Joseph as the leading figure in what is, at the end, a united family, cared for by him and perhaps assured by him before his death that God would restore them to the land which he had promised on oath to their ancestors. Thus, while the beginning of Exodus has now a clear narrative link with the stories of the patriarchs, the end of Genesis reaffirms the theme of the yet to be

---

the 'fourth generation' in Gen. 15.16, which is Deuteronomistic or later, he (ibid., p. 259) assigned most of the passage to his '*D-Bearbeitung*'. The only exceptions appear to be (both!) the statements about Joseph's age in vv. 22b and 26a (p. 257 n. 88), which he thought might belong to a different *Bearbeitung*. It is notable that in Rendtorff's consideration of the chronological notices in Genesis, to which Blum refers here, these two statements stand clearly apart from the major groups of such notices distinguished by Rendtorff (*Problem*, pp. 135-36). In the light of this formal difference and the significance of '110 years' in Egyptian texts of some antiquity (cf. Vergote, *Joseph en Égypte*, pp. 200-201 [with refs.]) it is perhaps not as 'surprising' as Rendtorff found it that these verses have commonly been attributed to the older sources of the Pentateuch. In *Studien* Blum reverted to his initial view that several redactional layers were represented in vv. 22-26: v. 24 is from KD, v. 22a is from P, vv. 22b, 25-26 are from the 'Joshua 24 Bearbeitung' (pp. 363-65: v. 23 is not explicitly mentioned here). This analysis is simplified somewhat in 'Literarische Verbindung', pp. 148-51, where (in agreement with Schmid and Gertz) Blum finds no place for KD in the passage (or anywhere in Genesis) and divides it between P (vv. 22-23) and the later 'Hexateuch redaction' (vv. 24-26), to which Exod. 1.6 with its repeated notice of Joseph's death is also now attributed.

fulfilled divine promise which provides the theological bridge to the narratives which follow. Contrary to what at first appears to be the case, therefore, the non-Priestly Exodus story does in fact begin against the background of a strongly theological understanding of the situation of the people and their future destiny.

In the Priestly source the Joseph-story did not appear, and so Exod. 1.1-5 will have been the immediate sequel of a series of passages which bring the story of Jacob to its conclusion (Gen. 46.6-7; 47.5-6a, 7-11, 27b-28; 48.3-6; 49.1a, 28b-33; 50.12-13). Jacob and his family have come to Egypt and prospered, the divine promise of progeny and land has been recalled, Ephraim and Manasseh have been recognized as full members of the family/tribal alliance, and Jacob himself has been buried in the family tomb at Machpelah. Now the transition is made to the beginning of the history of the people Israel (Exod. 1.7) by a renewed listing of the tribal ancestors (cf. Gen. 35.22b-26) as those who made the journey, with their families, to Egypt with Jacob. In recent years a strong case has been made for seeing Exod. 1.1-5 (and v. 7) as belonging properly to the Priestly story of Jacob rather than the Exodus story. This is already suggested by the *waw* ('And') with which v. 1 begins in the Hebrew and the recapitulation of details from the Jacob-story in it. But P. Weimar has pointed also to what he sees as the carefully structured composition of the Priestly Jacob-story, with its three symmetrical parts ('Aufbau und Struktur der priesterschriftlichen Jakobsgeschichte', *ZAW* 86 [1974], pp. 174-203 [200-201]). On the one hand Exod. 1.1-5 forms an *inclusio* around the whole narrative with the list of Ishmael's sons in Gen. 25.12-17; on the other it parallels the list of Esau's descendants in Genesis 36, which also follows a (briefer) account of Esau's exploits under a general *toledot*-heading (cf. Gen. 36.1 with 37.2). Too much should perhaps not be made of patterns such as this, which often owe more to the eye of the beholder than the author's intention, but the tendency for sections of the Priestly narrative to end with a list of descendants (as exemplified in the two passages in Genesis mentioned by Weimar) is sufficiently widespread to lend some support to Weimar's case.[5] Such an ending to the Jacob-story

---

[5] Coats seems to agree: in his study of Exod. 1.1-14 as a 'structural transition' he describes vv. 1-6 as 'a summary conclusion for preceding traditions' (pp. 130-31), which defines the organization of the people who entered Egypt. As

underlines the tension between the situation in which the family of Jacob finds itself (prosperous in a foreign land), on the one hand, and its origin (they 'came' to Egypt) and the destiny promised to it (the possession of the land of Canaan; cf. Gen. 48.4) on the other. This may well have been intended by P as a reflection on the situation of the Jews in exile in Babylon.

> 1 And[a] these are the names of the sons of Israel[b] who came to Egypt – with Jacob they came, each man and his household[c]: 2 Reuben, Simeon, Levi, [and] Judah[d], 3 Issachar[e], Zebulun and Benjamin, 4 Dan and Naphtali, Gad and Asher. 5 The total of all those persons who were descended from[f] Jacob was seventy persons[g], as Joseph was already in Egypt[h]. 6 Now Joseph died, and all his brothers and that whole generation[i].

Notes on the Translation

a. The introductory ו (cf. Lev. 1.1; Num. 1.1) links Exodus formally to the preceding book of Genesis. In translations (so already in LXX and Vulg: see Text and Versions) it is commonly overlooked as a result of the secondary subdivision of the Tetrateuch into four separate books.

b. Here, in contrast to v. 7 and most other places, בני ישראל must refer to the immediate descendants of Jacob, Israel being his alternative name according to Gen. 32.28 (JE) and 35.10 (P). This usage is most common in the older source-material of Genesis, where it has traditionally been attributed to J (cf. also Exod. 32.13 MT), but it occurs in P three times in the set formula בכור ישראל (Exod. 6.14; Num. 1.20; 26.5) and possibly once elsewhere (Gen. 46.8).

c. The inverted word-order, with the subject preceding the verb, and asyndeton are typical of circumstantial clauses (JM §155nc, 159c).

d. The use of ו with the last item in a list (or part of a list) and not the others is a common alternative to the preferred repetition of it with each item after the first (JM §177o: also in v. 3). Here the construction in MT serves to distinguish the first four sons of Leah who were born before the sons of Bilhah and Zilpah from those born afterwards. But it is likely that this copula was not in the original text (see Text and Versions on the reading implied by LXX and Vulg).

such it bridges the gap, in an abbreviated form, between Jacob and his family in Canaan and Israel in Egypt, i.e. it performs the same function as, and summarizes, the Joseph-story.

e. The punctuation of יִשָּׂשכָר is a *Qere perpetuum*, at least in the Ben Asher tradition, which implies a consonantal text with only a single *sin* (presumably understanding the name as an imperfect Niphal of the verb סכר). The Ben Naphtali text reads יְשַׂשְׂכָר (cf. BDB, p. 441a; *Ges18*, p. 503a), and the Samaritan pronunciation *yāšīšākar* (*Ges18*) retains the repetition of the sibilant character which is implied by the Samaritan mss. At Qumran this is also the normal spelling (4QGen-Exod[a], 4QExod[b] ad loc., 4Q484): on the possible etymologies see *ABD* 3, p. 577.

f. Lit., 'came out from the thigh of', where 'thigh' is presumably a euphemism for the genitalia: the same idiom appears in Gen. 46.26 and Judg. 8.30: compare also the oath-ritual in Gen. 24.2, 9; 47.29. To render 'hip' here for the sake of a connection with Gen. 32.26, 32-33 (Siebert-Hommes, *Let the Daughters*, pp. 31, 39) ignores the different uses of Heb. ירך. For the construct relation expressing motion after a participle cf. JM §121n.

g. Heb. נפש, used as often for the whole person (or even animal, Gen. 2.19), and not just for a spiritual 'soul'. This usage is particularly common in Priestly and related texts (cf. BDB, p. 660), but it is also found elsewhere in Biblical Hebrew (cf. Wolff, *Anthropologie*, pp. 41-44 [ET, pp. 21-22]; *THAT* 2, 88-90 = *TLOT* 2, pp. 755-56).

h. The inverted word-order (cf. note c) points to a subordinate status for the clause: 'Joseph being (already) in Egypt', i.e. the number is seventy if he (and his family) are included (cf. Childs, Houtman).

i. Heb. דור is used, like Eng. 'generation', both for a period of time and (as here) for all those who are alive at a particular time (cf. Gen. 7.1; Judg. 2.10). In view of the sequel in v. 8 it is natural to see the Egyptians being included as well as the Israelites.

Explanatory Notes

1. The introductory 'And', though contrary to the best English style, is a reminder that the books from Genesis to Numbers form a single literary composition. At the same time the compiler underlines the transition to a new episode in his story by recapitulating in a few words the situation which had been reached in the closing chapters of Genesis, to set the scene for what is to follow. Once more the names of the tribal ancestors, the sons of Jacob/Israel, are listed, recalling the 'family history' of Genesis 12–50 as a whole, but specifically their journey to Egypt in a time of famine, with all their dependents and livestock (Gen. 46.5-7 JE/P). A much fuller account of the family is included in Gen. 46.8-27, a probably later passage to which there are several similarities in these verses, both in MT and in the secondary witnesses to the text (see Text and Versions). The heading to the list in this verse begins with a formula, 'These are the names...', which is widely attested in Priestly passages in the Pentateuch (Gen. 25.13 etc.), but also in 2 Sam. 5.14; 23.8; 1 Kgs 4.8. For 'came to Egypt' of Jacob and his sons cf. Gen. 46.6, 8, 26-27; 47.5LXX; 48.5 (all P), and in other connections, e.g., Gen. 12.11, 14; 41.57 (all JE). The formula 'each man with his household' occurs only here in the Pentateuch, but cf. 1 Sam. 27.3 and 2 Sam. 2.3. The stylistic device whereby a word is repeated as part of a more precise specification (here 'who came...they came') has been shown by M. Paran to be a frequent and distinctive characteristic of Priestly style (*Forms of the Priestly Style*, pp. 47-97; cf. McEvenue, *Narrative Style*, who calls it a 'short-circuit inclusion' [e.g. pp. 43, 51-52]), and he cites the very close parallel to this example in Gen. 7.16 (p. 67). As he acknowledges, however, this device is also found occasionally in non-Priestly passages in the Pentateuch.

2-4. The listing and sub-division of the names of Jacob's sons is according to their mothers: the sons of Leah (vv. 2-3a), a son of Rachel (v. 3b), the sons of Bilhah, Rachel's maidservant (v. 4a) and the sons of Zilpah, Leah's maidservant (v. 4b). The arrangement is almost identical to that of the list in Gen. 35.23-26, where (unlike here) the names of the mothers are included: only in the inclusion of Joseph and in the absence of the further sub-division of the sons of Leah in MT (see Note d above) does that passage differ from this one. Both these passages follow, in relation to the maidservants' children, the order of the narrative in Genesis 29–30, and this passage also does so, in the MT, in the separation of Leah's sons into two groups. 1 Chr. 2.1-2 is also very similar, except for the strange position of Dan there. The much fuller list of the descendants of Jacob in Gen. 46.8-27 is structured in a broadly similar way, but there the descendants of each maidservant are included immediately after those of her mistress, so that vv. 8-18 deal with Leah's side of the family and vv. 19-25 deal with Rachel's side. This difference is an argument against the view (see the introduction to this section) that this list is based on that in Genesis 46.

5. The reckoning of all the descendants of Jacob as seventy (by implication at this stage of the story) elaborates the statement that each of the brothers had a household (v. 1) or family of his own – even Benjamin, whose youth was a prominent theme of the Joseph-story (cf. Gen. 43.8; 44.30-34). The figure 'seventy' is found elsewhere in Gen. 46.27 (at the end of a detailed list, complete with sub-totals) and in Deut. 10.22 (where no further details are given). In the extant form of the biblical narrative it is natural to see this figure as a reference back to Gen. 46.27 (this is certainly how it was understood by those – see the notes on Text and Versions – who amended the figure to 'seventy-five'), but in the light of Deut. 10.22 and other occurrences of the figure 'seventy' such a specific and precise interpretation may not have been originally intended. Seventy is the number of the elders of Israel (24.1), the vassals claimed by Adonibezek of Jerusalem (Judg. 1.7), the sons of Gideon (Judg. 8.30 etc.), the descendants of Abdon (Judg. 12.14), the sons of Ahab (2 Kgs 10.1) and, in Ugaritic mythology, the sons of Asherah (*KTU* 1.4.6.46: cf. F.C. Fensham, 'The Numeral Seventy in the Old Testament and the Family of Jerubbaal, Ahab, Panammuwa and Athirat', *PEQ* 109 [1977], pp. 113-15, for further parallels and discussion)[6]. It was clearly from one point of view a figure for a large company, but it was not a great multitude and in Deut. 10.22 it is used of the large family which in the course of time grew into a great people: it corresponds there to the 'few in number' of Deut. 26.5 who became 'a great nation'. The meaning here may be the same; cf. the reference in v. 7 to growth into a great and mighty people. Not all the family of Jacob had come down to Egypt with him; Joseph, the author concisely reminds us, was already there – the story has been told at length in Genesis 37–45.

6. The reference to Joseph's death, in the present form of the text, also belongs to the recapitulation or résumé of what was previously narrated, in this case at the very end of the book of Genesis (50.26, a verse drawn originally from a different source-document: see the introductory remarks above). Joseph is mentioned again in v. 8 and in 13.19. For the death of a leading figure marking the transition to

---

[6] The number of the descendants of Shem, Ham and Japhet in Gen. 10 was also reckoned at seventy (B.Sukkah 55b, Midr.Tehillim 9: cf. Blenkinsopp, *Pentateuch*, p. 144), and this calculation may be behind the Masoretic form of the text of Deut. 32.8, which states that the boundaries of the nations were fixed according to the number of the sons of Israel (בני ישראל as in v. 1 here). The reading in 4QDeut[j] (בני אלהים: *DJD* XIV, p. 90, pl. xxiii, fr. 34), which appears to lie behind LXX's υἱῶν (mss and OL ἀγγέλων) θεοῦ and is probably older, makes reference to the same mythological tradition as is attested at Ugarit. Tg[j] (translated in S.R. Driver, *Deuteronomy* [ICC; Edinburgh, 3rd ed., 1902], pp. 355-56) appears to know both readings.

a new cycle of tradition Vriezen compared the somewhat similar language of Judg. 2.8-10 ('Exodusstudien', pp. 335-39; cf. also Josh. 1.2). Having briefly narrowed its concerns to this one person, the résumé reverts to the larger picture: 'and all his brothers and that whole generation'. Houtman has noted that the reference to Joseph's 'brothers', the sons of Jacob, is the last appearance in Exodus of the family setting which dominated Genesis 12–50 (p. 229: for the character of these chapters as 'family narratives' see Westermann, 'Arten der Erzählung in der Genesis', in his *Forschung am Alten Testament* [Neukirchen, 1964], pp. 9-91).

Text and Versions

ואלה (1.1) The *waw* of MT is supported by SP, Tg^{O,J,N}, Sy and two very late Greek mss. The remaining Greek and all the Latin witnesses do not represent it. 4QExod^b is not extant at the beginning of the verse, but 4QpalGen-Exod^l reads אלה (without *waw*) at the beginning of a line. The possibility that the preceding line contained a majuscule *waw* (*DJD* IX, p. 26) cannot be excluded, but it is not supported by any other examples from this manuscript.

יעקב (1.1) 4QExod^b and LXX add אביהם, harmonizing with Gen. 46.8.

ויהודה (1.2) Almost all LXX witnesses and Vulg have no equivalent to the *waw*, thus treating all the sons of Leah and Rachel listed here as a single group concluded by Benjamin, and a minority of LXX witnesses do not have καί also before Benjamin and Naphtali, thus eliminating the other subdivisions of the sons of Jacob which are present in MT. By contrast (and in part with the same effect), the copula is inserted before all the names which do not have it in MT by SP in vv. 2-3, by Sy in vv. 2-4 and by Eth and (in three cases out of four) Ar in vv. 3-4. 4QpalGen-Exod^l and 4QExod^b, so far as they are extant, support MT in this respect, but 4QGen-Exod^a may agree with the SP reading in the two cases (both in v. 3) where it survives. It is probable that the nuanced use of the copula in MT is more original than the readings which consistently use it or do not use it, but the reading attested by LXX and Vulg may be the most original of all: it is difficult to see why the copula would have been omitted in this one place, whereas its addition can be explained by a wish to reflect the narrative of Genesis 29–30 more closely.

ובנימן (1.3) 4QExod^b inserts יוסף before this word and omits v. 5b (see below), incorporating Joseph into the main list of Jacob's sons as in Gen. 46.8-27 (and 35.23-26), but in contradiction to the heading here.

ויהי (1.5) SP ויהיו, which fits more smoothly with the context and especially with the collective sense of נפש here. The reading is doubtless secondary: nothing can be based on the plural forms in the ancient Versions. The Qumran mss are not extant at this point, but the uncertain reading of the

130   EXODUS 1–18

singular participle [יֹ]צֵא in 4QpalGen-Exod¹ fr. 39 (*DJD* IX, p. 47) would presumably reflect a different kind of attempt to create consistency.

יֹצְאֵי יֶרֶךְ יַעֲקֹב (1.5)   LXX ἐξ Ἰακώβ. In Gen. 46.26 and Judg. 8.30 the same Heb. idiom is precisely rendered, which suggests that here LXX may have had a different *Vorlage*, perhaps מִיַּעֲקֹב (for the abrupt construction cf. Num. 3.12; Josh. 12.4), rather than simply being paraphrastic. 4QExod[b] also seems likely, from the space available, to have had a shorter text here (*DJD* XII, p. 85, proposes לְיַעֲקֹב, as in Gen. 46.26 [cf. v. 27]: but LXX does not use ἐξ there).

שִׁבְעִים (1.5)   The figure 'seventy' is supported by SP, Tg[O,J,N] and Sy, but 4QGen-Exod[a] has נפש וחמש [שבעים] and 4QExod[b] has חמש ושבעים (see already Cross, *Ancient Library*, p. 137 n. 31). The total of 'seventy-five' has long been known from LXX here and, derivatively, Acts 7.14. The same figure occurs in LXX at Gen. 46.27, in a passage which makes it clear that the inclusion of five additional members of Joseph's family in the LXX (inserted on the basis of Gen. 50.22-26 and other passages) is the cause of the larger figure. No Qumran mss contain Genesis 46, but it may be presumed that a similar development took place in Hebrew texts of that passage. The number 'seventy-five' is clearly secondary, both because of the compilation of names from different passages in Genesis 46LXX and because in the two Qumran mss that exhibit the reading the position of the numeral חמש, 'five', differs, once before שבעים and once after – a classic indication of a secondary reading.[7]

ויוסף היה במצרים (1.5)   These words are omitted in 4QExod[b] (which includes Joseph in v. 3: see the note above) and are placed at the beginning of the verse in LXX. MT is supported by SP, 4QGen-Exod[a], 4QpalGen-Exod¹ and the other Versions. Cross argued that the reading of 4QExod[b] was the most ancient, citing (cf. the previous note) the divergent placing of the longer reference to Joseph in LXX and MT etc. (*Ancient Library*, p. 137 n. 31, followed in *DJD* XII, p. 85). When the variant is as long as this, however, it is unlikely that two scribes would add it independently in exactly the same words, and it is most probable (unless it originated as a marginal gloss) that it was moved by LXX (or its *Vorlage*) from where it is in MT to what seemed a more appropriate position, adjacent to the other names. The objection to the reading of 4QExod[b] is that it is in outright contradiction to v. 1: Joseph did not go to Egypt either with Jacob or with a household. It is inconceivable that the original author of these verses would have included his name in the main list.

---

[7] Against D. Barthélemy, 'Les tiqquné sopherim et la critique textuelle de l'Ancien Testament', in *Congress Volume: Bonn* (VTSup 9; Leiden, 1963), pp. 285-304, who claimed that to see 'seventy-five' as more original was 'plus économique' (302).

Chapter 1.7-22

The Growth of Israel Despite Egyptian Countermeasures

Whereas vv. 1-6 provided a résumé or summary of events narrated at the end of Genesis, vv. 7-22 represent the opening of the Exodus story itself. Egypt is now ruled over by a new king (v. 8) and he is the initiator of the action throughout this section: he, or those who either obey or disobey his orders, are the subject of most of the main verbs. Four times in all he or 'the Egyptians' launch hostile measures against the people of Israel (vv. 8-11, 13-14, 15-16, 22), twice in the form of hard labour and twice in attempts to eradicate the male children as soon as they are born. After the first and third of these measures, however, their futility is underlined by a reference to the continued increase in numbers of the Israelites (vv. 12, 20), picking up the theme of a large and growing population which is introduced at the beginning of the section (vv. 7 and 9). This theme, which thus appears as a counterpoise to the Egyptian mistreatment of the people throughout the section, clearly takes up a major aspect of the promises to the patriarchs in Genesis (see the note on v. 7), and there is at least an implication of divine action in it (explicit in v. 21). But from here on it almost entirely disappears (12.37 is a rare reappearance of it) – it has served its purpose, in fact the dual purpose of transforming the family of Jacob into a great people and giving a preliminary indication that Pharaoh's grand plans can be thwarted – and the following narrative is dominated by the oppression of God's people and the struggle for their release. It is significant that there is no indication that the labours of the people were discontinued and that when the Hebrew midwives refuse to carry out Pharaoh's orders (v. 17) he simply puts the matter into the hands of his own people (v. 22).

From a formal point of view the whole passage is narrative, with waw consecutive imperfect forms contributing the main connecting links everywhere except in v. 7 (where the S-V word order introduces the new episode in the story) and in v. 12a (where durative imperfects express the progressive growth in numbers). In vv. 8-10 a speech by Pharaoh sets the narrative in motion; a further speech by him in vv. 15-16 is intended to do the same, but fails because of the midwives' refusal to obey him, and a disputation follows in vv. 18-19; after Pharaoh's final speech (v. 22) no explicit indication is given of whether his orders were obeyed or not, but the beginning of the following section (2.1-10) seems to assume that they were.[1] G.W. Coats (pp. 21-29; cf. 'Structural Transition', pp. 129-42) recognises the two main parts of the passage (see below) as both functioning as expositions or introductions for what follows: vv. 7-14 (as well as vv. 1-6) for the Exodus traditions as a whole, and vv. 15-22 for the Moses adoption narrative. While there certainly is a link to ch. 2 by means of the threat to young infants, this should not obscure the fact that all of ch. 1 is a narrative about the people as a whole, whereas ch. 2 (and also chs. 3–4) has a narrower primary focus on Moses. A distinction can perhaps be made between vv. 15-21 and v. 22, with the latter making the transition to 2.1-10 (cf. Weimar, 'Exodus 1,1–2,10', pp. 183-84).

The passage falls into three sections: a brief statement about the growth in Israel's numbers (v. 7); the imposition of forced labour on them by the Egyptians (vv. 8-14); and the attempt to eliminate all their newborn males (vv. 15-22). The language of v. 7 is full of terms which recur in Priestly passages in Genesis (see the Explanatory Note) and vv. 13-14 fit awkwardly in their context – they repeat the essence of vv. 11-12 and after them a new kind of oppression is introduced without any explanation – as well as displaying some linguistic features that reappear in the major Priestly passage in 6.2-9. These verses are therefore generally agreed to contain extracts from P, and the argument in relation to vv. 13-14 favours the view that P was an independent source-document and not a redactional layer, as is sometimes thought (see for discussion of E. Blum's version of this latter approach my essay 'Reflections', and more generally the Introduction, section 4[ii]).[2] This need not mean that the whole of these verses is from P. The word 'and became…

---

[1] This is a frequent feature of biblical narrative: cf. Gen. 12.13; Josh. 10.18-19; and further W. Baumgartner, 'Ein Kapitel vom hebräischen Erzählungsstil', in H. Schmidt (ed.), *EYXAPIΣTHPION* (FS H. Gunkel; FRLANT 36; Göttingen, 1923), pp. 145-57 (146-48).

[2] For fuller discussion of the Priestly section of this passage see Weimar, *Untersuchungen*, pp. 25-36; Gertz, *Tradition und Redaktion*, pp. 352-54.

strong' (*ʿāṣam*) in v. 7 is not found elsewhere in P and a related adjective occurs in v. 9. This word may have stood in a non-Priestly introduction to the narrative, perhaps with 'they multiplied' ('many' in v. 9 is related to it): so Wellhausen, *Composition*, pp. 61, 68-69; Holzinger ('Man kann fragen...'), Eissfeldt, Beer, Van Seters, *Life of Moses*, pp. 19-20 (Weimar [*Untersuchungen*, p. 36] attributed these words to a source used by P).

Schmidt (pp. 11-12) rejects this view and sees 'and became...strong' as a late redactional addition based on v. 9 (as also in v. 20 – see below). It is true, as he says, that 'and became...strong' alone would not fit well between the non-Priestly material in vv. 6 and 8, but it is not difficult to imagine a somewhat fuller text, similar to but not as long as the P version in the rest of v. 7, from which the redactor might have drawn a word which made the link to what follows stronger; and such a text would help to bridge the chronological gap which otherwise remains between vv. 6 and 8 in the non-Priestly material. C. Levin attributes the whole of v. 7 (like v. 6) to a late redactional level, noting that it repeats Gen. 47.27 (P) and combines elements of Priestly and 'Yahwistic' vocabulary (*Der Jahwist*, p. 315). Neither of his arguments is compelling. As for vv. 13-14, it has commonly been thought (cf. Wellhausen, *Composition*, pp. 61-62, 68-69; Holzinger, Eissfeldt, Beer) that the detailed specification of the work 'on clay and bricks and on all kinds of work in the fields' (or even the whole of v. 14a: Carpenter and Harford-Battersby) was out of place in P and must be derived from one of the other sources; or alternatively that these words come from a late redactor who gathered together from elsewhere such information as he could find about the nature of the Israelites' labours in Egypt (cf. 5.7-19; Deut. 11.10: so Schmidt). But such lists are very much in the repertoire of P, as is the repetitive summary at the end of v. 14, which Wellhausen unnecessarily wanted to link directly to v. 13 (ibid.) and others have attributed (at least) in part to a redactor (Holzinger, Eissfeldt, Noth). The reasons given are not sufficient in this case to justify further subdivision.

The remainder of the section comprises two brief but coherent narratives, in which no significant basis can be found for the interweaving of two parallel accounts (contra, for vv. 8-12, Wellhausen, *Composition*, p. 69; Baentsch [pp. 1-2], Eissfeldt [L and J], and Beer). It is more generally held that while vv. 8-12 are from J, vv. 15-22 are (substantially at least) from E (so Wellhausen and most others: Van Seters, *Life*, pp. 23-29, seems to regard vv. 15-22 as entirely J, but his arguments are mainly based on v. 22). The two narratives do not presuppose one another, and a series of indicators associate the sub-units with passages in Genesis attributed to the two sources (see e.g. Holzinger, pp. 1-2; Beer, p. 15) and perhaps distinguish them from one another (the size of the population implied; the use of 'Israelites' in vv. 8-12 and 'Hebrews' in vv. 15-22). To the items commonly mentioned may be added the references to the fear of God in vv. 17 and 21 (see the Explanatory Note on v. 17).

The end of the second narrative shows some signs of multiple authorship, though these have been differently interpreted. God's favour to the midwives is recounted twice (vv. 20a and 21b), which led Eissfeldt to attribute v. 20a to E (cf. 'God') and the rest of the passage to his L. Wellhausen, on the other hand, found v. 20b intrusive between the references to the midwives and attributed it to J (with which its language seemed to cohere; cf. v. 9), and likewise v. 22, which he took to be a variant on vv. 15-21 (so also Noth, p. 12, ET, p. 23; L. Schmidt, 'Vorpriesterliche Verbindung', p. 34). The former suggestion, however, creates a doublet with v. 12 (unless with Wellhausen, but without good grounds, one attributes it to E or with Carpenter and Harford-Battersby treats the whole of v. 14a as J, so that v. 20b provides the antithesis to it and not to Pharaoh's first measures), while the latter (as Holzinger saw, p. 2) is both unnecessary and runs counter to the apparent link between v. 22 and 2.1-10, which is generally attributed to E. Schmidt (pp. 18-20) defends the E origin of v. 20bα (cf. Gen. 50.20) but attributes 'and became very strong' to a redactor, as he does in v. 7. The argument has more to be said for it here, not least because of the curious switch from a singular subject and verb to a plural one immediately afterwards. Schmidt sees v. 21 as a secondary elaboration of v. 20a on the basis of v. 17 (which is possible: but see the Explanatory Note on v. 21 for a different view) and remains undecided whether v. 22 is from J or E, just as he does for 2.1-10 (cf. p. 64).

The upheavals in Pentateuch criticism of the past decades have understandably not left the analysis of this passage untouched. Already in Schmidt's commentary (the relevant fascicle was published in 1974) a tendency to ascribe brief 'intrusive' elements to a redactor rather than seeing them as fragments of major source-documents has been observed. Others have increasingly extended this approach so as no longer to envisage the combination of parallel source-documents at all.[3] Blum originally did not examine the composition of 1.7-22 in detail, but he leant towards the view that it was ('apart from isolated later compositional elements') all derived from a single *vita Mosis*, which originated in the late monarchy period and formed the main narrative basis for the Deuteronomistic composition in Exodus (*Studien*, pp. 216-17: on this point 'Literarische Verbindung', pp. 146-48, apparently reaffirms his earlier

---

[3] On the following paragraphs see also my essay 'The Transition from Genesis', esp. pp. 69-71.

view). The 'compositional elements' to which he refers are, first, v. 8, which with v. 6 he saw as a Deuteronomistic 'bridge' between the patriarchal era and the story of the Exodus (pp. 102-103 [so also Carr, *Fractures*, p. 272 n. 112]: more recently [in 'Literarische Verbindung', pp. 148-49] Blum has accepted the view of Schmid and Gertz [below] that both verses are post-Priestly); and, second, (most of) the Priestly vv. 7 and 13-14, which in line with his overall theory he regards as part of a compositional layer rather than a source: for him these verses (like vv. 1-5) give the opening of the Exodus-story a 'compositional "rigidity"' of its own and bring the account of Pharaoh's oppression of Israel to an impressive climax by the five occurrences of the root ʿbd in vv. 13-14 (pp. 239-42: for criticism of Blum's view of P see my 'Reflections', and subsequently Carr, *Fractures*, pp. 118-29, and Schmid, *Erzväter*, pp. 53-54 [with references in n. 54], 372).

Konrad Schmid, who maintains that a literary link between the patriarchal narratives and the Exodus story was created for the first time by P, to which he attributes vv. 7 and 13-14 (op. cit., pp. 70-71, 234 n. 362), regards the whole of the rest of Exod. 1 as post-Priestly (pp. 69-73): older material begins only with the story of Moses' birth and adoption in ch. 2. The arguments for this remarkable conclusion (which is, however, essential if Schmid's overall theory is to stand) are as follows: (i) Exod. 1.1-8 consists in essence of repetitions of material from the end of Genesis, which are likely to have been required only when Exodus was made into a separate book (so also Levin, *Jahwist*, p. 315); (ii) vv. 6-8 constitute the real link between Genesis and Exodus, and within it v. 7 is the central element; (iii) v. 7 anticipates and is presupposed by the motivation for Pharaoh's action in vv. 9-12 and the reference to the population increase in v. 20; (iv) vv. 15-21 are a secondary redactional addition to the preceding narrative, designed to counter its xenophobic polemic – the God-fearing midwives being understood to be Egyptians ('cf. also explicitly Josephus, *Ant.* 2.9.2'), despite the counter-indications in 'MT', which are attributed to a subsequent 'Israel-centred narrowing' of the story's perspective. These arguments are full of holes: (i) the repeated material is in fact confined to vv. 1-6, and to some extent v. 7, as Schmid subsequently allows. As for vv. 1-5, it has already been argued (see the introduction to vv. 1-6) that it is probably the 'parallel' in Gen. 46.8-27 which is the later of the two passages, while the overlap between v. 6 and Gen. 50.26 (as Schmid recognises [p. 70], Exod. 1.6 adds some new information) fits well into a series of doublets at the end of Genesis in the non-Priestly material. In any case, the occurrence of repetition need by no means imply that the Pentateuch had by now been 'divided up' into separate books: this is clear from the case of Gen. 47.27 and Exod. 1.7, both regularly attributed to P, in which no such division existed. (ii) It is by no means clear that vv. 6-8 comprise a single unit of which v. 7 is the original core: v. 6, as has often been noted (cf. Schmidt, p. 10), breaks the sequence between vv. 1-5 and v. 7, while v. 7 breaks the natural link between v. 6 and v. 8 (ibid., pp. 12-13). Moreover, there is nothing to suggest that vv. 6 and 8 are dependent upon v. 7. (iii) First, it should be noted that v. 20 in no sense presupposes v. 7: it repeats part of its content and is therefore likely, if anything, to be of an independent origin. As for vv. 9-12, it is not merely to preserve a theory that commentators since Wellhausen have suggested that in v. 7 'and became...strong' is a portion of the non-Priestly narrative introduction to v. 9, but because in the context of a verse which is otherwise entirely made up of familiar Priestly expressions this word stands out like a sore thumb. Nor does v. 9 necessarily require such an explicit basis in the narrative as v. 7 provides: it is a common stylistic device in popular narrative for a situation to be first introduced in the words of a speech by one of the characters (cf. Gen. 50.24: so Carr, 'Genesis in Relation to the Moses Story: Diachronic and Synchronic Perspectives', in A. Wénin [ed.], *The Book of Genesis* [BETL 155; Leuven, 2001], pp. 273-95 [291]). (iv) Schmid's account of vv. 15-21 is pure speculation based on a disputable and probably mistaken view about the ethnicity of the midwives (see the Explanatory Note on v. 15). It is, in fact, natural to link the restrained references to population increase in Exod. 1.9-12 and 20 to the non-Priestly promise-texts in Genesis (so Carr, ibid., pp. 292-93, where further objections to Schmid's view can be found). Not only is Schmid's extreme conclusion about Exodus 1 unjustified: a closer examination of the evidence here undermines his whole theory.

J.C. Gertz has put forward a view of the development of Pentateuchal tradition which is in general terms quite similar to that of Schmid, though founded much more on a detailed study of the text of Exodus 1-14 (*Tradition*: for the acknowledged proximity to Schmid see pp. 5, 385). In relation to the present passage, however, Gertz takes a much more traditional view, attributing most of vv. 11-22 to an 'old Exodus narrative' (vv. 20b-21a are regarded as redactional) and emphasising their coherence, both as a unit and in relation to the Moses-story which follows. Gertz attributes vv. 8-10 to the 'Endredaktion' which combined the P source with an older Exodus-story, like Schmid on the grounds that it presupposes v. 7 (on this argument see the discussion above), but also apparently because the Hithpael of $ḥkm$, 'deal wisely' (v. 10), is only otherwise attested in Qoh. 7.16 and Sir. 10.26 – where the occurrences are so few and there are no other 'late' linguistic features in the speech this does not count for very much – and because of tensions between vv. 8-10 and 11-12 which earlier scholars had attributed to different sources or traditions. The 'tensions' are, however, not that significant and the result of Gertz's analysis is to leave the measures taken against Israel without any explanation and indeed to leave the whole 'old Exodus story' without an introduction. Finally, Gertz claims that vv. 8-10 presuppose the combination of forced labour and infanticide, which were originally separate, but this would (even if true) be no justification for attributing them to the *Endredaktion* rather than the 'old Exodus story'.

The older view, that vv. 8-12 come from J and vv. 15-22 from E, which has been largely reaffirmed in the studies of L. Schmidt ('Vorpriesterliche Verbindung') and Baden ('From Joseph to Moses'), remains most likely. Indeed for vv. 8-12, which are presupposed in 2.11-23aα, a passage which has clear connections to the distinct J narrative in chs. 3–4, it is practically certain. The case for an E origin for vv. 15-22 remains strong, but the passage lacks the direct narrative links to later passages that would confirm it. Nevertheless Baden has recently argued that this story has to be understood as a functional parallel to vv. 8-12 rather than a continuation of it – both demonstrate the inability of Pharaoh's interventions to prevent the growth of the Israelite population – and highlighted the typically E association of 'the fear of God' with divine approval (pp. 134, 139-41). To push further back into the origins of the tradition is difficult. At the heart of it there appears to be a historical memory of oppression in Egypt (vv. 11-12), which is described in language that has some echoes of Israel's own monarchy and which is reproduced also by P (vv. 13-14). Both the introduction to this recollection and the story which follows it appear to belong more to the genre of popular *Sage*, with, on the one hand, a picture of Pharaoh's court which is both unrealistic and caricatured and, on the other, an admiration for the ingenuity, boldness and uprightness of very ordinary members of the community (the midwives) (for features in vv. 15-21 shared with other 'deception stories' in the OT see R.C. Culley, 'Structural Analysis: Is it Done with Mirrors?', *Int* 28 [1974], pp. 165-81 [171-81]). The reference to 'Hebrews' may point to a north Israelite origin for at least vv. 15-22.

The theological dimension of the passage should not be overlooked. It is implicit especially in the references to the people's increase in numbers, indeed initially in their formation as a people (see the Note on v. 7; cf. v. 9); it is explicit in the rewarding of the midwives for their courageous 'fear of God' (vv. 17, 20-21). In addition Weimar has pointed out that the antithesis between life and death in vv. 15-21 (or better 15-22), which he regards on unconvincing structural grounds as the central 'bridge' passage of the opening of the book in 1.1–2.10, anticipates one of the major themes of Exodus, namely the liberation of Israel and the death of many Egyptians ('Exodus 1,1–2,10', pp. 192-93, 200-204).

7 *The Israelites were fruitful and spread everywhere*[a], *they multiplied* [and became] *exceedingly*[b] [strong], *and the land was full of them*[c]. 8 A new king arose over Egypt, who had no knowledge of Joseph[d], 9 and he said to his people: 'See, the people [of the Israelites] are too many and too strong for us[e]. 10 Come then[f], let us deal wisely with them; otherwise they may multiply and, in the event of war[g], they may even[h] be added to[i] our enemies, fight against us and go up[j] out of the land.' 11 So they put overseers of labour gangs[k] in charge of them, to cause them hardship by the tasks which they imposed. They built cities with storehouses[l] for Pharaoh[m], Pithom and Ramesses.[n] 12 But the more hardship they caused them[o] the more they multiplied[o] and the more they increased[o], so that [the Egyptians] were in dread[p] of the Israelites. 13 *So the Egyptians imposed labour*[q] *harshly*[r] *on the Israelites,* 14 *and made their lives bitter*[s] *by their hard labour, on clay and bricks*[t] *and on all kinds of work in the fields – all the labour for them*[u] *to which they harshly subjected them*[v]. [15 Then the king of Egypt said to the Hebrew midwives[w], one of whom was called Shiphrah and the other Puah – 16 he said, 'When you are helping the Hebrew women to give birth, you must look at the sexual organs[x]: if it is a boy, you must kill him, but if it is a girl she may live[y]'. 17 But the midwives feared[z] God and did not do as the king of Egypt ordered them, but let the boys[aa] live. 18 The king of Egypt called the midwives and said to them: 'Why[bb] have you done this, and let the boys live?' 19 The midwives replied to Pharaoh: 'Because[cc] the Hebrew women are not like the Egyptian women, for they are strong[dd]: before the midwife comes to them they give birth[ee]'. 20 God dealt kindly with the midwives, and the people multiplied and became very strong. 21 So[ff], because the midwives feared God, he gave them households[gg]. 22 But Pharaoh ordered all his people: 'Every boy who is born[hh] you shall throw[ii] into the Nile[jj], but every girl you shall allow to live'.]

Notes on the Translation

a. Heb. וישרצו. The verb שָׁרַץ and the related noun שֶׁרֶץ are almost always used of animals which appear in large numbers, especially small ones (Deut. 14.19), rather than humans: e.g. of fish in Gen. 1.20-21 and of the plague of frogs in Exod. 7.28JE. Where the verb is used of humans (only here and in Gen. 9.7P), there is probably an implied comparison to the way in which some kinds of animals congregate in great numbers. For the combination with 'were fruitful' and 'multiplied' cf. Gen 8.17P as well as 9.7.

b. Literally 'very very' (במאד מאד). Elsewhere only in Gen. 17.2, 6, 20 (all P) and Ezek. 9.9; 16.13 (the repetition of מאד without the ב is more widespread). For other examples of intensification by repetition see JM §141k.

c. For the use of the accusative pronoun with a passive (Niphal) verb here see JM §128c.

d. The precise sense of לא ידע, 'had no knowledge of', here is debated. As well as its straightforward cognitive meaning Heb. ידע has, especially with a personal object, stronger senses such as 'acknowledge' and 'care for' (see in addition to the lexica *TWAT* 3, 498-500 = *TDOT* 5, pp. 468-70; *THAT* 1, 689-99 = *TLOT*, 508-21). Hence it has been suggested that the behaviour of Pharaoh may be due not merely to factual ignorance (as a result of the lapse of time, perhaps: so Schmidt, p. 32) but to deliberate disregard (Tg[O,J,N,F], Rashi; cf. Houtman, pp. 222, 234-36: Pharaoh 'refused to honour the memory' of Joseph out of 'disregard'). The problem with this is that, with perhaps only one exception (Deut. 33.9), this extension of meaning seems to be limited to divine–human relationships: where human relationships are involved other idioms are used.

e. The traditional rendering (still favoured by Houtman and the NRSV) is 'more in number and stronger than us', giving מן its frequent comparative sense: in this case Pharaoh's statement would presumably have to be understood as hyperbole. But the translation given here, which is based on a well-known Heb. idiom (BDB, p. 582b, JM §141i; cf. Gen. 26.16), is equally possible and generally preferred today (e.g. Childs, Schmidt, RSV, NJPS, REB). עצום and the related verb עָצַם can also mean '(be) numerous', but the meaning 'strong' is well established for the root in classical Heb. (cf. Deut. 8.17; Isa. 40.29: *Ges18*, pp. 1001-1002; *TWAT* 6, 310-26 = *TDOT* 11, pp. 289-303) and is very appropriate here (and in vv. 7 and 20) after רב and רבה. Cognates in Ug. also have the meaning 'power(ful)' (*DULAT*, pp. 197-98). 'Strength in numbers' is evidently meant by the present phrase.

f. Heb. הבה, the emphatic singular imperative of יהב, 'give', a verb which is rare in Hebrew, though frequent in Aramaic. Here, as in Gen. 11.3-4, 7; 38.16 (all J), it is used idiomatically as a hortatory interjection, even with reference to a plural addressee.

g. The exact reading and translation of this phrase are uncertain. MT תקראנה (from קרא II = קרה, 'meet, befall, happen') is a third (or second) person fem. pl. form which could only agree with the singular subject מלחמה if the latter were taken in a collective sense, 'wars' (so Schmidt: cf. Tg[N]), but a single episode seems to be intended. Cassuto suggested that the form should be read as a third person fem. sing. with an energic ending, as found sometimes in Ugaritic and Arabic: so also JM §61f, comparing תשלחנה in Judg. 5.26 (see also B. Lindars, *Judges 1–5* [Edinburgh, 1995], p. 278). This rare form, if it is indeed the original reading, must have become unintelligible already in antiquity, as the ancient Versions give it no support but (apart from Tg[N]) render the alternative reading preserved in SP, which seems more likely to be original (see Text and Versions). M. Dahood, 'Hebrew–Ugaritic Lexicography IX', *Bib* 52 (1971), pp. 337-56 (348-49), regarded it as a Hophal of קרא I with an energic ending, in the sense 'when war is declared'. But neither the Hiphil nor the Hophal of קרא I is attested; קרא I is never used with מלחמה as its object; and the proposal involves a purely conjectural change to the vowels.

h. Heb. גם הוא. These words are generally ignored by recent translators and commentators, despite their strongly emphatic character. On such combinations see Muraoka, *Emphatic Structures*, pp. 47-48, 63-65; on גם ibid., pp. 143-46, and C. H. J. Van der Merwe, *The Old Hebrew Particle* gam (ATS 34; St Ottilien, 1990), and 'Old Hebrew Particles and the Interpretation of Old Testament Texts', *JSOT* 60 (1993), pp. 27-44. The possible interpretations can be subdivided into two major types, depending on whether גם marks הוא alone for focus or the whole clause, and each of these has two alternatives: (i) 'they *too* will be added...' (i.e. as well as some other possible new threat); (ii) same translation, but implying only 'as well as the existing enemies' (McNeile, p. 3, seems to favour one of these); (iii) 'they will, *moreover*, be added...' (so Houtman, with the nuance, 'make matters worse' [p. 237] or 'going from bad to worse' [p. 14]); (iv) 'they will *even* be added...' (i.e. strange as it may seem). Muraoka holds that an 'additive' meaning is nearly always involved with גם, though he recognises that the resemblance to the linked expression may not be total (so that 'in his turn' may be more correct than 'also' in Gen. 4.4), but occasionally there may be emphasis too. Van der Merwe also identifies 'additive' instances, but views them in his 1993 article (p. 36) from a discourse-analysis point of view as serving to signal 'the extent of a coherent text'. But he recognises another group of occurrences, e.g. Josh. 2.24, where גם focuses on a whole sentence and is best translated 'moreover'. Since no other potential enemy is mentioned in the context (i) is excluded; (ii) is weak (it probably lies behind the non-translation of modern English versions [cf. Vulg, Tyndale]) and lacks a clear parallel; there seem to be no examples of (iii) where גם is followed by the redundant/emphatic personal pronoun (Gen. 32.19; Exod. 4.14 and 1 Kgs 1.6, which are in Van der Merwe's list (art. cit., p. 37 n .37), are all cases where the pronoun is the subject of a nominal clause and Exod. 10.25 is [i] or [ii]). That seems to leave (iv) as the most probable interpretation.

i. Heb. ונוסף. The common translation 'join (sc. our enemies)', implying an alliance, may assume more than the Hebrew verb allows: there are no other examples of the stronger meaning in BH. For *ysp* Niphal = 'join' in Qumran Heb. see *DCH* 4, p. 235.

j. Heb. עלה is commonly used for departure from Egypt, esp. where a journey to (the higher ground of) Canaan is in view; cf. 13.18 (also Gen. 13.1; 45.25; 50.5: and see Schmidt, p. 4, for similar expressions in Egyptian). The Hiphil is frequently used of Yahweh's promise to bring Israel (back) to Canaan (Gen. 46.4; 50.24; Exod. 3.8, 17), so that Pharaoh's plan can legitimately be seen as direct (even if not at this stage intended) opposition to

Yahweh's declared purpose (cf. his aim that Israel should not 'multiply'). The view that עלה could mean 'become masters of (the land)' (M. Lambert, 'Notes exégétiques', *REJ* 39 [1899], pp. 299-303 [300], followed by Beer, Noth, Sarna and NEB/REB, NRSV) is based on no solid evidence and is now generally discounted (cf. K. Rupprecht, 'עלה מן הארץ (Ex 1₁₀ Hos 2₂): "sich des Landes bemächtigen"', *ZAW* 82 [1970], pp. 442-47; *THAT* 2, 278 = *TLOT*, 887; B. Renaud, 'Osée II 2: *'lh mn h'rṣ*: essai d'interprétation', *VT* 33 [1983], pp. 495-500): Hos. 2.2 is not an example, *pace* Wolff ad loc. The meaning 'rise (from the ground)' (NJPS) is in principle possible (cf. BDB, p. 748b), but scarcely fits the present context, as the Israelites have not yet been oppressed (cf. Sarna). The straightforward meaning is best.

k. 'Overseers' (Heb. שׂר; cf. 2.14) are simply 'officers' of a particular kind: for more specific terminology see 5.6. 'Labour gangs' (Heb. מסים) refers, except in LBH (Esth. 10.1), to the labourers themselves rather than to their (forced) labour itself (cf. BDB, pp. 586-87): the use of the singular in 2 Sam. 20.24; 1 Kgs 4.6; 5.28; 12.18, as well as in Heb. inscriptions (*AHI* 4.202[?] and 100.782), is presumably collective. Akk. *massu*, which occurs in the West already in the Alalakh tablets and in an Amarna letter from Megiddo (EA 365: cf. *AHw*, p. 619, and Schmidt) means 'corvée labourer': its origin is as obscure as that of the Heb. word, and perhaps both are loans from a third language (but scarcely from Egyptian where the technical sense is unknown).

l. Heb. ערי־מסכנות. The defining noun occurs seven times in BH (elsewhere 1 Kgs 9.19 and five times in Chr.) and caused problems to LXX and Vulg (see Text and Versions). The meaning 'storehouses' is clearly indicated by the context in 2 Chr. 32.28 and by Tg⁰ (from which Tyndale and AV's 'treasure cities' is ultimately derived) and Sy here. For occurrences in Aramaic ostraca of the Persian period from Idumaea see A. Lemaire, 'Der Beitrag idumäischer Ostraka zur Geschichte Palästinas im Übergang von der persischen zur hellenistischen Zeit', *ZDPV* 115 (1999), pp. 12-23 (13). Rashi and before him Menachem ben Saruk associated the term with Heb. *swkn*, 'steward', in Isa. 22.15 (from the root *skn*, 'be of service'), which has a Phoenician cognate (cf. *DNWSI*, pp. 785-86). But the precise meaning 'storehouse, depot' is attested for the very similar Akkadian word *maškantu* (from *šakānu*, with Heb. *s* corresponding to the Neo-Assyrian pronunciation of Akk. *š* as in Heb. סרים, סרנון etc.; cf. A.R. Millard, 'Assyrian Royal Names in Biblical Hebrew', *JSS* 21 [1976], pp. 1-14; for ninth-cent. examples of the correspondence in Aram. see *KAI* [5th ed.] 309.7, 18), and the Heb. word is thus most likely to be a loanword.[4]

---

[4] Recently a fresh case has been made for an occurrence of the Akk. word meaning 'granaries' in an Amarna letter from Palestine (EA 306.31: K.J. Baranowski, 'The Biblical Hebrew "Store Cities" and an Amarna Gloss', *VT* 67 [2017], pp. 519-27). The possible implications of this for when the word was borrowed into Heb. remain difficult to assess.

m. פרעה is a loanword from Eg. *pr ʿ3*, originally 'the great house', i.e. the royal palace, then used by metonymy as a title for the king from the fifteenth cent. B.C. until Ptolemaic times (see in more detail *ABD* 5, pp. 288-89). In Heb. it is equivalent to 'the king of Egypt' (1.15, 17 etc.), but it is never used in the pl.

n. Heb. וְאֶת־רַעְמְסֵס. Elsewhere (e.g. 12.37) the name is spelt רַעְמְסֵס, which is close to the pronunciation presupposed in Greek transcriptions of the name. Unless the variant form here is simply pausal, it could (in what is probably an older part of the Exodus narrative) in this respect preserve a more precise reproduction of the original Egyptian pronunciation; cf. Helck, 'Tkw und die Ramses-Stadt' (in the Explanatory Note), p. 43.

o. The three verbs are examples of the use of the Heb. imperfect for durative, especially progressive, action in the past (cf. JM §113f-g).

p. Heb. ויקצו. The meanings 'loathe' (so LXX, Aq, Vulg, RV mg, Childs, NEB/REB here) and 'dread' (BDB – cf. Tgg, Sy [and ὁ συρ, ὁ ἑβρ in Wevers], Schmidt, Houtman, NJPS, NRSV here) for the verb קוץ are clearly distinguished in biblical usage by the prepositions which follow the verb (ב in all cases of the former, מפני in all cases of the latter) as well as by contextual factors (note the presence of words referring to fear in Num. 22.3 and in the context of Isa. 7.6, 16 [cf. vv. 2 and 4]). This distinction was generally overlooked by the translators of LXX, Sy and Vulg (though note LXX at Isa. 7.16), but Tg⁰ shows some awareness of it. It is likely that the verb itself (which seems not to be attested outside Heb. and Aram.) refers to a strong repugnance whose precise character is defined by the preposition which follows it. Both of the closest parallels (Num. 22.3; Isa. 7.16) reflect fear at the approach of a large hostile mass (cf. רב in Num. 22.3 with ירבה here).

q. Heb. ויעבדו, Hiphil of עבד, as in 6.5P. This root is a *Leitmotif* of the Priestly narrative of the Exodus: in the next verse the verb (in Qal) occurs again and the noun עבדה three times; the latter reappears in 2.23 and 6.6. The verb and the noun both have a wide range of meaning, extending from the work of a free man through a subject's service to his ruler (or a foreign king) to slavery (in addition to the lexica see *THAT* 2, 188-91, 195-200 = *TLOT*, 824-26, 828-31, and the survey by Houtman, pp. 43-45). Schmidt and Houtman hesitate to use the term 'slavery' in the present context (contrast Childs). But despite the wider usage noted above and the difference between slavery and forced (corvée) labour required by a ruler (usually for a limited time), the terms translated 'harshly' and 'subjected them' in this and the following verse (see Notes r and v below) leave no doubt that the Priestly writer intended to represent the situation of Israel in Egypt as one of abject humiliation (compare also the phrase 'house of bondage [lit. of slaves]' in 13.3 etc.).

r. Heb. בפרך, an expression found also in v. 14, but elsewhere only in Lev. 25.43, 46, 53 and Ezek. 34.4. In Leviticus 25 it is used of the harsh treatment of slaves that may not be inflicted on fellow-Israelites; in Ezekiel it refers to the cruel, uncaring rule exercised over Israel by their own 'shepherds' or rulers. The word therefore fits a situation where a person or group is at the mercy of a powerful master whose rule cannot be challenged. The curious interpretation as 'mockery' in some of the Versions (see below on Text and Versions) has no obvious basis. In MH פֶּרֶךְ also refers to grinding or crushing (cf. the verb פָּרַךְ in MH and its cognate in later Aram.) and this could well explain, by metaphorization, the biblical usage of the word (so Rashi: cf. Ar. acc. to BDB) and the meaning 'injustice' which develops from a different starting-point in Akk. in the Neo-Assyrian/Neo-Babylonian period for *parku*, *perku* and *pariktu* (*AHw*, pp. 833b, 834a, 855a: von Soden s.v. *perku* conjectures an Aramaic basis for this, and a verb פרך occurs once in Official Aram. with the verb חבל [*KAI* 260.6; cf. *DNWSI*, p. 938: 'break, damage']).

s. Heb. וימררו. The normal interpretation, 'made bitter, i.e. unpleasant' is supported by the ancient Versions (see below). C.H. Gordon suggested, on the basis of the parallelism of *mrr* and *brk* in Ugaritic and cognates in Arabic and Aramaic, that מרר here (and in Judg. 18.25) has the meaning '(make) strong', referring (cf. v. 12) to the paradoxical growth of the Israelites under their hard labour (*UT*, pp. 438-39, no. 1556; cf. Schmidt, p. 4, and for a possible Egyptian cognate W.A. Ward, 'Egypto-Semitic *MR*, "be bitter, strong"', *UF* 12 [1980], 357-60). This proposal was refuted at length by D. Pardee ('The Semitic Root *mrr* and the Etymology of Ugaritic *mr(r)*‖*brk*', *UF* 10 [1978], pp. 249-88 [esp. 258]; cf. *VT* 35 [1985], p. 114 n. 5), who found no basis for the meaning 'strong' in a general sense in either Ugaritic or Hebrew. The meaning 'strengthen' has been reaffirmed for Ugaritic in *DULAT*, pp. 577-78, but in any case the object חייהם here makes the normal Heb. sense '(make) bitter' much more probable. On its metaphorical uses see P.D. King, *Surrounded by Bitterness* (Carlisle, 2012), pp. 322-54.

t. Heb. חֹמֶר can mean either 'clay' (e.g. Jer. 18.4, 6: so LXX, Tgg, Vulg, Luther, Tyndale, Baentsch, Schmidt, Houtman here) or specifically 'mortar' (Gen. 11.3: so BDB, *HAL*, *DCH*, *Ges18* here, also Nachmanides, AV, RV, NJPS, REB, NRSV, Childs, Sarna), clay being the main ingredient of mortar in antiquity (cf. Wright, *Ancient Building*, pp. 348-60, 408-13; A.J. Spencer, *Brick Architecture in Ancient Egypt* [Warminster, 1979]: includes a wide-ranging catalogue of buildings made with bricks; Kitchen, 'Brickfields'). The former sense is more common, but חֹמֶר is never certainly used of clay for making bricks (Nah. 3.14 and Job 13.12 are possible instances, but a different sense is more likely in both cases). The order of the words perhaps favours the translation 'clay': they worked with clay to make the bricks (cf. 5.6-19), and with bricks to build the cities. Houtman suggests a hendiadys ('making bricks from clay'), which is also possible.

u. The את which introduces this phrase is puzzling: 'namely' is more commonly represented in Heb. by ו (the 'explicative *waw*': BDB, p. 252a, cf. D.W. Baker, 'Further Examples of the Waw Explicativum', *VT* 30 [1980], pp. 129-36 [p. 131 deals with the use before a concluding summary]) or ל

(BDB, p. 514b). A variety of explanations have been suggested. Cassuto took את here as the preposition 'with', following Rashbam, but a reference to further kinds of work is not likely to be intended here, nor does את have the instrumental sense of the ב in the preceding phrases. So את must be the so-called *nota accusativi*. Its use to mark the subject of a sentence, which became more widespread from the sixth century onwards (see R. Polzin, *Late Biblical Hebrew*, pp. 32-37, 110-11: the attempts by Blau and Muraoka to explain the examples differently are not convincing), is not relevant here (because כל עבדתם is not the subject of a clause), unless this and one or two similar examples (see below) are to be regarded as a yet further development from the idiom. BDB, p. 85b, and Joüon §125j(1) (still in JM §125j) cite other cases of את 'resuming loosely some other preposition' or 'before a noun in apposition to a noun with a preposition' (Jer. 38.9; Ezek. 14.22b; 37.19b; Zech. 12.10; 1 Kgs 6.5; Ezek. 43.17). Muraoka (*Emphatic Words*, p. 156 n. 136) objects that this view is 'hardly acceptable', but does not say why. The final example, Ezek. 43.17, is certainly not a real parallel. Of the rest Jer. 38.9, Ezek. 14.22b and Zech. 12.10 could all be explained in the way to be mentioned next (which Muraoka there prefers), and the inclusion of Zech. 12.10 assumes a (small) emendation. But Ezek. 37.19b and 1 Kgs 6.5 are much stronger evidence for such an idiom, even though in the latter verse two alternative readings may have been combined in MT. J. Blau cited Exod. 1.14 as one of a few places where an antecedent (not being in the accusative) which corresponds to the object of a relative clause has the *nota accusativi* prefixed to it ('Zum angeblichen Gebrauch von *'ēt* vor dem Nominativ', *VT* 4 [1954], pp. 7-19 [11-12]: cf. GK §117l, Dillmann, p. 9, and Muraoka, p. 156): the best of the parallels cited are Num. 35.6; Ezek. 14.22b; Zech. 8.17, but of these it is only in Ezek. 14.22b that a preposition required by the context has been 'suppressed' by the את. Probably, therefore, the present instance is one where the two idioms coincide, like Ezek. 14.22b (and Jer. 38.9 and Zech. 12.10). It is notable that all the closely parallel passages cited seem to originate in the sixth century or later, which suggests a similar date for the present verse. The suffix ם- might be subjective ('their labour') or objective ('labour for them'): the close parallel in 6.6 supports the latter.

v. The idiom found here, in which one person or group 'works by means of' (ב עבד) another, is limited to contexts referring to slave-labour (so explicitly in Lev. 25.39; cf. v. 46 and Jer. 34.9-10), forced labour required by kings (Jer. 22.13; 25.14; 27.7; 30.8; Ezek. 34.27) and the use of animals (Deut. 15.19). If, as seems likely, the Deuteronomy reference is the oldest of these occurrences, it may indicate the degradation implied in the use of this idiom with reference to human labour (which again is a feature limited to what seem to be sixth-century texts).

w. Or, taking מילדת in a full participial sense rather than as a noun, 'those who acted as midwives for the Hebrew women'. This would allow the possibility of the midwives being Egyptian, but in what follows (and in its two other occurrences in BH, Gen. 35.17; 38.28) מילדת is clearly a noun. LXX and Vulg's genitives (see Text and Versions) offer a different way of reaching the same sense, but at the cost of an emendation to the vowels of MT. On 'Hebrew' here and in Exodus generally see the notes below on v. 15.

x. Heb. האבנים, a dual form which occurs in MT only here and in Jer. 18.3. There the reference is clearly to the potter's wheel, which incorporated two superimposed flat stones (cf. Heb. אבן) forming a bearing on which the working surface rotated (see *BRL*, pp. 345-46; *ABD* 5, pp. 427-28; King and Stager, *Life*, pp. 134-36). The word possibly also occurs at Isa. 65.3 (cf. 1QIs[a], Sy) and Qoh. 3.5 (see Tsevat below). Interpretations of the present occurrence understand it to refer either to stones or a stool (cf. Tgg and Rashi) on (על) which the pregnant woman sat or to the genitals of the mother herself or of the child being born, on the basis of a similarity of the female *labia* to the pair of stones in the potter's wheel or of the testicles of a male child to small stones in the scrotum. Most EVV. have continued to follow the former view, but the 1931 American Translation (according to Childs) followed the latter, and NEB/REB has 'as the child is delivered' (cf. Tyndale), which is akin to the paraphrases of LXX and Vulg (cf. Sy 'kneeling', a posture sometimes adopted for giving birth: see in Ugaritic *KTU* 1.12.1.26). In modern times the 'birthstool' interpretation has been supported by reference to Egyptian and other Near Eastern texts and artefacts (for a valuable up-to-date review see K. McGeough, 'Birth Bricks, Potter's Wheels and Exodus 1,16', *Bib* 87 [2006], pp. 305-18, with bibliography [to which add J. Wegner, 'A Decorated Birth-Brick from South Abydos: New Evidence on Childbirth and Birth Magic in the Middle Kingdom', in D. Silverman et al. (eds.), *Archaism and Innovation: Studies in the Culture of Middle Kingdom Egypt* (New Haven and Philadelphia, 2009), pp. 447-96]; further Schmidt, pp. 5-6). But it has also been strongly criticised (Baentsch ad loc.; A. Cohen, 'Studies in Hebrew Lexicography', *AJSL* 40 [1923–24], pp. 153-85 [156-59]): the birthstool would be invisible if the woman was sitting on it, and in any case would not reveal the sex of the child; there is no reference to the custom elsewhere in the Bible; the Egyptians used bricks, not stones; the distinctive pointing suggests that 'two stones' is not the meaning (Cohen argues for the meaning 'lap' in Jer. 18.3). McGeough avoids two of these difficulties by concluding that the place where the child was placed after the birth is meant (pp. 314-15, a possibility also considered by Wegner, pp. 477-78; cf. Brongers in H.A. Brongers and A.S. van der Woude, 'Wat is de Betekenis van *'ābnāyim* in Exodus 1:16?', *NedTT* 20 [1965–66], pp. 241-54 [247-49]), as in Papyrus Westcar (ET in W.K. Simpson, *The Literature of Ancient Egypt* [New Haven, 1972], pp. 15-30) and that האבנים is not etymologically related to אֶבֶן: the resemblance to האבנים in Jer. 18.3 is, he suggests, cultural and not physical. The alternative view, that the child's (or the mother's) genitalia are meant, has also received considerable support from e.g. Baentsch, Ehrlich, M. Tsevat ('Some Biblical Notes', *HUCA* 24 [1952–53], pp. 107-14 [109-10]), Houtman and Propp.

Some rabbinic comments on this verse (*MRI* [Lauterbach 2, p. 39]; Exod.R. 1.14; Eccl.R. 3.7) may point the same way (less likely the obscure variant of 1QIs[a] [cf. Sy] cited by Tsevat). Schmidt notes biblical evidence that, not surprisingly, midwives did observe a child's sex (Gen. 35.17; 1 Sam. 4.20). A more general reference to the newborn children is obtained by seeing האבנים as a variant form of הבנים with prosthetic *aleph* (van der Woude, 'Betekenis', pp. 249-52), but the other proposed occurrences of this form are unconvincing (cf. Brongers, ibid., pp. 252-54). An important factor in the difficult choice between the two main alternatives is the interpretation of the words which precede האבנים. If it means 'birthstool', they must be taken as a continuation of the temporal clause: 'and you see (them, sc. the Hebrew women) on the birthstool', which is weak. On the other hand, a comparison with Exod. 5.21 (the only close parallel) shows that על + ראה means 'examine, check', which gives very good sense here if followed by a word referring to the distinguishing criterion, i.e. the genitals of the newborn child.

y. For the permissive ('may') use of *waw* consecutive and the perfect see JM §119w (cf. §113l). Heb. וחיה (rather than the expected וחיתה read by SP) is explained as an ancient form of the 3rd fem. sing. derived from the original root *חיי, which was here treated as a Double Ayin verb (GK §76i). The omission of Dagesh may be due, as GK suggests, to pausal lengthening (so also BL §57t").

z. Heb. ותיראן is one of several 3rd feminine plural forms in vv. 17-19 in which the expected final *he* is omitted in MT (for other exx. see GK §47l; Bergsträsser, *Grammatik* 2, §5a, took these forms to represent a shorter alternative ending – compare Note aa on 2.20).

aa. The plural of ילד can refer to sons and daughters (as in 21.4), but where the context requires (e.g. Zech. 8.5; Ruth 1.5 as well as here) it may mean 'boys': the singular appears always to be used of boys.

bb. Heb. מדוע, as in 2.18; 3.3; 5.14; 18.14, whereas in 2.13 etc. 'why' is למה. Here the king is clearly speaking sharply to the midwives, which contradicts A. Jepsen's theory ('Warum?', in F. Maass [ed.], *Das Ferne und Nahe Wort* [FS L. Rost; BZAW 105; Berlin, 1967], pp. 106-13) that מדוע was used either simply to request information or to indicate amazement or sympathy, whereas למה expressed reproach or complaint (see Schmidt, p. 44, and J. Barr, 'Why? in Biblical Hebrew', *JTS* N.S. 36 [1985], pp. 1-33 [esp. p. 5], where it is also noted that the E source [as traditionally identified] has a greater propensity to use מדוע than J [pp. 10-12]).

cc. Heb. כי, which is ignored in many translations, ancient and modern, makes good sense in response to 'Why…' in v. 18. To take it as merely introducing the direct speech (Schmidt, p. 6) is less natural.

dd. Heb. חיות, which is now generally derived from *חָיָה, a by-form of חַי (stative participle?) which occurs only here in BH but may well be the basis for forms in MH with *qamets* in the first syllable. This interpretation (advocated by Ibn Ezra) may go back to the Palestinian Targumim. For the sense of 'abundant life' compare the similar use of חי in 2 Sam. 23.20K; Ps. 38.20, and of the verb חיה in Deut. 8.3b etc. (BDB, p. 311a; *TWAT* 2, 884-88 [*TDOT* 4, pp. 333-36]). The interpretation 'animals', given in B.Sotah 11b and Exod.R. 1.16 and favoured by Ehrlich (p. 261) and Houtman, would require the vocalisation חַיּוֹת and (probably) a prefixed כ. Another Jewish tradition (ibid., Symm, Rashi), which is probably presupposed in the renderings of Tg°, Tg^J (second rendering) and Vulg (possibly also Sy: see Text and Versions) saw here a MH word for 'midwife', but this again would require a different vocalisation, and the sense obtained is improbable (it is notable that Rashi found it necessary to add כ, 'like'). In modern times the same MH word has been held, in the sense of 'a woman in labour', to justify the translation 'when they are in labour' (Holzinger; Ges-B [14th ed.], p. 203 [it is given up in the 15th, p. 224, and the 16th, pp. 226-27, offers all the options]; G.R. Driver, *ZAW* 67 [1955], pp. 246-48; NEB/REB; C. Albeck, *Einführung in die Mischna* [Berlin, 1974], p. 210; *Ges18*, p. 344: cf. perhaps LXX, Aq, Theod); but the vocalisation remains a problem, and Driver's similar interpretation of חיתם in Ps. 78.50 has nothing in its favour. Siebert-Hommes, *Let the Daughters*, pp. 101-10, proposes 'life-producers', but gives no adequate argument for this and overlooks some factors which favour 'lively'.

ee. Frequentative use of the perfect consecutive referring to the present (JM §119q) or (recent) past (JM §119u-v), equivalent to an imperfect. The *waw* is the *waw apodosis* after the preceding temporal clause (JM §176f-g: a further example appears in v. 21 after a causal clause).

ff. Heb. ויהי is generally followed by a temporal clause and contributes little or nothing to the meaning of the sentence: here, unusually, the following clause is causal and the main clause 'he gave them households' specifies more closely what was meant by 'dealt kindly with' in v. 20 (or possibly refers to a further act of divine favour). On the possible summarising character of v. 21 see the Explanatory Note below; for some remarks on the 'macrosyntactic' role of ויהי see Gibson, *Syntax*, pp. 97-99.

gg. Literally, 'made them houses': 'them' is in fact להם, with the masculine suffix (contrast להן in v. 18), but such a lapse of concord is quite frequent (cf. JM §149b and, e.g., Exod. 2.17). The metaphorical use of this idiom for the continuation and growth of a family is well attested (1 Sam. 25.28; 2 Sam. 7.11; 1 Kgs 2.24; cf. [with בנה] Deut. 25.9; 2 Sam. 7.27; 1 Kgs 11.38; Ruth 4.11).

hh. The rare form ילוד (for the construct state יליד is used) is evidently equivalent in meaning to a passive participle and is now generally regarded as a participial form of the passive Qal with geminated middle radical (cf. Bergsträsser, *Grammatik*, 2, §15c [citing זרוע in Lev. 11.37 and Isa. 61.11 as a parallel]; Meyer §68.3c; *HAL*, p. 394, *Ges18*, p. 465 [not *DCH* 4, p. 222, and JM §58b]; cf. Driver, *Samuel* [2nd ed.], p. 262).

148   EXODUS 1–18

ii. M. Cogan, 'A Technical Term for Exposure', *JNES* 27 (1968), pp. 133-35, proposed that Heb. השליך has the weaker sense 'expose' as in Gen. 21.5 and Ezek. 16.5 (and possibly elsewhere cf. *HAL*, p. 1415), like Akk. *nadû*. But the context here is against it.

jj. Heb. יאר is a loan-word from Egyptian (*ytrw* > *yrw*) which also appears in Neo-Assyrian documents (*ANET*, p. 296). In addition to the lexica see *TWAT* 3, 385-90 (*TDOT* 5, pp. 359-63). As well as its frequent use in the singular for the Nile (as here and in 4.9 etc.), the word is used in the plural for 'streams', both of the Nile and (Isa. 33.21) more generally. No doubt this appellative use (cf. LXX ποταμόν here), which is also found in Egyptian, is the reason for the common attachment of the definite article, as here.

Explanatory Notes

7. The growing family (cf. Gen. 47.27, where two of the same verbs are used as here) now reached such a size that 'the land was full of them'. This is clearly seen in the present text as the cause of the Egyptians' counter-measures (vv. 9-10). But the language of this verse is strongly reminiscent of passages in Genesis which command mankind to 'be fruitful and multiply' (1.28; 8.17; 9.1, 7), to 'spread everywhere' (9.7) and even to 'fill the earth' (9.1). The same Heb. word (*'ereṣ*) is rendered, appropriately, by 'earth' in Gen. 9.1 and by 'land' (sc. of Egypt) here. In Gen. 1.28 and 9.1 the increase of mankind is traced to God's 'blessing', and the same is no doubt implied here too. The sequel to Gen. 9.1 and 9.7 is the list of the descendants of Noah's sons, who represent the nations of the earth in their entirety. It is plausible then to see the present verse as describing the transformation of Jacob's family into a people (cf. vv. 9, 20), who will henceforth be known as 'the Israelites' (lit. 'the children of Israel', cf. above on v. 1 and see below, vv. 9, 12-13). This transformation has also been prepared for in Genesis by God's specific promises to Abraham, Isaac and Jacob, where much of the same vocabulary appears (Gen. 17.2, 6; 35.11; 48.4; cf. 28.3), including the ideas of blessing (17.16; 28.3; 35.9; 48.3) and peoplehood (17.4-6, 16; 28.3; 35.11; 48.4). All these passages come from the Priestly source (cf. in the texts cited from Gen. 12–50 the recurrence of the name 'God Almighty/El Shaddai'). The same idea is found in non-Priestly passages too (Gen. 12.1-3; 15.5; 22.17; 26.4; 28.14; 46.3), but the terminology is not so similar there. So the present verse must originally have formed part of the Priestly source and expresses (though without any explicit cross-reference) the fulfilment of God the Creator's promise to the patriarchs (for this major theme of the Priestly source see especially W. Brueggemann, 'The Kerygma of the Priestly Writers', *ZAW* 84 [1972], pp. 397-413 [also in Brueggemann and Wolff, *Vitality*, pp. 101-113], though to describe it as the 'kerygma' is an exaggeration and Brueggemann underrates the universal significance of the passages in Gen. 1–11). The one phrase in this verse which does not have a background in the Priestly promise texts in Genesis is 'and became...strong' (Heb. *wy'ṣmw*). It does appear in Gen. 26.16 and the related adjective *'ṣwm*, 'strong', occurs in a non-Priestly promise text in Gen. 18.18. In addition, both verb (v. 20) and adjective (v. 9) occur later in Exodus 1, each time in direct connection with the verb 'multiplied' (*rbh*) or the related adjective 'many' (*rb*), but in passages which there is no reason to attribute to the Priestly source. It is therefore at least possible that 'became...strong' comes from the non-Priestly introduction to the Exodus-story, in which 'multiplied' might also have stood (cf. Van Seters, *Life of Moses*, pp. 19-20, following Wellhausen and Gressmann): but Schmidt may be right to attribute 'became...strong' (and the words 'and became very strong' in v. 20) to the redactor who combined the two versions together (pp. 12, 19). On other occurrences of 'strong', especially joined with 'many', see the note on v. 9. In view of these associations its meaning here and later in the chapter could also be '(became) numerous'.

8. The focus on Joseph in particular (and by implication his achievements) links this verse to v. 6 and the (non-Priestly) Joseph-story in Genesis 37–50. The text is entirely vague about the length of time which has elapsed since Joseph's death (v. 6). The only indication is the fact that in the next verse (as in v. 7) there has been time for the family to grow into a people, which requires a much longer period than a single generation. Other passages specified the period as 400 or 430 years (Gen. 15.13; Exod. 12.40-41) or four generations (Gen. 15.16; cf. Exod. 6.16-20, according to which Moses and Aaron are great-great-grandsons of Jacob): on the LXX and SP variants at Exod. 12.40-41, which effectively limit the period spent in Egypt to 215 years, see the notes on Text and Versions there. Likewise, as elsewhere in Genesis and Exodus, the text has nothing to say about the name of this first (cf. 2.23; 4.19) Pharaoh of the oppression (but see below on v. 11). The purpose of the verse is no doubt to signal, and explain, the impending change in the fortunes of the Israelites: with the passage of time the memory of Joseph's wise and beneficial rule has passed away and his family are no different from any other group of foreigners. But from a historical point of view it is not difficult to see why the question has been raised whether the 'Exodus group' really had such a close connection with the family whose flight to Egypt is narrated at the end of Genesis, the more so as Genesis has near its end an account of most of the family returning to Canaan to bury Jacob (50.1-13), even if only temporarily (vv. 5, 8, 14, 22, 24-26). It is true that the renaming of Jacob as 'Israel' in Gen. 32.27-28 (non-P) and 35.9-10P (cf. 46.1; 47.29-31; 48.8-14, 21) appears to establish a connection between the two 'blocks' of narrative, and the two names for the patriarch are already known to Hosea (12.13). But the very existence of the two names for one 'person' points to a complex if early development in the tradition.[5]

9. Pharaoh introduces his plan with an observation about the numbers of the Israelites, thus indirectly acknowledging the effect of the divine promises in Genesis (cf. v. 7). But he does so in relation to Egypt: they are 'too many and too strong for us' (less likely but linguistically possible: 'they are more in number and stronger than us' – see Note e on the translation above), and as such they pose a threat, which is more fully explained in the next verse. The expression 'the Israelite people' (*ʿm bny yśrʾl*) is unique and conflates two very common terms for Israel in the book of Exodus, 'the people' (*hʿm*) and 'the Israelites' (*bny yśrʾl*, lit. 'the children of Israel', as in v. 7). Probably only one of these terms originally stood here and, since the references to the Israelites in vv. 9-12 are all singular, this must have been 'the/a people'. Perhaps 'See, a people which is...' would be a possible beginning for Pharaoh's speech: otherwise some defining element would be needed (e.g. 'This people...' or 'The people of Israel...'). The addition of 'the Israelites' (*bny yśrʾl*) would be a redactor's device to achieve consistency among the different elements out of which this chapter was formed: the plural verbs of SP and the Versions are a further stage in the same process. The terms 'many' and 'strong' occur together elsewhere twelve times in BH (Num. 32.1; Deut. 7.1; 9.14; Isa. 8.7; 53.12; Joel 2.2, 11; Amos 5.12; Mic. 4.3; Zech. 8.22; Pss. 35.18; 135.10;

---

[5] See e.g. de Vaux, *Histoire ancienne*, pp. 160-69, 594-95 (ET pp. 169-77, 648-49); A. de Pury, 'La tradition patriarcale en Genèse 12–35', in id. (ed.), *Le Pentateuque en question* (Le Monde la Bible; Geneva, 1989), pp. 259-70.

Prov. 7.26), either linked by 'and' or in parallel phrases. The word-pair is also attested in Ugaritic (*KTU* 1.3.1.12; cf. *RSP* 1, p. 338, no. 516), and it is neither distinctively Deuteronomistic (the combination of 'great' [*gdwl*] with 'strong' is more characteristically Deuteronomistic [Gen. 18.18(?); Deut. 4.38; 9.1; 11.23; 26.5; Josh. 23.9: otherwise only Num. 14.12; Dan. 11.25]) nor exclusively late (cf. Isa. 8.7; Amos 5.12).

10. To teach Egyptian rulers to 'deal wisely' was the goal of the mass of 'Instruction' literature, of which much has survived (cf. *ANET*, pp. 412-25). The way in which Pharaoh here invited 'his people' to share in his plan (cf. 'us', 'our' and 'us' – a further 'us' probably lies behind 'in the event of war', see Note g on the translation above – and the plural verbs in vv. 11-14) is hard to reconcile with the concentration of political power in Egypt in the king's hands: in this respect the focus on Pharaoh's sole responsibility in vv. 15-22 (as also in ch. 5 and elsewhere) is more realistic. The scenario which Pharaoh fears is that in a time of war the Israelites, yet further increased in numbers, might become an additional source of opposition to his army and 'go up out of the land'. The first part of this is reasonable enough – the loyalty of a non-Egyptian element in the population could not necessarily be relied on – but a rationale for Pharaoh's fearing the departure of Israel from his land at this stage is lacking, for Israel is not yet a valued source of forced labour, as it is at the time when Moses later finds Pharaoh unwilling to let Israel leave the land even temporarily (the Rabbis seem already to have sensed the problem: see B.Sotah 11a). This has led to attempts to find a different meaning for the verb 'go up' (see Note j on the translation), but without success. It is most likely that Pharaoh is here presented prematurely in his classic role as the one who seeks to stand in the way of Yahweh's intention to bring his people to Canaan (for which cf. Gen. 46.4; 50.24), just as he seeks to prevent any further multiplication of the people in accordance with Yahweh's promise (Gen. 12.2 etc.). His failure to do the latter (cf. v. 12) would already raise doubts about his ability to do the former, and more generally about his 'wisdom'.

11. The narrative jumps to the execution of Pharaoh's plan, which involves forced labour on his cities for the storage of produce. The language recalls some aspects of the account of Solomon's building activities in 1 Kings 9, where both 'labour gangs' (vv. 15, 21) and 'cities with storehouses' (v. 19) are mentioned again, and the word 'overseer' (śr) also appears (vv. 22-23). But the overall character of that passage is quite different from this one and it is implausible to suggest that v. 11 is modelled on 1 Kings 9 (so Van Seters, *Life of Moses*, p. 24) or to use the shared terminology as an argument for a Solomonic date for this part of the narrative (Schmidt, pp. 21, 39). The specific task assigned to the Israelites, if not the terminology used, in fact corresponds more closely to the measures introduced by Joseph to combat famine in Egypt according to Gen. 41.34-36, 47-49, 55-56 (cf. 47.13-26). Both the use of foreign labour for such projects and the names given to the cities fit well into what is known of Egypt under the Nineteenth Dynasty. Two Ramesside papyri (Leiden Pap. 348 and 349) mention the employment of 'Apiru (on whom see more generally the notes on v. 15) by state officials as haulers of stones for the building of a fortress or a temple (for translations and references see Loretz, *Habiru-Hebräer*, p. 39 with nn. 157-61; cf. *TGI*, p. 35, Noth, *Geschichte*, p. 108 [ET, p. 113]: E. Wente, *Letters from Ancient Egypt* [Atlanta, 1990], pp. 123-24, renders the key phrase in P.Leiden 349 differently, 'who are drawing [water from] the well of Pre of Ramesses II'). A stele of Ramesses IV from Wadi Hammamat includes '800 'Apiru of the tribes of ꜥnt [Anat?]' among workers in the state quarries there (*TGI*, p. 36; cf. Loretz, p. 40; Noth, ibid.), and an apparently Nineteenth-Dynasty ostracon identified by G. Posener in Strasbourg also mentions 'Apiru among stoneworkers (see H. Cazelles, in *POTT*, pp. 14-15, where a drawing and transcription are given, and for further references to this text Loretz, op. cit., p. 40 n. 170: see more generally D.B. Redford, in Frerichs and Lesko [eds.], *Exodus*, p. 59). Although the terminology used in Exod. 1.11 is not distinctively Egyptian, the enforced use of native labour on building projects is well attested in Egypt of the New Kingdom period, especially at Deir el-Medina near Thebes in southern Egypt (cf. Kitchen, *Pharaoh Triumphant*, Chapter 9, with refs. on pp. 257-58; Weimar and Zenger, *Exodus*, pp. 105-10). It would not be surprising if from time to time individuals or groups of foreign origin were forced into this kind of labour. (The Egyptian evidence for brick-making in particular will be more fully considered in the commentary on ch. 5 below.)

Pithom is a form of the Egyptian expression 'Per-Atum', 'the house/temple of Atum', Atum being the primordial Egyptian god. His great cultic centre was at Heliopolis/On (the site is in the northeast suburbs of modern Cairo) and a minority view holds that this ancient city is meant by Pithom here (see E.P. Uphill, 'Pithom and Raamses: Their Location and Significance', *JNES* 27 [1968], pp. 281-316, and 28 [1969], pp. 115-39 [292-99]). But its Egyptian name was On (cf. Gen. 41.45, 50; 46.20), not Pithom/Per-Atum, and the biblical tradition seems to place the later Israelites' sojourn further to the north-east in the Eastern Nile Delta (see below). Possible sites for Pithom have therefore generally been sought in this region, where the worship of Atum is also attested (cf. Pap. Anastasi VI.51-61 = iv.11–v.5; *ANET*, p. 259, *TGI*, p. 40). The choice has appeared to be between two sites in Wadi Tumilat, a shallow valley extending west from modern Ismailiya: Tell el-Maskhuta and Tell er-Retabeh (for earlier discussions of the evidence see E.L. Bleiberg, 'The Location of Pithom and Succoth', *The Ancient World* 6 [1983], pp. 21-27, and my 'Was there an Exodus?').

Tell el-Maskhuta is situated 10 mi. west of Ismailiya: ancient monuments, some of which proved to be from the time of Ramesses II, were observed there from the late eighteenth century onwards and excavations by E. Naville in 1883 brought to light remains of a temple of Atum, 'storehouses' and structures from the Roman period (E. Naville, *The Store-City of Pithom and the Route of the Exodus* [London, 1885], with several plates of inscriptions from the site). Subsequent investigations by J. Clédat and especially the excavations directed by J.S. Holladay (1977–85) have added much new information and made it clear that the site lay unoccupied between a period in the Middle Bronze Age (c. 1750–1625) and the very end of the seventh century B.C. (see the full summary by Holladay in 'Maskhuta, Tell el', *ABD* 4, pp. 588-92, with bibliography). There can be no doubt, therefore, that the Ramesside monuments were brought there secondarily from another site. Evidence from the seventh century and later confirms that at this time the site was known as 'Per-Atum Ṭukw', a name which can plausibly be seen as reflected in the biblical toponyms Pithom and Succoth (for the appearance of the latter name in an Egyptian context see Exod. 12.37 etc.).

Tell er-Retabeh, which is less well known, is located 9 mi. west of Tell el-Maskhuta. It was first excavated by Flinders Petrie in the early twentieth century: he reported evidence of occupation in the Egyptian Middle Kingdom period and under Ramesses II and Ramesses III (including a temple), but nothing later (W.M.F. Petrie, *Hyksos and Israelite Cities* [BSAEP 12; London, 1906]:

brief summary in *IDB* 3, p. 821; see further Uphill, 'Pithom and Raamses', 299-301, and H. Goedicke, 'Ramesses II and the Wadi Tumilat', *Varia Aegyptiaca* 3 [1987], pp. 13-24). Further excavations were conducted at the site by H. Goedicke in the late 1970s, with similar results (see the summary and references in Hoffmeier, *Israel in Egypt*, pp. 119-20, with notes). A relief found there by Petrie shows Ramesses II striking an Asiatic before the god Atum, which suggests that Atum was worshipped at the site in the New Kingdom period, perhaps at the temple discovered by Petrie (*RITA* 2 §34 [p. 58]; detailed discussion in *RITANC* 2, pp. 107-10); and an inscription from the site refers to an official (Ramesside?) who was responsible for 'storehouses' (see Uphill, pp. 300-301).

Prior to Naville's excavations at Tell el-Maskhuta the dominant view was that Pithom was at Tell Abu Suleiman, 35 mi. west of Ismailia (see the references to Lepsius [1849 and 1883] and Edwards [1882–83] in Naville, op. cit., pp. 2-3, 29-31). Naville, on the basis of the Ramesside monuments, his other finds, a passage of Herodotus (2.158) and literary evidence relating to the Graeco-Roman toponym Heroopolis, proposed that Tell el-Maskhuta was the site of Pithom and this view has been widely followed (cf. W. Helck, '*Ṯkw* und die Ramses-Stadt', *VT* 15 [1965], pp. 35-48 [35-40]; after him Herrmann, *Israels Aufenthalt*, pp. 44-45 [ET, p. 26], Schmidt, p. 36, Weimar-Zenger, *Exodus*, p. 118, Davies, *Way of the Wilderness*, p. 79). Even after D.B. Redford's questioning of the antiquity of Pithom as the name of a town ('Exodus I 11', *VT* 13 [1963], pp. 401-18; severely criticised by Helck, art. cit.) and Holladay's demonstration that there was no Ramesside occupation at the site, there is good reason to conclude (see above) that in later periods (from c. 600 B.C. onwards) it was known as Per-Atum/ Pithom and that it is what Herodotus referred to as Πάτουμον τὴν Ἀραβίην πόλιν. The key question is whether another site in the vicinity may have been known by that name in earlier times.

The identification of Pithom with Tell er-Retabeh was first proposed by A. Gardiner in a 'Note on Pithom and Heroonpolis' in *JEA* 5 (1918), pp. 267-69 (cf. 19 [1933], p. 127) and was adopted – before the recent debate about the merits of Tell el-Maskhuta – by, e.g., Noth (*Geschichte*, p. 107 n. 2 [ET, p. 112 n. 2]), Bright (*History*, p. 111), and Wilson (*ANET*, p. 259 n. 5). More recently it has been supported by H. Goedicke ('Papyrus Anastasi VI 51-61', *Studien zur altägyptischen Kultur* 14 [1987], pp. 83-98, with qualifications),

M. Dijkstra ('Pithom en Raämses', *NedThT* 43 [1989], pp. 89-105), F. Yurco (in Frerichs and Lesko [eds.], *Exodus*, p. 55 n. 62), Hoffmeier (*Israel in Egypt*, pp. 119-21) and cautiously by Kitchen, *RITANC* 2, pp. 108-110. Although there is no explicit evidence that the site was ever known as Pithom, it apparently had a temple of Atum (a Per-Atum) in the Ramesside period and the significance of the site for Ramesses II has been underlined by Goedicke, who has also argued that it is referred to in P.Anastasi V, xix.3–xx.6; VI, 51-57 (artt. citt.). According to Goedicke and Hoffmeier the Ramesside monuments at Tell el-Maskhuta were probably brought there from Tell er-Retabeh. It is a plausible suggestion that Pithom in Exod. 1.11 originally referred to Tell er-Retabeh, whether or not this conformed to normal Egyptian nomenclature at the time, which points to the relative antiquity of the biblical narrative at this point (on which see the ensuing discussion of the name Ramesses), since at a later date the name clearly referred to Tell el-Maskhuta. It is possible to argue, as Redford and Holladay do, that the only clear extra-biblical evidence for Pithom as a town-name comes from the later period and refers to Tell el-Maskhuta, and that therefore this element of the biblical narrative must likewise be late, but the argument is not totally compelling, in view of the evidence relating to Tell er-Retabeh.

The identification of Ramesses has also been debated (see below), but in this case the much greater quantity of both textual and archaeological evidence has led in recent years to a consensus. The extensive source-material for the reign of Ramesses II (cf. K.A. Kitchen, *Ramesside Inscriptions* [Oxford, 1968–90]; *RITA*, *RITANC* [volumes on Ramesses II, 1996, 1999]) frequently refers to his new royal city in the Nile Delta, Pi-Ramesse (see the surveys of the evidence by A. Gardiner, 'The Delta Residence of the Pharaohs', *JEA* 5 [1918], pp. 127-38, 179-200, 242-71, and more briefly Uphill, 'Pithom and Raamses', pp. 15-23; examples in *ANET*, pp. 470-71; summaries in Kitchen, *Pharaoh Triumphant*, pp. 119-23, E.F. Wente, *ABD* 5, 617-18, M. Gitton, 'Ramses', *DBS* 9, pp. 1117-21). Of particular interest in the present context are the passages which refer to the great granaries of Pi-Ramesse: it is said to be 'full of food and provisions' and 'its granaries are (so) full of barley and emmer (that) they come near to the sky' (*ANET*, pp. 470, 471; cf. Weimar-Zenger, *Exodus*, pp. 118-20). After early identification with both Tell el-Maskhuta (Lepsius, resulting in the naming of a modern railway station nearby) and Tell er-Retabeh (Petrie), A. Gardiner briefly championed the claims of Pelusium on the Mediterranean coast (thereby reviving a traditional interpretation which can be traced back to the first cent. A.D.: cf. my *Way of the Wilderness*, pp. 13, 19, 21). But following the excavations at Tanis (San el-Hagar) begun by P. Montet in 1929, he, Gardiner and many others (e.g. Bright, *History*, p. 111 [cf. p. 54]) came to understand the numerous Ramesside monuments found at the site as indications of its identity with Pi-Ramesse (cf. Gardiner, 'Tanis and Pi-Ramesse: A Retractation', *JEA* 19 [1933], pp. 122-28). At the same time, however, excavations were begun a little to the south at Qantir and Tell el-Daba and in 1954 A. Alt put forward the influential proposal that Tanis and Qantir/Tell el-Daba were respectively the religious and the administrative parts of Pi-Ramesse (*Die Deltaresidenz der Ramessiden* = *Kleine Schriften* 3, pp. 176-85: followed by Herrmann, *Israels Aufenthalt*, pp. 45-46 [ET pp. 26-27]; Schmidt, pp. 37-38; Weimar-Zenger, *Exodus*, p. 119). This theory, and the identification with Tanis *tout court*, proved to be untenable when closer examination established that the Ramesside monuments at Tanis were not in their original location (Uphill, 'Pithom and Raamses', pp. 23-39). It is now agreed that Pi-Ramesse (like the earlier Hyksos capital Avaris) was at Qantir/Tell el-Daba and that the Ramesside monuments now at Tanis were taken from Qantir/Tell el-Daba to there when, in the mid-twelfth century B.C., Tanis took over the role of major political centre in the eastern Delta. It is this later pre-eminence of Tanis which is reflected in the biblical references to its Hebrew equivalent Zoan (*ṣōʿan*) as the site of events associated with the Exodus (Ps. 78.12, 43). Excavations at Tell el-Daba from 1966 to 1969 and from 1975 to the present and at Qantir have confirmed these conclusions and brought to light further archaeological evidence of the Hyksos capital and of the New Kingdom structures in the area (cf. M. Bietak, 'Avaris and Pi-Ramesse', *PBA* 65 [1979], pp. 225-89 [also published separately]; *Avaris: The Capital of the Hyksos* [London, 1996]; and esp. id. and Forstner-Müller, 'Topography'.

The reference to Ramesses by name seems likely to be an early element of the biblical tradition. Doubts raised by D.B. Redford about the omission of the original Pi (or Per) of the name and the spelling of the main element with *samekh* rather than *shin* ('Exodus I 11') were answered by W. Helck ('*Ṯkw* und die Ramses-Stadt'). The fact that Pi-Ramesse ceased to be a place of any importance in the mid-twelfth century (cf. p. 47), even though the memory of Ramesses II himself was maintained for centuries (Kitchen, *Pharaoh Triumphant*, pp. 227-31) makes it unlikely that it would have first come to the notice of Israelites at the time, say, of the Babylonian exile. This may have some relevance for the treatment of Pithom as well. While a late origin for that element of the tradition is in principle possible, in view of the use of the name for Tell el-Maskhuta in the Babylonian and Persian periods, its association with Ramesses favours an identification which makes it too a relatively early feature of the tradition. As indicated above, such an identification seems to be available in relation to Tell er-Retabeh. In some more recent studies the antiquity of the mention of both places here has again been questioned on archaeological and linguistic grounds (Van Seters, 'The Geography of the Exodus'; Redford, 'The Land of Ramesses', in P.J. Brand and L. Cooper [eds.], *Causing his Name to Live* [Leiden, 2009], pp. 175-77; L.L. Grabbe, 'Exodus and History', in Dozeman et al. [eds.], *Book of Exodus*, pp. 61-87 [71-74]; B.U. Schipper, 'Raamses, Pithom, and the Exodus': A Critical Evaluation of Exodus 1:11', *VT* 65 [2015], pp. 265-88). Fuller evidence about the equivalences of Egyptian and Semitic sibilants has been assembled by J. Hoch (*Semitic Words in Egyptian Texts of the New Kingdom and Third Intermediate Period* [Princeton, 1994]), but there continues to be some indication of variation in the earlier period (cf. Hoch, p. 270); alternatively it would not be surprising if the old spelling of Ramesses had been a little garbled or adjusted over the centuries. Further, the new alternative scenario presented by Schipper for the origin of the place-names in the context of later Egyptian expansion into Palestine at the end of the seventh century (pp. 276-82) is highly speculative (and in part improbable): in any case the older narrative is scarcely as late as this.

12. The key terms of the first two clauses in this verse are drawn from the preceding context (esp. 'multiply' in v. 10 and 'cause them hardship' in v. 11), but the combination expresses the exact opposite of what had been intended to happen and calls in question the 'wisdom' of the plan proposed by Pharaoh in vv. 10-11. The narrative thus expresses the same unexpected turn of events as Prov. 16.25. The third verb, 'increased' (Heb. *pāraṣ*), often carries the connotation of 'spread abroad' when it has this meaning, as in Gen. 28.14; Isa. 54.3; Job 1.10; 1 Chr. 4.38. The first of these verses is part of Yahweh's promise to Jacob, and the verb is used of Jacob's own prosperity in Gen. 30.43 (cf. v. 30). Here the same promise may be in view (so Schmidt, p. 40; Van Seters, *Life of Moses*, p. 21), just as the verb 'multiplied' picks up the vocabulary of the promises to the patriarchs (see on v. 7) and one of their major themes. Therefore, although there is no explicit theological explanation of the Israelites' continued growth in numbers in Egypt here, it is strongly implied that the unexpected outcome is a result of Yahweh's declared purpose. But this is not known to the Egyptians and should not be seen as the reason for their 'dread': like the two closest parallels to the use of Heb. *qwṣ* here (Num. 22.3; Isa. 7.16), it is due to the presence of a large (potentially) hostile mass (cf. vv. 9-10).

13-14. In the following verses the Egyptians (or their king) appear to impose two additional measures to counter the continuing growth in the Israelite population. First, they increase the severity of their forced labour (cf. 'bitter' and 'hard labour' in v. 14; 'harshly' in vv. 13-14; and the widening of scope implied by 'in the fields' in v. 14), whether or not (see Note q on the Translation) it should technically be described as slavery. But then, without waiting to see if this has any effect, they devise a plan to prevent a new generation of males from reaching maturity. The redundancy of the narrative is probably to be explained by the combination of extracts from different versions of the story (see the introduction to this section): linguistic features (see the notes on the translation, and below) favour the attribution of vv. 13-14 to the Priestly source, as its parallel to vv. 8-11(12), and of vv. 15-21(22) to one of the older sources, where it introduced the Moses stories which begin at 2.1. The phrase 'hard labour' is relatively rare: it recurs in the Priestly speech of God to Moses in 6.8 and occurs elsewhere only in Deut. 26.6; 1 Kgs 12.4 = 2 Chr. 10.4; Isa. 14.3. In the last three passages it refers to Solomon's rule and the Babylonian exile. The occurrence in Deut. 26.6 is part of the Deuteronomic amplification of an older cultic formula (A.D.H. Mayes, *Deuteronomy* [NCB; London, 1979], pp. 334-35; E. Nielsen, *Deuteronomium* [HAT; Tübingen, 1995], pp. 237-40). It is at least possible that the reference to Solomon's rule (which derives ultimately from north Israelite circles) is the most ancient of these occurrences and the model for the others. On 'clay and bricks' see the notes on ch. 5. Work 'in the fields' most naturally refers to agricultural labour (for this meaning of *śdh* cf. Gen. 37.7; 47.24;

Exod. 22.4-5; Lev. 27.16-24), though care of Egyptian livestock is perhaps also a possibility (Gen. 47.6, 16-18; Exod. 9.3-6 [cf. *śdh* in v. 3]). Working on another man's land was perhaps especially humiliating, both in contrast to the expected possession of family land and for those used, as the Israelites had been, to the freedom of shepherds tending their own flocks. An allusion to work on the land in Egypt appears in a different context in Deut. 11.10, but it is not clear there whether the Israelites were working for themselves or for others (though n.b. 6.21) or indeed whether the 'you' refers to them at all rather than being general and indefinite (for which see examples in GK §144h and JM §155h).

15. As a more drastic response to the failure of his plan, the 'king of Egypt' (cf. vv. 17-18; v. 19 has 'Pharaoh', probably a free variation) attempts to prevent any further increase in the male Israelite population (as potential warriors [cf. v. 10]?) by ordering their midwives to practise selective infanticide. They are called 'Hebrew midwives' (or 'midwives of the Hebrew women': see Text and Versions). The term 'Hebrew' is used twice more in the following verses (vv. 16 and 19: also in v. 22 in SP and some of the Versions), four times more in ch. 2 (vv. 6-7, 11, 13) and six times in the formula 'the God of the Hebrews' in chs. 3–10 (see the Explanatory Note on 3.18). The explanation for the use of this alternative name for the Israelites (as it appears to be) has been much debated, particularly since the discovery, from the nineteenth century onwards, of non-biblical texts referring to *ʿpr* or *ḫabiru*. The interpretation of these latter terms too is controversial.[6] Two preliminary points may be noted about the biblical occurrences of 'Hebrew'. The first is that very often, but not always, in narrative it is (as here) a term used by non-Israelites and in conversation with them, as has often been noted. It is not so often observed that the distribution of the term is quite restricted (in addition to the Exodus passages mentioned already, five times in the first part of the Joseph story [Gen. 39–43, beginning with 'the Hebrew slave' in 39.17], six times in connection with a law about the emancipation of slaves [the oldest being Exod. 21.2, where see the Explanatory Note], eight times in 1 Samuel [mainly in chs. 4, 13 and 14] and additionally in Gen. 14.13 and Jonah 1.9),

---

[6] A possible new reference to 'Hebrews' has now been detected in a Moabite inscription from c. 800 B.C.: A.L. Bean et al., 'An Inscribed Altar from the Khirbet Ataruz Moabite Sanctuary', *Levant* 50 (2018), pp. 211-36 (217, 219, 229).

and most of these passages are in one way or another associated with the northern tribes or the northern kingdom of Israel. Negatively it should be noted that the term is absent from Deuteronomy (except for the special case of Deut. 15.12, where it is likely to be derived from the earlier parallel in Exod. 21.2), from Deuteronomistic editorial material, and from Priestly texts. Further study is needed of this distribution pattern, but a provisional conclusion could be that the term was current among northern Israelites, especially as one which was known to be used or understood by foreigners speaking about them, and this might then be one factor in determining the traditio-historical background of Exod. 1.15–2.22.

The origin of the term, as indicated, remains a matter of dispute. O. Loretz (*Habiru-Hebräer* [BZAW 160; Berlin, 1984]) is a recent exponent of the view that it is a purely national designation used only in late texts for the members (and forebears) of the post-exilic Jewish community. According to him it is ultimately derived from *ḥabiru/ḥapiru*, but the meaning is quite different and no historical conclusions can be deduced from its use in the Old Testament. The articles by N.P. Lemche in *ABD* ('Ḥabiru, Ḥapiru', 3, pp. 6-10; 'Hebrew', 3, p. 95), while cautious, are more positive. He questions the late date given to many of the OT references and notes especially Exod. 21.2 as 'a testimony of the survival in Israel of an age-long societal connection'. He too accepts a link of 'Hebrew' with *ḥabiru* and believes that 'some aspects of the former social meaning of the expression have survived almost everywhere in the OT where the expression is used' (p. 95; cf. Lemche, '"Hebrew" as National Name for Israel', *StTh* 33 [1979], pp. 1-23; N. Naaman, 'Ḥabiru and Hebrews: The Transfer of a Social Term to the Literary Sphere', *JNES* 45 [1986], pp. 271-88; in his *Die Vorgeschichte Israels* [Stuttgart, 1996], pp. 50, 62-63, 141-45, Lemche plays down the possibility of a historical connection, but appears not to rule it out altogether). Thus the notion of 'refugees' or 'outsiders' may have been preserved for a time in Exodus too in the use of the term 'Hebrew'. For this purpose it is not necessary to suppose (as e.g. R. de Vaux did: *Histoire ancienne*, pp. 106-12, 202-208 [ET pp. 105-12, 209-16] that *ḥabiru* itself was an ethnic term: it is sufficient if the 'Israelites' in Egypt 'were part of a much wider group of people' (ibid., p. 207 [ET p. 215]) who were defined by their social situation rather than by their ethnicity. It is perfectly understandable that from its use almost exclusively of Israel in the early narratives of the OT (1 Sam. 14.21 is the only clear [but very significant] exception; cf. also the reference to 'the sons of Eber' in Gen. 10.21) that it came to be used as an alternative to 'Jew' in later times (see further my 'Was There an Exodus?' and the bibliography mentioned above, also the discussions of M. Weippert, *The Settlement of the Israelite Tribes* [London, 1971], pp. 63-102, and H. Cazelles, 'The Hebrews', *POTT*, pp. 1-28; the relevant non-biblical texts were collected by J. Bottéro, *Le problème des Ḥabiru* [CahSA 12; Paris, 1954]; see also his article 'Ḥabiru', in *RLA* 4, 14-27 (with a list of texts to 1971), and *Dialogues d'histoire ancienne* 6 [1980], pp. 201-13] and by M. Greenberg, *The Ḥab/piru* [AOS 39; New Haven, 1955]).

The midwives, who are the heroines of this section of the story, are immediately made prominent by being named. The names themselves, although not found elsewhere in the Bible, are both plausible Semitic forms. Shiphrah means 'fair(ness)' in Job 26.13 and is related to words in Hebrew and Aramaic meaning 'pleasing, beautiful' (see the lexica, esp. *HAL*, p. 1509, where references to Amorite names are given). Puah was explained by Noth (*Israelitische Personennamen*, 10.204) from the Hebrew root yp^c = 'shine', but a more attractive view relates it to Ugaritic $pġt$ = 'girl' (Gordon, *UT*, 2081), which is used as a proper name for Danel's daughter in the Aqhat text (*KTU* 1.19.1.34 etc.). The names are thus a strong argument against the view that the midwives were Egyptian women (see the discussions in Houtman, pp. 251-52, where this view is followed, and in Gertz, *Tradition*, p. 373 n. 103, where it is [convincingly] rejected). The fact that there are only two of them has been variously explained: older views saw them as leaders of guilds (Ibn Ezra, B. Jacob) or as all that were needed in the light of v. 19 (Dillmann); more recently the number has been attributed to a version of the story which envisaged only a relatively small group of Israelites (e.g. Noth, p. 12 [ET, p. 23]) or to the 'laws' of *Sage* (Schmidt) or, better, to a general simplicity and lack of precise realism (Houtman; cf. Gunkel, *Genesis*, pp. xxxiv-xxxvi [= *Legends*, pp. 47-52]). Modern data about birth-rates in Africa (50 per thousand of population per annum) and midwives' 'productivity' suggest that two midwives would suffice for a population of about 8,000.

16. The exact nature of the instructions given to the midwives depends on the interpretation of the rare Heb. *'obnayim* (see further Note x on the Translation). The translation 'sexual organs' given here can find some support in later Hebrew, and is preferable to the older view that a form of the traditional 'birthstool' on which the mother squatted or knelt is referred to (for ancient evidence see F. Weindler, *Geburts- und Wochenbettsdarstellungen auf altägyptischen Tempelreliefs* [Munich, 1915], *NERTOT*, pp. 35, 39, and H.E. Sigerist, *A History of Medicine*, 1 [New York, 1951], pp. 242-43 and pl. 26). Schmidt notes biblical evidence that, not surprisingly, midwives did observe a child's sex (Gen. 35.17; 1 Sam. 4.20). That midwives should be expected to turn such homely observations to the service of such a brutal royal plan only emphasises the king's cruelty.

17. Undeterred by the king's authority and power, the midwives do not carry out his instructions. The explanation given for this is that 'they feared God'. This is not simply equivalent to 'having moral norms' (Weinfeld, *Deuteronomy*, p. 275, who equates it with 'conscience' in passages like this: compare his erroneous view [p. 274] that 'in the wisdom literature...[it] is synonymous with wisdom'), but represents the religious attitude which has as one of its consequences the observance of moral norms (Schmidt – cf. *THAT* 1, 771 = *TLOT*, p. 573). Siebert-Hommes, *Let the Daughters*, p. 113, points out the specific link with respect for human life in Gen. 20.11; 42.18. For 'the fear of the Lord' as a response to specific actions or words of Yahweh later in Exodus; cf. 9.20; 14.31; 20.20 (and compare Gen. 22.10). But here and, e.g., in 18.21 'the fear of God' (*sic*) reflects the existence of an 'unwritten law', which even non-Israelites can be expected to recognise and follow (cf. Gen. 20.11; 42.18; Deut. 25.18). This is apparently a distinct and probably earlier idea than the association of 'the fear of the Lord' with obedience to the revealed commandments of Yahweh, as found in numerous passages in the Deuteronomic literature and in Leviticus (on which see Weinfeld, *Deuteronomy*, pp. 274, 279-81; *THAT* 1, 774, 777 = *TLOT*, pp. 575-77). In Genesis and Exodus 'fear of God' appears to be the main religio-ethical theme of the passages traditionally ascribed to the Elohist source: see Wolff, 'Thematik', pp. 59-72 (62-67); ET in Brueggemann and Wolff, *Vitality*, pp. 67-82 (70-75); for the question of whether wisdom or early prophetic usage lies behind this see *THAT* 1, 777 = *TLOT*, p. 577 and the references there to S. Plath and J. Becker's discussions). L. Derousseaux, *La crainte de Dieu dans l'AT* (Paris, 1970), Chapter 4, suggested that the moral concept of the fear of God therefore originated in the northern kingdom (cf. *TWAT* 3, 880, 888-89 = *TDOT* 6, pp. 301 n. 74, 309-11). There is also some evidence for the 'cultic' (or religious loyalty) use in early northern prophetic texts (1 Kgs 18.3, 12; 2 Kgs 4.1; Hos. 10.3); some have even seen a moral nuance in these passages (*TWAT* 3, 889 = *TDOT* 6, p. 310), but this seems less likely. H.F. Fuhs (*TWAT* 3, 889 = *TDOT* 6, p. 311) appears to favour the view that the ethical usage derives originally from the wisdom literature, but it remains a question whether the early examples there actually refer to ethical behaviour rather than a religious attitude *per se*. For a Sumerian text linking the 'fear' of a god with ethics as well as cult see *COS* 1, p. 570.

18-19. The midwives' reply to Pharaoh's indignant question asserts a physical superiority on the part of the Hebrew women ('strong', literally 'lively', is preferable to other translations that have been offered: see Note dd on the translation) and seems to satisfy him. It is, however, clearly a trick based on a lie and this has led to an impassioned debate among Jewish and Christian commentators about when, if ever, lying is morally justifiable (cf. Childs, pp. 23-24; Klopfenstein, *Die Lüge*, pp. 339-40). In the present context that is not an issue and the midwives' statement appears, like their original action, to be viewed with divine favour (cf. v. 20a). Such use of trickery by a weaker party to outwit a stronger one is a commonplace of folklore and is not infrequent in older biblical narratives. The fact that such action is regarded here as compatible with 'the fear of God' sheds interesting light on the parameters of the latter term.

20-21. The narrative reaches a provisional climax with the rewarding of the midwives by God, curiously interrupted by a further statement about the increase in the numbers of the people as a whole which uses the vocabulary respectively of vv. 12 and 7. The formulation of v. 21, with its repetition of the statement about the midwives' fear of God from v. 17, provides a summarising and didactic conclusion to the episode. The midwives' reward is large families, appropriately enough: there is no need to embellish the story further by suggestions that they had previously been barren or that their families were particularly distinguished.

22. Thwarted by the failure of his previous schemes, Pharaoh issues an edict to the whole Egyptian people. The distinction between males and females is the same as before (for the possible motive see on v. 16). His instructions omit the crucial words '(born to) the Hebrews', which the Samaritan text and some of the Ancient Versions supply (see the note below), but the imagined context leaves no real doubt who is meant. Nothing explicit is said about the carrying out of this measure, but the actions of Moses' mother in 2.2-3 presuppose that the danger had to be taken seriously.

Text and Versions

פרו וישרצו וירבו (1.7)   LXX ηὐξήθησαν καὶ ἐπληθύνθησαν καὶ χυδαῖοι ἐγένοντο begins with its standard equivalents for the Qal of פרה and רבה in Genesis (1.22, 28; 8.17; 9.1, 7; 35.11; 47.27; cf. 17.20; 28.3; 48.4) and delays its equivalent for the rarer שרץ (Wevers, *Notes*, p. 3). χυδαῖος (from χέω, 'pour out') occurs only here in LXX: its meaning is generally 'common, ordinary, vulgar' (cf. NETS; LSJ, pp. 2012-13), but that hardly fits the context. More probably, like the adv. χύδην, it has the sense 'overflowing, widespread' here (see the excellent note of *BAlex*, pp. 74-75), which fits this occurrence of שרץ well. The Three preferred harmonising renderings based on its more common use of animals as in 7.28 (cf. O'Connell, *Theodotionic Revision*, p. 290).

ותמלא הארץ אתם (1.7)   LXX ἐπλήθυνεν δὲ ἡ γῆ αὐτούς erroneously took ותמלא as Piel (not Hiphil, as Wevers, *Notes*, p. 3) and then gave מלא the sense of רבה: the Three properly corrected the verb to a passive form of πληρόω (cf. Tgᴼ, Sy, Vulg).

חדש (1.8)   TgF has the interpretation 'at the beginning' (sc. of his reign), which TgJ combines with the literal rendering of the other Tgg. LXX ἕτερος is 'good Greek' for 'new' according to Walters, who cites Plato, *Phileb.* 13a in support (p. 215): the Three nevertheless preferred καινός.

את־יוסף (1.8)   Almost all Sy mss have *lh lywsp*, with the idiomatic additional pronoun (cf. Brockelmann §216): only 5b1 omits *lh* to remain close to Heb.

הבה (1.10)   The Versions, in line with the plural addressee in the context, render by plural imperative forms rather than by a corresponding interjection. SP agrees with MT, as does 4QGen-Exodᵃ, the only Qumran ms. to contain this verse.

תקראנה (1.10)   On attempts to make sense of MT see Note g on the translation. SP reads תקראנו, '(when war) befalls us', which fits the normal usage of קרא/קרה better: the only example of its being used absolutely for 'happen' is in the participle in Isa. 41.22, which may be a special case. 4QExodᵇ reads

תקרנו (not in *DJD*),[7] agreeing in sense with SP but spelt according to a derivation from קרה rather than קרא. LXX συμβῇ ἡμῖν, Sy *nmṭyn*, Vulg *ingruerit contra nos*, Tg⁰ יערעינגא and Tgʲ יארע יתן all presuppose the SP reading. Only Tgᴺ ערע סדרי קרבא, '(when) battle lines are drawn', seeks to render MT (the marginal readings and the variants in Tgᶠ relate not to this phrase [as implied in McNamara's apparatus] but to the end of the verse [cf. the *editio princeps*]). MT's reading, which is probably an error, could be due to confusion with other words nearby which end in *he*.

ונלחם בנו (1.10)   Tgᴺ adds 'and set a king over them'.

Throughout vv. 10-12 the Versions use plural forms to refer to the Israelites, in contrast to the singulars of MT, SP (except in v. 11aβb, where it has the plural) and 4QGen-Exodᵃ. Plural forms are also found in 2QExodᵃ, where it survives in v. 12. These renderings, and the Hebrew variants, are clearly *ad sensum* and do not represent the original text. In the case of SP in v. 11aβb the temporary divergence may be due to misunderstanding of the suffix of בסבלתם as referring to the Israelites.

וישימו (1.11)   LXX (apart from a minority of witnesses) and Vulg have a singular verb here (but not for the subsequent acts of Egyptian oppression in vv. 11-12), attributing the appointment of the overseers to Pharaoh alone, rather than to the Egyptian 'people' (v. 9) as a whole, as in MT, SP and the other Versions. There is no relevant evidence from Qumran. The singular form fits the dominant role of Pharaoh in the rest of the Exodus narrative, but that is a good reason for regarding it as the inferior reading.

מסכנות (1.11)   LXX ὀχυράς and Tgᴺ תליל give the meaning 'strong, fortified' (Tgʲ combines the renderings of Tg⁰ – on which see Note l above – and Tgᴺ), using words that render the root בצר in Deut. 3.5 and 28.52 and probably guessing (wrongly) at the meaning. The traces in 2QExodᵃ are not sufficient to show whether it had a reading different from MT. Aq's σκηνωμάτων and the (*urbes*) *tabernaculorum* of Vulg no doubt rest on a mistaken association of the word with the root שכן, which is sometimes rendered by σκηνόω (and compare the rendering of מסכנות in the A-text at 1 Kgs 9.19).

את־פתם ואת־רעמסס (1.11)   To transliterations of the Hebrew names LXX added Ὤν, ἥ ἐστιν Ἡλίου πόλις, known from Gen. 41.45-50; 46.20 as the home of Joseph's father-in-law Potiphera. The rationale for the addition is unclear, unless it was to claim for the Israelites the credit for (re?)building another once great Egyptian city, which is also mentioned in some prophetic passages (see *ABD* 3, pp. 122-23): Eusebius, *Onom.* 176.4-6, saw the problem that Genesis itself presupposes the existence of the city before Jacob and his sons came to Egypt and preferred the MT reading, which he will have

---

[7] Cf. E. Tigchelaar, 'On the Unidentified Fragments of *DJD* XXXIII and PAM 43.680: A New Manuscript of *4QNarrative and Poetic Composition*, and Fragments of *4Q13, 4Q269* and *4QSb(?)*', *RQ* 21 (2003–2004), pp. 477-85 (483).

known from the *obelus* in Origen's Hexapla. The possibility of some connection between the LXX reading and third-century predecessors of the Jewish communities around the temple of Leontopolis and at Demerdash, both in the vicinity of Heliopolis, and with traditions linking the Israelites and Moses specifically with the Heliopolis region deserves investigation (for details see W. Horbury and D. Noy, *Jewish Inscriptions of Graeco-Roman Egypt* [Cambridge, 1992], pp. xvi-xxiv and *passim*; see further J. Schwartz, *BIFAO* 49 [1950], pp. 68-82, esp. 78ff., and for a different view my *Way of the Wilderness*, pp. 8, 95 n. 4). In the Palestinian Targum the cities named in MT are represented by the names of places in the Delta still known in late antiquity, Tanis and Pelusium: see my *Way of the Wilderness*, pp. 13, 19, 21-22.

ירבה (1.12)   SP יפרה, 'became fruitful', a verb used earlier in v. 7: the variant involves the substitution of one letter and its interchange with the adjacent one. The Versions, 2QExod^a, and 4QGen-Exod^a all read or imply a form of רבה at this point. The SP reading may be due to confusion with the next verb יפרץ, which also follows כן.

יפרץ (1.12)   2QExod^a reads ישרצו (on the plural form see the note above on vv. 10-12), from שרץ, with which רבה is more frequently paired (cf. v. 7 and other references in Note a there). LXX (ἴσχυον, which is followed in many mss [including B and M] by σφόδρα σφόδρα [from v. 7? cf. perhaps 2QExod^a])[8] gives the meaning 'grew strong' and Sy and Tgg add this, which might point to a Vorlage יעצם or ועצם, again as in v. 7 and also in v. 20. These readings are certainly inferior to the new but contextually appropriate word in MT and SP.

ויקצו (1.12)   LXX ἐβδελύσσοντο, Aq. ἐσικχαίνοντο and Vulg *oderunt* all give קוץ the meaning 'loathe', which it has when followed by ב. Tgg and Sy (cf. ὁ σύρος and ὁ ἑβραῖος as cited by Wevers ad loc.), with their use of the root עוק, 'be distressed, fear', give the correct meaning here. LXX, Tgg and possibly 2QExod^a (cf. in addition to the space available the inclusion of מצרים in the repetition of v. 12b which appears after v. 14, on which see below) add 'the Egyptians' to make clear the change of subject.[9]

בפרך (1.13-14)   While most of the Versions give the expected rendering 'violently, harshly', Theod (<ἐν> ἐμπαιγμῷ: Lev. 25.43, 46; Ezek. 34.4

---

[8] Wevers (*Notes*, p. 6; cf. *THGE*, p. 239) regards the longer text as secondary, grouping it with other instances where the text tradition expands the text as it left the hands of the translator. But, given the frequency of harmonisation with MT (hexaplaric and non-hexaplaric) in the textual tradition and the weak attestation of the shorter text here, the longer text may go back to the OG (cf. the edition of Rahlfs).

[9] In *DJD* XII, p. 18, the text of 4QGen-Exod^a, which is damaged after ויקוצו, is erroneously reconstructed on the basis of this variant and another attested by many LXX witnesses (but not the original Greek according to Wevers) to produce a much longer ending to the verse than in MT: the editor has apparently confused the occurrences of בני ישראל in vv. 12 and 13.

similarly), Symm (ἐντρυφῶντες: Ezek. 34.4 εὐφραινόμενοι) and Vulg (*inludentes eis*) on v. 13 give the sense 'with mockery'. This corresponds to early midrash in Jos., *AJ* 2.202 and possibly *LAB* 9.10 (cf. Salvesen, *Symmachus*, pp. 63-64): the linguistic basis, if any, for it remains obscure.

וימררו (1.14) 4QGen-Exod[a] reads the singular, against all other witnesses. This is apparently an accidental error: while a reference to Pharaoh is possible (cf. vv. 11, 15), an explicit mention of the new subject would be expected.

At the end of v. 14 2QExod[a] repeats v. 12b and probably (in a preceding lacuna) some of v. 12a (*DJD* III, p. 49). The aim of this secondary material must be to explain why there is a need for the further measures initiated by Pharaoh in v. 16. A similar addition was made in the LXX miniscule 14 (see Wevers's apparatus: cf. Exod.R. 1.13 init.). For the same reason Tg[J] inserted a *haggadah* in which a dream of Pharaoh is interpreted by his magicians Jannes and Jambres to mean that an Israelite child is to be born who will destroy all Egypt: a very similar explanation is given in Jos., *AJ* 2.205 (for other parallels see *AramB* 2, p. 162).

למילדת העבריח (1.15) LXX, ταῖς μαίαις τῶν Ἑβραίων, and Vulg, *obsetricibus Hebraeorum*, read למילדת as in the construct state, against the vowels of MT (לְמְ instead of לַמְ) and thus left the ethnicity of the midwives undefined (see the discussion above in the Explanatory Note). For העבריח the original reading of 5b1 (as in most other mss of Sy) was *'bryt'* but 'a much later corrector' has changed this to *mṣryt'*, as in Josephus's description of the midwives as 'Egyptian' (*AJ* 2.206-207; cf. Koster, p. 107).

שפרה...ופועה (1.15) Ms 5b1 of Sy unusually departs here from MT by inverting the order of the midwives' names, probably accidentally by parablepsis: the phrases that precede them are even more similar in Syr. than in Heb. Tg[F,J] identify them with Jochebed and Miriam respectively.

האבנים (1.16) So also SP: 4QGen-Exod[a] האב[נים]. Tg[O, J] מתברא, 'birthstool' (cf. Tg[J] at Num. 12.12 [in an expansion of MT]; Targum Jonathan at 2 Sam. 22.5), Tg[N] מתבריא (pl.). LXX (ὦσιν πρὸς) τῷ (var. τὸ) τίκτειν, and Vulg *partus tempus* (*advenerit*) paraphrase, as does Sy *m' dbrkn*, 'when they are kneeling', with greater recognition of the physical situation of women giving birth. B. Stade ('Miscellen: 15. "Auf jemandes Knieen gebären" Gen. 30,3. 50,23. Hiob 3,12 und אָבְנָיִם Exod. 1,16', *ZAW* 6 [1886], pp. 143-56 [154-56]) saw Sy as support for emending to הַבִּרְכַּיִם, 'the knees' (but of the attendant: cf. Gen. 30.3 etc.); Beer proposed to read הִבָּנְתָן (Niphal inf. cons. of בנה plus suffix in the sense of 'become a mother' as in Gen. 16.2; 30.3) on the basis of LXX. But it is unlikely that these common words would have been changed into the rare form in the Heb. witnesses (cf. Schmidt, p. 6).

היא (1.16) The only place in Exodus where *BHS* (i.e. Codex L) does not have the Kethibh הוא (for which see 3.8 etc.) for the feminine pronoun. The number of such exceptions in the whole Pentateuch is generally given as eleven (GK §32l, JM §39c, apparently on the basis of the Masora, but *BHS*/L exhibits a number of additional instances [Gen. 19.20; 40.10; Lev. 5.11; 13.6; 20.18 as well as here]: Gen. 14.2; 20.5; 38.25, Lev. 11.39; 13.10, 21; 16.31;

20.17; 21.9; Num. 5.13-14). For discussion of the reason for the strange Kethibh elsewhere see the grammars cited and Note n on the translation of 3.1-12.

וחיה (1.16) There are probably three readings to consider: MT (on which see Note y on the translation above; cf. Tg^(J,N)), SP וחיתה (which is the regular feminine form) and 4QExod^b, which probably read [וחיי]תנה (2nd person pl. feminine perfect consecutive Piel of חיה, 'you shall keep (her) alive', with full orthography at the end [cf. אליהנה for אלהן of MT in v. 19]). The third reading may well have been the *Vorlage* of LXX περιποιεῖσθε αὐτό (though Wevers, *Notes*, p. 8, apparently sees the imperative as a free rendering of MT; likewise *BAlex*, p. 78, emphasising stylistic considerations), Tg^(O,Nmg), Sy and Vulg MT, as the most difficult reading, is surely original; SP is a typical linguistic simplification, and the third reading (with its equivalents in the versions) involves a more drastic reformulation of the clause to match the way in which the treatment of the boys is expressed.

מלך מצרים (1.18) SP has פרעה here (cf. v. 19), though no such variant appears in v. 15. Here SP's reading leads more smoothly into the introduction to the midwives' response in v. 19.

למילדת (1.18) 4QExod^b adds העבריות, in conformity with v. 15, no doubt secondarily (cf. Sah).

הדבר (1.18) SP inserts the 'missing' את to make the grammar more regular.

חיות (1.19) So also SP. The Versions' renderings fall into three main groups (cf. Salvesen, *Symmachus*, pp. 64-65): Symm μαῖαι, Sy ḥyt', Vulg *obsetricandi habent scientiam* and possibly Tg^O, ḥkmyn, 'wise', understand it as 'midwives' (cf. MH); LXX τίκτουσιν, 'bear, are in labour', reflects a different use of the same MH word; and Tg^(N,F) translate by חיין, 'lively', while a medieval corrector of Codex Ambrosianus (F) has ὑγίαινον, 'were healthy'. Tg^J combines the first and third of these alternatives in a double rendering, and Aq's λοχαῖ<αι> (Sy^hex yldt') and Theod.'s ζωογονοῦσιν are probably best taken as alternative ways of expressing the second meaning without using a verb which elsewhere in the passage represents ילד. Salvesen's note on Theod is largely on the right lines, but overlooks the fact that Theod is a reviser of LXX who no doubt sought a way of giving some weight to the root חיה while retaining the overall sense offered by LXX. All these renderings are based on the consonants of MT. The only Qumran ms. to provide even indirect evidence is 4QExod^b, in which there seems to be insufficient space for the phrase חיות הנה. Cross therefore suggests that these words are a gloss added in MT and the Hebrew underlying most of the Versions (*DJD* XII, p. 86), but not in the *Vorlage* of LXX. As shown above, LXX can be seen as a rendering of the consonants of MT: there is no need to envisage a different *Vorlage*, such as חלות (Beer) or לדנה(ת?) (Cross). Nevertheless LXX reflects an understanding of the phrase which makes it virtually redundant (Eth actually omits it altogether, and a few other witnesses omit καὶ ἔτικτον at the end of the verse), as synonymous with וילדו, and such an understanding of the MT reading may have led to its omission in 4QExod[b] (or its archetype) and Eth. This is at least as likely as Cross's reconstruction of the history of the text.

הַמְיַלְּדֹת[20] (1.20)   Tg[N,F,J] add that it was the answered prayers of the Hebrew women which were responsible for the early births.

לַמְיַלְּדֹת (1.20)   Sy (except 5b1, which agrees with MT) adds *mṭl dʿbd ptgmʾ hnʾ*, 'because they did (f.pl.) this thing', supplying an explanation that was evidently felt to be lacking (though surely implied by the context). The addition is probably from the secondary stage of the Peshiṭta tradition.

וַיִּרֶב (1.20)   SP pl., conforming to the verb which follows; likewise several older mss of Sy, Tg[J,N] – compare the use of the plural *ad sensum* by various witnesses in vv. 10-12. The other versions (and 5b1 of Sy) follow MT's singular form, which is doubtless original.

וַיְהִי (1.21)   According to Cross (*DJD* XII, p. 87), possibly omitted by 4QExod[b]. LXX has no equivalent but this is not evidence of a shorter *Vorlage*: see Wevers, *Notes*, p. 16, on 2.11 (note also the lack of an equivalent to ויהי in v. 10 in LXX); Vulg similarly, but it has no equivalent in ten out of sixteen comparable instances in Exodus 1–20. Sy follows Heb., and 5b1 keeps even closer to it than the other mss in its rendering of the conjunctions.

וַיַּעַשׂ (1.21)   LXX ἐποίησαν (cf. Tg[F] עבדו) implies a plural verb, presumably with the midwives as the subject, 'they made themselves houses'. On the confused hexaplaric evidence see the helpful note of Salvesen, *Symmachus*, p. 65 n. 8: she is surely right to conclude that Symm and Aq read ἐποίησεν in conformity with the sing. of MT, which is also supported by SP, Tg[O], Tg[J,N] (in their actual rendering of the Heb.: they use a plural verb [as does Tg[F]] in their additional matter), Sy and Vulg. Wevers (*Notes*, p. 10) suggests that LXX's plural is due to the preceding plural verb and the influence of 'conventional wisdom'. It is difficult to choose between the two readings.

בָּתִּים (1.21)   Tg[N,F,J] add that these were the royal house and the high-priestly house.

כֹּל (1.22)   5b1 and some later mss of Sy prefix *d* (*recitativum*).

הַיִּלּוֹד (1.22)   4QGen-Exod[a] reads היל[ד], with defective writing of the form in MT. SP and LXX (4QGen-Exod[a] is unfortunately not extant at this point) agree in specifying (probably secondarily) that it is 'Hebrew' children who are meant, as in Jub. 47.2, 'to them': the same specification is found in Tg[O,J,N] (with the form [א]ליהודאי: this equivalent for עברי is regularly used in Exodus 1–10 by Onkelos and Pseudo-Jonathan, but by Neofiti only here).

הַיְאֹרָה (1.22)   SP היאר, without *he locale*, as with המים in 7.15. But the variation is not consistent and sometimes the ending is found in SP and not in MT (e.g. 4.20): see *GSH* §148d. The shorter form may be more original here.

תַּשְׁלִיכֻהוּ (1.22)   SP תשליכון, with *nun paragogicum* (cf. תחיון) but without the idiomatic resumptive suffix: probably another simplification of the language (cf. on וחיה in 1.16), though at the cost of the special emphasis on the treatment of the boys in MT. The resumptive pronoun is not represented in LXX, so that it is possible (though no more) that it was translated from a *Vorlage* like SP here.

Chapter 2.1-10

The Naming of Moses

In the midst of the renewed threats to the existence of the people descended from Jacob (1.22), the focus of the narrative is now concentrated on a particular family. The story serves to introduce the figure of Moses, who will be the divinely appointed leader of the Israelites in their escape from the oppression described in ch. 1 and the central human character in the narratives to follow. The individual focus is maintained (with the brief exception of 2.11) until 2.23 and more especially 3.7, where it is incorporated into the continuation of the dominant national epic narrative. The main story-line in 2.1-10 tells of Moses' birth to a Levite family, his preservation through the kindness of an Egyptian princess (whose behaviour contrasts sharply with that of her father in ch. 1 and his successor in later chapters) and his adoption and naming by her. A subsidiary plot-line (vv. 4, 7-10a), which may well be a secondary development (see below), tells of Moses' temporary restoration to the care of his natural mother. The narrative form predominates, being interrupted only by a brief dialogue in vv. 6b-8a and by further short speeches in vv. 9a and 10bβ. Grammatically the female characters predominate through most of the story, as is to be expected from the subject-matter: the main verbs are third person fem. sing. throughout, except for v. 1 and v. 10a. But, although his name does not appear until v. 10, Moses is everywhere at the centre of the narrator's (and the characters') interest, whether he is referred to by a noun ('son', 'child' or 'boy') or a pronoun ('he', 'him', 'his' or 'this'). These indirect references to him create a certain curiosity in the reader/hearer: who *is* this child and what will become of him? (for fuller analysis [not always well-founded] of the structure of the narrative and references to other literary studies of it see Siebert-Hommes, *Let the Daughters* Live!)

The narrative shares features with other descriptions of the birth and naming of a child in the OT (see the references in the note on v. 2 and the brief comments of Schmidt, p. 54), but it is distinctive because of the abnormal context of danger and the separation of the naming of the child from its birth. In addition M. Gerhards has noted that, as the account of the origin of a future leader of Israel, this passage is especially close in its function and length to the birth stories of Samson and Samuel (Judg. 13; 1 Sam. 1: *Aussetzungsgeschichte*, pp. 115-17). Elements of the story can be closely paralleled in ancient legend and legal practice. The closest and most commonly cited parallel is the 'Birth Legend of Sargon of Akkad' (*ANET*, p. 119; *COS* 1, p. 461), the story of a powerful king of the third millennium B.C. which is preserved in Neo-Assyrian and Neo-Babylonian copies (see B. Lewis, *The Sargon Legend: A Study of the Akkadian Text and the Tale of the Hero who was Exposed at Birth* [ASORDS 4; Cambridge MA, 1980]; more briefly Longman, *Fictional Akkadian Autobiography*, pp. 53-60, 70-72; Gerhards, pp. 149-264). Sargon is represented as the son of an unknown father and a high-priestess, who abandoned him in the river Euphrates:

> She placed me in a reed basket, she sealed my hatch with pitch.
> She left me to the river, whence I could not come up.
> The river carried me off, it brought me to Aqqi, drawer of water.
> Aqqi, drawer of water, brought me up as he dipped his bucket.
> Aqqi, drawer of water, raised me as his adopted son.
> Aqqi, drawer of water, set (me) to his orchard work. (*COS*, loc. cit.)

It was from here, Sargon says, that he was taken, through the love of the goddess Ishtar, to be king of Agade (Akkad). It is now generally agreed that this is a legend composed in the reign of Sargon's namesake Sargon II of Assyria in the late eighth century B.C. (cf. Longman, p. 58; Hallo, in *COS* 1, p. 401). While the similarity between (parts of) the Moses-story and the Assyrian text has been widely noted since it first publication in 1872 (see the short review of research in Gerhards, pp. 149-54, in addition to the discussions in the commentaries), most scholars have hesitated to infer that the former is directly dependent on the latter. This was, however, argued by E. Otto ('Mose und das Gesetz. Die Mose-Figur als Gegenentwurf politischer Theologie zur neuassyrischen Königsideologie im 7. Jh. v. Chr.', in id. [ed.], *Mose, Ägypten und das Alte Testament* [SBS 189; Stuttgart, 2000], pp. 43-83) and his argument has been followed and extended by Gerhards (pp. 187-264). Both scholars go on to infer from the likely origin of the Sargon-story in the time of Sargon II that Exod. 2.1-10 cannot have been composed earlier than the seventh century B.C. Gerhards in fact sees its adaptation of the Sargon text in the wider context of the

Exodus story as a polemical response to the Babylonian empire and its conquest of Judah, with the additions in vv. 4, 7-10a being part of a 'restoration' rewriting later still. This is surely to read too much of later political history into the narrative, and the very differences between the two stories which are described in terms of 'adaptation' make the older view that saw shared motifs in them rather than direct dependence more likely. The majority of the passage relates the paradoxical origin of Moses much more directly to the Egyptian context of the Exodus tradition than to later contacts with the empires of Assyria and Babylonia.

Other parallels are listed and discussed by D.B. Redford, 'The Literary Motif of the Exposed Child (cf. Ex. ii 1-10)', *Numen* 14 (1967), pp. 209-28, and Lewis, *Sargon Legend*, pp. 149-209, but they are not so close.[1] Two which are of greater interest because they relate precisely to the region of the Nile Delta are about the hiding of the god Horus from his enemy the god Seth (Redford, *Numen* 14 [1967], pp. 221-23; one is reproduced by Propp, p. 156). While probably too late (one text is Ptolemaic) or too different to have been a direct influence on the biblical story, they do indicate familiarity in Egypt with some elements shared with it. In the light of this, as well as more general considerations and the Egyptian loanwords in v. 3, it may be doubted whether the very limited similarities to the Sargon Birth Legend require any direct literary relationship to it. But they may well point to a similar fictional character and motivation for the biblical passage.

Childs ('The Birth of Moses') has shown that the story also makes use of a motif which is frequently referred to in non-biblical legal texts: the hiring of a nurse specifically to look after a foundling, who is usually adopted into his new family (see the notes on vv. 7-9 and 10 and the references there). This nurse motif belongs to what has been described above as 'the subsidiary plot-line' of the story, which is given a special twist by the roles assigned to Moses' sister and mother in it (see the note on v. 4 for the 'sudden

---

[1] The story of the Persian king Cyrus, which is cited by Noth (p. 16, ET, p. 27) and Blenkinsopp (*Pentateuch*, pp. 147-48), is really quite different: it involves a child of the royal line whom the king, Astyages, seeks to have killed, but Cyrus is preserved by being switched with the dead newborn child of a cowherd (Herod. 1.108-13; for a variant recalling the story of Romulus and Remus see 1.122).

appearance' [Noth, p. 14, ET, p. 25] of the sister). The story may well have been formed in two stages, the first (perhaps building on a recollection that Moses' name was Egyptian: for this see also Schmid, pp. 156-57 with n. 617) glorifying the origins of Israel's great leader and providing a Hebrew explanation of his name, and the second ensuring that it was not just a foreign woman who was involved in his earliest upbringing.

The parallels to the motifs of the story are not sufficiently close or distinctive to determine its place of origin and the Egyptian loanwords and scenery, while noteworthy, probably do not go beyond what might have been common knowledge at the royal courts of Israel and Judah. The reticence of the story-teller about divine intervention is reminiscent of wisdom literature and narratives related to it like the Joseph story. The story is hardly likely to be from P, but beyond that its literary provenance has proved difficult to determine conclusively.

In traditional source criticism the passage was generally attributed to the Elohist source (or to its equivalent, like Knobel's 'Rechtsbuch', *Num.-Jos.*, pp. 532, 602, and Dillmann's 'B'). This was the view of Carpenter and Harford-Battersby, Holzinger, Baentsch, McNeile, Gressmann and Childs. A key element in the argument has been the use of *'āmāh*, 'maidservant', in v. 5 (see Carpenter/Harford-Battersby 1, pp. 187 and 190, for the strikingly different distribution of this word and its synonym *šiphāh* in the Pentateuch), but Holzinger and Baentsch also noted the 'feminine' form of the inf. cons. in v. 4 as a feature of E, following Dillmann and GK §69m note 2. Wellhausen already suspected, because of the inconsistency between vv. 1-2 and v. 4, that two versions of the story might have been combined together in the familiar text (*Composition*, p. 69), and on this basis Eissfeldt, Beer/Galling and Fohrer (*Überlieferung*, pp. 18-19) divided it between L/J[1]/J and E. But since the 'sister' version is incomplete, it is better seen as a supplement to the original story, whether at the oral (Gressmann, Noth, Schmidt) or less likely at the written (Gertz, *Tradition*, p. 376; Gerhards, pp. 47-50) stage of composition. Rudolph (*Elohist*, pp. 3-4), Noth, Hyatt, Van Seters, Propp, Friedman (*Hidden Book*, pp. 127-28) and Graupner (*Elohist*, pp. 40-42) attribute the whole passage to J, doubting the arguments in favour of E (according to A. Jepsen, 'Ama[h] und Schiphcha[h]', *VT* 8 [1958], pp. 293-97, 425, *'āmāh* and *šiphāh* have different original meanings and so cannot serve as source-markers: the same was argued earlier by B. Jacob [see Jepsen, p. 425]) and seeing a strong connection with either preceding or following sections which they attribute to J. Schmidt understandably remains undecided (p. 64). The argument of Jacob and Jepsen is weakened by the fact that both words are used to refer to the same persons in Genesis (Hagar in chs. 16 and 21; Zilpah and Bilhah in chs.

29-31), but the quite wide use of *'āmāh* outside the Pentateuch means that it is not a decisive pointer to E. The validity of the distinction for identifying Elohistic passages has, however, been reaffirmed in the thorough discussion of Gerhards, pp. 98-105. His application of this conclusion only to a 'secondary' section of 2.1-10 is due partly to an unnecessary literary sub-division of the passage (pp. 47-50) and partly to his view that 1.22 (which leads into 2.1-10) belongs for stylistic reasons with 1.8-12 (J: p. 38). More generally Baden has provided some new reasons for attributing 2.1-10 as well as 1.15-22 to E ('From Joseph to Moses', pp. 138-42).

Those recent Pentateuchal scholars who do not think in terms of J and E at all attribute the passage to a relatively early stage of composition. Blum includes it in his pre-Deuteronomistic 'Vita Mosis' source (*Studien*, pp. 216-17) and Gertz assigns it to his 'non-Priestly narrative' (*Tradition*, pp. 375-76), while Konrad Schmid sees it as the beginning of his 'Exodus-narrative' (*Erzväter und Exodus*, pp. 153-57). There are certainly no indications of Deuteronomistic or Priestly authorship. Van Seters (*Life of Moses*, pp. 24-29, in attributing the story to his 'late Yahwist', relies entirely on arguments against its having once existed as an independent narrative.

It does indeed seem unlikely that this story would have existed alone, since its purpose is precisely to explain the origins and name of the future leader of Israel. At the same time it comes rather curiously to a conclusion and nothing is made of Moses' upbringing at the Egyptian court later on (at least not in the biblical narrative itself: later tradition was more inventive: e.g. Acts 7.22). It is not an essential prelude to the following episodes which take Moses to Midian, though some (perhaps briefer) reference to Moses' origin could be expected before them. On the other hand, it does presuppose a situation of danger like that described in 1.15-22: Schmid's attempt to dispense with this by supposing that Moses, like Sargon, was illegitimate (*Erzväter und Exodus*, pp. 154-55) is certainly imaginative, but has no real basis in the narrative. The very brief and otherwise inconsequential notice in 1.22 was almost certainly composed with 2.1-10 to provide such a background: Pharaoh's previous attempt at genocide had been thwarted by the midwives. But 1.22 itself seems to presuppose at least 1.15-20(21). It is possible that 1.22–2.10* was added secondarily to it and a more extensive narrative into which it led, but there is no strong argument against the whole narrative in 1.15–2.10 being from a single hand. The features which have been held to point to an Elohistic and 'wisdom' origin support such a view, and to them could be added the use of the term 'Hebrew' in 1.15-19 and 2.6. The reference to

Moses as a Levite in 2.1 may suggest a possible background for the composition of the narrative, as may the recognition that not all Egyptians were oppressors.

Beyond this, the account of the naming of Moses by the Egyptian princess in v. 10 probably provides a clue to the intended purpose of the whole of vv. 1-10, the more so in view of the fact that it does not (as noted already) generate any further progression in the overall plot. It has been suggested that the passage is designed to explain how Moses came to have what is almost certainly a name with an Egyptian origin (for this see below Note w on the translation and the comments on v. 10), even though his parents were both Israelites (I. Willi-Plein, 'Ort und literarische Funktion der Geburtsgeschichte des Mose', *VT* 41 [1991], pp. 110-18; Levin, p. 319). Yet, as Gerhards has pointed out (pp. 136-48), this presumes that the non-Hebrew character of the name was known to the writer and perhaps his audience, which is by no means certain. In fact there is no sign of it, either in v. 10 or earlier: the recurrent mention of a 'son' or 'child' (the likely meaning in Egyptian), on which Willi-Plein lays much emphasis (pp. 115-18), is only to be expected in a story such as this one. When the Egyptian princess explains the name, she provides it with a Hebrew, not an Egyptian, etymology. It is better, with Gerhards, to see this element of the story against the background of two similar accounts of the birth and naming of Israelite leaders, Samson (Judg. 13) and especially Samuel (1 Sam. 1). In both cases the birth-stories point to the future eminence and role of the child concerned, just as Moses is more specifically named 'the drawer out' or 'rescuer' here (see Note x on the translation). This does, as it happens, fit in very well with the prominence of Moses' activity in passages attributed to E (cf. 3.10, for example).

There is no explicit theological statement in this story – for that we must wait, in the older narrative to which it belongs, until ch. 3. But slowly and tentatively, from humble and precarious beginnings, an opening is made for the story of the liberation of the oppressed people of God. In unexpected ways a child who had at first to be hidden is preserved from danger, and at the end his name breaks into the anonymity of the other characters with an explanation that speaks of his rescue 'from the waters'. Such a 'rescue from the waters' is a commonplace of the psalms of thanksgiving and in one place it is expressed by the same Hebrew verb that is used here (Ps. 18.17). For a moment, at least, there is a glimmer of light in the darkness. There is no miracle, in the strict sense, here: only the careful provision of a mother, the patience and courage of a sister, and the compassion (v. 6) of a foreign princess – the last as close as the Old Testament comes to a 'good Samaritan' – but it is by such actions that the great tale of the Exodus is inaugurated.

1 A man of the house[a] of Levi went and took (sc. as his wife) a/ the daughter of Levi[b], 2 and the woman conceived and bore a son. Seeing that he was a fine child[c], she hid him for three months. 3 But then she could hide[d] him no longer, so she got a papyrus[e] box[f] for him and daubed it[g] with asphalt and pitch[h]. She put the child in it and placed it in the reeds[i] by the bank of the river Nile. 4 His sister took up position[j] at a distance, to learn[k] what would happen[l] to him. 5 Then the daughter of Pharaoh came down to wash by the river Nile, while her attendants walked beside the river[m]. She saw the box among the reeds and sent her maidservant and she brought it (to her). 6 She opened it and [n]when she saw him – the child – and that it was a little boy crying[n], she felt sorry for him and said, 'It is one of[o] the Hebrews' children'. 7 His sister said to Pharaoh's daughter, 'Shall I go and call a nurse[p] from the Hebrew women, so that[q] she can nurse the child for you?' 8 Pharaoh's daughter said to her, 'Yes'[r]. So the young woman[s] went and called the child's mother. 9 Pharaoh's daughter said to her, 'Take[t] this child and nurse him for me, and I will pay your wages'. So the woman took the child and nursed him[u]. 10 When the child/little boy had grown[v], she brought him to Pharaoh's daughter and he became her son, and she called his name Moses[w], 'because', she said, 'I lifted[x] him out of the water'.

Notes on the Translation

a. On the meaning 'family, household' see 1.1, Note ee on 1.21 and BDB, pp. 109-110. With proper names בית is commonly used to refer to a social unit of some importance and this may be the narrator's point here. The phrase בית־לוי recurs only in Num. 17.23, Zech. 12.13 and Ps. 135.20 (הלוי), all late texts.

b. MT's את־בת־לוי can apparently only be rendered 'the daughter of Levi'; even if GK §117d too quickly disposes of some cases where את precedes an indeterminate object (contrast JM §125h) and there are some examples where a noun in the construct state before a determinate noun has indeterminate meaning (GK §127e, JM §139b-c: but the cases cited all perhaps have special explanations which do not apply here), there seems to be no case where both את and a proper name in the genitive are present. This fits the Priestly genealogy of Moses in 6.20 and Num. 26.59, but it seems inappropriately specific here. Blum (*Studien*, p. 231 n. 12) draws attention to the possibility of a 'cataphoric' (i.e. forward-looking) use of the definite form, as with the definite article in 2.15, 3.2 etc. (cf. GK §126q-r), which would justify the renderings of RSV 'a daughter of Levi', NEB, NIV, REB, NRSV 'a Levite woman', in terms of the immediate context. See Text and Versions for the alternative reading ('one of the daughters of Levi') implied by LXX, which is less likely to be original.

c. Literally 'she saw him, that he was good, fine'. The use of the redundant pronoun 'him' reflects a common construction with verbs of perception (GK §117h, JM §157d).

d. The Hiphil form appears to be indistinguishable in meaning from the more common Qal (used in v. 2) and is perhaps just for variety. On the dagesh (*dirimens*) in the *tsade* see GK §20h.

e. Heb. גמא, which from its usage elsewhere in the OT (Isa. 35.7; Job 8.11; cf. Tg°, Vulg) is clearly a kind of reed, is recognised as a loanword from the Egyptian *qm3* (*HAL*; *WÄS* 5, 37: cf. T. Lambdin, 'Egyptian Loan Words in the Old Testament', *JAOS* 73 [1953], pp. 145-55 [149]). Papyrus (*Cyperus papyrus*) was prolific in Lower Egypt in antiquity and was used for many purposes, including the making of boats (*ABD* 2, p. 814: cf. Isa. 18.2). For designation of the material from which something is made by the construct relationship see GK §128o.

f. Heb. תבה, used elsewhere in the OT only of Noah's 'ark' but in later Heb. more generally and especially of the place in the synagogue where the Torah scrolls are kept, is also apparently a loanword from Egyptian (*HAL*), either *db3t*, 'box, coffin' (*WÄS* 5, 561), or *tb.t*, 'chest' (*WÄS* 5, 261): compare LXX θῖβιν, 'basket', here (LSJ, p. 801, with several attestations in papyri), which is probably derived from the same source. The fact that it has to be opened (v. 6) implies that it had a lid or cover.

g. The object suffix is here unusually written without Mappiq (cf. GK §58g, 91e for other examples).

h. According to Schmidt, who cites the first-cent. Greek medical writer Dioscurides (1.72-73), Heb. חמר and זפת refer respectively to products of mineral and vegetable origin (pp. 69-70). Both words are rare in BH. But the meaning of חמר, 'asphalt', is clear from Gen. 14.10 (the presence of חמר in the 'Vale of Siddim', near the Dead Sea, which was famous for its asphalt and named Asphaltitis after it) and its occurrence in Gen. 11.3 coheres well with the use of asphalt as a building material in Mesopotamia (cf. Wright, *Ancient Building* 1, p. 376). The other biblical occurrences of זפת (twice in Isa. 34.9) are not decisive for 'pitch', but the Versions' renderings in these passages and the cognates leave no doubt (cf. *HAL*, *Ges18*). LXX renders the phrase by ἀσφαλτοπίσσῃ, indicating the use of a mixture of the two materials, which is attested by Pliny, *HN* 24.41.

i. Heb. סוּף, which is most common in the place-name יַם־סוּף, 'Red Sea, Sea of Reeds' (10.19 etc.), is here and in three other places (v. 5; Isa. 19.6; Jon. 2.6) used as a common noun. Its general meaning is given by the association with קָנֶה in Isa. 19.6, but elsewhere the ancient translators seem to have been unfamiliar with it, seeing it as referring to the water rather than a plant: cf. B.Sotah 12a-b: 'R. Eliezer said: The Red Sea. R. Samuel b. Nachman said (12b): (It means) reeds (אגם), as it is written [cites Isa. 19.6]'. Of course אגם and its cognates usually mean 'pool' (see Rashi below), with אגמון being used for the vegetation which grows in them, but R. Samuel's argument seems to imply that he was using it to refer to the vegetation, for which there are some limited parallels in both BH (Jer. 51.32) and MH (but according to Jastrow not 'reeds'). The meaning 'reeds' for סוּף was known to the translator of the Bohairic version (perhaps significantly: see below) and to Jerome (*Ep.* 78.9), and Rashi (on Exod. 13.18) defined it as 'a marsh (אגם) in which reeds (קנים) grow'. Interestingly this corresponds to LXX's use of ἕλος, 'marsh' for סוּף in Exod. 2.3 and 5 (cf. Pesh. *rqq'*). From the nineteenth cent. on discussion of the meaning of סוּף has been dominated by the view that it is a loanword from the Egyptian *ṯwf* (*WÄS* 5, 359), which is generally translated 'reeds' or 'papyrus', and is frequently used with reference to the Nile delta region (on the implications of this for the identification of יַם־סוּף see the commentary on 10.19). W.A. Ward has questioned this widespread view, but he accepts that there is a connection and argues that both the Egyptian and the Heb. words are derived from a Canaanite ('Phoenician') original *sawp*: the borrowing into Egyptian would have had to have occurred before the time of Seti I, since *ṯwf* occurs in texts from his reign ('The Semitic Biconsonantal Root *sp* and the Common Origin of Egyptian *čwf* and Hebrew *sûp*: "Marsh(-Plant)"', *VT* 24 [1974], pp. 339-49 [346-49]). This is certainly possible, since there is plenty of evidence for the settlements of Semites precisely in the Eastern Delta area from the early second millennium onwards. Ward also points out that *ṯwf* sometimes refers to 'marsh-plants' in general and even (especially in Coptic) to 'papyrus' specifically (pp. 339-43), and the same may well be true of Heb. סוּף. The context in Jon. 2.6 in fact suggests an even wider meaning, 'water-plants' (so also *HAL*: cf. my *Way of the Wilderness*, p. 71). That סוּף could also mean 'marsh' in Exodus 2, as Ward states (p. 343) and some older interpreters thought (see above), is less likely. It is not *ṯwf* alone, but *pa-ṯwf*, that means 'the marshes' in Egyptian (Ward, pp. 341-43); and a reference to vegetation is clear in the two other occurrences of the common noun in BH and not a problem in Exodus 2.

j. Heb. ותתצב is a 'strange' form (Ibn Ezra). It is evidently intended as an imperfect consecutive form of יצב/צבב, 'stand, take up position', as was recognised by most of the Versions (LXX 'watched' is probably a free rendering: cf. Wevers, *Notes*, p. 13). But the vocalisation fits none of the regular patterns, and the attempts of König (1, pp. 429-30) and J. Blau ('Über die t-Form des

Hip'il im Bibelhebräisch', *VT* 7 [1957], pp. 385-88 [387]) to explain it are unsatisfactory. Blau groups it with other putative cases of a Hitaf'al conjugation (passive of Hiphil) in BH (cf. the Hittafal in Mishnaic Hebrew, but as Blau acknowledges this is due to Aramaic influence), but they can all be better explained in other ways (and they have no consistent vocalisation). In this particular case Blau cannot account for the absence of any trace of the radical *yodh* or *nun*. Most likely the consonantal text is corrupt through the omission of *yodh* and the Hithpael form, which is found in five other passages in Exodus, originally stood here, as it does in SP (so GK §71, BL §52t, BDB [p. 426], *HAL* [p. 408] etc.).

k. דעה is here the infinitive construct of ידע, which elsewhere is דעת. Such forms in ה- are occasionally found with other verbs, both Pe Waw (GK §69m) and more generally (§45d). GK notes that unusual forms of the infinitive are especially characteristic of passages that have traditionally been ascribed to the E source (§69m note 2).

l. The Heb. imperfect is used in a subordinate clause to express an occurrence which is future from the point of view of characters in the narrative (GK §107k, JM §113b).

m. Circumstantial ('background') clause (GK §156, cf. §141e; JM §159d, 166h).

n-n. MT here has sometimes been found to be repetitive and pleonastic: some ancient witnesses (cf. Text and Versions) omit 'him' and some modern commentators have regarded either it (Wellhausen) or 'the child' (Baentsch, Ehrlich) as secondary. But there may be both linguistic and literary reasons for the fulness of expression. Grammatically the (suffixed) pronoun 'him' may be regarded as idiomatically anticipatory (for other possible examples see GK §131m, JM §146e), as more frequently occurs in Aramaic and post-biblical Heb.; and the הנה-clause (in which the subject pronoun is presumably omitted, for which cf. JM §154c) is probably equivalent to an object clause linked to 'she saw' (JM §177i). As a description of the progression from sight to sound to response ('she felt sorry') the sequence makes for an unusual vividness, which is secured in other ways elsewhere in the narrative. The alternation of 'child' (ילד) and 'little boy' (נער) is less likely to be due to a wish to keep exactly seven occurrences of the former word in this story (Propp, p. 151), especially as the last one is textually doubtful (see Text and Versions on v. 10), or to נער being more gender-specific (Rashbam: the singular of ילד is always used of boys) than to 'register': נער seems to have carried the overtone of affection, at least when used of a very young child, rather like a diminutive, hence our 'little boy' (cf. Judg. 13.7-8 and esp. 2 Sam. 12.16 [beside ילד in v. 15 and elsewhere in the passage]: these passages, and others, also make clear that the use of נער for a newborn child is not at all exceptional, although it is overlooked in *HAL*).

o. Literally 'from' (מן): for the partitive use see BDB, p. 580b; cf. 6.25.

p. Literally 'a woman, a nurse' (for מינקת used nominally see Gen. 24.59, 35.8 etc.). Such cases of apposition are particularly common with the words איש and אשה (JM §131b): cf. v. 14 below.

q. Simple *waw* with the imperfect indicating purpose: GK §165a.

r. Literally, 'Go', with the repetition of a preceding verb as the characteristic way of giving a positive answer (E.L. Greenstein, 'The Syntax of Saying "Yes" in Biblical Hebrew', *JANES* 19 [1989], pp. 51-59 [54-55]).

s. Heb. עלמה, which has cognates in several Semitic languages and a masc. equivalent עלם in Heb., refers to a young woman who is ready for marriage (Gen. 24.43), sex (Prov. 30.19) and child-bearing (Isa. 7.14). Unlike נערה: there is no evidence that it could refer to a young child, nor is there any support (not even in LXX παρθένος in Gen. 24.43 and Isa. 7.14) for the idea that it carries the specific connotation of virginity, unlike at least some occurrences of בתולה (the clearest are in legal texts [e.g. Lev. 21.3, 13-14]: in general usage the reference may have been, as with עלמה, to age, so G.J. Wenham, '*bᵉtûlāh* "A Girl of Marriageable Age"', *VT* 22 [1972], pp. 326-48; *TWAT* 1, 872-77 = *TDOT* 2, pp. 338-43). There is no basis for G. Gerleman's idea ('Die sperrende Grenze. Die Würzel *ʿlm* im Hebräischen', *ZAW* 91 [1979], pp. 338-49 [345-47]) that עלמה means 'outsider, unknowing' or for the view, proposed by C. Dohmen (*TWAT* 6, 167-77 = *TDOT* 11, pp. 154-63), that it means 'an alien, foreign woman'.

t. Heb. הֵילִיכִי. The form with *ṣere* in the initial syllable is unique for the Hiphil of הלך, which is widely attested in its normal form. The meaning 'take' as distinct from 'lead' is rare, but attested in 2 Sam. 13.13; Zech. 5.13; Qoh. 5.14. The MT vocalisation is probably due to a misreading of an original *waw* (as *mater lectionis*) as *yodh*, perhaps through the influence of the form והיניקהו shortly afterwards (GK §69x). SP and a Geniza ms. (ap. *BHS*) have a form without *mater lectionis* in the initial syllable, probably reflecting a survival of the older spelling. The analysis into two words, הא = 'behold', and לכי = 'to you, yours', which is found in Jewish tradition, presupposed by Sy and favoured in modern times by Ehrlich and the NEB ('Here is the child': see Brockington, p. 9), has against it both the absence of the letter *aleph* and the presence of the object marker את before הילד, since it is not used after particles but only after verbs.

u. Heb. ותניקהו. The MT vocalisation of the *taw* with *shewa* rather than *ṣere* is irregular and perhaps an error. It would have to be attributed to the forward movement of the tone (GK §70e) unless, with BDB, p. 632, a unique instance of a by-form נוק for the regular ינק, which is used elsewhere in the context, is seen here. But that is unlikely.

v. גדל can mean 'grow', without necessarily having the connotation of 'grow big, grow up', as is clear from its use in Gen. 21.8 of a child that was ready to be weaned. Emendation (see Text and Versions) is therefore unnecessary.

w. The name of Moses is now generally thought to be Egyptian in origin (B. Jacob is a rare dissenter: pp. 29-31). In Egyptian *msy* means 'bore, was born', an element which occurs in numerous names of Pharaohs (e.g. Thutmose, Ramese) and *mose* itself is found both as an abbreviated form of such names and as a word for 'child' (see *WÄS* 2, 137-40; Griffiths, 'The Egyptian Derivation of the Name Moses', *JNES* 12 [1953], pp. 225-31). A problem was formerly seen in the correspondence of Heb. *shin* and Egyptian *ś*: elsewhere the latter is represented by Heb. *samekh* – cf. רעמסס in 1.11 (A. Gardiner, *JAOS* 56 [1936], p. 194). But there are numerous examples of the equivalence of Egyptian *ś* and Hebrew/Semitic *š* according to Griffiths, pp. 229-30, alongside those where *ś* = *s*: see now the fuller study of Hoch, *Semitic Words* (referred to in the note on 1.11), which confirms that the transcription with *shin* was an ancient one, and for a later review of the debate, with some additional observations, Hoffmeier, *Israel in Egypt*, pp. 140-42. On this view 'Moses' could have been a shortened form of a name which originally began, like those mentioned above, with the name of an Egyptian god. The earliest Greek spelling of it, Μωυσῆς (whence Lat. Moyses and Fr. Moïse), with a diphthong in place of the long *ō*, has been attributed to late Egyptian pronunciation, as attested with other names in the papyri (*HAL*, p. 607a, cf. Blass-Debrunner §38 and Mayser 1, pp. 138, 185). The quest for an Egyptian explanation of the name began already in Hellenistic Judaism, as Philo and Josephus bear witness: Philo, *De Vita Mosis* 1.17; Jos., *c.Ap.* 1.286; *AJ* 2.228. All three passages cite the Egyptian for 'water' in Greek transliteration as μωυ, and the final one adds that ἐσης means 'those who are being saved', an explanation which can be correlated in various ways with words in Egyptian and Coptic (see Griffiths, p. 226).

x. Heb. משׁיתהו. The Heb. verb (משׁה) used here in the Qal occurs elsewhere in BH only in the Hiphil (2 Sam. 22.17 ‖ Ps. 18.17), where the context is the rescue of the psalmist from the (metaphorical) waters that threaten him. In the Versions (q.v.) there is some support for the rendering 'draw, pull out' found in the lexica, but several of the renderings are less specific, perhaps due to the rarity of the word. There are no clear cognates, but some different specialised uses of similar words in Aramaic may be based on an original sense 'remove' (cf. 'glean', 'choose', 'sweepings' in Syriac; also possibly in OffAram [in Ahiqar 99] in the sense 'choose' or 'remove' [cf. *DNWSI*, p. 613 (for *mḥy₃*)]; Jastrow (p. 852), 'draw', for B.Bathra 153a, seems less secure). The sense 'wash' in JAram is more likely to be based on 'rub' and so not to be relevant. If the interpretation of משׁה in Isa. 63.11 as a participle of this verb (mentioned by Ibn Ezra: cf. W.A.M. Beuken, *Jesaja IIIB* [De Predeking van het Oude Testament; Nijkerk, 1989], pp. 14-15; NEB, REB) is preferred to other explanations of a difficult phrase, it would point to the more general meaning, since the object would be עמו, 'his people'. Whatever the exact sense, the form of the name is a masculine active participle ('lifter' or 'drawer') and so it is only loosely related to the explanation.

Explanatory Notes

1. Within this story, and probably in the larger source-document to which it originally belonged (see the Introduction), the husband and wife are, unusually, never named: they and the other equally anonymous characters in this story are only important for the part which they play in the origin of the leader who will himself not be named until the end (2.10). All that we are told is that both parents came from the 'house' or family of Levi. The clues to the significance of this lineage that might have been provided by the references to Levi in the narratives and poetry of Genesis (29.34; 34.25-31; 49.6-7) are probably less important for understanding it than the knowledge which the first hearers of the story would have brought from their contemporary situation: that the Levites were and had long been a group within Israel with a special responsibility for its religious life (cf. Exod. 32.28-29; Deut. 33.8-11; Judg. 17.7-13; 1 Sam. 2.27-28). The later laws of Deuteronomy and the Priestly Source were to underline this special role of the 'tribe' of Levi, and some prophetic oracles referred to it too (e.g. Jer. 33.17-22; Mal. 2.4-9; 3.1-4). The Levite origin of Moses' family is also mentioned in 4.14 and assumed in Judg. 18.27-31 and it provides an important clue at least to the origin of this strand of the narrative and possibly also to the specific character of the 'Hebrew' group whose experiences were the source of the Exodus tradition itself.

2. The account of the birth of this child both resembles and differs from a fairly standard pattern for such accounts in the Old Testament (e.g. Gen. 16.4+15; 21.1-3; 25.21-26; 29.32-35; 30.5-21, 23-24; 35.16-18; 38.3-5; Judg. 13.24 (cf. vv. 3 and 7); 1 Sam. 1.19-20; 2 Kgs 4.17; Hos. 1.3-9; Ruth 4.14: cf. Schmidt, p. 54). They are occasionally preceded by a reference to the 'taking' of the mother by the father, as in v. 1 here (so Hos. 1.3; Ruth 4.14), to sexual intercourse between the couple (absent here: but cf. Gen. 16.4; 30.4, 16; 38.2; 1 Sam. 1.19; Ruth 4.13) and to divine assistance (again absent here, but see e.g. Gen. 21.1; Ruth 4.13). The mention of conception is present in most cases (omitted in Gen. 30.10, 12, 21; 35.16; 38.5; Judg. 13.24). It is practically universal for the naming of the child to follow, normally by the mother (e.g. Gen. 29.32-33, 35: in v. 34 *qārā'* is probably indefinite subject equivalent to a passive [GK §144d-e: NRSV] with the same meaning), but occasionally by the father (Gen. 16.15; 21.3; 25.26 [unless the 3rd masc. form is again indefinite]; 38.3; implied by the masculine imperatives in Hos. 1.3, 6, 8, but the prophet is surely a special case) or by both parents (Gen. 25.25), and exceptionally by the women of the village (Ruth 4.17). A rare case where no naming takes place is 2 Kgs 4.17, where the child, although he is the focus of the narrative in vv. 18-37, is not a major figure in the larger context. The absence of reference here to sexual intercourse and to divine assistance is not unusual enough to attract special notice in itself (though the latter is certainly in line with the overall tendency of this story to avoid direct reference to God, however much his providence may be presumed to be in the background). The delay in the naming of the child is, however, extraordinary, as is the naming by someone other than (one of) the parents (v. 10). The pattern is so regular in this regard that the hearer/reader of this story is bound to ask: 'What is the child's name? Why is it not named by its parents?' This element of tension (*Spannung*) in the story is generally overlooked: but it, as well as the danger to which a newborn child was exposed according to 1.22, drives the narrative towards its conclusion.[2] The hiding of the child clearly presupposes at least one of the measures taken by Pharaoh to eliminate Israelite children, presumably the second (1.22), since the first is recognised to have failed (1.17). It is implied that the child was at first kept out of sight in the house of its parents (for the assumption that the Israelites in Egypt lived in houses rather than tents cf. 12.7, 23, 27).

3. The steps taken to protect the child have a strong Egyptian colouring, with as many as four words of Egyptian origin being used (see the Notes on the translation of 'papyrus', 'box' and 'reeds' and Note jj on 'the Nile' in 1.22). Papyrus or reed boats were well known in Egypt (Isa. 18.2), Israel (Job 9.26), Mesopotamia (cf. Lambert and Millard, *Atra-ḫasīs*, pp. 12, 126-29), and until recently in the British Isles ('coracles'). Here the reference is to a papyrus box, however, which was sealed to make it watertight and safe on water. 'The papyrus was a particularly useful

---

[2] It surely renders the idea that the naming of the child is an 'appendix' and no real part of the narrative (Childs, p. 19, against Noth's tentative suggestion [p. 15, ET, p. 26], that the whole story might be an aetiology generated by the explanation of the name) untenable. See the introduction to this section. The reason for the delay is that Moses' name is to be related to the story of his rescue rather than his birth, which is of only incidental importance.

plant of which scarcely any part was wasted...the stems...when separated into rind and pith were turned respectively into a fibre used for boxes, mats, ropes, and cord, and into a smooth, supple, thin writing material of great durability' (*IGECBM*, p. 16; cf. 221).[3] The unusual mention of both asphalt and pitch seems excessive and may have been intended to emphasise the extreme care taken by the mother. Propp has reasonably questioned the Egyptian background for the sealing of the box as 'the Egyptians seem not to have used such caulking on their vessels', and suggests that this motif may have come from Mesopotamian tradition, specifically a Flood story (p. 149; cf. pp. 159-60). Many have found a closer parallel to it in the 'Birth Legend of Sargon of Akkad' (see the introduction to this section). But it is probably not necessary to look so far afield, since both substances were available in the Levant (see note h) and shipbuilding was practised by the Phoenicians and, according to 1 Kgs 9.26-28; 10.22; 22.48-49, by the Israelite kings too, probably with Phoenician help. Pitch was apparently used by the Phoenicians to waterproof their ships, and very likely by the Israelites too. The Heb. word for 'box' itself, apart from other more general features of the story, has suggested (cf. the note on Sy in Text and Versions) a parallel with the biblical Flood story, since it is also used for Noah's ark (and only there apart from this passage in BH), which was also sealed with pitch (Gen. 6.14).[4]

4. The story up to this point might lead the reader to think that the child is his parents' firstborn, yet now it emerges that he has an older sister, old enough to be designated in v. 8 by a term that implies that she was in her teens (see Note s on the translation). This is presumably what led to the rabbinic tradition that what is described in v. 1 is a remarriage or a reunion of the parents (see the note on Text

---

[3] An example of a reed box is illustrated and described in *British Museum. A Guide to the Fourth, Fifth and Sixth Egyptian Rooms, and the Coptic Room* (London, 1922), pp. 264-65 (no. 2561); on papyrus and reed boxes see also A. Lucas and J.R. Harris, *Ancient Egyptian Materials and Industries* (London, 4th ed., 1962), pp. 130-31.

[4] A photograph of 'a rolled Egyptian papyrus...covered with pitch' in the British Museum (no further details are given), dated to a late period and reproduced s.v. 'Papyri and Ostraca' in *IBD*, p. 1144, indicates the occasional association of the materials (if the identification of the black material is correct) in a much less expected context!

and Versions there). Other biblical passages presuppose that Moses has a sister, Miriam (Exod. 15.20-21 [indirectly: she is 'Aaron's sister']; Num. 26.59; 1 Chr. 5.29 [EVV. 6.3]: Num. 12 passim; 20.1; Deut. 24.9; Mic. 6.4 do not mention the relationship), though they do not specify that she was older than him. According to Exod. 7.7 and also Num. 33.39 combined with Deut. 34.7, Moses' brother Aaron was older than he was, but these verses do not belong to the main old narrative tradition. In modern times (see Schmidt, pp. 51-58, and the introduction to this section) the unexpected appearance of the sister has been the basis for both source-critical and traditio-critical subdivisions of the passage, and it is possible that at one time the story circulated without vv. 4 and 7-10a.

5-6. The narrative assumes that the royal palace, as well as the Hebrew settlement where the child was born, was close to the river (as do 7.15; 8.16). This is consistent (for the palace) with the location of Pi-Ramesse (see the note on Ramesses in 1.11) at Qantir on the Pelusiac branch of the Nile and specifically of the main royal palace and its associated structures, of which traces have been uncovered in recent excavations (see Bietak and Forstner-Müller, 'The Topography', pp. 40-42 with fig. 5; E.B.P. Pusch, 'Pi-Ramesse-geliebt-von-Amun, Hauptquartier einer Streitwagentruppe. Ägypter und Hethiter in der Delta-Residenz der Ramessiden', in A.E. Eggebrecht [ed.], *Antike Welt in Pelizaeus-Museum. Die Ägyptische Sammlung* [Mainz, 1993], pp. 126-43). The unnamed princess is accompanied, as one might expect, by her attendants and her 'maidservant', who is there to do her bidding. The attendants (נערה) are perhaps more like 'ladies-in-waiting', for companionship as much as service (cf. Esth. 2.9; 4.4, 16). In the OT they are not the unique privilege of royalty: women of standing like Rebekah (Gen. 24.61) and Abigail (1 Sam. 25.42) had them too (cf. Prov. 9.3; 27.27; 31.15). The fact that they are regularly mentioned in the plural suggests that they did not have the special administrative responsibilities implied by some uses of the equivalent masculine term (see on this J. Macdonald, 'The Status and Role of the Naʻar in Israelite Society', *JNES* 35 [1976], pp. 147-70: the term is found several times on inscribed seals, see *AHI*, p. 442). An Egyptian princess was, potentially at least, a figure of considerable influence: she might if she had no brother be married to a prince from a subsidiary wife to establish his right to the succession, or she might be married to a foreign king (so at least in

1 Kgs 3.1), or even exceptionally take the throne herself. As such she would be educated and have high-ranking advisors (cf. Aldred, *The Egyptians*, pp. 182-84 with ill. 19). The sympathetic portrayal of the princess in this story contrasts, no doubt deliberately, with the cruelty and obstinacy of Pharaoh himself in the surrounding narratives. In fact (v. 6) she consciously defies her father's edict: it may perhaps be implied that only through the intervention of one so highly placed could a Hebrew child be preserved in these times. The child is referred to here, and perhaps also in v. 10, by the term נער in its ordinary familial sense (see Note n on the translation for its use even of very young children and the affectionate nuance which it seems to have carried in such cases). Jewish tradition deduced (cf. Exod.R. 1.24) that the child's nationality was apparent from its being circumcised. Circumcision was not in fact a uniquely Israelite custom in the Near East (as acknowledged in Jer. 9.25-26; cf. de Vaux, *Institutions* 1, pp. 78-82; ET pp. 46-48) and it was apparently practised by the Egyptians, though according to recent research in distinctive ways (evidence in *ANET*, p. 326, and *ANEP*, no. 629; see also *ABD* 1, p. 1025; J.M. Sasson, 'Circumcision in the Ancient Near East', *JBL* 85 [1966], pp. 473-76). It is more likely that either the child's appearance or clothing or its perilous situation was imagined to have betrayed its origin to the princess.

7-9. These verses, which some take to be part of a secondary expansion of the story (see on v. 4 and the introduction to this section), develop two interrelated themes that are also present in the main plot: the courage and inventiveness of the child's female relatives and the provision for the child's needs by an unexpected twist to events which, as in ch. 1, is not explicitly attributed to divine intervention but is readily so understood. The employment of wet-nurses was familiar in ancient Egypt, even in the royal family (Aldred, *The Egyptians*, p. 184), as well as among the Israelites (Gen. 24.59; 35.8; 2 Sam. 4.4; 2 Kgs 11.2; Isa. 49.23), and Childs showed that there was a consistent pattern of contract for the hiring of a nurse over two millennia ('The Birth of Moses', pp. 112-14), to which this narrative closely conforms. Even more interesting is the sequence found in some Sumerian texts (the series *ana ittišu*), in which a foundling child is taken into care, placed in the charge of a nurse (who is paid), adopted and taught a trade (Childs, pp. 111-12). On the possible contribution of these texts to the tradition-history of the passage see the introduction to this section.

10. The age at which Moses was brought back to Pharaoh's daughter is not stated ('had grown' is not very specific and unlike v. 11 it clearly does not mean 'fully grown' here), but the context suggests that it was when he was weaned. A variety of ancient evidence points to this being after about three years: the Sumero-Akkadian legal series *ana ittišu* (B. Landsberger, *Die Serie* ana ittišu [MSL 1; Rome, 1937], pp. 43-47 [iii.45-50]; cited by Childs, 'The Birth of Moses', p. 111); the Instruction of Ani (*ANET*, p. 420); 2 Macc. 7.27 (cf. Jos., *AJ* 2.230). The formula 'he became her son' probably implies Moses' adoption by the Egyptian princess, as most modern commentators (including Cassuto, p. 20) have agreed and as the naming of Moses by her at this point confirms (see on v. 2 for this as a characteristically parental role). Clear evidence of the practice of adoption in Israelite society is hard to find, although it was common elsewhere in the ancient Near East (see Schmidt, pp. 72-73, and the thorough recent survey by F.J. Knobloch in *ABD* 1, pp. 76-79; and for the specific case of a foundling Childs, 'The Birth of Moses', pp. 111-15; S. Franke and G. Wilhelm, 'Eine mittelassyrische fiktive Urkunde zur Wahrung des Anspruchs auf ein Findelkind', *Jahrbuch des Museums für Kunst und Gewerbe, Hamburg* 4 (1985), pp. 19-26; and M. Malul, 'Adoption of Foundlings in the Bible and Mesopotamian Documents: A Study of Some Legal Metaphors in Ezekiel 16.1-7', *JSOT* 46 [1990], pp. 97-126). The strongest cases in the OT occur in a foreign milieu (here and Esth. 2.7) and, according to some, in the patriarchal narratives (Gen. 15.1-2; 30.3-13; 48.5-6). The divine sonship of the Davidic kings (2 Sam. 7.14; 1 Chr. 17.13; 22.9 [EVV. 10]; 28.6; Pss. 2.7; 89.27-28 [EVV. 26-27]) is best understood in terms of adoption, but the royal theology could well be based on a foreign model rather than a native one. Objections to the interpretation of this verse in terms of adoption have a long history (see on Text and Versions) and have been made in modern times by R. de Vaux (*Institutions* 1, p. 85, ET, p. 51), B. Jacob and Houtman (both ad loc.), but the reasons given are not sufficient to outweigh the clear implications of the terminology used here.[5]

---

[5] Later rabbinic law did not recognise the practice of adoption, but there are a number examples of it from antiquity, where Jews presumably followed the common practice of their neighbours (e.g. a contract from Elephantine [E.G. Kraeling, *The Brooklyn Museum Aramaic Papyri* (New Haven, 1953), no. 8], an

Only now is the identity of the child revealed, and in a most surprising way. The explanation provided for the name 'Moses' is, like many others in the OT, an imprecise 'folk etymology' and is based on a poetic word that is rare in Biblical Hebrew (see Note x on the translation). Within the present narrative it serves an important structural purpose (see the Introduction). Such explanations of names are particularly common in Genesis and they are also frequent in other cultures (for an overview and analysis see J. Fichtner, 'Die Etymologische Ätiologie in den Namengebungen der geschichtlichen Bücher des Alten Testaments', *VT* 6 [1956], pp. 372-96, who emphasised their antiquity as part of oral tradition; more recently they have been understood as literary devices, cf. Y. Zakovitch, 'A Study of Precise and Partial Derivation in Biblical Etymology', *JSOT* 15 [1980], pp. 31-50, and H. Marks, 'Biblical Naming and Poetic Etymology', *JBL* 114 [1995], pp. 21-42 [esp. 29-33 on this passage]). In fact the name is almost certainly of Egyptian origin, meaning 'born' or 'child' (see Note w on the translation), which has led to both speculation about Moses' possible ethnic origin and arguments for the authenticity of his original association with the Exodus story. Some have argued that Moses actually was an Egyptian or an Egyptianised Semite and that he brought with him some form of (perhaps monotheistic) Egyptian religious belief which, with adaptation, formed the basis of his teaching and so of Israelite Yahwism (the classic example is Sigmund Freud's *Moses and Monotheism*, first published in German in 1939, but the idea goes back to the Hellenistic period and was popular again in the eighteenth century: see J. Assmann, *Moses the Egyptian* [Cambridge MA, 1997]). More cautiously Moses' Egyptian name has been seen as an argument for his original association with the Exodus tradition (e.g. R. Smend, *Jahwekrieg und Stämmeverband* [FRLANT 84; Göttingen, 1963], pp. 88-93, ET pp. 124-28; id., 'Mose als geschichtliche Gestalt' [1993], in *Zwischen Mose und Karl Barth: Akademische Vorträge* [Tübingen, 2009], pp. 1-25 [20-22]; Nicholson, *Exodus and Sinai*, pp. 58-61, both against the

---

epitaph from Leontopolis [W. Horbury and D. Noy, *Jewish Inscriptions of Graeco-Roman Egypt* (Cambridge, 1992), no. 34] and some Roman catacomb inscriptions [D. Noy, *Jewish Inscriptions of Western Europe, 2: The City of Rome* (Cambridge, 1995), nos. 25, 246, 489, 531]).

denial of this by M. Noth). There is a curious irony in the fact that the narrative attributes the giving of a name which is now thought to be Egyptian (though here explained as Hebrew) to an Egyptian princess. Does this perhaps derive from a distorted memory of Moses' actual origins?

Text and Versions

וילך (2.1)   This 'rather odd' opening (Van Seters, *Life of Moses*, pp. 26-27; but he notes the parallel in Hos. 1.3) is replaced in LXX by ἦν δέ, which may just be part of LXX's 'free...stylistic improvement' of the Hebrew of the verse (Wevers, *Notes*, p. 12). But the correspondence to ויהי, which often begins a narrative elsewhere (e.g. Judg. 13.1; 1 Sam. 1.1 – cf. Job 1.1), is at least noteworthy.

את־בת לוי (2.1)   So also SP, 4QGen-Ex[a], Sy and Tg[O.N.J]. LXX τῶν θυγατέρων Λευί, '(one) of Levi's daughters' (harmonised with MT in some 'Byzantine' mss) can scarcely be based on MT (contra Wevers, loc. cit., and Propp, p. 148) and probably renders a variant Heb. מבנות לוי (Schmidt: cf. the comparable phrase in MT and LXX at 6.25, and for the Heb. idiom 2.6 below), which arose as a way of easing MT's reading. The latter can of course be understood in terms of the Priestly genealogy of Moses (6.20; cf. Num. 26.59), further elements of which were incorporated in Tg[FJ (cf. Nmg)]. Tg[J] has an even fuller text which represents this as a *re*marriage of Amram to Jochebed and gives further details from Rabbinic tradition (see the refs. in *AramB* 2, p. 164 n. 3). Vulg *accepta uxore stirpis suae* is a free paraphrase which might be based on either MT or LXX.

ותלד בן (2.2)   Tg[J] records the tradition that the birth took place after only six months.

ותרא (2.2)   LXX renders with plural verbs in vv. 2b-3a, assuming that the father would be involved in the concealment too.

טוב (2.2)   LXX ἀστεῖον, presumably 'good-looking' here (cf. Sy *špyr*, Vulg *elegantem*), specifies the sense in which טוב is being used. Aq (ὅτι ἀγαθός) and Theod (ὅτι καλός) revert to more common equivalents and the grammatical structure of MT. Tg[J] takes טוב to mean 'likely to survive', presumably in the context of the child's premature birth.

שלשה (2.2)   4QGen-Ex[a] has the construct form שלשת. While both absolute and construct forms of the numerals from 2 to 10 may stand before a noun (GK §134a-b), in Genesis and Exodus the latter is always preferred in the temporal expression 'three days' and the former otherwise. A pedantic scribe may perhaps have assumed that 'three months' should be constructed like 'three days': for further examples of grammatical pedantry in this passage see the textual notes on vv. 4, 7, 9 and 10.

הצפינו (2.3) Tg^J gives the reason as the Egyptians' careful surveillance, as stated in Jub. 47.3; Philo, *Vit. Mos.* 1.10; B.Sotah 12a; Exod.R. 1.20 etc. (*AramB* 2, p. 164 n. 8). SP הצפנהו exhibits the older form of the suffix as again in 4.28 (see Text and Versions on שלחו there).

ותקח לו (2.3) SP and LXX add 'his mother', a specification which is the more necessary in LXX after its use of plural verbs in vv. 2b-3a.

תבת גמא (2.3) LXX θῖβιν, 'basket', on which see Note f on the translation and Lee, *Lexical Study*, p. 115. Aq(?) and Theod rendered more precisely κιβωτὸν παπύρου and the latter word was taken up into some hexaplaric witnesses. For גמא Tg^J has טונס, a *hapax* for which CAL follows Levy's conjecture that it is derived from Gk. δόναξ (also δοῦ-), 'reed', hence also *AramB* 'rushes'. Sy *'rq'*, 'juniper, acacia, box-wood', evidently implies the kind of box that would be found outside Egypt. But *'rq'* is also the word that is used in Gen. 6.14 of Noah's ark, and since Sy elsewhere renders גמא accurately (Isa. 18.2; Job 8.11) the translator must have deliberately identified the material as the same, perhaps for typological or other theological reasons.

ותשם^{20} (2.3) 4QEx^b apparently had ותשים here, very much against the normal Qumran (and Masoretic) pattern for *waw* cons. and imperfect (see Qimron, p. 45). This variant may, however, be linked with the preceding insertion in the scroll of ותואמר לשפחתה לכי, 'and she said to her maidservant, "Go..."', after which ותשים could be a final simple *waw* with the imperfect/jussive (cf. v. 7): 'so that she might place...' In any case, according to this reading, which seems to be unique, it was not the child's mother but her servant who put the box in the water. As Propp comments (p. 144), this is more likely to be deliberate midrash than a misplaced variant on v. 5, as Cross thought (*DJD* XII, p. 89).

בסוף (2.3) Sy *brqq'*, 'in the shallow water', as also in v. 5. The Versions generally miss the precise meaning of סוף: LXX ἕλος, 'marsh-meadow', Vulg *carectum*, 'sedge-bed', Tg^O יערא, 'thicket', Tg^{N,F} אפרה, 'meadow'. Aq's παπυρεῶνι (whence Vulg *papyrione* in v. 5 and cf. Tg^J גומייא) is the best ancient rendering here.

ותתצב (2.4) SP reads ותתיצב, which is probably correct. No Qumran ms. is extant at this point. Most of the Versions point to the meaning 'stood/stationed herself', though the Targums by their use of √עתד also include the idea of readiness. LXX κατεσκόπευεν, 'kept a look-out', might seem to point to a form of √רגל, which the verb renders several times elsewhere. But given the freedom of LXX's rendering, it is more likely to be an imaginative elaboration of MT (cf. *BAlex*, p. 81). Tg^J names the sister as Miriam on the basis of Num. 26.59, an identification first explicitly made in Jub. 47.4 and M.Sotah 1.9: see also the discussion in *MRI* (Lauterbach 2, pp. 81-82) on 15.20. Tg^J had already identified Miriam, with Jochebed, as one of the two midwives in 1.15, in line with B.Sotah 11b.

לדעה (2.4) Two Qumran mss (4QGen-Ex^a and 4QEx^b) read the more regular form לדעת, as does SP (two mss cited by von Gall [his text is in error at this point; cf. Baillet, 'Corrections', p. 28], as well as all those in Crown's text,

Camb. Add. 1846 and those printed by Sadaqa and Tal). The unusual form in MT is clearly more original. Some LXX mss have ἰδεῖν (instead of μαθεῖν), no doubt in consequence of the mistranslation at the beginning of the verse.

ונערתיה (2.5)   LXX αἱ ἅβραι αὐτῆς: ἅβραι is the pl. of a word used in Hell. Gk. for the favourite servant of 'a lady in high society' and Wevers aptly compares its use in LXX Esther and Judith (*Notes*, p. 14). But the theory that it is a Semitic loanword (ibid.) has been abandoned: see *BAlex* on Gen. 24.61 and R.S.P. Beekes, *Etymological Dictionary of Greek* (Leiden, 2010) 1, p. 6 for its native Gk. origin.

את־האמתה ותקחה (2.5)   In 4QEx^b there is room at the end of the verse, on a section of the scroll which does not survive, either for a space before the next verse (as before vv. 5 and 7) or for an expansive variant such as בת־פרעה or את־התבה (*DJD* XII, p. 88). The only variants in the Versions at this point are the plural form of the noun in Sy and possibly Tg^N and the derivation of אמתה from אַמָּה = 'forearm (, cubit)' implied in Tg^O,J: for the latter interpretation as an alternative to the normal one see B.Sotah 12b; Exod.R. 1.23. In Tg^J this is part of a more extensive expansion about a plague affecting Pharaoh's daughter (who is named Bithiah here after 1 Chr. 4.18: in Jub. 47.5 [cf. Jos., *AJ* 2.224] she is called Tharmuth): for fuller accounts of this tradition see the references in *AramB* 2, p. 164, and Houtman (artistic representations).

ותפתח (2.6)   SP adds the object suffix, probably secondarily. No Qumran ms. is extant at this point. Both LXX and Vulg abbreviate the first half of the verse, but probably presuppose MT.

ותראהו (2.6)   The object suffix of MT is omitted by 4QEx^b (ותראה) and SP (ותרא), and there is no clear equivalent to it in LXX, Tgg and Vulg. But Sy presupposes it and, while it is redundant, for that very reason it is more likely to have been omitted by a scribe than secondarily added.

בכה (2.6)   LXX adds ἐν τῇ θίβει, but there is no room for בתבה in 4QEx^b, and the addition is probably merely stylistic, like *in ea* in Vulg.

עליו (2.6)   4QEx^b, SP and LXX all add בת־פרעה after this, quite naturally: but since no explanation can be offered for its omission in MT, the shorter text is presumably original.

ותינק (2.7)   4QEx^b reads the perfect consecutive, which would normally have a straightforward future sense (cf. LXX, and וקראתי earlier in the verse) instead of the implication of an intention in MT (overlooked in *DJD* XII, p. 89, but picked up in Vulg *quae nutrire possit*). A choice between the two readings is difficult. Tgg and Sy all use *waw* with the imperfect, but may intend only a future sense. Since the context requires an expression of purpose and MT expresses it in a way that might have puzzled some scribes, 4QEx^b should probably be seen as a secondary simplification of the grammar.

בת־פרעה (2.8)   The omission of the subject by Vulg (which also abbreviates הילד to *eius*) is of little weight compared with its attestation in the major witnesses (which include 4QEx^b for this phrase).

הֵילִיכִי (2.9) Both SP (הלכי) and 4QEx[b] (לכ-ה-) point to a Hiphil imperative of הלך, while being unclear about its vocalisation, and such a form is also presupposed by Tgg and probably Vulg. LXX διατήρησον, however, is not a plausible equivalent and may be a guess based on the context. Sy *h' lky*, 'Behold, to/for you...', presupposes a division into two words which has been favoured by both traditional Jewish exegesis (B.Sotah 12b; Exod.R. 1.25; Rashi) and some modern scholars. But it can hardly be right (see Note t on the translation above).

הֵילֶד[20] (2.9) SP regularises the grammar by placing את before it, and this correction evidently also stood in 4QEx[b], although only the tops of the letters are visible for most of this line. The presence of ית in Tg[NJ] and of *l* in Sy might, but need not, be further support for this reading (Tg[O] lacks ית and clearly goes with MT), but it is a typical secondary element of the fuller texts.

וַיִּגְדַּל (2.10) Ehrlich and Beer proposed the emendation וינמל (Niphal), but there is no problem with MT.

הֵילֶד (2.10) SP has הנער, as all Heb. witnesses do in v. 6 (see Note n-n on the translation above). No Qumran ms. survives at this point and the Versions give no indication of a different word from before. But since it is more likely that a scribe would introduce the word used in the preceding verses here, for consistency, than a different one, the reading of SP might well be original.

לְבַת (2.10) Most mss of SP have אל instead of ל, perhaps because of the motion involved; the same variation occurs with verbs of speaking in 3.14, 8.5 and 10.17. The 'less regular' ל is probably to be preferred in each case.

וַיְהִי לָהּ לְבֵן (2.10) Most of the Versions translate the phrase verbatim, presumably implying Moses' adoption by Pharaoh's daughter (so explicitly Vulg: cf. Jos. *AJ* 2.232). But Tg[J], והוה לה חביב הי כביר, 'he was loved by her like a son', avoids this implication (cf. Exod.R. 1.26), presumably as being offensive.

Chapter 2.11-22

From Egypt to Midian

This unit is delimited by the connecting formula 'In those (many) days' in vv. 11 and 23 and, at the end, also by the temporary interruption in the focus on Moses. The introductory formula in v. 23a belongs with this unit (so Propp), as it reports the lifting of the threat to Moses' life posed in v. 15 (cf. 4.19). The division after v. 22 is traditional: it corresponds to an 'open section' in MT and an empty line in a Qumran manuscript (4QpalGen-Ex^1). The narrative consists of a series of brief episodes, the first two set in Egypt and the rest in Midian, but they are tightly bound together into a single coherent sequence. There are not two units here but one: v. 15 provides an explanatory transition between the two 'scenes', using the same device of the repetition of a verb in a different sense as in vv. 10-11. The narrator is economical with details and generally only those which are essential to the development of the plot are given. There is little explicit indication of either the characters' attitudes and motives or the narrator's evaluation of the characters' actions, but some insight into the former is provided by Moses' quest for secrecy in v. 12 and by the short 'disputation' dialogues in vv. 13-14 and 18-20.

The unit culminates in Moses' marriage, which led Coats, for example, to describe it as the 'Moses Marriage Story'. But the continuation of the story of Moses makes it unlikely that this is the real goal of the unit (although Moses' family are occasionally mentioned further on) and in fact it ends not with Moses' marriage but with the birth of his first son, whose name is made to point (by an artificial etymology, as in v. 10) to the wider situation in which Moses finds himself, that of a 'displaced person' among desert tribesmen. Moreover, the 'Egyptian' scenes are more than merely a linking passage (Schmidt, p. 80), since they foreshadow Moses' later relations with the Egyptians and his own people. In its present context at least, the function of the passage is clearly to explain by means of a variety of narrative material how Moses came to be in the vicinity of the 'mountain of God', where he had his first decisive encounter with Yahweh (ch. 3).

Nevertheless the marriage connection to the Midianites may well be the most ancient component of the passage, as both G.W. Coats ('Moses in Midian', *JBL* 92 [1973], pp. 3-10) and Schmidt have argued. It is true that there is some similarity between vv. 16-22 and Genesis 24 and 29, which could be explained either by all three passages drawing on a common 'type-scene' of oral tradition (Culley, *Structure*, pp. 41-43; Alter, *Art*, pp. 52-58) or by the use of a larger traditional sequence of episodes by the main author of the Jacob-story and the Exodus author in chs. 2–4 (R.S. Hendel, *The Epic of the Patriarch: The Jacob Cycle and the Narrative Traditions of Canaan and Israel* [HSM 42; Atlanta, 1987], pp. 133-65; cf. Propp, pp. 241-43). Direct modelling of this part of Exodus on the Jacob-narrative is also a theoretical possibility (Van Seters, *Life of Moses*, pp. 31-33), though the considerable differences between them in plot as well as geographical setting make this unlikely (cf. Schmidt, p. 84). It is clear that Moses' foreign marriage later became something of an embarrassment, certainly by the time of Deuteronomy which omits all reference to it (note also the criticism in Num. 12.1), and this speaks against its being a late tradition (against Van Seters, *Life of Moses*, pp. 29-34). It is also presupposed by the strange and probably ancient episode recounted in 4.24-26. The existence of variant traditions about the nationality of Moses' wife (cf. Num. 12.1; Judg. 1.16; 4.11) was cited by Noth as an argument against the originality of the specifically Midianite tradition about his marriage (p. 19, ET, pp. 30-31; cf. *ÜGP*, p. 186), but Schmidt is correct to point out that, given the hostility of the Israelites to Midian as early as the Judges period (Judg. 6–8, with later references back to it, e.g. Isa. 9.3: the traditions in Num. 25.6-17 and 31.12 are of more dubious historical value), attempts to dissociate Moses from such a close relationship to Midian could easily have led to the generation of the other traditions (*Exodus, Sinai und Mose*, pp. 110-12). Noth held that it was the tradition 'that Moses experienced his first encounter with God on the mountain of God in Midian' that was the primary one, though in line with his general scepticism about Moses he did not believe that this was a historical element in the Exodus events themselves (pp. 19-20, ET, pp. 31-33). As Schmidt implies (pp. 110-11 n. 162), Noth was almost too determined to fragment the tradition, and the specific tradition of Moses' marriage to the daughter of a *priest* of Midian encourages the belief that this was closely associated with his experience at the mountain of God from the start – the more so because the extant text does not (at least in chs. 2–3) say anything about any initiation of Moses by Reuel/Jethro into the worship of Yahweh: if anywhere this appears only later, in ch. 18, where further discussion of the 'Midianite hypothesis' will be needed. But for the time being it seems very reasonable to take the two traditions – of marriage and encounter with God – as having been united from the beginning.

T.C. Butler ('An Anti-Moses Tradition', *JSOT* 12 [1979], pp. 9-15) has suggested that behind this passage lie two narratives which once formed part of an 'anti-Moses tradition', which also comprised Exod. 4.24-26 and the two main sections of Exodus 18 and may have been directed against the Gershonite priesthood of Dan (see the Explanatory Note on vv. 21-22). This is perhaps easier to believe for vv. 11a-14 than for vv. 16-21a, since any note of criticism in the latter passage has been completely muted. In the former passage it is not difficult to see 'a desire for power and position' (Butler, p. 10) comparable to that which is attributed to Moses in Num. 16.3. Butler's case is weakened, however, by the fact that he has to read into the other passages mentioned the criticism of Moses which he finds there. But his theory remains an intriguing conjecture.

As with the preceding section, there is an interesting parallel narrative in ancient Near Eastern literature. The Egyptian Story of Sinuhe (*ANET*, pp. 18-22; *COS* 1, pp. 77-82), which is set in the Middle Kingdom period (c. 2035–1668 according to Aldred, *The Egyptians*, p. 9), from which the two main manuscripts come, tells how after the death of Sesostris I a royal official fled from the palace, for reasons which are not clear, and made his way into the desert east of the Nile Delta, where he found refuge with 'Asiatic' herdsmen before proceeding on his way northwards:[1]

---

[1] In his survey of ancient autobiographical literature T. Longman notes that this text is generally regarded by specialists as an authentic record of its author's experiences (*Fictional Akkadian Autobiography*, p. 201); *ABD* 6, p. 51, seems more doubtful about this.

I set out at night. At dawn I reached Peten. I halted at 'Isle-of-Kem-wer'. An attack of thirst overtook me: I was parched, my throat burned. I said, 'This is the taste of death'. I raised my heart and collected myself when I heard the lowing sound of cattle and saw Asiatics. One of their leaders, who had been in Egypt, recognised me. He gave me water and boiled milk for me. I went with him to his tribe. What they did for me was good. (*COS* 1, p. 78)

Later Sinuhe is received by a Canaanite ruler who, on learning that he is loyal to the new Pharaoh, takes him into his family:

He set me at the head of his children. He married me to his eldest daughter. He let me choose for myself of his land, of the best that was his, on his border with another land. It was a good land called Yaa... (*COS* 1, p. 79)

Eventually, now in old age, Sinuhe is summoned back to Egypt by the king. He leaves his new family behind in Canaan and is received at court and is provided with all the accompaniments of nobility.

Although the plot of the story is quite different, it shares a number of motifs with the Moses-story, and especially this passage, which are noteworthy and indicate the realism of some of its details. There is no reason to think that the author of this passage used the story of Sinuhe as a model, but there is a general similarity of genre and subject-matter which might shed some light on the background of the biblical narrative.

There has been widespread agreement in the attribution of this passage to the J source (or its equivalent, Knobel's 'Kriegsbuch' [cf. *Num.-Jos.*, p. 548]), with the exception of minor additions. Reference has been made to vocabulary items (*'ākēn*, v. 14, 'the troughs', 'where?', 'why?') and to similar motifs in Genesis. A contrast with ch. 18 (presumed to be E) has been seen in the reference to only a single son here (cf. 4.24-26). What might seem to be a strong reason for preferring J to E, namely the designation of Moses' father-in-law here as Reuel rather than Jethro (as in 3.1), has not been used (except by Propp, p. 170), apparently because of the very widespread view that it is a secondary addition to the narrative. But, as Gertz rightly points out (*Tradition*, p. 378), the addition of this name (if it is secondary at all: see the Explanatory Note on v. 18 for a different view) is likely to have occurred when 2.15/16-22 had not yet been joined to 3.1, in other words it was a feature of the narrative in its early form. As such it can and should play a part in arguments about the source to which the narrative belonged (or did not belong).

Dillmann and Holzinger, with a slight divergence over the boundary, attributed the first part of the passage to E, apparently because they saw close links between it and vv. 1-10. But the reason is weak and not sufficient to override the coherence of the passage as a whole. Smend (*Erzählung*, pp. 121-22), followed in the main by Eissfeldt (L) and Beer, assigned most of the passage to his J^1 source (parts of vv. 14-16 = J^2): Fohrer took a similar view for vv. 15b-22 (*Überlieferung*, pp. 24-28: N), while dividing vv. 11-15a between J (mainly) and E. But the case for invoking a separate narrative strand here is no stronger than it is elsewhere. Occasionally it is suggested that phrases in vv. 15 (Wellhausen, Gressmann, Noth) and 19 (Gressmann) may have been added to the main narrative, but the reasons given overlook possible stylistic features. The more recent Pentateuchal scholarship has also attributed the passage to a relatively early level of composition in the book of Exodus, like vv. 1-10. It certainly lacks any features of the later sources or redactional layers in the Pentateuch. But a thorough analysis of the earlier material probably requires a distinction between 2.1-10, which are closely linked to the E story in 1.15-22, and 2.11-22, which stand apart from the E material in chs. 3 and 18 and presuppose 1.8-12 in vv. 11-14. It is not impossible, as McNeile thought, that 2.11 was the beginning of J's account of Moses' activity, though it could have been preceded by a brief notice of his birth like 2.1-2a. But we presumably need to suppose that here as elsewhere E has only been partly preserved (cf. Noth, p. 23, ET, p. 35; Graupner, *Elohist*, pp. 8-11), as some kind of 'bridge' would be needed between its Egyptian material in 2.1-10 and the encounter with God in Midian in 3.1ff.

The bareness of this narrative which was noted earlier, not surprisingly, leaves little scope for religious or theological reflection. In a sense Moses becomes progressively less plausible as a future leader and liberator of his people as the narrative proceeds. At its end he has found a new home far from his own people, and his marriage into the family of a (presumably) pagan priest, while of enormous interest for the history of religion, seems to have rendered him totally unsuited for any role within his own people's religion. The sequel is anything but expected, but once it is known the chain of events in this passage, paradoxically, takes on a character that is inescapably providential.

11 In those days Moses, having grown up[a], went out to his fellow-countrymen[b] and observed[c] the labours imposed on them. He saw an Egyptian striking a Hebrew, one of[d] his fellow-countrymen. 12 Turning this way and that[e] and seeing that there was no one around, he struck the Egyptian down and hid[f] him in the sand[g]. 13 The next[h] day he went out and saw[i] two Hebrews fighting, and said to the one who was in the wrong[j], 'Why[k] are you beating your companion?' 14 He replied, 'Who made you an official[l] and judge over us? Are you proposing[m] to kill me, as you killed the Egyptian?' Moses was afraid, for he thought[m], 'The matter must[n] have become known'. 15 When Pharaoh heard of this matter, he attempted to kill Moses. So Moses fled, to escape from Pharaoh, and he dwelt in the land of Midian.

He sat down by a well[o]. 16 Now the priest of Midian had seven daughters, and they came and drew water[p] and filled the troughs[q] to water their father's flock. 17 Then the shepherds came and drove them[r] away. But Moses got up and came to their defence[s] and watered their[r] flock. 18 When they went home to Reuel their father, he said: 'Why[t] have you come home so early today?' 19 They replied[u], 'An Egyptian[v] – he rescued[w] us from the power of the shepherds and he even actually drew water[x] for us and watered the flock'. 20 He said to his daughters, 'So[y] where is he? Why ever[z] did you leave the man behind? Invite[aa] him to have a meal[bb]'. 21 Moses agreed[cc] to stay with the man and he gave Zipporah his daughter to Moses. 22 She bore a son, whose name he called Gershom, for he said: 'I have been a displaced person[dd] in a foreign land'.

Notes on the Translation

a. Here גדל clearly represents the contrast between a child and an adult, as in Gen. 21.20; 25.27; 38.11, 14, etc., as distinct from the relative growth of a young child (v. 10).

b. Literally 'his brothers'. The wider sense here (as again at the end of the verse and in 4.18, and frequently elsewhere, especially in Deuteronomy: cf. *TWAT* 1, 205-10 [206-207] = *TDOT* 1, pp. 188-93 [190-91]; *THAT* 1, 98-104 [99-100] = *TLOT*, pp. 73-77 [74-75]) expresses a feeling of solidarity and concern as well as membership of the same community.

c. So REB. Heb. literally 'looked on' (AV, RSV), with the preposition ב, implying 'look at with interest' (BDB, p. 907), as distinct from the simple direct object construction, which would be rendered by 'saw' (NEB, JB, NRSV). On the idiom see further E. Jenni, *Die hebräischen Präpositionen, 1: Die Präposition Beth* (Stuttgart, Berlin and Cologne, 1992), pp. 242-57; J.A. Emerton, 'Looking on One's Enemies', *VT* 51 (2001), pp. 186-96 (192-94).

d. Literally 'from' (cf. Note o on 2.6).

e. For כה (here idiomatically repeated as in Num. 11.31) meaning 'here' (rather than as normally, 'thus') cf. Gen. 22.5; 31.37; Num. 23.15 (twice); 2 Sam. 18.20; Ruth 2.8. BDB, p. 462, notes that this meaning occurs 'chiefly in E'.

f. A different Heb. word (טמן) from 2.2-3 (צפן), and one which is particularly (but not only) used of burying something in the ground (cf. Gen. 35.4; Deut. 33.19; Josh. 7.21-22; Isa. 2.10; Jer. 13.4-7; 43.9-10; Job 40.13, as well as numerous references to the hiding of a trap, e.g. Ps. 35.7).

g. Heb. חול is almost always the sand on the seashore (Gen. 22.17 etc.). But Deut. 33.19 seems to have the sand of the desert in mind (so in later Heb. also: cf. Jastrow, p. 433). In OffAram חל is used of the 'beach' beside the Nile (Cowley 26.7, cf. *DNWSI*, p. 372), which could well be meant here.

h. Lit. 'second', but biblical reckoning is usually inclusive, hence 'next', cf. Gen. 47.18 and *HAL*, p. 1482. Elsewhere (e.g. 18.13; 32.30) ממחרת, 'on the morrow', is used.

i. Heb. והנה, lit. 'and behold'. The various idiomatic uses of the deictic particle and relevant references are well set out by Houtman, pp. 18-19, and D.J. McCarthy, 'The Uses of *wᵉhinnēh* in Biblical Hebrew', *Bib* 61 (1980), pp. 330-42. Here it seems to be not much more than an equivalent to a verb of seeing: perhaps there is also an element of surprise (Childs, p. 30: cf. McCarthy's category of 'excited perception' [pp. 332-33]).

j. Heb. רשע sometimes as here refers to a person who is not necessarily 'wicked' in a general sense but is the 'guilty' party in a particular situation, just as its opposite צדיק can mean 'innocent' as well as 'righteous' (cf. *THAT* 2, 816-17 = *TLOT* 3, p. 1264). The context for such specific uses is often judicial (Exod. 23.1, cf. JB 'guilty'; Deut. 25.1-2 [with the related verb as well]), but it need not be so (cf. Exod. 9.27), and it is not clear that the narrator here regards the situation as (yet) a judicial one (v. 14 is certainly not decisive).

k. Heb. למה, as in v. 20, in both cases with the critical tone that Jepsen (see Note bb on 1.18) claimed to be characteristic of its occurrences.

l. Literally 'a man (Heb. איש) (who is) an official (שׂר)', the two nouns being in apposition, with the second defining the referent more precisely than the first (GK §131b). The idiom is particularly common with איש and אשה (JM §131b), cf. e.g. Lev. 21.9; Judg. 6.8). Against this background the suggestions of A.D. Crown, who took איש here and in 1 Kgs 2.2 to mean 'king' ('An Alternative Meaning for איש in the Old Testament', *VT* 24 [1974], pp. 110-12), and M. Dahood, who saw it as a vocative ('Vocative Lamedh in Exodus 2,14 and Merismus in 34,21', *Bib* 62 [1981], pp. 413-15 [413-14], with the *lamedh* before it taken as the sign of the vocative), lose their force. On שׂר as a frequent and general term for state officials of all kinds see U. Rüterswörden, *Die Beamten der israelitischen Königszeit. Eine Studie zu śr und vergleichbaren Begriffen* (BWANT 117; Stuttgart, 1985), and more briefly R. Kessler, *Staat und Gesellschaft im vorexilischen Juda: vom 8. Jahrhundert bis zum Exil* (VTSup 47; Leiden, 1992]), pp. 176-86. 'Official and judge' may be virtually a hendiadys, as giving judgment seems to have been an important role of (some) officials (see further the Explanatory Note on v. 14).

m. Literally 'saying' and 'said', but in the context best taken, even without the explicit phrase 'in your/his heart' (as in Gen. 8.21; 17.17; 27.41 etc.), as referring to unspoken thoughts (as, e.g., in Gen. 20.11; 26.9; see further *TWAT* 1, 358-59 = *TDOT* 1, p. 333).

n. 'Must' represents the force of the asseverative particle אכן, in its straightforward, non-adversative sense 'surely' (cf. Muraoka, *Emphatic Words*, pp. 132-33). Propp detects a note of surprise (p. 165), but this is unjustified.

o. Probably a case of the 'anticipatory' use of the article, on which see GK §126q-s, JM §137m-n. Alternatively, with Houtman (p. 306), it might mean '*the* well in the area' (cf. perhaps '*the* shepherds' in v. 17), but it is unlikely that there would be only one.

p. The form in MT is unusually defective: for some similar examples of omission of *yodh* see GK §75w. Many SP mss in von Gall insert an *aleph* or *he* where the *yodh* would be (see the notes on Text and Versions).

q. Heb. רהטים, as in Gen. 30.38, 41. The meaning 'troughs' is clear from the context, the Versions and cognate words in Akkadian (*rāṭu*, *AHw*, pp. 963-64) and Syriac, but opinions differ over the etymology of the word: BDB, p. 923, compared it and its cognates to Arabic *rahaṭa*, which can mean 'be collected' (cf. Freytag 2, p. 201), but *HAL*, pp. 1113-14, following Wagner, *Aramaismen*, saw it as a loanword from Aramaic, where it was derived from *rhṭ*, 'run' (cf. Heb. רוץ: the cognates are listed in *HAL*, p. 1126). A difficulty with this is that in Akkadian 'run' is *râṣu*, indicating Proto-Semitic *rwẓ*, whereas the noun *rāṭu* points to Proto-Semitic *r(h/w/y)ṭ*. But the explanation from Arabic is also far from secure.

r. The suffix is in each case masculine, although the reference is to the shepherdesses, as quite frequently occurs (cf. Note gg on 1.21). Curiously the verb in between has a feminine suffix.

s. Heb. ויושען. 'Saved' scarcely does justice to the rich meaning of ישע, and English versions rightly avoid that rendering here. It should especially be noted that the absence of the preposition 'from' (מן) after the verb here is typical of the majority of its occurrences (see J.F.A. Sawyer, *Semantics*, pp. 70-71, and the full analysis of all instances in Biblical Hebrew by J.K. Aitken, SAHD entry ישע, 3. Syntagmatics A.6), which supports the view that הושיע denotes primarily 'the bringing of help to someone rather than the actual rescuing or removal of them from danger' (Aitken, art. cit., 6. Exegesis A.1). Where הושיע is used of a situation of conflict, the usage of the related noun ישועה later in Exodus (14.13; 15.2 – see the commentary there) suggests that the reference is to defensive rather than offensive intervention (cf. Vulg *defensis puellis* here). This would include the few forensic uses of the root, but they are to be seen as a specialisation of the general use rather than as representing the original sense (Aitken, art. cit., 6. Exegesis B.1 and 2; contra Sawyer, *Semantics*, pp. 94-95 etc.).

t. Heb. מדוע, apparently just seeking an explanation without any overtone of criticism: contrast the use of למה in v. 20. Jepsen's distinction (see Note bb on 1.18) seems to work well here.

u. Defective writing of the third pers. pl. fem. imperfect, as in 1.17-19: see Note z on 1.17.

v. The fronting of the subject expresses the unexpectedness of the event, whether the appearance of an Egyptian at all in the desert or the intervention of an Egyptian (man) on behalf of tribal women (cf. GK §142a; Muraoka, *Emphatic Words*, p. 33: the cases where איש as subject is non-emphatically fronted [ibid., p. 34] all seem to represent a 'generic' use of איש).

w. Heb. הציל means 'remove from a state of danger' and is here as often followed by an explicit reference to the cause of danger introduced by the preposition 'from' (מן) (see J.K. Aitken, SAHD entry נצל Hiphil, 3. Syntagmatics A.3; 7. Conclusion A.1 and 2). The inclusion of the word 'power' (or perhaps 'violence') (יד) is normal when the danger comes from a person (as in 3.8; 18.9-10: cf. חרב in 18.4 and the full data in Aitken, art. cit., 3. Syntagmatics A.4).

x. The infinitive absolute construction underlines the speakers' surprise (also expressed by גם, 'even') at the extent of the stranger's help (cf. Muraoka, *Emphatic Words*, p. 88). It is odd that the action thus doubly emphasised by them is not mentioned at all by the narrator in v. 17.

y. Heb. ויאמר. For the inferential use of *waw*, especially at the beginning of a speech, see BDB, p. 254b.

z. זה (with *Dagesh Forte conjunctivum*, GK §20c) is used as an enclitic to strengthen interrogatives and other words (GK §136c-d; Muraoka, *Emphatic Words*, pp. 134-37: 'to bring out the speaker's keen interest').

aa. An analogous short form of the imperative fem. pl. occurs in Gen. 4.23 and may also underlie the defective consonantal text at Ruth 1.9, 12 and 20 (cf. Bergsträsser, *Hebräische Grammatik* 2, §5a). BL (§51a', 54r) explains these forms by the loss of an original short final vowel.

bb. Simple *waw* plus imperfect/jussive expressing purpose (JM §116d).

cc. Heb. יאל Hiphil, in the majority of its occurrences, means 'resolve, deign, agree' (*HAL*, p. 365; *Ges18*, p. 431), the last of which fits the present context well. A group of imperative uses of the verb expresses an invitation or polite request (Judg. 19.6; 2 Kgs 5.23; 6.3; cf. Job 6.28; 2 Sam. 7.29 par.), and the present instance in effect represents the response to such an invitation (cf. Houtman, p. 314: 'accepted the invitation'). The nuances of this meaning have been well captured by E. Jenni in an illuminating comparison with the near synonym אבה. יאל Hiphil represents the intentionality of a positive decision (as an 'internally causative' Hiphil), while אבה expresses a state of willingness that may or (more often) may not be present in a particular case (as is well exemplified by the conditional use in Isa. 1.19): see '"Wollen" und "Nicht-Wollen" im Hebräischen', *Hommages à André Dupont-Sommer* (Paris, 1971), pp. 201-207; more briefly in *THAT* 1, 22 = *TLOT* 1, pp. 16-17. The etymology of יאל is still not established: the view in both *HAL* and *Ges18* that it is a by-form of a root אול = 'be in front' fits the meaning 'begin' in Deut. 1.5 (a meaning which was seen much more widely in antiquity – see Text and Versions), but the relation between that meaning and the more common ones, as well as the sense 'persist' which appears in Josh. 17.12; Judg. 1.27, 35; Hos. 5.11, is not at all clear.

dd. Cf. 18.3. On the status of the גר in Israelite society see de Vaux, *Institutions* 1, pp. 116-18, ET, pp. 74-76, and more recently C. Van Houten, *The Alien in Israelite Law* (JSOTSup 197; Sheffield, 1991), and C. Bultmann, *Der Fremde im antiken Juda* (FRLANT 153; Göttingen, 1992): unlike a נכרי he was a permanent or semi-permanent member of the local community. Bultmann has argued on the basis of the Deuteronomic laws that originally it was dislocation rather than foreignness which was the essence of being a גר and that most early references are to displaced and landless Israelites rather than foreigners (p. 213). Examples like Judg. 19.16 and 2 Sam. 4.3 certainly show that the former were included. It is only in later texts that a גר is by definition a non-Israelite (e.g. Exod. 12.48; Isa. 56.3, 6-8) and the rendering 'foreigner' becomes possible, if not totally precise: 'resident alien' is better, as in 12.19, 48-49 (see the notes there). In the present case Moses happens to be a non-Midianite, but it is as a 'displaced person' who has been accepted into the local community that he refers to himself as a גר.[2]

Explanatory Notes

11-12. The opening of the unit ('In those days') establishes a link between the figure of Moses and the wider situation of his people's oppression described in ch. 1 (Schmidt, Houtman). This is briefly continued in the references to their 'labours' and their 'brotherly' relationship to Moses later in v. 11. Moses, now a grown man and according to the present context still apparently living in Pharaoh's palace, goes out to where the Israelites are at work and sees an Egyptian, plausibly but not certainly an overseer, beating a 'Hebrew' (the Heb. need not mean more than that, although it is the same verb that is used for killing [as v. 14, where the verb is more

---

[2] It has been claimed that the word occurs in an early inscription recently discovered at Khirbet Qeiyafa (cf. Schmidt, p. 511), but the decipherment and interpretation of the letters in question remain much in doubt: 'The reading of the two first letters is very uncertain, perhaps *gimel* and *resh* in an upside-down position, yielding the word *gr*, provided no letter is missing before and after' (A. Yardeni, in Y. Garfinkel and S. Ganor, *Khirbet Qeiyafa 1. Excavation Report 2007–2008* [Jerusalem, 2009], p. 260).

specific, makes clear] in v. 12). The term 'Hebrew' is shared by this episode (and v. 13) and those that have preceded it in 1.15–2.10: given the conclusions which we have reached about these sections in the Introduction, it was used in both the non-Priestly sections of the narrative. Similarly, but more distinctively, the term 'labours' links it to 1.11. The 'sand' in which Moses hides the body of the Egyptian is unlikely, given the geographical context, to be that of the seashore: either the neighbouring desert or the 'beach' beside one of the branches of the Nile may be meant (see Note g on the translation). The narrator shows no interest in the moral questions about Moses' action which have concerned later commentators (on whom see Childs, pp. 33-42; Houtman, p. 301): the story is briefly told and is presented as a link in the chain of events which will eventually bring Moses to Midian (v. 15).

13-14. The next link in the chain of episodes arises from Moses' attempt to settle a dispute within his people (as distinct from protecting them from outside oppression). It is assumed by the narrator that one party is in the wrong (see Note j on the translation) and that Moses knows which it is. The word used for 'Why?', as in v. 20, may lend an accusing note to his question, as often elsewhere; cf. Gen. 44.4; 1 Sam. 22.13 and H.J. Boecker, *Redeformen des Rechtslebens im Alten Testament* (WMANT 14; Neukirchen, 2nd ed., 1970), pp. 42-43, 176-77. Boecker's description of such accusations as 'pre-judicial' (*vorgerichtlich*) is, however, misplaced: only exceptionally are any formal legal proceedings in view. Even here the accused man fears immediate violence rather than legal proceedings. The implied answer to his first question is 'No one'. Moses' own question is posed *in mediis rebus*, not *post eventum* like a judicial investigation. Nevertheless there must be sufficient in common between it and judicial procedure to give point to the terms of the accused man's question. The similarity lies in the authority claimed by Moses in his attempt to stop the fight and in his (conciliatory?) use of a form of words (especially 'Why?') which was no doubt also used in judicial (or quasi-judicial) investigations, as in the passages cited above. The association of 'official' with 'judge' is found also in Amos 2.3 and Prov. 8.16 (cf. the parallelism of *zbl* and *ṭpṭ* in Ugaritic noted by Cassuto ad loc.) and is confirmed by two Hebrew inscriptions in which an appeal is made to an official (*śr*) to decide a case in favour of the writer, one from Yavneh Yam/*Meṣad Ḥašavyahu* (*AHI* 7.001) and the other of unknown provenance (*AHI* [vol. 2] 99.008). It is also possible that 'official' here refers to the role of the 'overseers' mentioned in 1.11, where the same word (*śr*) is used.

15. Finding himself in fresh danger, his attempt at secrecy foiled, Moses flees not only from the palace but from Egypt altogether, and settles down 'in the land of Midian'. The name 'Midian' and its gentilic 'Midianite' occur nearly seventy times in the OT, but not at all in contemporary non-biblical literature (for specialist studies see J.F.A. Sawyer and D.J.A. Clines, *Midian, Moab and Edom* [JSOTSup 24; Sheffield, 1983], esp. the essays of Bawden, Rothenberg and Glass, Knauf and Payne; E.A. Knauf, *Midian: Untersuchungen zur Geschichte Palästinas und Nordarabien am Ende des 2. Jahrtausends vor Chr.* [ADPV; Wiesbaden, 1988]; more briefly *ABD* 4, pp. 815-18). The biblical references can be divided into three main groups. The largest is the 'Transjordanian' group, with specific associations with Moab and Edom (Gen. 36.35; Num. 22-31 [14x]; Josh. 13.21; 1 Kgs 11.18; 1 Chr. 1.46), but Midianites also apparently cross into western Palestine from further north (Gen. 37.28, 36; Judg. 6–9 [29x]: there are references to the latter episode in Isa. 9.3; 10.26; Ps. 83.10). Secondly, there is an 'Arabian' group, which includes the genealogical lists in Gen. 25.2, 4; 1 Chr. 1.32-33 and two prophetic passages (Isa. 60.6; Hab. 3.7: the latter is part of a description of a theophany of Yahweh and so of particular interest). Thirdly, there is a 'Moses group', to which the present verse belongs and additionally Exod. 2.16; 3.1; 4.19; 18.1; Num. 10.29. The attitudes to Midian reflected in the three groups of passages are quite distinct, respectively negative, neutral and positive. The 'Moses-group' is not entirely lacking in geographical parameters, since it is implied that Midian could be reached from Egypt and that it was also in the vicinity of 'the mountain of God' (Exod. 3.1; 18.1-5; cf. 4.19, 27 and Num. 10.29-33), which may originally have not been identical with Mount Sinai/Horeb (see the notes on 3.1) and which appears to lie within 'three days' journey' (c. 60 miles) of Egypt (cf. 3.12 with 3.18). Given the wide geographical spread of these three groups of texts, it is understandable that some scholars have proposed that 'Midian(ite)' was an umbrella term for a wide range of desert tribes, like the later Nabataeans, who were bound together into some kind of alliance (O. Eissfeldt, 'Protektorat der Midianiter über ihre Nachbarn im letzten Viertel des 2. Jahrtausends v. Chr.', *JBL* 87 [1968], pp. 383-93; W.J. Dumbrell,

'Midian – A Land or a League?', *VT* 25 [1975], pp. 323-37). But two kinds of evidence from outside the Bible have been drawn upon to argue that the original heartland of Midian, to which the 'Moses group' of texts and 1 Kgs 11.18 may or must be held to refer, lay east of the Gulf of Aqaba (so with much geographical and archaeological detail Knauf, *Midian*, pp. 1-42). First there are occurrences of what is apparently the same name in Greek writings. The geographer Ptolemy mentions two towns in north-west Arabia called Μαδιάμα and Μοδιάνα (*Geog.* 6.7.2, 27), one of which Josephus appears to refer to in one of his accounts of the Exodus story (*AJ* 2.256-257). Of these one can with some confidence be identified with the oasis of al-Badʿ, east of the Gulf of Aqaba, with which later Arabic traditions about the Midianites are associated (G. Hort, 'Musil, Madian and the Mountain of the Law', in R. Iltis [ed.], *Jewish Studies for G. Sicher* [Prague, 1955], pp. 81-93). A study by H. von Wissmann (*P-W*, supp. 12, pp. 525-52) identified the other place with Qantara, 50 mi. SSW of Tebuk. Although this evidence is late, it fits into the general picture given by the 'Arabian' group of texts (also of a late or uncertain date) in the OT mentioned above. Evidence of much earlier settlement in this region has come to light from archaeological surveys and limited excavation. This evidence, conveniently summarised by P.J. Parr in 'Pottery of the Late Second Millennium B.C. from North-West Arabia and its Historical Implications', in D.T. Potts (ed.), *Araby the Blest. Studies in Arabian Archaeology* (Copenhagen, 1988), pp. 73-89 (more briefly in *ABD* 5, pp. 594-96), points to a people who had a substantial fortified settlement at Qurayya, c. 80 mi. SE of Aqaba, during a period which included the thirteenth and twelfth centuries B.C. Their activities (as attested by a distinctive kind of painted pottery) extended south-east to the great oasis of Teima, west to the Gulf of Aqaba, and north-west to the Egyptian copper-mines at Timna in Wadi Arabah. Parr infers that the location and size of Qurayya points to involvement in the incense trade and probable contact with Egypt on this account. Whether this quite short-lived civilisation bore the name 'Midianite' remains no more than a conjecture, based on place-name evidence from 1000 years later, and its bearing on our understanding of 'Midian' in this verse and the rest of the 'Moses group' of passages is not decisive. The 'Transjordanian' group of texts indicates that Midianites were encountered well beyond the region in which the distinctive 'Qurayya' pottery has been found, and the geographical indicators in the 'Moses group', imprecise as they are, should therefore not be discounted out of hand or regarded as merely the result of the secondary combination of the references to Midian with the main Exodus and Sinai traditions. There may have been Midianite groups in the north and west of the Sinai peninsula (to which 1 Kgs 11.17-18 may well refer: de Vaux, *Histoire*, p. 315, ET, pp. 332-33); indeed there is a variety of evidence for 'Shosu' or 'Asiatics' in this region in the second millennium B.C., including the proto-Sinaitic inscriptions at the Serabit el-Khadim mines, the story of Sinuhe and other Egyptian texts, and the name 'Midian' may have been used for some or all of them too. To see the 'Midian-tradition' of Exodus and Numbers as originally separate from the Exodus-tradition and to relate it to a 'heartland' further to the east is difficult to justify: it lacks independent motifs and it is everywhere tightly bonded into the main narrative (Schmidt, *Exodus, Sinai und Mose*, pp. 110-30).

16-17. The 'well' (v. 15) in this case provided not only (presumably) water for the traveller but, more important for the development of the story, a place of meeting with the local inhabitants. This is a common theme of biblical narrative and no doubt corresponded to a real aspect of ancient life, both in towns and in the desert. The motif (which has been described as a 'type-scene' by Alter, *Art*, pp. 50-58, building on observations of Culley, *Studies*, pp. 41-43) is developed more fully and with a different background in Gen. 24.10-51; 29.1-14 (cf. also 1 Sam. 9.11-14). A more distant parallel occurs in the Egyptian story of Sinuhe (see the introduction to this section). The Genesis stories, like this one, end in a betrothal, but the motif receives distinctive expression here through the characterisation of Moses' host and the description of Moses' own action. The host is 'the priest of Midian', whose role is emphasised by the fact that he is initially unnamed (see on vv. 18-20 for his different names): the title recurs in 3.1 and 18.1, each time at the beginning of an important episode. This association with a presumably pagan priest, which ends in a marriage to his daughter, caused embarrassment to traditional commentators and translators (and probably to the Deuteronomic and Priestly writers of the Old Testament, who avoid mention of it), but is of great historical importance for the origins of Yahwism (see the introduction to the commentary on 18.1-12). The precise status and role of a Midianite priest, whether as a sheikh or as a general religious functionary like the Arabian *kahin*, are of no interest to the narrator here (but see further the commentary on ch. 18) and presently not matters about which there is any direct non-biblical evidence (de Vaux, *Histoire*, pp. 319-20, ET, pp. 337-38). Moses' action is consistent with his protection of the weaker or injured party in vv. 11-14: it also replaces the family connection in Genesis 24 and 29 as the means by which he gains access to the local community.

18-20. The following dialogue takes place at the Midianite priest's home, the nature of which is not specified – a tent seems most probable. The priest's name is given as Reuel here, whereas it is Jethro in 3.1 and 18.1 (cf. also 4.18 [twice] [where MT has 'Jether' the first time: cf. LXX Ἰοθορ throughout]; 18.2, 5, 6, 9, 10, 12) and in Judg. 4.11 Moses' father-in-law is called Hobab (and regarded as a Kenite, not a Midianite; cf. Judg. 1.19), who in Num. 10.29 is the son of Reuel. Clearly there were different traditions in circulation about Moses' wife's family which were drawn on by the source-documents that underlie the final text of the Pentateuch and the historical books. The name Reuel is of a common theophoric type incorporating the element *ʾēl*, which may be either a divine name ('El', the chief god of the Canaanite pantheon: on him see *DDD*, 522-33) or an appellative ('[a/the] god'). It appears as a Hebrew name only in late sections of the OT (Num. 2.14 [but in other passages MT gives this name as Deuel and there are also variants in the Versions]; 1 Chr. 9.8), but is attested as an Edomite personal and tribal name both in the OT (Gen. 36 [5x]; 1 Chr. 1.35, 37) and in an inscription from Tell el-Kheleifeh (no. 6043: cf. J.R. Bartlett, *Edom and the Edomites* [PEFMS 1; Sheffield, 1989], pp. 219-20). The name may also occur in North Arabian inscriptions (Thamudic and Safaitic: cf. G. Ryckmans, *Les noms propres sud-sémitiques* [Louvain, 1934–35] 1, p. 249: further references in *ABD* 5, pp. 693-94). Noth (pp. 24-25, ET, p. 37), Schmidt (pp. 85-86) and many others see the name as secondary because it does not appear at the beginning of the narrative in v. 16, but this is a weak argument – the narrator begins with the most important information and adds further detail as the story proceeds (cf. the name of Zipporah in v. 21) – and it is hard to imagine a later scribe adding such an unusual name.

Presumably the reason for Reuel's questions is that normally his daughters' return was delayed by the interference (Heb. *yad*, 'hand', here in the sense of 'power' as, e.g., in 14.30-31) of the shepherds. The apparent difference between the narrative in v. 17 and what they say in v. 19 can readily be explained by assuming that after the shepherds 'drove away' the young women they watered their own flocks with (some of) the water in the troughs – that was presumably the point of their action. It is scarcely necessary to assume exaggeration on the part of the young women (Houtman). The short-term hospitality to which Reuel feels obligated was a commonplace particularly of (semi-)nomadic society (Houtman, pp. 313-14, provides a useful bibliography, to which add *ABD* 3, pp. 299-301) and is exemplified especially by Abraham (Gen. 18.1-18: compare also the story of Sinuhe referred to above). Moses' action would only have added to this sense of obligation.

21-22. There is an unexplained transition from the invitation to a meal (v. 20) to a longer stay which leads to marriage. But Moses' situation as a fugitive rather than a traveller (like Jacob in Gen. 29) clearly required more than a temporary solution and the canonical narrative (at least in its present form) passes over the details. Moses is now no longer an honoured guest but a 'displaced person' (see Note dd on the translation) accepted into the nomadic community in the same way that such persons were provided for in Israelite custom and law. According to de Vaux (*Institutions* 1, pp. 25-26, 116 = ET pp. 11, 74) a similar custom prevailed among the pre-Islamic Arabs, and Robertson Smith interestingly adds that this involved receiving the protection of the local god and probably some participation in the local cult (*Religion of the Semites* [London, 3rd ed., 1927], pp. 76-77). The name Zipporah occurs again in 4.25 and 18.2, but not elsewhere in the OT: the masculine equivalent is the name of a Moabite in Num. 22.2 etc. It is presumably related to צפור, 'bird', and comparable to other names that allude to birds and animals (see further *HAL*, p. 983). The marriage has been compared to the *beena* type, where the husband joins the wife's clan and she does not leave her father's house (so J. Morgenstern, '*Beena* Marriage [Matriarchat] in Ancient Israel and Its Historical Implications', *ZAW* 47 [1929], pp. 91-110 [92]: for details of the custom see briefly de Vaux, *Institutions* 1, pp. 51-52, ET, pp. 28-29). It is true that later Jethro brings Zipporah and her children to Moses after the Exodus (18.5-6), but even this passage says that Moses had 'sent her away' and, whatever exactly that means, it presupposes that she had lived for a time with Moses. In addition, 4.20 and 4.24-26 indicate that, when Moses left Jethro, his wife and child(ren) did so too. The similarity to the *beena* marriage is due simply to Moses' temporary situation (cf. W. Plautz, 'Zur Frage des Mutterrechts im Alten Testament', *ZAW* 74 [1962], pp. 9-30 [23-24]; Houtman, p. 315).

The name Gershom (like Gershon, on which see below) seems likely to be related to the verb גרשׁ (with -m and -n as formative elements), though the negative connotations in most of its occurrences are a problem. Perhaps in the noun מגרשׁ there is a more positive sense, 'drive', so that the names could originally have denoted 'a keeper (or driver) of animals'. The etymology in the text (see further Note dd on the translation) is certainly not original: compare the treatment of the name Moses in v. 10. The name Gershom reappears (after 18.3) in Judg. 18.30, where it is the patronymic of the priest of Dan whose ancestry, in the original text, is traced to Moses (a widespread variant 'Manasseh' is recognised to be secondary), several times in 1 Chr. 6 as the name of Levi's son who is elsewhere known as Gershon, and in Ezra 8.2 as a descendant of Aaron's son Phinehas. The occurrence in Judges 18 is particularly significant and points to a northern Israelite priestly connection for this element of the tradition about Moses (cf. Noth, *ÜGP*, p. 202). It has been suggested that the 'Gershonites' who form one of the three sub-divisions of the Levites in the Priestly source may be the degraded remnants of this once honoured priestly family. It is possible that the curious story in 4.24-26, in which the blood of the (unnamed) son of Moses and Zipporah saves Moses' life, also derives from the traditions of this northern priestly group.

Text and Versions

בימים (2.11)   4QExod[b] and LXX add הרבים as in the unique phrase in v. 23. The reading could be original (with omission by homoeoteleuton in MT and SP), but the reference to a long interval is less appropriate here than there and casual harmonisation is more probable.

אחיו (2.11)   LXX adds here and at the end of the verse (where Sy also has it) 'the sons of Israel', to remove any ambiguity. It is clearly a secondary expansion: it was not present at the end of the verse in 4QExod[b] and there is scarcely room for it in the lacuna earlier in the verse.

בסבלתם (2.11)   LXX, Vulg, Tg[O,J] and Sy all render by singular nouns, which suggests that the *defectiva scriptio* of Heb. was misread as singular before its vocalisation was fixed in writing. In MT בסבלתם is always in the plural and the *plene* writing of most SP mss (contra von Gall) supports this.

ויפן...איש (2.12)   Tg^J, and to some extent Tg^F, have here a midrashic interpretation designed to justify Moses' action, which is also found in Exod.R. 1.29, along with other similar material.

והנה (2.13)   Before it 4QExod^b has וירא and Tg^J and most mss of Sy support this reading. But in view of the general freedom of Tg^J its evidence counts for little and the omission of *whz'* in 5b1 and 7a1 makes it doubtful, even unlikely, that the original Sy translation included the word. LXX ὁρᾷ may simply render והנה (cf. Gen. 27.6; Exod. 9.7; 14.10), though ὁρᾶν alone does render וירא והנה in Gen. 24.63; 26.8; Josh. 5.13. The addition of וירא in 4QExod^b is much easier to understand (especially with so many occurrences of וירא in the context) than its omission by the other witnesses, and it should be regarded as secondary.

שני אנשים (2.13)   Tg^J names them as Dathan (also in v. 14) and Abiram, no doubt especially because of Num. 26.9 (cf. also 16.26). An extended list of their crimes, including this one, appears at Exod.R. 1.29.

רעך (2.13)   Almost certainly (though the traces are very slight) 4QExod^b had את here before the object (cf. v. 16). Such 'improvements' to the grammar are frequent (see the note on 2.9).

ויאמר (2.14)   4QExod^b, like Tg^J and Sy, adds the indirect object לו.

לאיש שר (2.14)   LXX has no equivalent to לאיש, rendering the Heb. idiom freely. The O-text added εἰς ἄνδρα, following (as is now clear) Theod and Aq: cf. Wevers' edition, p. 75.

ושפט (2.14)   SP has ולשופט: evidently an early variant, as it is present in 4QExod^b, but the repetition of the preposition, while common, is unnecessary (JM §132g) and therefore to be viewed as secondary.

הרגת (2.14)   LXX and Sy add 'yesterday', in line with ביום השני in v. 13. Both versions may have done this independently, or Sy may have drawn on LXX at this point, as it does elsewhere (e.g. 25.2; cf. Weitzman, *Syriac Version*, p. 71). The fuller text is unlikely to be original, in any case: on the variant readings of the Jewish revisers (which omit ἐχθές) in this verse see O'Connell, *Theodotionic Revision*, pp. 9-12, 181, 261-62.

ויירא (2.14)   4QExod^b adds the unusual form מואדה (for מאד: see Qimron, pp. 69, 117; Charlesworth, *Graphic Concordance*, p. 388). The combination is a common one (12x in MT, e.g. Exod. 14.10) and could have been added here either by accident or to dramatise the narrative.

אכן (2.14)   So MT, SP, 4QExod^b, Tg^{O,J} and Sy. The other Versions, as often, were perplexed by this particle: LXX has εἰ οὕτως (cf. 1 Sam. 15.32), apparently reading הכן and analysing it as *he interrogativum* plus כן; Vulg has *quomodo* (cf. Jer. 3.20), probably thinking of איך and its extensions איכה and איככה, 'How?' (the meaning fits the context); Tg^N has הא כען, 'Behold, now...', which also fits the context and could be a crude analysis of ה/אכן as if it were Aramaic.

וישב^{20} (2.15)   LXX prefixes ἐλθὼν δὲ εἰς γῆν Μαδιάν, which looks like a smoother alternative version of the preceding clause, without the repetition of וישב. Sy actually has precisely such a rendering for the preceding clause: *w'zl l'r'ᵒ dmdyn*. Ehrlich (*Randglossen*, p. 265), followed by A. Aejmaleus, *On the Trail*, p. 104 (= *ZAW* 99 [1987], p. 80) and G.F. Davies, *Israel in Egypt*, pp. 120-21, believe the LXX reading to be original, with MT due to homoeoteleuton. The longer text is, however, out of order and would if original invite an analysis in terms of the combination of parallel sources (cf. the fuller LXX text in Gen. 47.4-6). A more plausible alternative, 'the simplest explanation' according to Propp (p. 162), is to see MT and Sy as representing two alternative readings (Sy being more original) and LXX as a combination of the two (so already Cross in *DJD* XII, p. 90). Against this may be set the argument of Wevers (*Notes*, p. 19), which explains all the variations from MT in terms of the translators' handling of the text(s) before them. The crucial issue is whether one can more easily believe that Sy alone had a sight of the Ur-Text or that it has smoothed out what it found in LXX and MT. The latter seems to be more likely (cf. Weitzman, *Syriac Version*, p. 61: later examples of a similar move have been noted in Saadya and the NJPS by M. Greenberg, *Understanding Exodus* [New York, 1969], p. 46 n. 2). The 'difficult' text of MT is far from impossible and, as Propp points out, the recurrence of וינדל in vv. 10-11 marks a similar 'seam' between episodes.

ולכהן (2.16) Tgg and Peshitta avoid the cognate Aramaic words, which are reserved for Jewish (and Christian) priests. Tg⁰·ᴺ use רבא/ה, 'chief', and Tgᴶ the more domineering אונים, 'lord', eliminating the idea that Moses was associated with pagan religion (cf. *AramB* 2, p. 165 n. 22; 6, p. 139 n. 22). Sy's *kwmr'* meant 'priest' in a wide sense and did not have the special connotations of *khn'*.

בנות (2.16) After this word in 4QExodᵇ there are traces of letters before a lacuna, which appear to be from the word רועות, fem. pl. part. Qal of רעה, 'tend (sheep etc.)'. LXX, ποιμαίνουσαι τὰ πρόβατα τοῦ πατρὸς αὐτῶν, involves a similar expansion of the text, perhaps based as elsewhere on a *Vorlage* like 4QExodᵇ.[3] But there is insufficient space in the lacuna there for the Hebrew equivalent of the whole LXX plus, and *DJD* XII, p. 88, restores simply [צאנו]. There may also be room for the accusative particle before it, as before צאן later in the verse in this ms. (see below). The longer wording, in its various forms, is similar to 3.1 and may have been derived from there (cf. also Gen. 29.9).

ותדלנה (2.16) The original SP reading must be ותדלאנה, attested by nearly all the mss in von Gall, as well as Sadaqa, Tal and Crown, and in conformity with דלא אל in SP at v. 19. As elsewhere (cf. v. 17) von Gall mistakenly preferred the reading identical to MT.

---

[3] The Greek mss actually include the name Ιοθόρ in this verse, which Aejmalaeus (ibid., p. 103) is inclined to see as derived from a divergent *Vorlage*, perhaps one that preserved an older form of the narrative in which traces of parallel sources were still visible. Wevers, on the other hand, explains Ιοθόρ as a late gloss (*THGE*, pp. 239-40).

הרהטים (2.16) The majority of SP mss spell this word with *heth* in place of the second *he* (cf. the reading רחטנו of Kethibh at Song 1.17 in MT), but the variability of the gutturals in Samaritan Hebrew (and Aramaic) texts is well known (cf. *GSH* §12) and in this case the following emphatic letter may have contributed to the variation.[4]

צאן (2.16)   SP and 4QExod[b] insert the accusative particle את before it (cf. Tg⁰ יה), conforming to strict grammar, as in 1.18 and 2.9.

ויבאו...וינרשום (2.17) Sy renders by participles, perhaps suggesting repeated or continuing action (like the imperfect in a number of Greek mss), which was stopped by Moses' intervention.

ויקם (2.17)   Tg[J] adds 'in the power of his strength': for the phrase cf. Gen. 44.13.

ויושען (2.17)   The original SP reading was probably ויושיענה, with Tal, Crown and the largest group of mss in von Gall. LXX adds καὶ ἤντλησεν αὐταῖς, conforming secondarily to v. 19.

אביהן (2.18)   Tg[J] prefixes אבוה, 'the father of', reconciling the divergent names Reuel and Jethro by assuming that Reuel is Zipporah's grandfather (cf. the further additions in vv. 20-21 and Sifre Num. 78 [Horowitz, p. 72]).

ויאמר (2.18)   LXX, Vulg and Sy (except 5b1) have 'to them' afterwards (compare the similar addition in some witnesses at 2.14).

מהרתן בא (2.18)   The unusual idiom has understandably led Vulg and Sy to paraphrase, in the latter case with the substitution of 'watered' for 'came'.

ותאמרן (2.19) SP writes with the normal *plene* ending ה-. Sy (except 5b1) adds 'to him' after it, as in vv. 14 and 18.

מיד (2.19)   LXX has no equivalent for יד, גם or the infinitive absolute and does not distinguish הציל here from הושיע in v. 17. This 'bare rendering', as Wevers points out (*Notes*, p. 21), has the effect of creating (with LXX's modification of v. 17) a total parallel between what happens and what is said.

דלה דלה (2.19)   SP spells with final *aleph* (cf. *GSH* §12a, 83a). Tg[J] renders 'only one drawing he drew', incorporating the miraculous interpretation of the Heb. found in Exod.R. 1.32, where Moses also draws water for the shepherds (cf. 'the flock(s)', not '*our* flock' in Heb.): see further *AramB* 1B, p. 6.

לנו (2.19)   Vulg *nobiscum*, 'with us', which is a curious rendering of the Heb. Possibly it refers to the interpretation in Exod.R. 1.32, which takes the *lamedh* as the sign of the object: 'Us too he drew out, for the shepherds had thrown us into the water, and he brought us out'. This is logical, once the correct interpretation of לנו, limiting Moses' action to the women's flock, is rejected (see the last note).

אל־בנתיו (2.20)   No equivalent in Vulg, removing the indirect object rather than adding it. Tg[J] reads 'the daughters of his son', presupposing the same distinction between Reuel and Jethro as in v. 18.

---

[4] For מור[ב]תה in the *editio princeps* of Tg[N] מור[כ]תה should be read: cf. the mg. and *Michael Klein on the Targums*, p. 222.

ואיו (2.20)   SP ואיה, with the old writing of the 3rd m.s. suffix which is found in some pre-exilic Moabite and Hebrew inscriptions (cf. GK §9c, 91e; Gogel, *Grammar*, pp. 156, 164). This has a strong claim to be the original reading.

עזבתן (2.20)   Many SP mss (inc. Sadaqa, Tal and Camb. Add. 1846) have עזבתין, but the ending is Aramaic and must be secondary. In this case von Gall was right to follow the minority which agree with MT.

קראן (2.20)   Sy prefixes *zlyn*, f.pl. imp. P^eal of *'zl*, 'Go!', to make explicit the daughters' need to return to where they had left Moses at the well.

Tg^J has a long addition before its rendering of 2.21, in which Moses' confinement in a pit for ten years and his discovery of his staff (which appears without prior explanation in 4.2) in Reuel's garden are described. For further comment and references see *AramB* 2, p. 166 nn. 26-29.[5]

ויואל (2.21)   The SP reading is ויאל, which Ben Hayyim took to be equivalent to ויחל, 'began' (Z. Ben Hayyim, 'Observations on the Hebrew and Aramaic Lexicon from the Samaritan Tradition', in *Hebräische Wortforschung* [FS W. Baumgartner; VTSup 16; Leiden, 1967], pp. 12-24 [13-15]). The Sam. Tg. mss gloss this variously as אתרשי, 'was allowed', which might be based on the normal senses of יאל Hiphil, with a theological dimension presumed, and אפרש, 'declared', which, if not a textual error, might be a weakened version of 'swore', based on reading the defective form as the Qal of אלה, as also happened in Vulg. The latter alternative is close to Symmachus's ὥρκισε, 'made him swear', with Reuel as the implied subject and Moses as the object, an interpretation which is more fully expounded in *MRI* on 18.2-3 (ed. Lauterbach 2, pp. 168-69) and Exod.R. 1.33 and involved taking the (plene?) form as the Hiphil of אלה. The other versions give either 'desired' (Tg^{O,J}, Sy) or 'began' (Theod, Tg^N and probably LXX, which has no separate word for ויואל here but often renders the verb by ἄρχομαι elsewhere), an interpretation which is also known to Exod.R. 1.33. A further interpretation mentioned there is 'spent the night', which seems also to be presupposed by LXX in Josh. 7.7 (unless there is a double rendering of וישב there) but does not fit the context here well. For further discussion see Salvesen, *Symmachus*, pp. 67-69.

בתו (2.21)   Tg^J has 'the daughter of his son' (cf. the note on אביהן in v. 18).

למשה (2.21)   SP reads לאשה afterwards, 'to be his wife', making explicit the sense of נתן (cf. LXX). Sy (except for 5b1) has '(as) wife' in place of 'to Moses', with *lh*, 'to him', added earlier in the sentence to pick up the reference to Moses at the beginning of the verse. Tg^N and some LXX mss also add 'to him' earlier in the verse, anticipating the repeated naming of Moses at its end.

---

[5] This and other Jewish (and one Samaritan) interpretations of Moses' staff were examined in B. Elfick's unpublished dissertation, 'The Staff of Moses', to which he has kindly given me access. He points out (pp. 43-44) that elements of Tg^J's description of the staff are already to be found in *MRI* (Lauterbach 2, pp. 131-33: on 17.6).

ותלד (2.22)   LXX prefixes ἐν γαστρὶ δὲ λαβοῦσα ἡ γυνή, conforming this verse to the account of Moses' own birth in v. 2. Aejmalaeus (*On the Trail*, pp. 102-103) suggests that both here and at the end of v. 21 the longer text is original, MT having suffered from homoeoteleuton twice (cf. Propp, p. 170). This is ingenious, but where common formulae are involved standardisation is more likely.

בן (2.22)   Tg^J pedantically adds דכר, 'male'.

ויקרא (2.22)   Tg^N, as well as some mss of Sy, reads the fem. form, making the mother name the child, as often in Genesis, but in contradiction to the explanation given for the name.

גרשם (2.22)   The name appears in several different forms: LXX and Vulg have 'Gersham', Tg^O has 'Gershem', and Sy has 'Gershon', with the interchange of *mem* and *nun* creating the same name as that of Levi's first son (6.16 – see also the Explanatory Note on vv. 21-22). According to *DJD* IX, p. 27, 4QpalGen-Ex^l had the same pronunciation as MT but wrote the name *plene*. But the top of the fragment is very difficult to read, and the restored *waw* could presumably just as easily be a *yodh*.

גר (2.22)   Tg^N adds ותותב, corresponding to the frequent association of גר with תושב elsewhere (esp. Gen. 23.4).

נכריה (2.22)   Tg^J adds the pleonastic דלא דידי, 'which is not mine'. A longer addition in Sy and numerous mss of LXX and Vulg brings in a reference here to Moses' second son Eliezer from 18.4. The translation technique of the main Greek version of the plus points to the use of vocabulary from the Jewish revisions of LXX, and the manuscripts in which it occurs include especially those which were formerly believed to contain the Lucianic recension (but see the main Introduction, section 2b for the problems involved in identifying the L-text). It is possible that this variant goes back to a divergent Hebrew *Vorlage*. See more fully my article 'A Fragment of an Early Recension of the Greek Exodus', in E.A. Livingstone (ed.), *Studia Evangelica* VII (Berlin, 1982), pp. 151-56.

MOSES' COMMISSIONING AND APPROACH TO PHARAOH (2.23–7.13)

CHAPTER 2.23-25

GOD'S CONCERN FOR HIS PEOPLE ISRAEL

This short section is marked as a separate paragraph in MT and 4QpalGen-Ex[1], but in SP it is joined to 3.1-6. It consists of two apparently unconnected parts: the first part of v. 23 (to be precise, v. 23aα) reports the death of the king of Egypt and the remainder contains a somewhat repetitious (almost poetic in its multiplicity) account of the Israelites' pained cry for help in their distress and the initial reactions of God to it. The brevity of v. 23a (as we shall refer to it here) is comparable to the similar 'death notice' in 1.6 and in its content it is the counterpart of 1.8, which once followed 1.6 and reports the accession of this king. It is linked to the content of the preceding narrative by the mention of the attempt by 'Pharaoh' to kill Moses in v. 15, but the main connection is made by the contemporaneity implied by the opening phrase 'During that long period'.

The remainder of the passage reverts for a moment to the continuing sufferings of Israel in Egypt and introduces, for the first time in Exodus, an explicitly religious dimension to the portrayal of the people as a whole (such a dimension has been briefly visible in the specific case of the midwives in 1.17-21). Unlike the chapters which follow, this does not involve any citation of direct speech in either direction. Although such speech is presupposed in the final clause of v. 23, the other expressions used denote (or may do so in the case of 'cried out') inarticulate cries of pain and distress. The response of God, although not yet formulated in words, points unmistakably forward to his impending action.

The lack of any logical connection between the two parts of this section is best explained by editorial activity, and the connection of v. 23a with 1.6, 8 and of vv. 23b-25 with 1.14 ('labour') and with 6.3-5 (virtually the whole of v. 24) justify their usual attribution to respectively the older material in the Pentateuch and the Priestly source.[1]

In traditional source criticism v. 23a was almost always attributed to J: but Knobel saw it as a transitional link from the Jehovist redactor (*Num.-Jos.*, p. 579) and Smend (*Erzählung*, p. 122), Eissfeldt and Beer (pp. 8-10) assigned it to J¹/L),[2] like the preceding verses. But already Wellhausen made two observations that have subsequently been much discussed and variously evaluated, namely that 2.23a belongs closely with 4.19 and that in the LXX, which may preserve a more ancient form of the text, the words of 2.23a appear (also) between 4.18 and 4.19 (*Composition*, p. 71). Wellhausen concluded, as W.H. Schmidt has done much more recently (p. 89), that 2.23a had originally stood before 4.19 and was moved to its present position by a redactor. But a more popular view was that 4.19 (and according to McNeile much of the following verses to v. 26) belonged immediately after 2.23a before Moses' encounter with God at Horeb (so Carpenter and Harford-Battersby, Gressmann, Hyatt; similarly Eissfeldt and Beer in the context of the L/J¹ source): for how could it be that Yahweh would seek to kill the one whom he had called to lead his people out of Egypt (4.24)? Noth originally held that 3.1–4.18 were secondarily inserted in the J source between the two related verses (*ÜGP*, p. 221 n. 549: much earlier B.D. Eerdmans had thought likewise and according to Schmidt Noth was followed in this by K. Koch and A. Reichert). Although Noth abandoned this view by the time he wrote his commentary (pp. 21-22, ET, p. 33), it has been revived in a different form by Blum, who attributes 3.1–4.18 to the author of K_D. Gertz finds more continuity between 2.23a and elements of ch. 3, but still holds that prior to the composition of the main 'non-Priestly' narrative 2.23a formed part of a 'story of Moses' youth' which also included 1.15–2.22, 4.19 and possibly 4.20a,

---

[1] Two recent exceptions to this consensus are Coats (p. 33), who attributes the whole passage to J, and Van Seters (*Life*, pp. 65-67), who sees it, with 4.19-20, as the later Priestly frame for the J account of Moses' encounter with Yahweh in 3.1–4.18. Coats gives no reason for his view, and those given by Van Seters are unconvincing outside the context of his own overall approach to the text. On the older views of von Rad and Weimar that vv. 23b-25 are not a unity see below.

[2] Fohrer, however, followed the consensus here (pp. 25, 30). Noth in his Exodus commentary (pp. 22-23, ET, pp. 34-35) linked v. 23a to 4.18E, although in *ÜGP*, p. 31, he had associated it like others with 4.19J. Wellhausen and Holzinger were undecided about the source, and so is Propp.

24-26 (but not 3.1–4.18). The choice between these alternatives will depend on the treatment of chs. 3–4. It may even be that the association between 2.23a and 4.19 has been given exaggerated significance. It need not necessarily imply that the two verses were once adjacent to one another, especially as they differ in what they say about who has died ('the king of Egypt' vs. '*those* who were seeking your life'): this is more natural if the verses were not designed to stand alongside one another and even, perhaps, belonged to different sources. The LXX text in 4.18-19 is not necessarily more original than MT (cf. Wevers, *Notes*, p. 51).

To anticipate our conclusions below about 4.17-20, where we follow the view that two parallel versions have been intertwined and that vv. 17-18 and 20b are from E and vv. 19-20a (reading 'his son') are from J, it is most reasonable to see v. 23a (like Noth in his commentary) as being the E parallel to 4.19, leading originally (before the insertion of the Priestly part of this section) into 3.1.

In the verses normally attributed to P, it is not generally noticed that it is only v. 24 which corresponds closely in vocabulary and theme to other Priestly passages, especially 6.5, and the language is remarkably full and repetitive. If anything vv. 23b and 25 have more in common with the non-Priestly account of God's words to Moses in 3.7-9 (cf. 'outcry', 'seen' and 'know' there). It might therefore be suggested that the beginning and end of this section are from the redactor who combined P with the older source-material (i.e. PentR). However, one would expect such a redactor to use the same variant for 'cry' as his parent source (i.e. *ṣāʿaq* and not *zāʿaq* in v. 23b) and, if we are right in our interpretation of 'see' and 'know' in v. 25 (see the Explanatory Note), the meaning of these verbs is different here from what it is in 3.7-9.

The repetitiveness of the language was traced by von Rad (*Priesterschrift*, pp. 42-43) and P. Weimar (*Untersuchungen* [1973], pp. 51-70) to compositeness in the Priestly material. More recently the attempt has been made to explain it liturgically and theologically. The divine response in 6.2-8 and its anticipation here in v. 24 focus on the theological motifs of God's awareness of his people's troubles and his 'remembering' of the covenant made with their ancestors (Gen. 17). But vv. 23b and 25 indicate that this was provoked by an utterance of the people which moved from inarticulate 'groaning' to a cry for help (*šawʿāh*), and that God's reaction itself moved on to an active concern for his people. All of this is expressed in the language typical of the book of Lamentations, communal laments and thanksgivings, as both Schmidt (pp. 96-98) and Boyce (*Cry*, pp. 61-68) have shown (for details see notes b, d and f on the translation). In other words, alongside the reassurance provided by the Priestly covenant theology, these verses offered an ancient and authoritative *exemplum* of God's readiness to hear when his people cried out to him from a situation of trouble and great distress. Such a combination of theology and encouragement to liturgical lament would have been particularly apt in the exilic situation to which the Priestly Work seems to be addressed, and the extension of the pericope by repetition probably reflects a kind of homiletical purpose. Combining together insights of Schmidt and Boyce (who both record their debt to J. Plastaras's *The God of Exodus* [Milwaukee, 1966]), we may indeed view important elements of the P narrative in Exodus 1–15 as presenting a sequence based on liturgical practice: situation of need (1.13-14); lament by the people and divine response (2.23b-25); oracle of deliverance (6.2-8); narrative of deliverance (14.1-29*; cf. 15.19). If this is correct, P was not only (as generally recognised) prescribing in the laws about the tabernacle the need for a restoration of temple worship according to its own principles; it was also lending powerful encouragement to the practice of cultic lament in the situation of Babylonian supremacy.

As Propp points out (p. 178), while these verses uncover the divine reality which has been largely hidden in the narrative so far, from a literary point of view their inclusion by the redactor (PentR) somewhat spoils the sudden transition in the older narrative from Moses' apparent uselessness in the desert to the dramatic appearance of God to him in ch. 3. Yet even after 2.25 it is not at all clear *how* God's care for his people is going to be turned into action on their behalf, and to that extent a considerable element of suspense and uncertainty remains in the final form of the text.

> 23 [During that long period[a] the king of Egypt died.] *The Israelites groaned[b] because of their labour and cried out[c], and their cry for help[d] because of their labour came up to (the) God[e]. 24 God heard their moaning[f], and God remembered his covenant with Abraham, Isaac and Jacob: 25 God watched over[g] the Israelites and God knew (them)[h].*

Notes on the Translation

a. No exact parallel to this phrase occurs in BH: the closest is above in v. 11. As distinct from the similar phrases combined with מִן or מִקֵּץ in Josh. 23.1; Jer. 13.6; Ezek. 38.8, this one indicates that an event occurred within a (specified) long period rather than at the end of it. On the precise reference of 'that' (lit. 'those (days)', Heb. הָהֵם) see the Explanatory Note.

b. Heb. וַיֵּאָנְחוּ, a verb generally found in late and poetic texts, expressing distress at personal pain or national destruction. In Boyce's useful typology of such words it is grouped with others (including נאק: see v. 24) which denote a non-verbal, non-directed expression of pain (*Cry*, pp. 16-22; cf. *THAT* 2, 570-71 = *TLOT* 3, pp. 1089-90), apparently at the lower end of the vocal range (contrast ילל etc.). It is used several times of responses to the fall of Jerusalem to the Babylonians, whether anticipated (Ezek. 21.11-12) or past (Lam. 1.4, 8, 11, 21-22). By contrast Deutero-Isaiah speaks of its replacement by rejoicing (Isa. 51.11, cf. 35.10).

c. The verb זעק appears to be indistinguishable in meaning from the variant form צעק, which occurs in 3.7, 9; 14.10, 15, as well as in some references back to the Exodus story (Num. 20.16; Deut. 26.7; Josh. 24.7): according to Boyce it can express both the cry of pain and the cry for help (*Cry*, pp. 22-24: likewise *THAT* 2, 569-70 = *TLOT* 3, p. 1089).

d. Heb. שׁוְעָה and the cognate verb are frequent in the Psalms and in Job, and an addressee is generally implied even when not formally expressed (e.g. Pss. 5.3; 119.147): Boyce (*Cry*, p. 18) is undoubtedly correct to see in it a specialised word for a 'cry for help'.

e. Heb. הָאֱלֹהִים, with the definite article, as also in 1.17 and 21, whereas the other occurrences in both contexts lack the article. Such variation is found elsewhere too (e.g. Jon. 3.8-10; 4.7-9), but no difference in meaning seems to be intended.

f. Heb. נַאֲקָתָם. The root נאק, with its variant אנק, refers several times to the groaning of the wounded (Ezek. 26.15; 30.24; Jer. 51.52; Job 24.12), but אֲנָקָה is also used of prisoners in the context of the capture of Jerusalem by the Babylonians (Pss. 79.11; 102.21). The present occurrence is picked up in God's revelation to Moses in 6.5. Otherwise the closest parallel is in Judg. 2.18 (Dtr1, according to A.D.H. Mayes, *The Story of Israel between Settlement and Exile: A Redactional Study of the Deuteronomistic History* [London, 1983], p. 78).

g. For the strong sense of ראה as 'watch over' cf. Ps. 138.6; Job 37.24 ('cares for').

h. The absolute use of Heb. ידע without an object(-clause) is very unusual and many commentators therefore adopt the LXX reading 'was known/made himself known' (but see Text and Versions). The citation of Gen. 18.21 by M. Greenberg in support of MT (*Understanding Exodus*, p. 54; cf. Childs, p. 28)

220   EXODUS 1–18

is not quite apposite, as the suppressed object is hardly the same there. Here it is most likely to be either (as D. Winton Thomas proposed with reference to the Arabic version ['A Note on וידע אלהים in Exod. II 25', *JTS* 49 [1948], pp. 143-44]) the people themselves (cf. Hos. 13.5) or, less likely, their situation (compare with Blum, *Studien*, 240 n. 43, Gen. 35.22: וישמע ישראל). The use of ידע in the fuller sense 'care (for)' is well known (e.g. Amos 3.2; Ps. 1.6: cf. *TWAT* 3, 498-500 = *TDOT* 5, pp. 468-70; *THAT* 1, 689-99 (692) = *TLOT*, pp. 508-21). 'God knew' is both clear in its implication and arresting in its brevity, and the occurrence of ראה and ידע (without an object) in a similar sense is paralleled in Ps. 31.8 (Thomas, loc. cit.). Cf. also Deut. 9.24.

Explanatory Notes

23. The two parts of this verse contain statements which seem to lack any logical connection: the death of the king of Egypt who initiated ill-treatment for the people (1.8-10, 15-16, 22) would if anything have been a cause for thanksgiving. Rabbinic exegesis (see Text and Versions) could only make a link by tendentious translation and haggadic expansion. It is more probable that the juxtaposition of unrelated statements is due to the combination of material from different sources by an editor (see the introduction to this section). The 'long period' during which the king died could be the period of persecution described in ch. 1, but the more immediate context is Moses' stay in Midian and it is to this that a similar verse later on refers (4.19). According to the Priestly chronology (7.7) Moses would have been approaching eighty years of age by this point, but such precise reckoning is not a concern of this strand of the narrative.

The reaction of the Israelites to their 'labour' (for the term cf. 1.14; 6.6, 9) is described in three expressions which move from an inarticulate cry of pain and distress to a specific request for help (see notes b-d on the translation). 'Groaned' is a word that is often used of the exiles' response to the Babylonian capture of Jerusalem (see note b), whereas 'cried out' is a variant pronunciation (with z in place of $ṣ$) of the word that is most often used for the Israelites' cry to God in Egypt, both in Exodus (e.g. 3.7) and elsewhere (see the references in note c). The slight variation may in this case be due to linguistic change, as the form with z is found in Aramaic and predominates in later Biblical Hebrew (from the sixth century on). 'Came up', as in 2 Kgs 19.28 and Jon. 1.2, like 'came' in Gen. 18.21; Exod. 3.9; 1 Sam. 9.16; Lam. 1.22, implies that God has heard their cry, so that there is some repetition between this verse and the next.

24-25. But it is in the following verses that God's response is explicitly and fully expounded, in four parallel clauses, with 'God' emphatically repeated as the subject in each case, rather than being represented simply by the third-person verbal form. The language used in the first two clauses (v. 24) anticipates almost *verbatim* the wording of God's declaration to Moses in 6.5 (and in part 6.3-4), so that the case for attributing this verse at least to the Priestly source is overwhelming. 'Moaning' is another word used to refer to the lamentations of the survivors of the Babylonian capture of Jerusalem (see Note f on the translation). In the following phrase an explicit theological link is made with God's covenant with the patriarchs in Genesis, and in the first place with the Priestly account of the covenant with Abraham in Genesis 17, which is reaffirmed to Jacob at Bethel in Gen. 35.11-12. The idea of God 'remembering' his covenant (in an active and not merely cognitive sense; cf. B.S. Childs, *Memory and Tradition in Israel* [London, 1962], pp. 31-44) is also Priestly (Gen. 9.15; Exod. 6.5) and was taken up in the Holiness Code (Lev. 26.42, 45). The covenant with Abraham had in considerable measure been fulfilled (see the notes on 1.7), but the promise of the land of Canaan remained outstanding and it is this, as well as God's promise to be the God of Abraham's descendants (Gen. 17.7-8), which is now seen to call for the release of the Israelites from their bondage in Egypt. Here too, therefore, as well as in 6.2-9, there is a strong indication that P's perspective included Israel's onward journey to the promised land and did not end with the revelation at Sinai, as a number of scholars have recently proposed (see further H.-C. Schmitt's rebuttal of this view in the article cited in the introduction to 6.1-9). In the completed text of the Pentateuch words like these naturally also recall the older version of the covenant with Abraham in Genesis 15 and the various texts which refer to an 'oath' to the fathers, some of which include a specific promise of release from Egypt (e.g. Gen. 50.24). But it should be noted that both this verse and 6.5 refer not only to the covenant being remembered but to God's hearing of the distress of the Israelites in Egypt. The latter theme has of course been developed already in v. 23b and it is a well established part of the tradition (cf. 3.7; Deut. 26.7 etc.).

The language of v. 25, which elaborates further aspects of the divine response to Israel's suffering, exhibits a brevity which has puzzled interpreters, arguably from very early times, and led to different readings and even to proposals to emend the text (see Text and Versions). It is at first sight natural to take the verbs 'saw' and 'knew' as referring to God's perception of the Israelites' distress, like 'heard' in v. 24 – the more so as these very verbs are so used in the following declaration by God to Moses (3.7, 9). But then the absence of specific reference to the distress or cry becomes striking, so that either ellipsis is assumed or emendations are proposed: as Propp observes, such a view is also inconsistent with the order of the verbs in vv. 24-25 (the perception should precede at least God's remembering of his covenant), so that *hysteron proteron* has to be assumed (p. 179). All this points to the need to understand the verbs in a different way which allows them to be seen as the outworking of God's faithfulness to the covenant. In fact both verbs can be so used ('watch over', 'care for': see notes g and h on the translation). Such a rendering makes it less probable that there is (as is often thought) a cross-reference between this verse and ch. 3, which is of importance for discussion about the composition of these chapters (see the introduction to this section).

Text and Versions

A few words of these verses are preserved in the second or third cent. A.D. Oxyrhyncus fragment published by Sirat, Oxford Heb.d.89(P) i (see the main Introduction, end of pp. 26-27). What survives corresponds exactly to the consonants of MT.

בימים (2.23) LXX, Vulg and Sy render 'after', as though Heb. read מן הימים, as in Josh. 23.1; Ezek. 38.8 etc. Even if such a *Vorlage* existed, as the more common idiom it is less likely to be original. 4QpalGen-Ex¹ is not extant at this point, but SP and Tgg support MT.

וימת (2.23) Tgʲ reads 'was smitten with leprosy', which according to Rabbinic exegesis (Exod.R. 1.34) was equivalent to death (cf. Num. 12.12; Isa. 6.1). Tgʲ's addition of a royal command to kill the Israelite firstborn is no doubt to provide an immediate motivation for the 'groaning' which follows (so Exod.R. ibid.).

מן העבדה (2.23) Tgᴼ,ʲ, some LXX mss and Sy add that the labour was 'hard' (קשה); cf. 1.14 and 6.9, from where this secondary elaboration clearly derives.

ויזעקו (2.23)   SP has the alternative spelling with צ, which is regular elsewhere in the Pentateuch except for Gen. 18.20 (where SP also has צ). 4QpalGen-Ex¹ has צ here too, showing the antiquity of this reading, but as a normalisation of the spelling it is scarcely original.

אל (2.23)   Tg^{O,N} replace with the common substitute (ל)קדם, but Tg^J has 'to the high heavens of (the Lord)' (cf. *TWNT* 5, 511-12, 521-22 = *TDNT* 5, pp. 512, 521-22), and then 'he said in his Word to deliver them (from the bondage)', anticipating the statements in the next verse. Reference to heaven is found in other Targumic contexts where prayer is involved (cf. *AramB* 2, p. 163 [on Exod. 1.19], for references).

וישמע (2.24)   Tg^{O,J,N} have a passive formulation followed by קדם יוי and (in Tg^{O,N}) surprisingly the object marker ית, which must reflect a similar construction to the occasional appearance of an object marker after passive verbs in Hebrew (see Note u on the translation of 10.1-20). A similar ית occurs in Tg^J in the next clause.

נאקתם (2.24)   Oxford Heb.d.89(P) i preserves the first three letters of the word, which is sufficient to provide ancient support for the MT spelling. SP has נקאתם, as also in 6.5: the variation occurred easily when *aleph* was no longer pronounced, as also in other words (*GSH* §20a). Aq (followed by Symm) replaced LXX's τὸν στεναγμόν by τῆς οἰμωγῆς, since he reserved the former to render אנחה (cf. Jer. 51.33 = MT 45.3). Tg^O rendered by קבילתא, appropriately used by all the Tgg for שועה in v. 23, but here (and in 6.5) involving a change from the meaning of MT.

ויזכר (2.24)   Tg^N adds 'in his godly compassion', no doubt to avoid the impression that God's remembering of his covenant was purely cerebral.

את יצחק (2.24)   SP reads ואת, adding the copula in the middle of a list as in 1.2-3 (see the notes there). There is a lacuna in 4QpalEx¹ at this point, but several of the Versions (LXX, Sy, Vulg, Tg^J) also have an additional 'and' here, which may in some cases at least reflect knowledge of a *Vorlage* like SP. As Wevers observes (*Notes*, p. 24), the rendering of the preposition את by πρός (at the beginning of the list, as also in Gen. 6.18; 17.19, 21) reflects a more prescriptive view of the covenant than the Heb. does, like the (standard) rendering of ברית itself by διαθήκη rather than συνθήκη in LXX.

וירא (2.25)   LXX and Vulg render by verbs meaning 'watch over, have regard for', which are used of divine protection in classical literature, and this very likely is the sense of ראה here (cf. BDB, p. 907, s.v. 6d-e). Tgg, with the usual passive paraphrase (employing גלי in its weaker sense of 'be known'), add a closer definition of the object as the 'oppression' of the Israelites (cf. 3.7 and MT at 1 Sam. 9.16): so also Ehrlich by explicit emendation of MT, but this is based on a misunderstanding of the Heb. (see the Explanatory Note).

וידע אלהים (2.25)   LXX ἐγνώσθη αὐτοῖς, taking the verb as a passive form (Niphal or, more plausibly if the וידע of MT's consonantal text is original, Hophal as in Lev. 4.23, 28) and reading אליהם for אלהים, with the metathesis of one letter in the consonantal text. While the translator may well, as generally thought, have been motivated by the lack of an object in MT and the possibility of a link to the imminent self-revelation of God in ch. 3, it is notable that he introduces passive forms of γινώσκω at a number of other places in the Pentateuch, both where MT has a form of יעד (Exod. 25.22; 29.42; 30.6, 36; Num. 17.19) and where (as here) ידע is used in the Qal (Deut. 9.24). On the basis of this rendering a number of commentators (e.g. Hyatt, Schmidt, Blenkinsopp [*Pentateuch*, p. 150] – Propp seems undecided) reconstruct the original text as ויודע אליהם, but both the difficulty (but not impossibility) of MT and the evident determination of the LXX translator to introduce a 'revelatory' theology wherever possible make this unlikely. For further discussion, and defence of the MT reading, which is supported by Oxford Heb.d.89(P) i and the other witnesses, see Weimar, *Untersuchungen* (1973), pp. 56-69. Tg^{O,N} got round the difficulty by substituting a reference to God's intention to deliver Israel (cf. 3.8), which is included by Tg^J in v. 23; here Tg^J provides the verb with an object in the form of a 'secret repentance' on the part of the Israelites, which is one of a number of explanations of the phrase given in the Midrashim (*MRI* [Lauterbach 2, p. 196], on 19.2; Exod.R. 1.35-36).

Chapter 3.1-12

Moses' Commissioning by God

The section 3.1–4.17 (which the Masoretes treated as a single unit), like 2.23b-25, takes the reader forward from the circumstances that made the deliverance of the Israelites a necessity and prepared the way for it, to what may be called the prelude to the story of the Exodus itself. Like its Priestly parallel in 6.2–7.7 (which is the direct continuation of 2.23b-25) it responds to the dire situation of the Israelites described in ch. 1, and it also continues the story of Moses' early life recounted in 2.1-23a. From now on these two strands of the narrative are to be inextricably one: there is no 'biography of Moses' separate from the deliverance of his people by Yahweh. The 'call of Moses' (on the characteristics of the narrative and its parallels see below) is to be Yahweh's human agent in the deliverance of his people, so that it can even be said that he will 'bring them out' (vv. 10, 11, 12), a term that is more often used of Yahweh himself in relation to the Exodus (e.g. 6.6-7, 20.2). But Moses is no volunteer, at least from now on (contrast 2.11-15 perhaps): the initiative lies with Yahweh, who appears to him, Moses is anything but a compliant figure (3.11; cf. 4.10, 13), and throughout it is the care of Yahweh for his people and his powerful intervention that drives the story on.

Within the larger section four sub-sections can be distinguished: 3.1-12, the primary commissioning of Moses; 3.13-15, the answer to Moses' question about the divine name; 3.16-22, the detailed elaboration of Moses' task; and 4.1-17, a series of objections by Moses, with Yahweh's replies. One immediately noticeable characteristic of the whole section is its character as a dialogue: Moses has nearly as many utterances as Yahweh, even if they are generally quite brief. This is one important difference from the Priestly version in 6.2–7.7, where (as generally in P) divine speech is much more predominant. Another is its location. Whereas in P God speaks to Moses in Egypt (so explicitly 6.28), the scene of this call in dialogue form is 'the mountain of God' in the desert, named in 3.1 as Horeb and explicitly equated in 3.12 with the mountain to which Israel as a whole will come after the Exodus: it is from this place, where the prophet Elijah is also said to have had a decisive encounter with Yahweh (1 Kgs 19), that the events of the Exodus are set in motion.

The section as a whole, while apparently lacking any Priestly elements, is not an original literary unity and its first part (vv. 1-12) has long been seen as having drawn on two separate narrative sources, to which subsequent passages also belong.

Wellhausen established the main lines of the division that became standard, attributing vv. 2-4a, 5, 7-8 to J and vv. 4b, 6, 9-12 to E (*Composition*, p. 70).[1] His apparent attribution of v. 1 to J (less the name 'Jethro') was quickly reversed (Carpenter/Harford-Battersby, Baentsch, Holzinger, Gressmann: so more recently Childs and Propp). But Smend introduced a subdivision of the verse which has been widely accepted, with v. 1abα being from J and v. 1bβ (from 'and [he] came...') being from E (*Erzählung*, p. 116: so also Eissfeldt, Beer [both like Smend in the context of a threefold division of the older material of Exodus], Noth, Hyatt, W.H. Schmidt, Kohata [pp. 15-28], L. Schmidt ['Diachrone und Synchrone Exegese am Beispiel von Exodus 3-4', pp. 228-34], Graupner). Such a view is almost bound to regard the name 'Jethro' as secondary, and it may be better to attribute all or most of v. 1 to E, as Noth (pp. 25-26, ET, p. 38) and Kohata think possible: Baden is more confident about this (pp. 74, 120-21). Doubts were expressed early on about the originality of the descriptions of the land in v. 8aβb (Baentsch, Holzinger: contra Carpenter/Harford-Battersby, Smend (p. 116 n. 1), Eissfeldt), the phrase 'out of the bush' in v. 4bβ, and the second half of v. 12. Such elements continue to be attributed to either R[JE] or a Deuteronomistic redactor (along with other phrases, such as the references to Pharaoh in vv. 10-11: so Noth, Kohata, L. Schmidt, Graupner, all in the context of a view which denies E any part in chs. 5–11), probably unnecessarily: there is a limit to what can be affirmed with confidence about the redactional history of passages like this. Distinctive approaches within this broad tradition of analysis are taken by Weimar (*Berufung*, Chapter 4), who detects a third narrative strand in vv. 1-6 and in 4.2-4; by H.-C. Schmitt ('Redaktion des Pentateuch im Geist der Prophetie', *VT* 32 [1982], pp. 170-89 [185-86]; cf. 'Berufungsschema', pp. 211-13), who

---

[1] Hupfeld had carried his separation of material from 'J' and 'E' only to the end of Genesis (*Quellen*, pp. 101-95), while Knobel attributed all of ch. 3 to the *Rechtsbuch* (~E), despite the variation in the nomenclature for God (pp. 22-24; cf. *Num.-Jos.*, p. 532).

views the J strand as a prophetic elaboration of the original E narrative; and by Propp, who inverts the usual attribution of the doublets in vv. 7-9 in line with his distinctive treatment of the rest of the chapter (pp. 192-93).

The division into two (or more) parallel strands was contested by B. Jacob and Cassuto and within a literary-critical approach by Rudolph (*"Elohist"*, pp. 6-15]). Rudolph took the view, first put forward by B.D. Eerdmans, that the tensions between Exod. 3.1–4.18 and its surrounding context were due to its being a separate (and largely unitary) composition which was incorporated into his narrative by the J writer (see on this view and Noth's change of mind about it the introduction to 2.23-25). Other tensions, within 3.1-12, were dealt with by Rudolph in ways that suggest special pleading: he deleted 'God' in v. 4b, moved v. 9 to after v. 15, and claimed that the use of 'God' in v. 11 was conditioned by the imminent revelation of the divine name in v. 14 (but if so, why was 'God' not used in vv. 2, 4a and 7?). He also regarded 3.8b and 3.12b as redactional additions, the latter because he held that Horeb (v. 1) was not identical to Sinai, having adopted an arbitrary emendation of MT in Exod. 33.6.

The beginnings of a revival of Rudolph's approach can be seen in an excursus in H.H. Schmid's *Der sogenannte Jahwist* (Zurich, 1976), pp. 41-43, where in the wider context of a late dating of the J document he briefly alludes to reasons for doubting the analysis of Exodus 3–4 into two parallel accounts. A much fuller investigation into the structure and unity of Exodus 3–4, using the methods of the general study of narrative, was undertaken in the Rome dissertation of Fischer, *Jahwe unser Gott*. This laid great stress on the coherence of the narrative and concluded that there were no tensions within it which required the hypothesis of multiple sources. At most Exod. 4.1-17 might have been a somewhat later addition to ch. 3. Within 3.1-12 he argued that the variation in the divine names contributes to a variegated, rich portrayal of God (pp. 224-28), but the argument in relation to 'God' is purely lexical and pays no attention to its use elsewhere in historical and revelatory contexts (cf. Exod. 20.1!). It may be true to say that Exodus 3–4 is 'coherent' (p. 201), but the claim that nothing in it could be displaced without disrupting 'the logic of the narrative' (p. 202) is exaggerated and there remain tensions within it which are most likely to be explained by the combination of sources and/or redactional reworking.

In his *Studien* Erhard Blum gave Exod. 3.1-12 (and indeed chs. 3–4 as a whole) a key place in the 'composition layer' (p. 19) of the pre-Priestly Exodus narrative (his K_D). In line with a brief remark of Rendtorff's (*Problem*, pp. 88-89, ET, p. 112), Blum rejected the arguments for source-division here, citing counter-arguments of B. Jacob, M. Greenberg and M. Rose (pp. 22-26), and saw no basis for envisaging minor redactional additions if the whole passage is regarded (as he does) as a Deuteronomistic composition (pp. 26-27, 32-35), albeit one based to some extent on a 'Moses-biography' on which the (later) author of Exodus 18 also drew. This last hypothesis might point to a view like that of H.-C. Schmitt noted above, but Blum does not specifically separate out what was in the 'biography' and what was added by the Deuteronomistic author here.[2]

Van Seters, like Blum, regards Exod. 3.1-12 as a unity, discounting arguments for a division into separate sources or layers (*Life of Moses*, pp. 35-46), and attributes it all to his exilic Yahwist, because of what he sees as dependence on Josh. 5.13-15 in vv. 4-6 and on Deuteronomistic and prophetic (Jer. 1) call-narratives in vv. 7-12. A similar unitary view, but with an even later date, is advocated by Otto ('Die nachpriesterschriftliche Pentateuchredaktion im Buch Exodus', in Vervenne [ed.], *Studies*, pp. 61-111, esp. 101-11) and K. Schmid (*Erzväter und Exodus*, pp. 189-209, 367-71), who see the whole passage as post-Priestly (and dependent on P) and belonging to the final redaction of the Pentateuch. By contrast Levin (*Jahwist*, pp. 326-31) and Gertz (*Tradition*, pp. 254-305) believe that it is possible to identify in parts of vv. 1-8 an original narrative which Levin calls 'J' and Gertz 'the non-Priestly narrative', to which the remainder of the passage was added by later redactors. An important difference between them is that Levin's J also includes texts from Genesis, while Gertz's 'non-Priestly narrative' does not.

The idea that 3.1-12 is dependent on P is certainly to be rejected, for lack of evidence.[3] Equally the attribution of parts of the passage to a very late redactional layer is based not so much on strong arguments as on an almost doctrinaire preference for redactional ('supplementary') explanations over source-critical ('documentary') ones. Nor will a 'unitarian' approach to the passage do, since for all the success of the redactor(s) in forming an intelligible narrative there remain unevennesses and duplications here which are much more likely to be due to the combination of parallel accounts than to the revision of one original account (see the Explanatory Notes for details). The distinction between (extracts from) a J account in vv. 2-4a, 5, 7-8 and an E account in vv. 1, 4b, 6, 9-12, subject to minor redactional modifications whose extent can no

---

[2] In a more recent article ('Literarische Verbindung') Blum still regards Exod. 3.1-12 as substantially a unity deriving from KD and he rejects suggestions of others (such as Otto, K. Schmid and Gertz: see below) that it is dependent, in part or in whole, on the Priestly narrative (his KP). But KD now begins for him at Exod. 1 (not Gen. 12) and ends at Deut. 34 (p. 155), and as a consequence the reference to the three patriarchs in 3.6 is regarded as a later addition (as also in 3.15 and 4.5): see pp. 139-40.

[3] As shown by Blum, 'Literarische Verbindung', pp. 124-27; likewise T.D. Dozeman, 'The Commission of Moses and the Book of Genesis', in Dozeman and Schmid, *A Farewell to the Yahwist?*, pp. 107-29.

longer be definitively ascertained, not only provides a plausible account of the origin of this passage, but offers some valuable clues (according to the criterion of 'narrative continuity') for the analysis of the remainder of chs. 3–4.

In the earliest form-critical study of the OT the similarity of this passage to other 'call-narratives', such as those of Gideon, Manoah and Jeremiah was already noted (cf. Gressmann, *Mose*, pp. 43-44, 47-48). Subsequent studies, especially by E. Kutsch,[4] have made it possible to identify a recurring narrative structure in Exodus 3(–4), Judges 6, 1 Samuel 9–10 and Jeremiah 1, in which most or all of the following elements occur: (i) introductory setting of the scene; (ii) commissioning; (iii) objection to the commission; (iv) reassurance (answer to the objection); (v) sign. W. Richter noted a sixth element, a reference to a national crisis, which appears in the first three examples but not in Jeremiah 1 (*Die sogenannte vorprophetischen Berufungsberichte* [FRLANT 101; Göttingen, 1970], pp. 139, 143-45). This adds weight to Gressmann's observation about the psychological realism of the hesitation of the one called in each case.

Although some writers have one-sidedly emphasised the parallels to prophetic call-narratives (Noth, Hyatt, Childs: so especially F. Stolz, 'Zeichen und Wunder. Die prophetische Legitimation und ihre Geschichte', *ZTK* 69 [1972], pp. 125-44 [138-39], and Schmid, *Der sogenannte Jahwist*, pp. 19-43), Moses' role here is wider than that of a prophet and more closely comparable to those of Gideon and Saul, whose commissionings are described in Judg. 6 and 1 Sam. 9-10. Van Seters has argued that these parallels still indicate an exilic origin for the pattern of narrative, because they form part of the Deuteronomistic History (*Life of Moses*, pp. 42-46), but there is good reason to see the sections in question as forming part of the older source-material of Judges and Samuel (so, e.g., Schmitt, 'Berufungsschema', pp. 205-207, 210). Estimates of the antiquity of these 'non-prophetic call-narratives' have varied: Richter dated what he saw as the earliest of them (1 Sam. 9–10) to the reign of Saul (*Berufungsberichte*, pp. 176-77); W.H. Schmidt (pp. 123-29) followed a suggestion of L. Schmidt (*Menschlicher Erfolg und Jahwes Initiative* [WMANT 38; Neukirchen, 1970], pp. 37-52, 88-97; cf. 'Diachrone und synchrone', pp. 228-34) in dating them to the ninth century; and most recently

---

[4] 'Gideons Berufung und Altarbau Jdc 6,11-24', *TLZ* 81 (1956), pp. 75-84 (79-80), taking up suggestions of W. Zimmerli, *Ezechiel* (BKAT; Neukirchen, 1955-69), pp. 16-18 (ET, 1, pp. 97-98). For further bibliography see Childs, p. 47, Schmidt, pp. 123-24, and Coats, pp. 41-42.

Schmitt ('Berufungsschema') has proposed a date shortly after the fall of Samaria in 722. He holds, with others, that both in Judges 6 and in 1 Samuel 9–10 the pattern is found in a secondary expansion of the underlying narrative but, as noted above, that this layer is pre-Deuteronomistic: there is no hint in these sections that the crisis to which the commissioned leader is to respond is a punishment for sin. Schmitt also notes a close similarity between Gideon's lament in Judg. 6.13 and Psalm 80, which he rightly sees as related to the sufferings of the northern kingdom. But whether that psalm is to be dated after 722, as Schmitt and some others believe, rather than before the fall of Samaria is more doubtful: the most likely reference for the 'man/son of man' in v. 18, in view of the descriptions of him, is a still-reigning king of the northern kingdom. One might then better see the three 'call-narratives' as related to the northern kingship ideology which seems to lie behind Hosea's critique of kingship in passages such as 8.4 and 13.10-11. Schmitt's observation (214-15) that a reference to the weakness of God's chosen instrument occurs in a royal context (albeit of a different kind and in relation to a Judaean king, Solomon) in 1 Kgs 3.7 might lend this view some support.

On the possible relationship of the J narrative of Moses' commissioning to this schema see the introductions to 3.16-22 and 4.1-17.

The canonical form of this passage, and its two sources as usually reconstructed, all exhibit strong links with earlier and later parts of the biblical narrative of Israel's origins. Was this always the case? The most significant attempts to identify an older form of the tradition were made by Gressmann and Noth. According to Gressmann, in both the J and E strands it was possible to identify in vv. 1-6 the remains of an older, once independent 'legend of discovery' (*Entdeckersage*) which told of Moses' discovery of Yahweh's dwelling-place (and in E also of his name) (*Mose*, pp. 21-39; cf. id., *Anfänge*, pp. 30-32). Its expansion into the present 'call legend' (*Berufungssage*) took place when the ancient legends were being collected together. This is substantially the position also of Noth, except that for him Moses' appearance in the original legend, as well as any connection with Yahweh and Mount Sinai, is firmly excluded (*ÜGP*, pp. 219-22, cf. 151-55; for the reference to Gressmann see p. 221 n. 547). In both Noth's theory of five originally independent Pentateuchal 'themes' is the key factor in the argument. Schmidt, who like others does not accept this theory (cf. his *Exodus, Sinai und Mose*, Chapter 7), is more cautious: he, like Childs (p. 55), insists that the original Israelite story is the call-narrative, to which the 'discovery-legend' is subordinate, and he gives serious consideration to the differences as well as the similarities between this story and the cult-legends in Genesis and (like Gressmann) to the possibility that Moses and Yahweh may have been named in the earliest version of the burning-bush narrative (*Exodus* [BKAT], pp. 110-20; cf. *Exodus, Sinai und Mose*, pp. 38-39). Perhaps it is better to see the similarities to Genesis at the level of motifs rather than genre. If there is an element in 3.1-12 that corresponds to the cultic aetiologies it is more likely to be found in v. 12b (and in Exod. 24) than in vv. 1-5. This tends to suggest that Gressmann's 'discovery-legend' never existed at all and that vv. 1-5(6) simply form a special kind of introduction, in the form of a theophany, to the account of Moses' call.

An important theological characteristic of each part of the section 3.1–4.17 is the explicit connection now made between the God who appears to Moses and the preceding narrative that is now included in the book of Genesis (specifically chs. 12–50). There have been hints of this before (see the notes on 1.1-7; and cf. Gen. 50.24), but now there are repeated references to Yahweh's relationship to Israel's ancestors (3.13), sometimes explicitly named as Abraham, Isaac and Jacob (3.6, 15, 16; 4.5); and twice Israel is titled, for the first time, as Yahweh's 'people' (3.7, 10). The theme which is even more strongly emphasised in the Priestly references to the patriarchal covenant (2.24; 6.4-5) is thus clearly present here too. The forthcoming deliverance of Israel from Egypt is naturally also prominent (vv. 8, 10-12), as is the fact that it is not regarded as an end in itself but as leading to a greater goal. There may be some significance (even for the extent of the sources in question) in the fact noted by Gressmann (*Mose*, pp. 46-47) that in this passage J speaks of the destination as the land of Canaan (v. 8; cf. v. 17), while E places its emphasis on the return to the mountain of God (v. 12). In these ways the passage not only occupies a key place in the plot of the Exodus narrative: it highlights some central themes in the theology of the Pentateuch, and there is more to come in vv. 13-15.

1 [Now as Moses[a] was tending[b] the flock of Jethro his father-in-law, the priest of Midian, he led the flock beyond[c] the wilderness and came to the mountain of God, to Horeb.] 2 The angel of Yahweh appeared to him in a flame[d] of fire from the midst of a thorn-bush[e], and when he looked he saw that the bush was burning in the fire but the bush was not being consumed[f]. 3 So Moses said, I must turn aside[g], so that I may look[h] at this great

sight (and see) why the bush does not burn away[i]. 4 Yahweh saw that he turned aside to look, [and God called to him from the midst of the bush. 'Moses, Moses!', he said. 'I am here', said Moses.] 5 'Do not approach me[j]!', he said, 'Remove[k] the sandals from your feet, for the place on which you are standing is holy ground indeed[l].' 6 ['I am the God of your father', he said, 'the God of Abraham, the God of Isaac and the God of Jacob.' Moses covered his face, because he was afraid to look at God.] 7 'I have surely seen', Yahweh said, 'the troubles of my people which is in Egypt, and I have heard their outcry because of their taskmasters – indeed[m] I know their pains. 8 I have come down to rescue them from the power of the Egyptians and to bring them up from that[n] land to a land which is good and broad, to a land which flows with milk and honey[o], to the (dwelling-)place of the Canaanites, the Hittites, the Amorites, the Perizzites, the Hivites and the Jebusites. 9 [And now, know that[p] the outcry of the Israelites has reached me, and I have also seen the oppression to which the Egyptians have subjected them[q]. 10 So now go, and let me send you[r] to Pharaoh to bring out[s] my people the Israelites from Egypt. 11 'Who am I', Moses said to God, 'to go[t] to Pharaoh and bring out the Israelites from Egypt?' 12 '(You shall,) for[u] I will be with you', he said, 'and this will be the sign for you that it is I who have sent you – when you bring the people out from Egypt, you (pl.) shall worship God on this mountain.']

Notes on the Translation

a. The subject 'Moses' is unusually placed before the verb (cf. 1.7), to mark the beginning of a new episode in the narrative by the provision of some 'background' information. F.I. Andersen, *The Sentence in Biblical Hebrew* (The Hague, 1974), pp. 79-80, calls this an 'episode-initial circumstantial clause' (cf. Gen. 4.1 and many other examples); A Niccacci, *The Syntax of the Verb in Classical Hebrew Prose* (JSOTSup 86; Sheffield, 1990), pp. 36-40, 58, prefers the term 'antecedent construction'. The narrative proper begins with v. 1b.

b. The combination of the Heb. verb 'to be' (היה) with the participle often indicates a continuing action in the past (GK §116r, JM §121f).

c. Heb. אחר, usually 'after' or 'behind' (11.6); the longer form אחרי is used for 'beyond' in Deut. 11.30. This meaning is more often represented by either עֵבֶר or (מ)האלה.

d. Possibly 'as a flame...', with the preposition ב taken as *beth essentiae* (GK §119i, followed by Childs). But 'the angel of the Lord' is generally conceived as having a human form (Judg. 13.6), if any. Heb. לבת, a unique form, is taken in BDB to be a contraction of להבת (which SP reads). Schmidt compares the contraction of בהם to בם: a closer parallel may be מלכת in 1 Kgs 5.25 (if for מלאכת: J. Joosten, pers. comm.). Rashi compared לבתך in Ezek. 16.30 as a form of לב, 'heart', with the feminine ending and suggested that this was used here in the sense 'midst', which לב itself sometimes has. But the text in Ezek. 16.30 is not certain (a word cognate with Akk. *libbātu*, 'anger', may be involved) and all the Versions support the meaning 'flame'. Ehrlich conjectured בלב, but this does not explain the origin of the attested readings. More likely is a recent suggestion that the form in MT is a unique occurrence of a word derived not from the root להב but from a root לבה (cf. MH לבה, 'kindle', [in Nithpael] 'blaze') or לבב (*HAL*, pp. 490-91 gives a cognate in Ethiopic, to which Propp, p. 199, adds Akk. *labābu*, 'rage', perhaps originally 'burn') = 'burn'.

e. Heb. הסנה, now again identified with the bramble (cf. LXX, Vulg: R. Tournay, 'Le nom du "buisson ardent"', *VT* 7 [1957], pp. 410-13, and other refs. in Schmidt, p. 156; *HAL*, p. 718) after a period in which equation with *Cassia senna* was popular by way of Arabic *sina* (Ges-B; Noth, p. 27, ET, p. 39). The thorny character of the plant is confirmed not only by the Versions but by the cognate *snyʾ* used in Ahiqar 165-66 (cf. the context). The word possibly occurs in the Copper Scroll (3Q15) 11.4, as well as in Deut. 33.16: see the Explanatory Note. The definite article here is probably 'anticipatory', referring to the thorn-bush which is to be a prominent feature of the pericope (see Note o on 2.15). It is less likely that 'the well known thorn-bush' is meant (Schmidt, p. 115; Houtman, p. 339; Propp, p. 199), though Deut. 33.16 may indicate that in some circles (not necessarily those in which this narrative was composed) a thorn-bush was a well known feature of early Yahwism.

f. Heb. אכל. Although once viewed as a Pual participle without the usual preformative *mem* (e.g. GK §52s, with some hesitation; BDB), this and similar forms are now parsed as the participle of the passive Qal, to be associated with its perfect and imperfect which are similarly vocalised: so first J. Barth, *Die Nominalbildung in den semitischen Sprachen* (Leipzig, 1894), p. 273, subsequently BL §381ʹ-pʹ, Bergsträsser, *Grammatik* 2, 15a-c, Meyer §68.3, JM §58, *IBHS* §22.6.

g. Heb. אסרה, from סור, 'turn aside, depart': the weak sense 'go there' (Houtman), 'go forward' (Muraoka, in JM §105c) does not seem to exist for this verb. The addition of נא, usually a precative particle, is rare where the cohortative expresses self-encouragement as here, but cf. Isa. 5.1. In such cases it adds 'a forceful nuance' (JM §105c, who refer to C. Rabin's view that the particle has the same origin as the second energic in Arabic), hence the rendering 'must' here (following Childs).

h. Heb. ואראה, which could be rendered as a second cohortative (there being generally no distinction between cohortative and imperfect in Lamed

He verbs: GK §75l), 'and let me look', but the expression of a purpose (for this use of *waw* and a cohortative or jussive see JM §116a-e) fits the context and is confirmed by the final infinitive in v. 4.

i. Heb. בער, used in v. 2 to mean '(was) burning', can also mean 'be burnt up, burn away' (cf. Judg. 15.14; Isa. 1.31; Sir. 8.10). The occurrence of both meanings side by side is unusual, but the preceding 'was not being consumed' (v. 2) removes any ambiguity. There is therefore no need for D.N. Freedman's conjecture that לא is here an asseverative particle ('The Burning Bush', *Bib* 50 [1969], pp. 245-46): and, as Propp points out, 'the wonder... is not the combustion, but the non-consumption of the bush' (p. 200). The imperfect representing a durative action in present time is especially frequent in questions (JM §113d; cf. 5.4, 15) and may have an almost modal nuance.

j. Lit. 'hither', Heb. הלם, a word found elsewhere mainly in dialogue in older narratives (Gen. 16.13[?]; Judg. 18.3; 20.7 [and perhaps 14.15]; 1 Sam. 10.22; 14.16, 36, 38 [possibly also 33: cf. LXX]; 2 Sam. 7.18; Ruth 2.14: Ps. 73.10 is the only example in poetry, but the text is doubtful). The Ug. cognate cited in *HAL*, p. 239, and *Ges18*, p. 279, is used differently, as a deictic particle (like Heb. הנה) in narrative (cf. Gibson, *CML*², p. 145).

k. Only here and in the very similar passage Josh. 5.15 is Heb. נשל used of the removal of a sandal: in the legal procedures described in Deut. 25.9-10 and Ruth 4.7-8 and in the mourning ritual of Isa. 20.2 different verbs are used (חלץ and שלף) which suggest a gentler and more deliberate action ('pull off'). The other occurrences of נשל imply a more abrupt movement. This linguistic difference confirms that Exod. 3.5 and Josh. 5.15 have nothing to do with the legal procedure.

l. In the *casus pendens* construction, with the subject being resumed by the closing pronoun הוא, the latter gives emphasis to the element immediately preceding it, i.e. in this case the predicate: 'Moses is *solemnly* reminded[?] of the sanctity of the spot where he happens to be standing' (Muraoka, *Emphatic Words*, p. 76; cf. JM §154i).

m. Heb. כי is most likely emphatic here as sometimes elsewhere (cf. BDB, p. 472; *HAL*, p. 448); a causal rendering does not fit the context (likewise Schmidt, Childs, Propp). Some recent studies have played down the emphatic usage of כי outside certain specific types of expression (Muraoka, *Emphatic Words*, pp. 158-64; JM §164b; Aejmelaeus, 'The Function and Interpretation of כי in Biblical Hebrew', in *On the Trail,* pp. 166-85), but their alternative explanations are often much less probable.

n. ההוא with the *Qere perpetuum* to give the required feminine form, as in 8.15; 12.15, 12.19; 22.26 (twice); 31.13, 14 (twice); 17 (but not 1.16 in L), generally in the Pentateuch and occasionally elsewhere (GK §17c, 32l; JM §39c). SP always has the correct feminine consonantal form, and so apparently do the biblical scrolls from Qumran (for details see J.A. Emerton, 'Was there an Epicene Pronoun *hūʾ* in Early Hebrew?', *JSS* 45 [2000], pp. 267-76 [270 n. 1]). An old view, which has recently been revived, holds that the feminine arose from a time when the same form was used for the masc. and fem. of the 3rd person pronoun/demonstrative, but this view should be rejected according to Emerton ('Epicene Pronoun') and it is generally held now that it is due to some kind of scribal quirk which affected the Masoretic tradition at a certain stage. However, S.E. Fassberg has argued that there was more variation in dialectal forms of the pronoun (as with the 3rd f.pl. suffix in Bib. Aram.) and that הוא could represent a genuine spelling (and pronunciation, whether epicene or distinct) from the time (c. 450 B.C. in his view) when the text of the Pentateuch 'crystallised' ('The *Kethiv/Qere* הִוא, Diachrony, and Dialectology', in C.L. Miller-Naudé and Z. Zevit [eds.], *Diachrony in Biblical Hebrew* [Winona Lake, 2012], pp. 171-80).

o. For the construction of a participle (or adjective) in the construct state followed by a nomen rectum ('genitive') of nearer definition see GK §128x-y, JM §121m. Cognates of דבש in Ar. and Aram. refer (also) to sweet syrup made from dates and other fruits, but the only explicit reference to its source in the OT connects it with bees (Judg. 14.8).

p. Heb. הִנֵּה, drawing the attention of the hearer to a fact, 'often one upon which some suggestion or proposal is to be founded' (BDB, p. 244, s.v. b[*a*]).

q. Lit., 'with which the Egyptians have oppressed them'. The relative clause is an extension of the simple 'internal accusative' (*figura etymologica*) construction (on which see GK §117p-r, JM §125q-r), with a second object of the person(s) affected. For a close parallel cf. Deut. 8.1.

r. The verb after simple *waw* must be analysed as a cohortative (for the omission of the ending ה- before an object suffix see BL §48c), which may then be rendered as such (as here) or understood in a final sense (GK §108d), 'so that I may send you'. Since the command to 'go' and the 'sending' are simultaneous, the former is preferable. The inferential use of *waw* (Houtman: 'therefore') is not appropriate for this *waw*, but suits well the *waw* at the beginning of the verse (cf. our 'So'). S.E. Fassberg has shown that in general 'the lengthened imperative is used when the action of the verb is directed to the speaker (usually motion towards the speaker)'. Occasionally it 'marks a more general relationship to the speaker', as when it is followed by a first person verb ('The Lengthened Imperative קָטְלָה in Biblical Hebrew', *Hebrew Studies* 40 [1999], pp. 7-13 [10-11]: here the command and Yahweh's sending express the same meaning in different ways (cf. Isa. 6.8).

s. After a cohortative an imperative often expresses a consequence or even an intention (GK §110i: so Vulg, Schmidt, Houtman and NRSV here). See also on Text and Versions below.

t. Heb. כִּי is here consequential, literally '(so) that I should go...'

u. The initial Heb. כִּי might be understood as emphatic ('Surely...'), but recent studies have urged that this use of כִּי should only be appealed to when other more familiar ones are impossible (see Note m above). Houtman apparently regards it as an (unnecessary) introduction to the direct speech, as he does in 1.19 and 2.10 (p. 34: so also Schmidt, and cf. LXX). This is possible. An elliptical causal meaning also fits the context. One possibility is that the words introduced by כי are the continuation of what God was saying in v. 10 before (on this view) Moses interrupted him. Alternatively, as in the translation above, words responding directly to Moses' objection may be left unexpressed, only the reason why it is invalid being stated (for this kind of ellipsis cf. Isa. 28.11; 49.25; Pss. 44.24; 130.4). Rashi takes a similar view, supplying 'It is not your responsibility but mine' (cf. the similar readings cited by Propp, p. 203).

v. Or, perhaps, '"I will be" is with you', anticipating the use of אהיה as a proper name in v. 14b (and Hos. 1.9?).

Explanatory Notes

1. The focus of the narrative reverts to Moses, as in 2.1-22, after the interruption in 2.23-25. But although Moses' marriage to a daughter of 'the priest of Midian' is assumed here (cf. 2.21-22), the name of his father-in-law is different: instead of the unique Reuel of 2.18 (and perhaps Num. 10.29) he is here called Jethro, as also in 4.18b and seven times in 18.1-12.[5] There are several other names ending in -ô in the OT (cf. Noth, *Personennamen*, pp. 38-39). This name is presumably related to the meaning 'abundance' of the common Hebrew root: other names derived from it (cf. BDB, p. 452) are attributed to an Ishmaelite (1 Chr. 2.17 and prob. 2 Sam. 17.25) and an Edomite (Gen. 36.26; 1 Chr. 1.41) as well as to some Israelites, who include a son of Gideon (Judg. 8.20). The difference in name must go back to divergent oral traditions, and may well reflect the use of a different (or additional) source-document by the compiler here.[6] According to our source-analysis (cf. Carpenter/Harford-Battersby, Childs: see further the introduction to this section) this verse belongs to E.

The geography implied, however vaguely, depends on the location presumed for Midian (see the discussion in the note on 2.15). It appears to be assumed that a region of 'wilderness' ('dry pasture' rather than 'desert') lay between Midian and 'the mountain of God', which is here identified with 'Horeb', the name given to

---

[5] 'Jether' in 4.18a MT: cf. LXX Ιοθόρ throughout, even twice in 2.16 and once in 18.14, where MT has no name.

[6] The attempt of W.F. Albright, 'Jethro, Hobab and Reuel in Early Hebrew Tradition', *CBQ* 25 (1963), pp. 1-11, to reconcile the different names given to Moses' father-in-law is no more successful than earlier harmonisations.

the mountain of revelation and covenant in Deuteronomy (1.2, 6, 19; 4.10, 15; 5.2; 9.8; 18.16; 28.69: cf. 1 Kgs 8.9; 19.8). In Exodus 'Horeb' appears only here and in 17.6 and 33.6; the name 'Sinai' is much more common (see the notes on 19.1). The expression 'the mountain of God' appears in three other places in Exodus (4.27; 18.5; 24.13), as well as in 1 Kgs 19.8, where it is again equated with Horeb (in Ezek. 28.14 and 16 the context is mythological; in Ps. 68.16 the reference is to Bashan, possibly in a superlative sense; related phrases in Ps. 68.17 and Dan. 9.20 have Jerusalem in mind). Despite the explicit equation with Horeb in two places, the possibility has been raised that the Exodus passages might originally have had a different mountain in view (see the discussion in my *Way of the Wilderness*, pp. 68-69, with nn. 33-36). In the other three passages Aaron is always present as well as Moses, and it has been thought that it was originally he alone who acted there as the mediator between Israel and God (and the Midianites?), being later supplanted in this role by Moses. A further important issue is the meaning of 'God' (*h'lhym*) here. Is it to be understood, as in both Priestly (e.g. 2.23-25; 6.1) and non-Priestly passages (e.g. below, vv. 4, 6, 11-15), as a less explicit title for Yahweh before his name is 'revealed'? Or is it in this expression a genuine plural, giving the meaning 'the mountain of the gods', which may also be appropriate in Ezek. 28.14, 16 and Ps. 68.16 (though in these places the definite article is lacking)? In the former case a mountain specifically sacred to Yahweh would be meant, and this would be a strong argument for identification with Mount Sinai, since Sinai was Yahweh's original 'home' according to Judg. 5.5; Ps. 68.8, 17. In the latter case a mountain with more general sacred associations could be meant, comparable but not identical to 'Mount Lel' in the Ugaritic texts (*KTU* 1.2.1.14, 20).[7] Unless 'God' is used in two different senses without any indication in this passage, the former explanation must

---

[7] R.J. Clifford, *Cosmic Mountain*, pp. 42-43, reads *'il* for *ll* there, which makes the parallel even closer to the Exodus expressions, the more so if it is accepted, as seems to be implied by some passages in Genesis, that the use of (*h*)*'lhym* in non-Priestly texts was seen as a 'safer' alternative to *'l* (see my '"God" in Old Testament Theology', in A. Lemaire [ed.], *Congress Volume: Leiden, 2004* [VTSup 109; Leiden, 2006], pp. 175-94 [186]). But Clifford's proposal has received little support (note, however, Cross, *Canaanite Myth*, p. 37, and Del Olmo Lete, cited s.v. in *DULAT*, p. 498).

be preferred and its corollary, that this mountain is to be equated with Mount Sinai, makes best sense of the occurrence in 24.13 as well as of the identification with Horeb here. Both these features could of course be due to harmonisation of originally disparate traditions, and Noth argued just that for the word(s) 'to Horeb' here, because their occurrence at the end of the sentence is so 'lame' (p. 20, ET, p. 32: cf. his remarks on 17.6). This view is followed by Schmidt (pp. 136-37),[8] but the word-order is not a serious problem and 1 Kgs 19.8 is very similar. It is understandable in the context that the epithet of the mountain should precede the name of the place. The name 'Horeb' itself never occurs in the same context as 'Sinai' and evidently belongs to a different strand (or strands) of the Pentateuch. Whether it is a term of exactly the same scope as 'Sinai' is unclear: it is preceded by 'Mount' in the Hebrew text only in Exod. 33.6, so that it has been regarded as the name for the ('dry') region, as distinct from the specific peak, where the covenant was made. Why some passages would refer to a region rather than a specific peak is not clear, but such an explanation would make good sense of Exod. 17.6, which seems to precede arrival at the actual mountain. L. Perlitt has argued that the name 'Horeb' was first introduced in a late (i.e. exilic) level of Deuteronomy, to avoid the undesirable associations which 'Sinai' might then have had with the Babylonian god Sin and the regions of Midian and Edom ('Sinai und Horeb', in H. Donner et al. [eds.], *Beiträge zur alttestamentlichen Theologie* [FS W. Zimmerli; Göttingen, 1977], pp. 302-22, esp. 306-18). The explanation is an attractive one if the texts can all be dated so late, but if the Exodus occurrences of 'Horeb' are earlier, one may perhaps have recourse to the fact to which Deuteronomy itself bears witness (and which is independently confirmed by non-biblical texts), that different populations knew the same place (specifically a mountain) by different names (Deut. 3.9: cf. 2.11, 20).

2-3. The English word 'angel' is preferred to distinguish a heavenly 'messenger' (the real meaning of Heb. *ml'k*) from an earthly one, and it is a common role of such a being to bring a message from God to human beings. As such the 'angel' is a spokesman for God just as a human messenger was for an earthly king or leader, and he would normally deliver the very words of God to a human recipient

---

[8] So already tentatively Carpenter/Harford-Battersby 2, p. 83n. But many commentators pass over the point in silence.

(e.g. Gen. 16.10; 21.18; 22.15-17). An angel might also act as God's representative or intermediary in other ways (on this see the note on 14.19). In some passages God and his messenger/angel are clearly distinguished (cf. 23.20, and especially 33.2-3), but more often the narrator slips from one to the other almost unconsciously: 'The sender is present in the one sent' (Houtman, p. 336). So here it is 'the angel' who appears but it is Yahweh/God who speaks (vv. 4, 7). Later in this narrative the 'appearance' is said to be of Yahweh himself (3.16; 4.1, 5): the expression provides an important connecting link between elements of the narrative drawn from the J source here. See *TWAT* 4, 896-903 = *TDOT* 8, pp. 317-24, *DDD*, 81-108, and the additional bibliography in Houtman, p. 337 n. 30. Recently there has been some support for the translation 'a(n) messenger/angel of the Lord' (Schmidt, p. 103; Houtman). This is grammatically possible (GK §127e, JM §139c) and some passages do speak of more than one such angel (Gen. 19.1, 15; 28.12; 32.2). In some later texts a number of angels are named (so Gabriel and Michael in Dan. 8.16; 10.13 etc.; and many more in post-biblical literature, cf. Tg^J here), and there is some evidence of a multiplicity of messenger-gods in the ancient Near East, though this is by no means the rule (*DDD*, 82-83). The majority of the OT references suggest that a single unnamed heavenly figure was understood to be involved (cf. especially the reference to 'my angel' in Exod. 23.23; 32.34).

The divine name appears here for the first time in Exodus and for the first time in the narrative since Gen. 39.23 (in Gen. 49.18 it occurs in a poem). It then recurs in v. 4a, at the end of a short section which narrative continuity shows to be a unity. For the expression 'the angel of Yahweh' in the Pentateuch cf. Gen. 16.7-11; 22.11, 15; Num. 22.22-35. References to angels have traditionally been seen as more characteristic of the Elohist source (cf. Gen. 21.17; 28.12; 31.11; 32.2), but this can only be a matter of degree, if that.

Childs has suggested that the first half of v. 2 is a kind of superscription for the story which follows, like Gen. 18.1 (pp. 49-50, 53;1 so also Schmidt). Westermann (*Genesis 12–36*, p. 335 = ET p. 277), like others, takes this view of Gen. 18.1 (or more precisely of 18.1a), and compares Gen. 22.1a as another example. In both cases Westermann attributes an interpretative purpose to the superscription, and he regards 18.1a at least as literarily secondary. Childs is concerned to rebut excessive subdivision of the passage

(Richter) and to explain the otherwise premature appearance of the angel: a description of the chronological sequence begins only with v. 2b. If this is correct, v. 2b would have to be translated as a coordinated sentence: 'He (sc. Moses) looked, and to his amazement (Heb. *hnh*) the (a?) bush was burning...' The difficulty with this view is that v. 2a is needed as part of the narrative sequence, and there is nothing in what follows that takes up the idea of an appearance of (the angel of) Yahweh. A more straightforward reading of the passage is possible: Moses sees the form of the angel in the burning bush, he realises that unusually the bush is not being burnt up by the fire, so he leaves his path to investigate more closely, and at this point God/Yahweh begins to speak to him. Given the likely composite nature of the passage (see the introduction to this section), it must remain uncertain how the episode unfolded in its original form(s), but in its present form it makes better sense as a sequential narrative.

Where a visible form is attributed to 'the angel(s) of Yahweh' it is a human form, even one that is at first indistinguishable from that of a human being (Gen. 18.2 etc. [cf. 19.1, 15]; Num. 22.23, 31; Judg. 6.11 [cf. 22]; 13.6; Zech. 1.8 [cf. 9]; 1 Chr. 21.16). The present case is exceptional in the association of the appearance of the angel with fire, though Judg. 13.20 has an angel (hitherto in human form) disappear in a flame (*lhb*), and fire is a frequent manifestation of the presence or appearance of Yahweh himself (cf. 19.18; Num. 11.1; 16.35; Deut. 4.12 etc.; 5.4 etc.). Recently the rendering 'appeared... *as* a flame of fire' (*beth essentiae*: see Note d on the translation) has become popular (so Propp as well as Childs), but it introduces unnecessarily an abnormal inanimate form for the angel. Propp has a perceptive observation on the overlap in function between the angel in the OT and images in the ancient Near East: in very different ways both are localised manifestations of divine presence (pp. 198-99; cf. B. Sommer's characterisation of the angel as one kind of 'a small-scale manifestation of God's own presence' [*The Bodies of God and the World of Ancient Israel* (Cambridge, 2009), pp. 40-44]).

Whatever the precise identity of the 'thorn-bush' (see Note e on the translation), it must be of some significance that the particular word used here (Heb. *snh*) appears in the OT elsewhere only in Deut. 33.16, in the phrase (referring to Yahweh) 'who dwells in the bush' (*škny snh*). At the very least, if as some suppose (e.g. Cross and Freedman, *Studies*, p. 116) the reading there was originally *s(y)ny*, 'Sinai' (as in Deut. 33.1), the Exodus story could be the basis for the MT reading in the poem. But the Vss give no support to such an emendation, and its attestation in a few (late) Samaritan manuscripts cited by von Gall is of little significance. M.A. Beek, in a review of the interpretation of the verse, suggested that it was a relic of nomadic tradition, comparing the similar collocation of (thorn-)bush, desert and 'the angel of Yahweh/God' in Gen. 21.15-19 and 1 Kgs 19.4-8.[9] Despite the special characteristics of Exod. 3.2-6, these parallels are important and Deut. 33.16 suggests that behind Exodus 3 there may lie a tradition in which Yahweh had an enduring association with a sacred tree in the desert. The bush or tree which burns but is not consumed is the subject of numerous legends from the Levant and elsewhere and explanations in terms of electrical phenomena have been proposed (cf. W.R. Smith, *Religion of the Semites* [London, 3rd ed., 1927], p. 193 [additional material on pp. 562-63]; Gressmann, *Mose*, pp. 23-31; Houtman, pp. 344-45; briefly, Noth, p. 27, ET, p. 39). It has also been suggested that the episode took place in a vision (see Houtman for references), but there is no positive indication of this in the text.

4. Although the contents of the two parts of the verse fit smoothly together, it is probable that from the middle of the verse material from the E source has been incorporated. This is not simply because of the word 'God' in v. 4b, though the appearance of an explicit subject so soon after 'Yahweh' in v. 4a would be surprising in a single-strand narrative, and the attempt of Cassuto (p. 32) to explain the variation in the divine names here as due to Moses' loss of direct knowledge of Yahweh fails to account for the occurrences of the divine name in vv. 2 and 7. There is in addition a striking stylistic parallel between the dialogue in v. 4b and those in Gen. 22.11 and 46.2 (in the latter case there is a further parallel with v. 6: see the note there): in all three passages the name of the addressee is repeated and the latter replies 'I am here'. Both the other passages use predominantly the divine title 'God' (though in Gen. 22.11 it

---

[9] 'Der Dornbusch als Wohnsitz Gottes (Deut. xxxiii 16)', *OTS* 14 (1965), pp. 155-61.

is 'the angel of the Lord' who addresses Abraham: for different explanations of this deviation see Gunkel, *Genesis*, pp. 238-39, and Westermann, *Genesis 12–36*, pp. 441-42, ET, pp. 360-61), so this formula seems to be a distinctive feature of the E source (Gen. 22.1 is also similar). In Gen. 22.11 the repetition of the name expresses urgency, but this is not so obviously the case in 46.2. Here, in the present form of the text, a note of urgency can be seen (Houtman, p. 345), but the continuation in E material is with v. 6 and originally it may have been more a sign of divine authority, as in Gen. 46.2 (and 1 Sam. 3.4, 10).

5. The divine approach to Moses (vv. 2, 4) is accompanied by a warning that Moses must not approach too close to Yahweh: his curiosity (v. 3) threatens to violate the mystery of Yahweh's appearing. The language of this verse recurs with only minor differences in Josh. 5.15, which concludes the account of an encounter between Joshua and a (presumably angelic or divine) figure called 'the commander of the army of Yahweh' (Josh. 5.13-15): there Joshua is told, 'Remove the sandal from your foot, for the place on which you are standing is holy indeed'. The whole incident, which is placed just before Joshua's campaigns begin with the siege of Jericho, has some similarity with the present one, but it lacks the extensive divine speeches that are found here and perhaps serves in its present context simply to reinforce the instructions and assurances given to Joshua in Josh. 1.1-9 and 6.2-5. On the other hand the present passage lacks the military features which are natural enough in the Joshua context: the tasks before the two leaders are of a different character. But the similarity of the instructions serves to underline not only a general parallelism between them, but the fact that for both of them an encounter with the divine world on 'holy ground' was an essential part of their preparation.

'Holy' is a term whose associations in the OT are principally with cultic worship. In Exodus as a whole there are 102 occurrences of words belonging to the root *qdš*, 'holy' (a figure exceeded only in Leviticus and [just] Ezekiel), so that it plays a prominent part in the religious thought of this book and conversely Exodus is one of the main texts where the meaning of this word-group needs to be explored.

Excursus on 'Holy' and Related Terms in Exodus

See in general N.H. Snaith, *The Distinctive Ideas of the Old Testament* (London, 1944), Chapter 2; *THAT* 2, 589-609 = *TLOT* 3, pp. 1101-18; *TWAT* 6, 1179-1201 = *TDOT* 12, pp. 521-45; J.G. Gammie, *Holiness in Israel* (OBT; Minneapolis, 1989); P.P. Jenson, *Graded Holiness* (JSOTSup 106; Sheffield, 1992); B.J. Schwartz, 'Israel's Holiness: The Torah Traditions', in M.J.H.M. Poorthuis and J. Schwartz [eds.], *Purity and Holiness: The Heritage of Leviticus* [Jewish and Christian Perspectives 2; Leiden, 2000], pp. 47-59; J.W. Kleinig, *Leviticus* (Concordia Commentary; St Louis, 2003), pp. 4-13; M.B. Hundley, *Keeping Heaven on Earth* (FAT 2/50; Tübingen, 2011), esp. pp. 70-81, 87-93.

Four derivatives of the root *qdš*, 'holy', occur in Exodus: (i) the verb *qādaš*, 'be/become holy' (28x), e.g. 29.37, 'shall become holy', but most often in forms which mean 'make holy, consecrate' (25x, chiefly in the Piel; e.g. 13.2); (ii) the adjective *qādôš*, 'holy', which occurs just twice (19.6; 29.31); (iii) the noun *qōdeš*, 'holiness' (70x), which is often used as an alternative way of expressing the adjectival idea 'holy' (e.g. 3.5, literally 'ground with holiness') or, as abstract for concrete, representing an object or place that is holy (e.g. 28.29, lit. 'the holiness'); (iv) the noun *miqdāš*, 'holy building', i.e. 'sanctuary or shrine' (15.17; 25.8). The total of 102 occurrences is, however, not evenly spread through the book: 86 of them are in the thirteen chapters which describe how the tabernacle is to be built (chs. 25–31) and how it was supposedly built (chs. 35–40), thus confirming the primary connection of these words with cultic worship and in Exodus with the Priestly source, from which these chapters derive. The other 16 occurrences are also mainly in the context of ritual and worship (possible exceptions are 15.11; 19.6; 22.30: see the notes on these passages), but the fact that they belong to other sources and layers of the text confirms, as we would expect, that this word-group also had a wider use outside the specifically Priestly (P) school.

Older accounts of the meaning of 'holy' tended to focus narrowly on etymological theories about the original meaning of the root. About half the chapter on 'The Holiness of God' in Snaith's book is concerned with etymology, though this includes discussion of the etymology of other words outside the *qdš*-group. For the latter he cites two main theories, one arguing for an original meaning 'bright, clear' and the other for 'separated, cut off'. He shows that the first of these is unfounded and opts for the second. But he then makes a very important observation, which is in fact much more in line with modern linguistic approaches: OT usage shows that the 'holy' is not so much that which has been separated *from* other things as that which has been separated or dedicated *to* God: it has a positive rather than a negative connotation. This can be confirmed from the combinations in which the *qdš* group of words are used. The phrase 'holy to the Lord' is frequent (11x in

Exodus, many more elsewhere), while these words are never linked with the preposition *mn*, 'from', in Exodus and there are only two certain places in the whole OT where this happens (Lev. 16.19; 2 Sam. 11.4; in 2 Sam. 8.11 the *mn* probably expresses origin rather than separation). What is holy thus essentially 'belongs to God'. A further clue is the frequency with which causative forms of the verb *qādaš*, in the sense 'make holy, consecrate', occur. This strongly suggests that holiness, in the human world, is not a natural state but a status into which things have to be brought by being consecrated or dedicated. This is generally something which humans do, but there are three places in Exodus where it is said to be the action of God (20.11; 29.44; 31.13), and there are more elsewhere. 31.13 is especially noteworthy because it speaks of God as the one who makes Israel holy (cf. also 19.6), which is perhaps to be seen as the theological foundation for all Israel's acts of 'making holy'.

What kinds of persons and things can be '(made) holy'? In the order in which they appear in Exodus they are 'ground' (3.5), the firstborn (13.2), the whole people (19.10, 14), Mount Sinai (19.23), the sabbath day (20.8), Aaron (28.3), his sons the priests (28.41), the parts of a sacrifice that were reserved for the priests (29.27), the altar (29.37) and the tent of meeting (29.44). Examination of the individual contexts would show that not only are these persons and things related to cultic worship but their consecration itself is generally brought about by a ritual act of some kind. In many ways 'sacred' would be a less ambiguous term to use than 'holy' for that which is handed over in this way to God for use in worship.

A further aspect of holiness, which is most apparent in the Priestly sections of Exodus (and other books), is that it can be a matter of degree: there is not simply an opposition between what is and is not holy (on this see further below), but also between what is more and less holy, that is, there can be 'grading' (on this see especially Jenson's book above). This may be, but need not be, designated terminologically by reference to that which is 'holy' or 'most holy' (lit. 'holy of holies', *qōdeš q^edāšîm*) and it is most clearly evident in the spatial dimension of worship. The further one proceeds from the outside world to the innermost shrine of the tabernacle or desert shrine, whose construction is described in Exodus 25–31, 35–40, the greater the degree of holiness and the greater the strictness about the relevant regulations, for example about who is permitted access. The grading of temporal, personal and ritual dimensions of worship and their respective regulations are intimately related to this fundamental division of space. The whole ordering of cultic worship constitutes a complex 'symbolic system' which has its own rationale and 'message' to the community.

A final, linguistic, aspect of the concept of holiness is the wider 'semantic field' to which the *qdš* group of words belong (on this see more fully Jenson, *Graded Holiness*, Chapter 2). The most closely related terms are conveniently summarised in Lev. 10.10: the priests were 'to distinguish between the holy and the common, and between the unclean and the clean'. We have here two opposed pairs. The opposite of the holy is 'the common' (Heb. *ḥōl*): this essentially means 'that which has not been dedicated to God's use'. In Exodus there are two occurrences of the related verb *ḥālal*, which (in the Piel and occasionally the Hiphil) means 'to make common' or to undo the 'making holy' of something (Exod. 20.25; 31.14). The other opposed pair, 'clean' (*ṭāhôr*) and 'unclean' (*ṭāmēʾ*) are not synonyms of 'holy' and 'common': in their primary sense they are subdivisions of the 'common' (e.g. the meat of animals which may and may not be eaten according to Lev. 11), but they also apply to persons, either 'holy' or 'common' (i.e. priests or laymen), according to whether they are polluted by contact with something 'unclean': if they are, they are unfit to take part in cultic worship. The criteria for such pollution and the means for dealing with it (e.g. by sacrifice or by ritual washing) are not dealt with in Exodus, but mainly in Leviticus: in Exodus the word 'unclean' does not occur at all, and 'clean' appears mostly in combination with 'gold', in the sense 'pure gold', with no other metal mixed in with it. One other member of the semantic field occurs in Exodus: the verb *ḥāram* (22.19, in Hophal). This refers to a special kind of dedication to God which involves the total destruction of the dedicated object. It is best known from the treatment of the Canaanites in the book of Joshua in line with the Deuteronomic law (Deut. 7.2 etc.). In Exod. 22.19 it refers to the punishment of an Israelite [?] who sacrifices to a god other than Yahweh: NRSV translates 'shall be devoted to destruction'. This seems to be a very different kind of dedication from that which the 'holy' group of words denotes, although in the case of the burnt offering the treatment of the offering was externally not so different.

Holy places are often structures built by humans (though even then the common belief is that a deity has designated the site: e.g. Ps. 132.13-14), but they may also be natural spaces associated with the presence or appearance of a deity, as here. A similar presumption lies behind the instructions in 19.10-13, 21-24, which relate to the theophany before the people on Mount Sinai, and according to 3.1, 12 the same mountain is involved here. It appears to be implied that it was already sacred to Yahweh before Moses came there (cf. the expression 'mountain of God' in v. 1 and Jos., *AJ* 2.264), although the alternative view that it became holy by the appearance of (the angel of) Yahweh is not easy to exclude. The narrative certainly shows no interest in any pre-Mosaic sanctity of the place, e.g., as a Midianite place of pilgrimage, but that is only to be expected.

The removal of footwear is evidently understood as an act of reverence, as for example in Islam today, but surprisingly the only other reference in the OT to such behaviour with this motivation is in the similar (and perhaps related) passage Josh. 5.15. The removal of a sandal in a legal transaction (Ruth 4.7) and going barefoot as an act of (self-)humiliation or mourning (Deut. 25.9-10; 2 Sam. 15.30 etc.) are evidently distinct customs from this one. In post-biblical times it was believed that the priests entered the temple barefoot in obedience to Moses' example (Exod.R. 2.6), but there is nothing to this effect in the OT itself.

6. The opening 'he said' appears at first to be redundant (NRSV's addition of 'further' attempts to overcome the awkwardness): in the present form of the text it marks the transition from the preliminary instructions to Moses (v. 5) to the divine self-introduction that follows, but it could also be a sign of the combination of extracts from different sources: this verse is traditionally ascribed to E (and so would lead on directly from v. 4b), and v. 5 to J. The common form of divine self-introduction in the OT includes the divine name, often followed by an attributive phrase or phrases (see e.g. 6.2 and 20.2 and the notes on these verses; also the classic essay of W. Zimmerli, 'Ich bin Jahwe', ET in his *I Am Yahweh*, pp. 1-28). Here it is absent (or rather deferred: cf. vv. 15-16), and the wording in its two parts is closer to formulae which appear in the patriarchal narratives in Genesis. For 'I am the God of your father' compare Gen. 26.24; 28.13 (both with 'Abraham' intervening between 'the God of' and 'your father'); 46.3: similar phrases appear in Gen. 31.53; 46.1; 50.17. In 28.13 the divine name also appears, and in 46.3 'God' (*h'l*). These formulae represent the continuing relationship of a god with the patriarchal family which is a characteristic of the Genesis narratives and which A. Alt and others have seen as a true reflection of a central element in the religion of Israel's forebears (e.g. Alt, *Der Gott der Väter* [BWANT 3/12; Stuttgart, 1929], ET in *Essays*, pp. 3-77; Cross, *Canaanite Myth*, Chapter 1). Despite the severe criticisms of Alt's theory, among others, by M. Köckert (*Vätergott und Väterverheissungen* [FRLANT 142; Göttingen, 1988]), this element is so distinctive within the religion of the OT that it remains difficult to attribute it entirely to the invention of later stages in the tradition (likewise R. Albertz, *Religionsgeschichte*, pp. 49-53 = ET 1, pp. 26-29 [cautiously]; Moberly, *The Old Testament of the Old Testament*, pp. 193-98; A. Pagolu, *The Religion of the Patriarchs* [JSOTSup 277; Sheffield, 1998], in the context of a wider investigation of the religious practices portrayed in Genesis). Outside the OT the closest parallels are with formulae in trading contracts of Assyrian colonists in Cappadocia from the nineteenth cent. B.C. and texts relating to the city of Qatna in Syria (eighteenth–fourteenth cent. B.C.).[10] Addressed to Moses 'I am the God of your father' represents the continuation of this family-based religion among the Israelites in Egypt, which is, in the absence so far of any national dimension to their faith, only to be expected. Joshua 24.14 could be an allusion to this, unless it is intended as a reference to the presumed worship of Egyptian gods by Israel's ancestors. In Exod. 15.2 'my God' and 'my father's God' are emphatically identified with Yahweh in a celebration of the escape from the Egyptians at the 'sea', and whoever exactly is envisaged as the speaker there it is likely to be an ancient poem which reflects the memory that such family-based religion was dominant not only among the 'patriarchal' groups in Canaan but among the early (proto-)Israelites in Egypt, as 18.4 also suggests. Moses' father remains unnamed (as in 2.1: contrast 6.20), presumably because he did not have the importance for the tradition that the succession of patriarchs did in Genesis (though even there the father is not always named: cf. Gen. 46.1, 50.17).

The following phrases, like 2.24; 3.13, 15-16; 4.5; 6.2-8, identify the god who appears to Moses with the god (or gods) of those patriarchs, implying a connection with a much more ancient period of history according to the biblical chronologies and narrative sequence. It is not clear from this verse alone how much is meant to be read into the connection. Some of the most recent Pentateuchal criticism has argued that such links were made, even in the non-Priestly material, only at a very late stage of the composition of the Pentateuch (see the introductions to this and the next sections of the text), but this is highly improbable and there is no compelling reason to regard the words 'the God of Abraham, the God of Isaac and the God of Jacob' as secondary. Against the background of Gen. 50.24, which may well belong to the same source as this verse, an allusion to the promises to the patriarchs (perhaps especially Gen. 46.3) is likely.

Moses' fear when he realises that it is God who has appeared to him (for the delay in such realisation cf. [in relation to Yahweh's angel] Judg. 6.22; 13.21) corresponds to the widespread view in subsequent books (but not it seems in the patriarchal narratives)

---

[10] De Vaux, *Histoire*, pp. 257-59, ET pp. 270-71. Ug. *ilib* is probably not to be translated 'god of the father' (cf. *DDD*, 836-40 [J.F. Healey]; *DULAT*, p. 52).

that to see God or his angel placed human beings in danger of death (Judg. 6.22; 13.22; Isa. 6.5). Elsewhere in Exodus a similar view appears in 33.20 (though v. 22 uniquely makes this not apply to Yahweh's 'back'), but in 24.10-11 the leaders of Israel are (exceptionally: cf. v. 11a) allowed to see God without any dire consequence (so at least in the MT: but see Text and Versions on these verses). On the similar fear of hearing God's voice see the note on 20.19. Such beliefs are not just a relic of 'primitive mentality': they express a sense of the otherness and transcendence of God in relation to humans which continues to find a place in the most philosophical and spiritual types of theology. Yet the OT also preserves, in the consonantal text at least, traces of a different view in the context of a more intimate meeting of human and divine, both in the case of prophets (e.g. Amos 7.7) and in worship (Exod. 23.15 [cf. SP in 17); 34.20, 23-24; Isa. 1.12; Pss. 11.7; 17.15). In the latter cases the Masoretes have generally vocalised the text in such a way as to rule out such an understanding, and even the original consonantal text has been thought to be no more than an idiom for meeting with God (cf. Houtman, p. 51), based either on usage with regard to humans or on the language appropriate to the representation of a god by an image, or indeed both (for fuller studies see F. Nötscher, *'Das Angesicht Gottes schauen' nach biblischer und babylonischer Auffassung* [Würzburg, 1924]; J. Reindl, *Das Angesicht Gottes im Sprachgebrauch des Alten Testament* [Leipzig, 1970]; and the more recent and wide-ranging article of S. Chavel, 'The Face of God and the Etiquette of Eye-Contact: Visitation, Pilgrimage and Prophetic Vision in Ancient Israelite and Early Jewish Imagination', *JSQ* 19 [2012], pp. 1-55).

7-8. These verses provide a first explicit indication of the purpose of Yahweh's appearance to Moses (in the form of his 'angel' or messenger) in v. 2: to make known his awareness of Israel's situation in Egypt and his intention not only to rescue them from there but to bring them to the land of Canaan. The first two parts of this message are repeated in vv. 9-10, which lead on directly to vv. 11-12, where the divine title 'God' is used instead of the divine name itself. The repetition is a clear basis for attributing vv. 7-8 and vv. 9-10(12) to different versions of the episode (this seems to have been first explicitly mentioned by Beer, p. 9 [cf. Noth, p. 22, ET, p. 34]: on the recent questioning of this source-division see the introduction to this section), presumably J and E respectively.

The wording used in v. 7 to describe the Israelites' suffering is distinct from the Priestly language in 2.23-25 ('outcry' is similar to 'cried out' in 2.23, but the initial root letter is different), and in two cases correlates closely with the surrounding non-Priestly narrative. For 'troubles' compare the related verb *ʿānāh* Piel, 'cause hardship', in 1.11-12. No 'outcry' is mentioned there, but one could be expected in such circumstances according to Exod. 22.21-22. The expression 'taskmasters' is used in ch. 5 for what are called 'overseers of labour gangs' in 1.11: it is clear from 5.14 ('the taskmasters of Pharaoh') that Heb. *nōgēś* is being used here as a term for a kind of official (cf. Isa. 60.17; Zech. 10.4; Job 3.18; 39.17), and not to mean 'oppressors'. The word 'pains' is not found elsewhere in Exodus: it appears mainly in poetry of the exilic and later periods and its only other occurrence in a narrative text is in 2 Chr. 6.29 (a modification of the corresponding Kings passage). The three cognitive verbs, 'seen', 'heard' and 'know', do correspond to the wording of 2.24-25, but the two latter verbs seem to be used in a different way there (see the Note) and the explicit reference to the patriarchal covenant is missing here. Despite appearances, it is being emphasised again, God is fully aware of the sufferings of 'my people'.

This is the first time in Exodus, and indeed in the Pentateuchal narrative, that such an expression is used. From now on it becomes frequent, especially in the divine demand which Moses repeatedly brings to Pharaoh to 'let my people go' (5.1; 7.16, 26; 8.16; 9.1, 13, 17; 10.3-4), but also in other contexts (3.10; 5.23; 7.4; 8.18-19; 9.14; 15.16; 18.1; 22.24; 32.11, 12, 14; 33.13, 16; cf. the similar implication of 'my son' in 4.22). Most of these verses are prior to the making of the covenant at Mount Sinai and even to the Exodus itself, so that the relationship is not thought of as based on these events. For the most part it is simply assumed to exist (apart from the Priestly texts which speak of the patriarchal covenant: 2.24; 6.5) and where there is a reference to its origin (15.16), it is vague. In context it is of course explained by the Israelites' presumed descent from the patriarchs (cf. vv. 6, 13, 15, 16) and less transparently by the title 'the God of the Hebrews' (v. 18 etc.: see the Note there). The expression, at least as used here, perhaps expresses a quasi-familial relationship between Yahweh and Israel (cf. the use of *gāʾal* in 15.13 as well as 'my son' in 4.22) which is assumed always to have existed, without any clear idea of when or how it began. In such a context the later making of a covenant would be for the regulation of the relationship rather than its creation. This 'theology of the Exodus' is, according to N. Lohfink, an achievement of the Yahwist: 'Der Jahwist deutet also die alte Erzähltradition von der

Herausführung aus Ägypten mit Hilfe des Ausdrucks עם׳ יהוה ('Beobachtungen zur Geschichte des Ausdrucks עם׳ יהוה', in H.W. Wolff [ed.], *Probleme Biblischer Theologie* [FS G. von Rad; Munich, 1971], pp. 275-305 [295]). It is certainly prominent in passages attributed to J, but its presence in the Elohistic verse 3.10 (and 18.1) as well may point to an earlier origin (cf. also Exod. 15.13, 16). For the wider use of the expression 'the people of Yahweh' and equivalents see Lohfink, art. cit.; *THAT* 2, 302-307 = *TLOT* 2, pp. 904-107 (with some critique of Lohfink); *TWAT* 6, 187-93 = *TDOT* 11, pp. 171-77.

The descent of God (v. 8) is an already established fact according to all the textual witnesses (on SP see Text and Versions: the pointing of it in the apparatus of *BHS* is wrong), and may be compared to similar statements in Gen. 11.5 (cf. v. 7) and Exod. 19.18. Yahweh's coming intervention involves his active presence on earth on behalf of his people, but it is implied here to be an intermittent presence: his permanent dwelling is above, in heaven. 'Rescue' (Heb. *nṣl* Hiphil) is a word that connotes removal from danger or trouble (see Note w on the translation of 2.18), here defined as the 'power' (Heb. *yd*, lit. 'hand') of the Egyptians. 'To bring...up' is not simply an alternative to 'to bring out' (*yṣ*ʾ Hiphil: cf. vv. 10-12) that is preferred by certain authors (on this aspect see the summary in Schmidt, pp. 152-53), but a term that has the destination in the highlands of Canaan in mind (cf. Note j on the translation of 1.10). But in view of a recent tendency to find evidence of Deuteronomistic redaction in Exodus 3 it is worth noting that the preferred term in Deuteronomy is not 'bring up' (only Deut. 20.1) but 'bring out' (over 20x).

The description of the land of Canaan as 'good and broad' is unique. 'Good' (*twbh*) is so used several times in Deuteronomy (e.g. 8.7) and elsewhere only in Num. 14.7 and Josh. 23.16, but 'broad' only (with 'rich', Heb. *šmnh*) in Neh. 9.35. 'Good' may refer to either the beauty ('fair') or more likely the fertility of the land (BDB, pp. 373-74, gives numerous examples for both meanings, but prefers the second here). The idea of Canaan as a large land is represented by related expressions in Gen. 13.17; Deut. 12.20; 19.8 (cf. Isa. 8.8), and more specific descriptions of its boundaries are given in Gen. 15.18; Deut. 11.24; Josh. 1.3-4 and elsewhere (e.g. Num. 34.1-12). In what follows these two attributes are expanded with greater detail. 'Milk and honey' (a widespread phrase: see my 'KD in Exodus', p. 411, for a list) are not the staple crops of Canaan: the triad of 'grain, wine and oil' (Hos. 2.10 etc.) is a better indication of its true agricultural potential (cf. Baly, *Geography*, pp. 97-103).

From the point of view of the settled farmer milk and honey are the meagre diet which is all that remains in a devastated land (Isa. 7.15, 21-22: cf. 23-25), and it is among the Bedouin that they are most valued as a delicacy (A. Musil, *Arabia Petraea* [Vienna, 1907–1908] 3, pp. 156-58). The phrase used here is 'a picture of Palestine as seen from the desert' (Baly, *Geography*, p. 98), with the emphasis probably falling on the abundance indicated by 'flowing' (for further discussion and bibliography see Schmidt, pp. 164-65).[11] But the pleasantness of milk and honey continued to resonate even in later times (cf. Song 4.11). The idea that milk and honey are viewed as the food of gods and that Canaan was being depicted as a kind of paradise is no longer popular: rightly so, as the parallels are too distant.

The list of six peoples who inhabited Canaan (which is repeated identically in v. 17) is one of nearly twenty such lists in the OT. The same six peoples (though not always in the same order) are included in thirteen of these passages (Exod. 3.8, 17; 23.23; 33.2; 34.11; Deut. 20.17; Josh. 9.1; 11.3; 12.8; Judg. 3.5: in Deut. 7.1; Josh. 3.10; 24.11 the Girgashites are added [on whom see *ABD* 2, p. 1028: for related personal names in Ugaritic and Punic see *Ges18*, p. 228], making a round figure of seven), giving this group a classic character. It is noteworthy that outside Exodus it appears only in Deuteronomic/Deuteronomistic literature. A larger list is found in Gen. 15.20 (ten) and in Ezra 9.1 (eight), a different list in Neh. 9.8 (Girgashites in place of Hivites) and a shorter list in Exod. 13.5 (omitting the Perizzites); 1 Kgs 9.20; 2 Chr. 8.7 (omitting the Canaanites). All the names in the 'classic' list appear individually in non-Priestly passages in Genesis: the Canaanites in 12.6 (etc.) as a general term, the Hittites in 10.15 (ch. 23 etc. are P), the Amorites in 48.22 as a general term and elsewhere, the Perizzites in 13.7 and 34.30 (with the Canaanites), the Hivites in 34.2, and the Jebusites in 10.16. In fact all of them except the Perizzites (but with the Girgashites) occur in the J Table of Nations in Gen. 10.15-17, which would be a natural source from which they might (selectively) have been drawn.

---

[11] E. Levine, 'The Land of Milk and Honey', *JSOT* 87 (2000), pp. 45-57, relates the expression especially to good grazing ground, which would be attractive to wandering pastoralists and the pastoral component in a dimorphic society. But he also recognises that it would then belong to the 'archaisms' which survived from an early stage of Biblical Hebrew (p. 50 n. 14).

The most thorough and insightful study of this whole group of passages remains that of T. Ishida ('The Structure and Historical Implications of the Lists of Pre-Israelite Nations', *Bib* 60 [1979], pp. 461-90).[12] A subsequent essay by K.G. O'Connell added much valuable information on the textual variants in these lists, but it is itself now in need of supplementation with evidence from Qumran that was published both before and after O'Connell wrote (as well as, for completeness, with the evidence from the ancient Versions other than LXX).[13] Moreover, its main general conclusion, that the appearance of seven (or more) names, including the Girgashites, in most of the passages concerned in the Samaritan Pentateuch and at least some of the LXX witnesses is more original than the shorter text of MT (cf. the title of the essay), is certainly to be rejected. O'Connell's view that the same accidental error (which he calls haplography), i.e. the omission of the Girgashites in the MT tradition, occurred sixteen times independently is highly improbable: it is much more likely that the variation between the textual traditions is deliberate and that it is due to a desire to incorporate everywhere the full list of seven names that appeared in Deut. 7.1 (see also Text and Versions on this verse and 3.17).

The MT (which is the basis for the summary given above and for Ishida's discussion) thus appears to represent the most original version of the lists available to us. From this Ishida drew some important conclusions of lasting value (though not all of his conclusions are valid). He divided the lists into five categories: (a) the 'six-name' lists, with the 'seven-name' and 'five-name' lists treated as secondary variations of these; (b) short lists of 'representative nations' (Gen. 13.7; 34.30; Exod. 23.28; Judg. 1.4-5); (c) lists arranged geographically (most clearly Num. 13.29; Josh. 5.1; 11.3, but also Gen. 15.19-21); (d) the (J) Table of Nations (Gen. 10.15-18, with its par. in 1 Chr. 1.13-16); (e) lists in later sources, derived from the 'six-name' lists. Ishida noted that the distribution of names between the first and second halves of the 'six-name' list is generally consistent and that the internal order is less regular in the first half, where names appear which were used as general terms for the whole pre-Israelite population, than in the second half, where names for specific peoples occur. The variation in the first half can, he argues, be related to evidence from non-biblical sources for the terms used successively to describe the whole country: second millennium texts refer to it as 'Canaan', while terms related to 'Amorite' (Amurru) and 'Hittite' (Hatti) begin to be used in Assyrian records of the ninth and eighth centuries. Thus the oldest forms of the list began with 'the Canaanites' (Exod. 3.8, 17; 33.2; cf. Judg. 3.5), and the promotion of 'the Amorites' and especially 'the Hittites' to the beginning reflects the later

---

[12] The classic study of E. Meyer, *Die Israeliten und ihre Nachbarstämme* (Halle, 1906), pp. 328-38 (cf. 477-78), which is often referred to, goes into only some of the problems.

[13] 'The List of Seven Peoples', pp. 234-41.

terminology (so especially Deut. 7.1; 20.17; Josh. 9.1; 12.8, which can be dated to the seventh and sixth centuries). Although Ishida does not say this, the use of 'the Hittites' as a generic term in the Priestly texts in Genesis would follow naturally from this. Ishida sees the origin of the six-name lists in a need to establish Israelite identity as the possessors of the land in propaganda of the Solomonic period and views the texts in groups (b) and (c) as being slightly earlier than this and providing the basis for them. The list of peoples, like the story as a whole, has a pan-Israelite perspective, which much current scholarship can see only as the product of Deuteronomic ideology. But the period of the United Monarchy (assuming that there was one!) is just as plausible a background for it and Ishida is able to point to some features of the names in the list (and its predecessors) which connect particularly with the time of David (for details see below).

The names of the first three peoples in the list can readily be related to names in non-biblical texts of the OT period (though that does not straightforwardly settle their meaning here: note also their use together [synonymously?] in Ezek. 16.3), while the last three names are only attested in the OT, despite attempts to find parallels to them elsewhere. *Canaan* is a general term for a region that embraced Palestine and Lebanon (the region later known as 'Phoenicia') in both cuneiform and Egyptian texts of the later second millennium B.C. (for details see A.R. Millard, in *POTT*, pp. 30-33) and in the OT (Gen. 10.15-19; Num. 34.2-12). It is used alone for the region occupied by the Israelites in Exod. 6.4 and 13.11 (cf. 15.15; 16.35) and often elsewhere. At the head of the list here it could be intended as an inclusive term embracing all the other peoples, but the use of the gentilic in some places with a narrower reference to the inhabitants of the coastal plain and (sometimes) the Jordan valley (Num. 13.29; Josh. 5.1; 11.3) perhaps provides a more natural understanding of this passage. The *Hittites* are now best known from archaeological evidence as a major power of the second millennium B.C. centred in Asia Minor and some city-states in northern Syria, once part of their empire, maintained the name into the first millennium, as some biblical passages attest (e.g. 1 Kgs 10.29; 2 Kgs 7.6). Later still, from the eighth century onwards, the Assyrians used 'the land of Hatti' for an increasingly large area in Syria and Palestine, and it is probable that this lies behind the use of 'Hittites' as a general expression for the inhabitants of Canaan in the Priestly source (Gen. 23; 26.34; 27.46; also in Ezekiel [16.13]) and perhaps the prominence given to Hittites in some passages in Deuteronomy (7.1; 20.17) and Joshua (9.1; 12.8). But in lists like the present one the basis is likely to be a population element in the (southern?) hill-country (Num. 13.29; Josh. 11.3), from which some noted individuals are mentioned in narratives about David (1 Sam. 26.6; 2 Sam. 11 passim). This latter group may well have had nothing to do with the Hittites from the north (so H.A. Hoffner, in *POTT*, p. 214). The *Amorites* appear frequently in the OT as a major component of the pre-Israelite inhabitants of the land, and in some passages they even appear to comprise the totality of the population (e.g. Gen. 15.16; Josh. 24.15). But where different names are associated with parts of the land, the Amorites are confined to the hills of western Palestine, sometimes with other peoples (Num. 13.29; Josh. 5.1; 11.3), and to Transjordan (e.g. Num. 21.21-32). Texts from Mesopotamia and Syria refer to '(the land of) Amurru' but the relationship of the changing uses of this term to the OT expression is very complex and scholarly theories about it are legion (see the excellent survey and discussion by M. Liverani in *POTT*, pp. 100-33). The once popular association of the term 'Amorites' with a presumed 'Amorite migration' southwards and eastwards from Syria c. 2000 B.C. has largely been given up, though Liverani (p. 102) still maintained that the name had been applied to the inhabitants of Canaan in the first half of the second millennium. The problem with this is that there is no evidence outside the Bible, even in the Amarna latters, of its referring to anywhere so far south: the references are to a region in Syria, at first inland but then, in the thirteenth and twelfth centuries, also including part of the coast (see Liverani, pp. 116-19), and one biblical passage uses the term 'Amorite' in just this way (Josh. 13.4-5). A natural suggestion might be that the earliest uses of 'Amorites' to refer to people in Canaan applied to migrants from Syria who were displaced from their homeland by the political and demographic upheavals c. 1200 B.C., whom the 'Exodus-group' of '(proto-)Israelites' found already settled in the hills and in Transjordan (cf. Meyer, *Israeliten*, p. 478 n. 1, just as B. Mazar suggested for some other groups in the list: 'The Early Israelite Settlement in the Hill Country', *BASOR* 241 [1981], pp. 75-85). But it is impossible to go into the wider archaeological and historical issues here. From the ninth century onwards 'Amurru' began to be used by the Assyrians as a comprehensive term for Syria and Palestine and it is therefore possible that in passages like Gen. 15.16 and Josh. 24.15 (but hardly the present passage) this later usage was read back into the accounts of earlier times. Little is known of the *Perizzites*, and their name has often been seen as an originally appellative term for 'villagers' or 'outsiders' (so already Gunkel, *Genesis*, p. 174; more recently H.M. Niemann, 'Das Ende des Volkes der Perizziter', *ZAW* 105 [1993], pp. 233-57; in relation to some passages only, N. Naaman, 'Canaanites and Perizzites', *BN* 45 [1988], pp. 42-47). The more specific references to them (Gen. 13.7; 34.30; Josh. 17.15; Judg. 1.3-4) relate to the central hill-country; and the ending *-izzi* has been thought to be Hurrian in origin (J. Blenkinsopp, *Gibeon and Israel* [SOTSMS 2; Cambridge, 1972], p. 18 with n. 19). The *Hivites* are specifically connected with Shechem (Gen. 34.2) and Gibeon (Josh. 9.7; 11.19), but also with southern Syria (Judg. 3.3: cf. Josh. 11.3; 2 Sam. 24.7), which may indicate their ultimate origin (for fuller discussion see Blenkinsopp, *Gibeon and Israel*, pp. 14-21).[14] The non-Israelite population of Gibeon continued to be a distinctive element in the time of David according to 2 Sam. 21.1-9, where they are called 'Amorites' (v. 2).

---

[14] LXX reads 'Horites' in Gen. 34.2 and Josh. 9.7.

The *Jebusites* are mentioned several times as the pre-Israelite inhabitants of Jerusalem (e.g. 2 Sam. 5.6, 8), a place with especially important links to the narrative of David's reign, and Jebus is sometimes given as an alternative name for Jerusalem (Judg. 19.10-11; 1 Chr. 11.4-5). J.M. Miller suggested that this was in fact a place a few miles north of Jerusalem, whose inhabitants had occupied Jerusalem shortly before David's time ('Jebus and Jerusalem: A Case of Mistaken Identity', *ZDPV* 90 [1974], pp. 115-27), but both the narratives in which the name Jebus appears are late and it is probably an artificial toponym derived from the gentilic. The Jebusites remained in Jerusalem until the reign of David: for a brief account of the archaeological evidence from the twelfth and eleventh centuries see A.G. Auld and M. Steiner, *Jerusalem I: From the Bronze Age to the Maccabees* (Cambridge, 1996), pp. 30-33.

9-10. These verses, which are closely linked together, bring a repeated declaration of God's awareness of the Israelites' situation (v. 9) and of his intention to secure their release, now specifically through the actions of Moses (v. 10).[15] This alternative account is apparently derived from a different version of the episode. It is closely linked, both by the continuity of the dialogue and by specific expressions such as 'send you' and 'bring my people/the Israelites/ the people out of Egypt', to vv. 11-12, in which the divine title 'God' is used as in v. 6. This whole section has therefore generally been assigned to the E source. On the formal similarities of vv. 9-12 to other 'call-narratives' see the introduction to this section. While v. 9 uses the same word 'outcry' as in v. 7 (see the Note there), a different word, 'oppression' (Heb. *lḥṣ*: see Note q on the translation for the repetition of the root in the following clause) describes the Israelites' situation. This is a close synonym of 'troubles' ($^{co}nî$) in v. 7 (see the Note there), with which it is linked several times (Deut. 26.7; Ps. 44.25; Job 36.15). It is used of the oppression of one individual by another (Exod. 22.20; 23.9; Pss. 42.10; 43.2; 56.2), of hostility between Israel and other peoples (Judg. 2.18; 4.3; 6.9; 10.12 etc.; Isa. 19.20; Jer. 30.20; Amos 6.14; Ps. 44.25) and

---

[15] Each verse begins with the connective 'And now': such close repetition of 'now' (Heb. *ʿattāh*) is paralleled elsewhere (Josh. 22.4; 1 Sam. 25.26; Neh. 6.7: cf. Josh. 14.10, 12) and is no reason to regard the first occurrence as belonging to the separate account in vv. 7-8, 16-17 (contra, e.g., Eissfeldt and Weimar [*Berufung*, p. 49]). The inferential use (see on 4.11-12) does not fit 3.9 if it is the beginning of E's version, but the epistolary use of *wʿt* in inscriptions (see the list in *AHI*, pp. 467-68) and biblical instances such as 1 Sam. 25.7; 2 Kgs 5.6; 10.2 (see also *HAL*, pp. 853-34) point to a possible 'introductory' use of the particle.

specifically of the bondage in Egypt (Deut. 26.7); and it frequently leads to an 'outcry' (Exod. 22.20-22; Deut. 26.7; Judg. 2.18; 4.3; 10.12; 2 Kgs 13.4; Isa. 19.20), which Yahweh hears and responds to. The language of this verse is thus, like 2.23-24 (see the Notes there) and 3.7-8, closely related to that of individual and community laments and the divine response to them, and the memory of the Exodus deliverance itself was a natural source of confidence in such prayers (e.g. Pss. 77.12-21; 80.8-11).

The introductory imperative 'Go' (here in the lengthened form) is very common at the beginning of any kind of instruction, whether human or divine, and it occurs frequently in Exodus in God's instructions to Moses (cf. 3.16; 4.12, 19, 27 etc.). Here it is reinforced by 'now', lending it additional urgency, as in 5.18 and 32.34 (Houtman 1, p. 359). God's 'sending' of Moses to Pharaoh is a central theme of the next few verses, as is to be expected in a passage which is designed to establish his authority before Israel and Pharaoh. Although such sending is the hallmark of a prophet (who is viewed as a messenger of God: Isa. 6.8 etc.), it is also characteristic of other kinds of human agent of God: see Gen. 45.5; Judg. 6.14; 1 Sam. 15.18. Here Moses is assigned the role which is elsewhere generally ascribed to God himself, 'to bring out...the Israelites from Egypt' (cf. 6.6-7; 20.2), but he can only do this because of his divine commission: there is no hint of a human leader acting independently of God. Moses' role, but also its divine origin, were similarly understood by Hosea (12.14). Here too the Israelites are called 'my people' (cf. v. 7), and if (as seems likely) these verses are the original continuation of v. 6, the basis of this designation in the relationship of the people's ancestors to God will have been already indicated in the underlying (E) source.

11. Moses' demurral serves to underline the greatness of the task which he has been given as well as his own sense of inadequacy for it. On expressions of this type see G.W. Coats, 'Self-Abasement and Insult Formulae', *JBL* 89 (1970), pp. 14-26. The function of the formula depends on whether the subject in the first element is the speaker, as here, or a third party, as in Exod. 5.2, for example.

12. God's reply both reassures Moses by the promise of his 'accompanying presence' and confirms to the reader that the decisive factor in what follows is not the abilities of the human agent but the power of God. The notion of God being 'with' an individual or the people as a whole is widespread in the OT and apparently a feature which is largely distinctive from the beliefs of Israel's neighbours:

for detailed discussion see H.D. Preuss, '...ich will mit dir sein!', *ZAW* 80 (1968), pp. 139-73. Preuss distinguishes there between the original context of such promises in the stories of the patriarchs on their journeys and the early Israelites in their wars and a more general application to protection and help by God which developed later in the narratives about Joseph and David (cf. also *TWAT* 1, 485-500 = *TDOT* 1, pp. 449-63). It is the uses of the expression in narrative rather than discourse which give the clearest indication of what it was thought to imply (e.g. Gen. 21.20; 31.5-7; 39.2-3). In the present context the formula is broadly related to a journey, but the promise relates more specifically to what will happen after Moses has returned to Egypt and thus belongs to Preuss's second stage of development.

The additional reassurance provided by a 'sign' is a common feature of the commission by God of a leader (cf. Judg. 6.17, 36-40 [Gideon]); 1 Sam. 10.1-13 [Saul]), and in Exod. 4.1-9 (J) Moses himself is given three signs to perform to convince the Israelites that he has been sent by God. There has been, and continues to be, much discussion about what the sign referred to here is. An early but obscure indication of its importance is given by the citations of v. 12b in two fragments of 4QReworked Pentateuch (4Q158 fr. 2.16; fr. 4.2), which respectively make it central to what Moses reports to Aaron in Exod. 4.28 and see it (as a commandment, cf. fr. 4.1) as the validation for the act of worship described in Exod. 24.4-6. LXX (see Text and Versions) possibly dissociated the sign from worship on the mountain and identified it with something in the preceding context. Tg^J sees the worship as a response to the lawgiving in Exodus 19ff. and probably equates it with that described in ch. 24. In Exod.R. 4 these two lines of interpretation are combined: the sign is taken to be God's presence with Moses (cf. NJPS), seen in its effects, while the giving of the Torah (taken to be implied by 'you shall *serve* God', a different rendering of Heb. *ʿābad*) provides the rationale for the Exodus. Somewhat similarly Rashi (with a symbolic application to Moses) and Ibn Ezra see the sign as the burning bush and the final words of the verse as indicating the goal of the Exodus as being respectively the lawgiving and the worship in Exodus 24 which culminated in the making of the covenant. Rashi also records an interpretation which combined the two elements in Exod.R. 4: Moses' success (the result of God's presence with him) will be the sign that there is more to come, namely the lawgiving on the mountain, seen as a parallel to the sign in Isa. 37.30. While Heb. *ʿābad* can refer to the general service of God which includes the keeping of the commandments (Deut. 10.12-13; 13.5; Mal. 3.14; Job 21.15), there is no reason why a statement about this should be limited to 'the mountain of God' and the sense 'worship' is therefore to be preferred, with 4QRP and Ibn Ezra.

In modern times the formulation of v. 12b (especially 'God' in the third person in divine speech) has led some commentators to view the text as damaged (e.g. Noth) or revised by the redactor who combined the sources J and E (Schmidt), the original sign having been removed in either case. There is probably no need for such drastic solutions to the problem. Childs (pp. 56-60) has pointed the way to a plausible solution, both by his insistence that the asyndeton after 'sent you' requires that the sign be found in what follows rather than in what precedes and by his distinction between signs in the context of a prophecy (his Type A) and signs in the context of a commissioning (Type B). The examples of the latter (Gideon and Saul) occur in close proximity to the commissioning itself and precede the deliverance promised. This type of sign is therefore not involved here (despite Childs's attempt to find some room for it by a contorted reference to the burning bush). A precise study of Type A indicates that, while sometimes the performance of the sign precedes the fulfilment of the prophecy (1 Kgs 13.3; 2 Kgs 20.9; cf. Deut. 13.2-3), this need not be the case and the sign may be equated with the fulfilment of the prophecy (1 Sam. 2.34; 2 Kgs 19.29; Jer. 44.29). Then it rather declares that fulfilment to be 'significant', in that it confirms the faithfulness and reality of God, and by implication also the credentials of his messenger, as here with Moses ('that I have sent you'). So Moses and the Israelites must wait, according to this verse, and trust God's promise through Moses, without the prior guarantee that they might desire. Only when they come (back) to Mount Sinai/Horeb will they *know* that it is God who sent Moses, i.e. not even the Exodus itself is understood here as the decisive confirmation of this, against 14.31 (J), but somewhat in line with 19.9 (E! cf. 20.20?). According to Schmidt (p. 168), citing Schottroff, it is the revelation of God's name in vv. 13-15 that provides the true legitimation in advance for Moses: in that case this is the true equivalent to the 'confirmatory signs' given to Gideon and Saul, but it does not mean that the 'sign' in v. 12 refers to the divine name, as Coats proposed (p. 37).

While it is attractive to correlate the words of the promise with a specific later episode in the story, such as Exod. 18.1-12 or 24.1-11 (or even 32.1-6?), this is perhaps to lose sight of the openness of the saying in its present context: it simply places worship at the climax of the coming deliverance, a key theological statement that is independent of any particular 'fulfilment'. One might compare 'Let my people go, that they may worship (Heb. *ʿābad*) me/sacrifice/ celebrate a feast to me' later in both early strands of the narrative (5.1 etc.; cf. 3.18). In any case, it is revealing that it is a reference to worship which leads Moses to ask about the name of the god who is speaking to him (v. 13), since it is a theme to which the answer to that question will return (v. 15b).

Text and Versions

אחר (3.1) The Vss (except Tg^{J,N}) render freely, no doubt puzzled by the rare usage. LXX ὑπό probably intended 'beside', for which LSJ gives parallels: none such exist for Wevers' proposal (*Notes*, p. 25) 'into the far reaches of', which like Vulg *interiora (deserti)* is perhaps based more on knowledge of the actual geography. Some LXX mss, Tg^O and Sy have the weak '(in)to'. Tg^O adds 'to a place of good pasture', without a clear linguistic basis, but in accordance with an early tradition (see refs. in *AramB* 2, p. 167 n. 2), and Tg^J combines this with Tg^N's literal rendering of אחר.

הר אלהים (3.1) LXX has no equivalent to אלהים, perhaps motivated by the same reverential concern that led the Tgg to paraphrase 'on which the glory (of the Shekinah, Tg^N) of the Lord was revealed', but more likely because it seemed premature before God's appearance there: Wevers (*Notes*, p. 25) observes that later in Exodus the translator follows MT (4.27 etc.).

וירא (3.2) The Tgg use the more specialised אתגלי, 'was revealed'.

מלאך יהוה (3.2) Vulg has simply *dominus*, perhaps reflecting the intense theological discussion in the early Church about whether 'the angel' and 'God' were the same or different.[16] Tg^J adds the name Zaganzagel: see *AramB* 2, p. 167 n. 4 for other forms of the name elsewhere.

אליו (3.2) SP places this directly after וירא, which is the 'tidier' word-order. The same order is followed in LXX and Vulg, perhaps reflecting their *Vorlage*. The looser construction of MT is probably more original.

בלבת (3.2) SP בלהבת, adapting to the regular word: see Note d on the translation. 4QpalGen-Ex^l preserves only the final ת of this word. On the curious interchange in LXX's ἐν πυρὶ φλογός (paralleled in Parmenides fr.

---

[16] Cf. M. Kraus, 'Jerome', pp. 31-33, who also notes Exod.R. 2.3 and *PRE* 40 for Jewish equation of the angel with God.

8.56) see P. Katz (Walters), "Ἐν πυρὶ φλογός", *ZNW* 46 (1955), pp. 133-38; cf. *Text*, pp. 322-24.

מתוך (3.2)   LXX has simply ἐκ, a common rendering of this Heb. word by the translator of Exod. (cf. 2.5; 3.4; 9.24).

בער (3.2)   The main Vss render straightforwardly, but Aq and Symm modify LXX's rendering, probably to emphasise the contrast between 'burn' here and 'consumed' at the end of the verse (cf. Sy *mtgwzl' bh nwr'*). The ms. of Tg^J has מטריב (cf. טריב in v. 3), from a root apparently meaning 'burn' that is otherwise unknown except for two occurrences of a noun = 'boil, inflammation' (cf. Levy, p. 318; Jastrow, p. 553) in Tg^J's expansion of 2.5 (cf. perhaps BH √צרב, the equivalence being possible where Arabic would have *z* [Moscati, pp. 28-29]). CAL gives the basic meaning as 'be leafy' (cf. *DJPA*, p. 230), but then has difficulty in finding an apt interpretation here (esp. in v. 3). As noted in *AramB* 2, p. 167, nn. 5 and 7, the *editio princeps* read forms of the more common שרב = 'burn' here and in v. 3. See also the next note.

איננו אכל (3.2)   While Tg^O simply uses Aram. אכל, Tg^{N,F(V)} and Sy have יקד, which can mean 'be burned up' (cf. LXX's shift to κατεκαίετο): Tg^J typically combines the two. Tg^F has 'was moist/green and (so) was not burned', providing a reason for the phenomenon (likewise for לא־יבער in v. 3): the word for 'moist' is מרטב, and its similarity to the unusual word for 'burn' in Tg^J might point to one of them being due to a scribal error. At any rate the margin of Tg^N, which records the same rendering as Tg^F but with מטריב, succumbed to such confusion.

אסרה־נא (3.3)   SP אסור, without the cohortative ending, as often (cf. *GSH* §64a). 4QpalGen-Ex^1 agrees with MT. LXX, Vulg and Sy have no equivalent to נא; the Tgg render with words for 'now'.

המראה (3.3)   Symm replaces LXX's ὅραμα (which often refers to dream-visions: LSJ) with θέαμα, which has implications of a 'spectacle' and was used of the seven 'wonders of the world' in Str. 14.2.5 and Plut. 2.983e.

יבער (3.3)   Most of the Vss naturally use the same word for 'burn' here as for אכל at the end of v. 2, indeed more appropriately. Only Tg^J preserves the same rendering for בער in the use of its curious שרב. Tg^F (cf. Tg^{Nmg}) again inserts מרטב, less appropriately here.

יהוה (3.4)   SP (and Sam. Tg.) reads אלהים, evidently assimilating to the divine title in the next clause. All other witnesses support MT, including 4QpalGen-Ex^1.

אלהים (3.4)   LXX (except the hexaplaric F^b) has κύριος, by assimilation to the preceding divine name. Tgg also have the divine name, in line with their regular practice of substituting it for אלהים when used alone, from Gen. 1.1 onwards. The insertion of ממריה ד before it in Tg^N and מלאכיא ד in its margin might be related to the underlying אלהים, but the former is of course a common expansion in the Tgg (cf. Chester, *Divine Revelation*, pp. 293-313, and e.g. vv. 8 and 17 in Tg^N) and especially appropriate where there is a verb of speaking as here. Vulg omits אלהים as otiose, but Sy agrees with MT.

הנני (3.4)   LXX has the rather abrupt τί ἐστιν;, which contrasts with the literal rendering of the same expression in Gen. 22.1 (ἰδοὺ ἐγώ): Aq and Theod correct accordingly. Whereas the other Tgg translate normally, Tg^N inserts 'Moses replied in the language of the temple' and retains the Heb. form (so also in Gen. 22.1: for further refs. see *AramB* 2, p. 18 n. 3).

ויאמר (3.5)   The following *lh* in most Sy mss (but not 5b1) is a secondary inner-Syriac expansion.

נעליך...רגליך (3.5)   Some mss of both MT and SP read singular forms, as in MT at Josh. 5.15 (though there is a plural variant there too). LXX and Vulg have sing. equivalents for נעליך. Tg^{O,J,F} have forms which could be either sing. or pl., but Tg^N and Sy clearly support MT. Evidently Heb. idiom permitted both sing. and pl. forms (and a mixture of the two, cf. Isa. 20.2), but the weight of evidence favours pl. readings here.

אשר...עליו (3.5)   LXX rendered ἐν ᾧ (cf. Vulg *in quo*), but already the citation in Acts 7.33 reflects approximation to Heb. (ἐφ' ᾧ), which was taken further in Aq's ἐπ'αὐτόν. The Acts citation is also closer to Heb. in its rendering of בלבת אש in v. 2 by ἐν φλογὶ πυρός (see further the textual notes on vv. 6-8, 10 below).

אדמת (3.5)   All the Tgg render by אתר = 'place' (as for המקום), and so does Sy, an interesting example of similarity if not a direct relation to the Targum tradition (cf. my *Way of the Wilderness*, pp. 16-17, 97 nn. 6-8).

הוא (3.5)   SP היא, by attraction to the gender of the predicate אדמת, as also sometimes in Masoretic Heb. (GK §145n n. 3, JM §149c, 150m). Tg^J adds 'and on it you are to receive the Law to teach it to the children of Israel', anticipating chs. 19ff. (cf. 3.12).

ויאמר (3.6)   LXX adds αὐτῷ.

אלהי אביך (3.6)   SP has the pl. אבו(תי)ך, linking to what follows. The same reading appears in Acts 7.32 and in a few LXX witnesses (probably influenced by the Acts citation). Tg^J has אלקיה (דאבוך), as it usually does when אלהים is used in construct or suffixed forms, presumably for reverential reasons.

אלהי יצחק (3.6)   SP prefixes a *waw*, in line with its practice with lists of names (cf. on 1.2-3). The converse omission of 'and' before 'the God of Jacob' in Sy and Vulg is no more likely to be original.

מהביט אל האלהים (3.6)   So also SP and Sy, but the other Vss in different ways exclude the possibility that Moses might actually look at God: by using a different preposition (Vulg *contra*; Tg^Nmg קדם), a different verb and a different preposition (LXX κατεμβλέψαι ἐνώπιον), or an additional noun or nouns (Tg^O באיקר שכינתה דייי; Tg^N בצית איקר שכינתא דייי; Tg^J בצית יקרא דיוי). On the Targumic use of 'glory' and 'presence' as intermediate terms see Chester, *Divine Revelation*, pp. 313-22.

ויאמר יהוה (3.7)   LXX adds πρὸς Μωυσῆν; Tg^J has no equivalent to יהוה.

ראה (3.7)   SP ראו, an alternative spelling for the inf. abs. of Lamed He verbs, which is found sometimes in MT (GK §75n). Tg^{O,J} use circumlocutions, as often, for this and the other two verbs of perception in the verse; Tg^N does so only for 'know', but its mg. records a very full circumlocution for 'have seen'.

נגשׂיו (3.7) LXX⁰, Tg⁰·ᴶ·ᴺ and Sy have 3rd pl. pronouns or suffixes, as also for מכאביו (where the remainder of the LXX tradition agrees), but they are only rendering (as we have done) *ad sensum*. MT's variation between pl. and sing. in this verse (which is supported by SP; Vulg harmonises the other way), as the more difficult reading, must be more original, but it is tempting to see it as a clue to secondary expansion of the verse (cf. 2.24; 3.9; 6.5), especially as v. 8 reverts consistently to sing. forms. In place of the suffixed participle נגשׂיו Tgᴶ·ᴺ appear to read an abstract noun 'bondage, oppression', while Vulg has an expanded paraphrase.

מכאביו (3.7) The noun is read as sing. by SP, LXX, Vulg, Tg⁰·ᴺ and Sy, but Tgᴶ and a reading of the LXX ms. Fᵇ which Hatch and Redpath and *AramB* 2, p. 18 n. 6 attribute to Symm support MT. Its plural form is more appropriate to the context and with only a *yod* to differentiate between the two readings an error on the part of the other witnesses is not difficult to envisage. Vulg links the whole final clause of the verse to v. 8, perhaps to resolve the difficulty noted above (Note m on the translation) about its initial כי. The otherwise precise rendering (though with minor variations from LXX) of the verse in Acts 7.34 omits this clause and the two preceding words.

וארד (3.8) SP וארדה, with the rare addition of the 'cohortative' ending (*GSH* §64a), but no change of meaning (cf. Sam. Tg. איעה [*GSA* §44c]). Such forms of the *waw* consecutive are frequent at Qumran: see Qimron, p. 44, and e.g. 1QIsᵃ at Isa. 40.6. *BHS* oddly points the *waw* with shewa in its apparatus. Tgg paraphrase with 'revealed myself' as in Gen. 11.5, 7; Tgᴶ has in addition 'today to you' (i.e. Moses), and Tgᴺ has 'by my Word' (במימרי).

להצילו (3.8) LXX, Tg⁰·ᴺ again have third pl. pronouns or suffixes, as also later in the verse. Tgᴶ has a second m. si. suffix, probably an error due to its plus just before, and adds 'by my Word' (במימרי) here.

להעלתו (3.8) LXX has ἐξαγαγεῖν αὐτούς (cf. Vulg *educerem*) and then adds καὶ εἰσαγαγεῖν αὐτούς before 'to a land' to express the full sense of the Heb. verb. Tgᴺ has a 2nd pl. object pronoun (anticipating v. 17), but this is corrected towards MT by the mg. The citation in Acts 7.34, which agrees with LXX for the first clause of the verse, breaks off at this point and resumes at v. 10.

ההוא (3.8) SP ההיא, as usual not having MT's peculiar form (on which see Note n on the translation). Tgᴶ adds מסאבתא, 'unclean' (cf. Ezek. 20.7).

מקום (3.8) Vulg *loca*, for the different territories of the peoples just mentioned. Tgᴺ and most mss of Sy read 'the land', again, but 5b1 has *'tr'*, 'the place' with MT, and probably this is the original Peshiṭta reading (cf. Koster, *Peshiṭta of Exodus*, p. 63).

רחבה (3.8) Sy interchanges this with טובה, possibly because 'good' is explained by the clause that follows. Tgᴶ amplifies to 'wide (פתייא) in regions', perhaps because פתייא could otherwise be ambiguous.

חלב ודבש (3.8) Tg^N has 'good crops, clean like milk and sweet like honey', to match the better known produce of the land.

הכנעני... (3.8) The six names occur as in MT in Vulg, Tg^{O,J} and Sy, with only minor divergences. Tg^J and Sy have plural forms (*ad sensum*) throughout (as do LXX and Tg^N), and so does Tg^O for the first two names and the last two (and also the middle two in several mss and edd.). Vulg has no 'and' before 'Perizzites', thus dividing the names into two groups. Tg^J has '(the place) where...live', perhaps to avoid the idea of ownership implied in MT. Tg^N diverges from the rest only by the accidental repetition of 'Amorites' after 'Perizzites'. The significant variation in the list is the inclusion of (ו)הגרגשי in some major witnesses, to bring the list up to the classic figure of seven nations listed in Deut. 7.1 (see also the Explanatory Note). K.G. O'Connell, who lists the textual variants in SP and LXX for this and the numerous comparable passages, has argued that here and elsewhere the longer text is more original ('The List of Seven Peoples'). From Qumran O'Connell cites only the (fragmentary but decisive) evidence for the longer text in 4QpalEx^m at Exod. 34.11: to this needs to be added (a) for a longer text, 4QGen-Ex^a at Exod. 3.8, 4QEx^b at Exod. 3.17 (apparently), 4Q128, 140, 144, 145 (phylacteries), 4QDeut^j, 4QpalEx^m at Exod. 13.5, and the citations of Exod. 34.11 and Deut. 20.17 in 11QTemple^a, cols. 2.2-4 and 62.14-15 respectively; (b) for the shorter text MurPhyl, 8Qphyl, 34SeyPhyl, 4Q130 (phylacteries), 4QEx^e at Exod. 13.5 and (apparently) 4QDeut^{k2} at Deut. 20.17. Elsewhere the surviving text is too fragmentary to be decisive. That 'the Girgashite' is a secondary addition and not the original reading here is indicated by the fact that the name appears in different places in the list: in SP it is placed after 'the Perizzite' (so also in Codex Vaticanus and two minor LXX witnesses), while in 4QGen-Ex^a (which generally keeps very close to MT) and the rest of the LXX tradition (which Wevers judges more original than Vaticanus at this point [*THGE*, p. 175: contra Rahlfs]) it comes after 'the Hivite'. 4QGen-Ex^a also inverts 'the Amorite' and 'the Perizzite'. SP omits the *waw* before החתי, which also (like Vulg) perhaps links the first three names into a group, while 4QGen-Ex^a has no *waw* before החוי and הגרגשי, which links its last four names into a group.

ועתה (3.9) Vulg *ergo*, 'therefore', is inappropriate here but reflects its frequent and justifiable use to render ועתה in other contexts (e.g. 5.18; 9.19; 19.5; 33.13).

באה (3.9) Tgg and Sy render 'has come *up*', a natural modification and one perhaps encouraged by the similar expression in 2.23.

אלי (3.9) Tg^{O,J} as usual render 'before me'.

וגם (3.9) The גם is not rendered in either LXX or Vulg. According to Wevers (*Notes*, p. 30) this is the regular practice of the Exodus translator; in Vulg an equivalent is found in only three places in Exodus (2.19; 12.38; 19.22) out of seventeen. In contrast, both these Versions generally render גם explicitly when it occurs alone in Exodus.

ראיתי (3.9) Tgg have as usual '...is revealed before me'.

לכה (3.10) SP לך, without the emphatic ending, as frequently (*GSH* §64a).

פרעה (3.10) LXX adds βασιλέα Αἰγύπτου, combining the two titles which usually appear as alternatives except in Priestly texts (e.g. 6.11, 13).

והוצא (3.10) 4QGen-Ex^a agrees with MT, but SP reads והוצאת, second m.si. *waw* consecutive perfect. Such a text could be the basis for LXX καὶ ἐξάξεις and Tg^N ותפק, though they might just as well be a rendering of MT, whether it is taken as an imperative (see Note s on the translation: so most likely Vulg: *ut educas*) or as an infinitive absolute substituting for a perfect consecutive (GK §113z). The ואפק(י) of Tg^{O,J} (cf. Sy) may be taken either as a first si. imperfect ('and I will bring out': so Wevers, *Notes*, p. 31; *AramB* 7, p. 8) or as a second person m. si. imperative of the Aphel of נפק. The former would be a possible interpretation of הוצא as an infinitive absolute, but it is unlikely, unless Moses in the next verse is to be credited with a misunderstanding. As far as the Heb. text is concerned, the more difficult reading of MT and 4QGen-Ex^a should certainly be preferred.

בני ישראל (3.10) Tg^N adds לפרוקין, 'as (or "to be") redeemed people': this addition is found often elsewhere in Tg^N (cf. v. 11 and *AramB* 2, p. 19 n. 9).

ממצרים (3.10) LXX expands to ἐκ γῆς Αἰγύπτου, i.e. מארץ מ', as found sometimes in MT (e.g. 4.20; 5.12; 6.26). For the addition cf. v. 11 and also (e.g.) 4QEx^c at 12.40.

אל האלהים (3.11) Tgg as usual have 'before the Lord'.

אנכי (3.11) In place of LXX εἰμι Theod and Aq have ἐγώ εἰμι, their regular equivalent (see the notes on 4.23 and 8.25).

אוציא (3.11) Tg^N has אסק, 'bring *up*', assimilating to the verb used in v. 8 and elsewhere. The same reading is found in ms. 5b1 of Sy.

בני ישראל (3.11) Sy has 'those of the house (בית) of Israel', perhaps for variety.

ויאמר (3.12) LXX amplifies with ὁ θεὸς Μωυσῇ λέγων, Vulg with *ei*, and the oldest ms. of Sy (5b1) with *lh*, to which the other mss add *ʾlhʾ* as a second-stage clarification.

אהיה עמך (3.12) Tg^{O,J} characteristically have 'My Word (*memra*) will help you'; Tg^N simply inserts 'my Word' in apposition to 'I'.

את העם (3.12) LXX τὸν λαόν μου assimilates to v. 10.

תעבדון (3.12) LXX καὶ λατρεύσετε is puzzling: if καί = 'and', it suggests that the sign is God's presence with Moses (as in Exod.R. 4) rather than worship on the mountain (Wevers, *Notes*, p. 31). But it might simply mean 'also' (NETS). Either way it is unlikely that the *Vorlage* included a *waw*, since it would have to be followed by a perfect form to maintain the future sense. Vulg *immolabis* (sing. referring to Moses alone?) is also surprising, as Moses does not perform the sacrifice in Exod. 24.5 (except in 4Q158 fr.4.4, apparently), but scarcely sufficient on its own to be the original reading;

likewise Sy 5b1 *nplḥwn* ('*they* shall worship': the other mss = MT), which has some minority LXX support. In each case the variant may aim at consistency with the earlier part of the verse (Wevers, *Notes*, p. 32).

את האלהים (3.12) Tgg, as usual, have 'before the Lord': the same paraphrase also appears in Sy here. Tg^J adds 'because you will receive the law', echoing its anticipation of the lawgiving in v. 5.

There is evidence (though the whole verse is not preserved in either case) that 3.12 was included out of context in the 'Reworked Pentateuch' ms. 4Q158 after Exod. 4.28 (fr. 2.16) and 24.3 (fr. 4.2), essentially as it appears in MT. It was clearly regarded as a key verse by the author of this work.

Chapter 3.13-15

Moses' Question about the Name of God Answered

This short sub-section is made into a tightly constructed unity by its explicit concern with what Moses is to 'say to the Israelites' (vv. 13, 14b, 15a) and with the name of God (vv. 13, 15b). Formally it consists of a question by Moses in v. 13 and no fewer than three replies of God, each introduced by the usual formula 'and (…) said' and in three cases out of the four with the explicit designation of both the speaker and the addressee (the one exception, v. 14b, may indicate that it is meant to be taken very closely with the preceding utterance, as its contents also suggest). The deity is referred to by the narrator throughout as 'God' ($[h\bar{a}]^{ʾ}l\bar{o}h\hat{i}m$).[1]

These verses are also closely linked by theme and vocabulary to the preceding context, or at least parts of it. References to God 'sending' Moses appear in vv. 10 and 12, and v. 6 has already introduced God as the God both of Moses' own father and as the God of the patriarchs. While hitherto Moses' mission has been directed specifically to Pharaoh (vv. 10-11), the Israelites have also been

---

[1] It is difficult to see any semantic significance in the prefixing of the definite article in v. 13 (as previously in vv. [1], 7, 11 and 12) but not in vv. 14-15 (as in v. 4), as R. Rendtorff tried to do more generally in an appendix to his 'El als israelitische Gottesbezeichnung', *ZAW* 106 (1994), pp. 4-21. It appears that $^{ʾ}l\bar{o}h\hat{i}m$ as a singular was variously treated as a common noun which needed the article to make it specific and as a title which as the equivalent to a proper name did not need, or could not have, the article prefixed to it. The only observable distinction in this passage is the purely grammatical one that when $^{ʾ}l\bar{o}h\hat{i}m$ is the subject of a verb it has no article, and when it is not it does. This principle also holds in Exod. 1.17-21, and generally in Judges and 1 Samuel at least (in two cases $^{ʾ}l\bar{o}h\hat{i}m$ as subject has the article [Judg. 13.9a; 1 Sam. 10.7], and there are more cases [e.g. Judg. 18.5] where it lacks it when not the subject, though in all of the latter it is prefixed by *b*, so that they could represent no more than a later reading of the text, when the 'rule' had been forgotten). But it is not universal: for further cases where $^{ʾ}l\bar{o}h\hat{i}m$ as subject has the article see Gen. 20.6; 22.1; Exod. 19.19; 20.20-21, all mentioned by Rendtorff; and no doubt there are more.

clearly in view (vv. 9-11) and it is no surprise to learn that Moses sees himself as also 'sent' by God to them in v. 13. The narrator's use of 'God' rather than the divine name here continues the practice of vv. 1, 4b, 6, 11 and 12. At first sight there is also continuity with what follows, since the absence of any new speech-formula at the beginning of v. 16 implies that vv. 16-22 are the continuation of the speech of God which begins in v. 15. A Qumran ms. (4QEx^b) has an empty space before v. 15, indicating that its scribe saw this as the decisive break in the passage. However, this appears to be the sole case of such a division in the textual tradition and there are powerful arguments from the content of the passage against such a view. On the one hand it has already been seen that v. 15 represents the closure of the unit that begins with the question in v. 13. On the other, v. 16-17 introduce several new themes, such as the meeting with the elders of Israel and the replacement of talk about Moses being 'sent' by the claim that God/Yahweh has 'appeared' to him. These verses also reintroduce the theme of the land to which Yahweh will bring the Israelites, with its descriptions, which has not been mentioned since v. 8. These changes are well emphasised by R.W.L. Moberly, who summarises as follows: '...by the end the speech is hardly any longer answering the question of 3:13...a marked shift comes at 3:16...' (*The Old Testament*, pp. 16-17). Moberly's perception of these differences is the more significant in that he does not recognise any division into sources in ch. 3, although he does speak generally of the 'complex prehistory' of 3.13-22 (p. 20).[2]

The verses in 3.1-12 from which this sub-section takes its departure have all been attributed earlier to the E source, so that its origin will naturally be the same. The 'new beginning' and the overlap between vv. 15a and v. 16a, together with the references back to v. 8 (J) in v. 17 indicate that the following verses belong to a parallel account of Moses' commissioning which came from the J source, where the revelation of Yahweh's name was not an issue, because it was assumed by that author (anachronistically) that the name Yahweh had long been known and did not need to be specially revealed at the Exodus (Gen. 4.26; 15.7 etc.). The process of interpretation which this involved is again well described by Moberly

---

[2] Cf. Fischer, *Jahwe Unser Gott*, pp. 83-91, who also regards the chapter as a literary unity.

(*The Old Testament*, Chapter 2): he is only at fault in failing to recognise that this anachronism was present in only one constituent element of the tradition which was incorporated into Genesis, because he does not allow the existence of a separate E source (or stratum) there either. The view taken here about 3.13-15 as a whole was the usual one at least from the time of Wellhausen (*Composition*, p. 70) until quite recently, so that in essence it could contribute to knowledge of Israelite religion at least in the northern kingdom prior to the rise of classical prophecy.

The coherence and unity of these verses was maintained by Smend (*Erzählung*, p. 117) and Eissfeldt, but from early on the repeated speech-formulae in vv. 14-15 led to either v. 14 (already by Carpenter/Harford-Battersby) or v. 15 (by Baentsch and [v. 15a only] Holzinger) being regarded as a secondary addition. The debate about which verse is more original (and sometimes further subdivisions) has continued to the present day.[3] The most recent detailed discussion is by Gertz (*Tradition*, pp. 294-98, but see the critical remarks of Blum, 'Literarische Verbindung', pp. 126-27), who argues against a separation between vv. 14 and 15 (see below, n. 14, for other recent advocates of the unity of the passage, to which should be added those who regard the whole chapter as a unified composition: Fischer, *Jahwe Unser Gott*, pp. 41-45, 134-47; Moberly; Seitz). While Gertz's argument partly depends on his view that vv. (12αβb)13-15 are a late redactional supplement to vv. 7-12aα, 16-17 (v. 15 is needed to make a 'bridge' between vv. 14 and 16), in other respects it does not (no contradiction between vv. 14 and 15, but a careful exposition of the nature of the God revealed in his name). The late date given to these verses by Gertz (for which cf. Van Seters [exilic J], Schmid [post-P redaction] and Kaiser [exilic E source]) is in part based on questionable wider conclusions about the composition and sources of the Pentateuch (on which see the main Introduction). The more specific arguments of Gertz are not at all conclusive: the passage does not arise solely out of the 'sign' in v. 12αβb but from the implication in vv. 10-12 that Moses will have to confront the Israelites as well as Pharaoh, and in any case there is no need to regard v. 12αβb

---

[3] See the lists of supporters of the main alternatives in Schmidt, pp. 131-34; M. Saebø, 'Offenbarung oder Verhüllung? Bemerkungen zum Charakter des Gottesnamens in Ex 3,13-15', in J. Jeremias and L. Perlitt (eds.), *Die Botschaft und die Boten: Festschrift für Hans Walter Wolff* (Neukirchen, 1981), pp. 43-55 (46 n. 11); Gertz, *Tradition*, p. 296 n. 285: to which add Childs, pp. 69-70 (v. 14 from R[JE]); Saebø, op. cit., pp. 45-48 (v. 14, and also v. 15b, secondary); O. Kaiser, *Der Gott des Alten Testament*, 2 (Göttingen, 1998), pp. 96-98 (v. 14 secondary); L. Schmidt, 'Diachrone und Synchrone', pp. 233-34; K. Schmid, *Erzväter und Exodus*, pp. 207-209; Graupner, *Elohist*, pp. 21-22 (all seeing v. 15 as additional).

as so late; v. 15 cannot have been designed to act as a redactional 'bridge' to v. 16, since like the rest of vv. 13-15 it anticipates the command given by Yahweh in v. 16 (so Gertz himself on p. 294!); the attribution of v. 6a, from which v. 13 takes up its designation of God, to the *Endredaktion* is based on a particular interpretation of its connection with Gen. 46.1-5 (pp. 270-80) which is by no means compelling; and the argument that the revelation of the name plays no part in the later non-Priestly narrative, but only in Exod. 6.2-8P, overlooks both the numerous occurrences of the divine name in the following chapters (including passages attributed to E) and the lack of any echo in this passage of the specific language of P (a point that Gertz himself acknowledges in relation to v. 15, p. 296 n. 283: see more generally Blum, 'Literarische Verbindung', p. 127). There is no more force in Van Seters' claim (*Life of Moses*, pp. 46-48) that the passage is dependent on Ezek. 20.5-6, which locates the utterance – not the revelation – of the name in Egypt, not in the desert, and on Deutero-Isaiah, to which there are only very general similarities and the direction of any dependence is therefore impossible to determine; or in the comparison of v. 15b to the language of the Jerusalem temple cult as found in the exilic/post-exilic Psalms 102 and 135 (the language of the present passage is arguably more primitive than that of the psalms in question – see the Explanatory Note – and could just as well derive from Bethel as from Jerusalem [cf. perhaps Hos. 12.6]).

In contrast to both the recent revival of a unitarian approach to the chapter and the attribution of these verses to a late redactor, it is much more plausible to see in the anticipation here of the instruction to Moses to meet with the Israelites in vv. 16-17 and the 'new beginning' which those verses represent evidence of two parallel accounts of the 'call of Moses' which were imperfectly combined by a redactor: in short, additional evidence to that found in vv. 1-12 for the validity of a source-critical approach to this crucial chapter.

The form and possible background of these verses have been fruitfully investigated by Moberly on the basis of a remark by Childs (p. 69): see Moberly's *The Old Testament*, pp. 18-21. He rightly notes the difference between the question posed in v. 13 and Moses' objections to his calling elsewhere (e.g. v. 11), and the difference is even more apparent in the answer he receives, which goes far beyond his own personal situation. The formulation in terms of a question posed by others and the instruction about what 'you shall say' to them is closely parallel to the 'children's question' in Exod. 12.26-27; 13.14-15; Deut. 6.20-25; Josh. 4.20-24. The difference is that the present case is the narrative of a specific episode which accommodates the other, 'foundational' aspect of the passage (see the Explanatory Note on v. 15), but the didactic tone identified by Moberly is comparable to the texts referring to the children's questions. This tone is consistent both with the centrality of the subject-matter to Israel's faith and with the at first sight strange prefacing of the explanation to the declaration of the name itself (see also the comparison with narratives of the naming of places and people in the Explanatory Note on v. 14).

Theologically these verses serve a number of purposes. They reinforce Moses' authority to speak to his people in Egypt, and ultimately to Pharaoh as well. They attest to the belief (which is in all probability historically correct) that Israel's ancestors first entered upon the worship of their God by the name Yahweh at the time of the formative events of the Exodus and establish this as the name by which he is above all to be known in future. Finally and most distinctively, they interpret this name as embodying an assurance of his presence and faithfulness as one who is both the 'God of the fathers' from their past and the God who will lead them into a new future.

> 13 Then Moses said to God, 'When[a] I come[b] to the Israelites and say to them, "The God of your fathers has sent me to you", they will say to me, "What[c] is his name?". What shall I say to them?' 14 God said to Moses, 'I will be (there) as I will be (there)'[d], and he said, 'This is what you shall say to the Israelites, "It is I-will-be-there who has sent me to you".' 15 God in addition said to Moses, 'This is what you shall say to the Israelites, "It is Yahweh, the God of your fathers, the God of Abraham, the God of Isaac and the God of Jacob, who has sent me to you". This[e] is to be my name for ever[f], this shall be my designation[g] for all ages[h].'

Notes on the Translation

a. Heb. הנה. The common rendering 'If' (e.g. NRSV; cf. Childs, pp. 48, 50, but contrast p. 66) implies some doubt about Moses' intentions. The lexica give 'if' as a possible meaning for (ו)הנה (cf. C.J. Labuschagne, 'The Particles הֵן and הִנֵּה', in *Syntax and Meaning* [*OTS* 18 (1973)], pp. 5-12; D.J. McCarthy, 'The Uses of w^e *hinnēh* in Biblical Hebrew', *Bib* 61 [1980], pp. 330-42 [336-37]), but some of the grammars are firmly against it (GK §159w, n. 1; JM §167; contra Meyer §122.3a). It may be more correct to say that (ו)הנה always has its 'deictic' or 'perceptive' meaning, but that the combination of clauses sometimes makes it 'in effect' equivalent to a conditional particle, as

D.M. Stec argued for הן ('The Use of *hēn* in Conditional Sentences', *VT* 37 [1987], pp. 478-86). But in a good many cases at least 'When' would represent the implied meaning better than 'If', and so here. The asyndeton before the second מה makes it preferable, if not necessary, to keep what follows as an independent sentence.

b. Heb. בא, the Heb. participle following הנה as it often does in discourse as well as in prophecy to indicate imminent action: cf. 7.17; 8.25; 17.6.

c. The use of מה (rather than מי as in Judg. 3.17) makes no difference to the meaning: Gen. 32.28 and Prov. 30.4 show that an enquiry about someone's name can be formulated in either way (so e.g. Childs, Schmidt, against those who argue that מה implies a question about the meaning of the name).

d. Heb. אהיה אשר אהיה, generally regarded as an example of the *idem per idem* construction which is quite common in BH as well as in other languages, where a verbal form is repeated after the intervention of the relative particle אשר (or equivalent), as for example in 1 Sam. 23.13: ויתהלכו באשר יתהלכו, 'they wandered wherever they could go'. S.R. Driver commented neatly that the construction is used 'where either the means, or the desire, to be more explicit does not exist'.[4] The main alternative to this view in modern times is based on the fact that the verb in a relative clause may sometimes be attracted to agree in person with the verb in the main clause, as in Gen. 15.7 and Exod. 20.2 (cf. GK §138d; JM §158n), so that the meaning is 'I am he who is (or "will be")': so, e.g., R. de Vaux, 'The Revelation of the Divine Name YHWH', in J.I. Durham and J.R. Porter (eds.), *Proclamation and Presence: Old Testament Essays in Honour of Gwynne Henton Davies* (London, 1970), pp. 63-75. But none of the passages where this construction appears is a true parallel to this one (note specially the absence of an expressed antecedent for אשר here), as was forcefully demonstrated by B. Albrektson, 'On the Syntax of אהיה אשר אהיה in Exodus 3:14', in P.R. Ackroyd and B. Lindars (eds.), *Words and Meanings: Essays Presented to David Winton Thomas* (Cambridge, 1968), pp. 15-28, who gives references to both recent and earlier scholars who have favoured the alternative interpretation. See the Explanatory Note on v. 14 for further discussion of the meaning of these words. The proposal to read one or both of the verbs as a (causative) Hiphil and so find here a reference to creation (as in one strand of Targumic interpretation: see Text and Versions) was advocated by P. Haupt, W.F. Albright, D.N. Freedman, F.M. Cross and, in a modified form, W.H. Brownlee ('The Ineffable Name of God', *BASOR* 226 [1977], pp. 39-46: see also Holzinger, p. 12, for much earlier advocates of such a view), but it involves an unwarranted emendation of the text and now belongs only to the history of the subject (see the discussions in Childs [pp. 62-64] and Schmidt [pp. 105, 173]). See below on v. 15 for the equally groundless view that the name Yahweh originally meant 'he who created…'

---

[4] *Samuel*, pp. 185-86; cf. JM §158o. Further examples occur in Exod. 16.23; 33.19.

e. The antecedent of זה might theoretically be either the name Yahweh alone or the combination of it with the titles which follow. But the former is much more likely, both on general grounds and in the light of OT usage elsewhere (e.g. 6.3; 15.3).

f. Heb. לעלם, as in similar formulae elsewhere, denotes an indefinitely long period of time, but without the connotations of 'eternity' (cf. the note below on the parallel phrase). The defective writing is quite common (20x according to BDB, p. 761), and no basis for the correlation with עלם = 'hide' proposed, with the implication of ineffability, in Exod.R. 3.7 and Rashi ad loc.

g. Heb. זכרי. זֵכֶר generally means 'memory, remembrance', with the special sense sometimes of 'renown, fame' (Isa. 26.8; Hos. 14.8 and probably Ps. 135.13). The only really close parallel to the sense required here, which must be 'designation', as that by which someone is remembered, is Hos. 12.6, where זכר appears in a formula in which שם is often used (e.g. Amos 5.8). Attempts to distinguish between the referents of שם and זכר here (Childs, Propp) are probably mistaken.

h. לדר דר. Straightforward repetition (as distinct from the alternative idiom which links the nouns by *waw*, e.g. Pss. 102.13; 135.13) can indicate the superlative degree (GK §133l, followed by Schmidt), hence 'the remotest generation(s)', but may also indicate totality (GK §123c: cf. Propp), so '(throughout) all ages', and this seems more probable here. The parallelism of phrases containing דר(ו)ר with עולם is very frequent, and appears already in Ugaritic, where the repetition of *dr* without *w*, as here, is normal (see Propp, p. 205, for references). In BH the only exact parallels to the idiom are Exod. 17.16 (of the past: see Note u on the translation of 17.8-16) and Prov. 27.24 (with לעולם in parallel).

Explanatory Notes

13. Unlike Jacob (Gen. 32.29) and Manoah (Judg. 13.17), Moses does not directly ask the name of his heavenly interlocutor. For him, it seems, the identification provided in v. 6 (which is alluded to here) is sufficient. It is the people who will expect to know something more, he says. Why should this be so? Prior to God's reply (vv. 14-15) various answers are possible. Perhaps it is because the ancestral deity previously had no name, only an epithet or epithets, as A. Alt argued was originally the case for the gods of the patriarchs in Genesis and as v. 6 seems to imply. Perhaps it is because the ancestral deity did have a name, but Moses did not (any longer) know what it was because of his long separation from his people during his life at the Egyptian court and his stay in Midian (so C.R. Seitz, 'The Call of Moses and the "Revelation" of the Divine

Name: Source-Critical Logic and its Legacy', in C.R. Seitz and K. Greene-McCreight [eds.], *Theological Exegesis: Essays in Honor of Brevard S. Childs* [Grand Rapids, 1999], pp. 145-61 (150-52); Blum, 'Literarische Verbindung', pp. 126-27). In the first case, he anticipates that his people will need the more intimate knowledge mediated by a name before they will be ready to venture on an attempt to break free from their bondage. In the second case, a kind of test may be envisaged in which Moses has to prove himself as an authentic leader of his people by his knowledge of the name of their God.[5] On this view it is still a question what answer the people might expect to hear, for different passages in Genesis (usually assigned to the sources J, E and P) give different names to 'the God of their fathers': Yahweh (e.g. Gen. 14.22), 'God Almighty' (*'ēl šadday*: e.g. Gen. 17.1) and 'God' or El (e.g. Gen. 46.3). Given that the present passage is from the E source (see the Introduction), the last of these might most likely have been in the mind of the original author, but once the Pentateuch began to grow into its present form the other answers would become possible. Within the immediate context, however, a different approach may be more appropriate. On the one hand the question may just be a literary device to draw forth the answers in vv. 14-15, which associate in advance the revelation or at least an especially momentous declaration of the divine name with God's impending deliverance of his people from Egypt (compare Moberly's correlation with the use of such questions on the part of children as a didactic method, discussed above in the Introduction). But could this not have been done by a more direct question from Moses himself? It may therefore be better to see the question as the natural sequel to God's words to Moses in v. 12 about 'worship on this mountain', which by the use of a plural verb imply the involvement of the people as a whole. It is worship, in its various forms of praise and prayer, which especially requires the knowledge of a name by which to address the deity; and it is often thought (see the Note there) that the second half of v. 15 also has particular reference to the future use of the name in worship.

---

[5] Against this view, which has been revived by Seitz, see the powerful and apposite arguments of R.W.L. Moberly, *The Old Testament*, pp. 60-65. It is also quite unable to deal with the strongly 'foundational' conclusion in v. 15b, on which see below.

14. Strictly speaking the first reply of God is for Moses' own hearing, while his second reply (v. 14bβ) is what is for transmission to the people, both because of its introductory formula and because it takes up the wording of Moses' question in v. 14. These utterances have been the object of very varied interpretations which, not surprisingly in view of the fact that they purport to give the meaning of God's own name, have been strongly influential on Jewish and especially Christian theology and philosophy (see Text and Versions and the bibliography given there, especially the survey by Childs). This is particularly true of the interpretations which find here a reference to God as Being, 'He who is' (so LXX [on which see Fritsch, pp. 22-23] and in part Vulg: cf. some renderings in the Palestinian Targum tradition). But such renderings lack a sound linguistic foundation (see Note d on the translation for modern discussion of this approach) and have been gradually superseded by a more literal rendering of the Heb., such as 'I will be who (or what) I will be' and 'I am who (or what) I am',[6] as already in the Jewish revisers of LXX, Aq and Theod, Vulg in part, and then decisively in the European vernacular versions from the sixteenth century onwards.[7] The repeated verb-form (Heb. *'ehyeh*), which is also used in v. 14b, is the first person singular of the imperfect Qal (simple prefix-conjugation) of the verb *hāyāh*, 'be'. The most common use of the Heb. imperfect is to represent the future tense, but it can also be used for a repeated or continuing action or state (GK §107; JM §113), hence the variation in modern translations between a future and a (timeless) present rendering. The latter has been more popular, probably because it seems more fitting to represent the eternal nature of God. But the future, which was preferred by Luther, Pagninus and Tyndale, is more obviously appropriate to the general surrounding context of God's promises to his people about their future and is also supported by the appearance of the same verbal form in v. 12, where it clearly means 'I will be (with you)'. Indeed the occurrences here in v. 14 very likely take up and

---

[6] The still familiar 'I am that I am' of AV, RV and REB originated in the 'Great Bible' of Miles Coverdale (1539) and uses 'that' in a now obsolete way as an equivalent to '(the one) who'.

[7] A translation is avoided altogether in Tg⁰, Sy and other parts of the Palestinian Targum tradition, as well as in NJPS.

amplify that statement as an interpretation ('exegesis' – see below) of the divine name Yahweh itself.[8]

Whether the verb is regarded as future or (timeless) present in tense, there remain questions about the precise meaning of *hāyāh*, 'be', here and about the implications of its double use in combination with the relative 'who' or 'what'. *hāyāh*, like the verb 'to be' in English, can be no more than the copula, linking the subject of the sentence to an attribute or state that belongs to it (so e.g. in Exod. 6.7, 'I will be your God'). But it sometimes has the stronger sense of 'stay, remain', as in Jer. 32.5 and Ps. 89.37, and can therefore even by itself (without the 'with' of v. 12) express the idea of God's abiding presence as well as his 'being' (so 'be there', F. Rosenzweig here). Some modern Old Testament scholars have wanted to go beyond this to speak of the divine protection and action on behalf of his people which are the consequences of Yahweh's 'being with' them. But the vagueness or better undefinedness and generality of v. 14 is the distinctive characteristic of this particular 'exegesis of the divine name' and is not to be lost sight of. If this richer meaning is adopted, the relative is best translated by 'as', which is a rare but possible meaning for Heb. *ᵃšer* (BDB, p. 83b; *HAL*, p. 95; *Ges18*, p. 111; *DCH* 1, p. 434: e.g. Exod. 10.6; 14.13b; 34.18), rather than 'who' or 'what'. The attention drawn by this exegesis to Yahweh's presence also fits in well with, and provides a foundation for, the rich development of this theme in the later chapters of Exodus (see my 'The Theology of Exodus', in E. Ball [ed.[, *In Search of True Wisdom: Essays in Old Testament Interpretation in Honour of Ronald E. Clements* [JSOTSup 300; Sheffield, 1999], pp. 137-52).[9]

---

[8] Compare the similar assurances given in Gen. 26.3 and 31.3, and referred to in 28.20 and 48.21, with the (timeless?) present expressed without the verb 'to be' in Gen. 28.15). The importance of v. 12 for the understanding of v. 14 was well emphasised by J.R. Lundbom, 'God's Use of the *idem per idem* to Terminate Debate', *HTR* 71 (1978), pp. 193-201, who lists the few scholars before him who had noted this point (p. 198 n. 23). To them should now be added Schmidt, pp. 177-79. The approach taken here differs, however, from that of Lundbom's article as a whole, which regards v. 14 as a closure and v. 15 as a later addition. Exod. 33.19, which he regards as a support for his view of the rhetorical function of the *idem per idem* construction, rather undermines it, because of the continuation of the dialogue there, as here.

[9] R. Bartelmus, *HYH. Bedeutung und Funktion eines hebräischen 'Allerweltswortes'* (ATS 17; St Ottilien, 1982), is opposed to such a 'fuller' meaning of *hyh*,

The complex construction in v. 14a is an example of an idiom which is quite frequent in Hebrew (and also Arabic), the so-called *idem per idem* construction (see Note d on the translation). This implies a degree of vagueness or indifference on the part of the narrator or speaker. So Houtman takes the phrase here to be equivalent to 'I am whosoever I am. What does it matter who I am?', that is, it involves an evasive refusal to give an answer to the question asked by Moses in v. 13 (p. 95). He compares the places where a person is confronted by a divine being, asks its name and gets no answer (Gen. 32.30; Judg. 13.17-18). On this view v. 15 presumably has to be attributed to a different source or layer of redaction. Other recent commentators, however, such as Childs and Schmidt, have seen a much stronger and richer meaning here, expressing the consistency and actuality of God in whatever circumstances (compare the similar theological example in 33.19). The use of the *idem per idem* construction with the verb 'to be' may indeed lend it a different nuance from elsewhere. A. Alt discovered a closely similar expression (Eg. *wn[n]y wn.kwy*) in the early Egyptian Instruction for King Merikare, ll. 94-95 ('Mitteilungen. 1. Ein Ägyptische Gegenstuck zu Ex 3 14', *ZAW* 58 [1940/41], pp. 159-60: see also Herrmann, *Israels Aufenthalt*, pp. 21, 79-80, ET pp. 9, 53-54, 80 n. 5; Schmidt, p. 178), which has been variously translated as 'I am in that I am the irrevocably existing one' (Herrmann, p. 79 n. 5, ET p. 80 n. 5), 'I am while I am' (J.A. Wilson, *ANET*, p. 416), and '(I) shall be what I am' (M. Lichtheim, *COS* 1, p. 64). The speaker is the Pharaoh and his words express his determination and constancy in his campaigns against the Bedouin of the Sinai desert (Lichtheim understands them as the continuation of the preceding oath-formula). The surviving copies of the Instruction for Merikare are from the New Kingdom period, so the turn of phrase, which though grammatically different seems not too far in sense from ways in which Exod. 3.14 has been understood, may have continued to be current in the period of the Exodus. But it remains most unlikely that the Elohist writer would

---

both here and elsewhere (esp. pp. 106-14, 226-35), and renders v. 14a simply 'I will be whoever I will be'. His systematic linguistic analysis is to be welcomed and his criticisms of earlier scholarship are often well placed, but he is too reluctant to recognise a range of meanings for the verb, as the evidence seems to require (e.g. Exod. 9.3).

have been familiar with this possible Egyptian precedent for his interpretation of the divine name.

God's words to Moses are best seen as one of several examples of the 'exegesis of the divine name' in the book of Exodus.[10] It may seem strange that the 'exegesis' in this case precedes the reference to the divine name itself in v. 15 (which some scholars indeed regard as a secondary addition to the passage: see the introduction to this section). But it in fact corresponds to one way in which names are explained elsewhere in the OT, with the giving of the name following rather than preceding the explanation of it.[11] God first gives an assurance to Moses, and then he provides the name which embodies that assurance for ever.

In v. 14b *'ehyeh*, 'I will be (there)', functions grammatically as a name, or at least a substitute for a name, the divine name Yahweh. Here the explanation or exegesis is tied even more tightly to the name being explained, in the one-to-one correspondence of two very similar forms. The most noticeable difference that remains is between the prefix *'e-*, which stands for 'I', and the prefix *ya-*, which can represent 'he'. This naturally arises from the origin of the explanation in the direct speech of the deity, while the name itself is (understood to be) a form appropriate for use by his worshippers, i.e. 'he will be (there)'. The variation between *y* and *w* as the second root-letter reflects only the more and less common forms of the verb 'be' in Hebrew.[12] Childs (p. 69) and Schmidt (p. 178) point out that the unqualified use of *'ehyeh* in v. 14 expresses a clear commitment of God to his people, which is probably a further argument against those who would read v. 14a as an evasive answer to Moses' question.

---

[10] On this approach to Exod. 3.13-15; 6.2-8 and 34:5-8 see further my essay 'The Exegesis of the Divine Name in Exodus'.

[11] See 'Form II' in Fichtner, 'Die Etymologische Ätiologie', pp. 379-82, e.g. Exod. 15.23; Josh. 7.25-26. On the insertion of interpretative material before what is interpreted see also M. Saebø, 'Offenbarung', pp. 47-48.

[12] The fact that *hwy* or *hwh* is regular in Aramaic (and also in Amorite: cf. H.B. Huffmon, *Amorite Personal Names in the Mari Texts* [Baltimore, 1965], pp. 72-73, 159-60) may well be significant for the linguistic milieu in which the name Yahweh originated, if it is in fact derived from this verb (which is not certain).

Although v. 14 has been the focus of so much discussion about its meaning and its contribution to biblical (and dogmatic) theology, it should be remembered that its etymologising explanation of the divine name is hardly ever (if at all) referred to elsewhere in the OT. One interpretation of Hos. 1.9, which goes back to W. Robertson Smith, finds an allusion to it there (see my *Hosea* [NCB; London, 1992], pp. 59-60, for details), but it is not the only possible way of understanding that verse. There may also be an allusion to it in Ps. 124.1-2.[13] But other ways of defining the identity and nature of Yahweh are much more common, especially his role as the God of the Exodus (Exod. 20.1 etc.): for further (but not exhaustive) discussion see my essay, 'The Exegesis of the Divine Name in Exodus', referred to above.

15. This verse finally, with something of a fanfare, provides a direct answer to Moses' question in v. 13 by unveiling to him the name Yahweh itself, on which v. 14 has already provided an etymological commentary. This is its first occurrence in speech in Exodus (for the narrative use of it see 3.2, 4, 7) and, more strikingly, its first such occurrence anywhere in the Elohistic material (in Gen. 20.18; 22.11 [cf. v. 15], 14 it is probably a later addition [or part of one]), which, like the Priestly account in 6.2-3, preserves clearly the memory that it was only at the time of the Exodus that the ancestors of Israel became familiar with the name: for further discussion of the origins of Yahweh-worship see e.g. de Vaux, 'Revelation', pp. 49-63, and *Histoire*, pp. 321-37, ET, pp. 338-57; Cross, *Canaanite Myth*, pp. 44-75; J. Kinyongo, *Origine et signification du nom divin Yahvé à la lumière de récents travaux et de traditions sémitico-bibliques* (BBB 35; Bonn, 1970); K. van der Toorn, *DDD*, 1711-30, esp. 1717-23; O. Kaiser, *Der Gott des Alten Testaments*, 2 (Göttingen, 1998), pp. 67-104 (esp. 81-87); and M. Leuenberger, *Gott in Bewegung: Religions- und theologiegeschichtliche Beiträge zu Gottesvorstellungen im alten Israel* (FAT 76; Tübingen, 2011). The 'fanfare' is made up first of the titles 'God of your fathers' (taken up from the question in v. 13) and 'the God of Abraham…' (as in God's initial self-introduction to Moses in v. 6) and secondly of the declaration in v. 15b, on which see below. The phrase 'has sent me to you' is also repeated from v. 13

---

[13] A.A. Macintosh (personal communication): see also the notes on 9.3 below.

(and v. 14b) and the introductory formula 'This is what you shall say to the Israelites' is identical to that in v. 14b. In these ways v. 15 is clearly the climax of the section vv. 13-15, and its opening words 'God in addition said' underline the staged progression in God's responses in vv. 14-15. Although it may have seemed that God was not going to give a straight answer to Moses' question, now in fact he does. The triple repetition of 'God/he said' in vv. 14-15 without any response from Moses has often been seen (see the introduction to this section) as clear evidence of a succession of additions to an originally shorter text, but an alternative view is that it is a stylistic device: there are numerous examples of this where there can be no question of the combination of different sources or redactional expansion (e.g. Judg. 11.36-37; 1 Sam. 17.34-37; 2 Sam. 11.7-8: for fuller lists and discussion see S. Bar-Efrat, *Narrative Art in the Bible* [JSOTSup 70; Sheffield, 1989], pp. 43-45; G. Fischer, *Jahwe Unser Gott*, pp. 41-45; Moberly, *The Old Testament*, p. 18 with n. 19). Such a device seems to be especially common in dialogue between God and Moses, as in Exod. 32.7-10 and 33.19-23 (noted by Fischer, p. 45). Various suggestions have been made about the intended effect: a pause for a response or reflection by the one addressed (or for reflection by the speaker), the addition of a new aspect of the topic or a new argument, the expression of heightened emotion at a critical point in the life of an individual or the people. Here the repeated introductions could be designed both to divide up the different stages of God's reply and to give an appropriate 'slowing up' of the dialogue at a very solemn moment of revelation of his nature and purpose. The examples in chs. 32–33 are open to similar explanations.[14]

The verse, and the section, ends with a statement which goes far beyond the present situation of Moses and the Israelites, beyond even the return to the mountain for worship promised in v. 12 (cf. Schmidt, p. 180). It is to be understood, like v. 14a, as addressed to Moses alone, in view of its use of the divine first person (whereas the words which Moses is given to transmit to the people refer to God in the third person: so Childs, p. 80). These words thus give the episode a foundational, one might say aetiological, character: they define the way in which Israel is to refer to, address and indeed

---

[14] Recent supporters of the unity of vv. 14-15 are Van Seters, *Life of Moses*, pp. 47-48; Propp, p. 193 (hesitantly); and Gertz, *Tradition*, pp. 297-98.

worship their God throughout their future history. This is reflected in the actual usage of the Old Testament, where the divine name is by far the most frequent way in which God is referred to, even though other expressions continued to be used alongside it and even instead of it.[15] A close parallel to the expressions used here has been noted in Ps. 135.13, a late Jerusalem psalm (so e.g. Kraus, *Psalmen* [BKAT; Neukirchen, 5th ed., 1978], p. 1074), which might suggest a liturgical background for the present passage (and of course a late date). Recently it has then been cited as an argument for a Judaean origin for the verse and so by implication against its belonging to a presumed north Israelite (E) document (Schmidt, p. 133, followed by others). However, the Exodus passage is likely to be the older, because of its use of the rare and apparently more ancient expression for 'for all ages' (see Note h on the translation). The background of the expression may be illuminated by a consideration of its distinctive form: 'This is...for ever/for all ages'. Such 'inauguration formulae' occur in a variety of forms, especially in Priestly laws (e.g. Exod. 12.14), but the closest parallels seem to be Ps. 48.15 (a confession by worshippers that God [i.e. Yahweh] is their God for ever and ever) and in Ps. 132.14 (a declaration by Yahweh himself that Jerusalem would be his resting-place for ever). The form of the latter expression (including the use of divine speech) is especially close to those used here: compare also Gen. 28.17 for the designation of Bethel as 'the house of God', though without 'for ever'. Thus, not surprisingly, the language of 3.15 is similar to that used in accounts of the foundation of a sanctuary, the other key element in the worship of a deity alongside his/her name.

Text and Versions

הָאֱלֹהִים (3.13) Tgg as usual read the divine name, with the normal periphrasis 'before the Lord' after a verb of speaking. Two mss of the Old Latin read *dominum*, but the remainder of the LXX tradition agrees with MT.

---

[15] E. Jenni, *THAT* 1, 704 = *TLOT* 2, pp. 523-24, counts 6828 occurrences of the name in the Hebrew Bible; in addition there are around 370 places where the noun שֵׁם is used to refer to the divine name: A.S. van der Woude, *THAT* 2, 936-37 = *TLOT* 3, pp. 1349-50, and further 949-63 (*TLOT* 3, pp. 1357-67) on the ways in which the name itself is used.

להם (3.13) Although the evidence is faint and damaged, 4QEx^b appears to have read אליהם here as at the end of the verse (not יהוה as *DJD* XII, p. 21 [contrast pp. 90, 92], reports: the final letter in the photograph is clearly *mem*). LXX πρὸς αὐτούς could indicate the same variant in its *Vorlage*, as elsewhere in Exodus 1–3 ל after a verb of speaking is generally rendered by a dative, but προς αὐτούς in 2.9 suggests that the translator's practice was not rigid in this.

אלהי אבותיכם (3.13) The divine name is added before this in Sy (except 5b1), in a number of LXX miniscules and in two OL mss (but not in 4QEx^b: see previous note), by a thoughtless assimilation to the similar phrase in v. 15. Tg^J has the divine name here but not at this point in v. 15, which looks more like a deliberate alteration (to avoid any suggestion that the name itself is new?). SP and 4QGen-Ex^a agree with MT. A large number of LXX mss (inc. B) read '*our* fathers', perhaps a deliberate change, as it also appears widely in vv. 15 and 16, rather than (as might otherwise be thought) an itacistic corruption.

לבני ישראל (3.14) SP, 4QEx^b and (according to *BHS*) many Masoretic mss read אל for ל (cf. perhaps *ad filios* in one OL ms.), no doubt conforming to the idiom elsewhere in these verses. But the variation in MT and 4QGen-Ex^a is most likely to be original.

אהיה שלחני (3.14) Wellhausen (*Composition*, p. 70 n. 2), followed by e.g. Holzinger and Gressmann, wanted to emend אהיה to יהוה, without any ancient support, because of the 'impossibility' of one verb being the subject of another verb. But the first verb is here functioning as a name, which is a gloss on the well-known name Yahweh, and there is no need for a change: any awkwardness is a deliberate result of the 'decoding' of the name that is going on here.

At the end of 3.14 4QEx^b (but not 4QGen-Ex^a) has an empty space to the end of the line, indicating a division in the text at this point.

Excursus:
The Renderings of אהיה אשר אהיה *and of* אהיה *in Exodus 3.14*
in the Ancient Versions

This is a small part of the history of interpretation of Exod. 3.14, on which there appears to be no comprehensive study (see Childs, pp. 82-87, for an overview: a useful account of early and medieval interpretations is given in P. Vignaux et al., *Dieu et l'être* [Études augustiniennes; Paris, 1978]). See further W.R. Arnold, 'The Divine Name in Exodus iii.14', *JBL* 24 (1905), pp. 107-65, esp. 110-23; and the Appendix to my 'The Exegesis of the Divine Name in Exodus', which covers some more recent renderings as well.

LXX has ἐγώ εἰμι ὁ ὤν, 'I am he who is'. J.W. Wevers suggests that the rendering of the second אהיה is chosen because of the need to provide an intelligible equivalent for 'אהיה has sent me' later in the verse, which is translated ὁ ὤν ἀπέσταλκέν με, 'He who is has sent me'. 'It is doubtful whether one should understand ὁ ὤν as anything more than this straightforward attempt to make an acceptable Greek version of the Hebrew; it is not a philosophic statement; it is rather a religious affirmation.'[16] He does not comment on the fact that LXX uses the present tense here whereas it has used the future ἔσομαι to render אהיה in v. 12, and the theological, even philosophical, element of the translator's reasoning is surely underestimated by Wevers. LXX's sensitivity to God's visibility in Exod. 24.9-11 led to a substantial rewriting of the text, and here the translator seems to have taken advantage of the opportunity to give the God of the Jews a status which would match the claims which philosophers made for the fundamental reality of the universe (cf. Fritsch, pp. 22-23, 64). Philo, at any rate, was not blind to the door which this had opened (cf. *De vita Mosis*, 1.75). Aq and Theod gave a more literal rendering of the Hebrew: ἔσομαι ὃς ἔσομαι, 'I will be who I will be'. Vulg is similar, only in the present tense: *ego sum qui sum*, 'I am who I am'. But in v. 14b it retains the equivalent to LXX's ὁ ὤν: *qui est*, 'He who is'. The Aramaic Versions vary in their handling of these words. Sy and Tg⁰ simply transcribe the Hebrew words, without any attempt to translate them. Whether this is out of reverence or puzzlement is not clear. The same expedient is followed in part by two representatives of the Palestinian Targum tradition: Tgᴺ in v. 14a and its marginal readings and Tgᶠ in v. 14b.[17] The other Targumic renderings expand the text to bring out a richer meaning, but in three different ways:

Pseudo-Jonathan:	14a	דין דאמר והוה עלמא אמר והוה כולא
		He who spoke and the world came into being, spoke and everything came into being.
Fragmentary Targum:	14a (V)	דין דאמר לעלמא הווי והווי ועתיד למימר ליה הווי והווי
		He who said to the world,[18] 'Be', and it came into being, and who will again say to it: 'Be', and it will be.

---

[16] *Notes*, pp. 33-34.
[17] Ms. P diverges from the other mss in reading *hwʾ d*, 'It is he (who sent me)' instead of *ʾehyeh*. Here, as in v. 14a (see below), P is closer to Tgᴺ than the other FT mss.
[18] Ms. P adds *mn šyrwyʾ*, 'at the beginning', here (cf. Tgᴺ in v. 14b). The first marginal reading for this verse in Neofiti agrees almost entirely with Tgᶠ as preserved in mss B and V.

Neofiti margin 2°:	14a	אנא הוויתי עד לא איתברא עלמא ואנא הוויתי מן דאיתבריה עלמא ואנא הוא דהוויתי בסעדכון בגלותא דמצראי ואנא הוא דעתיד למהווי בסעדכון בכל דר ודר

I have existed before the world was created and have existed after the world has been created. I am he who has been at your aid in the Egyptian exile, and I am he who will be at your aid in every generation.

Pseudo-Jonathan:	14b	אנא הוא דהוינא ועתיד למיהוי (שדרני לותכון)

I am he who was and will be[19] (he has sent me to you).

Neofiti:	14b	מן דאמר והוה עלמא מן שרויא ועתיד למימר ליה הווי ויהווי (הוא שלח יתי לוותכון)

The one who said and the world came into existence from the beginning; and is to say to it again: Be, and it will be (he has sent me to you).

Tg^J in v. 14b simply spells out the implications of the use of the Hebrew imperfect tense to express a recurring action or state as a testimony to the eternal being of God (this is not very different from what is implied in LXX), and the first part of the marginal reading cited from Neofiti achieves a similar effect in a different way. Early evidence of this interpretation can probably be found in the book of Revelation: ὁ ὢν καὶ ὁ ἦν καὶ ὁ ἐρχόμενος (1.4, 8; cf. 11.17). In v. 14a Tg^J sees the phrase as identifying God as the Creator and uses a divine title which is found elsewhere in Tg^F and more widely in rabbinic literature.[20] This interpretation is given an eschatological extension in Tg^F on v. 14a and in Tg^N on v. 14b.[21] The second part of the Neofiti margin rendering relates the past and future being of God specifically to his deliverance of his people.

---

[19] Clarke's text reads *lmykwy*, but this cannot be correct. Ginsburger has *lmyhwy* and this is the reading of the ms. (J. Joosten, pers. comm.).

[20] See *AramB* 2, p. 168, n. 21.

[21] On these renderings see further C.T.R. Hayward, *Divine Name and Presence: The Memra* (Totowa, 1981), pp. 16-20; Chester, *Divine Revelation*, pp. 207-208, 301-308; and other references given in *AramB* 2, p. 20, n. 13.

עוד אלהים (3.15)   4QEx[b] inverts these words and the word-order of LXX may reflect such a *Vorlage*. SP and 4QGen-Ex[a] agree with MT. In Genesis and Exodus עוד precedes and follows a nominal subject with almost equal regularity: for a case of the latter in MT see Exod. 4.6. A decision about the original reading is impossible.

כה (3.15)   4QGen-Ex[a] has כי (an SP ms. has the same variant in v. 14), which might be due to the similarity of *he* and *yodh* in the palaeo-Hebrew and Samaritan scripts or to the frequency with which forms of אמר are followed by כי (e.g. 2.10; 3.12; 4.25). It is clearly an error.

אלהי־יצחק (3.15)   SP and 4QGen-Ex[a] have ואלהי, giving a fully connected list (cf. the notes on 1.2-4). 4QEx[b] agrees with MT, while LXX καὶ θεός perhaps points to a *Vorlage* with *waw*. The asyndetic reading is again likely to be more original. 4QEx[b] reads ישחק with ש (i.e. *sin*) by dissimilation from the emphatic צ, as in MT four times elsewhere and regularly in Sy.

ואלהי־יעקב (3.15)   Sy omits the *waw*, but it is usual at the end of a list.

זכרי (3.15)   Symm has ἀνάμνησίς μου in place of LXX's μνημόσυνον, keeping closer to the wording of the Heb.

לדר דר (3.15)   SP has the more common idiom לדר ודר as do some Masoretic mss according to *BHS*. It might be significant that LXX's strange γενεῶν γενεαῖς only occurs elsewhere in Isa. 58.12 and 60.15 where MT has דור ודור, but the Isaiah translator may have drawn his rendering from here without regard to the niceties of Heb. idiom (cf. D.A. Baer, *When We All Go Home: Translation and Theology in LXX Isaiah 56–66* [JSOTSup 318; Sheffield, 2001], p. 25, with references in n. 8, for the Isaiah translator's use of the Greek Pentateuch as a source: he does not deal with this particular case). The rarer (but evidently traditional: see Note h on the translation) idiom of MT must be original.

Chapter 3.16-22

Yahweh's Instructions to Moses

This section continues God's words to Moses in v. 15, but now the subject is no longer the name by which he is to be known but the commands and assurances which he gives to Moses. These include messages which Moses is to bring, first to the Israelite elders (vv. 16-17) and then, with their support, to Pharaoh (v. 18b). In each case Moses is told what the response to his words will be (vv. 18a, 19), and in the case of Pharaoh this leads to further assurances of what Yahweh himself will do, which will change Pharaoh's mind and enable the Israelites to leave Egypt with plentiful possessions. The effect of this, especially in vv. 19-22, is to give Moses (and the reader) a selective preview of the story that follows, as far as ch. 12.

So presented the passage coheres well from a literary point of view. Certain pairs of verses are inseparable from one another (vv. 16-17, 19-20 and 21-22) and the later verses, including v. 18, clearly depend on what has preceded. One could imagine that vv. 18, 19-20 and 21-22 were secondarily added to vv. 16-17 in one or more stages, but there is nothing in this passage taken alone that requires such a view. As for its relation to the earlier part of the chapter, vv. 16-17 largely take up the language of vv. 7-8, while on the other hand the instruction to Moses to go and speak to the people's representatives seems unnecessary after Moses has already anticipated that he will need to speak to the people in v. 13. The natural conclusion to draw, then, is that this passage (with vv. 7-8) comes from a different underlying source from vv. 13-15 (and vv. 9-12, on which they depend).

In the earliest critical commentaries on Exodus (e.g. Knobel, Dillmann) the passage was regarded as substantially a unity, and Childs returned to this view, attributing it all to J. Wellhausen, while impressed by the unity of 3.16–4.17, saw E 'motifs' in vv. 21-22 (*Composition*, pp. 70-72), and by about 1900 the view had become standard that vv. 16-18 were from J and vv. 19-22 from E, with grammatical aspects of E being noted in vv. 19-20 and a connection with 11.1-3 in vv. 21-22 (Carpenter/Harford-Battersby, Baentsch, Holzinger: similarly later McNeile and Hyatt). Smend, followed by Eissfeldt, Beer and Fohrer, attributed vv. 16-20 to J^2 and vv. 21-22 to his extra source J^1 (L, N), the latter being seen by Eissfeldt at least (pp. 32-33) as a duplicate of 11.2-3E and as part of a sequel (*sic*) to 4.24-26. Subsequent critical opinion was, however, more strongly influenced by the view of Gressmann (*Mose*, pp. 21 n. 1, 50; *Anfänge*, p. 28) that only vv. 16-17 belonged to an old source (J), while the remainder, as a 'preview' of coming events, was late and dependent on the following narrative (so already Jülicher: see further Rudolph, Noth, W.H. Schmidt, Weimar [with some characteristic variations], Kohata, L. Schmidt ['Diachrone und Synchrone', pp. 228-30], Graupner). Fohrer's arguments against this view (*Überlieferung*, p. 31 n. 17) will be noted below. In the most recent developments in Pentateuchal criticism the passage has again been regarded as a unity, though a relatively late (Blum [KD]; Van Seters [exilic J]) or a very late one (K. Schmid [R^P!]). A mixed view is found in Levin (*Jahwist*, pp. 327-30: vv. 16-18, 21-22 exilic J, vv. 19-20 J^S) and Gertz (*Tradition*, pp. 299-305): vv. 16-17, 21-22 'pre-P', vv. 18-20 'Endredaktion'). In the last two cases the presumed secondary status of the plague-narrative plays a part in identifying the later material.

Both the subdivision of the passage and its dating are based mainly on comparisons with other passages in Exodus, and so our conclusions about these topics will depend, to some extent at least, on the anticipation of later discussions. Recently L. Schmidt (art. cit.) has made much of the fact that vv. 18-22 are not presupposed in chs. 5ff.: this appears to relate mainly to a supposed incompatibility between vv. 19-20 and the nature of Moses' complaint (and Yahweh's answer) in 5.22–6.1, as though Moses would not complain so if he had been warned in advance of Pharaoh's obstinacy. This observation may demand too much logic of the narrative, and in any case Moses' words make as good sense on the basis that he had been promised stronger action by Yahweh as if he had not: Yahweh had indeed as yet not raised a finger to deliver his people (5.23). The '*Now* (Heb. *'attāh*) you shall see...' of 6.1 could well deliberately pick up the words which Yahweh had spoken earlier to Moses.

An assessment of the view of Gressmann and others that vv. 18-22, as an extended preview of future events, must be late can only be made on the basis of a careful form-critical analysis of the passage and a comparison with similar passages elsewhere. It has already been pointed out that as a whole vv. 16-22 comprise not only statements about the future but also instructions about what Moses or the people are to do. This combination of elements is sufficient to distance the passage from a comparison with salvation-prophecy, as proposed by W.H. Schmidt (p. 180) and Van Seters

(*Life of Moses*, pp. 97-99),[1] and also with Gen. 15.13-16 (e.g. L. Schmidt), which in any case looks forward to events in a much more distant future than is the case here. Equally these verses do not fit the pattern of a call-narrative, prophetic or otherwise, that was discussed in connection with vv. 1-12 (see Weimar, *Berufung*, Chapter 2, passim). Closer analogies are in fact to be found, as Fohrer has seen (*Überlieferung*, p. 31 n. 17; also Weimar, *Berufung*, pp. 100-101), in the narratives of Genesis and Exodus and also in Joshua, Judges and 1 Samuel, where a leader of the people is given often detailed assurances about what is to happen and also instructions about what to do (see e.g. Exod. 7.14-19; 16.4-5; 17.5-6; Josh. 6.1-5; Judg. 4.6-7; 7.9-11; 1 Sam. 9.15-16). The present passage, it is true, has in view a longer sequence of events and thus represents a literary development of its own, but it should be set against the background of (early) Hebrew narrative rather than prophetic speech. In line with the general emphasis in J on Yahweh rather than Moses, the latter is not given an overall commission to be the leader of his people but instructions about particular actions that he must take. This also keeps the passage close to the more limited focus of the related divine speeches listed above.

The section of this passage where a 'preview' element is most pronounced is in vv. 19-20, and it is understandable that several scholars have picked out these verses as being later intrusions into the passage (Carpenter/Harford-Battersby, Baentsch [citing Jülicher], McNeile, Levin, Gertz). But it may be doubted, in the light of the discussion above, whether this factor deserves as much attention as it has had. Most of the passage may be attributed to an early level in the J material. There is no more need to envisage redactional elaboration in vv. 16-17 than in vv. 6-8. But vv. 21-22, like their parallels in 11.2-3a and 12.35-36, are probably from a later redactional level (see the introduction to 11.1-10) and these two verses may well be much later than the others (see the Explanatory Note).

---

[1] Van Seters's other arguments for a late date are also unconvincing. It is far from clear that vv. 16-17 are dependent on Ezek. 20.5-6 (the language of that passage is quite different and it surely itself depends on an older account of the Exodus story) and the reference to 'elders' can just as plausibly be explained from what was known or believed to have been the case in earlier periods (see the Explanatory Note on vv. 16-17).

Theologically the passage serves to underline both the supremacy of Yahweh over Egypt and the privileged position of Moses in the Exodus narrative. Both the overall purpose of Yahweh, to liberate his people and establish them in a good land (vv. 16-17), and particular aspects of his plan to accomplish this purpose are described. His plan includes both a trick (v. 18), which nevertheless has a genuine religious dimension to it, and the use of his power (vv. 19-20) and his influence on the minds of the Egyptians (vv. 21-22) to secure the release of his people and the spoils of victors. In this way the cultured and powerful Egyptians are both outwitted and humbled. Moses does not only act as Yahweh's intermediary before the people and Pharaoh (vv. 16, 18): he is privileged with a knowledge of what is to come (vv. 19-22), which is only shared with the people in general terms (v. 17). This foreshadows his position of a trusted servant which will be crucial in later episodes in the narrative (and cf. Num. 12.6-8).

16 'Go and gather the elders of Israel and say to them, "The LORD the God of your fathers has appeared to me, the God of Abraham, Isaac and Jacob[a], saying, 'I have indeed seen and am concerned about[b] you and what is being done to you in Egypt 17 and I have resolved[c] (that) I will bring you up out of the oppression of Egypt into the land of the Canaanites, the Hittites, the Amorites, the Perizzites, the Hivites and the Jebusites, into a land that flows with milk and honey[d]'". 18 They will heed[e] what you say and you shall go, you and the elders of Israel, to the king of Egypt and you (pl.) shall say to him: "The LORD, the God of the Hebrews, has met[f] with us, so now let us go[g] a journey of three days into the wilderness and sacrifice to the LORD our God". 19 But I know that the king of Egypt will not allow[h] you to go[i]. Yet forced by a strong hand he will surely (let you go)[j]. 20 So I will stretch out my hand and strike the Egyptians with all my wonders which I will do in their midst[k], and after that he will let you go[l]; 21 [and I will make the Egyptians look with favour on this people[m], and it will turn out that when you go[n] you will not go empty-handed[o]: 22 each woman will ask[p] her neighbour and her house-guest[q] for objects[r] of silver and gold and for clothes, and you shall put them on your sons and daughters[s] and so you shall plunder[t] the Egyptians.]'

Notes on the Translation

a. The construct form אלהי is not repeated before the second and third names as it is in vv. 6 and 15 (and in 4.5): for this abbreviated format with the patriarchal triad cf. 1 Kgs 18.36; 1 Chr. 29.18; 2 Chr. 30.16, and more generally GK §128a, JM §129b (the latter noting a particular tendency in LBH to omit the repetition, though earlier examples are also found: e.g. 1 Sam. 23.7; 2 Sam. 19.6).

b. Heb. פקד פקדתי, with the strengthening inf. abs. The remarkably varied nuances of meaning of פקד, from 'muster (an army)' and 'command' to 'observe closely' to 'miss' and 'punish' (on which see *THAT* 2, 466-86 = *TLOT* 2, pp. 1018-31; *TWAT* 6, 708-23 = *TDOT* 12, pp. 50-63) seem to be held together by the idea of careful observation which leads to appropriate action, with 'attentiveness' as the central semantic component which may be extended by either a 'perception' or an 'action' component. The closely related occurrence of פקד in 4.31 represents attentive perception, as both the wider context and the following ראה indicate, and the same will be the case here. Yahweh's assurance to the elders thus summarises and deepens what has already been said to Moses alone in vv. 7-9, where the verbs of perception and cognition 'see, hear, know' are prominent and the Israelites are referred to as 'my people' in v. 7. The same meaning is also possible in Gen. 50.24-25 (cf. Exod. 13.19), where the potential risks following Joseph's death are what is immediately in view, despite the common preference for an 'action' rendering such as 'visit' (AV etc.) or 'come to' (NRSV): cf. *TWAT* 6, 714 = *TDOT* 12, pp. 54-55, 'God will surely take an interest in you...' for 50.24; J. Lübbe, 'Hebrew Lexicography: A New Approach', *Journal of Semitics* 2 (1990), pp. 1-15 (8), who places all these passages under his 'meaning b)' for פקד, 'be concerned, pay attention'.

c. Lit. 'said', Heb. אמר (see Text and Versions for LXX's renderings), vocalised by MT as part of the divine speech. Since Moses is reporting what he has heard (cf. vv. 7-9), the reference must then be to a divine declaration prior to that (in the divine council? or in divine solitude?). The reference may also be to a mental act, for which the full expression is (אמר בלב(ב, but there are a number of cases where (בלב(ב is omitted and the sense is clearly 'thought': with reference to God cf. Jer. 3.7, 19; Ps. 95.10. It is more difficult to find parallels to the sense 'decided', which would be the most appropriate mental act here, but Gen. 8.21 (with בלבב) is a striking example. In this case the 2nd pl. address to Israel in the words said will be due to their inclusion within the words given by Yahweh for Moses to transmit to Israel.

d. See Note o on the translation of 3.1-12 for the syntax of this phrase.

e. Heb. שמע followed by לקול is a rarer alternative to the idiom with בקול, and it can mean 'heed' (e.g. Gen. 3.17; 16.2) as well as 'obey'. It too, however, is normally associated with an action in response to what has been said and the only clear parallels for the sense 'accept as true' are in Exod. 4.8-9, where

הַאֲמִין occurs nearby. A subordinate understanding of this clause is preferred, e.g., by Heinisch, Noth and Houtman ('*If* they heed...': cf. GK §112kk, 159g) and by Calvin (*Et postquam audierint*: cf. GK §164b). While this is grammatically possible, it is characteristic of this divine speech to present the ensuing events as an assured sequence of actions and reactions. There is no inconsistency in any case between what is said here and the outcome in 4.31 (cf. Schmidt, p. 180).

f. Heb. נִקְרָה, Niphal of קרה (see Text and Versions for variant readings and translations). Houtman renders 'appeared, showed himself', but this is to assimilate what is said here too closely to the visual language of v. 16 and elsewhere (cf. Tg^N). The verb is used in the Qal of an event that 'happens' to a person or group (cf. 1.10) and in the Niphal chiefly of an 'encounter' or meeting between two or more persons, one of whom may as here be a god (cf. 5.3 and Num. 23.3-4, 15-16: in Deut. 22.6 the subject is exceptionally an object). For detailed discussion of the meanings of this root see *THAT* 2, 681-84 = *TLOT* 3, pp. 1169-71, and *TWAT* 7, 172-75 = *TDOT* 13, pp. 159-62. The element of 'chance' has probably been exaggerated in modern interpretation, and there are strong reasons against assuming it in the theological use of the verb (see *TWAT* 7, 173-74 = *TDOT* 13, pp. 160-61, and note especially Num. 23.15 where Balaam's intent is quite clear)[2].

g. Heb. נֵלֲכָה־נָּא. *Dagesh forte conjunctivum*, in accordance with GK §20f and 29e.

h. Heb. יתן, with נתן in the sense of 'permit' (cf. BDB, p. 679a). The construction with a following infinitive is found mainly in passages that have been attributed to E (Gen. 20.6; 31.7; Num. 20.21; 21.23; 22.13: cf. Carpenter/Harford-Battersby 1, p. 192 [no. 118]), but also elsewhere: Exod. 12.23 (J); Josh. 10.19 and (with slight variation) Job 9.18; 2 Chr. 20.10.

i. Heb. לַהֲלֹךְ, a rare instance of a 'regularly formed' infinitive of הלך Qal instead of the usual form לָלֶכֶת (see also Text and Versions). The other instances are Num. 22.13 (also preceded by נתן in the sense of 'permit'), 14, 16 (all E); Job 34.23; Qoh. 6.8-9.

j. Heb. וְלֹא בְּיָד חֲזָקָה. There are early textual variants for this phrase, which have been adopted by many commentators, but this 'most difficult reading' is likely to be the original one (see Text and Versions). But what can it mean?

---

[2] Barr (pp. 102-103, 335, no. 288) mentions with apparent approval C. Rabin's view that קרה/א here and in 5.3 means 'has asked (us) to hold a banquet' (see 'Etymological Miscellanea', *ScrHier* 8 [1961], pp. 384-400 [399]), with cognates meaning 'invite (to a feast)' in Ar. and Eth. and 'offer' (a sacrifice) in Ug. (presumably the passage in view is *KTU* 1.19.4.22-29). Rabin was seeking further support for the interpretation of כרה...ויכרה in 2 Kgs 6.23 as a borrowing of this root from Akk., where *qerītu* means 'feast' (for which see e.g. Cogan and Tadmor ad loc.). But the use of the Niphal and the preposition על in Exodus makes such a derivation unlikely here, whatever may be the case in 2 Kings, and the parallel uses of קרה in Num. 23 provide a much more straightforward basis for interpretation.

A literal translation would be 'and not by a strong hand' or, if the *waw* is understood emphatically (BDB, p. 252, s.v. 1.b,c; GK §154a n.1[b]), 'and that not by a strong hand' or 'and also not by a strong hand', and so more idiomatically 'not even by a strong hand'. A clearer way of expressing this meaning would have been by the use of (ו)גם followed by לא, but the Heb. here could probably bear this sense. It has, however, been objected that such an interpretation is in conflict both with the immediate context (the effect of Yahweh's 'strong hand' in v. 20) and by the use of the very same idiom to reinforce Yahweh's promise in 6.1 (cf. 13.9).[3] In reply it has been claimed that 3.19 refers to something different (which failed: Moses' strong appeal, or the first nine plagues) from Yahweh's effective intervention which is promised in v. 20 (see the references in Houtman, p. 378); and that a later modification by Yahweh (in 6.1) of what he had said earlier is tolerable if we do not impose too strict a requirement of theological consistency on the narrative (so P. Addinall, 'Exodus III 19B and the Interpretation of Biblical Narrative', *VT* 49 [1999], pp. 289-300). The first of these explanations seems unduly subtle, as it is difficult to see the expression 'a strong hand' as not including the 'hand' of Yahweh; while the second suffers from the fact that unless 3.19 is read in that artificial way there is a contradiction not only between two statements of Yahweh at different points in the narrative (which would indeed be tolerable from a literary point of view at least) but between two statements in successive verses.

A second possibility, which has received support in some recent commentaries (Schmidt, Houtman, Propp) is that ולא can itself bear the meaning 'unless' which others have sought to obtain by emendation on the basis of LXX and Vulg (see Text and Versions: such a variant reading is now attested in 4QExod[b]). Schmidt (p. 106) cites a number of scholars who have taken this view and mentions 1 Sam. 20.12-15 as a passage in which a more straightforward rendering of ולא is problematic. It is not clear that any of the six occurrences of ולא in 1 Sam. 20.12-15 means 'unless', and to be fair Schmidt does not say that they do, only that they show different meanings that ולא may have. Houtman simply refers to an article by E. Puech in support of the rendering 'unless'. Puech identified a case of ולא meaning 'except' in an Aramaic ossuary inscription (the first case of such a meaning in Aramaic) and claimed support for it in a number of examples in Biblical Hebrew ('Un emploi méconnu de *wl'* en araméen et en hébreu', *RB* 91 [1984], pp. 88-101): Exod. 3.19; 1 Sam. 2.3; 2 Sam. 13.26; 2 Kgs 5.17; Ps. 22.3. None of these is a secure case of the meaning 'except': if we set aside the passage presently under discussion, better sense can be obtained for the next two passages in other ways and in the remaining two the MT vocalisation (which is supported by LXX

---

[3] Even if in 6.1 the 'hand' is taken to be an expression for Pharaoh's own violent expulsion of the Israelites (cf. 11.1; 12.31), the tension with 3.19 understood in this way remains a problem, precisely because the expression in both places is left unspecific.

and Vulg) as well as the context favour the usual interpretation 'and if not, then...', while the Peshitta (*m' dl'*) and Targum (*wl'*) in fact give no support to the meaning 'except' (or even 'but on the contrary', as Puech proposed). Puech also mentions some further possible parallels, but of these only 1 Sam. 20.2 (which will be discussed below in connection with the arguments of Ska and Propp) even comes close to being apposite. Despite the weakness of the argument based on Hebrew Puech's interpretation of the Aramaic ossuary text does seem plausible, and knowledge of such a usage might help to explain why some early interpreters of Exod. 3.19 remodelled the text to give it a clear conditional form. Propp (p. 207) sees these early interpretations as evidence for the true meaning of MT, citing as additional support the commentary of Luzzatto, an article by J.-L. Ska and three biblical passages that have already been mentioned. Two of these (2 Sam. 13.26 and 2 Kgs 5.17) have already been discounted because they represent a different idiom which cannot be involved here. The third is 1 Sam. 20.2 and it is also the verse which Ska ('Note sur la traduction de $w^e l\bar{o}$' en Exode III 19b', *VT* 44 [1994], pp. 60-65, esp. 62, 64-65) regards as the closest parallel to Exod. 3.19. But it is arguable that it too represents a different idiom from that presumed by those who render ולא by 'unless' here. A literal translation of the relevant part of 1 Sam. 20.2 (following the Qere readings as most modern scholars do) would be: 'See my father does not do anything, great or small, and not (ולא) uncover my ear (i.e. tell me about it)'. The clause introduced by ולא indicates a distinct action from the previous one, and the force of the first לא carries over to this clause as well, so that the two clauses naturally combine into a single assertion, as the idiomatic rendering 'without disclosing it to me' (NRSV) shows. Exodus 3.19 is different, because there is no verbal expression in the ולא clause, and the verb that has to be supplied is the one from the preceding clause, so that the action is the same as there, only modified by the new adverbial expression. The fact that a different idiom is involved becomes clear if a comparable paraphrase to that given for 1 Sam. 20.2 is employed: '(he) will not allow you to go without allowing you to go by a strong hand'. This does not make good sense, nor is it equivalent to the meaning 'unless', which Propp is seeking to justify. One might of course argue that the two cases, though different, are similar enough for it to be arguable that in Exod. 3.19 (but apparently nowhere else in Biblical Hebrew) ולא does mean 'unless', but the difficulties suggest that it may be better to seek a solution in a different direction.

Ska's article in fact points in such a direction, despite its references to the rendering 'unless'. Curiously he misrepresents a key piece of evidence which supports a different approach, namely the reading of the Samaritan Pentateuch.[4] Ska cites it as if it represented the same interpretation of the sentence

---

[4] He is not alone in this: Propp (p. 186) describes it as 'nonsensical', but he misunderstands its meaning; and Puech (p. 94) treats it as arising from a scribal error.

as the 'unless/except' indicated by LXX and Vulg (p. 61; cf. Knobel, p. 33, who adopts it as the original reading in this sense). But הלוא, taken literally, makes the end of the verse into a question, presumably an elliptical one: '(Will he) not (allow you to go) by a strong hand?', which is equivalent (as often elsewhere: cf. BDB, p. 520, and esp. Exod. 4.11) to a strong assertion: '(he will) surely (allow you to go) by a strong hand'. It is quite frequent for לא alone, without the interrogative particle, to bear the same meaning (cf. BDB, p. 519a, s.v. 1.a [*e*]), and Ska quotes a number of such cases in his article: Exod. 8.22; 1 Sam. 20.9, 12 (cf. v. 14a); Ezek. 16.43, 56 (cf. v. 47).[5] In all of these, as in Exod. 3.19, לא is preceded by *waw*. If לא is taken to be equivalent to הלוא here and the *waw* is understood adversatively, a translation which fits the context is readily obtained: 'but (he will) surely (allow you to go) by a strong hand'. This seems to be the explanation of the MT which is least open to objection, and so it has been followed in the translation given above. The conclusion of Ska's article and his amplified translation (p. 65) are very similar, but his insistence on the presence of an 'if (not)' is unnecessary and probably unjustified. Of course the overall sense of the verse implied by our rendering is very close to that implied by a rendering with 'unless' or 'except' (a further reason why both early and more recent interpreters have been attracted by it), but that, it would seem, is not because ולא can by itself bear that meaning but because of semantic equivalence at the level of the sentence (deep structure).

k. Heb. בקרבו, with the masculine sing. suffix referring to the people of 'Egypt' (GK §122i), whereas in e.g. 10.7 the feminine gender refers to the effect of the plagues on the land, which is generally explicitly in view in the later narrative. Note, however, the construal of מצרים as feminine in what is clearly a reference to the people in 12.33.

l. Heb. ישלח, Piel of שלח, perhaps a deliberate echo of the Qal at the beginning of the verse. Here the briefer expression (contrast v. 19) which becomes the focus of the ensuing chapters (cf. 4.21, 23; 5.1-2 etc.) is introduced for the first time.

m. Literally 'I will give [or perhaps better "put", a possible sense of Heb. נתן] favour towards this people [construct relationship expressing an "objective genitive"' (GK §128h)] in the eyes of the Egyptians'. The idiom is found in both the related passages later in Exodus (11.3; 12.36) and also in Gen. 39.21: it expresses the divine providence which enables someone to 'find

---

[5] Ska drew attention to the LXX renderings of ולא by ἐάν/εἰ μή, as in Exod. 3.19, in 1 Sam. 20.14b, 15; Ezek. 16.56. In the first of these LXX has misunderstood the Hebrew and its καὶ ἐάν (no μή) may be based on reading לא as the hypothetical conditional particle לוא. The other two instances also involve mistranslation and the best explanation is perhaps that the translator wrongly saw here cases of the idiom where וְלֹא means 'if not, then…', which LXX recognised e.g. at 2 Sam. 13.26 and 2 Kgs 5.17.

favour in the eyes of' another, as the common phrase has it (for the expression of such favour by the 'face' or 'look' see *TWAT* 3, 26 = *TDOT* 5, pp. 24-25).

n. Heb. תֵּלֵכוּן, with *nun paragogicum* in pausal position (note also the vowel lengthening) in the subordinate clause, whereas in the following main clause the normal form is found in non-pausal position (cf. JM §44e). It is noteworthy that in Exodus 1–10 at least such forms are more common with the 2nd pl. imperfect (cf. 1.22; 3.12, 21; 4.15; 5.7; 9.28, 30) than they are with the 3rd pl. (4.9 [perhaps deliberate intensification after 4.8]; 9.29).

o. Heb. רֵיקָם. Although this adverb occasionally has the general sense 'in vain, without effect' (e.g. Isa. 55.11), its most common meaning is as here 'with empty hands' (cf. 23.15; 34.20).

p. Heb. שׁאל, which can mean 'borrow (for temporary use)' (cf. 22.13). It is so understood here and in 11.2; 12.35 (cf. the Hiphil in 12.36) by some (see in general Childs, pp. 175-77; Houtman, pp. 382-86; and in a defence against anti-Semitic interpretation, B. Jacob, pp. 346-59, ET, pp. 337-46). Among English versions the AV and NJPS translations have 'borrow', and there is a rabbinic precedent for this (Esth.R. 7.13). But there is little sign of it in modern English commentaries, except where some uncertainty about the exact meaning is expressed by Childs (p. 176) and Houtman (pp. 382-83). In Germany, although it is not followed in Luther's translation, it enjoyed much popularity between about 1900 and 1970 (Holzinger, pp. 15, 39; Gressmann, *Anfänge*, pp. 44, 49; Eissfeldt; Beer, p. 58; Noth, p. 73 (on 11.2-3), ET, pp. 93-94[6]. Heinisch (p. 56) is a rare exception in this period, but later Schmidt does not mention it, and Vriezen rejected it in his study of the meaning of וינצלו later in the verse (see below). The rightness of this rendering is generally taken for granted by those who adopt it, but Noth makes it explicit that for him it is a deduction from the reference to the 'plundering' of the Egyptians, presumably as something which they underwent unwillingly. One possible line of argument against the rendering 'borrow' is therefore to question the translation 'plunder' for נצל Piel here, as Jacob, Vriezen and Gradwohl have done (see below). But their alternatives are all problematic. Even so, it is doubtful whether the idea of 'plundering' need lead to the rendering 'borrow' for שׁאל: if the Egyptians gave what they were 'asked' for, this could still be represented as a kind of plundering of the former oppressors. The 'plunder' is in any case metaphorical, not literal. It should also be noted that neither here nor in the later passages in Exodus is this motif directly linked with the Israelites' desire to make a short journey into the desert, for which 'borrowing' might be appropriate (it is only in the polemical passage in Esth.R. 7.13 that this happens).

q. Heb. גרת ביתה. For the construction see JM §121n. The 'house' is presumably the neighbour's (cf. NRSV), as it is less likely that an Egyptian woman would be staying in an Israelite's house.

---

[6] Cf. Fohrer, *Überlieferung*, p. 43; G.W. Coats, 'Despoiling the Egyptians', *VT* 18 (1968), pp. 450-57 (453).

r. Heb. כְּלִי, according to standard Heb. style repeated before both 'genitives' (GK §128a), which as often designate the material out of which the 'objects' are made (GK §128o). The noun כְּלִי (for which cf. 3.22; 12.35; 35.22) is a regular formation from a root כלה (cf. BL §72h' for similar forms) and it was once associated with Heb. כָּלָה = 'be complete etc.' (BDB, p. 479, following Gesenius). More recently the view of J. Barth has been preferred as being better able to account for the narrower range of meaning in cognate languages: this proposes derivation from a separate root כלה which would be a by-form of כול = 'contain' (*HAL*, p. 456; *TWAT* 4, 179-80 = *TDOT* 7, p. 170; *Ges18*, p. 548). Even if this is correct, the much wider application to tools, weapons, jewellery etc., as well as 'vessels' in BH (for later Heb. cf. M.Kelim passim) might have been due to the (mistaken?) view that כְּלִי was related to כָּלָה = 'be complete etc.'; and occurrences in Ug. and (probably) Moabite suggest that even outside Heb. the meaning was not limited to 'vessel' (for a useful recent review of the cognates see B. Becking 'כְּלִי – 'vessel, utensil etc.' [on the KLY website, www.otw-site.eu/KLY/kly.php – version updated 24 March 2011], pp. 20-22). Here כְּלִי is sometimes taken to refer specifically to 'ornaments' or 'jewellery' (so e.g. *DCH*; cf. NRSV at 3.22 and 12.35, but at 11.2 it has 'objects'), perhaps because of an association with the (Priestly) use in that sense in 35.22. But there is no reason to exclude a reference in 11.2 and 12.35 to other precious objects such as cups and platters. It is only here in 3.22 that the instruction to 'put them on' the children may point to the more specific sense.

s. This is a regular idiom for 'putting on' clothes etc. (Gen. 24.47; 41.42; Lev. 8.8; Ruth 3.3).

t. Heb. נצל: Piel, which occurs in the related verse 12.36, in 2 Chr. 20.25 where it refers to acts of plundering, and in Ezek. 14.14 where it is used in MT as a unique alternative to the Hiphil (14x in Ezek., 4x in Ezek. 14) in the sense 'save, deliver'. Even if the reading in Ezek. 14.14 is secure (there have been proposals to read the Niphal or Hiphil: cf. LXX), it is most improbable that 'save' is the meaning here (despite the argument of Jacob, pp. 356-59, ET pp. 344-46; so also Fischer, *Jahwe Unser Gott*, p. 168, with reference to Y.T. Radday, 'The Spoils of Egypt', *ASTI* 12 [1983], pp. 127-47; for an early example see Text and Versions), and interpreters since the LXX have understandably taken their cue from the occurrence in 2 Chr. 20.25. It is true that, as Jacob pointed out, the unexpressed object there is the booty and not the defeated enemy. But the use of the Hithpael in Exod. 33.6 with an object of the jewellery 'stripped off' suggests that in these meanings נצל could be used with a double object, one of the person and one of the thing (for the general point see GK §117cc-gg), and so also with either alone. T.C. Vriezen ('A Reinterpetation of Exodus 3.21-22 and Related Texts', *JEOL* 23 [1973–74], pp. 389-401 [397-99]) proposed the translation 'take away, remove'. It could indeed be that it is other words in 2 Chr. 20.25 that convey the idea of 'booty' (cf. שללם) and that the Piel of נצל simply meant 'took away, removed'. This fits a few other uses of the root where 'save, deliver' is not the obvious meaning (the Hiphil in Gen. 31.9, 16; Hos. 2.11). However, in all these cases the removal of objects is a severe loss to the owner and that element of the meaning surely carries over into the context here and in 12.36, especially as the expressed object designates the person affected. If 'plunder' is too strong and too militaristic, perhaps 'appropriate the property of' will do. Vriezen's comparison to the tribute given to the victor by a defeated foe is less plausible as an account of the sense of נצל (which is never used in such contexts) than, perhaps, as a clue to how the episode as a whole may have been understood. Similarly the proposal of R. Gradwohl ('*Niṣṣal* und *Hiṣṣil* als Rechtsbegriffe im Sklavenrecht', *ZAW* 111 [1999], pp. 187-95) that נצל Piel is a technical expression from the law about slaves, meaning 'cause (the Egyptians) to pay the reward owed', while superficially attractive (cf. ריקם in v. 21 and in Deut. 15.13), fails to provide a convincing sense for the verb that can be related to its uses elsewhere. The Hiphil in Gen. 31.9, 16, which Gradwohl adduces in support (pp. 193-94), is not relevant because Jacob is not a slave but a hired labourer (cf. 30.32-33) and Laban's fault is the breach of an employment 'contract'.

Explanatory Notes

16-17. God's words to Moses continue with a command to him to go back to Egypt and inform the people (more specifically, their 'elders' – see below) about his encounter with their God and the message which he has received from him. This instruction seems almost unnecessary after v. 13, where Moses has already assumed that he will need to speak to his people, and it probably comes from a different strand of the narrative from vv. 13-15 (see the introduction to this passage). Its wording in fact has very close affinities to vv. 7-8: God's seeing, 'bring up', 'oppression', the names of the peoples that occupy Canaan, and its description as 'a land that flows with milk and honey' (see the notes on those verses for detailed comments on these expressions). Moses is thus sent as a messenger of God to repeat what he has been told to those whose cry has been heard and whose deliverance is near. Such repetition is frequent in ancient story-telling, for example the Ugaritic myths and legends, where messages are involved. But there are several new features here compared with vv. 7-8. (i) The people are represented by their 'elders'. Such elders were a widespread element in the leadership of ancient Near Eastern society (cf., briefly, de Vaux, *Institutions* 1, pp. 212-13, ET, p. 138; more fully, with references, *TWAT* 2, 644-45 = *TDOT* 4, pp. 126-27, and Reviv [below], Chapters 8–9), and it is not surprising that they are mentioned frequently in the Pentateuchal narrative (cf., in addition to v. 18 and the closely associated 4.29, Exod. 10.9; 12.21; 17.5-6; 18.12; 19.7; 24.1, 9, 14; Num. 11.16, 24-25, 30; 16.25; in Gen. 50.5; Num. 22.4,7 foreign elders are mentioned). Although Noth thought that 'elders' were an older component of the Exodus tradition than Moses himself (*ÜGP*, pp. 179-80), more recent scholarship has seen the references to them as shaped by the practices or interests of later times, whether in royal government (H. Reviv, *The Elders in Ancient Israel* [Jerusalem, 1989], p. 29) or in the exiled community (J. Buchholz, *Die Ältesten Israels im Deuteronomium* [GTA 36; Göttingen, 1988], pp. 33-38, 42-54; so also Van Seters, *Life of Moses*, p. 48). A reference like the present one scarcely needs any such special explanation, and Reviv (p. 30) recognises that the wider analogies strongly suggest that already in the 'pre-settlement' period elders would have played an important role in leadership. This will be the status quo into which the figure of Moses is introduced here. (ii) The divine titles 'the god of your fathers' and 'the god of Abraham, Isaac and Jacob' match those in v. 15, except for the abbreviated form of the latter (for which see Note a on the translation): compare 4.5. The emphasis on continuity with the past is again natural as Moses addresses his people for the first time. The separation of the second title in the Hebrew (see the translation) and the lateness of the parallels to its abbreviated form (see note a) have been taken as signs of a secondary addition (Holzinger, p. 8; Gertz, *Tradition*, p. 295), but the former point at least is not compelling, especially in a sentence where the subject and one of its attributes precedes the verb: to delay the verb further would (though possible: cf. v. 15) be very awkward (cf. Blum's doubts about this argument on stylistic grounds: 'Literarische Verbindung', p. 140). (iii) That Yahweh 'appeared' to Moses (a point taken up in 4.1, 5) is presumably a reference back to v. 2, with the usual implication that 'the angel of Yahweh' is not distinguishable from an appearance of Yahweh himself (see the note on vv. 2-3). (iv) The expression of Yahweh's 'concern' (see Note b on the translation) brings out what can be implicit in his 'seeing' Israel's sufferings (see the note on 2.24-25). The verb used here (*pāqad*) makes an important connection with the end of Genesis (50.24-25), where it is also (as here) used with the reinforcing infinitive absolute (for the connection see Propp, p. 193). We have argued earlier (see the introduction to 1.1-6) that Gen. 50.22-24 belongs with Exod. 1.6 as part of the J narrative: here in 3.16 what was there promised in the future tense is declared to have become a reality, and there is the same association as there with the names of the patriarchs and (in v. 17) the 'bringing up' (*'ālāh* Hiphil) of the Israelites to the land of Canaan.

18. According to this verse Yahweh himself instructs Moses and the elders to go to Pharaoh ('the king of Egypt', as also in v. 19: cf. 1.15, 17-18; 2.23, later alone only in 5.4 and 14.5; elsewhere in Exodus 'Pharaoh' is found [115x]) and prescribes what they shall say. In fact he is here given the title 'the God of the Hebrews', which is used alone in 5.3 and then recurs with the divine name (as here) in 7.16; 9.1, 13; 10.3, but nowhere else in the OT. This surprising alternative to the generally more widespread 'the God of Israel' (used in 5.1, as well as 24.10; 32.27; 34.23) is clearly related to the designation of the Israelites as 'Hebrews' in chs. 1–2 (see the note on 1.15) and provides evidence of 'narrative continuity' which clarified the composition of this section of the book (see the introduction to this section). In the present context it is clearly a title for Yahweh and not a different (anonymous?) god, but the question has been raised, especially in relation to 5.3, whether it may once have referred in an older form of the Exodus tradition to a different god who was revered by (proto-)Israelites in Egypt (so apparently K. Koch, 'Die Hebräer vom Auszug aus Ägypten bis zum Grossreich Davids', *VT* 19 [1969], pp. 37-81 [55, 62]; H. Schmid, 'Jhwh, der Gott der Hebräer', *Judaica* 25 [1969], pp. 257-66, esp. 262ff.). There are references to 'the gods of the Ḫabiru' in some of the Hittite treaties from the later second millennium (see, e.g., *ANET*, p. 206 [Mitanni]; *COS* 2, pp. 98 [Amurru], 105 [Tarḫuntašša]); but not apparently in the Hittite treaty with Egypt (contra Schmid, 'Gott der Hebräer', p. 262: for further references see M.P. Gray, 'The *Ḫâbirū*-Hebrew Problem in the Light of the Source Material available at present', *HUCA* 29 [1958], pp. 135-202 [152-53, 178], and M. Weippert, *Die Landnahme der israelitischen Stämme in der neueren wissenschaftlichen Diskussion* [FRLANT 92; Göttingen, 1967], p. 73 n. 3, ET, p. 70 n. 53), which might seem to lend some concrete authenticity to the phrase. But in the context of even an earlier version of the Exodus story than we now possess (see further the comments on ch. 5) there is no need to understand the phrase as anything other than a way of referring to Yahweh which would have been considered intelligible to Pharaoh, and the hypothesis that a different god was once referred to has not found widespread acceptance (cf. Schmidt, p. 260). All that the title implies is that these 'outsiders' have their own god, distinct from the Egyptian gods, who is defined by his relationship to the Hebrews rather than by the name of a shrine or a mythical role and requires their worship outside the boundaries of Egypt. Yahweh's instructions are first carried out in 5.3 (in 5.1 the wording of the request is different). The message is given in slightly different terms again in 7.16, 26; 8.16; 9.1, 13; 10.3: in all of these Heb. *'ābad* = 'worship' is used, whereas here and in 5.3 the verb is *zābaḥ* = 'sacrifice' and in 5.1 it is *ḥāgag* = 'hold a feast'. The 'journey of three days' is only mentioned here and in 5.3 (separately, and perhaps secondarily, also in 8.23): the wording of the other passages is more closely related to 4.23. The present verse is the direct continuation of vv. 16-17 and cannot have existed separately from them. 'A three days' journey' is a common and probably imprecise phrase for a significant but relatively short journey which at normal ancient rates of travel would be about 50-60 miles (see the discussion in G.I. Davies, 'The Significance of Deuteronomy 1.2 for the Location of Mount Horeb', *PEQ* 111 [1979], pp. 89-97). This means that either a place in the north of the Sinai peninsula was being envisaged or the phrase was deliberately (and deceptively) chosen to try to reassure Pharaoh that his workmen would not be away for too long (on possible implications for the locations of mountains held to be sacred in early Israel see my *Way of the Wilderness*, pp. 67-69). Of course the implication that the Israelites would be absent for only a short period of religious duty (such as are known to have been permitted to Egyptian workmen at Deir el-Medina: see references in Kitchen, *Ancient Orient and Old Testament* [London, 1966], p. 157) was deceptive in any case (it is perhaps significant that the form of request used elsewhere is entirely open-ended, as though to avoid any charge of deception).

19-20. Moses is again told not only what he must do but what its consequences will be (cf. v. 18a). Yahweh 'knows' that Pharaoh will not agree: this is not, however, because (as other passages say: 4.21; 7.3) he is going to 'harden' Pharaoh's heart. References to Yahweh's 'knowledge' appear, e.g., in Gen. 20.6; 22.12; Exod. 2.25; 3.7; 4.14; 32.22; Deut. 2.7, but not elsewhere in the Pentateuch (except Gen. 3.5) to his knowledge of future events. This is, however, presupposed in Gen. 15.13-16 and Deut. 31.20-21. Pharaoh's refusal to release Israel appears initially in 5.1-2 and then repeatedly in the plague narratives of chs. 8–11. Yahweh's plan to use a 'mighty hand' to overcome his resistance is recalled in 6.1, and Pharaoh's final capitulation occurs, after the slaying of the firstborn, in 12.31-32. The description of the plagues as *niplā'ōt*, 'wonders', is not found again in Exodus (or in Deuteronomy), though 15.11 uses the related word *pele'*, perhaps with the plagues in mind. The word translated 'wonders' elsewhere in Exodus and Deuteronomy is *mōptîm* (see the note on 4.21). Where *niplā'ōt* is found as a term for the plagues is in certain Psalms (78.4, 11-12, 32; 105.2,5,7; 106.22), which may be significant for the passage's origin.

21-22. This is the fullest of the three passages to refer to the 'plundering' of the Egyptians (cf. 11.2-3a; 12.35-36): the reference to divine favour appears in all three, but Yahweh's further instruction to Moses (11.2) is briefer and includes neither the references to clothing and the children nor the expression 'plunder', and the execution of the command in 12.35-36 also omits the children. The additional mention of Israelite men in 11.2 is unique. The fact that this particular motif is anticipated here, out of all the many details of the later narrative, demands some explanation. It might be seen as having an apologetic purpose, by lending divine support to an action that would otherwise be regarded as unethical, but this would be sufficiently provided for by 11.2. It is more likely that, like the events mentioned in the preceding verses, it was seen (by one writer at least) as a very significant part of the narrative, either because it underlined the supremacy of Israel and their God over the Egyptians (which the term 'plunder' might support [so Van Seters, *Life of Moses*, p. 98] – though see Note t on the translation – and cf. the 'mighty hand' of v. 19 and 6.1) or because it provided the materials for use in worship in the desert, whether licit (Exod. 25-31) or illicit (Exod. 32). The even more distant anticipation of this aspect of the Exodus in Gen. 15.14, which uses different language ('great possessions') and is not necessarily from the same stage of composition, seems to understand it in the former way (cf. also Ps. 105.37, 43-44).[7]

---

[7] G.W. Coats (cf. n. 7) argued that the motif of 'despoiling the Egyptians' was the climax of an alternative version of the Exodus tradition in which the final plague, the slaying of the firstborn, did not appear. But there is no need to see these elements as mutually exclusive (see Van Seters, *Life of Moses*, pp. 97-99). A. Malamat found at least an analogy for the 'despoiling' and perhaps even an Egyptian allusion to it, in the Elephantine stele of Sethnakht (c. 1190 B.C.: cf. *RITA* 5, pp. 7-8), which refers to the payment of 'silver and gold' to some 'Asiatics' by the leaders of a rebellion against him and the subsequent flight of the

For discussion of the ethical problem thought to be raised by these verses and other aspects of the history of their interpretation see the bibliography in Note p on the translation and S.M. Langston, *Exodus Through the Centuries* (Oxford, 2006), pp. 116-19. A striking point of detail here is that, unlike at least one version of the plague stories (cf. 8.18 etc.) as well as the final chapters of Genesis, it is assumed that the Israelites live among the Egyptian population rather than in a separate place, and even possibly that they have Egyptian lodgers in their houses. This makes it probable that these verses and those related to them in chs. 11–12 are secondary additions to the main non-Priestly narrative of the Exodus (see the fuller discussion in the introduction to 11.1-10). The other passages are both intrusive in their contexts and these verses, which combine details from them both, may have been added later still. At that stage, perhaps with knowledge of the Priestly expression in 35.22, the word 'objects' (Heb. $k^e l\hat{e}$) may have been understood to mean specifically 'jewellery', as 'putting them on' the Israelites' children suggests (cf. AV, RV, JB, NEB, REB): see further Note r on the translation and Text and Versions.

Text and Versions

ואספה (3.16)   Most mss of Sy omit the *waw* (perhaps a 'stylistic improvement' of the translation), but 5b1 (as ever closer to MT) and the other Versions have it. It is indispensable in the Heb. construction.

זקני (3.16)   LXX, τὴν γερουσίαν, and Tg[N], חכימיא, as elsewhere (inc. v. 18) equate the elders respectively with a political body known from the Greek world and the rabbinic leadership of later Judaism (on the latter see *AramB* 2, p. 169 n. 23). Aq restored a more literal translation, which is also preferred by the other Tgg here.

ישראל (3.16)   בני is prefixed (unnecessarily and surely secondarily) in most mss of SP, 4QExod[b], LXX* and Sy, conforming the expression to the immediate context (cf. vv. 13-15) and to 4.29, where the fulfilment of this command is recounted. An early correction towards MT is reflected in a citation in Justin, *Dial.* 59.2. In v. 18 (q.v.) support for the insertion of בני is much weaker, and it is likely that in both places the original text lacked it.

---

rebel party ('The Exodus: Egyptian Analogies', in Frerichs and Lesco, *Exodus*, pp. 15-26 [22-25]). The similarity of this episode, however, is not close and (like other attempts to fit the Exodus into the same period) hardly a basis for historical argument (see my 'Was there an Exodus?', pp. 34-36).

אלהם (3.16) 4QExod^b, which is generally prone to full spelling, here agrees with SP in reading אליהם.

נראה (3.16) All the Tgg read 'has revealed himself', as usual, and are joined on this occasion by Sy, except for 5b1, which coincides with MT.

יצחק ויעקב (3.16) Most SP mss simply prefix *waw*, but two of those cited by Crown additionally add אלהי before these two names, in line with the overall textual tradition in the previous verse. The same expansion is found in 4QExod^b (which as in v. 15 has the spelling ישחק), LXX and Vulg.

פקד פקדתי (3.16) All the Tgg render 'have remembered', following a standard rabbinic interpretation of פקד: cf. *AramB* 2, p. 169 n. 24, and B. Grossfeld, 'The Translation of Biblical Hebrew *pqd* in the Targum, Peshitta, Vulgate and Septuagint', *ZAW* 96 (1984), pp. 83-101. Sy has the same rendering, indicating its closeness to rabbinic tradition.

ואת־העשוי (3.16) The Sy ms. 5b1 and some later mss omit the *waw*. LXX and Vulg render freely 'what happened', while Tg^J ('the humiliation which...') and Tg^N ('what the Egyptians did...') are more specific.

ואמר (3.17) SP and 4QExod^b read the cohortative form ואמרה, but with no difference of meaning (see the note on וארד in 3.8). LXX^B and some other mss have εἶπεν, which has been taken (cf. *BHS*) as evidence for a (perhaps more original) *Vorlage* ויאמר, but it is probably due to inner-Greek corruption, with the original reading εἶπα (LXX^A etc.) and its Atticising equivalent εἶπον (LXX^{F,M} etc.) reflecting the same Hebrew as MT (so Wevers: cf. *Notes*, p. 36). Tg^{J,N} add 'by my [Tg^N 'his'!] Memra' (cf. on v. 12).

אעלה (3.17) Tg^N, Sy, Vulg and LXX^O subordinate this verb to the previous one, but probably as a free rendering rather than on the basis of a different Heb. from MT.

מעני מצרים (3.17) Tg^{O,N} and Sy render 'from servitude to the Egyptians', making the suffering more specific in line with (e.g.) 2.23 (as in v. 7) and treating מצרים as a reference to the people rather than the land (so also LXX, Tg^J for the latter).

הכנעני וג׳ (3.17) SP and LXX add והגרגשי after והפרזי: cf. v. 8, where LXX has it after החוי. Here LXX (if Wevers is right to regard the reading of LXX^{F,M} as the most original extant Greek text: cf. *THGE*, p. 175) has 'the Hivites' in third place in the list for a reason that remains elusive, but if the order in v. 8 is compared it seems most likely that it stood before 'the Girgashites' in the older 'LXX' tradition.[8] 4QExod^b may well have included 'the Girgashites' at the end of the list in view of the lacuna after והיבוסי (cf. *DJD* XII, p. 93, and for the Girgashites at the end of such a list Neh. 9.8). If so, the seventh name appears at three different places in those texts which have it here, a sure indication of its secondary character (see also the note on v. 8). Although most of the witnesses have the conjunction between all the names in the list, as in MT,

---

[8] The early fourth-cent. papyrus 866, like LXX^{BA}, did not have the Hivites in third place, but as either fourth or (more likely) sixth: the Perizzites come fifth.

there are cases of its omission at various points in SP (cf. the apparatus of von Gall), 4QExod^b and Vulg, probably due to (secondary) attempts to group the names in different ways.

זבת חלב ודבש (3.17)   Tgg render זבת by the paler עבדא, 'producing', as in v. 8. Tg^N has the same generalisation of the products as there, but this time without the description 'good' in the original text (it is inserted interlineally).

זקני ישראל (3.18)   Again here (cf. v. 16), some authorities insert בני before ישראל, but this time only 4QExod^b and Sy (except 5b1 and later mss).

מלך מצרים (3.18)   LXX inserts Φαραώ before this, producing the full form of the title, as it does throughout this chapter (though not regularly elsewhere), even where other witnesses have only one of the elements (Wevers, *Notes*, p. 36).

ואמרתם (3.18)   LXX and Vulg have the second person sing., in line with the fact that it is generally Moses alone who speaks (as a representative) to Pharaoh and no doubt with the intention of emphasising his role here. The less tidy reading of the other witnesses must be original. The change was easier to make because of the way LXX and Vulg understood נקרה later in the verse (see the note below).

יהוה (3.18)   LXX omits this, as do all witnesses in 5.3, where the instruction is fulfilled. Such harmonisation is certainly secondary.

העבריים (3.18)   The uncontracted form of the plural in MT is unique, and SP's העברים should be preferred.[9] The error could be due to dittography, influence of the feminine forms in 1.15-16, 19, or Aramaic influence. It is possible that the question in Exod.R. 3.8, 'Why did he call them Hebrews?', and the answer in terms of crossing the sea (ים) relates to the spelling variation and not the name as such: it was certainly observed by the Masoretes. Tg^{O,J} render as 'the Jews' as in chs. 1–2, anachronistically.

נקרה (3.18)   SP reads נקרא as in 5.3: the word does not survive here in any of the Qumran mss of Exodus, but נקרא is presupposed by the renderings in LXX, Vulg, ὁ ἑβρ and Tg^{O,J}, where אתקרי should be understood to mean '(has been) called', i.e. named, rather than 'happened' (with Chester, *Divine Revelation*, p. 141 n. 83 and *AramB* 2 ad loc.: cf. 5.3). The sense of the Heb. must be that of קרה – the interpretation as an active in LXX, Vulg and ὁ ἑβρ is inaccurate and shows that 'call' cannot be the meaning – and given that the spelling of this verb alternates between final *aleph* and *he* (see Text and Versions on 1.10) the inconsistency of MT may be more original. Tg^N and Sy (the agreement is again interesting) have 'has revealed himself' as in v. 16 for נראה, and this reading also appears in two early editions of Tg^O and the ms. followed in *AramB* 7.

---

[9] Note, however, that the uncontracted form כתיים occurs in three out of ten instances in MT and is presumably implied in the seven certain epigraphical occurrences of *ktym* (*AHI*, p. 388). Is this a special case?

ועתה (3.18) Omitted by SP and LXX, in agreement with the words spoken in 5.3 and probably due to pedantic harmonisation with them.

ליהוה (3.18) Tgg as usual have 'before the Lord'. LXX again omits יהוה, as it does in 5.3, although other authorities have it there. In this case the value of its reading can only be resolved in the light of an examination of 5.3 in its context (which is complex and repetitious), but the omission is again probably secondary. Rösel ('Reading and Translation', p. 421) suggests that it is because a foreigner is involved, as in Gen. 30.27; 31.49; Exod. 5.2-3; 10.11. But if so, the 'rule' is not consistently followed (cf. 10.10, 16, 17) and other factors seem also to be involved.

ואני ידעתי (3.19) Tg^{O,J} cautiously paraphrase 'it is revealed before me', in a variant of a regular formula (see Chester, *Divine Revelation*, pp. 20-21), but Tg^N (as well as Sy) renders literally.

להלך (3.19) 4QExod^b reads לל[כת], the normal form of the inf. constr. of הלך, instead of the rare form found in MT and SP, on which see Note i on the translation. Such secondary 'normalisation' of the grammar is a common feature of non-Masoretic textual traditions, esp. SP.

ולא ביד חזקה (3.19) Behind LXX ἐὰν μή and Vulg *nisi* (a similar meaning is given in the Madrid Polyglott text of Tg^O, in the margin of Tg^N, and in one, inferior, ms. of SamTg [A]) a variant reading אם לא, 'unless, except', has long been presumed to exist and many commentators in the past have regarded this as superior to MT (e.g. Kautzsch, Grätz, Baentsch, Eissfeldt, Beer, Childs; as possibly so McNeile, BHS: cf. *HAL*, p. 486). The appearance of כי אם with the same meaning at this point in 4QExod^b, a ms. which frequently has a text which could be a *Vorlage* of LXX, has on the one hand confirmed that LXX at least is probably based on a Hebrew variant here, but on the other hand presents a variant from which it is impossible to say that MT is derived by accidental error. In fact given these two readings, ולא and כי אם, the latter is clearly the easier one and therefore more likely to be due to deliberate scribal correction. This provides text-critical support for the tendency in recent commentaries (see Note j on the translation) for other reasons to retain MT and seek an explanation of it which is appropriate to the context. SP's הלוא, although also an easier and therefore probably secondary reading, very likely points to the correct explanation of MT as interrogative. One early ms. of SP (Camb. UL Add. 1846) reads הלוא ביד החזקה, 'Will he not by *the* mighty hand?', underlining what is already implicit in SP's הלוא, that the 'hand' is God's. Tg^N renders similarly, 'the hand that is mighty' (if the emphatic state ידא is understood definitely), but the preceding ולא indicates that like the other Tgg (and Sy) it understood the hand to be Pharaoh's: so most clearly Tg^J, which supplements its translation 'not because of his mighty strength' with the explanation 'but in order for his (i.e. God's) Memra to punish him with evil plagues and [v. 20] you will be detained there until...' (cf. Exod.R. 3.10 and *AramB* 2, p. 169 n. 30).

את ידי (3.20)   Tgg paraphrase, to avoid the anthropomorphism, with 'the stroke of my might' (Tg^N 'of my punishment').

ונתתי (3.21)   Only part of the first word survives for this verse in 4QExod^b, but the letter after *waw* is a clear *kaph*. *DJD* XII, p. 92, suggests that the third letter may be a final *nun*, but if so the origin of the reading remains obscure.

תלכון (3.21)   Tg^J adds מן תמן פריקין, 'from there as redeemed people', clarifying the sense and also making a neat balance and rhyme with its rendering of the next clause.

תלכו (3.21)   SP repeats the form with *nun paragogicum* (cf. *GSH* §63b for other such variations).

ריקם (3.21)   Von Gall gives this as also the reading of SP in his text, but a large number of the mss cited in his apparatus (likewise those used by Crown, Tal and Sadaqa, and Camb. Add. 1846) read ריקים, and only three have ריקם. The majority reading most likely represents the original SP text here (likewise at 23.15; 34.20; Deut. 16.16: at Gen. 31.42 and Deut. 15.13 ריקם is better attested). The form ריקים can be understood as the m.pl. of the adjective ר(י)ק, 'empty', i.e. presumably 'empty-handed', though no precise parallel to this use of the adj. exists in Hebrew. It may have arisen by over-enthusiastic 'improvement' of the text in places where a plural adjective would be grammatically possible (this is not the case where ריקם is the majority reading): it is less likely that the same error by metathesis occurred four times. Adjectival renderings appear in LXX, Vulg and Tg^{J,N}, but in each case the meaning of the adjective allows that they could be rendering ריקם.

ושאלה (3.22)   SP modifies and expands the text with wording drawn from 11.2 to include the men and the 'friends' of the women in the action.

משכנתה (3.22)   The majority of SP mss have משכינתה, which could be simply a plene spelling, but it is read as a Hiphil participle in the Sam. oral tradition (J. Joosten, pers. comm.) and should be preferred to von Gall's MT reading.

מגרת ביתה (3.22)   Again the majority of SP mss diverge from MT, reading מגירת ביתה, which is perhaps best understood as incorporating the feminine form of a common word for 'neighbour, housemate', as in Jewish Aramaic, מגיר(א) (cf. Tg^{N,F} for MT משכנתה here). Such an interpretation is facilitated and perhaps only made possible by SP's earlier use of the compound preposition מאת (from 11.2). At any rate this reading should be regarded as the standard SP text. The meaning 'housemate' is also given by LXX's συσκήνου, perhaps on the basis of the same Aramaic word. Symm has σταθμούχου, 'landlord', here presumably 'landlady', which may be what Vulg intends by its ambiguous *hospita*, but the interpretation owes more to logic than philology: the owner of a house being more likely to have been Egyptian and to have had objects of silver and gold. Tg^{O,J} render גרת by the word קרבית, 'near', which can mean 'a relative', but may here mean 'neighbour' (cf. Tg^J's addition 'of the wall'), thus avoiding the possible implication of MT that Egyptians and Israelites lived under the same roof (so Salvesen, *Symmachus*, p. 69). Tg^N combines this expression with תותבת, 'temporary resident' (cf. Heb. תושב), which is also used (alone) by Sy and seems to point to someone who actually lived in the Israelite woman's house.

כלי (3.22) The renderings in the Versions (e.g. LXX σκεύη, Vulg *vasa*) seem not to envisage the items of jewellery favoured by modern commentators.

כסף וזהב (3.22) The order is reversed in a group of LXX mss and in most mss of Sy, though not in 5b1, which agrees with MT as it does in two of the comparable cases in Genesis and Exodus (Gen. 24.53; 44.8), but not in Exod. 20.23. 5b1's general use (as here) of *ksp'* rather than the 'more modern' word *s'm'* to render כסף is also distinctive (cf. Koster, *Peshiṭta of Exodus*, pp. 70-72; Weitzman, *Syriac Version*, pp. 275-76, 289-90).

ושמתם (3.22) Tg^J העטרון, 'decorate', is a rare case of an ancient Version implying that jewellery was to be secured from the Egyptians.

ונצלתם (3.22) The 'strong' interpretation of נצל Piel as 'plunder' is followed by LXX, σκυλεύσατε, Aq, συλήσατε, and Vulg, *spoliatis*. Sy has the less military but still violent sense of 'shake out, clear out' (*nps*), which is represented in a Greek form known to Procopius of Gaza, probably from Eusebius of Emesa (so F. Petit, *La chaîne sur l'Exode*, II-III [TEG 10; Leuven, 2000], p. 111). Procopius also knew the milder interpretation still found in the Tgg, 'empty' (רוקן: i.e. the same root used by the Tgg at the end of v. 21 for ריקם). A reading of the same type is popular in the LXX tradition: συσκευάσατε, probably 'deceive' (so also Symm according to Salvesen, *Symmachus*, pp. 69-70, but the evidence is divided and Wevers attributes to him the original LXX reading: *Notes*, p. 39 n. 36). These latter readings are probably associated with the various attempts to defend the Israelites' action as justified rather than predatory. The Samaritan Greek version (in Wevers' apparatus) read καὶ διασώθητε ἀπὸ τῶν Αἰγυπτίων, taking the verb as Niphal and apparently reading מאת (by dittography) for the following את (cf. Pummer, 'Greek Bible', p. 297). There is no trace of this variant in Heb. mss of SP or in SamTg.

Chapter 4.1-9

Moses' First Objection Countered

The dialogue between Moses and Yahweh continues when it might be expected to have finished. Moses' intervention this time is in the form not of questions (as in 3.11 and 13) but of (negative) statements that relate once again, but in the opposite order, to the people's expected response when Moses returns to them and (in 4.10-16) to Moses' perception of his own capacity to fulfil his role. Yahweh's response is also different: not simply words of encouragement but the provision of additional support, in vv. 1-9 by means of miraculous signs and later by the use of an intermediary, Aaron, Moses' brother. This revised plan is then put into operation successfully at the end of the chapter (vv. 27-31).

The key motif in vv. 1-9 is whether the people will 'believe' (vv. 1, 5, 8, 9) that Moses has indeed met with Yahweh, who is the God of their ancestors and by implication their true God. Not one but three 'signs' are given to persuade them that this is the case, three being a favoured number of popular tradition, but also (cf. vv. 8-9a) a recognition of the difficulty that there might be in convincing the people. Nevertheless, the signs are not in any obvious order of impressiveness, and the final one does not involve the element of reversal that is present in the other two. The structure of the first two sign-narratives is in fact very similar, although there are distinctive elements in each case: the opening question and the reaction of Moses in vv. 2-5, the secondary action of Moses' withdrawal of his hand from inside his cloak, for which there is no explicit command, in vv. 6-8. The differences in the third case are considerable: in addition to the lack of reversal, there is no obedient action on Moses' part, no separate speech introduction, and the explanation precedes rather than follows the action and lacks the positive assurance found in the other two cases. It is a rather weak ending to the passage, not unlike the way that 1.22 is attached to 1.15-21.

The use of a miraculous sign or signs to authenticate the genuineness of a person's claim to contact with the deity is most closely paralleled, in the OT, in the legends about pre-classical prophecy: cf. 1 Kgs 13.3-5; 17.24; 18.36; 2 Kgs 1.10, 12; 5.8.[1] The law in Deut. 13.1-5 presupposes that such claims to authentication were common and subjects them to severe regulation. Isaiah 7.9-15 will have a similar background. This, rather than Egyptian magic (as illustrated, for example, by Papyrus Westcar: see the note on vv. 2-4), will be the more immediate background to these parts of the Moses tradition. Reference is sometimes made (e.g. Van Seters, *Life of Moses*, pp. 55-57) to the role of signs in the calling of Gideon (Judg. 6) and Saul (1 Sam. 10), but the purpose of these is to reassure the popular leader himself rather than the people more generally.[2]

Because of its links to 3.16-18, most critical scholars until the 1970s attributed this passage to the J source, either in its entirety (Wellhausen, *Composition*, p. 70; Dillmann, pp. 22-23 [his C source, but without making an original connection to 3.18], Carpenter/Harford-Battersby, Baentsch, McNeile, Rudolph, *Elohist*, p. 14, Childs) or with the exception of some later additions (Holzinger – vv. 5, 8, 9; Gressmann, *Mose*, pp. 42-45, 50, *Anfänge*, p. 35 – v. 9; Noth, pp. 22, 32, ET, pp. 34, 45-46 – vv. 5, 8, 9; Hyatt – v. 5).[3] It formed part of the third early source according to Smend (p. 118), Eissfeldt (p. 33), Beer and Fohrer (*Überlieferung*, pp. 29-30, 44-45), but their arguments against its being from the main J source were not strong (its 'derb populäre' character [Smend]; the failure to mention elders [Fohrer]; the contrast to the plague-stories [Eissfeldt]).

L. Schmidt, in an article first published in 1977 ('Überlegungen', p. 234) attributed the main body of the passage to a later redactor, with vv. 30-31a, and thought that that vv. 5 and 9 (but not 8) were later still. In the following years a group of scholars saw it, in whole or in part, as the work of R^{JE} in the late eighth or seventh century (Valentin, *Aaron*, pp. 138-39; Weimar, *Berufung*, pp. 59-65; W.H. Schmidt, p. 197; Kohata, *Jahwist*, pp. 83-84). A somewhat later background, in the exilic period, was advocated by Blum (*Studien*, pp. 32, 104) and Van Seters (*Life*, pp. 55-58). But already in 1982

---

[1] The verse following the first of these passages, 1 Kgs 13.6, recounts the healing of a diseased hand which is very similar to Exod. 4.7.

[2] Childs (pp. 144-49) notes the similarity between the (JE) plague-stories and prophetic legends of 'power' (as distinct from 'word'): that would be a parallel, though not identical, case to this.

[3] Eissfeldt, *Synopse*, p. 33, wrote that its origin had been disputed and that it was not often attributed to a source, but he gave no examples. See below on Knobel.

H.-C. Schmitt had argued, in the 'shadow' of Rendtorff's new suggestions about the composition of the Pentateuch, that these verses belonged to a very late redactional layer which was dependent on the Priestly section 2.23-25 ('Redaktion', pp. 181-82) and on the Priestly plague-narrative (p. 184). This very late dating has become increasingly popular in recent years (Levin, pp. 331-32; Otto, 'Pentateuchredaktion', pp. 101-106; Schmid, *Erzväter*, pp. 199, 203-205, 248; Gertz, *Tradition*, pp. 305-15; and now even Blum, in 'Literarische Verbindung', pp. 129-30).[4]

The change of perspective in scholarly estimation of this passage can be traced to two factors. One is R. Smend's article on the history of the verb *he*ᵡ*mîn*, 'believe' ('Zur Geschichte von האמין', in B. Hartmann et al. [eds.], *Hebräische Wortforschung* [FS W. Baumgartner; VTSup 16; Leiden, 1967], pp. 284-90). This at first left on one side the examples of *he*ᵡ*mîn* in Exod. 4.1-9, because they related to the truthfulness of a human being, to which there are a number of parallels (see the Explanatory Note on v. 1), rather than to faith in God (p. 285). Only after it had been concluded, because of uncertainty about the antiquity of other uses which refer to faith in God, that this was an innovation of the prophet Isaiah, were the cases referring to Moses brought into the discussion, again as part of a redactional layer, which included Exod. 14.31 and 19.9 and was deemed by Smend to be later than Isaiah, presumably because of the inclusion of Yahweh alongside Moses as the object of the people's trust in 14.31 (cf. 4.31). Whatever may be the case about the origin of the application of *he*ᵡ*mîn* to faith in God (and Smend's view is not as convincing as often seems to be assumed),[5] the uses in 4.1-9 with reference to Moses are a separate issue and scarcely a sure basis on which to date the passage after the time of Isaiah. One would imagine in fact that uses of *he*ᵡ*mîn* in relation to humans would be likely to precede the beginning of its use with reference to God, whenever that happened. Similar caution

---

[4] Propp is the only recent commentator to advocate a pre-exilic origin: he attributes the passage to E (p. 191). Graupner (*Elohist*, p. 19), who has no reason to treat the passage in detail, describes the whole of 4.1-17 as 'eine ausgestaltende Fortschreibung', which picks up from 3.11-12 and ignores 3.13-22(!): he evidently derives it from R^JE (pp. 61, 119), like W.H. Schmidt whom he follows elsewhere, and the curious arguments he puts forward seem to be taken from him (see his *Exodus*, pp. 192, 196).

[5] Caution is especially in place, lest (a particular view of) the history of a word be taken to represent the history of the concept which it denotes, since the latter may also be conveyed in other ways, e.g. by metaphors of Yahweh as 'rock' or 'refuge' (Ps. 18.3 etc.). Moreover, as H. Wildberger already pointed out (cf. *THAT* 1, 190 = *TLOT* 1, pp. 143-44), the use of *he*ᵡ*mîn* in Isa. 7.4-9 is probably based on earlier usage in oracles delivered to the king, as is well attested in Assyrian prophecy (see, e.g., *ANET*, p. 450; S. Parpola, *Assyrian Prophecies* [SAA 9; Helsinki, 1997], pp. 4, 7, 10 [cf. lxvi]; M. Nissinen, *Prophets and Prophecy in the Ancient Near East* [Leiden, 2003], pp. 102, 107, 110).

is expressed by A. Jepsen (*TWAT* 1, 331 = *TDOT* 1, p. 30): 'As far as the history of the word *he'emin* is concerned, its occurrences in the OT are much too scanty for anyone to be able to venture a reconstruction. Only detached observations can be made.'

The second factor is the appearance of similar 'wonders' in the plague-stories of ch. 7, and specifically the Priestly version of them, which has suggested to a number of scholars that 4.1-9 is modelled on and therefore later than the Priestly source or composition. Similar arguments have been put forward in relation to other parts of chs. 3 and 4 which have parallels in the Priestly sections of chs. 6–7 by scholars such as Otto and K. Schmid.[6] There is probably enough similarity between the Priestly and non-Priestly narratives of Moses' call to indicate some kind of relationship between them (cf. Schmidt, pp. 192-93), but the questions are: how extensive is it? what is its nature? and in what direction is dependence to be assumed? Only if it can be shown that Exodus 3–4, and specifically 4.1-9, are modelled on parts of chs. 6–7 is a post-Priestly origin for the former established. The case for a dependence of P on Exod. 4.1-9 has been presented by Schmidt (pp. 193-96), on whom Kohata (pp. 250-54) and Van Seters (*Life*, pp. 53-55) both depend. Many points that can be made are really indecisive for determining the direction of dependence, as Kohata in particular recognises, and sometimes the differences between the respective passages are so great that it becomes questionable whether there is a direct literary relationship between them at all rather than a shared oral tradition. One important difference is the inclusion in ch. 4 of Moses' temporary skin-disease. In view of the association of such afflictions with uncleanness it is surely much easier to understand why P would have omitted it than how a presumed even later redactor would have been able to add it to the sequence of actions performed by Moses. The absence of anything similar in the P plague-story also makes it necessary to assume that the redactor either invented the miracle out of thin air or, perhaps more likely, modelled it on what happens to Miriam in Numbers 12, which is of course a punishment. A further argument in favour of 4.1-9 being more original is that if P had this passage (or tradition) available to him it helps to explain why his plague-story begins in such a different way from that of J(E) (cf. Schmidt, p. 196). In the wider context, Blum has shown the inadequacy of the arguments for seeing Exodus 3 as dependent on Exodus 6 ('Literarische Verbindung', pp. 124-27). In 4.10-17, which might well on general grounds seem likely to be a case where the P parallel (6.12, 28-30; 7.1-2) is more original, as Valentin argued (*Aaron*, pp. 47-140), in view of the clearer motivation which P had for giving Aaron a prominent place in the Exodus

---

[6] This also seems to be what one of the pioneers of modern Pentateuchal criticism, Knobel, had in mind when he described 4.1-17 as consisting of 'imitations' and a 'free Je narrative' (p. 23). He of course, like most in his time, thought that 'P' was the oldest of all the sources, composed in the time of Saul.

story, the reference to Aaron as a Levite (הלוי) in 4.14 (but not in 7.1-2) needs to be carefully noted. In the context this should be an honorific title, but the laws about the priesthood in P which the redactor would *ex hypothesi* have known would have rendered it quite the opposite, and scarcely an expression which would at that time have been applied to Aaron (cf. Schmidt, p. 195; Kohata, p. 91; Van Seters, pp. 54-55).

In favour of a late redactional origin Otto cites the 'belief' strand, which he would now attribute elsewhere (4.31; 14.31; 19.9) to the PentR, who used it to build up authority for the revelation of the law at Sinai (a point taken up by Gertz) and the resemblance of Moses' obedience to Yahweh to the standard Priestly pattern of this. He also observes that Schmidt's comments about the numerous minor differences between 4.1-9 and the P parallels only have force if the redactor is seen as a wooden copyist, when there is reason to see him as a creative narrator. Schmid engages less in detailed argument, but makes a positive virtue out of the contrasts between the overall function and profile of the respective passages, since they lead to belief on Israel's part (4.30) but to unbelief in Pharaoh (7.13). The discussion of Gertz is, as always, much fuller: it begins with arguments based on connections with ch. 3, where he has already identified major contributions from EndR (his term for PentR), but then proceeds (after a lengthy demonstration of the literary unity of 4.1-17) to comparisons with the Priestly texts in ch. 7. He shows how the author of 4.1-9 could have adapted the Priestly texts to his purpose, and notes two specific arguments for the dependence of 4.9 on 7.14-22*: the Nile water miracle is out of place in the desert, so should be secondary there, and the word for 'dry ground' (Heb. *yabbāšāh*) is a Priestly word. He also considers in detail the reference to Aaron as a Levite (pp. 321-27) and argues from a review of other references to the post-exilic priesthood that the redactor may have been seeking a rapprochement from the 'Levite' side with the 'exclusive Aaronide' party (cf. Blum's reference in *Studien*, p. 362, to 'bridge-building' here). Blum observes in addition a parallel with the two accounts of the covenant with Abraham in Genesis 15 and 17, which he thinks confirms the purposefulness of the redactor in anticipating 'later' problems in the narrative.

Much of the argument on both sides is inconclusive. Clearly the author of 4.1-9 and P have carefully shaped the motifs they share in the interests of their different aims, but it is practically impossible to detect traces of one in the other, nor can an unanswerable account be given of why one version would have been composed after the other. Perhaps it is unavoidable that conclusions will be determined by decisions made about other passages, especially in ch. 3. The basis for a late dating in the 'belief' strand has surely been exaggerated. There may well be a case for regarding 4.9 as a secondary addition to the passage, and if so the use of *yabbāšāh* (rather than J's word *ḥārābāh*: Gen. 7.22; Exod. 14.21) would be an argument for dependence on P. But the rest of the passage can reasonably be attributed to a pre-exilic J, which would fit best with the setting when prophetic claims were supported by actions of this kind (see above). With vv. 10-12 it extends the parallel to E's account of Moses' commissioning in 3.9-15 (+4.17).[7]

Theologically, the concern with Moses' credibility as the bearer of Yahweh's promise of deliverance (3.16-20: cf. vv. 7-12) is central and taken up again at the end of the chapter (vv. 27-31, esp. v. 31). This is an important issue for the later part of the book (cf. 14.31; 19.9), where it is dealt with again in different, more impressive ways. While this is not the same as belief in the credibility of an informant on purely human affairs (as in Gen. 45.26 etc.), it is also not the same as faith in God absolutely, even if the two are understandably joined together in 14.31.[8] Moses is presented here in the guise of some of the pre-classical prophets, whose ability to perform 'acts of power' was seen as a demonstration of their divine authorisation. It was not a foolproof argument, as both the law in Deuteronomy 13 and the handling of the motif in the Priestly source (cf. 7.11-12, 22; 8.7) show, and it most likely reflects a fairly early and unsophisticated stage in the traditions about Moses. The identity of the God in whose name Moses speaks is naturally expressed not only by the divine name but by reference to the great figures of the past (v. 5), as in the words that Moses has been instructed to use (3.16, though the wording of this epithet [for which cf. 1 Kgs 18.36] is more precisely anticipated in 3.15). This emphasis on continuity has been an important theme of chs. 1–4, and it will reappear in the Priestly version in 6.2-8, but it is not mentioned again in the older material until 32.13 (cf. 33.1). The present, or from the point of view of later Israel, the narrative of the Exodus and the revelation at Sinai, now excludes attention to anything else.

---

[7] The contradiction between 4.17 (Moses performs 'the signs') and Aaron's role in the Priestly account of the plagues is a serious problem for the dependence of ch. 4 on chs. 6–7; and it may be doubted whether calling Aaron a Levite would be enough to challenge the Aaronides' primacy.

[8] H. Gross, 'Der Glaube an Mose nach Exodus (4.14.19)', in J.J. Stamm et al. (eds.) *Wort-Gebot-Glaube* (FS W. Eichrodt; ATANT 57; Zurich, 1970), pp. 57-65, fails to make this distinction clear and mistakenly reads 4.31 as a reference to faith in God.

1 Moses answered and said, 'But look\[a\], they will not believe me or accept what I say. For\[b\] they will say, "Yahweh has not appeared to you".' 2 Yahweh said to him, 'What is this\[c\] in your hand?' He said, 'A staff'. 3 He said, 'Throw it on the ground'. So he threw it on the ground and it became a snake; and Moses fled away\[d\] from it. 4 Yahweh said to Moses, 'Stretch out your hand and take hold of its tail – he stretched out his hand and took hold of it, and it became a staff in his hand – 5 so that\[e\] they may believe that Yahweh, the God of their fathers, the God of Abraham, the God of Isaac and the God of Jacob, has appeared to you'. 6 Yahweh said to him again, 'Please\[f\], put your hand inside your cloak\[g\]'. So he put his hand inside his cloak, and when he brought it out\[h\] he saw that the skin of his hand was diseased\[i\], like snow\[j\]. 7 He said, 'Put your hand back inside your cloak'. So he put his hand back inside his cloak, and when he brought it out from inside his cloak\[h\] he saw that it had become like his (normal) flesh again\[k\]. 8 (Yahweh said,)\[l\] 'If they do not believe you and do not heed what the former sign says\[m\], they will believe what the latter sign says\[m\]. 9 [If they do not believe even these two signs\[n\], or accept what you say, then you shall take some of the water of the Nile and pour it on the dry ground\[o\], and the water which you take from the Nile shall become\[p\] blood on the dry ground\[o\].]'

Notes on the Translation

a. Heb. וְהֵן. Some, e.g. Schmidt and Houtman, render '(What) if…' (cf. NRSV, 'But suppose…'), but it is controversial whether or how often הן bears this meaning in Heb., as it does in some dialects of Aramaic (including Biblical Aramaic). The lexica allow it and give examples, including this passage and 8.22 (BDB, p. 243b; *HAL*, p. 241b; *Ges18*, pp. 281-82; *DCH* 2, p. 572, '[when] followed by question functioning as apodosis of conditional sentence'): likewise GK §159w, but regarding it as a separate lexeme ('a pure Aramaism'), as הן never means 'behold' in Aramaic (this still seems to be true: see *DNWSI*, p. 286). JM §167l also regards this meaning as Aram. and gives a much shorter list, including only passages likely to be exilic or later (and not this one). The meaning 'if' is apparently not found in Ugaritic (cf. *DULAT*, pp. 342-43) or Phoenician (*DNWSI*, pp. 285-86), and the two instances in epigraphic Hebrew (*AHI* 2.21.3, 2.40.9) are both in (broken) contexts which there is no reason to regard as conditional. D.M. Stec ('The Use of *hēn* in Conditional Sentences', *VT* 37 [1987], pp. 478-86) examined all the alleged cases of *hēn* = 'if' in BH and concluded that 'Conditional sentences containing *hēn* are conditional not because of the presence of *hēn* but because of other syntactical considerations', the meaning of *hēn* itself always being 'Behold' (except for 2 Chr. 7.13, which is due to Aramaic influence) (p. 485). W.R. Garr's fuller study of the particle comes to much the same conclusion ('הֵן', *RB* 111 [2004], pp. 321-44 [336, 341]), but distinguishes הֵן more sharply from הִנֵּה: 'הִנֵּה presents; הֵן affirms or confirms' (343). In Exod. 4.1 there is no grammatical basis for a conditional rendering at all, because there is no plausible apodosis (one has to be supplied), as Childs saw: the basis for such a rendering comes from the desire to avoid too sharp a denial of what has been said in 3.18a (Houtman, pp. 389-90, who gives a list of older attempts to resolve the 'problem' in other ways) or from deductions from Yahweh's responses in vv. 5 and 8-9 (Schmidt, pp. 185-86). See further on Text and Versions.

b. Heb. כִּי. As a negative has preceded, the meaning could be 'But' (BDB, p. 474; JM §172c), as in Vulg.

c. Heb. מַזֶּה, which is probably more original than the regular מַה זֶּה of the Qere (see Text and Versions for SP). Such contraction into a single word is found elsewhere only in Isa. 3.15K; Ezek. 8.6K; Mal. 1.13; 1 Chr. 15.13 (unless MT is to be emended to a form of מִן) and 2 Chr. 30.3, the last two cases representing idiomatic and perhaps conversational uses of מַה. The contraction is not surprising, given the proclitic character of מַה (JM §37c) which frequently leads to the doubling of the following letter even when מַה is a separate word (see *DCH* 5, p. 150, for two further examples at Qumran, both like Ezek. 8.6 and here with a pronoun).

d. Heb. וַיָּנָס. Several modern translations offer alternatives to 'fled': 'drew back' (JB, NRSV), 'recoiled' (NJPS), 'drew back hastily' (REB: for this cf. G.R. Driver's comment on Judg. 6.11 in 'Problems in Judges Newly Discussed', *ALUOS* 4 [1962–63], pp. 6-25 [12], where he cited only הֵרִיץ in Gen. 41.14 as another way of saying 'move quickly'). There is no clear parallel for this meaning, nor do the lexica (or the Versions) support it. Sometimes the root נוּס means 'reach safety' (Jer. 46.6; Amos 9.1 – perhaps also 5.19) or in the Hiphil 'bring to safety, keep safe' (Exod. 9.20; Judg. 6.11; perhaps similarly the Hithpolel in Ps. 60.6 (*HAL*, *DCH*) if it is from נוּס and not from נסס, and the noun מָנוֹס means 'a place of refuge', so that 'reached safety' is a possibility. But מִפָּנָיו favours 'fled'.

e. It is clear that v. 5 is not part of the narrative but comprises words spoken to Moses (cf. אֵלֶיךָ), presumably as the continuation of the speech of Yahweh in v. 4a: but there is no indication that direct speech has been resumed in most of the textual witnesses (see, however, Text and Versions), which is unusual (though cf. v. 8), and in any case why is the purpose clause delayed? A somewhat similar transition, also beginning with לְמַעַן, has been noted at Gen. 37.22b by Gressmann and Schmidt, but that is the other way round, with narrative resuming after a speech, and easier (cf. also Gen. 3.22-23). Here it is common (cf. RSV, NJPS, NRSV) to regard v. 4b as interposed within the words of Yahweh in vv. 4a and 5 to suggest vividly that Moses acts as he has been instructed even before Yahweh has finished speaking. In a lively dialogue omission of 'And he said' occasionally occurs elsewhere in OT narrative (cf. Josh. 24.(22-)23; 2 Sam. 18.(22-)23; 2 Kings 10.15 and Fischer, *Jahwe Unser Gott*, p. 175 n. 212).

f. Heb. נא, a particle of entreaty which is unexpected in a divine utterance (4QExod[b] adds it in v. 3 too); but cf. Gen. 13.14; 22.2; Exod. 11.2; Isa. 7.3, all as here in a command, but perhaps with an element of condescension or intimacy when God is dealing with his human servants (compare also the use by Elijah when speaking to his servant in 1 Kgs 18.43, but not before the king in v. 41: JM §105c n.2).

g. Heb. בחיקך. See Houtman's discussion (p. 394) and *TWAT* 2, 912-15 = *TDOT* 4, pp. 356-58: חיק refers to parts of the front of the body from the chest to the lap and is characteristically a place where a young child or animal can be held, or indeed a sexual partner embraced (e.g. Mic. 7.5). But this occurrence belongs, as the use of יצא and indeed בוא as its counterpart ('go *in*, put *in*': BDB, pp. 97, 99) shows, to a group of passages in which the reference is to the fold of a garment (Prov. 6.27; 17.23; 21.14: cf. Ps. 74.13Q): 'pocket' would be the modern English equivalent. The common semantic component of all the uses of חיק (including those without a human point of reference at all) seems to be 'something enclosed'.

h. The logical subordination of these clauses is indicated by the following exclamation והנה (cf. 9.7): see in general GK §164b.

i. Heb. מצרעת, still rendered 'leprous' in NIV and NRSV, despite the general recognition now that neither צרעת in the OT nor λέπρα in the NT nor related words referred to what is known as 'leprosy' today (so-called Hansen's disease). The majority of the OT references to this disease come in Leviticus 13–14, where it afflicts not only persons but house-walls and clothing, which are in consequence regarded as 'unclean'. It covered a range of disfiguring skin diseases. For fuller discussion see the references in Schmidt (p. 199) and Houtman (p. 395 n. 126), esp. E.V. Hulse, 'The Nature of Biblical "Leprosy" and the Use of Alternate Medical Terms in Modern Translations of the Bible', *PEQ* 107 (1975), pp. 87-105, and most recently H. Avalos, *Illness and Health Care in the Ancient Near East* (HSM 54; Atlanta, 1995), pp. 311-16, and J. Milgrom, *Leviticus 1–16* (AB; New York, 1991), pp. 816-26: also *ABD* 4, pp. 277-82, and M. Marrazza, 'Analisi Componenziale del lessema צָרַעַת in EA', *Materia Giudaica* 23 (2019), pp. 51-68 (with recent bibliography). Hulse points out that, since Leviticus 13 is concerned to distinguish צרעת from other similar afflictions, it does not give a full description of its main symptoms. Narrative accounts, especially this one, Num. 12.10-12 and 2 Kings 5, are actually more informative, he argues, and the comparison to a stillborn foetus in Num. 12.12 points to skin diseases in which scales form, like psoriasis. The resemblance to snow, as here, might make the same point, rather than whiteness being meant (the addition of 'white' in EVV. here and in Num. 12.10 and 2 Kgs 5.27 has no foundation in the Heb.). NJPS, 'encrusted in snowy scales', expresses this interpretation well. Our less specific rendering is based on NEB and REB. Marrazza concludes that, while 2 Kings 5 has a specific infection (scabies) in view, Leviticus 13–14 use צרעה as a generic term for various discolorations judged to be in need of ritual cleansing.

j. Heb. כשלג, 'like *the* snow', with the article appearing as often in comparisons and with substances (JM §137i). See also the Explanatory Note.

k. Heb. שבה כבשרו. For the sense of שוב as '*changed* back' the best parallels are in Job 33.25-26, where לאנוש צדקתו corresponds to כבשרו here. Possibly some of the collocations of שוב with עפר etc. (e.g. Gen. 3.19) involve the same sense; more generally cf. Ezek. 16.55; Ps. 80.4, 8, 20; Dan. 9.25. For the specific sense of healing cf. 1 Kgs 13.6; 2 Kgs 5.10, 14, though the idioms are slightly different there. The rendering 'restored like the rest of his body' (Vulg, NRSV; cf. Houtman, p. 397) is less likely.

l. The resumption of direct speech without an introductory 'He/Yahweh said' is most unusual in Hebrew narrative (but cf. v. 5 and Note e above; in the NT cf. Luke 5.14). Verse 7aβb could be regarded as virtually parenthetical, like v. 4b, but the continuation of Yahweh's speech to provide a third sign makes this less likely here, as does the use of the formal introductory והיה in v. 8.

m. Heb. קול, here denoting the meaning or content of the sign, an extension of the more natural use for the content of words spoken as, e.g., in Gen. 45.16; Deut. 5.28, and esp. in LBH (see references in *THAT* 2, 631-32 = *TLOT* 3, p. 1134), but there are similar extended uses in Ugaritic (*KTU* 1.100.2) and an early Punic inscription from Malta (*KAI* 61A, 5-6).

n. Wildberger translates 'believe *because of* these two signs, taking ל in the sense 'on account of' (BDB, p. 514, 5g) and so avoiding the idea of faith *in* signs or miracles (*THAT* 1, 188-89 = *TLOT* 1, p. 142 and bibliography there). This seems less likely: the formulation of the previous verse implies that the signs 'say' something which the Israelites are expected to 'believe', namely that Moses does indeed have a commission from God. For ל referring to belief in an utterance as well as a person see 1 Kgs 10.7; Isa. 53.1; Ps. 106.24; Prov. 14.15.

o. The use of the alternative forms יבשה and יבשת within a single verse is curious (for similar variation compare פיו and פיהו in v. 15): perhaps it is to avoid rhyme between two parts of the sentence. The latter form occurs elsewhere only in Ps. 95.5. In the first case the noun is used adverbially of direction (GK §118d, f).

p. MT's repetition of והיו (see also Text and Versions on the second instance) is due to the length of the intervening relative clause: cf. JM §176b, n. 2, and further parallels in Schmidt, p. 186.

Explanatory Notes

1. Just as Moses' question in 3.13 responds to Yahweh's words in 3.10-12, so here his rejoinder ('answered') picks up elements from Yahweh's speech in 3.16-22: Moses denies that the people will 'accept what he says', as Yahweh has promised in 3.18, anticipating that they will reject the truth of the claim that Yahweh has 'appeared' to him, which he has been instructed by Yahweh to make in 3.16. These two motifs continue in the following verses (vv. 5, 9), but they are overlaid and dominated by a new expression, 'they will not believe (Moses)' (see, in addition to v. 1, vv. 5, 8 and 9), and it is this which sums up the people's eventual positive response at the end of the chapter (v. 31). 'Believe' (Heb. $he^{\ast}mîn$) is not here an expression for faith in God, as it is in Gen. 15.6: it is Moses' credibility which is at issue, a point which LXX emphasised by several additions to its translation (see the textual notes on vv. 5, 8 and 9). More precisely, v. 5 too makes clear that the focus is on the specific claim that Yahweh has appeared to Moses, and the use of the preposition l (rather then b) after $he^{\ast}mîn$ is especially frequent when (as here) the truth of a report is involved (cf. Gen. 45.26; 1 Kgs 10.7/ 2 Chr. 9.6; Isa. 53.1; Jer. 40.14; Prov. 14.15: Jepsen, *TWAT* 1, 324-26 = *TDOT* 1, pp. 302-303).

2-5. Yahweh's response to the danger that the people will not believe Moses is to provide evidence ('signs', vv. 8-9) that will convince them, not to condemn them for rebellion as in Num. 14.11 and Deut. 9.23 (Wildberger, *THAT* 1, 192-93 = *TLOT* 1, p. 145, is mistaken to associate Exodus 4 with such passages, despite some overlap of terminology). Each of the three signs also looks forward to the subsequent narrative in which Moses confronts Pharaoh. Moses' staff (cf. 4.17, 20) is used in three of the plagues (Exod. 7.15, 17, 20; 9.23; 10.13) as well as at the Red Sea (14.16) and at Rephidim (17.5, 9).[9] Nothing is said about its origin: it is apparently presumed that a shepherd would have one to tend his flock (cf. Ps. 23.4). The opening exchange between Yahweh and Moses is similar to the beginning of some prophetic vision-reports (Jer. 1.11,

---

[9] In the P narrative strand Aaron's rod takes its place in four of the 'signs and wonders' (7.9-10, 12; 7.19; 8.1; 8.12-13), the first of which has some similarities to 4.2-4: see the introduction to this section on the relationship between the two passages.

13; Amos 7.8; 8.1), but the continuation is naturally quite different. From here on only Yahweh speaks: Moses responds with obedient action, at one point apparently before Yahweh has finished speaking (see Note e on the translation), which allows the episode to end appropriately with the statement of its purpose. This is formulated in a way that once again (cf. 3.15-16) underlines the continuity with the earlier story in Genesis. Although the theological component in the narrative excludes a purely magical interpretation of it, comparisons have been noted with snake-charming (Houtman, pp. 391-92, though with a recognition of the differences) and more plausibly with an Egyptian tale in *King Cheops and the Magicians* of a priest who turned a wax crocodile into a real one and then reversed the process (P. Westcar I.17-IV.17 (mid-second mill. B.C.): Schmidt, p. 189; ET in A. Erman, *The Literature of the Ancient Egyptians* [London, 1927], pp. 36-47 [36-38]).

6-8. The second sign concerns Moses' hand, which also plays a prominent part in the later Exodus narrative, both in the older material (9.22; 10.12, 21-22: cf. 17.11-12) and in the Priestly version (8.1-2, 13; 14.16, 21, 26). The pattern is similar: only Yahweh speaks, Moses responds obediently, and there is a concluding confirmation that the purpose of the sign is to bring about acceptance of what Moses has said. Although the disease which temporarily affected Moses' hand cannot have been 'leprosy' as it is encountered in the modern world, for which there is no evidence in Europe and the Middle East in the OT period (see also Note i on the translation), it is clear from the legislation in Leviticus 13–14 and narratives such as Numbers 12 (Miriam) and 2 Kings 5 (Naaman) that it was an unpleasant and repulsive affliction.

9. The third and final sign, like the first, finds an echo in Moses' confrontation with Pharaoh (Exod. 7.14-24), but it is on a much more limited scale, as befits its purpose here. The description of it is necessarily much briefer than those of the other two signs, because it could not be 'rehearsed' in the desert outside Egypt. A number of parallels to the conversion of water, including the Nile, to (the appearance of) blood are cited with references by Propp, pp. 348-49. There is no reason to see the signs as more than the demonstration of Moses' divine commission by means of miraculous power: Houtman lists the numerous ingenious attempts to find a deeper meaning in them, but he rightly rejects them (pp. 392-94,

398-99, 402-403). The word for 'dry ground' here (*ybšh/ybšt*) is the characteristic expression of Priestly texts in the Pentateuch (Gen. 1.9-10; Exod. 14.16, 22, 29: contrast the *ḥrbh* of the older narrative in 14.21 and Gen. 7.22 etc.) and lends some support to the view that v. 9 is a later addition to this passage (see the Introduction).

Text and Versions

והן (4.1)   LXX has ἐὰν οὖν, 'So if...', following the Aramaic/Aramaising use of הן (see Note a on the translation), but then has to supply as an apodosis τί ἐρῶ πρὸς αὐτούς, which Aejmelaeus thinks reflects the original Hebrew here (*On the Track*, pp. 104-105), but it is suspiciously identical to the end of 3.13 and probably secondary. Tg^N, אין, also seems to take הן as 'if' with an implied question (so the Sp. tr. and *AramB* 2, p. 21), unless אין is here the homonym that means 'indeed'. Its margin has והינון, 'But they...'. The other Versions (inc. Tg^{O,J}) render 'Look' or have no equivalent (Vulg).

בקלי (4.1)   SP reads לקולי, and Sy has *lqly* (elsewhere in Exod. it has *bql* for בקול all 5x). This brings the expression into a precise antithesis to 3.18 (cf. also 4.8-9), where see Note e on the translation. There may have been a sense that 'obedience' which is usually implied by בקול, was not exactly the issue here. There is no evidence for this word in the Qumran mss, but MT should be preferred as the less expected reading.

לא נראה (4.1)   LXX prefixes a ὅτι *recitativum* (cf. Sy 5b1 *dl'*, here for once departing from MT), but there appears to be no room for a כי here in 4QExod^b, so it is to be attributed to the translator's style (see Aejmelaeus, *On the Track*, pp. 44-48). Tgg render נראה by אתגלי, as in 3.16 and elsewhere.

יהוה (4.1)   Tg^{Nmg}, as in vv. 2, 5 and 6, inserts 'the Memra of' (cf. 3.12). LXX reads ὁ θεός, whereas it has the expected κύριος in vv. 2, 4, 5 and 6 (as well as 3.16). This might be due to the fact that it twice has no equivalent for יהוה in 3.18 (see the notes there for the relationship to 5.3) or perhaps, as Wevers suggests (*Notes*, p. 40), follow from the Israelites' presumed rejection of the revelation of the divine name to Moses: but it is a frequent variation in LXX (Propp, p. 187; see also 14.31) and wider factors may be involved. See the discussion by M. Rösel, 'Reading and Translation', esp. pp. 419ff., which suggests several reasons.

יהוה (4.2)   Vulg has no equivalent, but in its abbreviating style this is of no significance.

מזה (4.2)   SP spells as two separate words, מה זה, avoiding the rare contraction (see Note c on the translation) and a possible obscurity.

השליכהו (4.3)   4QExod^b has נא after it, but this finds no support elsewhere. It was probably added to match הבא־נא in v. 6, on which see Note f.

ואחז (4.4)   4QExod[b] has ויחזיק, in line with the execution of the command later in the verse. LXX and Tg[N] also use the same verb in their translations both times, but this need only reflect their own desire for 'balance' (Wevers, *Notes*, p. 41) or simplicity. Vulg, Tg[O,J] and Sy use different verbs and support MT.

זנבו (4.4)   Tg[F] has בית קוטנוי (cf. Tg[Nmg]), which Klein renders 'its tail portion' (*Fragment-Targums* 1, p. 123).

בו (4.4)   LXX τῆς κέρκου, a further example of its quest for 'balance' in this verse.

למען (4.5)   4QGen-Exod[a] survives sufficiently for vv. 4-5 to indicate that it had a slightly longer text than MT: the most likely reconstruction is that it added ויאמר יהוה at the beginning of v. 5 (like many LXX witnesses and Vulg's *inquit*), to ease the sudden change back to direct speech (*DJD* XII, p. 22).

יאמינו (4.5)   LXX πιστεύσωσίν σοι, emphasising that it is Moses' credibility which is at stake, as also in v. 8b.

אבותם (4.5)   Vulg strangely has *patrum tuorum* (a Deuteronomism!), Tg[J] the more adjacent and more suitable דאבהתכון, 'of your (pl.) fathers' (cf. 3.13, 15-16).

אלהי יצחק (4.5)   SP has a preceding *waw* (cf. LXX), as elsewhere in lists.

יהוה לו (4.6)   The text of Tg[N] omits יהוה here (cf. all witnesses in v. 3), but the majority reading is likely to be correct at the beginning of the new sub-section. 4QExod[b] has אליו for לו of MT and SP, with the same variation after אמר as in 3.13-14. A similar variant occurs in SP sometimes (see the textual note on 2.10), with the converse in 8.21 and 10.24. Sy mss, including 7a1, read *lh mry' lmwš'*, but 5b1 omits *lmwš'* and on this occasion the Leiden edition follows it. The addition is in any case bound to be secondary.

ויוצאה (4.6)   An impressive array of witnesses supports the inclusion of מחיקו after this (SP, LXX, 4QGen-Exod[a]; line-length suggests that 4QExod[b] must have read it too, so *DJD* XII, p. 93), but if it was original it is hard to see how it was omitted in MT etc., and harmonisation with v. 7 provides a good explanation for its secondary addition.

מצרעת (4.6)   LXX has no equivalent at all for this, for which apologetic reasons can be suggested in the context of Alexandrian allegations preserved by Josephus (*AJ* 3.265; cf. *c.Ap.* 1.228-320) that Moses was, like the other Israelites, afflicted with skin disease (on the true meaning of λέπρα/λεπρός see Note i on the translation).The substitution of 'white' for 'diseased' is already found in Philo (*Vita* 1.79) and Josephus (*AJ* 2.273), and is taken up in Tg[O] and Tg[J], in the latter with the addition of סגירתא, literally 'locked up', a common euphemism based on Lev. 13.4. The Three, Sy, Vulg and Tg[N] give the correct rendering, and this found its way via Origen's Hexapla into much of the Greek tradition.

ויאמר (4.7)   Sy (except for 5b1) adds *lh mry'* in line with the previous verse.

כבשרו (4.7)   LXX εἰς τὴν χρόαν τῆς σαρκὸς αὐτοῦ: although χροιά/χρόα can mean 'skin, surface', 'colour' fits the context better and this implies that LXX understood the likeness to snow in v. 6 to involve a dis-(or de-) coloration. Tg^J amplifies similarly with למיהוי ברייא, 'to be healthy/in its natural condition', Tg^N adds just the infinitive 'to be', and Tg^G (ms. A, a 'very early' [eighth–ninth cent. or earlier] fragment containing parts of vv. 7-11: Klein 1, pp. xxxvii, 172-73) simply reproduces the wording of MT, like Tg^O.

והיה (4.8)   4QExod^b begins the verse with למען, but nothing more is preserved. It could have stood in place of והיה – 'so that, if they will not believe..., then they will believe...' – to introduce the sudden direct speech in the same way as v. 5 in MT.

לך (4.8)   Sy omits, perhaps through parablepsis. To ease the return to direct speech Vulg inserts *inquit* before it. From the surviving letters it seems that 4QGen-Exod^a had a significantly shorter text of this verse than MT. The omission by homoeoarkton (not 'haplography') later in the verse suggested in *DJD* XII, p. 22, is probably too extensive, and a more likely alternative is that a scribe's eye slipped from the sequence (א)ול לך to the first לקל, which would have resulted in a coherent and concise sentence.

האת (4.8)[10]   Tg^N has נסיה here, which *AramB* 2 renders 'signs', whereas later in the verse it has the expected singular נסה (Tg^G נסא). Unfortunately Tg^G does not survive for the middle of the verse and Tg^J omits the whole verse by a clear case of homoeoarkton. נסיה is unlikely to be either a real plural or the singular of an otherwise unattested word for 'sign': it is presumably a copyist's error, arising either from the plural form in v. 9 or by metathesis from a plene writing ניסה.

והאמינו (4.8)   LXX πιστεύσουσίν σοι, perhaps to match לך earlier in the verse, but in any case again (cf. v. 5) highlighting Moses' credibility.

יאמינו (4.9)   LXX again adds σοι (cf. on vv. 5 and 8).

גם (4.9)   There is no equivalent in LXX and Sy, but גם is clearly attested in the remaining portion of 4QGen-Exod^a as well as the other witnesses.

ישמעון (4.9)   SP ישמעו, omitting the *nun paragogicum*, which it has against MT in 1.22 (for further examples of this variation in both directions see *GSH* §63b).

והיו (4.9, 2°)   SP יהיו, replacing the idiomatic perfect with resumptive *waw* (see Note o on the translation) by the simpler imperfect. Confusion between *waw* and *yodh* could have facilitated the change.

Chapter 4.10-17

Moses' Second and Third Objections Countered

Moses' further objections to his commission (and Yahweh's answers to them) focus on the issue of who is to speak to Israel on Yahweh's behalf, and how. The passage presupposes that Yahweh has already spoken to Moses (v. 10) and given him a message to deliver to Israel (vv. 15-16: 'the words...the people'). It thus shares the presuppositions of 4.1-9 (cf. v. 1) and connections with that passage can be found, not it is true at the beginning or indeed anywhere in vv. 10-12, but in vv. 15 ('what you are to do') and 17 (but see the Explanatory Notes). The passage consists of two halves, each comprising a short speech of Moses (vv. 10 and 13) and a longer one by Yahweh (vv. 11-12, 14aβ-17), in which the second half clearly arises out of the first (cf. the verbal echoes cited in the Explanatory Notes). The dialogue pattern established in vv. 1-9 is thus continued, but it concludes after v. 17 (cf. the *petuchah* and division of synagogue readings in MT), with Moses' departure and return to Jethro. 4.27-31 is its continuation (after the next *petuchah*).

There is an obvious affinity between the role of Moses (and Aaron) here and that of a prophet, and this is reinforced by some of the expressions used, which also appear in prophetic narratives and utterances (see the Explanatory Notes for details). Especially the seven occurrences of *peh*, 'mouth', and the six (not seven) of *dibber*, 'speak', noted by Childs (p. 70) focus attention on the words of Yahweh's representatives to a greater extent than in the narrative hitherto (cf. also *d^ebārîm*, 'words' in vv. 10 and 15). The content of the 'objection and its answer' element of a commissioning narrative (see the introduction to 3.1-12) thus has here a more distinctively prophetic character than in ch. 3, and a comparison in general with Jer. 1.6-10 is certainly appropriate, though neither in v. 6 nor in v. 9 is the wording as close to this passage in the Hebrew as might at first appear. The intermediary role of Aaron has no close parallel in Israelite prophecy, however: neither the 'servant' of the prophet (1 Kgs 19.21; 2 Kgs 5.20) nor the succession of Elijah by Elisha (2 Kgs 2) nor the role of Baruch (Jer. 36) is really comparable. A closer analogy, up to a point, is the transmission of prophecies by messenger and letter to the king of Mari: this process is sometimes represented as having been specifically commanded by the prophet in question (ARMT II.90, III.40, XIII.113, 114 = *ANET*, p. 624). Of course there it is the distance between the prophet and the king that makes an intermediary necessary, not any felt inadequacy on the part of the prophet (within the OT cf. Amos 7.10-11).

Not surprisingly, given the complex process of composition in the book of Exodus, there are other passages which employ similar motifs to this one. Moses' expression of inadequacy and the divine reassurance in vv. 10-12 find a parallel, in the context of Moses' mission to Pharaoh (cf. Carpenter/Harford-Battersby 2, p. 85; McNeile), in 3.11-12, while the topic of the passage as a whole is more briefly resumed in the Priestly account in 6.10-12+7.1-2, after Moses' report of his meeting with Yahweh has been rejected by the Israelites (contrary to 4.27-31): Moses, now sent to Pharaoh, complains that he is incompetent as a speaker ('of uncircumcised lips') and Aaron is introduced to act as his 'prophet'. The relationships between the three passages are, like other duplications in Exodus, important clues for literary-critical analysis.

The attribution of the passage to sources or redactional layers has followed a similar pattern to 4.1-9, but the introduction of Aaron into the narrative adds a new criterion for evaluation, which has been variously assessed.

Excursus: Aaron

Aaron is mentioned 347 times in the OT, more often than any human other than Moses and David (see the clear survey of the evidence in *ABD* 1, pp. 1-6). Many of these are in the Priestly source and in Chronicles, where Aaron appears as the first high priest, who is the ancestor of all those who have full priestly status (see further on this the commentary on 28.1-43). He also plays a prominent part in the Priestly plague narrative, acting as Moses' 'prophet' (7.1-2) and using his staff to perform 'wonders' (7.8-13 etc.), and he is associated with Moses in the leadership of the people and the reception and execution of many (but not all) of Yahweh's commandments (e.g. Lev. 11.1; Num. 1.17). References to him elsewhere are far fewer and generally less specific: within the Pentateuch Exod. 4.14, 27-30; 5.1, 4, 20; 8.4, 8, 21; 9.27; 10.3, 8, 16; 12.31; 15.20; 17.10, 12; 18.12; 19.24; 24.1, 9, 14; 32.1-3, 5, 21-22, 25, 35; Num. 12.1, 4-5, 10-11; Deut. 9.20; 10.6; as the ancestor of later priests Josh. 21.4, 10, 13, 19; 24.33; Judg. 20.28; Pss. 105.10, 12; 118.3; 135.19; in other contexts, generally in association with Moses Josh. 24.5; 1 Sam. 12.6, 8; Mic. 6.4; Pss. 77.21; 99.6; 105.26; 106.16; 133.2.

 Critical scholarship has attempted to define both Aaron's actual role in the earliest history of Israel and the history of 'Aaronide' priests prior to the legislation of P. Important landmarks in the history of research (see the brief summary of earlier research in Valentin, *Aaron*, pp. 14-25) are H. Oort, 'De Aäronieden', *ThT* 18 (1884), pp. 289-335; R.H. Kennett, 'The Origin of the Aaronite Priesthood', *JTS* 6 (1905), pp. 161-86; G. Westphal, 'Aaron und die Aaroniden', *ZAW* 26 (1906), pp. 202-30; Gressmann, *Mose*, pp. 257-83; Noth, *ÜGP*, pp. 195-99; H. Seebass, *Mose und Aaron. Sinai und Gottesberg* (Bonn, 1962); A.H.J. Gunneweg, *Leviten und Priester: Hauptlinien der Traditionsbildung und Geschichte des israelitisch-jüdischen Kultpersonals* (FRLANT 89; Göttingen, 1965), pp. 81-98; H. Schmid, *Mose. Überlieferung und Geschichte* (BZAW 11; Berlin, 1968); E. Auerbach, 'Das Aharon-Problem', *Congress Volume: Rome 1968* (VTSup 17; Leiden, 1969), pp. 37-63; Cross, *Canaanite Myth*, Chapter 8; A. Cody, 'Aaron, Aaronitisches Priestertum. 1. Im AT', *TRE* 1 (1977), pp. 1-5; Valentin, *Aaron*; J. Schaper, *Priester und Leviten im achämenidischen Juda* (FAT 31; Tübingen, 2000), pp. 169-73, 270-79. No convincing Semitic etymology for Aaron's name has been identified. Several suggestions for an Egyptian origin, as with the names of some other Levites, have been made (cf. Noth, *Personennamen*, p. 63; *HAL*, p. 19; Houtman 1, p. 75), but none has found general acceptance (cf. M. Görg, 'Aaron – von einem Titel zum Namen?', *BN* 32 [1986], pp. 11-17 [his own proposal is very speculative]; *Ges18*, p. 21). From Exod. 17.9-16 and 24.14 it has been deduced that Aaron was a military and judicial leader, from Numbers 12 and other passages that he was a prophetic figure. Opinion is divided over whether the priestly role perhaps implied e.g. in Exod. 18.12 and much more fully developed in P is original or the result of his adoption as eponymous ancestor by a priestly group in later times. Tensions with Moses have suggested to some that he was originally the leader of a rival group whose religious leadership came off worse in an amalgamation with the group led by Moses (Gressmann, Seebass, Schmid). It has often been suggested that Aaronide priests functioned at the Bethel sanctuary, because of the golden calf episode in Exodus 32 (Kennett, Gunneweg, Cross: also at Jerusalem according to Cross), but others have doubted this and held that the idea of an Aaronide priesthood was an invention of P (Auerbach). In either case there is room for speculation about the reasons for P's adoption of such a definition of true priestly descent, when it is clear that down to the exile it was Zadok who was regarded as the eponym of the Jerusalem priesthood (see the discussion in Schaper: cf. Ezek. 44). Valentin's detailed study cut the ground from under much of this kind of reconstruction by arguing that scarcely any of the references to Aaron are in fact earlier than P (see my review in *VT* 31 [1981], pp. 117-20). This is excessively negative (though certainly in line with the most recent scholarship), but it seems to have discouraged further investigation so far.

In the period down to 1975 the mainstream of critical scholarship, from Wellhausen on, saw 4.10-12 as the continuation of the J narrative and v. 17 as being from E (cf. v. 20 and references to Moses' staff elsewhere).

It was generally held that vv. 13-16 were not an original part of either source, since they contradicted vv. 10-12, and that they were added either by a secondary hand in J (Carpenter/Harford-Battersby, Rudolph, Noth) or by R^{JE} (so apparently Wellhausen [pp. 70-71], also Baentsch and McNeile) or by a redactor influenced by P (C.H. Cornill, *Einleitung in das Alte Testament* [Freiburg, 1891], p. 84; Holzinger, Gressmann).[1] Baentsch and Holzinger held that the addition began only after the words 'Yahweh's wrath was kindled against Moses', the former asserting what the latter must have presumed, that the original wording of Yahweh's reply had been suppressed.[2] Hyatt attributed vv. 13-16 to E, noting the prominence of Aaron in that source, and so in part perpetuated the main early alternative to the views discussed so far. For in 1912 Smend had challenged the consensus that these verses were a secondary addition and attributed the whole of vv. 10-17 to E (*Erzählung*, p. 117): he was followed in this, as in most other respects, by Eissfeldt (cf. p. 269*), Beer and Fohrer (pp. 29-30: with the qualification that vv. 11-13a were secondary, an alternative way of removing the tension that had been perceived between vv. 10-12 and vv. 13-16 [pp. 40-41]). Smend observed that Wellhausen's suspicion of the references to Aaron in ch. 4 was related to the evidently secondary appearance of Aaron in the older portions of chs. 7–11, but that these were in J material and in any case did not involve Aaron speaking. The true (and only) execution of the role given to Aaron here was, however, in 4.27-30. Moreover vv. 13-16 did not look redactional, and they prepared the way well for the prominent position that Aaron has later in E, and especially in ch. 32. They should therefore be attributed to E, and likewise vv. 10-12, which were closely related to them. The passage as a whole thus formed the sequel to 3.9-15.

---

[1] Childs simply described them as 'secondary' (p. 53).
[2] For a fresh suggestion about the original expression of Yahweh's wrath, based on these scholars' acute analysis of the text, see below, and further (with reference to the recent study of J.T. Willis) in the introduction to 4.18-31.

In recent years only a few scholars have attributed even a part of the passage to a main narrative account. Blum originally assigned vv. 10-12 and, apparently v. 17 (though he did not discuss it in detail), to his KD (*Studien*, pp. 27-28), but he regarded vv. 13-16 as a very late addition (cf. p. 362), because the role given to Aaron contradicted 3.18.[3] Van Seters attributes vv. 10-16 to J and v. 17 to P (like v. 20), and Propp sees the whole passage as E, particularly because of Aaron's role in 4.27-31 (cf. 'the mountain of God'). The majority of recent scholars regard the whole passage (along with vv. 1-9) as redactional, a view which was in fact first proposed by Knobel in 1857 (p. 23). They differ, however, in whether they date it before or after P.L. Schmidt led the way for the earlier dating, first in 'Überlegungen', pp. 234-35, and then in 'Diachrone und Synchrone', p. 238, where he explicitly included v. 17 in the redactor's contribution and argued that the passage is from R^{JE} and for the first time made Moses into a prophet needing appropriate legitimation.[4] This view was subsequently adopted by W.H. Schmidt (pp. 192-97) and Kohata (pp. 84-91: see also Graupner, p. 19), both of whom argued at length against a later dating. The latter, which had earlier been a minority view for vv. 13-16 (see above), had been revived by E. Auerbach (VTSup 17 [1969], pp. 38-40) and was then extended to the whole passage by H. Valentin in a full discussion (*Aaron*, pp. 47-140). Valentin's view initially met with little acceptance (but see above on Blum). In 1995, however, E. Otto began his argument for attributing the whole of 3.1–4.17 to the final redactor of the Pentateuch (PentR) with this passage ('Pentateuchredaktion', pp. 101-103; apparently without being aware of Valentin's work), arguing that it 'anticipated' not only P's account of Aaron's appointment but elements in the Sinai pericope and the conclusion of Deuteronomy which he attributed to the same redactor. This view of the whole passage as dependent on P has subsequently been taken up by K. Schmid (*Erzväter*, pp. 199, 205-206), Gertz (pp. 315-27) and Blum ('Literarische Verbindung', pp. 129-30).

In seeking to reach a considered view of the passage's origins, it may first be observed that recent scholarship has paid too little attention to the older consensus about the lack of harmony between v. 17 and vv. 1-9, as well as the abruptness of the transition to it from the main theme of vv. 10-16. It is surely of a separate origin.

---

[3] This is of course beside the point, because that verse is speaking about Moses' confrontation with Pharaoh, whereas 4.16 refers specifically to 'the people'. See below on Blum's more recent view.

[4] Schmidt had been preceded (except for v. 17) by A. Reichert in his unpublished Tübingen dissertation, 'Der Jehowist und die sogennanten deuteronomistischen Erweiterungen im Buch Exodus' (1972), e.g. p. 35. Reichert had also made use of the article of Smend (1967) in his discussion of 4.1-9 (pp. 28-29).

The rest of the passage hangs together tolerably well and as it stands it effects the necessary transition between vv. 1-9 and vv. 27-31. There is no 'contradiction' between vv. 10-12 and vv. 13-16, simply a progression in the plot. The mild (merciful?) expression of Yahweh's wrath in a way that looks more like a compromise with Moses' implicit refusal to speak to the people does, however, raise a suspicion that Baentsch and Holzinger were right to suppose that this was not the original continuation of the passage. The whole narrative would be much more coherent if it led quickly (by way of some of vv. 18-20) to Yahweh's attempt to kill Moses in v. 24, which was thwarted by Zipporah's circumcision of her son. In the present text this episode remains quite unmotivated. So vv. 14aβ-16 may well be an expansion of this narrative, which led to changes in vv. 27-31 (see the commentary there). There is no necessary connection with the inclusion of Aaron in the non-Priestly sections of Moses' appearances before Pharaoh (5.1 etc.), for which this passage makes no provision (though it is possible that it seemed to a later redactor to be a natural extension of Aaron's support for Moses before his own people).

When, and why, was this addition to the narrative made? The debate about its relation to the P parallel in 6.10-13; 7.1-2 is scarcely any easier to resolve than that over vv. 1-9, which was surveyed at length in the introduction to that section. Many of the arguments are quite inconclusive. The most likely clues to both the time and the motivation of the addition are in v. 14, but they seem to point in different directions. On the one hand it is rightly pointed out that all the other references to Aaron as Moses' brother come in Priestly or later texts, which implies a similar origin for this passage. This argument can be answered by the suggestion that 'brother' here means 'kinsman' in a broader sense (see the Explanatory Note), but this has the appearance of special pleading. The same might be said of the suggestion that might be made, that 'your brother' is a secondary addition based on P, though the difficulty of translating the verse may be (partly) due to its being over-full. The description of Aaron as a 'Levite', on the other hand, is difficult to reconcile with a Priestly or post-Priestly origin, though Blum and Gertz have attempted to find a possible context for it in the complex developments in the organisation of the temple personnel in the Persian period. Schaper unfortunately does not address the interpretation of this verse: although his detection of an upsurge in the Levites' status in the time of Nehemiah and Ezra (*Priester und Leviten*, Chapter 6) might provide a context for it, the fundamental distinction between Aaronide priests and other Levites remained in force and it would be very odd at that time to make Aaron, in effect, just a representative of the roles of the priestly tribe as whole. This description fits much better the situation envisaged in Deuteronomy and elsewhere (but probably older in its origin), where Levites as such had the status of priests. On balance it seems more likely that even this passage, which might seem to have a particularly strong claim to a (post-)Priestly origin, derives from an earlier period. Its motivation can only be guessed. It was scarcely needed to establish the future prominence of the Levites, when Moses' own birth from this tribe had already been affirmed (2.1) and their priestly role was to be established in Exod. 32.28-29. But if Moses was to have an assistant, and if Aaron's prominence in the Exodus story was to be given a formal basis, the prerogative of the Levites could perhaps best be safeguarded if his affiliation to this tribe was made explicit.[5]

Our provisional conclusion is therefore that vv. 10-14aα represent the continuation of the J account of Moses' commissioning by Yahweh, while v. 17 was originally part of another account of this, presumably deriving from E like the parallel narrative in 3.1-15* and finding its sequel in (v. 18 and) v. 20b. Verses 14aβ-16 were added later, most likely by the compiler of J and E, who brought the end of Moses' commissioning into its present form and also used the older accounts to produce his own version of its sequel in vv. 18-31*.

The various parts of this passage all address the issue of Moses' equipment by Yahweh for his coming tasks, which arises from his profession of his own inadequacy for them. Yahweh's response takes the form, in the earliest material, of an assurance that he will provide Moses with the words to speak and the ability to speak them (vv. 11-12) and the power, through his staff, to perform 'signs' (v. 17). This develops the characterisation of Moses as a quasi-prophetic figure, especially in 3.16-22 and 4.1-9, but in a way that is grounded in a theology of Yahweh as the creator and sovereign of all human life (v. 11). The closest parallel to this is in Amos 3.3-8. Moses' role is modified to some extent by the provision of Aaron to act as an

---

[5] See also the Explanatory Note on v. 14.

assistant and mouthpiece for Moses himself, who thereby acquires an even more exalted role (as 'God', v. 16). There is some similarity of intent to other passages which will emphasise the unique role of Moses as the recipient of divine revelation (Exod. 33.7-11 – note here the role of Joshua as his assistant – and Num. 12.6-8).

10 Moses said to Yahweh, 'If I may say so[a], (my) Lord[b], I am no speaker[c], and never have been in the past[d] nor since[e] you spoke to your servant, for[f] I am slow of mouth and of tongue[f'].
11 Yahweh said to him, 'Who gave[h] human beings mouths? or who makes[h] them dumb or deaf[i] or seeing or blind? Is it not I, Yahweh? 12 Now go, and I will be with your mouth and I will teach you[j] what you shall say.' 13 But Moses said, 'If I may say so[a], (my) Lord[b], please send (your message) by means of whoever you will send[k]'. 14 Yahweh's wrath was kindled against Moses [and he said, '(Shall I) not (send) Aaron your Levite kinsman?[l] I know that he can certainly speak. Listen, he is coming out[m] to meet you, and when he sees you[n], his heart will rejoice. 15 You shall speak to him and put the words into his mouth, and I will be with your mouth and his mouth. I will teach you both what you are to do, 16 and he shall speak on your behalf to the people. So[o] he shall be a mouth for you and you shall be God for him.] 17 [This staff you are to take in your hand, with which you shall perform the signs.]'

Notes on the Translation

a. Heb. בִּי. A polite introduction to words spoken to a superior, human or divine, which always appears before אֲדֹנָי (see next note and cf. v. 13). Earlier explanations of it as derived from a root ביי or בעה (cf. BDB, p. 106) have given way to the suggestion that it means 'On me (be the blame/consequences)' (*HAL*, p. 117; *Ges18*, p. 140; JM §105c n. 6), but it may be a mistake to look for any specific etymology (cf. Eng. 'Um').

b. Heb. אֲדֹנָי, vocalised as it usually is when it is a title for God, as it is in the consonantal text of the OT some 450 times (in Exodus see also 4.13; 5.22; 15.17; 34.9 [twice], all in direct address to God). This vocalisation is in general explained either from an original pausal form of the first person sing. suffix on the plural of אדון (for wider use of this 'plural of majesty' see JM §136d) or as an old afformative nominal ending, '*the* Lord' (for discussion see O. Eissfeldt, *TWAT* 1, 66-78 = *TDOT* 1, pp. 62-72; *DDD*, 994-98). There is a parallel difference of view over whether this vocalisation is late and artificial or very early, with Ugaritic analogues. Whichever is correct (and Eissfeldt may well be right to suggest that both uses are ancient, with the vocalisation perhaps being harmonised over time), in a passage like this one a pronominal interpretation and a 'normal' (i.e. non-pausal) vocalisation are probably to be preferred (cf. the use of בי and of the correlative עבדך later in the verse: so also Eissfeldt, p. 73 = p. 68).

c. Literally 'I am not a man of words', a unique expression in BH but conforming to the common attributive use of a *nomen rectum* (GK §128p; for other phrases with איש see BDB, pp. 35-36). The use of לא rather than אין in a noun clause is associated with the presence of a pronominal subject and a substantival predicate and conveys a more forceful negation of the latter (GK §152d; JM §160b-c).

d. Originally (א)תמול meant 'yesterday' (cf. 1 Sam. 20.27; Ps. 90.4; Job 8.9; possibly also at the end of Exod. 5.14: cf. Akk. *timāli/u*, *AHw*, pp. 1359-60) and שלשׁ(ו)ם will have meant 'the day before yesterday' as the 'third day' by inclusive reckoning (cf. Akk. *šalšūmī*, *AHw*, p. 1150), though its sole occurrence alone in BH (Prov. 22.20) is probably corrupt. In combination the two words form an idiom for '(in) the past, previously' more generally, as in 5.7-8, 14; 21.29, 36 and frequently elsewhere. The use of repeated גם here apparently emphasises the extent of the past time referred to, as also in 2 Sam. 3.17; 5.2.

e. Heb. מאז, which developed from its adverbial use, 'from then, from of old', into a pseudo-conjunction followed by a finite verb (as in 5.23 and 9.24) or a pseudo-preposition followed by a noun (Ps. 76.8; Ruth 2.7) or, as only here and in Lachish ostracon 3.7 (*AHI* 1.3.7), by an infinitive construct, with the sense 'since'.

f. Heb. כי could be rendered 'but' after the preceding negative (so Schmidt, Houtman, Propp: cf. Note b on 4.1-9), but Moses seems to trace his deficiency as a speaker back to its source in a weakness of his vocal organs.

g. For the grammatical structure of this expression see Note o on the translation of 3.1-12. As the case in 3.8, 17 shows, the repetition of 'slow' (כבד) in the Heb. here is not strictly necessary and may serve to give emphasis to Moses' lack of ability. On the implications of 'slow' see the Explanatory Note.

h. The variation between the perfect and imperfect of שׂם is appropriate to a distinction between the original creation of mankind (so Tg^j explicitly) and the varied endowments of individuals through time. The suggestion that שׂם might be a participle (Propp, p. 211: cf. LXX, Tg^O) and so also indicate a timeless present is less attractive. On the unique form of the imperfect ישׂום cf. GK §73b.

i. Heb. חרשׁ. Although the verb חרשׁ is often used for 'be silent', it never seems to refer to dumbness as such, and the adjective always means 'deaf' (so clearly here alongside אלם).

j. Heb. והוריתיך. On the vocalisation see GK §75ee.

k. The construction is *idem per idem*, as in 3.14 (see Note d on 3.13-15), 16.23 and 33.19, unusually without אשׁר (but see in general GK §155n and esp. Job 29.16). The example in 16.23 is especially similar in that the main verb is again an imperative, as it is also in 2 Kgs 8.1, and in all three cases the speaker is leaving the addressee(s) to do as he or they wish. Moses does not explicitly exclude himself, but his words convey an indifference on the part of Yahweh's chosen instrument which is sufficient to arouse the deity's wrath (v. 14). The presence of ביד should not be overlooked: it is the usual way of designating those through whom Yahweh speaks to his people, including Moses (cf. 9.35 and other refs. in BDB, p. 391, 'd'). So an object like 'message' (cf. Tg^J) must be understood with שלח here (cf. 2 Kgs 5.5; 20.12; Isa. 9.7), and the common translation (e.g. NRSV), '...send someone else', is wrong: better is NJPS, 'make someone else Your agent' (cf. Houtman, p. 413).

l. The syntax of Yahweh's reply is much more difficult to determine than might be assumed from the little discussion which it has received. Most common among recent translations is (i) 'Is there not your brother Aaron, the Levite?' (RSV: similarly RV, JPS, JB, W.H. Schmidt), with its personalised variant; (ii) 'Have you not a brother, Aaron the Levite?' (NEB: cf. REB, Houtman). But the grammatical basis of this is insecure, since הלא seems insufficient to provide the existential predicate. More in line with regular usage is (iii) 'Surely, Aaron is your brother, the Levite!' (Valentin: cf. AV), but this seems to tell Moses only what he (presumably) already knows. A recent innovation (iv) is the paraphrase 'What about your brother Aaron, the Levite?' (NIV, cf. NRSV), which fits the context but is hard to get from the Hebrew, except perhaps by way of (i)-(iii), which are themselves unsatisfactory. An older approach (v) was to take these words with what follows: 'I know Aaron thy brother the Levite that he can speak' (Tyndale, evidently from Luther's 'Weiß ich denn nicht, daß dein Bruder Aaron aus dem Stamm Levi beredt ist?'). This appeals to the idiom whereby the subject of an object clause after ידע (and also ראה) can be brought forward into the main clause as the grammatical object (GK §117h). The absence of את before אהרן is not a fatal objection to this view and the word-order, while uncharacteristic, could be for emphasis. An alternative (vi), also based on regular usage and followed here, is to supply a verb '(I shall) send' from the preceding context (v. 13: for ellipsis after הלא; see e.g. Exod. 33.16; 1 Sam. 9.20). On the alternative possible interpretations of אחיך and הלוי see the Explanatory Note.

m. The complications of the relationship with v. 27 are discussed by Houtman (p. 416). A simple grammatical solution is to see the participle יצא as referring to the imminent future (GK §116p, '...is about to come out': cf. LXX, Sy). Propp suggests, alternatively, that Yahweh had already summoned Aaron, but the report of this is deferred until later to avoid interrupting the dialogue between Yahweh and Moses (p. 214).

n. See Note h on 4.1-9.

o. Heb. והיה, literally 'So it shall be: he shall...', with the first verb impersonal, as often. For the asyndetic continuation cf. Gen. 4.14; Isa. 2.2 and GK §112y. Verse 16b provides a summary of what has been said in vv. 15-16a: hence the demarcation by והיה.

Explanatory Notes

10. Moses' second objection to Yahweh's commission (to which the third, in v. 13, is closely related) concerns his perception of himself as incompetent for the task (cf. 3.11, and later 6.12 and 6.30). Fittingly he uses a succession of deferential expressions in speaking to Yahweh: 'If I may say so...', '(my) Lord' (see Notes a and b on the translation) and 'your servant'.[6] '(My) Lord', Heb. *ᵃdōnāy*, is a title which was originally distinct from the divine name Yahweh (although the Jewish reading tradition, which was canonised in the vocalisation of the MT, later required its use as a reverential substitute for the divine name), which was derived from *'ādōn*, the ordinary word for a human lord or master (as, e.g., in 21.4-6). It thus expressed the respect due to Yahweh for his power and authority, as distinct from the various connotations of the divine name, which Moses first uses in addressing Yahweh in Exodus in 5.22. The acknowledgement of Yahweh's authority by Moses is greater, not less, if the form is understood here personally, '*my* Lord', as is certainly possible in direct address to Yahweh (as distinct from narrative) and to be preferred here. Moses' first statement that he is 'no speaker' simply disclaims any gift of eloquence (something highly prized, e.g. in Proverbs: cf. 15.23; 16.24; 25.11), but his reference to the 'slowness' (lit. 'heaviness') of his mouth and tongue have sometimes been taken to imply a physical impediment of his speech: so some of the ancient Versions (see Text and Versions), Philo, *Quis heres* 3-4 (as the effect of God speaking to him: in *Vita* 1.83 the same LXX phrase is understood to mean lack of eloquence), as well as later Jewish and Christian writers such as Theodoret (cited by McNeile) and Rashi. A widely favoured alternative was that Moses was no longer competent in Egyptian (Rashbam). J.H. Tigay's survey of a wide range of interpretations and comparative linguistic evidence from Arabic, Akkadian and Sumerian as well as Hebrew concluded that a physical speech impediment is referred to here ('"Heavy of Mouth" and "Heavy of Tongue": On Moses' Speech Difficulty', *BASOR* 231 [1978],

---

[6] On the deferential use of 'your servant' etc. see *TWAT* 5, 999-1000 = *TDOT* 10, pp. 392-93, where it is also pointed out that this usage is frequent in Hebrew inscriptions of the biblical period and that such language is often used in the context of a request.

pp. 57-67). This, he argued, is the implication of a similar expression in Gen. 48.10; the use in Ezek. 3.5-6 to refer to unintelligible foreign speech involves a transfer from a physical application such as is attested in several other languages; in Akkadian *kabātu* (the cognate to Heb. *kābēd*, 'heavy'), is used of various kinds of physical ailment; and the 'for' (Heb. *kî*) indicates that a reason for Moses' lack of eloquence is being given, not simply a restatement of it. Moreover, while in the present text of Exodus Moses at nearly eighty years of age (7.7) may have forgotten the Egyptian he once knew, this figure comes from the Priestly source and in the older source-material there is no indication that such a long period had elapsed since Moses' flight from Egypt. It is true that in the sequel there is no explicit reference to any healing of a speech impediment (Luzzatto, B. Jacob), but others (including Theodoret) have argued that this could simply be because God intended to maintain Moses' impediment to show his power. Propp accepts Tigay's view (p. 211), but Schmidt (p. 201) and Houtman (p. 408) reject it, the latter rendering Heb. *kî* by 'but' (cf. Note e on the translation), a possibility which Schmidt also entertains (p. 186). Since various metaphorical uses of 'heavy' are found in Hebrew (cf. *TWAT* 4, 17-19 = *TDOT* 7, pp. 17-19), there is no need to see a reference to a physical or psychological abnormality here. Most likely lack of competence is traced back to the physical organ(s) through which it should be manifested, and the divine assistance promised in v. 12 (cf. v. 15) is designed to remedy that kind of incapacity (cf. Jer. 1.6-7).

11-12. Yahweh's reply comprises a three-part question (v. 11) and a renewed command to 'go' (cf. 3.10, 3.16) which is reinforced by two assurances of assistance (v. 12). The two parts are linked by the inferential particle '(and) now' (Heb. *wᵉʿattāh*), for which cf. 3.9-10. It almost nears the sense 'therefore' in many places.[7] For both the form and the theology (Yahweh as creator) of v. 11 a wisdom background has been identified (Childs, pp. 78-79; more fully Schmidt, pp. 201-202), with convincing parallels in Proverbs and Job (cf. also Ps. 94.9). The use of the generalising 'human beings' (Heb. *ʾādām*) could point in the same direction. But, as the commentators have recognised, parallels also exist in prophecy,

---

[7] Cf. BDB, p. 774; H.A. Brongers, 'Bemerkungen zum Gebrauch des adverbialen *wᵉʿattāh* im Alten Testament', *VT* 15 (1965), pp. 289-99 (esp. 293-94).

especially in Deutero-Isaiah (cf. Isa. 40.12-13, 26; 45.21); and the general theme of the creation of man is of course handled in the J creation story in Genesis 2. A wisdom background (or a priestly one) might be envisaged for 'teach' in v. 12 (and v. 15), but the idea of Yahweh himself as the teacher of men is more characteristic of prophecy (Isa. 1.10; 2.3; 28.26; 30.20; 48.17; 54.13; Jer. 32.33) and psalmody (Pss. 25.12; 27.11; 86.11; 119.33, 102).[8] Both the command to 'go' and the reference to Moses' 'mouth' also use the language of prophecy, though the expression 'I will be with' (*'ehyeh 'im*) recalls most directly God's promise to Moses in 3.12 (cf. 3.14!), and could be heard as a specification of this. But earlier in Genesis, of course, similar assurances have been given in passages attributed to J (26.3; 31.3: cf. 28.15; 39.2-3, 21, 23), so that Levin could see them as a keynote of the Yahwist's message (p. 422).

13. Moses' response, what we have called his 'third objection', continues to use prophetic language: 'sending' is accomplished by the command to 'go' (v. 12), and the two verbs are often associated (e.g. 3.10; Isa. 6.8-9). He begins with the same deferential expressions that are used in v. 10, which is only one of a series of verbal links between vv. 10-12 and 13-16. But this time they lead into, not a statement about himself, but an imperative addressed to Yahweh, albeit one that is softened by the precatory particle *nā'*, 'please'. The closest parallels to this *idem per idem* construction (see Note k on the translation) indicate that formally it leaves Yahweh free to send whoever he likes, and it is only by implication that Moses seeks to exclude himself. Nevertheless the LXX and Targums reflect that implication in their translations and recent commentators all see Moses' words as a refusal (Childs, p. 79; Schmidt, p. 202; Houtman, p. 413; Propp, p. 213). Yahweh's anger (v. 14) surely confirms this.

14. Only here in Exodus does Moses himself incur Yahweh's wrath (for his wrath against the people see 32.10-12; Num. 11.1, 10, 33; against Miriam and Aaron in Num. 12.9) and it causes him no harm (contrast Deut. 1.37; 3.26; 4.21).[9] The translation of the following words is uncertain (see Note l), but the general sense is

---

[8] See further S. Witmer, *Divine Instruction in Early Christianity* (WUNT 2/246; Tübingen, 2008), pp. 7-27, with bibliography.

[9] The problem is noted at B.Zeb. 102a, and it is deduced from the following words and from 1 Chr. 23.14 that this was why Aaron was a priest and not Moses.

clear: Yahweh will make use of Aaron as his spokesman, for 'he can certainly speak'. Aaron is here mentioned for the first time in Exodus, hence the addition of the words 'your Levite kinsman', or alternatively 'your brother, the Levite'. Both elements of the description raise problems. Although Aaron is listed as Moses' brother in the later Priestly (P^S) genealogy in 6.14-25 (v. 20) and is so described in the P narrative in 7.1-2 and elsewhere, this is the only place in non-Priestly texts (to which this passage apparently belongs) where this happens, and in 15.20 Miriam is described as Aaron's sister without any reference being made to a relationship with Moses (this is explicit only in Num. 26.59[P] and 1 Chr. 5.29 [EVV. 6.3]). One might therefore prefer the wider use of Heb. *ʾāḥ* ('brother') for 'kinsman' here, as in 2.11 and 4.18 (cf. *TWAT* 1, 206 = *TDOT* 1, p. 190). But see also the introduction to this section for the view of some that at least vv. 13-16 are dependent on P, which would make the rendering 'brother' appropriate. The description of Aaron as 'the Levite' is at least theoretically ambiguous. It might simply designate him as a member of the tribe of Levi, like Moses' father and mother in 2.1, though the expressions there are different. That could be deliberate, to avoid confusion with the much more common use of the term to refer to someone with at least a potential cultic status, which represents the second possibility here. The history of the Levites' role in biblical times is complex (see, e.g., Gunneweg, *Leviten und Priester*; Cody, *History*; Schaper, *Priester und Leviten*) and depending on its age, the expression here could have been intended to refer to a potential priest (as in Judg. 17), a member of the priestly tribe (as in Deuteronomy) or a member of the *clerus minor* (as in P and Ezek. 44.9-14). The interpretation of it is complicated further by the possibility that this description of Aaron is designed to validate the role of a type of cultic functionary in later Israel and that it might allude to a group whose function was somewhat different from that generally attributed to the Levites in the OT, for example a teaching role (as proposed by Gunneweg, *Leviten*, pp. 65-77, 95-98, for the Judges ['amphictyonic'] period and later: cf. Deut. 33.10a). It is hard to see why it would be necessary to mention Aaron's tribal affiliation for its own sake, whereas some form of the second approach would (even if anachronistically) provide a basis for the otherwise unexplained assumption that Aaron 'can certainly speak'. Of the possibilities outlined the least likely is a reference to the *clerus minor* of exilic and later writings, since Aaron was there explicitly and sharply distinguished from it as the ancestor of those who were entitled to be priests in the full sense.[10] In the non-Priestly material Aaron's role is not that of a priest but that of an assistant to Moses, and it may be as such that he is here designated as a prototypical Levite and will shortly come to 'the mountain of God' (v. 27).

15-16. There (no movement is envisaged on Moses' part) Moses will transmit to Aaron God's message for the people (*hāʿām*, v. 16). The formula for this ('put [*śîm*] the words into his mouth') is one that is used elsewhere for one human being telling another what to say (2 Sam. 14.3, 19; Ezra 8.17), but it is also used of the divine inspiration of a prophet (Num. 22.38; 23.5, 16; Isa. 51.16; in 59.21 it seems to refer to words given by God to all the people),[11] so it fits smoothly with the description of the process in v. 16b as a 'god' (Moses) giving a message to his 'mouth' or prophet (Aaron). This language (which is made more explicit in the Priestly version in 7.1-2) is only possible because Moses himself has already been entrusted with a message from Yahweh (3.16-17) and because Yahweh extends his promises to Moses of assistance and instruction (v. 12) to include Aaron as well (v. 15b): the wording is almost identical, with the substitution of 'do' for 'say' presumably designed to include the 'signs' of vv. 1-9 (so explicitly vv. 28 and 30).[12]

17. 'Take this staff' sounds like words accompanying the handing over of a staff to Moses by God (cf. in a human interaction 2 Kgs 9.1-3). Although the 'signs' (*hāʾōtōt*, as in v. 9: the singular twice in v. 8) must in the present context refer to those in vv. 1-9 (so explicitly LXX), there is also some awkwardness in the statement here that the staff is to be used to perform all of them, whereas earlier Moses' staff was involved in only one of them, and then

---

[10] See the introduction to this section, however, for the view of Blum and Gertz that the description of Aaron as a 'Levite' was part of an attempt to reconcile opposed factions in the post-exilic temple.

[11] The alternative expression employing *nātan* appears only to be used in the latter sense (Deut. 18.18; Jer. 1.9; 5.14).

[12] But since vv. 1-9 have already 'taught' Moses about the signs, why would Yahweh still be promising this to him as well as Aaron now (the final two instances of 'you' in v. 15 are both plural). Is more general guidance about what to 'do' meant?

more directly than the instrumental 'with' (Heb. *b*) might suggest. The language used parallels more closely passages in the plague-narrative (7.15 [which has an explicit reference back to 4.2-3], 17, 20; 9.23; 10.13) and later references at the Red Sea (14.16) and Rephidim (17.5), but in all of these the staff is described as Moses' staff. The sequel to v. 17 is v. 20b, which also probably derives originally from a different old version of Moses' commissioning (see the introduction to this passage). 'This staff' is emphatically placed before the verb at the beginning of the sentence in the Heb. (with an 'and' to make the connection with what precedes, which we have as often left untranslated). In the fuller original version of this tradition something had presumably been said about the origin of the staff which might more strongly justify its description as 'the staff of God' in v. 20 (see the Note there) as well as in 17.9.

Text and Versions

בי (4.10) LXX δέομαι, Vulg *obsecro*, Tgg. בבעו, lit. 'with a prayer' (Tg^N [and probably Tg$^{G(A)}$]) added ברחמין מן קדמיך, as it did in v. 13: for other instances of this see *AramB* 2, p. 22 n. 4), Sy *b^{c} ʾnʾ mnk*, 'I beg of you', as elsewhere.

איש דברים (4.10) LXX ἱκανός, 'capable', freely. An early variant which was widely preserved is εὔλογος, normally 'reasonable', but perhaps capable of the sense 'speaking well' (cf. εὐλογία in Plato, *Rep.* 3, 400d). The earliest attestation is in Ezekiel, *Exagog.* 113 (though Jacobson [pp. 107, 204 n. 32] thinks this is from ἄλογος in LXX of 6.12, despite the other contextual links to Exod. 4). Philo three times cites the word, twice clearly in this context (*De sacr. Abel* 12; *Vita Mosis* 1.83), and once in a clear distinction from the use of ἄλογος elsewhere (*Quod det.* 38). This is surely to be regarded as one of those cases where Philo bears witness to early corrections of LXX towards MT (see also E. Bickerman, *Studies in Jewish and Christian History*, 1 [AGAJU 9/1; Leiden, 1976], p. 145). Later, Aq has ἀνὴρ ῥημάτων and Symm εὐλαλός, the latter also appearing in Syh and several other mss and probably representing Origen's reading. On Cyril's readings see Wevers, *THGE*, p. 109. Tg^{N,G} insert מרי, 'master of'.

כבד פה (4.10) LXX has ἰσχνόφωνος, lit. 'weak-voiced', as also for ערל שפתים in 6.30 (but not 6.12: see above): it can denote a speech impediment, cf. Vulg *inpeditioris (...linguae)* (it has no separate equivalent for פה). Aq βαρὺς στόματι renders both words literally, Tg^O יקיר ממלל, 'heavy in speech', only the first, Tg^{J,N,F} חגר פום, 'lame, halting of mouth', only the second but again suggesting a speech impediment, as does Sy *l^{c}g mmllʾ*, 'stammer in speech'.

כבד לשון (4.10) LXX βραδύγλωσσος and Vulg *tardioris linguae* both indicate slowness of speech. On the other hand Tg⁰ עמיק לשון (cf. the Heb. of Isa. 33.19), Tg^{J,F} קשי/ה ממלל and Sy *'ṭl lšnʾ* suggest obscurity and indistinctness. Tg^N חגר ממלל points again to a speech impediment.

אליו (4.11) LXX and Tg^N specify 'to Moses'.

פה לאדם (4.11) Tg^J has 'the speech of the mouth in the mouth of the first man', making an explicit link to the creation story: for similar interpretations cf. *AramB* 2, p. 171 n. 15.

או מי (4.11) One SP ms. cited by Crown (Camb. 713) reads ומי.

ישום (4.11) SP ישים, using the standard form of the imperfect Qal (see Note h on the translation). This may make it secondary (normalisation), though given the similarity of *waw* and *yodh* e.g. at Qumran the possibility of an error in MT remains. All the Vss render in the past tense, probably due more to the preceding context than to any formalised awareness of the 'preterite' use of the imperfect (on LXX cf. in general T.V. Evans, *Verbal Syntax in the Greek Pentateuch* [Oxford, 2001], pp. 136-40, against Wevers, *Notes*, p. 46).

אלם או חרש (4.11) LXX's δύσκωφον καὶ κωφόν, 'deaf and dumb', produces an inversion of the MT order, which the Three correct by substitution of μογιλαλόν, 'dumb', for the first word, κωφόν also admitting the meaning 'deaf' (Wevers, *Notes*, p. 46).

פקח (4.11) The reading פסח, 'lame', has been proposed, since the positive quality of seeing is surprising in the context and פסח appears together with the other three adjectives in Isa. 35.5 (S.T. Lachs, 'Exodus iv 11: Evidence for an Emendation', *VT* 26 [1976], pp. 249-50, following Graetz, McNeile and others: also Valentin, *Aaron*, p. 52). Though ingenious this is hardly necessary, especially as פקח may refer to both hearing and seeing (Isa. 42.20: cf. Schmidt, p. 186; Houtman, p. 411). The intriguing haggadah cited by Lachs only includes 'lame' in late versions (*MRI* [Lauterbach 2, p. 171] omits it) and is hardly likely to be based on a variant Exodus text (more likely Isa. 35.5), let alone an original one.

יהוה (4.11) LXX κύριος ὁ θεός, perhaps as Wevers suggests (*Notes*, p. 47) because of the creation context. B and some other mss do not have κύριος: is this really 'a careless mistake' (Wevers) or was Rahlfs right to see it as original?

אנכי אהיה (4.12) LXX has καὶ ἐγὼ ἀνοίξω, using the more specifically prophetic language found in Ezek. 3.27; 33.28. Propp wonders if a different *Vorlage* should be envisaged (p. 188), but this would only push the evident clarification of MT one stage further back. Tg⁰ has 'and my Memra will be', the other Tgg 'and I by/with my Memra will be': this illustrates well the development of a 'limited exegetical device' in Tg⁰ into a portrayal of 'one main mode of God's activity' in Tg^N which is judiciously expounded by Chester, *Divine Revelation*, pp. 308-13 (the citations are from pp. 312-13; *AramB* 6, pp. 25-29, only summarises the scholarly debate without any resolution of it).

C.T.R. Hayward (*Divine Name*, pp. 20-21) sees the takeover of אהיה from MT in Tg^N here as support for his view that the Memra expresses God's eternal presence, but as Chester points out (pp. 307-308) this interpretation is untenable. The appearance of אהיה here and elsewhere in Tg^N is more likely to be due to a focus on the (meaning of the) divine name itself than to the presence of מימרא.

עם פיך (4.12) Vulg oddly has 'in your mouth': elsewhere (e.g. Deut. 18.18) it is God's words that are put in a prophet's mouth. Tgg (other than Tg^O) go the other way, rendering less boldly 'with the speech of your mouth'.

והוריתיך (4.12) Von Gall gives the SP reading as והוריתך, which is supported among others by four early mss, including Cam. Add. 1846. But other early mss agree with MT (see the editions of Sadaqa and Tal, as well as Crown's text), as do many later ones, in line with *GSH* §62b. Aq's rendering καὶ φωτίσω σε uses his standard equivalent, based on a mistakenly assumed relation of the form to √אור (for further evidence see Salvesen, *Symmachus*, pp. 70-71).

ויאמר (4.13) LXX and Sy specify the subject as 'Moses' (cf. v. 11).

בי (4.13) LXX and the other Vss render as in v. 10, but Aq and Theod are preserved here as reading ἐν ἐμοί, thus anticipating the modern analysis of the form as preposition and 1st person suffix (for occurrences of this rendering, and the 'more intelligible' ἐπ'ἐμέ, in LXX of Judges and Kingdoms see Wevers, *Notes*, p. 47 n. 14). Tg^Nmg מנך is probably just an alternative reading for מן קדמיך in the main text (J. Joosten, pers. comm.): cf. Sy.

אדני (4.13) This time Tg^Nmg has רבוני, reading more into the Heb. than a simple substitute for the divine name. This equivalent to אדני is used by Tg^J in words addressed to Pharaoh in Gen. 44.19 and (in the plural) to Abraham's visitors in Gen. 19.2, but not apparently where אדני is used of God, despite the use of רבון for simple אדון in Exod. 23.17 (cf. also the prayer referred to in B. Yoma 87b).

שלח ביד (4.13) Tg^J adds 'your message', clarifying the sense. LXX's paraphrase προχείρισαι δυνάμενον ἄλλον, 'choose an able other (person)', more clearly excludes Moses himself. It may also be meant to recall his complaint that he is not ἱκανός in v. 10 and perhaps has a kind of textual basis in יד here (in the sense of 'power'), which is otherwise ignored. The general sense conveyed is close to that given by Tg^{O,N,F} (see the next note). Vulg, like many later renderings, simply ignores ביד.

אשר תשלח (4.13) Tg^{O,N,F}, 'who is worthy to send/be sent', replace the focus on divine choice with the fitness of the one sent. Tg^J and Tg^Nmg amplify this with an eschatological reference to, respectively, Phinehas (cf. *LAB* 48.1-2) or the Messiah. Such interpretations may have encouraged the Christological exegesis of this verse (see *BAlex*, pp. 99-100; Petit, *La chaîne sur l'Exode*, III [TEG 10; Leuven, 2000], pp. 124-27), which Vulg *quem missurus es* probably reflects (see M. Kraus, 'Jerome', pp. 29-31). Exod.R. 3.16 cites explanations in terms of an angel (as well as Aaron), and this term actually appears in the marginal text of Tg^N, ביד מלאכא משיחה דעתיד למשתלחא, though perhaps as an error for מלכא, 'the King'.

הלא אהרן (4.14)   LXX's οὐκ ἰδού is a regular equivalent for הלא (e.g. Gen. 13.9; Deut. 11.30; 32.34: also many times in source-formulae in Kings) and occurs with the same meaning in Acts 2.7. The syntactical analysis of the following words is no easier in the Versions than in MT. None of them can easily be taken in the sense favoured by Luther and Tyndale (see Note l on the translation, [v]), despite *AramB* on Tg^O. Vulg *Aaron frater tuus Levites* might best be rendered 'Your brother Aaron is a Levite', but the Douai translation (1916 ed.) has 'Aaron the Levite is thy brother'.

ידעתי (4.14)   Tg^{O,J} paraphrase with גלי קדמי, while Tg^N retains the MT sense (cf. Sy), all as at 3.19 and elsewhere.

דבר ידבר (4.14)   LXX adds σοι, 'for you', anticipating v. 16.

יצא (4.14)   LXX and Sy render as future (perhaps vocalising it as an imperfect), while Vulg and Tgg have a present tense (see Note m on the translation).

בלבו (4.14)   SP בלבבו. This is the only one of 46 instances of לב in MT Exodus where SP has לבב. SP's reverse variant in the one place where MT Exodus has לבב (14.5) is easier to understand, as a 'correction' to the regular form. SP also has לבב twice in 20.21b, but in both cases the form, with its context, is imported from Deuteronomy, where לבב is the predominant form. Here perhaps בלבבו is original, with MT having been conformed to the more common form. The readings of the Versions (including LXX's paraphrastic ἐν ἑαυτῷ) are of course no help in such a matter.

הדברים (4.15)   LXX and Vulg render 'my words', underlining what is already implied in v. 12.

אנכי אהיה (4.15)   The Versions have similar renderings for these and the following words to those employed in v. 12 (see the note there).

פיהו (4.15)   SP has פיו as earlier in the verse, presumably a secondary harmonisation. Both forms are quite widely attested (unlike with אב and אח: for lists of occurrences see Mandelkern, p. 944), but פיו is over twice as common as פיהו, which is only rarely used with the inseparable prepositions. This appears to be the only verse where both forms appear together.

והיה (4.16)   This introductory verb is not reproduced in LXX and Sy.

לפה (4.16)   Tg^{O,J,N,F} and Sy personalise with 'an interpreter' (*[m]twrgmn*), as does Exod.R. 3.17. In addition to its general use, this referred both to the oral translator of the synagogue readings and (perhaps more relevant here) the speaker (*^{x}morā'*) who enlarged upon the brief words of the teacher (*tannā'*).

לאלהים (4.16)   Tgg continue the echo of synagogue practice, perhaps, in designating Moses as 'teacher' (רב: Tg^O) or as one 'seeking instruction from before the Lord' (Tg^{N,F}: cf. 18.19) or both (Tg^J). This is comparable to the rabbinic interpretation of אלהים in some other passages as 'judges' (דיינא: e.g.

21.6). Reverential paraphrases are also found in LXX and Vulg ('[you shall be there] in relation to matters concerning God'), apparently understanding Heb. ל as 'concerning' rather than 'as'. Only Sy gives the natural rendering 'God/a god'.

המטה הזה (4.17) LXX adds τὴν στραφεῖσαν εἰς ὄφιν to make the connection with v. 3 (cf. later 7.15 in MT, which provided the wording here for LXX; and more generally 17.5).

האתת (4.17) Tg^N expands with 'wonderful signs' (נסי פרישתא: lit. 'signs of wonders').

Chapter 4.18-31

Moses' Return to Egypt

The transition from Moses' commission at the mountain of God (Horeb, 3.1) to his activity in Egypt is made here in a complex passage, in which four sub-sections can easily be distinguished. From a narrative point of view the transition is already complete at the end of the first sub-section (vv. 18-20): Moses returns to Egypt with the staff of God in his hand. The other three sub-sections (vv. 21-23, 24-26 and 27-31) each 'hang' on this thread of narrative, but they also bring their own distinct theological contribution: in them Yahweh is frequently named as speaker or agent, in ways that go beyond the programmatic instruction of v. 19. Each of these sections has its own particular theme and the question of their original association with each other and with other passages in Exodus remains to be determined, as does the question of the internal literary history of each one of them.[1]

Verses 18-20 are dominated by the idea of Moses' 'return', first to Jethro and then to Egypt: the verb 'return' (Heb. *šûb*) occurs four times and 'went/go' (Heb. *hālak*) three times. Moses' family, including his father-in-law, are again prominent, for the first time since 2.16-22 and 3.1, though Moses now has 'sons' (v. 20: cf. 18.3-4). The verses provide two alternative explanations for Moses' departure, which must, as is generally recognised, derive from two different versions of the story. In v. 18 Moses asks Jethro's permission to leave so that he can see how his family in Egypt are faring, and Jethro gives this his blessing; while in v. 19 (afterwards!) Yahweh tells Moses to go, because it is now safe to do so. An early and persistent explanation of this was to see v. 18, with v. 20b, as deriving from the E source and v. 19 with v. 20a as being from J (so first Dillmann apparently; and recently Propp and Graupner[2]).

---

[1] It is worth noting that this passage formed the point of departure for the theory of a third early source in Exodus: cf. Smend, *Erzählung*, pp. 117-20; Eissfeldt, *Hexateuchsynopse*, pp. 31-33; Beer, pp. 8-10.

[2] Knobel anticipated Dillmann in the attribution of vv. 18-19, but ascribed all of v. 20 to his *Kriegsbuch* (= J: *Num.-Jos.*, pp. 532, 548), while Wellhausen, in

An alternative view, which has recently become very popular, is to attribute the duplication to the insertion of the supposedly once separate narrative of Moses' call (3.1–4.18) into a context which originally knew nothing of it and spoke simply of Moses' flight to Midian, his marriage and his eventual return to Egypt (2.11-22+23aα; 4.19-26). This was first advocated by B.D. Eerdmans (so Blum, *Studien*, p. 20) and it has been taken up in various ways by others who have called in question the existence of two parallel early sources of the Pentateuch (Rudolph, Blum, K. Schmid, Gertz). Whereas Rudolph saw the insertion as occurring within the formation of his single early source (and Gertz has returned to this view), Blum and Schmid attribute it to later stages in the composition of the Pentateuch, whether KD, PentR or both (the last in Blum, 'Literarische Verbindung').[3] While it is true that 4.19 does in a sense 'pick up the story' from the end of ch. 2, this is no different from the way in which 4.18 does so from 3.1, at the beginning and end of the supposed 'insertion', and so it in no way excludes the possibility that between 2.23aα and 4.19 too an account of Moses' call may have intervened from the beginning at least of the literary stage of composition.

Since it is clear (contrary to the 'unitarians' of all colours) that within 3.1–4.18 parallel versions of Moses' call have been combined (whatever further redactional activity there may have been), the duplications on each side of it are best explained in the same source-critical terms, by the attribution of one strand to E and the other to J.[4] Verse 20b evidently presupposes v. 17(E), so it probably also derives from E. Verse 20a as it stands fits well with E's reference to two sons in 18.3-4, but the repetition of the same verb and of Moses' name is against its belonging to the same strand as v. 20b, and it is likely that the reading was originally 'his son' in the singular (cf. v. 25, and 2.22) and the sentence belongs (like v. 19) to J.

Composition, p. 71, who saw the need to divide v. 20, distributed vv. 18-19 in the opposite way. Levin and Van Seters also ascribed v. 18 to J.

[3] Noth was at one stage attracted by this idea (cf. *ÜGP*, pp. 31-32), but later (like Wellhausen, *Composition*, p. 71) abandoned it (cf. pp. 21-22 = ET, pp. 33-34). One might have expected it to be attractive to those arguing for a third early source, but from this section Smend, Eissfeldt, Beer and Fohrer only attributed 3.21–4.9 to the third source, on weak grounds and without any surviving narrative setting for these merely supplementary elements of the call-narrative, and so breaking the immediate connection between 2.23aα and 4.19.

[4] Van Seters (*Life*, pp. 64-67) gives v. 19 (as well as vv. 20-23) to P, as a desperate ploy to avoid an early parallel to J, despite the absence of any indicators of Priestly authorship and the lack of any priestly interest (rather the reverse, most likely, in view of Num. 25.6-17!) in the Moses/Midian tradition.

The connection of vv. 21-23 to part at least of vv. 18-20 is made by the opening of Yahweh's speech, 'When you go back to Egypt...' Formally the speech consists more of instructions (21aβ, 22-23) than of predictions (21b), so even more than for 3.18-22 the comparison with salvation-prophecy is inappropriate. These verses do, however, serve a similar function to 3.18-22, in pointing forwards to important matters later in the story, and they may have further purposes in addition to this.

> Sometimes v. 21 has been attributed to a different source or layer from vv. 22-23 (Dillmann, Holzinger [both with the idea that vv. 22-23 have been displaced from ch. 10 or 11: cf. SP at 11.4], Hyatt, Weimar, Propp), but there is no real basis for this, and the motif of Pharaoh's refusal to release (Heb. *šālaḥ* Piel) Israel is common to both what Moses is told to do and what he is to say. Occasionally the section has been assigned to an early source (E: Wellhausen, Fohrer; J¹/L: Smend, Eissfeldt, Beer), but its position after Moses' commissioning is complete in the older material and some aspects of its vocabulary are against this. Already Carpenter and Harford-Battersby saw the verses as redactional (R^JE: likewise McNeile), and this is now the dominant view, with their presumed date becoming progressively later. The presence of Priestly terminology is fully documented by Schmidt (p. 211), and Van Seters derives them from P (which he sees as a redactional layer). But elements from JE are also present, including the whole conception of the plagues as a trial of Pharaoh's willingness to release Israel (see further Schmidt, p. 212), so that a redactor who drew on both major elements of the narrative, P and JE, is likely to be responsible (i.e. PentR: so W.H. Schmidt, p. 212 [cf. Kohata, Graupner], L. Schmidt, 'Diachrone und Synchrone', pp. 246-50; Blum, *Studien*, p. 28 n. 100; K. Schmid, *Erzväter*, pp. 250-51; Gertz).

The addition thus provides a prelude to the whole plague-narrative as it now exists, combining the conceptions of it in JE and P; it also provides an explicit justification for the final plague, though with specific attention to Pharaoh's own firstborn; and it does so by introducing an image for Israel's relationship to Yahweh which is of major theological importance, that of sonship.[5] Given the dating, this writer did not create the image – he could draw especially on Hos. 11.1ff. – but he introduced it into the Exodus narrative as an even more powerful justification than others which are used

---

[5] See the full discussion in V. Huonder, *Israel Sohn Gottes* (OBO 6; Freiburg/Göttingen, 1975).

for Yahweh's care for Israel and his hostility to Pharaoh and the Egyptians.[6]

Verses 24-26 recount the strange episode of Yahweh's 'attack' on Moses and the sparing of him as a result of his wife Zipporah's circumcision of 'her' son. The fact that Moses was not originally named here (see Text and Versions for renderings that make the references to him explicit) means that the passage is tightly bound into its context. The reference to 'the way' and a 'lodging-place' in v. 24 makes a general connection with the journey-motif in vv. 18-20 and Moses' wife and child(ren) have been mentioned in v. 20(a). But the naming of his wife and the reference to a single child makes if anything a closer link to 2.21.

The meaning and purpose of this narrative, both in its present form and (in modern times) in a possible earlier context different from its canonical location have been much discussed (for full summaries up to the mid-1980s see Houtman, pp. 439-47, and his article 'Exodus 4:24-26 and its Interpretation', *JNSL* 11 [1983], pp. 81-105).[7] One strand of early Jewish interpretation saw the reason for the attack as Moses' failure to circumcise his son (see Text and Versions and Vermes as referred to there), but Jub. 48.2-3 attributed it to the evil angel Mastema's desire to protect the Egyptians from the consequences of Moses' mission. Some Christian interpreters discounted the neglect of circumcision and found the reason in other failings of Moses (on Theodoret and Procopius see briefly B.P. Robinson, 'Zipporah to the Rescue: A Contextual Study of Exodus iv 24-6', *VT* 36 [1986], pp. 447-61 [456 n. 17, 459]; cf. the further texts in F. Petit, *La chaîne sur l'Exode II, III* [TEG 10; Leuven, 2000], pp. 11-14, 134-40). Accounts of modern interpretations (Childs, Schmidt, Houtman) have distinguished three main approaches. (i) Wellhausen and others (including Childs, *Myth and Reality* [SBT 27; London, 2nd ed., 1962],

---

[6] The concern in these verses to justify the final plague by reference to Pharaoh's conscious refusal to release Israel was accentuated by the insertion of vv. 22-23 in SP before 11.4 and was probably one motive for all the extensive additions to the plague-narrative in SP and related texts from Qumran. I believe I owe this suggestion to Professor Magnar Kartveit, but in his book published after we first met he attributes the 'major expansions' in these texts to a desire to enhance the standing of Moses as a prophet and to reinforce the principle enunciated in Deut. 18 that true prophetic successors of Moses must be preachers of the law (*The Origin of the Samaritans*, pp. 265-88, 299). The two explanations need not be mutually exclusive.

[7] The fullest and most recent account is in J.T. Willis, *Yahweh and Moses in Conflict* (Bible in History 8; Berne, 2010).

pp. 59-65) have seen it against a background in which circumcision was normally practised on young men in preparation for marriage: on this view the story was originally an aetiological explanation for the Israelite adoption of circumcision in infancy, and provides an alternative explanation to that given by P in Genesis 17. (ii) Meyer, Gressmann and others reconstructed a purported original version of the *Sage* in which a night-demon, perhaps already identified with Yahweh, attacked Moses (?) in his quest for the *ius primae noctis*, but was deceived by Zipporah's circumcision of her husband and her daubing of the blood on the demon's penis. This was an aetiology of circumcision as a marriage-ritual. (iii) Morgenstern and Kosmala argued that originally Zipporah's child, not Moses, was endangered because he had not been circumcised.[8] All of these theories involve bold and unfounded speculations, whether about the practice of circumcision as a marriage ritual in the ancient Near East[9] or about a prior obligation to circumcise a child, of which there is no trace in the older Genesis material. No doubt the search for an explanation of the puzzling phrase 'bridegroom of blood' which is clearly an important focus of the story in its present form (cf. v. 26b), has been the driving motive for these speculations. More recent studies have responded to Childs's insistence (pp. 98-101) that exegesis should concentrate on the (equally difficult) question of the meaning of the story in its present context. Childs's own answer, that v. 26b shows that for the redactor 'the story does not explain the origin of circumcision, but rather circumcision explains the meaning of Zipporah's action' (p. 100), does not adequately account for Zipporah's words and the interest in them. Houtman (first in 'Exodus 4.24-26', p. 102) proposed that the story is about Moses' dedication or consecration for the task ahead of him, but this seems to make too little of the danger to his life and his escape from it. B.P. Robinson does address this issue ('Zipporah', pp. 457-58), but his suggestion that Zipporah thereby assumes the role of Jethro, so that Moses becomes her 'son-in-law', involves a contorted interpretation of Zipporah's action and produces a definition of her relationship to Moses which is far less appropriate than the normal rendering 'bridegroom' here. His correlation of the narrative with the story of Jacob in Genesis 32–33 and with the Passover in Exod. 12 do have some justification, but do not touch what seem to be the central concerns of this passage. His most fruitful

---

[8] So now A.J. Howell, 'The First-Born Son of Moses as the "Relative of Blood" in Exodus 4.24-26', *JSOT* 35 (2010), pp. 63-76, mainly because of the focus on the first-born son in vv. 21-23. While the article makes some acute observations, it can at most (see above) reflect the interpretation of 4.24-26 adopted by a late redactor, and in any case the idea that Gershom is by his circumcision made into a 'a relative to Yahweh' flies in the face of the 'to me' in v. 26, which must refer to Zipporah.

[9] The material collected by Propp in 'That Bloody Bridegroom', *VT* 43 (1993), pp. 495-518 (515-18), is all modern.

point is the clear rejection of Moses' failure to circumcise his son as the cause of Yahweh's displeasure and the suggestion that it lies rather in his 'weakly trying to evade the duty of confronting the Pharaoh', with reference to vv. 20 and 23 (p. 456) and also to v. 14 (pp. 452, 459).

R. and E. Blum ('Zippora und ihr *ḥtn dmym*', in E. Blum et al. [eds.], *Die Hebräische Bibel und ihre zweifache Nachgeschichte* [FS R. Rendtorff; Neukirchen, 1990], pp. 41-54) see the problem with which the narrative now deals as Moses' marriage to a non-Israelite and find support for this in Zipporah's words about 'a bridegroom of blood', where they suppose blood to signify (fictive) full membership of the same kin-group. But this does not seem to be part of the Old Testament symbolism of blood: the example which they cite from Judith 9.4 will reflect Greek ideas. A larger objection to this interpretation is that the story (like the wider context) gives no indication that Zipporah is the problem or that her integration into Israel was achieved by this episode. Most recently Propp has revived the suggestion that 'blood' refers to Moses' killing of an Egyptian in 2.12 (see the Note on v. 25), that this is what aroused Yahweh's anger and that the blood of his son's circumcision was accepted as expiation for this sin. This explanation is, however, improbable for both literary and legal reasons. It would surely be surprising, if expiation were needed, for it to be left until after Moses' commissioning as the divinely chosen leader; and there is no Israelite parallel for blood-guilt to be expiated in any remotely similar way. The whole idea seems quite alien to the narrative context.

It is surely better to seek for a motive for Yahweh's attack (if there is one at all) closer in the narrative, and Robinson's suggestion that it is Moses' reluctance to carry out Yahweh's commission may well be on the right lines. At the end of his survey and analysis of previous interpretations (see above, n. 7, pp. 201-14) J.T. Willis takes Robinson's approach a step further by noting that this is only one of a series of 'recurring conflicts between Moses and Yahweh' in the text of Exodus and subsequent books. Here Yahweh's response would be much more severe than it is elsewhere, in Exodus at least, but this may be the result of what Willis calls 'the strong misgivings' that Moses had about carrying out his commission (p. 203). Willis put forward his view (which he reinforces with elements of traditional Jewish interpretation) at the level of the final form of the text, but it is if anything more persuasive in relation to what was probably the original sequence of the written narrative at this point. We noted earlier (see the introduction to 4.10-17) that Yahweh's anger against Moses in v. 14a now finds only a very mild expression in its present sequel about the use of Aaron as an intermediary

(vv. 14b-16). Those verses are commonly regarded as secondary in their context, however, and it may therefore be this episode, separated from v. 14a by only a verse or so (vv. 19-20a) within vv. 18-20, which provided its original continuation. Such a view would provide both the missing outcome of Yahweh's anger and the missing explanation for his attack on Moses – neatly 'killing two birds with one stone', as it were. As for the story itself, its leading theme is clearly the sparing of Moses because of Zipporah's action, which at its simplest level involves the apotropaic use of blood in a way closely comparable to the Passover story. But why circumcision blood and why the saying about Moses being a 'bridegroom of blood'? The concluding statement by the narrator (or redactor) in v. 26b seems to presuppose that Zipporah's utterance of these words was well known to the story's hearers but not their occasion – hence the emphatic 'It was at that time' (Heb. *’āz*) at the beginning and the specification of the circumcision context at the end. The story thus served to fix this 'floating saying' about Moses' Midianite wife in a particular narrative context. What its original meaning was and what function, if any, it may have had in Israelite society (e.g. as part of a wedding ceremony) we have no means of knowing. As for the use of blood from a child's circumcision and its daubing on Moses' genitals, this seems unlikely to be something simply invented by the narrator to provide an occasion for the saying: for one thing, the motif and the saying are not very similar to each other (except for the element of blood), which suggests an independent origin for each of them. It is more likely that the story was intended, by the association with Moses' escape from death, to reinforce belief in the effectiveness of circumcision as a means for preserving life.

These verses have been almost universally attributed to J (or the 'third early source'), because of their archaic character[10] and the association with 2.21. Wellhausen (*Composition*, p. 71) also noted the inconsistency in location between them and v. 27 (which he attributed to E), where Moses is (still?) at 'the mountain of God'; and if v. 14a does provide the explanation for Yahweh's attack, that is a further link to J material. Even some of those recent scholars

---

[10] So especially Gressmann, *Mose*, p. 57, who described them as 'wie ein erratischer Block der Urzeit'.

who do not reckon with two parallel early sources have attributed these verses to a continuous narrative at a relatively early (pre-exilic) stage of composition (Blum and Blum, 'Zippora', pp. 53-54 n. 40; Gertz). A minority have favoured a redactional origin for them: Weimar ascribed them to JE (except for v. 26b: PentR), because of what he took to be cross-references to vv. 22-23 as well as v. 19a, but he overlooked the much more significant connections with 2.21. Robinson, Levin and Van Seters envisage an even later origin for the passage, Levin because he suspects that it may be a midrash based on Genesis 17 and the others mainly because of a supposed connection with vv. 21-23. These are not weighty arguments.

Verses 27-31 are notable both for the introduction of Aaron into the narrative (anticipated in the present text in vv. 14-16) and for the account of Moses' reception by his fellow-Israelites in Egypt (which resolves the issues raised earlier in 3.13 and 4.1). Verse 31 in particular brings the narrative to an interim conclusion, with the people's prostration in worship, as in 12.27.[11]

The connections with earlier sections in ch. 4 have inevitably affected the analysis of these verses. Wellhausen's attribution of vv. 27-28 to E and vv. 29-31 (without the references to Aaron) to J remained popular until the 1960s (with further subdivision by Smend and his followers), though some elements of it were questioned by Gressmann, Rudolph and Noth (for Noth see pp. 36-37, ET, p. 51; also *ÜGP*, pp. 31-32). Since then the widespread view that vv. 1-9 and 14(b)-16 are at the earliest from R^{JE} has led to a general acceptance that at the most only vv. 29 (without 'and Aaron') and 31b can belong to an early narrative source. L. Schmidt, W.H. Schmidt, Kohata and Graupner attribute the rest to R^{JE}, but others (e.g. Levin, Van Seters) date the whole passage much later. Propp is unusual in deriving it all from E, but this is his 'default' solution where he finds no basis for division (p. 59) and he also holds that Aaron's role was a special concern of E.[12]

The role attributed to Aaron in v. 30, as Moses' intermediary before the people, clearly presupposes vv. 14-16 and presumably derives from the same stage of composition (R^{JE} in our view). But, as observed in the Explanatory Note, the implication that Aaron also

---

[11] There is also some similarity to 14.31 and its liturgical sequel in the hymns of 15.1-18 and 15.21.

[12] On Aaron see the Excursus in the introduction to 4.10-17.

performed 'the signs' goes beyond what vv. 14-16 say and originally the verse probably referred to Moses alone ('Moses spoke... had spoken to him'). The same may well be true for v. 29. Apart from this there is no need to doubt the unity of vv. 29-31 (on the apparent problem in the sequence of verbs in v. 31 see the Explanatory Note), and the reference to 'the elders' links these verses to 3.16-18 (J). The assessment of vv. 27-28 is more difficult. The meeting of Moses and Aaron at the mountain of God and Moses' communication of what he had been told by Yahweh to Aaron could certainly be a further contribution of the redactor who added vv. 14-16 and the references to Aaron in vv. 29-30, but they could also be the basis from which he worked, and so part of an older narrative source. The reference to the 'signs' here too distinguishes these verses from vv. 14-16, but not from v. 17. An original connection with v. 17 would be more plausible. The mention of 'the mountain of God' must be connected to 3.1, which we have also attributed to E. It cannot be said that there is an awkward transition from v. 28 to v. 29, and there is thus some justification for the view that vv. 27-28 belong to the same account as the underlying text in vv. 29-31 (i.e. J). But the connections just mentioned, together with the abrupt reversal in Moses' location after v. 26, favour the view that they come from an alternative account, i.e. E.[13]

The passage is thus based on extracts from the two main narratives identified in earlier sections, with vv. 19-20a, 24-26 and most of 29-31 being taken from J and vv. 18, 20b and 27-28 from E. These were combined by a redactor who added (in accordance with his insertion of vv. 14-16 into the previous section) the references to Aaron in vv. 29 and 30. A much later redactor (PentR?) prepared the way for the combined (Priestly and non-Priestly) plague-narrative by the insertion of vv. 21-23, which also introduced to the Exodus narrative the notion of Israel as Yahweh's 'son' and its use as a

---

[13] It is true that vv. 18-26 imply that Moses has now left 'the mountain of God', so that it is surprising that Aaron finds him still there in v. 27. Possibly therefore vv. 27-28 originally stood between vv. 17 and 18 in the complete E narrative and they were moved to their present position just before vv. 29-31 by the redactor (R^{JE}), who wanted to make them part of his presentation of Aaron as the intermediary between Moses and the people. But a better explanation, which also fits 18.1-5, would be that, in this account at least, 'the mountain of God' was located between Midian and Egypt, so that Moses could pass it again on his return journey.

justification for the slaying of the Egyptian firstborn in the final plague.

As already noted, the recurrence of the verb 'return' in vv. 18-20 introduces the main theme of this passage: the return of Moses, now accompanied by Aaron, to Egypt and his appearance before the Israelite elders and the people as a whole. The conclusion in v. 31 marks the transition from Moses' dealings with his own people to his confrontation with Pharaoh, which begins in ch. 5. Within the narrative there are also three verbal 'echoes' which highlight 'sub-themes' which are handled in different ways by different sections of the passage. The first to be introduced is the threat to Moses' life, which is removed: initially with reference to human hostility (v. 19: cf. 2.15), but then from Yahweh himself (vv. 24-26). Secondly, there are the references to 'sons': of Moses (vv. 20, 25), of Yahweh (vv. 22-23) and of Pharaoh (v. 23). Thirdly, there is 'meeting', with the repetition of the same verb in vv. 24 and 27 to refer to Yahweh's and Aaron's very different encounters with Moses (cf. the contrasting verbs which follow), but also in Moses' meetings with Jethro (v. 18) and, accompanied by Aaron, with the people (v. 29). One important development in the plot which both main theme and sub-themes accomplish is the completion of the reintegration of 'the story of Moses' with 'the story of Israel', which were temporarily separated in ch. 2 (and, in terms of geography, also through most of chs. 3–4).

Theologically, the word of Yahweh and human responses to it continue to be central: in the case of Moses (vv. 19-20), of Pharaoh (vv. 22-23; cf. v. 21) and of the people as a whole (vv. 30-31; cf. v. 28). But he is also a God who acts by 'wonders' (v. 21) and 'signs' (vv. 28, 30), which also seek a response, and in wrath which can nevertheless be dispelled (vv. 24-26).

18 [So Moses went back[a] to Jether[b] his father-in-law and said to him: 'Please[c] let me go back to my kinsmen[d] in Egypt, so that I may see[e] whether they are still alive'. Jethro said to Moses, 'Go, and may it be well with you!'[f]] 19 Yahweh said to Moses in Midian, 'Go back to Egypt,[g] for all the men who sought your life are dead'. 20 So Moses took his wife and his sons, mounted them on a donkey and returned to the land of Egypt: [Moses took the staff of God in his hand.] 21 [Yahweh said to Moses, 'When you go back to Egypt, see,[h] you shall do before Pharaoh

all the wonders which I have given you power to do.ⁱ But I will make his heart stubbornʲ and he will not let the people go. 22 You shall say to Pharaoh, "Thus says Yahweh, Israel is my son, my firstborn, 23 and I said to you, Let my son go, so that he may worship me.ᵏ But you refused to let him go,ˡ (so) mark this: I am going to killᵐ your son, your firstborn."'] 24 As he wasⁿ on his way at a camping-place,ᵒ Yahweh came upon him and sought to kill him.ᵖ 25 But Zipporah took a sharp-edged stoneᑫ and cut off her son's foreskin and made it touchʳ his genitals.ˢ She said, 'For you are a bridegroom of bloodᵗ to me'. 26 So he left him (in peace).ᵘ It was at that timeᵛ that she said 'Bridegroom of blood', at the circumcision.ʷ 27 [Yahweh said to Aaron, 'Go into the wilderness to meet Moses'. So he went and came upon himˣ at the mountain of God, and he kissed him. 28 Moses told Aaron all the words of Yahweh with whichʸ he had sent him, and all the signs which he had commanded him (to do).] 29 Moses went,ᶻ [and Aaron,] and [they] gathered together all the elders of the Israelites. 30 [Aaron] spoke all the words which Yahweh had spoken [to Moses] and he performedᵃᵃ the signs in the sight of the people. 31 The people believed and, having heardᵇᵇ that Yahweh had shown concern for the Israelites and observed their affliction, they bowed down and worshippedᶜᶜ.

Notes on the Translation

a. Lit. 'went and returned'. The combination of הלך and שוב, as also in the same way later in this verse and slightly differently in vv. 19 and 21, is a common example of the way in which, when הלך is closely followed by another verb, especially a verb of motion (cf. Deut. 20.5-8, Judg. 21.23: also בוא in Num. 13.26), their meanings may virtually coalesce.

b. Elsewhere (even later in this verse) MT always has the longer form 'Jethro' (see on 3.1), but the shorter form is reflected in LXX and Tgᴼ. Its appearance (probably as an accidental error here) may be due to its familiarity in other texts as a personal name (for other cases of its use alongside a longer form for the same person see 2 Sam. 17.25; 1 Kgs 2.5; 1 Chr. 7.37-38: each time the shorter form occurs after the longer one, which suggests that a tendency to abbreviation could be involved).

c. נא: *Dagesh forte conjunctivum*, GK §20f.

d. Heb. אחי, with את here as elsewhere (e.g. 2.11) in a wider sense than 'brother'.

e. The imperfect/cohortative with simple *waw* probably expresses purpose (GK §108d): so Vulg.

f. Heb. לך לשלום, lit. 'go in well-being', a frequent departure formula: Judg. 18.6; 1 Sam. 1.17; 20.42; 2 Kgs 5.19 (alternatively the preposition ב may be used: 1 Sam. 29.7; 2 Sam. 15.9).

g. Heb. מצרים, a simple 'accusative' of direction (GK §118f) in MT: for the addition of the directional ending in some witnesses, as MT in vv. 20-21, see Text and Versions.

h. כל־המפתים אשר־שמתי בידך may be taken as a *casus pendens* which is resumed by the suffix on ועשיתם, with *waw* of apodosis (Schmidt, p. 208; Houtman, p. 429: cf. GK §143d, more fully JM §156). It is not the object of ראה, which is best taken as an interjection virtually equivalent to הנה (so BDB, p. 907b; also LXX according to Wevers, *Notes*, p. 52, and Vulg). The root of Heb. מופת (like its possible Phoenician cognate מפת: *DNWSI*, p. 674) is unknown. BDB associated it with a root אפה (pp. 68-69), but the Ar. cognate which they cited probably has a different origin (see the Addenda, p. 1120). Recent dictionaries leave the matter completely open (*HAL*, p. 529; *TWAT* 4, 750-51 = *TDOT* 8, p. 174; *Ges18*, p. 645).

i. Lit. 'put in your hand/power'. There could be a reference to the staff in Moses' hand (v. 20).

j. Heb. אחזק, so lit. 'make strong', traditionally 'harden'. In this kind of expression, which is frequent in chs. 7–11, לב, 'heart', would refer to Pharaoh's will (Tg^J, BDB, p. 525, '4'; *TWAT* 4, 437-38 = *TDOT* 7, pp. 423-25).

k. Heb. ויעבדני. The more general sense 'serve' is also possible, both here and in later instances of the demand to Pharaoh (7.16 etc.): it is the use of זבח elsewhere (3.18; 5.3) and other references to worship (e.g. 5.1) which has led translators to prefer 'worship'. For the *waw* expressing purpose cf. GK §165a and Text and Versions.

l. It is possible to regard this clause as in effect subordinate to what follows, according to common Heb. usage (cf. Note h on 4.1-9), and thus see it as giving the reason for Yahweh's declaration ('Because you refused...', cf. Schmidt's 'Da' at the beginning of the verse [p. 208]), hence our '(so)' after it. Older translations (see Houtman, p. 431) took the sequence as conditional: 'and if thou refuse to let him go...' (AV: cf. Luther and see Text and Versions). Some support for this could be had from passages cited in GK §159g, e.g. Ps. 139.11. It does, as the Vss cited show, require the translation of ואמר in the present tense, but that is also possible (GK §111u-v). The real objection to such a rendering is that nowhere else is the slaying of the firstborn seen as a threat that might be withdrawn, like some of the earlier plagues (e.g. 7.27): it is the final inexorable blow which follows on Pharaoh's resolute refusal to yield.

m. The Heb. participle referring to the imminent future (cf. LXX), as often in prophetic announcements of judgement, which also may be preceded by הנה (cf. GK §116p, e.g. Isa. 3.1).

n. Heb. ויהי. Not 'And it happened...' here, as an antecedent is required for the suffix on ויפגשהו. The absence of an explicit reference to Moses is nevertheless strange (one is added by Sy): the continuation would be easier if, as many believe, this verse originally followed v. 20a immediately. Subordination is again to be presumed (cf. Note h on 4.1-9).

o. Heb. במלון. On the definite article see Note o on 2.15 and compare Heb. הסנה in 3.2. Older translations such as Luther and AV (see also Text and Versions) rendered 'inn', following a use in MH, but none of the occurrences in BH is likely to refer to a roofed structure (unlike the fem. form מלונה in Isa. 1.8; 24.20, which means 'hut'): cf. e.g. Josh. 4.3, 8. Commentators since Gressmann (*Mose*, p. 58 n. 4) have wondered whether there is a deliberate play on words (or more) between מלון here and מולת in v. 26.

p. Heb. המיתו. It is much more common for בקש to be followed by the inf. constr. with ל, but Jer. 26.21 is one other case where it is omitted, by coincidence with the same form (see more generally GK §114m and, for cases where ל is omitted after other verbs, Exod. 2.3, 18).

q. Heb. צר. The only other certain occurrence in BH is Ezek. 3.9, which draws metaphorically on its hardness; this may also be the point in the use of a by-form צָר in Isa. 5.28. The reference to a sharp stone, and even a stone blade, is well supported by cognates in Ar. and Akk. (see BDB, p. 866; *HAL*, p. 985: *AHw*, pp. 1114-15, gives examples of both *ṣurru* and *ṣurtu* in the sense 'knife'). The forms in -*u*- in Josh. 5.2 (pl.), Ps. 89.44 and Job 22.24 (pl.) belong either to this word (cf. GK §93bb for analogies) or to a by-form (so *HAL*, pp. 953-54), but in any case to the same root *ṣrr*: this designates a particular kind of stone and small stones ('pebbles') in general (cf. צרור in 2 Sam. 17.13; Amos 9.9), whereas צור means a great rock or mountain. Joshua 5.2 (also about circumcision) and Ps. 89.44 share the idea of sharpness with this occurrence. צָר in Job 41.7 (cited tentatively in *HAL*, p. 985) is less certainly associated.

r. Heb. ותגע, 3rd f.s. *waw* cons. Hiphil impf. of נגע. The majority of uses of the Hiphil are in fact intransitive ('reach, come to'), and this would be contextually possible here, with the foreskin (ערלה) as (fem.) subject. But many of the intransitive uses reflect the predominance of this meaning in LBH, and an unmarked change of subject is unlikely when there is ambiguity. The causative meaning 'make...touch' (with obj. sometimes supplied from the previous clause: Isa. 6.7; Jer. 1.9) has two specific applications, both of which have been invoked here: 'smear, daub' (of blood, in Exod. 12.22) and 'bring down' (to the ground, of the destruction of a city or building: Isa. 25.12; 26.5; Ezek. 13.14; Lam. 2.2). The latter was favoured here by AV ('cast it at his feet') and has been revived by Houtman ('dropped it', pp. 435-36), but this idiom elsewhere requires a phrase meaning 'to the ground' and the references to blood in the context make Exod. 12.22 if anything the closer parallel.

s. Heb. רגליו, lit. 'feet' or 'legs'. The euphemistic use for 'genitals' is most clearly attested in Isa. 7.20 and perhaps 6.2 (*HAL*, p. 1106; *TWAT* 7, 336 = *TDOT* 13, p. 315): the other passages in BDB's longer list (p. 920) are probably not relevant (Heb. מימי רגלים in the Qere at 2 Kgs 18.27 par. Isa. 36.12 will reflect MH idiom, cf. Jastrow, p. 775: it is represented in Tg both times and in Vulg at Isa. 36.12). Here the references to circumcision in the context make 'genitals' very probable. For LXX's different rendering see Text and Versions. NEB omitted the word altogether, but REB has 'Moses' genitals'.

t. So literally Heb. חתן דמים, unless חתן had its other meaning, 'son-in-law' (as e.g. in Gen. 19.14): but this is not appropriate for Zipporah to use of Moses and still less of her child, as Propp understands it in v. 26 (p. 238). Heb. idiom allows the construct relationship to express, among other things, either an attribute (GK §128p-v), so 'bloody bridegroom', or a cause (GK §128x, usually with a participle or adjective), so 'bridegroom by means of blood'. In the former case the use of the pl. דמים might refer to blood shed in murder or the guilt resulting from it (for the use of this possibility by Propp see the Explanatory Note; and cf. איש דמים in 2 Sam. 16.7-8; Ps. 5.7). But although this is nearly always the case where the pl. is used elsewhere, in Lev. 12.4-5, 7 and Ezek. 16.6 it refers to a woman's bleeding in childbirth, and in Lev. 20.18 and Ezek. 16.9 to menstrual blood. Blood from the wound of circumcision might therefore be referred to here and indeed this seems most natural in the context. H. Kosmala, in a new interpretation of the whole passage, argued from the use of the cognate verb in Arabic (to which a Midianite's language might be close) to mean 'circumcise' that חתן here means 'one who has been circumcised', and the whole phrase 'a blood-circumcised one', comparing LXX's reading, on which see Text and Versions ('The "Bloody Husband"', *VT* 12 [1962], pp. 14-28 [25-28]; so already J. De Groot, 'The Story of the Bloody Husband [Exodus iv 24-26]', *OTS* 2 [1943], pp. 10-17 [13], with the sense 'circumcised by blood and *not* by a stone/knife'). Against this it is pointed out that mention of blood in connection with circumcision is superfluous (H. Schmid, 'Mose, der Blutbräutigam', *Judaica* 22 [1966], pp. 113-18 [114]) and that the meaning 'circumcise' is not attested for חתן elsewhere in Heb. (Schmidt, p. 230). Childs's objection that the Ar. verb means 'circumcise a bridegroom' (p. 98) seems not to hold, however, as different forms of the verb and different related nouns are used for either circumcision or relatives by marriage without any overlap (Lane, *Arabic–English Lexicon* 1/2, pp. 703-704), nor is there evidence from the Near East of circumcision as a marriage ritual: it was a separate ceremony, even when performed after infancy. These considerations also exclude the translation 'a bridegroom by means of blood', at least if it is meant to refer to circumcision. Willis's proposal (*Yahweh and Moses*, pp. 85-86, 211-13, following Meyers, p. 65) to associate the noun (or adjective?) חתן with Akk. *ḥatānu*, 'protect' (cf. *AHw*, pp. 335-36; *HAL*, p. 330), certainly fits in well with the implied effect of Zipporah's action, but remains speculative in the absence of other convincing examples of this meaning in Heb. (cf. *TWAT* 3, 291 = *TDOT* 5, pp. 272-73).

u. Heb. וירף, 3rd m.s. *waw* cons. Qal impf. of רפה. Although the common meaning of the Qal is 'sink down', it is construed with מן (Neh. 6.9) and

מעל (Judg. 8.3) to mean, in effect, 'cease'. Only here does it have a personal subject in this construction, but the implication (cessation of anger) may be similar to Judg. 8.3 (רוח). This is a more secure interpretation (and one broadly supported by LXX ἀπῆλθεν) than to presume that the Qal is used in the sense of the Hiphil as in Deut. 9.14 and Judg. 11.37 (probably with ellipsis of a word like 'hand[s]') to mean 'let go of'. In the context the 'him' is presumably Moses and the 'he' is Yahweh. For the variant reading of SP see Text and Versions.

v. Heb. אז cannot here mean 'after that, next' (Josh. 22.1 and 1 Kgs 3.16 are really the only places where it certainly has that meaning with reference to the past), since Zipporah has already spoken these words in v. 25. The sentence is the narrator's way of underlining the fact that this was the (first?) occasion when these presumably famous words were spoken.

w. Heb. למולת. The exact sense of the ל is uncertain: it may be temporal (as we have taken it), causal or referential (BDB, pp. 512-17, paras. 5 and 6). Whichever is chosen, the point is to link the saying specifically to the act of circumcision. The pl. מולת is curious, and the noun itself occurs only here in BH. Grammatically one might explain the pl. by comparison to its use to describe a ritual which has several parts (GK §124f).

x. Heb. ויפגשהו, exactly as in v. 24, but this time פגש lacks the connotation of aggression which it has there (for which cf. Hos. 13.8 and its use of a wild animal in Prov. 17.12). The echo may nevertheless be deliberate. The verb is used twice of Jacob's meeting with Esau in Gen. 32.18 and 33.8, the first time with an expectation of hostility, the second neutrally.

y. For the omission of the expected retrospective preposition and suffix cf. JM §158i and e.g. Deut. 7.19. Although no example of the full expression seems to occur in BH, it is likely from the occasional use of ב after verbs of motion to indicate 'what one takes or brings with one' (BDB, p. 89) that ב would be the preposition used with שלח in such a construction. In the following clause there is less difficulty in assuming an implied double accusative, of the person and the thing, with צוה (cf. the examples with הדרך such as Exod. 32.8).

z. The verb is sing. here, but pl. in the next clause, after Aaron has been mentioned. For the use of a sing. verb before a compound subject there are enough parallels (e.g. 8.8) for it not to be suspect (JM §150q; the transition to the pl. in the next clause is also well illustrated there).

aa. Commentators disagree over who the subject of 'performed' should be, Aaron (Childs, Houtman) or Moses (Schmidt, Propp). If the verse is taken in its nearer context, it must surely be Aaron; only if vv. 1-8 and 17 are brought into the discussion can Moses be considered, and even then it remains difficult to envisage a change of subject without any indication (e.g. והוא עשה).

bb. Heb. וישמעו, lit. 'and they heard', but Heb. style regularly uses coordinated verbs where subordination is intended (GK §111d, 164b) and here such an understanding is suggested by the unlikelihood of 'hearing' following 'believing' (so also e.g. Childs, Schmidt, Houtman, NRSV).

cc. Heb. וישתחוו. Traditionally such forms were derived from a Hithpalel stem of שחה (e.g. GK §75kk), but since the discovery of the Ugaritic texts, where similar forms occur and Š- is the regular causative prefix of the verb, many have analysed them as Hishtaphal forms of חוה (e.g. *HAL*, pp. 283-84). J.A. Emerton, 'The Etymology of *hištaḥᵃwāh*', *OTS* 20 (1977), pp. 41-55, gave strong reasons for retaining the older view, but see also Davies, 'A Note on the Etymology of *hištaḥᵃwāh*', *VT* 29 (1979), pp. 493-95. On the curious pointing of וי- see Note t on the translation of 12.21-27.

Explanatory Notes

18. The narrative now brings Moses back from the scene of his commission (3.1–4.17) to the home of his father-in-law, who is named Jethro (see Note b on the translation for the different forms of his name in MT here) as in 3.1 (cf. ch. 18 passim). His request for leave to go back to Egypt, which introduces the topic which dominates vv. 18-31, implies a sense of responsibility to Jethro, based both on family ties and employment. Moses' silence about the real purpose of his journey and his plausible but evasive explanation cohere with this attitude, whether we attribute them to fear of refusal or a wish to spare his family anxiety. Indirectly the request shows that the hesitation which has dominated the account of Moses' call has now been overcome. For parallels to Jethro's parting good wishes see the references in Note f on the translation.

19. The same topic is now introduced again as an initiative of Yahweh, with an explicit reference to the danger which brought Moses to Midian in the first place. 'In Midian' presupposes that Moses is with his family, yet it is strange for Yahweh's command to follow Moses' request to Jethro, and vv. 18 and 19 are often therefore assigned to different sources (see the introduction). Although Jewish tradition saw 'the men who sought your life' as a reference to the fighting Hebrews of 2.13-14 (see Text and Versions), the language ('sought your life', 'are dead') recalls more specifically that used in 2.15 and 2.23 to refer to Pharaoh. Only the plural is a difficulty, but even in 2.15 the involvement of Pharaoh's officials is likely to be assumed. Again, rather curiously, nothing is said of the reason for Moses' return which has been central for the past chapter and a half. But it could perhaps be taken for granted just because it has been so central, and the encouragement given in v. 19b may simply address an unspoken fear of Moses which could have deterred him on the point of departure.

20. It is notable that in the transmitted text Moses here has more than the one son referred to in 2.22 and 4.25. The statement is more in conformity with 18.3-4 (though there it is assumed that Moses' children [and his wife] were still in Midian), and it is likely that an original singular form ('his son') has been changed to the plural to agree with that passage (see Text and Versions). There were evidently multiple traditions on this point, just as there were about the name of Moses' Midianite father-in-law. The use of a donkey (LXX assumed that more than one would have been required: see Text and Versions) fits in with other biblical narratives, both about the early period (e.g. Gen. 42.26-27) and about the period of the monarchy (1 Kgs 2.40; 13.11-32), and with other evidence from the ancient Near East from the third millennium on (cf. Albright, *Yahweh and the Gods*, pp. 62-64; and the well-known illustration of Semitic tribes in the First Intermediate Period from Beni Hassan, e.g. in *POTT*, pl. III). See also Cansdale, *Animals*, pp. 70-74. The 'staff of God' (the phrase itself occurs only here and in 17.9) is naturally associated with the staff mentioned in v. 17, which looks like part of a commissioning scene. Its mention here makes clear that there is, after all, more to Moses' journey than a family visit (Houtman, p. 424). Gods in the ancient world, including Yahweh himself (Isa. 10.26; 30.32; Ezek. 20.37; Mic. 7.14; Ps. 23.4: in the last three cases the Heb. is *šēbeṭ*, not *maṭṭeh* as here), were sometimes portrayed as wielding a 'staff', and the Assyrian king Ashurnasiripal III claimed that his sceptre had been placed in his hands by the god Shamash (Luckenbill, *ARAB* 1, pp. 141-42, Year 1: not in *ANET*). Other texts speak of gods wielding weapons more generally or putting them in the hands of human kings (see the examples cited by Propp, p. 228), but these parallels are not so close. In the context 'the staff of God' is simply the one which God/Yahweh has instructed Moses to 'take' (v. 17), but it is difficult to parallel such a weak link between God and what is said to be 'his', and the suspicion remains that a fuller tradition about the divine origin of the staff once existed.[14] As the text stands, it is not easy to tell whether the staff was simply a means of wielding divine power or carried wider connotations of authority (for the latter see Coats, *Moses*, pp. 66-68). See further the

---

[14] Later tradition speculated that it came from Reuel's garden, and even that it was one of the original products of creation (see Text and Versions on Tg^j at 2.21 and here).

commentary on 7.9 and 9.23, which speak respectively of Aaron's and Moses' staffs.

21-23. The additional instructions given here to Moses about how he is to carry out his commission in Egypt read on the one hand like an afterthought, but also anticipate later events in a way similar to 3.19-22. Apart from that passage they relate most closely to 4.17, and it is no doubt the connection made there between staff and 'signs' that has led to their inclusion here, just after the reference to 'the staff of God' in v. 20. But while v. 21 does summarise significant elements of Moses' later confrontation with Pharaoh, and as such contains nothing distinctive, the words given to Moses in vv. 22-23 appear nowhere in the subsequent narrative (except in the Samaritan text, where they are included before 11.4[15]). They are of considerable theological interest and provide a justification for the slaughter of the firstborn in terms of the *ius talionis* or 'poetic justice'. At their heart is the conception of Israel as Yahweh's son (or 'child'), a unique description in the Pentateuch but one which reappears in Hos. 11.1-4, where (also in relation to the Exodus) the positive implications of the metaphor are developed, and in Jer. 31.9, 20 (perhaps dependent on the Hosea passage), where it is applied, specifically in terms of the 'firstborn', to Yahweh's future restoration of his people (cf. the use of the plural, 'sons/children', in similar ways in Deut. 14.1; 32.19; Isa. 1.4; 30.1, 19; 43.6; 63.8; Jer. 3.14, 19, 22; 4.22; Hos. 2.1 [1.10], and the rare designation of Yahweh as the 'Father' of his people in the Old Testament [Deut. 8.5; 32.6ff; Isa. 63.16; 64.8; Jer. 3.19; Mal. 2.10; Ps. 103.13-14; Prov. 3.11-12], along with the use of 'mother' language in Num. 11.12; Deut. 32.18; Isa. 46.3; 49.15-16; 63.9; 66.13).[16] The implications of an intimate relationship and a responsibility for the safety and well-being of the child which these passages contain fit well with the present context (see further Brueggemann, *Theology*, pp. 244-47, 258-59). This passage is often seen as the basis for the others (so Brueggemann, p. 245; also Huonder, pp. 24, 29), but its

---

[15] The passage is not extant in 4QpalExod^m, but it has been inferred from considerations of the space available that the longer text of SP was also represented in this manuscript here.

[16] For full discussion see W. Schlisske, *Gottessohne und Gottessohn im Alten Testament* (BWANT 17; Stuttgart, 1973); also more briefly Huonder, *Israel Sohn Gottes*, pp. 20-31.

terminology as a whole rather suggests that it is a late element of the book and itself draws on the other passages (see the introduction). The idea of Israel as Yahweh's son was retained in post-biblical literature, as in 4Q504, 3.4-7, where Exod. 4.22 is cited (see also Schmidt, p. 215, and more fully Huonder, *Israel Sohn Gottes*). It is no coincidence that this idea is linked here to Israel's responsibility to 'serve' or 'worship' Yahweh (Heb. *ʿābad*, v. 23), which will recur so often in the context of the demand for Israel's release (7.16 etc.): for such a duty of a son to his father was a commonplace of ancient Near Eastern expectations (Huonder, p. 27, with n. 1: cf. 2 Kgs 16.7; Jer. 10.20; Mal. 3.17).

24. The location of the ensuing episode at a 'camping-place' (cf. Josh. 4.3: a built structure is not implied by *mālôn* in BH) probably indicates an event in the night, which has led commentators to dwell on the similarity to Jacob's wrestling with an 'angel' by night (Gen. 32.22-32). The two episodes seem already to have been linked no later than the first century B.C. in a 'Rewritten Bible' text which reworked the Pentateuchal narrative. Five fragmentary copies of this work were found in Cave 4 at Qumran (4Q158, 364-67) and in one of them Exod. 4.27-28 immediately follow Gen. 32.25-32 (4Q158 fr. 1-2: *DJD* V, pp. 1-2). This probably means (as there is no particular connection between these passages) that Exod. 4.24-26 came before the extract from Genesis and that some kind of correlation was made between it and Genesis 32 in the original complete text. The introduction of an angel into this passage by LXX and Tgg (see Text and Versions) made them even more similar than they are in the MT. But the original narrator here is not interested in the timing of the episode concerning Moses, but rather in its spatial location: 'on the way' from Horeb and Midian to Egypt. Of course spatial location is also important in the Jacob episode, but in a different, more specific way. The verb 'came upon' (Heb. *pāgaš*) can refer to an encounter which turns out to be either hostile, as here, or friendly, as below in v. 27 (see Note x on the translation). No reason is given here for Yahweh's attack: either this means that there was no reason (Yahweh's actions are not always explained in the OT: cf. Gen. 4.4-5) or, more likely, the reason lies somewhere in the preceding context. The former alternative led to the description of Yahweh's action here as 'demonic' (see esp. P. Volz, *Das Dämonische in Jahwe* [Tübingen, 1924], pp. 3, 13, 15, who saw this as a widespread and theologically significant element in the OT): if the point has some validity, it is nevertheless not the last word in this episode (cf. Schmidt, pp. 233-34). For the possibility that there was originally a close link between this episode and Yahweh's anger in 4.14 see the introductions to this passage and to 4.10-17.[17] The traditional Jewish interpretation deduced from Zipporah's action in v. 25 that Yahweh's attack was due to Moses' failure to circumcise his son in accordance with the requirements of Genesis 17 (see the full discussion by Vermes in *Scripture and Tradition*, pp. 178-92): this is found already in *MRI* on 18.3 (second–third cent. A.D.), and it has been claimed to be older still (Vermes, pp. 179-84). The total omission of the episode in the Hellenistic Jewish sources (Artapanus, Ps-Philo, Philo and Josephus), however, suggests that it was still an enigma to many at that time. It is in any case hazardous to explain an episode which is likely to belong to an early layer of the tradition from a demand that is most evident in the later Priestly source: this may well skew our understanding of its original meaning (see further the discussion of vv. 24-26 as a whole in the introduction to this passage).

25-26. Like the beginning of v. 24, with its reference to the journey (presumably) from Midian to Egypt, v. 25 makes connections with v. 20 rather than vv. 21-23: Moses' wife (but now referred to by name as Zipporah, as in 2.21) and his son (but only one, again as in 2.21, whereas 4.20 as it stands mentions 'sons' in the plural, and oddly the child is referred to here as Zipporah's) are the persons explicitly mentioned. But Moses himself must surely be meant by both 'his' (*pace* Childs, p. 103) and 'you', for otherwise this verse has no connection with its context. It seems to follow that the child has not previously been circumcised, and Moses likewise, for the smearing of blood on his genitals (or 'legs': see Note s on the translation) constitutes a kind of circumcision by proxy. The whole process is understood in v. 26 as bringing an end to the threat to

---

[17] This is a much more serious possibility than F. Coppens's view that v. 24 continues the direct speech of vv. 21-23, with the object suffixes referring to Pharaoh's son ('La prétendue aggression nocturne de Jahvé contre Moïse, Séphorah et leur fils', *ETL* 18 [1941], pp. 68-73): despite his appeal to Joüon §1181 the verbs cannot be construed as futures, as his interpretation requires. For further criticism see Robinson, 'Zipporah', p. 455 n. 15.

Moses' life, in a very similar way to what is said about the blood of the passover lamb in 12.7, 12-13, 22-24. But why does Zipporah describe Moses as a 'bridegroom of blood' as she does this? And why does the narrator pick out this saying for special comment in v. 26? The phrase appears to mean 'a bloody bridegroom' (for a discussion of alternatives see Note t on the translation). Propp suggests seeing this as a reference to Moses' killing of an Egyptian in 2.12 (pp. 234-38, following P. Middlekoop, *South-East Asian Journal of Theology* 8 [1967], pp. 34-38: see also his own article 'That Bloody Bridegroom' [above, n. 9]), although he thinks that the phrase was also applied to the child in a different sense in v. 26 (and prior to the creation of this aetiology for it). It is true that this would provide the missing explanation for Yahweh's attack on Moses (punishment for his bloodguilt) in v. 24, but is it likely that the author would have seen Moses' killing of an Egyptian as culpable homicide? It is more likely in the context that the blood referred to here is blood from the wound of circumcision seen as having the power to ward off the danger that threatened Moses, and there is no need for it to mean anything different in v. 26. Yet, as Propp and others have seen, it is very likely that the Hebrew phrase, *ḥᵃtan dāmîm*, here rendered 'bridegroom of blood', was current at the time of the original telling of the story and required an explanation, preferably an impressive one linked to the people's origins such as this episode gives it. Whether its original *Sitz im Leben* was a marriage ceremony or a circumcision ceremony, and what it meant in that context, can no longer be determined with any certainty: for some suggestions see the introduction to this section.

27. This verse, like those which follow it, seems to presuppose that Moses has not left the mountain of God (for which see on 3.1). If so (the only alternative is that the mountain lay 'on the way' from Midian to Egypt), this contradicts the narrative in vv. 18-26 and suggests that v. 27 (and 28) belongs to a different account from them (see n. 13 on the introduction for further discussion). Yet it is curious that Yahweh only now instructs Aaron to meet Moses, whereas in v. 14 he says that Aaron is (or soon will be) already on his way (see Note m on the translation of 4.10-17). The difficulty cannot be resolved by translating 'Yahweh said' here as a pluperfect (so Böhl [acc. Houtman, p. 450], Buber-Rosenzweig, NEB), since a different word-order would be required for this, as Childs has seen (pp. 93, 104), and Schmidt's suggestion that Yahweh is represented as speaking simultaneously to Moses and Aaron (p. 238) is impossible, given the narratives which separate the two episodes. The present sequence is easier to understand if, as argued earlier, vv. 14-16 are a secondary insertion (see the introductions to this section and to 4.10-17).

The kiss is a common gesture of greeting or farewell between members of the same family and sometimes others in the Old Testament: the examples in Gen. 33.4 and 45.15 are especially similar to this one. There need be no implication of ranking here (cf. Houtman, p. 451, against Ehrlich: for useful reviews of all the evidence see *IDB* 3, 39-40, and *TWAT* 5, 676-80 = *TDOT* 10, pp. 72-76).

28-30. The remainder of the journey back to Egypt is recounted very briefly at the beginning of v. 29: the rest of these verses is concerned with the words and signs given by Yahweh. They certainly can be read as the fulfilment of Yahweh's instructions to Moses in vv. 14-16, although on the one hand the reference to the 'signs' in vv. 28 and 30 goes beyond what is prescribed there and recalls rather vv. 1-9 (and in v. 28 perhaps 3.12, which 4Q158 introduced here: see Text and Versions);[18] and on the other hand it is only v. 30a which indisputably presupposes vv. 14-16. The remainder could and perhaps should be seen as following on from 3.7–4.9 (or part of this sequence). The gathering of the 'elders' (v. 29) recalls 3.16-18 in particular. The implication of v. 30 as it stands is certainly that Aaron performed the signs (see Note aa on the translation): the oddness of this in connection with vv. 1-8(9) and especially v. 17 may well be evidence that the reference to Aaron in the first half of the verse is secondary and depends on the insertion of vv. 14-16.

31. The reference to 'the people' at the beginning of this verse at first seems to contradict the previous focus on the elders, but it is prepared for by the performance of the signs 'in the sight of the people' in v. 30b. Less easy to reconcile with unity of composition is the sequence in the original, 'believed...heard...bowed down and worshipped', the more so as connections are made here with two

---

[18] 'Commanded' (Heb. *ṣiwwāh*) in v. 28 also departs from the specific vocabulary (though not the content) of the earlier part of the chapter: in fact apart from P passages this verb only occasionally appears in the Exodus narrative (18.23; 19.7; 32.8; 34.4).

different passages, respectively 4.1-9 (as in v. 30b) and 3.7-8, 16-18 (as in v. 29).[19] However, these passages are all likely to belong to the J source, and if v. 31 is translated as we have done (see Note bb on the translation), it is possible to see the verse as the work of a single writer who brings out the people's twofold response to act and word with a flourish and a chiastic reversal of the order in the previous verse. The highlighting of the theological basis for this response, which is paralleled in P's narrative in 2.23-25, is an important thematic element of the older narrative here and, as Schmidt notes (p. 236), the concluding reference to worship uses a combination of verbs which is frequent, both in passages normally assigned to J (Gen. 24.26, 48; 43.28; Exod. 12.27; 34.8; Num. 22.31) and elsewhere (e.g. 1 Kgs 1.16, 31).

Text and Versions

וילך...וישב (4.18) Sy inverts the verbs, producing an alternative version of the combined sense.

יתר (4.18) So also Tg⁰ and LXX (Ιοθόρ: but this is its rendering of the name everywhere). SP and the other Versions have the normal spelling יתרו.

חתנו (4.18) LXX τὸν γαμβρὸν αὐτοῦ, 'his relative by marriage' (for which many mss have the more precise τὸν πενθερὸν αὐτοῦ: from Symm. according to Wevers, *Notes*, p. 25 n.1), and Vulg *cognatum suum*, 'his relative', perhaps use the vaguer terms (as in 3.1) to avoid a contradiction over the name of Moses' father-in-law.

לו (4.18) LXX had no equivalent, but many mss add αὐτῷ.

אלכה נא ואשובה (4.18) None of the Versions clearly reflects the cohortative form, rendering the verbs as futures, and נא is either ignored (LXX, Vulg, Sy) or rendered by words meaning 'now' (Tgg). Sy (exc. 5b1) has no equivalent to the conjunction.

ואראה (4.18) Vulg *ut videam* indicates the expression of purpose implied by the Heb.: the other Versions render by a simple future.

בשלום (4.18) LXX ὑγιαίνων, reflecting the classical use of the imperative of this verb as a parting greeting. The Three preferred a more literal rendering (εἰς εἰρήνην or ἐν εἰρήνῃ). After 4.18 LXX adds its version of 2.23a, probably, as Wevers suggests (*Notes*, p. 51) to ease the 'abruptness' of the transition to Yahweh's instruction in v. 19, or at least to clarify the

---

[19] LXX's rendering 'rejoiced' for 'heard' can be traced to a small variation in the Heb. (see Text and Versions), which perhaps arose from consciousness of this problem.

שֻׁב (4.19)   LXX ἄπελθε seems imprecise, but ἀπέρχομαι is used a number of times to represent שׁוּב (e.g. Gen. 3.19: see further Hatch and Redpath, pp. 121-22) and it perhaps had a secondary meaning 'go *back*' (as in two of the examples cited in LSJ). Sy again inverts the verbs, as in v. 18.

מִצְרָיִם (4.19)   SP adds the directional ending ה- (cf. the form in v. 21), as do some Masoretic mss according to *BHS*.

מֵתוּ (4.19)   Tg^J 'they are considered as dead people', with an expansive explanation 'they have been emptied and have gone down from their wealth [i.e. become impoverished]'. The 'men' are identified with Dathan and Abiram in Jewish tradition, who were seen as the 'Hebrews' who Moses stopped fighting in 2.13-14 and also the 'supervisors' of 5.20 (B.Ned. 64b; Gen.R. 71.6; Lam.R. 3.2: cf. Text and Versions on 2.13 for Tg^J's earlier naming of them). Accordingly, since they were to appear again later in the story, they could not really be dead, but were regarded 'as if' dead. See further Text and Versions on 10.28-29.

הָאֲנָשִׁים (4.19)   LXX has no explicit equivalent, but this will be due to Greek idiom.

הַמְבַקְשִׁים אֶת נַפְשֶׁךָ (4.19)   Tgg paraphrase in various ways to make clear that this means 'to kill' Moses.

אִשְׁתּוֹ...בָּנָיו (4.20)   LXX has no specific equivalent to the possessive suffixes (Greek idiom does not require one), but Origen added αὐτοῦ after τὰ παιδία, from Symm according to Sy^h. A number of commentators have emended בניו to the sing. form to agree with v. 25 (e.g. Wellhausen, Holzinger). The textual tradition lends no support to this change, unless the mysterious insertion of τὸ παιδίον in v. 19 by papyrus 866 of LXX is a misplaced marginal variant for v. 20. Even so, the pl. form of the suffix is probably a secondary harmonisation (by the sole addition of a *yodh*: it might even have originated accidentally) to fit with the later mention of two sons in 18.3-4 (like the addition made to 2.22 in some of the ancient Versions: see Text and Versions there).

הַחֲמוֹר (4.20)   LXX τὰ ὑποζύγια, plural, no doubt reasoning that the noun could be collective in meaning (Wevers, *Notes*, p. 51), as it is in Gen. 32.5, and that more than one donkey would be needed.

וַיָּשָׁב (4.20)   Sy (except 5b1) adds *lm'zl*, 'to go', pairing the two verbs as in vv. 18-19, and in the same inverse order that it introduced there and uses again in v. 21.

אַרְצָה (4.20)   SP omits the directional ending here, as frequently with אֶרֶץ in the construct state (cf. *GSH* §148d): otherwise, its reading would have a strong claim to be the more original one (as being *difficilior*). LXX, Vulg, and Sy (exc. 5b1) all exceptionally have no equivalent to ארצה here (cf. LXX in

Gen. 48.5; Exod. 5.12; 9.24; Vulg in Exod. 10.15), but this may be because hitherto in Exodus מצרים has always been used alone. For LXX see *THGE*, pp. 238-39.

את מטה האלהים (4.20)   Clearly the concept of 'God's staff' caused anxiety, perhaps because of mythological parallels (see the Explanatory Note and Propp, p. 228), to some of the translators (though not to Exod.R. 8.1, which speaks without apology of God handing 'his sceptre' to Moses in 4.17), who resorted to paraphrase: LXX τὴν παρὰ τοῦ θεοῦ; Tg^{O,N,J} 'with which the miracles were done before the Lord'. Tg^J adds legendary details about the rod already given by it in 2.21, and also the fact that 'it was of sapphire from the glorious throne, its weight was forty seahs' (for this see the texts cited in *AramB* 2, p. 172 n. 20).[20]

בלכתך לשוב (4.21)   LXX renders both verbs by participles in a genitive absolute construction, sacrificing a little precision to smoother Greek style (though not according to classical models: cf. Wevers, *Notes*, p. 52). Vulg *revertenti* curiously links these infinitives to ויאמר, as though Heb. read בלכתו. Sy again inverts the verbs, as in vv. 18-19.

ראה (4.21)   Vulg *vide ut* clearly sees the words that follow as a *casus pendens* belonging with ועשיתם, and Wevers argues (*Notes*, p. 52) that LXX did so too, despite the αὐτά that follows ποιήσεις. SP adds את before כל to conform to strict grammar, as it does in 1.18; 2.10, 16, and so perhaps took כל־המפתים as the object of ראה: otherwise there would be a curious mixture of the *casus pendens* and the extraposed object constructions (see generally on the issue Muraoka, *Emphatic Words*, pp. 95-97; JM §156c).

שמתי (4.21)   Sy *ʿbdt* might be 1st person ('I did') or 2nd person ('you did'), in either case referring back, imprecisely, to the actions previously done in 4.1-9 rather than to the power given to Moses to do them in the future. LXX ἔδωκα may simply mean 'I put', as elsewhere in LXX (Muraoka, *Lexicon*, p. 125: a Semitism?).

בידך (4.21)   LXX and Sy (except 5b1) render freely with the pl.

אחזק (4.21)   The majority of SP mss (including the early ones: cf. Tal, Sadaqa, three of Crown's and Camb. 1846) read אחזיק. The Hiphil is also widely attested instead of the Piel in 14.4, 17 and ויחזק in several other verses could be read as a Hiphil form. This might imply a use of the Hiphil for 'make stubborn' which is not attested in Masoretic Hebrew. The fact that כבד is used in the Hiphil with a similar meaning could be responsible for this development. Tgg, as they will later, all use *tqp*, cf. Aq and Theod ἐνισχύσω. To avoid a reference to 'hardening' this early in the story Symm has θρασυνῶ

---

[20] Earlier very positive developments of the references to Moses' staff were made in Ezek., *Exagoge* 68-82 (a vision of a φῶς γενναῖος on a throne who gives Moses not only his sceptre but a crown) and *LAB* 19.11 (it will be like the rainbow promised to Noah): cf. Elfick, 'The Staff of Moses', pp. 23-26.

לבו (4.21)   Tgʲ יצרא דליביה, 'the inclination of his heart', pointing aptly (cf. Note j on the translation) to 'will' as the meaning of לב here.

בני בכרי (4.22)   LXX υἱὸς πρωτότοκός μου (noun plus adjective); the Three more exactly add μου after υἱός.

את בני (4.23)   LXX τὸν λαόν μου, which the Three naturally correct to agree with MT. LXX is harmonising with the normal form of the demand addressed to Pharaoh (esp. 7.16 etc.), but in so doing it destroys the force of the reasoning intended here.

ויעבדני (4.23)   LXX ἵνα and Vulg *ut* clearly pick up the expression of purpose by simple *waw* here. Tgg, as usual, safeguard the divine majesty by replacing the suffix by 'before me'.

ותמאן (4.23)   LXX and Sy render as a condition: 'if you are not willing…', mistakenly conforming to 9.2 (see Text and Versions there). But Aq καὶ ἀνένευσας, Symm ἠπείθησας (cf. Salvesen, *Symmachus*, p. 72), and σὺ δὲ οὐκ ἐβούλου in the majority of mss, like Vulg *noluisti*, reflect the accusation in the past tense in MT (so also Tgᴺ). The inverted participial construction in Tgᴼ and Tgʲ is not so clear (see the different renderings in *AramB* ad loc.): it might perhaps imply the conditional interpretation.

אנכי (4.23)   Aq and Theod are credited with the rendering ἐγώ εἰμι here (LXX as expected ἐγώ), on which see Barthélemy, *Dévanciers*, pp. 69-78, and O'Connell, *Theodotionic Revision*, pp. 19-22: it is regular for אנכי in the 'καιγε recension', Aq and Theod and apparently derives from rabbinic speculation about the opening word of the Decalogue (Barthélemy, pp. 74-78).

לשלחו (4.23)   Sy (except 5b1) has 'my son' in place of the suffix.

הרג (4.23)   LXX ἀποκτενῶ and Vulg *interficiam* rightly see the participle as referring to the future here.

בנך בכרך (4.23)   LXX again (as in v. 22) represents only one of the suffixes, this time the first one (likewise Vulg here). The Three add σου after πρωτότοκον to match MT.

ויהי (4.24)   Sy (except 5b1) adds 'Moses'.

במלון (4.24)   LXX ἐν τῷ καταλύματι, a word with a variety of meanings (cf. Lee, *Lexical Study*, p. 99; *BAlex*, pp. 103, 175) but probably implying a building, as do Vulg *in diversorio*, Tgᴼ בבית מבתה, Tgᴶ·ᴺ בבית אבתותא/ה, and Sy *byt bwth*.

יהוה (4.24)   LXX ἄγγελος κυρίου, Tgᴼ·ᴶ מלאכא די', and Tgᴺ מלאכא מן קדם יי' substitute an angelic figure for Yahweh himself (cf. Exod.R. 8.1). In Jub. 48.2-3 the attack is attributed to the evil 'prince Mastema' and an angel is Moses' deliverer. On the Jewish interpretation of vv. 24-26 generally see G. Vermes, *Scripture and Tradition*, pp. 178-92. Theod, Symm, Vulg and Sy agree with MT; Aq is curiously credited with ὁ θεός.

המיתו (4.24) Sy again adds 'Moses'. Tg^J has an extensive plus to give already here the reason that Moses had been prevented by Jethro from circumcising Gershom, although in the case of his second son Eliezer agreement had been reached to circumcise him. For other, fuller versions of this explanation of the episode see the references in *AramB* 2, p. 172 n. 23, esp. *MRI* on 18.3. Tg^{N,F,G} refer to it only in v. 26.

ויקח (4.25) Vulg inserts *ilico*, 'at once', to strengthen the connection with v. 24 (cf. Exod.R. 5.8: מיד, 'at once').

צר (4.25) The distinction from צור, '(large) rock', seems to be missed by Aq πέτραν and perhaps Vulg *petram* (cf. *OLD*), though the latter's additional *acutissimam* (from Theod. ἀκρότομον) suggests a wider use of the loan-word to refer to flakes of stone. Sy *ṭrn'* (of which the טנרא of the Tgg seems to be a metathesised by-form: the affixed *n* is more likely to be original than an infixed one, cf. Moscati, p. 82) = 'flint'. LXX ψῆφον simply means 'small stone, pebble': it is not clear what Symm thought to gain by the addition of πετρίνην, unless perhaps the idea of roughness, which the context requires.

ותכרת (4.25) LXX περιέτεμεν and Vulg *circumcidit* use the specialised words rather than a generic word like the *gzr* preferred by the Aramaic versions.

בנה (4.25) Tg^J names Gershom explicitly, an example of the clarification that is characteristic of its rendering of this verse (cf. also 2.13).

ותגע (4.25) The *plene* form ותגיע of the Hiphil (for which see *GSH* §11aκ, 78d, 94e) is attested as the SP reading by several mss in von Gall, all of those used by Crown and Camb. 1846. LXX καὶ προσέπεσεν, 'she/it fell', is probably based on the meaning 'touch, reach', which the Hiphil as well as the Qal can have and which is reflected more precisely by Symm καὶ ἁψαμένη, Theod καὶ ἥψατο and Vulg *tetigitque*. Sy w^{e}ḥdt, 'she took hold of', seems to be a further development which may be based on LXX: προσπίπτω can mean 'prostrate oneself' and even 'embrace'. The Tgg use קרב, which can also mean 'touch', in most (perhaps all) cases in a causative sense 'bring near, offer', with the foreskin as the explicit (Tg^J) or implied (Tg^{O,N,F,G}) object (in Tg^{O,N} an intransitive sense, 'she/it came near', is also possible: so Vermes, *Scripture and Tradition*, pp. 181, 183, and *AramB* 7, pp. 11-12, for Tg^O). Tg^{Nmg} has ותלקת (i.e. ושלקת, 'threw'), which provides some background for AV's 'cast it at his feet' (see Note r on the translation).

לרגליו (4.25) LXX simply πρὸς τοὺς πόδας, which is idiomatic if the possessive can easily be understood (αὐτοῦ is added by many mss, as by Symm and Theod), but it could theoretically refer to 'Moses or the angel [cf. v. 24LXX] or her son' (Wevers, *Notes*, p. 55). Most likely the feet of the angel are meant (Vermes, *Scripture and Tradition*, p. 180). Vulg and Sy likewise retain the imprecision of MT, but Tg^O (which in fact has the paraphrastic לקדמוהי, 'before him') and the other Tgg explicitly identify the feet as those of the angel, who is now given the attribute 'Destroyer' or 'of destruction' (only ms. V of Tg^F lacks this), which derives from the Heb. המשחית of 12.23.

כי (4.25) There is no explicit equivalent in LXX, Vulg, Tg^{O,J,F,G} and Sy, but Tg^N has ארום. The other Versions presumably treated it as a superfluous introduction to the direct speech.

חתן דמים אתה לי (4.25) Aq, Symm, Theod, Vulg and Sy reproduce MT (with which SP agrees) precisely, but LXX and Tgg either paraphrase freely or had a different *Vorlage*. According to Vermes, *Scripture and Tradition*, pp. 179-84, they all represent a common early tradition of exegesis and theology which saw Moses' life being saved by the 'sacrificial' blood of circumcision (for similar ideas cf. Tg^J on Ezek. 16.6 and Lev.R. on 17.11, both of which attribute the same saving power to the blood of circumcision as to the blood of the Passover lamb). This is clearly the tenor of the Tgg (see also their versions of v. 26): Tg^O 'by this blood of circumcision a bridegroom has been given to us' (Vermes, p. 181, and *AramB* ad loc. [cf. *AramB* 2, p. 172 n. 25] render as a wish, but אתיהיב is surely a perfect); Tg^J (following, as in the Pal. Tg. texts, a reference to Jethro's interference with the circumcision of Gershom) 'so may this blood of circumcision atone (יכפר) for my bridegroom'; Tg^{N,G} 'and now may this blood of circumcision atone[21] for the sins of this bridegroom'; Tg^F likewise, but with 'so' in place of 'now' and in ms. P with 'so that it may save this bridegroom from the hands/power of the angel of death' instead of 'for...bridegroom'. LXX ἔστη τὸ αἷμα τῆς περιτομῆς τοῦ παιδίου μου is identical to and probably derived from its rendering of v. 26b: for its basis and perhaps different implications from the Tgg see the discussion there.

וירף (4.26) LXX (apart from B and other mss which omit the whole verse by homoeoteleuton) has καὶ ἀπῆλθεν, 'and he departed',[22] Vulg *et dimisit*, which can mean 'and he left (him)' (cf. Symm, Theod). Closer to the precise meaning of MT are Tg^{O,J} with ונח, 'left off', and ופסק, 'ceased', respectively. The Pal. Tg. texts and Sy use the Aphel of רפי, 'let go of', which would be more appropriate if the Heb. were Hiphil, as some have in fact suggested. All the Tgg except Tg^O make the subject explicit, whether as מלאך חבלא (Tg^J), מלאכא (Tg^N), מחבלא (Tg^{F,G}; Tg^{Nmg} has this as well as מלאכא). Tg^F subordinates this clause to the following one by beginning with וכד, 'and when'.

ממנו (4.26) SP ממנה, 'from her', i.e. Zipporah, a reading which has a little support in the Greek tradition. The subject of וירף may then be Moses (cf. 18.2 and Salvesen, *Symmachus*, pp. 74-75). 4QGen-Exod^a appears to agree with MT (though the remains are very slight), as does all the other versional evidence.

---

[21] The Neofiti ms. reads וכפר, 'and...has atoned'. which might be compared to Tg^O's perfect, but the editors propose reading יכפר as in Tg^{J,F,G} and *AramB* translates accordingly.

[22] Wevers' idea that it means 'she departed' (i.e. Zipporah: *Notes*, pp. 55-56) is theoretically possible, but unlikely.

אז (4.26)   Tgg and Sy render as expected 'then', but LXX διότι, Symm, Theod ὅτι and in effect Vulg *postquam* all depart from the normal meaning of אז, making a causal link between Zipporah's words and God/the angel's departure.

אמרה (4.26)   The Tgg other than Tg⁰ elaborate to 'praised and said', to fit the exclamatory paraphrase which follows.

חתן דמים למולת (4.26)   Literal renderings of MT are found in Aq (preserved for דמים למולת only), Symm, Theod, Vulg (where *ob circumcisionem* is noteworthy) and Sy. LXX and the Tgg again paraphrase, but in different ways. LXX's ἔστη τὸ αἷμα τῆς περιτομῆς τοῦ παιδίου μου (found also in the previous verse), 'the blood of my child's circumcision is staunched' (for this use of ἵστημι see Luke 8.44, following Vermes, *Scripture and Tradition*, p. 180), apparently read חתן as if it were חתם, lit. 'sealed' but 'closed up' in Lev. 15.3, as does more clearly the ἐσφράγισε attributed here to ὁ ἑβρ; and it adds τοῦ παιδίου μου contextually without support in the Heb. In LXX there is no ritual manipulation of the foreskin: these (repeated) words are what causes (cf. διότι) the angel to desist from attacking Moses, after the bloody act of circumcision has been completed on the child (the difference from the Targumic theology is well brought out by Salvesen, *Symmachus*, pp. 73-74). The Tgg apparently proceed from an understanding of MT to mean 'a bridegroom of the blood of circumcision' (cf. Salvesen, p. 74), i.e. a bridegroom who benefits from the blood of circumcision. Tg⁰, 'but for this blood of circumcision the bridegroom would have been condemned to death (קטול – cf. v. 24)', restricts its elaboration of this to reflection on Moses' situation, while the other Tgg, with slight variations of wording, generalise it into an encomium of circumcision as such and introduce a further reference to the Angel of Destruction (or Death): 'How precious is this blood of circumcision, which saved the bridegroom from the hands of the Angel of Destruction!' (Tgᴶ). Cf. *MRI* on 18.3 and Exod.R. 5.8 for similar praise of circumcision. It is the blood itself which 'saves', or 'atones', as these texts say in v. 25.

לאהרן (4.27)   4Q158 includes some of v. 27a in its expanded version of the Pentateuch (immediately preceded by verses from Genesis 32, probably because of their similarity to vv. 24-26), and adds a superfluous לאמר here. This was clearly not present in 4QGen-Exodᵃ.

משה (4.27)   Sy (except 5b1) adds 'your brother' (cf. 4.14).

בהר האלהים (4.27)   Sy (except 5b1) adds 'Horeb', as in MT at 3.1. Tg⁰ᴶ have instead 'at the mountain on which the glory of the Lord was revealed', as they (and Tgᴺ) have at 3.1. Here Tgᴺ has 'at the mountain of the Lord's sanctuary'. בית מקדשא is a common Targumic designation for the Jerusalem temple (cf. Tgᴶ on Isa. 2.2 and Tgg other than Tg⁰ at Exod. 15.17), and the use of it here (and at Num. 10.33) by Tgᴺ⁽ᶠ⁾ is surprising, apparently reflecting an equation in some sense of Jerusalem with Sinai/Horeb and an emphasis on the latter as a place of cult rather than the theophanic significance which is prominent elsewhere, even in Tg^N (Chester, *Divine Revelation*, pp. 159-65; also Hayward, *Divine Name*, pp. 107-109, where Jub. 8.19 is cited for this). There could be dependence on Exod. 3.5 and some interpretations of 15.13.

וישק לו (4.27) LXX καὶ κατεφίλησαν ἀλλήλους makes this a mutual greeting, perhaps conforming the narrative to the social customs of a different world (cf. examples of bilateral kissing in *Joseph and Asenath* 4.1-7; 20.1-4; 21.7; 22.9, and more generally *ABD* 4, pp. 89-92).

יהוה (4.28) Tg^J האילין, 'these' (for the 'article' see Stevenson, p. 18: it is a distinctive feature of Jewish Aramaic [exc. OTA], presumably derived from Heb.), which is probably a scribal error arising from the frequency with which this word follows פיתגמיא in Tg^J (cf. Gen. 4.8; 32.25; 43.7; 48.1 etc.): the divine name is needed to be the antecedent of the pronouns which follow.

שלחו (4.28) So 4QGen-Exod^a, Mur1 and probably 4Q158, which also has part of 3.12 (referring to the 'signs') after this verse, a typical 'cross-reference' of this document (cf. fr. 4 on Exod. 24.4-6). Some SP mss, however, including Camb. 1846 and those used by Sadaqa and Tal, have שלחהו, with the older form of the suffix which MT only rarely has after the third person m.s. perfect, except with Lamed He verbs (JM §62c, e; 79k). For similar divergences in SP cf. 2.3; 20.8; 32.20 and *GSH* §55bγ (p. 245). LXX ignored the suffix for simplicity of expression, but the hexaplaric mss reflect it with αὐτόν; Tg^N adds the divine name again after the verb (but then omits the rest of the verse).

צוהו (4.28) Vulg has no equivalent to the suffix. Tg^J and Sy (except 5b1) add *lmʿbd*, 'to do (them)', probably independently influenced by the combination which is most common in Deuteronomy, but found also in Exod. 35.1, 29; 36.5.

וילך (4.29) SP simplifies the grammar, no doubt secondarily, by reading the plural (cf. Vulg, Sy). The other versions and Mur1 agree with MT.

את־כל־זקני בני ישראל (4.29) LXX had no equivalent to כל (πᾶσαν is added in hexaplaric and other mss), or perhaps saw it as implied in its rendering of זקני by γερουσίαν, as in 3.16, 18; Tg^N, again as there, has חכימיא, 'the sages' (on both see Text and Versions on 3.16).

וידבר (4.30) Some early mss of Sy (but not 5b1) add 'to them'.

הדברים (4.30) LXX adds ταῦτα (cf. Tg^J in v. 28): the mss which omit it do not include the main hexaplaric witnesses (only 376), which suggests a different origin for this 'Masoretic' reading.

יהוה (4.30) LXX ὁ θεός, as earlier for יהוה in 4.1, 11 (perhaps): cf. Wevers, *Notes*, p. 57 for other examples, which include v. 31. But cases of this variation continue beyond ch. 5 (cf. 6.26; 8.25-26; 9.5; 10.7, 11) as Wevers recognises elsewhere (p. 89: cf. *THGE*, p. 241). A tendency to increase the number of occurrences of ὁ θεός/ (ה)אלהים) would not be surprising: but then the question is why such a process was not carried through more consistently. See further Text and Versions on 3.18.

ויעש (4.30)   Some Sy mss read a plural form, as do some of LXX, to avoid the implication that Aaron alone performed the signs, which would contradict v. 17: the *b* family of mss solved the problem by inserting Μωυσῆς.

האתת (4.30)   Tg^N נסייא, as earlier in the chapter, making no distinction from its rendering of המפתים in v. 21.

ויאמן (4.31)   SP has the plural form (as do Tg^N and Sy [exc. 5b1]), conforming (unnecessarily: see Note z on the translation) to the following verb. The edition of Mur1 (which usually agrees with MT) gives its reading as ויאמן, but it is difficult from what remains to exclude the possibility of a plural form.

וישמעו (4.31)   LXX ἐχάρη, implying that it read וישמחו, with interchange of gutturals: but the apparent illogicality of MT may have led to the 'correction'. 2Q2 [ו]ישמעו provides early support for MT.

פקד (4.31)   Tg^{O,J,N} and Sy have 'remembered' as at 3.16. Tg^N also amplifies with 'in his good mercies'.

יהוה (4.31)   So also 4QGen-Exod^a and SP. LXX ὁ θεός (see the note on v. 30).

כי ראה את־ענים (4.31)   Tg^{O,J} paraphrase with 'that their bondage was revealed before him', to avoid the idea of God seeing: for 'bondage' cf. 3.7 (Sy has the same both here and there). Tg^N, which is generally similar, has *ṣ'rwn*, 'pain, trouble', instead, which is closer to MT (again as in 3.7).

ויקדו וישתחוו (4.31)   L has a dagesh in the penultimate *waw* of וישתחוו, one of its occasional special errors noted by *BHS*. LXX and Sy (except 5b1) add 'the people' as subject and Sy (except 5b1) also has 'before the Lord' at the end. Tg^N expands וישתחוו into אודן ושבחן, following its tendency to introduce explicit references to praise (see *AramB* 2, p. 25 n. 16).

CHAPTER 5.1-23

MOSES AND AARON'S FIRST, FRUITLESS, ENCOUNTER WITH PHARAOH

The scene shifts to Pharaoh's palace, where vv. 1-9 and 15-18 are presumably located (note 'went in' [vv. 1, 15] and 'came out' [vv. 10 and 20] marking the beginnings and ends of these sections). The subdivision of the chapter is difficult, because it consists of a series of interconnected dialogues, but a division into vv. 1-5 (Moses and Aaron, Pharaoh), 6-18 (Pharaoh, the taskmasters and the Israelite supervisors) and 19-23 (the supervisors, Moses, Aaron and Yahweh) perhaps has the most to be said for it (for the use of dialogue in biblical narrative see Alter, *Art*, pp. 63-87). The final section only reaches its conclusion in 6.1, after which both ancient tradition and modern source criticism have observed a break (see the introduction to 6.1-9). This is a widely accepted analysis of the chapter, except that v. 19 is normally attached to the second section (which some commentators also divide after v. 14): it is a transitional verse with links in both directions. The modern chapter-division was probably designed to secure a connection between the two divine speeches at the beginning of ch. 6 and we have retained this to underline the artificiality of the canonical narrative at this point. Houtman's placing of the division between major sections after 5.21 has the merit of keeping all the renewed 'conversation' between Moses and Yahweh together (his next section ends at 7.13), but it badly obscures the way in which Moses' complaint in v. 23 arises directly from events earlier in ch. 5.

The dialogues in ch. 5 are mainly contentious ones, and exhibit features of a dispute (for details see Coats, pp. 52-53), which arises from Moses and Aaron's attempt to bring an end to the forced labour described in partly different terms in 1.7-14 (cf. 2.12-14; 3.7-10). Their immediate impulse is derived, as v. 3 makes explicit, from Yahweh's commissioning of Moses in 3.1–4.17, and there is no direct causal link with the previous section: hence the purely temporal connection by the adverb 'afterwards' in v. 1. There is in fact a much stronger connection to the plague-story of chs. 7–11, which can be seen both in the wording of the demand with which ch. 5 opens and in the impasse with which it ends, as well as in the explicit future tenses of 6.1. To describe it as a 'redactional bridge' linking the older traditions of Moses' call and the plague-story (Van Seters, p. 70, summarising Childs, with whom he does not agree) does not do justice to the role of Pharaoh's refusal here in provoking the transition from words to action which takes place in ch. 7, as is emphasised both in 6.1 and in 7.14-17. In that sense the chapter is 'a – necessary – preparation and introduction for the plague-cycle... Pharaoh's harsh reaction provides the legitimation for the plagues' (Schmidt, pp. 255, 265).

The chapter itself makes coherent sense, though it has some characteristics which have led to a variety of hypotheses about both its literary composition and the origin of the tradition represented here.

> Knobel was unable to reach a view about its origin, but Wellhausen saw it as a unity, all from the J source, while noting some variation in the vocabulary and what he called 'an abundance of expression here and there, for example in vv. 4-5' (*Composition*, p. 72). Those hints were taken up by his successors, who agreed (except for Holzinger) that vv. 1-2 were from E and v. 3 was from J (or *vice versa* according to Dillmann), because of the evident duplication between vv. 1 and 3, but they disagreed about the analysis of the remainder of the chapter. Further duplication was seen in vv. 4-5 (see the Explanatory Note on these verses), but whereas Carpenter/Harford-Battersby, Baentsch, McNeile and later Hyatt attributed v. 4 to E and the rest of the chapter to J, Smend (*Erzählung*, pp. 123-24) and his followers Eissfeldt, Beer and Fohrer (pp. 55-60) gave v. 4 to J and v. 5 to E and then divided the remainder of the chapter between the two sources, in a minute and over-ambitious analysis which was based largely on variations in vocabulary. Gressmann's more sensitive analysis (which has, however, been mainly ignored) saw v. 5 as redactional and intended to replace v. 4 and then divided the chapter as follows: J – vv. 3-4, 6-9, 13, 22-23; E – vv. 1-2, 10-12, 14-21 (6.1) (*Mose*, pp. 61-66). It was widely thought (and still is today) that some or all of the references to 'Aaron' and to the 'supervisors' were secondary. Rudolph's treatment of the passage was a turning-point: apart from the minor additions just mentioned he argued that the chapter is a unity, from J. In this he has been closely followed (apart from v. 4) by Noth, W.H. Schmidt, Kohata, Särkiö (*Exodus und Salomo*, pp. 69-77) and Graupner, and also by Van Seters and (ironically) by Propp, who now attributes the whole chapter to E. A single old narrative source for the chapter (J) is also envisaged by Floss (*Jahwe dienen*,

pp. 228-30), Weimar (*Berufung*, pp. 82-84) and L. Schmidt (*Beobachtungen*, pp. 5-7), but they attribute all or most of vv. 1-2 to a redactor of JE. Some recent studies, which otherwise treat the chapter as unified and early, have seen 5.22–6.1 as a redactional addition linked to chs. 3–4, whether by KD (Blum, *Studien*, p. 19) or by a very late redactor (K. Schmid, *Erzväter*, p. 251). Finally, two contemporary scholars regard vv. 1-2 as the earliest part of the chapter (but still not part of the oldest Exodus narrative), with the remainder being added at a very late stage (Levin, p. 330; Gertz, *Tradition*, pp. 335-45).[1]

The arguments for the redactional (or compositional) origin of 5.22–6.1 based on links to chs. 3–4 stand, or rather fall, with the views of Blum and Schmid about those chapters. Like other parts of 5.3–6.1, the links are with sections of those chapters which we have attributed to J, and so there is no difficulty (in the absence of other arguments against their originality here) in regarding these verses as an integral part of the chapter. Levin gives no reason for a late origin for 5.3–6.1 except for the connection with 3.18, to which the same considerations apply. Gertz's discussion is as usual much fuller, but no more persuasive (pp. 337-45). The claimed 'dependence' on vv. 1-2 ignores the completely different language used in vv. 1 and 3; the cross-references (*Querbezügen*) to '(key)-texts of the *Endredaktion*' such as 3.18-20, 11.1 and 14.11-12, 31 are only such if Gertz's very questionable conclusions about these passages are accepted (and in some cases they could as easily be dependent on ch. 5, if there is any literary relationship at all); and his view that 5.3–6.1 was designed to facilitate the integration of the P account of the call of Moses loses sight of the fact that (as will be more fully argued in the commentary on 6.1-9) 6.1 does not at all lead one to expect a recommissioning of Moses (especially one that makes no reference to Pharaoh's refusal) but rather immediate (cf. the emphatic initial 'now' [Heb. ʿattāh]) action from Yahweh to make Pharaoh change his mind. The very slight verbal parallels between 5.3–6.1 and 6.2-9 can readily be explained in other ways.

On the other hand, the separate origin of 5.1-2 from most if not all of the rest of the chapter is a valid insight of earlier scholarship which needs to be retained. In view of the sharply different terms in which the request for leave is put, it is astonishing that Rudolph's harmonising exegesis has had so much influence, even on those like Noth and W.H. Schmidt who reckon with two old narrative sources elsewhere in Exodus. The outcome is most clearly seen in Graupner's book on the Elohist, which makes the absence of any story of conflict between Moses/Yahweh and Pharaoh into a key element

---

[1] Aurelius, *Fürbitter*, pp. 16-67 (cf. 204, 207), earlier attributed 5.3–6.1 to a Deuteronomistic revision of the Exodus story.

of E's theology of the Exodus, which proceeds by stealth rather than by confrontation. In fact, just as v. 3 (and what follows it) is the expected fulfilment of what Yahweh commands in J (3.18), so vv. 1-2 follow on from 3.9-10 and 4.27-28 (E).[2] Since it is these verses which are clearly taken up in 7.14-16, the consequences for the literary analysis of the plague-story are considerable and will need fresh investigation later. But it begins to appear that, so far from lacking a plague-story, as a number of recent scholars have thought, it must be the E source (and not J) which is responsible for key elements in the confrontation between Moses/Yahweh and Pharaoh in chs. 7–11.

Whether further elements of the E account of Moses' first confrontation with Pharaoh have been taken up in 5.4ff. remains uncertain. It is certainly possible that one of the parallel responses of Pharaoh in vv. 4-5 derives from E and the difficulty of explaining why a redactor would have added either one of them favours this possibility. The use of 'the king of Egypt' alongside 'Pharaoh' in v. 4, as in 1.15-21, which is generally attributed to E, would support the attribution of the verse to E, as would the mention of Aaron alongside Moses. But on the whole the thematic continuity with what follows is probably decisive for both verses belonging to J. There is no argument for seeing verses later in the chapter as being from E: here Rudolph's critique of Smend and Eissfeldt was well-founded. The references to Aaron and the associated plural forms in vv. 4-5 and 20-21 are then presumably due to R^{JE}.

The background and origin of the tradition have been discussed from several points of view. Early in the twentieth century it was noted that the description of brick-making could be correlated with and illustrated by evidence that was coming to light from ancient Egypt. A wall-painting showing various aspects of the manufacture of bricks from the tomb of the vizier Rekhmire (fifteenth cent. B.C.) was often referred to (conveniently available in *ANEP*, p. 115: official publication in N[orman] de G. Davies, *The Tomb of Rekh-mi-Rēʿ at Thebes* [Publications of the Metropolitan Museum of Art, Egyptian Expedition 11; New York, 1943], pp. 54-55, pls lviii-lix; cf. N[ina]

---

[2] The alternative possibility that most of 5.1-2 might be a secondary introduction to the chapter (from R^{JE}?), paving the way for the terms used in chs. 7–11, is not obviously superior and has been effectively answered by Gertz, *Tradition*, pp. 109-11.

de G. Davies, *Paintings from the Tomb of Rekh-mi-Rēʿ* [Publications of the Metropolitan Museum of Art, Egyptian Expedition 10; New York, 1935], pls xvi-xvii, xxiii). The fullest account of the relevant Egyptian material is given by Kitchen, 'Brickfields' (several of the texts referred to have now been published in Kitchen's *Ramesside Inscriptions*): see also C.F. Nims, 'Bricks Without Straw?', *BA* 13 (1950), pp. 22-28 (includes an account of traditional brick-making techniques in modern Egypt); for further references see Note t on the translation of 1.7-22. The written evidence goes back to the Abusir papyri of the Old Kingdom and the Reisner, Kahun and Gurob papyri and the Kerma stele of the Middle Kingdom. From the thirteenth century B.C., P. Anastasi III and IV and the Louvre 'Leather Roll' of the 5th year of Ramesses II (records of the building of the 'Great Stable' at Thebes) provide the most vivid evidence. Stages of manufacture and materials are referred to (Reisner, P. Anastasi III and 'Leather Roll'), as are supervisors at both a low level (Reisner, 'Leather Roll' – cf. Rekhmire) and a higher level (Abusir, Gurob), targets/quotas (P. Anastasi III – 'making their quota of bricks daily' [3.1-3] – 'Leather Roll' [with reference also to deficits]), the use of straw (Reisner, P.Anastasi IV) and the recording of the numbers of bricks made and used on particular structures (Kahun and Gurob, Kerma stele, Deir el-Medina ostraca, 'Leather Roll'). The organisation of the work-force was no doubt similar to the better attested situation of the tomb workmen at Deir el-Medina, on which see J. Cerny, *CAH³*, II/2, pp. 620-26. There were scribes who kept a diary and recorded absentees and reasons for absence. There were regular days off on the 10th, 20th and 30th days of each month, as well as for major religious festivals (gaps in the 'Leather Roll', cols viii-ix may be due to such 'holidays'). Most of the Egyptian evidence relates to Egyptian workmen (where it is possible to tell), but the Rekhmire painting includes Syrians and Nubians (with a caption referring to 'captives') and P. Leiden 348 speaks of Nubians being rounded up to form a labour-force. The general correspondences with the narrative in ch. 5 are thus close, though presumably practices were similar in and around Israelite cities where there was much building in brick, such as Lachish. However, if records of this were kept, they have not survived.[3]

---

[3] The Yavneh-Yam inscription (*AHI* 7.001) is only loosely related.

An early date for elements of the narrative has been claimed on other grounds. M. Noth observed that vv. 6-19 are unusual in the Exodus story, because here (unlike vv. 1-4) it is not Moses (and Aaron) who deal(s) with Pharaoh on behalf of the Israelites but subordinate leaders (Heb. *šōṭ^erîm* – see the Note on v. 6), and he saw this passage as a relic of an early stage in oral tradition when Moses was not yet linked to the Exodus story (pp. 38-40, ET, pp. 53-55; cf. *ÜGP*, pp. 76-77, 179). The idea that Moses was a latecomer to the Exodus tradition has not found wide acceptance (for arguments against it see e.g. Smend, *Jahwekrieg*, Chapter 7, Nicholson, *Exodus and Sinai*, pp. 58-60, and Schmidt, p. 253). In this particular narrative the issue at stake (which is not the liberation of Israel but a worsening of their conditions of work) makes it natural that others should first be involved (so already Smend, *Jahwekrieg*, pp. 90-91, ET, p. 125), and it should be noted that it provides the opportunity for a renewed intervention by Moses in vv. 22-23.

Noth also associated with his argument the fact that the request to Pharaoh in v. 3 is based on a meeting which the Israelites (not Moses alone) have had with their God, summoning them (it is implied) to celebrate a festival to him in the desert. This collective encounter is distinct, he argued, from the account of Moses' call, in which he meets Yahweh as an individual (pp. 40-41, ET, pp. 55-56). On this basis others have built the hypothesis that this element of the narrative belonged originally to a separate group of Israel's ancestors from the main 'Exodus' group, who perhaps associated themselves with a 'mountain of God' distinct from Sinai/Horeb and with Aaron rather than with Moses (and maybe even with a god other than Yahweh): H. Seebass, *Mose und Aaron: Sinai und Gottesberg* (Bonn, 1962), pp. 83-100; H. Schmid, *Mose: Überlieferung und Geschichte* (BZAW 110; Stuttgart, 1968), Chapters 3 and 5 – compare also Noth, *ÜGP*, pp. 150-55. The familiar narrative of the Exodus and subsequent events would then be the result of a conflation of the traditions of the different groups. It is a tantalising possibility, but the supposedly distinct strands are now so tightly woven together that it is difficult to be confident in any reconstruction of a separate origin for them. Moreover Midian, which has some important associations with the 'alternative tradition' (especially in Exod. 18), is also intimately linked with the story of Moses and his call. Schmidt may therefore be correct to conclude that such speculation is to be rejected, while nevertheless recognising that the references to a festival or to worship in the desert outside Egypt are a very ancient part of the Exodus story (cf. pp. 251-54: for him it is the account in Exod. 18.10-12 which is most significant, see also his discussion in *Exodus, Sinai und Mose*, Chapter 7).

More recently a somewhat later episode in Israel's history has been thought to have shaped this part of the narrative, namely Solomon's subjection of the northern tribes to forced labour (1 Kgs 5.27: EVV. 13), his son's ill-advised threat to increase rather than lighten the severity of their bondage (1 Kgs 12.3-14) and their secession from Judah (12.16-19). Smend seems to have been the first to suggest a relationship between the two narratives (*Jahwekrieg*, pp. 91-92, ET, pp. 125-27), but subsequently the idea was greatly elaborated by F. Crüsemann (*Der Widerstand gegen das Königtum* [WMANT 49; Neukirchen, 1978]), R. Albertz (*Religionsgeschichte*, pp. 72, 217-19, ET, pp. 43, 141-43) and others. Albertz even suggested that it was the rebellion of the northern tribes that first gave rise to a developed Exodus narrative. See also the monograph of Särkiö, *Exodus und Salomo* (1998), pp. 69-77. There is of course a good deal of evidence that the Exodus was the key theme of Yahwism in the northern kingdom. But while it is certainly possible that features of the Exodus story have been drawn from more recent experiences under the monarchy, and even perhaps that this particular episode is modelled on the events of Rehoboam's reign, the stories of the Exodus and the northern kingdom only resemble one another at certain points and a wholesale generation of the one by the other is improbable.

Van Seters is sceptical about this approach for a different reason, namely that it places the origin of the story too early (*Life*, pp. 71-73). Solomon was not the only king to use corvée labour (cf. Jer. 22.13), and the building materials used by Solomon were stone and wood, not brick. Brick was, however, the main material employed by Nebuchadnezzar in his rebuilding of Babylon in the sixth century. Moreover, the term $šōṭ^erîm$, which occurs four times in Exodus 5, is otherwise characteristic of 'late Dtr passages'. These features of the story seem at first sight to fit much better with Van Seters's theory of a Yahwist author of the exilic period. Of course Van Seters has chosen to ignore the evidence mentioned earlier for brick architecture in Egypt and in Israel, and it is only in a footnote (p. 73 n. 28) that he acknowledges the occurrences of *šōṭ^erîm* in Deuteronomic laws which are scarcely all 'late Dtr' and which may well reflect administrative terminology of the monarchy period. Once again his argument for an exilic date for the Exodus narrative proves on closer examination to be less telling than at first sight.

The impact of both strands of the narrative in this chapter is well summed up in Moses' prayer in vv. 22-23, even though it probably related originally only to vv. 3-21: after the confident hopes at the end of ch. 4, Pharaoh's utter refusal to let Israel take time off to worship their God and his increasing of their burdens leads to despondency and protest. Here for a moment the story dwells (more than in ch. 1) on the slave's experience of an apparently unchangeable situation, in which any challenge to powerful authority only makes matters worse. Even Moses himself feels discredited – 'Why ever did you send me?' (v. 22) – and humiliated in the face of a power whose absoluteness is underlined by the constant repetition of its demands throughout vv. 6-19: 'a day's output each day' (vv. 13, 19). A somewhat different note is struck in vv. 1-2, which may well once have led on directly to the story of the plagues in ch. 7. Here it is Pharaoh's defiant rejection of the word of Yahweh that remains in the foreground, justified as he sees it by the fact that he knows nothing of this God. The lines of battle between the god-king and 'the God of Israel' are being laid out.

Both strands of the narrative call for release from labour for the sake of worship 'in the wilderness'. This may be of historical as well as theological significance. At any rate it establishes the closest connection between the liberation from foreign power and oppression which is the leading theme of this part of Exodus and the need for Israel to worship their own God as he requires. It is a connection that will be repeatedly underlined in the remainder of the book (cf. 20.1-2), and it has already been introduced in 3.12, where the first sign promised to Moses that God has sent him is the assurance that he and his people would worship God 'on this mountain'. In the present narrative it is sometimes suggested that the reason given for Pharaoh to release Israel is a mere pretext, a deceitful ploy. There is an element of deception, to begin with at least, but this lies in what is not said rather than in what is said, which reflects the universal biblical conviction that the life of the people of God depends on their worship of him (cf. v. 3).

1 [Afterwards[a] Moses and Aaron went in and said to Pharaoh, 'Thus says Yahweh, the God of Israel: Let my people go, so that[b] they may celebrate a festival for me in the wilderness'. 2 Pharaoh said, 'Who is Yahweh, that[c] I should obey his command, by letting[d] Israel go? I do not know Yahweh, and moreover[e], as for Israel, I will not let them go'.] 3 They said, 'The God of the Hebrews has met[f] with us. Let us go, please[g], a journey of three days into the wilderness, so that[h] we may sacrifice to Yahweh our God, lest he come against us with pestilence or sword'. 4 The king of Egypt said to them, 'Why, Moses [and Aaron], will you distract[i] the people from their work? Go to your labours!' 5 Pharaoh said, 'See the people of the land are now many – will you[k] have them cease[l] from their labours?' 6 That day Pharaoh commanded the taskmasters of the people[m] and their supervisors[n], saying, 7 'You shall no longer[o] give the people straw for making bricks as you have previously: let them go and gather stubble as straw[p] for themselves! 8 But you shall impose upon them the same quota[q] of bricks as they made previously – you shall not reduce it[r]. For they are lazy[s]: that is why they are crying out, saying, "Let us go, let us sacrifice to our God!" 9 Let the work be a heavy burden on these men, and let them attend[t] to it and not attend to lies[u]!' 10 The taskmasters of the people and their supervisors went out and said to the people, saying, 'Thus says Pharaoh, "I am not giving you straw: 11 you go and get straw for yourselves from wherever you can find it, for no reduction is made in your work'. 12 The people dispersed throughout all the land of Egypt to gather stubble[v] for straw, 13 for[w] the taskmasters were pressing them, saying, 'Complete your work, a day's output each day, as you did when you had straw!' 14 The supervisors of the Israelites whom Pharaoh's taskmasters appointed over them were beaten, with the words[x]: 'Why have you failed to complete your appointed task[y] recently[z], to make bricks as you did before?' 15 The supervisors of the Israelites went in and cried out to Pharaoh, saying, 'Why do you treat your servants like this? 16 No straw has been given to your servants but "Bricks!", they are saying[aa] to us, "Produce (bricks)!" Look, your servants are being beaten, but the fault is your people's[bb]!' 17 He said, 'You are lazy – lazy[cc]! That is why you are saying, "Let us go, let us sacrifice to Yahweh!" 18 Now go and work[dd]: straw will not be given to you, but you shall deliver[ee] a regular quota[ff] of bricks.' 19 The supervisors of the Israelites saw that they[gg] were in trouble when it was said[hh], 'You shall not reduce the number of bricks: a day's output each day!'

20 They confronted Moses [and Aaron], who [were] standing[ii] in their way when they came out from Pharaoh's presence, 21 and they said to [them], 'May Yahweh examine [you][jj] and judge! For [you] have brought us into bad odour[kk] with Pharaoh and his servants, so as to put[ll] a sword in his hand[mm] to kill us.' 22 Moses returned to Yahweh and said, '(My) Lord[nn], why have you done harm to this people? Why ever[oo] did you send me? 23 For[pp] ever since I went in to Pharaoh to speak in your name, he has done harm to this people – and you have certainly not delivered your people.'

Notes on the Translation

a. Heb. אחר(ו) is used in both instructions (Gen. 18.5) and narrative (Gen. 10.18; 30.21) for the next stage or sequel of an action. In the latter case the intervening period may be left vague, as it is here (cf. Num. 12.16; Judg. 1.9; 1 Chr. 2.21). So while a connection is certainly made with what has preceded, the expression is not decisive for the delimitation of units in the text (contra Childs, p. 94).

b. Heb. ויחגו. Simple *waw* can express purpose (GK §165a), as in 2.7; 3.3, 10, 18; 4.18, 23. But where a modal form precedes, as here and in 2.20, it is also possible to render the verb as a further cohortative or jussive: 'and let them celebrate...'

c. It is more common for the consecutive clause in such a question to be introduced with כי, as in 3.11 (cf. BDB, p. 566). But the multivalent conjunction אשר occasionally has a consecutive sense (e.g. Gen. 13.16; 22.14: Houtman, p. 11).

d. 'Gerundival' use of the inf. constr. לשלח (GK §114o).

e. Heb. וגם. At first this looks like a case of emphatic גם, which is often followed by an anteposed object as here (see Muraoka, *Emphatic Words*, pp. 143-44). But here it probably relates to the whole clause, in an additive and perhaps climactic sense (GK §153), as in 3.9.

f. Heb. יקרא, with the etymologically less correct spelling for יקרה, which appeared in 3.18 (MT). But the verb is spelt with *aleph* also in 1.10, as well as in לקראת (as often) in 5.20.

g. See Note c on 4.18-31.

h. See Note b.

i. See Text and Versions for the alternative reading of SP and 4QExod[b]. Heb. פרע is used in a variety of senses covered by the idea of 'let loose, let go' (in Judg. 5.2 a homonym meaning 'lead' may be involved, for which there are cognates in Ar. and Ug.). The construction with a personal object recurs only in 32.25 (in a different kind of context: cf. the Niphal in Prov. 29.18 and the only other use of the Hiphil in 2 Chr. 28.19) and the syntagm with מן only here. Overall it is a word that most often conveys a tone of disapproval (cf. its use in Proverbs).

j. Heb. ממעשׂיו, i.e. pl. For מעשׂה as a term for the Israelites' labours in Egypt cf. v. 13: appropriately there too this neutral word is put on the lips of Egyptians. For its use of daily work elsewhere cf. 23.12 and Ezek. 46.1.

k. Verse 5b is generally understood as an ironic statement or question without interrogative *he* (JB, Schmidt, Houtman); cf. GK §112cc and e.g. Num. 16.10.

l. Heb. שׁבת can mean 'cease' as well as 'rest': for the use with following מן cf. Jer. 31.36; Ezek. 16.41; 34.10 (both Hiphil as here); Hos. 7.4; Lam. 5.14. Propp (p. 154) aptly compares *lpny šbt* in the Yavneh-Yam inscription (*AHI* 7.001.5-6).

m. In vv. 10, 13 and 14 Heb. נגשׂ is clearly an 'occupation' word ('taskmasters': cf. Job 3.18), and the following שׁטריו here (cf. v. 10) indicates that it has the same sense here. The *beth* before the object can be compared to its use after משׁל, for example, and simply indicates authority (BDB, p. 90).

n. Heb. שׁטר, 'official', apparently a loan-word, cf. Akk. *šaṭāru* = 'write', although no example of a similar nominalised part. has appeared in Akk. (for some late attestations in Jewish Aramaic and (?) Punic see *DNWSI*, p. 1123). In BH only משׁטר in Job 38.33 and a PN in 1 Chr. 27.29 may be related: for a possible occurrence of the verb in an inscription from Hazor see *AHI* 24.012.1. The noun שׁטר is frequent in BH (25x), and is used in a variety of administrative contexts (see the Explanatory Note for details and discussion), but not outside this chapter for 'supervisors' of corvée labour. Verse 14 makes clear that they were Israelites appointed by the Egyptian taskmasters to organise the work-force and ensure its productivity.

o. MT האספון. The Masora noted that the א is 'not read': for the unusual writing of this form of יסף cf. 1 Sam. 18.29 and probably Job 27.19 (conversely forms of אסף and other Pe Aleph verbs are sometimes written without the expected א: GK §68h). GK §23i notes examples of א added after a final long vowel and calls them 'early scribal errors'. Examples of this 'fuller orthography' are now well known from Qumran (cf. Qimron, p. 21). But in medial position the phenomenon appears to be limited to this verb, and accidental confusion with the similarly pronounced imperfect forms of אסף is the most likely explanation.

p. Heb. תבן...וקששׁו: in v. 12 the expression is fuller, לקשׁשׁ קשׁ לתבן, and the meaning may well be the same here. There might, however, be a deliberate difference, as the verb קשׁשׁ is used in Num. 15.32-33 and 1 Kgs 17.10, 12 for gathering something other than קשׁ (sticks). Pharaoh's instructions may therefore have been to 'gather straw', as the normal material for brickmaking, while v. 12 reflects the labourers' ability only to gather קשׁ. On the difference between תבן and קשׁ see the note on v. 12.

q. Heb. מתכנת: both this word and the related תכן, which appears in v. 18, also occur in Ezek. 45.11, where תכן seems to mean 'quantity' and מתכנת the action of 'measuring'. The same sense for מתכנת fits in its other occurrences in Exod. 30.32, 37 and 2 Chr. 24.13, although in each case the context gives it a special nuance. The idea of a 'standard' measure or composition is common to all these passages (and probably the use of the related verb by Ezekiel) and this appears also in the slightly different use here for a 'quota' or fixed assignment of output (cf. Text and Versions).

r. For the masc. suffix referring to the fem. noun מתכנת see GK §135o.

s. Heb. נרפים, Niphal part. m.pl. of רפה (the same form twice below in v. 17). Houtman, following Ehrlich (cf. Vulg *vacant*), interprets this to mean that the workmen did not have enough to do, not that they were intrinsically lazy (p. 468: but his rendering 'lanterfanten/are lazy bums' does not bring out this view clearly). *HAL*, p. 1191, 'schlaff, untätig', also retains this as a possibility. In the absence of other occurrences of the Niphal the best guide to the meaning, in addition to the context, is likely to be the Hithpael (cf. JM §52c), which is used three times of culpable inaction (Josh. 18.3; Prov. 18.9; 24.10). The long-accepted rendering as 'lazy', which is also very appropriate to the context, should therefore be retained.

t. We have (like *BHS*) adopted the reading וישעו (from שעה) of SP and 4QExod[b], which is also presupposed by some of the Versions (see Text and Versions), in preference to MT's ויעשו, which Childs, Schmidt, Houtman and Propp retain. The latter would have to mean 'and let them work (on/in it)', but such an absolute use of עשה is paralleled only in Neh. 4.10. A direct contrast with the use of the same verb in the next clause is much more likely (cf. Amos 5.4-5 for this kind of word-play).

u. Lit. 'words of falsehood' (שקר). Houtman renders 'harmful' (sc. to Pharaoh), citing (p. 472) Klopfenstein, *Die Lüge*, pp. 138-42 (cf. pp. 321-22, and *THAT* 2, 1010-19 = *TLOT* 3, pp. 1399-1405) for the view that lying is condemned in the Old Testament for its harmfulness to the community and its relationship to Yahweh rather than for its transgression of the sanctity of truth. Whether this be so or not, it should not affect the translation of שקר, which is clearly 'falsehood, deceptiveness'. A better case might be made out for the sense 'disloyalty', which the related verb can bear (cf. Gen. 21.23), but such uses of the noun שקר itself are hard to find.

v. Here a distinction between Heb. קש and תבן is clearly made: since קש can be used 'for' or 'as' תבן it is the same kind of material but of a different origin. This is borne out by the other occurrences of these words. Outside this passage, which is the only biblical reference to its use in brick-making, תבן is most often food (so certainly in Isa. 11.7; 65.25) or bedding for animals (Gen. 24.25, 32; Judg. 19.19; 1 Kgs 5.8 [EVV. 4.28]). It is, in other words, a useful by-product of the harvest. Only in Job 21.18, where it is parallel to מץ (probably 'chaff' – cf. the association with a threshing-floor in Hos. 13.3), does it possibly refer to a waste-product (Jer. 23.28 and Job 41.19 are both inconclusive). קש, by contrast, is nowhere else put to any profitable use: in half its sixteen occurrences it is burnt (e.g. Exod. 15.7) and in four more it is blown by the wind (Isa. 40.24; 41.2; Jer. 13.24; Ps. 83.14). While the latter might suggest the threshing-floor and a reference to 'chaff' (i.e. the small pieces of residue from the process of winnowing), this need not be the case, and burning is more likely to point to the 'stubble' left in the fields (which might be quite long according to Schmidt, p. 262: see also his references to *BRL* and Dalman). מץ, which clearly means 'chaff', is never burned in the Old Testament.

w. The following words are a classic circumstantial clause, introduced by *waw* and including a participle as predicate (JM §159d: cf. Driver, *Tenses*, pp. 195-211; Andersen, *Sentence*, pp. 77-91; *IBHS* §37.6).

x. Heb. לאמר may introduce words spoken to the subject of the sentence as well as words spoken by them (cf. v. 19 below and other exx. in BDB, p. 56a).

y. Heb. חק, although most familiar as a word for 'decree, ordinance', can also refer (unlike חקה, apparently) to a portion or a due that is prescribed by authority: cf. Gen. 47.22, Lev. 6.11 and other exx. in BDB, p. 349; also *TWAT* 3, 150-52 = *TDOT* 5, pp. 141-42.

z. Heb. גם תמול גם היום. This pairing is much less common than the preceding תמול שלשם: in BH it appears only in 1 Sam. 20.27, where it has its literal meaning of 'yesterday or today' (cf. vv. 24-26 with v. 27a: 2 Sam. 15.20 makes a different, contrastive use of תמול and היום). Given the idiomatic wider use of תמול שלשם to mean 'formerly' (as also here), it is most probable that the rarer phrase could also be used generally, to mean 'latterly' or 'recently'.

aa. A participle with unexpressed subject (GK §116s-t) may presuppose a subject from the preceding context (so often after הנה) or the subject may be indefinite (GK §144i). In the actual words of the supervisors there is no such preceding context, and an indefinite (or passive) sense is implied. But to the reader, of course, it is quite clear who they mean.

bb. These words have been variously understood, often with a slightly different reading (see Text and Versions). The difficulties are that the vowels of חטאת indicate either a 2nd s.f. or a 3rd s.f. (cf. GK §44f, 74g) perfect (consecutive) verb, neither of which seems appropriate to the context, and that חטא is not elsewhere construed with a direct object of the one sinned against (contra LXX), but only in other senses (neither Prov. 20.2 [*HAL*, p. 293] nor 8.36 [mentioned but discounted by Schmidt, p. 244] is a clear parallel). It is also not clear whether עמך (if that is the true reading) means the Israelites (like עבדיך) or the Egyptians. The only way to understand MT as it stands is to assume that עמך is the subject and that the use of the 3rd s.f. form is due to the collective nature of the subject (GK §145k, cf. 122s): so apparently Tg⁰, 'your people sin against them'.[4] But elsewhere this construction seems only to be attested with non-personal subjects. Rashi took חטאת as a noun = 'sin',

---

[4] Propp (p. 257) acutely notes that עם appears to be feminine in Judg. 18.7 and Jer. 8.5, but in both places MT is likely to be corrupt.

lit. 'your people are a sin', with the same meaning, in line with GK §141b-c. This analysis of חטאת seems to be presupposed by Aq, Symm and Theod and by the J-text of the Sam Tg, but the standard vocalisation for it would be חֲטָאת. In recent times Rashi's explanation has been adopted by Sarna, Houtman and Propp and it provides good sense in the context without change to the consonantal text of MT. See Text and Versions for possible evidence of a (probably secondary) reading לְעַמְּךָ.

cc. Whether the repetition of נרפים indicates intensification (e.g. REB, 'lazy, bone lazy': cf. GK §123e) or rhetorical effect is debatable: the separation of the occurrences, however, favours the latter.

dd. Heb. עבדו. The verb, like the related words in vv. 9, 11 and 16, can refer to slavery (e.g. 21.2, 6: for an overview see Houtman, pp. 43-45, as well as the dictionaries), but that is no more than an overtone here. The issue of whose servants/slaves Israel will be has been anticipated in 3.12 and the late addition of 4.23, but only becomes focused on this expression from 7.16 onwards.

ee. The matching of two forms of נתן as well as the similar-sounding nouns תבן and תכן underlines the harshness of Pharaoh's demand, although in essence it is no different from what has been stated in other words in vv. 7-8, 10-11, 13 and 16. The unusual *dagesh* in the *nun* of תתנו is a peculiarity of Codex L (cf. BHS). It may, as Propp avers, be a scribal error, but there are parallels in just such a pausal position (see GK §20i, BL §23c). Dotan, who recognises that there are errors in L (e.g. in 4.31: cf. his Appendix A), nevertheless retains the *dagesh* here. But BL Or.4445 appears not to have it.

ff. See Note p. The expression here is indefinite (though SP and Vss make it definite): the reference must be to a standard daily quota (cf. the paraphrase in vv. 13 and 19), whereas in v. 8 the related noun refers to *the* quantity previously delivered.

gg. On the unusual reflexive use of the pronoun אתם see GK §135k. It may be connected with the somewhat abbreviated form of expression here after ראה, for which cf. Gen. 7.1. Rashi took אתם to refer to all the Israelites, but this seems less natural.

hh. See Note x above on v. 14.

ii. The participle נצבים, 'standing', qualifies the object of the main verb, Moses and Aaron, not the subject, 'they' (as rabbinic tradition [e.g. Exod.R. 5.20] and Rashi, followed by Houtman [pp. 480-81], supposed): in addition to the word-order, this is indicated by the fact that the supervisors are moving, not standing still.

jj. יֵרֶא is the regular form of the 3rd s.m. jussive Qal of ראה, although in most Lamed He verbs the masc. form retains the *hireq* of the imperfect, while the fem. takes *ṣere* (GK §75p, JM §79i). The idiom with על recurs only in 1.16: here the following וישפט suggests the idea of a judicial enquiry, for which the more common terms seem to have been דרש and חקר.

kk. So NRSV, with an English idiom that closely resembles the wording of the Heb. metaphor, 'you have made our smell foul in the sight of Pharaoh...' (for באש in this metaphorical sense see e.g. Gen. 34.30).

ll. Inf. constr. indicating consequence (JM §124l).

mm. Reading בידו with SP, LXX and Vulg: see Text and Versions.

nn. Heb. אדני, see Note b on 4.10-17.

oo. Heb. למה זה, see Note z on 2.11-22. Here, as in chs. 1–2, there seems to be no difference in meaning between למה (vv. 4, 15, 22) and מדוע (v. 14): cf. Note bb on 1.7-22.

pp. For Heb. *waw* introducing a causal clause 'in a light and elegant manner' cf. JM §170c.

Explanatory Notes

1. The continuation of the narrative brings Moses and Aaron into Pharaoh's presence without any indication of how they secured an audience with him. Their address to Pharaoh is a direct and uncompromising demand in the name of their God, 'Yahweh the God of Israel'. They use the prophetic 'messenger formula' (see especially Westermann, *Grundformen*, pp. 70-91 = *Basic Forms*, pp. 98-128), which occurs frequently not only in the oracles of the canonical prophets (e.g. Amos 1.3) but in the accounts of confrontations between earlier prophets and the kings of Israel in the books of Samuel and Kings (e.g. 1 Sam. 15.2). As Westermann showed, this formula has its origin in the delivery of a message from one human being to another (as in v. 10 below). The title 'the God of Israel' is most common in the historical books, later parts of Isaiah and especially in Jeremiah, where it occurs 49 times, often in introductory formulae like this one. There are a few other notable occurrences of the title in the Pentateuch (Gen. 33.20; Exod. 24.10; 32.27 [an identical introductory formula to this one]; Num. 16.9), but it is not used again in the Exodus-story strictly defined. Even the reference to the people absolutely as 'Israel' is not as widespread as might be expected in Exodus (only otherwise in the phrase 'the elders of Israel' [3.16, 18; 12.21; 17.5-6; 18.12; 24.1, 9] and in 4.22; 5.2 [twice]; 9.4, 7; 11.7; 12.15; 14.5, 25, 30 [twice], 31; 15.22; 17.8, 11; 18.1, 8-9, 25; 19.2; 24.4; 32.4, 8, 13; 34.27), the preference being for combinations such as 'the children of Israel (most often) and the 'congregation/camp/house of Israel' or the designation as 'Hebrews' (so below in v. 3: cf. the note on 1.15). The verb 'let go'

(Heb. *šillaḥ*) can have a specific reference to the manumission of slaves, but when it does it seems always to be followed by *ḥopšî*, 'free', to make the sense clear (e.g. 21.26-27). Here the sense appears to be more general (cf. the distinction in *HAL*, p. 1402b): whether or not in narratives such as this the Israelites' situation is regarded as slavery, Pharaoh is in the context not being asked for a permanent liberation, but a temporary release from their obligations, it would seem, for a particular purpose. The demand as a whole is a variation on a formula which is a recurring feature of the plague-stories, 'Let my people go, so that they may worship/serve me!' (7.16 etc.), and which already appeared in an adapted form in the late addition in 4.23 ('Formula B' in the Excursus below).

Excursus on the Demand to Pharaoh

The request for the Israelites to be allowed to desist from their labours so as to go and offer worship to Yahweh in the wilderness is formulated in two quite distinct ways, which we may call Formula A and Formula B (for fuller discussion see Floss, *Jahwe dienen*, pp. 181-235). Each employs language which also occurs elsewhere in the accounts of the negotiations between Moses (and Aaron) and Pharaoh, but only (apart from 4.23 PentR) in passages from the older source-material: there are of course no negotiations in P!

Formula A is introduced, in its full form, by a reference to a prior encounter (*qārāh/qārā'* Niphal) between the speakers (Moses and the elders in 3.18; Moses and Aaron in 5.3) and 'the God of the Hebrews' (named as Yahweh in 3.18). The initial request employs a first person pl. cohortative form of the common verb 'go' (Heb. *hālak*) with the precative particle *nā'* ('please'), which is amplified by a probably vague (see the note on 3.18) indication of the distance involved ('three days' journey') and the specification of 'the wilderness' as the destination. The purpose is given by a cohortative form of the verb 'sacrifice' (*zābaḥ*) introduced by simple *waw* and with the indirect object 'Yahweh our God', backed up in 5.3 by a further purpose clause (introduced by *pen*, 'lest'), expressing the fear that otherwise this God will bring death to his people. Shorter versions (summaries) of this formula, comprising only the two cohortatives and the indirect object ('our God' in v. 8; 'Yahweh' in v. 17) appear later in ch. 5 as citations of the request by Pharaoh (see further Floss, *Jahwe dienen*, pp. 201-203). All the main elements of the formula also occur (without the introduction and with slight variation of order and form) in 8.23 (EVV. 27), as part of a response to Pharaoh's suggestion that the Israelites should sacrifice to their God within the land of Egypt. The imperfect (not cohortative) form of *hālak* also appears (twice) in 10.9 in a further response of Moses to Pharaoh. The verb 'sacrifice' (*zābaḥ*) is more frequent, at least in ch. 8, where it occurs in various forms in vv. 4, 21, 23 (twice), 24 and 25, sometimes in combination with 'let go', one of the key terms of Formula B (vv. 4, 24, 25).

Formula B represents a more forthright demand in the name of Yahweh, who is sometimes (in 7.16; 9.1, 13; 10.3) additionally referred to as 'the God of the Hebrews', introduced by the messenger formula (in 7.16 by a 'sending formula' instead). It begins with the imperative 'Let go' (*šalaḥ* Piel) and 'my people' as the direct object ('my son' in 4.23), and the purpose is given by an imperfect/jussive form of the verb *ʿābad*, which can mean both 'worship' (the primary meaning here, to judge from other expressions used in the context) and 'serve' (which may well be a significant undertone), with a suffix 'me' referring to Yahweh.[5] In 5.1 and 7.16 (the first two instances in the main sequence) 'in the wilderness' is added, and in 5.1 the verb 'celebrate a festival' (*ḥāgag*) is used instead of *ʿābad* (see further below in the main text). The formula occurs at the beginning of each section but one of the main plague-narrative (7.16, 26 [EVV. 8.1]; 8.16 [EVV. v. 20]; 9.1, 13; 10.3 – the exception is the plague of darkness [10.21-28], on which see the introduction to 10.21-29), and understandably it does not appear in the dispersed account of the killing of the firstborn (11.4-8; 12.21-27, 29-33): the time for negotiation was now past.[6] In addition to the late adaptation of it in 4.23 and the occurrence in 5.1, which are discussed further in the introduction to this section, a paraphrase of the formula is addressed to Pharaoh by his own courtiers in 10.7, picking up its last regular occurrence in 10.3. In this case too, elements of the formula also occur independently in the narratives of confrontation between Pharaoh and Moses (or rather Yahweh). The verb 'let go' is of course the *Leitmotif* of the whole section (including its Priestly components: cf. 6.11; 7.2; 11.10), at first negatively but increasingly more positively in relation to Pharaoh's response: 5.2; 6.1, 11; 7.2, 14, 27; 8.4, 17, 24-25, 28; 9.2, 7, 17, 28, 35; 10.4, 10, 20, 27;

---

[5] Floss argues strongly that originally (but this seems to mean a pre-J stage of the tradition) the meaning in the central group of texts in chs. 7–10 is 'serve' and not 'worship', and he develops the theological implications of this richly (*Jahwe dienen*, esp. pp. 230-35). The opposite view is maintained by I. Riesener in *Der Stamm* עבד *im Alten Testament: eine Wortuntersuchung unter Berücksichtigung neuerer sprachwissenschaftlicher Methoden* (BZAW 149; Berlin, 1979 [but completed in 1975 without knowledge of Floss]): cf. p. 172, where he speaks of 'die Teilnahme an einem bestimmten Kult', and pp. 167-69, where a fuller treatment is given (though without discussion of an alternative), beginning with 3.12: the main texts (J) refer to worship and 13.5, 20.5 and 23.24 are later. L. Schmidt is much more critical of Floss in his *Beobachtungen* (1990): see the notes passim. Kohata, p. 115, largely agrees over the very late redaction in ch. 10 but not about 5.1-2 (p. 149).

[6] For examination of this formula in the context of larger narrative patterns see Floss, *Jahwe dienen*, pp. 183-88 (cf. Noth, p. 52, ET, p. 69; Fohrer, pp. 63-65).

11.1, 10; 12.33; 13.15, 17; 14.5 (note also the anticipations in 3.20 and 4.21, 23). In almost every case the word 'people' (or an equivalent) appears as its object (there is no explicit object in 7.27 and 9.2). The verb *'ābad*, 'worship' or 'serve', with Yahweh as object occurs five more times in these chapters, but interestingly only towards the end of the plague-story (10.8, 11, 24, 26; 12.31: cf. 3.12).

This first demand addressed to Pharaoh speaks of the 'celebration of a festival' (Heb. *ḥāgag*) in the desert, in contrast to the more general references to worship or sacrifice elsewhere. The related noun 'festival' occurs in the later negotiations between Moses and Pharaoh in 10.9. In other contexts the word (cf. *TWAT* 2, 730-44 = *TDOT* 4, pp. 201-13), which is cognate with Ar. *ḥajj*, 'pilgrimage' (specifically to Mecca), is used for the great annual festivals of Israelite worship (e.g. 23.15-16; 34.18, 22: cf. 12.14; 13.6) and with particular reference to the autumn festival as '*the* festival' (e.g. 1 Kgs 8.2). Elsewhere in the story there are the expected references to animal sacrifices (esp. 10.25-26), but the requirement for all ages to be present (10.9) conflicts with the normal requirement that only the adult males should attend (23.17; 34.23), perhaps because of the role which the festival plays in securing the liberation of the whole people (but note also 1 Sam. 1.3-5). Below, in v. 3, non-observance of the festival is seen as a cause of danger to the people. The celebration of the festival 'in the desert' is also unusual, but can be explained by the fact that Yahweh is not a native Egyptian god and by the (relative) proximity of his holy mountain to Egypt. It is surely this mountain that is envisaged as the location of the festival, as is already hinted in 3.12. The later chapters of Exodus contain three narratives of worship at Mount Sinai/Horeb: the celebration of the Exodus with Jethro the priest of Midian in 18.12; the composite account of covenant-making and theophany in 24.1-11, and the story of the golden calf in ch. 32, in which the word *ḥāg* actually occurs (v. 5). Attempts have been made to identify the 'festival' referred to here with one of these, most often the first (Schmidt, pp. 251-53) or the last (Houtman, pp. 460-61), or with the Passover. The latter is the least likely in the present narrative context, since it is celebrated at the time of departure from Egypt, not 'in the desert', but it is possible that in the underlying tradition a spring festival for pastoralists which later developed into the Passover was intended.

2. Pharaoh's twofold refusal to release (Heb. *šillaḥ*) Israel is backed up by a question and a statement which probably express the same state of affairs: that Pharaoh has not previously heard of the god Yahweh. The temptation to see here a stronger sense of 'know' (Heb. *yādaʿ*: cf. *THAT* 1, 694-99 = *TLOT*, 2, pp. 517-20; *TWAT* 3, 499-500 = *TDOT* 5, pp. 469-70), such as 'acknowledge', should probably be resisted (cf. 1.8), although lack of acquaintance with a god would necessarily imply the lack of any regard for him. Naturally this is the starting-point for a process by which it is intended that Pharaoh should come both to know and to acknowledge Yahweh in the specific case of the demand for the release of his people, and this is expressed explicitly by the use of the verb *yādaʿ* later in Exodus (so Childs, p. 105, citing 8.18 [22], 9.29 and 11.8 [read '7']: to these may be added 7.5P, 17; 8.6 [10]; 9.14; 14.4P, 18P).[7]

3. The fuller and more diplomatic presentation of the request for leave by Moses and Aaron (who are in the context the antecedents of 'they') corresponds to 'Formula A' as defined above. It is not a direct answer to Pharaoh's question, although the title 'God of the Hebrews' would presumably have meant more to him than either 'Yahweh' or 'the God of Israel' (see the note on 1.15) and it can be read as a second stage in the confrontation that has already begun in v. 1. But the fact that most of it corresponds exactly to Yahweh's instructions to Moses in 3.18 (where see the notes) makes it a strong possibility that at an earlier stage of the tradition these words were the opening request that was made to Pharaoh in one version of the story. It is certainly to them that Pharaoh refers back later in the chapter (vv. 8, 17), rather than to the words of v. 1. It would then be possible and perhaps necessary to understand the 'they' differently, most probably of Moses and the Israelite elders (cf. 3.18; 4.29). The consequences of disobedience to the divine summons have not been mentioned before: 'pestilence' (*deber*) and 'sword' (*ḥereb*) appear later in Exodus as respectively a threat to the Egyptians (9.3, 15) and a threat from them (5.21; 18.4), and they are paired together as dangers that threaten a people in

---

[7] Cf. Schmidt, p. 259: 'So schlägt jene Jahwe herausfordernde Frage das für den Fortgang der Handlung entscheidende Thema an; Ex 7-14 bilden gleichsam die erzählerisch ausgestaltete Antwort.'

Amos 4.10 (cf. Lev. 26.25; Ezek. 28.23; 33.27), as well as appearing with 'famine' (*rāʿāb*) in a more widespread triad (23x in Jeremiah and Ezekiel: cf. *TWAT* 2, 133-35 = *TDOT* 3, pp. 126-27). The general idea that failure to worship a deity would risk his or her wrath is a commonplace of ancient Near Eastern religion.

4-5. Here as later in the passage Pharaoh rejects the request as a pretext for idleness (cf. vv. 8, 17). Viewed against the background of contemporary Egyptian evidence (see the introduction to this section), this seems severe, as Egyptian workmen were commonly allowed time off to take part in religious festivals. But an absence of a week or more might well have seemed excessive. Both the argument and the terminology of v. 5 are at first puzzling. Why are the numbers of the people (which certainly recall statements in ch. 1: vv. 7, 9, 12, 20) relevant to the Pharaoh's decision? Presumably it is because the loss of a large component of his work-force would make a noticeable difference to progress on the building work. Schmidt (p. 260), however, thinks that as in 1.9 Israel's numbers are perceived as a danger by Pharaoh.[8] The expression 'the people of the land' is also a surprising, and unparalleled, way to speak of the Israelites in Egypt: one would expect it to refer to the whole population of Egypt or the native Egyptians, as it does in Gen. 42.6 (cf. Neh. 9.10). Concern at the oddness of the phrase here is probably the reason for the variant texts of SP and some LXX mss (see Text and Versions). Elsewhere in the OT it generally means the whole population of a country or district, sometimes in distinction from the king and other leaders, and it is mainly used of the population of Judah in the monarchy period (e.g. Jer. 1.18).[9] If MT is retained, there are three possible ways of understanding it. (i) It may have a derogatory sense, 'the common people, the masses', on the lips of Pharaoh, who refers to the Egyptians as 'my people' in 8.4, 9.27 and

---

[8] There is certainly no need for Ehrlich's unfounded emendation to *nirpîm*, 'lazy', as in vv. 8 and 17, which was favoured by Gressmann.

[9] The thesis of E. Würthwein, *Der ʿam haʾarez im Alten Testament* (BWANT 69; Stuttgart, 1936: followed by G. von Rad in his *Deuteronomium-Studien*), which saw it as a political term for the Judaean aristocracy, was criticised by E.W. Nicholson in 'The Meaning of the Expression עם הארץ in the Old Testament', *JSS* 10 (1965), pp. 59-66, and de Vaux, *Institutions* 1, pp. 111-13, ET, pp. 70-72, and is now accepted, if at all, only for a minority of occurrences (esp. 2 Kgs 11.14-20). T. Willi, *Juda-Jehud-Israel* (FAT 12; Tübingen, 1995), pp. 11-17, is unusual in still regarding it as an institution, which survived the exile.

12.31. Such a use is hard to parallel in the OT, except in Ezra 4.4, where it is opposed to ʿm-yhdh and may refer to non-Jews. Houtman (p. 48), on this basis, thinks that it can even mean 'the foreigners, strangers', but this seems improbable. (ii) If the narrative in vv. 3-19 is either based on an extract from a north Israelite account of the revolt against Rehoboam or written with that situation very much in mind (see the introduction to this chapter), the phrase may be an unconscious (or even deliberate) borrowing from the terminology which might be appropriate in that very different situation (the dialogue in the Judaean account in 1 Kgs 12 several times uses the expression 'this people' to refer to the northern tribes). (iii) Propp takes the phrase in its natural sense in the context, as a reference to 'the Egyptians', and suggests that either Pharaoh speaks of the Israelites like this 'to assert his authority over them' or he means that Moses and Aaron's proposal is undermining the regular labour provided by his own people (p. 254).

It is odd to find two separate replies by Pharaoh in these verses, each introduced by 'the king of Egypt/Pharaoh said…' A number of commentators have therefore taken the second 'said' in the sense 'thought', which Heb. *ʾāmar* can bear, most often with 'in (his) heart' added but also alone (e.g. 2.14: cf. BDB, p. 56a; *TWAT* 1, 358-59 = *TDOT* 1, p. 333, and on this passage Holzinger, p. 17; Noth, p. 38, ET, p. 53; Schmidt, pp. 242-43; Van Seters, p. 74): it is suggested that Pharaoh would not wish to share his reasoning with the Israelites. This is perhaps a more powerful consideration if the SP reading, '(they) are more numerous than the people of the land' is followed in v. 5, as most of the scholars mentioned do. The occurrence of 'will *you* have them cease' later in the verse, however, suggests that Pharaoh is still speaking to Moses and Aaron (though see Text and Versions for the alternative [but probably secondary] reading 'we' of LXX). While a repetition of '(he) said' with the same subject is not impossible (see the notes on 3.14-15) and we might argue (with Graupner, *Elohist*, p. 63) that v. 4 looks backwards while v. 5 looks forward, it could also be an indication of the use of two sources or of an editorial addition (see further the introduction to this section).

6-9. Pharaoh now turns away from Moses and Aaron and gives new instructions to those who have charge of the Israelite workmen. The two designations for them refer to a higher and lower level of authority, the former native Egyptian and the latter Israelite, as the following verses (esp. vv. 14-16) make clear. Parallels to this system have been found in Egyptian administrative documents (see the introduction to this section). Although the Egyptian officials are given the title 'taskmasters', here the narrator deliberately identifies them as the cause of the Israelites' distress by the use of an expression which involves a slightly different construction that draws attention to the common meaning of the verb, 'oppress, treat harshly' (cf. 1 Sam. 13.6[, 14.24]; Isa. 3.5; 53.7; 58.3). The subordinate officials are designated by a term, $šōṭēr$, which occurs elsewhere mainly in Deuteronomy (7x), Joshua (5x) and Chronicles (6x: also in Num. 11.16 and Prov. 6.7). There are also nine instances of it in the Dead Sea Scrolls (see *DCH* 8, pp. 333-34), all apparently based on biblical precedents. Several times it appears in a list of leaders of the people, without any clear pointer to the role involved, but elsewhere the $šōṭ^erîm$ seem to be attached as subordinates or assistants to those of higher rank, in much the same way as here (Deut. 16.18; 1 Chr. 23.4; 26.29 [judges]; Deut. 20.5-9; Josh. 1.10; 3.2 [military commanders]), and this is probably the meaning in the lists as well. Curiously for such a term, it never occurs in Samuel or Kings or in prophecy: this could be by chance, with such junior officials not needing to be mentioned, but since the word seems to be a loan from Akkadian (see Note n on the translation) and most of the occurrences are in relatively late portions of the OT (Deut. 16.18 and 20.5-9 are perhaps the earliest), it may reflect the borrowing of the term from Assyrian or Babylonian administrative terminology in the later pre-exilic period (for further discussion see J.P.M. van der Ploeg, 'Les $šōṭ^erîm$ d'Israël', *OTS* 10 [1954], pp. 185-96; M. Weinfeld, 'Judge and Officer in Ancient Israel and in the Ancient Near East', *IOS* 7 [1977], pp. 65-88 [83-86]; U. Rüterswörden, *Die Beamten der israelitischen Königszeit* [BWANT 117; Stuttgart, 1985], pp. 109-11). On Egyptian evidence for the use of straw and other vegetable materials in brick-making and for daily 'targets' or 'quotas' see the introduction to this section.

10-13. Although the taskmasters and supervisors use the 'messenger formula' (see on v. 1), they do not repeat Pharaoh's words verbatim. 'Throughout the land of Egypt' is no doubt an exaggeration for effect: but the reference to the use of stubble in place of straw, which is quite explicit here (see Note p on the translation for the ambiguity of v. 7), implies the need to scour the fields for the material needed.

14-18. In these circumstances the failure of the Israelites to meet their quota of brick-production does not need to be specifically recounted: as often in biblical narrative, the implication of the taskmasters' words and actions is sufficient. Beating of an Israelite workman has already been mentioned in 2.11 (and note the batons in the overseers' hands in the Rekhmire tomb painting). Here it is the native Israelite supervisors who are held responsible and it is they who seek relief, presumably by the restoration of the straw supply, from Pharaoh himself. Some commentators (e.g. Noth, p. 34, ET, p. 48; for an explanation see Baentsch, pp. 39-40) find it surprising that the supervisors are not already aware of Pharaoh's attitude, given their earlier appearance before him, and suggest that the earlier references to them in vv. 6 and 10 are secondary glosses. The fact that the method of their appointment is only explained here could support this view. On the other hand the addition of them in vv. 6 and 10 is not easy to explain, and a complaint after they themselves had been beaten for the failure of their countrymen is natural enough, even if they had been directly instructed by Pharaoh before. More surprising, perhaps, is the fact that Moses and Aaron do not lead the protest, and this is what gave rise to Noth's theory that this episode derives from a very ancient stage of the tradition when Moses had, according to Noth, not yet become part of the Exodus story (see the introduction to the chapter on this).

19-21. The reaction of the supervisors to Pharaoh's refusal to soften his new demands (the key part of which is repeated in v. 19) is focused especially on their own dire situation as those who are held responsible for the delivery of a regular supply of bricks. It is they who have already felt the brutality of their superiors (vv. 14, 16), and when they speak of the danger that Pharaoh will 'kill us' in v. 21 it is logical to see the primary reference as being to themselves, rather than to the people as a whole. The accusation in the first half of the verse can also be seen as referring to their own loss of respect from the Egyptians. This helps to explain the vehemence of their attack on Moses and Aaron in v. 21, which is perhaps anticipated by the choice of Heb. *pāgaʿ*, 'confronted', for it has already been used in v. 3 ('come against') for the hostile reaction from Yahweh which is feared if his worship is neglected. Although both the expressions which they use, 'examine' (cf. Note jj on the translation) and 'judge', are technically neutral, there is no doubt of what verdict they expect and seek. Nevertheless this is not strictly a 'curse'

(Houtman, p. 482): it is close to the wording of some individual laments (for 'see' and 'judge' together cf. Ps. 35.22-24; Lam. 3.59), but the direct address to Moses and Aaron is even closer to David's words to Saul in 1 Sam. 24.16 (EVV. 15).

The fact that Moses and Aaron are brought into the dispute only at this late stage, and are waiting outside while others protest to Pharaoh, has been seen as a further reason for thinking that they played no part in the most ancient version of the Exodus story. It is certainly unusual, but it does provide an opportunity for an early introduction of the motif of 'rebellion' against their leadership, which becomes very prominent in the wilderness narratives (cf. Coats, *Rebellion*). Another possibility is that the narrative derives originally from a different situation, namely the breakaway of the northern tribes after the death of Solomon (for fuller discussion of these possibilities see the introduction to this section).

22-23. Moses' 'return' to Yahweh (alone, despite his close association with Aaron in vv. 20-21 and earlier in the chapter) is not primarily to be understood in a geographical sense, but as in 32.31 of a resumption of the conversation that was last mentioned in 4.19 and 4.21-23. The fact that in 9.29-33 Moses goes out of the city to pray to Yahweh (8.12 and 30 are not so precise) may mean that he is thought of as doing so here too: cf. Propp, p. 258, who compares Balaam's temporary withdrawal from Balak in Num. 23.3 and 15 (where 'return' is used in the context of Balaam's rejoining Balak). The Balaam narratives in several ways reflect a similar kind of prophetic behaviour to what is said about Moses. Moses addresses Yahweh not with the divine name itself (the NRSV is wrong to capitalise 'Lord' in v. 22) but, as in 4.10, 13, with the deferential '(my) Lord' ($^{a}d\bar{o}n\bar{a}y$: see the notes there), but without the particle *bî*, 'If I may say so', that was used earlier. This is deliberate (the insertion of equivalents to *bî* here in some renderings is a mistake: see Text and Versions), for although Moses still recognises Yahweh's authority he now complains to him about the failure of his mission to Pharaoh. The use of 'Why?' to introduce an accusing question is characteristic of the laments in the Psalter (e.g. 10.1; 22.2) and the prayers of Jeremiah which are modelled on them (Jer. 14.8-9; 15.18; 20.18): on the second occasion a stronger form, with the emphasising particle *zeh*, here rendered 'Why ever...?', is used as in Jer. 20.18. In view of the Psalms parallels there is no need to presume any dependence on Jeremiah (contra Van Seters, p. 75). Moses complains on behalf of the whole people, not just the supervisors, first for the worsening of their situation (vv. 22-23a) and then for the non-fulfilment of Yahweh's promise (3.7) to 'deliver' Israel from the power of Egypt (v. 23b). A different aspect of the structure of the complaint is that it begins and ends with Yahweh's own (in)action (vv. 22, 23b), but centres on the fact that in the human interaction between Moses and Pharaoh the outcome has been quite the opposite of what was hoped for (v. 23a). There is undoubtedly some tension between this aspect of the complaint and the warnings in 3.19-20 and 4.21-23 that Pharaoh would refuse to let Israel go, the more so as Yahweh's reply in 6.1 does not criticise Moses for his failure to heed these warnings. It is argued in the introduction to 4.18-31 that 4.21-23 is a very late addition to the narrative, but this is not so clearly the case for 3.19-20 (despite the arguments of a number of scholars). The justification (if one is needed) for Moses' complaint could be that no warning had been given that things would get worse for Israel before they got better, and it is this worsening in their situation ('done harm', Heb. *hēraʿ*, twice) which is at the forefront of what Moses says and what causes him once again to question his own commission ('sent': cf. 3.10-11, 13; 4.1, 10, 13), just as Jeremiah later doubted his (the verb 'send', however, does not appear in Jeremiah's complaints about the failure of his mission, which are focused rather on the validity of the divine 'word' and Yahweh's deception of him).[10] One might describe the question raised as one of 'theodicy' (Aurelius, *Fürbitter*, pp. 160-67), but this is no reason to attribute the section to a Deuteronomistic editor (ibid., pp. 204, 207): community laments stretching back into the monarchy period (cf. Ps. 80) express the same sense of abandonment and questioning.

---

[10] The expression 'speak in your/his name' (v. 23) does recur in Jer. 20.9, and the combination is in fact rarer than might be expected (otherwise only Deut. 18.19-20, 22; Jer. 29.23; Zech. 13.3; Dan. 9.6; 1 Chr. 21.19). But given the frequency of 'in the name of' in the sense of 'on behalf of' (including prophetic contexts like 1 Kgs 22.16; 2 Kgs 2.24), not too much should be made of the similarity.

Text and Versions

ואחר (5.1) The Vss. render 'after this', but probably without a different *Vorlage* from MT and SP, which seem to be supported by 4QGen-Exod[a], though little of the word survives.

באו (5.1) LXX has a sing. verb, perhaps imitating the idiom of 4.29. Its εἰσῆλθεν, like the other Vss, takes the Heb. in the sense 'entered' rather than 'came'. LXX also brings 'to Pharaoh' forward to this clause, resuming with αὐτῷ in the next, probably for stylistic reasons: the hexaplaric mss and others follow MT.

ויאמרו (5.1) Tg[J] has a sing. verb.

עמי (5.1) Tg[N] עמא, 'the people' (as in 7.26), although it elsewhere follows MT in this formula. The rendering is perhaps influenced by 4.30-31.

ויחגו (5.1) Vulg *ut sacrificet* reflects the language of 3.18 and 5.3.

לי (5.1) Tg[O,N] 'before me', with the usual avoidance of a direct relation to God; Tg[J] 'make (*'bd*) a festival for me' either achieves this in another way or is not troubled by the problem.

מי יהוה (5.2) Tg[O,J] paraphrase, 'the name of the Lord was not revealed to me', perhaps with reference to the rabbinic tradition about 'the book of the gods' noted below (so *AramB* 7, p. 13 n. 2), but more likely to avoid the blasphemy implied by Pharaoh's 'stark' question (Chester, p. 225). In LXX ἐστιν seems to correspond to יהוה, which is only represented (by κύριος or θεός) in secondary witnesses. Perhaps LXX read הוא, as *BHS* and Wevers, *Notes*, p. 59, reasonably presume in view of the frequent correspondence elsewhere (e.g. 3.5; 8.15; 12.11), but the translation may just be free here.

אשמע בקלו (5.2) Tg[O,J] paraphrase, 'receive his word'.

ישראל (5.2) For the first occurrence, but not the second, LXX has τοὺς υἱοὺς Ισραηλ, reflecting the expression normally used thus far in MT also (only 4.22 has had ישראל alone).

לא ידעתי (5.2) Tgg paraphrase variously: Tg[O] uses the same substitute as for מי יהוה earlier in the verse (it is if anything closer to the present expression); Tg[J] has an explicit reference to not finding the Name in 'the book of angels' and then 'I do not fear/worship him' (the latter being very similar to the handling of 'know the Lord' in the Tg at Jer. 31.34; Hos. 2.22; 4.1); while Tg[N] puts the statement into the 3rd person to preserve some respect for Yahweh (Chester, ibid.).

אשלח (5.2) LXX has present ἐξαποστέλλω (cf. the participial construction in Tg[N] and Sy), which Wevers, *Notes*, p. 59, plausibly sees as an indication of the 'adamance' of Pharaoh's refusal.

ויאמרו (5.3) LXX adds αὐτῷ, and Sy (except 5b1) begins the speech with the divine name.

העברים (5.3) Tg[O,J] 'the Jews', Tg[N] 'the Hebrews', both as earlier in Exod.

נקרא (5.3) So also SP. LXX and Vulg derive from קרא = 'call', apparently ignoring the Niphal form (as in 3.18: so still Luther, but AV has 'met'); Tg[J] similarly, 'his name was called', but the inserted subject allowed the passive form to be represented. Tg^N and Sy have 'revealed himself', again as in 3.18 (Sy is important evidence of the antiquity of this interpretation), while the evidence for Tg^O is again divided between this reading (*AramB*) and 'has been called, named (upon us)' (אתקרי: Sperber – see the textual note on 3.18). The true meaning of MT here, as in 3.18, (first?) appears in Ibn Ezra's longer commentary on both passages (Rottzoll 1, pp. 119, 153).

במדבר (5.3)   SP has the synonymous המדברה, but places it before דרך שלשת ימים. Mur 1 has דרך after נא, so (as expected) supports MT, as does the order of words in the Versions, except for a few mss of LXX which also invert the expressions, perhaps independently: closer association of a directional phrase with the verb may have seemed more appropriate.

ונזבחה ליהוה (5.3)   LXX omits יהוה, as in 3.18, but the fragmentary remains of 4QGen-Exod^a and 4QExod^b both attest it, as does SP. Tgg, as usual in expressions like this, represent ל by קדם; Tg^J adds 'the sacrifices of the feast' to make the object explicit.

בדבר או בחרב (5.3)   LXX, Symm, Theod, Vulg ignore the ב each time (whose presence is attested in the very slight remains of the verse in 2Q4 as well as SP), making these dangers the subject of ויפגענו, rather than Yahweh himself: Aq represented the preposition and therefore, like Tgg and Sy, implies God as subject. The subj. of פגע is generally personal. LXX and Tg^{O,J} use general terms, 'death or slaughter' (according to Wevers θάνατος is the regular equivalent for דבר in LXX), whereas Aq, Symm, Vulg and Tg^N have literal renderings (cf. Text and Versions on 9.3). Theod and Sy compromise, with 'death' and 'sword', but the latter curiously inverts them. The repeated agreements between Greek and Aramaic sources are noteworthy.

תפריעו (5.4)   SP and 4QExod^b read תפרידו, 'will you separate' (the other Qumran mss do not survive for this word). The Vss probably all presuppose MT (for details see Wevers, *Notes*, p. 61; Salvesen, *Symmachus*, p. 75): the characteristic equivalents for √פרד are not used. The variant does not reflect a known usage of √פרד and 'release' is more to the point than 'separation' here. It may have arisen in the palaeo-Heb. script, in which *daleth* and *ayin* could be quite similar; the use of מן after the Niphal of √פרד (though not the Hiphil) may have encouraged the misreading.

את־העם (5.4)   LXX τὸν λαόν μου, which (as Wevers, *Notes*, p. 61, points out) creates a direct challenge to Yahweh's claim in v. 1. Neither this variation nor LXX's free renderings later in the verse are supported by other witnesses.

ויאמר (5.5)   Sy (exc. 5b1) adds *lhwn*, following v. 4.

עם־הארץ (5.5)   The problematic phrase (see the Explanatory Note) is made easier in SP by the reading מעם, '(more numerous) than the people of the land', i.e. the Egyptians. Childs and Schmidt adopt this, but it leaves רבים without an explicit subject, which is scarcely possible. B and some other LXX mss have no equivalent to הארץ (similarly the first hand of Tg^N) and Propp finds this reading 'fairly attractive' (p. 245). But according to Wevers it is a secondary Greek reading, attributable to the oddness of the longer phrase here and the frequency of העם/ὁ λαός alone elsewhere in Exodus (*THGE*, p. 252: cf. v. 4).

MT, which is clearly supported by 4QExod^b (the other Qumran mss do not survive at this point), should be retained (so also Houtman and, in the end, Propp). Vulg has an unusually full text which seems to involve a double rendering of הארץ...הן (see also the next note).

והשבתם (5.5) LXX μὴ οὖν καταπαύσωμεν seems, first, to presuppose a different *Vorlage* והשבתנו (for the confusion of the suffixes owing to the use of a ligature cf. R. Weiss, 'On Ligatures in the Hebrew Bible [ם = נו]', *JBL* 82 [1963], pp. 188-94, and Tov, *Textual Criticism*, p. 249: in the first two of his examples the reading ם- is clearly preferable). The meaning must be not, as Wevers, *Notes*, p. 61, proposes (also *BAlex* 2, p. 107), 'we shall certainly not let them rest' (which would require οὐ μή), but 'let us not give them rest' (cf. OL *non* [for *ne*] *ergo demus eis requiem*; also Eth as cited in Wevers's apparatus): LXX has here again (cf. its τὸν λαόν μου in v. 4) increased the harshness of Pharaoh's reply, by turning what can be regarded as a question into a strong resolution in the negative. The underlying Heb., which could be rendered, 'and shall we give them rest (from their toils)?', makes the verse less of a repetition of v. 4 (and note the lack of any 'to them' after ויאמר this time) and leads well into Pharaoh's instructions to his officials in v. 6. But MT also makes good sense and it is supported by all the other surviving witnesses. Vulg *quanto magis si dederitis* again (see the previous note) expands and reinforces Pharaoh's words.

ביום ההוא (5.6) LXX had no equivalent (the gap was filled in the hexaplaric and some other witnesses: cf. also the rendering attributed to ὁ ἑβρ [Aq? Theod?] in Syh^mg), but the words are present not only in MT and SP but in 4QGen-Exod^a and 4QExod^b (the only surviving witnesses from Qumran). The omission in LXX might be due to its close association of vv. 5 and 6 (see above), which made the phrase unnecessary.

את־הנגשים בעם (5.6) The reading is supported by 4QExod^b as well as SP. The Vss ignore the ב and treat הנגשים as a nominalised part. referring to Egyptian officials (cf. vv. 10, 13, 14), 'taskmasters' (cf. EVV.): LXX's ἐργοδιώκταις is paralleled in a third-cent. B.C. papyrus (see further Lee, *Lexical Study*, pp. 96-97; *BAlex*, p. 90).

ואת־שטריו (5.6) LXX has καὶ τοῖς γραμματεύσιν, as often elsewhere: here, as Wevers (*Notes*, p. 62) suggests, the reference could be to the 'overseers who kept the record of works and therefore in charge of the corvée'. Sy similarly *wlsprwhy*. Tg^O,J use a general word for an 'officer', but Vulg (*exactoribus*) and Tg^N (וית־דחקיהון) have words with negative connotations more appropriate to הנגשים and perhaps due to an interchange of their renderings of the two words: from v. 10 in Tg^N and from v. 14 in Vulg the equivalents are reversed. The close parallel of the changing renderings in the two Vss may be due to Jerome's Jewish advisers knowing a text (or at least a tradition of interpretation) like Tg^N.

האספון (5.7) SP has תוסיפון, the regular form from יסף, and the Vss all agree in deriving the form from this verb. Even a marginal note in MT (cf. *BHS*) notes that the א is 'not read'. LXX paraphrases slightly (and uniquely), using an impersonal passive construction (perhaps imitating the form of an official decree?), which makes the Hebraism seem even odder in Greek: many mss (including *O*) correct to agree with MT's 2nd pl. active.

תבן (5.7)   LXX ἄχυρον/α, 'chaff' (as in vv. 10-13, 16, 18); Vulg has *paleas* the first time (again as in vv. 10ff., from OL), with the same sense, but *stipulam*, 'straw, stubble', the second, probably reflecting the literal sense of קשש (and perhaps its rendering by the Three: see below).

הלבנים (5.7)   SP omits the article, which is certainly dispensable here. 4QExod^b, the only Qumran ms. to preserve the word, agrees with MT and as elsewhere may give the *Vorlage* for LXX (εἰς τὴν πλινθουργίαν): similarly Tg^J and Sy, whereas לבנין in Tg^{O,N} seems to agree with SP. Since this is the first mention of bricks in Exodus since 1.14, the definite form could be regarded as the *difficilior lectio* and so as original.

וקששו (5.7)   SP reads the imperfect/jussive, but the mss are almost equally divided between יקששו and ויקששו: three of Crown's and Cam. Add. 1846 (after an erasure?) have the former, while the texts of Sadaqa and Tal support von Gall's preference for the latter. A *waw* seems to be needed and the first SP reading is probably an error, but it is difficult to choose between the other two, as both give the required sense. LXX renders by συνάγω, a non-specific word, but the other Vss (including the Three) reflect the etymological association with stubble in various ways (Vulg by using a different word for תבן, see above).

את־מתכנת (5.8)   LXX σύνταξιν, Tgg סכום, Sy ḥwšbn' all support the rendering 'fixed, agreed quantity': Vulg's *mensuram*, 'quantity', is more general.

תמול (5.8)   4QExod^b has כאתמול, with the alternative longer form of the adverb (which does not occur in MT in the Pentateuch but appears 5x in 1–2 Samuel and 3x elsewhere) and the prefixed preposition כ. The form could be a misplaced variant on the previous verse where כתמול appears: here it only makes sense if the adverbial phrase is taken with the following verb תשימו (so perhaps Tg^N [with היך] and Sy [ʾyk]). But the reading which differs from the previous verse (MT, SP) is surely original. LXX renders the phrase loosely καθ'ἑκάστην ἡμέραν, 'each day', which is more likely to be a rendering of MT than the variant (Wevers' view that LXX here refers to 'the present [i.e. new] arrangement' [*Notes*, p. 63], presumably because of the present tense ποιοῦσιν, is hardly compelling).

תשימו...תגרעו (5.8)   The original LXX apparently had second person sing. verbs (so mss A and B), although most witnesses have the pl. As Wevers sees (*Notes*, p. 63), the translator probably overlooked the fact that Pharaoh was addressing his officials (did he assume that the addressee was Moses?). Propp (p. 246) thinks the *difficilior lectio* might be original, but this would only be possible if it were a relic of a different version of the story in which Pharaoh dealt directly with (?) Moses.

ממנו (5.8)   4QExod^b adds דבר, probably assimilating to v. 11. The longer text may also be behind οὐδέν in LXX (which does not render ממנו): Vulg's *quicquam* was simply taken over from OL.

נרפים (5.8)   Vulg *vacant* implies the interpretation 'have nothing to do'; LXX's σχολάζουσιν and the *bṭl* of the Aramaic Vss. could mean this, but can also bear the moral sense 'lazy'. Cf. v. 17.

צעקים (5.8)   4QExod[b] has only some letters of this word but clearly begins it with the *he* of the def. art. This cannot be right: it may have arisen from a fuller writing of the preceding הם and a subsequent mistake in word-division (*DJD* XII, p. 95).

נזבחה (5.8)   4QGen-Exod[a] and 4QExod[b] both read 'ונ (cf. LXX, Vulg, Tg[N]): such additions of the copula are generally secondary.

לאלהינו (5.8)   Tgg amplify as in v. 3 (q.v.).

ויעשו (5.9)   SP and 4QExod[b] have (ו)ישעו, as later in the verse, and LXX's use of μεριμνάω both times points to a similar *Vorlage* (cf. Sy *nrnwn*). 4QGen-Exod[a] lacks this part of the verse. MT is supported by Vulg *expleant* and by Tg[J,N], which also use two different verbs. Tg[O] has יתעסקון both times ('let them busy themselves'), and is cited in support of וישעו here by Wevers, *Notes*, p. 64, and *DJD* XII, p. 95. But it could apparently render עשה too (cf. Tg[J], which uses it here but רחץ later in the verse), so possibly Tg[O] chose it precisely because of its versatility to render both verbs in MT (*AramB* has no comment on this). *BHS* may be right to omit Tg[O] from its list of supporters of the alternative reading.

ואל (5.9)   SP has ולא (this is the only case of such variation cited in *GSH* §155b), which may be designed to strengthen (GK §107o) or generalise the command. 4QExod[b] clearly read as MT, though the text is damaged; 4QGen-Exod[a] does not survive for this word. In 12.22 the variation between MT and SP is the other way round.

שקר (5.9)   LXX, Tg[O] and Sy render as 'empty, vain', which *AramB* 7, p. 13 n. 9, sees as less offensive to Israel than the stronger (and probably more accurate) rendering 'lying', as in Vulg, Tg[J,N].

ויצא (5.10)   So also SP and 4QGen-Exod[a] (4QExod[b] does not survive): LXX κατέσπευδον αὐτούς, 'they were urging them on', as for אצים in v. 13, so implying a *Vorlage* ויאצו (with metathesis). It is an error: 'urging on' cannot precede the instruction in v. 11. LXX and Vulg abbreviate their renderings of the subjects of the verb. Most Vss render them as in v. 7, but Tg[N] inverts its equivalents there, which corresponds better to MT.

ויאמרו (5.10)   SP and 4QExod[b] read וידברו, probably a stylistic change before the following לאמר. The word does not survive in 4QGen-Exod[a], but the Vss support MT.

לאמר (5.10)   Tg[J], Sy and Vulg omit, an alternative way out of the repetition of forms of אמר.

קחו (5.11)   4QExod[b] וקחו, cf. Vulg *et colligite* and the note on נזבחה in v. 8.

תמצאו (5.11)   Many LXX mss (and OL) have a plus here from the end of v. 18, probably to provide a better introduction to the כי-clause (Wevers, *Notes*, p. 65, observes the problem but curiously fails to mention the variant).

מעבדתכם (5.11) LXX ἀπὸ τῆς συντάξεως ὑμῶν, using the word that renders more specific terms in vv. 8, 14 and 18. Tg[N] has a plural form, 'your labours': this can only be paraphrase, as עבדה is not used in the pl.

ארץ (5.12) No equivalent in LXX, as in 4.20 (where Vulg and Sy also have none), whereas in 3.10-11 LXX has the longer expression against MT. In chs. 1–5 all witnesses generally have just מצרים. There is no clear pattern to the variation: perhaps the non-Priestly material originally had the shorter expression everywhere (from ch. 6 onwards the longer form is more consistently attested, at least in P material).

קש (5.12) Most Vss render appropriately, but Vulg omits (*ad colligendas paleas*: *palea* is its equivalent for תבן) and Sy has (*lmqš*) *qšt' dtbn'*, 'stubble *of* straw', perhaps because Sy *qšt'* has a wider use for 'loose remnants' and Heb. ל could be taken as indicating the genitive.

והנגשים (5.13) Aq 'corrected' LXX's ἐργοδιῶκται to εἰσπρᾶκται, which he used also in Job 39.7 for נגש. It appears to be a coinage of his, based on εἰσπράσσω, 'exact' (taxes etc.), with which he sometimes represents the verb נגש.

אצים (5.13) SP אצוים might be a part. from a by-form אצה (cf. *HAL*, p. 23), but the possible evidence of a form אצה in MH (cf. Jastrow, p. 32) is dubious. Propp (p. 247) cites a neat suggestion of K.G. O'Connell that it might be a conflation of MT with אצום, '(they) urged them', which might be the *Vorlage* of LXX (below). SamTg renders as if it were אצו. Perhaps then the origin of the SP reading (despite its appearance in all SP mss and [J. Joosten, pers. comm.] in the Sam. oral tradition) lies in an early error: in Gen. 19.15 SP has the same reading for this verb as MT. Both SP (בעם: for the ב cf. Gen. 19.15) and LXX (αὐτούς: so also apparently 4QExod[c] [אתהם]) add an object (one may also have stood in the long lacuna in 4QExod[b]: cf. *DJD* XII, pp. 94-95): the fact that they did so differently argues for the originality of MT, and אוץ is often used intransitively.

דבר יום ביומו (5.13) Sy (except 5b1, which has *'yk bkl ywm*) reads *'yk bklzbn*, 'as always', as in v. 19, most likely a misunderstanding of MT (or perhaps a defective form of LXX, reading simply καθ' ἡμέραν) rather than evidence of a different *Vorlage*.

התבן (5.13) SP adds נתן לכם, and all the Vss have renderings corresponding to this. Very likely it appeared in 4QGen-Exod[a] (cf. *DJD* XII, p. 24) and 4QExod[b] (ibid., p. 94) as well. With Schmidt and Houtman (against Propp) we regard it as a secondary (though very early) expansion of the text, modelled on v. 16: while it makes an easier text, it is not essential to the sense, and instead of the periphrastic combination of היה and part. one might have expected the Niphal inf. בהנתן in the classical language (cf. however GK §116r and specifically Gen. 34.25; Jer. 39.15 and Zech. 7.7).

שטרי (5.14) Vulg *qui praeerant operibus* at last reverses its equivalents for the two levels of officials (cf. *exactoribus* for נגש later, which may draw on Aq's equivalent noted on the previous verse). But its rendering of the first half of the verse is otherwise free and even misleading.

בני ישראל (5.14)   LXX prefixes τοῦ γένους, according to Wevers to clarify that these officials are themselves Israelites (*Notes*, p. 66). γένος occurs only once elsewhere in Exodus, at 1.9, where it renders עם before בני ישראל: the normal equivalent for עם is λαός.

חקכם ללבן (5.14)   LXX τὰς συντάξεις ὑμῶν τῆς πλινθείας, a free rendering of MT: the pl. συντάξεις presumably reflects the individual quotas of each supervisor; the conversion of the inf. ללבן into a noun makes the construction of the rest of the verse disjointed.

גם תמול (5.14)   LXX has no equivalent, perhaps regarding the reference to 'yesterday' as superfluous and even contradictory. But see Note z on the translation for an explanation of the fuller reading of the other witnesses.

אל־פרעה (5.15)   Tgg and Sy all use קדם, 'before', in place of אל, just as Tgg do when God is addressed: this suggests that Aram. idiom (and the absence of a direct equivalent to Heb. אל) may be involved in the use of קדם generally (Jastrow, p. 1266, gives cases of צוח with both על and ק(ד)ם; Payne Smith, p. 34, says that *'l* or *mn* is possible after *bgn*: perhaps then *qdm* was taken over from the Targumic idiom, though id., p. 490, cites its use after verbs of motion).

למה (5.15)   Tg^N adds כען, 'now', apparently to intensify the question: cf. v. 22 where it appears both when למה is followed by זה and when it is not.

תעשה (5.15)   Tg^O and Sy render as an impersonal passive, 'is it done', perhaps to avoid a direct challenge to Pharaoh: the consonants could be read as 3rd fem. sing. Niphal imperfect.

לעבדיך (5.15)   LXX τοῖς σοῖς οἰκέταις: the choice of this 'less servile' equivalent (as in v. 16a: v. 16b has παῖδες) might be thought of as a deliberate departure from δοῦλος by the translator to make the Israelites' case stronger, but it seems to conform rather to the translator's general preference in Exodus for οἰκέτης or παῖς as equivalents to עבד, except when it refers to Pharaoh's courtiers or to Moses or the patriarchs as servants of Yahweh, where θεράπων is used (e.g. 4.10; 5.21). The general avoidance of the δοῦλος word-group (except for particular cases like 6.6; 13.3, 14; 20.2, and the verb δουλεύειν) in the LXX Pentateuch (in contrast to later books) is noteworthy. Vulg with *servos* (contrast OL *domesticis*) seems to aim at greater consistency, for which the Three provided a precedent (see on v. 16). See also Wevers, *Notes*, p. 46 (on 4.10).

לעבדיך (5.16)   Vulg *nobis*, replacing the deferential language with its denotation. Later in the verse Vulg renders עבדיך more precisely (by *famuli tui*, an occasional alternative to Vulg's usual *servus* which appears only here in Exodus), but puts the verb (*caedimur*) in the 1st person to indicate the reference clearly, as elsewhere (e.g. 5.21) Pharaoh's עבדים are his courtiers. Vulg's renderings follow the use of δοῦλος by the Jewish revisers (on their treatments of the whole verse see O'Connell, *Theodotionic Revision*, pp. 16-18, 174, 253, 289).

עשו (5.16)   Tg^N has עבדך עבדו: עבדך is an error which was corrected by the second word: see *Michael Klein on the Targums*, p. 226.

חטאת עמך (5.16)   See Note bb on the translation. Tg⁰, 'your people sin against them' (cf. SamTgA), is based on the vocalisation of MT, as is Tg^N, 'Pharaoh and the people are sinning', although it adds a direct accusation of Pharaoh himself (cf. its rendering of the indefinite אמרים by 'you say'). LXX (ἀδικήσεις οὖν τὸν λαόν σου), Sy (wḥṭʾ ʾnt ʿl ʿmk) and Vulg (et iniuste agitur contra populum tuum, again preferring a passive formulation) take עמך as the object of the verb, referring to the Israelites, and Schmidt and Childs follow this view. The future of LXX is surprising in the context, though not unnatural as a rendering of the perfect consecutive. Possibly (cf. OL) it was intended as a question. The Three, Tg^J and SamTgJ all take חטאת as a noun (ἁμαρτία[ν]; עובתה ;חובתהון [with ע representing ח]), like Rashi, but differ in their treatment of עמך. Aq (λαῷ σου) and Theod (εἰς τὸν λαόν σου) presuppose a *Vorlage* לעמך (cf. Wevers, *Notes*, p. 67 n. 20), which might also justify the renderings of LXX, Sy and Vulg, with the expected ל after חטא. But this is the easier reading and must be secondary. Symm (ἔχεις) probably vocalised עִמָּךְ, 'with you', which may also be the sense intended by SamTg's עמך (Salvesen, p. 76; cf. the Sam. reading tradition [J. Joosten, pers. comm.]), unless it reflects entirely the same interpretation as Rashi. Tg^J, 'of your people', sees עמך as *nomen rectum* and has to add 'is great and going up (increasing?)' to complete the sentence. Of these only the reading עִמָּךְ, 'with you', is a serious alternative to MT, but its attestation is very weak.

ויאמר (5.17)   LXX and Sy add 'to them' and Sy also adds 'Pharaoh', as often to specify the participants in dialogue.

נרפים (5.17)   For the second occurrence LXX has σχολασταί, which has clearly negative overtones, 'idlers'. Vulg, however, with both occurrences represented by *vacatis otio*, avoids direct criticism, as in v. 8.

נזבחה (5.17)   Some SP mss prefix *waw*, and a similar (surely secondary) connection is made in many LXX mss, Vulg and Tg^N. Tg^J adds an object as in vv. 3 and 8.

ליהוה (5.17)   Tgg, as before, have קדם in place of ל. LXX and Tg^J have 'our God' in place of the divine name, no doubt assimilating to Pharaoh's earlier accusation in v. 8.

עבדו (5.18)   Vulg and Sy (except 5b1 and two other mss) prefix 'and', but the asyndetic reading is better attested and superior.

לבנים (5.18)   SP prefixes the def. art., and the Vss understand similarly (inc. Vulg *consuetum numerum*). The change may be based on the similar phrase in v. 8, but the contexts are different (cf. Note ff on the translation) and MT is the preferable reading here. The absence of את here in SP as well as MT is a further argument for this.

אתם ברע (5.19)   Five SP mss read אתם ברעה, but the sense is no different. LXX (ἑαυτοὺς) ἐν κακοῖς employs a Greek idiom used also in Esth. 7.7; Sir. 12.8; 20.9 and is not evidence of a different *Vorlage*. Propp finds the construction difficult and proposes to read ברעתם, comparing 2 Sam. 16.8 (p. 248), but the change from MT is considerable and unnecessary (see Note gg on the translation).

תנרעו (5.19) MT is supported by LXX (the 3rd sing. variant is due to inner-Greek corruption: see Wevers, *Notes*, p. 69), Tgg and Sy, but SP has ינרע, 3rd sing. Niphal imperfect and Vulg *minuetur* renders similarly. This approximates to the wording of v. 11, whereas MT is close to v. 8. The choice is difficult, but MT has slightly the stronger support.

דבר־יום ביומו (5.19) Sy again renders loosely, with *'yk dbkl ywm* (close to the rendering of 5b1 in v. 13).

נצבים (5.20) LXX ἐρχομένοις, which Propp thinks arose from a corrupt *Vorlage* יצאים (p. 248). This is hardly necessary: the translator may simply have been influenced by the much more common use of לקראת after a verb of motion (only after יצא otherwise in Exod. 7.15 and Num. 22.34).

מאת־פרעה (5.20) SP inserts פני before פרעה, matching 10.11, whereas MT is paralleled in Gen. 47.22. מעם is more common than either in Exodus (8.8 etc.). Tg^J and Tg^N (and some mss of Tg^O) and Sy have קדם, but this is probably due simply to Aram. idiom. LXX ἀπὸ Φαραώ and Tg^{O,G} מלות seem to support MT, but a decision between the two readings is difficult. As Propp notes (p. 248), the accidental omission of the first of the two words beginning with *pe* could have produced MT secondarily, but one hesitates to favour a reading supported only by SP.

ירא (5.21) SP יראה, as it has for ירא in Gen. 41.33. SP does admit apocopated forms, esp. in waw consecutive, but there are cases e.g. of רבה where the jussive remains unshortened (cf. *GSH* §84aβ, 98aβ). It is true (cf. Schmidt, p. 244) that SP could be read as Niphal (and see below), but there is no need to do so (and SamTg does not). Tgg employ יתגלי, 'let...be revealed', mostly with God (the Memra in Tg^G and Tg^{Nmg}) as subject, as if the Heb. were Niphal = 'appear', but in Tg^J with 'our humiliation' supplied as in 3.16 as what is seen by God and as far as the verb is concerned assuming the vocalisation of MT (cf. Chester, *Divine Revelation*, pp. 79-80, 175-76, 223-24, who discusses the connection with judgement).

יהוה (5.21) LXX ὁ θεός, continuing its avoidance of the divine name in this chapter (cf. v. 17).

וישפט (5.21) In Tg^{G,J} this is understood in the stronger sense of 'condemn, punish', probably on the basis of עליכם being understood as an expression of hostility (cf. *AramB* 7, p. 15 n. 12). But 'judge' is retained elsewhere, inc. Exod.R. 5.21.

הבאשתם את־ריחנו (5.21) LXX with ἐβδελύξατε ('made loathsome': see the correction to LSJ in *Suppl.*, p. 68) τὴν ὀσμὴν ἡμῶν paraphrases, hence Aq, Symm ἐσαπρίσατε, 'made rotten'. Tg^{N,G} also paraphrase, introducing the idea of a bad 'name'. Sy *'b'štwn lrwḥn* also avoided the explicit idea of a 'bad smell', perhaps using *rwḥ'* with suffix as a substitute for the obj. pronoun (similarly Tg^{Nmg} according to *AramB* 2, p. 27, note s).

לתת־חרב (5.21) Tg^J prefixes 'because you caused them' (reading דגרמתון for Clarke's הון- [with Ginsburger]) and Sy has *lmtln lḥrb*, apparently 'so as to give us to the sword', probably both to avoid the unlikeliness of a literalistic reading of MT.

בידם (5.21)   'In their hand', i.e. those of Pharaoh and his courtiers. Only Tg^O represents this exactly, but 'into their hands' of Tg^{G,J,N} and Sy is probably based on it too, with an interpretative pluralising of the noun. SP has בידו, meaning Pharaoh, and both LXX's εἰς τὰς χεῖρας αὐτοῦ and Vulg's *ei* support this reading, which may well be original: it is with Pharaoh that the decision lies, and MT could be due to a pedantic assimilation to the composite expression earlier in the verse.

אל־יהוה (5.22)   Tgg have קדם(ל), but this may just be a linguistic equivalent in view of the similar usage for אל־פרעה in v. 15.

אדני (5.22)   Before κύριε LXX^B has δέομαι, corresponding to 4.10, 13, but this unique reading is clearly a secondary development in the Greek tradition. Tg^{N,G} also insert a phrase equivalent to Heb. ב from there, one of several indications in this verse of the close association of these two Pal. Tg. mss and their distinctness from Tg^J. The addition overlooks the change of tone here compared with ch. 4.

למה זה (5.22)   SP prefixes a *waw*, and similar additions are found in LXX, Tg^{J,N} (but not Tg^G) and Sy. But the reading will be secondary. LXX's (καὶ) ἵνα τί (sometimes with τοῦτο etc. added) is its regular equivalent for למה זה throughout the Pentateuch (except for Gen. 18.13): the translator may therefore have seen this expression as alluding to (lack of) purpose rather than cause.

בשמך (5.23)   Tg^{N,G} 'in the name of your Memra': compare the similar addition in Tg^N at 34.5 (where ויקרא is taken to refer to Moses praying), and Chester's conclusion that the concept of Memra is closely related to that of 'name' in Num. 6.27 as well as to light in Exod. 12.42 (*Divine Revelation*, p. 312; cf. also p. 31 on Gen. 12.7).

הרע (5.23)   Tg^{O,J} and Sy render impersonally ('it was bad/worse'), as does Propp, while the other Vss (inc. Tg^{G,N}) have the expected 'he has done harm'.

הצל (5.23)   Neither LXX nor Vulg represent the inf. abs., unusually for the former (and Sy^h adds ῥυόμενος from Aq, Theod) but as a standard practice of the latter (only 3.16 has an equivalent in Exod. 1–14). The other Vss (inc. Sy) do represent it.

Chapter 6.1-9

God's (Renewed) Promise of Deliverance to Moses and Israel

This section comprises two speeches of Yahweh/God to Moses (vv. 1, 2-8) and a brief narrative of Moses' transmission of God's promise to the Israelites and their disregard of it, which it is natural to see as the sequel to God's instruction to Moses in v. 6. The first speech, with the divine name in its introduction, is clearly the conclusion of the dialogue at the end of ch. 5, with the pronoun 'them' referring back to 'your people' at the end of 5.23. Both the Jewish and the Samaritan manuscript traditions make a major division in the text after 6.1, and not after 5.23: unfortunately none of the Dead Sea manuscripts survives at this point, so it is impossible to confirm its antiquity, but it is likely. The second speech, ascribed to 'God', begins abruptly ('also' in NRSV is not in Heb.) with a formal self-introduction (v. 2b) and continues with a recollection in vv. 3-4 of God's dealings with Abraham, Isaac and Jacob under the name 'El Shadday' (traditionally rendered 'God Almighty': see the notes on v. 3) and a general assurance that the Israelites' sufferings are known and of concern to him. On this basis Moses is instructed to announce to the Israelites that God is about to secure their release from servitude and bring them to the promised land of Canaan. Both the speech as a whole and Moses' message for the Israelites are framed by the phrase 'I am Yahweh', which serves both as an emphatic announcement of God's name and as a comprehensive statement of his involvement in Israel's historical origins.

Unlike the shorter speech in v. 1, this speech has no specific connection with ch. 5 and it makes no reference to the setback suffered there or, indeed, to Moses' earlier commission and instruction by Yahweh in 3.1–4.17. The lack of any reference to a journey between vv. 8 and 9 implies that it is located in Egypt rather than at the mountain of God in the desert. It is in fact the beginning of a section of the Exodus narrative (6.2–7.13) which duplicates, with some variations and abbreviation, much of the contents of 3.1–5.1

(see the introductions to the following sections for further details). At the same time it has close parallels of wording and content both with passages in Genesis (esp. ch. 17, the second account of the covenant with Abraham: see further the detailed notes on each verse) and with shorter sections earlier in Exodus (1.13-14; 2.23b-25), as does v. 9.

It is not surprising, therefore, that an early summary of the biblical narrative omitted everything between 5.21 and 7.10 (Philo, *De Vita Mosis* 1.90) and that modern critical scholarship has detected different hands at work here (see the clear account of the arguments in Schmidt, pp. 270-72).[1] The different origins of v. 1 and vv. 2-9 are common ground: even Houtman, who emphasises as always the coherence of the final text, seems to imply that 6.2 was not originally written to follow 6.1 (p. 496).

Accounts of v. 1 naturally follow the approaches taken by scholars to ch. 5, though its role as a starting-point for the plague-story is also emphasised by some (Dillmann, Gressmann [*Mose*, p. 66 n. 6]). Knobel attributed it to R^{JE} (*Num.-Jos.*, p. 569), but Wellhausen was the first of many to assign it to J (so recently Van Seters, p. 76), which is likely to be correct. Baentsch thought that it might be from E because of the undefined (!) object pronouns ('them') and the verbal parallels in 3.19(!) and 11.1, and Gressmann and Propp advocated such an origin with more confidence but less argument. Smend, Eissfeldt and Fohrer (but not Beer, who followed the LXX reading) divided it between J and E, on the basis of supposed doublets within the verse (cf. Holzinger). Those who attribute the end of ch. 5 (Blum, L. Schmidt [*Beobachtungen* (1990), pp. 5-7], Levin, Schmid) or even most of the chapter (Gertz) to a redactor not surprisingly judge similarly for 6.1. Kohata (p. 29) and W.H. Schmidt (p. 247) regard only the occurrences of the phrase 'through mighty power' as from a (Deuteronomistic) redactor in a verse which is mainly from J (likewise Graupner, p. 64). The force of the reply and its inner coherence is, however, much weakened by the omission of these phrases, and Exod. 3.19 and Num. 20.20 are plausible pre-Deuteronomic parallels.

The Priestly origin of vv. 2-9 as a unit is generally regarded as assured, and with good reason (so recently Gertz, pp. 237-51). As already noted, there is both narrative continuity and verbal overlap with a series of other passages in Genesis and Exodus, and these

---

[1] Indeed its importance for the wider source-critical enterprise is such that Carpenter and Harford-Battersby could describe it as 'the real key to the composition of the Pentateuch' (*Hexateuch*, 1, p. 33).

are uniformly attributed to P. On the other hand, it lacks a strong narrative connection with the non-Priestly account in 3.1–5.1 and appears rather as an alternative version of the divine speech to Moses in 3.6-22.

Nevertheless there have been recurring questions about whether all of it formed an original part of P. Already Knobel saw v. 8 as an addition by J (pp. viii, 48; cf. *Num.-Jos.*, p. 548), which for him was a later supplement to the *Grundschrift* (= P), for much the same reasons as have more recently been urged again (see Kohata, *Jahwist*, pp. 29-34): supposedly non-Priestly vocabulary items such as *hēbîʾ*, 'bring into', *nāśāʾ yād*, 'swore' (but note Num. 14.30), and *môrāšāh*, 'possession', and the lack of reference to an oath elsewhere in P.[2] Dillmann also thought that elements of his 'C' (= J) had been worked into vv. 6-12: in particular he thought that v. 9b formed a better sequel to v. 1 than to v. 9a (p. 55), though it is hard to see why, as Holzinger pointed out. Klostermann and Kayser, who were followed by S.R. Driver (*Introduction*, p. 151), thought that vv. 6-8 were from the redactor who incorporated the Holiness Code, but their arguments were answered by Carpenter and Harford-Battersby (cf. McNeile, pp. xiv-xv) and Baentsch, though the latter still ascribed these verses to a secondary stage of P, with the possibility (first suggested by Kuenen) that another Priestly account of the Exodus had been drawn upon. Otto revived Klostermann's view ('Forschungen', 10 n. 45), but has been answered by Gertz (pp. 245-50). Fohrer (p. 52) seems to have had such views in mind when he drew attention to Ezekiel as a possible source for P of a number of the expressions which were thought to support editorial intervention. These include the phrase *bizrôaʿ nᵉṭûyāh* in v. 6, which W.H. Schmidt thinks may be from a (very late) Deuteronomistic redactor (pp. 275-76; cf. Kohata, pp. 28-29): it appears in Ezek. 20.33. In recent times Kohata (see above) has argued forcefully for a later origin for v. 8, adding to the earlier arguments from vocabulary the claim that the land-theology of v. 8 goes against what is found elsewhere in P, where the land has already been 'given' to the patriarchs (so even in 6.4). This argument (which seems to be based on the *Habilitationsschrift* of G.C. Macholz) will not do, as it overlooks the numerous references to the patriarchs as landless aliens in the land of Canaan (6.4: see the Explanatory Note) and the need therefore to distinguish between the senses in which Yahweh 'gives' the land, according to P, to the patriarchs and to Israel at the time of the conquest (which one might call a gift by anticipation, or even by legal claim, and a gift in actuality: *de iure* and *de facto*, perhaps).[3] An additional issue is raised by

---

[2] Smend, *Erzählung*, p. 125, cited some of these expressions as evidence for later reworking of P (cf. Eissfeldt, p. 269*).

[3] This distinction is well picked up by Schmitt, 'Jahwenamenoffenbarung', who speaks of the 'zwei Zeiten der Landgabe'. See further the Explanatory Note on v. 8.

K. Schmid (p. 262), although he does not want to use it as an argument for a separate origin for v. 8 (see also below): this concerns the use of *môrāšāh* rather than *ᵃḥuzzāh*, 'holding', which Kohata notes, but without drawing attention to the view maintained by Schmid that these expressions refer respectively to full possession and usufruct: the Priestly view being that Yahweh remains the true owner of the land and Israel is just a permanent tenant (cf. Lev. 25.23). However, such a distinction of meaning between the terms does not seem to be borne out by the dictionaries (cf. *Ges18*, p. 36). Schmid himself provides a strong structural argument in favour of the unity of vv. 2-8 by pointing to the chiastic arrangement of references to the patriarchs and the land on the one hand (vv. 2-4; 8) and the Israelites in Egypt and their deliverance on the other (vv. 5; 6-7) (pp. 260-61), to which there is a close structural parallel, with a shift of theological focus, in 29.45-46.

I. Knohl has argued that not only vv. 6-8 but the whole of vv. 2-8, and indeed its continuation as far as 7.6 is from the 'Holiness School' (HS), which revised the basic P account and in particular added the Holiness Code in Leviticus 17–26 (*Sanctuary of Silence*, p. 17 n. 24, cf. p. 61: Knohl's general conclusions are summarised on pp. 101-10). On the one hand this circumvents the arguments of earlier scholars and implicitly Schmid against a later origin for v. 8 or vv. 6-8 alone; on the other hand it is itself founded on very weak arguments, like much of Knohl's attempt to find the work of the Holiness School all over the Pentateuch. He cites three expressions: *sᵉbālāh*, 'burden', in vv. 6-7, the four occurrences of *ᵃnî yhwh*, and the recognition-formula in v. 7. Of these the first and last do not appear in Leviticus and the examples of the last which Knohl attributes to HS in Exodus are very debatable. *ᵃnî yhwh* is certainly a prominent expression in Leviticus 17–26 (see the Excursus on v. 2), but it is found elsewhere, especially in Ezekiel, and therefore cannot be a decisive criterion for HS authorship. In any case to ascribe so much of the Priestly narrative to a second stage would leave the first stage rather lacking in theological exposition.

It appears most likely that the appearance of uncharacteristic idioms in this passage is largely due to the influence of Ezekiel on the Priestly author himself at this point (so recently in detail J. Lust, 'Exodus 6.2-8 and Ezekiel', in Vervenne [ed.], *Studies*, pp. 209-24, and Gertz, pp. 244-50).

Theologically v. 1, while closely related to 5.1-23, looks mainly to the future (cf. the tenses of the verbs) and forms an interpretative key to the plague-narratives and their purpose as a means of overcoming Pharaoh's opposition to the departure from Egypt. It is no doubt for this reason that in the familiar division into chapters it has been made into the opening of a new chapter. At one time it would have led straight into 7.14. 6.2-8 on the other hand, with its narrative sequel in v. 9, has a pivotal position in the whole theological structure of the Priestly source, which is closely comparable to that of 3.6-18(22) in the non-Priestly material. W. Zimmerli pointed out that for P the Exodus is seen not (as it is in Deuteronomy) as the prelude to the covenant at Sinai/Horeb but as (part of) the fulfilment of the covenant with Abraham, and 6.2-8, along with 2.23b-25, is the key evidence for this.[4] Zimmerli also noted that the 'covenant formula' in v. 7 takes on a distinctive character in P from its association with the building of the tabernacle as a place for Yahweh's presence to 'dwell' (Exod. 25.8), which is the central theme of P's Sinai narrative (cf. especially 29.43-46, which adds this to several of the themes of 6.2-8).[5] To these themes of the covenant with Abraham (and the other patriarchs) and the relationship between Yahweh and his people, now conceived as his presence among them, are added the revelation of the divine name and the fulfilment of the promise of the land of Canaan. This draws attention to another important theological aspect of these verses, which is their role as an 'exegesis of the divine name', which is based on the sequence of the canonical 'saving acts' of Yahweh on Israel's behalf.[6] As Zimmerli correctly saw, this new handling of traditional themes answered precisely to the theological needs of the exilic age in which it originated. By it the radical questioning of Israel's relationship to her God which was set off by the failure of Israel to observe the demands of the Sinai covenant could be circumvented, and in a way which gave a central place to the Jerusalem cult and its rituals in Yahweh's future purpose for his people.[7] In line with this,

---

[4] 'Sinaibund und Abrahambund', in his *Gottes Offenbarung* (Munich, 1963), pp. 205-16; see more briefly my essay, 'Covenant, Oath and the Composition of the Pentateuch', in A.D.H. Mayes and R.B. Salters (eds.), *Covenant as Context* (FS E.W. Nicholson; Oxford, 2003), pp. 71-89 (72-73).

[5] See Rendtorff, *Bundesformel*, pp. 20-27, 59-64, ET pp. 14-22, 57-62, although the special features of the Priestly theology are obscured by Rendtorff's view of P as a supplement to the older Pentateuchal material rather than a separate source and by his reluctance (with his pupil E. Blum) to distinguish between the views of P and the Holiness Code in Lev. 17–26. On this see further my essay cited above (n. 4), pp. 82-86.

[6] See on this my 'Exegesis of the Divine Name', pp. 146-48.

[7] Cf. in general J. Van Seters, 'Confessional Reformulation in the Exilic Period', *VT* 22 (1972), pp. 448-59.

the recognition-formula in v. 7b, which Ezekiel had used repeatedly with reference only to the judgement and subsequent restoration which he foresaw (e.g. Ezek. 5.13; 16.62), is related to the events of the Exodus and their immediate sequel.

In the redacted text of the Pentateuch the fresh impetus of the Priestly theology, which brought together Jerusalem cult traditions and the traditional *Heilsgeschichte*, was inevitably softened. The mediating position of the Holiness Code and the integration of the non-Priestly Sinai-traditions of a covenant and its renewal made restoration dependent upon repentance and a more broadly conceived notion of holiness. In Exodus the Priestly 'keynote' revelation to Moses became little more than a confirmation of the assurances already given to Moses in ch. 3. In its immediate context, however, it could serve as an elaboration of the much shorter divine speech in v. 1 and so with it prepare the way for the dramatic events that were to follow in the plague-story.

1 Yahweh said to Moses, 'Now you shall see what[a] I will do to Pharaoh, for[b] through mighty power he will let them[c] go and through mighty power he will drive them[c] out of his land.' 2 *God spoke to Moses and said to him: 'I am Yahweh. 3 I appeared to Abraham, to Isaac and to Jacob as El Shaddai ('God Almighty')*[d] *but by my name Yahweh*[e] *I was not known*[f] *to them. 4 I also*[g] *established*[h] *my covenant with them, to give them the land of Canaan, the land of their residence as aliens, in which they lived as aliens. 5 I have also*[g] *heard the groaning of the Israelites, whom*[i] *the Egyptians compel to labour*[j]*, and I have remembered my covenant. 6 Therefore say to the Israelites: "I am Yahweh, and I will bring you out from subjection to*[k] *the burdens imposed by the Egyptians and I will rescue you from labour for them*[j]*. I will set you free*[l] *with my outstretched arm and with great acts of judgement*[m]*. 7 I will take you to myself for a people and I will be your God, and you will know that I am Yahweh your God, who brought you out from subjection to*[k] *the burdens imposed by the Egyptians. 8 And I will bring you into the land which I swore*[n] *to give to Abraham, to Isaac and to Jacob, and I will give it to you as a possession*[o]*. I am Yahweh."'* 9 Moses took this message to the Israelites, but they did not listen to Moses, because of their indignation[p] and their burdensome labour[j].

Notes on the Translation

a. Heb. אשר, in the sense 'that which', as in 4.12: the relative clause is in effect the object of the verb (GK §138e), and in such cases אשר is often preceded by את (e.g. 4.15: cf. SP here).

b. Heb. כי, in its causal sense, with Schmidt and Propp. NRSV 'Indeed', suggesting the 'emphatic כי' (see Note m on 3.1-12); Houtman 'that', apparently in the sense 'so that', which is possible (cf. BDB, pp. 472-73), but not necessary, since the 'mighty power' picks up what Yahweh is going to 'do'. A more likely alternative would be 'namely that' (BDB, p. 471).

c. The object suffixes have no antecedent in the sentence, but clearly refer back to לעם הזה and עמך in 5.23 and indicate the close connection between the two verses.

d. Heb. ב is here commonly recognised as an example of the *beth essentiae* (cf. GK §119i, JM §133c, and e.g. Exod. 18.5; Deut. 26.5). Propp appears to differ, translating 'in', 'to emphasise that Yahweh was not fully equivalent to God Shadday', the latter being 'a partial manifestation' of Yahweh (p. 271). But this seems very close to what e.g. Schmidt (p. 268) considers to be the implication of the *beth essentiae*: cf. his quotation from Brockelmann, *Syntax* 106g, 'to express the attribute in which a person shows himself'. In Priestly texts the construction is chiefly found modifying an object of a verb, e.g. Num. 18.10, 26, cf. Ezek. 45.1; 47.22, showing how it is (to be) regarded. The best commentary on the meaning here must be Gen. 17.1b: Yahweh appears (וירא) to Abraham and introduces himself with the name El Shaddai (cf. 35.9-11, with the recollection from the human point of view in 48.3).

The interpretation of שדי remains an enigma. Some OT occurrences link it closely with the verb שדד, 'devastate' (Isa. 13.6 = Joel 1.15), and probably understood it to mean 'the Devastator'. Such a meaning would also fit the contexts in Ps. 68.15, Ruth 1.20-21 and some verses in Job. But it does not suit the other passages so well (nor the PNs Ammishaddai and Zurishaddai in Num. 1.6, 12 etc.) and it may be a meaning that was etymologically deduced specifically by the prophet(s) concerned (cf. Koch, '*Šaddaj*', pp. 328-29). Two passages in Ezekiel (1.24 10.5), which include the one occurrence of the full title outside the Pentateuch, refer to the 'voice' of שדי (אל) and 10.5 mentions his 'speaking'. The inclusion of this title or name in the introduction to two of the oracles of Balaam (Num. 24.4, 16) might be associated with this and both verses actually speak of the 'vision of שדי': 'speaking' and 'appearing' are also the two main characteristics of אל שדי in P. It is of course possible that the 'voice' in Ezekiel (as in Isa. 30.30 and Ps. 29 with Yahweh) means the sound of thunder and so associated the title with phenomena of nature. The renderings of the title in the ancient Versions (see Text and Versions for details) are not of much help, as it seems that they were baffled by it. The now popular 'God Almighty' goes back only to one of several equivalents used by the Greek translation of Job and is by no means a sure guide to the meaning: it also lacks a convincing etymological basis.[8] Scholars have sought assistance from the related languages: by far the most promising parallel is the relatively recent discovery of a word *šdyn* in the ninth- or eighth-century Aramaic (?) Balaam text from Tell Deir ʿAlla in the east Jordan valley (ed. J. Hoftijzer and G. van der Kooij, *Aramaic Texts from Deir ʿAlla* [Leiden, 1976]; for translations and brief discussion see K. Smelik, *Writings from Ancient Israel* [Edinburgh, 1991], pp. 79-88; *TUAT* II/1, pp. 138-48 [Hoftijzer]; *COS* 2, pp. 14-45 [B. Levine]), where it occurs in close conjunction with *ʾlhn*, 'gods', in Combination 1, 7-8.[9] The Transjordanian provenance of this text, together with the occurrences of שדי in Numbers, Job and Ruth, may provide a clue to the ultimate origin of the divine title. Compare also the occurrences in Thamudic and Palmyrene cited by Niehr in *TWAT* 7, 1082-83 = *TDOT* 14, pp. 423-24. While the word is at Deir ʿAlla a generic term rather than a title for a particular deity, it may have stood for a general divine characteristic, like קדוש, 'holy', in Hebrew, which can be used in the plural of gods in general (Ps. 89.6, 8) as well as in the singular of Yahweh himself (e.g. Isa. 6.3). But what that characteristic may have been remains elusive (a recent survey of suggestions is given by Propp 2, pp. 760-61; cf. also Schmidt, p. 282, Houtman, pp. 100-102, *TWAT* 7, 1078-1104 = *TDOT* 14, pp. 418-46 [Niehr/Steins], and *DDD*, 1416-23 [E.A. Knauf, very speculative]). The most popular views in recent times have been those which associate שדי with an Akk. word for 'mountain', *šadû* (Cross, *Canaanite Myth*, pp. 52-60, also in *TWAT* 1, 273-75 = *TDOT* 1, pp. 255-57) or a Ug. word for 'field' (*šd*, in the sense of 'open country', cf. Heb. שדה: M. Weippert, 'Erwägungen zur Etymologie des Gottesnamens *ʾEl Šaddaj*', *ZDMG* 111 [1961], pp. 42-62, also in *THAT* 2, 873-81 = *TLOT* 3, pp. 1304-10; note also possible occurrences of a DN *šd* in Ugaritic and Phoenician discussed by A. Caquot, 'Une contribution ougaritique à la préhistoire du titre divin Shadday', *Congress Volume: Paris* [VTSup 61; Leiden, 1995], pp. 1-12 [cf. Niehr, *TWAT* 7, 1080-81 = *TDOT* 14, pp. 420-21]). Neither is very satisfactory: in the first case because of the lack of any parallel in a religious context and in both because of difficulties in the equivalence of Semitic sibilants.

e. The grammatical status of Heb. שמי יהוה, which is surprising in connection with the first person sing. Niphal verb נודעתי (on which see Note f), can be explained in two ways. It may be a case of the 'double subject', where the grammatical subject of the verb is amplified by a more specific word, usually with a pronoun suffix which makes the connection clear (GK §144l-m: e.g.

---

[8] Note Koch's insistence, based on his attention to the text with by far the largest number of occurrences of שדי: 'Der *Šaddaj* des Dialogs [sc. of Job] ist nicht der Allmächtige...sondern eher der göttliche "Allernächste"' (*VT* 26 [1976], p. 316.

[9] A Heb. pl. form of this word may underlie לְשֵׁדִים in Deut. 32.17 (J. Joosten, pers. comm.).

Isa. 26.9): 'I, that is my name Yahweh, was not known to them'. Or it may be a noun (phrase) used adverbially (i.e. where a preposition might be present) to indicate the aspect of a subject which is active or affected (GK §117s-t, JM §126g: e.g. Ezek. 11.13): 'By my name Yahweh I was not known to them'. The former explanation offers a closer parallel in terms of word order and the pronoun suffix and is preferred by Schmidt and (following W.R. Garr, 'The Grammar and Interpretation of Exodus 6:3', *JBL* 111 [1992], pp. 385-408) Propp (pp. 261, 272). But the latter, which is adopted by Childs and Houtman and favoured by JM, fits the contrast in the context better (which also explains the 'fronting' of the phrase).

f. Heb. לא נודעתי, Niphal perfect of ידע (on Vss, which at least assume a reading of the verb as Hiphil, see Text and Versions). The translation 'did not make myself known' is also possible (cf. Ruth 3.3; Isa. 19.13; Ezek. 20.5, 9) and recognised by all the dictionaries (cf. also GK §51f and JM §51c for a similar use of the Niphal as reflexive of Hiphil with other verbs). But most often the Niphal of ידע is passive and this fits the context here well too. To avoid the apparent contradiction between this statement and verses in Genesis which imply a knowledge of the name Yahweh (e.g. 4.25; 14.22; 15.7), it is sometimes suggested that ignorance of the name's meaning rather than the name itself is meant (so already Rashi), or that לא stands for הלא (cf. 3.19; 8.22: also GK §150a), thus making the statement into a (rhetorical) question (e.g. G.R. Driver, 'Affirmation by Exclamatory Negation', *JANES* 5 [1973], pp. 107-14 [109]), or that לא is not the negative but an affirmative or emphatic particle (like *l* in Ugaritic: see *HAL*, pp. 485-86, for the possible existence of such a particle in Heb.: but Muraoka, *Emphatic Words*, pp. 113-23, is doubtful). The first suggestion makes an artificial distinction, while the other two take insufficient account of the contrast with the first part of the verse. See further the Explanatory Note, Moberly, *Old Testament*, pp. 55-59, and Garr, 'Grammar and Interpretation'.

g. Heb. וגם. There is in vv. 4 and 5 (which also begins with וגם) a clear two-stage progression from the initial self-introduction of Yahweh as the God who had 'appeared' to the patriarchs, which makes 'also' the appropriate translation, rather than an emphasising particle like 'even' or 'indeed' (against Childs, p. 108 [cf. 110], who renders 'Now' in v. 5, and Schmidt, who has 'Freilich' [cf. Eng. 'Of course'] to express both a contrast with v. 3b and emphasis on what follows): see Note h on 1.7-22 for references and further discussion. Houtman (pp. 500-501) and Propp (p. 261) see in the repeated וגם a case of the possible meaning 'both...and' (which Houtman elevates to 'not only...but also'), but this strengthens the link between vv. 4 and 5 at the expense of that with v. 3 (and v. 2).

h. Heb. הקמתי, lit. 'made to stand'. Although sometimes used of 'maintaining' a covenant already made, whether by man (2 Kgs 23.3; Jer. 34.18) or by God (Lev. 26.9; Deut. 8.18; Neh. 9.8), in the majority of cases the meaning is, as it clearly is here, to 'make' a covenant (so in Gen. 6.18; 9.9, 11, 17; 17.7, 19, 21; Ezek. 16.60, 62). This is thus the characteristic idiom of P, whereas elsewhere כרת and occasionally other verbs are used (see M. Weinfeld, *TWAT* 1, 787-88 = *TDOT* 2, pp. 259-61, although his classification of some instances is questionable). Even the book of Ezekiel sometimes uses כרת. The reason for P's choice of הקים may perhaps have been to avoid the connotations of a covenant-making ritual like those described in Gen. 15.9-11, 17-18; Jer. 34.18-20.

i. This is the most common meaning of Heb. אשר and it is appropriate to the context, with אתם as the regular resumptive pronoun (GK §155c, JM §158f): so Childs, p. 108, Schmidt, p. 268, also Luther, AV, NIV, NRSV. Houtman (p. 501) and Propp (p. 273) advocate the meaning 'because', in agreement with NJPS, though the former actually gives 'whom' in his translation. Both scholars attribute a different rendering, 'that', to Rashi (cf. the Silbermann translation), but Rashi's insertion of הנואקים in his paraphrase is equally compatible with 'because'. It is really only when it is added that the rendering of אשר by a conjunction becomes plausible: for MT itself 'whom' is much to be preferred.

j. Heb. מעבדים. This and עבדה (קשה) in vv. 6 and 9 pick up precisely the language used in 1.13-14, another Priestly passage; see notes o, p and t there for the clear intention of the Priestly writer to refer to Israel's labours as slavery.

k. Heb. מתחת, lit. 'from under': cf. the similar idioms in 18.10 and Hos. 4.12, and the uses of תחת alone in BDB s.v. II.1.c-e.

l. Heb. וגאלתי אתכם. The specialised legal use of גאל, often translated 'redeem' here (e.g. AV, NRSV), is particularly well attested in Leviticus 25, Numbers 35 and the book of Ruth, where the nominalised participle גֹּאֵל is used for the 'kinsman' who has a particular responsibility to rescue or avenge a member of the family who has got into trouble or even been killed (see *THAT* 1, 383-94 (J.J. Stamm) = *TLOT* 1, pp. 288-96, *TWAT* 1, 884-90 = *TDOT* 2, pp. 350-55, and the works of Stamm, Johnson and Jepsen referred to there; also the SAHD database entry). In addition to a general sense of 'restore, recover', the legal use with reference to a (debt-)slave in Lev. 25.47-54 would have a particular appropriateness to the portrayal of the Israelites' situation in Egypt as slavery by P (see Note j above). There is, however, no sense of a price being paid here – the following expressions introduced by ב are instrumental in a quite different way – and for that reason 'set free' is to be preferred to 'redeem' as a translation.

m. Heb. בשפטים גדלים. The noun שֶׁפֶט occurs elsewhere in the Pentateuch at Exod. 7.4 (the identical phrase to here), 12.12, Num. 33.4 (modelled on Exod. 12.12), so in passages belonging to or dependent on P; and also 10 times in Ezek. (5.10, 15 etc.) and at Prov. 19.29 and 2 Chr. 24.24. A rarer form שָׁפוֹט may occur at Ezek. 23.10 and 2 Chr. 20.9. Apart from the last passage these words always occur in the pl. and refer to 'acts of judgement', generally done by God. But in Prov. 19.29, which may be the oldest of these passages, שׁפטים probably refers to human punishments (cf. the par. מהלמות). In other texts (and in Ezek. 5.8; 18.8; 39.21) משׁפט is sometimes used in a similar way. The phrase here is perhaps an ethical reworking of the Deuteronomic יד חזקה, which often follows בזרוע נטויה.

n. Here נשׂאתי את־ידי, lit. 'lifted up my hand', rather than the standard expression נשׁבעתי which is used in 13.5, 11; 32.13; 33.1. This formula is used in a variety of contexts reflecting different meanings of the gesture described (cf. BDB, p. 670a; *TWAT* 5, 640 = *TDOT* 10, p. 37), but as a reference to an oath it appears only in Ezekiel (7x in ch. 20, plus 36.7; 44.12; 47.14), here and in Num. 14.30 (both P), Deut. 32.40 (exilic?) and Neh. 9.15 (perhaps also Ps. 106.26). In all these passages it refers to God swearing an oath, but הרים is used in a similar way in Gen. 14.22 of a human being. Presumably the idiom is based on a contemporary custom, but the linguistic evidence points to a context in the exilic period and perhaps it has a Babylonian origin, though the corresponding Akkadian phrases seem not to be used in an oath context (unless *nīšu* I.4 [*AHw*, p. 797], 'Gebetsbeschwörung', means this, but it is more likely an incantation: *RLA* 2, 305, is firmly against the derivation of *nīšu/nēšu* II from *našû* and *AHw* ibid. agrees).[10] Whatever its origin, the prominence of gods' names in oath-taking and the phrase אל־שׁמים in Deut. 32.40 strongly suggest that the action originally expressed a recognition of the god(s) in whose name the oath was taken. In a divine oath, as here, such notions would of course not apply.

o. Heb. מורשׁה. Grammatically it is the (secondary) complement, but without the ל that can be used in such cases (cf. לאלהים, לעם in v. 7 and 4QGen-Ex[a] here: GK §117ii, 119t). The noun occurs mainly in Ezekiel (7x: otherwise only [metaphorically] in Deut. 33.4) and like other derivatives of the root ירשׁ it can refer to land which is violently seized and occupied (Ezek. 25.4). It refers to the possession of the land of Canaan by Israel (or more precisely the population remaining in Judah) in Ezek. 11.15 and 33.24. As here it is generally seen as the gift of Yahweh. The related verb is used by P in Gen. 28.4, with a contrast as here (v. 4) to ארץ מגרים (cf. Lev. 20.24; Num. 32.21, 39; 33.52-53, 55), but in such a context P prefers to speak of the land as an אחזה (Gen. 17.8; 48.4; Lev. 14.34), the same word that is used for the land at Hebron purchased by Abraham as a burial place (Gen. 23.4 etc.). This was an important term of property law (see further F. Horst, 'Zwei Begriffe für

---

[10] *Ges18*, p. 849, seems to imply that there might be parallel idioms for oath-taking in Ugaritic and OAram, but the passages cited in *DULAT* 2, p. 648 (*KTU* 1.14.2.22 [=75] and par.) and in *DNWSI* 2, p. 762, turn out to be different in meaning. *RSP* 2, pp. 387-88, cited in *HAL*, p. 684, compares an Akkadian text (RS 15.10:11, *PRU* 3, p. 311), but the context does not clearly indicate the meaning 'swear'.

Eigentum [Besitz]: *nahalā* und *'ªhuzzā'*, in A. Kuschke [ed.], *Verbannung und Heimkehr* [FS W. Rudolph; Tübingen, 1961], pp. 135-56).

p. Heb. מקצר־רוח is seen variously (cf. *HAL*, p. 1052; Wolff, *Anthropologie*, pp. 36, 64, ET, pp. 18, 37) as 'impatience' (BDB, p. 894; Childs, p. 109, with the additional suggestion that there is a hendiadys with the following phrase) or 'faintheartedness, brokenness of spirit' (Schmidt [p. 288], NRSV: cf. Vss and Text and Versions). The phrase (and the noun קֹצֶר) occurs only here in BH, but there are related idioms employing the verb קָצַר and the adjective קָצָר. Those with the noun נֶפֶשׁ could well support the interpretation 'fainthearted', or perhaps better 'weariness' (Num. 21.4; Judg. 16.16; Zech. 11.8: cf. Houtman, Propp, also *KTU* 1.16.6.34, 47 and *DULAT* 2, pp. 716-17), but the contrast between ארך אפים and קצר־רוח in Prov. 14.29 suggests more the notion of 'short-tempered' (cf. קצר אפים in 14.7) and the other occurrences of this combination in Mic. 2.7 (in a complaint) and Job 21.4 (almost 'indignation') seem to mean the same (and the opposite ארך רוח in Eccl. 7.8 and Sir. 5.11 points to this too). If taken with the following phrase here 'indignation at their burdensome labour' will be the meaning intended. However, if רוח and נפש are interchangeable, then a meaning like 'weariness' could be adopted, which does fit the context well.[11]

Explanatory Notes

1. These words of Yahweh are clearly his response to Moses' complaint in 5.22-23: the repeated pronoun 'them' has nothing to refer back to in the verse itself and presupposes the link to 'your people' in 5.23. The focus on Pharaoh also corresponds closely to the theme of ch. 5 as a whole and to the particular focus on his behaviour in 5.23 (in contrast to the complete disregard of him in the verses which follow, until v. 11). But it is because of what Yahweh will 'now...do' to him that Pharaoh will relent. There can be no real doubt in the context that the 'mighty power' (the phrase repeated for effect) is Yahweh's, as in 3.19 (against Van Seters, p. 76,

---

[11] R.D. Haak, 'A Study and New Interpretation of *qṣr npš*', *JBL* 101 (1982), pp. 161-67, distinguishes well the different meanings of *qṣr(t) npš* in Ug. (subjective, 'impatience' [or perhaps 'indignation'], in *KTU* 1.40.14-15 etc.; objective 'weak', in *KTU* 1.16.6.34, 47): all other accounts of the idiom (even *DULAT*) are faulty in some way. But his treatment of the OT occurrences ignores the possible distinction between רוח and נפש in Heb. and misunderstands both Mic. 2.7 and Job 21.4. There seems in fact to be no precise equivalent in Heb. to the objective meaning found in Ug.

who thinks it is Pharaoh's: cf. others cited in Schmidt, p. 244).[12] Not only will he let Israel go (Heb. *šillaḥ*, cf. 3.20, [4.21, 23] 5.1-2), but he will 'drive them out' (Heb. *gērēš*). The progression from release to forcible expulsion is found also in partly different words in 12.33 after the slaying of the Egyptian firstborn, and the word *gērēš* itself is used with reference to the Exodus in 11.1 and 12.39 (in other contexts in 2.17 and 10.11).

2. The narrator now refers to the deity as 'God' (Heb. *ᵉlōhîm*), not 'Yahweh' as in v. 1.[13] Since the focus of the following divine speech is on his redeeming purposes, the traditional explanation of variation in the divine names, that 'God' refers to divine judgement and 'Yahweh' to divine mercy, does not work. Rashi nevertheless sustained this approach by finding criticism of Moses (*mišpāṭ*, 'judgement') expressed in it, because of his harsh words spoken to Yahweh in 5.22-23. But why then is 'Yahweh' used in the actual response to Moses in v. 1? As is more fully argued in the introduction to this section, a source-critical explanation of the variation is much more satisfactory: the use of 'God' corresponds to the normal practice of the Priestly source in narrative hitherto, from Gen. 1.1 to Exod. 2.25 (see further my essay '"God" in Old Testament Theology', *Congress Volume: Leiden* [VTSup 109; Leiden, 2006], pp. 175-94, esp. p. 184). The words 'I am Yahweh' here have their original function as a self-introduction of the deity, most likely derived from (cultic) prophetic speech (cf. Pss. 50.7; 81.11).[14] On their use later in the passage see the notes below on vv. 6-8. Here they begin a formal address to Moses which (unlike v. 1) stands on its own and makes no reference to the immediately preceding

---

[12] A neat but unlikely alternative is Cassuto's suggestion (p. 74: based on Rashi) that the first time the 'mighty power' (lit. 'hand') is Yahweh's and the second time Pharaoh's: cf. the use of the related verb *ḥāzaq* in 12.33 (NRSV 'urged', lit. 'was strong').

[13] See Text and Versions for evidence of the reading 'Yahweh' here, which is less significant than it at first appears.

[14] See the classic essay of W. Zimmerli, 'Ich bin Jahwe'; also K. Elliger, 'Ich bin der Herr – euer Gott' (1954), in his *Kleine Schriften zum Alten Testament* (Neukirchen, 1966), pp. 211-31. For the formula's origin in prophetic rather than priestly utterances see J.W. Hilber, *Cultic Prophecy in the Psalms* (BZAW 352; Berlin and New York, 2005), pp. 132-33, and my 'Exegesis of the Divine Name', p. 148. Similar formulae are frequent in other Near Eastern texts: see the examples cited by Propp, p. 271.

context, neither to Pharaoh's intransigence nor to Moses' complaint nor indeed to Yahweh's earlier commissioning of Moses in very similar terms (3.1–4.17). In the originally independent Priestly source their significance will have been even greater, because here for the very first time the name 'Yahweh' is uttered, fittingly by Yahweh himself: hitherto the only names or titles spoken by anyone in Priestly texts have been $^{ʾe}lōhîm$ (Gen. 9.6, 16; 17.7-8; 28.4) and 'God Almighty' (ʾēl šadday: cf. v. 3 and the notes there).

Excursus on the Phrase 'I Am Yahweh'

In Hebrew the phrase has just two words, 'I' and 'Yahweh', with the verb 'to be' (as usual in the present tense) not being expressed. This does lead to uncertainty in some contexts where a first person verb follows, as to whether the meaning is 'I am Yahweh, I…' or 'I Yahweh…' (i.e. apposition). In the great majority of cases, including all those in Leviticus and Ezekiel and the five cases in Exodus 6 (vv. 2, 6, 7, 8, 29), the shorter form of the pronoun 'I' ($^{ʾa}nî$) is used (200x); only in eleven cases is 'I' represented by ʾānōkî (Exod. 4.11; 20.2, 5; Deut. 5.6, 9; Isa. 43.11; 44.24; 51.15; Hos. 12.10; 13.4; Ps. 81.11). As a formula of self-introduction 'I am Yahweh' is actually comparatively rare: Gen. 15.7; 28.13; Exod. 6.2, 6, 29; Lev. 18.2; Judg. 6.10; Ezek. 20.5 (with ʾānōkî Exod. 20.2/Deut. 5.6; Isa. 44.24; Ps. 81.11). In the largest number of cases it is an emphasising formula in the middle or at the end of a divine speech, and it is in this group of examples that the possibility or even likelihood of an appositional use arises. This group comprises Exod. 6.8; 12.12; 15.26; Lev. 11.44-45 and 49 cases in Lev. 17–26; 7 cases in Numbers; Deut. 29.5; Isa. 27.3; 60.22; 61.8 and 15 times in chs. 40–55; Jer. 17.10; 32.27; 18/19? cases in Ezekiel; Zech. 10.6; Mal. 3.6 (102/103 in all; with ʾānōkî in Exod. 20.5/Deut. 5.9; Isa. 43.11; 51.15; Hos. 12.10; 13.4). The other large group, which is concentrated especially in Exodus and Ezekiel, is the 'recognition-formulae', where the phrase is preceded by 'you/they shall know that': Exod. 6.7; 7.5, 17; 8.18; 10.2; 14.4, 18; 16.12; 29.46; 31.13; 1 Kgs 20.13, 28; Isa. 45.3; 49.23, 26; 60.16; Jer. 9.23; 24.7 (with a distinctive pronoun in the preceding clause); 71 (*TWAT* 3, 502 = *TDOT* 5, p. 471) cases in Ezekiel; Joel 2.27; 4.17.[15]

---

[15] On this group see especially W. Zimmerli, *Erkenntnis Gottes nach dem Buch Ezechiel. Eine theologische Studie* (ATANT 27; Zurich, 1954), ET in *I Am Yahweh*, pp. 29-98, and more briefly *THAT* 1, 697-99 = *TLOT*, 2, pp. 519-20; *TWAT* 3, 501-507 = *TDOT* 5, pp. 471-76.

It is noteworthy that the formula with ˣ*nî* is strongly concentrated, though not exclusively so, in the Priestly sections of the Pentateuch (including H), Ezekiel and Deutero-Isaiah. Further, while all three main uses of it appear in Exodus (including this passage) and Ezekiel, only the first two uses appear in the Holiness Code (the recognition-formula is absent). This might be taken as evidence that H is the earliest of the three texts, but there are in fact now good reasons for dating H later than the *Grundschrift* of P and *a fortiori*, on the usual view, later than Ezekiel. The relationship of Exodus 6 to Ezekiel (esp. ch. 20) is therefore of special importance in exploring the background to this passage.

3-4. That God/Yahweh 'appeared' to the patriarchs is stated several times in Genesis (12.7; 18.1; 26.2, 24; 35.1 [cf. v. 7, 'revealed himself' (Heb. *gālāh*)]), but that he did so using the title 'God Almighty' (Heb. *ʾēl šadday*) only in 17.1, 35.9 and 48.3, all passages attributed to the Priestly source. These verses relate to Abraham and Jacob, but not to Isaac, who is mentioned only briefly in texts that are clearly Priestly (21.3 [cf. 17.16-19], 4-5; 25.9, 19-20, 26b, 34-35; 28.1-9; 31.18b; 35.27-29). It is possible therefore that the Priestly writer had Gen. 26.2, 24 in mind here, though this need not mean that he incorporated ch. 26 into his work and the implication of that chapter that the patriarchs knew the name Yahweh clearly runs contrary to what is said later in this verse. The inclusion of Isaac in other aspects of the Priestly writer's conception of patriarchal religion is made clear in Gen. 17.19 (covenant) and 28.3-4 (familiarity with the name 'God Almighty' and the terms of the covenant with Abraham), but nowhere except here is a reference made to an appearance to him: it seems as though both Isaac (28.4) and Jacob (35.12) regard the initial appearance to Abraham as the decisive one. It is of course possible that a passage like Gen. 35.9-13 was omitted by the Pentateuch redactor, but it is just as likely that the Priestly writer here treated Abraham, Isaac and Jacob as a triad without feeling the need to provide a full account of each one's story.

The divine name/title which is normally translated into English as 'God Almighty', following the Vulgate *Deus omnipotens* (Heb. *ʾēl šadday*),[16] appears only seven times in the Bible (elsewhere in Gen. 17.1; 28.3; 35.11; 43.14; 48.3; Ezek. 10.5).[17] It combines one

---

[16] On this title see especially Koch, '*Šaddaj*'.

[17] In SP and LXX also at Gen. 49.25, but the reading is probably secondary. It is commonly thought that Gen. 43.14 is due to a late redactor.

of the Heb. words for 'God/god' with a divine title *šadday* which occurs on its own 41 times in the Bible (Gen. 49.25MT; Num. 24.4, 16; Isa. 13.6; Ezek. 1.24; Joel 1.15; Pss. 68.15; 91.1; 31 times in the poetry of Job [5.17 etc.]; and Ruth 1.20-21). Its distribution suggests a wide, if sporadic use, but the occurrences in sources connected with the Jerusalem temple (Ezekiel, Joel, Ps. 68) are likely to be the most significant indicators of the immediate origin of the Priestly writer's formula. The idea that it was an ancient title could have been reinforced by texts like Gen. 49.25 and Num. 24.4, 16, in all of which it occurs in parallel with the word *ʾēl*. The Priestly writer may also have been aware of the other titles including *ʾēl* in Genesis and have taken up this similar expression from Ezek. 10.5 to provide a more distinctive title for the God of the patriarchs than the common word for 'God/god', *ʾelōhîm*, which had been used by the Elohist writer, while avoiding the titles in Genesis themselves because of their association with particular, now discredited, cultic centres.[18] The original meaning of *šadday* remains very uncertain (see Note d on the translation and the entries in *THAT/TLOT* and *TWAT/TDOT* referred to there). Does this mean, then, that 'in Israel the divine designation was received as a pure personal name with no knowledge of its "original" (etymological) meaning' (*TWAT* 7, 1085 = *TDOT* 14, p. 426) and that it was used as such in the biblical period, so that it should in fact be simply transcribed as 'Shadday' in modern translations? Some biblical sources, in different ways, do seem to be comfortable with it as 'another name' for Yahweh (or El): there is no biblical text in which it can be said to be the name of a different deity. Perhaps here in Exodus the point was to recognise it and delimit it (with 'El') as 'another name' for Yahweh but firmly to relegate its legitimate use to the distant past. This would accord with the total avoidance of it in the Deuteronomic and (most of) the prophetic literature.

The second half of v. 3 is virtually a parenthesis, underlining the use of a different name by the God who now introduces himself as Yahweh in his dealings with the patriarchs: 'I also' at the beginning

---

[18] The avoidance of *ʾēl ʿelyôn*, 'God Most High' (Gen. 14.18-20, 22), which appears in a context related to Jerusalem and is echoed in numerous Jerusalemite psalms (e.g. 46.5; 47.3) is more puzzling but perhaps due to the clear Canaanite background which it has in Gen. 14. Alternatively it is possible that Gen. 14 is, as some have thought, a passage of a later origin than P but perhaps with a similar aim.

of v. 4 (cf. Note g on the translation) most naturally picks up from the first half of v. 3. The statement that the name Yahweh was not known to the patriarchs contradicts numerous passages in Genesis, where the name is freely used, but it conforms to what is presupposed in Exod. 3.13-15 (see the notes there for a defence of the view that this is indeed the implication of that passage). The Priestly writer was therefore not making a new distinction between the religion of the patriarchs and that of the Exodus period and later; in fact, he was continuing to maintain (no doubt for his own reasons) the importance of a distinction which is generally agreed to reflect historical reality, in contrast to the 'reading back' of later usage in the passages in Genesis referred to (see also Note f on the translation, and on the theological issues Moberly, *Old Testament*).

The retrospect about God's dealings with the patriarchs continues in v. 4 with a brief account of the covenant which he established with 'them'. The reference is especially, as in v. 3, to Genesis 17, where the same wording appears (vv. 7, 17, 19; cf. vv. 2, 4): although God speaks there only to Abraham, it is made explicit that the covenant is made not only with him but with his 'offspring', and that 'throughout their generations' (v. 7: then with specific [and in the context limited] application to Isaac and his offspring in vv. 19 and 21). The focus of the covenant promises is concentrated here on the gift of the land of Canaan (cf. Gen. 17.8; 28.4; 35.12; 48.4), although in what follows the establishment of a special relationship between God and his people (Gen. 17.7) is also recalled (v. 7). The promises made to Abraham that his descendants would become a great people (Gen. 17.2, 4-6 – cf. v. 20; 28.3-4; 35.11, 48.4) are no doubt regarded as having been already fulfilled (cf. Exod. 1.7P) in the multiplication of 'the children of Israel', to whom attention will shortly turn. The placing of the Exodus story so consciously in the context of the covenant with the patriarchs is a major theological development of the tradition by the Priestly writer (cf. also 2.24-25) – not, probably, in the sense that no such link had been made before (cf. Gen. 15: though it is common to see that passage as later than P today), but in the sense that for P, writing most likely in the aftermath of the disaster of 586, it is on the covenant with Abraham that Israel's future now depends, with its easily fulfilled condition of circumcision, not on a covenant at Horeb/Sinai as in Deuteronomy (and probably the older tradition in

Exod. 19–24), with its severe demands which according to prophets and historians Israel had failed to fulfil (e.g. 2 Kgs 17.7-20; Jer. 11.1-8; Ezek. 20.1-38).[19]

The phrases describing the land of Canaan as 'the land of their residence as aliens, in which they lived as aliens' also draw on the language of the Priestly sections of Genesis, where the expression 'their residence as aliens' (Heb. *megurîm*: Gen. 17.8; 28.4; 36.7; 37.1 [in 47.9 it is used differently]) is particularly characteristic of P (cf. also the noun *gēr* in Gen. 23.7 and the verb *gûr* in 35.27: the latter is also frequently used of the patriarchs in non-Priestly sections of Genesis, but everywhere of places *outside* the land of Canaan itself). The language used equates the patriarchs with the landless 'strangers' or 'foreigners' (*gērîm*) whose presence among the Israelites is frequently presupposed and legislated for in biblical law (see Note dd on the translation of 2.11-22, and the references there): there is a deliberate contrast with the future ownership of the land in v. 8.

5. The wording of this verse coincides closely with the account already given in 2.24(P) of God's response to Israel's distress ('groaning' here as there is Heb. *neʾāqāh*, not 'cry', *seʿāqāh*, as in 3.7). The only significant difference is the insertion of 'whom the Egyptians compel to labour', which is modelled very closely on the language of 1.13(P). It is made clear (as it was in 2.24) that God's imminent action is based both on compassion for his people and on his faithfulness to his covenant with their ancestors, which cannot be fulfilled if they are not set free from Egyptian oppression (on 'remembered' see the Explanatory Note on 2.24-25).

6-8. The 'Therefore' at the beginning of these verses not only explains why Moses is to speak to Israel but indicates that the theological basis for what he is to say lies in what has already been said in vv. 3-5 about the covenant with the patriarchs and Yahweh's hearing of his people's groaning. The message for the people begins with the divine self-introduction, as in v. 2. The promise of the coming deliverance is emphatically declared in the three clauses which make up the remainder of v. 6. The first two of these are

---

[19] See further the bibliography in Schmidt, pp. 266-67, esp. W. Zimmerli, 'Sinaibund und Abrahambund: ein Beitrag zum Verständnis der Priesterschrift', in his *Gottes Offenbarung* (Neukirchen, 1963), pp. 205-16.

virtually synonymous and focus on the Israelites' release from their labours: the initial 'I will bring you out' makes clear at the outset that the means for this will be removal from the land and picks up a classic expression for the Exodus deliverance (cf. Exod. 20.2; Deut. 26.8) which will appear again in v. 7.[20] The final clause in v. 6 differs both in the wider connotations of the verb used and in the indication of the violent means which Yahweh intends to use against the Egyptians. The verb 'set free' (Heb. *gā'al*, commonly rendered 'redeem') has its background in family law and refers to the intervention by a relative to rescue (and occasionally to avenge) a person who has fallen on hard times, and even into slavery (Lev. 25.47-54: see further Note 1 on the translation). The use of *gā'al* with reference to the Exodus is said by Stamm to be an exilic, post-Deuteronomic development (*THAT* 1, 389-90 = *TLOT* 1, p. 293), but both Exod. 15.13 and Ps. 78.35 probably represent earlier attestations of it; and for a theological use of the verb before the exile the occurrence of the name Gaaliah in several Hebrew inscriptions is decisive (cf. *AHI*, p. 321; *AHI* 2, p. 149); according to some also Khirbet Lei Inscription A (*AHI* 15.006.2), but Renz (*Handbuch* 1, p. 246) and others read the letters differently. The closing words of the verse (cf. 7.4) speak of action that is both powerful and punitive: 'judgements' expresses the specifically Priestly view of the plagues as punishments for Pharaoh's intransigent refusal to let Israel go, and represents a deliberate reformulation of the traditional formulae expressing Yahweh's superior power (cf. 6.1; Deut. 26.8 etc.). Verse 7 shifts attention from events to a lasting condition, from outward circumstances to the religious status and understanding of which they are the foundation. A version of what is often called the 'covenant-formula',[21] in a form that is actually much closer to the language used of a human marriage (e.g. Gen. 4.19; Deut. 7.3), establishes the two-sided relationship that is to exist between Yahweh and Israel (partly anticipated in the promise to Abraham in Gen. 17.7-8). But the Exodus is also the basis for

---

[20] On the relation of this expression to 'bring up' (3.8, 17) see Schmidt, pp. 152-53; also J.N.M. Wijngaards, 'הוציא and העלה, a Twofold Approach to the Exodus', *VT* 15 (1965), pp. 91-102, and W. Gross, 'Die Herausführungsformel', *ZAW* 86 (1964), pp. 425-53.

[21] See the detailed discussions in R. Smend, *Die Bundesformel* (Theologische Studien 68; Zurich, 1963), and Rendtorff, *Bundesformel*.

the 'knowledge' that this relationship exists: in contrast to other examples of the 'recognition-formula', the basic wording 'that I am Yahweh' is expanded by the addition of 'your God', as well as the relative clause (expressed by a Hebrew participle) defining him as the God of the Exodus.[22] In v. 8 the theme of divine action is taken up again, in the promise to bring Israel into the land of Canaan and (here again a lasting consequence is in view) to give it into their possession. The passage thus takes a two-fold view of the gift of the land to Israel, which is already evident in Genesis. Abraham and the other patriarchs had known the land only as a place in which they resided as aliens (*gērîm*: cf. v. 4), except for the burial place at Hebron which belonged to them as a 'possession' (*ªḥuzzāh*: Gen. 23.9, 20, cf. v. 18). But they had received the sure promise that one day it would be theirs for ever (Gen. 17.8) and Moses is to reaffirm this to the people as the gift which Yahweh would give to them once he had liberated them from Egypt.[23] Again, with the characteristic Priestly idiom for an oath (see Note n on the translation) referring back to the covenant promise of v. 4, the Priestly theology explicitly grounds the basic realities of Israel's existence in the covenant with Abraham. The speech of God concludes with 'I am Yahweh', clearly in a different function from earlier and probably as a reminder of the God whose faithfulness and power undergird what has been said (cf. 12.12 and numerous cases in Leviticus and Numbers: see the Excursus on v. 2). It can also be seen as an example of P's liking for the 'circular inclusio' identified by M. Paran, *Forms of the Priestly Style*, pp. 49-97; cf. McEvenue, *Narrative Style*, pp. 157-60, who detects it (as a 'palistrophe') in Genesis 17.

9. In contrast to 4.31 the Israelites do not accept (lit. 'hearken to') the message of deliverance which Moses brings here, so weighed down are they by their present servitude. The phrase 'burdensome labour' echoes exactly that used in the Priestly narrative section in

---

[22] On the recognition-formula itself see W. Zimmerli, *Erkenntnis Gottes* (above, n. 15). The formula is also applied (without 'your God') to the Egyptians in Exodus (7.5, 17; 8.18; 14.4, 18); but for Israel as the subject see 10.2, 16.12 (again with 'your God'), 29.45-46 (which is very close to the wording here) and 31.13.

[23] For this as the destiny of the people according to P, with implications for the extent of the original Priestly narrative (cf. Deut. 32.48-52), see Schmitt, 'Jahwenamenoffenbarung', esp. pp. 146-50.

1.14a. The exact meaning of the preceding phrase, lit. 'shortness of spirit' (Heb. *rûaḥ*), is debatable (see Note p on the translation). The closest parallels (Mic. 2.7; Job 21.4; Prov. 14.29) and the use of the opposite phrase 'long of spirit' (Eccl. 7.8; Sir. 5.11) suggest that the meaning should be 'indignation' or 'impatience'. A slightly different expression, 'shortness of soul/life' (Heb. *nepeš*), has the meaning 'discouragement, faintheartedness' (e.g. Num. 21.4), which leads some commentators (Schmidt, Houtman, Propp – cf. Rashi) to attribute a similar meaning to the phrase here. On the whole it seems better to retain the regular meaning of the phrase: the surprisingly negative reaction of the exiles to Deutero-Isaiah's message of hope (cf. Isa. 42.18; 45.9-11; 49.4) shows how good news is not always welcomed. Indeed in view of what we noted earlier about the echoes of exilic lamentation in a Priestly text (see the notes on 2.23-25), it is possible that just this background played a part in shaping the Priestly narrative here. It is of course also the case that the people's reaction has much in common with the attitude expressed by their superiors in 5.21 (cf. 14.11-12), and like other aspects of the Priestly narrative (see the notes on the following sections) it may have been inspired by that older tradition or something like it: Ezekiel also spoke (in exile) of a refusal of Israel to hear Yahweh's word in Egypt (20.8).[24]

Text and Versions

יהוה (6.1) Tg^G and Tg^Nmg prefix 'the Memra of' (cf. 5.21).

עתה (6.1) SP אתה, emphatic 'you', probably in origin an accidental error arising from the weakening of the gutturals. All the Vss read 'now'.

חזקה (6.1) On both occasions Camb. 1846, apparently alone out of all SP mss (including SamTg), prefixes the def. art., presumably to identify '*the* mighty power' as that of Yahweh. On the second occasion LXX (cf. Sy) replaces the whole phrase (as again in 32.11) with ἐν βραχίονι ὑψηλῷ, its regular equivalent for בזרוע נטויה in Deut. (also below in v. 6, no doubt its

---

[24] Kohata, *Jahwist und Priesterschrift*, pp. 321-26, curiously overlooks the older tradition in ch. 5 (and 14.11-12) in maintaining that the idea of Israel's disobedience (or unbelief) is new in P. Nevertheless her understanding of it within the Priestly narrative scheme is valid: it emphasises that Yahweh does not need his people's response to bring about their deliverance (another reflection of the exilic situation?) and their recognition of him only comes later (16.12; 29.45-46).

immediate source), which is 'stylistically a great improvement' (Wevers, *Notes*, p. 72). LXX seems to have had a liking for this phrase, as it is introduced four times into the translation of Deuteronomy where it is absent in MT (3.24; 6.21; 7.8; 9.26) and the same will have happened here: MT's 'non-Deuteronomic' repetition of ביד חזקה will be original (for the use of repetition in Hebrew poetry see Watson, *Poetry*, pp. 275-79; in prose dialogue 32.18 offers a good parallel).

יגרשם (6.1)   Most mss of Sy render with *npq* (cf. 10.11; 11.1; 12.39) but 5b1 has *nsq*, 'bring up', the verb used to represent עלה Hiphil, e.g. at 3.8, which is no closer to MT here. Both renderings are governed by the context: in 2.17 (*trdyn*) Sy shows that the precise sense of גרש was known to it.

אלהים (6.2)   SP reads יהוה, cf. Vulg *dominus*. LXX agrees with MT, but some witnesses (including the Lyon ms. of OL) have κύριος. The Leiden ed. of Sy gives *mry'* as its reading, following the majority of mss, but as both 5b1 and 7a1 (as well as 9l6) have *'lh'* the latter could well be the original reading. Tgg have the divine name (in Tg[G,Nmg] preceded by 'Memra'), but this is their normal equivalent for אלהים as well as יהוה (cf. Gen. 1.1). It is not surprising that at various stages of the tradition it should have been thought that the speaker of the words 'I am Yahweh' should be designated as Yahweh in the introduction to them, but the *difficilior lectio* of MT and LXX is clearly the original one.

יהוה (6.2)   Tg[O] adds 'who revealed myself to you in the midst of the bush and said to you, "I am Yahweh"', thus providing the reference back to ch. 3 which is so conspicuously lacking in the Heb.

וארא (6.3)   SP וראה, a case of *waw* consecutive of a Lamed He verb without the normal shortening, as often in SP (see Text and Versions on 5.21), and as occasionally even in MT (GK §49e, 75t). Tgg and Sy 'revealed myself', in Tg[G,N] with 'by my Memra' added.

אל יצחק (6.3)   SP, as often in lists, prefixes a *waw* (cf. LXX, Sy).

באל שדי (6.3)   This difficult expression (see the Explanatory Note) is variously rendered by the Vss (see the synopsis in F. Zorell, 'Der Gottesname "Šadday" in den alten Übersetzungen', *Bib* 8 [1927], pp. 215-19). Tg[O,J] simply transcribe it, as Tg[O] does with אהיה in 3.14; Sy likewise with the addition of *'lh'*, '(the) God' (which is its rendering of שדי often when it occurs alone). LXX has θεὸς ὢν αὐτῶν, where ὢν probably represents Heb. ב, 'as' (cf. Note d on the translation), and θεὸς αὐτῶν follows the pattern of the renderings of this expression in Genesis (e.g. 17.1, ὁ θεός σου), which are probably based on inspired guesswork and the context. Even where שדי occurs alone in the MT of Genesis (49.25), LXX renders by ὁ θεὸς ὁ ἐμός (though its *Vorlage* may have read אל שדי here too, like SP); and similarly Num. 24.4, 16 and Isa. 13.6 have (ὁ) θεός (without a possessive). These renderings might reflect awareness of the fact that *šdy[n]* was a general expression for deities in the wider cultural context. Elsewhere, apart from places where the divine title is not recognised at all (Ezek. 1.28; Joel 1.15; Job 27.10; 29.5; 37.23) LXX offers a variety of equivalents, some of which show the (relatively) early origin of interpretations found in other Vss: transliteration (Ezek. 10.5), 'the God of heaven' (Ps. 90[91].1; cf. 67[68].15), (ὁ) ἱκανός (Job 21.15; 31.2; 40.2; Ruth 1.20-21: based on the etymologising analysis into שׁ = 'who' + דַי = '[is] sufficient'), κύριος (Job 9x: the translator's preferred rendering for divine titles even where the *Vorlage* is not יהוה), παντοκράτωρ (Job 5.17 etc.: 15x in all, mainly in the second half of a verse), ὁ τὰ πάντα ποιήσας (Job 8.3) (see also Wevers, *Notes*, p. 73; *TWAT* 7, 1103 = *TDOT* 14, p. 446). The rendering of Aq here is given by Eusebius as ἐν θεῷ ἱκανῷ, with the etymological analysis of שׁדי (*Dem. Ev.* 5.13.5). The mg. of Codex Ambrosianus of the LXX (F^b) gives, without an ascription, ἐν ἰσχυρῷ ἱκανῷ, which corresponds to what it has at Gen. 43.14, 48.3 and (in part) 49.25: this involves rigorous etymologising of אל as well (cf. the homonym meaning 'strength': BDB, p. 43), which would be characteristic of Aq (cf. Swete, *Introduction*, pp. 40-41 for examples), but it appears from the listings in Hatch and Redpath at least that F^b's reading was the regular equivalent for אל שׁדי in all the Three. Eusebius may therefore have modified Aq's rendering in his citation (combining it with LXX). Vulg *in Deo omnipotente* employs its most frequent equivalent, based on παντοκράτωρ, which is the basis for the common English translation 'Almighty'. Tg^{F,G,N} have 'the God of heaven', as in LXX Pss.

ושׁמי (6.3) Tg^N adds תקיפא, 'mighty', and Tg^G adds קדישׁא, 'holy'. Sy, according to the Leiden ed., read *wšm*, apparently without the suffix, following 5b1 and other early mss, while 7a1 and later mss indicate the suffix. The preferred reading reflects the practice of some scribes not to write the silent *yod* of the 1st sing. suffix (J. Joosten, pers. comm.).

יהוה (6.3) Vulg uniquely (except for Judith 16.16!) represents the divine name by *Adonai*, for reasons that can only partly be understood. Tg^J adds 'except by the presence of my Shekinah'.

נודעתי (6.3) LXX ἐδήλωσα, Vulg *indicavi*, Tg^{O,F,N}, Sy 'made known, showed' all render as if the verb were Hiphil, but this would be the easier reading even if it were certain that it existed in Heb.: SP = MT, and there is no evidence from Qumran.

וגם (6.4) Both LXX (as in v. 5) and Vulg have only the simple copula (in v. 5 Vulg lacks even that).

הקמתי (6.4) The Aram. versions employ the cognate verb, probably in the sense 'make, establish', though 'confirm, fulfil' is also a possibility for the Pael in Tg^N. LXX and Vulg clearly intend the meaning 'make', the former by using ἵστημι, its favoured equivalent even in this idiom (e.g. Gen. 6.18; 9.11) – a Semitism?

כנען (6.4) LXX here has τῶν Χαναναίων, one of only four places in the Pentateuch where כנען is so rendered (cf. Gen. 36.2; Lev. 14.34; Num. 13.2), probably due to influence from 3.17.

מגרים (6.4)   LXX παρῳκήκασιν employs a member of the regular and appropriate word-group that it uses for derivatives from גור (cf. Lee, *Lexical Study*, pp. 60-61), but avoiding the neologism παροίκησις used in Gen. 28.4 and 36.7 (on which see Lee, p. 49). The perfect will represent the state of being a πάροικος, which is appropriate to its representation of a noun, whereas the aorist in the following phrase (with its [emphatic?] καί) perhaps represents the act of settling in the land (contra Wevers, *Notes*, p. 74).[25] Vulg *peregrinationis* (cf. *fuerunt advenae* for גרו) emphasises the patriarchs' foreign origin more than their insecure settlement in the land. The Aramaic versions use the precise equivalent תותב, with the corresponding verb in the Tgg to render גרו (probably a denominative rather than, with Jastrow, p. 602, an Ittaphal of יתב) but the more bland '*mrw*, 'lived', in Sy. See also Text and Versions on 16.35.

שמעתי (6.5)   Tg⁰ paraphrases with 'has been heard before me', but with a masc. part. and the object marker ית oddly following; Tg⁽ᴶ⁾ was probably originally similar (or read גלי, 'has been revealed', like Tg^{Nmg}) if its peculiar קימי is an abbreviated form for קדמי (so *AramB*) or a scribal error, but the verb has been omitted. Tg^{N,G} follow the wording of MT, like the other Vss.

נאקת (6.5)   So also 4QGen-Ex^a, but SP has קאנת with metathesis, as in 2.24: see Text and Versions there. Sadaqa's נאקת here must be a printing error (cf. *GSH*, p. 49 n. 74).

אשר (6.5)   Both LXX and Vulg render with sing. forms of the relative pronoun (though OL has 'how'), indicating that they take the antecedent to be נאקת rather than בני ישראל. The indeclinable *d* of the Aramaic versions is ambiguous, but there is support for the LXX-Vulg interpretation in the renderings of Tg⁰ in *AramB* and of Tg^G by Klein. This interpretation is only possible (and even then it seems forced and less straightforward than 'whom') if the Greek and Latin words used to render נאקה (and the latter itself) could have an extended meaning of 'cause of groaning, pain'. LS does give two possible examples of this for *gemitus* (Verg., *Aen.* 2.413, Lucr., *De Rer. Nat.* 5.1196) and a similar sense for στεναγμός might be supported by the unique use of it for Heb. צרה in Jer. 4.13 (though the translator could well have intended the normal sense 'groaning' there, and there seems to be no support anywhere else for a meaning 'pain, distress'). But since נאקה itself seems always to refer to an utterance of pain (including a prayer of complaint, in MH: hence presumably its rendering by קבלתא in the Tgg), such an interpretation by the translator would have to be regarded as erroneous. It remains unclear why there has been such widespread support (cf. also Note i on the translation) for

---

[25] This is similar to the understanding of the tenses here in T.V. Evans, *Verbal Syntax in the Greek Pentateuch* (Oxford, 2001), pp. 150-52, where Wevers's explanation is also regarded as unsatisfactory.

the less obvious renderings of אשר here, unless the translators just overlooked the idiomatic use of the resumptive pronoun אתם.

מעבדים (6.5) A reference to enslavement is seen here by LXX (καταδουλοῦνται) and possibly by Tg^{J,N} and Sy, which employ the cognate Aram. verb; Tg^O renders by מפלחין, 'make...work', and Vulg has the general *oppresserunt*.

ואזכר (6.5) So also Mur 1, though only parts of the letters remain: SP has ואזכרה, with its characteristic use of the longer form without any difference of meaning (see Text and Versions on 3.8). Tg^N adds ברחמין, 'in compassion', to bring out the nature of the divine remembering here (so more fully in 2.24), but there seems to be insufficient room for this in the lacuna in Tg^G.

בריתי (6.5) LXX (alone) has the 2nd pl. pron. ὑμῶν (4QGen-Ex^a gives an early attestation of MT's 1st sing. suffix): cf. Wevers, *Notes*, pp. 74-75, who points out a few examples of a similar 'objective genitive' referring to those with whom God makes his covenants (e.g. Deut. 4.31): they are mainly in later OT texts or in Greek. Here the continuing validity of the covenant for the Exodus generation receives additional confirmation by the change.

לכן (6.6) LXX βάδιζε, 'go', as for לך in 4.18-19, and presumably due to a misreading of the לכן which all other witnesses attest (inc. Mur1 and 4QGen-Ex^a), unless its *Vorlage* was damaged. Tg^N has 'With an oath', seeing לכן as including the adjective כן, 'true' (for which cf. 10.29; and cf. LXX ms. F^b, εἰς τὸ βέβαιον, here) and in accordance with rabbinic exegesis which compared 1 Sam 3.14 (cf. Exod.R. 6.4. and other refs. in *AramB* 2, p. 28 n. 5). The latter is alluded to by Rashi and Ibn Ezra here.

אני יהוה (6.6) LXX secondarily introduces the words to be spoken with λέγων, as it does elsewhere even where MT lacks לאמר (cf. 3.12; 7.1; 9.8). Sy adds *'lh'*, 'God', after the divine name as it does in v. 3 after אל שדי.

אתכם (6.6)[10] Tg^{N,G} add פריקין, 'free, redeemed', to clarify the meaning.

סבלת (6.6) So also Mur1 and 4QGen-Ex^a, but not SP, despite von Gall's (mis)judgement: see the other editions, Camb. 1846 and Baillet, 'Corrections', p. 32, all supporting סבלות (as in v. 7). Tg^{O,J} prefix '(from the midst of) the oppression of', probably to convey the force of מתחת, while Vulg *ergastulo*, 'workhouse', as in v. 7 makes the word (regarded as a singular) into the name of a place. LXX τῆς δυναστείας (cf. v. 7 καταδυναστείας) and Tg^N, Sy '(the yoke of) slavery', render freely: Tg^N seems to interchange its renderings of this word and מעבדתם later in the verse (as Tg^G may also have done), perhaps to give greater prominence to the release from slavery (cf. the wording of Exod. 20.2 etc.).

וגאלתי (6.6) The rendering 'redeem, ransom' is well established in the Vss here.

מעבדתם (6.6) Tgg render 'labour' (but see above on Tg^N), while LXX, Vulg and Sy have 'slavery'.

בזרוע נטויה (6.6) Tg^N and Sy have 'a mighty hand' as in v. 1, but Sy also has a rendering of the phrase in MT. The use of 'high' for נטויה in LXX, Vulg, Tg^O,J and Sy may be an anti-anthropomorphism (see *AramB* 7, p. 15 n. 6): only Tg^G renders it precisely.

ובשפטים (6.6) So also 4QGen-Ex^a. SP has the more regular ובמשפטים, no doubt secondarily (in view of the similarity of ב and מ at Qumran, the original error might have been accidental: the variant occurs in 7.4 but not in 12.12 or Num. 33.4). LXX renders in the sing. to represent 'a great judgement' in the abstract rather than individual plagues (Wevers, *Notes*, p. 75); by contrast Tg^N,G emphasise the number by adding 'rows of' (cf. 7.4).

ולקחתי (6.7) Tgg paraphrase, in accordance with their treatment of לי (see below): Tg^O,J 'I will bring you near', Tg^N,G 'I will separate you' (a formula used elsewhere in cultic contexts acc. *AramB* 2, p. 29 n. 6: cf. the insertion of 'holy' later in the verse).

לי (6.7) LXX renders it twice, once with the verb and once with 'a people', thus emphasising even more the divine association with Israel (Wevers, *Notes*, p. 76). By contrast Tg^O,J 'before me' and Tg^N,G 'for my Name' preserve the divine transcendence.

לעם (6.7) LXX λαόν, before which the Three add εἰς = MT, a reading widespread in Greek mss (also OL: cf. Vulg *in*). Tg^G qualifies with 'holy' (cf. 19.6) and Tg^N adds 'of holy ones'.

והייתי (6.7) Tg^N,G 'and my Memra will be...', surely a clear case of the 'theologically developed' use of the expression envisaged by Chester, *Divine Revelation*, pp. 311-13.

לאלהים (6.7) Tg^N,G add 'a Redeemer', noted as an especially important title for Tg^N by Chester, ibid., p. 353 (see also the next note).

המוציא (6.7) Again Tg^N,G introduce the idea of redemption, by adding either a finite verb or (as in v. 6) a participle from פרק.

סבלות (6.7) Von Gall's text of SP again gives a defective spelling here, against most of his mss, Camb. 1846 and the more recent editions, and is clearly in error. LXX καταδυναστείας adds a pejorative element to its paraphrase in v. 6 (cf. Wevers, *Notes*, p. 76): the other Vss render as in v. 6.

אשר (6.8) LXX εἰς ἥν, Vulg *super quam*, following a literal understanding of the following phrase, as if the deity stretched out/raised his hand towards Canaan, like the different Heb. idiom in (e.g.) Isa. 49.22.

נשאתי את־ידי (6.8) Tg^O,J paraphrase with 'promised by my Memra' (the latter here referring to the spoken word [cf. Chester, *Divine Revelation*, pp. 308-309]), avoiding the anthropomorphism and clarifying the meaning. For the same reason no doubt the phrase is replaced in 4QGen-Ex^a by [י]נשבעתה. Tg^N,G content themselves with clarification by adding בשבועה (cf. v. 6!) to their rendering of the MT wording. The other Vss, Mur1 and SP agree with MT. LXX's rendering of נשאתי by ἐξέτεινα is free and only used in this idiom elsewhere at Num. 14.30 and Neh. 9.15.

יצחק (6.8)   LXX and Sy prefix 'and'.

מורשה (6.8)   So also Mur1 and SP, but 4QGen-Exᵃ prefixes a ל (not commented on in *DJD* XII, p. 26), tightening up the grammar (see Note o on the translation) and assimilating to most of the uses of מורשה in Ezekiel (cf. LXX[106] here εἰς κατάσχεσιν). LXX ἐν κλήρῳ is a frequent phrase, but only renders מורשה here: it presumably means 'as an inheritance, allotment' (for the use of ἐν see Muraoka, *Lexicon*, p. 182: here too, as with σημεῖον in Gen. 17.11; Exod. 12.13, it may in fact be equivalent to εἰς). The Aram. Vss. render with words for 'inheritance' (on Tg^N's presumed double rendering ירתו ואחסנה and its possible background see *AramB* 2, p. 29 n.7), but Vulg has, perhaps rightly, the more general *possidendam*.

אני יהוה (6.8)   Tg^G (cf. Tg^Nmg) has אמר in place of אני: cf. Tg^N at 12.12. Such a conclusion to a divine speech never occurs in the MT Pentateuch: it is much more characteristic of prophetic speech (2 Kgs 20.17 par.; Isa. 45.13; 54.1; 65.25; 66.21, 23 etc.).

כן (6.9)   Vulg renders freely with *omnia*.

אל־משה (6.9)   Tg^N,G expand with 'the words of Moses'.

מקצר־רוח (6.9)   LXX ἀπὸ τῆς ὀλιγοψυχίας, 'fainthearteness', cf. Tg^O, Vulg; the other Tgg, Sy and Aq rendered more literally with words meaning 'shortness' but with the same sense. Contrary to what Wevers says (*Notes*, p. 78) Aq's rendering of רוח (πνεύματος) is preserved: cf. the apparatus of both the Cambridge and Göttingen editions.

מעבדה קשה (6.9)   Most of the Vss render with a straightforward reference to 'hard labour' as in 1.14: Tg^O,G expand slightly with 'because of the labour which was heavy upon them', perhaps to emphasise that it was harsh rather than difficult. Sy's šwʿbdʾ (qšyʾ) perhaps has the connotation of slavery (cf. its use of the term in vv. 6-7). Tg^J has 'because of the difficult foreign worship which was in their hands', taking עבדה in its cultic sense and alluding to the tradition of Israelite idolatry in Egypt which is already found in Ezek. 20.7-8 (and Josh. 24.14) and is taken up in exegesis of the verse in *MRI* on 12.6 (Lauterbach 1, p. 38) and Exod.R. 6.5. Grossfeld (*AramB* 7, p. 16 n. 10) suggests that such a reference stood in Tg^O, but this is pure speculation: in fact it is more likely that Tg^O is repudiating such an interpretation.

After this phrase SP adds (unnoticed by *BHS*): ויאמרו אל משה חדל נא ממנו ונעבדה את מצרים כי טוב לנו עבד מצרים ממותנו במדבר.

Apart from the introductory formula these are essentially (נא is not present there in MT, though it is in SP) words which the people say in 14.12 that they had spoken to Moses 'in Egypt'. This no doubt seemed the most likely occasion for their utterance and they could also usefully supply the expression, missing in MT, of the people's reaction to Moses' message. This plus is cited as being present in 'the Samaritan edition' in the margin of the Syrohexaplar (see the apparatus of Wevers' edition of the LXX here). It is the first of several substantial pluses in the SP text of Exodus, some of which are already attested in biblical mss from Qumran (see on 7.18 and in the Introduction to this commentary). But neither of the mss which survive at this point, Mur1 and 4QGen-Ex^a, included this material.

The two Qumran mss do confirm the antiquity of a division in the text at this point (cf. the *petuchah* of MT and the paragraph-break in SP). In 4QGen-Ex^a v. 10 begins on a new line, and it is clear that the wording of MT would not fill anything like the whole of the previous line: the last word to survive is מקצר, but there is room for about another 30 characters (not enough, however, for the SP plus: see *DJD* XII, pp. 10, 26). In Mur1 not only does v. 9 finish before the end of a line, but the whole of the following line was left blank.

CHAPTER 6.10–7.5

MOSES' OBJECTION AND ITS ANSWER
(INCLUDING: GENEALOGY OF AARON
AND THE AARONIDES)

From a narrative point of view this section covers the preparations for Moses' (second) confrontation with Pharaoh, following Yahweh's declaration (also for the second time) of his intention to liberate Israel from Egypt and Moses' (now unheeded) transmission of this to the Israelites. The sequel to the preparations (7.6-7) is often linked to this section (so the Masoretic divisions), but since these verses already begin the account of the confrontation with Pharaoh they are here taken with the next section of the narrative.

It is immediately evident that a large part of this section is not narrative at all, but belongs to the *Gattung* of genealogy (vv. 14-25), the only such section in the book of Exodus (unless the list of the sons of Jacob/Israel in 1.1-5 be counted as such). It begins with the descendants of Reuben and Simeon (vv. 14-15) as if it were going to be a genealogy of all the twelve tribes, like the list in Gen. 46.8-27, but its larger part is concerned only with Levi and the Levites (vv. 16-25) and with them it concludes. Genealogies and other kinds of tribal lists are a prominent feature of certain biblical books – especially Genesis, Numbers, 1 Chronicles and Ezra-Nehemiah – and the concern with ancestry and legitimacy which they reflect is a common feature of both non-literate and literate cultures. The studies of R.R. Wilson and M.D. Johnson have shown, on the basis of wide cultural comparisons, that the biblical genealogies are far from being simple records of family history: they were related to central social, institutional and political issues and elements of them at least were fabricated to represent relationships and rights that had built up through time. As such they had a regulative role at the time when they were produced and subsequently.[1]

---

[1] Wilson, *Genealogy and History in the Biblical World* (New Haven, 1977); Johnson, *The Purpose of the Biblical Genealogies* (SNTSMS 8; Cambridge, 2nd ed., 1988).

Not all societies preserve such documents, however, and within the ancient Near East there are few if any close parallels to Israel's genealogies. Reference is sometimes made to king-lists from Egypt and Mesopotamia (e.g. *ABD* 2, pp. 929-30), but these are at best a special case with its own unique character and motivations. Elsewhere it was certainly common for seals and other kinds of inscriptions to record an immediate patronym, but it was much rarer for more than one further generation to be added and very little with the complexity of the main biblical genealogies appears to be extant. Some examples of priestly genealogies are known from both Mesopotamia and Egypt and they were probably used to support the legitimacy and power of the priests.[2]

As shown in the detailed notes, the Levite part of the genealogy has a particular focus on the high-priestly line derived from Aaron, to such an extent that even Moses' descendants are completely ignored. This will concern us again later on, when we consider the purpose and background of the genealogy and its inclusion at this point. For the moment we need to note that the genealogy is surrounded by verses which also name Aaron alongside Moses, and in one case mention him before Moses (vv. 13, 26-27). Both this and the rather crude attempts to link the genealogy to the surrounding narrative in vv. 26-27 make it clear that all these verses belong closely with the genealogy itself. Verses 29-30, to which v. 28 is a rather rough introduction (despite the traditional division of the Hebrew text: see the notes on v. 28), virtually repeat what has already been said in vv. 10-12 and so prepare the way, after the genealogy, for the introduction of Aaron in 7.1-2. This feature too, therefore, is closely connected with the concerns of the genealogy.

From the beginnings of biblical criticism it has been recognised that all (or most) of 6.10–7.5 belongs broadly to the Priestly strand of the Pentateuch and also that within this section at least two stages of composition need to be distinguished.

---

[2] Wilson, pp. 117-19, 125-29. Valuable evidence in shorter genealogies from Sippar and Borsippa is ingeniously used to reconstruct the lineages of priestly families in A.C.V.M. Bongenaar, *The Neo-Babylonian Ebabbar Temple at Sippar: its administration and its prosopography* (Istanbul, 1997), pp. 443-46, 460-63, 469, 474-75, 480, and C. Waerzeggers, *The Ezida Temple of Borsippa: Priesthood, Cult, Archives* (Leiden, 2010), pp. 77-90 (with frequent attestation of the term *bīt-abi*), 731-43, but these archives apparently do not include comprehensive genealogical texts.

Knobel still thought that the whole section was an original part of P (his 'Elohist') and he rejected early suggestions that the genealogy was intrusive and secondary.³ His only doubt was about the unique use of the term 'prophet' (*nābî*) in P in 7.1. In Dillmann's revision of the commentary v. 12b (like v. 9b) was attributed to J, without good reason, and Dillmann also sought to secure a direct connection between 6.10-12a and 6.30b–7.5 by supposing a rearrangement of the text: according to him the genealogy (6.14-27) originally stood after 7.5, followed by 6.13, and 6.28-30a was composed to maintain the narrative connection when the genealogy was moved to its present position. Others have also held that the genealogy once stood elsewhere: Wellhausen (tentatively for 6.16ff.) before 6.2, Bacon (for 6.16-25) after 1.5, Beer after 7.7. But they could not explain why it would have been moved from these 'better' positions to a 'worse' one. That it was originally absent from P and was introduced by a redactor was already held by A. Kayser (cf. Wellhausen, *Composition*, p. 62) and by the time of the publication of the Oxford *Hexateuch* this was becoming generally accepted (cf. Baentsch, Holzinger). To begin with, the placement and composition of the genealogy was regarded as incompetent (Carpenter/Harford-Battersby, Baentsch, Smend), but Childs marks the beginning of a more sympathetic interest in it by speaking of its being 'carefully inserted', albeit still by an author later than P (p. 111). This was taken further in W.H. Schmidt's detailed investigation of its sources and the process by which it reached its present form (pp. 295-301). In the surrounding narrative sections Smend had used the criterion of non-Priestly vocabulary to call in question the originality of at least part of 7.3 and this and other arguments have more recently again been raised. Kohata saw 7.3b as an addition (*Jahwist*, pp. 34-37: a view which Schmidt [p. 318] gently rejects), and L. Schmidt (*Studien zur Priesterschrift*, pp. 3-4) and Gertz (*Tradition*, pp. 252-54) hold that the whole verse is secondary.⁴

The relationship of the original narrative sections (6.10-12, 7.1-5) to the surrounding non-Priestly context has until recently been assessed on the basis of the general view that P was the later of two (or more) narratives which were each originally composed to stand on its own. Thus the similarity to 4.10-16 was attributed to the Priestly writer's adaptation of the older version. Smend

---

³ A. Marx has revived the view that the whole of 6.13-30 forms part of the original P composition ('La généalogie', 326). But his many valuable observations, while they show that the incorporation of the genealogy at this point was a purposeful and in some ways carefully executed undertaking (see below), are insufficient to outweigh its clumsy and over-repetitive framing, which is untypical of P's normal practice. The features noted could just as easily be attributed to a later redactor.

⁴ Steingrimsson, *Vom Zeichen*, pp. 30-32, argued that both the references to divine intervention (7.3b, 7.4aβb) and the recognition-formula (v. 5) were secondary additions, but this is to press the idea of 'inconsistency' to unjustifiable extremes.

(pp. 124-25: cf. already Baentsch, p. 53) added the observation that 7.1-2 was merely imitative because there is no reference to Aaron speaking (only acting) in P (contrast 4.28-30 in JE). W.H. Schmidt examines more fully the signs of dependence on the older narrative in Exodus, but also on Deuteronomy (pp. 317-20) and on earlier prophecy (pp. 324-25). Blum (in relation to the dependence of 6.9-12 on 5.20-21 [*Studien*, p. 236] and to 6.14-27 [specifically 6.20] being 'a kind of inner-biblical midrash' on (the MT of) 2.1 [p. 231 with n. 12]) and Van Seters (by arguing that 7.1-7 leads into the combined JEP plague-narrative [pp. 105-106]) take such dependence as support for their view that P was composed as a supplement to JE.

Knohl departs from the widespread consensus in a different way: he attributes only 6.13 (possibly) to the original P narrative (as a link between 2.25 and 7.8) and the rest to two stages of his 'Holiness School' redaction (p. 61). 7.1-6 and either 6.10-12 or 6.29-30 belong, like 6.2-8, to a first stage of 'HS', while 6.14-25 and its framework were added at a second stage coinciding with the final version of the Korah story in Numbers 16–17. Most recently K. Schmid (*Erzväter*, p. 242) and Gertz (*Tradition*, pp. 315-21) have, in line with their general approach, seen this passage as the source of its parallels in ch. 4, which they attribute to the 'Endredaktor'.[5]

The main narrative here certainly, as all except Knohl agree, belongs to P. 6.12, which presupposes the divine instruction in 6.10-11, picks up the earlier reference to the people's refusal to hear Moses in 6.9. 7.1-2 is Yahweh's answer to Moses' objection in 6.12 and takes further his commission in 6.10 to go to Pharaoh. 7.3-5 anticipates the difficulties which this will encounter and speaks in terms closely related to 6.6-7 about Yahweh's subsequent action. The intervening verses, 6.13-30, while they share in P's distinctive desire to give prominence to Aaron and his descendants and exhibit some features of P genealogies in Genesis (see the detailed notes), show clear signs of being a later addition, as even those like Childs who see their inclusion here as deliberate and careful have acknowledged. Some structural features are closer to the genealogies in Chronicles than those in Genesis, and the section creates an awkward break between Moses' objection in 6.12 and its answer in 7.1-2, which the repetition of 6.10-12 in vv. 28-30 only makes more obvious. Suggestions that the genealogy once stood somewhere else in the narrative, while not convincing in themselves, reflect its intrusiveness here.

---

[5] Schmid seems indifferent to the common distinction (shared by Gertz, pp. 251-52) between two stages of Priestly composition here (pp. 99, 197, 198-99).

440 EXODUS 1–18

The secondary nature and detailed construction of vv. 13-30 have most recently been elaborated by W.H. Schmidt (pp. 295-301). According to him (see the summary on p. 299) the nucleus was an already existing Levite genealogy, as the inclusion of some names which are of no significance here or elsewhere confirms. Schmidt reconstructs this genealogy by simple subtraction of the 'narrative' elements in vv. 16b, 18b, 20, 23 and 25. This has the odd effect of leaving no reference to Amram's descendants (as well as Hezron's) at all, whereas Izhar's are continued for a further two generations to the sons of Korah. If he is right, the source looks like a Korahite genealogy, which would have been reshaped with a no doubt polemical intention (cf. Num. 16–17). While this is possible, the underlying document may already have included the names of Amram's descendants as far as the sons of Aaron (and originally Moses?) in v. 23, with only the extension to the next generation (Phinehas) being part of the reshaping of the list (cf. the distinctive anteposition of the subject in v. 25?). It also seems likely that the document would have included descendants of Hebron (cf. 1 Chr. 23.19), and it is of course possible that it was much more extensive, but there is no way of knowing this. At any rate (as Marx has more fully seen: 'La généalogie', pp. 321, 327-29) two features of the present text are clearly due to a desire to draw attention to Aaron and his descendants, namely the information about the lengths of life for Levi, Kohath and Amram (vv. 16b, 18b, 20b) and the marriages of Amram, Aaron and Eliezer (most of vv. 20 and 23 and [?] all of v. 25), and these will represent an adaptation of the original document. The information provided at the beginning about the 'clans' of Reuben and Simeon is less extensive and may well have been derived from a different source (its similarity to Gen. 46.8-11 and Num. 26.5-6, 12-13 has often been noted). On the motivations implied by the contents of the genealogy see further below.

The verses which follow it (6.26-30) were presumably composed by the redactor who incorporated it. This is generally held to be the case (so also Schmidt) for v. 13, but its reference (presumably as part of a summary of Moses' and Aaron's activity) to Aaron's mission to the Israelites does not fit the Priestly context and recalls 4.14-16, which makes its attribution to a still later redactor more probable. If this is correct, the transition to the genealogy was originally even more abrupt than it is now.

The other (possibly) later element in the passage which needs discussion is 7.3 (cf. Gertz). Objections have been raised to the 'premature' announcement of the hardening of Pharaoh's heart and the presence of 'non-Priestly' vocabulary, specifically the use of Heb. *qāšāh* Hiphil instead of the usual P expression *ḥāzaq* Qal or Piel (cf. 7.13, 22; 8.11, 15; 9.12; 11.10) and the appearance of Heb.

ʾōt, 'sign', alongside *môpēt*, 'wonder' (which is used in P in 7.9 and 11.10), *ʾōt* in the sense of an act of God's power being characteristic of the non-Priestly narrative (in the plague-story cf. 8.19 and 10.1-2). Neither of these arguments is compelling. Announcements of what is to come are characteristic of all the divine speeches in Exodus and the mention of the hardening of Pharaoh's heart only draws out what is already presupposed in the declaration (in 6.6 and 7.4, verses whose Priestly origin is not disputed) that the Israelites' release will be accompanied by 'great judgements'. There is of course an issue about the apparent manipulation of Pharaoh by Yahweh that is implied by the expression here, but that in itself is not any more alien to the Priestly account than the non-Priestly one (cf. 9.12; 11.10). As for the vocabulary argument, it is worth noting that Gertz at least did not rate it very highly in his discussion of 6.6-8 and it is hypercritical to limit an author's choice of language too narrowly. The wording of a programmatic speech like 7.1-5 may well vary from the narrative which it introduces (the expression 'lay my hand on' in v. 4 is not used again in the story either). Ezekiel, to whose language P is often close, uses the adjective *qāšeh* alongside *ḥāzāq* (Ezek. 2.4; 3.7). The combination of *ʾōt* and *môpēt* is most characteristic of Deuteronomy (e.g. 4.34) and may be another example of the adaptation of Deuteronomic vocabulary by the Priestly writer in his more theological discourses (cf. the note on 6.6 and more fully W.H. Schmidt, pp. 275, 279, 318-20).[6]

Van Seters has argued (*Life*, pp. 100-12), in the context of his general view of P as a supplement to the older narrative, that 7.1-7 and 11.9-10 form a framework not to the Priestly plague-stories alone but to the combined, complete plague-narrative which was produced by their addition to the older J stories.[7] Part of Van Seters'

---

[6] A stronger argument for redactional activity might be the separation of the 'hardening' from Pharaoh's refusal to hear in v. 5, but this can readily be attributed to a wish to highlight the decisive factor in the situation by placing it first (see our translation and the Explanatory Note).

[7] Cf. the earlier view of J. Ska (1989), to which Van Seters refers. But in his large book on the Pentateuch (first published in Italian in 1998; ET *Introduction to Reading the Pentateuch* [Winona Lake, 2006]) Ska was prepared to speak of at least the 'relative' independence of P (pp. 146-61; cf. 147, 212 on 7.1-5), as a result of his abandonment of the view that there was any earlier connected narrative of Israel's origins.

discussion is concerned with the relationship of the Priestly plague-stories themselves to their context and this will be dealt with in its proper place later on. On the framework he gives three reasons for thinking that it cannot apply only to the Priestly revision (pp. 105-106; cf. 112): (i) the instructions to Moses and Aaron to speak to Pharaoh are never fulfilled in P, but only in the non-Priestly ('J') version; (ii) the statement about Yahweh 'increasing' the number of signs and wonders (v. 3) does not cohere with the fact that P taken by itself contains fewer plagues than J; (iii) in P material the hardening of Pharaoh's heart and his refusal to listen does not (as in J) follow a demand and the ending of a plague, and is a mere 'cliché' which simply rehearses what has been said in 7.1-4. These arguments have been effectively refuted by Gertz (pp. 84-88; W.H. Schmidt seems not to deal with them specifically). He observes that in the non-Priestly version too Aaron does not perform the role prescribed for him in 7.1-2 (10.3 is the closest to it), so the combined narrative is scarcely a better 'fit'; and that in the episodes that are entirely Priestly (8.20-23 and 9.8-12) the failure to include an account of negotiations is inexplicable if the imagined *Bearbeiter* was proceeding on the principles assumed by Van Seters. Moreover (on this see Schmidt, pp. 325-26), the fulfilment of the commission in 7.1-2 (cf. 6.11) can be found in 7.6 (cf. v. 7b) or 7.9 – indeed the statement that Pharaoh 'did not listen to them' in 7.13 only makes sense if a demand for Israel's release is in fact implied in one of these verses (there is at this stage no non-Priestly text for it to refer back to [5.1-3 is too far away]!). The argument about the number of plagues misrepresents the meaning of the text: the verb here (*rābāh*, Hiphil) does not mean 'increase' but 'multiply' (so e.g. NRSV) and certainly does not refer to the number of plagues in different versions of the story. Van Seters' third argument overlooks the different intention of the Priestly Exodus narrative as a whole (the 'contest motif') and the general tendency of the Priestly writer to abbreviate the narrative and concentrate on (what seemed to him to be) its essential features. There is no serious discrepancy between 7.1-5 and the Priestly sections which follow it.

The religious interest of this section involves both Yahweh's dealings with Pharaoh and the internal hierarchy of Israel. Pharaoh is to be presented, as in the non-Priestly material (5.1-3), with Yahweh's demand for his people's release from bondage (6.10, 7.2; cf. 6.13, 29). But here too Pharaoh's refusal is both anticipated and even said to be the result of Yahweh's own sovereign power (7.3-4). It is that power, not Pharaoh's own decision, which brings about the Exodus: only then will the hostile Egyptians recognise Yahweh for who he is (7.5). Within Israel Moses' own leadership, so recently introduced in the Priestly material (6.2-8, esp. v. 6), is at first undercut by his own experience of failure and sense of inadequacy (6.12, cf. v. 30). But in 7.1-2 it is both strengthened ('I have made you a god to Pharaoh') and reinforced by the supporting role given to Aaron. The original Priestly narrative said no more at this point about Aaron's long-term significance: only in ch. 28 was his status as the gloriously attired ancestor of all true priests introduced.

The insertion of the genealogy in vv. 14-25 took the promotion of Aaron and his descendants significantly further (on the general function of biblical genealogies see above, pp. 436-37). Its purpose can be seen in its position, scope and detailed elaboration. It serves primarily to introduce and locate the high-priestly line within the tribal structure of early Israel (cf. Marx, 'La généalogie', pp. 326-35). It is placed at the point where Aaron is about to enter the Priestly Exodus story: once that is understood its placing is entirely logical. For its scope focuses attention on the priestly line. The special status of the Levites is underlined by the space given to them and the fact that the genealogy ceases with them. But it is only the line of Aaron which is traced through to a fifth generation (Phinehas) from the tribal ancestor. The focus on this line of descent is sharpened by the addition of the ages at death of Levi, Kohath and Amram and the details of the marriages of Amram, Aaron and Eliezer. There is no comparable interest in Moses here, only enough to indicate that Aaron had the distinction of being his brother (cf. 7.1-2), and their sister Miriam was originally not mentioned here at all (but see Text and Versions on 6.20), unlike Num. 26.59. The genealogy clearly has its origin in the context of exilic and post-exilic reorganisation of the priesthood under Aaronide leadership, like the list in 1 Chr. 5.27-41. Aaron's marriage into a leading Judahite family no doubt served to enhance the social standing of priesthood in that situation (see the Note on 6.23).

Yet unlike 1 Chr. 5.27-41 and more like the complementary list that follows it in 1 Chr. 6.1-15, the genealogy here spreads more widely than the high-priestly line. As was already noticed in the Middle Ages (Rashbam: cf. Cassuto, p. 87), the names of other Levites who would appear in the Pentateuchal narrative are included, whether their action was praised, like Mishael and Elzaphan (Lev. 10.4-5), or condemned, like Korah (Num. 16). The conclusion with Phinehas (cf. Num. 25.6-13) is also dictated by the extent of the Pentateuchal narrative. All of these names appear only in the Priestly sections of the Pentateuch, where Aaron's sons (Nadab, Abihu, Eleazar and Ithamar) also have a prominent place in the narrative (Lev. 10.1-11). It seems therefore that the compiler of the genealogy subtly combined his clear intention to highlight the origins of the Aaronide priesthood with a more literary purpose of introducing and placing the main characters in the (Priestly) narrative which was to follow.[8]

> 6.10 *But/so[a] Yahweh spoke to Moses as follows[b]:* 11 *'Go in, speak to Pharaoh the king of Egypt, so that[c] he may let the Israelites go from his land'.* 12 *Moses spoke in the presence[d] of Yahweh as follows: 'Look[e], the Israelites did not listen to me – how then[f] will Pharaoh listen to me, when I am so ill-prepared to speak (lit. of uncircumcised lips)?'[g]* 13 [*Thus[h] Yahweh spoke to Moses and to Aaron and commanded them (to go)[i] to the Israelites and to Pharaoh king of Egypt, to bring out the Israelites from the land of Egypt.*] [14 *These are the heads of their fathers' houses[j]. The sons of Reuben, the firstborn of Israel: Hanoch and Pallu, Hezron[k] and Carmi. These are the clans of Reuben.* 15 *The sons of Simeon: Yemuel and Yamin and Ohad and Yakin and Zohar and Shaul the son of a Canaanite woman[l]. These are the clans of Simeon.* 16 *These are the names of the sons of Levi according to their generations/genealogy[m]: Gershon and Kohath and Merari. The years that Levi lived were 137[n] years.* 17 *The sons of Gershon: Libni and Shimei according to their clans.* 18 *The sons of Kohath: Amram and Izhar,[and] Hebron and Uzziel. The years that Kohath lived were 133[n] years.* 19 *The sons of Merari: Mahli and Mushi. These are the clans of the Levites[o] according to their generations/genealogy[m].* 20 *Amram took Jochebed his aunt[p] to be his wife and she bore him Aaron and Moses. The years that Amram lived were 136[n] years.* 21 *The sons of Izhar: Korah and Nepheg and Zikri.* 22 *The sons of Uzziel: Mishael and Elzaphan*

---

[8] The late Priestly origin of vv. 14-25 is confirmed by the overlap in not only content but the use of formulae with Priestly sections of Numbers to which N.A. Wormell has referred as 'Numbers-P' in her (as yet) unpublished dissertation, 'Composition'.

*and Sitri. 23 Aaron took Elisheba, the daughter of Amminadab and sister of Nahshon, to be his wife, and she bore him Nadab and Abihu, Eleazar and Ithamar. 24 The sons of Korah: Assir and Elqanah and Abiasaph. These are the clans of the Korahites. 25 Eleazar the son of Aaron took^q one of the daughters of Putiel to be his wife, and she bore him Phinehas. These are the heads of the fathers(' houses)^r of the Levites according to their clans. 26 It was^s Aaron and Moses to whom Yahweh said, 'Bring the Israelites out of the land of Egypt according to their tribal divisions'^{t}. 27 They are the ones who spoke to Pharaoh the king of Egypt to bring the Israelites out of Egypt, it was^s Moses and Aaron. 28 On the day that Yahweh spoke^u to Moses in the land of Egypt, 29 Yahweh spoke to Moses as follows^b: 'I am Yahweh, speak to Pharaoh the king of Egypt all that I shall speak to you'. 30 But Moses said in the presence^d of Yahweh: 'Look, I am ill-prepared to speak^g; how then^f will Pharaoh listen to me?']
7.1 (So) Yahweh said to Moses, 'See, I have made^v you a god^w to Pharaoh, and Aaron your brother shall be your prophet. 2 You yourself shall speak all that I command you^x, and Aaron your brother will speak to Pharaoh that he should^y let the Israelites go from his land. 3 But I myself^z will harden Pharaoh's heart^{aa}. Even though I multiply my signs and wonders in the land of Egypt, 4 Pharaoh will not listen to you and so I will lay my hand^{bb} on the Egyptians and I will bring out my tribal divisions, my people the Israelites, from the land of Egypt with great acts of judgement. 5 Then the Egyptians will know that I am Yahweh, when I stretch out my hand against/over the Egyptians and bring out^{cc} the Israelites from their midst.'*

Notes on the Translation

a. The Heb. conjunction *waw* can have adversative or consecutive force in addition to its normal (and often otiose) connective function (cf. BDB, pp. 252-54; JM §118h, 172a), depending on the context. Either would be possible here, but simple succession ('Then...') may be all that the narrator intended.

b. Heb. לאמר, with *dagesh forte conjunctivum* according to GK §20c n.2: לאמר is a special case of a word that is neither a monosyllable nor accented on the first syllable where (after משה with a conjunctive accent) this appears (cf. v. 29).

c. Heb. וישלח, with simple *waw* and the imperfect/jussive to express purpose (JM §116d): so LXX, Vulg.

d. The idiom דבר לפני is rare in BH: BDB, p. 181, cites only Num. 36.1; Judg. 11.11; 1 Kgs 3.22; Esth. 8.3 in addition to this verse (v. 30, which is modelled on it, should be added), all with reference to a superior (in Judg. 11.11 it is Yahweh). It is much more frequent as a periphrasis in Tg⁰ (cf. *AramB* 6, pp. 21-22, and e.g. Exod. 3.11, 12; 4.10). An alternative view, that Moses is here speaking not to Yahweh but to himself, is proposed by J. Joosten, 'L'agir humain devant Dieu. Remarques sur une tournure remarquable de la Septante', *RB* 113 (2006), pp. 5-17 (12 n. 19).

e. Heb. הן, as again in v. 30. The context here would allow a periphrasis with 'If...', but see Note a on 4.1-9 for the view that in BH (unlike Aramaic) הן itself does not actually *mean* 'if'.

f. For the inferential use of *waw* in discourse see BDB, p. 254b, s.v. 4, and e.g. 2.20.

g. In Heb. a noun-clause introduced by *waw*, here introducing the circumstances which validate the preceding statement (cf. Vulg *praesertim cum*): JM §159d cites Gen. 15.2 and 44.34 as similar circumstantial clauses. The expression ערל־שפתים (again in v. 30, but not elsewhere) involves an epexegetical genitive of respect (GK §128x-y). Similar metaphorical expressions apply ערל, 'uncircumcised' to the ear (Jer. 6.10), the heart (Lev. 26.41; Jer. 9.25; Ezek. 44.7, 9 – cf. Deut. 10.16; Jer. 4.4) and a tree whose fruit is not to be eaten (Lev. 19.23): see *TWAT* 6, 386-87 = *TDOT* 11, pp. 359-61, which takes the phrase here to mean that Moses does not feel 'equipped to carry out God's commission'. In a Priestly context (cf. Gen. 17, which was clearly in mind earlier in the chapter, and also Exod. 12.48) the idea of exclusion from the covenant could easily be in mind, but the remedy proposed in 7.1-2 suggests something less, namely a functional deficiency, as in the equivalent expression in 4.10. The exact basis of the metaphor remains unclear. There seems to be no etymological evidence for any meaning other than 'uncircumcised' for ערל (cf. BDB, *HAL*). There might be a clue in the concentration of occurrences in Ezekiel 28–31, where it refers to dead people, apparently those slain in battle: might it have acquired the sense 'unburied' and so 'despised' (cf. the references in *HAL*)? A 'dead' ear etc. would make some sense. Yet the connotations of circumcision seem to be alive enough for Deut. 10.16 and 30.6 to use מול for the remedy there (cf. Jer. 4.4, with 'remove the foreskin of your hearts' in parallel). Perhaps then it is the notion of 'covering' which is the basis for the metaphors, so 'closed, unresponsive'. It is notable that all the occurrences are close in date (late seventh/sixth cent.) and an origin with Jeremiah or the Deuteronomists with reference to the heart looks most probable.

h. The verse appears to be a summary of the two commissions given to Moses (Aaron is added proleptically with 7.1-2 [and perhaps 4.14-16] in mind) in vv. 6-8 and 10-11, so the *waw* indicates not succession but a conclusion (cf. e.g. Gen. 2.1 and JM §118i, *IBHS* §33.2.1d).

i. The use of צוה with אל appears to be a conflation of two normally distinct idioms with equivalent meaning, 'to command to go to' and 'to send to' (cf. GK §119ee-gg on such 'pregnant' constructions). In most of the few similar cases with צוה the verb to be understood is 'to say' (cf. BDB, p. 846, s.v. 4a, c): the closest parallel is perhaps Esth. 4.5 (where על is used in place of אל, as elsewhere in LBH examples, though not in Esth. 4.10).

j. Heb. ראשי בית־אבתם, so that the translation could be 'the heads of their fathers' house', with 'their' referring to Moses and Aaron and the 'house' to the tribe of Levi (cf. Houtman, pp. 515-16). But 'their' could also refer to the 'Israelites', who are actually mentioned nearer the end of v. 13, and the genealogy does begin as if it is going to cover the whole people (proceeding from Exod. 1.1-5: cf. also Gen. 46.8-11 which contains the same names as vv. 14-16 here). The plural of בית־אב is in fact consistently בית־אבות, with the *nomen regens* oddly kept in the singular as though בית־אב were a compound noun (cf. GK §124r, with very few other examples, mostly including the word בית). On its distribution and meaning see the Explanatory Note.

k. The omission of *waw* before this name breaks up a long(ish) list into two parts (though no such need seems to have been felt with the six sons of Simeon in v. 15 or with a list of four [in MT – see Text and Versions] in v. 18). Similar divisions in Exod. 1.4 and 6.23 can be correlated with different mothers and future destinies respectively, but no such distinction can be appealed to here.

l. Heb. הכנענית. The same expression occurs at the corresponding point in Gen. 46.10 (but not in 1 Chr. 4.24). Such a gentilic with the def. art. would normally be preceded by a name (cf. 1 Chr. 2.3): here it may perhaps be explained by the same 'proleptic' use of the article as in 2.15 and 3.2 (GK §126q-r: in Num. 25.6 with a gentilic again), hence the English 'a' (as in e.g. AV, JPS, NRSV: Luther, JB have 'the').

m. Heb. לתלדתם. Cf. v. 19, at the end of the general section on Levi, which extends to his grandsons. In 28.10 it apparently refers to the sequence of the tribal names and Houtman suggests that 'the order of their birth' is the point here too (pp. 251, 516). The basic meaning 'generations' fits well, but a reference to an 'account of a man and his generations', as in Genesis (BDB, p. 410), i.e. a genealogy, is also possible.

n. On the order of the numerals, which is characteristic of P, see GK §134i.

o. Heb. הלוי. The gentilic adjective is commonly used collectively in the sing., especially in Deuteronomy and Joshua, but also in some Priestly passages (cf. Num. 3.20, 32; 18.23; 26.57; also the similar use of הקרחי in v. 24 and Num. 26.58). Such a usage is frequent with gentilics generally (cf. 3.8, 17 and GK §126m). In P the plural form is more common (e.g. v. 25 and 38.21) and likewise in Chronicles, probably reflecting an emphasis on the Levites' (inferior) function rather than their descent, but it also occurs in Deuteronomy (e.g. 18.7) and the Dtr History.

p. Heb. דדתו, which in its two other occurrences means 'uncle's wife' (Lev. 18.14; 20.20): a father or mother's sister is referred to as such, not with דדה, in Lev. 18.12-13; 20.19. This would make Jochebed the (former) wife of either Gershon or Merari. But Num. 26.59 makes her a daughter of Levi (cf. Exod. 2.1MT and Text and Versions there), i.e. presumably a sister of Amram's father Kohath, implying that meaning for דדה here (which Tg⁰ makes explicit). The situation in other languages (cf. 'aunt' in English) shows that such a dual meaning need not be a problem; and the number of occurrences in BH is too small to support a challenge to it. The variations in some of the Vss are probably due to legal scruples rather than further linguistic ambiguity (see Text and Versions).

q. The word-order is unusual, with the subject preceding the verb (contrast the similar sentences in vv. 20 and 23). There can be a variety of reasons for this: 'the action is not successive or is not represented as such' (JM §118d-g); emphasis or contrast (§155*n*b; cf. Vulg *at vero*); religious concerns (§155*n*e); a new beginning (§155*n*d): see in general Muraoka, *Emphatic Words*, pp. 28-41. The last of these seems most likely to provide a factor to distinguish this sentence from those which preceded: it is the succession of Eleazar by Phinehas which really established the high-priestly line (cf. the covenant with Phinehas in Num. 25.12-13 and the list beginning in 1 Chr. 5.30, with a series of inversions of subject and verb).

r. Heb. אבות. Here an abbreviated form of בית־אבות (v. 14), with the same sense 'families' (as e.g. Num. 31.26).

s. This seems the most likely rendering of the unusual sing. pronoun הוא (contrast הם at the beginning of v. 27) which both concludes the genealogy and resumes the instruction given in v. 13 (cf. BDB, p. 216, s.v. 6). After the genealogy has been allowed to run its course as far as Phinehas and the sons of Korah, its connection with its place in the narrative is reaffirmed by recalling names which were last mentioned in vv. 20 and 25 respectively. There is a similar use of הוא in 2 Chr. 28.22. The parallels cited by Schmidt (p. 311) are not so close.

t. Heb. על־צבאתם. צבאת is used again of the people as a whole in 7.4 and in 12.17, 41, 51. From its general use outside the Pentateuch (mainly in the sing., except for the expressions יהוה/אלהי־צבאת) it is clearly a military term and the pl. here relates to the use of the sing. to refer to the 'division' (or 'company') of each tribe in Numbers 2 and 10 (which might itself be an attempt to clarify the meaning of the name/title יהוה־צבאות in a particular way, although P does not use it): cf. *TWAT* 6, 872-73 = *TDOT* 12, pp. 212-13, for the military background, which also lies behind the use of דגל and מחנה in Numbers 2.

u. The use of ביום in the construct state before a finite verb (not an inf. constr., as might be expected) makes the following sentence into a virtual *nomen rectum*: such a construction is particularly common with expressions of time, as in Hos. 1.2 and, according to some, Gen. 1.1 (cf. GK §130d). For a closely similar case see Num. 3.1.

v. Or 'I make you', taking נתתי as a 'performative perfect' (cf. GK §106i, JM §112f-g and more fully I. Zatelli, 'Pragmalinguistics and Speech-Act Theory as Applied to Classical Hebrew', *ZAH* 6 [1993], pp. 60-74 [70-71]).

w. Heb. אלהים, where לאלהים would also be possible after נתן in the sense of 'make, appoint', just as it is after היה in the sense of 'become' (6.7).

x. Heb. אצוּךָ, with the energic form of the suffix, as often in pause (GK §58i, l).

y. Heb. ושלח, perfect consecutive. The normal meaning, 'and he will let… go', runs counter to the immediate sequel, in which Pharaoh's refusal to comply is anticipated (vv. 3-4): in fact in P Pharaoh never does comply (cf. 11.10). It is therefore common to translate the expression here as purposive (cf. LXX, Vulg: see Text and Versions). There is, however, little basis in Heb. witnesses for a reading וישלח (ibid.). But there are a few places where the perfect consecutive may express purpose (cf. GK §112q, citing Gen. 1.14-15), and this seems to be a usage that is specially favoured in Priestly texts, as a comparison of Exod. 8.12 and 9.8 (P) with 9.22 and 10.12 (non-P) shows (JM §119m). But Joosten, *Verbal System*, pp. 293-301, does not find it necessary to envisage such a use of the perfect consecutive.

z. Heb. אני. The emphatic subject-pronoun marks a contrast and the reversion to speech about Yahweh's own action, as distinct from the human activity in v. 2. The connotations of the conjunction *waw* vary considerably in this speech. In והרביתי it is probably epexegetical (Waltke/O'Connor §39.2.4), beginning an elaboration in detail of the initial declaration; in ולא־ישמע it is adversative again (we have paraphrased with a concessive expression) and in ונתתי it is consequential (BDB, p. 254, s.v. 4).

aa. Heb. אקשה את־לב פרעה. The expression is unusual (see the Explanatory Note): the closest parallel, in Deut. 2.30, uses רוח instead of לב (Exod. 13.15, cited as a parallel by Gertz, pp. 252-53, involves a different idiom). קשה Hiphil is used with לב in Ps. 95.8 and Prov. 28.14 of human obstinacy, similarly the adjective קָשֶׁה in Ezek. 3.7 (where, as in 2.4, it is coupled with חזק).

bb. Heb. ונתתי את־ידי. There is no exact parallel to what is presumably an idiom for taking violent action (see the list in *DCH* 4, p. 84); Ezek. 39.21 (with שים) comes closest (cf. also 2 Kgs 11.16||2 Chr. 23.15, with the dual ידים). In the following verse the more common נטה is used.

cc. For the coordination of a temporal inf. cons. with a perfect consecutive cf. GK §112v, 114r.

Explanatory Notes

10-12. There are tight logical connections between this brief narrative of Moses' being sent to Pharaoh and the context which precedes and (originally more directly) follows. He is sent to Pharaoh (who is here mentioned for the first time in the Priestly Exodus narrative: earlier cf. Gen. 41.46; 47.5-11) as the ruler of 'the Egyptians' from whose oppression Israel is to be set free (6.5-7; cf. 1.13-14). It is Israel's failure to 'listen to him' (v. 9) which is the first reason that Moses gives for his hesitation to face Pharaoh (v. 12); and it is that hesitation which makes necessary Yahweh's amended plan for the approach to Pharaoh in 7.1-2, which originally followed immediately on these verses (see the introduction to this section). It is unusual that Moses speaks 'in the presence of Yahweh' (v. 12): apart from v. 30 (which is dependent on this verse) and Judg. 11.11 (and perhaps 2 Kgs 19.15, where the verb is 'prayed': but Isa. 37.15 has 'to') the expression is more characteristic of the language of the Targums. In fact the expression 'Moses spoke to Yahweh' never appears in P: on the very rare occasions when there is a reference to Moses (and once Aaron) addressing Yahweh either the preposition 'with' is used (Exod. 34.34-35; Num. 7.89) or no formula at all (Num. 16.22). In interhuman dialogue speaking 'in the presence of' another is always a sign of the latter's superiority (Num. 36.1; 1 Kgs 3.22; Esth. 8.3). The expression 'of uncircumcised lips' (Heb. ^{ca}ral $s^ep\bar{a}t\bar{a}yim$) is also unusual (paralleled only in v. 30) and striking (see Note g on the translation). It has generally been understood along the same lines as the expression in 4.10, to mean a physical or intellectual deficiency (see Text and Versions), but the association of most of the metaphorical uses of 'uncircumcised' with disobedience and unresponsiveness to Yahweh has led some to see an acknowledgement of a deeper unfitness to act as Yahweh's spokesman (so especially Propp). Yet there is no hint in what follows that Moses needs purification or forgiveness before he can resume his speaking role ('I make/have made you a god' in 7.1, if anything, suggests the opposite), and a case for the usual view could be based on the clearly non-religious application to a tree in Lev. 19.23 and on the likely meaning of what may well be the earliest metaphorical use of 'uncircumcised' in Jer. 6.10 – something like 'thick-ears'.

13. It seems at first glance that this verse is the natural sequel to Moses' reluctance to go to Pharaoh to seek Israel's release, with Aaron being introduced to give him added support. But the formulation departs from the direct address to Moses (and Aaron) which is elsewhere characteristic of P (as well as the non-Priestly material), and the fuller, more specific account of Aaron's supporting role in 7.1-2 produces a much stronger continuation of the narrative. The reference to a sending of Aaron to Israel introduces a role for him in which P otherwise shows no interest and it seems to be an echo of the non-Priestly passage in 4.14-16, thus bringing together both occasions of the partnership of Moses and Aaron which appear in the completed text of Exodus. The verse must therefore belong to the stage when (or after) the Priestly and non-Priestly accounts were combined together, and is a summary (partly by anticipation) of the process by which Yahweh's word was brought first to the Israelites and then to Pharaoh (see Note h on the translation). Its inclusion here was probably designed, by the reference to Aaron, to ease the rather abrupt transition to the genealogy which follows, which the interpolator had overlooked (see on vv. 26-30 for his more careful integration of the genealogy with the subsequent narrative).

14-15. Verses 14-25 present genealogical material which is chiefly concerned with the origins and early stages of the high-priestly line that proceeded from Aaron (see 28.1 and the introduction to this section). But the genealogy begins, not with the priestly tribe of Levi, but with his two elder brothers, Reuben and Simeon, the former being specifically designated here as Israel's (i.e. Jacob's: cf. 1.1) firstborn son. The intention at this point is not simply to show that the high-priestly line is genuinely Israelite (though that may have been an issue at the time of writing), but to emphasise the seniority of Levi among the sons of Jacob. Judah, whom it was well known came after Levi (cf. 1.2), is not mentioned at all here (but see the note on v. 23). Since Reuben had been discredited in ancient tradition (Gen. 35.22; 49.4; cf. 1 Chr. 5.1-2) and Simeon had been incorporated into Judah (Josh. 19.9), there could be little challenge, from a genealogical point of view, to the primacy of Levi which the priests were no doubt glad to claim for other reasons as well. The antecedent for '*their* fathers' houses' is a matter of debate (see Note j on the translation). Holzinger (p. 19) found it sufficiently obscure to propose moving v. 14 to after v. 16b, but that does not explain why it came to be placed at the head of the list. Cassuto (p. 85), who is followed by Houtman (pp. 515-16), sees the antecedent as being Moses and Aaron, who have been mentioned in v. 13. This would certainly correspond both to the surrounding context, with its focus on these leaders (cf. especially vv. 26-27), and to the concern of the genealogy itself with the family of Moses and especially Aaron. Yet in the nearer context 'the Israelites' as a whole have been mentioned most recently (this is even more the case [cf. v. 12] if v. 13 is a very late addition to the text, as argued above), and it is not only the opening with Reuben and Simeon but later sections of the genealogy which range more widely, into other parts of the tribe of Levi, than the family of Moses and Aaron (cf. vv. 17, 19, 21-22, 24).

Hence Schmidt (p. 297) and Propp (p. 275) have argued with good reason that the initial heading should be understood with reference to the whole people. The fact that, while what is given is too wide for just the family of Moses and Aaron to be meant, it is too narrow to cover the whole people is not a strong objection, for it is due to the interpolator's intention to make only an extract from the kind of full genealogy that underlies Numbers 26 and Gen. 46.8-27. The allusion to such a full genealogy would still have served his purpose well.

On the terminology for the sub-divisions of tribes and the thinking behind it see above all de Vaux, *Institutions* 1, pp. 17-23, ET, pp. 4-8, but as he recognises the terminology could be fluid.[9] Here 'father's house' or 'family' (Heb. *bêt-ʾāb*) appears to be equivalent to 'clan' (*mišpāḥāh*: cf. vv. 17, 19, 24-25), rather than a sub-division of it. This will be due to the idea, which is also reflected in other ways, that the social structure of the community in later times was grounded on the development of small family units in the people's earliest history. Thus the hierarchical term 'heads' here and in v. 25 also alternates with the generational expression 'sons': it is those who were heads of households in early times who (it is supposed) have given their names to sub-tribal units later on.

Excursus on heads of fathers(' houses)

The 'father's house' or (extended) family was a key element of Israelite social structure from early times and the primary context for the life (and death) of the ordinary individual (cf. Wolff, *Anthropologie*, pp. 309-13, ET, pp. 214-16). References to it abound in the older layers of narrative texts such as

---

[9] See also J.R. Bartlett, 'The use of the Word ראש as a Title in the Old Testament', *VT* 19 (1969), pp. 1-10; D. Smith, *The Religion of the Landless: The Social Context of the Babylonian Exile* (Bloomington, 1989); S. Bendor, *The Social Structure of Ancient Israel: The Institution of the Family from the Settlement to the End of the Monarchy* (JBS 7; Jerusalem, 1996); H.G.M. Williamson, 'The Family in Persian Period Judah: Some Textual Reflections', in W.G. Dever and S. Gitin (eds.), *Symbiosis, Symbolism and the Power of the Past: Ancient Israel and its Neighbors from the Late Bronze Age through Roman Palestine* (Winona Lake, 2003), pp. 469-85; D. Vanderhooft, 'The Israelite *Mishpaha* in the Priestly Writings and Changing Valences in Israel's Kinship Terminology', in D. Schloen (ed.), *Exploring the Long Durée* (FS L.E. Stager; Winona Lake, 2009), pp. 485-96; A. Faust, *Judah in the Neo-Babylonian Period: The Archaeology of Desolation* (SBLABS 18; Atlanta, 2012), pp. 106-108.

Genesis (e.g. 12.1), Judges (e.g. 6.15), Samuel (e.g. 1 Sam. 9.20) and Kings. By contrast the title 'head of a father's house' is missing entirely from these books, as well as in the prophets. 'Heads' in the sense of leaders within the nation are occasionally mentioned there (Judg. 10.18; 11.8-9, 11; Hos. 2.2; Mic. 3.1, 9, 11), but not 'heads of families'.[10] It is likely that the term 'elders' was used instead (see below, and also the note on 3.16). Although the expression is used of earlier periods in Priestly texts in the Pentateuch, Joshua and Chronicles, the first uses of it with reference to a (more or less) contemporary reality are in the books of Ezra and Nehemiah. Here it always appears in the abbreviated form 'heads of fathers' (the expression 'father's house', *bêt-'āb*, occurs only in Ezra 2.59 = Neh. 7.61; Ezra 10.16; Neh. 1.6; 10.35 [also in Esth. 4.14 in a late text]), which implies that at a time earlier than the middle of the fifth century the full expression must have been current. Its origin may, however, not be much before this, both because of its absence from the older narratives and because both Ezekiel (e.g. 8.1) and the Aramaic documents in Ezra (5.5, 9; 6.7-8, 14) use 'elders' for the lay leaders of the community. Ezra 8.1, at the beginning of the list of those who returned to Judah with Ezra (vv. 1-14) is a classic instance of the application of 'heads of fathers' to the laity, and it is so used both in the (probably later) account of the first beginnings of the rebuilding of the temple (Ezra 1.5; 2.68 [cf. Neh. 7.69-70]; 3.12; 4.2-3) and in accounts of the times of Ezra and Nehemiah themselves (Ezra 10.16; Neh. 8.13). It also appears in lists of priestly personnel in Neh. 11.13; 12.12, 22, 23 (and likewise in the list of post-exilic priests and Levites in 1 Chr. 9.13 and 33-34; of laity in v. 9). Because of this predominance in lists of priests (and Ezra 8.1-4 was presumably compiled by a priest, Ezra) and the large-scale use of the expression in the temple-focused works of P and the Chronicler, it is plausible to think that the title (in its fuller form) originated in a priestly milieu, perhaps in the period of exile and in the context of the need then to redefine claims to the priesthood by the creation of genealogical documents.

Even in Priestly texts the expression is not very common. It appears twice here in Exodus (in v. 25 in the abbreviated form), never in Leviticus, six times in Numbers and five times in Joshua 14-22. In Num. 1.4, 7.2 and 17.18 and in Josh. 22.14 the tribal representatives (Heb. *nᵉśî'îm*) are identified as 'heads of fathers' houses' (in the full form): Num. 25.15 applies the expression to a Midianite. The shorter form is used with the same meaning in Num. 31.26 and 32.28. Elsewhere in Joshua it is always the shorter form that is used, and that only at the beginning and end of the lists of tribal inheritances: they distribute the inheritances with Eleazar and Joshua according to 14.1 and 19.51 and the same leading group is approached by the heads of the fathers(' houses) of the Levites in 21.1 in connection with the allocation of the Levitical cities which

---

[10] The numbers of occurrences elsewhere are: 2x in Exodus; 6x in Numbers; 5x in Joshua; 14x in Ezra-Nehemiah; 24x in Chronicles.

follows. There is therefore no attempt anywhere here to integrate this 'office' into the lower levels of the tribal organisation: the model of lay leadership from the post-exilic situation is simply applied to the early history from Sinai to the settlement in Canaan.

In Chronicles the use of the expression is much more extensive and thoroughgoing in its application. Whatever its significance may be, it is worth beginning by noting that the distribution of the longer and shorter forms of the expression largely follows a regular pattern. The longer form occurs (apart from a single exception in 1 Chr. 24.4) only in 1 Chronicles 1–9, mainly in some of the genealogies of the 'secular' tribes (Gad, East Manasseh, Issachar, Benjamin [first list: 7.7, 9]: in 5.24 it appears in a heading which is identical to Exod. 6.14a. The longer form also appears twice in the lists of post-exilic priests and laity in ch. 9 (vv. 9 and 13). In both kinds of text the expression is applied to 'family heads' lower down in the tribal organisation than is the case in Numbers and Joshua. The absence of the title from the genealogies given here for Judah and Levi should perhaps be noted.

Only a few occurrences of the shorter form of the title (which we may recall is the standard one in Ezra and Nehemiah) appear in 1 Chronicles 1–9 and they are all in the last two chapters, either in the second Benjamin list (8.6, 10, 13, 28) or in the post-exilic lists, in a curious paragraph which seems to give the heading and conclusion of a list which has not survived (9.33-34), unless v. 34 is the conclusion of the whole Levite list beginning in v. 14 and the equivalent of v. 13 at the end of the list of priests. But the shorter form is widely used (and with the exception of 24.4 universally) from 1 Chronicles 10 onwards, both in the lists of temple staff in 1 Chronicles 23–26 and in the subsequent narrative. In the latter the reference is to leaders of the people as a whole (2 Chr. 1.2; 19.8; 23.2; 26.12: cf. 1 Chr. 26.26 and 27.1), as found occasionally in Ezra–Nehemiah and in Numbers–Joshua. Here too there seems to be a process of equation and assimilation of the people's leadership in earlier times to that of the post-exilic community. The occurrences in 1 Chronicles 23–26 (apart from 26.26) naturally relate to the hierarchy of the priests and Levites and appear in the Levite genealogy (23.9, 24, which is parallel but not entirely identical [see below] to Exod. 6.16-25), the list of priestly divisions (24.6, 31: note also the longer form in v. 4), and a supplementary list of non-ritual duties of the Levites (26.21, 32). As in 1 Chronicles 1–9, these 'heads' are leaders of sub-divisions of a tribe rather than of the whole tribe, and so so more aptly described as 'heads of families'.

The examination of terminology in the foregoing Excursus places the form of the heading to this genealogy in v. 14a closer to 1 Chronicles 1–9 than to anything elsewhere in the Priestly corpus, not so much because of the use of the full form of the title as because of the very precise parallel in 1 Chr. 5.24 and its application to lower levels of tribal organisation. The contents of vv. 14b-15 (like vv. 16-25) have parallels both elsewhere in the Pentateuch and in Chronicles. The second generation of Reubenites and Simeonites is treated in Gen. 46.8-10, Num. 26.5-14 (with a continuation into a fourth generation, which leads to a reference to Korah, as here in vv. 21 and 24) and 1 Chr. 5.3 and 4.24 (both again with a continuation into further generations, but differently). The names are completely identical in Gen. 46.8-10, but only for Reuben's sons in Num. 26.5b-7, 12-14 and 1 Chr. 5.3 and 4.24: for Simeon's sons there are several differences in each case. For the introductory reference to Reuben himself, 1 Chr. 5.3 is the closest: the other passages both differ slightly. The concluding reference to the 'clans' of each tribe does not appear in Gen. 46.9-10 and 1 Chr. 5.3 and 4.24, but Num. 26.7a and 14a have an almost identical formula, differing only in the use of the gentilic instead of the personal/tribal name. No one of these passages can be regarded as the sole source of this one (or *vice versa*) in a straightforward way, but the exact correspondence of the names in Gen. 46.8-10 and Exodus 6 does associate these passages especially closely, while the divergent lists in Num. 26.12-13 and 1 Chr. 4.24 agree very closely with each other, differing only in the fourth name, where Numbers 26 agrees with Genesis 46 and Exodus 6, while 1 Chronicles has Jarib. They both also omit the reference to Shaul's Canaanite mother. The difference over the opening name – Jemuel (Genesis, Exodus) vs. Nemuel (Numbers, 1 Chronicles) might be due to accidental error, but the other differences are less easily so explained.

16-19. A separate section of the genealogy, dealing with the tribe of Levi, begins here and is introduced (in a way that the Simeon section in v. 15 is not) by a heading which is differently formulated from that in v. 14: 'heads of fathers' houses' are not mentioned, but 'names' and 'generations' are. Concluding formulae in vv. 19 and 25 bring this section to a preliminary and final close. The formula in v. 19 is similar to those in vv. 14 and 15, but also has the additional reference to 'generations'. 'These are the names' is particularly common as a heading in Genesis (5x) and Numbers (9x, out of a total of 26), where some of its occurrences are related to this one in other ways (Gen. 46.8; Num. 3.2-3, 18; cf. Exod. 1.1 and 1 Chr. 6.2), although nowhere else does it introduce a Levite list (Num. 3.17 is the closest: 'And these were the sons of Levi by their names'). 'By their generations' (*ltldtm*) is always found in name-lists and, apart from this passage and Gen. 10.32 and 25.13, only occurs (7x) in

1 Chronicles 1–9. A similar phrase is used in Exod. 28.10 of the arrangement of the tribal names on the high-priest's ephod. The phrase 'by their clans' (v. 17; cf. v. 25) is much more common, especially in Numbers and Joshua, but also in Genesis: surprisingly it occurs only twice in Chronicles. The formulaic language of these verses thus has a variety of affinities in passages of a similar kind, but taken as a whole it is only in Genesis and 1 Chronicles 1–9 that a complete set of parallels can be found.

As for the names themselves, those of Levi's three sons occur in the same order in comparable lists in Gen. 46.11; Num. 3.17; 26.57; and 1 Chr. 5.27, 6.1. But Genesis 46 contains no information about their children, Num. 26.58 lists the five names that it provides (in gentilic form) as a single group of 'clans' and then adds that Kohath was the father of Amram, while 1 Chr. 5.28 mentions only the four sons of Kohath, in the same order as here, in keeping with its narrowing focus on the high-priestly line. Numbers 3.18-20 and 1 Chr. 6.2-4, however, have exactly the same names as here and also share some of the same formulaic language. But this passage is exceptional in that for both Levi and Kohath the lengths of their lives are given: this, together with the similar information given for Amram in v. 20 serves to focus attention on the high-priestly line (cf. the data in vv. 20, 23 and 25 about the wives of Amram, Aaron and Eleazar), but it may also have been designed to play a part in chronological calculations about the duration of the sojourn in Egypt, in the context of the figures of 400 and 430 years given respectively in Gen. 15.13 and Exod. 12.40 (see further Houtman's comments [pp. 511-14] and Text and Versions both here and at 12.40). The formula employed for this is similar to those used in death-notices in the Priestly narrative in Genesis (23.1; 25.7, 17; 47.28: Gen. 35.28, Num. 33.39 and Deut. 34.7 are different).

20. After the preliminary conclusion in v. 19b the genealogical structure is interrupted, as it is in vv. 23 and 25, by a narrative section about the marriage and children of Amram, the father of Moses and Aaron. In this way the high-priestly line receives further highlighting. The only parallels to this verse are Num. 26.59 and 1 Chr. 5.29, both of which add the name of Miriam at the end of the list of Amram's children. Only in the former verse is Jochebed mentioned, where she is described as Levi's daughter (cf. Exod. 2.1) rather than as Amram's aunt (the two descriptions are of course equivalent, though see Note p on the translation). Numbers 26.59 is part of a secondary addition (vv. 58b[?], 59-61) to the Levite paragraph (vv. 57-58, 62) in the census-list of the tribes, which may itself be a supplement to the main list. This addition draws, like 26.9b-11, on the non-Priestly narrative as well as Priestly texts and is probably part of an even later reworking of the Pentateuch than Exod. 6.14-25. The name Jochebed is generally thought to be formed from a short form of the divine name Yahweh (as in many other names) and Heb. *kābēd*, 'heavy', probably here in the sense 'glorious' (for similarly formed names in Akkadian and Phoenician cf. *Ges18*, p. 451). If this explanation is correct, the name would be one of only two incorporating the divine name which is attributed to figures said to have been born before the Exodus: the other is that of Joshua (Heb. *yᵉhôšûaʻ*), which P pointedly (and against the true etymology) makes into a post-Sinai adaptation of the non-theophorous name Hoshea (Num. 13.8, 16). In Jochebed's case it may have been felt appropriate that the mother of Moses and Aaron should have a Yahwistic name, especially in view of the reference to Yahweh as the 'god of his father' in Exod. 3.6 and 15.2. At the late stage when this genealogy was added to the story (see the introduction to this section) the force of the Priestly doctrine in 6.3 may have been reduced (or perhaps Levi was thought to be better informed than his forebears!).[11] The ambiguity of Heb. *dōdāh*, like English 'aunt', is such that we cannot be sure whether a (former) wife of Gershon or Merari (Amram's uncles) is meant or, as Num. 26.59 certainly assumes, an otherwise unnamed sister of Amram's father Kohath (see Note p on the translation). A marriage with either would be a transgression of the Levitical laws (cf. Lev. 18.12-14, 19-20), and in the tradition the meaning of *dōdāh* is frequently 'stretched' to avoid this (see Text and Versions). For the author of the genealogy this seems to have been less important at this point (the laws had not yet been enacted) than the securing of a wholly Levitical ancestry for Moses and Aaron (cf. 2.1). Amram's age at death was most likely originally given as 136 (so also Propp, p. 264: see Text and Versions).

---

[11] The alternative suggestion, that Jochebed is not a Yahwistic name but a name formed simply from a verbal imperfect (like Isaac and Jacob, for example), is less likely because of the vocalisation (cf. Propp, p. 277).

21-22. The Kohathite genealogy is continued (those of Gershon and Merari are of no further interest for this author) with the descendants of Izhar and Uzziel (but not Hebron). The reason seems to be that some of them reappear later in the Priestly narrative: Korah in Num. 16.1 etc. and Mishael and Elzaphan in Lev. 10.4-5. The formulaic structure is very simple, similar to vv. 18-19. 1 Chronicles 6.22-23 (like Num. 16.1) has the same ancestry for Korah as here, but 6.7 makes him a descendant of Kohath via an Amminadab who is not otherwise mentioned (there is also a divergence between the lists of Korah's descendants in 1 Chr. 6.7-8 and 6.22: see below on v. 24). 1 Chronicles 23.18-22 gives the names of descendants of Hebron as well as Izhar and Uzziel (cf. 26.29-31), but they are different from or additional to those named here, probably because they are ascribed to a much later period. From the present list Nepheg, Zichri and Sithri appear nowhere else, which is evidence that this list was not created for its present position and purpose but drawn (most likely) from a more comprehensive document that has not been preserved (cf. Schmidt, p. 298).

23. A further verse in narrative form (cf. vv. 20, 25) advances the line of Amram by a further generation, but only with the wife and descendants of Aaron, not those of Moses. References to the latter appear in the Levite genealogy and list in 1 Chr. 23.14-17 and 26.24-25, but they are of no concern to this author. Aaron's wife Elisheba (the form 'Elisabeth' is due to an early textual error in the Septuagint tradition which affected Luke 1.5 etc.) is not mentioned elsewhere, but her father and brother are well-known members of the tribe of Judah: Nahshon was the 'prince' ($n\bar{a}\acute{s}\hat{\imath}$') of the tribe and his father is regularly named as Amminadab in Priestly texts (Num. 1.7; 2.3; 7.12-17; 10.14). According to 1 Chr. 2.3-17 (cf. v. 10) and Ruth 4.18-22 (cf. vv. 19-20) he was also an ancestor of King David. The high-priestly line is therefore given noble ancestry on both sides of the family. The special relationship of Aaron to Judah (obviously a key myth of the post-exilic social structure) was further underlined by the assignment of cities in Judah (as well as Simeon and Benjamin: i.e. the territory claimed by the post-exilic community) to the Aaronide priests in Josh. 21.9-19. Such a marriage outside the priestly tribe was not permitted for the high priest according to Lev. 21.14-15: again, as in v. 20, it may have been thought that the law did not apply to what was done before it was (supposed to have been) enacted.

The names of the four sons of Aaron appear in the same order (which implies that Nadab and Abihu were the eldest) in Num. 3.2, 26.60 and 1 Chr. 5.29. In Num. 3.3-4 the demise of Nadab and Abihu soon after their ordination in Lev. 10.1-7 is recalled, which resulted in Eleazar and Ithamar alone accompanying their father in his priestly activity. The names of Nadab and Abihu (but not their brothers) appear in a non-Priestly context, with Moses and Aaron and seventy elders, in Exod. 24.1-11, where they participate in a remarkable act of worship on Mount Sinai. Their inclusion in Priestly texts seems designed to be both an acknowledgement of this tradition and a polemic against it. The institutional implications of that tradition are regrettably totally hidden from us (no doubt deliberately).

24. A parallel line in the Kohathite genealogy is now also taken one generation further, in the descendants of Korah. Korah himself was the leader, according to Numbers 16, of a Levite revolt against the prerogative of the Aaronide priests and his death and that of his 250 companions was without doubt intended as a dire warning to any in the post-exilic temple personnel who considered making a similar challenge, and perhaps especially the temple-singers or gatekeepers known variously as 'the sons of Korah' (in Ps. 42.1 and other psalm-titles) and 'the Korahites' (1 Chr. 9.19; 26.1, 19; 2 Chr. 20.19). The rebels in Numbers 16 are never called Korah's sons and Num. 26.11 explicitly recognises their continued existence. Sons of Korah are not named anywhere else in the Pentateuch, but similar names to these appear in successive generations of descendants of Korah in 1 Chr. 6.7-8, 22; 9.19, evidently through a misunderstanding. 1 Chronicles 6.22 is part of the genealogy of Heman, one of David's leading temple-singers according to Chronicles.

25. The final narrative element, with the concluding formula, brings the genealogy to a close with the figure of Phinehas. His mother is not even named, and her father Putiel is completely unknown (see Text and Versions for later speculation about him). The closest parallels are the genealogical texts in 1 Chr. 5.30 and 6.35 (cf. Ezra 7.5), but Phinehas's ancestry is regularly given when he appears in narrative. His most famous exploit, which is probably the reason for his inclusion here, is his exemplary killing of an Israelite and his captive Midianite woman, which earned him according to Num. 25.10-13 the prize of a 'covenant of perpetual priesthood', that is a guarantee that the high-priestly line would continue among his descendants (cf. 1 Chr. 5.27-41). This is no doubt why no mention is made here of descendants of Aaron's other surviving son Ithamar: according to 1 Chr. 24.1-6 they were a significant division of the priesthood, presumably in post-exilic times (cf. Ezra 8.2).

26-27. These verses, framed by statements that are similar but also significantly different, are designed to tie the preceding genealogy into its present narrative context. The precedence given to Aaron in v. 26 (only elsewhere in Num. 3.1) reflects the concentration on his descendants in the latter part of the genealogy, whereas the reversion to the normal order, with Moses first, in v. 27 recognises his priority in the Priestly narrative, and especially in 7.1-2. Both verses ascribe to Moses and Aaron the task of 'bringing the Israelites out of (the land of) Egypt', as in v. 13, which was later added to the interpolated passage: elsewhere in P it is Yahweh himself who promises to do this (7.4; cf. 6.5-6), but cf. Exod. 3.10-12 (E) for Moses in this role. The expression 'their tribal divisions' (Heb. *ṣibʾōtām*: see Note t on the translation) is probably drawn by the redactor from 7.4, where see the note.

28. The Heb. is literally 'And it happened/was on the day...', which is a characteristic opening to a new stage in a narrative and supports the view taken in the translation that this verse is the introduction to vv. 29-30. There is, however, considerable evidence, some of it very ancient, for the view that v. 28 was seen as belonging with v. 27 and not v. 29. MT has a *petuchah* after v. 28 but not before, and SP is similar with its *qiṣṣāh*. This division is already marked by an incomplete line of text ('open section') in 4QpalEx^m, the only Qumran manuscript which survives at this point (*DJD* IX, pp. 72-73).[12] Among early and medieval Jewish commentators, on the basis of a motif found already in the Mekhilta of Rabbi Ishmael (on Exod. 12.3: Lauterbach 1, p. 22), Tg^J completes the unfinished sentence by an addition relating to Aaron (see Text and Versions), which must connect it with v. 27. Nachmanides also followed the

---

[12] The Leiden edition of the Peshitta, on the other hand, places a division marker before v. 28 but not after it. The facsimiles of LXX A and B show no break between vv. 27 and 28; A has an empty space after v. 28 and a paragraph marker after v. 29, while B has a paragraph break after v. 28, as in the Hebrew traditions. The divisions, if any, in the manuscripts of the other ancient Versions (except Tg^J) remain to be explored.

division in MT and saw v. 28 as reaffirming the primacy of Moses, in case vv. 26-27 might seem to imply that Moses and Aaron were equal. But Rashi firmly stated that v. 28 goes with what follows, and Ibn Ezra agreed, citing Deut. 2.16-17 as a parallel, which are also separated by a traditional division marker in MT (and SP).[13] Cassuto and the modern Jewish translations, as well as the vast majority of non-Jewish renderings, follow this view. But Eerdmans (as cited by Houtman, pp. 521-22) gave weight to the traditional division in supposing that the interpolation ended with v. 28, though he presumed that it had a (different) continuation in the document from which it was extracted. This, as Houtman sees, is rather far-fetched. Houtman himself (p. 522) follows Ehrlich in treating v. 28 as a free-standing conclusion to the preceding paragraph and regarding the subject of 'happened/was' as the situation of the house of Levi described in the genealogy: 'That was their position at the time that...' Such an interpretation requires a lot of the reader, and the connection of v. 28 with v. 29 makes much better sense, even if it does produce a rather repetitive sentence. It was perhaps this latter feature which led to the early (mistaken) subdivision of the text.

29-30. This is a much abbreviated recapitulation of the dialogue between Yahweh and Moses earlier in the chapter (cf. vv. 2, 10-12). The correspondence to the wording of v. 12 is particularly close, which is not surprising, as the purpose of the repetition (*Wiederaufnahme*)[14] is to provide 7.1 with the rationale which it had before the insertion of the genealogy and the related material in vv. 13-27. The one substantial change from v. 12 is that Moses now gives his own deficiencies as the only reason for doubt about the effectiveness of his mission: they are brought forward to the beginning of his response and Israel's refusal to listen to him in v. 9b is passed over completely. Apart from possible apologetic motives, this served to bring the Priestly account into closer agreement with the non-Priestly version in 4.10 (though note Moses' fears expressed in 4.1).

7.1-2. Yahweh's response to Moses' objection actually has two parts, which affect the status of both Moses and Aaron. Moses himself is first elevated to the status of a god in relation to Pharaoh,

---

[13] Cf. Rottzoll, pp. 188-89.
[14] See the classic study of C. Kuhl, 'Die Wiederaufnahme – ein literarkritisches Prinzip?', *ZAW* 64 (1952), pp. 1-11.

despite his previous failure and lack of rhetorical training. There is, in other words, no question of any diminution in Moses' position as a result of the new arrangements, rather the reverse. At the same time Moses is, as ever, firmly subordinated to Yahweh himself, who 'commands' (v. 2) what he is to say. Aaron's role is defined in explicitly prophetic terms (more clearly so than the references to Aaron as Moses' 'mouth' in 4.16). The use of this language needs careful evaluation for its bearing on the nature of Old Testament prophecy. This verse is often cited as providing a classic definition of what a prophet is, namely a spokesman for God in his dealings with men (and especially rulers). This does indeed correspond to much of the evidence in the narrative and prophetic books and also to the other key passage in Deut. 18.18-20. But the relatively later date of the Priestly Work should be borne in mind: it bears witness to an understanding of prophecy (or an aspect of prophecy) which may not have been universal in early times. Equally the application of the term 'prophet' (Heb. *nābî'*) to Aaron here is sometimes seen as a sign of the displacement of prophecy from its central role in Israelite religion and the transfer of authority to the priesthood (cf. Lev. 10.11 for P's view of the teaching authority of the priests). That is probably to make too much of a statement with limited purpose, and one which may just as well be based on an acceptance of the validity of true prophecy (on the dependence of P on other aspects of prophecy see Schmidt, pp. 324-25).

3-5. The remainder of this divine speech is marked off by the emphatic use of the independent personal pronoun 'I' (as in 6.5) as a statement of the divine action which is to follow (vv. 3-4) and its consequences for the Egyptians' 'knowledge' (v. 5): compare 6.6-8, with its statement in v. 7 about the 'knowledge' of the Israelites which will follow from Yahweh's action. 'Harden' here is, exceptionally in Exodus, Heb. *qāšāh* hiphil (cf. *qāšeh*, 'hard, difficult, stubborn'):[15] elsewhere (except 13.15, where Pharaoh himself is the subject) *ḥāzāq* piel (lit. 'make strong') and *kābēd* hiphil (lit. 'make heavy, unresponsive') are used. The author may have chosen the most unambiguous negative expression to begin with (so Wilson,

---

[15] See Note aa on the translation. Propp's suggestion (p. 282) that the verb here means 'give courage' hardly conforms to its usage elsewhere, no more than Weimar's claim (*Exodusgeschichte*, pp. 209-10) that it has a neutral sense (which Deut. 2.30 certainly does not support).

'Hardening', pp. 23, 31). In the subsequent Priestly narrative it is first said that Pharaoh's heart, i.e. will, 'was hard', i.e. determined (*ḥāzāq* qal: 7.13, 22; 8.15) and only later that Yahweh made it hard (9.12, 11.10, 14.4, 8). The opening statement may therefore refer to the final stages of Yahweh's dealings with Pharaoh: what follows details the actual sequence which events will follow – many signs and wonders, Pharaoh's refusal to obey, the final blow in the slaying of the firstborn and the liberation of the Israelites. This is preferable to seeing the 'hardening' as the beginning of the sequence (Schmidt, p. 326);[16] and while one could translate '(so) that I may increase my signs and wonders...' (Childs, Houtman), this involves a rare Hebrew construction (see Note y on the translation) and is not necessary. Alternatively the causative expressions in P, both here and from 9.12 onwards, may owe their location to the wish to emphasise at these points God's control of Pharaoh all along. (In the non-Priestly account it is only in ch. 10 [vv. 1, 20, 27] that such expressions occur, where they may be intended as a response to Pharaoh's earlier defiance.)

The climax of the speech is that 'the Egyptians will know that I am Yahweh...', an intention that is repeated in 14.4, 18 in the context of the sea-crossing. Here the anticipated occasion of this knowledge is probably more closely associated with the ensuing plagues and especially the killing of the firstborn (12.12-13, though the terminology there is different): the departure of the Israelites from Egypt is placed prior to the sea-crossing (12.41-42).[17] Egyptian recognition of Yahweh as a result of the plagues is a prominent theme of the non-Priestly account as well (cf. 7.17; 8.6, 18; 9.14, 29), though there it is often attributed to a redactional layer (cf. Carpenter/Harford-Battersby: not necessarily correctly). The 'knowledge' envisaged should probably not be limited to the mere experience of Yahweh's power (as Schmidt, p. 331, seems to hold): it includes an understanding that Yahweh is after all the power at

---

[16] Childs's translation and comment (pp. 109-10, 118, 172-73) seem to see vv. 3 and 4 as parallel (he does not elaborate the point), but this also seems less likely. But see also his further comments on pp. 139-40, where he makes a clear distinction between 'signs' and 'the blow' against the firstborn.

[17] Against Ska's view that the events of the sea-crossing are in view from v. 4aβ onwards ('Les plaies d'Égypte dans le récit sacerdotal (Pg)', *Bib* 60 [1979], 23-35 [24-27], cited by Van Seters, *Life*, p. 105).

work in events. The same recognition of Yahweh by non-Israelites (including the Egyptians) when he executes his vengeance and send his judgements is a central theme of Ezekiel's oracles against the nations (25.17; 26.6; 28.22-23; 29.6; 30.25-26; 32.15; 35.15; 38.23; 39.6-7): the temporal expressions ('when...') in several of these passages are very similar to the formula here. What distinguishes this recognition from that spoken of in 6.7 is the absence of the appositional phrase ('Yahweh) your God': the Egyptians still remain outside the special relationship between Yahweh and his people, even when they recognise him for who he is.

Text and Versions

וידבר (6.10)   LXX εἶπεν δέ, as though it read ויאמר: one of six such divergences from MT in Exodus (Wevers, *Notes*, p. 49, on 4.15), cf. v. 13 below. The use of אמר before לאמר would be unusual, but cf. 5.10; 7.8; 12.1; 31.12 etc. Wevers may be correct to suspect a variant *Vorlage* here. Mur1 has an empty line before where v. 10 would have stood and in 4QGen-Ex[a] וידבר begins a new line and probably followed an empty space ('open section') in the previous line (cf. MT's פ).

יהוה (6.10)   Tg[G] prefixes ד ממרה and this is taken up in Tg[Nmg] (cf. 6.1-2). Tg[N] repeats the beginning of v. 9 before v. 10 by paraplepsis due to homoeoarkton.

בא דבר (6.11)   Sy, rather freely, has *zl 'mr*, as if Heb. was אמר לך, a combination which does not occur elsewhere in Exodus but is found several times in Samuel–Kings, Isaiah and Jeremiah.

מארצו (6.11)   Tg[N] has an interlinear variant, 'from the land' (cf. the main text in v. 13 below). The unqualified form is rare with מן in MT (cf. 1.10; 12.33), but in Aramaic the variant could easily arise by interchange of ה and א.

וידבר...לאמר (6.12)   Sy *w'mr*, simplifying and showing the same preference for *'mr* as in v. 11.

אלי (6.12)   Tg[N] originally read 'to my words', but the mg has 'to me' as in the other Tgg.

ערל שפתים (6.12)   The Vss generally draw on their renderings of 4.10 to interpret this metaphorical expression: 'heavy of speech' (Tg[O]), 'with difficulty in speech' (Tg[J]), 'lame in speech' (Tg[N]), 'my tongue stammers' (Sy, borrowing more freely from 4.10), and without a verbatim parallel LXX ἄλογος, which Wevers notes must mean 'lacking verbal fluency' here, although its usual sense is 'mindless, irrational' (*Notes*, pp. 78-79): compare the unusual use of εὔλογος in a variant at 4.10, and a few examples of 'without speech' in LSJ, p. 72. The rendering not surprisingly gave rise to discussion in Philo and Origen: see *BAlex*, p. 113. Aq, Theod and Vulg gave literal renderings of Heb.: only Symm offered an independent interpretation of the idiom, οὐκ εἰμὶ καθαρὸς τῷ φθέγματι (as also in v. 30), with a correlation with Isa. 6.5 (where Symm's rendering is similar) and presumably the moral uses of the idea of (un)circumcision in Jeremiah and elsewhere (see Salvesen, pp. 77-78, whose general review of interpretations is valuable, and Note g on the translation).

וידבר (6.13) LXX again has εἶπεν δέ, as in v. 10: see the note there. Tg^{Nmg} adds a reference to the Memra.

ואל־אהרן (6.13) Tg^O, while using the עם which is idiomatic after 'spoke' in Aram. to refer to Moses (as do Tg^{J,N}, Sy here as well), uses ל before אהרן ('for'?), presumably to recognise the different roles given them according to 4.15-16 and 7.1-2.

ויצום (6.13) LXX συνέταξεν αὐτοῖς, the compound with συν being a frequent choice of the Pentateuch translators in this sense, even where צוה does not occur (e.g. 1.17; 9.12). Many mss add πορεύεσθαι or another word afterwards to ease the construction; this will also be the aim of Vulg's unique rendering of צוה by *dedit mandatum*. Tg^J 'solved' the problem by distinguishing between a 'warning concerning the Israelites' (√זהר being in some of its uses a passable equivalent for צוה; for other evidence of this interpretation see *AramB* 2, p. 176 n. 10) and a 'sending to Pharaoh', which at least does justice to the 'pregnant' use of צוה here (see Note i on the translation).

אל־בני ישראל (6.13) The original LXX omitted this phrase, probably due to homoeoarkton (in its *Vorlage*?) before (ו)אל־פרעה but possibly deliberately (Houtman), and as a result rendered הוציא by ἐξαποστεῖλαι, the verb naturally used (for √שלח) in v. 11 where only Pharaoh was involved. These errors were corrected in the manuscript tradition, in the first case by drawing on the renderings of Symm and Theod, in the latter apparently prior to Origen (Wevers, *Notes*, p. 79). In addition to MT, SP and the other Vss, there is just enough surviving to attest אל בני ישראל in 4QGen-Ex^a, which also exhibits a *vacat* after this verse (*DJD* XII, pp. 25-26, esp. fr. 29).

הוציא (6.13) Tg^{Nmg} adds 'set free, redeemed', as Tg^N does at 3.10 (see Text and Versions there) and elsewhere.

מארץ־מצרים (6.13) Tg^N has simply 'from the land' (cf. the interlinear variant in v. 11).

אלה (6.14) SP reads ואלה and LXX and Sy also have the conjunction (which Wevers, *Notes*, p. 79, considers 'textual', i.e. based on a *Vorlage* different from MT). The addition of such a link is much more likely to be secondary than its removal.

ראשי (6.14) LXX ἀρχηγοί (as quite often), but in the sense 'chiefs' rather than 'founders' (cf. its replacement by ἀρχαί in v. 25).

בית־אבתם (6.14) LXX οἴκων πατριῶν, 'houses of families', a slight paraphrase but close enough to have become LXX's standard equivalent. Vulg is freer (*principes*) *domorum per familias*, reflecting the segmented genealogy which follows. For *per familias* cf. v. 19, where it represents לתלדתם.

ראבן (6.14)   Sy curiously (but as elsewhere) has *rwbyl*, a transcription of the name which, according to Wevers, *Notes*, p. 80, also appears in the Ethiopic and Arabic versions, as well as the Syrohexaplar.

ופלוא (6.14)   LXX καὶ Φαλλούς, which Wevers, *Notes*, p. 80, takes as a 'Graecised' ending. But it may be due to a divergent *Vorlage*, as *aleph* and *samekh* could be quite similar in the palaeo-Hebrew script. The other Vss, and the occurrences of the name elsewhere support MT.

חצרון (6.14)   The Weber ed. of Vulg follows a minority of mss in reading *Aesrom*, but this is surely a conflation of the better attested readings *Esrom* and *Asrom*. Sy adds *waw* before the name, conforming to the pattern of most of the other lists in the passage.

משפחת (6.14)   LXX and OL render by words for 'family' in the singular, which would be a possible reading of the unvocalised text, although a surprising one after the preceding אלה. LXX's συγγένεια is one of no fewer than four equivalents for משפחה used in vv. 14-25, which correlate it either with בית־אב or with תלדת (συγγένεια is used for the latter in vv. 16 and 19). The Pentateuch translator(s) had a problem: φυλή had been used for משפחה throughout Genesis (8.19 etc.), but was clearly inappropriate here. It was only from the beginning of Numbers (1.20) that the very apt equivalent δῆμος, in the sense of 'township, commune', began to be used (on which see the refs. in Muraoka, *Lexicon*, p. 112, and A. Passoni dell'Acqua, 'Precisazione sul valore di δῆμος nella versione dei LXX', *Rivista Biblica* 32 [1982], pp. 197-214). Vulg, Tgg and Sy recognise the plural form here.

ימואל (6.15)   The reading is supported by all the main witnesses, including what remains of 4QGen-Exᵃ for this verse. Ms. B alone of LXX reads Ιεμιήλ, suggesting a *Vorlage* ימיאל, with confusion of *waw* and *yodh*. Vulg *Iamuhel* introduces an *h* to represent the medial *aleph*, as elsewhere (cf. *Ozihel* and *Misahel* in v. 22 and *Israhel* passim), while not doing so for a medial *he* or *heth* (cf. *Aaron* passim), a practice which is reminiscent of Catullus's Arrius (*carm.* 84)!

ואהד (6.15)   Many SP mss (including the earliest ones) read ואחד, with *heth* (cf. Tal and von Gall's apparatus; also Camb. 1846); the Aram. Vss support MT, but LXX and Vulg are compatible with either reading. The same divergence appears at Gen. 46.10.

ויכין (6.15)   Vulg does not represent the *waw*, dividing the long list into two groups of three. All the other witnesses agree with MT, which is probably original.

וצחר (6.15)   SP reads וצהר, with *he* (also at Gen. 46.10). LXX σάαρ, cited in *BHS*, is like Vulg inconclusive on this variation, but seems to indicate a different vocalisation, as with some other names in lists like this.

הכנענית (6.15)   LXX ἐκ τῆς Φοινίσσης, updating the geographical terminology as in 16.35 (but not, e.g., in 3.8, 17): 'Canaanite' was restored by the Three and consequently in some hexaplaric mss. Tgʲ records the tradition found in B.Sanh. 82b that this Simeonite was the Zimri of Num. 25.14, on the basis that בן here indicates his character (see also Tgʲ on Gen. 46.10).

משפחת (6.15) Only OL renders in the sing. here (Vulg *progenies* is ambiguous but probably pl.). LXX has πατριαί, 'families'.

שמעון[20] (6.15) LXX and Tg^N prefix 'sons of', as at the beginning of the verse, which may be connected with their pl. rendering of the preceding משפחת. 4QGen-Ex^a clearly did not have this insertion.

לתלדתם (6.16) LXX and Vulg use words for 'families' (as also in v. 19) which have already been used to render משפחה (contrary to their practice in Gen.). Tg^o borrows the Heb. word (cf. Tg^{N}int.), while Tg^{J,N} and Sy use words which can mean 'genealogy' as well as 'family' (יחוסין, *šrbt'*).

גרשון (6.16) LXX* Γεδσών, due to confusion between *daleth* and *resh* in (reading?) the *Vorlage*. The misreading became standard in later books (Wevers, *Notes*, p. 82), although the name was correctly transcribed in Gen. 46.10 (and in many mss here). Some LXX mss and Tg^N independently have a final -m, a common confusion.

וקהת (6.16) SP omits the *waw*, so that *waw* appears only with the final name in the list, a common practice (see Note d on 1.1-6). All the versions support MT on this (4QGen-Ex^a does not survive for this word), and repeated *waw* is characteristic of this passage generally. The standard English vocalisation of the name, 'Kohath' (so the AV and since), is not supported by the best mss or the Vss (German versions have remained closer to one or the other): it appears to derive from the pointing of the *qoph* with *hateph-qamets*, which according to BDB, p. 875, is found sometimes in van der Hooght's ed. of the text: on its rationale and early origin see I. Yeivin, *Introduction to the Tiberian Masorah* (SL Masoretic Studies 5; Chico, 1980), pp. 283-84.

חיי לוי (6.16) Sy apparently renders 'which Levi lived': cf. vv. 18 and 20 and the formula in Gen. 5.5.

שנה (6.16) LXX and Vulg do not represent this superfluous repetition. Tg^J adds after it: 'he lived until he saw Moses and Aaron, the liberators of Israel', which is (as *AramB* 2, p. 176 n. 13, points out) both unparalleled and in contradiction with 1.6 (and the period which Israel is supposed to have spent in Egypt). Such computations began in the Hellenistic period: cf. Demetrius fr. 2-3 (Charlesworth [ed.] 2, pp. 851-53), T.Levi 11-12 and 4Q559, which give different figures (on this see M.O. Wise, 'To Know the Times and the Seasons: A Study of the Aramaic Chronograph 4Q559', *JSP* 15 [1997], pp. 3-51, esp. 21-25, 28-33 on this passage).

בני (6.17) SP prefixes *waw*, as ובני appears elsewhere here at the beginning of a verse; likewise Sy, while LXX amplifies further with καὶ οὗτοι, as if the verse began (ו)אלה, like vv. 14 and 16. The (original) asyndetic text of MT no doubt represents the transition to a new generation.

גרשון (6.17) LXX again has Γεδσών, Tg^J (ו)גרשום (after י- in v. 16, probably just a slip, as Tg^J generally maintains the distinction between this figure and the similarly named son of Moses).

לבני (6.17) LXX and Vulg vocalise 'Lobeni': cf. Μοζέ for מִזָּה in Gen. 36.13.

למשפחתם (6.17) LXX οἶκοι πατριᾶς αὐτῶν, equating משפחה with בית־אב in v. 14, and ignoring the *lamedh* (cf. its rendering in v. 19).

ובני (6.18) Vulg simply *filii*, assimilating to v. 17 (as also in v. 19).

וחברון (6.18) SP and LXX (except hexaplaric and other mss) do not represent the *waw*, dividing the names into two groups of two (cf. MT at v. 14). Given the tendency of the tradition to add *waw*, this could be the original reading.

קהת[2o] (6.18) Tg[J] adds 'the pious one', no doubt because Kohath was the ancestor of Moses and Aaron (and Phinehas: see below).

שלש ושלשים (6.18) LXX has simply τριάκοντα, probably reproducing a *Vorlage* which had lost שלש by homoeoarkton (cf. Wevers, *Notes*, p. 83). Hexaplaric and other mss add τρια, afterwards in accordance with Greek grammar (cf. vv. 16 and 20).

שנה (6.18) Here (and in v. 20) LXX has ἔτη, but Vulg does not represent it. Tg[J] adds: 'He lived until he saw Phinehas – he is Elijah the high priest who is to be sent to the exiles of Israel at the end of days' (see *AramB* 2, p. 176 n. 14 for other evidence of Phinehas as an eschatological figure).

מחלי (6.19) LXX Μοολί, with the occasional representation of *pathach* by *omicron* in the vicinity of a guttural (cf. Γοθόμ in Gen. 36.11 and Νοεμάν in 46.21).

ומושי (6.19) LXX καὶ Ὀμουσί, where the initial *omicron* is due to transcription as well as translation of the Heb. *waw* (cf. Wevers, *Notes*, p. 84).

משפחת (6.19) LXX οἶκοι πατριῶν, with the latter word in the pl. (rather than the sing. as in v. 18) because all the three sub-divisions of Levi are now in view.

הלוי (6.19) LXX, Vulg, and Tg[O,J] ignore the article and treat this as a PN (cf. the end of vv. 14 and 15), while Tg[N] and Sy have plural forms implying a collective understanding of MT, in line with the expressions used in vv. 16 and 25.

לתלדתם (6.19) LXX, as in v. 16, has κατὰ τὰς συγγενείας αὐτῶν, perhaps referring to the three larger sub-tribal groups. Vulg (*familias*) and Tg[J] (לגניסתהון) introduce new 'family' words to avoid a repetition of their renderings of משפחה, but Sy has *šrbthwn* both times, utilising perhaps both its two meanings 'family' and 'generation'.

דדתו (6.20) Tg[O,J,F] (cf. Tg[Nmg]) give the straightforward equivalent of MT and SP's text, with Tg[O] having specifically 'his father's sister' in accordance with Num. 26.59. The remaining Vss use expressions equivalent to 'his cousin', with LXX specifying 'the daughter of his father's brother' (see also Demetrius fr. 2.19, in Charlesworth [ed.] 2, p. 852) and Tg[N] and Sy 'the daughter of his aunt/father's sister'. It was presumably thought impossible in some circles that Moses' parents married in defiance of the Levitical law (Lev. 18.14; 20.20).

לו לאשה (6.20) Tg[O,J] and Sy paraphrase slightly in different ways, as in vv. 23 and (except for Sy) 25.

ואת־משה (6.20)   SP and LXX add a reference to Miriam afterwards, with wording drawn from Num. 26.59: Exod. 2.4-9 assumes that Moses had an elder sister and 15.20 says that Miriam was the sister of Aaron, who was Moses' brother (or 'kinsman') according to 4.14 and 7.1. Most mss of Sy (not 5b1) add 'and Miriam' (but not 'their sister') either before 'Moses' (7a1, 8b1 etc.) or after it (7h13, 8a1 etc.). The shorter text of MT and the other Vss is to be preferred (although the text of 4QGen-Ex[a] breaks off at just this point, *DJD* XII, p. 26, is clear that there is no room in it for the additional phrase).

עמרם[20] (6.20)   As in v. 18 Tg[J] adds the epithet 'the pious one': *AramB* 2, p. 177 n. 16 notes traditions about Amram's righteousness, to which *LAB* 9 and the Aram. fragments of the *Testament of Qahat/Kohath* (4Q542) and the *Visions of Amram* (4Q543-548) may be added.

שבע (6.20)   SP שש, which is supported both by the Greek reading that is most likely to be original (so Wevers, *Notes*, p. 85, with references to other readings: the δύο of B which was preferred by Rahlfs is much less strongly attested) and by passages in the Aram. *Visions of Amram* (4Q543 fr. 1.3 = 4Q545 fr. 1 i 3). This may well be the original reading: MT, which is followed by the other Vss, is suspect because it repeats the number in v. 16.

שנה (6.20)   See on v. 18. After it Tg[J] adds 'He lived until he saw the sons of Rehabiah son of Gershom son of Moses'. This unique statement (though B.Baba Bathra 121b, cited by Houtman, goes even further) mistakenly confuses Moses' two sons: 1 Chr. 23.17 and 26.25 name Rehabiah as Eliezer's son.

ובני (6.21)   Here (and in vv. 22 and 24) Vulg does recognise the presence of *waw*, with its rather emphatic *quoque*, which is sometimes the equivalent of גם or עוד, but more often a stylistic addition or intensification, as here.

מישאל (6.22)   Sy *mnš'yl*, adapting to the interrogative particle in Syriac (cf. Lev. 10.4), though 5b1 retains the MT form. A, B, OL (ms 100) and other LXX mss omit, and Rahlfs followed them. Wevers, *THGE*, p. 252, sees this as an error in the Greek tradition, due to homoeoteleuton with the preceding Ὀζιήλ, and prefers the reading of those mss (inc. FM) which include it. All the other witnesses include the name: whether the omission took place in Heb. or Gk., it is secondary.

אלצפן (6.22)   SP אליצפן, which LXX and Sy support: the same variation occurs at Lev. 10.4. Elsewhere (cf. BDB, p. 45) MT also has the fuller spelling, and of course the shorter consonantal text could originally have been pronounced in the same way. Neither form occurs in epigraphic Heb., but similar variations in the spelling of other names occur both in MT and in inscriptions (cf. BDB, pp. 44-46; *AHI*, pp. 278-85, *AHI* 2, pp. 131-34): on the wider issue of medial *-î-* in names cf. M. Noth, *Personennamen*, pp. 33-36.

אלישבע (6.22)   LXX and Vulg transcribe 'Elisabe', although many mss of both have the final 't/th' which is familiar from Luke 1.5 etc., but due to (presumably early) dittography from the beginning of the following word θυγατέρα here (Wevers, *THGE*, p. 208).

לוֹ²ᵒ (6.23) Most of the early mss of Sy (5b1, 7a1, 8a1, 8b1) have no equivalent, but one is added in 7h13 etc. to agree with MT.

אֲבִיהוּא (6.23) So MT, SP and all the other Vss, but LXX has here and elsewhere Ἀβιούδ (Wevers, *Notes*, p. 87). Could this be ultimately due to confusion between *aleph* and *daleth* in a palaeo-Heb. ancestor of the *Vorlage*?

אֶת־אֶלְעָזָר (6.23) Sy spells *'ly'zr*, as normally for Moses' son. LXX, Vulg, Tg^N and Sy prefix 'and', making a continuous list as in other neighbouring cases. But the disjunction produced by its absence in MT, SP etc. has a good reason in the story in Lev. 10.1-7 and should be retained.

אַסִּיר (6.24) SP has אסור, by confusion of *waw* and *yodh*: Vss all support MT.

וְאֶלְקָנָה (6.24) Some SP mss and Sy have a final *aleph*; Vulg (cf. on v. 15) and Sy both have an initial 'H', which is remarkable.

וַאֲבִיאָסָף (6.24) SP and Sy ואביסף: the loss of medial *aleph* is a well-known phenomenon (GK §23f) and is attested for the name of this very person in 1 Chr. 6.8, 22; 9.19.

מִשְׁפְּחֹת (6.24) LXX introduces a new equivalent here, γενέσεις (as in v. 25 and four times elsewhere): it can mean both 'family' and 'generation', but is best known as the regular equivalent for תלדת in Genesis.

הַקָּרְחִי (6.24) So SP and, more or less, Vulg and Tg^N. But the remaining Vss simply repeat the proper name 'Korah', as most of the Vss also do with 'Levi' in v. 16.

וְאֶלְעָזָר (6.25) Vulg has *at vero* for the *waw*, reading the anteposed subject as an antithesis to the previous verse. Sy again spells the name as for Moses' son.

לוֹ¹ᵒ ²ᵒ (6.25) LXX omits the first occurrence as being semantically redundant, and Vulg omits them both.

פּוּטִיאֵל (6.25) Sy curiously spells *pntyl*. Tg^J prefixes '(of) Jethro, who is', a surprising equation in view of Jethro's foreign birth, but one that became popular (cf. *MRI* [Lauterbach 2, p. 164], and other refs. in *AramB* 2, p. 177 n. 18), perhaps because Jethro was a priest. Or was it the recurrence of 'daughters' in the pl. (cf. 2.16, 20) that led to it? Rashi cites an alternative tradition, which like the other he backed up by etymology, that this otherwise unknown figure was from the family of Joseph (B.Sota 43a; Baba Bathra 109b): see further Houtman, p. 519.

פִּינְחָס (6.25) Early editions of *BHS* misspell as פינהס.

רָאשֵׁי־אֲבוֹתָם (6.25) LXX ἀρχαὶ πατριᾶς, referring to the one 'family' of Levi (cf. v. 19 and, for the use of πατριά in the sing., v. 17).

הַלְוִיִּם (6.25) So also Vss, but SP has הלוי, assimilating to v. 19.

לְמִשְׁפְּחֹתָם (6.25) LXX again has (κατὰ) γενέσεις, as in v. 24, having used πατριά for אבות just before. Sy is not so deterred from using *šrbt'* again, as it did in v. 19 to render a different pair of words.

אַהֲרֹן וּמֹשֶׁה (6.26) Sy inverts the names, to conform to v. 27 (cf. v. 13).

יהוה (6.26) LXX ὁ θεός, as it has for the divine name 43 times in Exodus (Wevers, *Notes*, p. 89; *THGE*, p. 241). Here it may be due to the prominence of אלהים in v. 2, though the divine name has appeared several times since then in all witnesses.

הוציאו (6.26) LXX and Vulg paraphrase, assimilating to their renderings of v. 13. Tg^J (cf. Tg^{Nmg}) adds פריקין, 'redeemed', here for the first time, as the Pal. Tgg have done previously (see on 3.10 and 6.6).

על־צבאתם (6.26) For על Sy has *kwl*, perhaps due to a misreading of its *Vorlage*. LXX renders צבאתם by δυνάμει αὐτῶν in the sing.: this is its regular equivalent even where the Heb. noun is pl. (cf. 7.4) and the concrete meaning '(military) force' is well attested both in classical Greek and in LXX (cf. LSJ s.v. I.3 and Muraoka, *Lexicon*, p. 136). But here it may mean 'power': see on 7.4.

המדברים (6.27) Sy ignores the def. art. and has simply 'they spoke'.

להוציא (6.27) LXX καὶ ἐξήγαγον need not imply a different *Vorlage*, but simply a consequential understanding of the inf. (JM §124l)

ממצרים (6.27) So also 4QpalEx^m, LXX, Tgg and Sy, but SP and mss of LXX and Sy read מארץ־מצרים, assimilating to v. 26. On the LXX reading, where Wevers differs from Rahlfs, see Wevers, *THGE*, pp. 238-39.

הוא (6.27) Wevers (*Notes*, p. 89) takes LXX αὐτός to mean 'that is, namely', but he does not relate this to the normal senses of αὐτός. Perhaps 'Aaron himself...' (see the next note) is what the Greek was intended to mean, even if this can hardly be the sense of the Heb. Sy ignores the pronoun altogether.

משה ואהרן (6.27) LXX inverts the names, to correspond to v. 26 (the opposite of what Sy does there). The variation in MT etc. is in fact explicable (see the Explanatory Note). Tg^J adds the titles 'the prophet' and 'the priest' to indicate the future roles of Moses and Aaron as he saw them (in some tension with 7.1). 4QpalEx^m has spaces either side of this phrase, according to *DJD* IX, p. 93, because it is 'transitional'. MT has no division here: *DJD*, ibid., has been misled by the layout of *BHS*.

יהוה (6.28) Tg^{Nmg} prefixes 'the Memra of'.

מצרים (6.28) Tg^J adds 'Aaron was inclining his ear and he heard what he said to him', which makes v. 28 a (parenthetical) comment on vv. 26-27: cf. *AramB* 2, p. 177 n. 19 for a concern elsewhere to reconcile this verse with 12.1. At the end of this verse 4QpalEx^m has a division in the text, as do MT and SP, curiously separating what are two parts of a single sentence in Heb., albeit a repetitious one (see further the Explanatory Note on v. 28).

יהוה (6.29) Tg^{Nmg} again prefixes 'the Memra of'.

לאמר (6.29) Sy *w'mr lh*, 'and said to him', a substitution which seems more common than the use of the Syriac inf. (the latter only twice [3.16; 6.10] in Exod. 1–6). There is no need to envisage a different *Vorlage*.

כל אשר (6.29) LXX ὅσα, lit. 'as much as', could really include the idea of 'all', and is in fact a frequent equivalent for this phrase (cf. 9.19; 18.24 etc.).

לפני יהוה (6.30) Sy has simply *lmry'*, avoiding the unusual Heb. idiom as it did in v. 12.

הן אני (6.30) There are minor scribal errors in Tg^J and Tg^N, Sy's rendering *dyly*, 'Mine', is part of a free paraphrase (presumably 'My own tongue stammers') and 4QpalEx^m has a lacuna at this point. But SP and the other Vss support MT, which makes good sense.

ערל שפתים (6.30) The Vss generally render as in v. 12 (see the note there), but LXX has ἰσχνόφωνος, 'feeble-voiced', which is its equivalent to a different phrase with a similar meaning in 4.10 (see the note), instead of the rare (in this sense) ἄλογος used in v. 12.

ואיך (6.30) There is no equivalent to the *waw* in Sy and Vulg, but this is probably only a stylistic feature. Tg^J has וכדין, 'and thus', most likely a further scribal error (for והכדין, cf. v. 12 and Tg^N here).

ישמע אלי (6.30) SP ישמעני, harmonising with v. 12. *BHS* attributes the same *Vorlage* to 'Vrs', but the versional renderings are compatible with either reading, as אל after שמע is often rendered by a direct object (cf. 7.4, 13). In any case, the variation from v. 12 in MT (and 4QpalEx^m) is certainly original.

ויאמר יהוה (7.1) 2Q2 has a *vacat* before this verse, marking a major division; 4QpalEx^m has only a 'closed space'. Tg^{Nmg} as usual inserts 'the Memra of'.

אל משה (7.1) LXX adds λέγων, perhaps following 6.29, although there the main verb is דבר rather than אמר. Such additions are found occasionally elsewhere in LXX Pentateuch (cf. Hatch and Redpath, pp. 863-65, and the note on 6.6) and need not indicate a divergent *Vorlage*. Tg^J adds 'Why are you afraid?'

נתתיך (7.1) Most of the Vss give the appropriate sense 'made, appointed' but LXX and Sy have 'gave': probably in both languages this could mean 'appointed' (for Greek cf. a third-cent. BC papyrus cited in BAG, p. 192). Wevers (*Notes*, p. 92) observes that the Antiochene fathers regularly have τέθεικα in their citations of this verse, perhaps an indication that a distinct version circulated in Syria, even though it is not reflected in the ms. tradition here (or elsewhere according to Wevers: see the discussion of the 'Lucianic' recension in the Pentateuch in the main Introduction, p. 41). Tg^J adds 'already', referring back to the earlier narrative as it did in 6.2.

אלהים (7.1) LXX, Vulg, Sy and, more surprisingly, Aq and Symm render straightforwardly '(a) god'. Tg^O has רב, 'probably in the sense 'teacher' (cf. below on נביאך and above on its rendering in 4.16), while Tg^N combines it with שליט, 'ruler', in accordance with the application of אלהים to human rulers or judges which was formerly seen in Exod. 21.6 and elsewhere. Its margin preserves another rendering, רבון, 'lord', which has the same implication. Tg^J 'feared like his god', presents a different alternative again. On these and other rabbinic interpretations see the useful review by Salvesen, *Symmachus*, pp. 78-79.

נביאך (7.1)   Tg^{O,N} have 'your interpreter/translator' as they do in 4.16 for
פה (see the notes there on the background in synagogue practice).

תדבר (7.2)   LXX adds the 'necessary' (Wevers, *Notes*, p. 93) 'to him'
and Tg^J adds לאהרן. But the shorter and 'more difficult' reading of MT, SP,
4QpalEx^m and the other Vss must be original.

אצוך (7.2)   Tg^N has the verb in the perfect, no doubt alluding to Yahweh's
earlier instructions to Moses, but the mg has the present/future form of the
other witnesses.

ואהרן אחיך (7.2)   Vulg simply has *ille*, 'he', but hardly represents a divergent *Vorlage* from all the other witnesses (including 2Q2, in which ואהרן is the
only word to survive for this verse).

ושלח (7.2)   A Geniza ms. has וישלח according to *BHS*, presumably (purposive) simple *waw* with the imperfect. This agrees with 6.11, which could
be an argument for or against its originality. Owing to the frequent confusion of *waw* and *yodh*, dittography or haplography could be responsible for
the different Heb. texts. MT is supported by SP and 4QpalEx^m and at least
Sy among the Vss. LXX ὥστε ἐξαποστεῖλαι and Vulg *ut dimittat* have a
modal element in their translations (with Tgg this is possible but not certain),
and the immediate sequel seems to support such a sense, since Moses and
Aaron's request will not in fact bring about Israel's release. But ושלח itself
can probably be understood in this way (see Note y on the translation). So the
reading of the majority of the Heb. witnesses may be followed.

מארצו (7.2)   4QpalEx^m seems not to have this word (*DJD* IX, p. 73),
though some uncertainty exists. The shorter text would make sense (cf. 3.20),
and assimilation to 6.11 in the other witnesses is a possibility, as there is no
easy explanation of why the word would have been accidentally omitted in
4QpalEx^m (cf. Sanderson, *An Exodus Scroll*, p. 56).

ואני (7.3)   Vulg *sed ego*, with a strong contrastive interpretation of the
emphatic pronoun (but see Note z on the translation), cf. LXX ἐγὼ δέ.

אקשה (7.3)   LXX's σκληρυνῶ (cf. Soph. *Ant.* 473; Eur. *Andr.* 1261) and
Vulg's *indurabo* are especially apt for this Heb. verb and were used also for
the more common חזק (cf. 4.21), hence the English rendering of the whole
group of verbs (which also includes כבד, in LXX more often βαρύνω) as
'harden' (see the note on 4.21).

לב (7.3)   Tg^J prefixes 'the inclination (יצר) of', a characteristic modification
to indicate the volitional meaning of 'heart' here: see the list of parallels in
AramB 2, p. 178 n. 4, to which 4.21 should be added.

מופתי (7.3)   LXX does not repeat μου after τέρατα, as it can be understood, but it is added in Codex Alexandrinus and many hexaplaric and other
witnesses (with the note ὁ ἑβρ in Sy^{hex}).

ולא (7.4)   Clarke's edition of Tg^J omits this word, but Ginsburger has it,
so this is clearly due to an accidental error.

474   EXODUS 1–18

פרעה (7.4) Vulg again replaces with a pronoun (this time in the verb), as in v. 3.

ונתתי (7.4) LXX καὶ ἐπιβαλῶ renders less literally than in v. 1, and with a well-attested Greek idiom (see classical exx. in LSJ s.v. I.2 and Matt. 26.50): it is not clear why Wevers describes it as 'pejorative' (*Notes*, p. 93).

את־ידי (7.4) The Tgg paraphrase with 'the stroke(s) of my might/punishment', as they do with other references to God's 'hand' (cf. esp. 3.20 and Text and Versions there). Tg^J here keeps the word 'hand' along with the paraphrase and also prefixes a further gloss 'I will let loose deadly arrows against them' (for the expression cf. B.Taan. 25a: here the coming plagues are clearly meant). Yahweh's arrows are a symbol for his judgement e.g. in Deut. 32.23, 42.

את־צבאתי (7.4) Tg^J, as preserved, has no equivalent to this phrase, unless the gloss just referred to is somehow based upon it. LXX σὺν δυνάμει μου, perhaps puzzled by the triple apposition in MT (both Vulg and Sy add 'and' to assist), took את as the preposition and probably intended the sing. δυνάμει to represent an abstract sense ('power') which it attributed to צבאת here, and perhaps elsewhere. Wevers (*Notes*, p. 94) less convincingly thinks of Yahweh's 'heavenly host'.

בני־ישראל (7.4) Tg^J adds פריקין, 'set free, redeemed', as e.g. in 6.26.

בשפטים (7.4) SP, as in 6.6, has במשפטים, but 4QpalEx^m agrees with MT. LXX ἐν ἐκδικήσει, with the idea of vengeance or vindication, uses a word that never represents משפט (most often the root נקם) but is its choice on two other occasions for שפטים (12.12; Num. 33.4). The less common word, as in 6.6, is certainly original.

מצרים (7.5) SP prefixes כל, and LXX πάντες implies the same in its *Vorlage*. It seems unlikely that there is enough room in the lacuna in 4QpalEx^m for the extra word. There is no obvious verse to which the phrase could be assimilated (כל־מצרים occurs in 7.24; 9.11; 10.6; 12.30, but the contexts are different), but it is still most likely to be a secondary expansion of the text, emphasising the impact of the forthcoming events.

בנטתי (7.5) Neither LXX ἐκτείνων nor Vulg *qui extenderim* represent the temporal construction of Heb.: the descriptive expressions match more closely the participial conclusion to the recognition-formula in 6.7, which they may be imitating. Tg^{O,J} (like Sy) represent the verb נטה by רום Aphel, as elsewhere, but a little imprecisely; the combination with their renderings of את־ידי (see below) is awkward, and Tg^N dealt with this by using (even less precisely) שוי Pael, its equivalent for נתן in v. 4.

את־ידי (7.5) The best LXX texts have no equivalent to the suffix, since Greek grammar does not require one. Tgg render with the same periphrases as in v. 4, except that this time Tg^J omits יד altogether.

והוצאתי (7.5) Whereas the other Vss (except LXX) use either two past tenses (Vulg, Sy) or two futures (Tg^{O,J}) to translate בנטתי and this word, Tg^N curiously moves from a future to a past rendering here (cf. 6.7, where Tg$^{G(D)}$

seems to agree). This could be designed to place the 'recognition' clearly at the end of the sequence (cf. 14.4, 18).

ב בני־ישראל (7.5)   SP prefixes עמי, assimilating to v. 4. *DJD* IX, p. 73, says that there is insufficient space in the lacuna in 4QpalEx[m] for both this and בני, and it seems most likely that it did not read עמי. All the other witnesses support MT. Tg[J,N] add, as elsewhere, פריקין, 'set free, redeemed'.

Chapter 7.6-13

Staffs and Snakes

This section is tightly connected to its predecessor by the opening fulfilment formula and by the concluding words 'as Yahweh had said' (cf. vv. 3-4). In addition the entry into Pharaoh's presence (cf. 6.10-11) and the joint action of Moses and Aaron (cf. 7.1-2) pick up elements of Yahweh's instructions in the preceding narrative. Nevertheless it marks an important step forward in the action, from instruction and preparation to the actual confrontation with Pharaoh, and this is the basis for our subdivision of the narrative after v. 5 rather than after v. 7.[1]

The section itself has three components: a general statement that Moses and Aaron followed Yahweh's instructions (v. 6), an indication of the ages of Moses and Aaron when they confronted Pharaoh (v. 7), and an account of the first of the 'signs and wonders' performed before Pharaoh, which involves the transformation of Aaron's staff into a snake (vv. 8-13). The first two components are simple and straightforward (see the Explanatory Note for comments on their characteristics and parallels elsewhere): they provide a general introduction to the plague-story, and with its conclusion in 11.9-10 form a kind of frame for it.

The episode in vv. 8-13 is recounted in four stages (cf. Schmidt, pp. 352-53; Childs, p. 138, enumerates only three, but his parenthetical reference to the magicians adds a fourth): (i) Yahweh's instruction to Moses and Aaron (vv. 8-9); (ii) their fulfilment of this command, described in very similar words (v. 10); (iii) an unanticipated response by Pharaoh's magicians, and its outcome (vv. 11-12); and (iv) Pharaoh's stubborn refusal to listen to Moses and Aaron (v. 13). This pattern is very closely followed in two later episodes, dealing with the plagues of lice (or gnats) and boils (8.12-15 [EVV.

---

[1] Cf. Holzinger's comment that, because of the following v. 7, v. 6 is not an 'Abschluss' but an 'Einleitung' (p. 21). At first sight v. 8 seems still to belong to the preparatory stage, but such specific instructions are characteristic at the beginning of the individual sections in the plague-narrative.

16-19]; 9.8-12) and essentially the same wording also occurs in the episodes about water turned into blood (see 7.19, 20a, 21b, 22) and frogs (8.1-3, 11b). This comprises one of two (or possibly three) patterns of narration in the plague-narrative (on the other[s] see the introduction to 7.14-29). What is conspicuously missing from the present pattern (contrast e.g. 7.16-18) is a recurring instruction to Moses and Aaron about what they are to *say* to Pharaoh. This is not because they say nothing – the words (e.g. in 7.13) '(Pharaoh) did not listen to them' take for granted that they speak to him (as does the note in 7.7) – but the narrative does not repeat the original instruction to demand Israel's release given in 6.11 (cf. the more general instructions to speak to Pharaoh in 6.29 and 7.2). This was possible, either because the demand was thought in this strand of the narrative to have only been uttered once or because in these cases it was the same short demand each time, rather than the more elaborate warnings given to Pharaoh in the other type of narrative. This first episode differs from the others like it in certain respects: here, but not later, it is Pharaoh who (it is expected) requests a 'sign'; here (because it is the first in the sequence) he has to 'summon' his magicians; and the outcome of the magicians' intervention is different in each case (cf. 7.22; 8.3, 14-15a; 9.11).

The continuity, already noted, with the preceding narrative in 6.10–7.5*, which is itself linked to 6.2-9, makes it natural to attribute this section too to the Priestly source, and this has been the universal view of critical scholars since Knobel.

Only some minor or derivative issues need brief discussion. Knohl (pp. 61-62) attributes v. 6, like vv. 1-5, to his 'Holiness redaction'. Smend (*Hexateuch*, p. 125) attributed he chronological note in v. 7, with the others like it, to the final 'Bearbeitung' of the Hexateuch (cf. ibid., pp. 8-16, esp. 11-14), and (apparently independently) the same conclusion was reached by Rendtorff (*Problem*, pp. 131-33, 161-62) and Knohl (to judge by his exclusion of the verses from both P and HS on p. 61). Against this Weimar noted that the combination of the fulfilment formula in v. 6 with a chronological note is a recurrent structuring device of P, comparing 12.28+40 and Gen. 17.23-27 (*Exodusgeschichte*, pp. 222-23, 240; cf. Gertz, p. 58 n. 126, who adds Gen. 6.22+7.6 and Exod. 40.16-17a). Weimar saw it as a concluding formula, but it can also (as here) have a transitional function. There is in any case no good reason to see the chronological note as secondary here. Gressmann thought that vv. 8-13 must originally have followed the 'blood' episode, because its dramatic conclusion (v. 12b) comes too early in the narrative (but see our concluding reflections on this passage). The obvious similarity to 4.1-5 has led, in the context of recent study of Pentateuchal origins, to claims of dependence in both directions. The traditional view (taken here) that 7.8-13 was modelled on 4.1-5 is given a particular twist by Blum, who finds it impossible to deny that the sequence of similar sections in the plague-story (see above) once existed separately before their incorporation into his 'Priestly Composition' (KP), but sees 7.8-13 as composed by the author of KP as an introduction to them (*Studien*, pp. 245, 251-52): this, according to him, is why it includes the 'premature' swallowing of the magicians' staffs by Aaron's. L. Schmidt effectively refuted Blum's view (*Studien zur Priesterschrift*, pp. 13-14). On the other side K. Schmid (pp. 203-205) and Gertz (pp. 312-14) endeavour to show how 4.1-5 could have been produced on the basis of 7.8-13, as part of their view that the 'Endredaktor' was responsible for the creation of 3.1–6.1 as a 'preview' of the Priestly account which follows. Some remarks of Gressmann about the greater appropriateness of such 'magic' to the confrontation with Pharaoh (cf. *Mose*, pp. 88-89) might be cited in support of this view. But it remains at best unproven, and the alleged purpose of the redactor remains elusive: such duplications are more likely to have arisen from the combination of parallel accounts. Moreover, if the non-Priestly narrative were based on P, one would expect the reference back in 7.14 to use the word for 'snake' from 7.9-12 (*tannîn*), whereas in fact it uses *nāḥāš* from 4.3 (see further our introduction to 4.1-9 and *TWAT* 5, 394 = *TDOT* 9, pp. 366-67).

In terms of the overall plot, as Fohrer well observed (pp. 59-60), this episode performs a similar function to 5.1–6.1 in the non-Priestly material and it may draw for its inspiration on the story of the contest between Elijah and the prophets of Baal in 1 Kgs 18: it is the initial confrontation between the representatives of Yahweh and a powerful ruler, in this case a foreign one. At this stage it is not a question of a 'plague', but of a 'wonder' (v. 9), an act of special power to vindicate Moses and Aaron's authority, and it is consistent with this that Pharaoh is envisaged as asking for it. At first it seems that their power and that of Pharaoh's magicians are equally matched, but in the end Moses and Aaron triumph (v. 12b). Since Pharaoh nevertheless obstinately refuses to recognise their authority, the contest then moves on to a more serious and threatening level, both in the composite narrative (vv. 14ff.) and in the original sequence of Priestly plagues which begins in 7.19, where again Pharaoh's magicians are at first able to match the displays of Moses and Aaron (7.22; 8.3), before their final defeat (8.14-15a; 9.11).

6 *Moses, and Aaron, did*[a] *as Yahweh had commanded them: so they did*[b]. 7 *Moses*[c] *was eighty years old and Aaron was eighty-three when they spoke to Pharaoh.* 8 *Yahweh said to Moses and Aaron (saying)*[d]: 9 *When Pharaoh speaks to you saying, 'Give a sign to authenticate you'*[e], *you shall say*[f] *to Aaron, 'Take your staff and throw it (down)*[g] *before Pharaoh – let it become*[h] *a snake*[i]*'.* 10 *Moses, and Aaron, went in*[a] *before Pharaoh and they did*[j] *just as Yahweh had commanded. Aaron threw his staff (down) before Pharaoh and his servants, and it became a snake.* 11 *Pharaoh also summoned the wise men and sorcerers and they too, the magicians of Egypt*[k], *did the same with their spells*[l]. 12 *Each one threw his staff (down) and they became snakes. But Aaron's staff swallowed up their staffs.* 13 *Pharaoh's heart was stubborn; he did not listen to them, as Yahweh had said.*

Notes on the Translation

a. For the singular verb with plural subject (again in v. 10) see Note z on the translation of 4.18-31.

b. Repetitive formulae like this with כן, to emphasise conformity to Yahweh's commands, are a very frequent feature of the Priestly narrative (cf. Gen. 6.22; Exod. 12.28, 50; 39.32, 43; 40.16; Num. 1.54; 5.4; 8.20; 9.5; 17.26): they are an example of the structure which M. Paran has called 'the circular inclusio' (*Forms of the Priestly Style*, pp. 47-97 and 234, where the present idiom is treated among ways of concluding a pericope).

c. Verse 7 is a typical circumstantial or 'background' clause, indicating an aspect of the situation contemporary with the main action: cf. JM §159d.

d. Heb. לאמר. Although its use as here after another form of אמר seems particularly otiose, the combination is actually fairly common in BH (so 5.10 and also in other Priestly texts such as Gen. 9.8; Exod. 12.1; 31.12; 35.4; 36.5). See also Text and Versions.

e. Heb. לכם. In the context it seems best to take ל in a strong sense (cf. 3.12), rather than as just an example of the frequent idiom with a pronoun suffix after an imperative which adds little if anything to the meaning (for which cf. GK §119s, 135i, JM §133d and T. Muraoka, 'The So-called *dativus ethicus* in Biblical Hebrew', *JTS* N.S. 29 [1978], pp. 495-98).

f. Heb. ואמרת, i.e. the verb is sing., referring to Moses alone, whereas in v. 9a 'you' is pl. referring to both Moses and Aaron. It seems that despite the introductory formula in v. 8 it is still Moses whom Yahweh primarily addresses (cf. v. 2).

g. Heb. והשלך, imper. Hiphil of שלך. A downward movement is frequently involved in the use of this verb (e.g. Gen. 37.22; 2 Kgs 23.12; Ezek. 5.4) and it came to be used in later BH specifically for 'casting down' (cf. Jer. 9.18;

Ezek. 19.12; Lam. 2.1; 2 Chr. 25.12; Dan. 8.7, 11, 12). In the parallel in 4.3 this is made explicit by the addition of ארצה: it is perhaps significant for the date of the present passage that it was not felt to be needed here.

h. Heb. יהי. Driver took this as a final clause (*Tenses*, §152.2) but this would be more normal with *waw* preceding the jussive (cf. GK §109f, 165a; see also Text and Versions). Occasionally a jussive seems to be equivalent in meaning to an imperfect (GK §109k), though more often in poetry than in prose: Deut. 28.8 is the only close parallel, and it might justify the translation 'it will become' (cf. LXX, NRSV etc.). But the straightforward rendering adopted here is perfectly possible (and reminiscent of the divine commands in Gen. 1.3, 6, 14), and asyndeton is common in elevated speech (cf. JM §177a-f, and below in 7.14).

i. Heb. לתנין. This word is most often used of a large, mythological monster (so probably in Gen. 1.21), like its cognate *tnn* in Ugaritic (cf. *DULAT*, pp. 873-74): in Ezek. 29.2; 32.2 Pharaoh is compared to it. In two other places it appears to mean a poisonous snake (Deut. 32.33; Ps. 91.13, both times parallel to פתן, 'viper'), and this meaning is suggested here, though not established, by the use of נחש in the similar story in 4.1-4: נחש generally means 'snake', though it too occasionally refers to a mythological monster (cf. Isa. 27.1; Amos 9.3; Job 26.13). A more decisive consideration is the closer visual similarity of a staff to a (dead) snake. Jacob and Propp suggest specifically a cobra, which was a symbol of the Egyptian monarchy. Gressmann's 'crocodile' (*Mose*, pp. 88-89) seems to owe more to the Egyptian magical text which he compares than to the evidence of Heb. usage.

j. Codex L has ויעשו instead of the correct form ויעשׂו read by other authorities (Dotan's edition corrects the error: cf. p. 1230). The error may be due to the occurrence of the sing. form ויעשׂ a little earlier in v. 6.

k. Heb. חרטמי מצרים. This (or rather החרטמים alone) is the expression that is retained in the subsequent narrative (7.22; 8.3, 14-15; 9.11 [2x]). The contexts in which it is used (only Gen. 41.8, 24 and 7x in Daniel [4x Aram.] elsewhere) certainly give it connotations of foreignness (cf. Ibn Ezra), which is probably why it is introduced here with two native terms, the very general חכם, 'wise', and the specific מכשׁף, 'sorcerer' (Exod. 22.17; Deut. 18.10; Mal. 3.5; Dan. 2.2: cf. כשׁף in Jer. 27.9). In its occurrences outside Exodus חרטם is connected with the interpretation of dreams, but one of the words associated with it in Dan. 1.20 and 2.2 (cf. 2.10, 27; 4.4; 5.7, 11, 15), אשׁף, also has connections with magic (cf. Akk. *([w]āšipu)* and the biblical writers perhaps did not distinguish very clearly between the different kinds of religious specialists at foreign courts. The etymology of חרטם is disputed: BDB (Addenda, p. 1123) and (more precisely) H.-P. Müller (*TWAT* 3, 189-91 = *TDOT* 5, pp. 176-79) see it as an Egyptian loanword, but *HAL*, p. 339, reverted to the traditional association with Semitic words for 'beak, (elephant's) trunk' (further refs. in Childs, p. 128). Most recently *Ges18*, p. 396, and *DCH* 3, p. 400, prefer the

Egyptian basis (BDB's original derivation from Heb. חרט = 'stylus' [p. 355], hence 'engraver, writer', has been abandoned), and this seems most likely to be correct. Strictly the Eg. equivalent *ḥr-tb[i]* simply meant 'chief', but there is Eg. evidence for its specific use as a title for a magician, and it also appears as a loanword in some Neo-Assyrian texts. The phonological developments are explained adequately by Müller, loc. cit.

l. Heb. בלהטיהם. Where this word appears elsewhere in MT (cf. below in 7.22; 8.3, 14) it is spelt without the *he* (in Judg. 4.21 with a medial *aleph* instead, apparently as a vowel-letter), in accordance with its probable derivation from √לוט, 'wrap tightly, conceal'. The form with *he* is also attested in other textual witnesses elsewhere (see Text and Versions on the verses listed above), and such by-forms do occur occasionally in words from hollow roots (cf. רהיט and רהט in Cant. 1.17 [Q] and 7.6 if they are indeed related to רוץ, 'run'; more generally G.R. Driver, *Problems*, p. 7 n. 2). E. Lipiński, *La royauté de Yahwé dans la poésie et le culte de l'ancien Israël* (Brussels, 1968), pp. 223-24, finds the meanings 'surround, spell' in words that are usually attributed to the root להט, 'burn', but only Ps. 57.5 has any real plausibility and even there an alternative philological interpretation is possible (cf. *HAL*, p. 495; NEB). *Ges18*, p. 598, states that the form with *he* occurs in rabbinic Heb., but this seems to be based only on B.Sanh. 67b, where its occurrence here is explained by reference to the use of להט in Gen. 3.24 (cf. Exod.R. 9.11). The meaning(s) received further discussion from the medieval rabbis in their comments here and on v. 22 (cf. Rashi, Ibn Ezra, Nachmanides), but the Vss make no significant distinction between the different forms.

Explanatory Notes

6. The verse is a continuation of what has preceded, as the reference to Yahweh's command (cf. 6.10-11 [and its redactional echo in vv. 28-29] and 7.1-2) shows. The formula is a typical Priestly idiom which often concludes a section (see Note b on the translation): subdivision in the tightly constructed context is rather artificial, and many commentators take vv. 6-7 with the preceding section. We have done otherwise because the action summarised here already introduces Moses and Aaron's movement into Pharaoh's presence, which is eventually described in v. 9. It is probably not implied (as Noth, p. 54, ET, p. 71, suggested) that Moses and Aaron make a first appearance before Pharaoh at this point: the instruction in vv. 8-9 looks more like a further provision for their initial meeting with him, and the temporal clause in the next verse could as easily be anticipatory as retrospective.

7. Before the narrative (and Yahweh's instructions to Moses and Aaron) continues, a chronological note indicates that Moses and Aaron were already well advanced in years when they confronted Pharaoh. The figures given are consistent with those given in later notes of their total lifespan (Num. 33.39; Deut. 34.7), which have exactly the same form in Hebrew. Chronological notes of an identical form also appear in the stories of Abraham (Gen. 12.4; 16.16; 17.24-25; 21.5), Isaac (Gen. 25.20, 26) and Joseph (Gen. 41.46); elsewhere only in 1 Kgs 22.42 par.[2] It is difficult to be sure whether they are part of the original Priestly narrative or redactional: such chronological details are found both in the Priestly narrative itself (e.g. Gen. 5) and in redactional additions to it (Exod. 6.16, 18, 20). Aaron's seniority (also implied by the order of names in genealogical texts) is perhaps deliberately underlined to confirm his right to the priesthood in preference to Moses (and his descendants).

8-9. Yahweh's further instructions are addressed to both Moses and Aaron, although in what is said in v. 9b Aaron is spoken of in the third person (see also Note f on the translation), as in vv. 1-2. This might be seen as evidence that v. 9 was originally part of the speech addressed to Moses alone in vv. 1-5, and the 'and' with which it begins in LXX could be a vestige of this (see Text and Versions). On the other hand, as Propp (p. 321) well notes, there are several similar cases where the introductory reference to Aaron is ignored in the formulation of the divine speech which follows (Exod. 12.1; Lev. 11.1-2; 15.1-2; Num. 20.23-24), so not too much should be made of this feature here.

Aaron's staff is mentioned for the first time here (earlier Moses' staff has been mentioned, in a similar passage to this one [4.2-4], as well as a staff given to him by God [4.17, 20]): further references to it appear in 7.19; 8.1, 16 (but not 7.15: see the note there), all Priestly passages (see the introductions to the relevant sections), and in Num. 17.16-28 a 'staff of Aaron' turns into a living almond branch and is preserved to testify to his unique priestly privileges. That staff may be a new one (cf. vv. 2-3), but Aaron's staff here also marks him out as the holder of special power and authority.

---

[2] The expressions in e.g. Gen. 50.22, 26 and Josh. 24.29 are slightly different: those in Gen. 17.1, 26.34 and 37.1 are closer to the pattern here.

The first of the 'signs and wonders' (some authorities also have the dual terminology here: see Text and Versions) which Moses and Aaron perform before Pharaoh is distinctive in that (it is anticipated) Pharaoh requests it, as a way of validating Moses and Aaron's authority – the context presumes, though it does not state, that their authority to demand the Israelites' release is meant. It is also not a 'plague' as such, like those which follow, and it stands outside the standard reckoning of 'ten' plagues (first explicitly in Jub. 48.7, cf. v. 5: but this episode is also excluded from the summary in Ps. 105.26-36, which clearly knows [unlike Ps. 78.42-51] the Priestly version of the story as well as the older one). It is in fact very similar to the first of the 'signs' which Moses is given according to 4.1-9 in response to his fear that the Israelites will not believe him and which are actually performed by Aaron according to the present text of 4.30-31 (see the notes there). But there are notable differences. Some are due to the drastic abbreviation of the Priestly version (there is, for example, no reference to the reversal of the staff's transformation into a snake, although Jewish tradition [see Text and Versions] has seen it implied in the wording at the end of v. 12); but the word for 'snake' (if that is what it means; see Note i on the translation) is different (*tannîn* instead of *nāḥāš*) and the episode has a longer conclusion which is shaped by the introduction of the Priestly motif of the contest with the Egyptian magicians (see on vv. 11-12). The similarities and differences are best explained if the Priestly author knew the older version and adapted it to introduce his presentation of the plague-narrative. One aspect of the change emphasises the power of the divine word of command as in the Priestly creation story: 'Let it become (Heb. $y^eh\hat{\imath}$) a snake' preceding 'and it became ($way^eh\hat{\imath}$) a snake' (v. 8, as in 4.3), just like e.g. Gen. 1.3.

10. Now Moses and Aaron enter Pharaoh's presence and fulfil all that Yahweh has commanded them. The delivery of Yahweh's demands to Pharaoh (cf. 6.11 [29]; 7.1-2) is left unrecorded (though it is taken for granted in the words 'he did not listen to them' in v. 13), as is Pharaoh's request for a 'sign', because the emphasis falls entirely on the actions performed and Pharaoh's reaction to them (cf. 8.12-15 and 9.8-12). Pharaoh's 'servants' are mentioned only here in the Priestly plague-narrative, whereas they frequently appear in non-Priestly contexts (e.g. 7.20). They may be a secondary addition (Gertz, pp. 95-96), though it is hardly likely that Pharaoh was thought of as meeting Moses and Aaron alone.[3]

11-12. Pharaoh's reaction to the 'sign' is to call upon his own experts to do the same – the account is again abbreviated – and they succeed. Three separate terms are used for these experts, the last of which is probably Egyptian in origin (it appears as a loanword in Mesopotamian texts: see Note k on the translation) and is also used of the Egyptian interpreters of dreams in Genesis 41 and of similar Babylonian experts in Daniel 1–5.[4] The Priestly narrator seems readily to acknowledge that non-Israelite magicians could do such things (cf. also 7.22; 8.7), but distinguishes between their source of power ('their spells') and that of Moses and Aaron (the word of Yahweh). Indeed such practices of sorcery were known, but prohibited, in Israel (cf. 22.17). There is a fascinating account in an Egyptian text from the Greco-Roman period, cited by Propp (p. 322), of a similar contest between an Egyptian magician and a Nubian counterpart, in which the Egyptian is finally victorious (interestingly, it also combines super-normal abilities of perception with powers of sorcery, like the word translated 'magicians' here): for a translation see M. Lichtheim, *Ancient Egyptian Literature 3* (Berkeley and Los Angeles, 1980), pp. 138-51. No doubt this expresses what the Egyptians always expected to happen on such occasions. But the outcome here is unexpected, to the reader (who has been given no warning of how the episode might develop) as well as to the Egyptians: Aaron's 'staff', still in the form of a snake, swallows up all the magicians' 'staffs', presumably also still in the form of snakes. Such a defeat for the magicians does not recur in the first two of P's real plagues, only in the final two (8.14-15a; 9.11).

13. Despite this terrifying demonstration of the superior power of Moses and Aaron, Pharaoh adamantly refuses to yield. There is no mention of divine 'hardening' of his heart here (unlike v. 3a: cf. 4.21), only of divine foreknowledge (as in v. 4a). 'Stubborn' translates one of three Heb. words used of Pharaoh which have customarily (since the LXX and Vulg) been translated 'hard(en)'.

---

[3] The inclusion of Pharaoh's servants here is taken further in LXX (see Text and Versions).

[4] Holzinger thought that 'the magicians of Egypt' might be a gloss (p. 21: cf. Eissfeldt, p. 269*), but glosses usually explain an unfamiliar word rather than introducing one.

This is strictly the meaning only of the word (*qāšāh*) used in 7.3 (see the notes there): here *ḥāzaq*, 'be/make strong', is used (as also in 4.23; 7.22; 8.15; 9.12, 35; 10.20, 27; 11.10; 14.4, 8, 17). It is the term used throughout the Priestly narrative (except for 7.3), but the occurrences in 4.23; 9.35; 10.20, 27 are usually attributed to another stage of composition (or more than one).[5] Propp takes it in a positive sense, 'courageous, of firm resolve' (p. 323), but the occurrence of a related adjectival phrase in Ezek. 2.4 (*ḥizqê lēb*, lit. 'stubborn of heart': cf. 3.7) and the universally critical view of Pharaoh in the Exodus narrative confirm the usual negative interpretation (cf. *TWAT* 2, 856-57 = *TDOT* 4, p. 308). The 'heart' in this context will primarily refer to the will, as often elsewhere, though it would be artificial (from the point of view of Hebrew semantics as well as general psychological considerations) to make too sharp a separation between this and the cognitive aspect of the 'heart/mind' (cf. *TWAT* 4, 432-47 = *TDOT* 7, pp. 419-34, esp. 434 = 421). The focus on the will is particularly prominent in writings from the exilic period and later (ibid., 437 = 424; cf. the lists in BDB, pp. 523-25), which would include the Priestly writing but not, according to traditional critical opinion, the J and E sources. This may be a further aspect of an important distinction between the two/three accounts in Exodus: in P there is a clash of wills, Pharaoh's and Yahweh's, while in J Pharaoh's 'mind/intellect' is not perceptive enough (see Note a on the translation of 7.14-25) to recognise the significance of what he sees (see further the notes on 7.14), and the series of plagues seeks to bring him to a better understanding. The words 'he did not listen to them' recall Israel's response to Moses in 6.9; at the Exodus Israel is no more responsive to Yahweh than Pharaoh. This could be meant as a warning to the exiles of P's time (so Wilson, 'Hardening', p. 32), but it could equally be an encouragement to them, implying that for them too, despite the disobedience that had brought Yahweh's judgement upon them, his purpose to deliver and bless them once again remained unshaken (cf. the notes on 2.23-25 for further possible echoes of the exilic situation).

---

[5] For the third word (*kābēd*) see the notes on 7.14, and on the whole issue of the 'hardening' of Pharaoh's heart the Excursuses of Childs (pp. 170-75) and Propp (pp. 353-54), Wilson, 'Hardening', and most fully F. Hesse, *Das Verstockungsproblem im Alten Testament: eine Frömmigkeitsgeschichtliche Untersuchung* (BZAW 74; Berlin, 1955]).

Text and Versions

וַיַּעַשׂ (7.6) So also SP and 4QpalEx^m (4QGen-Ex^a does not preserve the beginning of the verse). All the Vss have a sing. verb except Sy, which accommodates to the plural subject.

יהוה (7.6)   Tg^Nmg reads 'the Memra of the Lord'.

אתם (7.6)   Vulg omits, rendering freely.

אהרן (7.7)   LXX added ὁ ἀδελφὸς αὐτοῦ, conforming to the expression in vv. 1-2; but many mss omit it (cf. Wevers, p. 95).

בן (7.7)   LXX and Vulg represent the Heb. idiom freely, without a direct equivalent to בן. For the second occurrence Sy^h attests the insertion of υἱός by Aq (as he no doubt did the first time too: Sy^h's text has it both times).

בדברם (7.7)   All the witnesses support the pl. suffix except LXX (ἐλάλησεν), which conforms precisely to what is commanded in v. 2. Many mss again agree with MT (but surprisingly few from the hexaplaric group).

ויאמר (7.8)   This reading is presupposed by all the Vss, but SP has וידבר, presumably to avoid two occurrences of אמר in the same sentence (cf. on 5.10). But such repetition is not uncommon (see Note d on the translation). None of the Qumran mss survives at this point. MT is to be preferred.

ואל (7.8)   Neither LXX nor Vulg has an equivalent to the second occurrence of the preposition, as is regular in Greek and Latin, but not in BH (cf. JM §132g).

לאמר (7.8)   Vulg and Sy have no equivalent (as in v. 9): this seems to be a regular practice of both in Exodus 1–10 after אמר (cf. 5.10) and an occasional one after דבר (cf. 6.12; contrast 6.10, 29). After other verbs לאמר always has an equivalent in Exodus 1–10 in both versions.

כי (7.9)   LXX καὶ ἐάν makes a connection that is not present in MT or the other witnesses and scarcely appropriate in the context. Might it be a relic of an originally closer connection with v. 5 (see the Explanatory Note)?

אלכם (7.9)   SP plene, and likewise 4QpalEx^m; in 4QGen-Ex^a the middle of the word is lost, but comparison with 3.13 suggests that there is room for the restoration אל[י]כם (contra *DJD* XII, p. 27, which restores according to MT).

לאמר (7.9)   Vulg and Sy again have no equivalent (see the note on 7.8).

לכם (7.9)   LXX ἡμῖν and Sy *ly* offer an 'easier' reference to Pharaoh himself. Vulg has no explicit equivalent, but may imply the same reading by its free rendering of תנו by *ostende*, 'show'.

מופת (7.9)   The normal sense 'wonder' is given by Tg^J, but the other witnesses appropriately introduce the idea of a 'sign', either by using equivalents with that meaning or (SP and LXX) by prefixing או אות, 'a sign or (a wonder)', in words identical to Deut. 13.2 and close to the formula used of the Exodus plagues elsewhere (e.g. Exod. 7.3; Deut. 4.34). Vulg, no doubt with an eye to the following narrative, uses the pl. *signa*. None of the Qumran scrolls survives at this point.

אהרן (7.9)   LXX again adds 'your brother', in line with vv. 1-2, one of several expansions in this verse derived from the context.

את־מטך (7.9) LXX (as in v. 10) and ms. 7a1 of Sy do not render the suffix (the Leiden edition, however, here follows the majority of Sy mss in a reading equivalent to MT). This could be simply because it is grammatically unnecessary, but the omission does also help to get round the problem of two (or more) different 'staffs' being involved in the Exodus narrative (see the Explanatory Notes on 4.17 and 4.20).

והשלך (7.9) The vast majority of SP mss have והשליך, which exhibits the fuller spelling of the imper. Hiphil which is found elsewhere in SP (cf. *GSH* §69c) and occasionally in BH (GK §53m): this is one of the places where von Gall's text mistakenly follows MT (which 4QpalEx^m and 4QGen-Ex^a support). Most of the Vss supply an object (but not Tg^O or Sy) and LXX also adds ἐπὶ τὴν γῆν from 4.3.

לפני פרעה (7.9) LXX adds καὶ ἐναντίον τῶν θεραπόντων αὐτοῦ, from v. 10b.

יהי (7.9) SP reads ויהי (no Qumran evidence survives) and LXX, Vulg, Tg^O and Sy also have 'and'. As the easier reading it is probably secondary: for MT see Note h on the translation. The verb is rendered as future by LXX, but jussive in Vulg: the Aram. renderings could be taken in either way.

לתנין (7.9) Most of the Vss have no difficulty in rendering by words for 'serpent' here: even LXX δράκων can bear that meaning. They presumably took 4.1-3 with its use of נחש as their guide (so Rashi, but not Ibn Ezra!). Aq, however, had κῆτος, to maintain consistency with LXX's rendering in Gen. 1.21; and Sy apparently intended 'dragon' with its *tnyn'* (the same word in Tg^N seems to have had a wider meaning, like its BH cognate). Tg^J adds חורמן, 'venomous', to heighten the drama (perhaps based on the parallelism of תנין with פתן in Deut. 32.33; Ps. 91.13) and also has a long addition comparing the subsequent 'cry' of the Egyptians to the 'cry' of the serpent (נחש) in Genesis 3 when its legs were cut off (cf. Tg^J on Gen. 3.14). The latter is perhaps an attempt to discern the reason why *this* wonder was chosen to warn Pharaoh.

ויבא (7.10) The Vss reasonably take this in the sense 'went in', apart from Sy. Tg^J surprisingly uses the Aphel of על(ל), but cf. 24.18 for the intransitive use. The sing. form is generally retained in the Vss, but in Sy only by 5b1 and 7a1: the Leiden ed. follows the majority reading (cf. Sy in v. 6).[6]

אל (7.10) There is strong support for the reading לפני: SP, LXX, 4QpalEx^m and 4QGen-Ex^a. Both *BHS* and *DJD* XII, p. 27, are inclined to explain it away by influence from the context, where לפני certainly is prominent (twice before פרעה in vv. 9-10). But although the normal expression in Exodus is בוא + אל (cf. 7.26; 9.1 etc.) the combination with לפני is also frequent, both with

---

[6] 7.10 is perhaps the most likely location for the unplaced fr. 37 of 4QExod^c (cf. *DJD* XII, p. 123), if it can be assumed that after פרעה in this fragment there was an omission by homoeoteleuton until the middle of v. 13: there are several other careless omissions in this ms. But there is no simple explanation for the surviving remains of the preceding line if this location is adopted.

reference to Yahweh (Exod. 28.30, 35; 34.34) and to a human king (2 Sam. 19.9; 1 Kgs 1.23, 28, 32; Esth. 8.1; 9.25). The Vss other than LXX support MT, but the weight of the other Heb. witnesses cannot easily be set aside. LXX, as in v. 9, added καὶ ἐναντίον τῶν θεραπόντων αὐτοῦ, to prepare the way for v. 10b.

וישלך (7.10)   Again von Gall's choice of the defective reading for his text may be questioned: more SP mss support it than in v. 9, but most of his early mss have וישליך, as do Sadaqa, all of Crown's mss and Camb. 1846. For the plene form cf. *GSH* §64c. Vulg's *tulit*, 'brought', is a weak rendering of Heb.

את־מטהו (7.10)   LXX again, this time joined by Vulg instead of Sy, ignores the suffix, according to 'good Greek style' (Wevers, *Notes*, p. 97).

לפני־פרעה (7.10)   In this and the following phrase Tg[J] renders לפני 'before the sight of', emphasising that Pharaoh and his servants saw what Aaron did.

עבדיו (7.10)   Sy here (but not in later occurrences) has *ḥ'rwhy*, 'his princes, nobles', correctly perceiving that Pharaoh's courtiers are meant: likewise Tg[G] and Tg[Nmg] 'his rulers'.

גם־פרעה (7.11)   LXX and Sy do not represent the גם.

לחכמים (7.11)   LXX τοὺς σοφιστὰς Αἰγύπτου is more specific and uses a word that had a widespread neutral meaning ('wise, expert') as well as its often derogatory use of the Greek 'Sophists', so 'experts' is a possible rendering here. *BAlex* 2, p. 37, however, notes that in LXX Daniel it is used exclusively of the Babylonian sages and argues for a pejorative meaning here too.

ולמכשפים (7.11)   LXX καὶ τοὺς φαρμάκους (as in 22.17), a rare word which seems like its more common cognates to refer to magic as well as drugs and poison; Vulg *et maleficos* (a word which already in Tacitus had the specific meaning 'sorcerer').

הם (7.11)   No equivalent in LXX, simplifying the sentence: the Three insert αὐτοί. Theod and Aq also characteristically render the preceding גם with καίγε (in place of LXX's καί: cf. O'Connell, *Theodotionic Revision*, pp. 181-82, 253, 275).

חרטמי (7.11)   The Aram. Vss use the same word as for מכשפים (*ḥrš'*), apparently taking הם as 'the latter'. LXX (followed by Symm, Theod) has a different word, οἱ ἐπαοιδοί, the Hellenistic form of a classical word for 'enchanter', which Aq replaced with κρυφιασταί, presumably 'experts in secret arts' (not 'interpreters of dreams', as in LSJ). Tg[J] adds the names of Jannes and Jambres, mentioned by it earlier in 1.15, a tradition already known to 2 Tim. 3.8, but also (without the name of Jambres) to CD 5.18, a passage of which three Qumran copies exist (4Q266 3 ii 6, 4Q267 2.2, 6Q15 3.2). For the fragments of the 'Book of Jannes and Jambres' see Charlesworth (ed.) 2, pp. 427-42, and A. Pietersma (ed.), *The Apocryphon of Jannes and Jambres the Magicians* (Leiden, 1994). Vulg goes astray here (but not in future occurrences of the word) in rendering *per incantationes*.

בלהטיהם (7.11) Some of the best SP mss read בלחטיהם, but this is only an example of the widespread interchange of the gutturals in Samaritan Hebrew (*GSH* §12h). The versional renderings fall into three groups: 'spells' (LXX, Tg^{N,G}, Sy); 'whispered words' (Tg^{O,J}, Aq: in Tg^J with the addition 'of their divinations/diviners' for precision); 'secret things' (Symm, Vulg – with etymological reference to √(לוט): cf. Salvesen, *Symmachus*, pp. 79-80.

מטהו (7.12) Sy adds 'before Pharaoh', an addition based on vv. 9-10 and the statement in v. 11 that the Egyptian magicians 'did the same' as Aaron.

לתנינם (7.12) Tg^J adds 'and at once they turned back to be as at the beginning', a midrashic expansion (for parallels see *AramB* 2, p. 178 n. 9) deduced from the statement that it was the magicians' 'staffs' that were devoured by Aaron's.

ויחזק (7.13) LXX normally renders חזק in Exodus by σκληρύνω (so already in 4.21; cf. its rendering of קשה in 7.3), meaning 'harden'. κατισχύω, which it uses here, does not have this meaning, but means 'prevail' and Wevers (*Notes*, p. 98) rightly invokes this sense here: 'Pharaoh won the first round', or thought he had. Symm follows the usual interpretation with ἀντέστη, 'resisted' (cf. Vulg *induratum est* and Salvesen, *Symmachus*, pp. 71-72). The Tgg use תקף Ithpa. here, lit. 'was strengthened', but it is a word that can refer to various kinds of mental states: Tg^O at least keeps to etymologically appropriate words for each of the three words for 'harden'. Sy *wʾtʿšn* has a similar range of meaning to תקף.

לב (7.13) Tg^J prefixes יצרא, 'inclination', as in 7.3.

שמע אלהם (7.13) Sy *šdr ʾnwn*, 'let them go', picking up the language of the end of 7.2 and elsewhere, or perhaps preparing the way for v. 14. All the other witnesses support MT (but no Qumran ms. survives at this point).

דבר (7.13) The equivalent is missing here in the ms. of Tg^J due to a scribal error: the expected דמליל appears in the other occurrences of the formula (7.22 etc.). LXX adds αὐτοῖς for no obvious reason.

יהוה (7.13) Tg^G and Tg^{Nmg} as usual add 'the Memra'.

MOSES AND AARON BEFORE PHARAOH
(THE FIRST NINE PLAGUES)
(7.14–10.29)

CHAPTER 7.14-25

THE PLAGUE(S) OF WATER TURNED TO BLOOD

7.14 is the introduction to the first main section of a new episode (vv. 14-18), which presents a further instruction to Moses to confront Pharaoh, this time with a warning of a coming catastrophe which will affect the river Nile itself: it will be turned into blood, and all the fish in the river will die. This is followed by a further divine speech, commanding Moses to instruct Aaron to bring about an even greater catastrophe of the same kind (though this time without any reference to the fish) for all the waters throughout the land (v. 19). These instructions are put into effect (vv. 20-21), but the Egyptian magicians are able to do the same, Pharaoh again makes no response and his people are forced to dig beside the Nile to find drinkable water (vv. 22-24). The final verse (v. 25) is best seen as a transition to the next episode, but it is included in this section (in accordance with the traditional section- and [Jewish] chapter-divisions) because of its reference to the Nile, which picks up the central theme of vv. 14-24.

The river Nile, with its annual inundation of the adjacent floodplain, made the development of the great Egyptian civilisation possible in a region where there is little or no rainfall (cf. Deut. 11.10; Herodotus, *Hist.* 2.13-14). Its origin was attributed to the god Re (or Aton), as was its role 'to maintain the people of Egypt' (*ANET*, p. 370; cf. 371 [*COS* 1, p. 46]; 13, 366, 369). On the one hand 'High Niles...refresh the hearts of the common people' (*ANET*, p. 379; cf. 416, 419 [*COS* 1, p. 67]), but a late text shows how failure of the Nile was remedied by a land-grant to the god

Khnum at Elephantine, near to where it was popularly believed that the Nile had its source (*ANET*, pp. 31-32 [*COS* 1, p. 131]). A 'Hymn to the Nile' of the Middle or New Kingdom period celebrated these beliefs, but it also made clear that there was no regular cult of the Nile, only it seems the presentation of offerings at the time of the inundation (*ANET*, pp. 372-73: see further *LexAeg* 4, pp. 480-500; *ABD* 4, pp. 1110, 1115; *DDD*, 1179-80; also H.F. Marlow, 'The Lament over the River Nile: Isaiah xix 5-10 in its Wider Context', *VT* 57 [2007], pp. 229-42 [232-33]). However, some Ramesside stelae at Gebel el-Silsile mention offerings also at the lowest level of the Nile and their dates seem to correspond to a period when there were increasing problems with low Niles and consequent food shortages (*LexAeg* 4, pp. 482, 498-500). One text, the Middle Egyptian 'Admonitions of Ipuwer', refers to the Nile turning to blood shortly after the inundation (*ANET*, p. 441 [*COS* 1, p. 94]), among other dramatic upheavals in the land.[1] There is clearly no direct connection between this description and the present passage, but both invite a search for a scientific explanation of the phenomenon.

Modern observation and science have offered a number of such explanations. Already in the nineteenth century the discoloration was being equated with a phenomenon in the early days of the Nile inundation in late June (Knobel, pp. 63-65: though he offered no scientific explanation and recognised that this had no harmful effect) or with a combination of the unpleasant smell in the weeks before the inundation, when the Nile turned greenish, with a reddening that was also known from elsewhere (e.g. 2 Kgs 3.22-23; Homer, *Il.* 11.52-54; 16.458-61) and due to certain kinds of fungi or algae, for example (Dillmann, pp. 72-73).[2] These explanations readily acknowledged that some features of the story, such as the death of the fish, were due to the storytellers' imagination.

A different, more apologetic, approach was exhibited by G. Hort's articles on 'The Plagues of Egypt' in *ZAW* 69 (1957), pp. 84-103, and 70 (1958), pp. 48-59, which sought to show that all ten plague-narratives (she did not discuss 7.8-13) were based on a connected

---

[1] Propp, pp. 348-49, cites further literary accounts from elsewhere in the ancient Near East.
[2] Flinders Petrie took a similar view (*Egypt and Israel* [London, 1911, repr. 1923, pp. 35-36), as did many others.

sequence of events for which she offered scientific explanations.[3] She rejected Dillmann's view, partly because of the regularity of the phenomenon and partly because the resulting discoloration is pink rather than blood-red. Instead she saw it as the extreme redness caused by earth particles brought down by a very high inundation combined with (somewhat as in Dillmann's explanation) the presence of bacteria and flagellates which deoxygenate the water at night and led to the harmful effects mentioned in the biblical narrative (*ZAW* 69 [1957], pp. 87-95). Because these factors are likely to be due to the waters of the Blue Nile, which rises in Ethiopia, she placed the onset of this plague later than Knobel, in July/August.

Hort's overall approach was rejected on literary grounds by Fohrer (pp. 75-79; cf. D.J. McCarthy, 'Moses' Dealings with Pharaoh: Ex 7,8–10,27', *CBQ* 27 [1965], pp. 336-47 [336-37]), but was still welcomed by J.K. Hoffmeier in 1997 (*Israel in Egypt*, pp. 146-49). However, in the meantime some other proposals had been put forward. Fuller evidence of harmful phytoplanktons (algae) and dinoflagellates was published in the early 1990s, much of it relating to salt water but some to fresh water. J.S. Marr and C.D. Malloy ('An Epidemiological Analysis of the Ten Plagues of Egypt', *Caduceus* 12/1 [1996], pp. 7-24 [9-10, 23 n. 10]; cf. H.M.D. Hoyte, 'The Plagues of Egypt: What Killed the Animals and the Firstborn?', *Medical Journal of Australia* 158 [1993], pp. 706-708) ascribed the plague to freshwater cyanobacteria. In *The Miracles of the Exodus* (London, 2003) C.J. Humphreys apparently combines Hort's idea about soil particles with a poisonous effect of salt-water dinoflagellates in the Nile Delta region as a tidal estuary. According to this the discoloration would extend throughout the land but the death of the fish would be confined to the Delta, the latter being the region to which the Exodus tradition is now seen to relate (pp. 114-18).

Given the complex history of tradition that lies behind the biblical text and the lack of any specific scientific (or even observational) data from the times and places that are likely to be involved (which are themselves not precisely known), it is out of place to speak with any confidence of an explanation for 'the plague' in this case or any

---

[3] Petrie (loc. cit.) also observed that the sequence corresponded to a realistic progression through the year, but he did not claim any causal links between the plagues.

of the others. At the most it is possible to say that certain natural phenomena might have contributed to the formation of the narrative (but we should probably not include the death of fish in estuary regions, since the Mediterranean as a whole is only minimally affected by tides and saline effects are limited to the outermost seaward limits of the Delta [e.g. R. Said, *The River Nile: Geology, Hydrology and Utilization* (Oxford, 1993), pp. 68-78; cf. *LexAeg* 1, pp. 1043-52]). But whether this was through a particular event or through knowledge of recurring phenomena by the storytellers cannot be determined, and so there cannot be any question of a scientific *proof* of the historicity of the tradition. The turning of Nile water into blood in 4.9, after it had been poured out on dry ground, can scarcely be explained in any of the ways suggested: it may well in any case be a secondary addition there (see the introduction to 4.1-9), based on the power attributed to Moses in this passage but without any knowledge of the underlying natural phenomena.

At first sight 7.14 makes a very natural sequel to vv. 8-13, which have demonstrated Pharaoh's unresponsiveness to Yahweh. But closer examination of vv. 14-18 reveals some significant differences in terminology from the preceding section and also a number of references back to the confrontation with Pharaoh in ch. 5 (see the detailed notes). It is only in v. 19, in parts of vv. 20-21, and in v. 22 that similarities to vv. 8-13 appear, most notably in the active involvement of Aaron and the Egyptian magicians, but also in a series of recurrences of the terminology used in vv. 8-13 (again see the detailed notes). The content of the passage too has some puzzling features: sometimes it is only the river Nile itself which is turned into blood, but elsewhere it is all the waters of Egypt; and the plague is brought about sometimes by Moses' staff, sometimes by Yahweh himself and sometimes by Aaron. In addition there are two separate references to Pharaoh's disregard of the plague, in vv. 22 and 23, and v. 20 leaves it very unclear who actually raised his staff to bring it about. It is not difficult to disentangle two different versions of the story, which are preserved virtually complete in the present text of Exodus, as well as what seem most likely to be extracts from a third similar account. At certain points, in vv. 17 and 20, the problems faced by the editor(s) who combined them are particularly clear. The two main components of the story are: (a) vv. 14-18, 20b-21a, 23-25; and (b) vv. 19, 20a, 21b and 22. As already noted, (b) is constructed in almost exactly the same way as 7.8-13 and can therefore be attributed to the Priestly source. Version (a), on the other hand, has numerous links to the non-Priestly narrative in ch. 5. This analysis of the story into two strands drawn from different earlier sources was first proposed by Knobel (pp. 53-54) and has been accepted by most scholars ever since.[4] The explanation is confirmed by the fact that it is possible to see similar patterns of narrative composition still in their original separate form later in the plague cycle: see on the one hand 8.16-28; 9.1-7 (13-35?); 10.1-20, 21-28 and on the other 8.12-15 and 9.8-12 (as well as 7.8-13).[5]

The only issue about the P material that requires some further discussion is whether it is, as most scholars have believed (including recently L. Schmidt, Levin, W.H. Schmidt, Propp and Gertz), part of an originally independent source or a supplement to the older narrative.

Of those who take the latter view Blum concedes that the four plague-stories normally attributed to P (see above: he does not include 7.8-13 in this) must have been taken by the Priestly author from an existing source: the character of these texts leaves no alternative. It is only features of some of the texts which he (following Noth against the great majority of commentators before and after him) attributes to P later in the plague narrative which make it possible for him to sustain in part his 'supplementary' view here (*Studien*, pp. 250-51). These features can readily be explained in a different, more convincing way (see the introductions to 9.13-35; 10.1-20, 21-29; and 11.1-10). Van Seters tartly comments that 'E. Blum...would like to have it both ways' (*Life*, p. 111), but his own discussion brushes aside the arguments against a supplementary view rather than answering them (*Life*, pp. 103-12: based on his earlier article 'The Plagues of Egypt: Ancient Tradition or Literary Invention?' in *ZAW* 98 [1986], pp. 31-39; cf. also 'A Contest of

---

[4] On the source-analysis of the plague-narratives in general see e.g. Carpenter/Harford-Battersby 2, pp. 88-89; Noth, pp. 52-54, ET, pp. 69-71; Fohrer, pp. 60-79; Steingrimsson, *Vom Zeichen*; W.H. Schmidt, pp. 349-67; L. Schmidt, *Beobachtungen*, pp. 58-85; *Priesterschrift*, pp. 10-19; Van Seters, *Life*, pp. 77-112. J. Kegler, 'Zu Komposition und Theologie der Plagenerzählungen', in E. Blum et al. (eds.), *Die Hebräische Bibel und ihre zweifache Nachgeschichte* (FS R. Rendtorff; Neukirchen, 1990), pp. 55-74, offers a discerning assessment of the themes and theology of the plague narratives in their final form.

[5] The story of the frogs (7.26–8.11) is another combined account, though the interweaving is not so intricate. It was natural that the editor would treat the episodes which were clearly about the same subject differently from those which had no exact parallel in the other account.

Magicians? The Plague Stories in P' in D.P. Wright et al. [eds.], *Pomegranates and Golden Bells* [Festschrift J. Milgrom: Winona Lake, 1995], pp. 569-80). He treats the limitation of Priestly authorship to the first four/five plagues as special pleading, designed to preserve the idea that P is an independent source (*Life*, p. 104), rather than giving even the slightest recognition to the fact (there is not even a footnote) that to ascribe later sections of the plague-narrative to P as he does was an innovation of Noth's which was refuted by Fohrer (pp. 63-70; cf. Childs, p. 131); and the clearly independent P accounts of staffs, blood, frogs, gnats and boils are declared summarily to 'have no independent status' and to 'hardly show any great originality' (*Life*, p. 111). Van Seters's main argument for a supplementary view of P here – 'the lack of coherence between the P framework and the series of Priestly wonders' (p. 106) – is groundless (see the introduction to 6.10–7.5; also Gertz, *Tradition*, pp. 84-94, and L. Schmidt, *Priesterschrift*, pp. 10-19 [against Blum]).

The non-Priestly version of the plague requires much fuller discussion, for it raises a major issue about the analysis of the plague-narratives as a whole and indeed about Pentateuchal origins more generally. From the late nineteenth century onwards it was observed that the references to Moses' staff in vv. 15, 17 and 20 and the alternative descriptions (as they were seen) of the plague as both a turning of the Nile into blood and the death of the fish in the Nile pointed to the combination of two alternative accounts of the episode. On this basis it became common to attribute vv. 15b (or even the whole verse), 17b, 20b and 23 to E, and the remainder to J.[6]

Rudolph (pp. 18-19) fully accepted the tensions in the text which had led to this view (against those who, like Eerdmans and Heinisch and more recently Houtman, Van Seters [*Life*, pp. 110-11] and Propp [p. 324], argued that the complexity in v. 17 had a theological or stylistic explanation), but he attributed it to redactional overworking of the J account, perhaps in part by R^P, because the intrusive material had no context or similarity to passages elsewhere. This explanation was taken up by Noth with more confidence (pp. 55-56, ET, pp. 73-74; cf. *ÜGP*, p. 32) and it has become the dominant view in recent scholarship, except for those (see above) who regard the non-Priestly

---

[6] So with occasional minor variations Carpenter/Harford-Battersby, Holzinger, Baentsch, Gressmann, McNeile, Beer, Fohrer, Hyatt and Childs. Wellhausen and Dillmann gave even more to E because they did not distinguish the alternative descriptions of the plague; Smend and Eissfeldt attributed this strand (minus v. 23) to J^1/L, because of links to passages in ch. 4 and the presence of non-E features, a variation given up in the analysis of the plague-narratives by Beer and Fohrer, who elsewhere follow their view.

account as a unity. At first the staff-references were attributed to R^{JE}, as the author of 4.1-17 (esp. vv. 1-5, 7): so E. Zenger according to L. Schmidt [below], p. 97 n. 20, Kohata (pp. 93-94), though she attributes the reference to blood at the very end of 7.17b (and therefore presumably also v. 20b) to R^P, L. Schmidt (*Beobachtungen*, pp. 4-10), along with vv. 16b-17a, and in effect Blum, who attributed them to his K$_D$ reworking of an older plague-story (p. 37 n. 141).[7] More recently, following W.H. Schmidt's lengthy discussion of the issue (pp. 379-82), the tendency has been to ascribe them to the 'final' editor of the Pentateuch (Graupner, pp. 64-66 [R^{JEP}], Gertz, pp. 98-113 [PentR]), despite Van Seters's telling objection (*Life*, p. 111) that this would involve the same redactor eliminating a reference to Aaron's staff (from P) and adding one to Moses' staff – and to what purpose?[8] It is only the turning of water to blood which has a possible origin in the Priestly narrative, but why then does the redactor complicate the story by limiting the phenomenon to the waters of the Nile? Although nearly all critical scholars have seen a literary division between the blood-plague in vv. 17b and 20b and the death of the fish,[9] it is in fact far from clear that this is the case (see the note on v. 17).

The choice between a redactional origin (most likely R^{JE}) and ascription to a parallel account (E?) remains difficult: the latter alternative depends largely on what is decided about the plague of darkness in 10.21-29 and to a lesser extent the references to Moses' staff in 9.23 and 10.13 (cf. also 17.5), which could provide the necessary context for an originally independent version here, which was only partly preserved. But in addition to such considerations, the join in v. 17 remains remarkably abrupt for a redactor reworking a single account: of the parallels cited by L. Schmidt (p. 8: 9.1-7; 11.1-8) neither is as abrupt as here, since they involve third-person references to Yahweh in divine speech rather than a shift in the referent of the first-person pronoun itself. An explanation in terms of parallel sources therefore remains a serious possibility.

---

[7] Van Seters (*Life*, p. 77 n. 1) also says they are secondary, contrary to what he says later (pp. 110-11): this is evidently a relic of the view which he says that he has now retracted (p. 110 n. 32).

[8] K. Schmid's view of this layer is hard to distil from his comments on pp. 146-48, but he evidently regards (some of?) it as post-P (p. 149).

[9] So also Steingrimsson in his impossibly complex reconstruction (pp. 66-68) and Levin (p. 336), both of whom think that the death of the fish belongs to the later of the two layers. Ps. 78.44 supports this (or a combined text) rather than the priority of the death of the fish alone.

Moreover, perhaps some reconsideration of the analysis and attribution of the non-Priestly sections is required in the light of decisions reached about earlier passages. Verses 14 and 17a pick up most closely from 5.1-2, which we have assigned to E, while v. 15(b) and v. 16(aα) are linked to 3.18, 4.1-5 and 5.3, which we have ascribed to J. On this basis the 'staff' sections in vv. 17 and 20 should be from J too, with the remainder of the non-Priestly text probably being from E (except v. 24?). Such a division of the text would identify a context (albeit an incomplete one) for the 'staff' passages as well as straightforward links to earlier chapters of Exodus for both strands of the non-Priestly text. Verse 15aα might also be from E: it duplicates the remainder of the verse, which could originally have continued directly from 6.1(J). It remains to be seen whether such a sub-division would create impossible problems for the analysis of the remainder of the plague-story or not – and the case for two independent sources for the non-Priestly narrative does not depend upon it.[10]

Despite the complexities behind what we may for simplicity call the 'JE' account, its narrative and theological profile and that of the Priestly version can be quite simply described. The latter follows precisely the pattern already seen in vv. 8-13: since Pharaoh is unimpressed by the 'wonder', which his magicians are able to imitate, Yahweh demonstrates his power through Moses and Aaron by the pollution of all the water-supply of Egypt. But again the magicians do the same and Pharaoh makes no response, as Yahweh had foretold. The (older) JE account differs from this in three main ways: Yahweh works through Moses alone, he is instructed to confront and speak to Pharaoh before he executes the plague on the river Nile, and there is no competition from Egyptian magicians. The scene is also briefly sketched and the impact of the plague on the Egyptian people is noted three times. The words that Moses hears and the message which he is given for Pharaoh make an explicit link to the earlier negotiations in ch. 5 and highlight the ignorance of Pharaoh which the plague ('this' in v. 17) is designed to overcome. But it is to no avail: despite 'this' (v. 23) Pharaoh remains implacable: Yahweh's plan seems to be thwarted once again.

---

[10] There is something of a problem in v. 16aβb, which uses language akin to 5.1-2. But perhaps it should be attributed to E too: it would form a good introduction to v. 17a.

The combination of the two (or more likely three) versions of the story leaves the structure of the JE account largely unchanged. Extracts from the Priestly version are added to the older instructions about the plague and its execution, but the main effect is dramatically to widen the scope of the transformation of water into blood. Nevertheless the impression that Pharaoh is still in control is significantly weakened by the inclusion of the Priestly observation that his continued stubbornness is 'as Yahweh had said'.

[In view of our overall conclusion (see the main Introduction, section 4[ii]) that the redactor of the non-Priestly accounts used the E version as the basis for his plague-narrative, to which he added shorter extracts from J, square brackets in the translations of 7.14–11.10 indicate portions from J as well as later redactional additions.]

14 Yahweh said to Moses, 'Pharaoh (lit. Pharaoh's heart) is slow to understand[a]: he has refused to let the people go. 15 Go to Pharaoh in the morning – he[b] will then be coming out to the water – and stand by the bank of the Nile to meet him. [The staff[c] which was turned[d] into a snake you shall take in your hand. 16 Say to him, "Yahweh, the God of the Hebrews[e]] sent me to you, to say 'Let my people go, so that[f] they may worship me in the wilderness'. But[g] you have still not taken any notice. 17 So this is what Yahweh (now) says: By this[h] you will know that I am Yahweh: I am going to strike[, with the staff which is in my hand,] the water in the Nile[i] and it will be turned into blood." 18 The fish in the Nile will die[j] and the Nile will stink, and the Egyptians will be loth[k] to drink water from the Nile.' 19 *Yahweh said to Moses, 'Say to Aaron, "Take your staff and stretch out your hand over the waters of the Egyptians, over[l] their rivers, their streams[m] and their pools, and all their stores of water[n], so that[o] they may become blood". There shall be blood all over the land of Egypt, even in vessels of wood[p] and stone.'* 20 *Moses and Aaron did just as Yahweh had commanded* [and he raised (his hand) with the staff[q] and struck the water in the Nile in front of Pharaoh and his servants,] *and all the water in the Nile was turned into blood.* 21 The fish in the Nile died[j], the Nile stank and the Egyptians could not drink water from the Nile. *The blood was all over the land of Egypt. 22 But the magicians of Egypt did the same with their spells[r] and Pharaoh's heart was stubborn: so he*

did not listen to them, as Yahweh had said. 23 Pharaoh turned[s] and went into his house and did not pay any attention even to this. 24 All the Egyptians dug for water[t] to drink around the Nile, because they could not drink from the water of the Nile. 25 Seven days were completed[u] after Yahweh struck the Nile.

Notes on the Translation

a. Heb. כבד, here used for the first time of the 'hardening' of Pharaoh's heart. See *THAT* 1, 794-812 = *TLOT* 2, pp. 590-602; Wilson, 'Hardening', pp. 18-36; *TWAT* 4, 13-23 = *TDOT* 7, pp. 13-22. The underlying meaning 'heavy' is comparatively rare (Exod. 19.16; Isa. 32.2; cf. the noun כֹּבֶד in Prov. 27.3), examples being greatly outnumbered by a variety of metaphorical uses, some positive (cf. the noun כָּבוֹד, 'glory, honour') and some negative. The combination with 'heart' (Heb. לב: see the Explanatory Note on 7.13) occurs eight times elsewhere in the OT: in the Qal, as here, in 9.7; in the Piel in 1 Sam. 6.6 (twice); and in the Hiphil in Exod. 8.11, 28; 9.34 (all with Pharaoh as the subject); 10.1 (with Yahweh as the subject); 2 Chr. 25.19 (with a human subject). There are also two examples of the Qal part./adj. in Sirach (3.26, 27). The sense of such 'heaviness of heart' can probably best be inferred from the similar usage for other human faculties: the eyes (Gen. 48.10); the ears (Isa. 6.10, 59.1; Zech. 7.11); speech (Exod. 4.10 [twice]). There it refers to inability to perform an organ's usual function (cf. Wilson, p. 22). Depending on whether the volitive or the cognitive function of the heart is in view, this could imply either stubbornness or lack of understanding (for the latter cf. Schmidt, p. 384, Wilson, pp. 14-22, Propp, p. 323). Most of the passages in question could be understood in either way, but the context in Sirach suggests a contrast between wisdom and the lack of it and this would also perhaps fit 2 Chr. 25.19 better. One who is 'heavy-hearted' would then be similar to, but perhaps not quite as bad as, the person who is חסר־לב, 'mindless' (Prov. 6.32 etc.). Such an interpretation would fit well with the prominence of the verb ידע, 'know', in reference to what Pharaoh needs to do in the plague-narratives (7.17; 8.6, 18; 9.14, 29; 10.7; 11.7). If correct this would mean that כבד in this context has a quite different meaning from חזק (on which see the Note on 7.13) and קשה (7.3), which do refer to stubbornness of will, with consequences for the understanding of the narrative strands in which they occur. It is true that the (usually self-)causative construction implies a definite decision or action, but even elsewhere biblical writers envisage a determined refusal to acknowledge truth: the 'fool' is culpable, not pitiable (cf. Prov. 1.22, 28; *TWAT* 4, 280-83 = *TDOT* 7, pp. 267-69).

b. Heb. הנה, without the subject pronoun that would be expected (see Text and Versions), as in 8.16. This abbreviated form of expression is quite common with the third m.s. pron. (and especially after הנה), less so with others (see GK §116s, JM §154c). הנה in this context seems to have a weak deictic sense, perhaps serving as little more than a marker for the circumstantial clause that follows (one might thereby justify the translation 'as he is coming out' of e.g. NJPS, NRSV), but embodying the 'participant perspective' identified by Andersen, *Sentence*, pp. 94-95.

c. The Heb. places the object first for emphasis, to reintroduce a topic that has not been mentioned for some time in the non-Priestly narrative (note also the use of נחש as in 4.3, not תנין as in 7.9-12).

d. Heb. נהפך, instead of the simple היה, 'become', in both 4.3 and 7.9-12, but as below in vv. 17 and 20 of the water turning to blood (which is also expressed by היה in 4.9). הפך Niphal is used both of things which change themselves (reflexive) and those which are changed by outside influence (passive), cf. BDB, pp. 245-46. It is not always easy to be sure which is meant, but here a passive interpretation seems most appropriate (cf. the Qal with Yahweh as subject in Pss. 78.44; 105.29).

e. The subj. precedes the verb, possibly just because this is an introduction to what follows (cf. JM §155nd, GK §142b). But Muraoka has identified a particular tendency for a divine subject to precede the verb, especially in reports of a theophany as here (*Emphatic Words*, p. 35; JM §155ne; cf. Gen. 31.29; 48.3). The effect is certainly to direct Pharaoh's attention from Moses to his god at the outset.

f. Heb. ויעבדני, final *waw* plus jussive/imperfect as e.g. in 5.1, which the present statement very likely paraphrases (see Note b on the translation there).

g. Heb. והנה. For הנה in an accusation cf. Jer. 6.10; Ezek. 22.6 (*THAT* 1, 506 = *TLOT* 1, p. 380): the particle perhaps expresses astonishment here, after the adversative *waw*, with which cf. Isa. 5.7b; 22.13 (cf. *IBHS* §40.2.1.e; also for the element of surprise Andersen, *Sentence*, pp. 94-96).

h. Heb. בזאת, with the fem. as often standing for the neuter in a summarising sense (cf. GK §136b, and more generally §135p; also the list of exx. in BDB, pp. 261-62), here with reference to what follows (cataphora), as often acc. BDB, p. 261, with ידע (a combination taken up in the Johannine ἐν τούτῳ...ὅτι [1 Jn 2.3 etc.]).

i. Heb. על־המים אשר ביאר, lit. '*over* the water...'. Heb. נכה Hi. is generally followed by a direct object (as in vv. 20 and 25), but occasionally the object is preceded by ב (e.g. 17.6; Num. 11.25; 1 Sam. 19.10 etc.; other prepositions such as אל and בין [and על in 1 Kgs 22.24; Mic. 4.14] are used to indicate a secondary effect). The only other case of על alone (apart from where it indicates the reason, as in Lev. 26.24) seems to be Jon. 4.8, of the sun on Jonah's head, perhaps because there is no physical contact. That may be the point here, just as elsewhere Moses or Aaron is commanded to 'stretch out' his hand or staff over the waters (v. 19) or the land (for other exx. see BDB, p. 755, s.v. 5).

j. The Heb. unusually has the subj. הדגה first, producing a chiasmus with the previous clause(s) and perhaps making the death of the fish a distinct event rather than the result of the water turning to blood.

k. Heb. ונלאו. The standard rendering of √לאה, 'be weary', is rather rare in the literal sense and only weakly supported by cognates in other Semitic languages (but see *Ges18* and *DNWSI*, p. 561, for a likely cognate (loanword?) in Jewish Aramaic). Psalm 68.10 and Isa. 16.12; 47.13 are the clearest examples of the Niphal, cf. Jer. 12.5 in the Hiphil and the derived noun תלאה, 'weariness, hardship'. A metaphorical use of mental or emotional weariness (sometimes equivalent to 'fed up') is much better attested, including probably all the examples of the Qal in BH as well as several of the Niphal and Hiphil (cf. *TWAT* 4, 410-11 = *TDOT* 7, pp. 395-96). Such a sense is found in combination with an inf. construct (Isa. 1.14; Jer. 6.11; 15.6; 20.9; Prov. 26.15), where it comes close to the meaning 'be unable' (LXX here: cf. the association with לא יכל in Jer. 20.9 and here [v. 24]), but probably more exactly 'be *no longer* able' (so *HAL*, Schmidt against *DCH*, *Ges18*), which fits the present context well, though perhaps without sufficient recognition of the negative feelings conveyed by the verb, hence our choice of 'be loth to'. Houtman's 'force themselves' (p. 34) has no real parallel.

l. Heb. על, without the conjunction, because the following list fills out the content of על־מימי־מצרים: asyndeton is common in such situations, which are essentially a variety of apposition (cf. Deut. 3.7 and other exx. in JM §131m).

m. The Heb. repeats the על, and without the conjunction (but see Text and Versions), according to a common way of constructing a list in which *waw* is only found with the final item (see Note d on the translation of 1.1-6, and JM §132g). יאר in the plural (as in the same sequence in 8.1: contrast the sing. elsewhere in this passage) reflects the appellative origin of this Egyptian loanword (see Note jj on the translation of 1.7-22). The plural is generally found in poetry and seven of the seventeen occurrences are in Ezekiel. Psalm 78.44 uses it in an allusion to the blood-plague in Egypt, a rare (unique?) case of that psalm coinciding with the Priestly version of the Exodus story.

n. Heb. כל־מקוה מימיהם, 'all their collection(s) of water', with the pron. suff. as often related to the nomen regens (or, one might say, the construct phrase as a whole: GK §135n). In Lev. 11.36 מקוה is a generic term for springs and cisterns and its position at the end of the list here suggests a similar comprehensive function in relation to the three expressions which have preceded it, together with other kinds of storage facility like those specified at the end of the verse (cf. the כל here). A collective sing. noun often appears after כל (GK §127c); for *waw* with such a comprehensive expression cf. 1.6; 8.20; 9.19; 10.6. מקוה and the related verb are used of the seas in Gen. 1.9-10. The later technical use of a pool for purification (e.g. M.Mikv. 2.2) does not occur in BH, and the specific term for an artificial pool there is מִקְוָה (Isa. 22.11: cf. Sir. 43.20; 48.17; 50.3); in Sir. 10.13 מקוה appears to have acquired the sense 'reservoir', and this may be present also in (some of) the Qumran occurrences listed in *DCH* 5, p. 460. The BH examples for the meaning 'source' included there (after M. Dahood) are very dubious.

o. Final *waw* as in v. 16 (cf. Note f).

p. Heb. ובעצים. *Waw* here has the stronger sense 'and also' (almost 'even': cf. the exx. in BDB, p. 253, s.v. 1g). עץ and the following אבן have the extended meaning of '*vessels* made of wood and stone' (cf. Text and Versions), as in the second occurrence of ועצים (with similar uses of other words for materials) in 1 Chr. 29.2 (cf. Lev. 15.12). Elsewhere in BH the pairing refers to building materials or to idols. For alternative interpretations here see Houtman 2, p. 37: it is doubtful if 'buildings' of wood and stone could be meant, as he suggests, or that the meaning is 'trees and stones, i.e. springs' (Schmidt and others, following Eerdmans).

q. Heb. וירם במטה. The expression appears to be unique, both in Exodus and more generally. רום Hiphil is elsewhere construed with a direct object of what is raised (so of the staff of Moses in Exod. 14.16). A similar use of ב with the object is found after some other verbs (GK §119q), but possibly 'his hand' is to be understood here by analogy with some uses of נטה (8.1, 13; without יד in Josh. 8.18 (בכידון): מטה as obj. in Exod. 8.12; 9.23; 10.13). Still the expression is odd and could be due to the conflation of two accounts (see the introduction to this section), like MT's unspecific reference to '*the* staff'.

r. Cf. Note l on the translation of 7.6-13. MT here has the expected form בלטיהם, but see Text and Versions.

s. Heb. ויפן. For פנה of turning away prior to departure cf. Gen. 18.22: in combination with הלך (and perhaps בא as here) it became virtually an equivalent for 'depart' (cf. Judg. 18.21; 1 Kgs 10.13).

t. The object of חפר, 'dig', may be the hole (often a well: e.g. Gen. 21.30) that is dug or what is sought for by digging (Job 3.21 and here: cf. with the more general sense 'search for' Job 39.29, but *pace* Houtman that is hardly the sense here).

u. Heb. וימלא. The sing. verb. before a plural subj. is quite common (cf. GK §145o). מלא is regularly used (normally in Qal and Piel) of the passage of time; the Niphal only occurs here in this sense, but its other uses are scarcely distinguishable from those of the Qal too. A set or expected period of time is usually involved (e.g. Gen. 25.24), but a more general use appears also in Ezek. 5.2, Dan. 10.3 and perhaps 1 Sam. 18.26 (if הימים means 'a year') and 2 Sam. 7.12.

Explanatory Notes

14. In contrast to vv. 8-9 Yahweh here speaks initially to Moses alone about how he (alone) is to approach and speak to Pharaoh: it is only in v. 19 that an instruction comparable to v. 9 appears.

This is the first of several indications that vv. 14-25 contain parts of at least two versions of the Nile plague, the first of which (beginning here) originally continued not the Priestly opening to the plague-narrative in 7.1-13 but the non-Priestly narrative of 5.1-23, which concluded with Yahweh's announcement of what he would 'do' (6.1) in response to Pharaoh's intransigence. The new speech-formula, in its original context, indicated the transition to a fresh phase of the story, perhaps after a short pause. The description of Pharaoh as 'slow to understand' (lit. 'Pharaoh's heart is heavy': see Note a on the translation) employs a different verb from those used in 7.3 ('harden') and 7.13 ('was stubborn') and draws attention to the corrective and disciplinary purpose of the plagues in this version of the story (cf. v. 17a). Pharaoh's refusal to release the Israelites will originally have been that recounted in 5.1-4, a passage with which there are several verbal correspondences here (for 'let... go' [Heb. *šlḥ* Piel] cf. 5.1-2: see further the notes on vv. 16-17), but in the present context a reference to v. 13 is natural. The verb 'refuse' (Heb. *m'n* Piel) and the related verbal adjective become a *Leitmotif* of the following narratives, where they appear in warnings to Pharaoh of the consequences if he continues to defy Yahweh's command (7.27; 9.2; 10.3-4: cf. earlier 4.23). Elsewhere the root is particularly common in the book of Jeremiah, where 12 of its 46 occurrences in the OT appear, in a variety of contexts, but in view of the number of occurrences elsewhere this is of no special significance for the origin of the non-Priestly Exodus narrative (which may well have inspired the wording of Jer. 50.33).[11]

15-16. The command to Moses to meet[12] Pharaoh 'in the morning' (as in 8.16 and 9.13; cf. 24.4; 34.2) probably implies that the instruction was given in the night, perhaps through a dream (so Houtman, Propp; Num. 12.6-8 distinguishes Moses' encounters with Yahweh from prophetic dreams). The meeting is to take place by the Nile; as in 8.16 no reason is given for Pharaoh's presence there (unlike that of a previous Pharaoh's daughter in 2.5, which was for her to

---

[11] See further *TWAT* 4, 616-18 = *TDOT* 8, pp. 44-46.

[12] Propp astutely suggests that the verb 'go' (Heb. *hlk*) is used when an outdoor meeting is envisaged (pp. 206, 326); presumably in contrast to the more frequent 'go in' (Heb. *bôʾ*), as in 3.18; 5.1, 23; 6.11; 7.10, 26; 9.1; 10.1, 3. In 8.16, where the meeting is again by the Nile, neither of these verbs is used.

bathe), but in this case the subsequent narrative requires it. All the great royal capitals of Egypt, like most of the other ancient settlements there, were close to the Nile: recent exploration and textual study has given a vivid picture of the ancient waterways and city buildings at Qantir in the eastern Delta region, which is now agreed to be the site of Pi-Ramesse (biblical Rameses), the capital in what is most likely to be the period to which the Exodus tradition refers (see the notes on 1.11 and further references in my 'Was there an Exodus?', p. 28). Moses is to take with him the staff which had turned into a snake: the Heb. word is *nāḥāš* as in 4.3, not *tannîn* as in 7.9-12, a further sign that the beginning of the Nile plague story was originally linked to earlier chapters rather than to 7.8-13. This staff, which is distinct from Aaron's staff (v. 19), reappears in vv. 17 and 20 in difficult contexts which suggest that the non-Priestly narrative itself has a complex literary history: see the Notes there and the introduction to this section.

Moses is told to begin his address to Pharaoh by recalling his previous encounter with him: his words are largely based on words found in 5.1 and 5.3 (cf. 3.18) and in fact unite elements of what we have called there 'Formula A' and 'Formula B'. Such intermingling of the two formulae is a recurring characteristic of the plague-narrative and its implications will be examined in the introductions to each section. Two features here are not characteristic of the earlier examples of either formula, although both are widely attested in the Exodus narrative as a whole. The first is the use of the verb 'send' (Heb. *šlḥ* Qal) of Moses' mission: it has appeared seven times in the account of Moses' commissioning in 3.1–4.17 (3.10, 12, 13-15; 4.13 (2x): i.e. in both the 'E' and the 'J' versions) and twice in the following narratives (4.28; 5.22), but this is its last occurrence in Exodus. The second feature is the displacement of more specific verbs denoting worship by 'serve' (Heb. *'bd*), as in 3.12 and 4.23 and then repeatedly in the non-Priestly plague-narrative (7.26; 8.16; 9.1, 13; 10.7), where the verb 'sacrifice' only appears in ch. 8, in two responses of Pharaoh to Moses and Aaron (8.4, 21) and in the dialogue that follows the second of these.

17-18. Like the reference to taking no notice (lit. not 'hearing') at the end of v. 16, the introduction to Yahweh's new message for Pharaoh picks up the language of the latter's reply to Moses and Aaron in 5.2: his 'I do not know Yahweh' there is answered by 'you will know that I am Yahweh', in the same 'recognition-formula' that has already been used in Priestly contexts in 6.7 (see the notes on 6.6-8) and 7.5 (the latter with reference to the Egyptians). Its appearance here and (with minor variation) in 8.18 is important evidence for its currency outside the main concentration of its occurrences in P and Ezekiel (cf. also 1 Kgs 20.13, 28). The actual announcement of the Nile plague oddly combines two different perspectives on it, since 'I am going to strike' must in the context imply Yahweh's own intervention (as is explicit in v. 25: cf. also the parallel expressions in 7.27; 8.17; 9.3, 9, 18; 10.4 [Wellhausen, p. 64]), whereas 'with the staff which is in my hand' equally clearly points to an action by Moses (cf. v. 15b). A popular solution to the problem limits Yahweh's own words to 'By this you will know that I am Yahweh' (cf. the punctuation in NEB, REB and NRSV), but Childs (p. 128) rightly describes this as 'artificial': 'By this' necessarily requires an explanation by the same speaker (as e.g. in 1 Sam. 11.2). The fact that Moses acts as Yahweh's representative no doubt gave (and gives) the present text a certain plausibility, but it remains extraordinary and unparalleled from a linguistic point of view, and it is most likely to be due to the combination of two different non-Priestly presentations of the story (in P it is Aaron's rod which is used, both here [v. 19] and elsewhere in the plague-stories). On the different possibilities for such an explanation see the introduction to this section: the awkwardness of the present text seems more likely to be due to the combination of extracts from two older accounts than to a redactor's amplification of a single account.

The description of the plague in vv. 17b-18 comprises a succession of four stages: the waters of the Nile will be turned to blood, the fish in the Nile will die, the Nile will stink, and the Egyptians will be loth to drink water from the Nile. A sequence of cause and effect is evidently envisaged and exactly the same pattern is followed in vv. 20b-21, with the same recurrence of the word 'Nile' (Heb. $y^e\,’ôr$). The latter is surely a deliberate way of highlighting the object of Yahweh's attack as the river which was so vital to all aspects of life in ancient Egypt: it is a very apt place for the non-Priestly plague-narrative to begin.[13] The sequence brings together two distinct

---

[13] A similar threat to the Nile (and therefore to Egypt), in the form of a drought, is portrayed in prophetic style in Isa. 19.5-10: see the recent study of H.F. Marlow, 'The Lament over the River Nile: Isaiah xix 5-10 in its Wider Context', *VT* 47 (2007), pp. 229-42.

motifs, each well grounded in the Egyptian background: the turning of the Nile to blood, with the consequence that it becomes undrinkable, as in the Admonitions of Ipu-wer (ii 10; *ANET*, p. 441, *COS* 1, p. 94), no doubt a reference to the periodic discoloration of the Nile which continues to the present day, and the death of the fish in the river, removing an important source of food (see the references in Schmidt, p. 385, and the 'Prophecy' of Neferti, 27-31: *ANET*, p. 445, *COS* 1, p. 108). A number of commentators have suggested that these two motifs belonged originally to two separate versions of the story, since either one alone would have been sufficient to make the Nile's water undrinkable (see the introduction to this section), but there are no signs of literary unevenness either here or in vv. 20b-21.

19. Moses' message for Pharaoh is followed by Yahweh's instructions which he is to pass on to Aaron, but surprisingly these have a much wider plague in view, affecting not only the Nile itself but all the water in the land of Egypt, even that contained in vessels of wood and stone (for this as the meaning of the last two words of the verse see Note p on the translation). This points to the incorporation here of part of a different version of the story and the precise verbal parallels with v. 9 mark it as a further extract from the Priestly account.

20-21. The account of the plague itself contains elements of both main versions of the story: the beginning of v. 20, with its mention of Aaron as well as Moses and the verbal parallel to v. 10, and the end of v. 21, with its reference to water turning to blood throughout the land, belong to the Priestly version; while the remainder, as already noted, follows very closely the wording of the warning to Pharaoh in vv. 17-18.[14] This combination of two versions of the story (or even three, if the second non-Priestly version identified in vv. 15 and 17 is included) is probably responsible for the long-standing debate (cf. Childs, p. 128) about who is the subject of the verbs 'raised' and 'struck' in v. 20. In the Priestly narrative the 'execution-formula' is usually followed by a specific verb with a

---

[14] A minor but significant variation in terminology which is maintained throughout this passage is the use of the verb 'turn' (Heb. *hpk* Niph.) in the non-Priestly version to describe the change from water to blood (vv. 17, 20: cf. v. 15 on Moses' staff), whereas the Priestly version uses 'become' (Heb. *hāyāh*: vv. 19, 21: cf. vv. 9-10).

named subject corresponding to Yahweh's command, usually Aaron (cf. v. 10; 8.2, 13: in 9.10 it is Moses): it is omitted here, apparently, to avoid contradicting the expectation encouraged by the preceding verses that it would be Moses who would use his staff over the Nile.[15] In fact, as both v. 17 and v. 25 suggest, one strand of the non-Priestly version attributed the striking of the Nile to Yahweh himself, and so originally Yahweh will have been the subject of 'struck' here too, before it was combined with the immediately preceding clause. In the latter 'raised' (Heb. *rwm* Hiph.) is a new verb in the present context and is found only here in the plague-narratives, but it appears with reference to Moses' staff in 14.16.

22-24. The imitation of the plague by the Egyptians (with no explanation of where they found water to turn into blood) and Pharaoh's continued stubbornness are described in v. 22 in almost exactly the same way as in the earlier Priestly section in vv. 11 and 13, except that this time there is no indication of the superiority of Moses and Aaron's power as in v. 12. In v. 23 Pharaoh's lack of response appears again, this time in language which in various ways recalls the opening (non-Priestly) verses of the section: he returns home from the visit to the Nile anticipated in v. 15 (but not actually recounted, as is typical of these narratives), it is literally his 'heart' that pays no attention (cf. v. 14) and 'even to this' (*zō't*) echoes in a contrasting way 'by this' (*zō't*) in v. 17. The presence of elements of two accounts (at least) of this plague is therefore visible right to its end. The final motif in v. 24 evidently belongs to the non-Priestly version because of its focus on the Nile and the specific connection with vv. 18 and 21. It exposes, as Houtman points out (p. 39), the contrast between Pharaoh's indifference and the dire straits of his people, but also their resourcefulness: there is no reason to assume that the search for clean water underground was a failure (against Houtman, p. 30).

25. The finale, with its reference to the Nile specifically, is again from the non-Priestly version and it leaves no doubt that the agent of the plague is Yahweh himself. The verse serves as a transition

---

[15] LXX and Sy add 'Aaron' as the subject here, and Tg^J specifies the rod which Moses is to take in v. 15 as Aaron's to remove the ambiguity (see Text and Versions). The medieval Jewish commentators (Rashi, Ibn Ezra, Rashbam, Nachmanides) also took Aaron to be the subject here, but debated why he had displaced Moses.

between this episode and the next;[16] it is the only case of a definite interval between the plagues being mentioned, and suggests that Pharaoh was being given time to reflect on what had happened before the onset of the remaining challenges to his power.

Text and Versions

ויאמר (7.14)   SP has וידבר as it did in v. 8 for MT's ויאמר and this time 4QpalEx^m is extant and supports the variant. דבר is frequently used in the Exodus narrative, but usually with לאמר or another form of אמר if direct speech follows (9.1, 32.7 and 33.7 seem to be the only exceptions in MT). Here the variant could be due to דבר יהוה at the end of the previous verse.

יהוה (7.14)   Tg^G and Tg^Nmg as usual add 'the Memra of'.

כבד (7.14)   LXX, Vulg and Tg^O reflect the change in terminology from v. 13 by using equivalents with a sense of 'heaviness', but the other Tgg and Sy keep to the same renderings, in the former case by using a word (תקף) which can mean 'heavy' as well as 'strong'.

לב (7.14)   Tg^J prefixes 'the inclination of', as in v. 13 etc.

מאן לשלח (7.14)   LXX τοῦ μὴ ἐξαποστεῖλαι (cf. OL *ne dimittat*), 'so as not to let go', probably read מאן as מ + אין, which occurs once in this sense with an inf. (Mal. 2.13), though without the ל. ל is, however, generally found after the vb. מאן, and the reading of MT, SP and the other Vss. (inc. Aq) is to be preferred.

העם (7.14)   SP prefixes את, 'improving' the grammar: 4QpalEx^m does not survive here. Tg^Nmg has a variant עמיה, 'his people': this is out of place (and not supported by Tg^G): the suff. may have come from the previous word in Tg^N.

אל־פרעה (7.15)   One ed. of SP (Sadaqa) reads לפרעה (a reading also cited from a late hand in another ms. by Baillet, 'Corrections', p. 29), with an interchange that is more widely attested elsewhere (cf. 8.21; 10.24): 4QpalEx^m agrees with MT, like the other SP mss Vulg has *ad eum*, abbreviating as often.

הנה (7.15)   4QpalEx^m prefixes *waw*, but SP agrees with MT. The Catena group of LXX mss also adds 'and', probably independently (cf. Wevers, *Notes*, p. 99), to produce a smoother text. After הנה SP and 4QpalEx^m add הוא as the subject of the participle, and LXX's αὐτός must reflect a similar *Vorlage*: this is the easier reading and so secondary, as Heb. idiom allows the omission of the pronoun (cf. Note b on the translation). Tg^N,G also have the independent pronoun, but probably for reasons of Aramaic grammar.

---

[16] As the paragraphing in the NRSV brings out well. There is therefore no need to arbitrate between those who see it respectively as the conclusion of what precedes and as the beginning of the next episode (to the adherents of each view listed by Childs [p. 128] may be added Houtman and the MT and SP section-divisions for the former and Propp for the latter).

המימה (7.15) SP lacks the directional ending, as in 1.22, but the variation is sometimes the other way round (see Text and Versions on 4.19-20). The shorter forms are probably more original where the witnesses are divided: the tendency of scribes was to make the meaning more explicit (cf. the previous note). Tg^{N,G} render 'by the river', anticipating the wording later in the verse; they and Tg^F also prefix 'to cool himself'. A different motive is provided by Tg^J's addition, 'to observe [reading למנטור with Ginsburger for the ms. reading למפטור, cf. 8.16] omens over the waters like a magus', from B.M.Qat. 18a. Rashi and other medieval commentators offered more practical explanations.

ונצבת (7.15) LXX* rendered precisely with καὶ στήσῃ (cf. the early papyrus 835), but Vaticanus has καὶ ἔσῃ. The origin of this variant may have been clarified by καὶ σὺ ἔσῃ in papyrus 866, which is more obviously a corruption of the true reading (Minutoli and Pintaudi, '*Esodo* [IV 16 – VII 21]', p. 47).

היאר (7.15) The Vss universally render this as a common noun, 'river' (so still Luther, AV and RV: RSV has 'the Nile'): cf. the use of the pl. in v. 19 and Note m on the translation.

והמטה (7.15) Tg^J 'the staff of Aaron', making an explicit link back to vv. 8-12 rather than 4.1-5 (see also the following note). This may be designed to avoid the suggestion of the original text that both Moses' and Aaron's staffs were involved.

לנחש (7.15) The renderings of LXX, Sy and Tg^O reflect the distinction in the words for 'snake' between this verse and 4.3 on the one hand and vv. 9-12 on the other. But the other Tgg use the same word throughout, and Vulg *draconem* (cf. OL) also reflects an indifference to the variation.

תקח (7.15) Sy *sb*, imperative, as at the beginning of the verse.

ואמרת (7.16) Sy *w'mr*, imperative, as in v. 15.

יהוה (7.16) LXX κύριος, = MT, now allowing the identity to be expressed, whereas in 3.18 it was ignored to conform to 5.3 (cf. Wevers, *Notes*, p. 100). Not too much should be made of this, since in LXX as well as MT the divine name has already been part of the confrontation between Moses and Pharaoh.

העברים (7.16) For the Tg renderings see Text and Versions on 5.3. Tg^G as usual agrees with Tg^N.

לאמר (7.16) Sy *w'mr*, perfect, avoiding the Heb. inf. construction (as of course LXX and Vulg do in a different way).

ויעבדני (7.16) LXX ἵνα and Vulg *ut* make the 'purpose' meaning clear. Vulg *sacrificet* is imprecise (as in 7.26; 8.16; 9.1, 13; 10.3) and presumably influenced by its rendering of זבח in 5.3 and 8.17 (in 4.23 it had the more specific equivalent *serviat*). Tgg as usual render the suffix 'before me'.

לא שמעת (7.16) Tg^{O,J} (and Tg^{Nmg}) render the verb with קבל to bring out the sense of 'obey' (*AramB* 6, p. 71 n. 1): cf. Vulg *audire noluisti* (with an echo of *non vult* in v. 14).

כה (7.17) Vulg *haec igitur* makes the implied connection explicit, as the καὶ νῦν of some LXX mss does more weakly (though reflecting ultimately the frequent use of ועתה in BH to make such a link (cf. 3.10; 4.12).

יהוה‎[lo] (7.17)   Tg[Nmg] adds 'the Memra of'.

באת‎ (7.17)   Tgg (except for Tg[O]) add different words with similar sounds to specify either a temporal (Tg[N,G] זמנא‎, 'time') or a causal (Tg[J] סימנא‎, 'sign') meaning: the latter is most likely correct, cf. גם לזאת‎ in v. 23.

ביאר‎ (7.17)   The corrector of ms. F of LXX has ῥείθρῳ, 'stream, channel' in place of the original translation's ποταμῷ, a correction which is regularly recorded from 1.22 onwards and serves to maintain the distinction between Heb. נהר‎ and יאר‎ in a manner typical of the Jewish revisers and especially Aq, to whom it is attributed in v. 19.

ונהפכו‎ (7.17)   Sy has *wnthpkwn wnhwwn*, 'and they turned and became', evidently not being comfortable with *hpk* Eth. alone for 'change into' (Payne Smith gives no examples, only one for the Peal). In vv. 15 and 20 *hwy* alone is used to render הפך‎ Niphal.

ביאר‎ (7.18)   SP agrees with MT, but 4QpalEx[m] has בת[ו]ך היואר‎ (and apparently the same in the expansion after this verse: see below). בתוך‎ represents 'an emphatic *in*, in the very heart and midst of' (BDB, p. 1063). It is used e.g. in Exod. 9.24; 11.4; 12.49; 24.18 and 6 times (with הים‎) in chs. 14–15, but only once of a river, in Ezek. 29.3, perhaps significantly for this variant, of Pharaoh as a (?) crocodile בתוך יאריו‎. In one other place, 11.3, a Qumran ms. (2Q2) has substituted בתוך‎ for ב‎, but it may have been influenced by the occurrence in 11.4. There are no variants in what is preserved of 4QGen-Ex[a] and 4QEx[c] here, but reconstructions based on line-length in the context suggest that both had a shorter text, probably due to homoeoteleuton between two of the three occurrences of יאר‎ in this verse.

ונלאו‎ (7.18)   LXX οὐ δυνήσονται 'probably comes close to what MT meant' (Wevers, *Notes*, p. 101), but is likely to be based on v. 24. The other Vss took up the physical sense of לאה‎ (cf. Note k on the translation): Vulg *adfligentur bibentes* made sense of it, apparently, by understanding לשתות‎ as a gerundive inf. Among medieval interpreters Rashi understood it freely to mean 'will weary themselves to seek healing for the waters' (cf. Sforno, 'to dig for water around the Nile', as in v. 24), but Rashbam and Ibn Ezra gave 'will not be able', the former comparing Gen. 19.11, as Saadya Gaon had earlier proposed.

מן־היאר‎ (7.18)   Here SP has the second of its longer expansions of the Exodus narrative (see the main Introduction, section 2b; and Text and Versions on 6.9), beginning with וילך משה ואהרן אל־פרעה ויאמרו אליו‎ in place of the first two words of v. 16 and then continuing with the remainder of vv. 16-18, with שלחנו‎ in place of שלחני‎ because of the introduction of Aaron as a co-speaker. It thus supplies an account of Moses' (and Aaron's) delivery of Yahweh's message to Pharaoh, which is not explicitly reported in MT and the witnesses that agree with it. Additions such as this were probably made to underline Pharaoh's full responsibility for what followed, since he had a warning of it. This text is reproduced exactly in the Sy[h]mg, and its two mss presumably provide the earliest attestation of the SP text as such, deriving from an earlier Greek version (see further R. Pummer, 'Greek Bible'). An even earlier witness is 4QpalEx^m: although only a few words survive in each line, it is clear that in it essentially the same addition appeared between vv. 18 and 19 of MT. Only the following variations occur: (a) ויאמר for ויאמרו in the introduction, which suggests that at this stage Aaron had not yet been introduced into the text here (the beginning of the addition almost certainly ['probably' according to *DJD* IX, p. 75] stood after the *vacat* at the edge of the preserved portion of the previous line: if ויאמר were the beginning, the *waw* would have been written in the *vacat* above according to the normal practice of this ms. [cf. *DJD* IX, p. 58, and v. 19 below]; unfortunately the word ו/שלחני does not survive); (b) [ו]בת[ן היואר for ביאר, as noted above; (c) מצריים is written *plene*. This kind of expansion of the Heb. text therefore originated no later than c. 100 B.C. (the date of 4QpalEx^m), apparently in a Jewish milieu.

יהוה (7.19) Tg^Nmg adds 'the Memra of', and so perhaps did Tg^G as elsewhere (there is a lacuna).

אהרן (7.19) LXX adds 'your brother': cf. its similar additions in 7.7, 9 and 8.1.

מטך (7.19) SP and 4QGen-Ex^a prefix את to 'improve' the grammar.

נטה (7.19) Tg^O,J and Sy have 'raise', conforming to v. 20.

ידך (7.19) SP and 4QGen-Ex^a again prefix את.

על־נהרתם (7.19) LXX and Vulg prefix 'and', not recognising that the three (or four) expressions that follow are in apposition to על־מימיהם.

על־יאריהם (7.19) The secondary prefixing of 'and' is more widespread in this case (SP, LXX, Vulg, Tg^O,N, Sy: Tg^G has a lacuna): only Tg^J agrees with MT. Tg^O, LXX, Aq and Vulg have the correct rendering 'channels, streams' and possibly Tg^J's ביציהון can have this meaning (cf. Jastrow, pp. 164, 183) as well as 'swamps' (see the next note), so that the emendation in the ed. prin. to פצידיהון, 'trenches, rivulets' (cf. *AramB* 2, p. 179 n. 14), would be unnecessary. In any case an imprecise rendering by words meaning 'well, spring' or 'pool, reservoir' is found in Tg^N,G and Sy and it would not be surprising, therefore, if Tg^J intended a similar (mis)understanding.

ועל־אגמיהם (7.19) The *waw* is not represented by Tg^J, but its evidence is scarcely sufficient for this to be the original reading. LXX and Vulg use words for 'swamps' and Tg^N's ביציהון could certainly mean this. According to Clarke Tg^J has שיקייאון (presumably for הון-; cf. Ginsburger), which means 'their pools' or 'their channels' (in the latter case one might think of an interchange in the renderings of this and the previous noun), while Tg^O,G and Sy use אגם/ *'gm*, which seems in both Heb. and Aram. to allow the meaning 'marshland' as well as the more clearly defined 'pools'.

ועל כל־מקוה מימיהם (7.19) Tg^O has בית כנישת for מקוה here and in Gen. 1.10; Lev. 11.36 (similarly Tg^J,N and Tg^G here): 'collecting-place' and perhaps '(man-made) reservoir', which may also be the implication of LXX συνεστηκὸς ὕδωρ (cf. Wevers, *Notes*, p. 102; *BAlex*, p. 120; Muraoka, *Lexicon*, p. 538) and Vulg *lacus* (unless it simply means 'lakes'). This interpretation would draw on a sense attested in post-biblical Heb. (see Note n on the translation). Sy *rmʾ*, 'pools', perhaps also has this in mind: it lacks an equivalent to כל by homoeoteleuton or by assimilation to the preceding phrases.

ויהיו (7.19) LXX ἔσται sing. could be due to the n.pl. τὰ ὕδατα Αἰγύπτου still being in mind as the subject (Wevers, *Notes*, p. 102) or, with the meaning 'there shall be blood', to the influence of the following phrase. In neither case is it necessary to envisage a *Vorlage* different from MT (and SP).

והיה דם (7.19) SP ויהי הדם, which LXX καὶ ἐγένετο αἷμα may also reflect, though the absence of a def. art. suggests that its (clearly erroneous, because premature: cf. v. 21) past interpretation is based on MT. The SP variant, unless due to accidental wrong word-division, is probably the result of a typical assimilation to the end of v. 21, but it is unlikely that it was intended in a past sense here: 'and let the blood be...' makes better sense (mss of SamTg offer both possibilities). Vulg *et sit cruor* could be based on the SP reading: the renderings of the Tgg and Sy are, however, compatible with MT.

ובעצים ובאבנים (7.19) Tg^{O,J} and Vulg add 'vessels of' to make the sense clear: the same explanation appears in a comment that has been thought to derive from Eusebius of Emesa (cf. *BAlex 2*, p. 120: but see also Petit, TEG 10, p. 166, who is doubtful). LXX τε...καί and Vulg *tam...quam* take the repeated *waw* as meaning 'both...and', which is probably not the sense here (see Note p on the translation); Tg^N and some mss of Sy (but not 5b1) omit the first *waw*, apparently missing its significance.

יהוה (7.20) Tg^{Nmg} adds 'the Memra of', as often: there is plenty of room for this in the lacuna in Tg^G. LXX and Sy add 'them', a typical expansion.

וירם (7.20) LXX and Sy add 'Aaron' (cf. Tg^J's addition in v. 15), with the subject specified as it is in 7.10 and 8.2. The shorter text of MT and SP is to be preferred: it and the divergence from the wording of the preceding instructions are probably due to the combination of different versions of the story here (see the introduction to this section).

במטה (7.20) SP במטהו, cf. the addition of 'his', i.e. Aaron's, in LXX, Sy (but not in 5b1) and Tg^N, conforming to the wording in v. 10 and especially 8.13.[17] Again the less specific reading of MT is probably more original and due to the use of non-Priestly material here.

ויך (7.20). All SP mss have this reading except for Camb. 1846, which has the fuller form ויכה. Although this form occurs ten times in MT (GK §76b), it never occurs in the Pentateuch and SP regularly writes ויך (*GSH* §96cβ). The variant spelling could be due to the fact that even this form was read with a final i-vowel (ibid.).

---

[17] On LXX see Elfick, 'The Staff of Moses', pp. 13-14.

ביאר (7.20) 4QExᶜ, here and in v. 21, omits the *aleph*, with a kind of defective orthography which occurs elsewhere at Qumran (cf. Qimron, pp. 25-26: the example of שׁרית[א] is especially similar). 4QpalExᵐ, however, regularly has the full spelling (e.g. v. 18). Fᵇ again attests Aq's rendering (ἐν) ῥείθρῳ (see the note on v. 17).

לעיני (7.20) Clarke's ed. of Tgᴶ has the otherwise unattested form לאחמי both times, but in 9.8 it has the expected למיחמי, which Ginsburger has here: the meaning is not affected.

ויהפכו (7.20) Sy has *whww lhwn*: the use of *hwy* follows its practice elsewhere and *lhwn* is the *dativus ethicus*, underscoring the entry into a state (like the second *lh* in 4.7: J. Joosten, pers. comm.): cf. Brockelmann §196.

כל...ביאר (7.20) Vulg has no equivalent to this expression, an extreme case of its tendency to abbreviate when the meaning is clear. The text of Tgᴺ also abbreviates slightly here, in a way similar to a variant in ms. 5b1 of Sy earlier in the verse.

הדם (7.21) 4QExᶜ reads דם, without the art., assimilating to v. 19 against all the other witnesses. Tgᴶ prefixes 'the plague of' (cf. 7.4-5; 8.13-15, 19; 9.11 for the introduction of this word). A trace of this addition has been found in Tgᴺᵐᵍ for v. 20.

חרטמי (7.22) LXX prefixes καὶ, 'also'. Most versions render the noun as in v. 11 (and later), but Vulg *malefici* is more precise than before (see the notes there) and Tgᴶ has 'astrologers', as also in 8.3, 14-15; 9.11, instead of 'sorcerers'.

בלטיהם (7.22) SP בלהטיהם (some mss again spell בלח-, with confusion of the gutturals) and so apparently also 4QExᶜ (cf. *DJD* XII, p. 105), the spelling which MT has in v. 11. The Vss. generally render as in v. 11, but Vulg this time has *incantationibus*, 'spells', which it used for חרטמי in v. 11 – again an improvement. Tgᴶ adds 'and they turned some of the waters of Goshen into blood', assuming (cf. 8.18, 26) that Aaron's action did not affect Goshen (cf. the addition of *lhwn* in v. 20 by Sy): no parallel to this tradition is known.

ויחזק (7.22) LXX ἐσκληρύνθη (already in 4.21) and Sy *'tʿby* ('swell, harden') recognise the metaphorical meaning of חזק here and regularly afterwards (contrast v. 13).

לב (7.22) Tgᴶ prefixes 'the inclination of' as elsewhere.

שמע (7.22) Symm προσέσχεν (with νοῦν understood, as commonly in both classical and LXX Greek: cf. LSJ s.v. προσέχω 4), 'heed' (not 'hold to', as Wevers, *Notes*, p. 104 n. 25, has), reflects the meaning more precisely than 'hear'.

דבר (7.22) LXX εἶπεν, Sy *'mr* (the latter also in v. 13) are probably translational variants rather than evidence of a different *Vorlage*. On LXX see Wevers, *Notes*, p. 90 (on 6.29): in 9.12 LXX diverges again with συνέταξεν (on which see Wevers, *Notes*, p. 9, with useful statistics). Vulg has *praeceperat*, 'commanded' here, as in v. 13 (cf. 1.17; 8.15, 19; 12.35: but not 9.12!), but this is unlikely to be correct.

יהוה (7.22) Tg^G (cf. Tg^Nmg) prefixes 'the Memra of', as often.

ויפן (7.23) While Tg^O,N render as expected (for N's כיון [Pael] CAL gives 'turn in a direction': cf. the instances cited in *AramB* 2, p. 32 n. 9a), T^Nmg has ואסתכל, in the sense 'looked' which is used in Tg^N for פנה in 2.12; Num. 12.10 (J. Joosten, pers. comm.), and Tg^J has 'relieved himself', based on a euphemistic use of פנה in MH and JAram: some Midrashim cited by Rashi gave this as the original reason for Pharaoh's walk by the river in v. 15.

כל־מצרים (7.24) Tg^J omits 'all', conforming to v. 21.

מים לשתות (7.24) LXX ὥστε πιεῖν ὕδωρ, as if the Heb. object could precede the infinitive: the meaning is much the same, the wording perhaps influenced by that in v. 21 (see also below). Tg^J adds 'but they did not find clear (water)', following the final clause of v. 21 (P) rather than what the J narrative probably intended here: for it only the water of the Nile itself was affected (v. 20).

ממימי היאר (7.24) LXX ὕδωρ ἀπὸ τοῦ ποταμοῦ slightly misrepresents the Heb. here, following instead the similar phrase in v. 21 (likewise 6k10 and late mss of Sy). The versions of the Three are preserved in entirety and, as usual, they correspond precisely to MT at both points where LXX diverges in this verse.

וימלא (7.25) SP וימלאו, with the pl. form to match the following pl. subject. The Vss all naturally render with pl. verbs, but could just as easily be based on the sing. reading, which is grammatically possible in Heb. (see Note u on the translation). SP's reading is a typical 'tidying up' of the grammar and as such secondary.

את־היאר (7.25) Tg^N prefixes 'the waters of' (cf. v. 24) and adds 'and he healed it'; Tg^J has 'and after this the Memra of the Lord healed the river' (cf. Tg^Nmg). The 'healing' of the waters after seven days is also found in several rabbinic passages (cf. *AramB* 2, p. 180 n. 20) and in Philo, *Vita Mosis* 1.101. This probably corresponds to the intention of the original narrator.

Chapter 7.26–8.11

The Plague(s) of Frogs

In modern editions of the Hebrew text, as also in (e.g.) German translations, this episode curiously crosses the boundary of two chapters, although there is no Masoretic section-division anywhere within it. English versions, however, (apart from NJPS, which follows the Hebrew editions) place the whole story in ch. 8, as do editions of the Septuagint and Vulgate.[1] The Samaritan version of the Hebrew does have a division after the first four verses (and another after the extra text which it inserts at this point: see Text and Versions), and so do two Qumran mss (4QEx^c, 4QEx^j, the first without the additional text, the second probably with it: *DJD* XII, pp. 105 and 150), but another does not (4QpalEx^m, although it probably did have the additional text: *DJD* IX, p. 76). The editorial division of the Hebrew text, whatever its exact origins, thus has some early precedent and is probably due to a presumed pause in the action prior to Yahweh's second address to Moses.[2]

As with the other episodes of the plague-narrative, the boundaries are clearly defined by the subject-matter. Within the passage it is equally straightforward to distinguish (i) a first address by Yahweh to Moses, with a message for Pharaoh (7.26-29); (ii) a second address by Yahweh to Moses, with instructions for Aaron (8.1); (iii) the coming of the plague (8.2-3); (iv) negotiations between Moses and Pharaoh about the removal of the plague (8.4-7); (v) its removal and Pharaoh's stubborn reaction (8.8-11). As elsewhere, no account is given of Moses' transmission of Yahweh's messages to Pharaoh and Aaron, except in the Samaritan version and texts related to it (see Text and Versions after 7.29 and 8.1). Moses is told to repeat the

---

[1] As a result the English verse-numbers from 8.5 onwards are four higher than those in the Hebrew printed texts.
[2] On the issue in general see my 'Dividing up the Pentateuch: Some Remarks on the Jewish Tradition', in D.A. Baer and R.P. Gordon (eds.), *Leshon Limmudim: Essays on the Language and Literature of the Hebrew Bible in Honour of A.A. Macintosh* (LHBOTS 593; London, 2013), pp. 45-59.

demand that Pharaoh release the people, or else Yahweh will bring a plague of frogs on Egypt. It is evidently presumed that Pharaoh refuses, and Moses is told to instruct Aaron to bring on the plague. He does so, but so do the Egyptian magicians. Pharaoh then asks Moses and Aaron to pray for the removal of the plague, promising then to let Israel go to worship Yahweh, and after some negotiations about its timing they do so. The frogs die, but when Pharaoh sees this he reneges on his promise.

At two points, at 8.1 and 8.4, the development of the narrative takes a surprising turn (see the Explanatory Notes on these verses), and it is precisely in the section between them (i.e. 8.1-3) that very close correspondences of language and content can be observed with earlier passages that are attributed to the Priestly source (cf. also v. 11b and the Note there), i.e. 7.8-13, 19-20a, 21b-22. The distinction between a Priestly version of the plague in 8.1-3, 11b and a non-Priestly version (usually attributed to J) in 7.26-29; 8.4-11a is already to be found with Knobel and has been accepted by critical scholars ever since, with only minor variations.

Even the newer approaches to Pentateuchal criticism of Blum, K. Schmid and Gertz have accepted this analysis (Blum, *Studien*, pp. 13-15, 36-37; 245, 250, 253; Schmid, *Erzväter*, p. 148; Gertz, *Tradition*, pp. 113-23). Occasionally elements of the 'missing' J account of the coming of the plague have been identified in 8.2b (Van Seters, *Life*, pp. 77-78) or 8.3b (Rudolph, p. 18; cf. Propp, p. 311). But these sections have no particular affinity with J and the expression 'the land of Egypt' is more characteristic of the Priestly account. It is therefore generally assumed that the redactor of J and P omitted the J description of the plague itself to avoid undue repetition, just as he did with the Priestly reference to Pharaoh's stubbornness in v. 11. A further implication of these apparent omissions is that, as most naturally understood, the frogs pericope becomes strong confirmation that the J and P accounts were originally independent, since each in turn seems to have been curtailed in the process of editing and neither as it survives is capable of being the basic narrative to which the other was just a supplement. More than a century ago there were suggestions that traces of a third parallel account could be detected in the passage (Wellhausen, *Composition*, pp. 63, 67; Holzinger, pp. 23-24), but they were based on flimsy linguistic arguments rather than clear signs of disunity and were not taken further. More serious questions were raised about redactional additions to the J account. It is generally thought that the references to Aaron in vv. 4 and 8 and the plural form of the verb 'Make supplication' in v. 4 are secondary and, given their position in the second half of the passage after Aaron's prominent appearance in the verses taken from P, it is logical to attribute them to the redactor who combined the two accounts.[3] In any case it is notable that it is in the context of intercession that Aaron is introduced into the older account, although it is still Moses who negotiates with Pharaoh and intercedes with Yahweh (vv. 5, 8b: cf. 9a, 'what Moses said'). Textual uncertainty and an impression of long-windedness have led some to doubt the originality of part or all of 7.28-29 (Gressmann, *Mose*, pp. 69-71; Fohrer, p. 64 n. 11 [with the additional argument that 'swarm' (Heb. *šāraṣ*) only occurs elsewhere in P: but cf. Ezek. 47.9 and Ps. 105.30); L. Schmidt, *Beobachtungen*, pp. 11-12; Gertz, *Tradition*, pp. 114-15). But the arguments are far from convincing and rest too much on the quest for a shorter version of the story which conforms more closely to the accounts of other plagues. Some variation is only to be expected. Much the same applies to the more widespread suggestion that 8.5-7 have been secondarily expanded (Carpenter/Harford-Battersby, Baentsch, Gressmann, Fohrer, Kohata, L. Schmidt, Levin, Gertz): the reasons given for redactional intervention could just as readily apply to the original author (for some such observations see Gertz, *Tradition*, pp. 115-17).[4] Steingrimsson's radical attribution of 7.26-28 (29) and 8.4-11a* to different layers of composition (*Vom Zeichen*, pp. 68-71) has understandably found no supporters.

If only a single non-Priestly account has been used here, with minimal editorial supplementation, to which of the parallel accounts detected in 7.14-25 is it related? Arguments from narrative continuity based on 7.26, 8.5 and 8.11 (see the Explanatory Notes) point to a connection with the E strand defined there (cf. vv. 14, 17a) and in 5.1-2. The only possible problem with this is the use of 'sacrifice' (Heb. *zābaḥ*) in 8.4, as distinct from 'worship' (Heb. *'ābad*) in 7.26 (and 16b), since it is characteristic of the J account in 5.3–6.1 (cf. 5.3, 8, 17). Gertz has recently drawn attention to this variation, which has generally been overlooked, and has used it as part of his argument that the whole of 8.4-9a is a *Fortschreibung* of the original end to the episode (*Tradition*, pp. 117-21). That is a possible, but very drastic, way to deal with the problem, and it is probably

---

[3] Further sporadic mentions of Aaron occur in 8.21; 9.27; 10.3, 8, 16; 12.31: these could be the work of the same redactor. It is, however, noticeable that all these references to Aaron occur in the main non-Priestly account of the plagues, which we have attributed to E. They might, therefore, like those in 4.27-28 and 5.1 go back to E itself.

[4] The most plausible candidate for a secondary expansion is 8.5b, which provides a pedantic exception in Moses' question to Pharaoh (cf. e.g. Noth) and is probably due to unnecessary harmonisation with v. 7b.

unnecessary. It may be recalled that 5.1 began by speaking of the celebration of a festival as the object of the proposed journey into the wilderness. There is no difficulty in this term being resumed successively by 'worship' (Heb. *'ābad*) and by 'sacrifice' (Heb. *zābaḥ*) as the narrative proceeds. Whereas Yahweh (and so Moses) uses the former in 7.26 (with its overtones of 'service' to Yahweh rather than Pharaoh), it is understandable that Pharaoh should concentrate on the ritual term in 8.4, since he has no intention of conceding that the Israelites are or shall become Yahweh's 'servants' rather than his own. The validity of this solution will of course have to be tested in the further episodes of the plague-narrative where *zābaḥ* is used, but provisionally it seems to require neither the attribution of the non-Priestly account to J nor the derivation of the dialogue in which it occurs from a supplementer of that account.

The redaction has therefore left the extracts from the two underlying accounts largely intact, apart from the omissions noted above to avoid undue repetitiveness. The only possible addition by the redactor may have been to give Aaron a (minor) role in the older material about the removal of the plague. Nevertheless the combined version involves significant departures from the plot of each of its component parts. The insertion of the Priestly extract introduces a human agent (and not Moses but Aaron) into the bringing about of the plague, and indeed allows a corresponding power to the Egyptian magicians, which seems to blunt the force of the challenge to Pharaoh. On the other hand the omission of the Priestly reference to Pharaoh's stubbornness at this point (where it usually appears even in the present text: cf. 7.22) and its deferral to v. 11 makes Pharaoh's lack of response the result of the removal of the plague as described in the non-Priestly version.

Theologically the new element in this episode is the recognition by Pharaoh that (whatever his own magicians may be able to do) it is Yahweh who has power over the plague and so is able to remove it, and that it is only Moses (and Aaron) who can intercede on his behalf with this powerful God. The sequel vindicates this calculation and provides Pharaoh with all the evidence that he needs to see that Yahweh is supreme and incomparable among the gods. But when the pressure is taken off him, he withdraws his permission to let the Israelites worship their God, showing double defiance and untrustworthiness. It seems that Yahweh's plan has been thwarted as a result of his mercy, in the face of a ruthless opponent.

7.26 Yahweh said to Moses, 'Go to Pharaoh and say to him: Thus says Yahweh, Let my people go, so that[a] they may worship me. 27 But if you refuse[b] to let them[c] go, behold I am going to afflict all your territory with frogs[d]. 28 The Nile will swarm with frogs and they will rise up and come into your house and your bedroom and upon your bed, and into the houses[e] of your servants and on your people[f] and your ovens and your kneading-bowls[g], 29 and even upon you[h] and your people and all your servants will the frogs come up[i].' 8.1 *Yahweh said to Moses, 'Say to Aaron, Stretch out your hand with your staff[j] over the rivers, the streams and the pools, and bring up[k] the frogs upon the land of Egypt'. 2 Aaron stretched out his hand over the waters of Egypt, and frogs came and covered the land of Egypt. 3 But the magicians[l] did the same with their spells, and they brought up the frogs upon the land of Egypt.* 4 Pharaoh summoned Moses and Aaron and said: 'Make supplication[m] to Yahweh, so that[n] he may remove the frogs from me and my people, so that[o] I may let the people go to sacrifice[n] to Yahweh'. 5 Moses said to Pharaoh, 'I yield the honour to you![p] From when[q] shall I make supplication[m] for you, your servants and your people, that the frogs[r] may be taken away from you and your houses and be left only in the Nile?' 6 He said, 'From tomorrow[s]'. He said, 'So be it, that you may know that there is none like Yahweh our God. 7 The frogs will depart from you, your houses, your servants and your people — only in the Nile will they be left.' 8 Moses and Aaron went out[t] of Pharaoh's presence, and Moses cried out to Yahweh about the frogs which he had inflicted[u] on Pharaoh. 9 Yahweh did what Moses said: the frogs died out from[v] the houses, the courts and the fields. 10 They were piled up[w] in countless heaps[x], and the land stank. 11 Pharaoh saw that the respite[y] had come and he refused to understand[z]. *He did not listen to them, as Yahweh had spoken.*

Notes on the Translation

a. Heb. ויעבדני. See Note b on 5.1-23.

b. The placing of the participle מאן (cf. GK §52s for the form) before אתה draws attention to it and the inappropriateness of such a response.

c. Heb. simply לשלח, but the pronominal object is easily understood from the preceding verse (GK §117f).

d. Heb. בצפרדעים. The def. art. here (and in 8.1) is anticipatory: see Note o on 2.11-22. צפרדע (collective sing. in 8.2 and Ps. 78.45: otherwise always pl.) occurs in BH only with reference to this plague (outside Exod. 7–8 only Pss. 78.45 and 105.30). It is probably a unique native quinqueliteral (onomatopoeic?) noun in BH (cf. BL §61hϵ), which alone preserves the full spelling, the cognates in Aram., Syr. and Ar. having one less consonant (see *HAL*, p. 983: Akk. *muṣa"irānu*, cited there, is perhaps unrelated).

e. Heb. ובבית, presumably collective (as in 8.20 with a similar *nomen rectum*), unless a single official residence for the courtiers is meant. Although not mentioned in the standard lists (GK §123b, JM §135c), בית seems often to have a collective meaning when followed by a plural *nomen rectum*: cf. בית־ אבתם in 6.14 and the notes there, also JM §136n and further possible examples in Prov. 14.11 and 15.25.

f. Heb. בעמך, so that 'your people' are in MT themselves an additional target of the frogs, a point which seems to be made again in v. 29 (cf. 8.4-6). See Text and Versions on vv. 28-29.

g. Heb. במשארתיך. The specific type of vessel meant is deduced from 12.34 (cf. Tg^{O,J,N}, Sy here): the sibilant is different from the word for 'leaven', though Propp thinks the pointing may be secondary (p. 326, taking up the suggestion first made by Geiger in 1857, which LXX may support). Ibn Ezra and Rashbam (both on 12.34) supported the reference to a utensil, which was adopted in AV and later versions (RV, NEB, NIV, REB: cf. Holzinger, W.H. Schmidt) in the expression 'kneading-troughs'. A wall-painting from the tomb of Ramesses III (reproduced in A. Erman and H. Ranke, *Aegypten und Aegyptisches Leben im Altertum* [Tübingen, 2nd ed., 1923], fig. 71; *IDB* 1, p. 340) might seem to support this. But the large container shown was probably designed to provide the quantity of dough required in the royal bakery, and in a domestic situation something smaller would be used. The ethnographic studies of G. Dalman (cf. *AuS* 4, pp. 46-47, 54) and archaeological comparisons (A.M. Honeyman, 'The Pottery Vessels of the Old Testament', *PEQ* 71 [1939], pp. 76-90 [84 with fig. 7]; J.L. Kelso, *The Ceramic Vocabulary of the Old Testament* [BASOR Supp. Stud. 5-6; New Haven, 1948], pp. 11, 13, 25 with fig. 13; cf. Amiran, *Ancient Pottery*, pp. 192-95, 201-206) support the rendering 'kneading-bowls', which has consequently gained in popularity (RSV, NJPS, JB, EÜ, NRSV, ESV).

h. Heb. בכה, with ה as a mater lectionis on the 2nd m.sing. suffix, as often in the Qumran scrolls (Qimron, p. 23) and occasionally elsewhere in MT (cf. GK §91d, 103g; also §44h for the ending of the 2nd m. sing. perfect of the verb, for which there are also epigraphic examples in Renz/Röllig, *HAE* II/2, p. 45).

i. Heb. יעלו. צפרדע is fem. (cf. 8.2, 5, 7), but here and in 8.9-10 the masc. form is used with it as the more common gender (GK §145o-p).

j. Heb. במטך. This word, which is not present in the execution-formula in v. 2 (in vv. 12-13 it is present in the execution but not in the instruction), replaces the prior instruction for Aaron to 'take' his staff in 7.19: the ב expresses accompaniment rather than instrumentality here (cf. BDB, p. 89).

k. Heb. העל, the apocopated imperative form, which is quite frequent with Lamed He verbs (GK §75gg [cf. cc]).

l. Heb. החרטמים. Codex L mistakenly has the vocalisation הֲחַ֫ (as again in 9.11b).

m. Heb. עתר Hiph. (see the Explanatory Note). An apparently related noun עָתָר, 'suppliant', is used in connection with sacrifice in Zeph. 3.10; 4Q173 1.4 [ע]תרות] (*TWAT* 6, 491 = *TDOT* 11, p. 460; *DCH* 6, p. 643) may contain another = 'supplication'.

n. *Waw* with the jussive expressing purpose (see Note b on 5.1-23).

o. *Waw* with the cohortative can also express purpose (GK §165a).

p. Heb. התפאר עלי. Literally 'get glory over me!' Here it is, to judge from the context, a (unique) conversational idiom expressing (ironic) submission, more specifically the right to choose when the removal of the frogs should begin. The closest analogy is the construction with על used in Judg. 7.2 and Isa. 10.15 of 'taking the credit' when it is not deserved, a slightly different kind of claim to superiority from what is implied here. NRSV 'Kindly' (cf. RSV) is inappropriate (cf. Childs, p. 128; Houtman, p. 48 [there is no 'Please' in his Dutch original]), and there is no need for the speculative philological suggestions in C. Rabin, 'Etymological Miscellanea', *ScrHier* 8 (1961), pp. 384-400 (397).

q. Heb. למתי, the combination with ל only here. As in למחר in v. 6, the ל here expresses the time *at which* something happens or is to happen (cf. BDB, pp. 516-17 [6]).

r. L's vocalisation הַצֲפַרְדְעִים, while perhaps possible (see GK §10g for some analogous extensions of the use of *ḥaṭeph-pathaḥ*), is out of line with the other occurrences of this form in the context, and probably a simple error: other mss have the normal vocalisation (cf. Note i).

s. Heb. למחר. Houtman takes the ל as emphatic (also in v. 19): '*Early* tomorrow'. In view of the common temporal use of the preposition (see note q), this is unlikely.

t. Heb. has sing. verb with composite subject: cf. 4.29 and Note z on 4.18-31.

u. Heb. שם. The meaning could be 'appointed' (cf. 9.5; 21.13), but after the emergence of the frogs a stronger meaning seems to be required, and 2 Kgs 11.16 uses שים with ל of laying hands 'upon' someone (cf. the construction with ב in Exod. 10.2; 15.26 and with על in 2 Kgs 18.14b). NRSV^mg (cf. RSV) gives 'as he [i.e. Moses] had agreed with Pharaoh' (cf. LXX, Vulg: see Text and Versions), taking אשר in its rare sense of 'as' (BDB, p. 83 [8e]), gives some doubtful examples: but see *HAL*, p. 94, where Exod. 34.18 is the strongest parallel). Even then it is hard to get the sense 'agreed' from שים alone.

v. Heb. וימתו...מן. For other examples of 'pregnant' constructions of מן with verbs that have no sense of movement or removal see BDB, p. 578, and GK §119ff. Here 'and ceased' has to be understood after 'died'.

w. Heb. ויצברו. There is no obvious subject in the context, so it is probably an impersonal third person pl. equivalent to a passive (JM §155b).

x. The repetition of חמרם expresses multiplicity: cf. GK §123e, JM §135e and especially Gen. 14.10 and Joel 4.14.

y. Heb. הרוחה, the def. art. referring back to Pharaoh's request in v. 4.

z. Heb. הכבד, lit. 'made heavy (his heart)' (cf. Note a on 7.14-25). The inf. abs. is used here in continuation of a finite verb: GK §113z notes this as being especially characteristic of later books, but some of its examples are likely to be early (Gen. 41.43; Judg. 7.19; 1 Sam. 2.28). The subject is generally assumed to be Pharaoh (as in 8.28; 9.34), but it could in theory be 'the respite'. However, the reference back to this passage in 8.28 (cf. גם there) confirms the usual view.

Explanatory Notes

26-29. The new section begins, like 7.14, with Yahweh's command to Moses to go to Pharaoh with a message about a further plague, this time of frogs. The place of meeting is not specified, but if the verb *bw'* has its stronger sense 'go in' (cf. v. 23) the implication is that Pharaoh is in his palace (cf. Beer, Noth) rather than by the Nile as in 7.15 (and 8.16): cf. 9.1, 10.1.[5] The change of scene helps to reduce the repetitiveness of the narrative. A more significant difference from the previous section is that the plague is only threatened if Pharaoh still refuses to let the Israelites go to worship Yahweh, rather than being a punishment for his prior refusal, as in vv. 14 and 16. The combination of warning and demand becomes a regular pattern from now on (cf. 8.16-17; 9.1-3, 13-14, 18; 10.3-6) until the final two plagues, where there is no opportunity for Pharaoh to change his mind. The omission of 'in the wilderness' from the demand (as in all subsequent cases [8.16; 9.1, 13; 10.3]: contrast 5.1, 3; 7.14) certainly does not mean that this requirement has been abandoned, as the negotiations in 8.21-24 show: the abbreviation is perhaps to focus attention on the act of worship itself rather than indicating any willingness to compromise on Moses' part.

Frogs are mentioned in the Old Testament only in this passage and in two psalms which summarise the plague-narrative (Pss. 78.45; 105.30). They are not specifically listed as 'unclean' in legal texts, but were presumably understood to be included among the

---

[5] 9.13 is not specific in either way, but 'rise up early in the morning' associates it with the passages that mention the Nile; in 10.21 Moses is evidently not with Pharaoh when he acts (cf. vv. 18, 24).

forbidden water creatures that lacked fins and scales (Lev. 11.10-12; Deut. 14.10). Some modern writers (though not apparently the classical Jewish commentators) have deduced that their presence would have polluted the land of Egypt and especially (v. 28) its preparation of food (Houtman, pp. 39-40; Propp, p. 326, though he shows more awareness of the objections to this). But the Israelite laws were about what animals could and could not be eaten, and at least while alive they were not a source of defilement otherwise. In Egypt Heqet, a goddess who was believed to assist women in childbirth and blow the breath of life into new bodies, was portrayed with the head of a frog, which suggests that there frogs were not seen as a religious threat (cf. Cassuto, p. 101; Houtman, pp. 43-44). The sheer unpleasantness and discomfort of frogs crawling everywhere is sufficient to justify their presence being seen as a plague. Psalm 78.45 attributes 'destruction' (Heb. *šḥt* Hiphil) to them, and later Jewish tradition took their effects much further (cf. Houtman, p. 41 n. 65 for references), including an equation with crocodiles (but this is rejected by Ibn Ezra: see Rottzoll 1, pp. 211-12, also Rashi on 8.2 and Cassuto, p. 101). The appearance of large numbers of frogs continues to be a regular phenomenon in Egypt when the Nile inundation recedes, but what is threatened here seems exceptionally severe. Compared with the (temporary?) transformation/discoloration of the Nile, the intrusion of this plague on to the land beside it and its occupants can certainly be seen as an intensification. Schmidt notes the complementarity of the lists of places and people in vv. 28-29 (p. 391): this is disturbed in MT, which reads literally 'and on (or among) your people' in v. 28, and the Septuagint reading is preferable (see Text and Versions). The typical 'oven' of biblical times (cf. Hos. 7.4-7) was a squat clay cylinder with converging walls and an open top, which was later developed into the *ṭābūn* of traditional Middle Eastern households (cf. Dalman, *AuS* 4, pp. 74-126). The 'kneading-bowl' (see Note g on the translation) was evidently portable (12.34) and presumably made of clay too.

8.1-3. The sequel to these instructions is not (except in the Samaritan and related texts: see Text and Versions) an approach by Moses to Pharaoh and an account of Pharaoh's reaction to Yahweh's demand, but further instructions, this time about what Moses is to tell Aaron to do, which also do not refer to any refusal on Pharaoh's part. Yahweh's threatened direct action (7.27) is transmuted into, or replaced by, Aaron's use of his staff. The previous focus on the

Nile alone as the source of the frogs (7.28: cf. later vv. 5 and 7) is extended to cover all areas of water in Egypt, in words that correspond exactly to 7.19, and the frogs spread throughout the land, just as the transformation of water into blood did in 7.19 and 21. The intervention of the magicians follows, just as in 7.11 and 22, with mention of their 'spells'. In the previous two cases this leads into a statement about Pharaoh's stubbornness, which is delayed here until v. 11.

4-7. Instead, and somewhat surprisingly, the success of the magicians leads Pharaoh to plead with Moses and Aaron to secure a respite from the plague, promising that if he is successful in this the people will be allowed to go and sacrifice to Yahweh. Throughout the ensuing dialogue the terminology that is used for the source of the frogs and those affected by them corresponds to 7.28-29 rather than to 8.1-3. Pharaoh's request is that Moses and Aaron should 'make supplication' to Yahweh on his behalf (so explicitly in v. 5: cf. v. 24 with a different Heb. preposition). The verb (Heb. *'tr* Hiphil)[6] is one that is never used of appealing to a human, only to God, and it is a recurrent expression in the plague-story (Hiphil also in vv. 24-25 and 9.28; 10.17; Qal, apparently without difference of meaning, in 8.26; 10.18). A similar use occurs in Gen. 25.21 (with a different Heb. preposition again), but the context does not make it clear whether words alone were the means of Isaac's appeal to God on behalf of Rebekah. In 2 Sam. 24.25 a passive (Niphal) form is used of appeasing Yahweh's wrath by sacrifice (21.14 is sometimes taken in a similar way, but it might refer to prayers rather than the preceding actions). In most cases, however, it is clear that prayer is meant, whether for oneself (e.g. Judg. 13.8) or, as here (and perhaps originally), for someone else.

It is Moses alone who takes on the responsibility of intercession and negotiates its precise terms (v. 5: cf. vv. 8b-9): Aaron simply accompanies him. Intercession is a frequent and even characteristic task of Moses outside the plague-narrative as well (among the bibliography cited by Schmidt [p. 336] see especially Aurelius, *Fürbitter*, for references and discussion, though he virtually ignores the plague-narrative: it is mentioned only briefly in passing, p. 164 n. 147). Already in 5.22-23 Moses protests effectively to Yahweh

---

[6] Cf. *THAT* 2, 385-86 = *TLOT* 2, pp. 961-62; *TWAT* 6, 489-91 = *TDOT* 11, pp. 458-60, and Note m on the translation.

that he is failing to fulfil his promise to deliver Israel from Egypt, and his intercession for them becomes a recurrent part of the narrative from the sea-crossing onwards (Exod. 14.15; 15.25; 17.4, 11 [with an action of raising his hands]; 32-34 passim; Num. 11.2; 12.13; 14.13-19; 16.22; 21.7; Deut. 9.18-20, 26-29; 10.10). It also found its way into psalmodic and prophetic texts (Pss. 99.6; 106.23; Jer. 15.1). Aurelius and Van Seters (*Life of Moses*, pp. 94-95) treat the motif as a late one, post-prophetic or even exilic, relying on the occurrences in Exodus 32–34 and the Deuteronomic/Deuteronomistic texts. But the incidental references to it elsewhere are too widespread for this to be its origin, whatever theological elaboration it underwent in later times. It is still likely (despite the questions raised by S.E. Balentine, 'The Prophet as Intercessor', *JBL* 103 [1984], pp. 161-73) that intercession was a function of early prophecy in Israel (cf. Gen. 20.7; 1 Sam. 12.23; 1 Kgs 17.20; Amos 7.1-6), and the beginnings of the Moses-tradition find a natural home in this context. The repeated use of the unusual verb ʿtr (cf. above) is scarcely explicable from the situations proposed by Aurelius and Van Seters.

Moses' invitation to Pharaoh (expressed with a playful deference: see Note p on the translation) to decide the time when the frogs will be removed (v. 5) is to be understood from the intention with which he agrees to Pharaoh's proposal in v. 6: 'that you may know that there is none like Yahweh our God'. Yahweh's power to intervene will be clearer if it is revealed at a prescribed time. 'Tomorrow', as Houtman well sees (2, pp. 49-50), indicates (as one would expect) an early removal of the frogs: 'next morning' is often the time for immediate action by humans, and also for God (so later in the plague-story in 8.19, 25; 9.5, 18; 10.4). The aim to teach Pharaoh that Yahweh is supreme continues from 7.17, except that this time it works through the removal of the plague rather than its imposition. Here it is not simply Yahweh's identity but his incomparability that is to be shown. None of Pharaoh's gods, it is implied, can act in this way. Such claims (cf. 15.11) are common not only for Yahweh but more widely in the ancient Near East (cf. C.J Labuschagne, *The Incomparability of Yahweh in the Old Testament* [Leiden, 1966]). In the Old Testament they are often made in the context of deliverance from trouble (e.g. 1 Sam. 2.1-2: cf. *TWAT* 4, 4-5 = *TDOT* 7, pp. 4-5), as also in the naming of a child as Micaiah or Michael (shortened to Micah on occasion), lit. 'Who is like Yahweh/God/El?'

8-11. The negotiations now being complete, Moses and Aaron leave Pharaoh's presence – not expelled, as later (10.11, 28), but to seek privacy for prayer, as already in 5.22 and again in 8.25-26; 9.29, 33; 10.18. The end of v. 8 naturally recalls that it was Yahweh who had sent the plague of frogs (cf. 7.27): the alternative translation 'as he had agreed with Pharaoh', despite its long pedigree, involves unnatural understandings of the Heb. (see Note u on the translation and Text and Versions). The death of the frogs ensues and is seen by Pharaoh as a 'respite', despite the piles of dead animals and the foul smell (presumably from the rotting flesh). The expression for his reaction in v. 11a uses the same Heb. words as in 7.14 (see Note z on the translation), whereas the wording of the second half of the verse corresponds exactly to 7.13 and 22. Thus the rather repetitious conclusion to this episode probably combines elements of both the versions that have been detected earlier in the passage (see further the introduction to this section).

Text and Versions

יהוה (7.26)   Tg^{Nmg} as usual prefixes 'the Memra of' to both occurrences.

בא (7.26)   The Vss in general support the interpretation 'go in', but Sy *zl* (as in 9.1) here employs its regular equivalent for הלך, 'go' (cf. 7.15, which may have influenced the rendering here). OL *vade* is similar.

ואמרת (7.26)   SP ודברת, a common variation (cf. 7.14 and Text and Versions there), perhaps here to avoid three occurrences of אמר in one verse. The Vss support MT.

עמי (7.26)   Tg^N has עמא, 'the people' (as in 5.1): it has עמי in 7.16 and 9.1, and is perhaps assimilating to 8.4 here.

ויעבדני (7.26)   Vulg has its regular equivalent *ut sacrificet mihi* (cf. 7.16 and Text and Versions there: OL *serviant* is notable for its 'underinterpretation'): for the singular verb, which is a possible interpretation of the MT consonants, cf. Sy *wnplḥny*. Tgg as usual render the suffix 'before me'.

נגף (7.27)   Tg^N and its mg render 'destroy' (with two different words), a strengthening of the threat in line with the effect of a later plague (8.20).

את־כל־גבולך (7.27)   LXX πάντα τὰ ὅριά σου employs the pl. that is usual in Greek, but in a sense which seems to have been extended by the range of meaning of גבול, which can mean both 'boundary' and 'territory'. Vulg *omnes terminos tuos* must follow its lead (by way of the OL presumably), since the expression is not natural in Latin.[7]

---

[7] Cassiodorus, *Ant.* 2.296, has *terras* (with v.l. *terram*), but he is translating Josephus!

בצפרדעים (7.27)   Most SP mss read as MT, but the Rylands ms. used by Crown spells the word consistently as צפורדע.

ושרץ (7.28)   LXX καὶ ἐξερεύξεται, 'vomit forth', is probably based on its understanding of שרץ in Gen. 1.20-21, where it renders with ἐξάγω, and will be the source of Vulg's more restrained *ebullient*, 'bubble up with'.

בביתך (7.28)   The SP reading is בבתיך, 'into your houses', despite von Gall's total silence about the variant (on which see already Baillet, 'Corrections', p. 30),[8] and LXX εἰς τοὺς οἴκους σου is probably based on a similar text. But it may simply be due to metathesis: the singular is more appropriate here.

בחדר משכבך (7.28)   SP has the pl. בחדרי משכביך, and again LXX has the same sense (likewise Tg^N). Wevers (*Notes*, p. 107) thinks that throughout LXX is correctly representing the collective meaning of the singular nouns. This time the pl. finds support in Ps. 105.30, though it does not refer specifically to bedrooms. Sy divides the words by an additional 'and'.

ועל מטתך (7.28)   SP מטתיך indicates a pl. by the form of the suffix, and 4QEx^c by the insertion of a *waw*: LXX follows suit.

ובבית (7.28)   Here a pl. sense does seem appropriate and the reading ובבתי is attested or reflected in SP, LXX, Vulg and Tg^N. But 4QEx^c agrees with MT, which can bear the required meaning (cf. Note e on the translation) and is probably original.

ובעמך (7.28)   LXX καὶ τοῦ λαοῦ σου implies a reading ועמך, without the ב, which avoids the anticipation of v. 29 and may well be correct (so Childs): בית may be an unusual case of a construct noun governing two linked *nomina recta* (GK §128a), and a scribe may have mistakenly copied the form in the next verse here (Houtman). After this word Tg^N repeats its rendering of ובכל-עבדיך in the next verse, by a clear case of paraplepsis, and this could also be the explanation for the additional בכל in 4QEx^j *if* it represents the MT form of the text (see further the notes on the following verses).

ובתנוריך (7.28)   LXX has inverted its renderings of this and the following word. Sy *wbt᾽wnyk*, 'and in your inner rooms', is strange, since תנור is not an obscure word and fits well with the following word, whose culinary associations Sy recognised. Similarity of sound is the most likely reason for the error.

ובמשארותיך (7.28)   Vulg *in reliquias ciborum tuorum* related the word (which occurs only four times in BH) to the root שאר = 'be left over', as it does also in Deut. 28.5, 17 (cf. LXX there and Tg^J in Exod. 12.34). LXX here has καὶ ἐν τοῖς φυράμασίν σου, 'dough', as also in 12.34 (likewise Vulg and Sy there), misreading the sibilant. See further Text and Versions on 12.34.

ובכה (7.29)   The curious plene spelling does not appear in SP; none of the Qumran mss preserves this word. Tg^J has 'in(to?) your body' (see the following notes).

---

[8] This is especially odd since von Gall prints the plural reading in the SP addition after v. 29.

528   EXODUS 1–18

ובעמך ובכל־עבדיך (7.29)   LXX again inverts the nouns and omits 'all', a secondary harmonisation in both cases with 8.5, 7 (cf. 7.28). Sy freely abbreviates to 'on all your people'. Tg^J inserts 'the body of' before 'your people' (cf. the last note).

יעלו (7.29)   Vulg *intrabunt*, repeating (the sense of) the wrong verb from v. 28, or perhaps relating the verb to Aram. עלל = 'enter'. The use of *ad* rather than *in* in the previous phrases shows that Vulg did not envisage the frogs entering the Egyptians' bodies, as Tg^J, with 'will prevail over' (perhaps derived from a different sense of Heb. עלה [cf. Deut. 28.43]) and the addition of 'the body' noted above, and Rashi inferred (cf. Exod.R. 10.3).

After 7.29 SP has an addition corresponding to vv. 26-28, beginning ויבא משה ואהרן אל פרעה וידברו אליו, i.e. with SP's use of דבר in place of אמר and the typical addition of Aaron (as also in the addition after 7.18). The actual delivery of Yahweh's message to Pharaoh is thus recounted. Sy^{hex} records this longer text, apparently without any representation of the ב before עמך in v. 28 (cf. LXX there), which may be of relevance for the origin of the Greek version (cf. Pummer, pp. 306-307, 310). It is likely that both 4QEx^j and 4QpalEx^m had this expansion: though the fragmentary surviving evidence is not decisive, indirect arguments based on reconstruction and, in the latter case, the analogy of better attested passages support it (cf. *DJD* XII, p. 149; *DJD* IX, pp. 66-67, 76). 4QEx^c, which is equally fragmentary at this point, clearly did not have it (*DJD* XII, p. 105).

אמר אל אהרן (8.1)   Tg^J omits, implying that the following words are addressed to Moses. In v. 2 Aaron responds and Tg^J's addition at the end explains why. LXX adds 'your brother' after אהרן as in 7.7, 9 and 19, and Sy joins it here.

נטה (8.1)   Tg^{O,J} and Sy have 'lift up' (cf. 7.20); Tg^N 'incline', following a different and less appropriate sense of נטה.

את ידך במטך (8.1)   LXX more logically (cf. Wevers, *Notes*, p. 108) puts the preposition with 'your hand'. Vulg simply omits 'with your staff'.

על־היארים (8.1)   SP prefixes a *waw*, unnecessarily, and the conjunction is also supplied by LXX and Vulg. Tg^J seems, as in 7.19 (see the notes) to interchange its rendering of this and the next phrase: Tg^{N,F} have the expected equivalents.

והעל (8.1)   A few SP mss, including two collated by Crown and Camb. Add. 1846, have the fuller form of the imperative, as elsewhere (*GSH* §89dγ).

על ארץ מצרים (8.1)   LXX omits, presumably as unnecessary (Propp suggests homoeoteleuton, p. 295): the hexaplaric mss follow Aq (or Theod?) and Symm in restoring it.

After 8.1 SP has ויאמר משה אל אהרן נטה את ידך במטך והעל הצפרדע על ארץ מצרים, an abbreviated account of Moses' delivery of the command to Aaron, which in its latter part is based more on v. 2 than on v. 1 (i.e. on the sequel to Aaron's response). This is the only case where an account of Moses addressing Aaron is added, probably because in 7.10, 20 and 8.13 it is assumed to be implied by the statement that '*Moses and* Aaron did so' (in 9.8 Moses and Aaron receive the command together).

ויט (8.2)   Tgg and Sy render the verb נטה as in v. 1.

את־ידו (8.2)   LXX and Vulg render freely, without the possessive.

ותעל הצפרדע (8.2)   LXX has a double translation, one maintaining Aaron as the subject and following the wording of v. 1 (and v. 3), the other rendering MT here, with ὁ βάτραχος in the sing. (though still presumably collective in meaning – cf. the pl. in the other Versions – rather than an anticipation of the later rabbinic tradition about a single frog which bred prolifically [for which see *AramB* 7, p. 19 n. 1]). Two groups of mss and some of the Egyptian versions have only the freer rendering: this could be due to homoeoteleuton (the second cent. AD papyrus 970 apparently already has the longer text, but might preserve an original reading which was corrected in the standard text. Tg^J expands to 'the plague of frogs'.

After 8.2 Tg^J has a long plus explaining that Moses himself did not punish the Nile either with blood or with frogs, because it had been the means of his preservation when he was a baby.

כן (8.3)   LXX and Sy add 'also', as all witnesses do in 7.11 and LXX alone does in 7.22.

החרטמים (8.3)   SP חרטמי מצרים, as all witnesses have in 7.22, likewise LXX οἱ ἐπαοιδοὶ τῶν Αἰγυπτίων. This will be a clarifying gloss: MT is supported by the other witnesses. Tg^J again, as in 7.22, represents the magicians as 'astrologers'.

בלטיהם (8.3)   SP again has the fuller spelling בלהטיהם (or בלח׳): see Text and Versions on 7.22 (and Note 1 on the translation of 7.6-13). MT preserves the more authentic form of the word.

את־הצפרדעים (8.3)   SP lacks the את, so in this case MT may be secondary: the tendency in the tradition was to add את where it was 'missing'. In SP ויעלו could be taken as Qal, matching the construction in v. 2 (cf. 7.28-29), but SamTg implies the Hiphil.

ויאמר (8.4)   Sy adds 'to them', as do some Greek and Latin mss.

העתירו (8.4)   LXX adds περὶ ἐμοῦ, 'for me', anticipating לך in v. 5 (cf. also v. 24).

אל־יהוה (8.4)   Tgg and Sy render 'before the Lord' as often elsewhere; similarly Tgg and later mss of Sy at the end of the verse.

ויסר (8.4)   The final sense is represented by a 3rd pers. imperative in LXX and by *ut* in Vulg. Probably Tgg and Sy intended a final sense too here (cf. *AramB* ad loc.). Tg^N has a pl. verb, presumably Peal with 'the frogs' as subject (cf. MT in v. 2).

ואשלחה (8.4)   SP ואשלח, in line with its widespread rejection of the cohortative ending (*GSH* §64a): MT is to be preferred. LXX and Vulg have futures here (unless *dimittam* is a subjunctive after the preceding *ut*), and the renderings in Tgg and Sy could intend a future sense as well as the expression of purpose.

ויזבחו (8.4) LXX καὶ θύσωσιν according to the better reading, which is a possible way to express purpose in later Greek (Wevers, *Notes*, p. 109: he cites Thackeray, p. 91; cf. BDF §369 for similar expressions in early Christian Greek). On the other hand Vss see the note on ויסר. Tg^J adds 'festival offerings' as in 5.3, 8, 17 (and later in 8.21, 23) for completeness.

לפרעה (8.5) SP אל־פרעה, which is possibly also what LXX πρὸς Φαραώ represents. The other Vss support MT. In 7.26 and 8.1 both SP and MT have אל, so perhaps SP is assimilating to that.

התפאר עלי (8.5) So also SP, but the Vss not surprisingly diverge on this difficult phrase. Only Tg^J renders literally. LXX τάξαι πρός με (πρός in the sense of 'concerning' renders על well) and Vulg *constitue mihi* guess from the context that a general word for 'order' is meant, Vulg being close to Sy and the second rendering in Tg^O, 'ask/set a time for yourself', which, however, specify the obvious object and ignore the suffix of עלי. Tg^O prefixes 'ask a mighty act for yourself', a less obviously relevant guess. Tg^{N,F} 'give me a סימן and trust me' represents a different approach which takes account of the suffix of עלי and perhaps generates the idea of trust from על, '(resting) on'. סימן, 'mark, sign', is virtually synonymous with 'time' here (might it even be an error for זמן?). By their paraphrases Tg^{O,N,F} and Sy all avoid any (self-) disparagement of Moses, in line with the treatment of similar texts in Gen. (see *AramB* 7, p. 19 n. 3).

למתי (8.5) Tg^J renders 'Whenever' (which the Aram. equivalent can also mean) and adds 'you ask'.

להכרית (8.5) Tgg 'to expel' (cf. Sy), which is probably also behind Vulg *ut abigantur* (LXX ἀφανίσαι keeps closer to Heb.). For the varied Jewish interpretations of הכרית see W. Horbury, 'Excommunication and Extirpation', *VT* 35 (1985), pp. 13-38 (31-34).

ומבתיך (8.5) Vulg renders in the sing. *et a domo tua*, likewise Tg^N with the addition of 'the men of': this accords with the corresponding sing. in MT in 7.28, but not with its pl. here and in v. 7, both of which will appropriately have other residences in view as well as the palace. SP adds ומעבדיך ומעמך, probably conforming to the list in v. 7 (though homoeoteleuton might be responsible for the shorter text in MT etc.). The plus is recorded in Sy^{hex} (Lagarde) and appears, perhaps independently, in the Clem. ed. of Vulg and one ms. of Sy. LXX inserts καὶ ἀπὸ τοῦ λαοῦ σου before its rendering of ומבתיך to achieve a similar purpose (naturally Sy^{hex} marks this with an obelus), and Tg^N's plus (above) does so even more economically.

רק ביאר תשארנה (8.5) Sy omits this entirely; all the other witnesses have it (Tgg render '*those which are* in the Nile...' here and in v. 7, which makes no significant difference), but it fits much better on its second occurrence in v. 7 than in Moses' question here and Sy may (even without textual support) have restored the oldest form of the text here.

ויאמר (8.6) Sy adds *lh* both times.

כדברך (8.6) So also SP according to von Gall, but this seems to be a mistake, as all the recent editions (and Camb. Add. 1846) read כדבריך, apparently with 'words' in the pl. LXX paraphrases and is of no value in determining the reading. Tg^N also has the pl., but the other Vss all render by a sing. In comparable contexts BH prefers the sing. noun where the suffix is second pers. sing. (Gen. 30.34; Num. 14.20; Judg. 11.10; 1 Kgs 17.13; 20.4) and the pl. where it is 2nd pl. (Gen. 44.10; Josh. 2.21; Jer. 42.4): the only definite exception to this rule is כדבריך in 1 Kgs 3.12 (where Solomon has made a longer speech), but in Ezra 10.12 K and Q are divided on this point. SP according to Tal's edition has the pl. in all five cases in the Pentateuch, so there may be a dialectal variation at work (cf. *GSH* §55bγ).

כיהוה אלהינו (8.6) LXX renders ἄλλος πλὴν κυρίου, a clear expression of monotheistic belief which goes beyond MT and accommodates to passages like Ps. 18.32 and Isa. 44.6, 21. The omission of 'our God' is part of this variation (cf. Wevers, *Notes*, pp. 110-11, and Text and Versions at 9.14). The Jewish revisers restored the missing phrase: the citation of them here is also interesting for its evidence that they retained the old practice of writing the divine name in its Hebrew form (cf. 12.42; 15.18; 22.10; 32.9: O'Connell, *Theodotionic Revision*, pp. 127-29).

ומבתיך (8.7) Vulg and Tg^N have the sing. as in v. 5 and are joined here by Tg^J and Sy, no doubt because the following nouns were taken to imply that this word refers to Pharaoh alone. But this consideration is not decisive, and the clear pl. הבתים in v. 9 (which even Vulg reflects) confirms the originality of the pl. which is present here in MT, SP and LXX. LXX itself adds καὶ ἐκ τῶν ἐπαύλεων afterwards, which it has for מן־החצרת in v. 9. The added phrase stands out in v. 7 through its lack of a possessive pronoun (only a few witnesses have one), and it is entirely omitted in a significant number of mss (including two uncials). But its presence in A and B may suggest that it was in the original translation, where it will have been introduced to match v. 9 more closely (Wevers, *Notes*, p. 111). There can, however, be no question of its being an original part of the Heb. text.

תשארנה (8.7) The identical endings of vv. 5 and 7 have led to the omission of vv. 6-7 in two LXX mss and one SP ms. – an excellent example of the effect of homoeoteleuton – and Sy^hex recorded, according to Wevers's apparatus (p. 129), that the Sam. Greek version omitted them too. The reason will be the same, whether this refers to the version as such or to the particular copy used by the 'Sam.' annotator. The *b* group of LXX mss has an addition here based on v. 24 and the beginning of v. 25, which was included in the text of the Complutensian Polyglott, a useful clue to the ms(s). used in the preparation of the latter (cf. Wevers's ed., p. 39, which identifies ms. 108, a member of the *b* group, as the Polyglott's main source for the Greek text of Exod. 1–34).

ויצא (8.8) Vulg *egressi sunt*, with a pl. verb for grammatical consistency as in 4.29 (but not 7.6).

מעם פרעה (8.8) 4QExᶜ preserves parts of four words in this verse, corresponding to MT, but פרעה was initially omitted by scribal error and was restored above the line (by a later hand according to *DJD* XII, p. 106).

ויצעק (8.8) Tgg and Sy have 'prayed', preferring the more specific word that is appropriate in this context (see further *AramB* 7, p. 21 n. 4), and characteristically add 'before' with the divine name.

על דבר (8.8) Tgg and Sy render by equivalent idioms for 'concerning, about', but LXX περὶ τοῦ ὁρισμοῦ, 'concerning the limitation' (sc. to the Nile, according to Moses' words in vv. 5 and 7)⁹ and Vulg *pro sponsione*, 'according to the promise' (sc. of Moses to Pharaoh), both take דבר in its regular sense of 'word' and elaborate this in terms of its content or character. This is an unnatural way to read the Heb., which may have arisen from these Vss's understanding of the following words (see the next note).

אשר שם לפרעה (8.8) Tgg and Sy render שם straightforwardly and probably correctly with שוי, 'appointed', or (Sy) ʾyty, 'brought', presumably with an easily supplied divine subject. LXX ὡς ἐτάξατο Φαραώ is more ambiguous: it is even possible to take Φαραώ as the subject (with reference back to v. 6: so *BAlex*, p. 124), though that would imply or assume a different *Vorlage* from MT and SP (פרעה, without ל). But Φαραώ may, as in the other witnesses, be in the dative case: while it is possible to use the Greek art. to make this clear (hence the τῷ in the majority text, though not the best mss, A B 970: cf. 8.15), it is not invariably used (cf. 6.10). This is Wevers's view (*Notes*, p. 112), though he oddly then renders the verb as a passive ('as was arranged for Pharaoh'), which is unlikely and unnecessary: either God or Moses could be the subject of ἐτάξατο, depending on whether it means 'appointed' or 'agreed'. After ὁρισμοῦ the latter is rather more likely, and it also probably corresponds to the meaning of Vulg's (*sponsione*...) *quam condixerat Pharaoni* (which clearly has Pharaoh as the indirect object).

יהוה (8.9) Tgᴺᵐᵍ as usual prefixes 'the Memra of'.

וימתו (8.9) Sy has *wmyt*, presumably a fem. pl. form.

מן־החצרות (8.9) SP, LXX, Vulg, Tgᴶ·ᴺ, Sy prefix 'and', as often in lists: Tgᴼ agrees with MT, which is to be preferred (4QExᶜ preserves a few words of this verse, but not these). The Aram. versions correctly render 'courtyards': LXX τῶν ἐπαύλεων here fails to distinguish חצר I from חצר II, which means 'villages'. The Greek word has a range of meanings, including 'country-house' (see LSJ), and this is probably the basis of Vulg's *villis*, which may have already stood in OL here and elsewhere. However, the meaning of *villa*

---

⁹ Most authorities agree on 'limitation' as the sense of ὁρισμός here: it is well attested in LSJ. Lust, however, gives 'the agreed time' (*Lexicon*, p. 339), which fits the other uses of the word in LXX: this has some point in the present context too (cf. vv. 5-6), but the need to understand 'for the removal of' makes it less likely than the straightforward sense here.

seems to have broadened considerably by the time of Jerome, to judge from its use elsewhere in Vulg (esp. the NT), and the choice of it to render חצר here may be due simply to that.

ויצברו (8.10) All the Vss render 'collected, gathered', except Aq with συνέχωσαν, 'heaped up', which represents the precise sense of the word in BH. There is some evidence that its meaning broadened in later Heb. (cf. Jastrow), which will explain the consistency of the other renderings – unless translators simply thought that the idea of 'heaps' was sufficiently indicated by the following words.

חמרם (8.10) Aq's (repeated) κόρους is due to confusion with חמר II, a dry measure (Wevers, *Notes*, p. 112 n. 14).

ותבאש (8.10) Tg^O 'and *they* decayed/stank on (the land)', a pedantic change of construction to identify the precise source of the smell.

והכבד (8.11) SP ויכבד, replacing the inf. abs. with the finite verb which it represents, a typical smoothing of the grammar and one which is frequently found in SP (cf. *GSH* §178 and e.g. Exod. 13.3). The Vss naturally employ finite verbs, but this need not mean that their *Vorlagen* agreed with SP. LXX and Sy make Pharaoh's heart the subject of a passive/stative verb (for Sy *w'by* see Text and Versions on 7.22), avoiding the impression of deliberate obduracy which MT and SP give (but see Note z on the translation).

דבר (8.11) Sy *'mr*, a common variation (but see the next note); Vulg *praeceperat*, as elsewhere (cf. Text and Versions on 7.22).

יהוה (8.11) Tg^{Nmg} as usual prefixes 'the Memra of'; Sy adds 'to Moses', perhaps to vary the repeated formula.

Chapter 8.12-15

The Plague of Lice

The structure of this section follows a pattern which is by now well established, though there is one major variation from it which is all the more significant because of the previous regularity. The pattern is set by 7.8-13 (see the introduction to that section) and can be discerned also in parts of the composite narratives about the plagues of blood and frogs (7.14-25; 7.26–8.11). It appears here (even in the precise wording to some extent) in the opening instruction to Moses, in the execution of the command by him and especially Aaron, in the coming of the plague, in a response by Pharaoh's magicians, and in Pharaoh's concluding refusal to let Israel go. The main difference is in the magicians' response: they again imitate Aaron's action, but this time instead of producing the same effect they fail and they acknowledge that the plague has come about through divine agency. Schmidt points out that the coming of the plague also indicates an element which is not in the divine command: it affects both 'man and beast' (vv. 13-14: cf. 9.9-10P). It is therefore a real 'narrative', not simply a stereotyped fulfilment of what had been declared in advance (p. 399). The nature of this plague bears some resemblance to the one which follows in 8.16-28 – both involve small insects – just as 9.1-7 does to 9.8-12, so that there is an element of duplication between them, while the form of the narratives is very different: this is very likely due to the combination of once separate accounts.

The features noted above have led to general agreement since Knobel that these verses are also part of the Priestly material.

Steingrimmson's 'A' (*Vom Zeichen*, pp. 184-85, 188-95) corresponds to this, and even Houtman concedes that the verses have a different origin from v. 11 (2, p. 53), in view of the 'abrupt transition' between them. Van Seters's view that they form part of a supplement to J has found little recent support (but see Dozeman) and it is strongly contested by K. Schmid (p. 147 n. 539) and Gertz (pp. 84-88). Even Blum recognises its original independence before it was incorporated into his 'P-Composition' (pp. 245, 250). The only other discussion has been about possible redactional expansions of the original account, which is certainly somewhat verbose. Evidence of a shorter text in v. 13 in LXX or significant mss of it has led to the view that either 'They did so' (BH^3, Rudolph, Beer, Noth, L. Schmidt) or (part of) the second half of the verse (Holzinger, Gressmann [*Mose*, p. 91], Gertz) is not original. But the shorter texts are probably due to the translators' desire to abbreviate rather than to a variant *Vorlage* (see Text and Versions), and the other arguments cited are not conclusive. The same is true of Steingrimmson's claim (pp. 81-82, 85) that '(the) lice came upon man and beast' in v. 13 is secondary, and of Levin's view that, as elsewhere, the references to the magicians are intrusive (p. 336). The only such proposal that deserves serious discussion is that v. 14b is what Noth called 'an inadvertent repetition of words from v. 13' (p. 47 n. 2, ET, p. 63: likewise Gressmann, Beer/Galling, Steingrimmson, L. Schmidt, Gertz). It is not quite the case that the clause 'makes no sense' here (Gertz, p. 80 n. 17), but it is difficult to explain, despite the suggestions of Rudolph, Houtman and W.H. Schmidt (p. 397: but on pp. 344-45 he seems to agree with Noth). The most likely explanation is that it provides a reason for what the magicians say in v. 15 (see the Note on vv. 14-15), but even then its awkwardness may point to its being an afterthought: the meaning of v. 15 would be clear enough without it.

In relation to the overall composition of the plague-story it is perhaps surprising that the final redactor did not interweave the Priestly and non-Priestly versions, as he did in the two preceding episodes. The fact that he did not do so is perhaps an indication that he did not regard them as sufficiently similar, and this is more understandable if he took the view that the creatures concerned were lice rather than gnats, which we have argued is also the more likely view on philological grounds (see the Explanatory Note on vv. 12-13).

With this episode the Priestly plague-narrative reaches a preliminary climax: even if Pharaoh remains unmoved, his magicians are convinced that divine power is at work through Moses and Aaron (v. 15).[1] To complete the overthrow of Pharaoh they (9.11) and indeed all the Egyptians will have to suffer more, much more. But Pharaoh's isolation, even among his own people, is beginning to emerge, as it does progressively also in the non-Priestly narrative (cf. 9.20-21; 10.7).

---

[1] Cf. Blenkinsopp, *Pentateuch*, p. 155.

536   EXODUS 1–18

12 *Yahweh said to Moses, 'Say to Aaron, Stretch out your staff and strike the dust of the earth and it shall become lice*[a] *throughout the land of Egypt'.* 13 *They did so, (and) Aaron stretched out his hand with his staff*[b] *and struck the dust of the earth and (the) lice*[c] *came upon*[d] *man and beast: all the dust of the earth became lice throughout the land of Egypt.* 14 *The magicians did the same with their spells to produce*[e] *(the) lice, but they could not do so. But the lice were on man and beast.* 15 *So the magicians said to Pharaoh, 'It*[f] *is the finger of a god'. But Pharaoh's heart was stubborn, so he did not listen to them, as Yahweh had said.*

Notes on the Translation

a. Heb. כנם, as also (spelt *plene*) in vv. 13b and 14a: see also Note c on v. 13. The only other definite occurrence is in Ps. 105.31, a reference to this episode (and probably this passage), but כמו־כן ימותון in Isa. 51.6 is sometimes taken as another (Goldingay and Payne ad loc. are doubtful, however). כנים also occurs in a list of the plagues in 4QParGenEx (4Q422) 3.8. The meanings 'gnat, mosquito' and 'lice, vermin' both have early attestation (see respectively Philo, *Vita Mosis* 1.107 [cf. Herod. 2.95] and Josephus, *AJ* 2.14.13: also Text and Versions) and the modern dictionaries are not unanimous either (BDB gives both, *HAL* and *Ges18* favour 'gnat, mosquito', *DCH* gives 'perh. **louse**' before citing other possibilities). The cognates proposed all favour 'lice, vermin', though only MH כנה is really close in form, and possibly the preposition ב with אדם and בהמה in vv. 13-14 is more likely to be used of this than a flying insect. כנים in Sir. 10.11(A) must from the context mean 'louse' (or even 'maggot': cf. REB here), but the reading seems to be corrupt and it could be related to MH כנימה instead (see Note c). On the basis of MH there seems to be more to be said for 'lice' (AV, NJPS) than for 'gnats' (NRSV). But McNeile (p. 50), favouring 'gnats', says that lice do not affect animals, on the basis of a non-specific reference to Macalister.

b. Heb. במטהו: on the force of ב here see Note j on 7.26–8.11.

c. Heb. הַכִּנָּם, a curious form which also appears in v. 14b (cf. also LXX's sing. τὸν σκνῖφα in v. 14a), where 4QpalEx[m] seems to have read הכנים, like SP which also does so here (see Text and Versions). MT vocalises הכנם as a m.pl. in v. 12 (for defective writing of the m.pl. ending cf. GK §87a and, e.g., חמרם in v. 10), and its different vocalisation here has been variously explained, either grammatically (BL §61kι note [p. 504]) or lexically, in relation to MH כנימה (GK §85t; *HAL* and *Ges18* give both explanations). It is surely most unlikely that the original author used two different words or forms so close together and the MT vocalisation here and in v. 14b must be regarded as artificial. The explanation for it, as both BDB, p. 487, and BL §61kι note suggest, is probably the fem. sing. verb ותהי which precedes it on each occasion: here (unnecessarily in view of the possible use of the fem. sing. verb in a collective sense: see the next Note) the Masoretes have constructed a singular form to agree with it, which was perhaps based on the alternative word כנימה that was in use in MH.

d. Heb. ותהי. Since עפר is masc. it cannot be the subject of היה in the sense of 'become' as in v. 12 and v. 13b, so the subject must (as in v. 14b) be הכנם and the meaning will be 'were' or better 'came', as often elsewhere (BDB, p. 225b, s.v. 'II'). For the (collective) use of the fem. sing. with a non-human pl. subject see GK §145k.

e. Heb. להוציא. Here clearly 'bring forth' in the sense of 'make, generate', as in the Priestly creation story (Gen. 1.12, 24) but also elsewhere several times (BDB, p. 425, s.v. 4.j). 'Remove' (Bekhor Shor and Jacob, p. 269) is theoretically possible (cf. Gen. 45.1), but it does not fit the context so well, as the magicians regularly attempt to repeat what Aaron has done, not to reverse it.

f. Heb. הוא, with the gender reflecting the use of the fem. to represent the neuter (GK §135p, but §136b says that the masc. form הוא is more common, so perhaps the Qere is an over-correction). For the *Qere perpetuum* with this form see Note n on 3.1-12. The gender (in MT at least) is against the interpretation of 'It' as a reference to Aaron's rod (Couroyer; Propp, p. 328).

Explanatory Notes

12-13. The account of this plague follows closely the pattern of the sections already attributed to the Priestly source (see the introduction to this section). A minor difference, probably just for variety, is that Aaron is commanded simply to stretch out his staff (the account of his action reverts to the fuller expression of 7.19 and 8.1: see also Text and Versions). The use of 'dust' (which may mean 'dry soil' [Noth]) shifts the focus from the water (7.19; 8.1) to the land: it is unlikely that the association of dust with the dead (Houtman) is in view, but its countless quantity (e.g. Gen. 13.16: Propp) could be. The nature of this plague has been disputed since early times, with 'gnats' being a favoured alternative to 'lice' since Hellenistic times (Artapanus fr. 3, 31 [Charlesworth (ed.) 2, p. 902]; Philo, *Vita Mos.* 1.107-108; later Origen, *Hom. in Exod.* 4.6: in modern times see especially McNeile and Beer/Galling). But the best philological evidence points to 'lice' being meant (see Note a on the translation, and Text and Versions: so RV and recently Houtman and Propp). Those who continue to render by 'gnats' (*HAL*, Schmidt, *Ges18*) make use of the prevalence of the latter in Egypt (noted by Herodotus 2.95: Houtman 2, p. 55, mentions 'dense swarms' in October and November in modern times) and the closer parallel to the following non-Priestly plague of flies which it provides. These are not decisive arguments: we do not know how familiar the Priestly writer was with Egyptian conditions, and a difference from the next plague may be more likely, even when a source-critical approach is taken (see the introduction to this section). In any case philological evidence, where it is available, should be determinative. Cansdale (*Animals*, pp. 229-31) suggests 'ticks'. Verse 13b is strictly unnecessary, but it exhibits the repetitiveness which is sometimes a feature of Priestly style: the two clauses introduce first the effect on both humans and animals and then the (expected, cf. v. 12) extent throughout the land.[2]

14-15. 'Did the same' must refer to the magicians' action rather than to its effect, since on this occasion they failed to produce any change ('they could not'). 7.12-13 indicates that they too had staffs, which they no doubt stretched out to the accompaniment of 'their spells' on each occasion. Recent commentaries and translations (Houtman, Schmidt, NRSV: cf. Propp) have rendered 'tried to (do the same)', but this cannot be justified linguistically. Verse 14b is repetitive (cf. v. 13aβ), but perhaps with good reason: after the account of the magicians' failure it is a reminder of the situation (see Note f on the translation) which they attribute in v. 15 to 'the finger of God'. The latter phrase is ambiguous, because Heb. *ᵉlōhîm* can be rendered either 'God' or 'a god' ('gods' is theoretically possible too, but less likely here because of the sing. 'finger'). Prior to the revelation to Moses in 6.2-8 P regularly used *ᵉlōhîm* to refer to 'God' (e.g. 2.23-35), and it is possible that he would envisage Egyptians using the word in this sense too. But he has also used the word as a common noun in 7.1 and will do so again in 12.12, so the weaker meaning is also possible, and perhaps more likely (cf. Houtman, Propp). Either way, the magicians acknowledge that Moses and Aaron are acting with divine support. 'Finger' is used by synecdoche for its (presumed) effect. It is much more common to speak of God's 'hand' in such cases (cf. 7.4: his 'finger' is elsewhere only

---

[2] Cf. McEvenue, *Narrative Style*, e.g. pp. 168-69 (on Gen. 17.9-14). Paran's treatment of the verse is doubly strange because he includes it with non-Priestly instances of *inclusio* (*Forms of the Priestly Style* [Heb.], p. 53).

the means of writing (31.18; Deut. 9.10), though the plural 'fingers' is used of his work of creation in Ps. 8.4. Probably, as in laws about sacrificial practice (29.2 etc.), the index finger, representing an act of pointing (cf. Isa. 58.9; Prov. 6.13), is meant, as sometimes where 'hand' is used (see the notes on 6.8). The idea that God's finger represented a lesser intervention than his hand formed the basis for some rabbinic commentary (see Text and Versions for references) and has recently been taken up again by Schmidt (p. 399), but it is probably just a different way of expressing the same belief in divine agency.³

The section concludes like earlier passages from P (cf. 7.13, 22; 8.11): even after his magicians' failure and their interpretation of the plague Pharaoh remains adamant. The words 'to them' in v. 15 have their closest antecedent in the magicians, who have indeed spoken on this occasion, and there might be a secondary allusion to that here. But the recurrence of the refrain throughout the Priestly plague narrative makes it likely that the primary reference is again to Moses and Aaron's words demanding Israel's release (6.10-12; 7.1-7).

Text and Versions

נטה (8.12)   Tg^{O,J} and Sy have 'lift up' (cf. 7.20; 8.1; likewise v. 13), due to the influence of a common formula; Tg^N's equivalent was accidentally omitted.

את־מטך (8.12)   So also Tgg, Sy, Vulg, but SP and 4QEx^c have את־ידך (במטך), presumably assimilating to the expression in v. 13 (cf. also v. 1). LXX's addition of τῇ χειρί, though not an exact rendering of the longer text, corresponds to what it has for it elsewhere and so it could be based on a variant *Vorlage*.

---

³ For a recent discussion of the idiom and its occurrences see G.A. Klingbeil, 'The Finger of God in the Old Testament', *ZAW* 112 (2000), pp. 409-15, who thinks it represents an extraordinary intervention of Yahweh's creative power. B. Couroyer, 'Quelques égyptianismes dans l'Exode', *RB* 63 (1956), pp. 209-19; 'Le "doigt de Dieu" (Exode, VIII, 15)', ibid., 481-95, had earlier noted that in Egyptian texts writing with the 'finger' as well as the 'fingers' (even of a god) was a common idiom, but that the 'finger' of a god could also be an object that looked like a finger, so that here Aaron's rod might be meant. Perhaps more plausible is a comparison with the pointing of a god's finger in judgement (cf. Amenemope, xix, 20-21 [*ANET*, p. 423; *COS* 1, p. 120] and other texts cited by Couroyer, p. 488).

וחך (8.12) Two early mss of SP (cf. Tal and Camb. 1846) have the fuller form והכה: such forms of Lamed He verbs are commonly preferred to apocopated forms in SP (*GSH* §64c) and this could be its original reading here.

והיה (8.12) SP has the jussive form ויהי, probably conforming the expression (as it does also in 7.19) to the pattern of the first episode in 7.9. Vulg *sint* also gives a jussive meaning, but the other Vss presuppose MT. LXX ἔσονται is probably not an unusual case of χῶμα being treated as a collective subject (Wevers, *Notes*, p. 113) but due to assimilation of the expression to v. 13aβ: 'there will be...'

לכנם (8.12) LXX and Vulg ignore the ל and treat כנם as the subject of והיה. SP has the plene form (ל)כנים, as it does throughout this section, and the editors attribute the same reading 'probably' to 4QpalEx^m (*DJD* IX, p. 77). The Vss diverge sharply in their interpretation of כן: LXX σκνῖφες (or σκνῖπες), which is transcribed *scinifes* in Vulg (and apparently OL) was from early times understood to mean a stinging insect (cf. Philo, *Vita Mos.* 1.107-108), hence 'gnat, mosquito'. But the exx. cited in LSJ, pp. 1612-13 point rather to a kind of vermin. This is in fact the interpretation of כנם supported by Tgg and Sy (Aram. קלמתא, קלמין, קלמו, *qlm*') and also by Jos., *AJ* 2.14.13 (φθείρ). LXX adds 'on man and beast', as in v. 13; Tg^J has an addition here comparable to that in v. 2 (see Text and Versions there), which explains that Moses himself could not strike the earth because it had been the means of his escape in 2.12.

ויעשו כן (8.13) LXX (followed by Beer) omits this clause, which appeared in the corresponding place in 7.10 and 7.20 but not in 8.2 (or 9.10). All other witnesses have it (including probably 4QpalEx^m and 4QEx^c, to judge from the space available) and the hexaplaric witnesses restore it, the majority with a singular verb (referring to Aaron alone) as also in Sy. Omission by homoeoarkton is the likely explanation of LXX's reading (Propp, p. 296). Lemmelijn, by contrast, considers it more original, attributing the majority text to an early scribal confusion with the beginning of v. 14 (pp. 165-66).

ויט (8.13) See the note on נטה in 8.12. Tg^N has וארכן as in v. 2 (see the note on 8.1).

את־ידו במטהו (8.13) Vulg *manu virgam tenens*, making a somewhat awkward sequence which some mss (followed in the Clementine ed.) have eased by reading *manum*, as the object of *extendit*. *manu* seems to have been taken over mechanically from the OL (cf. LXX τῇ χειρί), despite Jerome's modification of the rendering of במטהו.

ותהי (8.13) LXX, Vulg and Tg^N render (correctly) by a pl. verb, and LXX and Tg^N extend this understanding (incorrectly) to the following clause.

הכנם (8.13) SP reads הכנים, i.e. the normal pl. form, against the vocalisation of MT. None of the Qumran mss preserves the whole word here (the כ probably survives in 4QpalEx^l), but pl. renderings are used in LXX, Vulg, Tg^N and perhaps Tg^J and Sy. Only Tg^O clearly has a sing. form (cf. LXX in v. 14a) which supports the peculiar vocalisation of MT. Tg^J prefixes מחת, 'plague of', which provides a fem. sing. subject for the verb (likewise in v. 14).

באדם (8.13)   Sy and Tg^N have בבני־אנשא, a regular equivalent; Tg^J בבישרא דאינשא, 'on the flesh of men (and beasts)', is a clarifying expansion.

כל־עפר הארץ (8.13)   4Q365 reads בכול וג׳, a reading which also lies behind LXX's καὶ ἐν παντί... The intention, as Wevers well sees (*Notes*, p. 114), will be to make the account more realistic, with insects appearing *among* the dust of the earth rather than it all being transformed into insects. According to *DJD* XIII, p. 264, one Masoretic ms. has this reading (de Rossi 233 acc. Propp, p. 296), but its statement that Sy reads or implies בכל is an error: the oldest mss agree with MT and even the variant *wkwlh* (cf. *BHS*) only appears from the ninth cent. onwards. The omission of parts of the second half of the verse in some LXX mss will be due to abbreviation of the repetitive text, and is no basis for emendation of MT (contra Holzinger).

היה (8.13)   See above on ותהי for the renderings in LXX and Tg^N. Sy adds *lh*, which is presumably the 'emphasising' use of *l* with a reflexive pronoun: cf. perhaps the expansion in Tg^J, 'was changed to become', which (in contrast to the reading of 4Q365 and LXX) underlines the miraculous nature of the event.

ויעשו כן (8.14)   4Q365 had these words above the line and is not preserved where they would be expected to appear (*DJD* XIII, pp. 263-64). But there seems to be space either for them or for some additional material there.

החרטמים (8.14)   LXX and Sy prefix 'also' to improve the sense, as in 8.3 (see Text and Versions there). Tg^J adds 'sorcery' as a clarifying object.

בלטיהם (8.14)   4Q365 (like 4QEx^c in 7.22) reads the fuller form בלהטיהם, which is used throughout by SP and in 7.11 by MT.

להוציא (8.14)   LXX ἐξαγαγεῖν can mean 'produce' (Wevers, *Notes*, p. 114) as well as 'lead out'. Sy puts the infinitive and its object after 'could not', perhaps supposing that it was needed there more than after the formulaic beginning to the verse.

את־הכנים (8.14)   So MT, SP and most of the versions, and the traces of הכנים in 4QpalEx^l probably belong here. LXX has sing. τὸν σκνῖφα, which can be taken collectively, but its unique use of the sing. here raises the possibility that its *Vorlage* was defectively written at this point (cf. הכנם in MT in v. 13 and later in this verse and see Note c on the translation).

ותהי (8.14)   So also SP, but 4QpalEx^m curiously has the masc. form ויהי, perhaps out of puzzlement with the fem. form or recalling the corresponding form in SP at 7.19.

הכנם (8.14)   SP (as in v. 13) and 4QpalEx^m (which is the only Qumran ms. to survive for this word) read the plene form הכנים. The Vss render as in v. 13, with predominantly pl. forms.

באדם (8.14)   Sy renders as in v. 13; Tg^J elaborates the meaning of the preposition differently here by prefixing שלטא, 'was in control of'.

אל־פרעה (8.15)   Tg^J renders 'of Pharaoh', eliminating the explicit address to him: this would be more plausible if the preposition were ל rather than אל, as it is in the other Aram. renderings. So Tg^J here may best be seen as a secondary development within the tradition rather than an attempt to render the Heb. directly.

אצבע אלהים (8.15)   Tgg paraphrase the anthropomorphism (as they do even with יד in 7.4), in various ways: Tg^O 'a plague from before the Lord'; Tg^J 'not from the mighty power of Moses and Aaron, but a plague sent from before the Lord'; and Tg^N 'a finger of (om. mg.) might from before the Lord'. Some rabbinic interpretations showed less anxiety about the literal meaning (for references see *AramB* 7, p. 21 n. 6, and *AramB* 2, p. 35 n. 7), while Ibn Ezra and Rashbam proposed naturalistic explanations (which were refuted by Nachmanides) on the basis of אלהים being used rather than יהוה.

הוא (8.15)   SP reads the expected היא (as in the MT vocalisation). None of the Qumran mss survives at this point.

ויחזק (8.15)   Sy here renders by *wʾtqšy*, 'was hardened', for the first time: previously this verb was used only to render its cognate in 7.3. The reason could be consultation of LXX, which has ἐσκληρύνθη here as also elsewhere. Previously Sy has preferred words that render חזק and כבד more literally: *ʿšn* in 4.21; 7.13-14; *ʿby* in 7.22 and 8.11.

דבר (8.15)   Vulg again has *praeceperat*: see Text and Versions on 7.22.

Chapter 8.16-28

The Plague of Worms(?)

The nature of the next plague has been a subject of disagreement since antiquity, because the Heb. word *'ārōb* is only used of this episode. A Jewish interpretation that has been widespread since Josephus sees a reference to wild animals in general here (see Text and Versions on v. 17). The common translation '(swarm of) flies' lacks any etymological basis and recent study has suggested that 'vermin' (Houtman) or 'worms' may be meant (see Note h on the translation and the Explanatory Note on vv. 16-17). By contrast, the structure of this section is relatively simple, though it includes one new element. It begins with (i) an address by Yahweh to Moses (vv. 16-19), which is followed by (ii) an account of the plague (v. 20). There then follow (iii) negotiations between Pharaoh and Moses (vv. 21-25) and (iv) an account of the plague's removal and Pharaoh's reaction to it (vv. 26-28). There are close parallels throughout to the corresponding sections about the pollution of the Nile (7.14-25) and the frogs (7.26–8.11): see the Explanatory Notes for details. But this time there is no second address by Yahweh, as in 7.19 and 8.1, and the characteristic features and language of these verses (including the active role of Aaron) and also of 7.22 and 8.11b, which occupied the whole of the Priestly section 8.12-15, are entirely missing. On the other hand, for the first time the motif of a distinction between Yahweh's treatment of Israel and the Egyptians appears, based on Israel's separate dwelling in the land of Goshen (see the notes on vv. 18-19, and cf. 9.4-7).

There is thus no clear basis in this narrative for seeing it as due to the conflation of parallel accounts, and much critical analysis has agreed with more traditional commentaries in seeing it substantially as a unity, generally attributing it to J.

The inclusion of Aaron along with Moses in v. 21 (and the consequential use of a plural imperative – 'Pray' – in v. 24) can, as in v. 4, be readily attributed to the redactor who combined the older source(s) with the Priestly account.¹ On the other hand, the view that 'and your houses' in v. 17 is a later addition (Holzinger, Beer/Galling, Gertz) is hard to justify in view of the reference to 'houses' in v. 20. A number of commentators have seen the clause 'he will be coming out to the water' in v. 16 as an addition based on 7.15, because here it has no point: this time the plague has no particular connection with the Nile (so Carpenter/Harford-Battersby, Baentsch, Holzinger, Gressmann). But then why would a later redactor have added it? It is equally possible that the original narrator repeated the clause here to explain how Moses could have an encounter with Pharaoh. It has also been thought that the reason given for the exclusion of the land of Goshen from the plague in v. 18b is secondary (Wellhausen, Carpenter/Harford-Battersby, Baentsch, Holzinger, Gressmann), like similar verses which give the plagues an educational purpose. But, as with 7.17a and 8.6b, such a purpose in fact corresponds exactly to the best interpretation of the older account's view of Pharaoh's 'hardness of heart', that it was a (wilful) failure to understand that Yahweh was more powerful than he was.² Some scholars have found a doublet in vv. 18-19, and then argued that either v. 18a (Rudolph) or v. 19 (Kohata) is secondary. But in fact they complement one another, speaking first of the land and then of the people, as both L. Schmidt (*Beobachtungen*, p. 16) and W.H. Schmidt (p. 401) have seen.³ L. Schmidt (ibid.) regards the whole of vv. 18-19 as an addition, apparently because the distinction referred to between the Israelites and the Egyptians is not mentioned later in the passage. But it is probably taken for granted: 'as he had said' (lit. 'thus') in v. 20 is sufficient to indicate it.⁴

More far-reaching problems have been the subject of discussion in the account of the negotiations between Pharaoh and Moses in vv. 21-27. The abrupt, asyndetic, transition to 'make supplication for me' in v. 24, the fact that it appears at the end of Pharaoh's proposal rather than at the beginning as in v. 8 (cf. 9.28 and 10.17), and the use of the verb 'sacrifice' (Heb. *zābaḥ*) instead of 'worship' (Heb. *'ābad*) as in v. 16 (see vv. 21, 22, 23, 24, 25) have led several scholars to see these verses as alien to their context.

---

¹ The secondary addition of 'and Aaron' in v. 21 is made more likely by the use of a different preposition before it in MT (see Text and Versions). It is true that Lev. 10.6 exhibits a similar variation, but there 'and to his sons Eleazar and Ithamar' (and the conversion of the following verbs into plurals) may also be due to a modification of the original narrative.

² Note also the reference to the sparing of Goshen as a 'sign' in v. 19.

³ The impression of a doublet is due perhaps to the widespread emendation of פדת in v. 19 to פלה, which does recall והפליתי in v. 18. But a different solution to that problem is probably to be preferred (see Note j on the translation).

⁴ Nor is there any need for Holzinger's complex rearrangement of vv. 17b-19a: it is hard to imagine what kind of an 'accident' could have caused the disruption of the original text which he envisages.

Dillmann attributed them to his parallel 'B' account (the E of other scholars), Gressmann thought that vv. 21-22 originally stood after v. 28 and vv. 23-24a after 9.7 (he also envisaged the omission of some text after v. 24b and 9.7), and Noth (followed by Reichert, Floss and Levin [p. 337: for him the main account is itself only a secondary addition to J]) initially regarded vv. 21b-24a as a secondary expansion of the J account.[5] Gertz goes further: taking up the analysis of Steingrimsson (pp. 97-98), he points out that it would be strange if Pharaoh were able to secure Moses' willingness to 'make supplication' for him (vv. 26-27) if he had made no concession (*Tradition*, pp. 123-29, cf. p. 395), so that vv. 21-27 must be taken together as a unit. For him (because of the use of Heb. *zābaḥ* and because he judges the similar passage in 8.4-9a to be intrusive and late) that means that it should be attributed to the final redactor (EndR). His argument could of course lead to the retention of the whole section as part of the original narrative, if the objections noted above can be overcome. The abruptness of the wording in v. 24 and the different order in Pharaoh's proposal compared with 8.4 can surely be attributed to narrative considerations: here the narrator chooses to have Pharaoh respond immediately with a compromise proposal.[6] We have already discussed the change from 'worship' to 'sacrifice' in the introduction to 7.26–8.11, where we concluded that it need not be a sign of different authorship. Here it is true that 'sacrifice' occurs six times, so that it is more prominent. But that is due to the increased length and complexity of the negotiations: once Pharaoh has introduced the expression (probably to avoid any suggestion that Israel should 'serve' [the underlying sense of *ʿābad*] anyone but him) it is natural for Moses to continue to use it in his replies.

There therefore seems to be no basis for envisaging substantial secondary additions in this section. But since we have argued, both in relation to ch. 5 and in relation to 7.14-25, that there is evidence of two parallel accounts behind the present text, just as there is in chs. 3–4, there remains the question of the strand or source to which 8.16-28 belongs. In relation to 7.26–8.11 we concluded on the basis of narrative continuity (i.e. shared motifs and vocabulary) that the non-Priestly verses (7.26-29; 8.4-11a) belonged to the E strand, like

---

[5] *ÜGP*, p. 32, without explanation. Later, in his commentary (p. 59, ET, p. 77), Noth mentioned the abruptness in v. 24, but held that the section is original and part of the narrative's elaboration of the negotiations as it proceeds. Gressmann's rearrangement of the text is very speculative and actually produces a less coherent text than the present one.

[6] These problems evidently do not seem weighty to Gertz, since he attributes the whole of vv. 21-27 and 8.4 to the same redactor.

5.1-2 and 7.14-15aα, 16aβb-17a, 18, 21a, 23, 25. The correspondences with the earlier episodes here point the same way (see the notes on vv. 16-17, 18-19, 20-23), with one exception: the expression 'three days' journey' in v. 23 has occurred previously in connection with worship/sacrifice in the wilderness only in 3.18 and 5.3, which there is good reason to attribute to the J strand of the narrative. It could perhaps be argued that the E source independently introduced the motif here, not as part of the divine demand but as Moses' way of reassuring Pharaoh that the desert journey (5.1) would not be a long one. Yet it seems to make Pharaoh's insistence that 'you must not go far' (v. 24) unnecessary (unless Pharaoh is there reminding Moses of what he has said, or perhaps insisting on an even shorter journey outside the land): the dialogue would be smoother without it. On this basis we could, alternatively, suppose that the phrase was added when the J and E accounts were combined (or subsequently). Thus again the better preserved 'old' account of the plague can be attributed to E (with Propp).

Yahweh's attempt to convince Pharaoh to let Israel go is continued here by means of a further demonstration of his powerful presence in the land (vv. 22-23). But the 'argument' is reinforced by a new element, that the plague will not affect the region where the Israelites live (just as in vv. 10-11 it is the removal of the plague rather than its coming which is seen as the decisive factor). In this there is of course also evident that special care of Yahweh for his people which has already initiated a plan for their release (3.9-10) and will eventually culminate in its successful completion. But of this there can of course be no mention in the present dialogue with Pharaoh. In fact Moses' argument proceeds in a way that seems to make the respecting of Egyptian religious scruples a major concern (v. 22), even if its final purpose is the safety of Israel as they carry out their duty to their God. In the end it all comes to nothing: Pharaoh refuses to learn from what has happened, breaks his promise again (the repetition is underlined in both v. 25 and v. 28, as well as in the verbal echo of v. 11a in v. 28) and blatantly does not do what Yahweh has commanded (cf. v. 28b with v. 16b: also 7.14). At the same time the stature of Moses is further enhanced: not only as the true messenger of Yahweh (v. 20) but as a powerful intercessor with him (vv. 26-27: cf. vv. 12-13).

16 Yahweh said to Moses, 'Get up early[a] in the morning and take your stand[b] before Pharaoh – he[c] will then be coming out to the water – and say to him, "Thus says Yahweh, Let my people go so that[d] they may worship me. 17 For if[e] you do not let them go[f], then I will let loose[g] worms[h] against you, your servants, your people and your houses, and the houses of the Egyptians shall be full of the worms, and also the ground on which they stand. 18 But I will make an exception on that day of the land of Goshen, on which my people dwell[i], so that the worms shall not come there, in order that you may know that I Yahweh am in the midst of the land. 19 So I will make a distinction[j] between my people and your people: tomorrow this sign will occur."' 20 Yahweh did as he had said (lit. thus): masses of worms came into Pharaoh's house[k] and the houses[k] of his servants, and throughout the land of Egypt the land was being devastated[l] because of[m] the worms. 21 Then Pharaoh called Moses and Aaron and said, 'Go, sacrifice to your god in the land'. 22 Moses said, 'It is not safe to do so, for what we sacrifice[n] to Yahweh our God is an abomination to the Egyptians. If[o] we sacrifice what is an abomination to the Egyptians where they can see it (lit. in their eyes/sight), they will surely[p] stone us. 23 [Three days' journey] We will go[q] into the wilderness and sacrifice[q] to Yahweh our God as he tells us.' 24 Pharaoh said, 'I will let you go and you may sacrifice to Yahweh your god in the wilderness, only you must not go far[r] – make supplication for me'. 25 Moses said, 'Now I am going to leave[s] you, and I will make supplication to Yahweh, and the worms will depart from Pharaoh, his servants and his people tomorrow. Only let not Pharaoh again be deceitful[t] by not letting the people go[u] to sacrifice to Yahweh!' 26 Moses left Pharaoh and made supplication to Yahweh. 27 Yahweh did as Moses asked, and the worms departed[v] from Pharaoh, his servants and his people – not one remained. 28 But Pharaoh refused to understand[w] this time too and did not let the people go.

Notes on the Translation

a. Heb. השכם. This frequent idiom (cf. 9.13; 24.4; 32.6; 34.4; also Gen. 19.2 etc.) clearly means 'make an early start' (cf. the recurring combination with בבקר) and then more generally in Jeremiah 'show eagerness, do repeatedly'. The basis for this has long been held (cf. BDB, p. 1014) to be an original use for loading animals (cf. שכם = 'shoulder') at the beginning of a day's journey (so still *HAL*, p. 1383, with lit.). In Ug. (cf. *DULAT*, pp. 903-904) and Eth.

cognate words mean 'carry on the shoulder', and ESA *tkmtn* is said to mean 'first year of an eponym, entry into the office' (*HAL*, ibid.: the meaning 'set off [in the night]' in Eth. is less secure). This explanation has been criticised by W. von Soden ('Zum hebräischen Wörterbuch', *UF* 13 [1981], pp. 157-64 [161-62]) and more convincingly by R. Bartelmus ('*haškem w^elammed* – die "Unermüdlichkeitsformel" und die Etymologie von *hiškîm*', in W. Gross et al. [eds.], *Text, Methode und Grammatik* [FS W. Richter; St Ottilien, 1991], pp. 17-27; *TWAT* 7, 1328-30 = *TDOT* 14, pp. 682-84). Bartelmus takes a synchronic approach, avoiding etymological speculation, and concludes that the primary sense is 'be in a hurry, be earnest' and that early rising is only one specific instance of this. This could be correct, though it goes against the distributional evidence in Biblical Hebrew, where 'rise early' is widely (and without exception) attested in early/traditional narrative, whereas 'be earnest' is found predominantly in the Dtr. sections of Jeremiah, as well as in other probably later texts. If a connection with שכם, 'shoulder', is then still to be maintained, more note needs to be taken of the fact that in BH (and also in the occurrences of the Ug. verb in *KTU* 1.19.2.1, 6; 4.28, 36) it is almost always the carrying of a burden on human, not animal, shoulders that is meant. The original meaning might then be 'shoulder your load', that is, 'get ready for a journey or a task'.

b. Here the Hithpael of יצב is used, as in 9.13 (cf. 14.13; 19.17; 34.5), whereas in 5.20 and 7.15 (cf. 15.8; 17.9; 18.14; 33.8, 21; 34.2) the Niphal of נצב appears, apparently with much the same meaning (on the curious form in 2.4 see Note j on the translation of 2.1-10: probably read the Hithpael there too, with SP). But at least in some contexts יצב Hithpael 'expresses not the state of "standing" but the action of "taking up a position"' (*TWAT* 5, 560 = *TDOT* 9, p. 524).

c. Heb. הנה without any indication of the subject, as in 7.15, with יצא in a virtual future sense (see Note b on the translation of 7.14-25).

d. Heb. ויעבדני, with *waw* and the imperfect/jussive indicating purpose, as in 4.23 etc.

e. Heb. כי אם (cf. 9.1 and 10.4, in contrast to ואם in 7.27) is most naturally so rendered, though 'But if' (Schmidt: cf. Text and Versions) might be possible (cf. Jer. 7.5).

f. The periphrastic use of אין with the participle in place of a finite verb is quite frequent in the early chapters of Exodus (3.2; 5.10-11, 16: cf. also 33.15 and the elliptical expression in 32.32 [both conditional as here]). In such cases the subject is often pronominal (GK §159v), but not always: see the full account in Muraoka, *Emphatic Words*, pp. 102-11 (also JM §160g).

g. Heb. משליח. There is a clear play on words between the Piel and Hiphil participles of שלח here, which is made possible by the use of the periphrastic expression in the preceding clause. The Hiphil of שלח is much rarer than the Piel (and the Qal), occurring only five times in BH. It seems to be reserved for the divine infliction of something unpleasant on humans, a sense which can also be expressed by the Qal (cf. 9.14) and the Piel (e.g. Deut. 7.20), and may be regarded as a 'pseudo-Hiphil' like those listed in JM §54f.

h. Heb. את־הערב. For the definite article see Note o on the translation of 2.11-22. עָרֹב occurs in BH only in this passage and in the two psalms which refer to the same episode (Pss. 78.45; 105.31): it also appears in a summary of the plagues in 4Q422 3.8 (followed by [בב]היהמה) – cf. esp. v. 20 here). Some kind of animate creature is evidently meant (cf. בא in vv. 18 and 20), but there are no clear cognates. The still common interpretation 'swarm (of flies)' is based on words meaning 'mix, mixture' (Heb. ערב II), but only JAram ʿrbrwbʾ here and Syr. ʿarūbāʾ (Payne Smith, p. 427: and here Sy has to add *dkl gns* to suggest the nature of the plague; cf. *Thesaurus*, 2984: *miscella copia, colluvies*) may have (among others) the specific meaning 'a swarm (of vermin and insects)'. BH עֵרֶב in 12.38 and cognates in MH and Jewish Aramaic mean 'a mixed multitude of people' and could lend some support to the idea. But the explanation is precarious (cf. *Ges18*, p. 1010; *TWAT* 6, 357 = *TDOT* 11, p. 333). In Akk. *urbatu* II means 'a kind of worm' (*AHw*, p. 1428: cf. *HAL*, p. 832; *Ges18*, p. 1010; *TWAT* 6, 355, 357 = *TDOT* 11, pp. 331, 333), and this should perhaps be taken more seriously as a guide to the meaning (compare the conjecture 'lice' of F.S. Bodenheimer, *Animal and Man in Bible Lands* [Leiden, 1960], pp. 72-73): it could make better sense of the destructive effect of the עָרֹב (v. 20: cf. Ps. 78.45). The Vss seem to have been guessing (see Text and Versions – Philo [*Vita Mos.* 1.130-32] and Ezek. *Exagoge* 138 as usual follow LXX): they are divided between 'flies', 'a mixture' and 'wild animals' (the last already in Jos., *AJ* 2.14.3 (303)).

i. Heb. עמד, for which the general meaning 'remain, endure' is well attested (cf. 18.23; 2 Kgs 15.20), but 'dwell' seems to be paralleled only in Hag. 2.5 (of the spirit of Yahweh in the midst of his people).

j. Heb. פְּדֻת, a word occurring three times elsewhere in BH, always written plene פדות, in the sense 'redemption (by God)' (Isa. 50.2; Pss. 111.1; 130.7), and 16 times at Qumran (details in *TWQ* 3, pp. 261-63 [A. Gray]). This sense is defended here by some (e.g. Houtman, Propp: cf. Tgg), but it does not suit the context, especially the following בין, 'between', which requires a meaning like 'separation' or 'distinction' (as in the other Versions: see Text and Versions). A.A. Macintosh has argued that פדה is to be derived from a root פדד which is otherwise unattested in Hebrew but could be cognate with Syr. *pd* = 'strayed' and Ar. *faḍḍa*, 'was/became apart', and so could mean 'separation' ('Exodus VIII 19, Distinctive Redemption and the Hebrew Roots פדה and פדד', *VT* 21 [1971], pp. 548-55). However, the correspondence of consonants presumed would be irregular and the Heb. cognate of these verbs should be פז, which could well be the basis for BH מופז and פז, 'pure gold', i.e. 'separated' from impurities. Dillmann considered reading פָּלֻת, from √פלה (cf. v. 18), and many have adopted this emendation (cf. *BHS*), but it is not easy to see how textual corruption would then lead to פדה (and LXX did not render the verb פלה by 'separate' in v. 18: Propp, p. 329). A more likely original reading is פָּרֻדָּה (or פְּרֻדָּה) from √פרד, which is also common in BH in the sense 'divide' and is sometimes followed by בֵּין: MT could then be the result of virtual haplography, given the similarity of *daleth* and *resh* (Davies, 'The Hebrew Text of Exodus VIII 19 [EVV. 23] – An Emendation', *VT* 24 [1974], pp. 489-92: followed by Durham). One ms. of SP seems to attest a reading like this (see Text and Versions).

k. The sing. forms of בית here correspond to those in 7.28, just as the pl. in v. 17 does to those in 8.5 and 7. A collective interpretation of the sing. is possible, and likely in the second case here (cf. Note e on the translation of 7.26–8.11). The pl. forms probably include the house(s) of Pharaoh's courtiers, so there is no difficulty in rendering ביתה־פרעה here by 'Pharaoh's house' (to which ביתך in 7.28 will also refer).

l. Heb. תשחת. The use of the imperfect to express durative action in the past (rather than the participle), while less frequent than the iterative use, is recognised by both older (GK §107b-d: but not all the exx. are valid) and newer (JM §113f-g) grammars: Gen. 2.6 and Exod. 13.22 are clear examples. The attempt of Driver, *Tenses*, pp. 35-36 (approved by GK §107d), to reduce this idiom to a sub-set of the iterative use does not explain all the examples. השחית is a strong expression (cf. אכל in Ps. 78.45), which is often used of the devastation of land or crops (cf. Judg. 6.4; Mal. 3.11), but also of severe disease (1 Sam. 6.5).

m. For the simple causal use of מפני cf. 3.7, 9.11 and BDB, p. 818.

n. Probably the imperfect וזבח is to be understood as iterative, referring here to what is customary (GK §107g – so JB, JPS, NRSV), though a future interpretation (as in AV, RV, RSV, NEB) is also possible. As elsewhere the object precedes the verb for emphasis (cf. 7.15 and the note there).

o. Heb. הן probably never *means* 'if' (e.g. NRSV) as it does in Aram. (see Note a on the translation of 4.1-9), but this is a context in which a conditional understanding of the sentence is not just possible, as it is in 6.12 and 30 (see Note e on the translation of 6.10–7.5), but plausible. Nevertheless, since a condition can be expressed in Heb. 'by the simple juxtaposition of two clauses' (GK §159b), this would not demand that הן here means 'If' rather than 'Look'. On Garr's understanding of הן as 'affirmative' rather than 'presentative' (*RB* 111 [2004], p. 343], one might indeed do better to translate the clause 'Since we shall be sacrificing...' (cf. ibid., pp. 335-36).

p. Heb. ולא here introduces a question without the interrogative particle הֲ (GK §150a), lit. 'will they not stone us?' – unless it be supposed that לא here is not the negative but an asseverative particle as in other Semitic languages (so F. Nötscher, 'Zum emphatischen Lamed', *VT* 3 [1953], pp. 372-80 [esp. p. 375]). But Muraoka, *Emphatic Words*, pp. 113-23, finds this unproven except for a few passages, mainly in poetry, and explicitly rules it out for this passage (p. 118). Cf. Note j on the translation of 3.16-22 for a similar case.

q. The verbs here are imperfect and perfect consecutive (as later in 10.9), not cohortative like Moses' initial request (5.3) and references to it (3.18; 5.8,

17). This is appropriate to the new context of negotiations, in which Moses is in a stronger position. Since the imperfect can have a modal use (JM §113l-m), the rendering 'must' (e.g. JB, JPS, NRSV) is also possible, but it is not necessary.

r. The inf. abs. is a common way of strengthening a command (JM §123h, ja). For the adverbial use of the Hiphil followed by an inf. cons. (ללכת here) see JM §54d, 124n.

s. Heb. יוצא, the participle of the 'imminent future' (JM §121e), with which הנה is especially frequent.

t. Heb. התל. Hiph. inf. abs. of תלל II: sometimes rendered 'mock, trifle with' (cf. BDB, p. 1068), but the Hiphil forms all have the meaning 'deceive' (Sir. 13.7 can be added to those in BH: cf. also the noun מהתלות in Isa. 30.10 [BDB, p. 1122]; CD 1.18; 4Q266 2 1.22; 4Q438 12.1). It is the Piel forms, which are generally derived from a separate (by-?)form התל, which mean 'mock' (for an excellent review of the occurrences and discussion about the relationship between the forms and the meanings see *TWAT* 8, 662-71 = *TDOT* 15, pp. 672-81). The Vss (see Text and Versions) uniformly support the meaning 'deceive, lie', but the confusion of the two forms (roots?) is an old one (see *AramB* 7, p. 23 n. 12 for refs.), and persistent (cf. Childs, Houtman).

u. Heb. לבלתי. Followed by an inf. cons. this particle is the negative counterpart to ל, and here too 'the ל can have various values according to the context' (JM §124e). While it normally expresses purpose or consequence, it may also presumably make the inf. into the equivalent of a Latin gerund (so with ל alone, JM §124o) and this fits the present context best.

v. Heb. ויסר. The form is most likely Qal (like the perfect consecutive וסר in v. 25), but it could be the Hiphil, which is indistinguishable in this form (cf. Gen. 8.13: BDB, p. 694; JM §23b, 80k, n: cf. Text and Versions here, and Propp), giving the alternative rendering 'and he (i.e. Yahweh) removed the worms...' (cf. 8.4 of the frogs).

w. Heb. ויכבד...את־לבו, lit. 'made his heart heavy' (see the notes on 7.14). Here Pharaoh is clearly the subject and in view of the גם here, which assumes a previous similar statement, this should also be the interpretation in 8.11 (see Note z there).

Explanatory Notes

16-17. Again, as in 7.26-29, Yahweh sends Moses to Pharaoh to demand the Israelites' release and to announce a plague if he does not comply. Here and in the following verses the fact that Israel is 'my people' is even more strongly emphasised (vv. 16, 17, 18, 19). In addition to specifying the time, 'in the morning' (as in 7.15: implying a nocturnal visitation by Yahweh?), the common expression 'get up early' is introduced (cf. 9.13, and Note a on the translation here).

In other respects too the opening words resemble 7.15, but here there is no mention of a staff. There is a word-play in v. 17, as both 'let go' and 'let loose' are participles (of different conjugations) of the same verb (Heb. *šlḥ*): see Notes f and g on the translation. The exact nature of the plague is uncertain, as Heb. *ʿārōb* occurs only here and in related passages (Pss. 78.45; 105.31). Early explanations took it to mean 'dog-flies' (which has the widest scholarly support today), 'wild animals' (so famously in illustrated texts of the Passover Haggadah) and 'a mixture', the latter being due to the word's similarity to 'mixed multitude' in 12.38 and related words. Some interpretations have combined these possibilities (see Note h on the translation and Text and Versions). The suggestion 'worms' is adopted here because of an Akkadian parallel and the better fit with the location of the plague and the 'devastation' mentioned in v. 20 (cf. Houtman's 'vermin' and Propp's 'biting insects', with connections to 'lice': the latter was the explanation favoured by the biologist F.S. Bodenheimer).

18-19. A new element in the plague narrative appears here for the first time, a clear distinction between the treatment of the Israelites and the Egyptians, which recurs in the plagues of pestilence and hail (9.4, 6, 26: not, however, with the locusts or darkness in ch. 10) and reaches its climax in the death of the firstborn in ch. 12. Probably the same point was made again in v. 19 originally (see Note j on the translation), but the Hebrew texts have the word for 'redemption' here and, while this is likely to be an accidental error, it does lead to a theological 'deepening' of the narrative (Schmidt, pp. 345, 404), which the Targums elaborated in two different ways (see Text and Versions). The sparing of the Israelites reflects Yahweh's general care for them, but its purpose here is to reinforce the lesson to Pharaoh which the plague is designed to teach: that Yahweh is present and active in the midst of Pharaoh's land (for similar intentions earlier see 7.17 and 8.6, and later in 9.14-16; but not as such in ch. 10). In this sense it is a 'sign' (v. 23: cf. in relation to the Egyptians 4.17 (?) and 7.3, both in the plural; the expression is used in relation to the Israelites themselves in 10.1-2 [again with 'know']). The separate place where the Israelites live is here named 'Goshen' for the first time in Exodus: so again in 9.26, and much more often in the later chapters of Genesis (45.10; 46.28-29, 34; 47.1, 4, 6, 27; 50.8). This constitutes another important link between the non-Priestly narratives in Genesis and Exodus (cf. 'Joseph' in

1.6, 8), whose significance has been ignored by those who have recently argued that a literary connection between the patriarchal narratives and the Exodus story was only made at a late stage in the composition of the Pentateuch. The Genesis passages indicate not only the separateness of Goshen (46.34), but that it is close to the residence of Joseph, i.e. the capital (45.10), that it is good land within Egypt (45.18, 20: the Priestly terminology in 47.6a, 11 is slightly different and speaks of the 'land of Rameses'), that it is on a route from Canaan to the Egyptian capital (46.28-29) and that it is suited to shepherds (46.34). The LXX here and from Gen. 47.1 onwards simply gives a transcription of the name (in fact Γέσεμ, which departs slightly from the MT form, possibly through knowledge of a contemporary place-name, but see Text and Versions on v. 18). Earlier in the Genesis narrative it either adds the word 'Arabia' (45.10; 46.34) in the sense of a region in north-eastern Egypt (see below) or, where the word 'land' is not present in the Hebrew (46.28-29), renders Goshen as Ἡρώων Πόλιν (Heroopolis), the name of a well-known Hellenistic city in Egypt which has been firmly located at Tell el-Maskhuta in the Wadi Tumilat (see further my *Way of the Wilderness*, pp. 5-6, 8). Such a location fits the requirements of the biblical narrative well and also corresponds precisely to the region in which an Egyptian text of the thirteenth century B.C. states that nomads might be allowed to pasture their animals (*ANET*, p. 259; P. Anastasi VI, 51-61 [iv.11–v.5]).[7] Nineteenth-century attempts to find an Egyptian name equivalent to Goshen in the 20th nome south-west of Qantir/Ramesses (such as E. Naville, *The Shrine of Seft el-Henneh and the Land of Goshen* [London, 1887], based on a late topographical list in the temple at Edfu) were contested long ago by A.E. Gardiner, 'The Supposed Egyptian Equivalent of the Name of Goshen', *JEA* 5 (1918), pp. 218-23: for a recent summary see M. Görg, *NBL*, 1, pp. 903-904.[8]

---

[7] The place (or places) of the same name mentioned in Josh. 10.41; 11.16; 15.51 is evidently quite distinct, despite occasional suggestions to the contrary: see especially H. Cazelles, 'La localisation de Goshen: problèmes de méthode', *Autour de l'Exode (Études)* (Paris, 1987), pp. 233-39, who envisages the incorporation of a separate tradition about the deliverance of some elements of Israel from Egyptian control in Palestine.

[8] Görg himself favours an echo of the phrase *t3 n qsn.t*, 'land of affliction, hunger' in the Prophecy of Neferti, 35 (see *ANET*, p. 444; *COS* 1, p. 108: both 'desert'). But this hardly fits the description of the region in Genesis. Naville's idea

20-23. Pharaoh's response to the devastation of the land (v. 20) is to call for Moses and Aaron (for the latter cf. vv. 4 and 8) and to offer them (and presumably their people) leave to go and sacrifice to Yahweh, but only within Egypt, as Egyptian workmen would be expected to do for their gods. His assumption is presumably that this will cause Yahweh to relent and the plague to cease. The reply of Moses (who alone speaks, as usual) is surprising, since it is based not on Yahweh's demand but on Egyptian religious sensitivities and their likely effect. To translate 'It is not right' (e.g. NJPS, JB, NRSV, following Tgg and Sy: cf. 'meet' in AV, RV) in v. 22 does not fit what follows and in fact Heb. *nākôn* probably never means 'right' in the sense of 'proper, morally justified', although it can mean 'right' in the sense of 'true' (Gen. 41.32; Deut. 13.15; 17.4; Ps. 5.10; Job 42.7, 8). 'Expedient' or better 'safe' is what the context requires (cf. Luther's 'Das taugt nicht', perhaps, and probably in effect the 'It is impossible' of LXX and Vulg) and some basis for this can be found in the use of *nākôn* in Job 21.8 and the places where it means 'sure, firmly established' (2 Sam. 7.16, 26; 1 Kgs 2.45; Isa. 2.2; Ps. 93.2), though it remains unusual.[9] Moses is portrayed as being concerned about the consequences if the Israelites sacrifice in Egypt, literally, 'the abomination of the Egyptians'. This phrase was in the past (see Text and Versions) often taken, like the similar phrase in 2 Kgs 23.13b, to mean the gods whom the Egyptians worshipped, or more precisely the animals which represented them in the form of images.[10] But the genitive is more likely, in the light of similar expressions in Gen. 43.32 and 46.34, objective: 'that which the Egyptians regard as an abomination', i.e.

---

has been revived by Van Seters ('Geography', pp. 267-69), who answers Gardiner's objections and rejects D.B. Redford's association of Goshen with Gashmu of Qedar: he argues that the name was introduced in the eighth century B.C.

[9] *THAT* 1, 814-15 = *TLOT* 2, pp. 603-604, gives a good fourfold analysis of the meanings, but 'right', the third category in which Exod. 8.22 is placed, brings together a varied group of usages. *TWAT* 4, 95-107 = *TDOT* 7, pp. 89-101, is even less useful, as it concentrates mainly on the Hiphil and Polel forms of the verb *kûn* and on derived nouns. Gressmann's emendation to *nābôn*, 'sensible', is ingenious but probably unnecessary. Beer compared Judg. 12.6 for the sense 'impossible' (cf. Propp), but his 'Es schickt sich nicht' takes this in a moral sense.

[10] A modern variant of this view is that Egyptian sacrifices (which would be an abomination to Yahweh) are meant (Holzinger, p. 26), but this is clearly opposed to v. 22b (Holzinger significantly regards this as a gloss, but without good reason).

animal sacrifices. This does face the problem that in the second millennium B.C. the Egyptians seem to have been quite tolerant of Asiatic immigrants and their foreign cults (cf. Propp, p. 329) and indeed poultry and pieces of meat were often included in their own offerings (cf. Hyatt, p. 112; *ANET*, pp. 327, 417). It is only in later times, in the fifth century, that hostility on the part of Egyptians to animal sacrifices is actually attested: in Herodotus, *Hist.* 2.18, 41-46, and in the Elephantine papyri (Cowley, nos. 31-33: *ANET*, pp. 492-93).[11] Such attitudes may have been in existence for some time and an Israelite writer of the monarchy period could have been aware of them. Alternatively the author may have attributed to the Egyptians a similar intolerance of foreign practices to that which he knew to exist in Israel. This seems to be what has happened with the reaction which Moses is said to anticipate. Stoning is attested as the punishment for a serious offence in Israelite law and narrative (cf. also 17.4), but not elsewhere in the ancient Near East (cf. *TWAT* 5, 945-48 = *TDOT* 10, pp. 341-44). The writer evidently reflects the practice with which he was familiar.

Pharaoh's offer is therefore found unacceptable, and Moses insists on the need to worship Yahweh in the wilderness (cf. 5.1, 3; 7.16), which will only take 'a couple of days': the phrase 'three days' journey' (for which cf. 3.18, 5.3 – here it is placed at the beginning of the sentence for emphasis) is a frequent one in the Old Testament and represents a short journey, not necessarily precisely defined but of the order of fifty miles, to judge from its other occurrences (see further my 'The Significance of Deuteronomy 1.2 for the Location of Mount Horeb', *PEQ* 111 [1979], pp. 87-101 [89-97]).[12] The distance involved is far too little to reach any of the likely sites for Mount Sinai/Horeb (see my *Way of the Wilderness*, pp. 63-69) and, if this element of the tradition is not a mere ploy to win Pharaoh's agreement, the goal would have to be another mountain (or place) closer to Egypt, perhaps that referred to in some passages as 'the mountain of God' (cf. ibid., pp. 68-69). Moses also insists that Yahweh is to be worshipped according to his own requirements, which are yet to be revealed ('as he tells us': cf. 10.26b): there can therefore be no question of accommodating Egyptian scruples.

---

[11] For later references still see Propp, p. 430.
[12] See the introduction to this section for the possibility that the phrase may be a redactional addition here.

24-25. Pharaoh appears to concede all that Moses has asked – 'not...far' is consistent with 'three days' journey' (see above). Apart from his request for intercession (which is delayed by comparison with 8.4), he only insists on his prerogative to grant such leave: the 'I' in 'I will let you go' is reinforced by an emphatic independent pronoun (*'ānōkî*). When Moses replies in v. 25, he uses the same pronoun and, although it may not in itself be emphatic in the different grammatical construction there,[13] the rapid recurrence of the same form does have the effect of making Moses equally insistent on his power, in his case to secure the removal of the plague by his prayer. His concluding warning to Pharaoh not to be deceitful and break his promise (on this meaning for Heb. *tll* Hiphil and the closest parallels see Note t on the translation) recalls what had happened shortly before (cf. v. 11) and proleptically comments on what actually happens in v. 28.

26-28. Despite the effectiveness of Moses' prayer and the removal of the worms (however the ambiguous text is understood – see Note v on the translation – this is clearly implied to be Yahweh's doing), Pharaoh shows no more understanding on this occasion than before: the intention expressed in v. 18 has been to no avail. As in v. 11 the Heb. implies a wilful refusal to understand: Pharaoh closes his eyes to the evidence before him of Yahweh's power.

Text and Versions

ויאמר יהוה (8.16)   4QpalEx¹ had a *vacat* after v. 15, and both 4QpalExᵐ (not noted in *DJD* IX, pp. 60-61, 76-77) and 4Q365 probably had empty space at the end of one line and the beginning of the next, corresponding to the *setumah* in MT. Before יהוה here and later in the verse Tg^Nmg as usual inserts 'the Memra of'.

אל־משה (8.16)   4QpalExᵐ adds לאמר, which is only occasionally found in MT after another form of אמר (but see Note d on the translation of 7.6-13) and not present in any other witness here.

והתיצב (8.16)   4Q365 has והתצבתה, i.e. perf. cons., and Tgʲ translates accordingly, probably an independent stylistic improvement: all other witnesses support MT's imperative.

---

[13] Muraoka, *Emphatic Words*, pp. 138-40, suggests that it would be, but a comparison between the examples of pronoun suffix and independent pronoun following *hinnēh* in Exod. 1–10 does not bear this out (cf. 3.13).

הנה (8.16)   Vulg renders freely with *enim*. As in 7.15, SP adds הוא to complete the construction and LXX's αὐτός probably reflects a similar *Vorlage*, since Greek grammar does not require it. The Qumran mss do not survive for this part of the verse, but the word may have stood in 4QpalEx^m (which has it in 7.15) and 4QEx^c (*DJD* XII, p. 106, says 'there would have been room...' on the basis of the meagre remains), though probably not in 4Q365 (against *DJD* XIII, p. 264: its restoration oddly omits (ה)המימה, which would take up [at least] the space available).

המימה (8.16)   SP reads המים, omitting the *he locale* as in 7.15 (see Text and Versions there) and elsewhere. Tg^{J,N} add the same explanations for Pharaoh's promenade as they do in 7.15.

ואמרת (8.16)   Sy has the imperative, maintaining the construction earlier in the verse.

עמי (8.16)   SP and 4Q365 insert את for grammatical propriety and to match v. 17: the other Qumran mss do not preserve this part of the verse.

ויעבדני (8.16)   4Q365's *plene* orthography attests the plural form indicated by the vocalisation of MT. Vulg and Tgg render as in 7.16. All the uncial mss of LXX (followed by Rahlfs) add ἐν τῇ ἐρήμῳ, assimilating to 7.16, but Wevers regards the phrase as an early addition rather than part of the original translation (see *THGE*, p. 242). The alternative explanation of the shorter text in many miniscules would be that it is due to harmonisation with MT: no asterisks are reported, so it might be pre-hexaplaric (cf. *THGE*, p. 40). But even if the extra phrase goes back to a Heb. *Vorlage*, it is certainly secondary.

כי אם (8.17)   4Q365 has ואם (as in 7.27), a variant which might also be the basis for LXX's ἐὰν δέ (cf. Sy and perhaps Vulg *quod si*), though the translators could have modified MT independently: the point of the כי (to reinforce the command) is not immediately obvious, though cf. 9.2.

משלח (8.17)   LXX βούλῃ ἐξαποστεῖλαι, introducing a reference to Pharaoh's will, as elsewhere (cf. Wevers, *Notes*, p. 116).

משליח (8.17)   SP, 4QEx^c and 4Q365 read משלח, without the vowel-letter. In the case of SP at least this is not a defective spelling of the Hiphil/Afel (though such occasionally occur: cf. 6.7), but the Piel part., since in Lev. 26.22 SP clearly substitutes the Piel perf. for the Hiphil, apparently because the Hiphil with its distinct usage (see Note g on the translation) was no longer in use. This reading also appears in 11QpalLev^a (Freedman/Mathews, p. 46) and probably explains the Qumran readings here as well. Most of the Vss (not Sy) indicate the difference in meaning by using different forms of the same verb (Tg^o) or two different lexemes. As the rarer form MT is very probably original.

ובעבדיך (8.17)   Sy has no equivalent, probably by accidental omission through homoeoarkton.

ובבתיך (8.17)   4Q365 reads the sing. ובביתכה, as do Tg^J and many mss of Sy (inc. 5b1, but the Leiden ed. follows 7a1, 7a13 and 8a1 in reading the pl. of MT and SP). Tg^N has 'on the men of your house(hold)'. All these probably assimilate to the sing. in v. 20, failing to see that here the pl. includes (as in vv. 5 and 7) the residences of Pharaoh's courtiers.

את־הערב (8.17) LXX (followed by Philo and Symm) has κυνόμυιαν, 'dog-fly', but Aq and Theod have words for 'mixed' or 'mixture', as do the Aram. Vss, linking the word to a root in MH and Aram. of which only nominal derivatives occur in BH. Tg^J has throughout 'a mixture of wild animals', following an interpretation which is already attested in Josephus (see Note h on the translation: cf. Exod.R. 11.2 [beasts and birds combined] and Sy, 'a mixture of every kind [sc. of creatures]').[14] Vulg *omne genus muscarum* (cf. later in the verse *muscis diversi generis*) combined the two traditions of interpretation. There is a suggestion in *AramB* 2, p. 35, that the Aram. word used alone in Tg^{F,N} might mean 'vermin' (cf. Sokoloff, *Dictionary*, p. 418; CAL online 15.9.2008). Sam.Gk. had κόρακα, confusing this word with עֹרֵב = 'raven'.

וגם האדמה (8.17) Tg^O reproduces the wording of MT, and Sy 'like the land...' comes close to this. The other Tgg have ו(אוף) ית ארעא, as though the land was an additional object of a preceding verb: this seems to correspond to the occasional use of Heb. את with the subj. of a passive verb (for which see GK §121a-b, JM §128b). LXX καὶ εἰς τὴν γῆν and Vulg *et in universa terra* (cf. v. 12) are best understood as paraphrases which, with the following clauses, see the Heb. here as already limiting the plague to regions other than Goshen (cf. v. 18 and Wevers, *Notes*, p. 117).

הם (8.17) 4QpalEx^m, 4QEx^c and 4Q365 all read המה, which had become much the more common form at Qumran (compare the statistics in Qimron, p. 58, with those in [e.g.] *DCH* 2, pp. 563 and 566). SP has הם, which should be retained here.

והפליתי (8.18) Tg^O and Sy recognise the derivation from √פלה, but LXX παραδοξάσω,[15] Vulg *faciam mirabilem* and Tg^{J,N} 'I will do (signs and) wonders' treat the form as פלא Hiphil, as they also do in 9.4 (except for Tg^N). SP agrees with MT here but has הפלא in 9.4. The construction in 9.4 certainly favours the sense 'distinction' there, as does the continuation in the second half of 8.18 and v. 19 here.

גשן (8.18) LXX Γέσεμ, as in 9.26 and Gen. 47.1 etc. For other renderings see my *Way of the Wilderness*, p. 5. The interchange of final 'm' and 'n' is

---

[14] Propp notes that 'wild animals' are the object of the rare Hiphil of שלח in Lev. 26.22 (p. 328), which may be the 'clue' that led to this interpretation of ערב.

[15] For the meaning ('marquer d'un prodige') see *BAlex* 2, pp. 34-35: the relation of this word (which seems to be one of the few real Septuagintal neologisms) to παράδοξος and other words leaves no room for doubt. Curiously both Lust et al. (p. 351) and Muraoka (p. 434) give a primary sense ('to treat with distinction', 'to act in discriminating fashion') based on MT here rather than Greek philology (cf. LSJ, p. 1308 for these two passages). I am grateful to Dr J.K. Aitken for advice about this issue.

עמד (8.18) So also SP, but 4Q365 reads יושב, a more regular way of expressing the meaning intended (and therefore clearly secondary). The Aram. Vss reflect this sense with *ytb* (Sy) and שרי: LXX ἔπεστιν and Vulg *est* are weaker equivalents.

לבלתי (8.18) LXX ἐφ'ἧς οὐκ, a free rendering that takes up ἐφ'ἧς earlier in the verse and is perhaps based on a consequential rather than a final understanding of the infinitive construction (cf. Theod ὥστε μή, Vulg *ut non*).

בקרב הארץ (8.18) Two kinds of paraphrase are found in the Vss. Both LXX ὁ κύριος πάσης τῆς γῆς and the insertion of שליט in Tg^{O,J} see God's presence as implying his 'complete mastery' (Wevers, *Notes*, p. 118: *AramB* 7, p. 21 n. 7 cites the (medieval) midrash *Sekhel Tob*, Exod., p. 48, to similar effect). Similar additions are found in Tg^{O,J} at Deut. 3.24 and 4.39. On the other hand Tg^N ('whose Memra dwells...') and its mg ('the glory of whose Shekinah dwells...') introduce expansions that are used elsewhere (on the latter see Chester, *Divine Revelation*, pp. 320-22). Vulg and Sy render MT straightforwardly.

ושמתי (8.19) LXX καὶ δώσω is in general a rare equivalence, but there are six other exx. in Exodus (4.11, 15, 21; 9.5; 17.14; 21.13), matched by another seven in Isaiah 40–66. The rendering looks like a Hebraism based on the wider meanings of נתן (cf. Lee, *Lexical Study*, p. 11), but *BAlex* 2, p. 127, points to a possible basis in earlier Greek idiom.

פדת (8.19) SP writes פדות, like the other occurrences of the word in MT, but Camb. 1846 has an erasure (of ד?) between the *daleth* and the *waw* (and an unexplained space at the corresponding point in the SP plus below): probably evidence of a variant close to the emendation proposed in Note j on the translation. LXX, Vulg and Sy give the meaning 'separation, distinction' that is required by the context. Tg^N has פורקן, 'redemption' (but from a verb that can mean 'separate'), and Exod.R. 11.2 perhaps indicates how this was understood ('This teaches that Israel too deserved to be smitten with this plague, but God made the Egyptians their ransom', cited in *AramB* 7, p. 21 n. 8). Tg^{O,J} have a simpler theology, but have to rewrite the verse to achieve it: 'I will put redemption for my people and for your people *I will bring a plague*'.

למחר (8.19) LXX and Sy prefix 'and', but the asyndeton of MT etc. is both effective and idiomatic, esp. where the verb is deferred as here (cf. JM §177a).

האת הזה (8.19) LXX adds ἐπὶ τῆς γῆς, probably influenced by the wording of 9.5. Codex Vaticanus and family *f* have no equivalent to האות, and *BHS* implies that this is the original LXX reading (against both Rahlfs and Wevers: the omission of τὸ σημεῖον could be due to homoeoarkton).

560   EXODUS 1–18

After this verse SP again has a long addition (cf. on 7.18 and 7.29) corresponding to vv. 16b-19, in which Moses and Aaron take Yahweh's message to Pharaoh: the introduction is exactly as in 7.29b except for the use of אמר instead of דבר. There is also clear evidence of this plus at the top of col. IV of 4QpalEx^m (*DJD* IX, p. 77) – sections of Yahweh's instructions in vv. 16-19 are present at the bottom of the preceding column – and in Sy^hex (the precise wording is again very close to LXX, as at 7.29). There is no evidence to determine whether or not the plus appeared in any other Qumran ms.: in particular nothing remains of 4Q365 (which, like some other mss of 4QRP, often agrees with SP) between the beginning of 8.19 and 9.9.

יהוה (8.20)   Tg^Nmg prefixes 'the Memra of', as usual.

כן (8.20)   After this word SP has a paragraph break which is not in MT. It is possible, but not certain, that such a division was marked in 4QpalEx^m (*DJD* IX, p. 78).

ויבא (8.20)   Read as a Hiphil, continuing the divine subject, in Tg^J and Sy.

כבד (8.20)   Tgg and Sy have *tqyp*, probably 'mighty', though it can mean 'severe', which is closer to the metaphorical sense of כבד. SP and 4QpalEx^m add מאד, which follows כבד elsewhere in MT in this section of Exodus (9.3, 18, 24; 10.14; 12.38), but intensification of the plague is likely to be secondary here. Vulg *gravissima* is probably not based on this reading: it never represents Heb. כבד מאד elsewhere.

ביתה־פרעה (8.20)   LXX εἰς τοὺς οἴκους Φαραώ, a mistaken assimilation to v. 17 (see Note k on the translation). Vulg *domos* goes with both genitives, so is not textually significant. Tg^N בפלטורין דפרעה uses a more specific word derived from Lat. *praetorium* for the only time in Exodus; it is used several times in Genesis for Pharaoh's or Joseph's 'palace' (also in Tg^J in an expansion of Exod. 12.31, but not here).

בית עבדיו (8.20)   LXX again has the pl., as does Tg^N, in this case with more reason. But MT's sing. is supported by the other witnesses and is the more difficult reading. The Sebirin ובבית is a secondary easing of the syntax (cf. Tov, *Textual Criticism*, p. 64).

ובכל (8.20)   SP omits the *waw*, so that the phrase must be taken with what precedes rather than what follows (MT, Tgg), a natural consequence of its insertion of a *waw* before the following verb (see the next note). LXX, Sy and Vulg keep the 'and' here but imply the same sentence-division as SP.

תשחת (8.20)   SP prefixes *waw* (the 'and' here in LXX, Vulg, Sy could be due to a similar *Vorlage*) to remove the 'difficulty' of the unusual imperfect in past narrative by making it into the regular imperfect consecutive. MT, which is supported by Tgg, is certainly to be preferred. Symm ἐφθάρη (cf. Vulg *corruptaque est*), in place of LXX's (καὶ) ἐξωλεθρεύθη, may be designed to make an intertextual link with Gen. 6.11, where LXX uses this verb, as the simplex form is rare (cf. Salvesen, *Symmachus*, pp. 246, 270). Propp (p. 298) suggests that SP's Heb. variant might be due to the influence of the same verse.

הארץ (8.20) Tg^J 'the inhabitants of the land', perhaps as a result of its regular rendering of ערב by 'wild animals'.

אל־משה (8.21) SP למשה, following the more natural repetition of the same preposition in v. 4. Compare Lev. 10.6, where MT again has אל followed by ל and SP has אל twice as in v. 12. MT's 'mixed' construction is surely original.

ויאמר (8.21) LXX, freely, has λέγων here (contrast 8.4). Vulg and Sy add 'to them'.

זבחו (8.21) Tg^J amplifies here and in v. 25 with a reference to 'festival offerings' as in 5.3 etc.

לאלהיכם (8.21) Tgg and Sy have 'before' instead of 'to' and, with the exception of Tg^O, also introduce the divine name in line with v. 22.

בארץ (8.21) Tg^J and Tg^N specify the location more precisely by adding 'this' or 'of Egypt' (as do some mss of LXX and Vulg).

לא נכון לעשות (8.22) LXX οὐ δυνατὸν γενέσθαι and Vulg *non potest... fieri* render freely, without the moral element which the other Vss introduce (see the Explanatory Note).

תעבת מצרים (8.22) LXX and Theod render straightforwardly though in the pl., as do Vulg and Sy here (but not later in the verse: see below). Tg^O 'some of the cattle which the Egyptians worship', Tg^J 'some of the sheep which are the idols of the Egyptians', and Tg^N 'the idols of the Egyptians are an abomination (and) from them' (mg. 'the sheep are the abominations of the Egyptians [and] from them') all indicate a reference to the animal form of some Egyptian gods. A linguistic basis for this could be found in the occasional concrete use of Heb. תעבה for a foreign deity (e.g. 2 Kgs 23.13b). For pars. see *AramB* 2, p. 36 n. 13.

נזבח (8.22) The LXX witnesses are divided between future indicative θύσομεν and aorist subjunctive θύσωμεν (which occurs a few words later), and Wevers oddly regards the latter as original, against other edd. (see *THGE*, pp. 228-29). But it is hard to see what it could mean (Wevers's 'we would sacrifice' is scarcely convincing) and the future is more likely. In any case it makes no difference to the underlying Heb. Tgg prefix 'take' and as usual replace 'to' with 'before'.

הן (8.22) LXX, Aq, Symm, Vulg, Tg^{J,N}, Sy have the 'if' suggested by the context and Aram. usage, but Tg^J simply has 'behold' (הא) and Theod only καί (following a variant Heb. *Vorlage* according to O'Connell, *Theodotionic Revision*, p. 135; but later he suggests that it may be a scribal error [p. 255]).

את־תעבת מצרים (8.22) Here Vulg *ea quae colunt Aegyptii* and Sy *dḥlt' dmṣry'* indicate a reference to theriomorphic deities, like the Tgg earlier in the verse. Tg^{Nmg} by contrast reverts here to MT.

ולא יסקלנו (8.22) All the Vss (with some paraphrase in LXX and Tgg) give the intended positive meaning, presumably on the basis of treating the clause as interrogative.

דרך (8.23) Tg^N amplifies with 'the way of a journey of...'

נלך...וזבחנו (8.23)   SP reads the cohortative both times, as in 5.3, on which this verse is closely modelled (so the recent edd. and almost all mss: von Gall's נלך...ונזבח is a minority reading). Vulg clearly supports MT, which as an unusual expression that fits the context well is surely original. The evidence of the other Vss is not so clear, because the LXX witnesses are divided (but both Rahlfs and Wevers favour the future) and the Aram. imperfects of Tgg and Sy can have a modal as well as a future sense. After their equivalents to וזבחנו Tgg amplify as usual (see the notes on v. 21).

יאמר (8.23)   So also SP and most of the Vss; but LXX and Tg^N have the past tense, which might indeed have been expected in the light of ch. 3. But the imperfect is the more difficult reading and attested by the Heb. witnesses. On its meaning see the Explanatory Note.

וזבחתם (8.24)   Again the LXX witnesses are divided, between the aor. imper. καὶ θύσατε and the future καὶ θύσετε, which as the reading closer to MT is presumably secondary. The original reading anticipates the form of the commands which follow. Tgg as usual have 'before' with the divine name.

הרחק לא־תרחיקו (8.24)   LXX οὐ μακρὰν ἀποτενεῖτε is idiomatic Greek (Wevers, *Notes*, p. 121), employing the verb ἀποτείνω in its rarer intransitive use as in a similar phrase in Pl. *Gorg.* 458b.

העתירו בעדי (8.24)   LXX adds οὖν (cf. 'also' in Tg^N and Sy), to avoid the abrupt connection, and πρὸς κύριον, which 'makes Pharaoh recognise once again that the Lord is in control' (Wevers, ibid.).

משה (8.25)   Sy adds *lpr'wn*, making the addressee pedantically explicit, as in v. 21 and elsewhere.

הנה (8.25)   LXX unusually renders with ὅδε (Aq and Theod replace it with the regular equivalent ἰδού; Symm paraphrases), but this is found occasionally in the Pentateuch (otherwise only Judg. 9.31[A]), the closest parallels being Gen. 50.18, Exod. 17.6 and Num. 14.40. For the (virtually adverbial: cf. Wevers, *Notes*, p. 121, 'right now') usage here cf. LSJ s.v. I.2-3: the literary parallels are mostly poetic.

אנכי (8.25)   Theod and Aq expand LXX's ἐγώ to ἐγώ εἰμι, even with a finite verb immediately following, a device used in the *kaige* recension to distinguish between occurrences of אנכי and אני (cf. O'Connell, *Theodotionic Revision*, pp. 19-24, 281).

והעתרתי (8.25)   Tg^N ונצליה, as often in PTM (cf. Stevenson, p. 51), uses a first person pl. form to represent the sing.

אל־יהוה (8.25)   LXX πρὸς τὸν θεόν (as also in v. 26), although it has κυρίῳ for the divine name at the end of the verse. Tgg (also later in the verse) and Sy as usual have 'before'.

וסר (8.25)   Tgg, like the other Vss, agree with MT: the causative renderings of Tg^O and Tg^N in *AramB* here are surely erroneous.

מפרעה (8.25)   LXX ἀπὸ σοῦ, continuing the direct address earlier, as it does to the end of the verse (treating the second פרעה as a vocative).

מעבדיו (8.25) SP prefixes *waw*, to complete the syndesis: the Vss (except Tg°) all have 'and', probably an example of the common tendency for Hebrew texts and translations to exhibit independently the same 'improvements' rather than necessarily further evidence of a Heb. text different from MT (which would in any case be secondary).

ומעמו (8.25) Tg^N 'and from the people' (ומן עמא), though the *aleph* is probably just a scribal error for *he* due to the similar form later in the verse.

אל-יסף פרעה (8.25) Vulg has simply *noli ultra*, thus retaining at this point (though not earlier) the change to direct address in LXX (and probably OL, though no evidence for this phrase survives).

התל (8.25) The Vss (inc. Aq and Symm) uniformly have words for 'deceive, lie', as the context requires, and show no signs of the conflation of this sense with 'mock, make sport of' that appears elsewhere in them (cf. Note t on the translation).

שלח (8.25) Vulg freely *ut non dimittas*, again with the direct address to Pharaoh.

אל-יהוה (8.26) LXX again has πρὸς τὸν θεόν, as part of its emphasis that it is the supreme and only God with whom Pharaoh is confronted. Tgg and Sy have 'before' as usually with verbs of prayer.

יהוה (8.27) Here LXX reverts to κύριος, in keeping with the other Vss (though Vulg uses a pronoun here, as it does for 'Moses').

דבר (8.27) Tg^J adds בעותא to specify that it was a request.

ויסר (8.27) LXX, Vulg and Tg^{O,J} use transitive forms which show that they read this form as a Hiphil (Tg^N ועבר and Sy *wprq* could be either P^{e}al or Pael), not unnaturally after the divine subject in the previous clause.

מעבדיו (8.27) As in v. 25 SP and all the Vss except Tg° add 'and': the less smooth text of MT is again to be preferred.

לא (8.27) LXX and Sy add 'and', but the asyndesis of the other witnesses is very appropriate and surely original.

אחד (8.27) Sy, Tg^N and Vulg lexicalise the emphasis by adding 'not even'.

ויכבד (8.28) The Vss generally continue with their etymologising use of verbs meaning 'made heavy', but Tg^N as in 7.14 and 8.11 uses its equivalent for all the verbs of 'hardening', תקף, while Sy *qšy* follows its earlier rendering of קשה in 7.3. Vulg *et ingravatum est (cor pharaonis)* follows 7.14 rather than Heb. here, a misrendering that drew Augustine's criticism (*Qu.Ex.* 29): cf. his citation of what is presumably the OL's active rendering in *de grat. et lib. arb.* 45 (*PL* 44, 911).

את-לבו (8.28) Tg^J as usual prefixes 'the inclination' (see Text and Versions on 7.3).

שלח (8.28) LXX ἠθέλησεν ἐξαποστεῖλαι, emphasising again the involvement of Pharaoh's will (see the note on v. 17).

Chapter 9.1-7

Pestilence on the Animals

The boundaries of this section are clearly defined, like several others, by opening and concluding formulae, which are most closely paralleled in 7.26–8.11 and 8.16-28. But even here there are some divergences of detail. The main structure is also similar to these passages, with (i) an opening address of Yahweh to Moses (vv. 1-5: see the Explanatory Note on v. 5), (ii) a brief account of the plague (v. 6) and (iii) a statement of Pharaoh's reaction to the plague (v. 7). But this time there are no negotiations between Pharaoh and Moses and no intercession by Moses to remove the plague. In these respects the passage is more like 7.14-25. The introductory words of Yahweh (v. 1) say nothing about where and when Moses is to meet Pharaoh: in this they resemble most closely those in 7.26 and differ from 7.14-16 and 8.16. Unlike all three of these passages, there is no statement that the plague (or its removal) is designed to bring Pharaoh to knowledge, or rather recognition, of Yahweh (contrast 7.17; 8.6, 18). Nor is Aaron mentioned at any point. All these features have the effect of making this the shortest of the non-Priestly plague episodes so far: in fact it is the shortest of all the episodes generally attributed to this strand. At the same time it is not lacking in some elaboration of the bare minimum required to describe a plague: it dwells at some length (see below) on the distinction made in the scope of the plague between Egypt and Israel (for which cf. 8.18-19 etc.) and it contains in vv. 2b and 7a motifs which are found nowhere else (Pharaoh's 'holding on' to the people; and his investigation to see whether Israel has indeed been treated differently), both of which intensify the focus on Israel's experience (negatively and positively).

These variations justify W.H. Schmidt's observation that (to a much greater extent than the Priestly account) the non-Priestly account of the plagues was put together by a lively narrator who sustained the interest of his hearers and conveyed his theological teaching in different ways. There is some truth in the observation, made by R. Smend (*Erzählung*, p. 127) and others, that the first six plagues in this sequence form two successive groups of three, so that this episode corresponds in certain ways to the first, the turning of water in the Nile into blood and the death of the fish in it. But this does not explain all the special features of it, in particular the strong concentration on the distinctive treatment of Israel (a feature noted by Childs, p. 157, and Houtman, p. 68). In fact the omission of other motifs serves to give this one a greater prominence than it has anywhere else, except in the final plague, the death of the firstborn, and this is probably deliberate. A further effect of the relative brevity of this account is to accelerate the pace of the narrative: almost before one realises it Egypt has suffered a further blow and yet Pharaoh still remains intransigent.

Two other features of the passage deserve note. As Schmidt again has noted (p. 407), its links to the preceding section are not limited to the repetition of the 'distinction' motif, but make a neat continuation in various ways. As Moses has 'come out' from Pharaoh's palace (8.26), so now he is to 'go in' (v. 1). The possibility that Pharaoh will 'continue' to hold Israel (v. 2) recalls the fact that in 8.28 he had refused to release them 'this time too'. Then he 'refused to understand' (lit. 'made his heart heavy'), now 'he did not understand' (lit. 'his heart was heavy'). There are also signs of 'heightening' (Gn. *Steigerung*: ibid., pp. 409-10): the plague is not merely 'heavy' (Heb. *kābēd*, 8.20: '*masses of* worms') but 'very heavy' (9.3, *kābēd mᵉʾōd*: '*very* severe'). This motif may receive additional highlighting from the echoing use of the related verb, 'was heavy' (cf. above), in v. 7, as word-play has independently been suggested as a prominent device in 9.1-7 (Houtman, p. 68 n. 113, 71, 73; cf. Propp, p. 331, who refers to Cassuto). The most prominent example concerns the word for 'pestilence' itself in v. 3 and words for 'speak' and '(no)thing' and 'this' (lit. 'this thing') in vv. 1, 4, 5 and 6 (see the Explanatory Notes on these verses), but further cases have been detected in vv. 3 and 7 (see the Explanatory Notes). The passage thus seems to have been composed carefully with its context in mind and so to make a loud if brief impact at this point in the narrative.

It also hangs well together and has been generally seen as a literary unity (so explicitly Rudolph, p. 19; Gertz, p. 129). Critical scholarship has with very few exceptions attributed it entirely to the Yahwist source (J²: Beer) until the recent challenges to the latter's existence.

Holzinger (p. 26) and Gressmann (*Anfänge*, p. 39) saw the list of animals in v. 3 as a later addition,[1] and the latter saw the 'distinction' motif and the specification of the time as secondary developments as in 8.18-19 (*Mose*, p. 72), though possibly only in the sense that they did not belong to the original oral *Sage*. Noth initially attributed the passage to J (*ÜGP*, p. 32), but in his Exodus commentary (pp. 60-61, ET, p. 79) he took up the view (attributed by L. Schmidt, *Beobachtungen*, p. 102 n. 88, also to E. Meyer, *Israeliten*, p. 29) that the passage must as a whole be a secondary addition to J, because of its divergence from the accounts of other plagues and the third-person references to Yahweh in vv. 3-4. For similar reasons L. Schmidt attributed it to R^{JE} (pp. 19-22) and Levin (p. 337) and Gertz (pp. 130-31) to secondary elaboration of the non-Priestly plague-narrative. Levin is followed by Gertz in seeing an additional argument for this in the fact that the passage 'interrupts' the reference back from 'this time' in 9.14 to 'this time also' in 8.28. On the other hand the 'echo' might be less jarring if it were more distant, as it is with 9.1-7 in between, and in any case the speech to which 9.14 belongs seems to presuppose 9.1-7 at several points (see also the notes there). Noth's original arguments were effectively answered by Kohata (pp. 98-99) and W.H. Schmidt: as we have also noted, variation is characteristic of the non-Priestly plague narrative and it may well be due to a particular point which the narrator wished to emphasise here; while the unusual transition to third-person reference to Yahweh in v. 3 is no less abrupt in a supplementer's work than in part of the original composition. The only real 'solution' to it is Steingrimmson's view that vv. 1-2a and 2b-6 are from two different writers altogether (pp. 99-100), but that is no solution at all since, as he recognises, both his presumed strands are incomplete (p. 105). Much the same can be said of Levin's less drastic view (loc. cit.) that most of vv. 4-7 are secondary.

Apart from this, the section is so closely related to the main body of the non-Priestly plague-narrative that it must be from the same source-document. This (like Propp) we have argued to be the E source because of the close connections to 5.1-2 (rather than 5.3ff., which we have attributed to J). 9.1-7 raises one problem for such an attribution, the epithet 'the God of the Hebrews', which occurs in 5.3 and also in 3.18 (part of another J passage: cf. also 7.16). It is possible, however, that it was used occasionally by E (cf. 9.13; 10.3) as it was by J: the expression 'Hebrews' for the Israelites is used several times in 1.15-22, which is generally attributed to E. Alternatively, if our general argument about sources in this part of Exodus is sound, it could be regarded as a redactional expansion of the divine name in the original text.

---

[1] So perhaps also Rudolph, loc. cit., with reference to Kautzsch.

For the first time a plague is attributed to 'the hand of Yahweh', or even identified with it (v. 3). The name of Yahweh appears, equally unusually, twice more in the message which Moses is to bring to Pharaoh (vv. 4-5). The pestilence is also described as 'very severe'. Along with this solemn language it is repeatedly emphasised that the plague did not fall on the animals of the Israelites, so that a sharp distinction is opened up between the experience of Israel as the people of Yahweh (v. 1) and the Egyptians (as the people of Pharaoh), a distinction which contrasts with their present status but one which is to be much more terribly applied in the final plague in the sequence (12.29: cf. 11.4-7). Thus this fourth plague at the mid-point of the non-Priestly series corresponds not only to the first but to the last of the seven plagues in it. Despite this dramatic distinction, of which he makes himself specifically aware (v. 7a), and the precise timing of the plague (vv. 5-6), Pharaoh remains immoveable and so consequently do the people of Israel.

1 Yahweh said to Moses, 'Go in^a to Pharaoh and speak to him^b: "Thus says Yahweh, the God of the Hebrews, Let my people go, so that^c they may worship me. 2 For if you refuse to let them go and continue^d to hold on to them, 3 be sure^e that the hand of Yahweh is about to come^f against your animals^g which are in the open country, the horses, the donkeys, the camels, the cattle and the flocks, (as) a very severe pestilence. 4 But Yahweh will make a distinction between the animals of Israel and the animals of the Egyptians, and ^{h}nothing of all that belongs to^h the Israelites will die. 5 Yahweh has appointed a time, saying: Tomorrow Yahweh will do this in the land."' 6 Yahweh did this on the following day^i, and all the animals of the Egyptians died. But not one of the animals of the Israelites died. 7 Pharaoh sent (men to investigate)^j, and it was true^k, not even one^l of the animals of Israel had died. But Pharaoh did not understand^m and he did not let the people go.

Notes on the Translation

a. Heb. בא. The sense 'go in' (cf. LXX, Vulg, Tgg) is especially clear when בא is followed by a place that is entered (7.23; 8.20), but is probably to be assumed in all expressions of this kind (cf. 5.1, 15, 23; 6.11; 7.10, 26; 10.1, 3). The use of הלך in 3.10-11 and 7.15 is a less specific alternative.

b. The use of Heb. דבר immediately before direct speech is rare: elsewhere in Exodus it only occurs at 32.7, 13; 33.1.

c. See Note d on the translation of 8.16-28.

d. Heb. עודך, with the suffix representing the subject of the part. that follows, as more often with אין and הנה (both in 8.17): similar combinations occur especially in the formula 'While *x* was still speaking...' (Gen. 29.9; 1 Kgs 1.14, 22, 42; 2 Kgs 6.33; Esth. 6.14), but see also Gen. 18.22; Exod. 9.17; Job 2.3, 9. More generally on the use of עוד with suffixes see JM §102k and Exod. 4.18.

e. Heb. הנה. For the primary deictic meaning leading to emphasis cf. JM §164a and below Note k.

f. Heb. הויה, f. sing. part. of היה, regularly formed (except for the unusual *plene* orthography). The part. of היה occurs only here in BH, the present tense 'is' etc. being normally expressed by a nominal clause. Its use here may be due to either or both of two factors: the need to denote the imminent future (cf. GK§116p) and the stronger sense 'come' (for which cf. BDB, pp. 225-26).

g. Heb. מקנך. מִקְנֶה is lit. 'a possession', but it seems always to be used of domestic animals (and as a collective sing.): for other kinds of 'possession' קִנְיָן or מִקְנָה is found. Here and often מִקְנֶה is a very general expression, like בהמה, but in Num. 31.9, 32.26 and 2 Kgs 3.17 it occurs alongside בהמה, in the last case clearly referring to living creatures. Possibly in these passages the style is deliberately expansive.

h. For לא...דבר = 'nothing, not one' there are numerous parallels (e.g. Isa. 39.2: cf. also אין...דבר in Exod. 5.11), based on the wider use of דבר for '(some)thing': cf. BDB, p. 183, s.v. IV.6. מכל ל involves an ellipse of אשר or an unusual 'genitive' construction, for which the closest parallels are Gen. 39.4 (GK §130d) and 2 Chr. 30.17 (in most of the exx. in GK §155d a verb follows).

i. Heb. ממחרת, whereas in the preceding direct speech מחר is used: the distinction seems to be universal in BH, even in those places where מחר means 'in future' more generally (e.g. Exod. 13.14).

j. Heb. וישלח, without an explicit object, according to a frequent idiom (BDB, p. 1018, s.v. k): 1 Kgs 20.17 is especially similar.

k. Heb. והנה, with a similar emphatic function to v. 3 (see Note e), but here in a narrative context rather than in discourse.

l. Heb. עד־אחד, lit. 'up to one', as in 14.28, Judg. 4.16 (both with לא נשאר) and 2 Sam. 17.22, apparently a stronger expression than when אחד alone is used in 8.27 and 10.19 (compare the use of עד in a different expression in Deut. 2.5).

m. Lit. 'Pharaoh's heart was heavy': see Note a on 7.14-25.

Explanatory Notes

1-4. Yahweh's instructions to Moses correspond especially closely to those in 7.26-27a: only the verb 'speak' (Heb. *dibber*) and the epithet 'the God of the Hebrews' are different in v. 1. On the unusual use of the verb see Note b on the translation: Houtman suggests that it is preferred to prepare for the similar-sounding *deber*, 'pestilence', in v. 3 (p. 71). Yahweh has not been called 'the God of the Hebrews' since 7.16 (earlier cf. 3.18 – and the note – and 5.3), but the epithet recurs in 9.13 and 10.3. In v. 2 'and continue to hold on to them' is an expansion of the earlier formula which implicitly criticises Pharaoh's defiance (cf. 8.25) and responds to his latest refusal to 'let the people go' (8.28). This clause especially emphasises Pharaoh's responsibility (cf. Childs, pp. 157-58). From v. 3 MT refers to Yahweh in the third person, despite the messenger-formula in v. 1 (see Text and Versions for secondary readings which are grammatically more consistent): this sometimes happens also in prophetic oracles (e.g. Isa. 40.2), and here it may reflect the perspective of Moses' intended delivery of the message to Pharaoh (so Houtman, Schmidt). But the effect of the introduction of the divine name itself into the message should not be overlooked, especially in the awesome phrase 'the hand of Yahweh', which is used here for the first and only time in the plague-narrative (but cf. Num. 11.23). The expression is used generally to designate Yahweh's powerful intervention in a variety of contexts (cf. *THAT* 1, 672-73 = *TLOT* 2, pp. 501-502; *TWAT* 3, 446-51 = *TDOT* 5, pp. 418-23, both with reference to ancient Near Eastern parallels: see also J.J.M. Roberts, 'The Hand of Yahweh', *VT* 21 [1971], pp. 244-51), but its specific use in relation to a plague in 1 Sam. 5.6, 9 and 2 Sam. 24.14-15 deserves special note and may be traditional (cf. Schmidt, p. 408). There is also an echo of the 'mighty hand' of 3.20 and 6.1 (see the notes there). The verb 'come' is Heb. *hāyāh*, 'be, become', which frequently has this stronger sense in connection with the 'coming' of the word of Yahweh to a prophet, but also in other contexts (cf. 8.11; 10.13; 19.16 and further examples in BDB, p. 225, s.v. II, inc. 1 Sam. 5.9, 7.13 and 12.15 of 'the hand of Yahweh' in particular): compare also the use with Yahweh himself as subject discussed in the notes on 3.14 (Houtman, p. 71, and Propp, p. 331, see a further word-play here). The appropriateness of this use of the verb and the regular pattern of the announcements of the plagues by the participle expressing the imminent future combine to make this the only place in the Old Testament where the active participle of *hāyāh* occurs (see Note f on the translation), as noted by G.S. Ogden, 'Notes on the Use of הויה in Exodus IX 3', *VT* 17 (1967), pp. 483-84 (cf. id., 'Time and the Verb היה in O.T. Prose', *VT* 21 [1971], pp. 451-69; also R. Bartelmus, *HYH. Bedeutung und Funktion eines hebräischen 'Allerweltswortes'* [ATS 17: St. Ottilien, 1982], pp. 164-65). 'Pestilence' (Heb. *deber*: cf. *TWAT* 2, 133-35 = *TDOT* 3, pp. 125-27) has already been associated with Yahweh in 5.3: it is frequently mentioned as a means of divine judgement on Israel by the prophets and is even seen, personified, as part of Yahweh's entourage (Hab. 3.5, par. *rešep*, which is the name of a minor deity at Ugarit and elsewhere: cf. *TWAT* 7, 684-90 = *TDOT* 14, pp. 11-16). This plague at least is therefore not specifically appropriate to Egypt, although it will scarcely have been unknown there (H. Goedicke, *LexAeg* 5, 918-19, gives some ancient examples, but apparently of plagues on humans, so the concerns expressed by Holzinger, Beer and Houtman have some basis).

'Your animals' (the possessive suffix refers to a singular 'you') could be taken in a strong sense to imply that Pharaoh claimed the ownership of all the livestock in his country (Heb. *miqneh* is a general word for all kinds of domestic animal: see Note g on the translation), perhaps on the basis of the agreement supposedly made in a time of famine according to Gen. 47.15-17, where a very similar list of animals appears (only the camels of those mentioned here are missing: see below). However, such a claim is hard to parallel in Egyptian sources (cf. *OEAE* 2, p. 257, contra *LexAeg* 3, p. 486) and the Genesis narrative may not imply anything about the ownership of animals (47.26 refers only to Pharaoh's ownership of the land and his entitlement to a fifth of its produce). The expression may simply be based on Pharaoh's representative status as ruler of Egypt: below (vv. 4 and 6) reference is made to 'the animals of Egypt/the Egyptians'. The list of animals corresponds closely to other biblical lists and to the lists of booty in Egyptian texts (e.g. the account of Hittite 'tribute' sent to Ramesses II, *ANET*, p. 257b), except (it seems) for the camels, as Hyatt (p. 114) and Propp (p. 331, citing Firmage, *ABD* 6, p. 1139, and B. Midant-Reynes and F. Braunstein-Silvestre, 'Le chameau en Égypte', *Orientalia* 46 [1977], pp. 337-62) have noted. Camels are included in the list of

Abraham's possessions in Gen. 12.16, and Gen. 37.25 and Isa. 30.6 also imply that camels could be seen in Egypt, though not that they were owned by Egyptians. To speak of 'an anachronistic projection of Asian custom upon Egypt' here (Propp) goes too far, but the evidence for domesticated camels in Egypt before Hellenistic times is certainly very limited, whereas there are numerous references to them elsewhere in the Old Testament and Sennacherib includes them in his list of booty taken from Judah in the time of Hezekiah (*ANET*, p. 288). Once again Israel is to be spared the effects of this plague (cf. 8.18-19; 9.26; 10.23; 11.4-7) and this motif receives particular emphasis here (cf. vv. 6-7), the more so because other 'additional' motifs are missing in this comparatively short account (see the introduction to this section). Although no specific mention is made here of the Israelites' dwelling separately in Goshen (as in 8.18 and 9.26), the need for Pharaoh to 'send' investigators perhaps implies it. That the Israelites had their own animals in Egypt is a recurring motif in Genesis 46–47 and becomes a cause of dispute later in Exod. 10.24-26 (cf. 11.7; 12 passim; 17.3 and 34.3 are rare references thereafter, except where sacrifices are involved). In v. 4 they are referred to first as 'Israel' and then as 'the Israelites' (lit. sons/children of Israel'), designations which both recur, in the opposite order (thus producing a chiasmus) in vv. 6-7.

Excursus on Israel/Israelites in Exodus 1–20

In Exodus as a whole there are 123 occurrences of 'sons/children of Israel' and 47 other cases where 'Israel' occurs without a preceding 'sons/children of'. In the second half of the book, where Priestly sections predominate, the fuller expression is four times as common as the simple one, and in the Priestly sections of chs. 1–20 it is almost always used (exceptions are 6.14 [referring to Jacob] and 12.15 [in a standard phrase]). In the non-Priestly sections of chs. 1–20 the fuller expression is also frequent (c. 35x), but the simpler expression is often used too. The latter is exclusively used in ch. 18 and nearly so in the non-Priestly sections of chs. 14 and 17 (whereas 'sons/ children of Israel' is found in the Priestly verses). There is therefore evidence that 'Israel' alone was sometimes preferred in non-Priestly narrative (occurrences in chs. 24, 32 and 34 would add further weight to this), but if this was originally the case everywhere there must have been substantial modification of the wording when the different source-material was brought together (as seems to have continued later: see Text and Versions passim). Carpenter and Harford-Battersby suggest that according to their source-analysis J prefers

'Israel' alone as a name for the people (17x in Exodus vs. 4x in E),[2] whereas E prefers the fuller expression (1, p. 187). By contrast, our own different analysis (limited so far to Exod. 1–18) finds the usage of both the sources to be quite evenly balanced, with a very slight preference for 'Israel' alone in E and for 'sons/children of Israel' in J.

The alternation between 'Israel' and 'Israelites' in vv. 4-7 is notable but need not be the result of redactional activity. Although the half-verses in which 'the Israelites' occurs (vv. 4b and 6b) are both dispensable and v. 6b somewhat undermines the narrative tension by anticipating what Pharaoh is still to discover according to v. 7, the narrator probably just sought some variation of expression in the recurring references to Israel's livestock here. This is the more likely because the section as a whole displays a somewhat different structure from other plague-stories (see the beginning of the introduction to it).

5. This verse may be understood in two ways. It may represent a further utterance of Yahweh to Moses, following that contained in vv. 1-4 and perhaps (so Houtman, p. 72) separated from it by Moses' transmission of Yahweh's demand to Pharaoh and the latter's refusal to comply. Or it may be the continuation of the message which Moses has been instructed to give to Pharaoh in v. 1b. On the other occasions where the timing of the plague is stated (8.23; 9.18; 10.4) it is always part of the initial message to Pharaoh (8.6 concerns the removal of the plague, as the result of negotiations), so that is most likely what is intended here as well. 'This' in the Heb. here, as in v. 6, is *haddābār hazzeh*, literally 'this word, thing', so that there is a further similarity of sound to *deber*, 'pestilence', in v. 3 (Houtman, p. 68 n. 113; Propp, p. 331).[3]

---

[2] As it does according to them as a name for the patriarch Jacob (24x). For wider surveys see A. Besters, '"Israël" et "fils d'Israël" dans les livres historiques (Genèse – II Rois)', *RB* 74 (1967), pp. 5-23; H.J. Zobel, in *TWAT* 3, 990-94 = *TDOT* 6, pp. 401-404. Specifically on Exodus (1–14) see Besters, 'L'expression "fils d'Israël"', though his conclusion (p. 355) that all the supposedly 'old' (i.e. JE) occurrences of 'the sons/children of Israel' come from the Deuteronomists, P or later glosses is, with rare exceptions (1.9; 12.37), based on weak arguments. *THAT* 1, 783 = *TLOT* 2, p. 582, has a table giving a clear summary of the distribution of the fuller expression and 'Israel' in all combinations throughout the OT.

[3] Both Houtman and Propp suggest that 'nothing' in v. 4 (Heb. *lō'... dābār*), which is admittedly odd when applied to a living creature, also involves a word-play. But this is less likely.

6-7. The emphatic statement that 'all' the Egyptians' animals died as a result of the pestilence (v. 6) seems to be contradicted in 9.9, 19-25, 11.5 and 12.29 (cf. 13.15), where Egyptian animals are the victims of later plagues. 9.9 is less of a problem than the other passages, because it comes from the Priestly account of the plagues (see the introduction to 9.8-12). Houtman lists various explanations that have been suggested (pp. 69-70), but he holds that the problem probably did not concern the narrator. Most likely is an explanation based on the phrase 'in the open country' in v. 3: 9.19-21, 25 explicitly draw a contrast between what happened to animals 'in the open country' and those left indoors. Presumably here too there were survivors who had remained indoors. Pharaoh's 'mission of enquiry' (v. 7) raises hopes that he may relent when he discovers that Israel has been spared again from the effects of the plague. It takes the place of the motif of intercession in 8.4 and 8.24, probably because in this case there is no remedy: the damage has already been done. But the outcome is the same as before (cf. 8.11, 28), although this time the narrator does not underline the fact: he did not need to.

Text and Versions

יהוה (9.1)   For both occurrences Tg[Nmg] adds, as usual, 'the Memra of'.

בא (9.1)   While the other Vss give the probable meaning 'Go *in*' (cf. Note a on the translation), Sy has simply *zl*, 'Go'.

ודברת (9.1)   SP has ואמרת (as do some Masoretic mss acc. to Propp), which corresponds both to other episodes in the plague-narrative (7.16, 26; 8.16) and to regular usage (see Note b on the translation): LXX, Sy and Tg[N] diverge similarly from MT and the other Vss (inc. Tg[Nmg]) here, but the variant must be secondary (for an overview of all such occurrences in Exodus see Sanderson, *Exodus Scroll*, pp. 228-30: in 32.7 and 33.1 SP adds לאמר [as did 4QpalEx[m] in 32.7] in a similar context, but in 32.13 it agrees with MT).

ויעבדני (9.1)   Vulg *ut sacrificet mihi*, as before in 7.16 etc. (see also Text and Versions on 5.1); in the present context this accords well with the use of זבח in 8.21-25, but it is clearly not specifically the result of that. Tgg as usual represent the suffix by 'before me', except for Tg[Nmg] which has 'before him': this is a consistent variation, so not an accidental error, and will be due to treating the final clause as outside the direct speech of Yahweh.

כי (9.2)   LXX μὲν οὖν probably indicates 'but, however' (cf. Wevers, *Notes*, p. 124), which may be the meaning of כי אם in Jer. 7.5 and is suggested here by Vulg *quod (si)* and Sy *w*. In 8.17 LXX had ἐὰν δέ for כי אם, probably under the influence of ואם in 7.27. Tgg have the expected 'For'.

מאן (9.2) LXX μὴ βούλει (cf. Sy) as regularly in Exodus since 4.23. The same rendering occurs even outside the confrontation with Pharaoh (16.28; 22.16 in Exod.) and is evidently idiomatic Greek for 'refuse', not a weakening of the Heb. Symm nevertheless replaces it with the closer equivalent ἀπειθεῖς (cf. Vulg, Tgg).

לשלח (9.2) LXX supplies an explicit object τὸν λαόν μου from v. 1 (cf. Sy 'them').

מחזיק (9.2) Von Gall gives the SP reading as מחזק, but several mss (inc. Tal and Camb. 1846) have מחזיק and the defective writing may be due to the influence of standard Sam. pronunciation. LXX ἐγκρατεῖς is taken by LSJ and Lust as 'control, master', and Aq and Symm preferred more regular equivalents for 'hold on to'. But related words make it likely, as Muraoka and Wevers (*Notes*, p. 124) suppose, that ἐγκρατέω could also have this meaning.

יד יהוה (9.3) Tgg all have מחא, 'blow, plague', Tg⁰ in place of יד (and with a distancing 'from before' after it), the others as a clarifying addition, either before יד itself (Tgʲ) or before 'my punishment' in place of it and the divine name (Tgᴺ). Vulg *manus mea* also has a first person reference to God, against MT, as if the divine speech continued (compare the treatment of אצבע אלהים in 8.15 and Text and Versions there).

הויה (9.3) SP היה, presumably just a defective writing of the fem. s. part. Tgʲ amplifies 'is now to be let loose as has not happened (before)'; Tgᴺᵐᵍ has אתיא, 'is coming', with a unique rendering of the following words too, anticipating the statements found in MT at 9.18, 24; 10.6.

במקנך (9.3) SP במקניך, with the additional *yodh* reflecting the Sam. pronunciation, as elsewhere, rather than indicating a pl. form (*GSH* §55bγ). Vulg, rendering freely, has *super agros* for this word and the following clause.

בשדה (9.3) Tgᴺ has 'of the field', which the ed. corrects to agree with MT and the other witnesses. Sy *bmdbrʾ* should mean 'in the wilderness': as *dbrʾ* is a common word for 'field' (cf. vv. 19, 25, alternating with *ḥqlʾ*), perhaps *dbmdbrʾ* is an old mistake for *dbdbrʾ* (cf. Propp, p. 299: Urmia and Barnes's ed. agree with Leiden, which records no variant here).

בסוסים (9.3) LXX and Vulg add 'and' before each item in the following list and Sy before all except this word (thus preserving the distinction between the generic term and the species). SP and Tgᴺ subdivide the list by prefixing 'and' to the second and third and the second item respectively. Tg⁰·ᴶ follow MT, which is likely to be original.

דבר (9.3) LXX θάνατος, as generally elsewhere: 'death' is also the meaning given here by Tg⁰·ᴶ·ᴺ (cf. Text and Versions on 5.3). The basis for this widespread misinterpretation remains obscure: the Midrashim on this passage cited in *AramB* 7, p. 23 n. 4, are presumably based on it rather than its source. The Ar. and Akk. cognates cited by BDB, p. 184, and *HAL*, p. 203, meaning 'death, disaster' support a more general meaning, but instances in BH or Aram. remain elusive. Aq and Symm correct LXX to λοιμός, likewise

Vulg *pestis* and Sy *mwtn'*. (The latter word, which means 'pestilence' in other dialects of Aram. as well, may be a clue to LXX and Tgg's mistake: the translators' familiarity with it may have led them to assume that דֶּבֶר too was associated with the idea of 'death'.)

כבד (9.3)   LXX μέγας and Tg⁰ סני probably intend a reference to the numbers of those dying (see previous note): more precise renderings are provided by the other Vss (inc. Aq, Symm: βαρύς).

והפלה (9.4)   As in 8.18 (see Text and Versions there) LXX, Vulg and Tg^J render as if the verb were פלא, and here SP actually has והפלא. Tg^{O,N} (including the mg of Tg^N with its rare use of Aram. כסי in the sense 'distinguish' as in MH) and Sy support the MT reading, which the context surely requires. LXX's καὶ παραδοξάσω ἐγώ also assimilates to the first person form of 8.18; but the further assimilations to ἐν τῇ ἡμέρᾳ ἐκείνῃ there are secondary expansions in LXX^B etc. (Wevers, *THGE*, p. 242).

יהוה (9.4)   Tg^{Nmg} adds 'the Memra of'.

מקנה (9.4)   Vulg renders *possessiones* both times here (cf. on v. 7), but recognises the specific reference to animals in vv. 6-7.

ישראל...מצרים (9.4)   Both LXX (which has 'sons of Israel' here as later in the verse) and Tg^N (which is corrected by its mg) invert the names, probably independently, to bring the two references to Israel together.

ולא (9.4)   LXX omits 'and', producing an effective asyndesis, while Vulg *ut* makes what follows, logically, into a result clause.

מכל־לבני ישראל (9.4)   LXX, Tg^{Nmg} and Sy paraphrase, the first in a way that could imply that the Israelites themselves will be spared, the others more clearly by inserting the word בעיר. Sy also oddly has 'the house of Israel', a phrase which is only rarely found in the MT Pentateuch, mainly in Leviticus: see Propp, p. 185 (on 3.11) for other exx.

דבר (9.4)   LXX ῥητόν, as elsewhere only in 22.8, instead of its usual Hebraising rendering ῥῆμα (which is attested here according to Wevers's apparatus for Sam. Gk. [cf. Tg^{Nmg}'s literalising פתגמא], accompanied by the very idiomatic Greek οἷον δηποτοῦν ['of whatever kind']). Muraoka, *Lexicon*, p. 504, suggests that the meaning is '(nothing) stated', comparing Greek usage: the reference would presumably be to the animals listed in v. 3. Vulg *nihil omnino* and Sy *'p l' ḥd*, 'not even one', add emphasis, as also in v. 6.

וישם יהוה (9.5)   LXX καὶ ἔδωκεν ὁ θεός (cf. Sy): on ἔδωκεν see on 8.19 and Wevers, *Notes*, p. 126. ὁ θεός is surprising when κύριος follows later in the verse. Tg^{Nmg} as usual adds 'the Memra of' before each occurrence of the divine name.

לאמר (9.5)   Sy omits any equivalent, but apparently still sees the following words as a citation: 'Tomorrow (is when [*d*ʾ]…)'.

הדבר (9.5)   SP prefixes את to mark the def. obj., as in MT in v. 6. *BHS* cites a Geniza ms. which also has it: whether the presence of יה in Tg^J is textually significant is hard to judge.

בארץ (9.5)   SP has a long addition, with an introduction based on v. 1a (and with 'and Aaron' added as usual) after this word to indicate that the message given in vv. 1-5 (with the SP variants) was actually transmitted to Pharaoh. 4QpalEx^m preserves words corresponding to vv. 3-5 which lead into v. 6 and it is likely, in view of space considerations and the clearer evidence of an expanded text at 7.18 and 8.19, that this is part of the repetition of the message as in SP. But 4QpalEx^m does not share SP's addition of את before הדבר here. Sy^hex (L) also presents a rendering of the expansion: the wording is in several ways close to LXX (though 'Israel' and 'the Egyptians' are in the MT/SP order) and must be related to it in some way (cf. 7.29 and 8.19).

יהוה (9.6)   Tg^Nmg as usual prefixes 'the Memra of'.

בני־ישראל (9.6)   Sy again has the odd 'the house of Israel' (cf. on v. 4).

אחד (9.6)   Tg^N has אף לא חד, 'not even one' (cf. Vulg and Sy both here and in v. 4).

וישלח (9.7)   So also SP, probably 4QpalEx^m (cf. Sanderson, *Exodus Scroll*, pp. 249-52), Sy, Tgg, Vulg. LXX ignored it, although it renders the same idiom precisely in v. 27. Tg^J added 'scouts to see' (cf. Vulg *ad videndum*) to clarify the sense. A fourth cent. papyrus (Oxf 4), described by Wevers (*Exodus*, p. 16) as 'very Hebraising', is the sole Greek witness to present the text (secondarily) in its MT form here.

והנה (9.7)   LXX ἰδὼν δὲ Φαραὼ ὅτι, 'and Pharaoh seeing that' (with 'Pharaoh' betraying LXX's knowledge of the preceding clause in the Heb.), and Sy *whzʾ d*, 'and he saw that', paraphrase.

ממקנה (9.7)   Vulg *de his quae possidebat*: cf. its general renderings in v. 4.

ישראל (9.7)   SP and 4QpalEx^m prefix בני to conform to the previous verse (cf. LXX, Tg^J).

ויכבד (9.7)   The Vss render in their usual ways: see Text and Versions at 8.28.

לב (9.7)   Tg^J prefixes 'the inclination of' as elsewhere.

Chapter 9.8-12

Boils on Humans and Animals

The structure of this episode is broadly similar to that of 7.8-13 and 8.12-15 and the fragmentary sections in 7.19-22* and 8.1-3, 11b. Moses and Aaron are again instructed by Yahweh to perform an action which will lead to unpleasant consequences for the Egyptians, without any prior warning to Pharaoh (vv. 8-9). They perform the action, the unpleasant consequences follow, Egyptian magicians do not even attempt to imitate them (which they had failed to do in the preceding case in 8.12-15), but Pharaoh remains obdurate, 'as Yahweh had spoken'. But, as is more fully discussed in the Explanatory Notes, there are a number of differences from the earlier pattern, all of which can probably be related to the fact that this episode represents a climax (at least an interim one) in the plague-story. Moses and Aaron receive the instructions together, rather than Moses being instructed to transmit them to Aaron; Aaron this time does not act separately (and so his staff is not mentioned), but only (in a preliminary stage of the action) with Moses; the action is to be performed directly before Pharaoh (only previously in these sections in 7.8-13: in 7.20 the words 'in the sight of Pharaoh' belong to the parallel account); the magicians are totally overcome (even more so than in 8.12-15); Pharaoh's intransigence is now attributed directly to Yahweh; and there is a specific reference to Yahweh's earlier declaration 'to Moses' in 7.3. The effect of these changes, as is well noted by W.H. Schmidt (pp. 412-13), is above all to bring Moses himself into direct confrontation with the magicians (see esp. v. 11a) and with Pharaoh. The special features are not entirely without preparation: some link this episode closely to 7.8-13, and the final defeat of the magicians has already been anticipated in 8.14-15. In view also of the general features shared with all the earlier passages, there can be no question of this section being dissociated from them, and the major differences from the non-Priestly pattern remain.

It is therefore not surprising that since the beginnings of critical analysis of Exodus this section has been uniformly attributed to the Priestly source.[1] That it belongs to a different account from 9.1-7 is clear from the fact that according to v. 6 there were no Egyptian livestock left in the land to be affected by this plague, as vv. 9 and 10 both envisage (cf. Fohrer, p. 73). This observation is also a strong argument against the 'supplementary' view of scholars such as Van Seters, who hold that the Priestly account was composed from the outset to give the non-Priestly account a fresh dimension (see especially *Life of Moses*, pp. 103-12). Blum, *Studien*, pp. 242-56, partly avoids this problem (and others) by his hypothesis of a pre-existing 'priestly' account of the plagues which his K^P expanded with passages later in ch. 9 and in ch. 10. A full consideration of this view must await our examination of those passages, but Blum's hypothesis does of course raise questions about the literary context in which such a pre-existing account might have been formed and transmitted (see also the full critique of both Van Seters and Blum by Gertz, pp. 85-94).

The origin of the pericope evidently lies in knowledge of a malady that was widespread but especially associated with Egypt (see the Explanatory Note on vv. 8-9 and esp. Deut. 28.27).

Gressmann argued from the use of soot and what he saw as ill-fitting aspects of the account that it originally told of a plague of darkness, like 10.21-29 (which was at that time attributed to E), and that it was given its present form through the influence of the J account of the pestilence in 9.1-7 (*Mose*, pp. 91-93). But this reconstruction is unduly speculative and influenced by a rigid conception of the Priestly 'plagues' as *Schauwunder*. What could well be true is that here as elsewhere the Priestly narrator made use of the older series of plagues (in this case 9.1-7) as a pattern to follow, although only with considerable freedom and innovation (cf. Kohata, pp. 244-49). It seems to be Steingrimmson's view that 9.8-12 belonged to neither of the underlying sequences of plagues that were taken up by the Priestly narrative (A1 and

---

[1] Holzinger (p. 26) suggested that unevennesses in vv. 8 and 12 pointed to use of an E version, comparing 10.20, 27, but this has not been taken up by others and the parallels are now more often thought to indicate a Priestly (or post-Priestly) origin for the verses in ch. 10 (see the introductions to 10.1-20 and 10.21-29). Levin, as elsewhere, regards the reference to the magicians (i.e. 9.11) as secondary (p. 336), but he gives no reason and this would deprive the passage of a key element in its structure.

A2), but that it was composed to ease the transition between them, perhaps especially by the attribution of the hardening of Pharaoh's heart to Yahweh himself (see pp. 105-108). Against this it must be recalled that the passage shares much more of its structure with the preceding passages than with what follows and that the differences from that pattern are ones that fit well with its role as an interim climax. There is thus no justification for attributing it to a different literary stage from them.

It is generally thought that this episode is not referred to in either of the psalms (Pss. 78 and 105) which summarise the Exodus story in some detail (cf. Kohata, pp. 256-57). Recently both L. Schmidt (*Beobachtungen*, p. 89) and Gertz (p. 155 n. 302) have argued that Ps. 78.49-50 contains references to both the non-Priestly 'pestilence' in 9.1-7 and to this passage, on the grounds that humans are affected by the plagues described, as in 9.9-10. But this is by no means clear, as Ps. 78.48 refers to animals and the 'them' and 'their' of vv. 49-50 may and probably do have them in mind.

In the Priestly sequence of plagues this passage marks the clear end of the Egyptian magicians' efforts to match the power of Yahweh as shown through Moses and Aaron and a point at which Pharaoh's stubbornness is presented as no longer an attitude of his own devising but as the result of Yahweh's action (cf. 7.3). The die is fixed and the inevitable sequel is the final plague of the firstborn, as 12.1-20 (with its introduction in 11.[9-]10) spells it out. Nevertheless the theme of divine hardening extends also into the final episode of the Priestly Exodus story, the destruction of Pharaoh and his army at the crossing of the sea (14.4, 8, 17).

8 *Yahweh said to Moses and Aaron, 'You are to take[a] handfuls of soot from a kiln[b] and Moses shall toss it[c] up into the air[d] in the sight of Pharaoh. 9 It will become a cloud of dust[e] over all the land of Egypt, and it will turn into boils[f] on man and beast, which break out into blisters,[g] throughout the land of Egypt.' 10 So they took the soot from the kiln and stood before Pharaoh. Moses tossed it up into the air and it turned into blistering boils[h] which broke out on man and beast. 11 The magicians could not hold their ground[i] before Moses because of the boils, for the boils came on the magicians[j] as well as all (the rest of) the Egyptians. 12 But Yahweh made Pharaoh's heart stubborn and he did not listen to them, as Yahweh had spoken to Moses.*

Notes on the Translation

a. Heb. קחו לכם. The 'centripetal' *lamed* is a way of intensifying a command (and occasionally another verbal form) by stressing the involvement of the agent (JM §133d and notes).

b. Heb. פיח כבשן. The genitive expresses origin, a rare variety of its defining use which is not noted in the grammars, but cf. מטר השמים in Deut. 11.11. The whole phrase is an appositional indication of the material (GK §131d). פיח occurs only here and in v. 10 in BH, but according to *Ges18*, p. 1049, the meaning (as distinct, say, from 'ash') is confirmed from later Heb. and Aram. (cf. CAL s.v.). Houtman (p. 78) prefers 'ashes'.

c. Heb. וזרקו. The perfect consecutive often continues an imperative (GK §112r), though usually in the second person. The other cases with third person forms cited by JM §119m are probably simple futures (including 8.12), so not exact parallels.

d. Heb. השמימה. Lit. 'to the heavens', but with עוף it clearly refers to the 'air' or 'sky' (e.g. Gen. 2.19-20), so the same closer region can be readily intended here.

e. Heb. לאבק. The meaning seems always to be not 'dust lying on or composing ground' (BDB), but 'airborne dust' (Deut. 28.24; Isa. 5.24; 29.5; Ezek. 26.10; Nah. 1.3; perhaps also אבקה in Song 3.6b, cf. v. 6a): thus an etymological link with Ar. *'abaqa*, 'run away' (BDB, *HAL*), is possible.

f. Heb. שחין, always found in the sing. but evidently used collectively for 'boils'. Cognate verbs in Akk., Ug., Aram., Ar. and Eth. have the sense 'be hot' (*HAL*, p. 1356): in *KTU* 1.12.2.38 it seems to refer to an infection of the loins (*mtnm*: cf. *DULAT*, p. 813). In BH only the noun occurs. It is used in Leviticus 13 of an inflammation which may develop into 'leprosy' (צרעת: see the notes on 4.6) but in itself is not treated as unclean and may heal up (cf. v. 23). 2 Kings 20.7 (par. Isa. 38.21) mentions the cure of Hezekiah's שחין by the application of a fig-cake, in the context of an illness which was thought to be life-threatening (v. 1). Deuteronomy 28.27 includes 'the שחין of Egypt' among other unpleasant and incurable diseases which would afflict the disobedient, and v. 35 describes more fully שחין רע, which affects the whole body and head, but especially the legs, again incurable. The same expression is used of Job's affliction in Job 2.7, where the reference to scraping with a sherd may suggest itching as one symptom. His sitting in ashes certainly indicates humiliation, perhaps more (cf. Jer. 6.26; Ezek. 27.30; Jon. 3.6; Lam. 3.16); and his friends at first no longer recognise him (Job 2.12). The expression occurs several times in the Mishnah, chiefly in connection (as in Lev.) with the diagnosis of צרעת (M.Neg. 1.5-6 etc.: 9.1 suggests a use also of injuries causing non-infectious skin discolorations), but also as a factor in fitness for marriage (M.Ket. 3.5; 7.10), presumably in a severe form. Gen.R. 41.2 (Soncino ed., p. 333: on Gen. 12.17) indicates that eventually no fewer than 24 forms of שחין were distinguished. In the later Aram. dialects (and perhaps in Akkadian: see Y. Elman, 'An Akkadian Cognate of Hebrew *šəḥîn*', *JANES*

8 [1976], pp. 33-34) cognates were used of skin infections (cf. *HAL*, p. 1354) and שחנא באישא is attested twice in the Qumran Prayer of Nabonidus (4Q242 f1: 3.2, 6), where it may be a technical term for a specific ailment, as attested in Syr. (Payne Smith, p. 564). This could also be the case with שחין רע in Deut. 28.35 and Job 2.7. In the Qumran Job Targum שחין appears in Job 30.14 with no obvious justification in MT (11Q10 16.21). The translator probably took פריץ in the sense of 'calamity' and introduced שחין from 2.7. In the damaged parallel stich באישא[ ] may be the remnants of a similar expression: did the translator equate שאה with שאת = 'eruption, sore', which occurs several times in Leviticus 13?

g. Heb. פרח אבעבעת. The construction here, in contrast to v. 10 (see Note h), involves an 'accusative of result' (JM §125o: whether פרח = 'break out' is the same word as פרח = 'bud, sprout' remains an open question). אבעבעת occurs only here and in v. 10 in BH and seems to indicate an additional feature of the boils, presumably 'blisters' or 'pustules'. The *aleph* is prosthetic, since the Aram., MH and Akk. (*bubuʾtu*: H.R. Cohen, *Biblical Hapax Legomena in the Light of Akkadian and Ugaritic* [SBLDS 37; Missoula, 1978], p. 109; *AHw*, p. 135, with numerous occurrences; some meaning 'pus') cognates lack it.

h. Heb. שחין אבעבעת. Here שחין is probably in the construct state and אבעבעת indicates an attribute according to GK §128p-q. פרח this time has no associated accusative, just as in its similar uses in Leviticus 13–14. The clause can also be rendered 'and blistering boils appeared (lit. "were, came")…' (so Houtman, p. 79: cf. BDB, pp. 225-26 for the possibility of both renderings when ל [as in v. 9] is not present and esp. 8.13-14).

i. Heb. לעמד, lit. 'stand': for the sense required by the context, with following לפני, cf. Judg. 2.14; 2 Kgs 10.4; Esth. 9.2; Dan. 8.4 (other passages have בפני: cf. BDB, p. 764a).

j. The Leningrad ms. B19a is erroneously and impossibly vocalised בַּהַרְטָמִּם (cf. 8.3; and early editions of *BHS* printed a *he* in place of the *heth*), but the correct vocalisation בַּחַרְטֻמִּם is found in most mss and editions (including Dotan).

Explanatory Notes

8-9. The address to Moses and Aaron together is paralleled in the plague narrative only at its beginning and is a departure from the pattern established in 7.1-2 (and earlier 4.14-16): for other examples in Exodus see 6.13, 26 (both redactional); 12.1 (in Lev. 11.1; 13.1; 14.33; 15.1; Num. 2.1; 4.1, 17; 14.26; 16.20; 19.1 the formula is slightly different; in Num. 20.12, 23 it is the same as here). In earlier Priestly sections (see the introduction to this passage) Moses is to instruct Aaron what to do, but here they begin by acting together and then Moses performs the decisive action which brings about the plague. A preliminary stage is envisaged (not mentioned in the fulfilment in v. 10) in which the four handfuls of soot are miraculously transformed into a dust cloud covering the whole country (v. 9a). This bears some similarity to the 'magic' of earlier episodes (and to 4.1-6), which demonstrated Yahweh's power over material things. But this time, like the 'pestilence' of the parallel account (9.1-7), there is to be a plague in the normal sense and it is to afflict not only livestock but human beings (compare perhaps the escalation of Job's sufferings in Job 1–2, though the correspondence is not exact). 'Boils' (Heb. $š^eḥîn$: the word for 'blister' occurs only here in the OT – see Notes f and g on the translation) are mentioned elsewhere both as a physical ailment (Lev. 13.18 etc.; 2 Kgs 20.7 [= Isa. 38.21]; Job 2.7), which does not in itself make a person unclean,[2] and as a punishment for disobedience (Deut. 28.27, 35), when it is incurable. Possibly a different, more severe, variety of it is denoted by the phrase 'grievous boils'/'loathsome sores' in Deut. 28.35 and Job 2.7 (Heb. $š^eḥîn\ ra^c$ in both cases). In Deut. 28.27 the possibly milder form is described as 'the boils of Egypt', as if the disease had its origin there or was especially prevalent there. This could be simply a reference to the Exodus tradition as reflected also in this passage (cf. 'the diseases of Egypt' in Deut. 7.15; 28.60), but it may point to knowledge that such infections were generally widespread there (cf. Houtman, pp. 76-77). In Thucydides' account of the plague at Athens in the second year of the Peloponnesian War (430 B.C.), which includes some very similar symptoms (see Text and Versions on v. 9), he says that it originated in Ethiopia and spread first into Egypt and Libya, before extending into a large part of the Persian Empire (*Hist.* 2.48.1). The precise meaning of Heb. $š^eḥîn$ (if it had one) is not agreed, but the ancient Versions (including their renderings of the word for 'blister') point in the direction of 'boils' rather than some other diseases that have been suggested (for a list see Houtman, p. 76; also *ABD* 6, p. 11).

10-12. The account of the execution of the plague as usual follows the divine instruction closely, although 'in the sight of Pharaoh' (v. 8) is taken up by a corresponding verbal expression and the intermediate stage represented by the dust cloud (v. 9) is omitted. The former change emphasizes that here again, as in the

---

[2] Contrary to the assertions of Houtman (p. 74) and Propp (p. 332, cf. p. 331).

first Priestly plague pericope (7.8-13), Moses and Aaron confront Pharaoh directly. But the outcome is very different (v. 11): Pharaoh's magicians, who had already been unable to match Aaron's action on the previous occasion and had acknowledged his possession of divine power (8.14-15), are now totally unable to resist Moses (lit. 'stand before Moses': see Note i on the translation – many see a deliberate word-play with the identical Heb. phrase in v. 10) and themselves fall victim to the infection. That is enough for the narrator: he does not tell us that Pharaoh was affected, or that the Israelites were not, though both might be (and have been) inferred. His point here is that the contest between Yahweh's and Pharaoh's representatives is over, with the decisive defeat of the latter. It is all the more surprising, from a human point of view, that Pharaoh still does not give way, and perhaps that is why the narrator at this point reintroduces the ultimate theological cause of it for the first time in a Priestly text (or any text) since Yahweh's introductory declaration in 7.3 (cf. also the summary in 11.10), which the addition in this case (but not before) of 'to Moses' also recalls. The hardening of Pharaoh's heart by Yahweh is a theme that is taken up more extensively in the Priestly account of the sea-crossing (Exod. 14.4, 8; cf. 17: Gertz, p. 203).

Text and Versions

קחו (9.8)   4QpalEx^m prefixes לאמר, and LXX's λέγων may well be based on such a *Vorlage* (Wevers, *Notes*, p. 127). MT itself occasionally uses the speech-marker after a form of אמר (e.g. 5.10, 7.8, 12.1, 15.1), but where the witnesses are divided (SP agrees with MT here) the shorter text is likely to be more original.

חפניכם (9.8)   4QpalEx^m reads חפנכם, the sing. form (a defective writing of the pl. is less likely), implying that Moses and Aaron were each to take one handful of soot, thus magnifying the miracle. Against the agreement of all other witnesses this is not likely to be original.

פיח (9.8)   Vulg *cineris*, Tg^{J,N} and Sy render the rare Heb. word with words for 'ash', Tg^J with the addition (here but not in v. 10) of דקיק to preserve the idea of fine powder. But 'soot' as in LXX and Tg^O agrees more closely with the meaning of the cognates (see Note b on the translation).

השמימה (9.8)   So also 4QGen-Ex^a, if the small fr. 37 is correctly located here (there is no obvious alternative position for it). But SP and 4QpalEx^m agree, as often, in reading the form without directional *he*. See the note on 7.15 Text and Versions (המימה), where it is suggested that the shorter forms are likely to be original.

לעיני פרעה (9.8) Tgʲ has (פרעה) קדם and the first two editions of the Biblia Rabbinica printed this as the reading of Tgº (in agreement with one ms. against the לעיני of the rest). This is probably just a free rendering of MT. LXX adds καὶ ἐναντίον τῶν θεραπόντων αὐτοῦ as it does in 7.9-10, no doubt because it is clear from the sequel that Pharaoh was not alone.

והיה¹ᵒ (9.9) Both LXX and Vulg interpret this as a jussive rather than a future (as they more naturally do with וזרקו in v. 8), but the second occurrence is rendered as a future (ἔσται, *erunt*).

על כל־ארץ מצרים (9.9) 4QpalExᵐ omits the כל, against all other witnesses, probably by homoeoteleuton (Propp: but cf. Sanderson, *Exodus Scroll*, pp. 147-50, where the possibility that it has the original reading is left open). A trace of the *kaph* is said to be preserved in 4QRPᶜ (365), but the evidence is very slight. Little else of the verse survives in 4QRPᶜ, which appears to have had a shorter text in vv. 9-10, probably due to homoeoteleuton: a partial filling of the gap is fragmentarily preserved between the lines.

על־האדם (9.9) Tg^N and Sy here and in v. 10 insert *bny* before their renderings of האדם.

שחין (9.9) LXX ἕλκη can mean 'wounds' as well as 'ulcers', and knowledge of this rendering (via the OL?) probably accounts for Vulg's use of *vulnera* here: in Leviticus 13 and Job 2.7 it has the expected *ulcer*. Jerome no doubt thought that the precise meaning was sufficiently clear from the following words.

פרח אבעבעת (9.9) LXX φλυκτίδες ἀναζέουσαι and Vulg (*et*) *vesicae turgentes* follow the inverted order of these words in v. 10. φλυκτίς (or rather its classical equivalent φλύκταινα), like ἕλκος, appears in Thucydides' account of the Athenian plague (*Hist.* 2.49), but the accompanying verb there is not ἀναζέω (for which the closest pars. involve an outbreak of worms) but ἐξανθέω, which Symm uses here and LXX has regularly for פרח in Leviticus 13. Vulg's *turgentes*, 'swelling up', may be dependent on the use of *sgy* in the Aram. translation tradition.³ Sy *dnwphʾ dsgy* also follows the word-order of v. 10 but keeps closer than LXX and Vulg to its grammatical form. Tgg follow MT here, with the only significant variant being the addition in Tg^N of עבד, 'producing' (which the mg omits), to פרח, which it may have regarded as intransitive in line with most of its occurrences. All the Vss agree in rendering the rare word אבעבעת by words for 'blisters, pustules'.⁴

---

³ Aq's πεταζόμενα/αι, 'spreading out', is difficult to explain as πετάζω/πετάννυμι is generally used by him and in LXX in contexts of flight. It could assume the presence of a cognate of Aram. and MH פרח = 'fly', which is perhaps found in Ezek. 13.20 and in the nouns אפרח and פרחה in BH.

⁴ According to *AramB* 2, p. 37 n. *o*, and Sokoloff, *Dictionary*, p. 551, the word שלבוקיין used in Tg^{F,J,N,Nmg} (and spelt with *pe* in Tg^{J,N} here: in v. 10 Tg^N has a scribal error and Tgʲ spells with *beth*) is only found here and in CPA, but Jastrow, p. 1577, cites what must be a related verb שלבק in MH, which has a SamAram cognate meaning 'inflame' (CAL; it appears in some mss of SamTg at Exod. 3.3).

After this phrase LXX inserts ἔν τε τοῖς ἀνθρώποις καὶ ἐν τοῖς τετράποσιν (καί), corresponding to what follows its inverted equivalent in the Heb. of v. 10, despite the fact that the scope of the plague has already been stated earlier in the present verse. This makes it even clearer that the translator was slavishly using v. 10 in making his version of v. 9. The hexaplaric tradition naturally obelised the additional material here.

ויקחו (9.10)   LXX ἔλαβεν, putting the focus on Moses as later in the verse, but against v. 8.

ויעמדו (9.10)   LXX* had no equivalent to this, perhaps because it assumed that λαμβάνω, like Heb. לקח and נשא which it often renders, could have the sense 'carry'. ויעמדו, which is attested by all other witnesses, has no anticipation in the command in v. 8 (except for the implication of לעיני פרעה) but is needed here to complete the sense. Sanderson (*Exodus Scroll*, pp. 105-106) and Lemmelijn (pp. 172-73), however, regard ויעמדו as secondary.

השמימה (9.10)   SP has השמים, as in v. 8: see the note there. 4QpalEx^m does not preserve the word here. Sy adds 'in the sight of Pharaoh' from v. 8, as do LXX miniscules, but it is otiose after לפני פרעה.

פרח אבעבעת (9.10)   The Vss mainly employ the same expressions to render these words as in v. 9 (where see the notes). LXX and Vulg have them in the same order (though Vulg recognises the different genitive construction here), because they had based their renderings of v. 9 on this verse. Sy employs Syr. *prḥ* to render פרח but makes it begin a separate clause by the addition of *w*: this is just a free rendering, though with the slightly different meaning of 'spread'. The original hand of 4QRP^c (365) seems to have omitted the phrase (see the note on v. 9), but immediately before באדם it has רעות, 'painful' (cf. Jub. 48.5 according to *DJD* XIII, p. 265), which presupposes that its exemplar must have had it, though most probably with אבעבעת following פרח as it does in v. 9. In other words, whereas LXX and Vulg (and perhaps the Heb. *Vorlage* of LXX) assimilated the wording of v. 9 to v. 10, the exemplar of 4QRP^c seems to have done the opposite.

ובבהמה (9.10)   LXX employs τετράπους as its equivalent here, as in v. 9 (and already in 8.16-18 and ten other places in the Pentateuch), and this has a good basis in classical usage. But the preferred equivalent from v. 19b onwards is κτῆνος, which also does duty for Heb. מקנה etc. 4QRP^c, according to the reconstruction in *DJD* XIII, p. 265, added בכול ארץ מצרים from v. 9 at the end of this verse, which would fit with its harmonisation already observed in the previous note.

החרטמים (9.11)   LXX renders by φάρμακος both here and later in the verse, having previously used ἐπαοιδός: on both words see Text and Versions on 7.11. In Gen. 41.8, 24 LXX had used a third word, ἐξηγητής.

כי היה השחין בחרטמם (9.11)   Vulg *quae in illis erant* is a free paraphrase: a similar tendency appears in LXX^M and Sy. The latter has the stronger *sgy* for היה (cf. its rendering of פרח in v. 9). Tg^J as previously inserts 'the blow/plague of' before השחין (cf. 7.21; 8.2, 13-14) as a reminder that this is part of Yahweh's onslaught on Egypt.

מצרים (9.11)   LXX γῇ Αἰγύπτου, no doubt assimilating to the two occurrences of the longer phrase in v. 9. Wevers (*Exodus*, p. 141; *Notes*, p. 129, cf. Propp, p. 300) is mistaken to say that 4QRP^c (365) has the fuller expression – this part of the verse does not survive: he may have been misled by the restoration at the end of v. 10, on which see above. The variant is also attested in some Masoretic mss, but is surely secondary: it probably also involves a misunderstanding, because here מצרים must refer to the Egyptians.

ויחזק (9.12)   Sy *wqšy*, using the same verb (here in the Pael) as in 8.15: see Text and Versions there.

לב (9.12)   Tg^J, as usual in this connection, prefixes 'the inclination of': see Text and Versions on 4.21.

דבר (9.12)   LXX oddly has συνέταξεν: cf. 1.17 and 12.35 (where it is more appropriate) and Wevers, *Notes*, p. 9. Vulg similarly has *praeceperat* in a series of passages where it seems inappropriate (on which see Text and Versions on 7.22), but here it reverts to the natural *locutus est*.

אל־משה (9.12)   LXX^B and other mss have no equivalent and their shorter text was preferred by Rahlfs. Wevers prefers the reading τῷ Μωυσῇ of a larger number of mss which include A and M (for the argument see *THGE*, p. 253). Either way, the omission that produced the shorter text was presumably due to assimilation to the pattern in 7.13, 22; 8.11, 15.

After v. 12 4QEx^c has a *vacat*, which probably extended to the end of a line (*DJD* XII, p. 108). In 4QpalEx^m there is no direct evidence, but reconstruction based on two adjacent fragments suggests that there was an interval within a line (*setumah*), as in MT (*DJD* IX, p. 80).

CHAPTER 9.13-35

THE HAIL AND THE THUNDER

The boundaries of this section are clear, like most other episodes in the plague story: it begins with a new instruction from Yahweh for Moses to 'take your stand' before Pharaoh and concludes with Pharaoh's refusal, once again, to let the Israelites leave Egypt. There are section-divisions at the beginning and end in Masoretic mss, and 10.1 begins a new reading in both lectionary cycles. The mss also attest section-divisions before 9.13 and 9.22.[1] At Qumran open lines mark divisions before 9.13 and 10.1, and probably before 9.22, in 4QExod^c. 4QpalExod^l and 4QpalExod^m also have the open line before 10.1 (and 4QpalExod^l has an empty line there too) and the former may have had a short division before 9.27 (as 4QExod^c may also have done). It does not survive for 9.13 and 9.22; nor does 4QpalExod^m for 9.22 and 9.27, but before 9.13 it probably had a closed space. The Qumran evidence, so far as it goes, agrees with the medieval divisions, and there is some indication of an additional break before 9.27.

The intermediate breaks correspond well to the main sub-divisions of the episode: vv. 13-21 contain Yahweh's initial instructions to Moses to warn Pharaoh of the impending plague and the Egyptians' responses to this; vv. 22-26 recount Yahweh's command for the plague to begin, its occurrence and effects; and vv. 27-35 Pharaoh's reactions to the plague itself, first submissive and then recalcitrant. Within these sub-sections there are several close correspondences of form to earlier episodes (see for details the notes on vv. 13, 14, 22, 26, 27-28, 29-30, 33, 34-35), but also fresh elements of various kinds which serve to reveal more clearly both Yahweh's purposes and character and the religious dimension of Pharaoh's (and his courtiers') refusal to let Israel go (vv. 17, 20-21, 27, 30, 34). Compared with the immediately preceding episodes (9.1-7;

---

[1] Or. 4445 originally had no division before 9.13 (L, Maim. *setumah*) but a marginal note indicates a *petuchah* here.

8-12) the length and complexity of this section represent a striking change. The following section (10.1-20) is comparable to it in this respect, but its sequel (10.21-29) is briefer. Both these sections (see further the introductions to them) also share features with 9.13-35, some of which are not present in earlier episodes (cf. 9.22-23 with 10.12-13, 21-22; 9.27 with 10.16-17; and 9.35 with 10.20, 27).

Although the new elements in this section can be seen as no more than ways of enriching the narrative as it develops, some of them have been attributed by scholars to a more complex process of composition than before.

Some have pointed to 'deviations from narrative continuity' in vv. 14-16(17) and vv. 31-32 and to differences of expression and undue amplification in the account of the plague in vv. 22-26 (cf. v. 18, and Schmidt, p. 423). Verses 34 and 35 are a clear case of duplication, and v. 35 closely resembles the conclusions of the earlier plague-accounts that have been attributed to the Priestly narrative (see the Explanatory Notes on vv. 34-35), just as some features (but not all) of v. 22 recall the beginnings of those episodes. But the explanation of such 'clues' has taken, and continues to take, different forms, which are closely related to the developing history of Pentateuchal criticism in general. In the specific case of the plague-narrative as a whole some conclusions about the analysis of this section and the two which follow it may be decisive in the choice that is made between competing theories elsewhere.

From Knobel to Childs, almost without exception, source-critical explanations formed the basis for the analysis of the passage. Knobel distinguished between v. 35 (P, his *Grundschrift*) and the rest (initially ascribed by him to the Jehovist (*Ex.-Lev.*, p. 79), subsequently to E, his *Rechtsbuch* (*Num.-Jos.*, p. 504 – for him it was the only plague that did not belong to J, his *Kriegsbuch*, or P). Wellhausen (*Composition*, pp. 63-68) observed clear signs of parallel sources in vv. 18-24, distinguished by references to Yahweh's action which Moses announces and Moses' use of his staff respectively, so that at least vv. 22-23a and 35 belonged to E and the rest mainly to J. This pattern of division was followed by most commentators down to Childs, though with an increasing (but not unanimous) tendency to regard vv. 14-16, 19-21 and 31-32 as later additions to the J account, which could thereby be reduced to the scale and structure of J's earlier plague-accounts. The exceptions were Rudolph and Noth. Rudolph regarded vv. 22-23a and 35 as redactional expansions of the J account too (*Elohist*, pp. 19-20), while Noth initially treated these verses (except v. 22b) as parts of the J account itself (*ÜGP*, p. 32; cf. pp. 24-28). Later, however, he attributed them to P (*Exodus*, ET, pp. 70, 80: so also Blenkinsopp, p. 141). This later view of Noth's was followed by Steingrimsson (with the addition of vv. 24a, 25-26 to the P account) as part of what seemed at the time a complex combination of source-critical and redactional explanations of the passage (*Vom Zeichen*, pp. 108-30, 194-95). But most subsequent commentators have preferred what may broadly be termed a 'supplementary' account of the verses formerly attributed to E.[2] Blum (*Studien*, pp. 245-50) and Van Seters (*Life of Moses*, pp. 77 n. 2, 107) attribute them to the supplementary Priestly layer which they see as being overlaid, respectively, on a 'Deuteronomistic Composition' or an exilic Yahwist narrative. Indeed this passage and others like it (especially 7.17-20 and 10.12-13) are seen by them as decisive proofs that P was such a supplementary layer and not a once independent source. This view can claim support from close verbal parallels in earlier and later passages of P, but it overlooks some important differences, especially the central place of Moses', rather than Aaron's, staff here (v. 23). A more common view is therefore that, because the verses seem to presuppose elements of the J narrative as well as P, they should be ascribed to the final redactor of the Pentateuch (EndR/PentR: so Kohata, L. Schmidt, W.H. Schmidt, Graupner). For them the main narrative strand is from J or, according to L. Schmidt (for reasons given in *Beobachtungen*, pp. 26-30), from R^{JE}. Recently Levin (*Jahwist*, pp. 337-38) and Gertz (*Tradition*, pp. 132-52) have given the whole main narrative (including vv. 22-23a, 35) a much later origin, with EndR or even later, in connection with their view that 9.13-16 (with 11.8 and also 10.28-29 and parts of 11.4-7 according to Gertz) brought the J/non-Priestly series of plagues to a close. There are some attractions in this view, but even if objections to it cannot be overcome (see below) it does not necessarily lead to such a late dating of either the plague of hail or those which immediately follow it.

For a fresh assessment of such varied explanations of the composition of this passage it is important to begin by observing that it cannot be studied in isolation. As already indicated it shares, on the one hand, its basic structure and even verbal expressions with the preceding non-Priestly plagues. But it also exhibits new features, especially in vv. 22-23a and 35; in the first passage Moses (with his staff) is given a new role at the actual onset of the plague, while in the latter Pharaoh's resistance is described in a different way in a doublet of the normal non-Priestly expression in v. 34(b). Both these features reappear in the two following episodes (10.12-13, 20; 21-22, 27): in the plague of locusts they are again combined

---

[2] The exceptions are Houtman, who treats the whole passage as a 'homogeneous' story (2, p. 81); Propp, who thinks that v. 35 may be from a redactor (pp. 290, 313) but that the rest is all from E, like most of the non-Priestly plague narrative (pp. 314-15: p. 312 sees no significance for authorship in the distinctions noted by Wellhausen and others); and Dozeman, who in his commentary observes P additions to the earlier narrative in vv. 14, 27 and 29 (p. 233: in *God at War* [Oxford, 1996], pp. 28-29 n. 5, he mentions also a Dtr addition in v. 16b and the Priestly origin of v. 35b).

with features of the earlier non-Priestly pattern, while in the plague of darkness the new dimension of Moses' role begins the (much shorter) episode and most of the earlier non-Priestly features do not appear at all. These variations are clearly connected and could be explained in three ways: (i) the same non-Priestly writer as before introduced new elements into his presentation of the narrative as it reached its climax; (ii) the compiler drew on an additional older narrative source at these points; and (iii) the new elements are due to a redactor or supplementer of the main narrative sources. These are of course, successively, the views of older, traditional readings of the narrative, of critical scholarship between about 1870 and 1970, and of (much of) the scholarship of the past twenty-five years.

It should be noted that the role assigned to Moses' staff (or hand) is not limited to these three passages. Within the plague-cycle his staff has already appeared in 7.17-20 alongside Aaron's staff, and earlier it was mentioned in 4.1-5 and 4.17 (cf. v. 20) as a means for Moses to 'perform signs'. Later, at the crossing of the sea, Moses' staff (or hand) has a similar role in 14.16, 21, 26-27, and it is the means of bringing water out of the rock in 17.5-6 (with an explicit reference to 7.17-20) and in Num. 20.7-11. These passages need not necessarily all be from the same author, but they are presumably connected in some way, and decisions reached about their authorship will have a bearing on the present discussion.[3]

Attention also needs to be given to a different kind of consideration of the wider context, to which Gertz has recently given a prominent place in his argument for a redactional origin for the whole of the hail-plague. This is the view that 9.13-16 did not originally serve to introduce the hail-plague but formed the transition to the final plague, the death of the firstborn. The first to suggest this, in fact for vv. 14-17, appears to have been Holzinger (p. 27), who believed that (most of) these verses came from the J source but originally stood somewhere later on (perhaps before 11.4b: he does not seem to give a precise location). Later Rudolph, who assigned v. 14 to J (he regarded all of vv. 15-16 as later additions), took the

---

[3] In Num. 20.7-11 the staff is only said to belong to Moses in v. 11: in vv. 8-9 it is simply '*the* staff' and in v. 9 it is taken 'from before Yahweh', which is where Aaron's staff had been left in Num. 17.25-26. The 'his' in v. 11 may well therefore be a harmonising gloss (so, e.g., Carpenter/Harford-Battersby 2, p. 221 n. 11; Eissfeldt, *Hexateuch-synopse*, p. 42, who cites LXX in support).

same view, though in a rather curious way, because he believed that the hail, locusts and darkness were all parts of J, but that they were not part of the traditional narrative which J inherited:[4] they had previously been 'free-floating' traditions, and were incorporated for the first time by J (pp. 19-21). Rudolph also thought that 'all my plagues' in v. 14 (which Holzinger had regarded as a redactional gloss) originally stood in the singular, though it is not clear whether he means in the written form of J or the tradition behind it.

Most recently this idea has been taken up by Levin and Gertz. Levin sees 9.13-16 as implying that all the previous plagues would now be inflicted on Pharaoh himself and his closest associates, an account of which was displaced by the insertion of the death of the Egyptian firstborn and its prior announcement (11.4-7; 12.29-33). 11.8 was its original sequel (*Jahwist*, pp. 337, 339). Gertz's approach is less drastic and less speculative in that he sees the reference as being to the death of the firstborn and regards 10.28-29, 11.4-7* and 12.29-33* as part of the same redactional layer (*Tradition*, pp. 146-50). But he also, like Levin, draws the conclusion that the three intervening episodes (9.17–10.27) must be later additions.[5] That need not in itself, of course, mean that they are the pure invention of the 'final' redactor of the Pentateuch, as Gertz believes, and the inclusion of two of them in Psalm 78 as well as Psalm 105 is an argument against such a late origin for them. But more seriously it may be doubted whether 9.14 need or even can be taken in the ways suggested by these scholars. The plagues which are to follow are quite severe enough to represent the intensification implied (as Holzinger at least recognised when he came to explain the displacement of 9.14-17 to their present position: p. 27), and '*all* my plagues' is hardly capable of being referred to the single episode of the death of the firstborn. Of course it is possible to suggest that a singular expression originally stood in its place, but

---

[4] W.H. Schmidt (p. 423; cf. p. 363) shares this view, but like many others he regards all of vv. 14-16 as a redactional (for him R^JE) addition to J and sees these verses as referring to the purpose of 'all' the following plagues, which are also later than J (pp. 417-21: cf. 10.1b-2).

[5] In fact Gertz also believes that the pestilence in 9.1-7 is a later addition to the original series of plagues, because like Levin he thinks that the phrase 'this time' in 9.14 is meant to echo the same phrase in 8.28 (p. 149: Heb. *bappaʿam hazzōʾt*). This is a tenuous basis for argument, and such a connection is probably no more likely than it is in the case of the similar phrases in 9.27 and 10.17.

this is pure speculation: the fact remains that the text as we have it does not fit the proposed interpretation. Levin (see above) does take the plural seriously but his theory involves the reconstruction of a quite different finale for the plagues on a very flimsy basis. The conclusion must be that, whatever the origin of vv. 14-16, they were designed to refer, as they do now, to the hail-plague (and perhaps also to [some of] those that follow).

This still leaves the question of the origin of 9.22-23a and 35 to be discussed. More recent discussion (since Noth) has stressed the similarity of the formulae and vocabulary used to those of the Priestly source. The correspondences have been laid out with particular clarity by Blum (*Studien*, pp. 247-48) and Gertz (*Tradition*, pp. 132-34). Yet that is not the whole story: there are features in these verses which are not typically Priestly (Moses' staff; the second and third clauses of v. 35), which have recently led to the widespread attribution of them to the 'final' redactor of the Pentateuch (since Kohata). However, the role played by Moses and his staff in these verses and the two following episodes is not easily accounted for in this way: it looks much more like a different tradition that has been incorporated into the non-Priestly narrative at this point, as also seems to be the case in 7.17-20. As for the Priestly language, perhaps too much has been read into the similarities by recent scholars: if a staff is to play a part in the onset of a plague, 'stretching it out' is an obvious verb to use, and 'stubbornness of heart' is an expression with enough analogies elsewhere to make dependence on the Priestly narrative less than certain (Josh. 11.20; Jer. 5.3; Ezek. 2.4; 3.7-9). The correspondences within the same section of the Exodus tradition may make some relationship to the Priestly account likely, but it is just as possible that the Priestly narrator borrowed expressions from another (older) account (as seems quite often to be the case elsewhere: cf. Kohata) as vice versa.

Moreover, the doublets do point to the combination of two once independent accounts of the plague – not only in vv. 34-35 but in the overfull and confused descriptions of the hail-plague in vv. 22-25 – and the plague of darkness in 10.21-23, 27 shows what a full version of the alternative type might have looked like, as Wellhausen already observed (*Composition*, pp. 66-67) and Fohrer set out with even greater clarity (pp. 65-67; based on H.-P. Müller, 'Die Plagen der Apocalypse: eine formgeschichtliche Untersuchung', *ZNW* 51 [1960], pp. 268-78, apparently). Yet even among those who believe in two old narrative sources in the Pentateuch ('J' and 'E') there have been thought to be decisive objections to finding such duplication (in effect traces of a parallel E account) in the plague-narratives. L. Schmidt argued that in E there is no trace of Moses demanding Israel's release from Pharaoh or even meeting him, and so the presuppositions for a plague-story such as this are missing (*Beobachtungen*, pp. 23-24). Moreover, the use of the divine name 'Yahweh' in 9.22 is held to be contrary to the Elohist's practice. Graupner makes the same argument about the divine name and adds the fragmentary nature of these portions of text and the fact that Moses' staff is never described as 'the staff of God', as it is in 4.20 (*Elohist*, p. 65). Like others, he also believes that intertextual relations alone can explain the origin of these passages. W.H. Schmidt is more cautious, although he accepts the argument based on the divine name. But for him the absence in E of any encounter between Moses and Pharaoh is only 'possible' (p. 415). He recognises that 13.17 refers to Pharaoh's 'release' of Israel and that the E version of Moses' commission and his response to it (3.10-11) implies that he is indeed to go and meet Pharaoh. So it is only in a 'conjectured' older version of E that such an encounter might be missing: the present text positively leads us to expect one. Our own analysis of ch. 5 has reaffirmed an older view that both J and E are represented there (see the introduction to 5.1-23). Given Pharaoh's resistance there, it is actually to be expected that there would be a plague-narrative in both older accounts.

Those scholars of an earlier generation who took this view attributed the main body of the hail-plague account to J (like the previous non-Priestly plague-accounts) and the fragments of a parallel version to E. In our discussion of 7.14-26 we concluded that, contrary to the older view of that passage, the main narrative was from E and the references to Moses' staff from J. In consequence we have assigned the subsequent non-Priestly plague-narratives to E and the implication of this is that the essentially similar framework of the hail-plague is derived from E, and vv. 22-23a, 35 from J.[6] It is probable, as earlier scholars saw, that in vv. 23b-25 the description

---

[6] There is the possibility of assigning v. 35 to a later redactor familiar with P, but the appearance of similar language in 10.20 and especially 10.27, which seems to be part of a complete plague-story from the 'other early source', favours its attribution to J as well.

of the plague should be subdivided according to the links either with v. 18 (and 19-21) or with vv. 22-23a: this points to the attribution of vv. 24a and 25b (and possibly some elements of vv. 26-34: see the Explanatory Notes) to J as well.

Are there any problems with the attribution of the remaining verses to E? The use of the title 'the God of the Hebrews' (v. 13) has already been discussed in connection with its occurrence in 9.1. 'The land of Goshen' (v. 26) has already been mentioned in 8.18 and on numerous occasions in the last few chapters of Genesis (for a list of passages and discussion of geographical issues see the Explanatory Note on 8.18). All the Genesis passages were traditionally assigned to J, and on that basis it would not be difficult to add v. 26 here to the extracts from J: in 9.4-7, where the Israelite animals are spared in a passage attributed by us to E, Goshen is not mentioned. But the situation is not so simple: the mention of Goshen in 8.18 is in a passage which we attribute to E, while 10.23, which again distinguishes the place where the Israelites lived without naming Goshen, belongs to a section of the 'Moses' staff' version of the plagues and so is likely to be assigned by us to J. Nevertheless, the appearance of Goshen in two E passages is not an insuperable problem. For one thing, even the traditional analysis of the Joseph-story attributed very little of the narrative after Jacob's arrival in Egypt to E and nowhere there is anything at all said about the location of the family's settlement: for all we know, the putative original E version of the Joseph-story may have mentioned Goshen too. Secondly, and more to the point, most recent scholarship, even where the existence of old sources is recognised, has on the one hand been reluctant to subdivide the Joseph-story into two parallel strands and on the other has with good reason seen it as essentially a north Israelite composition. If this is correct, it is not at all difficult to see how the author of E could have been familiar with the name of Goshen.[7]

Some features of the main narrative here are actually easier to parallel in E than in J. The references to the 'fear of (the word of) the Lord' in vv. 20 and 30 fit well with what is generally recognised to be a pervasive theme of E (cf. 1.17, 21: more generally Wolff, 'Zur Thematik', pp. 62-67 [ET, 161-67]). The identification of Pharaoh's

---

[7] The 'echoes' of the J Flood Story noted by Levin (p. 338) and W.H. Schmidt (p. 426) are too insignificant to require common authorship.

defiance as 'sin' recalls the language of Abimelech's protest to Abraham (Gen. 20.9) and a later passage in Exodus (20.20), both normally ascribed to E. Even such a trivial idiom as 'get up early' is particularly frequent in passages elsewhere attributed to E (cf. Graupner, *Elohist*, p. 191 nn. 102 and 103).

A majority of critical scholars have regarded vv. 14-16, 19-21 and 31-32 as redactional additions to the main narrative. It is true that none of them is indispensable to its central plot, and vv. 31-32 are often said to be a piece of learned comment that is out of place where it stands (see, however, the Explanatory Note on these verses). Verses 19-21 complicate the plot and may seem to weaken the intended impact of the plague. But recent commentators have found their presence in the narrative (whatever date they ascribe to it) less intrusive, and their theological language fits well within the outlook of the E source. The commentary on Yahweh's plans in vv. 14-16, which emphasises his restraint as a means to his ultimate purpose of revealing his power not only to Pharaoh but throughout the world, certainly goes beyond earlier such explanations of the divine intention (e.g. 8.18). But the further the sequence of plagues proceeds, the more the need for such a complex explanation arises, and it is not in fact difficult to see these verses as an extension of those that have preceded. They may be the work of a redactor who was more reflective than the original narrator, but it is hard to be sure that this is the case. Provisionally we treat all three sections as parts of the original E narrative.

Within the general theological framework of the plague-narrative as a whole, this passage includes some notable innovations, as well as the reappearance (cf. 7.14, 17, 20) of Moses' role as the human controller of the plague in vv. 22-23a. Yahweh for his part is seen as a God who initially restrains his power in his dealings with human opponents like Pharaoh, but who is prepared to make a full onslaught upon him when this becomes necessary to achieve his purpose. This purpose is, as before, to secure the liberation and worship of his people (v. 13), but it is also to make Pharaoh recognise his uniqueness and power (vv. 14, 16a) and to win himself even wider fame (v. 16b). At the same time, he gives Pharaoh instructions that could spare him from the worst effects of the hailstorm (v. 19). What he requires of Pharaoh and his courtiers is now defined as 'fear' of him and his word, but the Egyptians' response remains deficient (vv. 20-21, 30). Nevertheless Yahweh once again relents and brings the storm to an end, in response to Pharaoh's declaration of submission and Moses' intercession on his behalf. The situation remains open, on Yahweh's side at least, for the conflict of wills to be resolved. But the prospect is darkened, both by the twofold reference in the present composite text to Pharaoh's inner resistance, as both folly and stubbornness (vv. 34-35), and by the use, for the first time in the plague-narrative, of the strongly laden word 'sin' to describe it. First Pharaoh's own words indicate an acknowledgement (admittedly limited: see the Explanatory Note) that he has done wrong (v. 27), and then the narrator himself solemnly underlines that Pharaoh's offences (and implicitly the punishment that they merit) have only been increased by this episode (v. 34a). The specific nature of Pharaoh's offence also receives its proper name in v. 17: 'acting arrogantly', a unique reflexive expression that draws upon language used for the building of embankments and siege-mounds (Heb. *sll*) to portray vividly the self-importance of a powerful ruler.

> 13 Yahweh said to Moses, 'Get up early[a] in the morning and take your stand[b] before Pharaoh and say to him, "Thus says Yahweh, the God of the Hebrews, Let my people go so that they may worship me[c]. 14 For this time I am sending[d] all (these?) my plagues[e] into your midst/upon you yourself[f] and on your servants and upon all your people, so that you may know that there is no one like me in all the earth. 15 For I could now have stretched out[g] my hand and struck[h] you and your people with the pestilence and you would have been wiped off[i] the earth. 16 But for this reason have I let you remain, to show you my strength and for my name to be declared[j] in all the earth. 17 If[k] you continue[l] to act arrogantly[m] against my people by refusing to let them go[n], 18 surely[o] I will straightaway tomorrow[p] cause a very severe downpour[q] of hail, such as has not occurred in Egypt from the day of its foundation[r] until now. 19 So now send, bring to safety[s] your animals and everything you have which is outside[t]: every man and beast which remains outside[t] and is not gathered together indoors[u] will die, when the hail comes down upon them."'[v] 20 Whoever of Pharaoh's servants feared the word of Yahweh made his servants and animals take refuge indoors, 21 while whoever paid no heed to the word of Yahweh left[w] his

servants and animals outside. 22 [Yahweh said to Moses, 'Stretch out your hand towards the heavens, so that hail may come in all the land of Egypt'. 23 Moses stretched out his staff towards the heavens, and Yahweh gave[x] thunder and hail, and fire came[y] on the earth,] and Yahweh brought a downpour of hail upon the land of Egypt. 24 [There was hail, with successive flashes[z] of fire amid the hail,] (which was) very severe, such as had never occurred in [all the land of] Egypt from the time when[aa] it became a nation. 25 The hail smote everything that was outside throughout the land of Egypt, man and beast; [and the hail (also) ruined[bb] all the plants of the field, and all the trees of the field it smashed[bb].] 26 Only[cc] in the land of Goshen, where the Israelites were, was there no hail. 27 Pharaoh sent and called Moses and Aaron, and said to them, 'This time[dd] I have sinned: Yahweh is in the right, and I and my people are in the wrong. 28 Make supplication to Yahweh – enough of[ee] immense thunder[ff] and hail! – so that I may let you go and you remain (here) no longer'. 29 Moses said to him, 'When I leave the city[gg], I shall stretch out my hands to Yahweh: the thunder[hh] will cease and the hail will not continue, so that you may know that the earth belongs to Yahweh. 30 But as for you and your servants[ii], I know that you do not yet fear Yahweh (who is) God[jj].' 31 Now the flax and the barley[kk] had been ruined[ll], for the barley was in the ear and the flax was in bud[mm]. 32 But the wheat and the emmer had not been ruined[ll], because they are late growths[nn]. 33 Moses went from the city out of Pharaoh's presence and stretched out his hands to Yahweh: the thunder ceased and the hail and rain(?)[oo] did not pour down on the land. 34 Pharaoh was afraid because the rain, the hail and the thunder ceased, but he continued to sin, and he refused to understand[pp], he and his servants. 35 [Pharaoh's heart was stubborn[qq] and he did not let the Israelites go, as Yahweh had spoken through Moses.]

Notes on the Translation

a. See Note a on the translation of 8.16-28.
b. See Note b on the translation of 8.16-28.
c. The *waw* in ויעבדני expresses purpose, as in the other occurrences of this formula (most recently 8.16 and 9.1). The defective writing of the pl. ending is also characteristic of the formula: on the variation between defective and full (*plene*) writing in general see briefly GK §8i-l and more fully F.I. Andersen and A.D. Forbes, *Spelling in the Hebrew Bible* (Rome, 1986: reviewed by

598   EXODUS 1–18

Barr in *JSS* 33 [1988], pp. 122-31) and J. Barr, *The Variable Spellings of the Hebrew Bible* (Oxford, 1989: reviewed by Tov in *JSS* 35 [1990], pp. 303-16).[8]

d. Heb. שֹׁלֵחַ, Qal part., used here not of the present but the imminent future (GK §116p). If it were not for בפעם הזאת the participle could be taken to refer to the whole sequence of plagues, past, present and future, and this would make the following את־כל־מגפתי easier. But vv. 15f. also seem to imply that a new intensifying of the onslaught is in view.

e. Heb. מגפתי: מגפה, from the root נגף, is used only here in Exodus (though the related נֶגֶף occurs at 12.13 and 30.12, both P). Like the verb נָגַף, 'strike, smite', it is used of military defeat (1 Sam. 4.17; 2 Sam. 17.9; 18.7), of individual suffering and of plague or pestilence. The latter meaning is particularly common in Priestly sections of Numbers, in Chronicles and in other late texts (Zech. 14.12, 15, 18; Ps. 106.29-30), but it is also found in 1 Sam. 6.4 and 2 Sam. 24.21, 25 and the verb is used in such a context in Exod. 12.23, 27 (not P); 32.35; Josh. 24.5. So it is not necessarily a mark of Priestly authorship (P in Exodus actually prefers other words for the plagues: cf. 6.6; 7.3-4) or a late date for the verse. See further *TWAT* 5, 227-30 = *TDOT* 9, pp. 210-13.

f. Heb. אל־לבך, lit. '(in)to your heart [or 'the heart of you']. The EVV. (and Luther) almost all take the phrase as a way of referring to Pharaoh's personal suffering (e.g. 'against you yourself' [REB], 'upon you yourself' [NRSV]), with only JB basing its rendering 'on you' on an emendation (presumably to בך). The interpretation is otherwise probably based on the assumption that אל here has the sense of על, which SP actually reads. לב is frequently used for 'self', but generally for states of mind rather than physical afflictions (the latter perhaps in 1 Kgs 8.38: cf. v. 37 and 2 Chr. 6.29). A collective interpretation of the suffix might be considered, 'into the midst of you', with לב understood metaphorically as it is sometimes used (e.g. בלב־ים in 15.8), but apart from Ps. 45.6 (where a literal sense is possible) the genitives tend to be inanimate. Moreover a shift from a collective 'you' to a personal 'you(r)' in the two following phrases is awkward, and the sequence does look like a variant of the formula already encountered in 7.29 and 8.17, beginning with בך. The variation here could then be seen (as the recent translations take it: note also JPS 'upon your person') as laying special emphasis on the effects on Pharaoh himself. But it remains an unusual idiom. See further Text and Versions.

g. A straightforward past translation of the perfects in this verse is excluded by the contradiction that this would create both with the preceding narrative (in v. 3 the דבר only touches animals) and with the following verses. The perfect is used here of a hypothetical possibility according to GK §106p. In Gen. 31.42 and 43.10 כי עתה introduces the apodosis of a hypothetical past

---

[8] Neither book deals with this specific case, but the general type of case is dealt with by Andersen and Forbes, pp. 201, 278 (Type 56: overall 60:40 preference for *plene*, but Exod. 1-11 strongly *defective*) and by Barr, pp. 25-32 ('Affix Effect').

condition, with כִּי being used as an emphatic particle (further examples in JM §167s), and it is possible that a (suppressed) protasis such as 'If I had wished' is understood here (so Gibson, *Syntax* §81c; Driver, *Hebrew Tenses*, §141). Even on this understanding the meaning 'For' for כִּי is contextually preferable here. Alternatively the perfects may represent 'hypothetical assertions' without any underlying condition, as occurs with כִּמְעַט in Gen. 26.10 (Waltke/O'Connor 30.5.4b: further examples in GK §106p), and in this case כִּי would even more likely mean 'For'. כִּי can of course itself be a conditional particle, but mainly in laws where it approximates to 'when': there seem to be no clear cases of its use in a hypothetical past conditional sentence.

h. Heb. וָאַךְ. A unique form. In the first person sing. *waw* consecutive of Lamed He verbs longer forms are normal (here וָאַכֶּה, as SP reads), but there are other examples of apocopation (GK §49e, 75t: cf. Gen. 31.10).

i. Heb. כחד Niphal is followed by מִן several times when it means 'be hidden' (cf. the Piel), but this is the only case with the sense 'be destroyed': a 'pregnant' sense with the additional idea of removal must therefore be assumed here, as sometimes elsewhere (GK §119ff: the use after the Hiphil in Ps. 83.5 is different).

j. When an inf. constr. has no explicit subject, the subject need not be the subject of the main clause and need not even be expressed elsewhere in the sentence (1 Sam. 18.19; Ps. 42.4). In the latter case especially 'the infinitive… is best rendered in English as a passive' (GK §115e n. 1). So while '(sc. for me) to declare my name' is the most obvious translation here, it is not the only possibility and the idea may well be that human beings throughout the earth should declare Yahweh's name/fame (for the expression with a human subject cf. Ps. 22.23; 102.22; for the idea of worldwide praise of Yahweh expressed in other ways e.g. Pss. 66.1, 4; 96.1; 98.4; 100.1).

k. There is no אִם and the verse could be understood as a statement in its own right (e.g. NJPS, NRSV). But a condition is often expressed without an introductory particle (GK §159b-k) and in the present context a conditional threat is expected (cf. 7.27; 8.16; 9.2).

l. As often the suffix attached to עוֹד represents the subject of the following participle (GK §100o).

m. Heb. מִסְתּוֹלֵל. The Hithpoel of סלל (cf. GK §54b for the metathesis) occurs only here in BH (there are later exx. in Sir. 39.24; 40.28), but a similar, though positive, use of the Pilpel appears at Prov. 4.8.

n. Heb. לְבִלְתִּי שַׁלְּחָם. Gerundive use of the inf. cons. (GK §114o).

o. Heb. הִנְנִי, used as often 'to reinforce affirmation' (JM §164a) rather than deictically in the narrow sense.

p. Heb. כָּעֵת מָחָר, a combination occurring 7 times elsewhere in BH, all in (source-material of) the Deuteronomistic History (1 Sam. 9.16; 20.12; 1 Kgs 19.2; 20.6; 2 Kgs 7.1, 18; 10.6). The variant in Josh. 11.6 מָחָר כָּעֵת הַזֹּאת clearly means 'tomorrow at/about this time' (cf. Lexx., NRSV etc., Text and Versions). That sense would make the threat more precise here than it has been earlier in the plague narratives (cf. 8.6, 19; 9.5; later cf. 10.4), which is of course possible. But כָּעֵת alone means 'now' (so clearly in Num. 23.23 and Judg. 13.23, and perhaps also in Judg. 21.22: in Job 39.18 it may be a conjunction), or 'about this time', and the order of the words in the idiom is rather against כעת defining מחר more closely (in Josh. 11.6 the order is the reverse). So perhaps it means 'imminently', as עתה often does. The issue is related to the even more difficult expression כעת חיה in Gen. 18.10, 14; 2 Kgs 4.16-17, where כעת is generally not translated 'about this time'.

q. Heb. מטר Hiphil (denom. from מָטָר) is used quite widely in a metaphorical sense of the (supposed) descent of materials other than rain (cf. 16.4; also Gen. 19.24; Pss. 11.6; 78.24, 27; Job 20.23), and the meteorological use here and in v. 23 is closer to the literal meaning than the others.

r. Heb. למן is most often (and perhaps most originally) found with a following עד(ו), as here and in 11.7, so that the ל can perhaps be understood to govern the whole expression in a temporal or other sense. The use of the abs. st. היום before the inf. cons. is peculiar (see also Text and Versions), but paralleled in 2 Sam. 19.25 and probably to be explained as a case of apposition (so BDB, p. 583; cf. GK §127f). הוסדה would normally be written with mappiq in the second *he*, but it was sometimes omitted (GK §91e) and this should not be regarded as an error.

s. Heb. העז, imper. Hiph. of עוז as in Isa. 10.31 and Jer. 4.6; 6.1, here in a straightforward transitive sense.

t. Heb. בשדה, lit. 'in the field', as again in vv. 21 and 25.

u. Heb. הביתה, lit. 'into the house(s)' (cf. v. 20).

v. The final two clauses of the verse, each beginning with *waw*, constitute the apodosis for the *casus pedens* which precedes, according to JM §177i-k; the first of them is best understood as temporally subordinate (JM §166b).

w. Heb. ויעזב, with *waw* of apodosis as in v. 19 (see Note v): in this case the *casus pendens* takes the form of an 'independent' relative clause (GK §138e, cf. JM §158l).

x. Heb. ויהוה נתן. The precedence of the subject is due to the change from the preceding clause and to draw attention to the divine origin of the phenomena, already affirmed in the divine speech of v. 18 (cf. 10.13).[9] The use of נתן without an indirect object is especially common when followed by קול, 'voice, sound', both of a human being or animal (Jer. 4.16: see further BDB, p. 679 [1.x]) and of God, where the use for thunder (as here) occurs several times (2 Sam. 22.14 = Ps. 18.14; Jer. 25.30; Joel 2.11; Amos 1.2).

y. Heb. ותהלך. Such 'regular' forms of the Qal imperfect of הלך are much rarer in BH than those apparently formed from a by-form *ילך and elsewhere occur only in poetry. A form ואהלך does, however, occur in Moabite (*KAI* 181, 14-15). In this case (as in Ps. 73.9) both the first and final vowels are also unusual (cf. GK §69x: 'offenbar dialektisch' according to BL §55g').

---

[9] For a slightly different explanation see Joosten, *Verbal Syntax*, p. 133 n. 27.

z. Heb. מתלקחת, lit. 'taking hold of itself'. The form occurs elsewhere only in Ezek. 1.4, also of lightning. The exact meaning is not certain: see BDB, p. 544 and Houtman 2, p. 91, for other suggestions, to which should be added the rabbinic interpretation 'enclosed' (cf. Propp, p. 334, who also understands the part. as passive), sc. like a flame in a crystal ball (e.g. Exod.R. 12: further refs. in Jastrow, pp. 717 and 1128). The clause as a whole is best taken as circumstantial and parenthetical, since כבד מאד goes most naturally with ברד, both grammatically and in the light of v. 18.

aa. Heb. מאז. For its use as a conjunction cf. 5.23; in 4.10 (see Note e on the translation there) it is used (as a 'pseudo-preposition') with an infinitive construct.

bb. The postponement of the verbs (and in the first case the subject) is probably for stylistic variation; it also corresponds to the fact that the impact on both kinds of vegetation was not mentioned in the warning of the plague in vv. 18-19, so that attention is properly drawn in this way to the additional extent of the disaster.

cc. Heb. רק, which is restrictive rather than adversative ('But') in meaning here, despite what 8.24-25 might suggest.

dd. Heb. הפעם. BDB, p. 822, distinguishes three meanings for הפעם among the other idioms involving this lexeme: (1) 'now' (Judg. 16.18); (2) 'this once' (Gen. 18.32; Exod. 10.17; Judg. 6.39; 16.28 [with הזה]: in all these cases אך or רק precedes); (3) 'now at length' (Gen. 2.23; 29.34-35; 30.20; 46.30; Judg. 15.3; 16.18 [again!]), with Exod. 9.27 seen as a variation of this: *now at length* (it is clear that) *I have sinned*'. It is, first of all, doubtful whether the parenthesis is necessary, as Pharaoh may perfectly well be acknowledging wrongdoing on the present occasion and not throughout the sequence of plagues. Its addition by BDB is probably due to the belief that these cases of the expression include the idea of a long period leading up to the present situation, indicated by 'at length'. But while this could be implied in some cases (Gen. 2.23; 30.20), it is not always (cf. Gen. 46.30; Judg. 15.3; 16.18), and the rendering 'this time' seems more generally applicable, usually with a contrast to preceding instances. 'Now' is probably best in Gen. 46.30, and perhaps in Judg. 16.18 ('this instant'?). But here 'this time' will fit very well: it may be illogical for Pharaoh to admit that he had been wrong in the most recent episode and not earlier, but it is perfectly understandable as a bargaining device. His plea in 10.17 takes a similar line (but the idiom there is slightly different because of the preceding אך, which as in the other cases in (2) lays more emphasis on the [rhetorically asserted] uniqueness of the present occasion). See *TWAT* 6, 706-707 = *TDOT* 12, pp. 47-48. The meaning here will not be significantly different from בפעם הזאת in 8.28 and 9.14.

ee. Heb. ורב מהית. For רב = 'enough, too much' see BDB, p. 913, 1f. There are two ways of explaining the syntax. The *waw* may introduce a circumstantial clause with causal meaning with the מן being either partitive (BDB, p. 580, 3), 'for there (has been) enough/too much of thunder etc. coming', or as BDB prefer comparative (pp. 582-83, 6d), like 1 Kgs 12.28, 'it is *more than that…*

(= there is enough of [thunder etc. coming])'; or ורב may be equivalent to a jussive (cf. Baentsch: for this as a possibility after an imperative as well as another jussive cf. Gen. 8.17; Jer. 48.26; GK §112r) and the מן may introduce a negative consequence with the infinitive, 'let it be enough, so that there is no more...' (BDB, p. 583, 7). In fact the first of these alternatives would imply the wish expressed by the second (like the English translation given), so that the sense is much the same either way.

ff. Heb. קלת אלהים: 'thunder(ings) of God' makes sense in view of v. 23 and the use of אלהים rather than יהוה by Pharaoh here could be because he is a non-Israelite (cf. 8.15). But אלהים can express the superlative (cf. JM §112r and references there; so perhaps already Tg⁰ here, and in modern times D.W. Thomas, 'A Consideration of Some Unusual Ways of Expressing the Superlative in Hebrew', *VT* 3 [1953], pp. 209-24 [210]: he cites some mediaeval and later rabbis who took this view elsewhere [211] but he is doubtful about this example [214-15]).

gg. A direct object after יצא is rare, but cf. v. 33 and Gen. 44.4.

hh. The S-P word-order here is notable: it is scarcely covered by the explanations given in GK §142a and is perhaps more akin to a *casus pendens*, delaying the words that Pharaoh wishes to hear.

ii. Heb. ואתה ועבדיך. It is possible for the subject of a clause that follows ידע to appear as its direct object in the main clause (Gen. 18.19; 2 Sam. 3.25: GK §117h), as with ראה in Exod. 2.2, and such an object could presumably be placed before the verb for emphasis. But the use of אתה (rather than אתך) shows that this is not the construction here. Rather is אתה ועבדיך a *casus pendens*, separated from what follows in the Masoretic punctuation by the major distinctive accent *athnach*. The effect is, however, the same: to give greater prominence to what can logically at least be described as 'the principal subject' (GK §143a-c; cf. JM §156a). The delay of the usual retrospective pronoun until a following subordinate clause is, however, very rare and perhaps unparalleled;[10] but the sense intended is readily conveyed because the main clause is so short.

jj. Heb. יהוה אלהים. In this formula (on which see further the Explanatory note on v. 30 and Text and Versions) אלהים is presumably in apposition to the divine name, as titles may be with the names of human beings (JM §131k: for אלהים as a 'title' for Yahweh elsewhere see Davies, 'Exegesis', p. 179; E. Blum, 'Der vermeintliche Gottesname "Elohim"', in I.U. Dalferth and P. Stoellger [eds.], *Gott nennen: Gottes Namen und Gott als Name* [Tübingen, 2008], pp. 97-119 [110, 115]).

kk. The precedence of the subject in the main (verbal) clauses of this and the following verse is due to the interruption of the narrative by reference to

---

[10] J. Joosten has drawn my attention to a close if not exact parallel in 21.13 (cf. W. Gross, *Die Pendens-Konstruktion im Biblischen Hebräisch: Studien zum althebräischen Satz 1* [ATS 27; St Ottilien, 1987], p. 118).

an already existing situation, which is best represented in translation by the use of pluperfect verbs (cf. GK §142a-b; JM §118d), and perhaps also (in the second case at least) to emphasise the contrasting effects of the hail on the different crops (JM §155n*b*).

ll. Heb. נכו...נכתה. These forms of נכה (which resume the uses of the Hiphil in the [partly different] more general description of the catastrophe in v. 25) are the only examples of the Pual in BH (the Piel does not occur at all),[11] the normal passive conjugation being the Hophal. The consonantal text could be revocalised as the Niphal, which occurs once (2 Sam. 11.15; also Job 30.8 from the by-form נכא); and the given forms could also be regarded as passive Qals (on which see JM §58), though Qal-like forms of נכה are only attested as adjectives and nouns in BH (cf. BDB, pp. 644, 646). Be that as it may (and the standard grammars and dictionaries find no difficulty with the Pual), the fem. sing. form with the composite subject in v. 31 may be explained either by agreement with the nearer subject (GK §146e) or as a collective use of the fem. sing. form (GK §145k). For SP's reading see Text and Versions.

mm. The precedence of the subjects in the subordinate clause (cf. Note kk) needs no explanation (despite reverse P-S order in the similar clause in v. 32), because it is in line with about two-thirds of all noun clauses according to JM §154f; ibid. §154fa indicates that the case in v. 32 is probably due to the pronominal subject. No special emphasis seems to be involved in either case. גבעל occurs only here in BH, but the meaning is not in doubt: the word occurs in MH and it will be a by-form of גביע, 'cup', which is used of bud-like features of the menorah in Exod. 25.33-34.

nn. On the word-order see Note kk. אפילת is a *hapax legomenon* in BH, but its meaning is clear. 'Late' fits the context well and is confirmed by Akkadian cognates (*apālu* II, 'be late', *uppulu* and *uppultu*, 'late', esp. of crops [cf. Houtman, p. 95; *AHw*, p. 1425]) and examples in post-biblical Heb. and Aram., as well as the Versions. Alternative suggestions such as 'dark, hidden' (BDB; Propp, following Ibn Ezra) and 'wondrous' (Exod.R. 12.6) are much less well founded.

oo. Heb. וממר. The absence of the article ('corrected' in SP: see Text and Versions) is perhaps responsible for the MT punctuation which sees the preceding והברד as a second subject of ויחדלו. One might wonder whether והברד וממר should be taken as a composite subject of נתך(לא־), though a singular verb following is very rare (GK §146d-e) and a 'double-duty' article does not seem to be found elsewhere. But perhaps the text is corrupt (see Text and Versions and the Explanatory Note).

pp. See Note a on the translation of 7.14-25.

qq. See Note j on the translation of 4.18-31.

---

[11] BL's reference (§59e) to Piel forms in 1 Kgs 20 is a mistake: they are clearly Hiphil. Jastrow, p. 910, cites specialised mercantile uses of the Piel/Pael in MH and Jewish Aramaic.

Explanatory Notes

13. The opening of this episode closely resembles those of the non-Priestly plague-narratives in 7.15-16, 26; 8.16; 9.1: the resemblance to 8.16 is especially close. The absence of 'Go in' (Heb. *bō'*), in contrast to 7.26 and 9.1, may indicate that Moses is to confront Pharaoh and demand Israel's release outside his palace this time (Propp, p. 333).

14. The continuation of Yahweh's words, however, takes a different course as the series of plagues approaches its climax. No specific plague is mentioned until v. 18 (contrast 7.17, 27; 8.17; 9.3), and the threat is no longer made explicitly subject to Pharaoh's refusal to release the Israelites (in this respect 7.17-18 at the beginning of the sequence is similar). Yahweh declares that he will send 'all (these?) my plagues' against Egypt (see Text and Versions on the likely original reading here). The 'all', as well as 'this time', suggests that a final onslaught on Pharaoh is being prepared to deal with his intransigence. Most naturally the plural 'plagues' would be taken to anticipate all the plagues that are still to come, including the death of the Egyptian firstborn in chs. 11–12 (for a review of the alternatives see Houtman 2, pp. 85-86, where a reference to the hail and its accompaniments [vv. 23-24] is preferred). A similarly extended view of the plagues is taken in 10.1-2. But there the focus is different, on future generations of Israelites rather than on Pharaoh alone, although the purpose of instruction ('so that…may know') is present in both places. Here the rationale, to demonstrate to Pharaoh Yahweh's uniqueness and power (cf. v. 16) continues a theme that has been present already in other non-Priestly narratives (7.17; 8.18; cf. 5.2). Dozeman (pp. 233, 236; cf. 197-99) has noted the similarity of this motif to the Priestly account's recurrent use of the formula 'that…may know that I am the Lord' (6.7; 7.5; 14.4, 18) and attributes it here to the Priestly author/redactor too. This is unlikely, both because the occurrences in non-Priestly texts show a much greater variety of language and because the Priestly formula is related specifically to the departure from Egypt rather than to the plagues. On the more general question of whether v. 14 (and vv. 15-16) is a secondary addition to the narrative see the introduction to this section.

15-16. Pharaoh is to be told that the leniency of his treatment thus far is not because of any weakness on Yahweh's part, but because Yahweh's purposes go beyond the mere liberation of his people. Yahweh 'could have' already delivered a overwhelming blow against Pharaoh (on this understanding of the Hebrew see Note g on the translation), but he has chosen to let him live: partly because he wants Pharaoh to see and acknowledge his power, and partly so that Yahweh's 'name' will be proclaimed throughout the world. As in the readiness that he has already shown to end a plague when Pharaoh agrees to his demands (8.17, 35: see also the notes on vv. 19-21), Yahweh deals patiently and mercifully with Pharaoh in the non-Priestly account. But here for the first and only time there is also a concern (and, on the part of the narrator, an interest) for the impact of Yahweh's treatment of Pharaoh on the wider world, not just Egypt (at least if Heb. *ʾereṣ* means 'earth' here and not just the 'land' of Egypt). The language used recalls that of some of the Psalms (for 'declaring Yahweh's name' in worship see Pss. 22.23; 102.22; for 'declaring' his glory 'among the nations' see Ps. 96.3) and Exod. 10.2 speaks about 'declaring' what Yahweh has done to future generations. 'My name' recalls the account of its revelation to Moses in 3.13-15 (see the Explanatory Note on 3.15 and cf. 6.2-3), and its celebration in a hymn of praise in 15.3 and in solemn (perhaps originally liturgical) declarations in 33.19 and 34.5, where it is 'exegeted' in terms respectively of the Exodus deliverance and of the attributes of Yahweh, especially his mercy.[12] Here, as sometimes elsewhere, 'name' is virtually synonymous with 'glory, fame, majesty' (cf. van der Woude, *THAT* 2, 958-60 = *TLOT* 3, pp. 1363-64). The idea that Yahweh's fame for the Exodus deliverance will reach other nations is probably implied in 15.14-16, but it is more widespread in the Deuteronomistic History (Josh. 2.8-10; 9.9; 1 Sam. 4.8; 6.6; 1 Kgs 8.41-42).

17-19. It is possible to read v. 17 as a condition or as a statement (see Note k on the translation). According to the former interpretation Yahweh allows Pharaoh one more chance to respond positively to his demand, as in most of the previous non-Priestly plague accounts (cf. also 10.4). On the latter view Pharaoh's persistent refusal to yield is given as the reason for a more severe plague.

---

[12] See further Davies, 'Exegesis'.

Pharaoh's behaviour is described for the first time as self-exaltation or arrogance, the pride of the ruler who thinks that he is above all threats to his position. The court eulogies of the Pharaohs preserved in many Egyptian texts (for example, but not only, from the reign of Ramesses II) certainly encouraged such an attitude on their part. This time Yahweh's intervention is to come in the form of a hailstorm of unprecedented severity. Hail is frequently mentioned in the Old Testament: it was a familiar phenomenon of stormy weather in Palestine (Ps. 148.8). But most of the references are to its role in divine judgements upon Israel or their enemies (Josh. 10.11; Isa. 28.2, 17; 30.30; 32.19; Hag. 2.17; Ps. 18.13 [but not 2 Sam. 22]; Job 38.22-23). In Josh. 10.11 and Ps. 18.13 it forms part of a theophany of Yahweh, and Dozeman has rightly pointed out the closeness of this language to that used of Baal/Hadad as the storm-god in the Ugaritic texts (pp. 235, 237). It is of course an ironic transformation of a myth that was designed to reassure the Canaanites of the Levant that the regularity of the winter storms which nourished their land was safe in the hands of the victorious deity. In Egypt hail is rare, like other forms of precipitation, but thunderstorms do occur, especially in the Delta area in the spring.[13] The idea of the 'foundation' (Heb. *yāsad*, normally used of buildings) of a nation is not found elsewhere in the Old Testament (for an equivalent expression see v. 24), but B. Couroyer has observed that such language is found in some Egyptian texts.[14] It might therefore be a further case of Egyptian influence on the language of the Exodus story (compare the notes on 2.3).

Unusually the announcement of the plague includes advice to Pharaoh about how to avoid its effects (v. 19), a further indication of Yahweh's merciful treatment of Pharaoh. At this point the concern is with livestock and human beings. It has often been observed that according to 9.6 all the Egyptian livestock had already perished in the previous non-Priestly plague, and various explanations for this apparent contradiction have been offered (see the Note on 9.6-7). There is an additional peculiarity within the present episode, since

---

[13] See Knobel, p. 81, and Dillmann, p. 87, for hail in Egypt between December and March.

[14] 'Un égyptianisme biblique: "Depuis la fondation de l'Égypte"', *RB* 67 (1960), pp. 42-48. The texts include the Tale of Wenamun (*ANET*, p. 27; *COS* 1, p. 91).

the impact of the hail comes subsequently to include plant life and vegetation as well (vv. 22, 25) and then to affect only the crops (vv. 31-32). Along with other indications of duplication, this may suggest that slightly varying accounts of the hail plague, from different sources, have been combined here.

20-21. As usual no account is provided (except in the Samaritan text and a related Qumran manuscript: see Text and Versions) of Moses' delivery of Yahweh's message to Pharaoh: it is taken for granted. The narrative also gives no explicit account of Pharaoh's response at this stage, but it is implied that he made no concession about Israel's release, while nevertheless ensuring that his 'servants' (i.e. the officials responsible for the care of livestock) were made aware (cf. 'send' in v. 19) of the warning that had been given. Among Pharaoh's officials there is a divided response: some take precautions, others do not. The language used by the narrator to describe the reasons for these responses is strongly theological but has no exact parallel in the Exodus story or indeed elsewhere. 'The word of the Lord' is almost always used as an expression for prophetic oracles (cf. *TWAT* 2, 118 = *TDOT* 3, p. 111); in Deut. 5.5 and a few other places (e.g. Num. 15.31) it refers to the commandments given through Moses. The prophetic use fits well with Moses' role here as the messenger of Yahweh to Pharaoh (cf. the 'messenger formula' in v. 13 etc.). Although it is very common in the Deuteronomistic History and in editorial passages in the prophetic books, it was hardly invented at such a late stage (cf. Num. 11.24; 1 Sam. 3.1; 9.27; 2 Sam. 16.23) and it is notable that the expressions of which it is the object here are replaced by others elsewhere (especially 'hear/obey' [Heb. *šāma'*] etc.: cf. *TWAT* 2, 117-18 = *TDOT* 3, p. 110). To fear Yahweh or God (1.17, 21; cf. 9.30; 14.31) is a common way of speaking of the respect that he is due, and that respect is also due to his word (cf. Amos 3.8; Hagg. 1.12). In Deuteronomy Israel is once urged to 'pay heed to' Yahweh's commandments (32.46; cf. 11.18), but this is not sufficient to make it a 'Deuteronomistic' idiom.

22. The coming of the hail is preceded by a motif which has not appeared hitherto in the non-Priestly portions of the plague-narrative (except briefly in 7.17, 20: see the Notes there): Moses is commanded by Yahweh to stretch out his hand towards the sky to make the hail begin. The closest parallels to this are in 10.12, where there is an explicit reference back to the hail, and 10.21. In the first two cases Moses is then said to stretch out his staff (v. 23

and 10.13), while in 10.22 he stretches out his hand. But there is also a similarity to the Priestly plague-stories in 7.19, 8.1 and 8.12, where Aaron is told to stretch out his staff to bring about a plague. For a consideration of the implications of these and other features of the verse for the composition of the passage see the introduction to this section.

23-25. Within these verses it is possible to distinguish descriptions of (i) Moses' action; (ii) the coming of the hail, with the accompaniment of thunder and (flashes of) lightning ('fire'); (iii) the severity of the storm; and (iv) its effects on humans, animals, plants and trees. The description of the storm is considerably amplified compared with the announcements of it in vv. 18 and 22 and the coming of the hail itself is mentioned three times. Some features of the description correlate closely with v. 18 ([iii] and parts of [ii] and [iv]) while others match elements of v. 22 ([i] and parts of [ii] and [iv]). There is much to suggest that here too different materials about the plague have been combined (Schmidt, p. 423: see further the introduction to the section). The role of Moses' staff, in conjunction with the coming of the storm, has been compared by Propp (p. 334) to that of Baal's 'lightning pole' (*'ṣ brq*) in a Ugaritic text (*KTU* 1.101.4; cf. *ANEP*, nos. 490 and 500). This might seem to strengthen Dozeman's argument (see above on vv. 17-19) for the portrayal of Yahweh here as the storm-god, but the fact that it is Moses who wields the staff, not Yahweh, undermines the parallel somewhat.

26. The sparing of the Israelites in Goshen recalls 8.18-19 (see the notes there) and 9.4, 6-7, but in this case it has not been anticipated in the announcement of the plague. The motif is not present in the next plague (locusts) but it reappears in 10.23 (darkness) and of course in the slaying of the Egyptian firstborn (11.7; 12.13, 23, 27).

27-28. Pharaoh's reaction to this plague bears some resemblance to what is said in 8.4 and 8.21-25, and even more to 10.16-17. Each time he summons Aaron (who plays no other part in this episode) as well as Moses and asks them to pray for the removal of the plague and here, in 8.4 and in 8.28 he promises to let Israel depart. There are minor differences even in these parts of his speech, which make the narrative less monotonous than it would otherwise be. Perhaps the most significant of them is the absence of any attempt on Pharaoh's part to place a limitation on the Israelites' departure (contrast 8.21, 24; 10.10-11). But it is in Pharaoh's opening acknowledgement of his wrongdoing that the main new development in his conflict with Yahweh appears, an attitude that will surface again in 10.16-17 (but not thereafter). The language is far-reaching and no doubt designed to impress Moses and Aaron. The form of the confession of sin (Heb. *ḥāṭā'tî*)[15] has been compared by Schmidt to a number of other passages (p. 347), but only Num. 22.34, Josh. 7.20 and 1 Sam. 26.21 are really similar, and it is not certain whether 1 Sam. 26.21 refers to a sin against Yahweh or David. Coats, who gives a different list of passages (including 1 Sam. 15.24, 30; 2 Sam. 12.13; 19.20-21; 24.10; 2 Kgs 18.14), describes the formula as 'a statement in the midst of juridical proceedings or in situations conceived judicially, in which a defendant formally acknowledges his or her guilt' (p. 159). In fact the only one of these passages which has a judicial context is Josh. 7.20: in most of the others the 'defendant' is confronted by a prophet or a king in a situation that is not formally judicial. It is presumably to Moses as a kind of prophet that Pharaoh submits here. The words that follow, especially 'in the right' (Heb. *haṣṣaddîq*) and 'in the wrong' (Heb. *hārᵉšā'îm*), have stronger associations with courts of law (e.g. Exod. 23.1, 7-8; Prov. 24.23-24), but even they can also be used in the context of a more informal dispute (Exod. 2.13; 1 Sam. 24.18). Too much should therefore not be made of the specifically legal background to this passage. Pharaoh's attempts to limit his own responsibility ('this time'; 'and my people') simply show that he still has much to learn. The reference to 'thunder' in v. 28 (and subsequently in vv. 29, 33-34) recalls vv. 23-24 in the part of the plague's description which we attribute to the alternative version. Even there thunder is not mentioned in the announcement of the plague (v. 22), presumably because it was seen as a regular accompaniment of a hail-storm. Its appearance only at the climax of the main account is therefore not surprising, though it is possible that it was added when the two accounts were combined.

29-30, 33. Moses' agreement (again, as in 8.5-9 and 8.25-26, he responds and acts alone) to intercede with Yahweh on Pharaoh's behalf is tempered by another reminder of what a respite is meant to teach Pharaoh (cf. 8.6) and a realistic assessment of the shallowness of his and his officials' change of mind (cf. the warning in 8.25).

---

[15] On the meaning of *ḥāṭā'* and related words see *TWAT* 2, 857-70 = *TDOT* 4, pp. 309-19 and *THAT* 1, 541-49 = *TLOT* 1, pp. 406-11.

'Moses is no naïve simpleton, easily duped by a false promise. By now, Moses knows what kind of person he deals with' (Houtman 2, p. 84). 'Fear of Yahweh/God' (probably only one of the expressions for God originally appeared here: see Text and Versions)[16] now emerges more clearly (cf. v. 20) as the positive attitude to which the process of divine instruction is meant to lead Pharaoh: it is not just a matter of new understanding but of humble submission to Yahweh. The gesture of stretching out (up? Heb. *pāraś*, whereas in vv. 22-23 it is *nāṭāh*) the hands to God in prayer (vv. 29, 33) is widely attested in the ancient world (cf. Keel, *Bildsymbolik*, pp. 294, 297-301 [ET, 316, 319-23]) and familiar from accounts of public prayer in the Old Testament (1 Kgs 8.22, 38, 54; Isa. 1.15; Pss. 44.21; 143.6; Ezra 9.5), but it occurs only here and (we argue: see the Explanatory Note there) in 17.12 with Moses' prayers in Exodus. 'Rain' (v. 33) has not been mentioned before (but it recurs in v. 34): it may be a misguided deduction from the verb 'rain' in vv. 18 and 23.

31-32. The additional description of the effects of the hail might have been expected to appear after v. 25, and its intrusiveness between Moses' agreement to intercede for Pharaoh and the intercession itself is often commented on and regarded as a reason for seeing it as a later supplement to the narrative (cf. Schmidt, pp. 423-24). But its position at least has been carefully chosen, as Houtman (2, p. 95) points out: the incompleteness of the devastation of the crops provides a specific explanation for Moses' suspicion in v. 30 that the Egyptians' reaction will not be lasting. Three of the crops mentioned are well known, but the fourth, 'emmer' (Heb. *kussemet*: for MH cf. Jastrow, p. 623), is sometimes differently identified. It is mentioned elsewhere as a border crop in Isa. 28.5 and at the end of a list of ingredients for making bread in Ezek. 4.9: it was also well known at Ugarit (*DULAT* 1, pp. 462-63). Most English versions have 'spelt' (cf. BDB, p. 493; so also, apparently, LXX and Vulg: on Tgg see Text and Versions), but the weight of modern botanical and lexicographical opinion favours 'emmer' (cf. I. Löw, *Die Flora der Juden* [Vienna, 1924–34], 1, pp. 767-76; M. Zohary, *Plants of the Bible* [Cambridge, 1982], pp. 74-75;

---

[16] J. L'Hour, '"Yahweh Elohim"', *RB* 81 (1974), pp. 524-56 (528-31), argued that the whole phrase was original and, like other occurrences of it (including those in Gen. 2–3), reflects a theology of Yahweh's lordship over the nations which was taken up in Jerusalem temple worship.

O. Borowski, *Agriculture in Iron Age Israel* [Winona Lake, 1987], pp. 87-91 [following M. Kislev, 'The identification of *Ḥiṭṭa* and *Kussemet*', *Leshonenu* 37 (1973), pp. 83-95, 243-52 (Heb.)]; *HAL*, p. 466; *Ges18*, p. 562; so NJPS, ESV, Hyatt [pp. 120-21]; Houtman [1, p. 157, tentatively]; Propp [p. 335]). Emmer (*Triticum dicoccum*) is 'hulled-grain wheat' which is native to the southern Levant, and 'was cultivated extensively in Eretz-Israel before the Iron Age' as well as in biblical times (Borowski, p. 91), whereas there is little if any evidence for the cultivation of spelt in ancient Palestine (see the full account in D. Zohary and M. Hoff, *Domestication of Plants in the Old World* [Oxford, 2nd ed., 1993], pp. 39-53). There is evidence from Egypt that barley and flax were among the earliest crops harvested there (cf. Hoffmeier, *Israel in Egypt*, p. 148), and that the Egyptian agricultural cycle as a whole was ahead of that in Palestine (Propp, p. 335). The precedence of the barley harvest over the wheat harvest is also reflected in the biblical cultic calendar (Exod. 34.22; cf. 2 Sam. 21.9; Ruth 2.23).

34-35. The conclusion to this episode contains another duplication, for Pharaoh's continued stubbornness is described twice, once in v. 34 and once in v. 35, and in different words. In particular, as our translation brings out, two different words are used for what is commonly called the 'hardening' of Pharaoh's heart: 'he refused to understand' (Heb. *kābēd*) and 'Pharaoh's heart was stubborn' (Heb. *ḥāzaq*). The former echoes the conclusions to other episodes of the main non-Priestly account (8.11a, 28; 9.7), and the mention of what Pharaoh 'saw' also recalls 8.11a. Verse 35 is similar to the conclusion of the Priestly accounts (7.13; 8.11b, 15; 9.12), but not exactly so, as the words 'and he did not let the Israelites go' are replaced there by 'and he did not listen to them'. The final phrase, 'through Moses' is also new: it is found in Priestly passages later in Exodus (34.29; 35.29) and in other books of the Pentateuch (e.g. Lev. 8.36), but always with reference to Yahweh's commandments. The use of 'through' (Heb. *bᵉyad*) in relation to a prediction, as here, finds its closest parallels, not surprisingly, in prophetic narratives in the historical books (1 Sam. 28.15, 17: more examples in BDB, p. 391). Houtman (p. 96) and others take this to refer to Moses' words in v. 30, but they are not a divine speech. If a specific reference is intended, it is more likely to be to verses like 3.19, 4.21 and 7.3-4. Much of v. 35 is also closely paralleled in the conclusions to the next two episodes (10.20, 27) as well as in 11.10b. On the scholarly

612   EXODUS 1–18

debate about the implications of these correspondences for the
origin of v. 35 see the introduction to this section. Amongst all the
formulaic language it should be noted that in v. 34 the narrator uses
the same word 'sin' to describe Pharaoh's response as Pharaoh
himself had used in v. 27 (and will use again in 10.16-17), leaving
no doubt about the seriousness of Pharaoh's situation.

Text and Versions

ויאמר (9.13) Vulg adds *quoque*, as it often does (e.g. 8.16), here perhaps
taking up the reference to divine speech in v. 12.

יהוה (9.13) Tg^{Nmg} prefixes 'the Memra of' to both occurrences, according
to its usual practice.

השכם (9.13) Vulg *consurge* as in 8.16, weakening the rendering of the
word from those of LXX (ὄρθρισον) and OL (*vigilare*), perhaps because its
mane already implied the early morning. The rendering is then phrase-for-
phrase rather than word-for-word.

העברים (9.13) Tg^{O,J} have as elsewhere in Exodus 'the Jews' and Tg^N joins
them here (as in v. 1), although its mg records the literal rendering 'Hebrews'.
On the variation see *AramB* 2, p. 37 n. 1.

עמי (9.13) Tg^N עמא, as it has at corresponding points in 5.1 and 7.26 (but
not 7.16; 8.16-17; 9.1). Here the preceding העם of v. 7 may have influenced it.

ויעבדני (9.13)   Vulg as before has *ut sacrificet mihi* (see Text and Versions
on 7.16). Tgg as usual render the suffix 'before me'. 4QpalEx^m has only a
few parts of words in this and the following verse, but space considerations
suggest that it may have had an extra word or two here. The other witnesses
give no clues but one possibility is that it added במדבר at the end of v. 13.

את־כל־מגפתי (9.14)   LXX συναντήματα can mean specifically 'calami-
ties' (cf. its use for נגע in 3 Kgdms 8.37 and perhaps the related verb in Exod.
5.3 and Deut. 31.29: also exx. in LSJ, p. 1696). But its frequency in a neutral
sense led to its replacement with θραύσεις (Aq and Theod) or πληγάς
(Symm), both being words often used for מגפה elsewhere in LXX. Tg^J 'a
plague from heaven'; Tg^{Nmg} has two alternative renderings, one a paraphrase
of MT (contra *AramB* 2, p. 38 n. *s*), the other making the element of punishment explicit.

אל־לבך (9.14)   MT is supported by LXX εἰς τὴν καρδίαν σου, so the
reading is early, but SP has על־לבך, which fits the context better, and Tg^N, Sy
render similarly, whatever their *Vorlagen* might have been. Tg^O has בליבך with
a similar meaning and the same preposition as MT uses in what follows. Tg^J
has a long addition which makes a distinction between one plague which is
about to come (see the previous note) and its effect in making Pharaoh realise
that all the plagues have a divine and not a human cause, based on taking

אל־לבך as 'into your heart/mind'. This is a measure of the difficulty of MT, but even the replacement of אל by על does not yield a straightforward text, and the witnesses cited above probably reflect attempts to ease the difficulty rather than the original text. See Note f on the translation for further discussion of the problems of MT. Adequate sense would be given by reading simply בך (as in 7.29 and 8.17: so probably JB here), but an explanation of the additional letters in MT (and probably presupposed elsewhere) is needed. Possibly אל was originally the short form of אלה, 'these', without the article as in Exod. 10.1; 1 Kgs 10.8; 22.23; Jer. 31.21 (cf. GK §126y): 'all these my plagues upon you...' The second *lamed* could be due to dittography (so Driver, p. 72; also Ehrlich acc. Houtman 2, pp. 85-86, Baentsch, Beer).

ובעבדיך ובעמך (9.14)   LXX's καὶ τῶν θεραπόντων σου καὶ τοῦ λαοῦ σου in the genitive attaches these words to לב/καρδίαν as a way of smoothing the syntax, but at the cost of close correspondence to its likely *Vorlage* and natural Greek idiom.

כמני (9.14)   LXX adds ἄλλος, as it did in 8.6 (see Text and Versions there).

שלחתי (9.15)   Although LXX and Vulg use subordinating participles to render this verb, it is clear from what follows (πατάξω...ἐκτριβήσῃ; *percuties...peribis*) that they understood this verse as a threat (prophetic perfects?), despite the difficulties this raises in the next verse. Sy, with two present-future participles and an imperfect, evidently intended the same.[17] Tgg, like the later Jewish commentators, recognised something like the potential interpretation but represented it in different ways: Tg^N used past tenses throughout (*AramB* 2, p. 38, adds '[almost]' to its translation); Tg^O amplifies with 'it was near before me that I would [Aram. פן] send...'; and Tg^J has 'if I had sent...it would have been just that...' ('I could rightly have...').

ידי (9.15)   Tgg paraphrase to avoid the anthropomorphism (cf. Text and Versions on 3.20 and 9.3).

ואך (9.15)   SP ואכה, without the apocopation and so the more regular first person sing. form.

בדבר (9.15)   As elsewhere (cf. Text and Versions on 5.3 and 9.3) the rendering 'death' is widespread in the Vss, but here Tg^N joins Sy in reading *mwt(ʾ)nʾ* (cf. Vulg *peste*; Aq, Symm). It may well have been knowledge of this word, which clearly means 'pestilence' but is derived from מות, 'die', that led to the use of words for 'death' (with their exegetical possibilities which are illustrated by the midrashim) in both Greek and Aramaic versions.

---

[17] Wevers, *Notes*, p. 131, claims that LXX's verbs 'are aorist subjunctives and must be translated as potentials and contrary to fact'. The parsing is theoretically possible, but the presumed meaning is questionable. The OL's rendering by Latin futures is against it, and Vulg and Sy may also have derived their unambiguous future renderings from what they took LXX to express.

ותכחד (9.15) Tg^N adds 'O Pharaoh' to make the reference of 'you' more direct.

ואולם (9.16) LXX simply καὶ, without any adversative particle, probably because its rendering of the previous verse in the future made it inappropriate here. The other witnesses all support ואולם.

בעבור זאת (9.16) Tg^{J,N} prefix a clause saying what was not the reason, i.e. to show kindness to Pharaoh. 4QEx^c apparently had a shorter text, probably due to homoeoarkton from the two occurrences of בעבור (*DJD* XII, p. 108).

העמדתיך (9.16) LXX renders freely in the passive, a variation already corrected in the citation of the verse in Rom. 9.17 and then also in OL and Vulg. Tg^N adds 'until now' (as also in its additional clause).

הראתך (9.16) SP הראיתך in all mss, not a perf. (as in Deut. 34.4), which is syntactically improbable, but the inf. with the fuller form of the suffix sometimes found in SP (*GSH* §55bγ). Tgg give the natural interpretation, 'to show you', but LXX (ἵνα) ἐνδείξωμαι ἐν σοί changes the point, so that Pharaoh becomes the means and not the beneficiary of Yahweh's demonstration of power. This is the text cited in Rom. 9.17, which helps to explain the retention of this interpretation in OL and Vulg. Most mss of Sy follow MT, but some were affected by the LXX/'NT' version.

כחי (9.16) Tg^N strengthens the sense by prefixing תקף.

ספר (9.16) LXX, Vulg and Sy appropriately render in the passive; Tg^O provides a general subject, 'that *they* may tell', while Tg^{J,N} make Pharaoh himself the intended subject (Tg^{Nmg} has a literal rendering of MT here).

שמי (9.16) Tg^O prefixes 'the power of', recalling its rendering of 'hand' in v. 15 and elsewhere; Tg^{J,N} add 'holy'. The majesty of the divine name is thus emphasised.

עודך (9.17) Many SP mss have a question-mark at the end of the verse (cf. AV, RV for this interpretation). Possibly the unexpected οὖν in LXX's ἔτι οὖν σύ points this way too: 'So are you still…?' Tg^N begins this verse like the next with הא, 'Behold', thus setting them in clearer opposition.

מסתולל (9.17) Only Tg^{J,N}'s 'claim superiority' comes close to the meaning of MT; Exod.R. 12.1 recognised its relation to מסלה, but saw this as supporting the interpretation given by Tg^O, 'oppress' (so also Rashi). LXX's ἐμποιῇ, 'you lay claim to', and Aq's more standard equivalent ἀντιποιῇ seem to be guesses. The other Vss found their clue in the similar statement (MT מחזיק) in v. 2 and rendered 'hold, detain' as there: the evidence is clearly set out by Salvesen, *Symmachus*, p. 80.

לבלתי (9.17) Vulg freely *et non vis*.

הנני (9.18) Sy represents only the pronoun, not 'Behold', and places the time-statements first.

ממטיר (9.18) LXX's ὕω (for which mss have the 'modernising' βρέχω: cf. v. 23) has an archaic character in Hell. Gk. and was perhaps chosen to fit the solemn divine speech (so Lee, *Lexical Study*, pp. 122-24, with exx. inc.

כעת (9.18)   The main versions all translate 'at this time/hour', but Tg^Nmg gives a hint at uncertainty with its ביומא הדין ו, 'this day and (tomorrow)'.

כבד (9.18)   LXX's πολλήν (cf. πολλή in v. 24) is 'corrected' by Aq and Symm to βαρεῖαν. כבד and its context appear in 4QEx^c as in MT, but *DJD* XII, p. 108, infers that there were omissions and variations elsewhere in the verse. This may be due to a misplacement of fr. 13: if it is placed on the left of the col. rather than the right, a text essentially identical to MT can be reconstructed for vv. 15-20, apart from an omission due to homoeoteleuton in v. 15.

למן היום (9.18)   SP למיום, avoiding the difficult article in MT (see Note r on the translation) and presumably a secondary smoothing of the grammar. No Qumran ms. survives at this point, but at the corresponding point in the repetition after v. 19 4QpalEx^m has the MT reading, an unusual but not unique case of its not anticipating an SP variant.

הוסדה (9.18)   SP היסדה, with the vestigial *waw* replaced by the *yodh* that is characteristic of most forms of this verb. This is not a universal tendency of SP (see the exx. in *GSH* §81fβ,δ, esp. Gen. 21.5), but in MT the *waw* is standard in the impf. and inf. Niphal (BDB, p. 414) and it should be retained. The Vss generally take יסד in the obvious metaphorical sense (Sy *'tbnyt* can be metaphorical), but Aq and Symm have the literal ἐθεμελιώθη for LXX's ἔκτισται. Tg^N's אזדמנת, 'was appointed, prepared', stands apart from the others, and the verb seems not to be used elsewhere in such a context: in Tg^N it is mainly used of 'coming together' in marriage or of 'meeting'. Perhaps this gives a hint at the translator's thinking here in terms of Egypt's being 'gathered together' as a people.

עד־עתה (9.18)   עתה (with the beginning of v. 19) is preserved in 4QEx^c. It is slightly odd that LXX (ἕως τῆς ἡμέρας ταύτης) and Vulg (*in praesens tempus*) give such full equivalents; it is presumably due to the prepositions, though more literal renderings are found in both Vss elsewhere.

ועתה (9.19)   LXX νῦν οὖν recognised the inferential character of the *waw*, and Vulg *ergo iam nunc* also rhetorically strengthened its rendering of ועתה.

שלח (9.19)   LXX's κατάσπευσον, 'urge on' (cf. 5.10, 13: but Wevers [*Notes*, p. 133] and *BAlex*, p. 133 [sic!] prefer 'hurry'), is a free interpretation (found only here) of שלח, perhaps due to a misunderstanding of העז as an infinitive (see the next note).

העז (9.19)   All the Vss render freely 'gather', using (except for LXX) the verb which they have for אסף later in the verse (the rendering is defended by Rashi and Leqah Tob ad loc. with ref. to Isa. 10.31 and Jer. 6.1). Most reflect MT's imperative, but LXX συναγαγεῖν subordinated העז to שלח, presumably reading it as an inf., which is also possible, though less likely in the absence of an intervening noun. Some SP mss read אחז, 'hold, grasp, catch', but the sense is probably too violent for the present context (cf. Isa. 5.29) and a double confusion of gutturals (cf. *GSH* §12 for the frequency of this in SP mss) and the rarity of עוז are probably responsible for this corruption.

מקנך (9.19)   So also 4QExᶜ (מ[קנך]), but SP has מקניך, the additional *yodh* being a scribal reflection of a fuller pronunciation (*GSH* §55bγ), as earlier in 9.16 (see the note on הראתך), rather than a pl. variant. Space considerations suggest that 4QExᶜ may have read את כל before this word (*DJD* XII, p. 108).

בשדה¹º (9.19) Tgᴺ באפי ברא, 'out in the open', a perceptive variation which is not, however, maintained for the second occurrence in the verse (where Vulg conversely shifts its rendering to *foris*).

כל־האדם (9.19)   Both LXX (γάρ) and Vulg (*enim*) supply a causal connection, which is left unexpressed (and more forceful) in the Heb. Vulg ignores כל here and apparently attaches it to the relative clause that follows to make a comprehensive expression: *et universa quae inventa fuerint*.

יאסף (9.19)   LXX εἰσέλθῃ, a unique equivalence which continues LXX's free renderings of the verbs in this verse.

וירד (9.19)   LXX πέσῃ, Vulg *ceciderit*, 'falls', again rendering freely. Sy has no equivalent to the idiomatic *waw* of the apodosis.

SP has another long addition after v. 19, recounting the delivery of Yahweh's message to Pharaoh. Its introduction is identical to that used after 9.5 (so not entirely parallel to Yahweh's instructions in v. 13) and then vv. 13bβ-19 follow with the minor textual variations of SP noted already. In 4QpalExᵐ words equivalent to parts of vv. 17-19 occur in a column which is only partly preserved, but the editors of *DJD* IX infer with good reason, from the analogy of the clearer cases after 7.18 and 9.5 and from the available space in cols. V-VI, that the ms. included the same expansion of the narrative (with minor variants as noted above) as SP and that the preserved material corresponding to vv. 17-19 is from it (it leads directly into words from vv. 20-21). Lagarde's text of Syʰᵉˣ also has the additional text, attributed to Sam as in the similar cases elsewhere, and here it is particularly clear that the Greek version presented is based on the often divergent wording of LXX in most places.

הירא (9.20)   Tgᴶ,ᶠ,ᴺᵐᵍ identify the one servant of Pharaoh who 'feared the word of the Lord' as Job (cf. Job 1.1): for other examples of this see *AramB* 2, p. 184 n. 15. Tgᴶ,ᶠ,ᴺᵐᵍ have a similar identification in v. 21: see below.

דבר (9.20)   Tgᴺ has no equivalent, thus conforming its rendering to the normal expression 'fear the Lord/God'.

עבדיו (9.20)   Tgᴺ שליטיו, 'his rulers'; this (or שלטון) is its regular rendering (cf. 5.21; 7.20; 8.20, 25, 27; 9.34; 10.1; 11.3) and it matches well the authority often entrusted to the עבד of a king: *AramB* 2, p. 32 n. 9, gives other examples and compares Exod.R. 18.1.

הניס (9.20)   LXX, Tgᴼ,ᴶ and Sy render freely 'gather', as for העז in v. 19. The precise meaning is, however, represented here by Symm (διέσωσεν), Vulg and Tgᴺ (cf. Salvesen, p. 81).

את־עבדיו (9.20)   LXX has no equivalent, which could be due to para-blepsis in either a Hebrew or a Greek text. But the same minus occurs also in v. 21, which may support Wevers' view that the omission was deliberate: 'presumably the servants could fend for themselves' (*Notes*, p. 134). Whatever its origin, the discrepancy with MT/SP was remedied by both the Three and mss of the hexaplaric and Catena groups, though curiously with different equivalents for עבד: δοῦλος and παῖς respectively. It seems that Origen did not always take his supplementary material from one of the Three. Lemmelijn (p. 174), like Sanderson (*Exodus Scroll*, p. 103), thinks that the shorter text of LXX is more original (cf. Propp, p. 301).

אל־הבתים (9.20)   Tg^N and Sy have 'house' in the sing., as in v. 19. Tg^F's באפי ברא corresponds to Tg^N's rendering of the first בשדה in v. 19, and must be an error of copying, since it belongs to the end of the following verse here (see the note below). A few SP mss read על for אל: three in von Gall, all of those used by Crown and Camb. Add. 1846. The majority reading (also in the editions of Sadaqa and Tal) must be preferred even within the Samaritan tradition (for confusion of gutturals see *GSH* §12), as אל is attested already in 4QpalEx^m and clearly fits the context better.

ואשר (9.21)   Tg^J (followed in Tg^{Nmg}) as in v. 20 makes an identification with an individual, in this case Balaam, who was one of Pharaoh's counsellors according to Exod.R. 1.9 and B.Sotah 11a (*AramB* 2, p. 184 n. 16).

לבו (9.21)   LXX had no equivalent to the suffix, but one was added in the hexaplaric witnesses.

אל (9.21)   This (or ל) is the normal idiom after (שׂים לב(ב, but SP's על is occasionally found in MT (Hagg. 1.5, 7 [var. אל]; Job 1.8). Sy also has ʿl, but this is due to the Syriac idiom that it uses. The idiomatic renderings of LXX (cf. Wevers, *Notes*, p. 135) and Vulg make it impossible to discover the preposition in their *Vorlagen*, but Tgg support אל. 4QpalEx^m does not preserve this part of the verse. SP is the more difficult reading, but the possibility of a confusion of gutturals (*GSH* §12) or the influence of later idiom (cf. the three exx. of על in Sir in *Ges18*, p. 1285) perhaps justifies the retention of MT.

את־עבדיו (9.21)   LXX has no equivalent, but the omission was supplied in the Hexapla, as in v. 20.

את־מקנהו (9.21)   Neither LXX nor Vulg represented the possessive suffix, but 'his/their' is easily understood. In this case Sy^{hex} specifically notes that the addition of αὐτου was according to the Three.

בשדה (9.21)   Tg^{N,G} render idiomatically by באפי ברא, 'out in the open', as Tg^N did in v. 19a and does again in vv. 22 and 25.

יהוה (9.22)   Tg^G prefixes 'the Memra of'.

נטה (9.22)   LXX, Vulg and Tg^{N,G} render as expected ('stretch out' or 'incline'), but Tg^{O,J}, Sy and probably Tg^{Nmg} have ʾrym = 'lift up', a freer rendering.

ויהי (9.22)   Most Vss render straightforwardly, but ms. 5b1 of Sy has wnḥwt, 'and (hail) will come down', which is clearly influenced by v. 19 – a good example of the kind of divergent reading which led scholars to see this ms. as a distinctive witness to the Peshitta translation.

כל־עשב השדה (9.22) LXX πᾶσαν βοτάνην τὴν ἐπὶ τῆς γῆς, using γῆ to render שדה, as it does in 10.5 and 15, rather than its usual πεδίον. On the 'corrections' of the Three and the hexaplaric mss see Wevers, *Notes*, p. 135 and n. 35: again, as with את־עבדיו in v. 20, it seems that Origen took his new material not from the Three but from LXX itself. The situation is complicated here by LXX's omission of the final two words of the verse, presumably as otiose, which Origen also needed to 'correct'.

Somewhere between the middle of v. 22 and the middle of v. 23 4QExᶜ must have omitted about half a line of text, as the vertical correspondences in fr. 16 are uneven: see *DJD* XII, p. 109, which provides two good alternative explanations for omission by parablepsis.

ויט (9.23) The versional renderings diverge as in v. 22: see the note there.

את־מטהו (9.23) LXX τὴν χεῖρα, conforming to the instruction in v. 22 and omitting the unnecessary possessive: the hexaplaric mss supply the latter but do not alter the noun. The other witnesses agree with MT.

יהוה^lo (9.23) Tg^G prefixes 'the Memra of', as it does later in the verse, where Tg^Nmg also has it.

קלת (9.23) LXX φωνάς, as in v. 28, apparently a Hebraism, as φωνή seems not to be used of thunder in classical or Hellenistic Greek (LSJ); a variant βροντάς (also in v. 28) and Vulg *tonitrua(s)* (so also some OL evidence) clarify the meaning.

ותהלך (9.23) LXX καὶ διέτρεχεν is more 'graphic' (Wevers), but LSJ, p. 416, cites some exx. of the use with (other) heavenly phenomena. Vulg has *discurrentia fulgura*, freely, as a third object of 'gave'; for the part. cf. Tgg and Sy, although they have it, like MT, as part of a separate clause. Tg^O,N and Sy keep close to the sense of MT, but Tg^J 'glowing', Tg^G 'consuming' (מתכלא; cf. Klein 2, p. 56, and CAL s.v. תכל) and Tg^Nmg 'leaping' (as in v. 24) elaborate.

אש (9.23) LXX's τὸ πῦρ is an exceptional case of the addition of the def. art. before this word, probably due to the mention of thunder just before.

וימטר (9.23) Tg^J,N and Sy have 'brought down', less graphically but as they (and there Tg^O) had in v. 18 for the same verb.

ארץ מצרים (9.23) LXX prefixes 'all', again conforming to the wording of v. 22.

ויהי (9.24) Sy 'and...was coming down (*nḥt*)' follows its rendering of וימטר in v. 23; cf. also the note on ויהי in v. 22. Vulg is very free in this verse, but its *ferebantur* probably corresponds to ויהי and also represents a more specific rendering of it. The use of a durative past tense in both Vss is probably an attempt to deal with the repetition of what had already been said in v. 23 (cf. LXX's ἦν [rather than ἐγένετο as in e.g. 9.10]).

ברד (9.24) SP's הברד may have been the *Vorlage* for LXX's ἡ (δὲ) χάλαζα (the use of the emphatic state in [all] Tgg and Sy is not necessarily textually significant, as it may represent an indefinite noun [Stevenson §8.2; Brockelmann §89]). The variant could be explained by assimilation to the articulated forms which appear later in the verse and in v. 25, but it is more likely that it is due to the fact that the coming of hail has already been reported in v. 23 of the present text, so that the absence of the article seemed inappropriate. MT should be retained as the *difficilior lectio*: it is probably a sign of the combination of multiple accounts of this plague (see the introduction to this section and also the previous note).

ואש (9.24)   LXX τὸ δὲ πῦρ again has the anaphoric article (cf. on v. 23), but this time without the support of SP.

מתלקחת (9.24)   The Heb. is most precisely represented by Aq συναναλαμβανόμενον, Symm ἐνειλούμενον (cf. Exod.R. 12) and Vulg *inmixta* (+ *pariter*?), but all of them give the Hithpael a passive rather than its usual reflexive sense.[18] The rendering 'flaming' (LXX, Sy, Tg^O)[19] is probably a guess from the context, while 'leaping' (Tg^{J,N}) is more imaginative and closer to what is likely to be the real meaning (see Note z on the translation).

כבד (9.24)   LXX repeats ἡ χάλαζα from the beginning of the verse to avoid any misunderstanding: there is no need to presume a repetition of הברד in its *Vorlage*.

מאד (9.24)   LXX intensifies with σφόδρα σφόδρα, which represents MT מאד מאד in 1.7 (and is added by LXX mss in the related 1.12). Vulg's paraphrase contains no explicit equivalent to מאד.

בכל־ארץ מצרים (9.24)   SP has simply במצרים, as in v. 18, and LXX* ἐν Αἰγύπτῳ implies the same reading (though it could be due to independent assimilation to v. 18 on the translator's part). The wording of MT is already reflected in a surviving piece of 4QEx^c, as well as in Aq's 'correction' and Sy (and also Tgg and Vulg), but its precise correspondence to v. 22 and the fact that an expression for the people rather than the land is needed in the following clause suggest that the fuller expression is secondary here (so also Propp, p. 302).

מאז (9.24)   The Vss render in the idiom of their own languages, but the use of the same expression, lit. 'from the *day* that', in Sy and Tg^G is especially striking.

לגוי (9.24)   LXX and Vulg reformulate the clause, making 'a/the nation' the subject and then departing further from MT (LXX adds ἐπ'αὐτῆς, sc. [the land of] Egypt). The intention seems to be to make the wording closer to that of v. 18. Tg^{J,N} add ומלכו, 'and a kingdom', but Tg^{Nmg} and Tg^G lack this: its precise purpose is unclear.

בכל־ארץ (9.25)   SP בארץ, in conformity to the expressions in vv. 22b and 23b; in v. 24 SP had במצרים, which may well be original there (see the note above). LXX ἐν πάσῃ γῇ and the other Vss agree with the reading of MT

---

[18] The addition of *pariter* leads M. Kraus to find Jerome's source in the tradition preserved e.g. in *PRK* 1.4, which sees a similar phenomenon in 'the fire of a lamp' ('Jerome', pp. 22-24).

[19] Klein restores the reading of Tg^G with that of Tg^O, but the basis for this is only an uncertain *lamed*.

(Sy *lklh ʾrʿ* takes the phrase as a direct obj. of הכה, but cases of ב being used in this way after הכה are very rare [BDB, p. 645-46: cf. Exod. 17.6] and את is used later in this verse). None of the Qumran mss preserves the phrase, and Lemmelijn does not discuss it. SP is probably secondary here.

את כל־אשר בשדה (9.25)   LXX has no equivalent, but SP and the other Vss agree with MT and the Three and Origen restored the phrase. There is no obvious basis for an omission of just these words by parablepsis, but LXX (or its *Vorlage*) may have found them superfluous in view of all that follows and so not reproduced them. Lemmelijn (p. 176) regards this as one of the few places where LXX preserves a superior text to MT, in view of the very similar phrase in v. 19 which MT etc. may have copied, but the argument is weakened by the fact that it occurs not in the announcement of the plague but in the instruction given to Pharaoh. In fact the whole of v. 25 is without a parallel in the earlier context.

ועד (9.25)   Most SP mss omit the *waw* (three of Crown's mss are the only ones cited as having it – *if* they are correctly recorded), as they do with the same phrase in 12.12 and 13.15, as well as Num. 3.13 where MT also has עד. In general SP has no aversion to ועד in other combinations with מן, and in 11.5 and 23.31 it even has it where MT has just עד. While both traditions exhibit some variation from place to place, SP seems to have aimed at consistency over this phrase, perhaps reflecting local idiom, and so is likely to be secondary here. There is no clear support elsewhere for a text omitting the *waw*: LXX's ἕως and Vulg's *usque ad* may simply follow Greek and Latin idiom respectively.

שבר (9.25)   Tg^J amplifies with ושריש, 'and uprooted (them)', but unlike the end of v. 24 its reading here is not shared by any of the other Tgg.

רק (9.26)   LXX πλήν can mean 'But' in later Greek (cf. *BAlex* 'cependant'), but its classical meanings 'except (that)' and 'only' continued in use (cf. LSJ, p. 1419; Muraoka, p. 463) and fit well here (cf. Note cc on the translation).

גשן (9.26)   For LXX Γέσεμ see Text and Versions on 8.18; here Sy^hex(T) has the correction (cf. Sy) as well as Vulg.

שם (9.26)   Most of the Vss simply supply 'were', but Tg^N and Sy both have the more specific 'dwelt' (compare the verbal agreement between Tg^N and Sy's renderings of מאז in v. 24).

לא היה (9.26)   Sy *dlʾ nḥt*: the *d* is difficult and was omitted by 8b1 and later mss. J. Joosten (pers. comm.) notes two other places where *d* occurs unexpectedly before a verb in Deut. 2.37 and Josh. 11.22: in both, as here, the sentence begins with an adverbial expression for 'only' and an ellipse of 'It was' can perhaps be inferred. The use of *nḥt* follows Sy's rendering of היה in vv. 22 and 24; here Vulg *cecidit* gave the same more precise sense.

ברד (9.26)   LXX ἡ χάλαζα, from the previous verse: with the preceding ἐγένετο the sense intended was probably 'the hail did not come'. It cannot be determined whether Vulg and Sy intended the same variation from the sense of MT.

וישלח (9.27) Tg^J adds 'agents', as in 9.7 and most similarly in 10.16.

ויקרא (9.27) Tg^J 'to call': the divergent early reading of ms. 5b1 of Sy (*qr'*) might, if read as a part., represent a similar avoidance of a succession of main verbs (cf. LXX's rendering of וישלח by a part.).

חטאתי (9.27) Tg^{O,Nmg} render with חוב, 'be guilty', which they and the other Tgg also have for הרשעים at the end of the verse. Tg^Nmg also adds 'in that I rebelled against the Memra of the Lord', making Pharaoh's offence explicit.

הפעם (9.27) According to one LXX ms. the Sam Gk had ἐν καιρῷ here, which LXX used for הפעם in 8.28 (but not here). Vulg *etiam nunc*, 'also now', apparently to avoid having Pharaoh imply that he had not sinned previously. The same concern may lie behind the addition of ידעית, 'I know', in Tg^J (see also the addition at the end of the verse) and of גלי, 'it is manifest/revealed', in Tg^Nmg, both of which could and probably should be taken with their renderings of הפעם, 'now'. In other words, what is new is not Pharaoh's guilt but his awareness of it.

ואני ועמי (9.27) Vulg has no *et* before *ego*, probably to make a more forceful contrast: Tg^N oddly has 'Pharaoh and the people', as though the words were the narrator's (Klein restores this for Tg^G too, but there is no evidence of it in the surviving text).

הרשעים (9.27) LXX has ἀσεβεῖς, using a word which had specifically religious overtones (appropriate here) in classical Gk. but is a common equivalent for רשע in LXX generally (e.g. Gen. 18.23, 25; Exod. 23.7: cf HR and *BAlex* 2, p. 134n.). Vulg *impii* can have a religious meaning but need not, so it (like Tgg. חייב) keeps closer to the precise sense of the Heb. Tg^J adds 'in each individual plague', again (cf. the note on הפעם) making clear the full extent of Pharaoh's acknowledgement of guilt.

העתירו (9.28) LXX adds οὖν περὶ ἐμοῦ, 'So...for me', as it did in 8.4 – the wording seems to be based on 8.24, where MT has בעדי. Tg^Nmg also expands, with כען, 'now, so'.

אל־יהוה (9.28) Tgg and Sy have 'before the Lord', with the usual distancing of God from human address.

ורב מהית (9.28) The Vss all paraphrase this difficult expression, missing the precise sense of the idiom and generally translating it as a wish. LXX and Vulg have 'May (voices of God [cf. on v. 23]/thundering) cease (to be/occur)...', and Tg^N has 'May he [sc. Yahweh] restrain the coming of...' The other Tgg also give the expression a theological dimension, by inserting 'before him' again, and render רב literally by סגי, either alone (Tg^{J,G}) or with the addition of 'respite' (רוח, Tg^O). Sy alone apparently did not understand the expression as a wish, but as a basis for the prayer: *w'yt 'tr' sgy qdmwhy dl'*, 'and/for there is a great possibility before him that (there will) not...' Possibly Tg^{J,G} understood 'much' in the sense of 'far' in view of the following מן.

קלת אלהים (9.28) LXX and Sy render literally and Vulg by *tonitrua Dei*; Tg^N and probably Tg^G diverge only by the insertion of 'from before'. But

Tg^J additionally characterises the קלה as 'of malediction' (לווט), an addition which is also present in Tg^O's unusually amplified rendering (עלנא קלין דלוט כאלין מן קדם ייי), where the 'like those…' may be based on the awareness that אלהים could have a superlative force (and probably does here: see Note ff on the translation). The idea of malediction appears also in vv. 33-34 in Tg^J (see *AramB* 2, p. 184 n. 19 for some further refs., to which Tg Isa. 13.1 may be added): it is a characteristic Targumic expression for judgement on Israel's enemies.

וברד (9.28) 2Q2 has ואש after this, cf. LXX καὶ πῦρ.[20] These readings correspond to the wording of v. 23 and especially v. 24 and could well be seen as due to secondary scribal addition of what was felt to be a missing element here (so Lemmelijn, pp. 177-78). But since the next word begins with the same three letters, it is also possible that it is the shorter text of MT, SP etc. that is secondary, having lost this word by homoeoarkton. The choice between these explanations may be affected by the conclusions reached about the composition of the passage (see the introduction to this section).

ואשלחה (9.28) Vulg *ut dimittam* (and perhaps the Aram. versions) captures the expression of purpose by this idiom well, unlike LXX καὶ ἐξαποστελῶ. SP omits the cohortative ending, as in 1.10; 3.3; 8.4, and elsewhere (see Text and Versions on 8.4).

ולא תספון לעמד (9.28) Vulg renders ולא by *et nequaquam*, a strong expression which it uses especially where the Heb. has יסף Hiphil (cf. 5.7; 14.13). *AramB* 2, p. 1184, renders Tg^J's version of the clause (which is identical to Tg^O) 'Do not delay any longer', apparently as an instruction to Moses and Aaron: this is a possible sense for Aram. עכב Ethpaal and might be correct, even for the original Heb. (though the *waw* makes a connection with the preceding clause more likely and the verb can mean 'be detained').

אליו (9.29) Vulg and some LXX mss have no equivalent, probably regarding it as unnecessary. 2Q2 has מושה directly after ויאמרו (the *plene* writing is characteristic of this ms.) and then breaks off, so it either omitted אליו or had it after מושה. Elsewhere in Exodus suffixed forms of אל more commonly come between the verb and its subject, but they can appear after the subject (for the variation see 34.31). 4QpalEx^l has משה immediately before כצאתי, like MT and SP, but it is not clear what it had before. Sy mss of the eighth cent. and later have *lpr'wn* after *mwš'*. There is insufficient evidence to support any reading other than that of MT (and SP).

כצאתי (9.29) So SP, 4QpalEx^l and the main Vss. Tg^{Nmg} has כד נפוק, apparently 'when we [Moses and Aaron?] go out', which might be related

---

[20] The omission of these words in ms. A is attributed by Wevers (*Notes*, p. 139) to homoeoteleuton (*sic*), but A does sometimes present readings that have been harmonised with MT (cf. *THGE*, pp. 40, 93-103) and this could just as well be the reason here.

to Pharaoh's request in vv. 27-28. But there is no echo of such joint action anywhere else here or in the following verses and more likely it is a case of the frequent use of the first person pl. form for the first person sing. in Galilean Aramaic (J. Joosten, pers. comm.: cf. Stevenson §18.13).

את־העיר (9.29)   Vulg *de urbe* and Tg^{Nmg}, Sy 'from the city' simply represent MT in the native idiom. Tg^J סמיך לקרתא, 'near the city' (so also in v. 33), is at first more puzzling, but reflects rabbinic interpretation of את as the preposition 'with' (*MRI* on 12.1 [1, pp. 3-4]; Exod.R. 12.7).

את־כפי (9.29)   SP and 4QEx^c have no את, perhaps conforming mechanically to כפיו in v. 33, but possibly preserving the older reading, as such 'omissions' are comparatively rare: much more often SP (etc.) seems to have added an את which is missing in MT (cf. *GSH* §180a-c). The unmarked object is especially common when it is an 'inalienable' part of the subject (J. Joosten, pers. comm.). Tg^{O,J} render כפי with ידי (cf. Sy) – the inclusion of כפי before it in Tg^{N,G} is presumably an accommodation to MT – and also add בצלו, 'in prayer', to clarify Moses' intention (also in v. 33: see *AramB* 2, p. 184 n. 21 for further instances).

אל־יהוה (9.29)   Tg^{O,J,N} as usual have 'before the Lord'.

הקלות (9.29)   Most SP mss (not Sadaqa or Camb. 713 acc. Crown) and LXX prefix 'and' (2Q2 is unclear), a reading which is certainly inferior to the anacoluthon of MT and 4QEx^c.

יחדלון (9.29)   4QEx^c has יחדלו, with the kind of 'normalisation' that is more common in SP: cf. 4.9; 15.14; 20.20; 22.21, 30 (2x) with the same ending, but such variation is by no means universal in SP or in 4QEx^c, which again diverges from MT in v. 30, while retaining הסְפון in v. 28 (for such inconsistency in biblical mss from Qumran, where the ending ון- is generally rare, see Qimron, p. 45).

הברד (9.29)   LXX adds καὶ ὁ ὑετός, preparing for the references to rain in vv. 33-34. The shorter reading of MT, SP and 4QpalEx^l is clearly preferable (Lemmelijn, p. 178, attributes it also to 2Q2 and 4QEx^c, but they do not survive at this point).

לא יהיה־עוד (9.29)   Vulg *non erit* with no equivalent to עוד, which elsewhere is represented by *ultra* after a negative (10.29; 14.13; 36.6). OL had *amplius* and the omission in Vulg is probably because it seemed unnecessary when (as it can be) לא יהיה is understood to mean 'there shall be no…' Sy renders היה, as earlier, by *nḥt*, 'fall'.

הארץ (9.29)   Tg^{Nmg,G} prefix כל, 'all', perhaps thinking of a verse like 19.5 (so Klein 2, p. 56).

ואתה (9.30)   Tg^{Nmg} adds 'O Pharaoh' for emphasis.

טרם (9.30)   The sense 'not yet' is well represented by LXX, Vulg, Tg^O and Sy (as later by Rashi); Symm has simply 'not', discounting even the possibility (Salvesen, pp. 81-82). The other Tgg seem not to recognise the correct sense here (although Tg^J does so in Gen. 2.5; 24.15; Exod. 10.7), and render by 'before': Tg^N על דקדם, lit. 'concerning what was before', i.e.

'formerly' (*AramB*);[21] Tg[Nmg] expresses the same sense by דעד לא (which Tg[N] has at Gen. 37.18), but also has a periphrastic rendering 'before [read עד לא] the plagues befall you (you do not fear...)'; Tg[J] has 'before (עד לא) you release the people'; Tg[G] has [קד , which Klein restores to [קד]ם עד לא]: this represents 'before' often in Tg[N]. The determination to render (ב)טרם always in the same way, which leads either nowhere or to a midrashic expansion, is reminiscent of the views of medieval commentators such as Ibn Ezra, Ramban and Bekhor Shur, which B. Jacob sought to reinstate (Gn. ed., p. 283), but to no avail.

תיראון (9.30) On 4QEx[c]'s spelling תיראו see the note on יחדלון in v. 29. Most of the Vss probably understand this in a positive sense (so clearly Tg[O,Nmg], with 'humble yourselves' [כנע]), but in Tg[J] it seems to be taken to mean 'you will have cause to fear, i.e. suffer'.

מפני (9.30) LXX and Vulg do not represent the preposition (although LXX normally does and Vulg does in Deut. 31.6), probably because fear of God is so often expressed by the direct object (e.g. 1.17, 21).

יהוה אלהים (9.30) Vulg, Sy and Tgg reflect the reading of MT (Tg[Nmg] as usual prefixes 'the Memra of' to the divine name), but SP has אדני יהוה, a divine title that is frequent in Ezekiel and occurs in the MT Pentateuch at Gen. 15.2, 8; Deut. 3.24; 9.26. The only other occurrence of it in SP alone is in Num. 20.13b, where it is derived from Deut. 3.24. It appears at Exod. 9.30 also in 4QEx[c], a ms. with a number of 'Samaritan' characteristics (though not the major pluses), and probably the reading is an inherited one. The LXX witnesses (apart from those which have the hexaplaric correction to MT) are divided between the readings τὸν κύριον (AM etc.) and τὸν θεόν (B etc.). Wevers points out that the articulation of κύριος when referring to God is very rare in LXX Exodus (*Notes*, p. 141), which should perhaps be taken as a sign that τὸν θεόν is more original (against the editorial decisions of both Rahlfs and Wevers here). Whether LXX's *Vorlage* was אלהים or יהוה is difficult to say in view of the occasions when LXX ὁ θεός corresponds to Heb. יהוה. The SP/4QEx[c] reading is most likely an amplification of an original יהוה. MT may perhaps be seen as a 'mixed reading' based on texts which had יהוה and אלהים respectively, but which of these is most ancient is impossible to say (cf. Propp, p. 303).

נכתה (9.31) SP נכו, as MT also has in v. 32; Tgg and Sy also have pl. forms, but are probably rendering *ad sensum*; the sing. in LXX (ἐπλήγη) and Vulg (*laesum est*) reflect knowledge of MT's more difficult reading (on which see Note ll on the translation), which is surely original.

אביב (9.31) Tg[O] uses the Aram. cognate, but the other Tgg use different words meaning 'early to ripen'. LXX παρεστηκυῖα, 'ripe' (cf. Lee, *Lexical Study*, pp. 56-57, and LSJ, p. 1341), Vulg *virens*, 'green, sprouting' and Sy *mhy knʾ*, 'striking root' (though *knʾ* strictly means 'stalk') render more generally.

---

[21] Klein (*Michael Klein on the Targums*, pp. 222-23) argues persuasively that either the edition or the ms. is in error and that the reading should be עד דקדם, as consistently elsewhere.

גבעל (9.31) Tg^J and Sy render 'had formed pods', while Tg^{O,G} have the Aram. cognate, as do Tg^{N,F} with the addition of ואתרת נצה, 'and had shed its blossom', to specify the stage of growth more closely. LXX σπερματίζον again uses a general equivalent, but Vulg (perhaps on the basis of an incompletely preserved Greek rendering]λακίζον) preserves the specific reference to the flax 'pods'.

4QEx^c has only a few letters of this verse, but enough to show that it had the final two clauses in the opposite order to the rest of the tradition. No doubt this was a change to match the order of the crops at the beginning of the verse, instead of the chiastic arrangement of the other texts.

והחטה (9.32) SP in general agrees with MT, but Camb. 1846 reads והחטתא, evidently a scribal error due to Aram. influence.

והכסמת (9.32) LXX and Vulg have words corresponding to 'spelt', and this is the traditional equivalent for Aram. כונתא as found in most of the Tgg and Sy. But the word occurs in several Egyptian Aramaic documents from the Persian period and there the translation 'emmer' has reasonably been adopted in *TAD* 3, p. xxxviii, and *DNWSI*, p. 521, presumably for the reasons cited in the Explanatory Note on vv. 31-32. Its meaning in the Aram. Vss is likely to be the same. Tg^G's וכופפייתא is unparalleled elsewhere and is perhaps simply a scribal error for וכונתא (so Klein 2, p. 56).

כי (9.32) Again most of the Vss render as expected: Tg^{Nmg}'s קלין, 'parched', hardly fits the context and is probably simply an error by metathesis from the reading לקין in the text.

אפילת (9.32) Tg^O renders with the Aram. cognate, the other Tgg and Sy with *lqyš*, LXX ὄψιμα, Vulg *serotina*, all with the meaning 'late (to ripen)'. The marginal variant הוויין לקישן in Tg^N that is recorded for v. 31 probably belongs here (the meaning is the opposite of what is required in v. 31), as it presents the two words in the opposite order to the text of Tg^N here (but an order corresponding to the final two clauses of Tg^N's rendering of v. 31).

את־העיר (9.33) The separation of the object from its verb was no problem for the Vss which had used a preposition already in v. 29 (Vulg, Sy, Tg^{Nmg} and Tg^J [סמיך: see the note there]), though Sy did interchange this phrase and the previous one. LXX resorted to a preposition (ἐκτός), and Tg^{O,N,G} simply followed MT.

כפיו (9.33) Tg^J added בצלו as in v. 29 (see the note there).

אל־יהוה (9.33) The Tgg have 'before the Lord' as usual. Sy prefixed 'to the heavens' to make the direction explicit, although it did not do so in v. 29.

הקלות (9.33) Tg^J added 'of execration' as in v. 28, where see the note.

מטר (9.33) Rain was not mentioned before in MT, so the indeterminate form was natural (so also Tg^N). LXX equally naturally has καὶ ὁ ὑετός (cf. the note on v. 29). Tg^{O,J} have 'the rain which was coming down' as a retrospective completion of the picture, and probably SP's והמטר was similarly motivated. It is not possible to be sure what Vulg *pluvia* and the מטרא of the other Aram. versions were meant to convey.

לא־נתך (9.33)   LXX and Vulg have weak equivalents meaning 'dripped' (cf. Wevers on LXX, *Notes*, p. 142) and add '(no) more' (ἔτι, *ultra*) in conformity to v. 29. Since Vulg has no equivalent to עוד there, it most likely followed LXX (via the OL) slavishly at this point. Tg^{N,G} 'did not come down' keep close to MT, except that Tg^G adds (apparently) ברגוז, 'in anger', as Klein (2, p. 56) notes that it does again in 14.24: here the addition will be an elucidation of Heb. נתך on the basis of its use of divine anger in Nah. 1.6 etc. Tg^{O,J} and Sy have 'did not reach', which alludes to a legend that the rain was suspended in mid-air: see *AramB* 2, p. 185 n. 24 for refs.

המטר והברד והקלת (9.34)   There is some variation in order in the transmission of these words. MT's order, which differs from any that has preceded and is the exact opposite of v. 33, is most likely to be original (it is shared by LXX*, Vulg, Tg^{O,J} and apparently 4QEx^c and 4QpalEx^l) and the other readings can be seen as attempts to conform at least in part to earlier verses. SP interchanges the first two nouns to agree with their order in v. 33. Tg^N puts והקלת at the beginning (but its mg corrects to MT), where it is in vv. 28, 29 and 33, while the Sy ms. 5b1 places it before והברד for the same reason. Tg^J again adds 'of execration' after והקלת (see the note on v. 28) and adds another verb for 'ceased' after it to divide up the long clause.

ויכבד (9.34)   Sy, Vulg, Tg^N and two LXX mss render by a passive, probably to simplify the grammar at the end of the verse: the attempt of LXX to do the same was less successful, because it gives the impression that Pharaoh made his servants' hearts stubborn as well as his own! The passive rendering could lend support to the view that וַיִּכְבַּד is the original reading (Propp, p. 303).

ויחזק (9.35)   For LXX ἐσκληρύνθη and Vulg *induratum* (*est*) cf. 8.15. Vulg adds *nimis*, a free intensification of Pharaoh's obduracy. Sy uses ʿbʾ here for חזק (as in 7.22; 14.17) instead of its most common equivalent qšʾ, the latter having been used for כבד in v. 34.

לב (9.35)   Tg^J prefixes 'the inclination *and*' in a small variation from its usual expansion of MT.

דבר (9.35)   Vulg as usual in these formulae has *praeceperat*: this would make sense if taken with the immediately preceding clause rather than (as was probably intended originally) with the stubbornness of Pharaoh. Sy *šlḥ* is not as different from MT as at first appears, as *šlḥ* means specifically 'to send *word*' in Syr. (other kinds of sending being represented by *šdr*).

ביד (9.35)   Both LXX and Tg^N render 'to Moses', assimilating to 9.12, the only other occasion in these formulae where Moses is mentioned.

Chapter 10.1-20

The Plague of Locusts

The story of the locust plague is clearly demarcated in the present text by the new introductory divine speeches beginning in 10.1 and 10.21, and these divisions are marked both in the great medieval manuscripts and in the Qumran biblical texts. In addition 4QExod^c had a division before v. 12 (as is likely also for 4QpalExod^m) and probably before v. 6b or v. 7. The episode is at two points (vv. 5, 15) directly linked to the preceding storm of hail, as well as sharing with it some features which do not appear in the earlier plagues (see the Explanatory Notes on vv. 12-15 and 16-17). Dozeman is therefore justified in suggesting that 'the pair of plagues should be interpreted as a single action of Yahweh in two stages' (p. 240). There are also close parallels of wording with the following plague of darkness (see the introduction to 10.21-29), so that it may even be proper to see these three plagues as a 'triptych' which together take the narrative forwards to its climax in the death of the firstborn. The structure of the locust plague also has a closer similarity to the hail plague than to any of the others before it: (i) Yahweh's instruction to Moses to confront Pharaoh, including a more general explanation of the purpose of the plagues (vv. 1-2: cf. 9.13-19); (ii) Moses' delivery of Yahweh's message to Pharaoh and its effects (vv. 3-11: cf. 9.20-21 [there the delivery of the message is presumed rather than narrated]); (iii) Yahweh commands Moses to bring on the plague by the use of his staff (v. 12: cf. 9.22); (iv) the plague is described (vv. 13-15: cf. 9.23-26); as are (v) the effects of the plague and its removal (vv. 16-20: cf. 9.27-35).

But even at the overall structural level there are features in this section which are quite new. Instead of Yahweh's message being declared in the opening address to Moses, it appears only in the initial confrontation with Pharaoh (vv. 3-6a). The actual description of this confrontation is also an innovation – in the earlier non-Priestly plagues it is taken for granted – and it leads on to the initiation of negotiations between Pharaoh and Moses at an earlier stage than hitherto (vv. 7-11). Particularly after this, it is curious that the negotiations at the end of the story include no explicit promise on Pharaoh's part to let the Israelites go to worship their God. These variations in narrative structure can plausibly be attributed to a desire to intensify further the conflict between Yahweh and Pharaoh as the climax approaches. But when the details of the narrative are examined more closely, other features become evident which have led most critical scholars to conclude that the construction of this episode is due to the work of more than one author.

Knobel proposed that the core of the narrative lay in vv. 12-20, which derived from his *Kriegsbuch*, like most of the other non-Priestly plagues (p. 86; *Num.-Jos.*, p. 548): he noted numerous variations in vocabulary from vv. 1-6, which he attributed (along with parts of vv. 12 and 15) to the *Jehowist*, for him the final redactor of the Pentateuch. He saw vv. 7-11 as being originally the conclusion of the hail plague, an idea which was taken up by Dillmann. But from Wellhausen onwards it became normal until very recently to attribute most of vv. 1-11 to J, but to suppose that the insertion of vv. 1b-2 by a redactor (a point on which Smend, Eissfeldt and Noth in his Exodus commentary dissented) had led to the displacement of the revelation of Yahweh's message from its original (and usual) place. Wellhausen also saw v. 12 as the beginning of a parallel account deriving from E, which was interleaved with the end of the J account and concluded with v. 20.[1] This analysis of the story remained the dominant view down to Childs's commentary of 1974, with Hyatt (p. 124) noting that the verses attributed to E gave 'a complete account of the coming of the plague'. In addition the original conclusion to the J version of the locust-plague had by 1900 (Carpenter/Harford-Battersby 2, p. 95) been 'discovered' in vv. 24-26, 28-29, where they are now attached to the plague of darkness (for discussion of this theory see the introduction to 10.21-29).[2]

The presence of an E strand was questioned by Rudolph in 1938 (*Elohist*, p. 21), who argued that there was no case for sub-division in v. 15 (following B. Eerdmans) and that the rest of the non-J material was due to later supplementation. Noth at first went even further from the consensus and attributed the whole of vv. 12-19 to J, treating only v. 20 as a supplement (*ÜGP*, p. 32), but in his Exodus commentary he reverted to a source-critical analysis of the passage, seeing vv. 12-13a and 20 as extracts from a Priestly version of

---

[1] This is strongly implied in *Composition*, pp. 66-67, even though not explicitly stated. Wellhausen was aware of some similarity in vocabulary between E and P (Q in his terminology at that time), which he had noted earlier in Genesis (p. 67).

[2] Although very widely accepted (even recently by Blum and Van Seters), this view was occasionally questioned (McNeile, p. 45; Noth, pp. 64-65, ET, pp. 83-84 – in *ÜGP*, p. 32, he oddly seems to accept the common view for vv. 28-29 alone).

the plague (p. 63, ET, p. 82: cf. pp. 61, 64 [ET 80, 83] on the preceding and following sections). This elimination of E was strongly criticised by Fohrer (p. 63 n. 9), chiefly because it overlooked the distinctive formal pattern of the plague-narratives attributed to E, and implicitly by Hyatt, but Noth's later views were taken up in a more extensive way by Steingrimmson, who assigned all the 'E' material to his A-group, which corresponds here to P (pp. 183, 208-209). Noth's attribution of vv. 12-13a and 20 to P was also taken up in the more influential studies of Blum (*Studien*, pp. 245-56, esp. 249-50 on verbal parallels in Priestly texts, including parts of ch. 14)[3] and Van Seters (*Life*, pp. 77 n. 2, 107), but in the sense of the overall perspective that they both adopt, namely that P was a supplementary layer and not an independent source. Both regard the remainder of the passage as belonging to an exilic narrative (KD or late J).

Three other approaches to the passage have been put forward in the most recent period of scholarship, all agreeing against the older consensus that no second, parallel version of the story can be detected here. One group attributes most of the passage to J, with vv. 1b-2 as before coming from a redactor ('R^JE') with a Deuteronomic/Deuteronomistic background, and vv. 12-13a and 20 being seen as the work of the very late redactor who combined the J and P sources together (PentR). The argument for this latter conclusion was developed most fully by Kohata (*Jahwist*, pp. 105-15), who is followed closely by L. Schmidt (*Beobachtungen*, pp. 35-37, adding v. 14a to the late layer), W.H. Schmidt (pp. 415-16) and Graupner (*Elohist*, pp. 64-66).[4] A second view, represented by Levin (pp. 337-38) and Gertz (pp. 138-41, 152-63), regards the whole passage, like the hail-plague, as belonging to a very late supplement to the Exodus narrative, either PentR (Gertz) or an even later stage (Levin, 'nachendredaktionell'). The argument is based partly on conclusions already reached about earlier passages, on which 10.1-20 is thought to be dependent, and partly on Kohata's conclusion about vv. 12-13a and 20, which is taken to be the *Grundlage* (Levin) or at least an inseparable part of the passage, which is treated as essentially a unity (Gertz).[5] The third approach shares Gertz's

---

[3] Blum apparently views v. 14a as also part of the Priestly layer (ibid., pp. 246 and 253 n. 86).

[4] Also H.-C. Schmitt, 'Tradition der Prophetenbücher in den Schichten der Plagenerzählung Ex 7,1 – 11,10', in V. Fritz et al. (eds.), *Prophet und Prophetenbuch* (Festschrift O. Kaiser; BZAW 185; Berlin, 1989), pp. 196-216 (211-16), together with all the other references to Moses' staff. K. Schmid does not discuss the analysis of the passage in detail but appears to regard it as mostly earlier than P (p. 148) and in its present form as close to sixth-century writings such as Deutero-Isaiah (pp. 144-45).

[5] Berner similarly regards the whole section as post-Priestly, but divides it between three separate redactional layers, all later than the addition of the hail-plague (*Exoduserzählung*, pp. 229-41, 261-66).

assessment of unitary authorship for the passage but either dates it much earlier (Propp, who attributes it like the other plagues to E) or refrains from exact dating (Houtman, p. 97; but vol. 1, p. 1, places the authorship of Exodus 'in the middle of the sixth century BC').[6]

Many of the issues and arguments raised in the analysis of this passage have already been discussed in connection with the hail-plague (see the introduction to 9.13-35) and there is no need to repeat that discussion here. Provisionally we may conclude that the earlier critics were correct to discern here too the combination of two parallel accounts (not just the supplementation of a single account), with the evidence for this being particularly clear in vv. 12-15. The main contribution is again from E, who here too (as in the hail-plague) constructs a more complex narrative than before as the climax of the sequence of plagues approaches. J, on the other hand, at least to judge from what is preserved, had a much briefer account of the plague (vv. 12-13a, 14-15*: see below on v. 20), perhaps again (as in 9.13-35) including no negotiations with Pharaoh himself.

Some assessment is needed, however, of the curious beginning to the main narrative and of the conclusion in v. 20, which this time does not form part of a doublet (unlike 9.34-35). There are three aspects to the oddity of vv. 1-2 within the wider context of the plague-story. First, only here (in v. 1) is the Hiphil of the verb *kābēd* (a verb which is elsewhere characteristic of the non-Priestly strand of the narrative) used of Yahweh's 'dulling' of Pharaoh's heart/mind.[7] This already creates a new dimension to Yahweh's activity in the whole narrative, indeed one that appears to contradict the purpose of the successive plagues that are sent to teach Pharaoh the error of his ways and, presumably, to make him agree to Moses' demands.

---

[6] Dozeman's commentary can be placed here, since he regards most of vv. 1b-2 as well as vv. 12-13a and 20 as part of the main narrative and assigns only details (the end of v. 2 and the references to Aaron) to a later Priestly hand. His main narrative layer ('non-P' is dated broadly to the exilic or post-exilic period (pp. 39-40). In *God at War* he distinguished between the main ('pre-exilic') story (p. 16) and 'possible' Deuteronomistic additions in vv. 1b-2 and 19 (ימה סוף) (p. 43).

[7] In 8.11, 28; 9.34 it is used of Pharaoh's (and in 9.34 also his courtiers') self-delusion.

Within the present section, the 'dulling' of Pharaoh's courtiers as well as Pharaoh himself sits uneasily alongside the courtiers' own response to Moses' warnings in v. 7. Secondly, the purpose of the plagues, no longer a device to persuade Pharaoh, is seen in a much longer perspective as being for the instruction of subsequent generations of Israelites. Apart from passing allusions to it in Num. 14.11 and 22, such an intention is more characteristic of Psalm 78 (note vv. 1-4) and a number of passages in Deuteronomy (see the footnote in the Explanatory Note). A similar concern about the teaching of the Exodus story in general to future generations appears in laws later in Exodus about the festivals of Passover and Unleavened Bread and in the ritual for the firstborn (12.24-27; 13.8-10, 14-16). This is certainly a different kind of concern from that which appears in 9.14-16 and there is no good reason to treat them as coming from the same author. When these two factors are combined with the third peculiarity of 10.1-2, namely the lack of any indication of what Moses is to do when he approaches Pharaoh, the case for a secondary origin for vv. 1b-2 becomes inescapable. They belong, like the verses in chs. 12–13 mentioned above, to a developing educational setting of some kind in Israel itself which like Deuteronomy, but not necessarily in dependence upon it, is concerned to use the Exodus story as a means of religious instruction, in what Hosea called 'the knowledge of God/Yahweh'. Psalm 78 appears to have extended this concern to include later epochs in the history of Israel. In view of the explicit association with Passover and Unleavened Bread, it is very tempting to find the primary *Sitz im Leben* of this instruction in these festivals. Presumably vv. 1b-2 have replaced specific instructions to Moses whose general character can be inferred from what follows.

The conclusion in v. 20 corresponds closely, though not exactly, to the wording of 9.35 and 10.27. The absence of a doublet like that in 9.34 makes its attribution to one of the underlying sources less certain, but this remains possible. There is certainly a close similarity to the language of P (which also moves from the use of the Qal of *ḥzq* to the Piel between 8.15 and 9.12) in the first half of the verse, but the second half picks up the terminology of vv. 3, 7 and 10 instead, which is more generally characteristic of the non-Priestly version. It is not immediately clear why a Priestly redactor should have intervened at this point in the narrative, when

P and non-P are otherwise generally kept separate (a direct overlap in subject-matter is responsible for the exceptions in 7.19-22 and 8.1-3, 11). So the more likely suggestion is that v. 20 belongs to one of the non-Priestly accounts, most likely J in view of what is to follow.

Together with the hail, the locust plague is said to make a complete devastation of the land of Egypt (vv. 5, 15), and like the hail it is of unprecedented severity (vv. 6, 14; cf. 9.18, 24) – indeed no subsequent plague of locusts has been like this one either (v. 14). The pressure applied to Pharaoh by Yahweh could not be greater. Even the threat of it is enough to break the resolve of his courtiers, and it seems for a moment Pharaoh himself. But each time he begins to yield, his inner resistance gets the better of him (vv. 10-11, 20). As in the preceding episode, and with an apparently greater sense of his personal responsibility before God (vv. 16-17: cf. 9.27), Pharaoh acknowledges that he has done wrong. But when the pressure is relaxed, the question put to him by Moses and Aaron on Yahweh's behalf remains unanswered: 'How long do you refuse to humble yourself before me?' (v. 3: cf. 9.17). Small wonder that one narrator concluded that Pharaoh's stubbornness must be part of a divine plan (v. 20) and that a later commentator saw the treatment of him and his countrymen by Yahweh as a stage-managed way of showing later generations of Israelites the fearful greatness of their God (vv. 1b-2).

1 Yahweh said to Moses, 'Go (in) to Pharaoh, [for it is I who^a have made him and his servants unable to understand, in order to produce^b these^c signs of mine in his/their midst^d, 2 and so that you may declare in the hearing of your son^e and your grandson^e how^f I dealt severely^g with the Egyptians and my signs which I produced among (against?) them, and you (pl.) shall know that I am Yahweh.]' 3 So Moses and Aaron went (in)^h to Pharaoh and said to him, 'Thus says Yahweh the God of the Hebrews: How long do you refuse^i to humble yourself before me? Let my people go so that they may worship me. 4 For if you refuse^k to let my people go, then I am going to bring^l locusts^m into your country^n tomorrow, 5 and they will cover the surface^o of the land and it will be impossible^p to see the land. They will eat up the remainder that escaped^q, which you had left after the hail, and they will eat up all the trees that grow up from the open country for you.

6 They will fill[r] your houses, the houses of all your servants and the houses of all the Egyptians, as[s] your fathers and fathers' fathers never saw, from the day when they came to be in the land until now.' Then he turned and went out of Pharaoh's presence. 7 Pharaoh's servants said to him, 'How long shall this man be a snare for us? Let the men go to worship Yahweh their God. Do you not yet know[t] that Egypt is ruined?' 8 So Moses[u] and Aaron[u] were brought back to Pharaoh and he said to them, 'Go, worship Yahweh your God. Who exactly[v] are those who will go?' 9 Moses said, 'We shall go with[w] our young ones and our old men, with[w] our sons and daughters, our sheep and our cattle we shall go, for it is a festival[x] of Yahweh for us.' 10 He said, [y]'May Yahweh be with you – as (little as) I will let you and your dependants go![y] Look, you have some wicked plan in view[z]. 11 Not so[aa] – you go, just the men[bb], and worship Yahweh, since that[cc] is what you are seeking.' With that they were expelled[dd] from Pharaoh's presence. 12 [Yahweh said to Moses, 'Stretch out your hand[ee] over the land of Egypt towards the locusts[ff], so that they may come up over the land of Egypt and eat up all the plants in the land, everything that the hail left'. 13 So Moses stretched out his staff over the land of Egypt,] and [gg]Yahweh drove[gg] an east wind[hh] into the land all that day and all the night. As soon as morning[ii] came, the east wind[ii] brought[jj] the locusts. 14 [The locusts came up over all the land of Egypt, and they settled[kk] in all the country of Egypt,] in great numbers – there had never been locusts like them before them, and there never will be the like again. 15 They covered the surface[o] of all the land so that the land became dark[ll]. [They ate up all the plants in the land and] all the fruit on the trees which the hail had left: [nothing green was left on the trees or on the plants in the open country all over the land of Egypt.] 16 Pharaoh hastened to call Moses and Aaron and said: 'I have sinned against Yahweh your God and against you. 17 But now forgive[mm] my sin, I pray, just this once[nn] and make supplication to Yahweh your God, so that he may remove from me just[oo] this deadly scourge[pp] (too).' 18 So he went out from Pharaoh's presence and made supplication to Yahweh, 19 and Yahweh turned it (i.e. the wind) into a very strong west wind[qq], and it carried the locusts away and drove them[rr] into the Yam Suf. Not a single locust was left in all the country of Egypt. 20 [But Yahweh made Pharaoh's heart stubborn[ss] and he did not let the Israelites go.]

[The precise sub-division between the sources in vv. 14-15 is not certain: see the Explanatory Note.]

Notes on the Translation

a. The independent pronoun is emphatic here, especially before the verb (GK §135a; more precisely in Muraoka, *Emphatic Words*, pp. 48-53, and JM §146a).

b. Heb. שׂתי. The sense 'make' (as distinct from 'put, place') is less frequent with שׂית than with שׂים (which is used in the corresponding phrase in v. 2), both with and without a second object: the closest pars. are Jer. 51.39, Hos. 6.11 and Ps. 104.20.

c. Heb. אלה, without the usual def. art. after a determinate noun, but the omission is regular after a pron. suffix (GK §126y).

d. Heb. בקרבו. The sing. suffix is generally understood to be collective (cf. Text and Versions and 'Pharaoh and his servants' earlier in the verse), but this is strange without a preceding collective noun as antecedent (as when מצרים precedes בקרבו in 3.20, a very similar context). Cassuto takes the reference to be to Pharaoh: '*in his midst*, that is in the midst of his country'. One might cite אל־לבך in 9.14 in support of this interpretation, but that phrase may well be corrupt (see Text and Versions there).

e. The sing. forms of the Heb. are commonly rendered in the pl. (cf. Text and Versions and e.g. NRSV), but the usage is perhaps not so much collective (the corresponding plural forms are after all common enough) as 'individualising', like e.g. the instructions in 13.8, 14 and Deut. 6.20-21; 7.3-4: it is more a feature of style than of grammar.

f. Heb. את־אשר. Since the Hithpael of עלל probably does not take a direct object (see the next note), this cannot be the introduction to an 'independent relative clause' (GK §138e) but opens an object-clause as an alternative to כי: GK §157c, BDB, p. 83 (8.a [a]), 'that, how'.

g. Heb. התעללתי. The occurrences of עלל in BH derive from at least two homonymous roots, as the cognates in other Semitic languages (for which see esp. *Ges18*, p. 972) make clear, but the meanings attributed to the most common root (עלל I) are varied and hard to correlate. There is even some disagreement in the standard lexica about what the meanings are. If the clear instances of 'glean' are left on one side, the remaining cases of the Poel are judged by *TWAT* 6, 152 = *TDOT* 11, p. 140, and *Ges18*, p. 972, to have an essentially neutral sense, 'treat, act', perhaps because this does seem to be true of two of the related nouns, מעלל and עלילה, however much they may be used (esp. in prophecy) to refer to evil actions.[8] On the other hand BDB, p. 759 ('act arbitrarily, severely'), *HAL*, p. 789, and *DCH* 6, p. 425, recognise an element of 'hurt' or 'violence' in at least some cases (likewise *THAT* 2, 464 =

---

[8] *Ges18* does find itself compelled, inconsistently, to introduce the idea of hurt (*Schmerz*) in its rendering of Lam. 3.51 (and perhaps in Isa. 3.12, where the text is doubtful).

TLOT 2, p. 1016). This is scarcely avoidable in Lam. 3.51, so that it seems that a verb which probably did originally mean simply 'act' (cf. the nouns and also the occurrence of the Poal in Lam. 1.12) developed a specialised sense of 'do harm'. This is relevant to the meaning of the Hithpael here and in its other six occurrences (Num. 22.29; Judg. 19.25; 1 Sam. 6.6; 31.4; Jer. 38.19; 1 Chr. 10.4). Here too there is disagreement between the lexica. There is a widespread view that 'make sport of, play with' is the meaning in all cases (cf. *HAL*, p. 789; *Ges18*, p. 972; *DCH* 6, p. 426, except for Judg. 19.25 ['abuse (sexually)']). But *TWAT* 6, 154 = *TDOT* 11, p. 141, gives 'abuse, mistreat' for all cases, without discussion of the more common view; cf. BDB, pp. 759-60 ('busy oneself with', so '*have made a toy* of Egypt' in Exod. 10.2, but 'deal wantonly, ruthlessly with' in the other instances). The latter approach fits well with the meaning of some cases of the Poel (cf. above) and it also suits all the contexts where the Hithpael occurs. On the other hand 'make sport of, play with' is very difficult to relate to the other meanings of the verb, and is probably not required by any of the contexts: even in Num. 22.29 it is quite possible that Balaam accuses his ass of 'mistreating' him. The noun תעלולים is sometimes associated with this meaning, but in both its occurrences (Isa. 3.4; 66.4) 'mistreatment' is possible. Why then is the meaning 'sport, play with' so popular? Two explanations are possible, and they are probably connected. The rendering 'mock' is popular in the Vss (see Text and Versions for details); and the meaning is also attested for later Hebrew and Jewish Aramaic (cf. Jastrow, pp. 1083-84; *CAL* [consulted 24 August 2017], however, offers nothing closer than 'have sexual relations with' and [for Syriac] 'pretend', both under the main sense of 'enter').

h. On the sing. verb with composite subject cf. 7.6, 10; 8.8 etc. and Note z on the translation of 4.18–31.

i. Heb. מאנת. Understandably עד־מתי, 'How long?', is more often followed by the imperfect (e.g. 10.7), but where it is to be emphasised that the action referred to continues from the past the perfect is used, as in other cases where a past action continues into the present (GK §106h; JM §112e): cf. Ps. 80.5; Prov. 1.22aβ; and after עד־אנה Exod. 16.28; Hab. 1.2. Joosten (*Verbal System*, p. 209) suggests that the sense is modal: 'How long *will you refuse*…?'

j. Heb. לענת. Pointed as a Niphal inf. cons., with elision of the prefixed *he* presumed by the Masoretes, as in a few other places (cf. GK §51l). SP has the same consonants; they could be read as the inf. cons. Qal, but the meaning 'humble oneself', although only attested here for the Niphal in BH, is perhaps more appropriately represented by a passive/reflexive form (cf. the Hithpael in Gen. 16.7 and perhaps the Pual in Lev. 23.29).

k. See Note b on the translation of 7.26–8.11.

l. Heb. מביא, the 'participle of the imminent future' (GK §116p; JM §121e), as elsewhere in the non-Priestly plague-narrative in 7.17, 27; 8.17; 9.3, 18: all preceded by הנה.

m. Heb. ארבה, the sing. being almost always used as a collective (of a single locust only in v. 19b, Ps. 109.23 and Job 39.20 [?]), though with sing. verbs following in v. 5 (also vv. 12, 14-15; but pl. in v. 6, for which cf. GK §145g). The word is commonly related to רבה, 'be many' (with prosthetic *aleph*), and its use in similes to express large numbers (Judg. 6.5; 7.12; Nah. 3.15b) would support this: there seems to be no alternative view.

n. Heb. גבול. בגבלך primarily means 'border', but is also used as a synonym for ארץ in the sense of a particular country or territory (cf. vv. 14 and 19 below; also 7.27 and 13.7).

o. Heb. עין, lit. 'eye', as again in v. 15 and in Num. 22.5, 11 (in the same phrase, again following כסה); it can also mean 'appearance, sparkle'. The basis for these metaphorical uses is not entirely clear, although they do all share the idea of 'the visible' (*THAT* 2, 265 = *TLOT* 2, p. 878, where it is pointed out that the more regular expression here would involve a metaphorical use of פנים, 'face').

p. Heb. יוכל, imperf. of יכל, here used with an indefinite subject, lit. 'one will not be able' (GK §144d-e).

q. The יתר is probably not a part of the residue (e.g. what had not been eaten: Houtman) but is qualified by הפליטה acc. to GK §128m.

r. Heb. ומלאו, i.e. Qal perf. cons. The Qal can be transitive, as well as meaning 'be full (of)' (BDB, p. 570). On the interpretation followed here, the locusts are now referred to in the pl. (contrast v. 5, and for the change cf. GK §145g). The other interpretation, which was once popular (see Text and Versions and Houtman), is less likely in the absence of a pronoun to refer to the locusts ('of them', 'with them').

s. Heb. אשר, in place of the normal כאשר: BDB, p. 83 (8.e) is dubious, but the sense 'as' is recognised in *HAL*, p. 95, and *Ges18*, p. 111, in a few cases including this one (cf. Sy). Deuteronomy 15.14 may be another example (cf. JB).

t. Normally the perfect of ידע would be used, but טרם and בטרם are (like עד sometimes) almost always followed (as here and in 9.30) by the imperfect, even when the reference is to the past (GK §107c, 152r). The rationale in these cases would seem to be neither duration (GK) nor a simple preterite (JM §113i-j), but the element of (non-)anticipation that is present in the conjunction/adverb.

u. The use of את with what appear to be subjects of the passive verb ויושב follows a quite widespread usage which is best explained by seeing the grammatical subject as the logical *patiens* of the verbal action: cf. e.g. Gen. 40.20 and most fully, J. Hoftijzer, 'Remarks concerning the use of the Particle *'t* in Classical Hebrew', *OTS* 14 (1965), pp. 1-99 (esp. pp. 14-15, 44). GK §121a-b and JM §128b prefer to see the use of את as being due to the passive verb being impersonal; but this is not always the case (cf. 2 Sam. 21.22; Jer. 36.22) and association with an impersonal active verb would be more readily explained in this way. In any case there is no reason to see את as conveying any special emphasis in this construction (see the careful review by Muraoka, *Emphatic Words*, pp. 146-58).

v. Heb. מי ומי, apparently a unique repetition in BH, which seems (unless it is purely emphatic) to invite a multiple reply. For the translation given see GK §137a.

w. Heb. ב here clearly indicates those who will accompany the adult males and females: cf. BDB, p. 89 (III.1.a-b), for this usage.

x. Cf. GK §127e.

y. At first sight Pharaoh's reply, which probably uses a regular formula of blessing (cf. 1 Sam. 20.13; 1 Kgs 1.37; Ruth 2.4; also *AHI* 8.021: Kuntillet Ajrud, Pithos B), appears to have a positive sense, and it was so understood in NEB. But the sequel in v. 11 makes it clear that it is ironic and represents precisely the opposite meaning: 'May the help of your God be *as far from you* as I am *far from* giving you permission to go forth with your little ones' (Cassuto, p. 125 [my italics]: cf. REB). Cassuto noted that the outcome makes its own ironic retort: 'in the end he will let them and their children go, and so the Lord will actually be with them' (cf. 12.31-32, with a recollection of this passage in 'as you said'). 'Little ones' or 'children' is, however, too narrow an interpretation of Heb טף, as v. 11 and 12.37 make clear (cf. *HAL*, p. 362, and P. Swiggers, *ZAH* 6 [1993], pp. 45-47).

z. Heb. נגד פניכם. The combination seems to be paralleled only in Isa. 5.21, where the sense is slightly different. More common is לנגד עיני, which can be used of having something in mind (e.g. Pss. 18.26; 36.2) and of a plan or purpose (Ps. 101.3).

aa. Heb. לא כן. The combination is well attested as part of verbal or nominal clauses (BDB, p. 486a): for the absolute (elliptical) use cf. Gen. 48.18, where the speaker again rejects a course of action that has been proposed.

bb. Heb. הגברים. It is not usual for an imperative to have a noun as subject – the jussive would be expected in such cases. A vocative interpretation might be considered ('O men'), but only Moses and Aaron are present (v. 8) and the reference must be wider than them. הגברים may perhaps best be seen as a noun in apposition to the pronoun subject of the verb which at the same time extends its reference (for some broadly similar phenomena see GK §126f, 131k-o).

cc. Heb. אתה. For the use of the fem. form of the obj. pronoun (which gains emphasis from its position before the subject) to refer generally to a preceding statement or request see GK §122q, 135p.

dd. Heb. ויגרש. The subject could theoretically be Pharaoh again, but his naming at the end of the verse makes it more likely that here the third person m.s. form has an indefinite force equivalent to a passive (GK §144d): cf. JPS, NRSV.

ee. Heb. נטה ידך, without את: cf. 9.5, 10.3 and for other examples of inconsistency in the use of את Muraoka, *Emphatic Words*, pp. 150-51, and JM §125f.

ff. Heb. בארבה. The usual preposition after נטה is על (cf. 9.22 and v. 21 below), but ב is sometimes used of direction towards with certain verbs (BDB, p. 89 [II.3]; the closest parallels would be נשא and קרב) and may be chosen here because על has appeared in the preceding phrase. Not only the definite article but the statement as a whole seem to assume that a swarm of locusts is already present to the east of Egypt.

gg. Heb. יהוה נִהַג. On the form of the verb see GK §64c-d. The precedence of the subject here (cf. 9.23) may simply be to make clear that a different subject is now to act (without any special emphasis or contrast: cf. GK §142a), but Muraoka has observed that such precedence of the subject is rather common when a divine agent is concerned and may have a religious basis (cf. *Emphatic Words*, p. 35; JM §155ne).

hh. Heb. רוח קדים. Presumably, as in the phrase ורוח הקדים later in the verse, קדים is a *nomen rectum*, defining the nature of the רוח (GK §128m); for קדים alone as meaning 'east wind' see e.g. Gen. 41.6.

ii. Where two successive subjects precede their verbs, 'rapid succession' is indicated (GK §164b[3]) and often the subordination of one clause to the other, e.g. Gen. 19.23; 44.3-4. JM §166j takes the second clause here as anterior to the first (cf. NRSV, Houtman), saying that 'the context' indicates this (the other examples of anteriority given all have *wayyiqtol* preceding), but מחר in v. 4 more naturally points to the locusts' arrival in the morning rather than in the night, and this is what the closest syntactical parallels also suggest.

jj. Heb. נשא, the third person m.s. form indicating that רוח is here viewed as masculine, as below in v. 19 (cf. חזק): *HAL*, p. 117, following K. Albrecht, 'Das Geschlecht der hebräischen Hauptwörter', *ZAW* 16 (1896), pp. 41-121 (42-44), lists 12 other definite examples of this in BH out of a total of 378 occurrences (some of which will be unclear as to the gender).

kk. Heb. וינח, from נוח Qal, which does not always have the sense 'rest, repose' (cf. Gen. 8.4; 2 Sam. 21.10); hence the (orthographically distinguished) Hiphil occurrences that mean 'place, put'.

ll. Heb. ותחשך. If the text is correct (and it probably is: see Text and Versions), the clause may be subordinate (indicating the result of the preceding action: cf. JM §169c), especially as it interrupts a sequence of clauses which have the same subject. Cf. v. 5, where a consecutive translation might also be appropriate (cf. NRSV and JM §169b, citing Isa. 8.10[?]).

mm. Heb. שא (in the sing. as if only Moses is addressed: cf. ויצא in v. 18), from נשא in the sense 'take away' (as literally in v. 19), hence of sins 'forgive' (as e.g. in Gen. 50.17 [also addressed to a human]; BDB, p. 671).

nn. Heb. אך הפעם. The def. art. with פעם, as with יום, can have demonstrative force: cf. 9.27 and Note dd on the translation of 9.13-35. As noted there אך or רק regularly precedes הפעם in such cases: on the 'restrictive' function of אך here see Muraoka, *Emphatic Words*, pp. 129-30.

oo. Heb. רק, on which see Muraoka, ibid., pp. 130-32, though he does not comment on this phrase. The sense must be 'only' in much the same sense as

אך is used earlier in the verse: in fact in Judg. 6.39 רק הפעם follows אך הפעם in a context which implies 'just once *more*'. So here the implication, if not the sense, may be 'just...too', sc. in addition to the previous time(s) when Yahweh has relented.

pp. Heb. את־המות הזה, lit. 'this death', the result being substituted for its cause. There appear to be no comparable uses of מות in BH, but in the story of Keret Ug. *mt* is twice used of what is elsewhere called an 'illness' or a 'plague' (*KTU* 1.16.6.1, 13; *CML*, pp. 100-101) and Gk. θάνατος is sometimes used in LXX for Heb. words meaning 'plague' (דבר: Exod. 5.3; 9.3, 15; Lev. 26.25; Num. 14.12; Deut. 28.21: cf. Lust et al., p. 201).

qq. Heb. הפך is occasionally used with two accusatives (cf. Lev. 13.10 [here the second is an adjective]; Ps. 114.8), the first denoting the prior state and the second the changed state (which is normally expressed with ל). Here the first accusative is to be understood from v. 13 ('it') and only the second appears.

rr. Heb. תקע is used often enough for forcing a weapon etc. into someone for it to mean 'forcibly convey' as well, but there are no close parallels in BH. Its alternative meaning 'blow' (on a musical instrument) might therefore be a better basis for its interpretation here (cf. Propp, p. 339).

ss. Heb. ויחזק: the causative Piel as previously in 4.21 and 9.12 and subsequently in 10.27; 11.10; 14.4, 8, 17; Josh. 11.20 (cf. the Qal in 7.13, 22; 8.15; 9.35).

Explanatory Notes

1-2. The new episode begins just like two earlier sections of the plague-story (cf. 7.26 and 9.1) but quickly departs from the general pattern: the regular statement of the message to be delivered to Pharaoh is missing. Instead Yahweh explains in more general terms why Moses is being instructed to approach Pharaoh on this and presumably the preceding occasions. The explanation proceeds in four stages which correspond to what are seen as a chain of actions, two performed by Yahweh and the third by the Israelites, and a final intended outcome, 'and you shall know that I am Yahweh'. The action to be performed by the Israelites, with its reference to future generations, lends the whole story a much more long-term purpose, which seems almost to lose sight of the present predicament of Israel in Egypt that has dominated the plague-narrative thus far. For the first time in the non-Priestly narrative the 'dulling' (Heb. *kbd* Hiphil) of Pharaoh's mind is attributed to Yahweh himself, and as in 9.34 (cf. v. 30) it is extended to 'his servants' or courtiers: the latter development sits uneasily with indications elsewhere in the surrounding context that some at least of Pharaoh's servants do indeed understand what is happening and react accordingly (9.20; 10.7). The prior action of Yahweh implies that Pharaoh's negative responses are predetermined, and accordingly Yahweh's severe treatment of him and the Egyptians more generally is probably no longer seen as the provision of 'signs' *for* them (cf. the use of different prepositions: 'in the midst' [v. 1], 'among' [or even 'against': Heb. *b*]) but for the Israelites of the present and future generations. This would contrast with the use of the same word (Heb. *'ōt*) in 8.19 and extend the provision of signs for Israel in the earlier chapters of the book (3.12; 4.8-9, 28, 30: 4.17 is not so clear) to include the plagues inflicted on Egypt.[9] At any rate the outcome is now that 'you', in the plural and referring to Israel, 'shall know that I am Yahweh', a formula which, while well known elsewhere, is only used in this way here in the non-Priestly Exodus story. Education is still a central purpose of it, but now in the sense that its recitation (v. 1b) is to teach subsequent generations of Israelites:[10] the attempt to educate Pharaoh (cf. 7.17 etc.), whose failure will soon be observed by his own subjects (v. 7b), becomes only part of the story that is to be told.

3-6. The narrative now returns to more familiar motifs, albeit in a new setting. Yahweh's message for Pharaoh includes the demand for his people's release (v. 3b) and the conditional threat of a plague, this time of locusts, which is described in some detail (vv. 4-6a). But instead of it being revealed to Moses without any account (except in the 'Samaritan' expansion of the narrative) of its delivery to Pharaoh, this time the narrator recounts the initial encounter with Pharaoh, and without any prior indication of what Moses and Aaron are going to say. This is clearly because of the negotiations which are shortly to take place in an effort to avert the plague (vv. 7-11),

---

[9] For this view of the plagues see also Num. 14.11, 22; Deut. 6.22; 7.19; 11.3; 26.8; 29.2; 34.11-12. The Priestly view is different again: the plagues are signs for the Egyptians, but from the beginning it is intended that they will not have their effect until the whole process of deliverance is complete (7.3-5; 14.4, 18). The 'sign' for the Israelites in P is Yahweh's dwelling in their midst in the sacred tent or tabernacle (29.45-46; cf. 6.7) and, even more explicitly, the regular observance of the Sabbath (31.12-17). The Passover law (12.13) uses the idea of a 'sign' in a different way.

[10] This theme is taken up again, in a different way, in 13.3-16 (with more references to 'signs' in vv. 9 and 16).

not merely to reduce its effects (as in 9.19-21) or to secure its removal (as in 8.4-7; 21-25; 9.27-30, and again in 10.16-18).[11] The additional scene in Pharaoh's palace enables the narrator to raise the reader's hopes that perhaps at last Pharaoh is ready to respond to Yahweh's warnings before they are put into effect. A more explicit indication that the narrative is reaching its climax and that this may be Pharaoh's last chance comes in the new opening of Yahweh's message with its accusing question 'How long?' (v. 3a), a phrase whose significance will be underlined by its use by Pharaoh's own servants in v. 7 (cf. also 'not yet' there, and Dozeman, p. 240).

The description of the threatened locust plague reinforces the impression that the screw is being tightened for Pharaoh with increasing severity. The allusions to the preceding context are unusually specific. The unprecedented hailstorm of 9.23-25 (cf. v. 18) had at least left some of the crops and trees standing (v. 5; cf. vv. 12 and 15). But there is coming a swarm of locusts (Heb. *ʾarbeh*) so unique that no vegetation will survive it, and like the frogs in 7.28-29 they will even come into the Egyptians' homes (v. 6a). Biblical Hebrew has a rich vocabulary for the locust and related insects (see e.g. Joel 1.4), but *ʾarbeh* is the most frequent and widely distributed of them. It is not certain whether the different words refer to different species, different stages of growth or both. Possibly they are sometimes used without any clear distinction of meaning. Their devastating effect on all kinds of vegetation has frequently been witnessed in modern times (e.g. in 1915 in Palestine [L. Bauer, 'Die Heuschreckenplage in Palästina', *ZDPV* 49 (1926), pp. 168-71] and in North Africa in 1988 [Hoffmeier, *Israel in Egypt*, p. 148]). Not surprisingly several references to such plagues occur in the OT: in addition to this passage and others alluding to it (Pss. 78.46; 105.34), in a covenant curse (Deut. 28.38: cf. the Sefire Treaty, *KAI* 222 A 27), in prophecy (Joel 1.4; 2.25) and in a prayer (1 Kgs 8.37 = 2 Chr. 6.28: cf. a Neo-Assyrian prayer for Sargon II, *COS* 1, p. 473).[12] Locusts are also frequent in comparisons, especially as being very numerous (Judg. 6.5; 7.12; Jer. 46.23; Neh. 3.15), but also for other reasons (Nah. 3.17; Ps. 109.23; Job 39.20: cf. *KTU* 1.2.10; 1.14.4.29). The Priestly dietary law permitted them to be eaten (Lev. 11.22; they are

---

[11] The connection is well seen by L. Schmidt, *Beobachtungen*, p. 39.

[12] In all the passages cited *ʾarbeh* occurs: for passages using other words see e.g. Isa. 33.4; Amos 4.9; 7.1.

not mentioned in Deut. 14.3-20, but v. 19 would seem to exclude them) and a wisdom saying recognised with admiration their instinctive ability to move together (Prov. 30.27). The descriptions of their activity in the present passage could easily have been taken from the writers' experience in Palestine (see also below on vv. 13 and 19).

Nothing is said of Pharaoh's initial response to the warning, but Moses' abrupt departure (v. 6b, perhaps echoing Pharaoh's in 7.23) and the reaction of Pharaoh's courtiers in v. 7 leave no doubt that it was unyielding.

7. The intervention of Pharaoh's servants is unexpected after their inclusion with him in v. 1 as the objects of Yahweh's bemusement, probably a further sign that a redactor has been at work in vv. 1-2. But the intervention is itself a new feature of the narrative, which goes beyond and no doubt arises from the response of some of Pharaoh's officials to Moses' previous warning in 9.20 and its evident success (9.25). Again Pharaoh is faced with the question 'How long?', but his servants initially temper their criticism of him by making Moses the source of their troubles (Heb. *zeh*, 'this', in the masculine form is likely to mean 'this man', rather than, as Propp [cf. LXX] suggests, 'this [situation]'). 'Snare' (Heb. *môqēš*) is originally a hunter's trap (Amos 3.5), but it is most often used metaphorically of a cause of death or ruin. Common sense makes it better to yield to Moses' demand, and in their parting shot these advisers turn their criticism on Pharaoh's own blindness, and show that they at least recognise ('know') how desperate the situation has become.

8-11. Pharaoh, it seems, sees the sense of this advice. Moses and Aaron are recalled and granted permission to leave. But Pharaoh is clearly suspicious about their real intentions (cf. v. 10b) and enquires further about who will participate in the worship. His revised plan (pursued in a different way in v. 24) is evidently to retain the Israelites' women and children as, in effect, hostages to ensure that the men do return to Egypt after their festival is over (Heb. *ṭap* in v. 10 means more than 'little ones' [NRSV: see Note y on the translation], as the contrast with the word for 'men' in v. 11 [Heb. *gᵉbārîm*, 'adult males'] shows). Moses' insistence on the attendance of the whole people because 'it is a festival of Yahweh' may have seemed devious to some readers of the story: the laws later in Exodus about such 'pilgrimage feasts' (Heb. *ḥag*) required only the adult males to be present (23.17; 34.23: cf. Deut. 16.16, although vv. 11 and 14 imply a wider participation). Pharaoh's refusal begins with the mocking irony that reasserts his superiority: he will decide who may leave. This brings the negotiations to a sudden end, and this time Pharaoh, apparently back in control, does not wait for Moses and Aaron to leave: they are expelled from his presence.

12-15. The initiative remains with Yahweh, nevertheless, and the coming of the locusts is set in motion in exactly the same way as the previous plague of hail (9.22-23): again Moses understands the stretching out of his 'hand' to mean the use of his staff. The description of the locust plague follows closely the wording of the warning in vv. 5-6 (note especially the recurrence of the rare phrase 'the surface [Heb. *'ên*, "eye"] of [all] the land' in v. 15), but with two significant variations. The locusts are now brought by the action of a 'natural cause', an east wind, albeit one stirred up by Yahweh himself (v. 13: cf. 14.21). The 'east wind' (Heb. *qādîm*, which is related to other words referring to the east) is frequently mentioned elsewhere in the OT as a source of drought and destruction, both in Egypt and more often in Palestine (e.g. Hos. 13.15): it corresponds to the Arabic *sirocco*, which also originally meant 'eastern'. Hebrew has only words for the main compass points, so that anything from north-east to south-east could be referred to as 'east', and this may be why the Septuagint translators, who knew where locusts generally came from in Egypt felt justified in using here a word meaning 'south wind' (see Text and Versions, and also the note on 'west wind' in v. 19). The second major variation from the warning in vv. 5-6 is that the activity of the locusts is confined to the open fields and nothing is said about their entry into the Egyptians' houses.[13] Unlike the three previous plagues in the non-Priestly account (8.18-19; 9.4-7, 26) and the next one (10.23) there is no reference to the Israelites being spared on this occasion: perhaps it was taken for granted in what is already a long and complex narrative.

There is less evidence of duplicate narration here than in 9.22-26 (v. 14a is the most obvious case), but the major variations from the warning given earlier and some lesser differences may be signs

---

[13] The five occurrences of the word 'all' in v. 15 ('nothing' is literally 'all... not') represent an understandable heightening of the description. The statement that 'the land became dark' (for the textual variants see Text and Versions) fits exactly descriptions of locust plagues given in modern times such as the 'black ravenous carpet' in the report cited by Hoffmeier, *Israel in Egypt*, p. 148, as well as the likely sense of Joel 2.2.

that a second version of the plague was used here too. The repeated mention of Moses and his staff is also a striking contrast to the main sequence of plague narratives and probably points in the same direction (see further the introduction to this section).

16-17. As before, but with an additional emphasis on haste, Pharaoh's reaction to the devastation of the plague is to seek an end to it through the intercession of Moses and Aaron.[14] Again, as in 9.27, he acknowledges that he has 'sinned' (does this refer in part to 9.34?), and here he takes all the blame himself, rather than sharing it with his people. Perhaps in the light of the fraught exchanges in vv. 8-11, Moses and Aaron are viewed as the offended party as much as Yahweh himself and it is Moses' forgiveness (see Note 14) that he seeks rather than Yahweh's. For him at least, the narrative is still being played out largely at the inter-human level: it is only Moses who deals directly with Yahweh. Two features of Pharaoh's request add to the sense that the sequence of plagues is reaching its climax (as observed, among others, by Childs, p. 160, and Houtman, p. 101): he twice in different words asks to be spared just one more time, and he refers to the plague, in a unique use of the Hebrew word, as 'this death' (see Note pp on the translation). To paraphrase this as, for example, 'this deadly scourge' is almost unavoidable, but the anticipation of what is soon to follow in 12.29-30 (cf. 11.4-6) is surely deliberate (compare also the statement of Pharaoh's servants in v. 7 that Egypt is already 'ruined'). The one motif that is missing here is any promise by Pharaoh of what he will do, in contrast to all the previous requests for Moses' intercession (8.4, 21; 9.28) and to Pharaoh's response to the next plague (10.24) and indeed the final one (12.31-32). Few commentators observe this: of those who do Houtman (p. 101) suggests that Pharaoh overlooked it because he was too upset, while Schmidt (pp. 431, 433) seems to view it in the light of vv. 24-26, which he regards as containing more of the conclusion to this episode (like others before him: see the introduction to 10.21-29).

18-19. The real surprise, which neither of the explanations just mentioned deals with, is that neither Moses nor Yahweh seems perturbed by the lack of any assurance that Pharaoh will now let Israel

---

[14] Aaron is only half-involved: not only is it Moses alone who makes the prayer (v. 18) but Pharaoh's plea for forgiveness is, in the older MT version (see Text and Versions), addressed to Moses alone.

go. Moses proceeds as before to intercede, and Yahweh as before removes the plague. It is as if by now both know that Pharaoh's assurances are worthless, yet even so his plea finds a response and the land is spared further devastation. There is of course some inconsistency with v. 15 in this, and it may be that these verses (and vv. 16-17) belong to a different strand of the narrative in which the destruction by the locusts was halted before it was complete.

The removal of the locusts, like their coming, is attributed to Yahweh's control of the wind, which is now turned in the opposite direction, apparently. The expression 'west wind' (Heb. *rûaḥ yām*) means literally 'wind of [probably "from"] (the) sea' and it occurs only here. But '(the) sea' is one quite frequent designation elsewhere for 'the west', as this is the direction in which the (Mediterranean) sea lies from the perspective of Palestine (so very clearly in Gen. 13.14 and 28.14, with the other three cardinal points of the compass). The fact that in Egypt (at least in the Nile Delta region) the sea lies to the north could have been overlooked by the narrator from his standpoint in, presumably, Judah or Israel, but any problem would be alleviated by the fact, noted above on vv. 12-15, that in Hebrew the main compass points have to cover a wide range, and so 'west' could include 'north-west', for example.[15] The place where the locusts are 'driven' is called in the Heb. Yam Suf. In the Septuagint and early Jewish and Christian literature in Greek and Latin this was equated with 'the Red Sea' and especially the two Gulfs of Suez and Aqaba/Eilat which surround the Sinai peninsula on the west and the east (cf. my *Way of the Wilderness*, pp. 6-9, 31, 39-43 for details). But 'Yam Suf' does not *mean* 'Red Sea', and the fact that Heb. *sûp* means 'reeds, vegetation' (as in Exod. 2.3) led to the adoption by Martin Luther (on the basis of Rashi's comment on Exod. 13.18) of the translation *Schilfmeer*, 'Sea of Reeds'. In the late nineteenth century it was argued by the Egyptologist H. Brugsch that the expression, so understood, was equivalent to an Egyptian term (now written *ṯwf[y]*, 'papyrus') and that it referred or could refer to one or more of the lakes east of the Nile Delta (cf. *Way of the Wilderness*, pp. 70-74: see also *TWAT* 5, 794-800 = *TDOT* 10, pp. 190-96). This conclusion has been widely adopted,

---

[15] It was not a problem for the Septuagint translators or for the Neofiti version of the Palestinian Targum, who rendered literally 'from the sea' (see Text and Versions).

either instead of or in conjunction with the traditional equation with (parts of) the Red Sea, and it is clearly of great relevance to discussion about the nature and location of the Israelites' 'crossing of the sea' when they left Egypt, a question which will be discussed later in this commentary. Here it is sufficient to observe that the stretches of water in question all lay to the east (or south-east) of the site(s) in the Nile Delta where the plague-narrative is set by its author(s). Schmidt apparently follows (p. 431) a view that the Gulf of Aqaba may be meant as the destination of the locusts, but this is some 200 miles away and it is more likely that one of the nearer bodies of water, either the Gulf of Suez to the south-east or one of the lakes to the east, is meant here. Removal to one of these would be quite sufficient to end the catastrophe in Egypt.

20. The wording here (including 'made stubborn', Heb. *ḥzq* Piel) corresponds closely to 9.35 and the ending of the earlier Priestly plague-stories (7.13 etc.), but the explicit attribution of Pharaoh's stubbornness to Yahweh has appeared only in 7.3 (Heb. *qšh* Hiphil) and 9.12 so far: it will recur in 10.27 and 11.10, and later in 14.4, 17.[16] In 9.35 the corresponding expression is clearly a duplicate of 9.34, and it is likely that here too it belongs to a different strand from the main narrative, which may not have ended on such a negative note (see further the introductions to this section and, more fully, the next).

Text and Versions

4QExod^c, 4QpalExod^l and 4QpalExod^m all show evidence of a major text-division between ch. 9 and ch. 10, in the latter two cases with a (mainly) blank line as well as an 'open' line before (*DJD* IX, pp. 30, 81; *DJD* XII, p. 109).

יהוה (10.1)   Tg^{Nmg} as usual prefixes 'the Memra of'. In LXX λέγων is added afterwards to introduce the direct speech, like similar participles in 3.12; 6.6; 7.1; 9.8; 12.43; 15.21; 18.6; 19.21 in Exodus 1–20.

בא (10.1)   See Note a on 9.1.

הכבדתי (10.1)   While most of the Vss employ the same equivalent as in 9.34, Vulg has *induravi*, probably because of its rendering of חזק in the adjacent 9.35. The same deviation from MT is found in some LXX (and OL) witnesses.

לבו...לב (10.1)   LXX and Vulg understandably represent לב only once. Tg^J prefixes יצר to לב both times, as e.g. in 9.34-35.

---

[16] In 10.1 the verb (Heb. *kbd* Hiphil) and the sense are different.

עבדיו (10.1) Tg^N has 'his rulers', but the mg corrects to agree with MT.

שתי (10.1) LXX rewrites the remainder of the verse, removing specific references to divine involvement (Wevers, *Notes*, p. 144), adding a note of hostility (*BAlex* 2, p. 135) and highlighting by the addition of ἑξῆς the succession of plagues that is to follow. Vulg *faciam* and Sy *ʿbd* also avoid the unusual idea of 'placing' signs, but in other respects follow MT more closely.

אתתי (10.1) 4QExod^c appears originally to have omitted the end of v. 1 and most of v. 2 by parablepsis (cf. ואת־אתתי in v. 2aβ) and then to have inserted the missing material above the line (*DJD* XII, p. 111: a less likely possibility is that the scribe accidentally omitted a line of text in his exemplar). Neither LXX nor Sy represents the pron. suffix; Tg^Nmg expands with 'and my wonders' in accordance with 7.3.

בקרבו (10.1) LXX ἐπ'αὐτούς (cf. Tgg, Sy) and Vulg *in eo* are most likely free renderings of the MT/SP text rather than (in the former case) pointing to a *Vorlage* בקרבם (Propp, p. 303).

ולמען (10.2) LXX has simply ὅπως, seeing what follows as the purpose of the 'signs' rather than of the 'dulling' of the Egyptians' hearts.

תספר (10.2) LXX has second person pl., as it does throughout the verse, conforming to the final verb in MT (so also in part Tg^N and Vulg).

באזני (10.2) Tg^O, Sy ('before') and Tg^J,N ('in the hearing of') render freely.

ובן־בנך (10.2) LXX καὶ τοῖς τέκνοις τῶν τέκνων ὑμῶν not only employs the pl. but detaches the phrase from the *nomen regens* באזני, by making it an indirect object of the verb.

את אשר (10.2) LXX ὅσα and Vulg *quotiens* render the Heb. freely.

התעללתי (10.2) Only LXX (ἐμπέπαιχα) gives the sense 'mock, make sport of' here: the other Vss are divided between the senses 'do' (generally; Sy, and with 'signs' added in the main clause, Tg^O,J) and 'wear out, confound' (Vulg, Tg^N). But, as *AramB* 7, p. 26 n. 2, points out well, the translators were apparently constrained here by a desire not to ascribe an inappropriate action to God, and in places where the verb has a non-divine subject (e.g. Num. 22.29) they used renderings like 'laugh (at)' (חייך: Tg^O), 'mock' (*bzh*: Sy; [*commereo* and] *illudo*: Vulg), 'act deceitfully' (שקר: Tg^J,N) and even 'took vengeance' (פרע: Tg^Nmg). See further Note g on the translation: given that (apparently) such meanings for עלל were current in post-biblical Heb. and Aram., the Vss may have imported them from contemporary usage when they were not present in BH.

ואת אתתי (10.2) Sy did not represent the possessive suffix; Tg^Nmg has 'the signs of my wonders' (cf. its version of v. 1).

שמתי (10.2) LXX, Vulg and Sy have 'did' rather than 'put'.

וידעתם (10.2) Vulg *et sciatis* treats this as a final clause, still governed by the *ut* in v. 1. Tg^Nmg has 'and they shall know', missing the difference from verses like 9.29, which refer to the Egyptians: but here Israel's descendants could be meant.

יהוה (10.2) SP adds אלהיכם, assimilating to the otherwise identical phrase in 6.7. The addition is recorded not only in the Heb. mss of SP but in the Sam. Greek version cited in Sy^hex (Wevers, *Exodus*, p. 149: see the next note).

After 10.2 SP adds ואמרת אל־פרעה and then, in its own slightly divergent form of the text (on which see the notes on the following verses), the wording of vv. 3aβ-6a, so including in Yahweh's instruction the exact words which Moses (with Aaron) is to speak to Pharaoh. This is the opposite to what SP does after 7.18, 7.29, 8.19, 9.5 and 9.19, where the 'missing' *fulfilment* of an instruction given by Yahweh is added, but the motivation is the same: to produce a narrative that has no awkward gaps. Essentially the same addition after 10.2 is attested in Sy^hex, though it is noteworthy that the added text is based, as elsewhere, on the fuller and sometimes divergent LXX version of vv. 3aβ-6a (for which see below in the notes). At Qumran 4QpalEx^l seems unlikely to have had this addition, though the possibility cannot be excluded (*DJD* IX, pp. 30-31), and 4QEx^c certainly did not have it. On the other hand there is strong indirect evidence that 4QpalEx^m, as elsewhere, did have the expanded text here and that the meagre remains of col. vi.27-29 represent the additional material, while those in vi.30-33 and vii.1-4 correspond to Moses and Aaron's actual address to Pharaoh in vv. 3-6.

ויבא (10.3) See the note on בא in 9.1. Here Tg^N, as well as Sy, has 'came'. Vulg's pl. *introierunt* and Sy *w'tw* accommodate to the composite subject rather than presupposing a divergent *Vorlage*, for which there is no other evidence.

אל־פרעה (10.3) LXX unusually has ἐναντίον, 'before', as in 7.10 (where the original Heb. may have been לפני: see the note there), treating the clause as an abbreviation of the fuller expression in e.g. 9.13 (Wevers, *Notes*, p. 145). 4QExod^c's insertion of במצר[ים] is quite unnecessary here and is probably part of the material inserted above the line to restore what the original scribe had omitted in v. 2 (see the note on אתה in 10.1 for 4QExod^c's carelessness in this passage). It is in exactly the right place before אתה ו[א] on the adjacent fr.

העברים (10.3) Tg^O has 'of the Jews' as usual, but Tg^J exceptionally renders 'of Israel' for no discernible reason.

מאנת (10.3) LXX and Sy render as usual 'you do not wish' (see the note on 9.2: Vulg's *non vis* is the regular form from *nolo*).

לענת (10.3) LXX's ἐντραπῆναί με, 'respect, reverence me', is a unique rendering of the (rare) Niphal of ענה III, but it is used for other verbs meaning 'be humbled' and Wevers rightly describes it as 'simple and elegant' (*Notes*, p. 146). Vulg's stronger equivalent *subici* seems to be based on an unattributed Greek rendering ὑπεῖξαι, 'yield, submit to', which is reflected in some OL sources.

מפני (10.3) Tg^N has 'before YHWH', probably from a wrong word-division (cf. Tg^J קדמי).

עמי (10.3) SP and 4QpalEx^l prefix את, assimilating to v. 4: 4QpalEx^m preserves only a few letters of this verse, so its reading is uncertain.

ויעבדני (10.3) Vulg *ut sacrificet*, as regularly since 7.16 (see the note there). Tgg as usual render the suffix 'before me'.

מאן אתה (10.4) LXX uses (μὴ) θέλῃς this time, perhaps for variety after (οὐ) βούλει in v. 3. There seems to be no sign of the distinction between the words noted in LSJ, p. 325 ('consent' vs. 'wish'). Vulg has the double rendering *resistis et non vis*, making the active refusal more evident, as it is in the Tgg.

את עמי (10.4) Vulg *eum*, for brevity.

הנני (10.4) A final ה[survives in 4QpalEx^m where this word would appear, leading *DJD* IX, p. 81, to suggest that the ms. may have had [אנכי] ה[נ]ה, as in the very similar sentence in 7.27 (cf. 7.17; 8.25). If so, the variant must be attributed to assimilation.

מביא (10.4) LXX adds ταύτην τὴν ὥραν, its rendering for כעת in 9.18, from where the expression may be drawn.

ארבה (10.4) The renderings in the Vss (LXX ἀκρίς; Vulg *lucusta*; Tgg (inc. Tg^F) גובא; Sy *qmṣʾ*) can all mean 'locust', even if they are sometimes used for other species as well. LXX adds πολλήν, which is its rendering for כבד in v. 14 (and 9.18): no doubt the threat is being conformed secondarily to the outcome.

בגבולך (10.4) LXX ἐπὶ πάντα (cf. Sy *ʿl klh*) τὰ ὅριά σου, implying בכל as in vv. 14 and 19 below, with further assimilation of the threat to the outcome.

את־עין הארץ (10.5) LXX (τὴν ὄψιν), Tg^{J,N} and Sy (the last simply using *ʿyn*) represent עין in a way close to its sense in Heb. without completely clarifying the meaning: only Vulg's *superficiem* does this. Tg^O, with עין שמשא (as in v. 15 and Num. 22.5), betrays some unease with the simple rendering and may intend something like Heb. תחת השמש: it is in any case followed by דארעא, which must indicate 'the sun's view *of the earth*' (rather than the opposite, as *AramB* 7, p. 27 n. 5, envisages).

ולא יוכל (10.5) LXX and Tg^N use second person verbs, presumably referring to Pharaoh, to clarify the indefinite Heb., but thereby introduce too much precision: much better is Sy's addition of *br ʾnšʾ*, 'a (son of) man', i.e. anyone.

ואכל (10.5) Tg^J renders (both times) with וישיצי, 'will destroy', a possible sense for אכל, but probably more than is intended here. The rest of v. 5bα is rendered precisely by Tgg, but very freely in LXX, Vulg and Sy, though without any clear indication of a *Vorlage* different from MT, with which SP agrees here (except for a variant הנשארות – pl. in apposition to פליטה? – in two mss).

את־כל העץ (10.5) Between כל and העץ SP has עשב הארץ ואת כל פרי, and most of this additional text is preserved in 4QpalEx^m.[17] The Vss agree with MT in not having the plus. It corresponds exactly to words in v. 15 (the

---

[17] Not enough of 4QEx^c survives for it to be clear whether it too had the 'SP' plus.

fulfilment of this threat), from which the fuller text probably took it (cf. the expansions in LXX noted in v. 4). Although it might seem that the MT reading here is deficient (in mentioning only the effect on trees), the preceding clause (which has no equivalent in v. 15) probably has the effect on other vegetation in view.

מן השדה (10.5) There is some divergence from MT's preposition in LXX ἐπί, Vulg *in* and Sy *b*, but this is due simply to a free rendering of essentially the same sense.

ומלאו (10.6) Most of the Vss render by a passive verb, implying that 'the houses' are the subject and the meaning is 'shall be full' (but see Note r on the translation). Only Vulg and possibly some mss of Sy, which have the ambiguous Peal form, give the sense 'shall fill' (with the locusts as the subj.).

ובתי כל־עבדיך (10.6) LXX does not represent כל here (cf. Sy: Propp, p. 304, follows this reading), but has καὶ πᾶσαι αἱ οἰκίαι for the next phrase. Wevers suggests that LXX's *Vorlage* may have had כל in a different place (*Notes*, p. 147), but the variation may be due to the translator. In any case it is unlikely to be original, since SP and 4QpalEx^m support MT, as do the other Vss (except for Vulg's free rendering), and a double occurrence of כל in the same Heb. construct chain is most improbable. Tg^N, as elsewhere, has the contextually appropriate 'rulers', but its mg reverts to the Heb. expression.

כל־מצרים (10.6) LXX ἐν πάσῃ γῇ Αἰγύπτου, breaking up the construct chain to create an adverbial phrase and adding γη to reinforce the local interpretation of מצרים, which is less likely here.

לא (10.6) LXX renders with οὐδέποτε, giving greater intensity, in keeping with what follows.

ואבות אבתיך (10.6) LXX οὐδὲ οἱ πρόπαπποι αὐτῶν, 'nor their great-grandfathers', preferring the idiomatic expression to strict verbatim accuracy.

היותם (10.6) Vulg *orti sunt* and Tg^{Nmg} הוון שריין, 'they dwelt', clarify the sense of Heb. היה here.

ויפן ויצא (10.6) LXX adds Μωυσῆς as subject, but many mss (inc. Alexandrinus) omit it, as did Symm, to conform to MT. Or was the addition a secondary development in the Greek tradition? LXX's ἐκκλίνας ... ἐξῆλθεν (without a second καί) follows good Greek style. Sy *whpkw npqw* (without 'and') follows a Syriac idiom for 'went back out', but this is not exactly what Heb. means and some mss read *whpkw wnpqw* which gives the correct sense of MT. They include 5b1, so this may be the original reading of Sy. The pl. forms are presumably intended to include Aaron (cf. v. 3), but the sing. of MT and SP is the more difficult reading and surely correct. Tg^N וזר, 'and he went quickly' (and the mg addition of וכון, perhaps 'and deliberately'), departs further from Heb. and may allude to a midrash (cf. *AramB* 2, p. 41 n. 5).

In 4QEx^c no text from v. 6 survives, but the space available suggests that there was a *vacat*, either after v. 6a (where SP has a division) or at the end of the verse (*DJD* XII, pp. 111-12).

ויאמרו (10.7)   LXX λέγουσιν δέ, using the historic present as occasionally in Exodus (cf. Wevers, *Notes*, p. 18; and more fully Evans, *Verbal Syntax*, p. 119 with n. 2).

עבדי פרעה (10.7)   Sy ʿbdwhy lprʿwn expresses the sense differently, 'his servants (said) to Pharaoh', presumably for stylistic reasons.

זה (10.7)   LXX, Vulg and Sy treat זה as neuter, 'this (situation)', for which זאת would be more normal. Vulg *patiemur* for לנו...יהיה is a consequential paraphrase. The specific reference to Moses is maintained by Tgg, with especial clarity in Tg^J's דין גברא, 'this man'.

למוקש (10.7)   Most of the Vss shift the metaphor from 'snare' to 'stumbling-block' (Tgg, Symm, Vulg, Sy). LXX's σκῶλον (to which Aq prefixed εἰς to represent the ל) does not mean this (*pace* Wevers, *Notes*, p. 148) but 'thorn', as *BAlex* 2, pp. 38-39, sees: it is used again for מוקש in Deut. 7.16 and Judg. 8.27. The Samareitikon's εἰς ἄτας, 'for ruin', interprets the metaphor well (cf. Salvesen, *Symmachus*, p. 82).

האנשים (10.7)   4QExc preserves most of this word, which is also attested by SP and most of the Vss: Tg^N's עמא (which was corrected by its mg) assimilates to the common wording as, e.g., in v. 3.

את־יהוה (10.7)   Tgg as usual have 'before the Lord'.

הטרם תדע (10.7)   Tg^O,J, Sy and Symm reflect the sense of MT precisely, and Vulg *nonne vides* is close to this. LXX, which had rendered טרם correctly by οὐδέπω in 9.30, gives a paraphrase here which seems to ignore it: ἢ εἰδέναι βούλει, 'or do you want to know [i.e. discover?]...?' The Samareitikon (πρὶν γνῷς, again different from LXX) and Tg^N read טרם in the sense of בטרם, 'before', but this does not fit the context.

כי אבדה מצרים (10.7)   Tg^J 'that *by his hand* the land of Egypt *is going to perish*' introduces a reference to the dream of Pharaoh about Moses' future victory which it had included at 1.15 (see Text and Versions there).

ויושב (10.8)   The majority of SP mss (inc. Tal and Camb. 1846) read וישב, but a few have וישוב (Qal? see Crown) or וישיב (Hiphil). The majority text should probably be read as Hiphil (indef. 3rd m.s.), with which the following nouns with את fit easily: MT is clearly the more difficult reading (see Note u on the translation) and to be preferred. LXX, Vulg, Sy and Tg^N all render with active verbs, but could be paraphrasing MT; Tg^O and Tg^J retain the passive, the latter with the addition of פקיד, which is perhaps a pass. part. as in *AramB*'s 'the order was given' (but פקיד is very often the equivalent of active forms of צוה in Tg^J).

ויאמר (10.8)   Tg^N ואמרו, probably miscopied from the beginning of v. 7.

עבדו (10.8)   Vulg uses *sacrifico* as elsewhere for עבד (as in v. 7: and see the note on 7.16). Tg^Nmg prefixes *waw* to avoid asyndeton.

את־יהוה (10.8)   Tgg (and here Sy) have 'before the Lord'.

מי ומי (10.8)   Vulg's *quinam* is probably its way of representing the emphasis implied by the duplication of מי (cf. its *quidnam* for מה־זאת in Gen. 12.18; 42.48). Sy prefixes ʾlʾ, 'but', to indicate Pharaoh's reservation.

652   EXODUS 1–18

ההלכים (10.8)   Neither Sy nor Sperber's text of Tg⁰ expressly represent the Heb. def. art., although several mss of the latter have דאזלין like Tg^J. There is probably no text-critical significance in the variation.

ויאמר משה (10.9)   Sy has *'mr lh mšh*, 'Moses said to him', without the initial *waw* and with a pronoun to refer to Pharaoh; the one ms. of Tg^J omits 'Moses'. These variants reflect no more than stylistic changes or, in the latter case, scribal error. In addition to SP, both 4QEx^c and 4QpalEx^m support the reading ויאמר.

בנערינו ובזקנינו נלך (10.9)   These words were originally omitted by homoeoarkton in 4QEx^c, but were subsequently added above the line. LXX and Vulg adapt the list of participants to the greater economy of Greek and Latin style, omitting the possessive and the preposition in most cases and also any equivalent to the second נלך.

בבנינו ובבנותנו (10.9)   Tg^J adds ניזיל, 'we will go', after its equivalent to this phrase, to create full symmetry.

בצאננו (10.9)   LXX καὶ προβάτοις, making the last four nominal expressions into a connected sequence.

חג־יהוה (10.9)   Tgg have 'a festival *before* the Lord' (cf. their treatment of the expression 'worship the Lord' e.g. in v. 8).

לנו (10.9)   LXX τοῦ θεοῦ ἡμῶν suggests a misreading of this as אלהינו, which Vulg *(Domini) nostri* only partly corrected towards MT (cf Sy^h). LXX^B* omitted the whole phrase, as did OL[104].

יהי (10.10)   So MT and 4QpalEx^m, and a jussive rendering is given in LXX, Vulg and Tg^O,J. But SP has the imperfect יהיה, 'will be', and Tg^N יהוי and Sy *nhw'* might be so understood. Both the strength of textual support and the morphological difference from אשלח in the comparative clause favour יהי as the original reading: יהיה etc. could be designed to 'smooth' the grammatical structure, as SP often does.

כן (10.10)   Tg^O,N have כען, 'now', leading to a temporal interpretation of כאשר. But this is not a regular meaning of כן (Neh. 2.16 is a possible instance) or of any word like it in BH. 4QpalEx^m and SP agree with MT, as do the other Vss (and Tg^O mss and Tg^Nmg).

יהוה (10.10)   Tgg (all) prefix 'the Memra of'.

עמכם (10.10)   Tg^O,J,Nmg (but not Tg^N itself) have בסעדכון, 'your helper', as elsewhere, clarifying the sense but also avoiding anthropomorphism.

ואת־טפכם (10.10)   LXX μὴ καὶ τὴν ἀποσκευὴν ὑμῶν; reads the words as a separate clause expressing an elliptical question: 'as I shall release you, shall I also (release) your dependants?' But it is much more likely that כאשר refers back to the preceding כן and that ואת־טפכם is a second object of אשלח, as the other Vss all understand it. The rendering of טף by ἀποσκευή is fully discussed by Lee, *Lexical Study*, pp. 101-107 (cf. *BAlex*, 2, p. 39), who shows that in Hellenistic Greek ἀποσκευή could mean (or include) 'human dependants' (usually of a soldier) as well as 'baggage'. Sy *'yqrtkwn*, 'baggage', may

ראו כי (10.10) Vulg *cui dubium est quod* is an imprecise paraphrase (did it read ראוּי?), while Sy's *ḥzw dyn dlm'*, 'But see/consider, lest...', is even further from the Heb. Tgg, with the exception of Tg^N, begin closer to MT but amplify freely (see *AramB* 7, p. 27 n. 7 for an extensive discussion of variant readings and interpretations).

לא כן (10.11) SP לכן, 'Therefore', is the easier reading (see Note aa on the translation) and it could have arisen from conflating the two words in MT (all other witnesses, inc. 4QpalEx^m, support the division) and treating the *aleph* as a vowel letter (cf. *GSH* §16a). Tg^J ('as you think') and Vulg *fiet* amplify the abrupt Heb.

לכו (10.11) LXX oddly has a 3rd pl. imper. here (which simplifies the clause) and a 2nd pl. for עבדו. Tg^J prefixes אלהין, 'but', to make the connection clearer.

את־יהוה (10.11) LXX renders by τῷ θεῷ in a common variation; SP agrees with MT, as do the other Vss (Tgg and Sy as often prefix 'before').

ויגרש (10.11) MT's (indefinite, equivalent to a passive) sing. form is reflected in Tgg, but SP, LXX and Sy have the pl., probably as a secondary change to make clear that Pharaoh himself is not the subject. The *Vorlage* of Vulg's passive rendering (*eiecti sunt*, to which *statim* is prefixed as a common way to enliven the narrative: cf. 34.2) cannot be determined.

יהוה (10.12) Tg^Nmg prefixes 'the Memra of'.

נטה (10.12) Tg^O,J and Sy have 'raise', assuming an upward movement, while Tg^N conversely has ארכן, 'incline, bend down' (so again in v. 13). All seek to add more precision than the Heb. merits.

ידך (10.12) SP prefixes את, conforming to the wording of v. 13. According to *DJD* XII, p. 112, there is probably insufficient room for this in 4QEx^c; in 4QpalEx^m there is inadequate evidence for a decision. LXX* did not represent the suffix, though most mss have σου.

בארבה (10.12) So also SP, and Tg^N, Sy and Vulg follow MT closely. Tg^O,J amplify slightly to express an intention, and LXX transfers the word to the next clause as the subject of ἀναβήτω, with the same result.

על־ארץ מצרים (10.12) For the second occurrence LXX omitted 'of Egypt' and Vulg gives simply *super eam* to avoid what was seen as an unnecessary repetition.

ואכל (10.12) Tg^J, as in v. 5, uses שיצי, 'destroy', probably over-interpreting the Heb.

עשב־הארץ (10.12) Almost all mss of Tg^O, like most of the other Vss, follow MT, but *AramB* 7, p. 26, presents the rendering 'plant *of the field*', following a reading that is only attested (presumably) in the early Vatican ms. (Eb. 448) used by the translator and in one edition (1492). The phrase occurs in MT in v. 15 (and also in 9.22, 25), so harmonisation must be a possible source of the variant here. Tg^N reads עשבא וארעא, 'the plants and the land', but the ed. is probably right to see this as a scribal error.

את כל־אשר (10.12)   SP reads ואת כל פרי העץ אשר, with the addition of words from v. 15 and as a result two parallel objects for ויאכל. The Qumran mss do not survive at the relevant point, but again *DJD* XII, p. 112, thinks it unlikely that 4QEx^c had the variant text. The latter is, however, followed in LXX, and Sy *wklmdm* produces a double object for the verb without the additional specification. Such assimilation is likely to be secondary.

השאיר הברד (10.12)   Vulg *residua fuit grandini* is a free rendering that follows closely its version of the slightly different Heb. expression in v. 5.

ויט (10.13)   4QEx^c reads the unapocopated form ויטה: such forms are found in other biblical mss from Qumran (Qimron, p. 45 n. 8) as well as occasionally in MT (GK §75t). Tg^{O,J} and Sy render by 'raise' as in v. 12 and are joined exceptionally here by LXX (ἐπῆρεν), probably because of the involvement of Moses' staff (cf. 7.20 and 14.16) and the variation in the next note but one.

מטהו (10.13)   SP reads ידו, conforming to v. 12: 4QEx^c does not preserve this part of the verse, but all the Vss agree with MT. In the very similar situation in 9.23 SP agrees with MT, whereas LXX made the change. In both cases the discordant readings of MT must be more original, but they do raise exegetical and perhaps literary-critical problems. Neither LXX nor Vulg represents the pronominal suffix here.

על־ארץ מצרים (10.13)   LXX εἰς τὸν οὐρανόν corresponds to 9.22-23 and/or 10.21-22. Lemmelijn considers this reading more original (pp. 185-86), which is unlikely, but since the translator generally harmonises command and execution he may have found the divergent text in his *Vorlage*.

ויהוה (10.13)   Tg^{Nmg} prefixes 'the Memra of'.

(ה)קדים (10.13)   For both occurrences LXX has νότον/ς, 'south wind' (as in Exod. 14.21), which could (as Wevers, *Notes*, p. 152, suggests) be due to the translators' knowledge of Egyptian conditions. The equivalence is occasionally found elsewhere in LXX, which may be due to the influence of the Pentateuch translation. The translators of the prophets and Job used καύσων, 'burning heat, wind', for קדים, capturing its character if not its direction, and Aq and Symm employ it here: similar equivalents appear in Vulg and Sy.

נשא (10.13)   Some SP mss, but by no means all (three of Crown's and Camb. 1846 agree with MT), read the fem. form נשאה, following the usual fem. gender of רוח. 4QEx^c agrees with MT, which there is no reason to change.

ויעל הארבה (10.14)   LXX ἀνήγαγεν αὐτήν took the verb as Hiphil, 'brought up', with the wind from v. 13 as subject and הארבה as object (freely rendered by αὐτήν). In the absence of את it is much more likely that הארבה is the subject, and the other Vss render accordingly.

כבד מאד (10.14) The space between the words remaining in 4QExᶜ seems insufficient for all of MT, and perhaps מאד was accidentally omitted here. Vulg *innumerabiles* is a neat equivalent and the end of the verse is concisely if a little freely reproduced.

כן (10.14) LXX has no equivalent to the first occurrence, which it probably regarded as redundant. Tgᴶ clarifies with קשיין (probably 'severe'), though the use of the pl. form is awkward in the context.

כמהו (10.14) LXX τοιαύτη is appropriate, but Aq and Theod sought more precision with ὁμοία αὐτῇ.

ואחריו (10.14) Sy *w'p...btrh*, 'and also...after it', expands for effect: some mss (including 5b1) omit the *waw*.

ויכס את־עין כל־הארץ (10.15) The Vss render variously as with the similar expression in v. 5: see the notes there. Here LXX has no equivalent to כל, while Tgᴺ has an additional 'all' before its rendering of עין.

ותחשך (10.15) So also SP and the renderings of Tgg and Sy. But 4QExᶜ has ותשחת, 'was destroyed', which was clearly the *Vorlage* for LXX ἐφθάρη and, with some paraphrase, for Vulg's *vastantes* (*omnia*). Both readings make sense, but ותשחת is a little more 'obvious' (cf. 8.20) and so MT and SP's vivid reading should be preferred (cf. Childs, p. 130; Propp, p. 305).

ויאכל (10.15) Tgᴶ again employs its more severe rendering by שיצי; Vulg *devorata est* (without 'all') gives an unnecessary passive form to the clause.

אשר הותיר הברד (10.15) LXX here renders in the passive, whereas in v. 12 it retained the active of the Heb. and in v. 5 it changed a passive expression to the active!

ובעשב (10.15) Sy *'p l' 'sb'* again makes a change for stylistic effect, as at the end of v. 14. LXX prefixes 'all' as often elsewhere: here it may be taken from earlier in the verse.

בכל־ארץ מצרים (10.15) Vulg *in cuncta Aegypto* abbreviates slightly.

וימהר (10.16) Vulg *quam ob rem festinus* strengthens the causal link between vv. 15 and 16 and uses the (generally poetic) adj. *festinus* well to express the adverbial function of מהר, with the 'calling' then as the main verb (*vocavit*).

לקרא (10.16) Tgᴶ ושדר פולין, 'and sent agents', the same clarification as was used for a different Heb. expression in 9.27.

ויאמר (10.16) LXX's λέγων almost implies that what follows were the words of the invitation. Sy adds *lhwn* to smooth the connection.

חטאתי (10.16) All the main Vss use verbs that imply Pharaoh's acknowledgement of his guilt. But Symm ἐσφάλην, probably 'I have erred, made a mistake', will have been chosen to avoid such an acknowledgement, as Salvesen sees (p. 83). Heb. חטא does occasionally have such a meaning (Prov. 19.2), but Symm evidently wished to present Pharaoh as never really penitent: cf. his rendering of 9.30 and the note there.

ליהוה (10.16) While Vulg and Sy use the same preposition here and for ולכם, Tgg and interestingly LXX make a distinction by using a word for 'before' in this case. The implication (which is a common one in other contexts in Tgg) is that God is not directly affected by human actions, they are simply observed by him. This is not the view of the Heb. here or in many other OT passages. But LXX makes the same adjustment quite frequently to avoid the notion of sin against God (e.g. Gen. 39.9; Exod. 32.33) and also, though less often, with other verbs (e.g. Exod. 3.6; 22.7). Although there are some Heb. examples in late biblical passages (cf. 6.12 and the article by Joosten cited in Note d of the translation of 6.10–7.5), Joosten has argued (ibid.) that this is more likely one of the situations where knowledge of Imperial Aram. has influenced Septuagintal Gk., since such phrases are much more widespread there.

שא (10.17) SP and 4QExᶜ have the pl. שאו, including Aaron as well as Moses, like the suffixes in v. 16 and the imper. later in v. 17, and LXX, Vulg and Sy have pl. forms too, perhaps on the basis of a pl. *Vorlage*. Tgg agree with MT in what is certainly the *difficilior lectio*. The other witnesses probably represent secondary attempts, perhaps independently, to secure greater consistency. It is notable that it is generally Moses who responds to Pharaoh's requests, as here in v. 18. LXX's προσδέξασθε, normally 'receive, accept', is strange where נשא clearly means 'forgive' (and Gen. 50.17a and Exod. 32.32 show that the translator[s] knew this sense of נשא) and seems to be an unthinking transfer from its use to render a different idiom with נשא in Gen. 32.21. Vulg *dimittite* is better (so also in Gen. 50.17b and Exod. 32.32), though somewhat lacking in specificity.

חטאתי (10.17) Tg^{O,N} (and possibly Tg^J) render as pl., amplifying Pharaoh's guilt.

אך הפעם (10.17) LXX ἔτι νῦν and Vulg *etiam hac vice* render as if עוד, not אך, were the first word, probably on contextual grounds. Sy *hn' zbn'* ignores the modifier (unless it is represented by *'p* at the beginning of the verse).

והעתירו (10.17) SP omits the initial *waw*, perhaps conforming to the asyndeton in 8.24 and 9.28: all other witnesses have a conjunction.

ליהוה (10.17) SP has אל יהוה, which could be secondary assimilation to the wording in v. 18. But עתר is invariably followed by אל of the addressee elsewhere (in 8.5 ל is used of the beneficiary), so it may be original, with MT's ליהוה (אלהיכם) being mistakenly copied from v. 16b. Tgg and Sy as usual render 'before the Lord'.

אלהיכם (10.17) Omitted, probably accidentally, in Tg^J.

את־המות (10.17) Most of the Vss render with words for 'death': LXX's use of θάνατος is the easier to understand because of its regular use as an equivalent for דֶּבֶר (cf. 5.3 and, for a possible explanation, Text and Versions on 9.3). Adaptation to the context is sought in Tg^N מותנא, 'plague' (which occurs as a variant in some mss of Sy), and the generic רוגזא, 'anger, trouble', in its mg.

ויצא (10.18)   Some mss of SP, LXX and Sy add 'Moses' as the subject; not Vulg, however: the attestation in *BHS* relates to the Clementine ed., but most of the early mss and the newest edd. do not have it.

אל-יהוה (10.18)   LXX πρὸς τὸν θεόν (though AM etc. have κυριον), an odd case of this variation directly after κύριον in v. 17. Perhaps the translator simply liked some alternation between the equivalent terms, as occurs also in 8.24-27. Tgg and Sy as usual have 'before the Lord'.

ויהפך (10.19)   The free renderings of Vulg (*flare fecit*) and Sy (*whpk 'yty*, 'and...brought back': for the idiom cf. v. 6) are probably due to their not recognising the rare use of הפך with only an expressed accusative of the product (see Note qq on the translation).

יהוה (10.19)   Tg^Nmg adds 'the Memra of'.

רוח-ים (10.19)   Most of the Vss give ים the sense of 'west' which it often bears (from the point of view of Palestine) as an indication of direction. But LXX, perhaps more aware of the geographical realities (though it uses θάλασσα elsewhere too where a direction is meant: Gen. 13.14; 28.14; Exod. 26.22, 27), gives ἀπὸ θαλάσσης (cf. Tg^N בימא, probably just conforming to MT, with ב perhaps indicating where the wind was 'turned around').

חזק מאד (10.19)   LXX σφοδρόν is for the whole phrase, similarly Vulg *vehementissimum*. σφοδρός is never used for חזק alone, for which ἰσχυρός and κραταιός are the normal renderings.

ויתקעהו (10.19)   All the Vss render with words for 'throw' (cf. Luther, AV, Houtman), although this meaning is hard to justify (see Note rr on the translation), except from the context.

ימה סוף (10.19)   SP reads ים סוף, without the directional ending, in line with its tendency (*GSH*, p. 428) to avoid this feature with nouns in the constr. state (cf. 4.20 and Text and Versions there). So the MT reading is probably original. LXX and Vulg as usual render with the expression 'the Red Sea' (cf. my *Way of the Wilderness*, pp. 6, 70), but the Aram. Vss retain Heb. סוף: apparently as a place-name, as סוף is not used in Aram. generally for 'reeds' (cf. CAL, consulted 4.4.2011).

לא (10.19)   LXX, Tg^Nmg and Sy prefix 'and' to avoid the asyndeton, but the narrator likes this stylistic feature (cf. v. 14) and both SP and MT preserve it.

אחד (10.19)   Vulg *ne una quidem* and Sy *'p l' ḥd* (as well as some minor witnesses) add further emphasis to the statement (cf. v. 15).

גבול מצרים (10.19)   LXX γῇ Αἰγύπτου, reflecting the more common expression of v. 15b. Vulg and Tg^N here render מצרים by 'the Egyptians'. Tg^J has additional material at the end to indicate that even salted locusts in jars were blown away by the wind (for the midrashic background see *AramB* 2, p. 187 n. 17).

לב (10.20)   Tg^J prefixes 'the inclination (יצרא) and', as in 9.35.

Chapter 10.21-29

Darkness

The limits of this section are firmly defined by 'open sections' (*petuchot*) in the medieval manuscripts at its beginning and end and by an open section at the beginning in both 4QpalEx^m and 4QEx^c. Neither of the Qumran manuscripts preserves the end of the passage. The break at the beginning is confirmed by the concluding refrain in 10.20 and by the transition from the end of the locust plague in 10.19 to the beginning of the darkness plague in 10.21. But there are complications at both ends. After v. 29 there is certainly a thematic break, as the darkness plague concludes with the usual formula in v. 27 and what appears to be the end of direct contact between Pharaoh and Moses in vv. 28-29; and 11.1 begins the introduction to the final plague, the death of the Egyptian firstborn (cf. 11.4-5). But closer inspection suggests that there is no *scenic* break between 10.29 and 11.1, or at least 11.4: Moses remains in Pharaoh's presence until he departs in 11.8. In modern times a closer link than first appears between parts of 10.21-29 and the preceding narrative has also been argued for, on the basis of the unusual structure of the passage and its complex relationship (or lack of one) to the alternative patterns that have been evident in the earlier episodes of the plague-cycle.

We must therefore look next at the plot structure of the passage and then at the discussion of its implications in modern critical scholarship. We may distinguish (i) Yahweh's instruction for Moses to bring on the plague and Moses' obedient fulfilment of this (vv. 21-22a); (ii) the coming of the plague and its effects (vv. 22b-23); (iii) Pharaoh's summoning of Moses and his agreement, on certain conditions, to let the Israelites leave (v. 24); (iv) Moses' rejection of the conditions proposed (vv. 25-26); (v) Yahweh's intervention, leading to Pharaoh's withdrawal of his permission for the Israelites to leave (v. 27); and (vi) Pharaoh's expulsion of Moses from his presence, which Moses readily accepts (vv. 28-29). This pattern of narrative has no exact parallel in the earlier parts of the plague story. There the Priestly and non-Priestly sections each have their own characteristic features and the distinction between them is easily seen. Here the beginning of the section (units [i] and [ii] above) has noticeable similarities to the 'Priestly' pattern (see the helpful charts in Blum, pp. 247-48, and Gertz, pp. 132-34, for example) and differs markedly from the usual non-Priestly pattern, which begins with Moses being sent to Pharaoh to tell him of the approaching plague. At the same time v. 23, with its fuller description of the effects of the plague and the explicit exclusion of the Israelites from them, is closer to the non-Priestly pattern. This is also true of the ensuing dialogue between Pharaoh and Moses (vv. 24-29), especially at its beginning where they discuss the terms on which Israel may be permitted to celebrate a religious festival outside the land (cf. 8.21-25; 9.27-30; 10.7-11). The finality with which the dialogue concludes, however, has no real parallel earlier, though 10.11 comes close to it. More striking is the difference in the timing of the negotiations here: previously they have been held when the plague was still at its height (or, in 10.7-11, anxiously awaited) and they are associated with Pharaoh's request for Moses to pray for its removal. Here, by contrast, the plague is already over and so there is no need for Pharaoh to ask Moses to pray. With one possible exception, however, the narrative does in itself make coherent sense as it stands, as is widely recognised, and not only by those who take a more 'holistic' view of Exodus (cf. Schmidt, p. 434). The exception is v. 27, where again language more typical of the Priestly account reappears (cf. 9.12 especially) and where the following 'Pharaoh said to him' in v. 28 would fit much better immediately after v. 26, in which Moses ('him') has just been speaking and Pharaoh would need to be reintroduced as the speaker: in the present context we would expect v. 28 to begin 'He said to Moses' (cf. Holzinger, Baentsch).

We begin our review of modern critical scholarship with Knobel, who attributed the whole passage, like the locust-plague and most of the non-Priestly plagues, to his *Kriegsbuch* (approximating to later 'J': cf. *Num.-Jos.*, p. 548). Wellhausen, however, was already alive to the distinctiveness of vv. 21-23 from the main pattern, because of the prominence of Moses' staff/hand and the difference from passages where Yahweh alone brings about the plague. He saw no break in vv. 21-27, which he attributed to E, but separated vv. 28-29 as being the original J continuation of v. 19 (*Composition*, pp. 63-64, 66-68). From here, by way of Dillmann's detection of some non-Elohistic features in vv. 24-26, a consensus gradually emerged that was to last until the 1970s, with only rare exceptions: vv. 21-23+27 were seen as from E and vv. 24-26+28-29 comprised the J conclusion of the locust-plague (so already Carpenter/Harford-Battersby, Holzinger [who still thought there was some E in vv. 24-25] and Baentsch). In relation to the latter verses the negotiations with Pharaoh were seen as the sequel to those in 10.8-11 and v. 28 was seen as connecting most naturally with v. 26 (cf. above). Smend (*Erzählung*, pp. 128-29) noted the difference in structure between vv. 21-23+27 and the other plague-accounts as a further argument for a separate origin for them. A first disturbance of the consensus was made by Rudolph (*Elohist*, p. 21), who claimed that vv. 21-23 were from a *Beischrift* of unknown origin, while v. 27 was an 'unnecessary' addition. Noth at first went further still (*ÜGP*, p. 32), regarding all of vv. 21-27 as a supplement to J, but without giving any reason why vv. 24-26 could not be from the original J account. In his Exodus commentary, however, he retained all of vv. 24-26+28-29 for J, and also v. 23, so that the passage preserved all but the beginning of a J darkness-plague; but he now attributed vv. 21-22+27 to P (pp. 64-65, ET pp. 83-84). The reason for the strange (and unexplained) division after v. 22 was perhaps to leave a section that could more reasonably be attributed to P, but it did not find any support subsequently. In fact Fohrer, Hyatt and Childs rejected Noth's approach *in toto* and returned to the earlier consensus. At first only Steingrimmson was attracted by Noth's general idea, but he regarded vv. 24-26+28-29 as later than his A-strand (= P), because they were 'unselbständig' and presented Moses in the same role as he had in the late addition in 10.1b-2 (pp. 148-54) – neither argument having much weight.[1]

The beginning of the most recent stage of analysis can again be found in Kohata's work (pp. 103-15; cf. pp. 122, 126). For her the whole passage is a single unit of a late redactional origin, as her decisions about 9.22-23 and 10.12-13 already lead one to expect. But she adds a number of specific arguments based on features of this section, and these will need to be carefully examined below. Her main discussion is concerned with vv. 21-27, but once they are assigned to EndR she understandably concludes that vv. 28-29 must be too. Only Levin (pp. 337-38) has followed Kohata completely, but her arguments have had a much wider effect in, for the time being, driving the division of the section between J and E from the field. Blum went back to Noth's analysis in effect, though in accordance with his general approach he saw the P sections as supplementary to the older (KD) account rather than as derived from an already existing source (the argument for this is weaker here than in the two preceding plagues). Van Seters takes a similar view about vv. 21-23, but finds difficulties in assigning v. 27 to P, apart perhaps from some of the wording (*Life*, pp. 107-108; cf. p. 87 n. 26). So most of vv. 24-29 is J for him, and the J account here, as earlier, includes an explicit statement

---

[1] Blenkinsopp's brief treatment (pp. 141, 154) also seems to follow Noth in dividing the passage between J and P.

about the hardening of Pharaoh's heart. But because he finds the transition from v. 26 to v. 28 'quite awkward', Van Seters takes up the view of F.V. Winnett that vv. 28-29 originally stood between 11.8a and 11.8b. This has, for him, the added advantage that he can simplify the analysis of ch. 11 and attribute the whole of 11.1-8 to J (pp. 77, 98-99). But it is a desperate measure and other solutions to the problems are more convincing (see below, and the introduction to 11.1-10). Conversely to Van Seters, Propp attributes v. 27 to P, while also regarding the rest of the passage as entirely older (pp. 313-14).

A larger group of scholars have built on Kohata's work while rejecting her view that the whole of the passage is from EndR. L. Schmidt accepts her view of vv. 21-23+27 as very late, but sees no reason not to retain the older view of vv. 24-26+28-29 as the end of the J locust-plague. This has now also become the view of W.H. Schmidt (pp. 434-37), who had supervised Kohata's dissertation, and of Graupner (pp. 64-66: for the J sections see p. 64 n. 200 [which should be numbered 201 and *vice versa*]). Gertz too, in his 'minimalist' reconstruction of the end of the plague-narrative that was added to the non-(and pre-)Priestly Exodus-story, includes vv. 28-29 in it, but as the direct sequel to 9.13-14: vv. 24-26 are assigned by him to EndR as part of vv. 21-27, which (like Kohata) he regards as a unity (pp. 163-66).

The unity of the whole passage has also found some support in recent years, so that the history of research given here comes full circle. This is clearest with Houtman, in line with his general reluctance to adopt source-critical solutions (p. 115: in n. 173 he shows his awareness of such views). K. Schmid does not discuss the passage in detail, but his general treatment of the non-Priestly plague-story suggests a unitary origin for it between Deuteronomy and the Priestly source (pp. 145-46, 148). Dozeman's commentary makes clear that the passage is entirely non-Priestly but he reckons with some unspecified 'addition of motifs over time' (p. 245).

In assessing the debate and attempting to reach some conclusions of our own, we may begin with the question of the passage's unity or disunity. Despite occasional suggestions about contradictions and unevennesses elsewhere (some not mentioned in the survey above), the major points which need to be considered here are the possibility of a 'seam' between vv. 23 and 24 and the apparent intrusiveness of v. 27 between vv. 26 and 28. In the latter case, as noted earlier, the designation of the subject and indirect object in v. 28 is surprising if it was written to follow v. 27, whereas v. 28 makes a smooth connection with v. 26. Although v. 27 does in its present position provide an explanation for Pharaoh's outburst in v. 28, it is not necessary and it could be argued that its character as 'comment' disturbs the lively alternation of the dialogue in vv. 24-26, 28-29 in a way that is not characteristic of the narrative as a whole.

Between vv. 23 and 24 it is not so obvious that there is a literary break. It is true that the words spoken by Pharaoh and Moses make no explicit reference to the period of darkness described in vv. 22-23. But this could be because here, unlike earlier such dialogues, there is no need for Pharaoh to ask for the removal of the plague: it has already ceased. If it is asked, why then is it necessary or appropriate for Pharaoh to negotiate at all, the answer could be that the three days of darkness, although now over, have made such an impression on Pharaoh that he fears what may happen next. Nevertheless, the fact that there are no textual connections between vv. 21-23 and vv. 24-26 does allow the possibility that they had originally separate origins, and this is a point to which we shall need to return.

Next we should consider again the form which the account of the plague itself takes. It is clearly very different from the main sequence of non-Priestly plagues that have preceded it. It lacks the opening instruction for Moses to go to Pharaoh: instead Yahweh instructs Moses to raise his hand and by this gesture to bring on the darkness. This in itself, as Wellhausen and Fohrer noted at length, involves a significant difference of conception from the accounts in which the plague is due to Yahweh's direct action, which is previously announced in a messenger-speech by Moses. Moses' own role is also very different, even if still governed by divine guidance and initiative. Therefore it is impossible to consider this passage as the straightforward continuation of the preceding sequence: it must be from a different author.

Here another important difference from the two immediately preceding plagues must be noted. Within them two passages of a very similar character to 10.21-23 appear, 9.22-23 and 10.12-13. Because of their position in the middle of a story that has its own coherent and complete structure, those passages can be, if taken alone, and have been understood as (late) redactional amplifications of an older narrative and not as part of a once independent account of the plagues as a whole. That option, however, does not exist here: without these verses there is no plague of darkness.[2] In other words the alien structure of this plague-story is a much stronger pointer to the derivation of this sequence of passages from an originally independent source-document than the two earlier examples of it

---

[2] Noth's attempt to find in v. 23 the remains of a J account of this plague has rightly found no support from other scholars.

on their own. It is perhaps conceivable that a redactor might, for the sort of reasons discussed in the final part of this introduction, decide to insert an additional plague before the final denouement in the death of the Egyptian firstborn. But is it likely that in doing so he would construct a new narrative pattern, and in fact one which places less rather than more emphasis on Yahweh's own power? Such an explanation could only be seriously considered if no other option existed.

In recent times the only such alternative that has been thought possible is that the plague of darkness is derived from the Priestly source or layer (so Noth, Steingrimsson, Blum, Blenkinsopp and Van Seters). There are indeed some notable similarities of wording to the Priestly plague-stories earlier in Exodus 7–10. But there are three major differences from them, even in vv. 21-23 (if the negotiations in vv. 24ff. are included there are even more), which make a Priestly origin highly unlikely. One is the total absence of Aaron from this passage: even in 9.8-12, where he has no active role, he is mentioned in an ancillary role (vv. 8, 10). The second is the focus on Moses' hand, which to judge from 9.23 and 10.13 probably implies the use of his 'staff'. While this is mentioned several times in non-Priestly passages (to which we shall return), it is found in P only in Num. 20.8-11, which is clearly modelled on the similar non-Priestly story in Exod. 17.1-7 (so recently R. Albertz, 'Das Buch Numeri jenseits der Quellentheorie. Eine Redaktionsgeschichte von Num 20-24 [Teil I]', *ZAW* 123 [2011], pp. 171-83 [175 n. 17]; see also Kohata, pp. 232-33). Thirdly, the elaboration of the description of the darkness, its effects and the exclusion of the Israelites from them is quite uncharacteristic of the short earlier Priestly plague-narratives.

As for the close correspondences of wording at certain points, the possibility of dependence by the Priestly writer on this passage (and those earlier in chs. 9–10) needs to be taken more seriously than it usually is. Already Wellhausen noted, with specific reference to the plague-narrative, that one of the two non-Priestly strands in it 'steht sachlich und sprachlich näher zu Q, *ein Verhältnis, welches sich gleicherweise in der Genesis constatiren lässt*' (p. 67 [our italics]). Such dependence of the Priestly writer on non-Priestly material is likely throughout the Pentateuchal narrative, even to the extent of imitation. We noted above the case of the two stories of Moses striking the rock to obtain water, but there are many more examples where behind P's distinctive and creative remodelling of the narrative an older basis can be discerned. In Exodus (and the related passages in Genesis) the idea that the name Yahweh was only revealed at the time of the Exodus is one such case, and the transformation of a staff into a snake in Exod. 4.2-4 and 7.9-12 is another. Of course the precise level in the non-Priestly tradition on which P depends may vary from case to case, as Kohata has argued in some detail (*Jahwist*, passim), but its use of older models is, as one would naturally expect, well attested. So similarity of wording in the present case need not imply Priestly authorship (or dependence of it on P): the plague of darkness may belong to an older level in the tradition from which P took certain motifs and terminology.[3]

If the Priestly origin of these verses is at best inconclusive and in fact involves some serious difficulties, the alternative view which was once generally held deserves reconsideration: namely that the plague of darkness comes from, and once brought to a conclusion, a second non-Priestly account of the plagues.

Although its origin in a *Beischrift* of limited scope, as suggested by Rudolph, remains a possibility, the more economical explanation is to connect it and other evidence of a second non-Priestly strand in the plague narrative (see the introductions to 7.14-25; 9.13-35; and 10.1-20) with the evidence, which Rudolph rejected, of two larger-scale parallel accounts of the Exodus-story and, perhaps, of Israel's origins more generally. The earlier arguments for such a view were that the passage and others like it embodied a distinct conception of how the plagues were activated, involving a direct action of Moses and his hand/staff; were characterised by a structure distinct from both the J and the P presentations; and, we may recall, were in the related passages in the plague-narratives made visible by the duplication and contradiction of features in the surrounding context. The objections raised against such a view by Kohata are in fact not difficult to overcome. The fact that the passages employ the divine name Yahweh is no problem at all after 3.13-15: to claim that (E) 'uses the divine designation אלהים throughout his narrative'

---

[3] J. Stacker has presented new arguments for a Priestly origin in 'Why Does the Plague of Darkness Last for Three Days? Source Ascription and Literary Motif in Exodus 10.21-23, 27', *VT* 61 (2011), pp. 657-76, but they are no more persuasive than those proposed before.

(p. 106) is both improbable and based on an unnecessarily limited identification of the remnants of E. The motifs shared with the main plague-narrative (ibid.: cf. p. 104 n. 73) in no way exclude the passage's attribution to a parallel account. The view that 'Weder J noch P, sondern die redaktionelle Bearbeitung kennt Moses Stock (7,15.17; 4,17.20b)' (p. 107) presupposes questionable attributions of the verses cited and overlooks Exod. 4.2-4. We have argued earlier that all these verses belong to the (older) non-Priestly narrative(s). That 'Pharaoh knows Moses' demand [sc. in vv. 24-26]' (p. 108) is not a problem when it is recognised that 5.1-23 contains extracts from two accounts of Moses' (and Aaron's) initial confrontation with Pharaoh. The number of plagues at different stages of the composition of the Pentateuch (pp. 113-14) is also not an objection to an early origin for the plague of darkness. The fuller older account ('J') is agreed to have seven plagues, including the slaying of the firstborn. When the second older account was combined with it (traditionally 'E'), this would indeed add one to the total (three of the plagues being included in both 'J' and 'E'), but there would still be seven leading up to the slaying of the firstborn in 'JE' and ten prior to the slaying of the firstborn in the final text after the addition of P. 'Significant numbers' are present throughout, therefore, and not only if the darkness plague is regarded, as it is by Kohata, as a very late addition to the series. In fact the biblical narrative itself never draws attention to these numbers – the first mention of 'ten' plagues comes in Philo of Alexandria (*Vita Mosis* 1.96) and *LAB* 10.1 – so not much need hang on them anyway.

If there is thus good reason to attribute the plague of darkness to a parallel older account of the plagues, how far in the present text does the account of it extend? This is not entirely certain. We concluded earlier that v. 24 could be the original continuation of v. 23, despite the lack of any linkage between the content of vv. 21-23 and vv. 24-26 (apart from the figure of Moses himself: but his omnipresence in the Exodus narrative makes him of little significance in such an argument). But if the wider context is taken into account, a link between vv. 23 and 24 becomes less likely. First, as is often pointed out, Pharaoh's proposal that the Israelites' children may now go with them but not their animals looks very like a variation on Pharaoh's 'last word' in vv. 10-11, so that it must be part of the same narrative as that. But the difference in form and conception between vv. 21-23 and 10.1-6 requires that they belong to different versions of the story. Secondly, if vv. 24ff. are the sequel to vv. 21-23, what is to be made of v. 27, which sits so awkwardly where it is? It would have to be seen as a redactional addition to the otherwise unitary text of vv. 21-29. The same would presumably apply to 9.35 and 10.20. But then it would be a remarkable coincidence that such additions were made precisely to the three passages in which non-standard introductions to plagues appear (9.22-23; 10.12-13; 10.21-22), especially in the case of 9.35, where the narrative already has a 'hardening' conclusion in v. 34.

It is therefore most likely that, as the old consensus held, v. 24 is not the original continuation of v. 23 but once represented a renewal of negotiations after the locust plague in the main plague narrative. Presumably v. 24 once followed v. 19 and Pharaoh's (slight) change of mind was due to the evidence of Yahweh's power in the removal of the locusts. Verses 21-23 and 27 comprised a part of the alternative account (presumably its conclusion) and they were spliced into the main narrative to add a further plague to the sequence which provided a particularly awe-inspiring transition in the combined story to the formal denouement in the slaying of the firstborn. The separation of v. 27 from the earlier part of the episode was a necessary consequence of the placing of the latter before the account of the renewed negotiations, but it was found (in one way) a very fitting position just before Pharaoh's abrupt rejection of Moses' counter-proposal, which it serves to explain in the present form of the text.

Since we have earlier found reason to assign the main non-Priestly plague-narrative to E, the same will apply to vv. 24-26+28-29. The darkness plague itself and the shorter sequence of plagues that concludes with it, which is elsewhere preserved in fragmentary form, will therefore have belonged to J.

Both narrative strands which are present in this passage end with a continuing deadlock in the struggle of wills between Pharaoh and Moses the representative of Yahweh. Neither a further demonstration of Yahweh's power nor Pharaoh's attempt to negotiate without yielding fully to Yahweh's demands is able to bring about a resolution to the impasse. In the combined text that we now have the crisis is if anything deepened. Pharaoh's ending of negotiations in v. 28 is for the first time attributed to Yahweh's influence over his mind; and the episode ends (as the locust episode had originally done in the main underlying account) with both Pharaoh and Moses announcing that from now on they have nothing more to say to one another. The time for persuasion and education is over: both have evidently failed.

This ending of one protracted 'act' in the drama of the Exodus narrative, which is at the same time the point of departure for the terrible but effective intervention that is to follow, is fittingly embodied, as Dozeman has recently pointed out, in the onset of three days of total darkness. This 'tenth plague' in the present form of the text is also to be seen as the first stage of a final triad of divine blows against Egypt which also includes the slaying of the Egyptian firstborn (11.1-12.51) and the destruction of the Egyptian army at the 'Red Sea' (14.1-15.21). In them too the Israelites are spared (cf. 10.23), and both narratives also include references to the night, as the time of slaughter in the first case (11.4; 12.12, 29-31, 42) and as its precursor in the second (14.20-21; cf. vv. 24, 27).[4] To all this the plague of darkness, with its various connotations (see the Explanatory Note on vv. 21-22), provides both an introduction and an interpretive key. And the initiator of it (v. 21), like the disasters which follow, is Yahweh, who declares in the context of a later act of deliverance which brings the overthrow of a proud and powerful enemy:

> 'I form light and create darkness,
> I make weal and create woe,
> I the Lord do all these things.' (Isa. 45.7)

21 [Yahweh said to Moses, 'Stretch out your hand towards the heavens, so that there may be darkness over the land of Egypt and people grope in darkness[a]'. 22 So Moses stretched out his hand towards the heavens, and there was thick darkness[b] throughout the land of Egypt for three days[c]. 23 People could not see each other, and no one arose from where he was[d] for three days[c]. But all the Israelites had light in their settlements[e].] 24 Pharaoh called to Moses and said, 'Go, worship Yahweh,

---

[4] But Dozeman's claim that the reference is to a 'single night' (pp. 203-204) does not work chronologically for the completed form of the narrative (cf. 12.37; 13.20: note also that the three days of darkness are finished before the final plague is even threatened), even if it might for an earlier stage of it.

only[f] your sheep and cattle shall be left[g] here. Your families[h] may go[i] too.' 25 Moses said, 'So you yourself[j] will provide us with sacrifices and burnt-offerings, and we will offer them[k] to Yahweh our God. 26 Our own animals[l] must go with us – not a single hoof shall remain behind – for some of them[m] we shall select[n] for worshipping Yahweh our God, and we ourselves[o] will not know how[p] we should worship Yahweh until we arrive there.' 27 [But Yahweh made Pharaoh's heart stubborn[q], and he was not willing[r] to let them go.] 28 Pharaoh said to him, 'Go away from me. You take care[s]: do not[t] come into my presence[u] again[t], for on the day that you come[v] into my presence[u] you will die.' 29 Moses said, 'You have spoken rightly[w]. I shall not come into your presence[u] again[x] any more[y].'

Notes on the Translation

a. Heb. ויֹמשׁ חשׁך. The verb is most likely jussive of מֹשׁשׁ, 'feel, grope', with simple *waw* again (as in ויהי) indicating purpose. A derivation from מושׁ I, 'depart, remove' (Tg[O,J]: cf. Text and Versions), does not produce a meaning that fits the context. H.P. Rüger, 'Zum Text von Sir 40 10 und Ex 10 21', *ZAW* 82 (1970), pp. 103-109 (esp. 108-109), having argued for the existence of a second root משׁשׁ meaning 'arrive' in Sir. 40.10 and Prov. 17.3 (with support from Ar. and MH: cf. *DCH* 5, pp. 567, 886), suggested that it might be present here too. The problem is that it would then add nothing to v. 21aβ and Rüger therefore understandably concluded that v. 21b must be a gloss on ויהי חשׁך earlier in the verse (see also Text and Versions). Given the rarity of the verb this seems very unlikely. A sense based on the regular meaning of מֹשׁשׁ is therefore to be preferred (cf. *HAL*, p. 617; *Ges18*, p. 762). In Judg. 16.26 (Qere), the only other occurrence of the Hiphil in BH, it has the expected causative sense and W. Fuss (*Pentateuchredaktion*, p. 247 n. 5; cf. Houtman, p. 123) proposed the meaning 'zum Tasten nötigen' here, leading to the translation 'and the darkness may compel (people) to grope' (cf. the use of the Piel for 'groping' like the blind in Deut. 28.29). חשׁך is then the subject of the clause, and there is no explicit object, which would be odd. It is therefore better to see the Hiphil as 'inwardly causative' (GK §53d-e) and either to presume an indefinite subject with חשׁך as the object (equivalent, as in many translations, to a passive: cf. LXX, Vulg and *IBHS*, p. 71 [4.4.2, citing Gen. 11.9]); or, perhaps better, to treat חשׁך as adverbial (which would make the absence of the def. art. easier) and render 'and people may grope in darkness' (cf. Text and Versions on Pal. Tg., also RV mg), an idea exactly paralleled in the use of the Piel (with adverbial חשׁך again) in Job 12.25. Propp's suggested emendation (p. 306) is then unnecessary.

b. Heb. חשך־אפלה. There appears to be no distinction in meaning between these words, although 'darkness' and 'gloom' are commonly used to translate them and so indicate the variation in the Heb. They are linked by 'and' in Joel 2.2 and Zeph. 1.15 (cf. 6Q18 f2 3) and appear in parallelism in Isa. 58.10; 59.9 (cf. 4Q422 3.9). אפלה and its cognates are mainly limited to poetry and the only other prose occurrences are in Deut. 28.29 and Josh. 24.7. Grammatically the combination of the two synonyms is an alternative way of expressing the superlative: cf. Isa. 2.10; Jon. 2.9; Ps. 43.4: GK §133i; JM §141m; *IBHS* 14.5b. In BH the other examples cited are all in poetry.

c. Heb. שלשת ימים, the adverbial use of a noun phrase to express duration of time (GK §118k), which can legitimately be referred to as an 'accusative of time' in view of the prefixing of את when such expressions are definite (cf. 13.7; Deut. 9.25).

d. Heb. מתחתיו, lit. 'from under him', cf. Zech. 6.12. More often תחת is used idiomatically (and perhaps historically) without מן to mean 'the place beneath' (cf. Ar. *taḥtun* in BDB, p. 1065), hence 'where someone stands' (cf. 16.29: all the exx. appear to involve a [reflexive] pronominal suffix).

e. Heb. במושבתם. For the use of ם- with a pl. noun ending in (ו)ת- as regular in earlier BH see GK §91n. The noun מושב itself, although frequent in P and other later texts, is well attested in earlier passages for 'dwelling-place' (Gen. 10.30; 27.39; Num. 24.21; Ps. 132.13) as well as in other senses. It generally forms its pl. in ת- (cf. GK §87p for other masc. nouns that do this): the pl. constr. st. מושבי in Ezek. 34.13 is exceptional.

f. Heb. רק can be either a restrictive adverb qualifying a nominal expression (cf. 8.5; 10.17) or an adversative conjunction introducing a whole sentence (Gen. 19.8; Exod. 8.24; and esp. in Deut. and Dtr., see exx. in BDB, p. 956). Both uses are possible here, but the former makes for a smoother transition to v. 24b.

g. Heb. יצג. Hophal impf. of יצג with assimilation of the initial *yodh* (GK §71), which only occurs here. The Hiphil usually means 'put, place', but in Gen. 33.19 it carries the additional sense of leaving something behind, which the context also requires here. In Sir. 30.18 the Hophal is used again in this way.

h. On the meaning of Heb. טף see Note y on the translation of 10.1-20.

i. Heb. ילך. The imperfect is permissive here (GK §107s).

j. Heb. גם־אתה, with the independent personal pronoun adding to the emphasis and contrast with what follows. 'So' is added to the translation to bring out the (probable) irony with which Moses begins his response (see the Explanatory Note).

k. Heb. ועשינו. The object 'them' can be understood from the previous clause. The perf. cons. only very rarely expresses purpose (cf. JM §119i [n. 2], m), so a simple future translation is most likely. The sense 'offer' for עשה is well attested (BDB, p. 794, II.4), including early exx. such as Judg. 13.16 and 2 Kgs 5.17).

l. The fronted position of the subject מקננו reflects its topical prominence in the dialogue (summarising צאנכם ובקרכם in v. 24), and the preceding גם is emphatic like the first one, with the *waw* perhaps having inferential force, 'Then'.

m. Heb. מהם is probably partitive (cf. BDB, p. 580, noting the frequency of such a use with לקח). The position of the object before the verb is possibly for emphasis (JM §155o; Muraoka, *Emphatic Forms*, pp. 38-39), but may be due simply to the retrospective pronoun (here in the form of a suffix): cf. Deut. 6.13.

n. Heb. נקח. לקח has virtually the sense of 'select' when it is used as the first stage in a sacrificial or ritual action, a special case of the wider use of a 'preliminary to further action' (BDB, p. 543): numerous exx. are included in the lists in *DCH* 4, pp. 568-69.

o. Heb. ואנחנו. The independent pronoun clearly has some rhetorical force, which may here be, as the translation implies, that even the Israelites cannot predict what their God in his sovereign freedom will require. But Muraoka's discussion (*Emphatic Forms*, pp. 47-59; cf. JM §146a-b) suggests that a more general 'emotional elevation' may be expressed by this idiom, and it seems in many cases that the 'emphasis' is not so much on the person(s) indicated by the pronoun as on the associated verbal action or state, here 'will not know'.

p. The adverbial use of מה is frequent (cf. BDB, p. 553) and supported here by Tg^N כמה. But BDB also includes this verse with Isa. 19.21 as rare cases where עבד is construed in the sense 'worship' with an acc. of the offering made (p. 713: so the other Vss and Houtman, p. 126). Even so 'how' is the more straightforward interpretation.

q. Heb. ויחזק: see Note ss on the translation of 10.1-20.

r. Heb. לא אבה. אבה is almost always used with a negative (52 out of 54x in BH), the positive equivalent being expressed by יאל Hiph. (*THAT* 1, 22 = *TLOT* 1, pp. 16-17). A distinction in meaning between לא אבה and מאן, 'refuse', which frequently appears in Moses' warnings to Pharaoh in Exodus 7–10 (e.g. 7.14), is hard to establish and Deut. 25.7 and Isa. 1.19-20 suggest that there is none. All that can be said is that, among sections of the OT where there are enough instances to be significant, מאן is four times more frequent in the Tetrateuch than לא אבה (which occurs also in Gen. 24.5, 8; Lev. 26.21) and in Jeremiah it is always used; while in Deuteronomy and Joshua–2 Kings לא אבה is considerably more frequent than מאן and in Chronicles it is always used.

s. Heb. הִשָּׁמֶר לְךָ, with 'centripetal *lamed*' focusing extra attention on the subject (JM §133d note) and retraction of the tone in the previous word leading to shortening of the final vowel (GK §29e-f).

t. Heb. אַל־תֹּסֶף. The vocalisation אַל for the negative particle in Codex L is a rare deviation from the norm (elsewhere only Deut. 2.9; Josh. 22.19; Jer. 51.3 [2x]; *Ges18*, p. 56a, also cites the hexaplaric transcription ελ in Ps. 31.2), and other mss and edd. read the expected אַל. A similar variation occurs occasionally in other words (GK §27p-q), so it should be regarded as an alternative spelling rather than (*DCH* 1, p. 271) an error. תֹסֶף, second person sing. m. jussive Hiphil of יסף, with retraction of the tone before another accented syllable (GK §69v), is the common idiom for repeating an action, as again in v. 29 (Note x).

u. Heb. ראוֹת פְּנֵי, lit. 'see my face', the same idiom in vv. 28b and 29 and, with reference to God, in 23.15. In none of the three examples here is the *nota accusativi* prefixed to the object: as Muraoka notes (*Emphatic Forms*, p. 150 n. 125), omission of the particle is particularly frequent before nouns determined by a pronominal suffix.

v. Heb. בְּיוֹם רְאֹתְךָ, with יוֹם as frequently in the constr. st. before an inf. constr. to indicate 'the day (or time) when…' (BDB, p. 400).

w. Heb. כֵּן, here clearly the adj. = 'right', used nominally and placed first for emphasis.

x. Heb. אֹסִף, defective writing for אֹסִיף.

y. Heb. עוֹד, added this time to יסף Hiphil, presumably for greater emphasis: the combination occurs in nearly 40 of the 173 occurrences of יסף Hiphil.

Explanatory Notes

21-22. In contrast to the two preceding episodes Moses is not first sent to Pharaoh to warn him of the impending plague (contrast 9.13; 10.1, 3), nor is there any mention of Aaron here. Instead Moses is instructed to act in a way that recalls the second stage of the two previous episodes, where after a preliminary response by Pharaoh and his courtiers to Moses' warning the catastrophe is brought on by means of Moses' raising of his staff either to heaven as here (9.22-23) or over the land of Egypt (10.12-13). In the full narrative context, therefore, there is an acceleration of the action in this case, which is also reflected in the lack of elaboration of the episode's basic structure later on. Although Moses' staff is not mentioned here, its use is probably assumed: in 9.22 and 10.12 the sequel implies this. The wording of both instruction and report are very similar to passages referring to Aaron and his staff which also begin an episode (e.g. 7.8-10), but this resemblance can be explained in more than one way and the specific mention of Moses' staff in other passages (4.2-4; 7.15-17; 14.16, 21; 17.5-6, 9) also needs to be taken into consideration in discussion about the origin of the present passage, on which see further the introduction to this section.

In the sequence of plagues the three days of even 'thick darkness' might seem like an anti-climax, and in terms of destructiveness and death it is true that it is nothing like as devastating as those which precede it. But many commentators have seen that its significance may be of a different kind, whether cosmic, mythological or in a broad sense eschatological (cf. Houtman's use of the word 'apocalyptic' on p. 116), depending on whether Israelite readers or the presumed Egyptian victims are primarily in mind. Within biblical literature the darkness before creation (Gen. 1.2; cf. Jer. 4.23) or the darkness which accompanies a theophany (Exod. 20.21; Deut. 5.23; 2 Sam. 22.12 = Ps. 18.12) or the Day of Yahweh in prophecy (e.g. Isa. 13.2; Joel 2.1-2; Amos 5.18-20) would lend such a phenomenon a deep sense of coming crisis. The very wording of v. 21b is similar to a comparison in the covenant curse of Deut. 28.29.[5] In terms of Egyptian religion such darkness was a sign of the weakness or the anger of the sun-god Re, with whom the Pharaoh was believed to have the closest of relations (see the texts cited by Propp, pp. 351-52, who includes other ancient Near Eastern parallels, and Dozeman, pp. 247-48). These associations were known to biblical writers (Jer. 46.25; Ezek. 32.7-8). Rather, then, than being a weak conclusion to the series of physical afflictions that reach their climax in the locust-plague, the coming of darkness is the prelude to the final undoing of Egypt. Dozeman has put it well: 'The plague of darkness is not simply one more plague in the assault on Pharaoh. It is, rather, a transition to the death of the Egyptian first-born. Darkness sets the stage for the midnight act of death, thus providing an introduction to the defeat of Pharaoh (p. 245; cf. Childs, p. 160).[6]

23. The impact of the darkness on the Egyptians is described in very vivid, if everyday, terms: ordinary life came to a standstill for three days. The very precise verbatim parallels to the 'three days of darkness' and people not seeing each other, which are cited by Propp (pp. 351-52) from a late Egyptian magical text (M. Lichtheim, *Ancient Egyptian Literature* 3 [Berkeley and Los Angeles, 1980], p. 144) and the Epics of Gilgamesh (XI.111: *COS* 1, p. 459) and Atrahasis (III.3.13: *COS* 1, p. 452) respectively are certainly striking,

---

[5] See in more detail *TWAT* 3, 265-76 = *TDOT* 5, pp. 248-58.

[6] Dozeman actually sees the darkness as the first of a final trio of episodes of conflict which also includes the destruction of Pharaoh's army at the Red Sea (pp. 203-206).

but are unlikely to be directly related to the biblical narrative. The Mesopotamian parallels are in the very different context of the Flood Story.

Again, as in several of the non-Priestly plagues (cf. 8.18; 9.4-6, 26), it is emphasised that the Israelites were unaffected by the withdrawal of light from the Egyptians. How this could happen is no more a concern of this narrative than it was before, and it is pointless to speculate. The recurrence of this motif here is of the greatest significance, because it too points symbolically forward to what is to come, a catastrophe from which the Israelites will be spared (cf. 11.7 etc.).

24. Apparently after daylight has returned,[7] Pharaoh summons Moses, who was mentioned in v. 18 as having gone out of Pharaoh's presence, presumably into the open air to judge from vv. 21-22. But it is common to see a literary break at this point (see the introduction to this section), even though at first sight the narrative reads very coherently. It is true that only here does Pharaoh summon Moses after the plague has ended, but that could simply be a narrative variation, associated with the place which this episode has within the story. The fact that Pharaoh has not been mentioned earlier in the section (Schmidt, p. 434) is not a strong argument, since it clearly forms part of a longer narrative in which Pharaoh and Moses are the main protagonists. Nor need Pharaoh's concession be seen as unnecessary after the darkness has ended (Kohata, p. 108): if its impact is likely to have been as great as suggested above (see the Note on vv. 21-22), it is entirely natural that Pharaoh should want to take steps to bring the impasse to an end. Nevertheless (see the introduction to this section) on closer examination it becomes likely that vv. 24-26 and 28-29 originally recounted the conclusion of the locust plague in vv. 1-19(20) and have now been spliced together with the darkness plague after its addition to the sequence. Even in the present context Pharaoh's terms for giving the Israelites leave to celebrate their festival look like an adjustment to his demands in vv. 10-11: he will keep their animals rather than their dependants as a guarantee of their return. Eventually (12.32) Pharaoh will allow the 'sheep' and 'cattle' to go too.

---

[7] The idea that Pharaoh summoned Moses while the darkness continued (Calvin) has no basis in the text and conflicts with the absence of any request for the removal of darkness in Pharaoh's words.

25-26. Moses' response, and in particular v. 25, has been understood in different ways. (i) Verse 25 may be saying the same thing as v. 26, that the Israelites need (all) their livestock for the requirements of worship – the repetition being for rhetorical emphasis (RSV; cf. Vulg). The problem with this is that the emphasis on Pharaoh at the beginning of v. 25 (lit. '*You yourself* [emphatic independent pronoun] shall also [Heb. *gam*] provide...') suggests that it is talking about other animals whom Pharaoh himself must or may provide for sacrifice. So (ii) some (e.g. Houtman) suggest that Moses' counter-demand is for animals from Pharaoh as well as the Israelites' own offerings, perhaps as a sign that Pharaoh too really does acknowledge Yahweh's lordship. The two occurrences of Heb. *gam* at the beginning of vv. 25 and 26 are then understood, as they can be, to mean 'Both...and' (so also Baentsch, p. 84). Others, however, such as Noth and W.H. Schmidt, (iii) see v. 25 as either ironic or a rhetorical question: 'So you yourself are going to provide...' or 'Are you yourself then going to provide...?' The *gam* in this case simply adds further emphasis to the statement or question, as it can do (cf. 1.11 and Note h on the translation of 1.7-22). (iii) is the most likely view: while it may be going too far to say, as L. Schmidt does (*Beobachtungen*, p. 49), that (ii) implies an understanding of v. 25 that is incompatible with v. 26, it does involve Moses in an additional demand which contributes nothing to his strategy for the Israelites' release and which is nowhere part of Yahweh's instructions to him.

The distinction between 'sacrifices' (Heb. $z^e b\bar{a}\d{h}\hat{i}m$) and 'burnt offerings' (Heb. *'ōlôt*), which occur together again in accounts of worship after the Exodus (18.12; 24.5), is that in the former case most of the animal's meat was consumed by the worshippers, while the latter, as its English name (based on the Greek ὁλοκαυτώματα) implies, was wholly burnt on the altar (see Lev. 1.1-17; 3.1-17 [where the $z^e b\bar{a}\d{h}\hat{i}m$ are called as often elsewhere *zebaḥ šᵉlāmîm*, 'a sacrifice of well-being', formerly translated 'peace-offering'], and de Vaux, *Institutions* 2, pp. 292-95, ET 415-18; A. Marx, *Les systèmes sacrificiels de l'Ancien Testament* [VTSup 105; Leiden, 2005], pp. 46-48).

27. A very similar statement occurs in 10.20, at the end of the account of the locust-plague, and the same Heb. verb (*ḥzq*) is used for 'stubborn' in 9.35, at the end of the hail-plague, as well as in earlier verses which conclude sections of the Priestly plague-story

(7.13; 8.11, 15; 9.12; cf. 11.10). The fact that it appears here before the end of the episode is due to the citation afterwards of the actual words of Pharaoh which embody his stubbornness (and Moses' reply), to which there is no equivalent in the other passages. On the significance of this verse for the origin of the whole passage see the introduction to this section: it was probably at one time the conclusion to vv. 21-23.

28-29. Pharaoh's reply is very abrupt, consisting of three short commands followed by a threat to Moses which goes beyond anything that he has said before. It is the end of any negotiations, as Moses' reply confirms, but Moses' departure is delayed by a further message from Yahweh to Pharaoh and does not take place until 11.8. A contradiction is sometimes thought to exist between these verses and 12.31-32, where Pharaoh does summon Moses (with Aaron) one more time to yield at last to his demands, after the death of the Egyptian firstborn. This is not so much a contradiction as a clever (or ironic) twist in the narrative, in which words spoken in the heat of anger are overtaken by events.[8] But any trace of inconsistency is also reduced by recognition of the idiomatic sense of 'see the face' here, as several commentators have observed (see Houtman 1, p. 51; Schmidt, p. 349: cf. *TWAT* 6, 647 = *TDOT* 11, p. 604). It commonly refers to being given an audience by a powerful figure, so that Houtman's 'Don't you dare to set one foot in my court again' is a very apt, if a little colloquial, rendering of it. In an extended sense the same idiom was used of entering the presence of God in a sanctuary, probably without any implication of either a visionary experience or the existence of an image in the temple: see further the notes on 23.15.

Text and Versions

Before 10.21 both 4QExod^c and 4QpalExod^m preserve evidence of an openended line, corresponding to the *petuchah* of the medieval mss.

ויאמר (10.21)   4QpalExod^m reads וידבר, a variation from MT sometimes (but not here) found in SP: see Text and Versions at 7.8, 14; 30.34; 31.12. In these verses 4QpalExod^m survives at the relevant point only in 7.14, and there it reads [ו]ידבר. Here all the other witnesses support MT.

---

[8] Cf. Childs, p. 201: 'The point of the story is to portray Pharaoh's complete capitulation'.

יהוה (10.21) Tg^Nmg prefixes 'the Memra of'.

נטה (10.21) So also SP, LXX and Vulg; the other Vss render as at 10.12 (see Text and Versions there: Tg^Nmg here agrees with Tg^O,J and Sy), as also in v. 22.

ידך (10.21) As in 10.12 SP prefixes את (cf. v. 22) and LXX does not render the suffix (see Text and Versions on 10.12).

ארץ מצרים (10.21) Sy (but not 5b1) prefixes *klh*, 'all (of it)', conforming to the effect in v. 22. In 4QpalEx^m the verse ends with מצר[ים], so that the words וימש חשך are omitted (as is their Greek equivalent in ms. 75). This is scarcely sufficient evidence to support Rüger's conjecture that these words are a secondary gloss (see Note a on the translation) or Propp's deletion of them as 'unintelligible' (p. 306).

וימש חשך (10.21) SP reads החשך, as one would expect after its mention earlier in the verse, but the undetermined form is the *difficilior lectio* and can be understood adverbially (see Note a on the translation and Tg^N's בחשוכא). The verb is associated with משש by LXX ψηλαφητόν and Vulg *tam densae* (sc. *tenebrae*) *ut palpari queant* (with the added idea of 'thickness' which is taken further in *Mekh. R.Shim.ben Yochai* and Exod.R. 14.3: cf. *AramB* 2, p. 43 n. 13) and also, in its sense of 'grope' (as a blind person), in Tg^N,F. Tg^O,J saw Heb. מוש, 'depart', here and implausibly identify the darkness referred to as that of night, so that the plague is located after daybreak (Tg^J specifically בקריצתא, 'at dawn') and is clearly distinguished from ordinary nightfall. Sy, either unaware of these explanations or unconvinced by them, has *n'mṭ* (from *'mṭ*, 'become dark'), which is probably a guess based on comparison with v. 22, where Sy uses the related *'mṭn'* for אפלה.

ויט (10.22) See the note above on נטה in v. 21.

ידו (10.22) Neither LXX or Vulg renders the suffix, as 'his' is easily understood.

חשך־אפלה (10.22) The construct relationship is recognised by Tgg and rendered by a genitive construction involving two near synonyms. LXX σκότος γνόφος θύελλα treated חשך and אפלה as two nouns in apposition (cf. Walters, p. 160, who notes the reluctance of the earlier Greek translators to use a genitive in such cases) and rendered them appropriately but then surprisingly added a third noun, θύελλα, 'storm, squall'. The same trio renders חשך ענן וערפל in Deut. 4.11 and 5.22 (LXX's *Vorlage* in 5.22 had probably, like SP, been assimilated to 4.11). There must be a connection between the translations of the three passages, and it is most likely that LXX Deut. took the phrase from here, since it fits the Deut. context less well (so Wevers, *Notes*, p. 156: for other views see *BAlex* 2, p. 140, and Lemmelijn, pp. 187-89). Vulg *tenebrae horribiles* paraphrases freely and Sy, also not reproducing the construct relationship, inserts 'and' between its renderings of the two nouns to make a smoother phrase.

לא ראו (10.23) LXX prefixes καί, to make a closer connection between cause and effect.

מתחתיו (10.23) Tg⁰ renders with the corresponding Aram. expression, while Tg^{J,N}, Sy and Vulg have the clearer 'from his place'. LXX ἐκ τῆς κοίτης αὐτοῦ, 'from his bed', is more specific.

ולכל בני ישראל (10.23) Tg^J renders ...בכל, a small variation in sense.

היה אור (10.23) Tg^J has an expansion explaining the different benefits for the righteous and the wicked (for which see respectively Exod.R. 14.3 and *MRI*, pp. 94-95 [on 12.27]); Tg^{Nmg} has a slightly different version of the former.

במושבתם (10.23) LXX (with the addition of πᾶσιν) and Vulg paraphrase; Tg^{Nmg} renders 'in their huts'; Sy (and Tg^J?) has a sing. form, which may either be collective or presuppose that the Israelites were all in a single settlement.

ויקרא (10.24) Tg^J prefixes 'At the end of three days' (cf. vv. 22-23): for other cases of such temporal precision in Tg^J see *AramB* 2, p. 187 n. 23.

אל־משה (10.24) 4QpalEx^m and SP have למשה ולאהרן (but Sadaqa has אל before משה like MT: an error?). Such variation between the prepositions is frequent (cf. 8.21): for more exx. see *GSH* §156a. Both אל and ל are found elsewhere with קרא (BDB, p. 895), with אל apparently being more common. The inclusion of Aaron is found also in LXX, Vulg, one Sy ms. (7h13) and Tg^N (but clearly not in 4QEx^c), possibly as a result of the plural verbs which follow: it will in any case be a secondary development. In v. 16 both the use of ל and the inclusion of Aaron are found in MT as well as SP, and this may well be the source of both variations here, by assimilation.

ויאמר (10.24) 4QpalEx^m may have read the pl., but if so it must be an error, perhaps due to the following pl. verbs. LXX has λέγων as in v. 16. Sy adds 'to him/them' as often elsewhere.

את־יהוה (10.24) The Tgg and Sy prefix 'before' as usual; LXX and later mss of Sy add 'your God' in conformity with vv. 25-26 and usage elsewhere (cf. Wevers, *Notes*, p. 156).

יצג (10.24) Vulg and Tg^{J,N} make the animals the subject and render MT accurately, but LXX, Tg⁰, Tg^{Nmg} and Sy have the pl. imper. 'leave', which is a paraphrase. Josephus (*AJ* 2.307) explains Pharaoh's insistence by recalling that the Egyptians' own animals had been destroyed.

גם (10.24) Sy (except 5b1 and 8a1) has *w'p*, but the copula is certainly secondary.

טפכם (10.24) On the renderings of LXX and Sy see the note on v. 10. Vulg's *parvuli* is again too narrow.

ויאמר (10.25) Vulg *ait*, a historic present, as frequently for ויאמר (60x in all in Exodus), and here in agreement with some LXX mss. Sy adds 'to him' as in v. 24.

גם (10.25) LXX has ἀλλὰ καί, a lively equivalent which Wevers describes as 'sensible' (*Notes*, p. 158). Most Vss take it with the emphatic אתה, as its position suggests, but Vulg places its *quoque* less aptly with the objects of the verb.

בידנו (10.25) Some mss of MT read בידינו in the pl. (cf. Tg^{Nmg}).

זבחים ועלות (10.25) LXX inverts the order, placing the burnt offerings first as in MT of 18.12 and 24.5 – perhaps also because they were regarded as holy in a greater degree (cf. M.Zeb. 5.4-8). Tg^{O,J} have נכסת קודשין, 'animals for sacrifices', as in 18.12, presumably distinguishing them from other kinds of slaughter: the phrase is elsewhere used for expressions referring to the שלמים (e.g. Exod. 24.5; 29.28; Lev. 3.1).

ועשׂינו (10.25) LXX and Vulg subordinate by the use of a rel. pron., the latter continuing with a subjunctive verb to indicate purpose. Vulg *offeramus* and Sy *wndbḥ* also introduce specific words for sacrifice.

ליהוה (10.25) Tgg (but not Sy) as usual have 'before the Lord'.

וגם מקננו (10.26) SP's מקנינו may simply be an orthographic variation: see the note on מקנך in 9.19. 4QpalEx^m appears to agree with MT here. Vulg *cuncti greges* renders freely, as in much of this verse.

תשׁאר (10.26) So also SP. MT is followed by Tg^{J,N}, Sy and Vulg, but 4QpalEx^m has נשאר, presumably a first person pl. Hiphil imperfect, and LXX and Tg^O presuppose this reading: 'we shall <not> leave…' Both readings are possible here. It is noteworthy that LXX and Tg^O also have active forms for יצג in v. 24, where the Heb. mss (inc. 4QpalEx^m) all agree. This might suggest that the more direct active forms have been substituted here too (and also in 4QpalEx^m) for an original passive. But alternatively one could argue that the passive form was original in v. 24 and the active here, with consistency being secondarily achieved in different ways in the different witnesses.

פרסה (10.26) Tg^O מדעם, 'anything', provides a plainer, generalising interpretation. Tg^J פרסתא חדא, Tg^N פרסת רגל and Sy *ʾp lʾ ḥdʾ ṭprʾ tnn* retain MT's vividness, but with amplifications for emphasis or clarity.

לעבד (10.26) Here Tg^N has למקרבא, 'to offer', whereas later in the verse it uses the more common equivalent פלח for נעבד: its mg, however, preserves the reading נקרבה there.

ואנחנו (10.26) After its rendering of the independent pronoun Tg^J adds 'shall not leave them', which may be based on Tg^O's equivalent for תשאר (cf. above). If so, this is a very clear example of Tg^J's dependence on both Tg^O and the Pal.Tg.

את־יהוה (10.26) LXX adds τῷ θεῷ ἡμῶν, pedantically conforming to the epithet earlier in the verse.

עד־באנו (10.26) LXX ἕως τοῦ ἐλθεῖν ἡμᾶς looks like a Hebraism, which contrasts with the freer renderings of infinitive constructions noted elsewhere by Lemmelijn, p. 149. Sy curiously renders עד by *mʾ*, which can mean 'when, after' but scarcely 'until': this may indicate that (unnaturally) it took the temporal expression with נעבד rather than with נדע.

ויחזק (10.27) The Vss employ their by now standard equivalents for this verb, including Sy *qšy* (cf. 9.12; 10.20): earlier its equivalences were not fully consistent (cf. 9.35 vs. 8.28 and 9.7).

יהוה (10.27) Tg^{Nmg} as usual prefixes 'the Memra of'.

את־לב פרעה (10.27)   Tg^J prefixes 'the inclination of' to this phrase, as elsewhere; Tg^N renders simply 'his heart', omitting (perhaps by scribal error) 'of Pharaoh', which the mg supplies.

לו (10.28)   LXX* had no equivalent, but αὐτῷ was added in some uncials and the hexaplaric and Catena groups of mss. Sy, like some LXX miniscules, has 'to Moses' instead after 'Pharaoh'. MT and SP doubtless preserve the original reading.

לך (10.28)   SP לך לך, i.e. with the addition of the emphatic suffixed *lamed* (as in MT of Gen. 12.1; 22.2). In 4QpalEx^m only [י]לך מעל [ ] is preserved, so it is impossible to tell whether it had the longer SP reading here. But the space available seems to make this more rather than less likely. Sy *zl lk* points the same way. The reading of MT and the other Vss could easily be due to haplography and the longer text of SP may well be original, although, as Propp points out (p. 307), it might be due to the influence of the following השמר לך.

אל־תסף (10.28)   LXX has no negative particle (although it does represent Heb.'s negatives in 23.21 and 34.12 after προσέχειν) and it may have understood אל in some other way or not understood it at all (Lemmelijn, p. 87: cf. Note t on the translation for the unusual vocalisation of אל in MT). But the similar expression in 19.12 (where admittedly MT and SP have no negative either) suggests that the negation could be supplied by the reader (Muraoka, p. 488). LXX also (like Tg^O and Vulg) makes אל־תסף grammatically dependent on השמר לך, with some loss of the abruptness of Pharaoh's commands.

ראות פני (10.28)   Sy already here uses the passive of *ḥzʾ* in the sense 'appear' for this idiom (see below on its occurrence later in the verse). Tg^J adds words specifying that Moses is not to continue speaking to Pharaoh as he has done and Tg^{N,F} make the same point more fully in place of the words about not seeing Pharaoh's face. These Tgg thus highlight that it is what Moses *says* that is so unwelcome to Pharaoh.

ראותך פני (10.28)   LXX (as also in v. 29), Vulg and Sy use passive forms here in the sense of 'appear'. Tg^{N,F}'s free translations again have no equivalent to the phrase.

תמות (10.28)   Tg^J, 'my anger will rage against you and I will hand you over into the power of those men who were seeking your life to take it', and the similar expansions in Tg^{N,F} connect Pharaoh's threat with the mention of Moses' enemies in 4.19, where Tg^{J,Nmg} say that they were not dead (as in MT) but weakened (see further the notes on the next verse and Text and Versions on 4.19). Josephus (*AJ* 2.310) states that Pharaoh was already angry.

ויאמר (10.29)   Vulg renders with the more precise *respondit*. Tg^{N,F} and Sy add 'to him' or 'to Pharaoh'.

כן דברת (10.29)   Tgg and Sy understood כן correctly to mean 'rightly, well'. LXX's εἴρηκας alone (with λέγω unusually as the equivalent of דבר: cf. Wevers, *Notes*, p. 160) has in fact not 'disregarded the כן' (Wevers, ibid.) but given a (probably colloquial) rendering that is based on כן = 'thus'. This recalls the σὺ εἶπας of Matt. 26.25 and similar expressions in the Gospels and confirms that they do mean 'Yes': cf. BAG, pp. 225, 471; BDF §441,3. Symm ὀρθῶς explicates the meaning accurately, but the οὕτω(ς) of Aq and Theod, which was adopted by Origen, led Vulg to a quite mistaken periphrasis: *ita fiat ut locutus es*.

After their translations of these words Tg[J,N,F] have long additions which begin with an explicit recollection of 4.19 and a warning that the withdrawal of the previous plague is no guarantee of Pharaoh's safety. Tg[N,F] develop this further with an anticipation of the tenth and final plague. Curiously after their expansions of 10.28 they refer to 4.19 in its MT form which affirms that Moses' enemies are indeed dead.

ראות פניך (10.29) LXX again paraphrases with a passive form, but εἰς πρόσωπον comes closer to the Heb. (for the Gk. idiom cf. Eur., *Hipp.* 720). The other Vss all render the phrase literally here.

www.ingramcontent.com/pod-product-compliance
Lightning Source LLC
Chambersburg PA
CBHW050313240426
43673CB00042B/1392